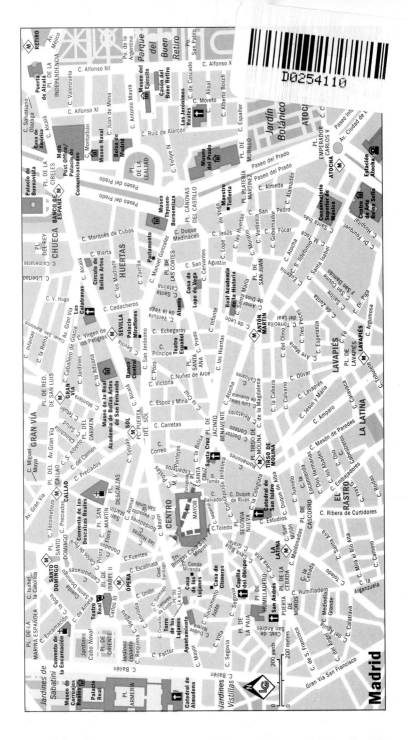
Madrid

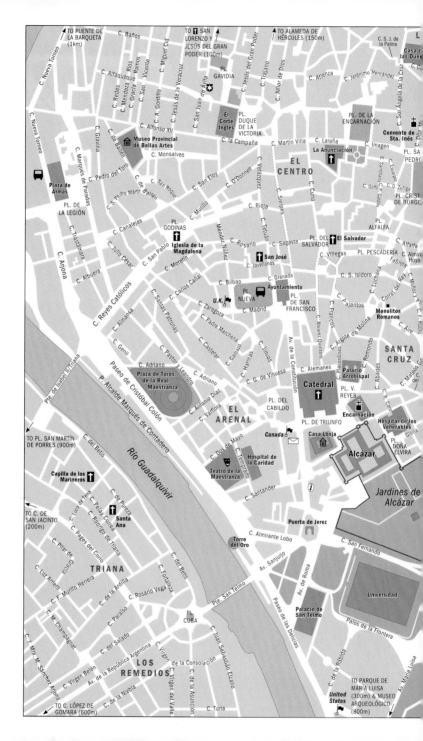

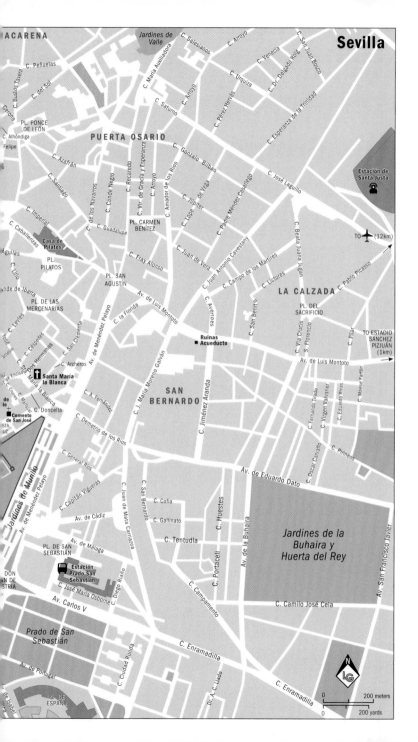

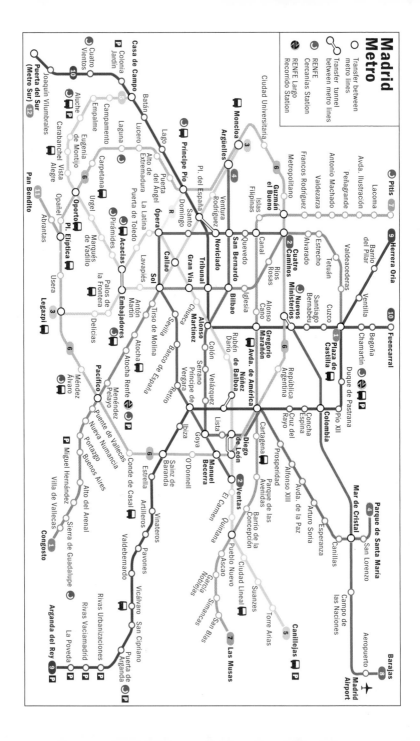

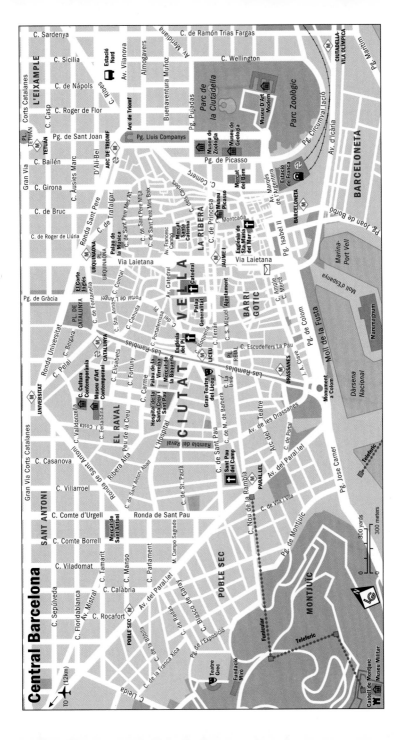

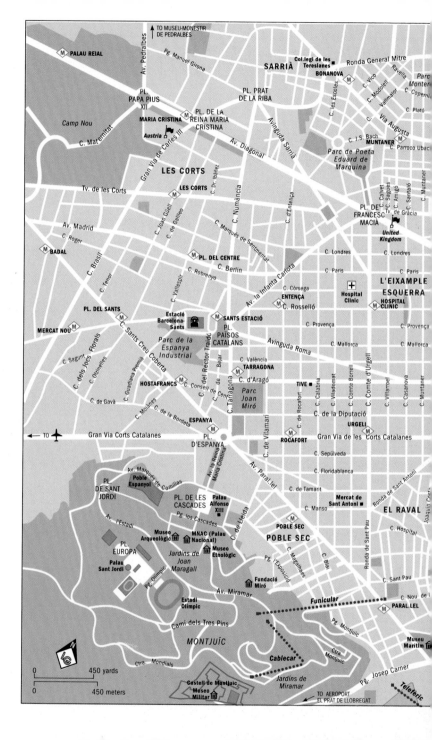

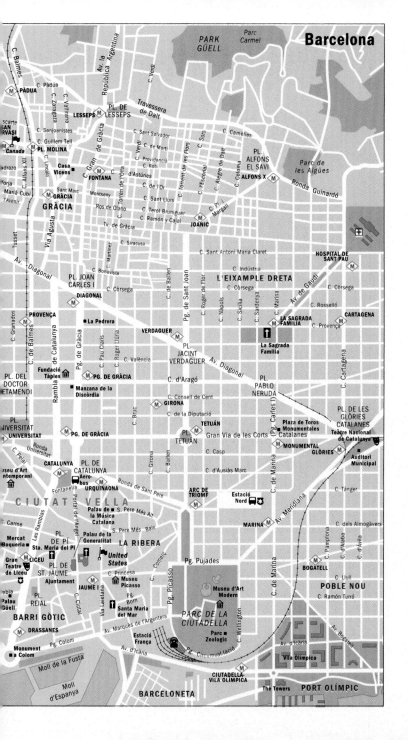

Barcelona Metro

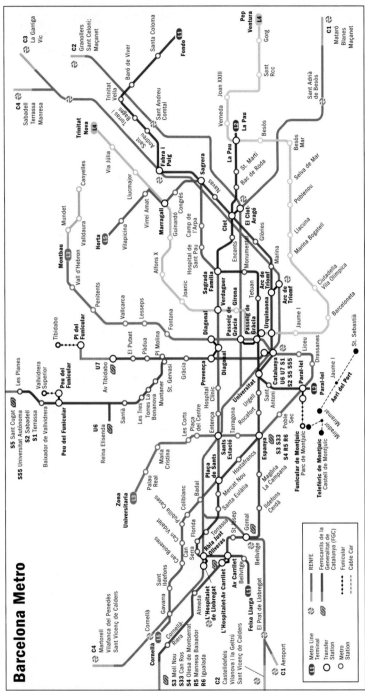

LET'S GO

■ THE RESOURCE FOR THE INDEPENDENT TRAVELER

"The guides are aimed not only at young budget travelers but at the indepedent traveler; a sort of streetwise cookbook for traveling alone."

—*The New York Times*

"Unbeatable; good sight-seeing advice; up-to-date info on restaurants, hotels, and inns; a commitment to money-saving travel; and a wry style that brightens nearly every page."

—*The Washington Post*

"Lighthearted and sophisticated, informative and fun to read. [Let's Go] helps the novice traveler navigate like a knowledgeable old hand."

—*Atlanta Journal-Constitution*

"A world-wise traveling companion—always ready with friendly advice and helpful hints, all sprinkled with a bit of wit."

—*The Philadelphia Inquirer*

■ THE BEST TRAVEL BARGAINS IN YOUR PRICE RANGE

"All the dirt, dirt cheap."

—*People*

"Anything you need to know about budget traveling is detailed in this book."

—*The Chicago Sun-Times*

"Let's Go follows the creed that you don't have to toss your life's savings to the wind to travel—unless you want to."

—*The Salt Lake Tribune*

■ REAL ADVICE FOR REAL EXPERIENCES

"The writers seem to have experienced every rooster-packed bus and lunar-surfaced mattress about which they write."

—*The New York Times*

"A guide should tell you what to expect from a destination. Here Let's Go shines."

—*The Chicago Tribune*

"[Let's Go's] devoted updaters really walk the walk (and thumb the ride, and trek the trail). Learn how to fish, haggle, find work—anywhere."

—*Food & Wine*

LET'S GO PUBLICATIONS

TRAVEL GUIDES

Alaska 1st edition **NEW TITLE**
Australia 2004
Austria & Switzerland 2004
Brazil 1st edition **NEW TITLE**
Britain & Ireland 2004
California 2004
Central America 8th edition
Chile 1st edition
China 4th edition
Costa Rica 1st edition
Eastern Europe 2004
Egypt 2nd edition
Europe 2004
France 2004
Germany 2004
Greece 2004
Hawaii 2004
India & Nepal 8th edition
Ireland 2004
Israel 4th edition
Italy 2004
Japan 1st edition **NEW TITLE**
Mexico 20th edition
Middle East 4th edition
New Zealand 6th edition
Pacific Northwest 1st edition **NEW TITLE**
Peru, Ecuador & Bolivia 3rd edition
Puerto Rico 1st edition **NEW TITLE**
South Africa 5th edition
Southeast Asia 8th edition
Southwest USA 3rd edition
Spain & Portugal 2004
Thailand 1st edition
Turkey 5th edition
USA 2004
Western Europe 2004

CITY GUIDES

Amsterdam 3rd edition
Barcelona 3rd edition
Boston 4th edition
London 2004
New York City 2004
Paris 2004
Rome 12th edition
San Francisco 4th edition
Washington, D.C. 13th edition

MAP GUIDES

Amsterdam
Berlin
Boston
Chicago
Dublin
Florence
Hong Kong
London
Los Angeles
Madrid
New Orleans
New York City
Paris
Prague
Rome
San Francisco
Seattle
Sydney
Venice
Washington, D.C.

COMING SOON:
Road Trip USA

SPAIN & PORTUGAL
INCLUDING MOROCCO
2004

CATHERINE M. PHILLIPS EDITOR
KATHRYN A. RUSSO ASSOCIATE EDITOR
R. KANG-XING JIN ASSOCIATE EDITOR

RESEARCHER-WRITERS
PETER M. BROWN
MEGAN CREYDT
MARLA B. KAPLAN
CAROLINE LUIS
NARESH RAMARAJAN
CHRIS STARR
SARAH THOMAS

TIM SZETELA MAP EDITOR
JENNIFER O'BRIEN MANAGING EDITOR

ST. MARTIN'S PRESS ✯ NEW YORK

Maps by David Lindroth copyright © 2004 by St. Martin's Press.

Distributed outside the USA and Canada by Macmillan.

Let's Go: Spain & Portugal Copyright © 2004 by Let's Go, Inc. All rights reserved. Printed in the United States of America. No part of this book may be used or reproduced in any manner whatsoever without written permission except in the case of brief quotations embodied in critical articles or reviews. Let's Go is available for purchase in bulk by institutions and authorized resellers. For information, address St. Martin's Press, 175 Fifth Avenue, New York, NY 10010, USA.

ISBN: 0-312-31999-1

First edition
10 9 8 7 6 5 4 3 2 1

Let's Go: Spain & Portugal is written by Let's Go Publications, 67 Mount Auburn Street, Cambridge, MA 02138, USA.

Let's Go® and the LG logo are trademarks of Let's Go, Inc.
Printed in the USA.

ACKNOWLEDGMENTS

LET'S GO

CATHERINE THANKS: Katie for putting up with what might have been the most anal retentive summer of your life and for sticking it out to the bitter end. It wouldn't have been the same without you, and I wouldn't have wanted it any other way. I look forward to wearing your shoes one day. Kang-Xing for being cheerful and efficient, the silent dependable machine. Jenn for listening to me and online voodoo, for Extreme Gulps and years of experience, and most of all for helping me see the bigger picture. Tim for his unfailing attention to detail and 3am surprises. No one will get lost now. To the RWs who made this book happen, and to Spain and Portugal for being there in the first place. I'll be back soon.

KATIE THANKS: Catherine for perfecting the art of graceful assertiveness, and being more on top of it at 4am than most ever are. For keeping me sane with cynicism, and for infusing us all with your passion for this book. Consin, for being the skinniest person ever to bridge the divide, and for doing it with an easy smile. Jenn and (sometimes) Jesse for eyes like a hawk, Tim for not faulting our lack of grids, and Team SPAM for never settling for less than stellar, while managing to stay witty and irreverant all the while. Mom, for the fire escape phone calls, and for helping me "dance" all the times that I lost the beat.

KANG-XING THANKS: Catherine for being an unbelievable editor (nothing gets past you!), for all your 24hr.-a-day work, and for the chocolate and oh-so-good Ultimate Bertucci. Katie, for being a great fellow AE and for your Spanish pop music. Jenn for your discerning eye, which helped make this book great. Jesse for filling in with distinction, for your crazy energy, and for your last-minute efforts. Tim for making all our maps super-spiffy. Anthony and Jandro—what can I say? You guys rule. Thanks also to my friends and parents for their support.

TIM THANKS: Catherine, Katie, and Kang-Xing, maó and maó thanks. To SPAM RWs, thanks for the numbered tour. And thanks of course to all of Mapland.

Editor
Catherine M. Phillips
Associate Editors
Kathryn A. Russo, R. Kang-Xing Jin
Managing Editor
Jennifer O'Brien
Map Editor
Tim Szetela
Typesetter
Jeffrey Hoffman Yip

Publishing Director
Julie A. Stephens
Editor-in-Chief
Jeffrey Dubner
Production Manager
Dusty Lewis
Cartography Manager
Nathaniel Brooks
Design Manager
Caleb Beyers
Editorial Managers
Lauren Bonner, Ariel Fox,
Matthew K. Hudson, Emma Nothmann,
Joanna Shawn Brigid O'Leary,
Sarah Robinson
Financial Manager
Suzanne Siu
Marketing & Publicity Managers
Megan Brumagim, Nitin Shah
Personnel Manager
Jesse Reid Andrews
Researcher Manager
Jennifer O'Brien
Web Manager
Jesse Tov
Web Content Director
Abigail Burger
Production Associates
Thomas Bechtold, Jeffrey Hoffman Yip
IT Directors
Travis Good, E. Peyton Sherwood
Financial Assistant
R. Kirkie Maswoswe
Associate Web Manager
Robert Dubbin
Office Coordinators
Abigail Burger, Angelina L. Fryer,
Liz Glynn

Director of Advertising Sales
Daniel Ramsey
Senior Advertising Associates
Sara Barnett, Daniella Boston
Advertising Artwork Editor
Julia Davidson

President
Abhishek Gupta
General Manager
Robert B. Rombauer
Assistant General Manager
Anne E. Chisholm

HOW TO USE THIS BOOK

ORGANIZATION. Coverage of Spain spirals out counter-clockwise from Madrid, ending in the Canary Islands. Coverage of Portugal starts in Lisbon and then runs south-to-north. Coverage of Morocco is focused on the coast and tailored toward short trips for those coming from Spain and Portugal.

PRICE RANGES & RANKINGS. Our researchers list establishments in order of value from best to worst. Our absolute favorites are denoted by the coveted Let's Go thumbs-up (👍). Since the best value does not always mean the cheapest price, we also give the price range for each listing.

PHONE CODES & TELEPHONE NUMBERS. Area codes for each city appear opposite the name of the city next to the ☎ icon and are always listed as part of local numbers. Phone numbers in text are also preceded by the ☎ icon.

PHARMACIES. Where relevant, we have listed a pharmacy in cities. Night pharmacies generally rotate; check the window of any pharmacy for the schedule.

MAPS & DIRECTIONS. In cities with maps, directions are omitted from listings. To find a particular listing, simply consult the map.

WHEN TO USE IT

TWO MONTHS BEFORE. The first chapter, **Discover Spain & Portugal**, contains highlights of the region, including Suggested Itineraries (see p. 5) that might help you plan your trip. The **Essentials** (see p. 9) section contains practical information on planning a budget, renewing a passport, booking tickets, etc., and has other useful travel tips.

ONE MONTH BEFORE. Take care of insurance, and write down a list of emergency numbers and hotlines. Make a list of packing essentials (see **Packing,** p. 27) and shop for anything you are missing. Read through the coverage and make sure you understand the logistics of your itinerary. Make any reservations necessary.

2 WEEKS BEFORE. Leave an itinerary and a photocopy of important documents with someone at home. Take some time to peruse the Life and Times sections for Spain (see p. 67), Portugal (see p. 618), and Morocco (see p. 755), which have information on history, culture, recent events, and more.

ON THE ROAD. The **Appendix** contains a glossary, a phrase book, a distance chart, a climate chart, and other sundry bits of info to help you on your way.

A NOTE TO OUR READERS The information for this book was gathered by *Let's Go* researchers from May through August of 2003. Each listing is based on one researcher's opinion, formed during his or her visit at a particular time. Those traveling at other times may have different experiences since prices, dates, hours, and conditions are always subject to change. You are urged to check the facts presented in this book beforehand to avoid inconvenience and surprises.

CONTENTS

RESEARCHER-WRITERS

Peter M. Brown *Portugal*

Armed with knowledge from his studies in Portuguese language and literature, Peter eagerly accepted the daunting challenge of revitalizing the Portugal coverage—all by himself. Having lived in Portugal for over a year, Peter coasted through his adopted country and sent back witty, comprehensive copy. With his original though slightly midwestern prose, he brought his region to life and showed Portugal who was boss. Now he is working in Kenya as part of an NGO. Who knows? There may be a *Let's Go: Kenya 2005.*

Megan Creydt *Madrid, Castilla La Mancha, & the Canary Islands*

A Wisconsin farm kid turned *Let's Go* researcher, Megan was well-prepared to tackle her route. A veteran of *Let's Go: Australia* and a former English teacher in the Canary Islands, she nonetheless approached this year's challenge with the attitude of an enthusiastic first-timer. Megan blitzed through Madrid's museums and tore through the Canaries, delivering concise, to-the-point coverage of Spain, from its heart to its farthest islands. Having conquered Madrid, she looks forward to spending more time in Barcelona.

Marla B. Kaplan *Andalucía & Extremadura*

Having both researched and edited for *Let's Go* in the past, Marla came back for more—and it just got better. Never afraid to throw down the gauntlet, this decorated veteran was authoritative, discerning, and utterly unaccepting of stagnant listings. With smoothies in tow, she uncovered a whole new Sevilla. Nothing got by this scholar of Spanish film and culture as she cruised the Costa del Sol and blew through Extremadura, a far cry from her previous travels in Ecuador, Mexico, Austria, and the Czech Republic.

Caroline Luis *Galicia, Asturias, & Castilla y León*

Asturian and Galician blood runs thick in Caroline's veins, and she covered her ancestral home with pizazz, making all the Luises proud. Caroline brought her background in art and architecture to bear on her route and crafted pertinent and amusing features in styled prose. By no means a homebody, Caroline has graced Peru, Australia, and Venezuela with her presence, not to mention various other parts of Spain. When stateside, she enjoys selling knives, playing varsity lacrosse, and dancing to Spanish music.

Naresh Ramarajan *Andalucía & Extremadura*

Spain seduced Naresh into foregoing his usual developing world travels. This expert in Arabic and north African literature and civilization exploded onto the scene, quickly learning Spanish and falling in love with the south's Moorish flavor. Whether off-roading through national parks, interviewing locals, or dodging storks, he never ceased to impress. Naresh spent last summer at the edge of the Sahara with a public health NGO before shipping off to India for *Let's Go: India & Nepal 2004.*

Chris Starr   *Cantabria, País Vasco, La Rioja, Navarra, & Aragón*

Writer-actor Chris Starr grew up eating *chorizo* and attending Basque festivals in his native Nevada. True to his Basque roots, he jumped at the chance to go "home" and struck out on his first true overseas adventure. Crazy bus schedules, rain, and technical difficulties didn't stop him from sending back perpetually side-splitting anecdotes. Chris enjoyed the Basque Country so much, he moved to San Sebastián and looks forward to having a drink with anyone who might be passing through, especially if it's on them. Look him up.

Sarah Thomas   *Murcia, Valencia, & the Balearic Islands*

Sarah followed an internship at the World Organization Against Torture in Geneva with a summer suffering on Spain's most beautiful beaches. If anything, this Spanish and English literature scholar was overqualified, having spent a semester in Madrid and backpacked throughout Spain, Italy, France, and Switzerland. Undeterred by hordes of cockroaches and tourists, she rolled along the coast and churned out stellar copy with aplomb. Her meticulous attention to detail and penchant for adventure will long be remembered.

CONTRIBUTING WRITERS

Stef Levner   *Editor, Let's Go: Barcelona 2004*

Megan Moran-Gates   *Associate Editor, Let's Go: Barcelona 2004*

Scott Michael Coulter   *Researcher-Writer, Let's Go: Barcelona 2004*

Emilie Faure   *Researcher-Writer, Let's Go: Barcelona 2004*

Manuela S. Zoninsein   *Researcher-Writer: Let's Go: Barcelona 2004*

Dr. Gloria Totoricagüena Egurrola received her Ph.D. from the London School of Economics and Political Science and is currently an Assistant Professor at the University of Nevada, Reno Center for Basque Studies in Reno, Nevada.

ASTURIAS & CANTABRIA
pp. 537-564

La Coruña
Bilbao
Oviedo
Santiago de
Compostela
ASTURIAS
Cangas de Onís
Santander
CANTABRIA

GALICIA
pp. 565-590

León
Burgos

Viana do
Castelo
Bragança
Valladolid

DOURO & MINHO
pp. 731-744
TRÁS-OS-MONTES
pp. 749-754
CASTILLA Y LEÓN
pp. 167-211

Porto

Salamanca

THE THREE BEIRAS
pp. 721-731
Segovia

Aveiro

MADRID
pp. 91-151

Coimbra
Madrid

PORTUGAL

RIBATEJO &
ESTREMADURA
pp. 700-720
Toledo

LISBON
pp. 634-671
EXTREMADURA
pp. 212-226
CASTILLA
LA MANCHA
p. 152-166

Lisbon
Setúbal
Mérida

ALENTEJO
pp. 690-699
Badajoz
Ciudad Real

Évora

Beja

Córdoba

Sevilla
ANDALUCÍA
p. 227-331

Lagos
Granada

Faro

ALGARVE
pp. 672-689
Málaga

ATLANTIC
OCEAN

Gibraltar

Algeciras

CANARY ISLANDS
pp. 591-617
Tangier
MOROCCO
pp. 755-770

TO
CASABLANCA

Spain & Portugal Chapters

PAÍS VASCO
pp. 509-536

FRANCE

ANDORRA
pp. 462-466

NAVARRA

• Vitoria

• Pamplona

LA RIOJA
&
NAVARRA
pp. 489-508

CATALUÑA
pp. 432-461

• Girona

• Logroño

LA RIOJA

• Zaragoza

ARAGÓN
pp. 467-488

BARCELONA
pp. 392-431

Sigüenza •

S P A I N

• Teruel

TO
MENORCA →

Cuenca •

Mallorca
• Palma

Valencia •

VALENCIA

BALEARIC ISLANDS
pp. 362-391

Ibiza

Eivissa/Ibiza

Formentera

Menorca

• Alicante

Ciudadela •

• Mahón

Murcia •

VALENCIA & MURCIA
pp. 332-361

MURCIA

MEDITERRANEAN SEA

ALGERIA

N

0   75 miles

0   75 kilometers

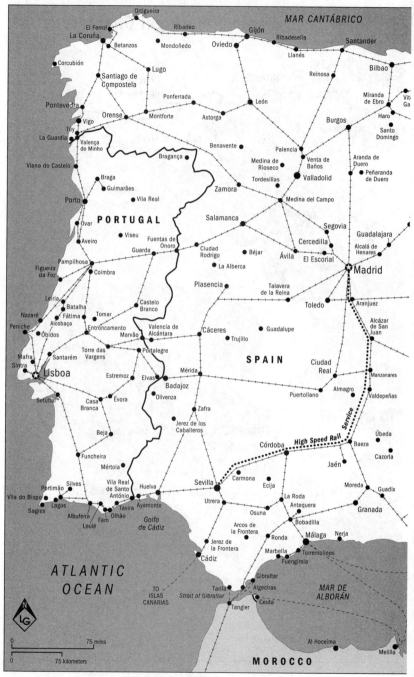

Spain & Portugal Transportation

ABOUT LET'S GO

GUIDES FOR THE INDEPENDENT TRAVELER

Budget travel is more than a vacation. At *Let's Go*, we see every trip as the chance of a lifetime. If your dream is to grab a knapsack and a machete and forge through the jungles of Brazil, we can take you there. Or, if you'd rather enjoy the Riviera sun at a beachside cafe, we'll set you a table. If you know what you're doing, you can have any experience you want—whether it's camping among lions or sampling Tuscan desserts—without maxing out your credit card. We'll show you just how far your coins can go, and prove that the greatest limitation on your adventure is not your wallet, but your imagination. That said, we understand that you may want the occasional indulgence after a week of hostels and kebab stands, so we've added "Big Splurges" to let you know which establishments are worth those extra euros, as well as price ranges to help you quickly determine whether an accommodation or restaurant will break the bank. While we may have diversified, our emphasis will always be on finding the best values for your budget, giving you all the info you need to spend six days in London or six months in Tasmania.

BEYOND THE TOURIST EXPERIENCE

We write for travelers who know there's more to a vacation than riding double-deckers with tourists. Our researchers give you the heads-up on both world-renowned and lesser-known attractions, on the best local eats and the hottest nightclub beats. In our travels, we talk to everybody; we provide a snapshot of real life in the places you visit with our sidebars on topics like regional cuisine, local festivals, and hot political issues. We've opened our pages to respected writers and scholars to show you their take on a given destination, and turned to lifelong residents to learn the little things that make their city worth calling home. And we've even given you Alternatives to Tourism—ideas for how to give back to local communities through responsible travel and volunteering.

OVER FORTY YEARS OF WISDOM

When we started, way back in 1960, Let's Go consisted of a small group of well-traveled friends who compiled their budget travel tips into a 20-page packet for students on charter flights to Europe. Since then, we've expanded to suit all kinds of travelers, now publishing guides to six continents, including our newest guides: *Let's Go: Japan* and *Let's Go: Brazil*. Our guides are still annually researched and written entirely by students on shoe-string budgets, adventurous travelers who know that train strikes, stolen luggage, food poisoning, and marriage proposals are all part of a day's work. Even as you read this, work on next year's editions is well underway. Whether you're reading one of our new titles, like *Let's Go: Puerto Rico* or *Let's Go Adventure Guide: Alaska*, or our original best-seller, *Let's Go: Europe*, you'll find the same spirit of adventure that has made *Let's Go* the guide of choice for travelers the world over since 1960.

GETTING IN TOUCH

The best discoveries are often those you make yourself; on the road, when you find something worth sharing, please drop us a line. We're Let's Go Publications, 67 Mt. Auburn St., Cambridge, MA 02138, USA (feedback@letsgo.com).

For more info, visit our website: www.letsgo.com.

DISCOVER SPAIN & PORTUGAL

SPAIN

Spain is colorful and playful, cultured and refined. It is a country offering equally generous portions of art, architecture, beaches, and nightlife. The people have a joyful, social lifestyle that they are eager to share, and the wildly diverse regions assure something for everyone. Art lovers flock to northeastern Spain to see trend-setting Barcelona, the rugged coastline that inspired Dalí, and Bilbao's shining Guggenheim Museum. Adventure-seekers trek through the dizzying Pyrenees and the Picos de Europa, while architectural enthusiasts explore the Baroque cathedrals of Galicia, Antoni Gaudí's Modernista conjurings in Catalunya, and the Arab intricacies of Andalucía. Flamenco, bullfighting, and *tapas*, Spain's most familiar cultural expressions, also hail from Andalucía, while Madrid, Barcelona, and Ibiza do enough insane, all-night partying to make up for every early-to-bed grandmother the world over. Spain is the perfect destination for first-time travelers, for seasoned adventurers, for families with children, or for college students in search of fast, easy fun. Once you're in Spain, you'll wonder why you never came before.

PORTUGAL

Sandwiched between Spain and the Atlantic Ocean, Portugal is often unjustly overshadowed by its Western European neighbors. Most people know it only as the inventor of sugary-sweet port wine and the former home of intrepid, globe-trotting explorers. Travelers who come to Portugal today will discover one of Europe's newest hotspots. Lisboa, the capital and largest city, has the country's most impressive imperial monuments, while the southern Algarve boasts spectacular beaches and wild nightlife, drawing backpackers in droves. Northern Coimbra crackles with the energy of a university town, and Porto surpasses even Lisboa in sophisticated elegance. Portugal's small inland towns retain a timeless feel, with medieval castles overlooking rushing rivers and peaceful town squares. Portugal's wild northern hinterlands, where some villages have not changed in nearly a millennium, are perhaps the country's most unique region; the land in Trás-Os-Montes is among the most pristine in all of Europe.

WHEN TO GO

Summer is **high season** (*temporada alta*) for coastal and interior regions in Spain, Portugal, and Morocco; winter is high season for ski resorts and the Canary Islands. In many parts of Spain and Portugal, high season extends back to **Semana Santa** (Holy Week; April 5-12 in 2004) and includes festival days. Tourism on the Iberian Peninsula reaches its height in August; the coastal regions overflow while inland cities empty out, leaving closed offices, restaurants, and lodgings. As a general rule, always make **reservations** if you plan to travel in June, July, or August.

Traveling in the **low season** (*temporada baja*) has many advantages, most noticeably lighter crowds and lower prices. Many hostels cut their prices by at least 30% , and reservations are seldom necessary. While major cities and university towns may burst with vitality during these months, many smaller seaside spots are ghost towns, and tourist offices and sights cut their hours nearly everywhere. During **Ramadan** in Morocco (Oct. 16-Nov. 13 in 2004), there is little activity outside the religious realm. For a temperature table, see **Climate,** p. 812. For a chart of **festivals** in Spain, see p. 82; in Portugal, p. 628; and in Morocco, p. 764.

WHAT TO DO

There are as many ways to see Spain, Portugal, and Morocco as there are places to go. One could search out every Baroque chapel, spend weeks trekking on some of Europe's best trails, or hop from city to city indulging cosmopolitan fantasies.

IT'S IN THE BLOOD

Spain, Portugal, and Morocco are *alive*. Two millennia of invaders have washed over these countries, resulting in a vibrant and eclectic culture filled with custom, religion, history, and an irrepressible energy. You can see it in Madrid's famous nightlife (p. 115), in the happy chaos of Fez's outdoor medina (p. 785), in the sidewalk cafes of Lisboa (p. 634), and above all in Spain's spectacular festivals. During **Carnaval** in Cádiz (p. 272), **Las Fallas** in Valencia (p. 332), the **Feria de Abril** in Sevilla (p. 239), and the infamous **San Fermines** in Pamplona (p. 499), there is no denying Spaniards' overwhelming cultural exuberance.

Still, like all passions, it's not entirely manic. Iberia's poignant expressions of heartbreak are often as blood-quickening as its celebrations. The ritually tragic emotions of flamenco and *fado* bring tears to the eyes of even the most macho of bullfighters, who in turn create their own tragedies of life and death on the bullring sand. Actual tragedy on a national scale scarred Spain during a good part of this century—Picasso's powerfully symbolic **Guernica** (p. 127) and the propagandistic **Valley of the Fallen** (p. 145) give travelers a taste of the pain of Fascism. All of this emotional heritage demands a break now and then. There is ample opportunity for peace and quiet here as well: the thin-aired reverence of **Montserrat** (p. 425), the calm of a rowboat in **El Retiro** (p. 139), or the surreal peace of **Park Güell** (p. 425).

ARCHITECTURE

From traditionally conservative to unconventionally decadent, the buildings and monuments of Iberia form a collage of architectural styles. The remains of ancient civilizations are everywhere—from the Celtiberian tower of **O Castro de Baroña** (p. 573) to Roman ruins like the aqueduct in **Segovia** and the amphitheater in **Mérida** (p. 219). Hundreds of years of Moorish rule left breathtaking monuments all over Iberia, including Granada's spectacular **Alhambra** (p. 316), Córdoba's **Mezquita** (p. 253), and Sintra's **Castelo dos Mouros** (p. 665). The Catholic church has spent immense sums of money to build some of the world's most ornate religious complexes, ranging from the pastiche of the **Convento de Cristo** (p. 717) to the imposing **El Escorial** (p. 144), from which the Inquisition was conducted. Spain's magnificent cathedrals can be Gothic, Plateresque, or just plain bizarre, as with Gaudí's magnificent, still-unfinished **Sagrada Familia** in Barcelona (p. 418), a brilliant climax of the Modernista style. Modern additions to Iberia's rich architectural landscape include Lisboa's expansive **Parque** das Nações (p. 659), Bilbao's shining **Guggenheim Museum** (p. 523), and Valencia's huge **Ciudad de las Artes y las Ciencias** (p. 338).

NATURE

Iberia's best-kept secrets are its sprawling national parks and soaring, snowy mountain ranges. **Andorra,** in the heart of the Pyrenees, has easily accessible glacial valleys, rolling forests, and wild meadows (p. 463). In northern Spain, the **Parque Nacional de Ordesa** (p. 483) offers well-kept trails along jagged rock faces, rushing rivers, and thundering waterfalls, and the **Parc Nacional d'Aigüestortes** (p. 334) hides 50 ice-cold mountain lakes in its 24,700 acres of rugged peaks and valleys. The **Picos de Europa** (p. 548) offer some of Europe's best mountaineering. Northern Portugal's **Parque Natural de Montesinho** (p. 752) is probably the most isolated, untouched land in all of Europe. Farther south, greenery-starved *madrileños* hike through the **Sierra de Guadarrama** (p. 149), and nature-lovers are drawn to Andalucía's huge **Parque Nacional Coto de Doñana** (p. 269), which protects nearly 60,000 acres of land for threatened wildlife. **Las Alpujarras** (p. 323), the southern slopes of the Sierra Nevada, are perfect for hiking among Spain's famous *pueblos blancos* (white towns), while trails in **Mallorca** (p. 364) and the **Canary Islands** (p. 591) juxtapose mountain peaks with ocean horizons.

BEACHES

It would be a shame to spend your *entire* time in Spain and Portugal beach-hopping, but if you were to insist, the options are virtually endless. Marc Chagall deemed the red-cliffed shores of **Tossa de Mar** (p. 436) "Blue Paradise." **San Sebastián's** (p. 510) calm, voluptuous Playa de la Concha attracts young travelers from around the world, while **Santander** caters to an elite, refined clientele. The beaches of **Galicia** (p. 565) curve around kilometers of crystal-green, misty inlets. On the **Balearic** (p. 362) and **Canary Islands** (p. 591), bronzed, glistening bodies crowd the chic beaches, and southern Spain's infamous **Costa del Sol** (p. 285) brings tourists to its scorched Mediterranean bays by the plane-load. The eastern **Costa Blanca** (p. 343) mixes small-town charm with ocean expanses, and the looming cliffs and turquoise waters of Portugal's southern **Algarve** (p. 672) adorn hundreds of postcards. In Morocco, beach-lovers flock to the former pirate cove of **Essaouira** (p. 801).

TOP TEN LIST

TOP 10 MERGERS & ACQUISITIONS

Invaders have, well, invaded Iberia for centuries. *Let's Go* brings you the countdown of beatdowns to help you plan your own invasion.

1. Head to **O Castro de Baroña** (p. 573) to see one of Spain's best-preserved Celtic villages.

2. Beautiful **Covadonga** (p. 551) in Asturias is in the heart of old Visigoth country.

3. Portugal's **Algarve** (p. 672) beaches attracted Phoenicians in the 9th century BC.

4. Berbers carpet the Atlas Mountains in Morocco, and you can, too, in the **Fez medina** (p. 785).

5. The Romans left more ruins in **Mérida** (p. 219) than you can shake a fasces at.

6. Hilltop **Toledo** (p. 152) hosted Jews, Muslims, and Christians in remarkable harmony.

7. The Moors set up shop in **Córdoba** (p. 253) until *la Reconquista*.

8. The French may have occupied **Casablanca** (p. 795), but the Americans filmed that silly movie.

9. Today, shoppers flood mountainous **Andorra la Vella** (p. 463) to plunder the duty-free shops.

10. At the turn of the 20th century, Gaudí and his *modernistes* took over the streets of **Barcelona** (p. 392).

DISCOVER

NIGHTLIFE

Nightlife in Spain and Portugal can be relaxing—sipping a cold beer in a local bar or people-watching in the town square. But who really wants that? Just setting foot outdoors is likely to lead to events of unabashed hedonism unlike anything you've ever experienced. With countless bars and clubs and an incredible, intoxicating energy, **Madrid** (p. 115) has earned international renown as one of the greatest party cities in the world. **Barcelona's** (p. 392) wild, edgy nightlife reflects the city's outrageous sense of style. Residents of **Sevilla** (p. 236) pack discos floating on the Río Guadalquivir to drink and dance the night away, and only on **Ibiza** (p. 383), the jetset's favorite party island, will you find the world's largest club filled with 10,000 decadent partiers. Student-packed **Salamanca** (p. 178) is a crazed, international game of "find-your-fling," and **Lagos**, Portugal (p. 672), has more bars and backpackers per square meter than any town in the world. If mint tea and all-male establishments sound appealing, Moroccan nightlife is right up your alley.

■ **LET'S GO PICKS**

BEST PLACE TO STUPIDLY ENDANGER YOUR LIFE: Pamplona (ES), during the infamous Running of the Bulls (p. 499).

BEST UNFINISHED BUILDING: La Sagrada Familia, Gaudí's masterpiece in Barcelona (ES). 120 years under construction, and counting (p. 418).

BEST PLACE TO LOSE YOUR WOMAN: Mallorca (ES), where Frédéric Chopin and George Sand spent a winter of passion and discontent (p. 362).

BEST PLACE TO HANDLE YOUR MONKEY OR CHARM YOUR SNAKE: Djema'a al-Fna, Marrakesh's (M) bizarre bazaar (p. 808).

BEST PLACE TO SEE A BURNING BUSH: Parque Nacional de Timanfaya, in the Canary Islands (ES), where volcanic fires burn just below ground (p. 613).

BEST PLACE TO SEE STONE PANCAKES: Sierra de Torcal, outside Antequera (ES), the closest thing Spain has to Mars (p. 307).

BEST PLACE TO ATTACK OTHER TOURISTS: Festa de São João, in Braga (PT), where for one evening in June, the entire town beats each other over the head with hammers (p. 742).

BEST PLACE TO SPOON A STRANGER: Refugio L'Atalaya, in the Parque Nacional de Ordesa (ES), where tight quarters make for fast friends (p. 483).

BEST EXAMPLE OF MEDIEVAL RECYCLING: 5000 unwitting skeletons went into the making of Évora's (PT) macabre **Capela dos Ossos** (p. 694).

BEST SINFULLY DELICIOUS DESSERTS: The heavenly **pastries** made by the cloistered nuns of Sevilla's (ES) Convento de Santa Inés (p. 245).

BEST PLACE TO SIT ON THE THRONE: Sintra's **Palacio de Pena** (PT), where Dona Maria II had a toilet lined in golden tiles (p. 665).

SUGGESTED ITINERARIES

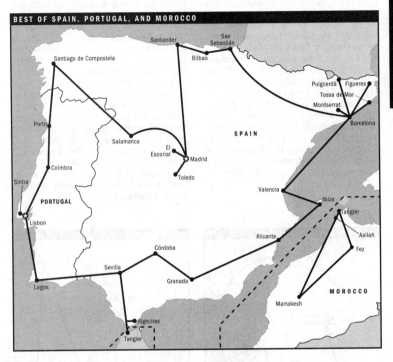

BEST OF SPAIN, PORTUGAL, AND MOROCCO

BEST OF SPAIN, PORTUGAL & MOROCCO (6 WEEKS) Start the party off in **Madrid** (4 days, 4 nights, p. 91), with daytrips to the reserved palace of **El Escorial** and the medieval streets of **Toledo** (p. 152). Visit the ancient center of **Salamanca** (2 days, p. 178) before traversing north to the mystical city of **Santiago de Compostela** (1 day, p. 458). Hop the border into **Portugal**, heading up to unpretentious **Porto** (2 days, p. 731). Continue down to the vibrant university town of **Coimbra** (1 day, p. 721). Immerse yourself in the sights, sounds, and cafes of **Lisboa** (2 days, 3 nights, p. 634) with a daytrip to the town of **Sintra** (1 day, p. 665). To the south lie the beaches and cliffs of the Algarve; stop in **Lagos** (2 days, p. 672) to dance the night away. Catch your shut-eye on the 7hr. bus from Lagos to **Sevilla** (2 days, p. 227) and prepare for a romantic stroll along the Río Guadalquivir. Delve deeper into Iberia's Arab roots and take a ferry from **Algeciras** to **Tangier, Morocco**, escaping immediately to the beaches of **Asilah** (1 day). Move inland to the imperial cities of **Fez** (2 days, p. 785) and **Marrakesh** (2 days, p. 804) with their enchanting medinas. Swing back through Algeciras and Sevilla to **Córdoba** (2 days, p. 253), with its gargantuan Mezquita, and **Granada** (2 days, p. 310), home to the world-famous Alhambra. Enjoy the beaches and vibrant nightlife in **Alicante** (2 days, p. 286). Hop over to **Ibiza** (1 day, p. 490) in the Islas Baleares for decadence, discos, and debauchery. Head back to the mainland and up the Mediterranean Coast to **Valencia** (1 day, p. 332), where the food—*paella* and oranges—rivals the new planetarium as Valencia's top attraction. Onwards to **Barcelona** (4 days, p. 392), one of Europe's most vibrant cities full of Modernista architecture and fierce nightlife. During the summer, sun on the beaches in **Tossa de Mar** (1 day, p. 436), or visit the monastery in **Montserrat** (1 day, p. 425). In the winter, a better bet is skiing in **Puigcerdà** (1 day, p. 452). Visit Spain's second most popular museum, the Teatre-Museu Dalí in **Figueres** (1 day, p. 446) before heading on to **San Sebastián** (2 days, p. 510) and **Bilbao** (1 day, p. 519), home to the Guggenheim. Enjoy the beaches and boardwalks of **Santander** (1 day, p. 444) for some relaxation on your final stop.

ning fields of Spain's Costa del Sol. Layover in **Marbella** (1 day, p. 291) for raging nightlife and celebrity-watching. Head inland to the cobblestoned streets and the incomparable Alhambra in **Granada** (2 days, p. 310) before cruising the coast up to **Alicante** (1 day, p. 286) and **Valencia** (1 day, p. 332). Display your tight tummy as you tan and frolic in **Ibiza** (1 day, p. 383). Venture north to Spain's coastal jewel, **Barcelona** (2 days, p. 392), a pleasure for art and nightlife lovers alike. Worthwhile daytrips in Cataluña abound: partake of **Tossa de Mar's** beaches (1 day, p. 436), admire breathtaking mountain views from **Montserrat** (1 day, p. 425), or say Hello Dalí in **Figueres** (1 day, p. 446). Grab a bus to the beaches and *tapas* of **San Sebastián** (2 days, p. 509). Next, it's on to **Bilbao** (1 day, p. 519), home of the Guggenheim Museum, before a final stop in the charming university town of **Salamanca** (1 day, p. 138).

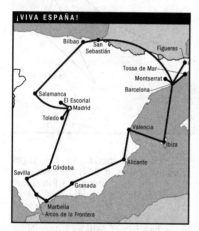

¡VIVA ESPAÑA!

SEE YA IN ANDALUCÍA

¡VIVA ESPAÑA! (3 WEEKS) Begin *la marcha* in **Madrid** (4 days, 4 nights, p. 91), with daytrips to **El Escorial** (p. 144) and **Toledo** (p. 152). Then speed down to **Córdoba** (2 days, p. 253), and on to **Sevilla** (2 days, p. 227). Board the bus to the peaceful *pueblo blanco* of **Arcos de la Frontera** (1 day, p. 270). Next, make your way south to the tan-

SEE YA IN ANDALUCÍA (2 WEEKS)

Whisk away from Madrid on the high-speed AVE train to **Córdoba** (2 days, p. 253) to tour the Mezquita mosque-turned-cathedral. Hop back on the AVE to **Sevilla** (3 days, p. 227) to inspect the three towers dedicated to gold, silver, and God. A quick trip down to Costa de la Luz yields the soft-sanded stretches of **Cádiz's** beaches (2 days, p. 272). Move into the heart of Andalucía and the classic *pueblo blanco* **Arcos de la Frontera** (1 day, p. 270). Marvel at the *gorge*-ous sights in **Ronda** (1 day, p. 255) before partying in the Costa del Sol resort town of **Marbella** (2 days, p. 291). Continue inland to **Gran-ada** (2 days, p. 310), where the Alhambra and Albaicín are sights for sore eyes. Mountain air awaits hiking from town to town in **Las Alpujarras** (1 day).

THE BEST OF PORTUGAL (2 WEEKS)

Begin in busy **Lisboa** (3-4 days, p. 634) and daytrip to fairy tale **Sintra** (1 day, p. 665). Head down to the infamous beach-and-bar town **Lagos** (2-3 days, p. 672) and spend an afternoon in **Sagres,** once considered the end of the world. Check out the creepy bone chapel in **Évora** (1 day, p. 690) and the mysterious convent in **Tomar** (1 day, p. 717). Slam shut those dusty books in the university town of **Coimbra** (2-3 days, p. 721) and take in the youthful fun. Finish in **Porto** (2 days, p. 731), home of fine artwork and sweet port wine.

INTO AFRICA (2 WEEKS)

Hop on a ferry from Algeciras (in Spain) to **Tangier.** Once on land, move directly to **Asilah** (1 day, p. 795). Decamp to the enchanting stone medina of

BEST OF PORTUGAL

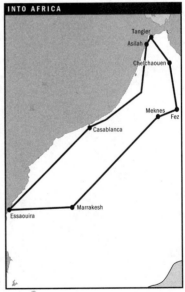

INTO AFRICA

Chefchaouen (1 day, p. 777) for sweet-smelling relaxation. Experience the dazzling imperial cities of **Fez** (3 days, p. 785), **Meknes** (2 days, p. 779), and **Marrakesh** (3 days, p. 804). Hit the beaches of **Essaouira** (2 days, p. 801) before cruising back up the coast to storied **Casablanca** (2 days, p. 795) on your way back to Tangier.

ESSENTIALS

FACTS FOR THE TRAVELER

ENTRANCE REQUIREMENTS
Passport (p. 11). Required of all foreign travelers.
Visa (p. 13). Required in addition to a passport of South Africans going to Spain, Portugal, or Morocco, and for anyone staying more than 90 days.
Work Permit (p. 5). Required of all foreigners planning to work in Spain, Portugal, or Morocco.
International Driving Permit (p. 49). Recommended for those planning to drive in Spain, Portugal, or Morocco.

EMBASSIES & CONSULATES

CONSULAR SERVICES ABROAD

The following listings are for Spanish, Portuguese, and Moroccan embassies and consulates in selected foreign countries. For listings of foreign embassies and consulates located in Spain, Portugal, or Morocco, consult our country-specific **Essentials** sections (p. 83, p. 629, and p. 765).

SPANISH

Australia: Embassy: 15 Arkana St., **Yarralumla,** ACT 2600; P.O. Box 9076, Deakin ACT 2600 (☎2 6273 3555; fax 6273 3918; www.embaspain.com). **Consulates:** Level 24, St. Martin's Tower, 31 Market St., **Sydney,** NSW 2000 (☎2 9261 2433; fax 9283 1695); 146 Elgin St., Carlton, VIC 3053 **Melbourne** (☎3 9347 1966; fax 9347 3580).

Canada: Embassy: 74 Stanley Ave., **Ottawa,** ON K1M 1P4 (☎613-747-2252; fax 744-1224). **Consulates:** 1 Westmount Sq., Suite 1456, Ave. Wood, **Montreal,** Quebec H3Z 2P9 (☎514-935-5235; fax 935-4655; www.docuweb.ca/spainincanada); Simcoe Place, 200 Front St., Suite 2401 **Toronto,** Ontario M5V 3K2 (☎416-977-1661; fax 593-4949).

Ireland: Embassy: 17a Merlyn Park, Ballsbridge, **Dublin** 4 (☎269 1640 or 283 882 7269; fax 269 1854).

New Zealand: Refer to the embassy in Australia.

South Africa: Embassy: 169 Pine St., Arcadia, P.O. Box 1633, **Pretoria** 0083 (☎12 344 3875; fax 343 4891). **Consulate:** 37 Shortmarket St., **Cape Town** 8001 (☎21 22 2415; fax 22 2328).

United Kingdom: Embassy: 39 Chesham Pl., **London** SW1X 8SB (☎0207 235 5555; fax 259 5392). **Consulates:** 20 Draycott Pl., **London** SW3 2RZ (☎0207 589 8989; fax 581 7888); Suite 1A, Brookhouse, 70, Spring Gardens, **Manchester** M2 2BQ (☎161 236 1262; fax 228 7467); 63 North Castle Street, **Edinburgh** EH2 3LJ (☎220 18 43 or 14 39; fax 226 45 68).

United States: Embassy: 2375 Pennsylvania Ave. NW, **Washington, D.C.** 20037 (☎202-728-2330; fax 728-2302; www.spainemb.org). **Consulates:** 150 E. 58th St., 30th fl., **New York,** NY 10155 (☎212-355-4080 or 355-4081; fax 644-3751); **branches** in Boston, Chicago, Houston, Los Angeles, Miami, New Orleans, San Juan (PR), and San Francisco.

PORTUGUESE

Australia: Embassy: 23 Culgoa Circuit, **O'Malley,** ACT 2606; P.O. Box 9092, Deakin, ACT 2600 (☎2 6290 1733; fax 6290 1957). **Consulate:** Level 9, 30 Clarence St., P.O. Box 3309, **Sydney,** NSW 2000 (☎2 9262 2199; fax 9262 5991; www.consulportugalsydney.org.au).

Canada: Embassy: 645 Island Park Dr., **Ottawa,** ON K1Y 0B8 (☎613-729-0883; fax 729-4236). **Consulates:** 438 University Ave., Suite 1400, **Toronto,** ON M5G 2K8 (☎416-217-0966; fax 217-0973; www.cgportugaltoronto.com); 904-700 W. Pender St., #904, **Vancouver,** BC V6C 1G8 (☎604-688-6514; fax 685-7042).

Ireland: Embassy: Knocksinna House, Knocksinna Road, Foxrock, **Dublin** 18 (☎289 4416; fax: 289 2849).

New Zealand: Embassy: Refer to the embassy in Australia. **Consulates:** 33 Garfield St., Parnell, P.O. Box 305, **Auckland** (☎649 309 1454; fax 308 9061); 21 Marion St., **Wellington** (☎644 382 7655; fax 382 7659).

South Africa: Embassy: 599 Leyds St., Muckleneuk, **Pretoria,** 0002; P.O. Box 27102, Sunnyside, 0132 (☎012 341 2340; fax 341 3975). **Consulates:** Barcley Sq., 296 Walker St., Sunnyside, **Pretoria,** 0002 (☎012 341 5522; fax 341 5690); Portuguese House, 1st fl., Ernest Oppenheimer Ave., 2198, Bruma, **Johannesburg;** P.O. Box 5092 (☎11 293 8206; fax 333 9009); Main Tower Suite 1005, Standard Bank Centre, 10th fl. Hertzog Blvd., Hereengracht, **Capetown,** 8001; P.O. Box 3433, Captetown 8000; 320 W. St., Suite 1612, P.O. Box 315, **Durban** 4000 (☎31 305 7511; fax 304 6063).

United Kingdom: Embassy: 11 Belgrave Sq., **London** SWIX 8PP (☎0207 235 5331, fax 245 1287; www.portembassy.gla.ac.uk/info/embassy.html). **Consulate:** Silver City House 62, Brompton Rd., **London** SW3 1BJ (☎0207 581 8722; fax 581 3085).

United States: Embassy: 2125 Kalorama Rd. NW, **Washington, D.C.** 20008 (☎202-328-8610; fax 462-3726 or 518-3694). **Consulates:** 630 5th Ave., Suite 801, **New York,** NY 10111 (☎212-246-4580; fax 459-0190); **branches** in Boston, Chicago, Coral Gables (FL), Honolulu, Houston, Los Angeles, Newark, New Bedford (MA), New Orleans, Philadelphia, Providence, Río Piedras (PR), San Francisco, and Waterbury (CT).

MOROCCAN

Australia: Embassy: 11 West St., **North Sydney,** NSW 2060 (☎2 9957 6717; fax 9923 1053).

Canada: Embassy: 38 Range Rd., **Ottawa,** ON K1N 8J4 (☎613-236-7391 or 236-7392; fax 236-6164; www.ambassade-maroc.ottawa.on.ca). **Consulate:** 1010 Sherbrooke West, Suite 1510, **Montreal,** QU H3A 2R7 (☎514-288-8750, fax 288-4859; www.consulatdumaroc.ca).

Ireland: Embassy: 53 Raglan Rd., **Dublin** 4 (☎353 1 660 9449; fax 1 660 9468).

South Africa: Embassy: 799 Schoeman St., Arcadia 0083; P.O. Box 12382, Hatfield 0028 **Pretoria** (☎12 343 0230; fax 343 0613).

United Kingdom: Embassy: 49 Queens Gate Gardens, **London** SW7 5NE (☎0207 581 5001; fax 225 3862).

United States: Embassy: 1601 21st St. NW, **Washington, D.C.** 20009 (☎202-462-7979; fax 265-0161). **Consulates:** 10 East 40th. St., 23rd fl., **New York,** NY 10016 (☎212-758-2625; fax 779-7441); 1821 Jefferson Pl. NW, **Washington, D.C.** 20036 (☎202-462-7979; fax 452-0106).

TOURIST OFFICES

SPANISH
Spain's official tourist board operates an extensive website at www.tourspain.es.

Canada: Tourist Office of Spain, 2 Bloor West, Suite 3402, **Toronto,** ON M4W 3E2 (☎416-961-3131; fax 961-1992; www.tourspain.toronto.on.ca).

United Kingdom: Spanish National Tourist Office, 22-23 Manchester Sq., **London** W1U 3PX (☎0207 486 8077; fax 486 8034).

United States: Tourist Office of Spain, 666 5th Ave., 35th fl., **New York,** NY 10103 (☎212-265-8822; fax 265-8864). Additional offices in **Chicago,** IL (☎312-642-1992), **Beverly Hills,** CA (☎323-658-7188), and **Miami,** FL (☎305-358-1992).

PORTUGUESE
The official Portuguese tourism website is located at www.portugal-insite.pt.

Canada: Portuguese Trade and Tourism Commission, 60 Bloor West, Suite 1005, **Toronto,** ON M4W 3B8 (☎416-921-7376; fax 921-1353).

United Kingdom: Portuguese Trade and Tourism Office, 22-25A Sackville St., 2nd fl., **London** W1S 3LY (☎0207 494 1517; fax 494 1868).

United States: Portuguese National Tourist Office, 590 5th Ave., 4th fl., **New York,** NY 10036 (☎800-767-8842 or 212-354-4403; fax 764-6137; www.portugal.org). Additional office in **Washington, D.C.** (☎202-331-8222).

MOROCCAN
The official website for tourism in Morocco is www.tourism-in-morocco.com. Address all correspondence to the Moroccan National Tourist Office.

Australia: 2/11 West St. North, **Sydney** NSW 2060 (☎2922 4999; fax 2923 1053).

Canada: 1800 Ave. McGill College, Suite 2450, **Montreal** QC H3A 3J6 (☎514-842-8111; fax 842-5316).

United Kingdom: 205 Regent St., **London** W1R 7DE (☎0207 437 0073; fax 734 8172).

United States: 20 East 46th St., Suite 1201, **New York,** NY 10017 (☎212-557-2520; fax 212-949-8148). Additional office in **Lake Buena Vista,** FL (☎407-827-5337).

DOCUMENTS & FORMALITIES

Carry one set of copies in a safe place, apart from the originals, and leave another set at home. Consulates also recommend that you carry an expired passport or an official copy of your birth certificate in a part of your baggage, separate from other documents.

PASSPORTS

REQUIREMENTS. All travelers need valid passports to enter Spain, Portugal, or Morocco and to re-enter their own countries. For citizens of some countries, neither Spain, Portugal, nor Morocco allows entrance if the passport expires in under six months. Returning home with an expired passport is illegal; fines may result.

NEW PASSPORTS. Citizens of Australia, Canada, Ireland, New Zealand, the UK, and the US can apply for a passport at any post office, passport office, or court of law. Citizens of South Africa can apply for a passport at any Home Affairs Office. Any new passport or renewal applications must be filed well in advance of the departure date. Most passport offices offer rush services for a very steep fee.

ESSENTIALS

ONE EUROPE. The idea of European unity has come a long way since 1958, when the European Economic Community (EEC) was created in order to promote solidarity and cooperation. Since then, the EEC has become the European Union (EU), with political, legal, and economic institutions spanning 15 member states: Austria, Belgium, Denmark, Finland, France, Germany, Greece, Ireland, Italy, Luxembourg, the Netherlands, Portugal, Spain, Sweden, and the UK.

What does this have to do with the average non-EU tourist? In 1999, the EU established **freedom of movement** across 15 European countries—the entire EU minus Ireland and the UK, but plus Iceland and Norway. This means that border controls between participating countries have been abolished, and visa policies harmonized. While you're still required to carry a passport (or government-issued ID card for EU citizens) when crossing an internal border, once you've been admitted into one country, you're free to travel to all participating states. Britain and Ireland have also formed a **common travel area,** abolishing passport controls between the UK and Ireland. This means that the only times you'll see a border guard within the EU are traveling between the British Isles and the Continent. For more important consequences of the EU for travelers, see **European Customs** (p. 13) and **Customs in the EU** (p. 14).

PASSPORT MAINTENANCE. If you lose your passport, immediately notify the local police and the nearest embassy or consulate of your home government. To expedite its replacement, you will need to know all information previously recorded, so it's a good idea to keep a photocopy of the page of your passport with your photo, as well as your visas, traveler's check serial numbers, and any other important documents. You will also need to show ID and proof of citizenship. In some cases, a replacement may take weeks to process, and it may be valid only for a limited time. Any visas stamped in your old passport will be irretrievably lost. In an emergency, ask for immediate traveling papers to re-enter your home country.

VISAS

As of August 2003, citizens of South Africa need a visa in addition to a valid passport for entrance to Spain, Portugal, or Morocco; citizens of Australia, Canada, Ireland, New Zealand, the UK, and the US do not need visas to visit Spain, Portugal, or Morocco for less than ninety days. Visas vary in cost based on the length of stay and can only be obtained with extensive documentation on your planned activity in the country. Applications are available at the nearest consulate or embassy for the country to which you are traveling. Generally speaking, visa applications must be filed in your home country. US citizens can take advantage of the **Center for International Business and Travel** (**CIBT;** ☎ 800-929-2428; www.cibt.com), which secures visas for travel to almost all countries for a variable service charge. For up-to-date info on entrance requirements before departure, contact the nearest embassy of Spain, Portugal, or Morocco. US citizens can also consult www.pueblo.gsa.gov/cic_text/travel/foreign/foreignentryreqs.html.

WORK PERMITS. Admission as a visitor does not include the right to work, which is authorized only by a work permit. Entering Spain, Portugal, or Morocco to study requires a special student visa. For more info, see **Alternatives to Tourism,** p. 57.

IDENTIFICATION

Always carry at least two forms of identification, including a photo ID; a passport combined with a driver's license or birth certificate is usually adequate. Never carry all your forms of ID together; split them up in case of theft or loss.

TEACHER, STUDENT & YOUTH IDENTIFICATION. The **International Student Identity Card (ISIC),** the most widely-accepted form of student ID, provides discounts on sights, accommodations, food, and transport; access to 24hr. insurance information (in North America call ☎877-370-4742, elsewhere call US collect ☎1-715-342-4104; www.isic.org); and insurance benefits for US cardholders (see **Insurance,** p. 27). The ISIC is preferable to an institution-specific card (such as a university ID) because it is more likely to be recognized and honored abroad. Applicants must be degree-seeking students of a secondary or post-secondary school and must be of at least 12 years of age. Because of the proliferation of fake ISICs, some services (particularly airlines) require additional proof of student identity.

The **International Teacher Identity Card (ITIC)** offers teachers the same insurance coverage and similar but limited discounts. For travelers who are 25 years old or under but are not students, the **International Youth Travel Card (IYTC)** offers many of the same benefits as the ISIC. Similarly, the **International Student Exchange ID Card (ISE)** provides discounts, medical benefits, and access to student airfares.

Each of these identity cards costs US$22 or equivalent. ISIC and ITIC cards are valid for roughly one and a half academic years; IYTC cards are valid for one year from the date of issue. Many student travel agencies (see p. 40) issue the cards, including STA Travel in Australia and New Zealand; Travel CUTS in Canada; usit in the Republic of Ireland and Northern Ireland; SASTS in South Africa; Campus Travel and STA Travel in the UK; and Council Travel and STA Travel in the US. For a listing of issuing agencies, or for more information, contact the **International Student Travel Confederation (ISTC),** Herengracht 479, 1017 BS Amsterdam, Netherlands (☎31 20 421 28 00; fax 20 421 28 10; www.isic.org).

CUSTOMS

Upon entering Spain, Portugal, or Morocco, you must declare certain items from abroad and pay a duty on the value of those articles that exceeds the allowance established by the country's customs service. Goods and gifts purchased at **duty-free** shops abroad are not exempt from duty or sales tax at your point of return and thus must be declared as well; "duty-free" merely means that you need not pay a tax in the country of purchase. Duty-free allowances were abolished for travel between EU member states on July 1, 1999, but still exist for those arriving from outside the EU. Upon returning home, you must similarly declare all articles acquired abroad and pay a duty on the value of articles in excess of your home country's allowance. In order to expedite your return, make a list of any valuables brought from home and register them with customs before traveling abroad. Also be sure to keep receipts for all goods acquired abroad. Spain and Morocco have value-added taxes which can be redeemed upon leaving the country. See the **Essentials** sections for **Spain** (p. 87) and **Morocco** (p. 767) for more info.

FURTHER RESOURCES

Australia: Australian Customs National Information Line (in Australia ☎1300 363 263, elsewhere ☎612 6275 6666; www.customs.gov.au).

Canada: Canadian Customs, 2265 St. Laurent Blvd., Ottawa, ON K1G 4K3 (in Canada ☎800-461-9999 (24hr.), elsewhere ☎1-506-636-5064; www.revcan.ca).

Ireland: Customs Information Office, Irish Life Centre, Lower Abbey St., Dublin 1 (☎878 8811; fax 878 0836; www.revenue.ie).

New Zealand: New Zealand Customhouse, 17-21 Whitmore St., Box 2218, Wellington (☎64 473 6099; fax 473 7370; www.customs.govt.nz).

South Africa: Commissioner for Customs and Excise, Private Bag X47, Pretoria 0001 (☎12 422 4000; fax 422 5186; www.sars.gov.za).

United Kingdom: Her Majesty's Customs and Excise, Passenger Enquiry Team, Wayfarer House, Great South West Rd., Feltham, Middlesex TW14 8NP (☎845 010 9000; www.hmce.gov.uk).

United States: US Customs Service, 1330 Pennsylvania Ave. NW, Washington, D.C. 20229 (☎202-354-1000; fax 354-1010; www.customs.gov).

MONEY

CURRENCY & EXCHANGE

The currency chart below is based on August 2004 exchange rates. Check the converter on financial websites such as www.bloomberg.com and www.xe.com for current rates.

CURRENCY		
1 AUS$ = 0.564 EUR = 5.808 DH	1 EUR = 10.449 DH = 1.804 AUS$
1 CDN$ = 0.651 EUR = 6.822 DH	1 EUR = 10.449 DH = 1.536 CDN$
1 NZ$ = 0.477 EUR = 4.996 DH	1 EUR = 10.449 DH = 2.096 NZ$
1 ZAR = 0.097 EUR = 1.011 DH	1 EUR = 10.449 DH = 10.357 ZAR
1 US$ = 0.851 EUR = 10.731 DH	1 EUR = 10.449 DH = 1.1758 US$
1 UK£ = 1.564 EUR = 16.379 DH	1 EUR = 10.449 DH = 0.705 UK£

It's generally cheaper to convert money in Spain, Portugal, or Morocco than at home. While currency exchange will probably be available in your arrival airport, it's wise to bring enough foreign currency to last for the first 24 to 72 hours of a trip. Travelers from the US can get foreign currency from the comfort of home: **International Currency Express** (☎888-278-6628; www.foreignmoney.com) delivers foreign currency or traveler's checks second-day (US$12) at competitive exchange rates.

When changing money, use only exchange bureaus with no more than a 5% margin between buy and sell prices. You lose money on every transaction, so **convert large sums, but no more than you'll need.**

If you use traveler's checks or bills, carry some in small denominations (the equivalent of US$50 or less) for times when you are forced to exchange money at disadvantageous rates. Bring a range of denominations since charges may be levied per check cashed. Store your money in a variety of forms; ideally, you should always carry some cash, some traveler's checks, and an ATM and/or credit card. All travelers should also consider carrying some US dollars (about US$50 worth), which are often preferred by local tellers. However, throwing around dollars for preferential treatment may be offensive, especially in Morocco, and it can attract thieves. It may also mark you as a foreigner and invite locals to jack up prices.

TRAVELER'S CHECKS

Traveler's checks are one of the safest and least troublesome means of carrying funds, though not always the best way to pay in Spain, Portugal, and Morocco. Outside major cities and tourist traps, most vendors prefer cash. **American Express** and **Visa** are the most widely recognized companies, offering a number of services.

While traveling, keep check receipts and a record of which checks you've cashed separate from the checks themselves. Also leave a list of check numbers with someone at home. Never countersign checks until you're ready to cash them, and always bring your passport when you cash them. Many establishments, especially banks, may require several IDs in order to cash traveler's checks. If your checks are lost or stolen, immediately contact a refund center

to be reimbursed; they may require a police report verifying the loss or theft. Ask about toll-free refund hotlines and the location of refund centers when purchasing checks, and always carry emergency cash.

American Express: Checks available with commission at select banks, at all AmEx offices, and online (www.aexp.com; US residents only). AmEx cardholders can also purchase checks by phone (☎888-269-6669). AAA (see p. 49) offers commission-free checks to its members. Checks available in US, Australian, British, Canadian, Japanese, and Euro currencies. *Cheques for Two* can be signed by either of two people traveling together. For purchase locations or more info contact AmEx's service centers: in Australia ☎800 68 80 22, in New Zealand ☎0508 555 358, in the UK ☎080 0587 6023, in the US and Canada ☎800-221-7282, elsewhere call US collect ☎1-801-964-6665.

Citicorp: In the US and Canada, call ☎800-645-6556, in Spain ☎900 97 44 30, in Portugal ☎800 84 41 40, in Morocco and elsewhere call US collect ☎1-813-623-1709. Traveler's checks available at 1-2% commission. Call 24hr.

Travelex/Thomas Cook: In the US and Canada call ☎800-287-7362, in the UK ☎800 62 21 01, elsewhere call the UK collect ☎4417 3331 8950. Checks available at 2% commission. There are no Thomas Cook offices in Spain; banks accept their checks, but charge commission. In Portugal, **Marcus & Harting** will cash checks commission-free in Faro, Lisboa, and the Algarve. In Morocco, **Credit de Maroc** will cash commission-free.

Visa: Checks available (generally with commission) at banks worldwide. For the location of the nearest office, call Visa's service centers: in the US ☎800-227-6811, in the UK ☎080 051 5884, elsewhere call the UK collect ☎44 0207 937 8091. Checks available in US, British, Canadian, Japanese, and Euro currencies.

CREDIT CARDS

Credit cards often offer superior exchange rates—up to 5% better than the retail rate used by banks and other exchange bureaus. Credit cards may also offer services such as insurance or emergency help and are sometimes required to reserve hotel rooms or rental cars. **MasterCard** (a.k.a. EuroCard or Access in Europe) and **Visa** (a.k.a. Carte Bleu or Barclaycard) are the most welcome; **American Express** cards work at some ATMs and in major airports.

Credit cards are also useful for **cash advances,** which allow you to withdraw euros or dirham instantly from associated banks and ATMs. However, transaction fees for all credit card advances (up to US$10 per advance, plus 2-3% extra on foreign transactions after conversion) tend to make credit cards a more costly way of withdrawing cash than ATMs or traveler's checks. In an emergency, however, the transaction fee may prove worth the cost. To be eligible for an advance, you'll need to get a **Personal Identification Number (PIN)** from your credit card company (see **ATM & Debit Cards,** below).

PIN NUMBERS & ATMS. To use an ATM or credit card to withdraw money from an ATM in Europe, you must have a four-digit **Personal Identification Number (PIN).** If your PIN is longer than four digits, ask your bank whether you can just use the first four, or whether you'll need a new one. **Credit cards** don't usually come with PINs, so if you intend to hit up ATMs in Europe with a credit card, call your credit card company before leaving to request one.

People with alphabetic, rather than numerical, PINs may also be thrown off by the lack of letters on European cash machines. The following handy list gives the corresponding numbers to use: 1=QZ; 2=ABC; 3=DEF; 4=GHI; 5=JKL; 6=MNO; 7=PRS; 8=TUV; and 9=WXY.

ATM & DEBIT CARDS

ATM CARDS. ATM (cash) cards are widespread in Spain, Portugal, and Morocco. Depending on the system your home bank uses, you can most likely access your personal bank account from abroad. ATMs get the same wholesale exchange rate as credit cards, but there is often a limit on the amount of money you can withdraw per day (around US$500), and unfortunately computer networks sometimes fail. There is also typically a surcharge of US$1-5 per withdrawal.

DEBIT CARDS. Debit cards can be used wherever the associated credit card company (usually Mastercard or Visa) is accepted, but the money is withdrawn directly from the holder's checking account. Debit cards often also function as ATM cards and can be used to withdraw cash from associated banks and ATMs. The two major international money networks are **Cirrus** (US ☎ 800-424-7787; www.mastercard.com) and **Visa/PLUS** (US ☎ 800-843-7587; www.visa.com). Most ATMs charge a transaction fee.

VISA TRAVELMONEY. This prepaid, PIN-protected card gives 24-hour access to your funds in local currency at more than 700,000 Visa ATMs worldwide, including Spain, Portugal, and Morocco. TravelMoney is safer than carrying cash and provides funds at favorable exchange rates. For local customer assistance or to activate a card in Spain, call ☎ 900 95 11 25, in Portugal ☎ 800 81 14 26. There is no number for local customer assistance in Morocco, but to activate a card call collect ☎ 410 581-9091.

GETTING MONEY FROM HOME

If you run out of money while traveling, the easiest and cheapest solution is to have someone back home make a deposit to your credit card or ATM card. Failing that, consider one of the following options.

WIRING MONEY. It is possible to arrange a **bank money transfer,** which means asking a bank back home to wire money to a bank in Spain, Portugal, or Morocco. This is the cheapest way to transfer cash, but it's also the slowest, usually taking several days. Note that some banks may only release your funds in local currency, potentially sticking you with a poor exchange rate; inquire about this in advance. Money transfer services like **Western Union** are faster and more convenient than bank transfers—but also much pricier. Western Union has many locations worldwide. To find one, visit www.westernunion.com, or call in the US ☎ 800-325-6000, in Canada ☎ 800-235-0000, in the UK ☎ 080 083 3833, in Australia ☎ 800 501 500, in New Zealand ☎ 800 270 000, in South Africa ☎ 0860 100 031, in Spain ☎ 902 11 41 89, in Portugal ☎ 800 20 68 68, and in Morocco ☎ 07 26 15 59. Money transfer services are also available at **American Express** and **Thomas Cook** offices.

US STATE DEPARTMENT (US CITIZENS ONLY). In dire emergencies only, the US State Department will forward money within hours to the nearest consular office, which will then disburse it according to instructions for a US$15 fee. If you wish to use this service, you must contact the Overseas Citizens Service division of the US State Department (☎ 202-647-5225; nights, Sundays, and holidays ☎ 202-647-4000).

COSTS

The cost of your trip will vary considerably, depending on where you go, how you travel, and where you stay. The most significant expenses will probably be your round-trip **airfare** and a **railpass** or **bus pass**. Before you go, spend some time calculating a reasonable per-day **budget** that will meet your needs.

STAYING ON A BUDGET. To give you a general idea, a bare-bones day (camping or staying in cheap hostels or pensions, buying food at grocery stores and markets) in Spain would cost about US$40 (€43), in Portugal about US$30 (€33), and in Morocco about US$20 (200dh); a slightly more comfortable day (sleeping in nicer hostels and the occasional budget hotel, eating one or two meals a day at a restaurant, going out at night) would run US$65 (€71) in Spain, US$50 (€55) in Portugal, and US$40 (400dh) in Morocco. Don't forget to factor in emergency reserve funds (at least US$250) when planning how much money you'll need.

TIPS FOR SAVING MONEY. Search out opportunities for free entertainment, split accommodation and food costs with other trustworthy travelers, and buy food in supermarkets rather than eating out. Bring a **sleepsack** (see p. 29) to save on sheet charges in hostels, and do your **laundry** in the sink (unless you're explicitly prohibited from doing so). With that said, don't go overboard with your budget obsession. Though staying within your budget is important, don't do so at the expense of your health or a great travel experience.

TIPPING, BARGAINING & TAXES

See the individual **Essentials** sections for **Spain** (p. 87), **Portugal** (p. 629), and **Morocco** (p. 767) for specifics on tipping, bargaining, and taxes in each country.

SAFETY & SECURITY

PERSONAL SAFETY

The following section is intended as a general guide; refer to the **Essentials** sections of **Spain** (p. 67), **Portugal** (p. 539), and **Morocco** (p. 662) for more detailed info.

EXPLORING. To avoid unwanted attention, try to blend in as much as possible. Respecting local customs (in many cases, dressing more conservatively) may placate would-be hecklers. Familiarize yourself with your surroundings before setting out, and carry yourself with confidence; if you must check a map, duck into a shop first. If you are traveling alone, be sure someone at home knows your itinerary, and **never admit that you're traveling alone.** When walking at night, stick to busy, well-lit streets; avoid dark alleyways. If you feel uncomfortable, leave as quickly as you can, but don't allow fear of the unknown to turn you into a hermit.

SELF DEFENSE. A good self-defense course will give you concrete ways to react to unwanted advances. **Impact, Prepare, and Model Mugging** can refer you to local self-defense courses in the US (☎800-345-5425). Visit www.impactsafety.org for a list of nearby chapters. Workshops start at US$50; full courses run US$350-500.

DRIVING. If you are using a **car,** learn local driving signals and wear a seatbelt. Children under 40 lbs. should ride in the backseat and only in a specially-designed carseat, available for a small fee from most car rental agencies. Study route maps before you drive, and if you plan on spending a lot of time on the road, you may want to bring spare parts. If your car breaks down, wait for the police to assist you. For long drives in desolate areas, invest in a cellular phone and a roadside assistance program (see p. 49). Be sure to park your vehicle in a garage or well-traveled area, and use a steering wheel locking device in larger cities. **Sleeping in your car** is one of the most dangerous (and often illegal) ways to get your rest.

ESSENTIALS

TERRORISM. While Spain, Portugal, and Morocco are relatively stable countries, there are some terrorist activities that travelers should keep in mind. The militant Basque separatist group ETA bombed a hotel in Benidorm and Alicante, Spain and has carried out attacks on government officials and other popular destinations in the past. Though the attacks are ongoing, they generally target specific public officials, and the threat to travelers is relatively small. There are no particular terrorist threats in Portugal.

Casablanca, Morocco, was bombed in May 2003. The perpetrators have still not been identified, and the potential for transnational terrorism remains relatively high. Travelers should be aware of tension in the region and exercise caution

> **!** **TRAVEL ADVISORIES.** The following government offices provide travel information and advisories by telephone, by fax, or via the web:
>
> **Australian Department of Foreign Affairs and Trade:** ☎ 13 0055 5135; faxback service 02 6261 1299; www.dfat.gov.au.
>
> **Canadian Department of Foreign Affairs and International Trade:** In Canada and the US call ☎ 800-267-6788, elsewhere ☎ 1-613-944-6788; www.dfait-maeci.gc.ca. Call for their free booklet.
>
> **New Zealand Ministry of Foreign Affairs:** ☎ 04 494 8500; fax 494 8506; www.mft.govt.nz/trav.html.
>
> **United Kingdom Foreign and Commonwealth Office:** ☎ 0207 008 0232; fax 008 0155; www.fco.gov.uk.
>
> **United States Department of State:** ☎ 202-647-5225; faxback service 647-3000; travel.state.gov. For the *A Safe Trip Abroad* booklet, ☎ 202-512-1800.

FINANCIAL SECURITY

PROTECTING YOUR VALUABLES. Spain and parts of Portugal are heavily touristed, encouraging a thriving pickpocket trade. Morocco is notorious for the prevalence of theft, even in hostel rooms and other "secure" places. To minimize the financial risk associated with traveling: first, **bring as little luggage with you as possible.** Second, buy a few combination **padlocks** to secure your belongings either in your pack or in a hostel or train station locker. Third, **carry as little cash as possible.** Keep your traveler's checks and ATM/credit cards in a **money belt** along with your passport and ID cards. Fourth, **keep a small cash reserve separate from your primary stash.** This should be about US$50 sewn into or stored in the depths of your pack, along with your traveler's check numbers and copies of important documents.

CON ARTISTS & PICKPOCKETS. In large cities **con artists** often work in groups, and children are among the most effective. Beware of certain classics: sob stories that require money, rolls of bills "found" on the street, mustard spilled onto your shoulder to distract you while they snatch your bag. **Don't ever let your passport and bags out of your sight.** Beware of **pickpockets** in crowds, especially on public transportation. Be alert in telephone booths and at ATMs: if you must say your calling card number, do so very quietly; if you punch in your pin number, make sure no one can look over your shoulder.

ACCOMMODATIONS & TRANSPORTATION. Never leave your belongings unattended; crime occurs in even the most demure-looking hostel or hotel. Bring your own **padlock** for hostel lockers, and ideally store valuables in hostel safes rather than more public, individual lockers.

Be particularly careful on **buses** and **trains;** horror stories abound about determined thieves who wait for travelers to fall asleep. Carry your backpack in front of you where you can see it. When traveling with others, sleep in alternate shifts. When alone, use good judgement in selecting a train compartment: never stay in an empty one, and use a lock to secure your pack to the luggage rack. Try to sleep on top bunks with your luggage stored above you (if not in bed with you), and keep important documents and other valuables on your person, preferably in a money belt, even while you are sleeping. If traveling by **car,** don't leave valuables (such as luggage or radios) in it while you are away.

DRUGS & ALCOHOL

Recreational drugs are illegal in Spain, Portugal, and Morocco. Any attempt to possess, buy, or sell marijuana in Spain or Portugal will definitely land you in jail or with a heavy fine. Morocco is infamous as a supplier of hashish to the Iberian Peninsula; don't be surprised if you are stopped and searched on your way into Spain. The Moroccan government enforces drug laws more strictly than most, and foreigners with drugs have regularly been arrested and severely punished.

HEALTH

Common sense is the simplest prescription for good health while you travel. Travelers complain most often about their feet and their stomach, so take precautionary measures: drink lots of fluids to prevent dehydration, and wear sturdy shoes and clean socks.

BEFORE YOU GO

In your **passport,** write the names of any people you wish to be contacted in case of an emergency, and list any allergies or medical conditions. Matching a prescription to a foreign equivalent is not always easy, safe, or possible, so carry up-to-date, legible prescriptions or a statement from your doctor stating the medication's trade name, manufacturer, chemical name, and dosage. While traveling, be sure to keep all medication with you in your carry-on luggage. For tips on packing a basic first-aid kit and other health essentials, see **Packing,** p. 29.

IMMUNIZATIONS & PRECAUTIONS. Travelers over two years old should be sure that their following vaccines are up to date: MMR (for measles, mumps, and rubella); DTaP or Td (for diphtheria, tetanus, and pertussis); OPV (for polio); HbCV (for haemophilus influenza B); and HBV (for Hepatitis B), although HBV is really only recommended for stays six months or longer. Adults traveling to Morocco on trips longer than four weeks should consider getting a Hepatitis A (or immune globulin) and typhoid vaccine four to six weeks before leaving. See the **Essentials** section for Morocco (p. 764) for more specific information on staying healthy during a stay in North Africa. For recommendations on immunizations and prophylaxis, consult the Centers for Disease Control (CDC) in the US or the equivalent in your home country, and be sure to check with a doctor for guidance.

USEFUL ORGANIZATIONS & PUBLICATIONS. The US **Centers for Disease Control and Prevention** (CDC; ☎877-FYI-TRIP/877-394-8747; fax 888-232-3299; www.cdc.gov/travel) maintains an international traveler's hotline, an international fax information service, and a comprehensive travel website. The CDC's booklet *Health Information for International Travel*, an annual rundown of disease, immunization, and general health advice, is free online or US$25 via the Public Health Foundation (☎877-252-1200). For quick information on health and other travel warnings, call the **Overseas Citizens Services** (☎202-647-5225, after-hours 647-4000; http://travel.state.gov/overseas_citizens.html). Info on medical evacuation services and travel insurance firms can be found on the US government's website at http://travel.state.gov/medical.html or the **British Foreign and Commonwealth Office's** site at www.fco.gov.uk. To find detailed info on travel health, including a country-by-country overview of diseases, try the **International Travel Health Guide** by Stuart Rose, MD (US$24.95; www.travmed.com). General health info is also distributed by the **American Red Cross** (☎800-564-1234; www.redcross.org).

MEDICAL ASSISTANCE ABROAD. If you are concerned about obtaining medical care while traveling, you may wish to employ special support services. *MedPass* from **GlobalCare, Inc.,** 6875 Shiloh Rd. East, Alpharetta, GA 30005, USA (☎800-860-1111; fax 678-341-1800; www.globalems.com), provides 24hr. international medical assistance and evacuation resources. The **International Association for Medical Assistance to Travelers** (IAMAT; in US ☎716-754-4883, in Canada 519-836-0102; www.cybermall.co.nz/NZ/IAMAT) has free membership, lists English-speaking doctors worldwide, and offers detailed info on immunization requirements and sanitation. If your regular **insurance** policy does not cover travel abroad, you may wish to purchase additional coverage (see p. 27).

Those with medical conditions (diabetes, allergies to antibiotics, epilepsy, heart conditions, etc.) can obtain a **Medic Alert** membership (first year US$35, annually thereafter US$20), which includes a stainless steel ID tag and a 24hr. collect-call number. Contact the Medic Alert Foundation, 2323 Colorado Ave, Turlock, CA 95382, USA (☎888-633-4298, outside US1-209-668-3333; www.medicalert.org).

ONCE ABROAD

ENVIRONMENTAL HAZARDS
Neither Spain, Portugal, nor Morocco has a very extreme climate; the biggest environmental threat for most travelers is the sun. Stay aware of how much time you're spending lying on Spanish beaches or sweating in Moroccan sand dunes. To avoid dehydration, avoid alcohol, caffeine, and salty foods. Be sure to drink plenty of fluids. Prevent sunburn by covering exposed skin and bringing sunscreen.

INSECT-BORNE DISEASES
Be aware of **mosquitoes** and other arthropods while hiking and camping, especially in wet or forested areas. Mosquitoes are most active from dusk to dawn. Wear long pants and long sleeves, tuck your pants into your socks, and buy a mosquito net. Use insect repellents containing DEET, and soak or spray your gear with permethrin (licensed in the US for use on clothing). Consider natural repellents that make you unattractive to insects, like vitamin B-12 or garlic pills. To stop the itch after being bitten, try Calamine lotion or topical cortisones (like Cortaid), or take a bath with a half-cup of baking soda or oatmeal. **Ticks,** responsible for Lyme and other diseases, can be particularly dangerous in forested regions, such as northern Spain and Portugal. Pause periodically while walking to brush off ticks using a fine-toothed comb on your neck and scalp. Do not try to remove ticks by burning them or coating them with nail polish remover or petroleum jelly.

> **Malaria:** Extremely limited risk, only in some rural parts of Morocco. Early symptoms include fever, chills, aches, and fatigue, followed by high fever and sweating, sometimes with vomiting and diarrhea. See a doctor for any flu-like sickness that occurs after travel in a risk area. Left untreated, malaria can cause anemia, kidney failure, coma, and death. To reduce the risk of contracting malaria, use mosquito repellent, particularly in the evenings and when visiting forested areas, and take oral prophylactics, like **mefloquine** (sold under the name Lariam) or **doxycycline** (prescription only).

Tick-borne encephalitis: A slight risk in the few forested areas of Spain and Portugal. A viral infection of the central nervous system transmitted by tick bites (primarily in wooded areas) or unpasteurized dairy products. While a vaccine is available in Europe, the immunization schedule is impractical, and the risk of contracting the disease is relatively low, especially if precautions are taken against tick bites.

Lyme disease: Also a slight risk in forested areas of Spain and Portugal. A bacterial infection carried by ticks and marked by a circular bull's-eye rash of 2 in. or more. Later symptoms include fever, headache, fatigue, and aches and pains. Antibiotics are effective if administered early. Left untreated, Lyme can cause problems in joints, the heart, and the nervous system. If you find a tick attached to your skin, grasp the head with tweezers as close to your skin as possible and apply slow, steady traction. Removing a tick within 24hr. greatly reduces the risk of infection.

FOOD & WATER-BORNE DISEASES

Prevention is the best cure: be sure that everything you eat is cooked properly and that the water you drink is clean. Peel your fruits and veggies and avoid tap water (including ice cubes and anything washed in tap water, like salad). Watch out for food from markets or street vendors that may have been cooked in unhygienic conditions. Other culprits are raw shellfish, unpasteurized milk, and sauces containing raw eggs. Buy bottled water, or purify your own water by bringing it to a rolling boil or treating it with **iodine tablets.**

▨ Traveler's diarrhea: Results from drinking untreated water or eating uncooked foods; a temporary (and fairly common) reaction to the bacteria in new food ingredients. Symptoms include nausea, bloating, urgency, and malaise. Try quick-energy, non-sugary foods with protein and carbohydrates to keep your strength up. Over-the-counter anti-diarrheals (e.g. Immodium) may counteract the problems, but can complicate serious infections. The most dangerous side effect is **dehydration;** drink 8 oz. of water with ½ tsp. of sugar or honey and a pinch of salt, try decaffeinated soft drinks, or munch on salted crackers. If you develop a fever or your symptoms persist more than 5 days, consult a doctor. Immediately consult a doctor for treatment of diarrhea in children.

Dysentery: Results from a serious intestinal infection caused by certain bacteria. The most common type is bacillary dysentery, also called shigellosis. Symptoms include bloody diarrhea (sometimes mixed with mucus), fever, and abdominal pain and tenderness. Bacillary dysentery generally only lasts a week, but it is highly contagious. Amoebic dysentery, which develops more slowly, is a more serious disease and may cause long-term damage if left untreated. Seek medical help immediately for both. A stool test can determine which kind you have. Dysentery can be treated with the drugs norfloxacin or ciprofloxacin (commonly known as Cipro). If you are traveling in Morocco (especially rural regions), consider obtaining a prescription before you leave home.

Hepatitis A: A viral infection of the liver acquired primarily through contaminated water. Symptoms include fatigue, fever, loss of appetite, nausea, dark urine, jaundice, vomiting, aches and pains, and light stools. The risk is highest in rural areas and the countryside, especially in Morocco, but it is also present in urban areas throughout Spain, Portugal, and Morocco. Ask your doctor about the vaccine (Havrix or Vaqta) or an injection of immune globulin (IG).

Parasites: Microbes, tapeworms, etc. that hide in unsafe water and food. **Giardia,** for example, is acquired by drinking untreated water from streams or lakes all over the world, including Spain, Portugal, and Morocco. Symptoms include swollen glands or lymph nodes, fever, rashes or itchiness, digestive problems, eye problems, and anemia. Boil water, wear shoes, avoid bugs, and eat only thoroughly cooked food.

Typhoid fever: Caused by the salmonella bacteria; common in villages and rural areas in Morocco. While mostly transmitted through contaminated food and water, it may also be acquired by direct contact with another person. Symptoms include fever, headaches, fatigue, loss of appetite, constipation, and a rash on the abdomen or chest. Antibiotics can treat typhoid, but a vaccination (70-90% effective) is usually recommended.

OTHER INFECTIOUS DISEASES

Rabies: Really only a risk for those who may be exposed to wild or domestic animals during their travel. Transmitted through the saliva of infected animals; fatal if untreated. By the time thirst and muscle spasms appear, the disease is in its terminal stage. If you are bitten, wash the wound and seek immediate medical care. A rabies vaccine, which consists of 3 shots given over a 21-day period, is only semi-effective.

Hepatitis B: A viral infection of the liver transmitted via bodily fluids or needle-sharing. Symptoms may not surface until years after infection. Vaccinations are recommended for health-care workers, sexually-active travelers, and anyone planning to seek medical treatment abroad. The 3-shot vaccination series must begin 6 months before traveling.

Hepatitis C: Like Hep B, but the mode of transmission differs. IV drug users, those with occupational exposure to blood, hemodialysis patients, and recipients of blood transfusions are at the highest risk, but the disease can also be spread through sexual contact or sharing items like razors and toothbrushes that may have traces of blood on them.

AIDS, HIV & OTHER STDS

For detailed information on **Acquired Immune Deficiency Syndrome (AIDS)** in Spain, Portugal, and Morocco, call the **US Centers for Disease Control's** 24hr. hotline at ☎800-342-2437, or the **Joint United Nations Programme on HIV/AIDS (UNAIDS)**, 20 av. Appia 20, CH-1211 Geneva 27, Switzerland (☎41 22 791 36 66; fax 22 791 41 87; www.unaids.org). Spain, Portugal, and Morocco may deny long-term residence to those who test HIV-positive, but they generally do not deny tourist, student, and work visa applications on the basis of HIV status, even when medical tests are required. Contact the nearest consulate.

Sexually transmitted diseases (STDs) such as gonorrhea, chlamydia, genital warts, syphilis, and herpes are easier to catch than HIV and can be just as deadly. **Hepatitis B** and **C** are also serious STDs (see **Other Infectious Diseases,** above). **Condoms** may protect you from some STDs, but oral or even tactile contact can lead to transmission. Warning signs include swelling, sores, bumps, or blisters on sex organs, the rectum, or the mouth; burning and pain during urination and bowel movements; itching around sex organs; swelling or redness of the throat; and flu-like symptoms. If these symptoms develop, see a doctor immediately.

WOMEN'S HEALTH

Women traveling in unsanitary conditions are vulnerable to **urinary tract** and **bladder infections,** common and very uncomfortable bacterial conditions that cause a burning sensation and painful (sometimes frequent) urination. To try to avoid these infections, drink plenty of vitamin-C-rich juice and clean water, and urinate frequently, especially right after intercourse. Untreated, these infections can lead to kidney infections, sterility, and even death. If symptoms persist, see a doctor.

Vaginal yeast infections may flare up in hot and humid climates. Wearing loosely fitting trousers or a skirt and cotton underwear will help, as will over-the-counter remedies like Monistat or Gynelotrimin. Bring supplies from home if you are prone to infection, as it may be embarrassing, if not difficult, to explain your predicament

INSURANCE ■ **27**

to a foreign druggist. Since **tampons, pads,** and reliable **contraceptive devices** are sometimes hard to find when traveling in rural areas of Spain, Portugal, and Morocco, consider bringing supplies with you.

Abortions are illegal in Spain, Portugal, and Morocco, except to save the life of the woman. Women considering an abortion while traveling can contact the **International Planned Parenthood Federation** (**IPPF;** ☎0207 487 7900; fax 487 7950; www.ippf.org) for guidance. In the US and Canada, the **National Abortion Federation Hotline** (in the US ☎800-772-9100, in Canada 800-424-2280; available M-F 9am-10pm) provides referrals.

INSURANCE

Travel insurance generally covers four basic areas: medical or health problems, property loss, trip cancellation or interruption, and emergency evacuation. Prices generally run about US$50 per week for full coverage; trip cancellation or interruption may be purchased separately for about US$5.50 per US$100 of coverage.

Medical insurance (especially university policies) often covers costs incurred abroad; check with your provider. **US Medicare** does not cover foreign travel. **Canadians** are protected by their home province's health insurance plan for up to 90 days after leaving the country; check with the provincial Ministry of Health or Health Plan Headquarters for details.

ISIC and **ITIC** (see p. 14) provide basic insurance benefits, including US$100 per day of in-hospital sickness for up to 60 days, US$3000 of accident-related medical reimbursement, and US$25,000 for emergency medical transport. Cardholders have access to a toll-free 24hr. helpline for medical, legal, and financial emergencies overseas (in the US and Canada ☎877-370-4742, elsewhere call US collect ☎1-715-345-0505). **American Express** (US ☎800-528-4800) grants most cardholders automatic car rental insurance (collision and theft, but not liability) and travel accident coverage of US$100,000 on ticket purchases made with the card. **Homeowners' insurance** often covers theft during travel and loss of travel documents (passport, plane ticket, etc.) up to US$500.

Council Travel and **STA** (see p. 40) can supplement your basic travel coverage. Other private insurance providers in the US and Canada include: **Access America** (☎800-284-8300; www.accessamerica.com); **Berkely Group/Carefree Travel Insurance** (☎800-323-3149; www.berkely.com); **Globalcare Travel Insurance** (☎800-821-2488; www.globalcare-cocco.com); and **Travel Assistance International** (☎800-821-2828; www.europ-assisstance.com). **Columbus Direct** (☎020 7375 0011; www.columbus-direct.net) provides insurance in the **UK**. In **Australia,** try **AFTA** (☎02 9264 3299).

PACKING

Pack lightly: lay out only what you absolutely need, then take half the clothes and twice the money. If you plan to do a lot of hiking, see **Camping & the Outdoors,** p. 32.

LUGGAGE. If you plan to cover most of your itinerary by foot, a sturdy **frame backpack** is unbeatable. (For the basics on buying a pack, see p. 32.) Toting a **suitcase** or **trunk** is fine if you plan to stay in one or two cities and explore from there, but a very bad idea if you're going to be moving around a lot. In addition to your main piece of luggage, a **daypack** (a small backpack or courier bag) is a must.

CLOTHING. No matter when you're traveling, it's a good idea to bring a warm jacket or wool sweater, a rain jacket (Gore-Tex® is both waterproof and breathable), sturdy shoes or hiking boots, and thick socks. Flip-flops or waterproof san-

dals are crucial for hostel showers. You may also want a nice outfit, as many nightlife sights will not allow jeans or sneakers. Remember also that if you plan to visit any religious or cultural sights, you will need appropriately respectful covering. Men should wear long pants and women should err to the side of modesty, covering shoulders, legs, and head.

SLEEPSACK. Some hostels require that you either provide your own linen or rent sheets from them. Save cash by making your own **sleepsack**: fold a full-size sheet in half the long way, then sew it closed along the long side and one short side.

CONVERTERS & ADAPTERS. In Spain and Portugal, electricity is 220 volts AC; most of Morocco runs on 220V as well, though some smaller towns still have 110V outlets. **Americans** and **Canadians** should buy an **adapter** (which changes the shape of the plug; US$10) and a **converter** (which changes the voltage; about US$20). **New Zealanders** and **South Africans** (who both use 220V at home), as well as **Australians** (who use 240/250V), won't need a converter, but will need a set of adapters. For more info on converters and adapters, check http://kropla.com/electric.htm.

TOILETRIES. Toothbrushes, towels, cold-water soap, deodorant, razors, tampons, and condoms may be difficult to find in rural areas; pack some extras. **Contact lenses** can be expensive and hard to come by, so stock up on extra pairs and enough solution for your entire trip. Don't forget your glasses and a copy of your prescription in case you need emergency replacements.

FIRST-AID KIT. For a basic first-aid kit, pack bandages, aspirin or other painkillers, antibiotic cream, a thermometer, a Swiss Army knife (although this can not be taken through airport security), tweezers, moleskin, decongestant, motion-sickness remedy, diarrhea or upset-stomach medication (Pepto Bismol or Immodium), an antihistamine (like Benadryl), sunscreen, insect repellent, and burn ointment.

FILM. Film and developing in Spain, Portugal, and Morocco can get expensive, so consider bringing along enough film for your entire trip and developing it at home. Despite disclaimers, airport security X-rays *can* fog film, so buy a lead-lined pouch at a camera store or ask security to hand inspect rolls of film. Always pack it in your carry-on luggage, since higher-intensity X-rays are used on checked luggage.

CELLULAR PHONES. A cell phone can be a lifesaver (literally) on the road; if you own a cell phone and are traveling abroad, it most likely will not work when you arrive at your destination. Companies like Cellular Abroad (www.cellular-abroad.com) rent cell phones that work in many international destinations, providing a more reliable option than attempting to pick up a phone in-country.

OTHER USEFUL ITEMS. For safety purposes, you should bring a **money belt** (a pouch that ties around your waist under your clothes) and small **padlock.** Quick repairs of torn garments can be done on the road with a needle and thread; also consider bringing electrical tape for patching tears. Doing your laundry by hand (where it is allowed) is both cheaper and more convenient than doing it at a laundromat, so bring **detergent**. Other items to bring: an umbrella, sealable **plastic bags** (for damp or dirty clothes, soap, food, shampoo, and other spillables), an **alarm clock,** safety pins, rubber bands, a flashlight, earplugs, and a small **calculator.**

ACCOMMODATIONS

For more specific information on accommodations, see the **Essentials** sections for **Spain** (p. 88), **Portugal** (p. 632), and **Morocco** (p. 769).

ESSENTIALS

HOTELS, HOSTALES & PENSIONES

Hotel and **hostal** singles in Spain cost US$22-30 per night, while doubles cost US$35-40. In Portugal rates run US$20-30. You'll typically share a hall bathroom; a private bathroom will cost extra. Smaller **pensiones** are often cheaper than hotels. If you make reservations in writing, indicate your night of arrival and the number of nights you plan to stay. The hotel will send you a confirmation and may request payment for the first night. Not all hotels take reservations, and few accept checks in foreign currency. Enclosing two International Reply Coupons will ensure a prompt reply (each US$1.05; available at any post office).

YOUTH HOSTELS

Youth hostels are generally dorm-style accommodations, often in single-sex large rooms with bunk beds, although some hostels do offer private rooms for families and couples. They sometimes have kitchens and utensils for your use, bike or moped rentals, storage areas, and laundry facilities. There can be drawbacks: some hostels close during certain daytime "lockout" hours, have a curfew, don't accept reservations, and impose a maximum stay, or, less frequently, require that you do chores. In Spain, a bed in a hostel will average around US$13-18 per night, while a night in a Portuguese hostel will be around US$10-15. Though there are fewer youth hostels in Morocco, they only cost about US$4 per night.

HOSTELLING INTERNATIONAL

Joining the youth hostel association in your own country automatically grants you membership privileges in **Hostelling International (HI),** a federation of national hostelling associations that offer accommodations at significantly cheaper prices than private lodgings. HI hostels are scattered throughout Spain, Portugal, and Morocco and many accept reservations via the **International Booking Network** (in the US ☎ 202-783-6161; www.hostelbooking.com). To research hostelling in Spain and Portugal, check out HI's website (www.iyhf.org) or these other comprehensive websites: www.hostels.com, www.hostalbooking.com, and www.hostelplanet.com. All prices listed below are valid for **one-year memberships** unless otherwise noted.

Australian Youth Hostels Association (AYHA), 422 Kent St., Sydney NSW 2000 (☎ 2 9261 1111; fax 9261 1969; www.yha.org.au). AUS$52, under 18 AUS$16.

Hostelling International-Canada (HI-C), 400-205 Catherine St., Ottawa, ON K2P 1C3 (☎ 800-663-5777 or 613-237-7884; fax 237-7868; www.hihostels.ca). CDN$35, under 18 free.

An Óige (Irish Youth Hostel Association), 61 Mountjoy St., Dublin 7 (☎ 1 830 4555; fax 830 5808; www.irelandyha.org). €25, under 18 €10.50.

Hostelling International Northern Ireland (HINI), 22-32 Donegall Rd., Belfast BT12 5JN (☎ 28 9032 4733, fax 28 9043 9699; www.hini.org.uk). UK£10, under 18 UK£6, family UK£20.

Youth Hostels Association of New Zealand (YHANZ), P.O. Box 436, Level 1, Moorhouse City, 166 Moorhouse Ave., Christchurch 1 (☎ 3 379 9970; fax 365 4476; www.yha.org.nz). NZ$40, under 17 free.

Hostels Association of South Africa, 3rd fl. 73 St. George's House, P.O. Box 4402, Cape Town 8000 (☎ 424 2511; fax 424 4119; www.hisa.org.za). ZAR79, under 18 ZAR40, lifetime ZAR299.

Youth Hostels Association (England and Wales) Ltd., Trevelyan House, Dimple Rd., Matlock, Derbyshire DE4 3YH (☎ 16 2959 2600, fax 16 2959 2702; www.yha.org.uk). UK£13.50, under 18 UK£6.75, families UK£27.

Scottish Youth Hostels Association (SYHA), 7 Glebe Crescent, Stirling FK8 2JA (☎87 0155 3255; fax 1330 8562; www.syha.org.uk). UK£6, under 18 UK£2.50.

Hostelling International-American Youth Hostels (HI-AYH), 8401 Colesville Rd., Suite 600, Silver Spring, MD 20910 (☎301-495-1240; fax 495-6697; www.hiayh.org). US$28, under 18 free.

UNIVERSITY DORMS

Many **colleges and universities** open their residence halls to travelers when school is not in session; some do so even during term-time. Getting a room may take a few phone calls and require advance planning, but the low room rates are worth it.

CAMPING & THE OUTDOORS

For more specific information on camping, hiking, and biking, write or call the publishers listed below to receive a free catalog. Campers heading to Spain and Portugal should consider buying an **International Camping Carnet.** Similar to a hostel membership card, it's required at some campgrounds and provides discounts at others. It is available in North America from the **Family Campers and RVers Association** and in the UK from **The Caravan Club** (see below). An excellent general resource for travelers planning on camping or spending time in the outdoors is the **Great Outdoor Recreation Pages** (www.gorp.com).

Automobile Association, A.A. Publishing. Orders and inquiries to TBS Frating Distribution Center, Colchester, Essex, CO7 7DW, UK (☎19 1223 7071; www.theaa.co.uk). Publishes *Caravan and Camping: Europe* (UK£9) and *Britain and Ireland* (UK£8), as well as big road atlases for Europe, including Spain.

The Caravan Club (☎013 4232 6944; www.caravanclub.co.uk). For UK£27.50, members receive equipment discounts, maps, and a monthly magazine.

Sierra Club Books (☎415-977-5500; www.sierraclub.org/books). Publishes general resource books on hiking, camping, and women traveling in the outdoors.

The Mountaineers Books (☎800-553-4453; www.mountaineersbooks.org). Over 600 titles on hiking, biking, mountaineering, natural history, and conservation.

NATIONAL PARKS

Spain and Portugal have quite an extensive national park system, including nature preserves and historic monuments, which offers numerous opportunities for hiking, mountaineering, and, generally avoiding the cities. Camping is usually forbidden within national park boundaries, but campgrounds can be found in most nearby towns. The general procedure is to stock up on equipment and supplies in nearby towns, stop by the visitors information center to pick up free maps, and head into the park. More detailed maps, with specific hiking or adventure information, can be purchased both at the visitors centers and in nearby towns.

WILDERNESS SAFETY

THE GREAT OUTDOORS. Stay warm, stay dry, and stay hydrated. The vast majority of life-threatening wilderness situations can be avoided by following this simple advice. Prepare yourself for an emergency, however, by always packing rain gear, a hat and mittens, a first-aid kit, a reflector, a whistle, high-energy food, and extra water for any hike. Dress in wool or warm layers of synthetic materials designed for the outdoors; never rely on cotton for warmth, as it is useless when wet. See **Suggestions for Hikers,** p. 549, for useful information on hiking. See **Health,** p. 22, for info about outdoor ailments and medical concerns.

Check **weather forecasts** and pay attention to the skies when hiking, since weather patterns can change suddenly. Whenever possible, let someone know when and where you are going hiking, either a friend, your hostel, a park ranger, or a local hiking organization. Do not attempt a hike beyond your ability—you may be endangering your life.

WILDLIFE. You may encounter Pyrenean bears roaming throughout the Pyrenees and on the many excellent hiking trails. Stay calm, and make sure to collect and properly dispose of all trash you generate at campsites to keep the bears at bay. Thousands of birds descend on the Parque Nacional Coto de Doñana every year during their annual migration; bring binoculars. The wildest wildlife in Spain, Floquet de Neu (Snowflake), Barcelona's famous albino gorilla, has recently been diagnosed with cancer.

CAMPING & HIKING EQUIPMENT

Good camping equipment is both sturdy and light. Camping equipment is generally more expensive in Australia, New Zealand, and the UK than in North America. Key components of a successful wilderness adventure in Spain, Portugal, or Morocco include a down or synthetic **sleeping bag** (with pad), a free-standing or dome **tent** with groundcloth, and an internal or external frame **backpack** with a waterproof cover. Haul your stuff around wearing **hiking boots** with good ankle support that can fit comfortably over two pairs of **wool socks.**

The promotion of outdoor activity equipment has burgeoned into quite a niche industry, offering many cumulatively expensive necessities. **Synthetic** layers, like those made of polypropylene, and a **pile jacket** will keep you warm even when wet. A **"space blanket"** will help you retain your body heat and doubles as a groundcloth (US$5-15). Plastic **water bottles** are virtually shatter- and leak-proof. Bring **water-purification tablets** for when you can't boil water. Although most campgrounds provide campfire sites, you may want to bring a small **metal grate** or **grill** of your own.

Virtually every organized campground in Europe forbids fires and the gathering of firewood, so you'll need a **camp stove** (the classic Coleman starts at US$45) and a propane-filled **fuel bottle** to operate it. Don't forget a **first-aid kit, pocketknife, insect repellent, calamine lotion,** and **waterproof matches** or a **lighter.**

The mail-order/online companies listed below offer lower prices than many retail stores, but a visit to a local camping or outdoors store will give you a good sense of the look and weight of certain items.

Campmor, 28 Parkway, P.O. Box 700, Upper Saddle River, NJ 07458, USA (US ☎888-226-7667; www.campmor.com).

Discount Camping, 880 Main North Rd., Pooraka, South Australia 5095, Australia (☎08 8262 3399; fax 8260 6240; www.discountcamping.com.au).

Eastern Mountain Sports (EMS), 1 Vose Farm Rd., Peterborough, NH 03458, USA (☎888-463-6367; www.ems.com).

L.L. Bean, Freeport, ME 04033, USA (in the US and Canada ☎800-441-5713, in the UK ☎08 0089 1297; www.llbean.com).

Mountain Designs, 51 Bishop St., Kelvin Grove, Queensland 4059, Australia (☎07 3856 2344; fax 3856 0366; www.mountaindesigns.com).

Recreational Equipment, Inc. (REI). Sumner, WA 98352, USA (in the US and Canada ☎800-426-4840, elsewhere 253-891-2500; www.rei.com).

YHA Adventure Shop, 19 High St., Staines, Middlesex, TW18 4QY, UK (☎17 8445 8625; fax 464 573; www.yhaadventure.com). The main branch of one of Britain's largest outdoor equipment suppliers.

ORGANIZED ADVENTURE TRIPS

Organized adventure tours offer another way of exploring the wild. Activities include hiking, biking, skiing, canoeing, kayaking, rafting, climbing, photo safaris, and archaeological digs. Tourism bureaus can often suggest parks, trails, and outfitters; other good sources for info are stores and organizations that specialize in camping and outdoor equipment like REI and EMS (see above).

Specialty Travel Index, (☎800-442-4922 or 415-459-4900; fax 415-459-9474; www.specialtytravel.com). Tours worldwide.

 ENVIRONMENTALLY RESPONSIBLE TOURISM. The idea behind responsible tourism is to leave no trace of human presence behind. A camp stove is the safer (and more efficient) way to cook than using vegetation, but if you must make a fire, keep it small and use only dead branches or brush rather than cutting vegetation. Make sure your campsite is at least 150 ft. (50m) from water supplies or bodies of water. If there are no toilet facilities, bury human waste (but not paper) at least four inches (10cm) deep and above the high-water line, and 150 ft. or more from any water supplies and campsites. Always pack your trash in a plastic bag and carry it with you until you reach the next trash receptacle. For more information on these issues, contact one of the organizations listed below.

Earthwatch, 3 Clock Tower Place #100, Box 75, Maynard, MA 01754, USA (☎800-776-0188 or 978-461-0081; www.earthwatch.org).

International Ecotourism Society, 28 Pine St., Burlington, VT 05402, USA (☎802-651-9818; fax 651-9819; www.ecotourism.org).

National Audubon Society, Nature Odysseys, 700 Broadway, New York, NY 10003 (☎212-979-3000; fax 979-3188; www.audubon.org).

Tourism Concern, Stapleton House, 277-281 Holloway Rd., London N7 8HN, UK (☎020 7753 3330; fax 7753 3331; www.tourismconcern.org.uk).

KEEPING IN TOUCH
BY MAIL

ESSENTIALS

See the **Essentials** sections for **Spain** (p. 89), **Portugal** (p. 633), and **Morocco** (p. 769) for more detailed information about mailing from abroad.

SENDING MAIL

Airmail is the best way to send mail home from Spain, Portugal, or Morocco. **Aerogrammes,** printed sheets that fold into envelopes and travel via airmail, are available at post offices. Write *par avion* on the front. Most post offices will charge exorbitant fees or simply refuse to send aerogrammes with enclosures. **Surface mail** is by far the cheapest yet slowest way to send mail. It takes one to three months to cross the Atlantic and two to four to cross the Pacific—good for items you won't need to see for a while, such as souvenirs or other articles you've acquired along the way that are weighing down your pack. Postage is readily available at local post offices or *estancos*. To the United States, postcards and letters generally cost about €0.70, and may take several weeks to arrive. For more information on mailing to your country from abroad, see the websites listed below.

Australia: www.auspost.com.au.

Canada: www.canadapost.ca.

Ireland: www.anpost.ie.

New Zealand: www.nzpost.co.nz.

United Kingdom: www.postoffice.co.uk.

United States: www.usps.com.

To send mail abroad from home, mark envelopes "air mail" or *par avion* or your letter or postcard will never arrive. There are several ways to arrange pick-up of letters sent to you while you are abroad. In addition to the standard postage system whose rates are listed below, **Federal Express** (in the US and Canada ☎800-247-4747, in Australia ☎13 26 10, in New Zealand ☎0800 73 33 39, in the UK ☎08 0012 3800; www.fedex.com) handles express mail services from most home countries to Spain, Portugal, and Morocco, but the fees can be substantially greater. For example, they can get a letter from New York to Madrid in 1 day for a whopping US$300, or in two days for a slightly more reasonable US$40; rates among non-US locations are similarly expensive (London to Madrid, for example, costs upwards of US$35).

RECEIVING MAIL

There are several ways to arrange pick-up of letters sent to you by friends and relatives while you are abroad. Mail can be sent internationally via **Lista de Correos** in Spain, **Posta Restante** in Portugal, or **Poste Restante** in Morocco to almost any city or town in Spain, Portugal, or Morocco with a post office and is fairly reliable. Mark the envelope "HOLD" and address it with the last name capitalized and underlined, like so:

Spain: <u>PHILLIPS</u>, Catherine; Lista de Correos; Post Office Street Address; City; Postal Code; SPAIN; PAR AVION.

Portugal: <u>RUSSO</u>, Katie; Posta Restante; Post Office Street Address; City; Postal Code; PORTUGAL; PAR AVION.

Morocco: Moroccan post offices often misplace or automatically return held mail. If you want to try, mail should be addressed as follows: <u>JIN</u>, KANG-XING; Poste Restante; Post Office Address; City; MOROCCO; PAR AVION.

The mail will go to a special desk in the central post office, unless you specify a post office by street address or postal code. As a rule, it is best to use the largest post office in the area, and mail may be sent there regardless of what is written on the envelope. It is usually safer and quicker, though a little more expensive, to send mail express or registered. When picking up your mail, bring a form of photo ID, preferably a passport. There is generally no surcharge; if there is one, it should not exceed the cost of postage. If the clerks insist there is nothing for you, have them check under your first name as well. *Let's Go* lists post offices in the **Practical Information** section for each city and town.

American Express travel offices worldwide offer a free **client letter service** (mail held up to 30 days and forwarded upon request) for cardholders who contact them in advance. Address the letter in the same way shown above. Some offices will offer these services to non-cardholders (especially AmEx Travelers Cheque holders), but call ahead to make sure. *Let's Go* lists AmEx office locations for most large cities in **Practical Information** sections; for a complete list, call ☎ 800-528-4800.

OTHER OPTIONS. DHL (in the US ☎ 800-225-5345, in Spain ☎ 902 12 24 24, in Portugal ☎ 218 10 00 99, in Morocco ☎ 212 297 20 20; www.dhl-usa.com) can get a document from New York to Madrid in 1-2 days for US$39.

BY TELEPHONE

CALLING HOME

A **calling card** is probably your cheapest bet. Calls are billed collect or to your account. You can frequently call collect without even possessing a company's calling card just by calling their access number and following the instructions. **To obtain a calling card** from your national telecommunications service before leaving home, contact the appropriate company listed below (using the numbers in the first column). To **call home with a calling card,** contact the operator for your service provider in Spain, Portugal, or Morocco by dialing the appropriate toll-free access number (listed below in the second column).

Let's Go has recently partnered with **ekit.com** to provide a calling card that offers a number of services, including email and voice messaging. Before purchasing any calling card, always be sure to compare rates with other cards, and to make sure it serves your needs (a local phonecard is generally better for local calls, for instance). For more information, visit www.letsgo.ekit.com.

PLACING INTERNATIONAL CALLS. To call Spain, Portugal, or Morocco from home or to place an international call from abroad, dial:
1. The **international dialing prefix.** To dial out of **Australia,** dial 0011; **Canada** and the **United States,** 011; **Ireland, Morocco, New Zealand, Portugal, Spain,** and the **United Kingdom,** 00; **South Africa,** 09.
2. The **country code** of the country you want to call. To call **Australia,** dial 61; **Canada** and the **United States,** 1; **Ireland,** 353; **Morocco,** 212; **New Zealand,** 64; **Portugal,** 351; **South Africa,** 27; **Spain,** 34; the **United Kingdom,** 44.
3. The **local number,** including the **city** or **area code.** *Let's Go* lists city and area codes as part of local numbers. Phone codes for cities and towns in Spain, Portugal, and Morocco are also listed opposite the city or town name, alongside the ☎ icon. If the first digit is a zero (e.g., 09 for Tangier), omit it when calling from abroad (e.g., dial 011 212 9 from Canada to reach Tangier).

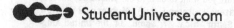

COMPANY	TO OBTAIN A CARD, DIAL:	TO CALL ABROAD, DIAL:
AT&T (US)	800-288-4685	**Spain:** 900 99 0011 **Portugal:** 800 800 128 **Morocco:** 002 11 0011
British Telecom Direct	800 34 51 44	**Spain:** 900 99 0044 **Portugal:** 800 800 440 **Morocco:** 002 11 0044
Canada Direct	800-668-6878	**Spain:** 900 99 0015 **Portugal:** 800 800 122 **Morocco:** 002 11 0010
Eircom (Ireland)	800 40 00 00	**Spain:** 900 990 353 **Portugal:** 810 800 353 **Morocco:** 002 11 0353
MCI (US)	800-444-3333	**Spain:** 800 09 9357 **Portugal:** 800 800 123 **Morocco:** 002 11 0012
Sprint (US)	800 877-4646	**Spain:** 900 99 0013 **Portugal:** 800 800 640 **Morocco:** No service.
Telecom New Zealand	0800 00 00 00	**Spain:** 900 99 0064 **Portugal:** 800 800 640 **Morocco:** No service.
Telkom South Africa	10 219	**Spain:** 900 99 0027 **Portugal:** 800 800 2700 **Morocco:** No service.
Telstra Australia	13 22 00	**Spain:** 900 99 6138 **Portugal:** 800 861 799 **Morocco:** No service.

You can usually also make **direct international calls** from pay phones, but if you aren't using a calling card, you may need to drop your coins as quickly as your words. Where available, prepaid phone cards (see below) and occasionally major credit cards can be used for direct international calls. (See the box on **Placing International Calls** (p. 35) for directions on how to place a direct international call.)

Placing a collect call through an international operator is even more expensive, but may be necessary in case of emergency. You can place collect calls through the service providers listed above even if you don't have one of their phone cards.

CALLING WITHIN SPAIN, PORTUGAL & MOROCCO

The simplest way to call within the country is to use a pay phone. **Prepaid phone cards** (available at tobacco stores and newspaper kiosks), which carry a certain amount of phone time depending on the card's denomination, usually save time and money in the long run—in fact, some phones only accept cards. The computerized phone will tell you how much time, in units, you have left on your card. Another kind of prepaid telephone card comes with a Personal Identification Number (PIN) and a toll-free access number. Instead of inserting the card into the phone, you call the access number. These cards can be used to make international as well as domestic calls. Phone rates tend to be highest in the morning, lower in the evening, and lowest on Sunday and late at night.

CALLING CARD OPTIONS

Many phone companies, such as **MCI WorldPhone,** provide services such as legal and medical advice, exchange rate information, and translation. **To obtain a calling card** from your national telecommunications service before you leave home, contact the appropriate company below.

Australia: Telstra Australia **Telstra Direct** (☎13 22 00).

Canada: Bell Canada **Canada Direct** (☎800-668-6878).

Ireland: Telecom Éireann **Ireland Direct** (☎800 40 00 00).

New Zealand: Telecom New Zealand (☎0800 00 00 00).

South Africa: Telkom South Africa (☎10 219).

United Kingdom: British Telecom **BT Direct** (☎800 34 51 44).

United States: AT&T (☎800-288-4685), **Sprint** (☎800-877-4646), or **MCI** (☎800-444-3333).

Before purchasing any calling card, always compare rates with other cards and make sure it serves your needs (a local phonecard is generally better for local calls, for instance). Let's Go provides a phonecard service through ekit. For more information, visit **www.letsgo.ekit.com**.

TIME DIFFERENCES

Spain is 1 hour ahead of Greenwich Mean Time (GMT) and 6 hours ahead of US EST. **Portugal** and **Morocco** are on GMT and 5 hours ahead of EST. Thus, when it is noon in New York, it is 5pm in Portugal and Morocco and 6pm in Spain. Spain and Portugal, together with the rest of Europe, switch to Daylight Savings Time about 1 week before the US does; they switch back at the same time. Morocco does not switch, and so is 4 hours ahead of US EST and 2 hours behind Spain in summer.

BY EMAIL & INTERNET

Email is quite easy to access in Spain and Portugal, but less so in Morocco. Though in some places it's possible to forge a remote link with your home server, this is a much slower (and thus more expensive) option than taking advantage of free **web-based email accounts** (e.g. www.hotmail.com or www.yahoo.com). **Internet cafes** and the occasional free Internet terminal at a public library or university are listed in the **Orientation and Practical Information** sections of major cities. Travelers with laptops can call an Internet service provider via a **modem**. Long-distance phone cards specifically intended for such calls can defray normally high phone charges; check with your long-distance phone provider to see if it offers this option. **Internet cafes** and the occasional free Internet terminal at a public library or university are listed in the **Practical Information** sections of major cities.

GETTING THERE

For country-specific information on traveling, travel organizations, and travel discounts within Spain, Portugal, and Morocco, see the **Transportation** sections for **Spain** (p. 84), **Portugal** (p. 630), and **Morocco** (p. 765).

BY PLANE

When it comes to airfare, a little effort can save you a bundle. If your plans are flexible enough to deal with the restrictions, courier fares are the cheapest. Tickets bought from consolidators and flying standby are also good deals, but last-minute specials, airfare wars, and charter flights often beat these fares. The key is to hunt around, to be flexible, and to ask persistently about discounts. Students, seniors, and those under 26 should never pay full price for a ticket.

ESSENTIALS

AIRFARES

Airfares to Spain, Portugal, and Morocco peak between mid-June and early September; holidays are also expensive. The cheapest times to travel are December and January, when it's freezing cold. Patching one-way flights together is a costly way to travel. Midweek (M-Th morning) round-trip flights run US$40-50 cheaper than weekend flights, but they are generally more crowded and less likely to permit frequent-flier upgrades. Traveling with an "open return" ticket can be pricier than fixing a return date when buying the ticket. Round-trip flights are by far the cheapest; "open-jaw" (arriving in and departing from different cities, e.g. New York-Madrid and Paris-New York) tickets tend to be more expensive. Flights between capitals or regional hubs—Madrid, Barcelona, Lisboa, Rabat, and Casablanca—tend to be cheaper.

If Spain, Portugal or Morocco is only one stop on a more extensive globe-hop, consider a **round-the-world** (RTW) ticket. Tickets usually include at least 5 stops and are valid for about a year; prices range US$1200-5000. Try **Northwest Airlines/KLM** (in the US ☎800-447-4747; www.nwa.com), **British Airways** (in the US ☎800-828-7797; www.britishairways.com) or **Star Alliance,** a consortium of 22 airlines including United Airlines (in the US ☎800-241-6522; www.star-alliance.com).

BUDGET & STUDENT TRAVEL AGENCIES

While knowledgeable agents specializing in flights to Spain, Portugal, and Morocco can make your life easy and help you save, they may not spend the time to find you the lowest fare—they get paid on commission. Travelers holding **ISIC** or **IYTC cards** (see p. 14) qualify for big discounts from student travel agencies. Most flights from budget agencies are on major airlines, but in peak season some may sell seats on less reliable chartered aircraft.

CTS Travel, 30 Rathbone Pl., **London** W1T 1GQ, UK (☎0207 290 0630; www.ctstravel.co.uk). A British student travel agency with offices in 39 countries including the US, 350 Fifth Ave., Suite 7813, **New York,** NY 10118 USA (☎877-28-6665; www.ctstravelusa.com).

STA Travel, 7890 S. Hardy Dr., Suite 110, Tempe, AZ 85284 USA (24hr. reservations and info ☎800-781-4040; www.sta-travel.com). A student and youth travel organization with over 150 offices worldwide (check their website for complete listing), including US offices in **Boston, Chicago, Los Angeles, New York, San Francisco, Seattle,** and **Washington, D.C.** Ticket booking, travel insurance, railpasses, and more. In the UK, walk-in office 11 Goodge St., **London** W1T 2PF (☎0207 436 7779). In New Zealand, Shop 2B, 182 Queen St., **Auckland** (☎09 309 0458). In Australia, 366 Lygon St., **Carlton** Victoria 3053 (☎03 9349 4344).

Travel CUTS (Canadian Universities Travel Services Limited), 187 College St., **Toronto,** ON M5T 1P7 (☎416-979-2406; fax 979-8167; www.travelcuts.com). Offices across Canada and the United States in **Seattle, San Francisco, Los Angeles, New York,** and elsewhere. Also in the UK at 295-A Regent St., **London** W1B 2H9 (☎0207 255 2191).

USIT, 19-21 Aston Quay, **Dublin** 2 (☎1 602 1600; www.usitworld.com). Ireland's leading budget/student agency has 22 offices throughout Northern Ireland and Ireland.

Wasteels, Skoubogade 6, 1158 Copenhagen K., Denmark (☎3314-4633; fax 7630-0865; www.wasteels.com). A huge chain with 180 locations in Europe. Sells Wasteels BIJ tickets (2nd-class international point-to-point train tickets with unlimited stopovers for those under 26) at a 30-45% discount (sold only in Europe). Locations in Iberia and Morocco are: Plaça de Catalunya, **Barcelona** (☎933 01 18 81); C. de Blasco de Garay, 13, **Madrid** (☎915 43 12 03); Rua dos Caminhos de Ferro, 90, **Lisboa** (☎218 86 97 93); 25 rue León l'Africain, **Casablanca** (☎02 314 060); 45 bd. Mohammed V, **Meknes** (☎05 523 062); pl. de la Marche Vert, **Tangier** (☎09 938 185).

✈ **FLIGHT PLANNING ON THE INTERNET.** Many airline sites offer special last-minute deals on the Web. For **Spain,** check Iberia (www.iberia.com), Spanair (www.spanair.com), and Air Europa (www.aireuropa.com); for **Portugal,** try TAP (www.tap-airportugal.pt); for **Morocco,** Royal Air Maroc (www.royalairmaroc.com). Other sites compile the deals for you—try www.bestfares.com, www.onetravel.com, and www.travelzoo.com. ▩ **StudentUniverse** (www.studentuniverse.com) and **STA** (www.sta-travel.com) sell student tickets and railpasses, while **Microsoft Expedia** (msn.expedia.com) and **Travelocity** (www.travelocity.com) offer full travel services. **Priceline** (www.priceline.com) allows you to specify a price and obligates you to buy any ticket that meets or beats it; be prepared for antisocial hours and odd routes. **Skyauction** (www.skyauction.com) allows you to bid on tickets.

COMMERCIAL AIRLINES

The commercial airlines' lowest published fare is the **APEX** (Advance Purchase Excursion) fare, which provides confirmed reservations and allows "open-jaw" tickets. Generally, reservations must be made 7 to 21 days ahead of departure, with 7- to 14-day minimum-stay and up to 90-day maximum-stay restrictions. These fares carry hefty cancellation and change penalties (fees rise in summer). Book peak-season APEX fares early; by May you will have a hard time getting your desired departure date. Use **Microsoft Expedia** (www.msn.expedia.com), or **Travelocity** (www.travelocity.com) to get an idea of the lowest published fares, then use the resources outlined here to try beat them. Low-season fares should be appreciably cheaper than the **high-season** (mid-June to August) ones listed here.

TRAVELING FROM NORTH AMERICA

Basic round-trip fares to Spain, Portugal, and Morocco range from roughly $400-$1200, depending on when you fly. Standard commercial carriers like **American** (☎800-433-7300; www.aa.com) and **United** (☎800-241-6522; www.ual.com) will probably offer the most convenient flights, but they may not be the cheapest, unless you manage to grab a special promotion or airfare war ticket. You will probably find flying one of the following "discount" airlines a better deal, if any of their limited departure points is convenient for you.

Icelandair: ☎800-223-5500; www.icelandair.com. Stopovers in Iceland for no extra cost on most transatlantic flights.

Finnair: ☎800-950-5000; www.us.finnair.com. Cheap round-trips from San Francisco, New York, and Toronto to Madrid, Málaga and Lisboa; connections throughout Europe.

TRAVELING FROM THE UK & IRELAND

Because of the myriad carriers flying from the British Isles to the continent, we only include discount airlines or those with cheap specials here. The **Air Travel Advisory Bureau** in London (☎020 7636 5000; www.atab.co.uk) provides referrals to travel agencies and consolidators that offer discounted airfares out of the UK.

Aer Lingus: In Ireland ☎0818 356 000; www.aerlingus.ie. Return tickets from Dublin, Cork, Galway, Kerry, and Shannon to Madrid. €102-244.

British Midland Airways: In the UK ☎087 0607 0555; www.flybmi.com. Departures from throughout the UK. London to Madrid and Barcelona (UK£90-110).

buzz: In the UK ☎087 0240 7070; www.buzzaway.com. A subsidiary of KLM. From London to Jerez and Murcia (UK£50-70). Tickets cannot be changed or refunded.

easyJet: In the UK ☎087 0600 0000; www.easyjet.com. London to Barcelona, Madrid, Málaga, Palma, and Mallorca (UK£47-136). Online tickets.

Go-Fly Limited: In the UK ☎090 6302 0150, elsewhere call UK ☎44 12 7966 6388; www.go-fly.com. A subsidiary of British Airways. From London to seven locations in Spain and Portugal, including Barcelona and Faro (return UK£53-180).

Ryan Air: In Ireland ☎08 18 30 30 30, in the UK ☎08 71 24 60 000, elsewhere ☎ 353 1249 7851; www.ryanair.ie. Offers 5 daily flights to Spain from Dublin, including Barcelona and Murcia. Also flies to Faro in Portugal.

TRAVELING FROM AUSTRALIA & NEW ZEALAND

Qantas Air: In Australia ☎13 13 13; in New Zealand ☎0800 808 767; www.qantas.com.au. Flights from Australia and New Zealand to London for around AUS$2400.

Singapore Air: In Australia ☎13 10 11; in New Zealand ☎0800 808 909; www.singaporeair.com. Flies from Auckland, Sydney, Melbourne, and Perth to Madrid.

Thai Airways: In Australia ☎1300 65 19 60; in New Zealand ☎093 770 268; www.thaiair.com. Auckland, Sydney, and Melbourne to Amsterdam, Frankfurt, and London.

TRAVELING FROM SOUTH AFRICA

Air France: ☎011 770 16 01; www.airfrance.com/za. Johannesburg to Paris; connections throughout Europe.

British Airways: ☎0860 011 747; www.british-airways.com/regional/sa. Cape Town and Johannesburg to the UK and the rest of Europe from SAR3400.

Lufthansa: ☎0861 842 538; www.lufthansa.co.za. From Cape Town, Durban, and Johannesburg to Germany and elsewhere.

Virgin Atlantic: ☎011 340 34 00; www.virgin-atlantic.co.za. Flies to London from both Cape Town and Johannesburg.

AIR COURIER FLIGHTS

Those who travel light should consider courier flights. Couriers help transport cargo on international flights by using their checked luggage space for freight. Generally, couriers must travel with carry-ons only and must deal with complex flight restrictions. Most flights are round-trip, with short fixed-length stays (usually one week) and a limit of a one ticket per issue. Most of these flights also operate only out of major gateway cities, mostly in North America. Courier flights to Spain are common; those to Portugal or Morocco are more scarce. Generally, you must be over 21 (in some cases 18). In summer, popular destinations require an reservation about 2 weeks in advance (though you can usually book up to 2 months ahead). Super-discounted fares are common for "last-minute" flights (3-14 days ahead).

TRAVELING FROM NORTH AMERICA

Round-trip courier fares from the US to Spain run about US$200-500. Most flights leave from New York, Los Angeles, San Francisco, or Miami in the US; and from Montreal, Toronto, or Vancouver in Canada. The four organizations below provide members with lists of opportunities and courier brokers worldwide for an annual fee (typically US$50-60). Alternatively, you can contact a courier broker directly; most charge registration fees, but a few don't. Prices quoted below are round-trip.

Air Courier Association, 350 Indiana St. #300, Golden CO 80401 USA (☎800-282-1202; www.aircourier.org). Ten departure cities throughout the US and Canada to Madrid (high-season US$150-360). 1yr. membership US$49.

International Association of Air Travel Couriers (IAATC), P.O. Box 980, Keystone Heights, FL 32656 USA (☎352-475-1584; www.courier.org). From North American to Western Europe, including Madrid. 1yr. membership US$45-50.

Global Courier Travel (www.globalcouriertravel.com). Six departure points in the US and Canada to Madrid. 1yr. membership US$40, 2 people US$55.

NOW Voyager, 315 W. 49th St., New York, NY 10019 USA (☎212-459-1616; www.now-voyagertravel.com). To Madrid (US$499-699). Usually 1 week max. stay. 1yr. membership US$50. Non-courier discount fares also available.

FROM THE UK & IRELAND

Although the courier industry is most developed in North America, there are limited courier flights in other areas. The minimum age for couriers from the **UK** is usually 18. **Brave New World Enterprises,** (www.nry.co.uk/bnw) publishes a directory of all the companies offering courier flights in the UK (UK£10, in electronic form UK£8). **Global Courier Travel** (see above) also offer flights from London and Dublin to continental Europe. **British Airways Travel Shop** (☎0870 606 11 33; www.british-airways.com/travelqa/booking/) arranges flights from London to destinations in continental Europe (specials as low as UK£60; no registration fee).

STANDBY FLIGHTS

Traveling standby requires considerable flexibility in arrival and departure dates and cities. Companies dealing in standby flights sell vouchers rather than tickets, along with the promise to get to your destination (or near your destination) within a certain window of time (typically 1-5 days). Call before your specific window to hear flight options and the probability that you will be able to board each flight. You can then decide which flights you want to try to make, show up to the airport at the appropriate time, present your voucher, and board if space is available. You may receive a monetary refund only if every available flight within your date range is full; if you opt not to take an available flight, you can only get credit toward future travel. Read standby flight agreements carefully; tricky fine print can leave you in a lurch. It is difficult to receive refunds, and clients' vouchers will not be honored if an airline fails to receive payment on time. To check on a company's service record in the US, call the **Better Business Bureau** (☎212-533-6200).

TICKET CONSOLIDATORS

Ticket consolidators, or **"bucket shops,"** buy unsold tickets in bulk from commercial airlines and sell them at discounted rates. Look for consolidators in the Sunday travel section of any major newspaper (such as the *New York Times*), where many bucket shops place tiny ads. Call quickly, as availability is extremely limited. Not all bucket shops are reliable, so insist on a receipt that gives full details of restrictions, refunds, and tickets, and pay by credit card (in spite of the 2-5% fee) so you can stop payment if you never receive your tickets.

    Travel Avenue (☎800-333-3335; www.travelavenue.com) searches for best available published fares and then uses several consolidators to attempt to beat that fare. **NOW Voyager,** (☎212-431-1616; fax 219-1793; www.nowvoyagertravel.com) arranges discount flights, mostly from New York, to Barcelona, London, Madrid, Milan, Paris, and Rome. Other consolidators are **Pennsylvania Travel** (☎800-331-0947); **Rebel** (☎800-227-3235; www.rebeltours.com); and **Cheap Tickets** (☎800-377-1000; www.cheaptickets.com). Yet more consolidators on the web include the **Internet Travel Network** (www.itn.com); **Travel Information Services** (www.tiss.com); and **TravelHUB** (www.travelhub.com). Keep in mind that these are just suggestions for starting your research; *Let's Go* does not endorse any of these agencies. As always, be cautious before you hand over your credit card number.

ESSENTIALS

CHARTER FLIGHTS

Charters are flights a tour operator contracts with an airline to fly extra loads of passengers during peak season. Charter flights fly less frequently than major airlines, make refunds particularly difficult, and are almost always fully booked. Schedules and itineraries may also change or be cancelled at the last moment (as late as 48hr. before the trip, and without a full refund), and check-in, boarding, and baggage claim are often much slower. However, they can also be cheaper.

Discount clubs and **fare brokers** offer members savings on last-minute charter and tour deals. Study contracts closely; you don't want to end up with an unwanted overnight layover. **Travelers Advantage,** Trumbull, CT, USA (☎877-259-2691; www.travelersadvantage.com; US$60 annual fee includes discounts and cheap flight directories) specializes in European travel and tour packages.

BY TRAIN

Rail travel is common and convenient throughout the European continent, though not in Morocco. Connections are made through France into Spain and Portugal.

SHOULD YOU BUY A RAILPASS? Railpasses were conceived to allow travelers to hop on trains wherever and whenever they wanted through Europe. In practice, it's not so simple. You still must stand in line to validate your pass, pay for supplements, and fork over cash for seat and reservations. More importantly, railpasses don't always pay off. If you are planning to spend extensive time on trains, hopping between big cities, a railpass would probably be worth it. But in many cases, especially if you are under 26, point-to-point tickets may prove a cheaper option.

EURAILPASS. Eurail (www.eurail.com.) is valid in Austria, Belgium, Denmark, Finland, France, Germany, Greece, Hungary, Italy, Luxembourg, The Netherlands, Norway, Portugal, the Republic of Ireland, Spain, Sweden, and Switzerland. It is not valid in the UK. Standard **Eurailpasses,** valid for a consecutive given number of days, are most suitable for those planning on spending extensive time on trains every few days. **Flexipasses,** valid for any 10 or 15 (not necessarily consecutive) days in a two-month period, are more cost-effective for those traveling longer distances less frequently. **Saverpasses** provide first-class travel for travelers in groups of two to five (prices are per person). **Youthpasses** and **Youth Flexipasses** provide second-class perks for those under 26. Eurail offers the **Selectpass,** which allows travel in your choice of 3, 4, or 5 adjoining countries for any 5, 6, 8, 10, or 15 days in a two-month period. Selectpass replaces the **Europass.** Passholders receive a timetable for major routes and a map with details on possible ferry, steamer, bus, car rental, hotel, and Eurostar discounts. Passholders often also receive reduced fares or free passage on many bus and boat lines.

> **! JUST SAY NO.** If you are planning on traveling in just Spain and Portugal, do not buy a Eurailpass. Train travel in these countries is less expensive than the rest of Europe, where passes can save you from paying for expensive train fares. A Eurailpass makes sense only for those planning to travel in other European countries as well.

SHOPPING AROUND FOR A EURAIL PASS. Eurailpasses are designed by the EU itself and are purchasable only by non-Europeans almost exclusively from non-European distributors. These passes must be sold at uniform prices determined by the EU. However, some travel agents tack on a US$10 handling fee, and others offer certain bonuses with purchase, so shop around. Also, keep in mind that pass prices usually go up each year, so if you're planning to travel early in the year, you can save cash by purchasing before January 1 (you have three months from the purchase date to validate your pass in Europe).

It is best to buy your Eurailpass before leaving; only a few places in major European cities sell them, and at a marked-up price. You can get a replacement for a lost pass only if you have purchased insurance on it under the Pass Protection Plan (US$10). Eurailpasses are available through travel agents, student travel agencies like STA and Council (see p. 40), and **Rail Europe,** 500 Mamaroneck Ave., Harrison NY 10528 (US ☎888-382-7245, fax 800-432-1329; Canada ☎800-361-7245, fax 905-602-4198; UK 09 9084 8848; www.raileurope.com) or **DER Travel Services,** (US ☎888-337-7350; fax 800-282-7474; www.der.com).

INTERRAIL PASS. If you have lived for at least six months in one of the European countries where InterRail Passes are valid, they prove an economical option. There are eight InterRail **zones,** one of which includes Spain, Portugal, and Morocco. The **Under 26 InterRail Card** allows either 21 days or one month of unlimited travel within one, two, three, or all eight zones; the cost is determined by the number of zones the pass covers (UK£159-259). If you buy a ticket including the zone in which you claim residence, you must still pay 50% fare for tickets inside your own country. Passholders receive **discounts** on rail travel, Eurostar journeys, and most ferries to Ireland, Scandinavia, and the rest of Europe. Most exclude **supplements** for high-speed trains. For info and ticket sales in Europe contact **Student Travel Center,** 24 Rupert St., 1st fl., London W1V 7FN (☎0207 437 8101; fax 734 3836; www.student-travel-centre.com). Tickets are also available from travel agents or major train stations throughout Europe.

BY BUS

Though European trains and railpasses are extremely popular, buses are another viable option for travel to Iberia.

Busabout (UK ☎0207 950 1661; fax 950 1662; www.busabout.com), is a hop-on hop-off network linking 70 cities and towns in Europe including London, Paris, Madrid, Barcelona, and Lisboa. Consecutive-day Passes and Flexipasses available. Consecutive-day standard/student passes range from US$339/309 for 2 weeks to US$1149/1039 for a season pass. Flexipass standard/student passes range from US$339/309 for 7 days out of 1 month to US$909/809 for 24 days out of 4 months.

Contiki Holidays (888-CONTIKI; www.contiki.com) offers a variety of European vacation packages designed for 18- to 35-year-olds. For an average cost of $65 per day, tours include accommodations, transportation, guided sightseeing, and some meals.

Eurolines (UK ☎15 8240 4511; www.eurolines.co.uk or www.eurolines.com). Largest operator of Europe-wide services with offices in **Madrid** (Estación Sur de Autobuses, C. Méndez Álvaro, 83; ☎915 06 33 60; fax 06 33 65) and **Barcelona** (Ronda Universitat, 5; ☎933 42 51 80; fax 18 59 97).

BY BOAT

FROM THE UK

Brittany Ferries: In the UK ☎087 0901 2400; www.brittany-ferries.com. **Plymouth** to **Santander, ES** (24-30hr., 1-2 per week, UK£80-145).

P&O European Ferries: In the UK ☎087 0242 4999; www.poportsmouth.com. **Portsmouth** to **Bilbao, ES** (35hr., 2 per week, UK£186).

FROM MOROCCO

For travel from Spain to Morocco, the most budget-minded mode is by sea. Spanish-based **Trasmediterránea** (in Spain ☎902 45 46 45; www.trasmediterranea.es/homei.htm) runs ferries on a shuttle schedule. Check online weekly schedules, or see p. 765 for more information.

BORDER CROSSINGS

The border between Spain and Portugal is oft-traversed. Portugal is easily accessible by plane or long-distance train from **Madrid** (p. 91) to Lisboa, and buses from **Sevilla** (p. 227) to Lagos. Closer to the border, trains run from **Huelva** (p. 253, easily accessible from Sevilla) and **Cáceres** (p. 212) to Portugal. Trains and buses run from **Badajoz** (p. 223), only 6km from the border, to Elvas and elsewhere. **Ciudad Rodrigo** (p. 188) lies only 21km from the border. In the north, trains run from **Vigo** (p. 575) to Porto; from **Túy** (p. 579), you can walk across the Portuguese border to Valença do Minho.

GETTING AROUND

BY PLANE

Many national airlines offer multi-stop tickets for travel within Spain, Portugal, and Morocco. These tickets are particularly useful for travel between the Spanish mainland and the Balearic and Canary Islands. Given the mountainous terrain of Morocco, flights are often the most efficient way to traverse the country. For more information on intra-country plane travel in **Spain** see p. 84, in **Portugal,** see p. 630, and in **Morocco,** see p. 765.

BY TRAIN

Trains in Spain and Portugal are generally comfortable, convenient, and reasonably swift. Second-class travel is pleasant, and compartments (seating 2-6) are great places to meet fellow travelers. Trains, however, are not always safe; for safety tips, see next page. For long trips make sure you are in the correct car, as trains sometimes split at crossroads. Towns listed in parentheses require a train switch at the town listed immediately before the parenthesis.

You can either buy a **railpass,** which allows you unlimited travel within a particular region for a given period of time, or rely on buying individual **point-to-point** tickets as you go. Many countries give students or youths (usually defined as anyone under 26) direct discounts on regular domestic rail tickets, and many also sell a student or youth card that provides 20-50% off all fares for up to a year.

RESERVATIONS. While seat reservations are required only for selected trains (usually on major lines), you are not guaranteed a seat without advance booking. Reservations are available on major trains up to two months in advance, and Europeans often reserve far ahead of time; you should strongly consider reserving during peak holiday and tourist seasons (at the very latest a few hours ahead). It will be necessary to purchase a **supplement** (US$10-50) or special fare for high speed or quality trains such as Spain's AVE.

OVERNIGHT TRAINS. Night trains have their advantages—you won't waste valuable daylight hours traveling, and you will be able to forego the hassle and considerable expense of securing a night's accommodation. However, night travel has its drawbacks as well: discomfort and sleepless nights are the most obvious. **Sleeping accommodations** on trains differ from country to country, but typically you can either sleep upright in your seat (for free) or pay for a separate space. **Couchettes** (berths) typically have four to six seats per compartment (about US$20 per person); **sleepers** (beds) in private sleeping cars offer more privacy and comfort, but are considerably more expensive (US$40-150). If you are using a railpass valid only for a restricted number of days, inspect train schedules to maximize the use of your pass: an overnight train or boat journey uses only one of your travel days if it departs after 7pm (you need only write in the next day's date on your pass).

DISCOUNTED TICKETS

For travelers under 26, **BIJ** tickets (Billets Internationals de Jeunesse; a.k.a. **Wasteels, Eurotrain**, and **Route 26**) are a great alternative to railpasses. Available for international trips within Europe as well as most ferry services, they knock 20-40% off regular second-class fares. Tickets are good for 60 days after purchase and allow a number of stopovers along the normal direct route of the train journey. Issued for a specific international route between two points, they must be used in the direction and order of the designated route and must be bought in Europe. The equivalent for those over 26, **BIGT** tickets provide a 20-30% discount on 1st- and 2nd-class international tickets for business travelers, temporary residents of Europe, and their families. Both types of tickets are available from European travel agents, at Wasteels or Eurotrain offices (usually in or near train stations), or directly at the ticket counter in some nations. For more info, contact **Wasteels**, Pl. de Cataluña, **Barcelona** (☎933 01 18 81); C. de Blasco de Garay, 13, **Madrid** (☎915 43 12 03); or Rua dos Caminhos de Ferro, 90, **Lisboa** (☎218 86 97 93).

BY BUS

Though trains are quite popular in the rest of Europe, buses are often a better option in Spain, Portugal, and Morocco. In Spain, the bus and train systems are on par; in Portugal, bus networks are more extensive, more efficient, and often more comfortable. In Morocco, buses are the easiest way to get around, even though some may run infrequently. See the **Essentials** sections of **Spain** (p. 86), **Portugal** (p. 630), and **Morocco** (p. 766) for country-specific details on bus travel.

BY BOAT WITHIN SPAIN

The following companies offer ferry service among the Canary Islands. See the section on transportation in the Canaries (p. 591) for more information.

Fred Olsen (☎922 62 82 00 or 902 10 01 07; www.fredolsen.es).

Naviera Armas (☎902 45 65 00; www.naviera-armas.com).

Trasmediterránea (24hr. ☎902 45 46 45; www.trasmediterranea.com).

Ferry service in the Balearic Islands is considerably less expensive than flights, but longer in duration. The following companies run boats to and around the Balearics. More information is on p. 363.

Balearia (☎902 16 01 80; www.balearia.com).

Buquebus (☎902 41 42 42 or 934 81 73 60).

Trasmediterránea (☎902 45 46 45; www.trasmediterranea.com).

Umafisa Lines (☎902 19 10 68 or 971 31 02 01).

BY CAR

Cars offer speed, freedom, access to countryside, and an escape from the town-to-town mentality of trains. Unfortunately, they also insulate you from the *esprit de corps* of rail traveling, and driving in major cities can be hair-raising. Although a single traveler won't save by renting a car, a group of four usually will. If you can't decide between train and car travel, you may benefit from a combination of the two; Rail Europe and other railpass vendors offer rail-and-drive packages.

Before setting off, know the laws of the countries in which you'll be driving. The **Association for Safe International Road Travel (ASIRT)** can provide more specific information about road conditions in Spain, Portugal and Morocco. ASIRT is located at 5413 West Cedar Lane #103C, Bethesda, MD 20814 USA (☎301-983-5252; fax 983-3663; www.asirt.org).

RENTING

You can rent a car from a US-based firm with European offices, from a European-based company with local representatives, or from a tour operator which will arrange a rental for you at its own rates. Multinationals offer greater flexibility, but tour operators often strike better deals. Most available cars will have standard transmission—cars with automatic transmission are difficult to find in Europe and much more expensive. Reserve well before leaving and pay in advance if possible. It is always significantly less expensive to reserve a car from the US than from Spain, Portugal, or Morocco. Ask your airline about special fly-and-drive packages; you may get up to a week of free or discounted rental. The minimum age to rent in Spain and Portugal is usually 25 with the larger agencies (Hertz, Avis) and 21 at smaller, local businesses. Minimum age in Morocco is almost always 21 (Hertz 23). At most agencies, all you need is a US license and proof that you've had it for a year, although in Spain you may need an international driver's license.

RENTAL AGENCIES. You can generally make reservations before you leave by calling major international offices in your home country. However, occasionally the price and availability information they give doesn't jive with what the local offices in your country will tell you. Try checking with both numbers to make sure you get the best price and accurate information. Local desk numbers are included in town listings; for home-country numbers, call your toll-free directory. Rental agencies in Spain, Portugal, and Morocco include:

Alamo (☎800-GO-ALAMO; www.alamo.com). Alamo has 149 offices in Spain and 13 in Portugal, including the airports of Barcelona, Lisboa, Madrid, and Sevilla. Frequent flyer deals available when flying on most major US airlines.

Auto Europe (US ☎888-223-5555; www.autoeurope.com). Offers car rentals in Spain, Portugal, and Morocco, as well flight and hotel bookings. Also rents cell phones to US citizens traveling in Europe.

Budget (☎800-527-0700; www.budget.com). Rentals in Spain, Portugal, and Morocco.

Hertz (in the US ☎800-654-3001, in the UK ☎087 0844 8844, in Australia ☎3 9698 2555; www.hertz.com). Rentals in Spain, Portugal, and Morocco.

Europcar (in the US ☎800-227-3876, in Canada ☎877-940-6900, in the UK ☎087 0607 5000; www.europcar.com, www.europcar.co.uk). Rentals in Spain, Portugal, and Morocco. One of the few services that will rent to those ages 21-24 in most locations.

Europe by Car (☎800-223-1516; www.europebycar.com). Student discounts.

COSTS & INSURANCE. Rental car prices start at around US$20 per day from national companies. Expect to pay more for larger cars and for 4WD, less for minis or at local agencies. Cars with **automatic transmission** are considerably more expensive than those with standard transmission (stick shift), and in some places, automatic is hard to find in the first place. It is virtually impossible, no matter where you are, to find an automatic 4WD. National chains often allow one-way rentals, picking up in one city and dropping off in another. There is usually a minimum hire period and sometimes an extra drop-off charge of a few hundred dollars.

Be sure to ask questions before leaving the agency, including the number of kilometers included with the rental cost, the cost of returning a car without a full tank of gas, and the type of insurance included with the rental fee. Most credit cards cover standard insurance, though you should double-check with your credit card company. If you rent, lease, or borrow a car, you will need a **green card,** or **International Insurance Certificate,** to certify that you have liability insurance and that it applies abroad. Green cards can be obtained at car rental agencies, car dealers (for those leasing cars), some travel agents, and some border crossings. Rental agencies may require you to purchase theft insurance in countries they consider to be high-risk. If you have a collision abroad, the accident will show up on your domestic records if you report it to your insurance company.

ON THE ROAD. Speed limits in Spain and Portugal are 60kph on main roads, 90kph on larger roads, and 120kph on highways. Police are often on the lookout for speeding tourists, and if you're caught you will face an on-the-spot fine. Petrol (gasoline) prices vary, but average about €0.85 per liter. Road conditions are fairly good throughout Spain and Portugal, with the most difficult conditions in the Pyrenees. Driving in Morocco can be difficult. For specific information on driving conditions, potential hazards, and car assistance see the country **Essentials** sections for Spain (p. 86), Portugal (p. 631), and Morocco (p. 767). Western Europeans use unleaded gas almost exclusively.

DRIVING PERMITS & CAR INSURANCE

INTERNATIONAL DRIVING PERMIT (IDP). If you plan to drive a car while in the region, you should have an International Driving Permit (IDP), though Spain, Portugal, and Morocco allow travelers to drive with a valid American, Canadian, or EU member license. It may be a good idea to get an IDP, in case you're in a situation (e.g. an accident or stranded in a small town) where the police do not know English; information on the IDP is printed in 10 languages, including Spanish, French, Portuguese, and Arabic. Your IDP, valid for one year, must be issued in your own country before you depart. When you are on the road, you will always be

> **!**
>
> **DRIVING PRECAUTIONS.** When traveling in the summer or in the desert, bring substantial amounts of water (a suggested 5 liters of **water** per person per day) for drinking and for the radiator. For long drives to unpopulated areas, register with police before beginning the trek, and again upon arrival at the destination. Check with the local automobile club for details. When traveling for long distances, make sure tires are in good repair and have enough air, and get good maps. A **compass** and a **car manual** can also be very useful. You should always carry a **spare tire** and **jack, jumper cables, extra oil, flares, a torch (flashlight),** and **heavy blankets** (in case your car breaks down at night or in the winter). If you don't know how to **change a tire,** learn before heading out, especially if you are planning on traveling in deserted areas; blowouts on dirt roads are exceedingly common. If you do have a breakdown, **stay with your car;** if you wander off, there's less likelihood trackers will find you.

asked to present your regular license in addition to your IDP. An application for an IDP usually needs to include one or two photos, a current local license, an additional form of identification proving that you are over 18, and a fee. To apply, contact the national or local branch of your home country's Automobile Association.

BY BICYCLE

Today, biking is one of the key elements of the classic budget Eurovoyage. With the proliferation of mountain bikes, you can do some serious natural sightseeing. If you are nervous about striking out on your own, **Blue Marble Travel** (in the US ☎215-923-3788, in Canada ☎519-624 2494, in France ☎01 42 36 02 34; www.bluemarble.org) offers bike tours designed for adults aged 20 to 50.

Many airlines will count your bike as your second piece of luggage, and a few charge extra. The additional fee runs about US$60-110 each way. Airlines sell bike boxes at the airport (US$10), although it is easier and cheaper to get one from a local bike store. Most ferries let you take your bike for free or for a nominal fee. You can always ship your bike on trains, though the cost varies.

Renting a bike beats bringing your own if your touring will be confined to one or two regions. *Let's Go* lists bike rental shops for most larger cities and towns. Some youth hostels rent bicycles for low prices. Some train stations rent bikes and often allow you to drop them off elsewhere.

BY MOPED & MOTORCYCLE

Motorized bikes don't use much gas, can be put on trains and ferries, and are a good compromise between the high cost of car travel and the limited range of bicycles. In Spain, they are an extremely popular method of transportation for locals, and they can be a fun alternative for tourist daytrips. However, they're uncomfortable for long distances, dangerous in the rain, and unpredictable on rough roads and gravel. Always wear a helmet, and never ride with a backpack. If you've never been on a moped, the windy roads of the Pyrenees and the congested streets of Madrid are not the place to start.

Before renting, ask if the quoted price includes tax and insurance, or you may be hit with an unexpected additional fee. Avoid handing your passport over as a deposit; if you have an accident or mechanical failure you may not get it back until you cover all repairs. Pay ahead of time instead.

BY THUMB

No one should hitch without careful consideration of the risks involved. Hitching means entrusting your life to a random person who happens to stop beside you on the road and risking theft, assault, sexual harassment, and unsafe driving. In spite of this, there are gains to hitching. Favorable hitching experiences allow you to meet local people and get where you're going, especially in areas where public transportation is sparse or unreliable. For instance, hitching in southern Spain, particularly in Andalucía, and northern Portugal is easier than hitching in Murcia and allows you to mingle with the locals. The choice, however, remains yours.

Where one stands is vital. Experienced hitchers pick a spot outside of built-up areas, where drivers can stop, return to the road without causing an accident, and have time to look over potential passengers as they approach. Hitching (or even standing) on super-highways is usually illegal: one may only thumb at rest stops or at the entrance ramps to highways. Finally, success will depend on what one looks like. Successful hitchers travel light and stack their belongings in a compact but visible cluster. Most Europeans signal with an open hand, rather than a thumb; many write their destination on a sign in large, bold letters and draw a smiley-face under it. Drivers prefer hitchers who are neat and wholesome.

Safety issues are always imperative, even for those who are not hitching alone. Safety-minded hitchers avoid getting in the back of a two-door car and never let go of their backpacks. They will not get into a car that they can't get out of again in a hurry. If they ever feel threatened, they insist on being let off, regardless of where they are. Acting as if they are going to open the car door or vomit on the upholstery will usually get a driver to stop. Hitchhiking at night can be particularly dangerous; experienced hitchers stand in well-lit places. Expect drivers to be leery of nocturnal thumbers (or open-handers).

> **HITCHHIKERS BEWARE.** *Let's Go* strongly urges you to seriously consider the risks before you choose to hitch. We do not recommend hitching as a safe means of transportation, and none of the information presented here is intended to do so. Women traveling alone should never hitch.

SPECIFIC CONCERNS

WOMEN TRAVELERS

Women exploring on their own inevitably face some additional safety concerns, but it's easy to be adventurous without taking undue risks. If you are concerned, consider staying in hostels which offer single rooms that lock from the inside or in religious organizations with rooms for women only. Communal showers in some hostels are safer than others; check them before settling in. Stick to centrally located accommodations and avoid solitary late-night treks or metro rides.

When traveling, always carry extra money for a phone call, bus, or taxi. **Hitching** is never safe for lone women, or even for two women traveling together. Choose train compartments occupied by other women or couples; ask the conductor to put together a women-only compartment if he or she doesn't offer to do so first. Look as if you know where you're going (even when you don't) and approach older women or couples for directions if you're lost or feel uncomfortable.

ESSENTIALS

Generally, the less you look like a tourist, the better off you'll be. Dress conservatively, especially in rural areas. Wearing a conspicuous **wedding band** may help prevent unwanted overtures. Some travelers report that carrying pictures of a "husband" or "children" is extremely useful to help document marriage status. Even mentioning a husband, father, or brother waiting back at the hotel may be enough to discount your potentially vulnerable, unattached appearance.

Your best answer to verbal harassment is no answer at all; feigning deafness, sitting motionless, and staring straight ahead will do a world of good. In extreme cases, the persistent can sometimes be dissuaded by a firm, loud, and very public "Go away!" in the appropriate language. In Morocco, however, it is more advisable to simply ignore advances, as local women do; rebuffs, or any kind of reaction, are often construed as playing hard to get. Don't hesitate to seek out a police officer or passerby if you are being harassed. Memorize emergency numbers in places you visit, and consider carrying a whistle or airhorn on your keychain. A self-defense course will not only prepare you for a potential attack, but will also raise your level of awareness and confidence (see **Self Defense**, p. 19). Refer to the **Essentials** section for **Morocco** (p.539) for more information on traveling there.

TRAVELING ALONE

There are many benefits to traveling alone, including independence and greater interaction with locals. However, a solo traveler is a more vulnerable target for harassment and street theft. Try not to stand out as a lone tourist, look confident, and be careful in deserted or crowded areas. If questioned, never admit that you are traveling alone. Maintain regular contact with someone at home who knows your itinerary. For more tips, pick up *Traveling Solo* by Eleanor Berman (Globe Pequot Press; US$17) or subscribe to **Connecting: Solo Travel Network** (☎604-886-9099; www.cstn.org; membership US$35). **Travel Companion Exchange**, P.O. Box 833, Amityville, NY 11701, USA (☎631-454-0880, in the US 800-392-1256; www.whytravelalone.com), will connect solo travelers with companions with similar travel habits and interests (US$48).

OLDER TRAVELERS

Senior citizens are eligible for a wide range of discounts on transportation, museums, movies, theaters, concerts, restaurants, and accommodations. The books *No Problem! Worldwise Tips for Mature Adventurers*, by Janice Kenyon (Orca Book Publishers; US$16) and *Unbelievably Good Deals and Great Adventures That You Absolutely Can't Get Unless You're Over 50*, by Joan Rattner Heilman (NTC/Contemporary Publishing; US$13) are both excellent resources. For more information, contact one of the following organizations:

ElderTreks, 597 Markham St., Toronto, ON M6G 2L7 Canada (☎800-741-7956; www.eldertreks.com). Adventure travel programs for the 50+ traveler in Morocco.

Elderhostel, 11 Ave. de Lafayette, Boston, MA 02111 USA (☎877-426-8056; www.elderhostel.org). Organizes 1-4 week "educational adventures" in Spain, Portugal, and Morocco on varied subjects for those 55+.

The Mature Traveler, P.O. Box 15791, Sacramento, CA 95852 USA (☎800-460-6676; www.thematuretraveler.com). Deals, discounts, and travel packages for the 50+ traveler. Subscription $30.

Walking the World, P.O. Box 1186, Fort Collins, CO 80522 USA (☎800-340-9255; www.walkingtheworld.com). Organizes trips for travelers 50+ to a variety of destinations, including Spain and Portugal.

BISEXUAL, GAY & LESBIAN TRAVELERS

Attitudes toward homosexuality in Spain, Portugal, and Morocco vary by region. Gay and lesbian travelers may feel out of place in the smaller, rural areas of Spain and Portugal, given the countries' strong Catholic religious heritage, but overt homophobia is rare. Larger cities, especially Madrid, Barcelona, and Lisboa have well-developed gay men's scenes, and the lesbian scene is growing rapidly. In Spain, Sitges and Ibiza are internationally renowned as gay party destinations, and Madrid has one of the most lively gay scenes in Europe, including the epic parties of *Orgullo Gay* in June. Most Spanish newsstands carry the *Guía Gay Visado*, a publication dedicated to gay bars, discos, and contacts in Spain. (See **Gay and Lesbian Services**, p. 104, for more information.) The website www.guiagay.com has similar information. The Portuguese website www.portugalgay.pt also similar offers listings in Portuguese and English. There is no gay community in Morocco. Lesbianism is almost unheard of and unrecognized; male homosexuality is illegal under Islamic and civil law.

Listed below are contact organizations that offer materials addressing some specific concerns. **Out and About** (www.planetout.com) publishes a biweekly newsletter addressing travel concerns and offers a comprehensive website addressing gay travel concerns.

Gay's the Word, 66 Marchmont St., London WC1N 1AB, UK (☎0207 278 7654; www.gaystheword.co.uk). The largest gay and lesbian bookshop in the UK, with both fiction and non-fiction titles. Mail-order service available.

Giovanni's Room, 1145 Pine St., Philadelphia, PA 19107, USA (☎215-923-2960; www.queerbooks.com). An international lesbian/feminist and gay bookstore with mail-order service (carries many of the publications listed below).

International Lesbian and Gay Association (ILGA), 81 rue Marché-au-Charbon, B-1000 Brussels, Belgium (☎2502 2471; www.ilga.org). Provides political information, such as homosexuality laws of individual countries.

▼ **FURTHER READING**

Damron Men's Guide, Damron Road Atlas, Damron's Accommodations, and The Women's Traveller. Damron Travel Guides (US$14-19). For more info, call ☎800-462-6654 or visit www.damron.com.

Ferrari Guides' Gay Travel A to Z, Ferrari Guides' Men's Travel in Your Pocket, and Ferrari Guides' Inn Places. Ferrari Publications (US$16-20).

The Gay Vacation Guide: The Best Trips and How to Plan Them, Mark Chesnut. Citadel Press (US$15).

Spartacus International Gay Guide 2002-03. Bruno Gmunder Verlag (US$33).

TRAVELERS WITH DISABILITIES

Wheelchair accessibility varies widely in Iberia but is generally inferior to that in the US. In Spain and Portugal, handicapped access is common in modern and big city museums. Access in Morocco is minimal.

Those with disabilities should inform airlines and hotels of their disabilities when making reservations. Call ahead to restaurants, museums, and other facilities to find out about the existence of ramps, the widths of doors, etc. **Guide dog owners** should inquire as to the quarantine policies of each destination. At the very least, they will need to provide a certificate of immunization against rabies.

ESSENTIALS

Rail is probably the most convenient form of travel for disabled travelers in Europe: many larger stations have ramps, and some trains have wheelchair lifts, special seating areas, and specially equipped toilets. Spain and Portugal's rail systems, however, have limited resources for wheelchair accessibility, especially in smaller stations. For those who wish to rent cars, some major **car rental** agencies (Hertz, Avis, and National) offer hand-controlled vehicles.

USEFUL ORGANIZATIONS

Mobility International USA (MIUSA; (☎541-343-1284, voice and TDD; www.miusa.org). Provides a variety of books and other publications containing information for travelers with disabilities.

Society for Accesible Travel & Hospitality (SATH; ☎212-447-7284; www.sath.org). An advocacy group that publishes free online travel information and sells a variety of print and alternative materials. Annual membership US$45, students and seniors US$30.

Directions Unlimited, 123 Green Ln., Bedford Hills, NY 10507 USA (☎800-533-5343). Books individual and group vacations for the physically disabled; not an info service.

MINORITY TRAVELERS

Because of demographic homogeneity, Spanish people experience little interaction with other races. The infrequent incidents of racism are rarely violent or threatening, just a little awkward. They occur out of naiveté, ignorance, or curiosity rather than insensitivity. Portugal, with its rich ethnic composition, is actively anti-racist, and minority travelers have little to fear. Morocco encompasses a diverse cultural and racial spectrum; visitors are defined more by their foreign ways than by their skin color.

TRAVELERS WITH CHILDREN

Family vacations often require that you slow your pace, and always require that you plan ahead. When deciding where to stay, remember the special needs of young children; if you pick a hostel or a small hotel, call ahead and make sure it's child-friendly. If you rent a car, make sure the rental company provides a car seat for younger children. **Be sure that your child carries some sort of ID** in case of an emergency or in case he or she gets lost.

Museums, tourist attractions, accommodations, and restaurants often offer discounts for children. Children under two generally fly for 10% of the adult airfare on international flights (this does not necessarily include a seat). International fares are usually discounted 25% for children ages two to 11. For more information, consult one of the following books:

Adventuring with Children: An Inspirational Guide to World Travel and the Outdoors, Nan Jeffrey. Avalon House Publishing (US$15).

Backpacking with Babies and Small Children, Goldie Silverman. Wilderness Press (US$10).

Gutsy Mamas: Travel Tips and Wisdom for Mothers on the Road, Marybeth Bond. Travelers' Tales, Inc. (US$8).

Have Kid, Will Travel: 101 Survival Strategies for Vacationing With Babies and Young Children, Claire and Lucille Tristram. Andrews McMeel Publishing (US$9).

How to take Great Trips with Your Kids, Sanford and Jane Portnoy. Harvard Common Press (US $10).

Trouble Free Travel with Children, Vicki Lansky. Book Peddlers (US$9).

DIETARY CONCERNS

Spain and Portugal can be difficult places to visit as a strict vegetarian; in Spain meat or fish is featured in the majority of popular dishes. Most restaurants serve salads, however, and there are also many egg-, rice- and bean-based dishes that can be requested without meat. Be careful, though, as some servers may interpret a "vegetarian" order to mean "with tuna instead of ham." Eating as a vegetarian in Morocco is easier, as bean-based stews and couscous dishes are widespread. The **North American Vegetarian Society** (☎518-568-7970; www.vegdining.com), has an excellent database of vegetarian and vegan restaurants worldwide.

Keeping **kosher** is difficult in Spain, Portugal, and Morocco. If you are strict in your observance, you may have to prepare your own food. Travelers who keep kosher should contact synagogues in larger cities for information on kosher restaurants. Good resources include the website www.shamash.org/kosher and the *Jewish Travel Guide*, by Michael Zaidner (Vallentine Mitchell; US$17).

ESSENTIALS

OTHER RESOURCES

Let's Go tries to cover all aspects of budget travel, but we can't put *everything* in our guides. Listed below are books and websites that can serve as jumping off points for your own research.

USEFUL PUBLICATIONS

The Broadsheet, monthly magazine aimed at English speakers in Spain. Features current cultural and social events, as well as news. Commercially oriented. Web edition at www.spainalive.com.

Contemporary Spain: A Handbook, Christopher Ross. Broad and informative discussion of Spanish politics, culture, society, and travel (US$20/£13).

Culture Shock! Morocco, Orin Hargraves. An extremely helpful guide to the salient cultural characteristics of Morocco, the differences between this culture and ours, and how to manage those differences (US$14/£10).

Culture Shock! Spain, Marie Louise Graff. With a comprehensive coverage of Spain's history, beliefs, festivals, and working conditions, this book navigates the visitor through local customs, bureaucracy, and eating and entertaining habits (US$14/£10).

Focus Magazine (www.focusmm.com), monthly online magazine about the Mediterranean world. Includes information on Morocco.

A Traveller's History of Spain, Juan Lalaguna. Helpful for those seeking more background historical and cultural background information about Spain (US$15).

Worst Case Survival Handbook: Travel, Joshua Piven and David Borgenicht. Finally someone has filled the void: 2 experts offer advice on such things as how to stop a runaway camel and how to navigate a minefield (US$15).

THE WORLD WIDE WEB

Almost every aspect of budget travel is accessible via the Web. Within 10min. at the keyboard, you can make a reservation at a hostel in Spain, Portugal, or Morocco, get advice on travel hotspots from other travelers who have just returned, or find out how much a train from Madrid to Barcelona costs. Listed here are some budget travel sites to start off your surfing; other relevant websites are listed throughout the book.

ESSENTIALS

THE ART OF BUDGET TRAVEL

How to See the World: www.artoftravel.com. A compendium of great travel tips, from cheap flights to self defense to interacting with local culture.

Rec. Travel Library: www.travel-library.com. A fantastic set of links for general information and personal travelogues.

Backpacker's Ultimate Guide: www.bugeurope.com. Tips on packing, transportation, and where to go. Also tons of country-specific travel information.

TravelPage: www.travelpage.com. Links to official tourist office sites through Europe.

INFORMATION ON SPAIN, PORTUGAL & MOROCCO

All About Spain: www.red2000.com/spain/index.html. Has an excellent photo tour of Spain, traveler's yellow pages, and information on major regions and cities.

Arab Net: www.arab.net/morocco/morocco_contents.html. Good historical, cultural, and tourist information on Morocco, including a list of links.

CIA World Factbook: www.odci.gov/cia/publications/factbook/index.html. Statistics on Spanish, Portuguese, and Moroccan geography, government, economy, and people.

CyberSpain: www.cyberspain.com. Has a wide variety of tourist and cultural info as well as links to other good sites inside and outside of Spain.

Geographia: www.geographia.com. Highlights, culture, and people of Morocco.

MadridMan: www.madridman.com. A site devoted entirely to the city of Madrid, with tons of useful info for visitors as well as history, culture, and current events sections.

Morocco Today: www.morocco-today.com. A comprehensive source of information on Moroccan current events, government, and society.

MyTravelGuide: www.mytravelguide.com. Country overviews, with everything from history to transportation to live web-cam coverage.

PlanetRider: www.planetrider.com. A subjective list of links to the "best" websites covering the culture and tourist attractions of Spain, Portugal, and Morocco.

Portugal-info: www.portugal-info.net. An excellent source for all types of information, from photos to wine descriptions to Portuguese personals.

Sí, Spain: www.sispain.org. Run by the Spanish Ministry of Foreign affairs, this site offers cultural and historical info, tourist info, and another great set of links.

SpainAlive: www.spainalive.com. From bars and concerts, to beaches and soccer, covers nightlife and recreation info for Spain's major tourism cities.

Spain Tourism: www.tourspain.es. The **official** Spanish tourism site. Offers national and city-specific info, an information request service, helpful links on all aspects of travel, cultural and practical info including stats on national parks and museums, and links to the biggest Spanish newspapers. In French, English, Spanish, and German.

Tourism in Morocco: www.tourism-in-Morocco.com. Helpful information on all aspects of traveling to and within Morocco, plus city-specific info.

AND OUR PERSONAL FAVORITE...

 WWW.LETSGO.COM Our newly designed website now features the full online content of all of our guides. In addition, trial versions of all nine City Guides are available for download on Palm OS™ PDAs. Our website also contains our newsletter, links for photos and streaming video, online ordering of our titles, info about our books, and a travel forum buzzing with stories and tips.

ALTERNATIVES TO TOURISM

When it comes to natural beauty, vibrant spirit, and rich history, it doesn't get much better than Spain and Portugal. Not surprisingly, these countries grace many a traveler's itinerary, but often only briefly. Unfortunately, the rapid pace of such a tour can cause you to miss the more subtle and nuanced aspects of these multifaceted countries. If you crave a more in-depth travel experience, you may want to consider some alternatives to conventional tourism. Studying, working, or volunteering are some options that can help you understand and appreciate life in Spain and Portugal in ways that a mere tourist might not. This chapter outlines some of the different opportunities available for individuals who want something other than the typical budget traveler experience.

VOLUNTEERING

Though Spain and Portugal are considered wealthy in worldwide terms, Portugal is one of the poorer countries in Western Europe. Both countries face the strain of absorbing large numbers of impoverished African immigrants and refugees into their economies. Morocco is one of the more affluent countries in Africa, but remains rather poor by to global standards.

Most people who volunteer in Spain, Portugal, or Morocco do so on a short-term basis, at organizations that make use of drop-in or once-a-week volunteers. These can be found in virtually every city and are referenced both in this section and in our town and city write-ups themselves. The best way to find opportunities that match up with your interests and schedule may be to check with local or national volunteer centers. A variety of short-term work is generally available, including jobs in construction, conservation, education, health, and law.

More intensive volunteer services may charge you a fee to participate. These costs can be surprisingly hefty (although they frequently cover airfare and most, if not all, living expenses). However, you can sometimes avoid high application fees by contacting the individual workcamps directly. Many people choose to go through a parent organization that handles logistics and frequently provides a group environment and support system. There are two main types of organizations—religious and non-sectarian—although there are rarely restrictions on participation for either.

AmeriSpan, P.O. Box 58129, Philadelphia, PA 19102-8129 USA (In US and Canada ☎ 1-800-879-6640, elsewhere ☎ 215-751-1986; www.amerispan.com). Provides listings of volunteer and internship opportunities in Barcelona and beyond.

Comisión Española de Ayuda al Refugio (CEAR), Fonthonrada 10-2, 08015 Barcelona, Spain (☎ 934 24 27 09; www.cear.es). The fundamental aim of this non-profit non-governmental organization is to protect the right to asylum, especially in Spain. Volunteer opportunities in outreach, legal assistance, translation, and human rights research.

Earthwatch, 3 Clocktower Pl. Suite 100, Box 75, Maynard, MA 01754, USA (☎ 800-776-0188 or 978-461-0081; www.earthwatch.org). Arranges 1- to 3-week programs in Spain to promote conservation of natural resources. Fees vary based on program location and duration; costs average $1700 plus airfare.

We at *Let's Go* have watched the growth of the 'ignorant tourist' stereotype with dismay, knowing that the majority of travelers care passionately about the state of the communities and environments they explore—but also knowing that even conscientious tourists can inadvertently damage natural wonders, rich cultures, and impoverished communities. We believe the philosophy of **sustainable travel** is among the most important travel tips we could impart to our readers, to help guide fellow backpackers and on-the-road philanthropists. By staying aware of the needs and troubles of local communities, today's travelers can be a powerful force in preserving and restoring this fragile world.

Working against the negative consequences of irresponsible tourism is much simpler than it might seem; it is often self-awareness, rather than self-sacrifice, that makes the biggest difference. Simply by trying to spend responsibly and conserve local resources, all travelers can positively impact the places they visit. Let's Go has partnered with **BEST** (**Business Enterprises for Sustainable Travel,** an affiliate of the Conference Board; see www.sustainabletravel.org), which recognizes businesses that operate based on the principles of sustainable travel. Below, they provide advice on how ordinary visitors can practice this philosophy in their daily travels, no matter where they are.

TIPS FOR CIVIC TRAVEL: HOW TO MAKE A DIFFERENCE

Travel by train when feasible. Rail travel requires only half the energy per passenger mile that planes do. On average, each of the 40,000 daily domestic air flights releases more than 1700 pounds of greenhouse gas emissions.

Use public mass transportation whenever possible; outside of cities, take advantage of group taxis or vans. Bicycles are an attractive way of seeing a community firsthand. And enjoy walking—purchase good maps of your destination and ask about on-foot touring opportunities.

When renting a car, ask whether fuel-efficient vehicles are available. Honda and Toyota produce cars that use hybrid engines powered by electricity and gasoline, thus reducing emissions of carbon dioxide. Ford Motor Company plans to introduce a hybrid fuel model by the end of 2004.

Reduce, reuse, recycle—use electronic tickets, recycle papers and bottles wherever possible, and avoid using containers made of styrofoam. Refillable water bottles and rechargable batteries both efficiently conserve expendable resources.

Be thoughtful in your purchases. Take care not to buy souvenir objects made from trees in old-growth or endangered forests, such as teak, or items made from endangered species, like ivory or tortoise jewelry. Ask whether products are made from renewable resources.

Buy from local enterprises, such as casual street vendors. In developing countries and low-income neighborhoods, many people depend on the "informal economy" to make a living.

Be on-the-road-philanthropists. If you are inspired by the natural environment of a destination or enriched by its culture, join in preserving their integrity by making a charitable contribution to a local organization.

Spread the word. Upon your return home, tell friends and colleagues about places to visit that will benefit greatly from their tourist dollars, and reward sustainable enterprises by recommending their services. Travelers can not only introduce friends to particular vendors but also to local causes and charities that they might choose to support when they travel.

Elderhostel, Inc., 11 Ave. de Lafayette, Boston, MA 92111-1746, USA (☎877-426-8056; www.elderhostel.org). Sends volunteers age 55 and older around the world to work in construction, research, teaching, and many other projects. Costs average $100 per day plus airfare.

Habitat for Humanity International, 121 Habitat St., Americus, GA 31709, USA (☎229-924-6935 ext. 2551; www.habitat.org). Volunteers build houses in over 83 countries, including Portugal, for anywhere from 2 weeks to 3 years. Short-term program costs range from US$1200-4000.

Idealist (www.idealist.org). Run by the organization Actions Without Borders, this site has worldwide job and volunteer listings, including some in Spain and Portugal.

Peace Corps, Office of Volunteer Recruitment and Selection, 1111 20th St. NW, Washington, DC 20526, USA (☎800-424-8580; www.peacecorps.gov). Opportunities in 70 developing nations, including Morocco.

Service Civil International Voluntary Service (SCI-IVS), 3213 W. Wheeler St., Seattle, WA 98199, USA (☎/fax 206-350-6585; www.sci-ivs.org). Arranges placement in work camps in Spain and Portugal for those 18+. Registration fee US$65-125.

Stop SIDA, C. Finlandià 45, 08014 Barcelona, Spain (☎900 06 01 60; www.stop-sida.org). Helps combat the spread of AIDS by providing info on AIDS prevention, offering support services, and promoting understanding.

Volunteers for Peace, 1034 Tiffany Rd., Belmont., VT 05730, USA (☎802-259-2759; www.vfp.org). Arranges placement in work camps in Spain and Portugal. Membership required for registration. Annual *International Workcamp Directory* US$20. Programs average US$200-500 for 2-3 weeks.

❗ HOW NOT TO GET SCREWED

Before handing your money over to any volunteer or study abroad program, make sure you know exactly what you're getting into. It's a good idea to get the name of **previous participants** and ask them about their experience, as some programs sound much better on paper than in reality. The **questions** below are a good place to start:

-Will you be the only person in the program? If not, what are the other participants like? How old are they? How much will you be expected to interact with them?

-Is room and board included? If so, what is the arrangement? Will you be expected to share a room? A bathroom? What are the meals like? Do they fit any dietary restrictions?

-Is transportation included? Are there any additional expenses?

-How much free time will you have? Will you be able to travel around?

-What kind of safety network is set up? Will you still be covered by your home insurance? Does the program have an emergency plan?

STUDYING ABROAD

Study abroad programs range from basic language and culture courses to college-level classes, often for credit. In order to choose a program that best fits your needs, you will want to research all you can before making a decision—determine costs and duration, as well as what kind of students participate in the program and what sort of accommodations are provided.

In programs that have large groups of students who speak the same language, there is a trade-off. You may feel more comfortable in the community, but you will not have the same opportunity to practice a foreign language or to befriend other international students. For accommodations, dorm life provides a better opportunity to mingle with fellow students, but there is less of a chance to experience the local scene. If you live with a family, there is a potential to build lifelong friendships with natives and to experience day-to-day life in more depth, but conditions can vary greatly from family to family.

Spain is one of the most popular destinations in the world for study-abroad students. To find out more, contact US university programs and youth organizations that send students to Spanish universities and language centers. Many programs cluster around Madrid, Sevilla, and Salamanca. While not many students think of studying abroad in **Portugal,** most Portuguese universities open their gates to foreign students. Study abroad is rare in **Morocco,** though programs are available.

Studying in Spain and Portugal requires a good deal of regulatory paperwork. Students planning to stay longer than three months must obtain a visa from their destination country's consulate. Those students studying only for the summer (i.e., for less than three months) need only a passport. Individual universities and programs have their own requirements, most of which involve a basic knowledge of the local language and a minimum grade point average.

Those relatively fluent in Spanish, Portuguese, French, or Arabic may find it cheaper to enroll directly in a university abroad, although receiving college credit may be more difficult. Some American schools still require students to pay them for credits obtained elsewhere. Most university-level study-abroad programs are designed as language and cultural enrichment opportunities, and therefore are conducted in the language of the country. Still, many programs offer classes in English as well as beginner- and lower-level language courses.

A good resource for finding programs that cater to your particular interests is **www.studyabroad.com,** which has links to various semester abroad programs based on a variety of criteria, including desired location and focus of study. When contacting individual programs, ask for the names of recent participants to get their evaluation of the program.

UNIVERSITIES

AMERICAN PROGRAMS

Academic Programs International (API), 107 E. Hopkins, San Marcos, TX 78666 (☎800-844-8124; www.academicintl.com). Programs available in Barcelona, Cádiz, Granada, Madrid, Salamanca, and Sevilla. Classes include international business, Spanish literature, and Spanish studies.

American Institute for Foreign Study, College Division, River Plaza, 9 West Broad St., Stamford, CT 06902 (☎800-727-2437, ext. 5163; www.aifsabroad.com). Organizes programs for high school and college study in Spanish universities.

Arcadia University for Education Abroad, 450 S. Easton Rd., Glenside, PA 19038 (☎866-927-2234; www.arcadia.edu/cea). Operates programs in Toledo.

Central College Abroad, Office of International Education, 812 University, Pella, IA 50219 (☎800-831-3629 or 641-628-5284; www.central.edu/abroad). Offers internships, summer-, semester-, and year-long programs in Granada.

School for International Training, Admissions, Kipling Rd., P.O. Box 676, Brattleboro, VT 05302 (☎800-336-1616 or 802-257-7751; www.sit.edu). Semester- and year-long programs in Spain and Morocco. Also runs the **Experiment in International Living** (☎800-345-2929; www.usexperiment.org), 3- to 5-week summer programs that offer high school students homestays, community service, ecological adventures, and language training in Spain.

Council on International Educational Exchange (CIEE), 633 3rd Ave., 20th fl., New York, NY 10017 (☎800-407-8839; www.ciee.org). Sponsors study abroad and volunteer programs in Spain.

International Association for the Exchange of Students for Technical Experience (IAESTE), 10400 Little Patuxent Pkwy. Suite 250, Columbia, MD 21044 (☎410-997-2200; www.aipt.org). 8- to 12-week programs in Spain and Portugal for college students who have completed 2 years of technical study.

Institute for the International Education of Students (IES), 33 N. LaSalle St., 15th fl., Chicago, IL 60602, USA (☎800-995-2300; www.IESabroad.org). Offers year-long, semester, and summer programs for college study in Barcelona, Madrid, and Salamanca. Internship opportunities. US$50 application fee. Scholarships available.

Institute of Spanish Studies, 17303 Southwest 80th Place, Miami, FL 33157 (☎888-454-6777; www.spanish-studies.com). Offers a range of courses in history, Spanish language, and literature. Students live with host families in Valencia.

PROGRAMS IN SPAIN & PORTUGAL

Universities in major cities like Madrid and Lisboa generally have options available for foreign students who wish to study abroad, but many other universities in smaller cities like Salamanca, Granada, and Coimbra also have active study abroad programs and host thousands of foreign students every year. Check with the individual school for specific requirements and enrollment procedures.

Universidad Complutense de Madrid, Vicerectorado de Relaciones Internacionales, Isaac Peral s/n, 28040 Madrid, Spain (☎913 94 69 20; www.ucm.es). Largest university in Spain. Hosts 3500 foreign students annually. Opportunities for study in a variety of fields with or without a specific study abroad program.

Universidade de Lisboa, Rectorate Al. da Universidade, Cidade Universitária, 1649-004 Lisboa, Portugal (☎217 96 76 24; www.ul.pt). Allows foreign students to enroll directly in most of its divisions.

Al Akhawayn University, Office of Admissions, Al Akhawayn University, P.O. Box 104, Ifrane 53000, Morocco (☎055 56 77 77; www.alakhawayn.ma) Welcomes direct enrollment by foreign students. Offers programs with an emphasis on Moroccan culture.

LANGUAGE SCHOOLS

Unlike American universities, language schools are frequently independently-run international or local organizations or divisions of foreign universities that rarely offer college credit. Language schools are a good alternative to university study if you desire a deeper focus on the language or a slightly less rigorous courseload. These programs are also good for high school students who may not feel comfortable with older students in a university program.

Arabic Language Institute in Fez, B.P. 2136, Ville Nouvelle, Fez 30000, Morocco (☎055 62 48 50). Specializes in standard Arabic and colloquial Moroccan Arabic.

Center for Cross-Cultural Study, C. Harinas, 16-18, 41001 Sevilla, Spain (☎954 22 41 07). Coordinates a variety of study-abroad programs in Seville and other parts of Spain. Students take classes either in the center or at the University of Seville. Offices also at 446 Main Street, Amherst, MA 01002-2314, USA (☎413-256-0011; www.cccs.com).

CIAL Centro de Linguas, Av. de República, 41-2° Esq., 1050-191, Lisboa, Portugal (☎217 940 448; www.cial.pt). Portuguese courses in Lisboa, Porto, and Faro.

Centro de Lenguas e Intercambio Cultural (CLIC), C. Albareda, 19, 41080 Sevilla, Spain (☎954 50 21 31; www.clic.es). Over 20 years of experience. Fourteen mix-and-match course programs in 8 levels. Twelve students max. per class. 2-week intensive courses (20hr.) begin at €270. Substantial discounts for longer sessions.

Don Quijote, C. Conde de Ibarra, 2, 41080 Sevilla, Spain (☎923 27 72 00; www.don-quijote.com). A huge language school chain in Spain and Latin America. Offers Spanish courses for all levels in Barcelona, Granada, Madrid, Málaga, Salamanca, Sevilla, and Valencia. Very social atmosphere. 2-week intensive courses (20hr. language plus 5hr. "culture") start at €360. €32 enrollment fee. Large discounts for longer sessions.

Eurocentres, 101 N. Union St. Suite 300, Alexandria, VA 22314, USA (☎703-684-1494; www.eurocentres.com), or in Europe, Head Office, Seestr. 247, CH-8038 Zurich, Switzerland (☎485 50 40; fax 481 61 24). Spanish language programs for beginning to advanced students in Barcelona, Madrid, Málaga, and Salamanca.

Language Immersion Institute, 75 S. Manheim Blvd., SUNY-New Paltz, New Paltz, NY 12561-2499, USA (☎845-257-3500; www.newpaltz.edu/lii). 2-week summer language courses (US$1000) and some overseas courses.

OTHER STUDY ABROAD OPTIONS

For those who are looking for something less traditional, these are only a few of the many exciting opportunities available.

ADENC, C. Sant Isidre, s/n, 08208 Sabadell, Spain (☎937 17 18 87; www.adenc.org). Catalan conservation group offers short summer courses on bird-watching, astronomy, biology, and other eco-tourism related topics.

Escuela de Cocina Luis Irizar, C. Mari, 5, 20003 San Sebastián, Spain (☎943 43 15 40; www.escuelairizar.com). Learn how to cook Basque cuisine at this culinary institute. Programs range from the comprehensive 2-year apprenticeship to week-long summer courses. Some of the summer courses may be taught in English.

Taller Flamenco School, C. Peral, 49, E-41002 Sevilla, Spain (☎954 56 42 34; www.tallerflamenco.com). Offers courses in *flamenco* dance (€180-240 per week) and guitar (€204 per week) with substantial discounts for longer commitments.

WORKING ABROAD

As with volunteering, work opportunities tend to fall into two categories. Some travelers want long-term jobs that allow them to get to know another part of the world as a member of the community, while other travelers seek out short-term jobs to finance the next leg of their travels. This section discusses both short-term and long-term opportunities for working in Spain and Portugal. Make sure you understand the requirements for **visas** and **work permits** for working in these countries, as they are often complicated. See the box on p. 13 for more information on visas. Travelers from within the European Union can work in any EU member country, but those from outside the EU need a work permit. All foreign workers in Morocco are required to have a permit.

LONG-TERM WORK

If you're planning on spending more than three months working in Spain or Portugal, search for a job well in advance. International placement agencies are often the easiest way to find employment abroad, especially for teaching English. **Internships,** usually for college students, are a good way to segue into working abroad, although they are often unpaid or poorly paid (many say the experience, however, is well worth it). Be wary of advertisements or companies that offer to get you a job abroad for a fee—the same listings are often available online or in newspapers, or may be out of date.

In **Spain,** the national employment service *(Oficinas de Empleo)* has a monopoly on the job-finding market; begin your search here. Many seasoned travelers, however, go straight to a particular town's Yellow Pages *(Las Paginas Amarillas)* or even go door-to-door in the town in which they are staying. In **Portugal,** the English-language weekly newspaper *Anglo-Portuguese News* carries job listings. In **Morocco,** contact your national consulate for a list of schools and organizations with openings. Additional resources for Spain and Portugal include:

Career Journal (www.careerjournaleurope.com). The *Wall Street Journal* publishes this online journal listing thousands of jobs throughout Europe. There are both short- and long-term jobs; part- and full-time jobs.

Escape Artist (www.escapeartist.com/jobs/overseas1). Provides information on living abroad, including job listings for Spain and Portugal.

Go Jobsite (www.gojobsite.com). Lists jobs for European countries, including Spain.

Resort Jobs (www.resortjobs.com). Self-explanatory and ridiculously cool. Short- and long-term jobs in some of the most beautiful places on the planet. Jobs include camp counseling, bartending, waiting tables, and working on a cruise ship.

Trabajos (www.trabajos.com). Provides job listings for all regions of Spain.

Working Adventures Worldwide (www.bunac.org). A database of programs which incorporate adventure travel and work.

TEACHING ENGLISH

Teaching English is one of the most popular jobs in Spain and Portugal for those craving a more long-term experience. For non-EU citizens, teaching English is likely one of the few options available that avoid the long and bureaucratic process of obtaining a work permit through a sponsoring company. However, even though the teaching job market in Spain has become one of the world's largest, it has recently begun to slow down. Non-EU citizens in particular may have difficulty immediately landing a job; it might be easier to find work in Portugal, especially in the north. Morocco generally has fewer jobs than Spain and Portugal. Still, with persistence, you should be able to find a job in the country of your choice.

Teaching jobs abroad are rarely well-paid, although some elite private American schools can pay somewhat competitive salaries. Volunteering as a teacher in lieu of getting paid is also a popular option; even in those cases, teachers often get some sort of a daily stipend to help with living expenses. Do not be deterred by the seemingly low salaries, particularly in Morocco, which has a low cost of living. You will be living on a different scale abroad, making low-paying jobs much more profitable. In almost all cases, you must have at least a bachelor's degree to be a full-fledged teacher, although college undergraduates can often get summer positions teaching or tutoring.

ALTERNATIVES TO TOURISM

Many schools require teachers to have a **Teaching English as a Foreign Language (TEFL)** certificate. Lack of the TEFL does not necessarily exclude you from finding a teaching job, but certified teachers often find higher paying jobs. Native English speakers working in private schools are most often hired for English-immersion classrooms where no local languages are spoken. Those volunteering or teaching in public, poorer schools, are more likely to be working in both English and Spanish, Portuguese, or Arabic. Placement agencies or university fellowship programs are the best resources for finding teaching jobs in Spain, Portugal, and Morocco. The alternative is to make contacts directly with schools or just to try your luck once you get there. If you are going to try the latter, the best time of the year is several weeks before the start of the school year. The following organizations are extremely helpful in finding a teaching job in Spain, Portugal, and Morocco.

Dave's ESL Cafe (www.eslcafe.com). Site dedicated to teaching English as a second language worldwide. Job listings and advice offered.

International Schools Services (ISS), 15 Roszel Rd., Box 5910, Princeton, NJ 08543-5910, USA (☎609-452-0990; www.iss.edu). Hires teachers for more than 200 overseas schools, several in Spain and Morocco; candidates should have experience teaching or with international affairs. 2-year commitment expected.

Teach Abroad (www.teach.studyabroad.com). Sponsored by Study Abroad, brings you to listings around the world for paid or stipended positions to teach English.

TeachAbroad.com (www.teachabroad.com). Features worldwide job listings including some in Spain, Portugal, and Morocco.

TESOL-Spain (www.tesol-spain.org). Non-profit association of English teachers in Spain. Site features a jobs board among its many resources.

AU PAIR WORK

Au pairs are typically women, aged 18-27, who work as live-in nannies, caring for children and doing light housework in foreign countries in exchange for room, board, and a small spending allowance or stipend. Most former au-pairs speak favorably of their experience and of how it allowed them to get to know a foreign country without the high cost of traveling. Drawbacks, however, often include long hours of constantly being on duty and mediocre pay (€55-60 per week). Ultimately, much of the au pair experience depends on the family you're placed with. The agencies below are good starting points.

Accord Cultural Exchange, 3145 Geary Blvd., San Francisco, CA 94121, USA (☎415-386-6203; www.aupairsaccord.com).

Au Pair Homestay, World Learning, Inc., 1015 15th St. NW, Suite 750, Washington, DC 20005, USA (☎800-287-2477; fax 202-408-5397).

Au Pair in Europe, P.O. Box 68056, Blakely Postal Outlet, Hamilton, Ontario L8M 3M7 Canada (☎905-545-6305; www.princeent.com/aupair).

Childcare International, Ltd., Trafalgar House, Grenville Pl., London NW7 3SA UK (☎+44 020 8906 3116; www.childint.co.uk).

InterExchange, 161 Sixth Ave., New York, NY 10013, USA (☎212-924-0446; www.interexchange.org).

SHORT-TERM WORK

Traveling for long periods of time can get expensive. Those with unlimited time but not unlimited money often work odd jobs for a few weeks at a time to finance another month or two of travel. Because the process for obtaining a work permit is often long, complicated, bureaucratic, and requires a prior job contract, few travelers seeking short-term work have one. For non-EU citizens, working without a permit is illegal in Spain and Portugal, but many establishments hire travelers illegally, particularly in highly seasonal resort areas. These jobs often include bartending, waiting tables, or promoting bars and clubs. Another popular option is to work several hours a day at a hostel in exchange for free or discounted room and/or board. Most often, these short-term jobs are found by word of mouth, or simply by talking to the owner of a hostel, restaurant, or bar. Many places, especially because of the high turnover in the tourism industry, are always eager for help, even if only temporary. *Let's Go* tries to list temporary jobs like these whenever possible; look in the practical information sections of larger cities, or check out the list below for some of the available short-term jobs in popular destinations. *Let's Go* does not recommend working illegally.

Intern Jobs (www.internjobs.com). Not only lists internships, but also includes many ideal short-term jobs like camp counseling and bartending.

Summer Jobs (www.summerjobs.com). A website mostly for those 25 and under (students) who are looking for summer jobs. The website also has listings for resources where students can find the most up-to-date job listings.

Bodega Tour Guide, in Jerez de la Frontera, Spain (see p. 266). Many of Jerez's famed sherry *bodegas* hire summer guides. Call the *bodegas* directly for more information.

ADVENTURE TRAVEL

Why bum around cathedrals and museums all day, when you could be out schlepping through national parks, frolicking with wildlife, or hanggliding above it all? The following sites organize rather extreme travel packages worldwide, including Spain, Portugal, and Morocco, and may be a good option for those seeking their inner backpacker. Nevertheless, there are plenty of opportunities for outdoor adventure in Spain, Portugal, and Morocco without going through an agency: wildlife preserves, hiking, rafting, climbing, canyoning, skiing, and surfing await.

Adventure Travel (www.adventuretravelabroad.com). Listings of adventure travel trips around the world.

Blue Dog Adventures (www.bluedogadventures.com). Runs unbelievably exciting tour and adventure expeditions around the world; activities offered include breaking horses, becoming a white water rafting expert, and roping cattle.

Global Eco and Spiritual Tours (www.globalecospiritualtours.org). Gives adventure travel tours, clearly with a focus on ecotourism and spirituality, around the world.

Working Adventures Worldwide (www.bunac.org). Lists programs incorporating adventure travel and work.

FOR FURTHER READING ON ALTERNATIVES TO TOURISM

Alternatives to the Peace Corps: A Directory of Third World and U.S. Volunteer Opportunities, by Joan Powell. Food First Books, 2000. (US$10)

How to Get a Job in Europe, by Sanborn and Matherly. Surrey Books, 1999. (US$22)

How to Live Your Dream of Volunteering Overseas, by Collins, DeZerega, and Heckscher. Penguin Books, 2002. (US$17)

International Directory of Voluntary Work, by Whetter and Pybus. Peterson's Guides and Vacation Work, 2000. (US$16)

International Jobs, by Kocher and Segal. Perseus Books, 1999. (US$18)

Invest Yourself: The Catalogue of Volunteer Opportunities. Commission on Voluntary Service and Action (☎ 718-638-8487).

Overseas Summer Jobs 2002, by Collier and Woodworth. Peterson's Guides and Vacation Work, 2002. (US$18)

Transitions Abroad. http://www.transitionsabroad.com/listings/work/resources/.

Work Abroad: The Complete Guide to Finding a Job Overseas, by Hubbs, Griffith, and Nolting. Transitions Abroad Publishing, 2000. (US$16)

Work Your Way Around the World, by Susan Griffith. Worldview Publishing Services, 2001. (US$18)

SPAIN

Imagine a parched central plateau surrounded by lush rolling hills, craggy snow-covered peaks, and glistening white sand beaches, a land where tradition and modern life collide with spectacular results, one whose glorious past is overshadowed only by its people's passion for living. This is Spain. Though travelers are drawn here by visions of flamenco dancers and bullfighting, these are but two sides of the country's personality. A banquet of civilizations and empires stretched out like the world's ultimate *tapas* bar, attended over a millennium by foreign invaders, artistic and literary geniuses, architectural masterpieces, and religious conflicts. Spain gorged itself, resulting in a cultural cocktail spiked with an enviable array of artistic and architectural treasures and an unmistakable flair for the celebratory. Modern Spain is a constellation of autonomous regions, each with its own character and often its own language. Speaking of "the Spains" as a whole is difficult, but there is a certain indefinable yet irrepressible spirit that binds the country together. Travelers who come here find breathtaking landscapes and priceless cultural riches along with some of the world's best nightlife and wildest festivals. Easily accessible and relatively inexpensive, Spain mesmerizes visitors with its vibrant energy and unforgettable hospitality.

HISTORY

With a history that spans over 50 constitutions, an endless array of amorphous kingdoms controlled by indigenous Iberians, Celts, Romans, Visigoths, Arabs, and French, and an empire that once spread to the Americas, Spain has emerged financially scarred but culturally enriched from its encounters as both colony and colonizer. Beginning in 1588, Spain began a long and arduous descent from world-class empire to Pyrenean pauper, during which its military defeats were matched only by its artistic and literary achievements.

RULE HISPANIA (PREHISTORY-476 AD). Spain was colonized by a succession of civilizations—**Basque** (considered indigenous), **Tartesian, Iberian, Celtic, Greek, Phoenician,** and **Carthaginian**—each of which left its mark cultural mark before the **Romans** dropped in with a vengeance in the 3rd century BC. Over nearly seven centuries, the Romans drastically altered the face and character of Spain, introducing their language, architecture, roads, irrigation techniques, and cultivation of grapes, olives, and wheat. A slew of Germanic tribes, including Swabians and Vandals, swept over Iberia, but the **Visigoths,** newly converted Christians, emerged above the rest. The Visigoths established their court at Barcelona in 415 AD and effectively ruled Spain for the next three hundred years.

PLEASE, SIR, MAY I HAVE SOME MOORS? (711-1492). Following Muslim unification, a small force of **Arabs, Berbers,** and **Syrians** invaded Spain in 711. Practically welcomed by the divided Visigoths, the Moors encountered little resistance, and the peninsula soon fell under the dominion of the caliphate of Damascus. Christian hero Roland blew his horn at **Roncevalles** in 778, but to no avail; the Umayyad Moors set up their Iberian capital in **Córdoba.** During **Abderramán III's** rule in the 10th century, some considered Spain the wealthiest and most cultivated country in the world. His successor, **Al Mansur,** snuffed out all opposition within his extravagant court and undertook a series of military campaigns that climaxed with the destruction of **Santiago de Compostela** in 997 and the kidnapping of its

Spain

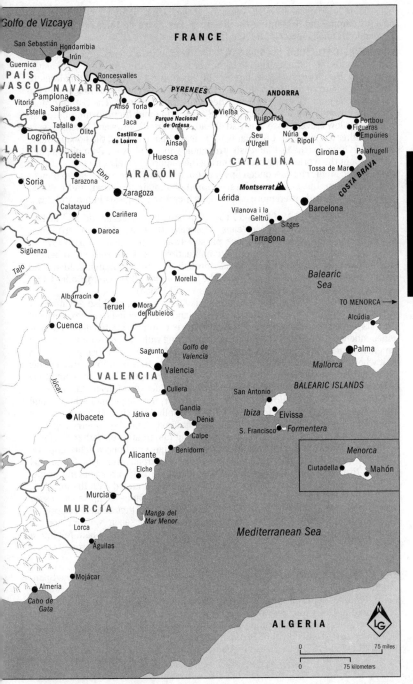

bells. The Christians needed 240 years to get them back, fighting a number of successful campaigns, including the battle of **Las Navas de Tolosa** (1212), until Fernando III finally took Córdoba in 1236.

LOS REYES CATÓLICOS (1469-1516). It took almost 750 years, if you count the 718 victory of the Asturian Don Pelayo over a Muslim army in Covadonga as the start of *la Reconquista* (Reconquest) of Spain, for the Christian kingdoms to "retake" Spain from the Moors. In 1469, the marriage of **Fernando de Aragón** and **Isabel de Castilla** joined Iberia's two mightiest Christian kingdoms. The Catholic Monarchs introduced the **Inquisition** in 1478, executing and then burning heretics, principally Jews (even those who had already converted). Jews and Muslims were forced either to convert to Christianity or to leave Spain. In 1492, the power couple captured Granada (the last Moorish stronghold) and swallowed Columbus's pack of lies about the world being round. During their approximately fifty years of rule, the Catholic Monarchs ensconced Spain as not only the prime European exponent of Catholicism, but also as an international economic, political, and cultural power—power made even more enduring by lucrative conquests in the Americas.

ENTER THE HABSBURGS (1516-1713). The daughter of Fernando and Isabel, **Juana la Loca** (the Mad), married **Felipe el Hermoso** (the Fair) of the powerful Habsburg family. When *Señor Hermoso* passed away after a game of *jai alai* (an apparently lethal lacrosse/racquetball combination), *La Loca* refused to believe that he had died and dragged his corpse through the streets screaming. Juana and Felipe secured their genetic legacy with the birth of the half-Habsburg **Carlos I,** better known as Holy Roman Emperor Charles V (1516-1556).

Felipe II (1556-1598) inherited not only his father's nose, but also a handful of rebellious territories in the Protestant Netherlands. He decided to annex Portugal after its ailing Dom Henrique died in 1580. One year later, the Dutch declared their independence from Spain, and Felipe began warring with the Protestants, spurring an embroilment with England's Elizabeth I. The war with the British ground to a halt when Sir Francis Drake totaled Spain's invincible **Armada** in 1588. Much of his European empire lost and wealth from the Americas sapped, Felipe retreated to **El Escorial** and sulked in its monastery through the last decade of his reign.

Felipe III (1598-1621) allowed his favorite adviser, the Duque de Lerma, to pull the governmental strings. In 1609, the two expelled nearly 300,000 of Spain's remaining Moors. **Felipe IV** (1621-1665) painstakingly held the country together through his long, tumultuous reign. Emulating his great-grandfather Carlos I, Felipe IV patronized the arts (painter Diego Velázquez and playwrights Lope de Vega and Calderón de la Barca graced his court) and architecture (the Parque del Buen Retiro in Madrid). Then the **Thirty Years' War** (1618-1648) broke out in Europe, and defending Catholicism drained Spain's resources. It ended with the marriage of Felipe IV's daughter María Teresa to Louis XIV of France. Felipe's successor **Carlos II El Hechizado** (the bewitched; 1665-1700), product of generations of inbreeding, was known to fly into fits of rage and epileptic seizures. From then on, little went right: Carlos II left no heirs because of his "problem," Spain fell into a depression, and cultural bankruptcy ensued. Rulers from all over Europe battled for the Spanish crown; the War of the Spanish Succession had begun.

THE REIGN IN SPAIN (1713-1923). The 1713 Peace of Utrecht ended the Spanish Succession ordeal (and Spain's possession of Gibraltar) and seated **Felipe V** (1713-1746), a Bourbon grandson of **Louis XIV,** on the Spanish throne. The king built ostentatious palaces to mimic Versailles and cultivated a flamboyant, debaucherous court. Still, Felipe competently administered the Empire, at last beginning to regain control of Spanish-American trade lost to northern Europe. **Carlos III** (1759-1788) was probably Madrid's finest "mayor," founding academies and beautifying the capital. Spain's global standing recovered enough for it to team with France to help the American colonies gain independence from Britain, aid symbolized by Captain Bernardo de Gálvez's victories in the American South.

As part of his world domination trip, **Napoleon** invaded Spain in 1808, inaugurating an occupation commensurate with the general's height that ended, ironically enough, when the Protestant Brits beat up the Corsican's troops at Waterloo (1814). This victory led to the restoration of reactionary **Fernando VII** (1814-1833), who sought to revoke the progressive *Constitución de Cádiz* of 1812. Galvanized by Fernando's ineptitude and inspired by liberal ideas in the new constitution, most of Spain's Latin American empire soon threw off the colonial yoke. Domestically, parliamentary liberalism was restored in 1833 upon Fernando VII's death and survived the conservative challenge of the first **Carlist War** (1833-1840); it would dominate Spanish politics until 1837, when the monarchy was so weakened that the first **Spanish republic** was proclaimed. Despite the political anarchy that ensued until the **Primo de Rivera** dictatorship in the 1920s, rapid industrialization and prosperity marked the last two decades of 19th-century Spain. During this period, the wealth produced by Catalunya's industrially-inspired *Renaixença* (Renaissance) financed Barcelona's **Modernista** movement in architecture and design. But Spain's 1898 loss to the US in the **Spanish-American War** cost it the Philippines, Puerto Rico, Cuba, and any dreams left of Latin American wealth.

Closer to home, Moroccan tribesmen rebelled against Spanish troops in northern Africa beginning in 1917, resulting in a series of embarrassing military defeats that further weakened Spaniards' morale and culminated with the **massacre** of 14,000 Spanish troops in 1921, an event which threatened the very survival of the monarchy. The search for those "responsible" for the disaster occupied aristocrats, bureaucrats, and generals for the next decade, throwing the country into political and social chaos. General Miguel Primo de Rivera brought both order and unprofessionalism to the situation, introducing Spain to dictatorship in 1923.

REPUBLIC & REBELLION (1931-1939). In April 1931, **King Alfonso XIII** (1902-1931) abdicated, disgraced by his support for the Primo de Rivera dictatorship and afraid of his own military, giving rise to the **Second Republic** (1931-1936). Republican Liberals and Socialists established safeguards for farmers and industrial workers, granted women's suffrage, assured religious tolerance, and chipped away at traditional military dominance. National euphoria, however, faded fast. The 1933 elections split the Republican-Socialist coalition, increasing the power of right wing and Catholic parties in parliament. Military dissatisfaction led to a heightened profile of the **Fascist Falange** (founded by Primo de Rivera's son José Antonio), which further polarized national politics. By 1936, radicals, anarchists, Socialists, and Republicans had formed a **Popular Front** coalition to win the February elections, though the victory was short-lived. Once **Generalísimo Francisco Franco** snatched control of the Spanish army, militarist uprisings ensued, and the nation plunged into war. The **Spanish Civil War** (1936-1939) ignited worldwide ideological passions. Germany and Italy dropped troops, supplies, and munitions into Franco's lap, while the US and liberal European states hid behind the Non-Intervention Treaty. The Soviet Union organized the International Brigades—an amalgamation of Communists and other leftist volunteers from all over Europe and the US—to battle Franco's fascism. But soon after, aid waned as Stalin began to see the benefits of an alliance with Hitler. All told, bombings, executions, combat, starvation, and disease took nearly 600,000 lives and forced nearly a million to emigrate. In April 1939, Franco marched into Madrid and ended the war.

FRANCO & THE NATIONAL TRAGEDY (1939-1975). As scientists, artists, intellectuals, and sympathizers emigrated or faced imprisonment and execution, dissatisfied workers and students took to the streets, fomenting regional discontent and international isolation. Groups like the **Basque ETA** resisted the dictatorship throughout Franco's reign, often via terrorist acts. In his old age, Franco tried to smooth international relations by joining NATO, courting the Pope, and encouraging tourism, but the **national tragedy** (as it was later called) did not officially end until Franco did in 1975. King Juan Carlos I (1975-), grandson of Alfonso XIII and nominally a Franco protégé, carefully set out to undo Franco's damage.

TRANSITION TO DEMOCRACY (1975-2000). In 1978, under centrist prime minister Adolfo Suárez, Spain adopted a new constitution and restored parliamentary government and regional autonomy. The post-Franco years have been marked by progressive social change. Although many women choose to fulfill more traditional roles, still more continue to chip away at the glass ceiling in the public sector, and Spain has one of the most active trade union cultures in Europe. Suárez's resignation in early 1981 left the country ripe for an attempted **coup** on February 23, when a group of rebels took over parliament in an effort to impose a military-backed government. King Juan Carlos used his personal influence to convince the rebels to stand down, and order was restored, paving the way for the charismatic **Felipe González** to lead the PSOE (Spanish Socialist Worker's Party) to victory in the 1982 elections. González opened the Spanish economy and championed consensus policies, overseeing Spain's integration into the European Community (now the EU) four years later. Despite unpopular economic stands, González was reelected in 1986 and continued a program of massive public investment that rejuvenated the nation's economy. By the end of 1993, however, recession and revelations of large-scale corruption led to a resounding Socialist defeat at the hands of the Partido Popular (PP) in the 1994 European parliamentary elections. **José María Aznar** has helmed the PP ever since, managing to maintain a fragile coalition with the support of the Catalan and Canary Islands regional parties. Though the PP won an absolute majority in 2000, their fearless leader Aznar intends to step down before elections in 2005, possibly to assume a larger role in EU affairs and to avoid further criticism of his pro-United States stance on affairs in the Middle East.

CURRENT EVENTS

Basque separatists in northwestern Spain have pressed on in their effort to establish an autonomous state. The movement's militant wing, **Euskadi Ta Askatasuna** (ETA; Basque Homeland and Freedom), is known for its terrorist activities; over 800 people have been killed since 1968, though their trademark car bombings commonly target specific politicians rather than innocent bystanders. In June 2002, authorities seized 288 pounds of dynamite near Valencia, charging ETA with planning to strike tourist spots along the Mediterranean coast. Finally, during a 2002 EU summit in Sevilla, ETA planted several car bombs in resort towns along the Costa del Sol and northern Spain, injuring several. In the fall of 2002, controversy ensued when the Spanish parliament banned **Herri Batasuna**, a pro-independence Basque political party that prime minister Aznar and others allege to be allied with ETA. The bombings of two hotels in heavily-tourist Benidorm and Alicante in July 2003 are only the most recent attempts to intimidate the Spanish government. Thankfully, ETA notified the hotels prior to the attacks, so injuries were minimal.

For the past three hundred years, Spain has fought an uphill battle to regain control of **Gibraltar**, a strategic 6km territory in the south currently under British rule. Despite considerable resistance from the Rock, which is overwhelmingly loyal to the crown, Britain's desire to improve relations with Spain has paved the way for some concessions. In November 2001, Spain and Britain vowed to resolve the Gibraltar issue by summer 2002, considering proposals such as joint Anglo-Spanish sovereignty and self-government. But Gibraltarians continue to delay agreements, registering their disapproval through massive pro-British marches and media campaigns against Spanish rule.

In July 2002, a handful of Moroccan soldiers "occupied" the goat-infested island of **Perejil** in Spanish territorial waters off Morocco, sparking an international event proportionate to Spain's role in international affairs. After withdrawing its ambassador and deploying nothing less than helicopters and a destroyer (all without consulting the UN), Spain removed the soldiers and their Morocco flag amid much fanfare and grandstanding. Its sovereignty and military prowess secured, Spain could once again direct its attention to pressing internal affairs, such as increased **immigration** from northern Africa and environmental protection.

PEOPLE & CULTURE

LANGUAGE

Castellano (Castilian), spoken almost everywhere, is Spain's official language. **Català** (Catalan) is spoken throughout Catalunya in the northeast and is the official language of Andorra. It has given rise through permutations to **valencià** (Valencian), the regional tongue of Valencia, and **mallorquí,** the principal dialect of the Islas Baleares. The once-Celtic northwest corner of Iberia gabs in **gallego** (Galician), which is closely related to Portuguese. Although more prevalent in the countryside than cities, Galician is now spreading among the young, as is **euskera** (Basque), spoken in País Vasco and northern Navarra. Tiny Asturias even has its own dialect, **bable,** spoken mostly among older generations.

City and provincial names in this guide are listed in Castilian first, followed by the regional language in parentheses where appropriate. Information within cities (i.e. street and plaza names) is listed in the regional language. For a **phrasebook, glossary,** and **pronunciation guide,** see p. 813.

RELIGION

The **Roman Catholic Church** has dominated everyday life in Spain since 1492, but there are still remnants of a strong **Jewish** and **Muslim** heritage. **Protestant** denominations enjoy begrudging tolerance, but the Catholic Church still reigns supreme even though congregations are increasingly grey-headed. Many towns still celebrate their patron saint's feast day as they have for hundreds of years. Treat churches, cathedrals, and **soccer** stadiums with respect, as most Spaniards are deeply religious and expect you to behave properly in sacred places of worship.

FOOD & DRINK

Spanish food's taste often ranks above appearance, preparation is rarely complicated, and many of the best meals are served not in expensive restaurants, but rather in private homes or streetside bars. All of this has begun to change, however, as Spanish food becomes increasingly sophisticated and cosmopolitan. Fresh local ingredients are still an integral part of the cuisine, varying according to each region's climate, geography, and history.

LOCAL FARE

ANDALUCÍA. Andalusian cuisine is the oldest in Spain, flavored with spices and prepared according to traditional methods brought by Islamic tribes during the first millennium. Centuries later, it was through Sevilla that New World products like corn, peppers, tomatoes, and potatoes first entered Europe. Andalusians have since mastered the art of *gazpacho*, a cool, tomato-based soup perfectly suited to the hot southern climate. The area is also known for its *pescadito frito* (fried fish), *rabo de toro* (bull's tail), egg yolk desserts, sherry wines, and tasty *tapas*. Spain's best cured ham, *jamón ibérico*, comes from the town of Jabugo, where black-footed pigs gain special flavor from daily oak acorn feasts.

CENTRAL SPAIN. Sheep share space with more of these prized pigs in nearby **Extremadura,** where the pastoral life has lent itself to *cocidos* (hearty stews), cheeses, and unique meals based on *migas* (bread crumbs). This type of dry-land "shepherd's cuisine" dominates central Spain. **Castilla La Mancha** is famous for its sheep's milk *queso manchego*, the most widely eaten cheese in Spain, while lamb and roasted game are essential parts of menus both here and in **Castilla y Léon.** *Escabeche*, an Arab tradition of sautéing with lemon or vinegar, has become a Castilian specialty, as has *tortilla española* (potato omelette) and *menestra de verduras*, a succulent vegetable mix. **Madrid** rivals Andalucía with its *tapas* offerings and renowned *cocido madrileño*, a heavy stew of meats, cabbage, carrots, and potatoes.

CANTABRIAN COAST. Farther north, the 800 miles of coastline fringing **Galicia** ensure that shellfish dishes are prepared to emphasize freshness. Octopus, spider crab, and mussels are popular here, as is *empanada gallega*, the Galician pastry filled with everything from pork to chicken to fish. In **Asturias,** dried beans rule the kitchen; *fabada asturiana*, a bean and sausage stew, is the best-known hearty dish for regaining strength after a long work day. Apples, *cidra* (cider), and cow's milk are also especially good here. **Cantabrian** sardines, tuna, and anchovies are among the best in Spain. Food in the **País Vasco** rivals that of Catalunya in national prominence. Popular dishes include *bacalao* (salted codfish), *angulas* (baby eels), and squid *en su tinta* (in its own ink). It was also in the Basque country that Spain's first gastronomic society was founded on January 1, 1900; these all-male cooking groups now number over 1,000.

NORTH CENTRAL. **Navarra** boasts the best red peppers in Spain, as well as the famous Roncal cheese; cooked game, sausages, and caldron stews are popular here. Neighboring **La Rioja** is known for its pork, vegetables, and above all *vino* (wine). **Aragón's** hearty cuisine reflects the region's varied character. *Migas de pastor* (bread crumbs fried with ham) and lamb chops are ubiquitous; more surprising treats include *chilindrón* (lamb and chicken stewed with red peppers) and *melocotones al vino* (sweet native peaches steeped in wine).

MEDITERRANEAN. In **Catalunya,** the Roman trilogy of olives, vineyards, and wheat dominates. Seafood, grilling, and unique sauces are key elements of many meals. **Valencia,** on the Mediterranean coast, has been the home of *paella* and oranges ever since Arab short-grain rice and American oranges were introduced to the area. Less than 200 years old, *paella* has evolved from a simple vegetable-rice dish to an increasingly elaborate mix of rice, vegetables, seafood, poultry, and meats.

MEALS & DINING HOURS

Spaniards start their day with a continental breakfast of coffee or thick, liquid chocolate combined with *bollos* (rolls) and *churros* (lightly fried fritters). Mid-morning they often have another coffee with a *tapa* to tide them over to the main meal of the day, *la comida*, eaten around 2 or 3pm. *La comida* consists of several courses: an appetizer of soup or salad; a main course of meat, fish, or a twist like *paella*; and a dessert of fruit, cheese, or sweets. Supper at home, *la cena*, tends to be light, usually a sandwich or tortilla consumed around 8pm. Eating out starts anywhere between 9pm and midnight. Going out for *tapas* is an integral part of the Spanish lifestyle; groups of friends will often spend several hours moving from bar to bar.

EATING OUT

While some restaurants are open from 8am to 1 or 2am, most serve meals from 1 or 2 to 4pm only and in the evening from 8pm until midnight. Some hints: eating at the bar is cheaper than at tables, and the check won't be brought to your table unless you request it. (*"La cuenta, por favor."*) Service in Spain is notoriously slow and at times frustrating. Many *bar-restaurantes* (and some *hostales*) have cozy *comedores* (dining rooms) on the premises. Diners will repeatedly come across three options. **Platos combinados** (combination platters) include a main course and side dishes on a single plate, plus bread and sometimes a drink. Spaniards commonly choose the **menú del día**—two or three dishes, bread, wine/beer/mineral water, and dessert—for the *comida*, a good deal at roughly €5-9. Those dining **á la carte** choose from individual entrees. Large *tapas*, often comparable in size to entrees, are called *raciones*.

DRINKY DRINKS

Cultivate your palate with the fine potpourri of Spanish wine. When in doubt among your choices, the *vino de la casa* (house wine) is an economical, often delectable choice. Also good are *vino tinto* (red wine), *vino blanco* (white wine), or *rosado* (rosé). For a taste, get a *chato* (small glass). Mild, fragrant reds are Spain's best vintages, but the crops of fine wines are vast. La Mancha's **Valdepeñas** are light, dry reds and whites, consumed without long aging. Catalunya's whites and **cavas** (champagnes) and Aragón's Cariñena wines pack bold punches. **Sidra** (alcoholic cider) from Asturias and País Vasco, and **sangría** (a red-wine punch with sliced peaches and oranges, seltzer, sugar, and a dash of brandy) are delicious alcoholic options. A popular light drink is *tinto de verano*, a cool mix of red wine and carbonated mineral water. **Jerez** (sherry), Spain's most famous wine, hails from Jerez de la Frontera in Andalucía. Try the dry *fino* and *amontillado* as aperitifs, or finish off a rich supper with the sweet *dulce*. The manzanilla produced in Sanlúcar has a salty aftertaste, ascribed to the region's saline soil.

Wash down your *tapas* with a *caña de cerveza*, a normal-sized draft-beer. A *tubo* is a little bigger than a *caña*, and small beers go by different names—*corto* in Castilla, *zurito* in Basque. Pros refer to **mixed drinks** as *copas*. Beer and Schweppes make a **clara**. A **calimocho**, popular with young crowds, mixes Coca-Cola and red wine. Older drinkers prefer **sol y sombra** (brandy and anise). Spain whips up numerous non-alcoholic quenchers as well, notably **horchata de chufa** (made by blending almonds and ice) and the flavored crushed-ice **granizados**. *Café solo* means black coffee; add a touch of milk for a *nube*; a little more and it's a *café cortado*; half milk, half coffee and you have *café con leche*.

CUSTOMS & ETIQUETTE

Although Spaniards are stereotyped as proud, they are generally polite, courteous, and kind to foreigners. Attempts at correct behavior will not go unnoticed; you'll be treated with cooperative friendliness if you make the extra effort.

TABOOS. As is to be expected, Spaniards take offense to critical comments about their country, their leaders, and their customs. Foreigners should be careful when approaching Spanish women; overly *macho* fathers, husbands, or boyfriends can be unusually sensitive and aggressive. Though dress in Spain is obviously more casual in the hot summer months than in winter, strapless tops on women and collarless t-shirts on men are generally unacceptable. Be cautious of shorts and flip-flops; they may be seen as disrespectful in some public establishments.

SPAIN

PUBLIC BEHAVIOR. Strongly individualistic, Spaniards are formally polite in mannerisms and social behavior. To blend in, it's a good idea to be as formal as possible upon a first meeting. Introduce yourself in detail, giving more than just your *nombre* (name). You'll be welcomed openly and made to feel at home if you mention who you are, where you're from, and what you are doing in Spain. Be sure to address Spaniards as *Señor* (Mr.), *Señora* (Mrs.), or *Señorita* (Ms.), and don't be surprised if you get kissed on both cheeks instead of receiving a handshake. Also, don't yawn or stretch in public; this is considered disrespectful, and your actions could garner some glares and grimaces.

TABLE MANNERS. Having a meal, whether at home or at a restaurant, is one of the most popular forms of socializing in Spain. The key to acceptance at a Spanish *mesa* is not imitating *how* Spaniards eat, but rather eating *when* they do. You'll encounter odd looks if you demand an evening meal at six o'clock. As for Spanish table manners, be sure to eat with both your fork *and* your knife in hand at all times, and make sure both hands are visible during the meal.

THE ARTS

From the dark solemnity of El Greco's paintings to the playful exuberance of Gaudí's buildings, Spanish art and architecture ranges from the austere to the ostentatious. While the tradition has been shaped by foreign influences, Spain's dazzling architecture, paintings, and literature are distinctly Spanish.

ARCHITECTURE

Spanish architecture is as impressive and varied as the civilizations that have ruled the Iberian peninsula. Remnants of Spain's glorious past dot the landscape, hinting at the wealth and power that once flowed through the land. Bold postmodern projects promise to maintain Spain's proud architectural tradition for years to come.

ANCIENT & EARLY MODERN. Scattered **Roman ruins** testify to six centuries of colonization. Highlights include some of the finest Roman ruins in existence: the aqueduct in Segovia, the theater in Mérida, and the town of Tarragona. Other vestiges of Spain's Roman past lie at the ruined towns of Itálica (near Sevilla), Sagunto (near Valencia), and Empúries (near Palafrugell).

After the invasion of AD 711, the **Moors** constructed mosques and palaces throughout southern Spain. Because the Qur'an forbids human and animal representation, Moorish architects thought of other ways to adorn their buildings, lavishing them with stylized geometric designs, red-and-white horseshoe arches, and ornate tiles. Intricate and elegant decorative work combined with courtyards, pools, and fountains created buildings destined to delight the senses. The spectacular 14th-century **Alhambra** in Granada, said to be one of the most beautiful buildings in the world, and the **Mezquita** in Córdoba epitomize the Moorish style. Long periods of peaceful coexistence between Islam and Christianity created two architectural movements unique to Spain—**Mozárabe** and **Mudéjar**. Christians living under Muslim rule adopted Moorish design elements to create the distinctive Mozárabe style. The more prevalent and striking Mudéjar architecture was created by Moors living under Christian rule in the years between the Christian resurgence (11th century) and the Reconquista (1492). Sevilla's Alcázar is an exquisite example of Mudéjar.

The **Spanish Gothic** style experimented with pointed arches, flying buttresses, slender walls, airy spaces, and stained-glass windows. The first Gothic cathedral in Spain was that of Burgos (begun in 1221). Along with those in Toledo and León, the cathedral of Burgos is one of the finest examples of the Spanish Gothic style.

Sevilla boasts the largest Gothic cathedral in world. Maestro Mateo's **Pórtico de la Gloria,** completed in 1188 in Santiago de Compostela, is considered one of the best examples of Spanish **Romanesque** sculpture.

THE RENAISSANCE. New World riches inspired the **Plateresque** ("silversmith") style, a flashy extreme of Gothic that transformed wealthier parts of Spain. Intricate stonework and extravagant use of gold and silver in interiors splashed 15th- and 16th-century buildings, most notably in Salamanca, where the university practically drips with ornamentation. In the late 16th century, Italian Renaissance innovations in perspective and symmetry arrived in Spain to sober up the Plateresque style. **El Escorial,** Felipe II's immense palace-cum-monastery, was designed by one of Spain's most prominent architects, **Juan de Herrera.**

BAROQUE. Opulence seized center stage in 17th- and 18th-century **Baroque** Spain. The Churriguera brothers pioneered the new **Churrigueresque** style which reflected the wealth and ostentation of the era. Wildly elaborate ornamentation with extensive sculptural detail gave buildings of this period a rich exuberance, most resonant in Salamanca's Plaza Mayor.

MODERN & POSTMODERN. In the late 19th and early 20th centuries, Catalunya's **Modernistes** burst on the scene in Barcelona, led by the eccentric genius of **Antoni Gaudí, Lluís Domènech i Montaner,** and **Josep Puig y Cadafalch.** Modernista structures defied any and all previous standards with their voluptuous curves and unusual textures. The new style was inspired in part by Mudéjar, but far more so by organic forms and unbridled imagination. **La Sagrada Família** and **La Casa Milà,** both by Gaudí, stand as the most famous examples of Catalan *Modernisme.*

In the mid-20th century, Catalan architect **Josep Lluís Sert** helped introduce European Modernism with his stark concrete buildings. Spain's outstanding architectural tradition continues today with current stars like **Ricardo Bofill, Rafael Moneo,** and **Santiago Calatrava,** who has become the most recent sensation with his elegant steel-and-crystal buildings in Valencia and unmistakable bridges in Sevilla, Mérida, and Bilbao. Spain has also acquired more than a few landmarks from foreign architects, including the stunning Guggenheim Museum in Bilbao by Frank Gehry.

PAINTING

Ever since primitive Spaniards put bones in berries and created the cave paintings at **Altamira,** Spanish painting has been enlightened by a series of luminaries snuffed out by several lulls. Flemish, French, and Italian influences often dominated the Spanish scene, but such heavy hitters as El Greco, Velázquez, Goya, and Picasso have forged a dazzling, distinctive, and hugely influential body of work.

MEDIEVAL & RENAISSANCE. In the 11th and 12th centuries, fresco painters and manuscript illuminators adorned churches and their libraries along the Camino de Santiago and in León and Toledo. **Pedro Berruguete's** (1450-1504) use of traditional gold backgrounds in his religious paintings exemplifies the Italian-influenced style of early Renaissance works. Not until after Spain's imperial ascendance in the 16th century did painting reach its **Siglo de3 Oro** (Golden Age; roughly 1492-1650). Felipe II imported foreign art and artists in order to jump-start native production and embellish his palace, El Escorial. Although he supposedly came to Spain seeking a royal commission, Cretan-born Doménikos Theotokópoulos, known as **El Greco** (1541-1614), was rejected by Felipe II for his intensely personal style. Misunderstood by his contemporaries, El Greco has received newfound appreciation for his haunting, elongated figures and dramatic use of light and color. One of his most famous canvases, *El entierro del Conde de Orgaz* (*The Burial of Count Orgaz*, 1586) graces the Iglesia de Santo Tomé in Toledo, the city whose landscape he so vividly painted beginning in 1597.

Felipe IV's foremost court painter, **Diego Velázquez** (1599-1660), is generally considered one of the world's greatest artists. Whether depicting Felipe IV's family or lowly court jesters and dwarves, Velázquez painted with naturalistic precision; working slowly and meticulously, he captured light with a virtually photographic quality. Nearly half of this Sevillian-born artist's works reside in the Prado, notably his famous *Las meninas* (1656; see **Museo del Prado,** p. 126). Other distinguished Golden Age painters include **José de Ribera** (1591-1652), **Francisco de Zurbarán** (1598-1664), and **Bartoloméo Esteban Murillo** (1618-1682).

FROM MODERN TO AVANT-GARDE. While Spain's political power declined, its cultural capital flourished. **Francisco de Goya** (1746-1828) ushered European painting into the modern age. Hailing from provincial Aragón, Goya rose to the position of official court painter under the degenerate Carlos IV. Dispensing with flattery, Goya's depictions of the royal family come closer to caricature, as Queen María Luisa's haughty, cruel jawline in Goya's famous *The Family of Charles IV* (1800) attests. His series of etchings *The Disasters of War* (1810-1814), which includes the landmark *El dos de mayo* and *El tres de mayo*, records the horrific Napoleonic invasion of 1808. Deaf and despondent in his later years, Goya painted more nightmarish and wildly fantastic visions, inspiring expressionist and surrealist artists of the next century. The Prado has a room full of his chilling *Pinturas negras* (*Black Paintings*, 1820-1823).

It is hard to imagine an artist who has as profoundly affected 20th-century painting as Andalucian-born **Pablo Picasso** (1881-1973). A child prodigy, Picasso headed for Barcelona, then a hothouse for Modernista architecture and political activism. Bouncing between Barcelona and Paris, Picasso inaugurated his Blue Period in 1900, characterized by somber depictions of society's outcasts. His permanent move to Paris in 1904 initiated his Rose Period as he probed into the engrossing lives of clowns and acrobats. With his French colleague Georges Braque, he founded **Cubism,** a method of painting objects simultaneously from multiple perspectives. His 1937 mural *Guernica* portrays the bombing of that Basque city by Nazi planes in cahoots with Fascist forces during the Spanish Civil War (see **The Tragedy of Guernica,** p. 526). A protest against violence and fascism, *Guernica* now resides in the Museo Centro de Arte Reina Sofía in Madrid (see p. 127).

Catalan painter and sculptor **Joan Miró** (1893-1983) created simplistic, almost child-like shapes in bright, primary colors. His haphazard, undefined squiggles rebelled against the authoritarian society of the post-Civil War years. By contrast, fellow Catalan **Salvador Dalí** (1904-1989) scandalized society and leftist intellectuals in France and Spain by supporting the Fascists. Dalí's name is now synonymous with **Surrealism.** A self-congratulatory fellow, Dalí founded the **Teatro-Museu Dalí** in Figueres, the second-most visited museum in Spain after the Prado.

Since Franco's death in 1975, a new generation of artists has thrived. With new museums in Madrid, Barcelona, Valencia, Sevilla, and Bilbao, Spanish painters and sculptors once again have a national forum for their work. Catalan **Antonio Tápies** constructs unorthodox collages and is a founding member of the self-proclaimed "Abstract Generation," while **Antonio López García** creates hyperrealist paintings.

LITERATURE

Iberian poets, playwrights, and authors have given the world some of its most iconic literary figures, from the inimitable Don Quixote to the unenviable Don Juan. Though these men and women of letters explore universal themes of faith, love, death, and honor, the contest between the pen and the sword ends with an inevitably tragic and unmistakably Spanish passion.

FROM THE MIDDLE AGES TO THE GOLDEN AGE. Spain's rich literary tradition blossomed in the late Middle Ages (1000-1500). The 12th-century *El Cantar del Mío Cid* (Song of My Cid), Spain's most important epic poem, chronicles national hero Rodrigo Díaz de Vivar's life and military triumphs, from his exile from Castilla to his return to grace in the king's court. No less integral to the national identity is **Fernando de Rojas's** *La Celestina* (1499), a tragicomedy beloved for the strong, witch-like female character who serves as literature's first go-between for star-crossed lovers Calixto and Melibea. *La Celestina* helped pave the way for picaresque novels like *Lazarillo de Tormes* (anonymous, 1554) and *Guzmán de Alfarache* (Mateo Alemán, 1599), rags-to-riches stories about *pícaros* (mischievous boys) with mostly good hearts. This literary form surfaced during Spain's **Siglo de Oro** (Golden Age), which spanned the 16th and 17th centuries. Poetry thrived in this era; some consider the sonnets and romances of **Garcilaso de la Vega** the most perfect ever written in Castilian. Along with his friend **Joan Boscán**, Garcilaso introduced the Italian (or Petrarchan) sonnet to Iberia. The Golden Age also bred outstanding dramatists, including **Pedro Calderón de la Barca** (1600-1681) and **Lope de Vega** (1562-1635), who collectively wrote over 2,300 plays. Both espoused the Neoplatonic view of love, claiming it changes one's life dramatically and eternally. Nothing could be more true for Don Juan Tenorio, the blasphemous title character of **Tirso de Molina's** (1580-1648) famed *El Burlador de Sevilla* (1616). **Miguel de Cervantes's** *Don Quijote de la Mancha* (1605-1615)—often considered the world's first novel—is the most famous work of Spanish literature. Cervantes relates the hilarious parable of the hapless Don and his servant Sancho Panza, who fancy themselves bold *caballeros* (knights) out to save the world.

ROMANTICS & ESSAYISTS. The 18th century brought a period of economic and political decline accompanied by a belated Enlightenment; one of the movement's most important figures was **José Cadalso**, author of the *Cartas Marruecas* (1789). The 19th century inspired contrasting variety, including the biting journalistic prose of **Mariano José de Larra**, **José Zorrilla's** romantic poem *Don Juan Tenorio* (1844), **Rosalía del Castro's** innovative lyrical verse, **Benito Pérez Galdós's** prolific realism, and the naturalistic novels of **Leopoldo Alas ("Clarín").** Basque essayist and philosopher **Miguel de Unamuno** and cultural critic **José Ortega y Gasset** led the **Generación del 1898,** along with novelist **Pío Baroja,** poet and playwright **Ramón del Valle Incán,** and poets **Antonio Machado** and **Juan Ramón Jiménez.** Reacting to Spain's defeat in the Spanish-American War (1898), these nationalistic authors argued that each individual must spiritually and ideologically attain internal peace before society can do the same. Unamuno and Ortega y Gasset influenced the **Generación del 1927,** a group of experimental lyric poets who wrote Surrealist and avant-garde poetry. This group included **Jorge Guillén, Federico García Lorca, Rafael Alberti,** and **Luis Cernuda.**

MODERN MARVELS. Spanish playwright and essayist **Jacinto Benavente y Martínez** (1922), poet **Vicente Aleixandre** (1977), and novelist **Camilo José Cela** (1989) have all received the Nobel Prize. Female writers, like Catalan **Mercè Rodoreda** and **Carmen Martín Gaite,** have likewise earned international critical acclaim. As Spanish artists are again migrating to Madrid, just as they did in the early part of the century, an avant-garde spirit—known as *La Movida*—has been reborn in the capital. **Ana Rossetti** and **Juana Castro** led a new generation of erotic poets into the 80s, for the first time placing women at the forefront of Spanish literature.

MUSIC

Flamenco, one of Spain's most clichéd and famous cultural attributes, combines *cante jondo* (melodramatic song), guitar, and dance. It originated among Andalusian gypsies and remains an extremely popular tradition that hypnotizes audiences all over the world even today. While it is possible to buy all manner of flamenco recordings, nothing compares to seeing a live performance. **Andres Segovia** (1893-1987) was instrumental in endowing the flamenco guitar with the same renown as the violin and the cello.

Pau (Pablo) Casals (1876-1973), Catalan cellist, conductor, composer, pianist, and humanitarian, was one of the most influential classical musicians of the 20th century. To promote world peace, Casals composed the oratorio *The Manger* (1960) and conducted it throughout the world. Hailing from Lérida, **Enrique Granados** (1867-1916) contributed the opera *Goyescas*, based on (oddly enough) paintings of Goya, and his own personal takes on the **zarzuela**, a form of light opera particular to Madrid. Lauded by music publishing house Schirmer as "the greatest Spanish composer of this century," Cádiz native **Manuel de Falla** (1876-1946) wrote the popular opera *El sombrero de tres picos* (*The Three-Cornered Hat*), which premiered in London in 1919 with stage design by Picasso. Another favorite de Falla work is the frequently-performed *Noches en los jardines de España* (*Nights in the Gardens of Spain;* 1914). Barcelona-born **José Carreras** and **Plácido Domingo** are recognized as two of the world's finest operatic tenors.

While youth throughout Spain covet American rock, there is considerable national pride in the Spanish version, which is plentiful and widespread. **Mecano** enthralls audiences around the world, and disco-goers dance all night long to pulsing **bakalao** (comparable to American house). Barcelona band **El Último de la Fila** and big-forum **Héroes del Silencio** are well worth a listen. **Ella Baila Sola** tops the best-selling charts, and other popular groups and soloists are **Presuntos Implicados, Los Rodríguez,** and **Manolo Tena.** We can't forget **Julio Iglesias,** beloved the world over, and of course, his handsome offspring **Enrique.** Yet even this familial duo has been overshadowed by the wildly popular **Las Hijas del Tomate** (**Los Ketchup**), with their summer 2003 hit "Aserejé."

FILM

Spain's first film, *Ría en un Café* (directed by Fructuos Gelabert), dates to 1897, and director **Segundo de Chomón** is recognized worldwide as a pioneer of early cinema. Surrealist **Luis Buñuel,** close friend of **Salvador Dalí,** produced several early classics, most notably *Un Chien Andalou* (1929). Later, in exile from Francoist Spain, he produced a number of brilliantly sardonic films including *Belle du Jour* (1967). Meanwhile, in Spain itself, Franco's censorship stifled most creative tendencies and left the public with nothing to watch but cheap westerns and bland spy flicks. As government supervision slacked in the early 1970s, Spanish cinema showed signs of life, led by **Carlos Saura's** dark, subversive hits such as *El Jardín de las Delicias* (1970) and *Cría Cuervos* (1975).

One of the greatest influences on Spanish film was not a filmmaker, but a politician: Franco's censors (1939-1975) defined Spanish film both during and after his rule. In 1977, in the wake of Franco's death, domestic censorship laws were revoked, bringing artistic freedom along with financial hardship for Spanish filmmakers, who found their films shunned domestically in favor of newly permitted foreign films. Depictions of the exuberant excesses of a super-liberated Spain found increasing attention and respect elsewhere. **Pedro Almodóvar's** *La ley del deseo* (1986), featuring **Antonio Banderas** as a gay man, captures the risqué themes of transgression and sexuality most often treated by contemporary Spanish cinema. **Penelope Cruz's** role as a pregnant nun in Almodóvar's Oscar-winning 1999 film *Todo sobre mi madre* garnered her almost as much attention as her recent fling with Tom Cruise. Other directors to look for in Spain include **Bigas Luna,** director of the controversial *Jamón Jamón* (1992); **Fernando Trueba,** whose *Belle Epoque* won the Oscar in 1993 for Best Foreign Film; **Alejandro Amenabar,** who has received international acclaim for his 1997 release *Abre los ojos;*

José Luis Cerda with his touching film *La lengua de las mariposas* (2000); and **Vicente Aranda's** adapted versions of Catalan Juan Marsé's novels *El amante bilingüe* (1993) and *Si te dicen que caí* (1989).

BULLFIGHTING

The national spectacle that is bullfighting dates in its modern form to the early 1700s. Bullfighting's growing popularity meant that Roman amphitheaters like those in Sevilla and Córdoba were restored, and bulls were bred to possess aggressive instincts. The techniques of the modern *matador* (bullfighter) were developed around 1914 by **Juan Belmonte,** considered one of the greatest matadors of all time (others include **Joselito, Manolete,** and **Cristina,** the first female matador).

A bullfight is divided into three principal stages: in the first, picadors (lancers on horseback) pierce the bull's neck muscles to lower his head for the kill; next, assistants on foot thrust *banderillas* (decorated darts) into his back to enliven the tiring animal for the final stage; finally, the matador has ten minutes during the *faena* ("task") to kill his opponent with a sword between the shoulder blades. He can be granted up to five extra minutes if necessary, but after that the bull is taken out alive, much to the matador's disgrace. On the other hand, if the matador has shown special skill and daring, the audience waves white *pañuelos* (handkerchiefs) to implore the bullfight's president to reward him with the coveted ears (and, very rarely, the tail).

Bullfighting has always had its **critics**—the Catholic Church in the 17th century felt that the risks made it equivalent to suicide. The argument for the late 20th century comes from animal rights activists and social workers who object to the cruel death of the bull or feel that bullfighting's prospects for social mobility lead many young men to premature deaths. Whatever its merits and faults, bullfighting is an essential and horny element of the Spanish national consciousness. ¡Olé!

THE MEDIA

NEWSPAPERS & MAGAZINES. *ABC*, tangibly conservative and pro-monarchist, is the oldest national daily paper. It jockeys with the more liberal *El País* for Spain's largest readership. *El Mundo* is a younger left-wing daily renowned for its investigative reporting. Barcelona's *La Vanguardia* serves a substantially Catalan audience, while *La Voz de Galicia* dominates the northwest. *Diario 16*, the more moderate counterpart to *El Mundo*, publishes the popular newsweekly *Cambio 16*, whose main competition is *Tiempo. Hola*, the original *revista del corazón* (magazine of the heart), caters to Spain's love affair with aristocratic titles, Julio Iglesias, and "beautiful" people. The nosier, less tasteful tabloid *Semana* has gossip galore and readers aplenty.

TELEVISION. Tune in to news at 3 and 8:30pm on most stations. Programming includes dubbed American movies, sports, melodramatic Latin American *telenovelas* (soaps), game shows, jazzed-up documentaries, and cheesy variety extravaganzas. If all else fails, try *fútbol* games or bullfights.

SPORTS

Fútbol is a nationally uniting and locally divisive passion for Spaniards. The 2002 World Cup enraged Spain, an early favorite, when the national team "lost" to South Korea due to a series of contested referee calls. You have not lived until you have shared a national victory (or defeat) with a bar full of unnervingly interactive Spaniards. Spanish teams—including decorated clubs Real Madrid, Barcelona, Valencia, and Deportivo de La Coruña—consistently appear in Euro-

SPAIN

pean championship series, often upsetting their trans-Pyrenean competitors. Real Madrid signed former Manchester United Spice Boy David Beckham in summer 2003, the latest jewel in a crown already studded with Brazilian icons Ronaldo and Roberto Carlos, Portuguese international Luis Figo, and French darling Zinedine Zidane. Spanish La Liga competition starts up every September, accompanied by full-color posters, pull-outs, and promos from Spain's two most visible sports dailies, *As* and *Marca*. If its centuries-old rivalries you've come for, don't miss a game between Real Madrid and Barcelona, Real Madrid and Atlético de Madrid, or Barcelona and Espanyol. *¡Viva España!*

The beat and the glory go on for Spanish sports. The retired 5-time consecutive Tour de France champion **Miguel Indurain**, a Navarrese hero and Spain's most decorated athlete, is remembered fondly by his fans. Old favorites like **Arantxa Sánchez-Vicario** (also retired) and **Conchita Martínez** and up-and-comers like **Carlos Moya** and **Alex Corretja** have made their names in tennis. Regional specialties spice the sports scene, including *cesta punta* (known internationally as *jai alai*) from the País Vasco, wind surfing along the southern coast, and skiing in the Sierra Nevada and the Pyrenees.

NATIONAL HOLIDAYS

The following table lists the national holidays for 2004.

DATE	HOLIDAYS
January 1	New Year's Day
January 6	Epiphany
March 1	Victory Day
March 19	Saint Joseph's Day
April 17	Maundy Thursday
April 18	Good Friday
April 20	Easter
May 1	May Day/*Fiesta del Trabajo*
May 2	Autonomous Community Day
July 6-14	Feast of San Fermín (Pamplona)
July 25	Día de Santiago (St. James's Day)
August 15	*La Asunción* (Feast of the Assumption)
October 12	*Fiesta Nacional de España* (National Day)
November 1	All Saints Day
November 9	Virgen de la Almudena
December 6	*Día de la Constitución* (Constitution Day)
December 8	*La Inmaculada Concepción* (Feast of the Immaculate Conception)
December 25	*Navidad* (Christmas)
December 31	New Year's Eve

RECOMMENDED READING

English-speaking scribes have penned several first-class Spanish travel narratives, ranging from the patronizing to the sublime. Richard Ford's witty *Handbook for Travellers in Spain and Readers at Home* (1849) is a favorite. Most time-honored classics are region-specific, including Washington Irving's *Tales of the Alhambra* and Bloomsbury Circle-expat Gerald Brenan's *South from Granada*. Look for Lucia Graves's account of her life in Mallorca titled *A Woman Unknown: Voices from a Spanish Life* (2000).

FICTION, SPANISH & FOREIGN. Start with the epic medieval poem *El Cantar del Mío Cid*. Alternatively, if you like reading about how a Spanish hunk steals the virtue of all the ladies in one medieval Spanish town, enjoy Tirso de Molina's *El burlador de Sevilla*. Dream the impossible dream and actually finish Cervantes's two-part über-classic *Don Quijote de la Mancha*. For gorgeous early 20th century prose, read Nobel laureate Benito Pérez Galdós. His tale of friendship, love, and betrayal in *El Abuelo* (made into a movie nominated for Best Foreign Film at the 2000 Academy Awards) will charm you with its prose and make you weep for its characters. To get a taste of Spain during the Franco regime, read Ana María Matute's wondrous account of growing up in *Primera Memoria*. Spain has also inspired a number of American and British authors. Ernest Hemingway immortalized bullfighting, machismo, and Spain itself in *The Sun Also Rises* and *For Whom the Bell Tolls*.

ART & ARCHITECTURE. The definitive work is Bradley Smith's *Spain: A History in Art*. For late 20th-century art, check out William Dyckes's *Contemporary Spanish Art*. If you want to splurge, go for Fred Licht's *Goya* (2001), a must-read for fans of the artist. Biographies of Pablo Picasso, Salvador Dalí, and Antoni Gaudí can be found with minimal fuss. Bernard Bevan wrote the standard text on Spanish architecture: *History of Spanish Architecture*. For the 1980s and 90s scoop, peruse Anatzu Zabalbeascoa's *The New Spanish Architecture*. If you really want to know your *arquitectura*, get your hands on *Spain: Contemporary Art and Architecture Handbook* by Sidra Stich.

HISTORY & CULTURE. James Michener's best-seller *Iberia* (1968) continues to captivate audiences with its thoroughness, insight, and style. *Barcelona*, by Robert Hughes, delves into the culture of Catalunya. George Orwell's *Homage to Catalonia*, a personal account of the Spanish Civil War, rivals *Iberia* and *Barcelona* in quality and fame. A handful of other historians and works stand out—Richard Fletcher's comprehensive *Moorish Spain*, J.H. Elliot's masterful *Imperial Spain 1469-1716*, Raymond Carr's *Spain 1808-1975*, and Stanley Payne's *The Franco Regime 1936-1975*. Finally, don't miss María Rosa Menocal's *The Ornament of the World* (2003) about the peaceful intersection of Moorish, Christian, and Jewish cultures in Toledo.

SPAIN ESSENTIALS

This section is designed to help travelers get their bearings once in Spain. For info about general **travel preparations** (including passports, money, health, packing, and more), consult **Essentials** (p. 11). Essentials also has important information for those with specific concerns. See **Alternatives to Tourism** (p. 57) for opportunities to study and work in Spain.

ENTRANCE REQUIREMENTS
Passport (p. 11). Required of all travelers.
Visa (p. 13). Required only of citizens of South Africa and all travelers staying more than 90 days.
Work Permit (p. 13). Required of all foreigners planning to work in Spain.
Driving Permit (p. 49). Recommended for those planning to drive.

EMBASSIES & CONSULATES

Embassies and consulates are usually open Monday through Friday, punctuated by *siestas*. Many consulates are only open mornings. Call ahead for exact hours.

Australia: Embassy: Pl. Descubridor Diego de Ordás, 3, **Madrid** 28003 (☎914 41 60 25; fax 42 53 62; www.embaustralia.es). **Consulates:** Gran Vía Carlos III, 98, 9th fl., **Barcelona** 08028 (☎934 90 90 13; fax 11 09 04); Federico Rubio, 14, **Sevilla** 41004 (☎954 22 09 71; fax 21 11 45).

Canada: Embassy: C. Núñez de Balboa, 35, **Madrid** 28001 (☎914 23 32 50; fax 23 32 51; www.canada-es.org). **Consulates:** Elisenda de Pinós, 10 **Barcelona** 08034 (☎932 04 27 00; fax 04 27 01); Pl. de la Malagueta, 2, 1st fl., **Málaga** 29016 (☎952 22 33 46; fax 22 40 23).

Ireland: Embassy: Po. de la Castellana, 46, 4th fl., **Madrid,** 28046 (☎914 36 40 93; fax 35 16 77). **Consulate:** Gran Vía Carlos III, 94, 10th fl., **Barcelona** 08028 (☎934 91 50 21; fax 11 29 21).

New Zealand: Embassy: Pl. de la Lealtad, 2, 3rd fl., **Madrid** 28014 (☎915 23 02 26; fax 23 01 71). **Consulate:** Travesera de Grácia, 64, 4th fl., **Barcelona** 08006 (☎932 09 03 99; fax 02 08 90).

South Africa: Embassy: C. Claudio Coello, 91, 6th fl., **Madrid** 28006 (☎914 36 37 80, fax 77 74 14; www.sudafrica.com). **Consulates:** C. Teodora Lamadrid, 7, 11th fl., **Barcelona** 08022 (☎934 18 64 45; fax 18 05 38); Las Mercedes, 31, 4th fl., Las Arenas, **Bilbao** 48930 (☎344 480 0328; fax 64 11 24); C. Albareda, 54, 2nd fl. **Las Palmas** 35008 (☎928 22 60 04 fax 22 60 15).

United Kingdom: Embassy: C. Fernando el Santo, 16, **Madrid** 28010 (☎917 00 82 00, fax 00 83 11; www.ukinspain.com). **Consulate-General:** Edificio Torre de Barcelona, Av. Diagonal, 477, 13th fl., **Barcelona** 08036 (☎933 66 62 00; fax 66 62 21). **Consulates:** Pl. Calvo Sotelo, 1-2, **Alicante** 03001 (☎965 21 61 90; fax 14 05 28); Alameda de Urquijo, 2, 8th fl., **Bilbao** 48008 (☎944 15 76 00; fax 16 76 32); Av. d'Isidor Macabich, 45, 1st. fl., Apartado 307, **Ibiza** 07800 (☎971 30 18 18; fax 30 38 16); Marqués de la Ensenada, 16, 2nd fl., **Madrid** 28004 (☎913 08 52 01; fax 08 08 82); Edificio Eurocom, C. Mauricio Moro Pareto, 2, 2nd fl., **Málaga** 29080 (☎952 35 23 00; fax 35 92 11); Pl. Mayor, 3D, **Palma** 07002 (☎971 71 24 45; fax 71 75 20); Po. de Pereda, 27, **Santander** 39004 (☎942 22 00 00; fax 22 29 41); Edificio Cataluña, C. Luis Morote, 6, 3rd fl., **Las Palmas** 35007 (☎928 26 25 08; fax 26 77 74).

United States: Embassy: C. Serrano, 75, **Madrid** 28006 (☎915 87 22 00, fax 87 23 03; www.embusa.es). **Consulate General:** Po. Reina Elisenda de Montcada, 23, **Barcelona** 08034 (☎932 80 22 27; fax 80 61 75). **Consulates:** Po. de las Delicias, 7, **Sevilla** 41012 (☎954 23 18 85; fax 23 20 40); C. Los Martínez Escobar, 3, Oficina 7, **Las Palmas** 35007 (☎928 27 12 59; fax 22 58 63); Dr. Romagosa 1-2 J **Valencia** 46002 (☎963 51 69 73; fax 52 95 65); Cantón Grande, 6-8 E, **La Coruña** 15003 (☎981 21 32 33; fax 22 88 08); Edificio Reina Constanza, Porto Pi, 8, 9D, **Palma** 07015 (☎971 40 37 07; fax 40 39 71).

TRANSPORTATION

Transportation to and within Spain is generally efficient, comfortable, and reliable. The easiest, quickest method of entering Spain is by plane, although Barcelona is well-connected to the European rail system. Despite the romanticized view of European train travel, buses offer the most extensive coverage and are the best option for short trips. Spain's islands are accessible by plane and ferry. For more specific info on island travel, see the **Islas Baleares** (p. 362) and the **Islas Canarias** (p. 591). For general info on traveling in the region, see **Getting There,** p. 39.

BY PLANE

All major international airlines offer service to Madrid and Barcelona, most serve the Balearic and Canary Islands, and many serve Spain's smaller cities. **Iberia** (in US and Canada ☎800-772-4642, in UK ☎45 601 28 54, in Spain ☎902 40

05 00, in South Africa ☎ 11 884 92 55, in Ireland ☎ 1 407 30 17; www.iberia.com) serves all domestic locations and all major international cities. **Aviaco** (www.aviaco.com), a subsidiary of Iberia, covers mostly domestic routes, with a few connections to London and Paris. Some fares purchased in the US require a 21-day minimum advance purchase. Iberia's two less-established domestic competitors often offer cheaper fares and are worth looking into. **Air Europa** (in US ☎ 888-238-7672, in Spain ☎ 902 40 15 01; www.air-europa.com) flies out of New York City and most European cities to Madrid, Málaga, Tenerife, and Santiago de Compostela. Discounts available for youth and senior citizens. No service Wednesdays or Sundays during the summer. **SpanAir** (in US ☎ 888-545-5757, in Spain ☎ 902 13 14 15; fax 971 49 25 53; elsewhere ☎ 34 971 74 50 20; www.spanair.com) offers international and domestic flights.

SpanAir and Iberia offer the following special flight packages for travel throughout Spain, and especially between the islands and the mainland.

Iberiabono España: One-way coupons good for all mainland airports and the Canary and Balearic Islands. Reservations must be made before arriving in Spain, and you must purchase your international return ticket before starting your trip. Minimum purchase 3 coupons. Mainland and Balearics: 3 coupons €200, 4 coupons €259. Mainland and Canary Islands: 3 coupons €348, 4 coupons €402.

SpanAir Spain Pass A: Good for flying to any airport within Spain, including Ibiza, Mallorca, or Menorca. No minimum stay; maximum stay 6 months. Reservations must be made before arriving in Spain. Valid for 1 year. Under 12 65% discount. Minimum purchase of 3 tickets €158; additional tickets €53. **SpanAir Spain Pass B** is the same as Spain Pass A, but also includes Lanzarote, Gran Canaria, or Tenerife. Three tickets €280; additional tickets €63.

BY TRAIN

Spanish trains are clean, relatively punctual, and reasonably priced, but tend to bypass many small towns. Spain's national railway is **RENFE** (www.renfe.es). Avoid *transvía*, *semidirecto*, or *correo* trains—they are very slow. The following list includes many types of trains you will find in Spain and their relative speed.

AVE (Alta Velocidad Española): High-speed trains dart between Madrid and Sevilla, Ciudad Real, Puertollano, and Córdoba. AVE trains soar above others in comfort, price, and speed. The 10am and noon trains are cheapest; student discounts available.

Talgo 200: Sleek trains zip passengers in air-conditioned compartments from Madrid to Málaga, Cádiz/Huelva, or Algeciras. It's more comfortable, possibly faster, and twice as pricey as Cercanías-Regionales trains. Changing a Talgo 200 ticket carries a 20% fine.

Grandes Líneas: RENFE's business unit for long distance travel. A wide range of lines including Euromed, Alaris, Arco, Talgo, and Trenhotel meet every traveler's needs.

Intercity: Cheaper than Talgo, but fewer stops. A/C and comfy. Five lines: Madrid-Valencia, Madrid-Zaragoza-Barcelona, Madrid-Alicante, Madrid-Zaragoza-Logroño-Pamplona, and Madrid-Murcia-Cartagena.

Estrella: A pretty slow night train that has *literas* (bunks).

Cercanías: Commuter trains from large cities to suburbs and towns, with frequent stops.

Regional: Like cercanías but older; multi-stop, cheap rides to small towns and cities.

There is absolutely no reason to buy a Eurail pass if you plan to travel only within Spain and Portugal. Trains are cheap, so a pass saves little money. For the most part, buses are an easier and more efficient means of traveling around Spain. Visit www.raileurope.com for more specific information on the passes below.

Spain Flexipass offers 3 days of unlimited travel in a 2mo. period. 1st-class €211; 2nd-class €164. Each additional rail-day (up to 7) €37 for 1st-class, €32 for 2nd-class.

SPAIN

Iberic Railpass is good for 3 days of unlimited 1st-class travel in Spain and Portugal for €217. Each additional rail-day (up to 7) €48.

Spain Rail 'n' Drive Pass is good for 3 days of unlimited 1st-class train travel and 2 days of unlimited mileage in a rental car within a 2mo. period. Prices €252-343, depending on how many travelers and type of car. Up to 2 additional rail-days and extra car days are also available, and a 3rd and 4th person can join in the car using only a Flexipass.

BY BUS

Bus routes, far more comprehensive than the rail network, provide the only public transportation to many isolated areas and almost always cost less than trains. They are generally quite comfortable, though leg room may be limited. For those traveling primarily within one region, **buses are the best method of transport.**

Spain has numerous private companies; the lack of a centralized bus company may make itinerary planning an ordeal. Companies' routes rarely overlap; it's unlikely that more than one will serve your intended destination. We list below the major national companies, along with the phone number of the Madrid office; you will likely use other companies for travel within any given region.

ALSA/Enatcar (☎902 42 22 42; www.alsa.es). Serves Madrid, Galicia, Asturias, and Castilla y León. Also to France, Italy, Morocco, Poland, and Portugal.

Alosa (☎934 90 00 00; www.alosa.es). Operating primarily in northeastern Spain, Alosa serves Barcelona, Huesca, Jaca, Lérida, and Pamplona.

Alsina Graells (☎954 41 88 11; www.alsinagraells.es). Primarily serves southern Spain, including Granada, Jaén, Sevilla, and Córdoba.

Auto-Res/Cunisa, S.A. (☎902 02 09 99; www.auto-res.net). From Madrid to Castilla y León, Extremadura, Galicia, and Valencia.

Busabout (www.busabout.com, see p. 45). Serves: Barcelona, Bilbao, Granada, Madrid, Pamplona, Salamanca, San Sebastián, Sevilla, Tarifa, Toledo, Valencia, and Zaragoza.

Daibus (☎902 27 79 99; www.daibus.es). To Algeciras, Madrid, Málaga, and Marbella.

Juliá Tours (☎913 35 18 97; www.juliatours.es). Iberia, Western Europe, and Morocco.

Linebús (☎902 33 55 33). Runs to Italy, France, Morocco, the Netherlands, and the UK.

Samar, SA (☎914 68 48 39; www.samar.es). To Andorra, Aragón, Portugal, and Toulouse (France).

BY BOAT

Ferries leave from **Algeciras** for **Tangier** and the Spanish enclave of **Ceuta** in **Morocco** (see p. 280) and from Valencia and Barcelona for the **Balearic Islands** (see p. 363). Ferries are also the cheapest, if longest and slowest, way to travel between the **Canary Islands** (see p. 591).

BY CAR

Spain's highway system connects major cities by four-lane *autopistas* with plenty of service stations. **Speeders beware:** police can "photograph" the speed and license plate of your car and issue a ticket without pulling you over. Purchase **gas** in super (97-octane), normal (92-octane), diesel, and unleaded. Prices are astronomical by North American standards, about €1.50-1.60 per liter. **Renting** a car in Spain is considerably cheaper than in many other European countries. Try **Atesa** (in Spain ☎902 100 101, elsewhere ☎902 100 515; www.atesa.es), Spain's largest rental agency. The Spanish automobile association is **Real Automóvil Club de España (RACE)**, C. José Abascal, 10, Madrid (☎915 94 74 75; fax 94 73 29). For more info on renting and driving a car, see p. 47.

BY THUMB

Hitchers report that Castilla and Andalucía are long, hot waits; hitchhiking out of Madrid is virtually impossible. The Mediterranean Coast and the islands are much more promising. Approaching people for rides at gas stations near highways and rest stops purportedly gets results. Let's Go does not recommend hitchhiking.

MONEY

	THE EURO (€)	
US $1 = €0.91		€1 = US $1.10
AUS $1 = €0.59		€1 = AUS $1.69
CDN $1 = €0.66		€1 = CDN $1.52
DH 1 = €0.09		€1 = DH 10.74
NZ $1 = €0.53		€1 = NZ $1.90
UK £1 = €1.44		€1 = UK £0.70
ZAR 1 = €0.12		€1 = ZAR 8.06

Banking hours in Spain from June through September are generally Monday through Friday 9am to 2pm; from October to May, banks are also open Saturday 9am to 1pm. Some banks may be open in the afternoon. **Banco Santander Central Hispano** often provides good exchange rates. For more info on money, see p. 15.

Tipping is not very common in Spain. In restaurants, all prices include service charge. Satisfied customers occasionally toss in some spare change—usually no more than 5%—but this is purely optional. Many people give train, airport, and hotel porters €1 per bag while taxi drivers sometimes get 5-10%. **Bargaining** is really only common at flea markets and with street vendors.

Spain has a 7% **Value Added Tax,** known as IVA, on all restaurant and accommodations. The prices listed in *Let's Go* include IVA unless otherwise mentioned. Retail goods bear a much higher 16% IVA, although listed prices are usually inclusive. Non-EU citizens who have stayed in the EU fewer than 180 days can claim back the tax paid on purchases at the airport. Ask the shop where you have made the purchase to supply you with a tax return form. For more general info on money in the region, see p. 87.

SAFETY & SECURITY

MEDICAL EMERGENCY☎112	LOCAL POLICE: ☎092. NATIONAL POLICE: ☎091. GUARDIA CIVIL: ☎061.

PERSONAL SAFETY. Spain has a low **crime** rate, but visitors can always fall victim to tourist-related crimes. Tourists should take particular care in Madrid, especially in El Centro, and in Barcelona around Las Ramblas. If visiting the Costa del Sol in a car, be aware of the fact that this area has seen increased **car theft** in recent years. If using a car in Spain you happen to experience car problems, be wary of people posing as Good Samaritans. Drivers should be extremely careful about accepting help from anyone other than a uniformed Spanish police officer or *Guardia Civil* (Civil Guard.) Travelers who accept unofficial assistance should keep their valuables in sight and at hand. For those travelers using public transportation, it is essential to be on the lookout for potential **muggings** and **pickpocketing.** Scams such as squirting mustard on clothing and asking for street directions are often employed for such purposes. For more **general safety tips,** see p. 19.

TERRORISM. Basque terrorism concerns all travelers in Spain and is a highly controversial issue both domestically and internationally. **ETA,** or Euskadi Ta Askatasuna (Basque Homeland and Freedom), is the militant wing of the Basque separatist movement. It was founded in 1959 to fight for Basque self-determination, concentrating on establishing the Basque region as its own independent country. ETA attacks have resulted in more than 800 deaths since 1968. In 1998, the Spanish government issued the **Declaración Lazarra,** which called for an open dialogue between all involved parties, and ETA publicly declared a truce eight days later. However, ETA ended the cease-fire after 14 months. It is blamed for 39 deaths since November 1999, and 26 car bombings since January 2001. ETA has historically aimed its attacks at the police, military, and other Spanish government targets, but in March 2001, ETA issued a communique announcing its intention to target Spanish tourist areas. Though several suspected ETA members have been arrested in recent months and the Spanish government has succeeded in preventing numerous attacks, the ETA has continued a relatively active terrorist campaign. In June 2002, the ETA carried out a series of bombings in resort towns along the Costa del Sol and in northern Spain during an EU summit in Sevilla. These attacks were followed up in the July 2003 bombings of a hotel in Benidorm and another in Alicante. While there may be some risk to travelers, the attacks are very targeted and are not considered random acts of terrorism.

HEALTH

There are no particular health risks associated with traveling in Spain. Be sure to be up to date on your vaccinations for tetanus-diphtheria, measles, and chickenpox. If traveling during flu season, which runs from November through April, add the flu shot to your case. The public health care system in Spain is very reliable; in an emergency, seek out the *urgencias* (emergency) section of the nearest hospital. For smaller concerns, it is probably best to go to a private clinic to avoid the frustration of long lines. Expect to pay cash up front (though most travel insurance will pick up the tab later; request a receipt) and bring your passport and other forms of identification. A single visit to a clinic in Spain can cost anywhere from €70-180, depending upon the service. You can visit the following site for the most recent updates on travel-related health concerns in Spain: www.mdtravelhealth.com/destinations/europe/spain.html.

Farmacias in Spain are also very helpful. A duty system has been set up so that at least one farmacia is open at all times in each town; look for a flashing green cross. Spanish pharmacies are not the place to find your cheap summer flip-flops or greeting cards, but they sell contraceptives, common drugs, and many prescription drugs; they can answer simple medical questions and help you find a doctor. For more general info on travel-related health concerns, see **Health,** p. 22.

ACCOMMODATIONS

PENSIONES, HOSTALES & HOTELES

Spanish accommodations have many aliases, distinguished by the different grades of rooms. The cheapest and barest options are **casas de huéspedes** and **hospedajes.** While **pensiones** and **fondas** tend to be a bit nicer, all are essentially just boarding houses. Higher up the ladder, **hostales** generally have sinks in bedrooms and provide sheets and lockers, while **hostal-residencias** are similar to hotels in overall quality. The government rates *hostales* on a two-star system; even establishments receiving one star are typically quite comfortable. The system also fixes each *hostal's* prices, posted in the lounge or main entrance. *Hostal* owners invariably dip below the official rates, especially in the off season (Sept.-May).

The highest-priced accommodations are **hoteles,** which have a bathroom in each room but are usually on the pricey side for the budget traveler. The top-notch hotels are the handsome **Paradores Nacionales**—castles, palaces, convents, and historic buildings that have been converted into luxurious hotels and often are interesting sights in their own right. For a *parador*, €75 per night is a bargain. If you have trouble with rates or service, ask for the **libro de reclamaciones** (complaint book), which by law must be produced on demand. The argument will usually end immediately, since all complaints must be forwarded to the authorities within 48 hours. Report any problems to tourist offices who may help you resolve disputes.

YOUTH HOSTELS

Red Española de Albergues Juveniles (REAJ), C. Galera, 1a, Sevilla 41001 (☎954 21 68 03, fax 21 18 49; www.reaj.com), the Spanish Hostelling International (HI) affiliate, runs 165 youth hostels year-round. Prices depend on location (typically some distance away from town center) and services offered, but are generally €9-15 for guests under 26 and higher for those 26 and over. Breakfast is usually included; lunch and dinner are occasionally offered at an additional charge. Hostels usually lockout around 11:30am and have curfews between midnight and 3am. As a rule, don't expect much privacy—rooms typically are dorm-style with four to 20 beds in one room. Call in advance to reserve a bed in high season (July-Aug. and during fiestas). A national **Youth Hostel Card** is usually required (see **Hostels,** p. 30). HI cards are available from Spain's youth travel company, **TIVE.** Occasionally, guests can stay in a hostel without one and pay extra, or pay extra for six nights to become a member.

ALTERNATIVE ACCOMMODATIONS

In less-touristed areas, **casas particulares** (private residences) may sometimes be the only option. **Casas rurales** (rural cottages) and **casas rústicas** (farmhouses), referred to as *agroturismo*, have overnight rates from €6-21. In the Pyrenees and Picos de Europa, there are several **refugios,** rustic mountain huts for hikers.

CAMPING

In Spain, **campgrounds** are generally the cheapest choice for two or more people. Most charge separate fees per person, per tent, and per car; others charge for a *parcela*—a small plot of land—plus per-person fees. Although it may seem like an inexpensive option, prices can get high for lone travelers and even for pairs. Campgrounds are categorized on a three-class system, with rating and prices based on amenity quality. Like hostels, they must post fees within view of the entrance. They must also provide sinks, showers, and toilets. Most tourist offices provide information on official areas, including the hefty *Guía de campings*.

KEEPING IN TOUCH

Some useful **communication information** (including international access codes, calling card numbers, country codes, operator and directory assistance, and emergency numbers) is listed on the **inside back cover.**

TELEPHONES. The central Spanish phone company is *Telefónica*. Most bars have pay phones, though they are often only coin-operated. The best way to make local calls is with a phone card, issued in denominations of €6 and €12 and sold at tobacconists (*estancos* or *tabacos*, identifiable by brown signs with yellow lettering and tobacco leaf icons) and most post offices. Ask tobacconists for calling cards known as *Phonepass*: €6 gives you 62 minutes on public phones for calls to the US. For an additional €6, get 150 minutes. International calls made using phone cards are cheap and easy; however, you may prefer to call home with an international calling card issued by your phone company. Numbers for obtaining calling cards from home are in the **Essentials** section (see p. 37).

FAX. Most Spanish post offices have fax services. Some photocopy shops and telephone offices (*Telefónica, locutorios*) also offer fax service, but they tend to charge more than post offices, and faxes can only be sent, not received. Cybercafes are also becoming increasingly popular places to send faxes at cheap rates.

MAIL. Air mail (*por avión*) takes five to eight business days to reach the US or Canada. Standard postage is €0.80 to North America. Surface mail (*por barco*), while considerably less expensive than air mail, can take over a month, and packages will take two to three months. Registered or express mail (*registrado* or *certificado*), is the most reliable way to send a letter or parcel home, and takes four to seven business days. Spain's overnight mail is not worth the added expense, since it isn't exactly "overnight." For better service, try private companies such as DHL, UPS, or the Spanish company SEUR; look under *mensajerías* in the yellow pages. Their reliability, however, comes at a high cost. Stamps are sold at post offices and tobacconists (*estancos* or *tabacos*). Mail letters and postcards from yellow mailboxes scattered through cities, or from the post office in small towns.

EMAIL. Email is easily accessible within Spain and much quicker and more reliable than the regular mail system. An increasing number of bars offer Internet access for a fee of €1.20-4.20. Cybercafes are listed in most towns and all cities. In small towns, if Internet access is not listed, check the library or the tourist office (where occasionally travelers may get access for a small fee). The website www.tangaworld.com lists nearly 200 cybercafes in Spain by location and name.

MADRID

The relentless summer sun parches sidewalks and sidestreets, blazing across a city filled with tremendous history and life. Casting a spell throughout Madrid, the dry air induces a hedonistic fever that rages at sunset. In this city of restless energy, the morning rush hour coincides with the move to after-hours clubs, and fervent activity seems to pause only for an afternoon siesta. *Madrileños* never stop enjoying life, leaving straight from work for the city's many plazas, *tapas* bars, and romantic parks, surviving on minimal sleep and living each day to its fullest. While tourists inundate the city, spending their days absorbed in its Old World monuments, world-renowned museums, and raging nightlife, Madrid's population of 5 million roams the labyrinthine neighborhoods with a simple and energetic joy.

Madrid's history does not read like that of rival European capitals. Although the city witnessed the coronation of Fernando and Isabel, Madrid did not gain importance until Habsburg monarch Felipe II moved the court here in 1561. Despite its considerable distance from vital ports and rivers, it immediately became a seat of wealth, culture, and imperial glory, serving as the center of Spain's 16th- and 17th-century Golden Age of literature, art, and architecture. In the 18th century, Madrid witnessed a Neoclassical rebirth as Carlos III embellished the city with wide, tree-lined boulevards and scores of imposing buildings. However, the 19th-century Peninsular Wars against Napoleon scarred Madrid and provided the bloody inspiration for some of Francisco de Goya's most famous canvases.

In 1939, Madrid was the last city save Valencia to fall in the Spanish Civil War. Though hostile to Franco's nationalism, the city served as the seat of his government. This time, its location—smack in the center of the country—was considered its greatest strength. Franco's death nearly 40 years later brought an explosion known as *la movida* ("shift" or "movement"). After decades of totalitarian repression, Madrid exploded in a breathtaking, city-wide release of inhibition. A 200,000-strong student population took to the streets and stayed there—they haven't stopped moving yet.

Today Madrid continues to serve as Spain's political, intellectual, and cultural center. It is neither as cosmopolitan as Barcelona nor as charming as Sevilla, but it is undeniably the *capital*—the wild, pulsing heart of Spain. Students, families, and artists flock here in pursuit of their dreams, and Madrid continues to grow as a city of opportunity. Its very architecture—with modern skyscrapers and shining industrial spaces expanding from narrow alleys and ancient plazas—epitomizes the mix of galvanizing history and intense passion for life that so defines Spain.

HIGHLIGHTS OF MADRID

SCOPE other travelers in **El Parque del Buen Retiro** (see p. 139).

FEAST on *tapas* at **Casa Botín,** the oldest restaurant in the world (see p. 118).

WINCE at the blood drawn from bulls and matadors at **Las Ventas** (see p. 113).

STROLL down the three *paseos* in leisurely, high-bourgeois style (see p. 140).

RIDE out to Aranjuez for **strawberries and cream** (see p. 148).

DANCE till dawn at killer club **Kapital** (see p. 129).

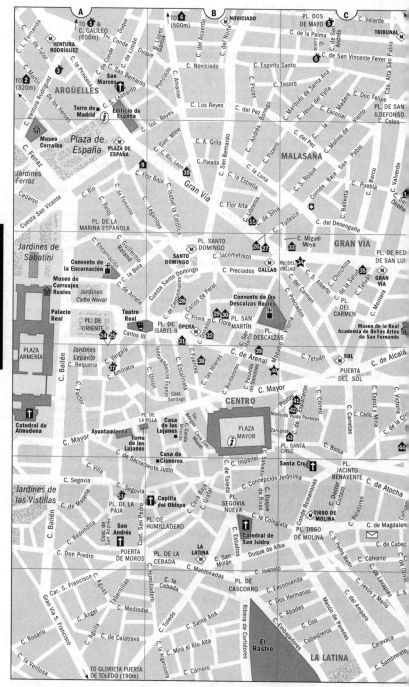

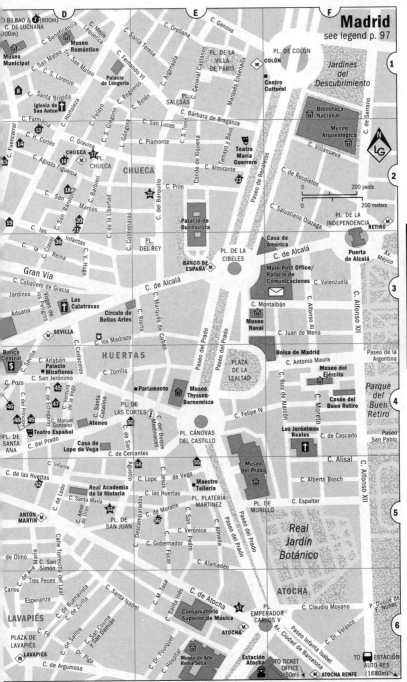

Madrid
see legend p. 97

D — **E** — **F**

TO BILBAO & 🚇 (800m)
C. DE LUCHANA (200m)

🏛 Museo Municipal

🏛 Museo Romántico

C. Beneficencia
C. Mejía Lequerica
C. Santa Teresa
C. Orellana
C. Genova

PL. DE COLÓN

Jardines del Descubrimiento

C. San Mateo
Trv. San Mateo
C. Fernando VI
C. Argensola
C. General Castaños
PL. DE LA VILLA DE PARÍS
🚇 COLÓN

Palacio de Longoria

C. S. Lorenzo
C. C. Pelayo
C. S. Gregorio
C. Regueros
C. Belén
PL. SALESAS
■ Centro Cultural

C. de Serrano

8

🏛 Iglesia de San Antón

C. Santa Brígida
C. Hortaleza
C. San Lucas
C. Bárbara de Braganza

🏛 Biblioteca Nacional

🏛 Museo Arqueológico

C. Farmacia

13

C. Fuencarral
C. H. Cortés
C. Gravina
C. Piamonte
C. Villanueva

14

C. Agusto Figueroa
16
17 PL. CHUECA
🚇
CHUECA
Conde de Xiquena
C. S. Tomé
C. Lanuza y Baus

Teatro María Guerrero

C. de Recoletos

15

18
CHUECA

C. Barbieri

C. Almirante

23

C. de Recoletos

19

C. San Bartolomé
20
21

C. Marcos

C. Prim

Paseo de Recoletos

0   200 yards
0   200 meters

36

C. las Infantas
C. de la Libertad
C. del Barquillo
22

Palacio de Buenavista

C. Salustiano Olázaga
PL. DE LA INDEPENDENCIA 🚇 RETIRO

C. la Clavel
C. la Reina
C. V. Hugo

PL. DEL REY

PL. DE LA CIBELES

Casa de América

C. de Alcalá

Puerta de Alcalá

Av. Méjico

Gran Vía

C. Caballero de Gracia

BANCO DE ESPAÑA 🚇

Main Post Office/ Palacio de Comunicaciones

C. Valenzuela

Jardines
Virgen de los Peligros

Las Calatravas 🏛

C. de Alcalá

C. Montalbán

C. Alfonso XI

C. Alfonso XII

Aduana

Círculo de Bellas Artes

🏛 Museo Naval

C. Juan de Mena

Banco Central 💲

C. los Madrazo

🚇 SEVILLA

HUERTAS

Bolsa de Madrid

Paseo de la Argentina

C. Ariabán
Palacio de Miraflores

C. San Jerónimo

C. Zorrilla

■ Parlamento

🏛 Museo Thyssen-Bornemisza

C. Antonio Maura

🏛 Museo del Ejército

Parque del Buen Retiro

45

C. Pozo

C. Sevilla

C. Cedaceros

C. Marqués de Cubas

C. Ruíz de Alarcón

C. de la Vega

Casón del Buen Retiro

46

47

C. de Echegaray

Ateneo

C. Santa Catalina

PL. DE LAS CORTES ℹ

C. del Duque de Medinaceli

PLAZA DE LA LEALTAD

C. Felipe IV

Los Jerónimos Reales ✝

C. de Cascado

Paseo San Pablo

48
49

🎭 Teatro Español

C. Manuel González

50

PL. DE SANTA ANA

C. del Prado

Casa de Lope de Vega

C. de San

PL. CÁNOVAS DEL CASTILLO

C. de Cervantes

C. Alisal

C. Alfonso XII

C. Infante

C. de las Huertas

52

Real Academia de la Historia

54

C. Lope de Vega

55

🏛 Museo del Prado

C. Alberto Bosch

C. de León

■ Maestro Tellería

C. Santa María

53

C. Amor de Dios

PL. DE SAN JUAN

C. las Huertas

PL. PLATERÍA MARTÍNEZ

C. Espalter

C. de Moratín

56

C. San Pedro

PL. DE MURILLO

ANTÓN MARTÍN 🚇

C. Descamparados

C. Santa Isabel

C. Verónica

C. Almeda

Paseo del Prado

Real Jardín Botánico

de Olmo
C. Ave María
C. San Simón

C. Gobernador

C. Fúcar

C. Alamadén

Tres Peces

C. de Buenavista

C. de Zurita

Carlos

Esperanza

LAVAPIÉS

C. Fe

PLAZA DE LAVAPIÉS

🚇 LAVAPIÉS

C. de Argumosa

C. M. Toca

C. Santa Inés

C. de Atocha

ATOCHA

C. Claudio Moyano

P. Duque de F. Núñez

C. Cosme
San Damián

Conservatorio Superior de Música

57

PL. EMPERADOR CARLOS V

Paseo Infanta Isabel

C. Dr. Velasco

C. Dr. Fourquet

🚇 ATOCHA

🏛 Museo de Arte Reina Sofía

Estación Atocha

Av. Ciudad de Barcelona

TO 🚉 ESTACIÓN AUTO RES

C. Dr. Piga

C. Hospital

TO TICKET OFFICE (50m)

🚇 ATOCHA RENFE (1680m)

1

2

3

4

5

6

MADRID

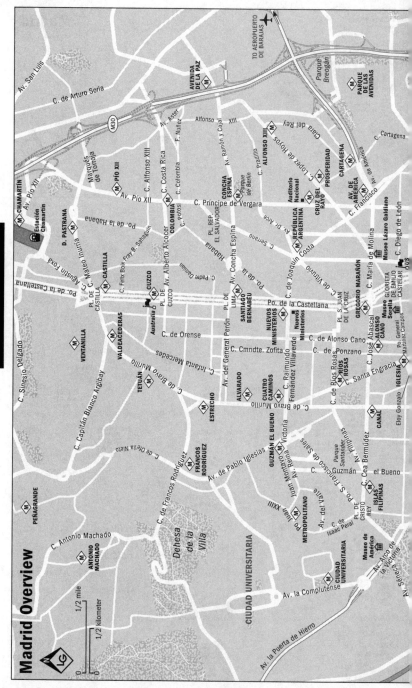

MADRID

Madrid Overview

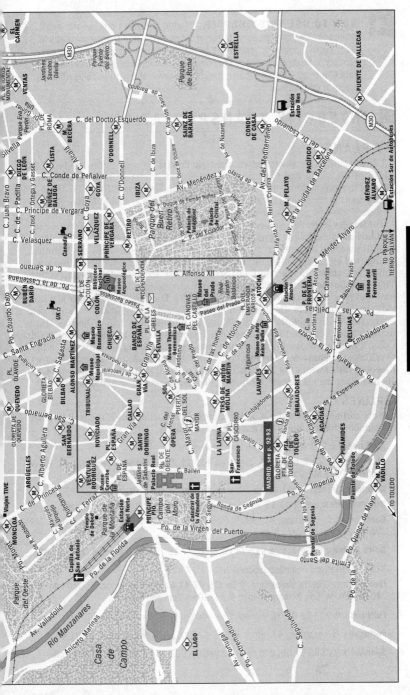

MADRID

> **HOW TO USE THIS CHAPTER.** Madrid is divided into several neighborhoods. We have grouped together all of each area's accommodations, food, sights, museums, and nightlife listings. General information on these aspects of Madrid, as well as shopping and specific listings for camping and entertainment (including sports, theater, concerts, and film) appears after the practical information.

■ INTERCITY TRANSPORTATION

BY PLANE

All flights land at **Aeropuerto Internacional de Barajas** (general info ☎913 05 83 43, 44, 45, or 46), 20min. and 13km northeast of Madrid. A branch of the **regional tourist office** in the international arrivals area has maps and info. (☎913 05 86 56. Open M-F 8am-8pm, Sa 9am-1pm.) **Luggage storage** (*consigna*) is available. (1 day €2.65, 2-15 days €3.30-4.65 per day, after day 15 €0.66-1.33 per day.)

The **Barajas Metro line** connects the airport to all of Madrid (€1.10). From the airport arrivals area, follow signs to the Metro (10min.). Take Line 8 (pink) to Nuevos Ministerios and switch to Line 10 (dark blue, dir: Aluche). At Tribunal, change to Line 1 (light blue, dir: Congosto), and two stops later you'll find yourself at Sol, smack in the middle of Madrid's best accommodations and sights. The green **Bus-Aeropuerto #89** leaves from the national and international terminals and runs to the city center. (☎914 31 61 92. Look for "EMT" signs just outside the airport doors. Daily 4:45, 5:17, 6:17am and every 15min. 6:17am-10pm; every 10min. 10-11:30pm; every 30min. 11:30pm-2am; €2.46.) The bus stops underground beneath the Jardines del Descubrimiento in **Plaza de Colón** (M: Colón). After surfacing in Pl. de Colón, walk toward the neo-Gothic statue that overlooks the **Paseo de Recoletos**. The Colón Metro station is across the street. Fleets of **taxis** swarm the airport. Taxi fare to central Madrid should cost €15-18, including the €4 airport surcharge, depending on traffic and time of day.

AIRLINES

Over 65 airlines fly in and out of Aeropuerto Internacional de Barajas. Below are the numbers for the most relevant airlines in Madrid.

Air Europa: ☎902 40 15 01; www.aireuropa.com.

Air France: Pl. de España, 18, 5th fl. (☎901 11 22 66; www.airfrance.es). M: Pl. de España. Open M-F 9am-5pm.

American Airlines: ☎902 11 55 70; www.aa.com. Open M-F 9am-6pm.

British Airways: ☎902 11 13 33; www.britishairways.com. Open M-F 9am-7pm.

Continental: C. Leganitos, 47, 9th fl. (☎915 59 27 10). M: Pl. de España. Open M-F 9am-6pm.

Delta Airlines: C. Goya, 8. ☎915 77 06 50 or 77 18 72, reservations 917 49 66 30.

KLM: Reservations and information ☎902 22 27 47.

Iberia: Santa Cruz de Marcenado, 2 (☎915 87 47 47; 24hr. reservations and info 902 40 05 00). M: San Bernardo. Open M-F 9:30am-2pm and 4-7pm.

Lufthansa: ☎902 22 01 01. Airport office open daily 5:15am-7:45pm.

Portugalia: C. Leganitos, 47, 6th fl. ☎915 42 21 61, reservations 902 10 01 45.

SpanAir: ☎913 93 67 40, info and reservations 902 13 14 15; www.spanair.com.

Madrid
see map p. 92-93

⌂ ACCOMMODATIONS

Albergue Juvenil Santa Cruz de Marcenado (HI), 4	B1
Hispa Domus, 18	D2
Hostal A. Nebrija, 9	A2
Hostal Abril, 15	D2
Hostal Aguilar, 45	D4
Hostal Alicante, 39	B4
Hostal Armesto, 50	D4
Hostal Cantábrico, 46	D4
Hostal Chelo, 19	D2
Hostal Esparteros, 42	C4
Hostal Gonzalo, 54	E5
Hostal Internacional, 47	D4
Hostal Lauria, 26	B3
Hostal Lorenzo, 36	D3
Hostal Madrid, 41	C4
Hostal Margarita, 27	B3
Hostal Medieval, 14	D2
Hostal Oriente, 31	B3
Hostal Palacios/Hostal Ribadavia, 12	C2
Hostal Paz, 30	B3
Hostal Portugal, 29	B3
Hostal-Residencia Alibel, 33	C3
Hostal-Residencia Carreras, 48	D4
Hostal-Residencia Cruz-Sol, 43	C4
Hostal-Residencia Domínguez, 8	D1
Hostal-Residencia Lamalonga, 11	B2
Hostal-Residencia Lido, 47	D4
Hostal-Residencia Luz, 38	B4
Hostal-Residencia Rios, 2	A1
Hostal-Residencia Rober, 32	B3
Hostal-Residencia Sud-Americana, 55	E5
Hostal R. Rodríguez, 44	C4
Hostal Santillan, 10	B2
Hostal Triana, 35	C3
Hostal Valencia, 24	A3
Hotel Villar, 49	D4
Hotel Mónaco, 20	D2
Los Amigos Backpackers' Hostel, 28	B3

🍴 BEST OF FOOD

Al-Jaima, 21	D2
Ananias, 1	A1
Arroceria Gala, 56	E5
Café de Oriente, 25	A3
Café Gijón, 23	E2
Café-Botillería Manuela, 6	C1
Casa Alberto, 52	D5
Cáscaras, 3	A1
Chez Pomme, 16	D2
El Estragón Vegetariano, 51	A5
La Granja Restaurante Vegetariano, 5	C1
Inshala, 37	A4
Osteria Il Regno di Napoli, 7	D1
El Rey del Barnio, 13	D2

⭐ BEST OF NIGHTLIFE

Acuarela, 17	D2
Big Bamboo, 22	E2
El Café de Sheherezade, 53	D5
Kapital, 57	E6
Palacio Gaviria, 40	B4
Pasapoga, 34	C3

MADRID

TAP Air Portugal: Pl. de los Mostenses, 13, 6th fl. (☎915 42 12 03; www.tap-airportugal.pt). Airport counter ☎913 93 82 53. Open M-F 9am-6pm.

USAirways: ☎901 11 70 73; www.usairways.com. Open daily 9am-3:15pm.

BY TRAIN

Two *largo recorrido* (long distance) **RENFE** stations, **Chamartín** and **Atocha**, connect Madrid to surrounding areas and the rest of Europe. Both stations are easily accessible by Metro. (For Atocha, avoid lost tourist syndrome and get off the Metro at Atocha-Renfe, *not* Atocha.) Call RENFE (☎913 28 90 20 or 902 24 02 02; www.renfe.es) for reservations and info. Buy your tickets at the stations or at the **RENFE Main Office,** C. de Alcalá, 44, at Gran Vía. (M: Banco de España. Open M-F 9:30am-8pm.) Schedules for **Regionales, Cercanías, AVE** (☎915 34 05 05), and **Talgo** trains are available at the stations and online.

Estación Atocha (☎913 28 90 20, 915 06 61 37, or 902 10 00 07). M: Atocha-Renfe. Ticket windows open 7:15am-10pm. No international service. **AVE** (☎915 34 05 05) high-speed service to the south of Spain, including **Sevilla** (2½hr., 20 per day 7am-11pm, €57-64) via **Córdoba** (1¾hr., €35-47). The cast-iron atrium of the original station has been turned into a simulated rainforest. Art galleries, boutiques, restaurants, and cafes provide additional diversions. **RENFE information office** in the main terminal (☎902 24 02 02). Open 7am-10pm daily. **Luggage storage** (€2.40-4.50), follow signs for *consignas automáticas,* upstairs from the rainforest (open daily 6:30am-10:15pm).

Estación Chamartín (☎913 00 69 69 or 902 10 00 07). M: Chamartín. Bus #5 runs to and from Puerta del Sol (45min.); the stop is just beyond the lockers. For international destinations, call RENFE or ☎934 90 11 22; for domestic destinations call RENFE (☎902 24 02 02; Spanish only). Ticket windows open 8am-10:30pm. Chamartín services both international and domestic destinations in the northeast and south. Most *cercanías* (local) trains stop at both Chamartín and Atocha. Major destinations include: **Barcelona** (7-10½hr., 10 per day 7am-11pm, €32.50-44); **Lisbon, PT** (9½hr., 1 per day 10:45pm, €47.50-67); **Paris, FR** (13½hr., 1 per day 7pm, €119-131). Chamartín is a mini-mall of useful services, including a **tourist office** (Vestíbulo, Puerta 14, ☎913 15 99 76; open M-Sa 8am-8pm, Su 8am-3pm), **currency exchange, accommodations service, post office, car rental, police,** and **luggage storage** (*consignas;* €2.40-4.50; open daily 6:30am-10:15pm).

BY BUS

Numerous private companies serve Madrid, each with its own station and set of destinations. Most buses pass through **Estación Sur de Autobuses** and **Estación Auto-Res,** both easily accessible by Metro. The Pl. Mayor tourist office has information on the most relevant inter-city buses. For more general info, see **By Bus,** p. 100.

AISA (☎902 42 22 42) runs to **Aranjuez** (45min.; M-F every 15-30min. 6:30am-11:30pm, Sa every 45min. 7:30am-11pm, Su 10 per day 8am-11pm; €3). International destinations include: **Czech Republic, France, Germany, Italy, Poland, Portugal, Romania,** and **Switzerland,** but flying can actually be cheaper. Contact **Eurolines** for more information. (Reservations: ☎902 40 50 40. Madrid office in bus station ☎915 06 33 60; www.eurolines.es. Open M-F 7am-11pm, Sa 7:15am-2pm, Su 9-10am and 10:15-11pm.)

Estación Empresa Alacuber: (☎913 76 01 04), on Po. de Moret. M: Moncloa. To **El Pardo** (20min., every 15min. 6am-1:30am, €1.05).

Estación Auto-Res: C. Fernández Shaw, 1 (☎902 02 09 99; www.auto-res.net). M: Conde de Casal. Info booth open daily 6:30am-1am. Tickets can be bought here daily 6am-1am. To: **Badajoz** (5¼hr., 9-10 per day 8am-1am, €21.70; express 4½hr., €25.50); **Cáceres** (4¾hr., 7-9 per day 8am-1am, €16.17; express 3½hr., €19.20); **Cuenca** (3hr.; M-F 8-10 per day 6:45am-10pm, Sa-Su 5-6 per day 8am-8pm; €8.86; express 2½hr.; M-F and Su 2 per day 10am and 6:30pm, Sa 1 per day 10am; €11.20); **Mérida** (4¼hr., 9 per day 8am-1am, €18.43; express 4hr., €22.20); **Salamanca** (3-3¼hr., 7 per day 8:30am-10:30pm, €9.89; express 2½hr., 14-15 per day 7am-9:30pm, €14.70); **Trujillo** (3¼hr., 11-12 per day 8am-1am, €13.59; express 3hr., €16.60); **Valencia** (5hr., 4 per day 1am-2pm, €19.23; express 4hr., 10 per day 7am-10:30pm, €23.20). **Luggage storage** €1.20 per bag per day.

Estación Empresa Continental Auto: Av. de América, 9 (☎917 45 63 00). M: Av. de América. To: **Alcalá de Henares** (40min.; M-Sa every 15min. 6:15am-10:45pm, Su every 30min. 7-9am and every 20min. 9am-11pm; €1.83); **Guadalajara** (1hr.; M-F every 30min. 7am-midnight, Sa-Su every hr. 7am-midnight; €3.31); **Toledo** (1½hr.; M-Sa every 30min. 6:30am-10pm, Su every 30min. 8:30am-midnight; €3.89.

Estación Autocares Herranz: C. del Rey, 27 (☎918 96 90 28), in the Intercambio de Moncloa. M: Moncloa. To **El Escorial** (50min.; every 15min. M-F 6:55am-11:30pm, Sa 9am-10:15pm, Su 9am-11pm; €2.85) and **Valle de los Caídos** via El Escorial (20min.; departs El Escorial 3:15pm, returns 5:30pm; round trip plus admission €7.70).

Empresa Larrea (☎915 30 48 00) to **Ávila** (1½hr.; M-F 8 per day 7:15am-8pm, Sa-Su 4 per day 8:30am-8pm; €6.26).

Estación La Sepulvedana: Po. de la Frontera, 16 (☎915 30 48 00). M: Príncipe Pío (via extension from M: Ópera). To **Segovia** (1½hr., every 30min. 6:30am-10:15pm, €5.51).

Estación Sur de Autobuses: C. Méndez Álvaro (☎914 68 42 00). M: Méndez Álvaro; Metro stop inside station. Info booth open daily 7am-11pm. **ATMs,** food, and **luggage storage** (bags €4.85) are available. National destinations include: **Albacete,**

Algeciras, Alicante, Aranjuez, Barcelona, Benidorm, Cartagena, La Coruña, Gijón, Lugo, Murcia, Oviedo, Santiago de Compostela, Segovia, Toledo, and Zaragoza. Check at the station or call for specific info on routes and schedules.

◪ ORIENTATION

The "Kilómetro 0" sign in front of the police station in **Puerta del Sol** marks the intersection of eight of Madrid's most celebrated streets and the starting point of the country's major highways. To make Madrid's infinite plazas and serpentine streets more navigable, coverage of the city is broken down into five major neighborhoods: **El Centro, Huertas, Malasaña and Chueca, Bilbao,** and **Argüelles,** all of which are within walking distance or a short metro ride of one another.

Most of Madrid's prominent sights, including the **Ópera** and **Plaza Mayor,** radiate from Sol in El Centro. Just west of Sol off C. Mayor, **Plaza Mayor** is the hub of activity for tourists and *madrileños* alike; the plaza houses both contemporary cafes and the churches and historical buildings of **Habsburg Madrid,** also known as **Madrid de los Austrias.** Farther west of Sol, by way of C. del Arenal, lies the reigning monument of **Bourbon Madrid,** the Palacio Real. This section of Madrid, also known as **Ópera,** hosts fantastic gardens and churches.

To the southeast of Sol lies **Huertas,** once the literary district and now the center for exploring the city's three great museums (see **Museums,** p. 146) or the lush **Parque del Buen Retiro** (see p. 139). Bordered by C. de Alcalá to the north, Po. del Prado to the east, and C. de Atocha to the south, the neighborhood is the home of traditional cafes, lively theaters, and intoxicating nightlife. Centered around **Plaza de Santa Ana,** Huertas is crowded with some of the best budget accommodations in the city, as well as some of the best traditional *tapas* bars.

Also south of Sol and west of Huertas is the area around the Metro stop **La Latina,** which has less prestige and fewer tourists than the rest of Old Madrid. Small markets line winding lantern-lit streets, perfect for an evening of gourmet tradition. **El Rastro,** a gargantuan ancient flea market, is staged here every Sunday morning. Farther south lies **Lavapiés,** a working-class neighborhood.

North of Sol, busy **Gran Vía** is the commercial center of Madrid, littered with fast-food joints and a handful of skyscrapers. Linked to C. de Fuencarral, it acts as the southern border of **Malasaña** and **Chueca,** both full of trendy restaurants and shops. Beyond Gran Vía and east of Malasaña and Chueca lies modern Madrid. Running the length of Madrid from **Atocha** in the south to **Plaza de Castilla** in the north, **Paseo del Prado, Paseo de Recoletos,** and **Paseo de la Castellana** pass the Prado, the fountains at **Plaza de la Cibeles** and **Plaza de Colón,** and the elaborate skyscrapers beyond Pl. de Colón, including the leaning towers of the **Puerta de Europa.**

The area northwest of Sol holds the **Plaza de España** and the soaring **Torre de Madrid,** the pride of 1950s Spain. Still farther northwest of Sol lie **Argüelles** and **Bilbao,** energetic neighborhoods spilling over from **Moncloa.** Both are student districts, filled with cheap eateries and neon nightclubs.

Madrid is much safer than most major European cities, but Puerta del Sol, Pl. de España, Pl. Chueca, and Malasaña's Pl. Dos de Mayo are intimidating late at night. As a general rule, avoid parks and quiet residential streets after dark, and always watch out for thieves and pickpockets in crowds.

MAPS

The free *Plano de Madrid* (street map) and *Plano de Transportes* (public transportation map) are fantastic. Pick them up at the tourist office in the arrivals area of the airport terminal or from any other tourist office. Public transportation info can also be accessed by phone (☎012) or by web (www.ctm-madrid.es). **El Corte Inglés** (see p. 103) offers a one-page map of Madrid. For a comprehensive map with street index, pick up the *Almax* map (€4.42) at any newsstand.

⌐ LOCAL TRANSPORTATION

METRO

Safe, speedy, and spotless, Madrid's Metro puts most major subway systems to shame. Trains run frequently; green timers above most platforms show increments of five minutes or less since the last train departed. The free *Plano del Metro* (available at any ticket booth) and the wall maps of surrounding neighborhoods are clear and helpful. Fare and schedule info is posted in every station.

Twelve lines, totaling more than 171km, connect Madrid's 158 stations, making the city incredibly easy to get around. Line 12, Puerta del Sur, now extends coverage to the Casa de Campo, Móstoles, and Getafe regions south of the city. Lines are distinguished by color and number. An individual Metro ticket costs €1.10, but frequent riders opt for the **bonotransporte** (ticket of 10 rides vaild for both the Metro and bus system) at €5.20. Buy them at machines at Metro stops, *estancos* (tobacco shops), or newsstands. Remember to hold on to your ticket until you leave the Metro—riding without one incurs outrageous fines. For more details, call **Metro info** (☎902 44 44 03) or ask at any ticket booth. For a comprehensive guide, visit www.metromadrid.es.

Trains run every day from 6am to 1:30am. Violent crime in Metro stations is almost unheard of, and women usually feel safe traveling alone. Pickpockets tend to do their best work in crowded cars, though. If you feel uncomfortable, avoid empty cars and ride in sight of the conductor. At night, avoid the stations to the north, which tend to be less frequented. Metro stations Chueca, Gran Vía, La Latina, Pl. de España, Sol, and Tirso de Molina can be intimidating after midnight if alone. These areas are usually busy all through the night with bar- and club-hoppers, but many crimes are reported in the area. Use caution and common sense.

READ THIS The **Guía del Ocio,** available behind the counter of any news kiosk, should be your first purchase in Madrid (€1). It has concert, theater, sports, cinema, and TV schedules, and lists exhibits, restaurants, bars, and clubs. Although it's in Spanish, alphabetical listings of clubs and restaurants are invaluable even to non-speakers. The *Guía* comes out on Thursday or Friday, so be sure that you're buying an up-to-date copy instead of last week's issue. For an English magazine with articles on new finds in and around the city, pick up **In Madrid,** distributed free at tourist offices and many restaurants. Live Music and Nightlife sections are basically an English-language translation of the *Guía*. **The Broadsheet,** free at bookstores, is a no-frills listing of English-language classifieds. The weekly **Segundamano,** on sale at kiosks, is essential for apartment or roommate seekers. Gay travelers will want to pick up the free magazine **Shanguide,** which lists activities and nightspots for every town in Spain, or buy **Zero** magazine at any kiosk (€3.95). **Minerva,** available at the Círculo de Bellas Artes, keeps you up to date on the art scene.

BUS

While the Metro makes the most sense for trips across Madrid, buses cover areas inaccessible by the Metro and are a great way to see the city. Like the Metro, the bus system is exceptionally well organized. Most stops are clearly marked, but if you want extra guidance in finding routes and stops, try the handy *Plano de Transportes*, free at the tourist office, or *Madrid en Autobús*, free at bus kiosks.

Bus fares are the same as those for the Metro, and Metro tickets can also be used on city buses. Buses run from 6am to 11:30pm. From midnight until 3am, the night bus service, **Búho** (owl), travels from Pl. de la Cibeles (and other marked routes) to the outskirts every 20min.; from 3-6am, they run every hour. Night buses (N1-N20), the cheapest form of transportation for late-night revelers, are listed in a special section of the *Plano*. For more info, call **Empresa Municipal de Transportes.** (☎914 06 88 10 or 06 88 00. Spanish only. Open 6am-midnight.)

TAXI

Taxis stream through Madrid around the clock. If one does not appear when you need it, or if you want to summon one to your door, call **Radio Taxi** (☎914 47 51 80), **Radio-Taxi Independiente** (☎914 05 12 13), or **Teletaxi** (☎913 71 37 11 or 71 21 31). A green *"libre"* sign in the window or a green light indicates availability. Base fare is €1.35, plus €0.63-0.81 per kilometer from 6am-10pm and €0.81-0.91 from 10pm-6am. Common fare supplements include: airport (€4); bus and train stations (€2); luggage charge (€0.50 per bag). Fare from the city center to the airport is €15-18.

Check that the driver starts the meter. If you have a complaint or think you've been overcharged, demand a *recibo oficial* (official receipt) and an *hoja de reclamaciones* (complaint form), which the driver is required to supply. Take down the license number, route taken, and fare charged. Drop off the forms and information at the **Oficina Municipal del Taxi**, C. Vallehermoso, 1, 2nd fl. (☎915 88 96 32; fax 88 96 35) or the **Ayuntamiento** (City Hall), Pl. de la Villa, 4 (info ☎010; ☎915 88 10 00) to request a refund. To request **taxi service for the disabled,** call ☎915 47 85 00 or 47 86 00. Rates are same as other taxis. If you leave belongings in a taxi, visit or call the **Negociado de Objetos Perdidos,** Pl. Legazpi, 7. (☎915 88 43 46 or 88 43 48. Open M-F 9am-2pm.) Drivers are obligated to turn in items within 48 hours.

CAR RENTAL

There is no reason to rent a car in Madrid. If congested traffic and nightmarish parking don't drive you into hysterics, aggressive drivers, annoying mopeds, and sky-high gasoline prices will. *Estancos* (tobacco shops) sell parking permits for designated street parking. If you plan to drive to destinations outside of Spain, a larger car rental chain is the best bet.

Atesa: Reservations: ☎902 10 01 01 in Spain, elsewhere 10 05 15; www.atesa.com. Offices: Gran Vía, 80, in Pl. de los Mostenses (☎915 42 50 15; fax 41 80 89); airport (☎913 93 72 32; fax 93 72 34).

Avis: Reservations: ☎902 13 55 31; www.avis.com. Offices: Estación de Atocha (☎915 30 01 68); Gran Vía, 80 (☎915 48 42 03); airport (☎913 93 72 22 or 93 72 41).

Budget: Reservations: ☎901 20 12 12; www.budget.com. Booth at airport.

Europcar: Reservations: ☎902 10 50 30; www.europcar.com. Offices: Estación de Atocha (☎915 30 01 94); airport (☎913 93 72 35).

Hertz: Reservations: (☎902 40 24 05 or 913 72 93 00; www.hertz.com). Offices: Estación de Atocha (☎915 06 04 97); Estación de Chamartín (☎917 33 04 00); Gran Vía, 88, #12 (☎915 42 58 05); airport (☎913 93 72 28 or 93 72 29).

MOPED & BIKE RENTAL

Fortunately for pedestrians, Madrid is not scarred by the moped mayhem that has taken over other parts of Europe. Though mopeds are swift and convenient, Madrid's stellar public transport system is more than sufficient for getting around. A lock and helmet are necessary. **Motocicletas Antonio Castro,** C. del Conde Duque, 13, rents mopeds starting at €26 per day or €120 per week, including unlimited mileage and insurance. €390 deposit required for 1-day rentals, €450 for 1-week rentals. Must be at least 21 and have an **International Driver's Permit.** (☎915 42 06 57;

M: San Bernardo. Open M-F 8am-1:30pm and 5-8pm.) For **bicycle rental**, try **Karacol Sport,** C. Tortosa, 8. (☎915 39 96 33. M: Atocha. Rental €15 per day; €40 deposit and passport. Open daily 10:30am-8pm, Th 10:30am-10pm, Sa 10:30am-2pm.)

🔲 PRACTICAL INFORMATION

TOURIST & FINANCIAL SERVICES

Tourist Offices: English is spoken at most tourist offices. Those planning trips outside the Comunidad de Madrid can visit region-specific offices within Madrid; ask the tourist offices below for their addresses. **Regional Office of the Comunidad de Madrid,** main office: C. del Duque de Medinaceli, 2 (☎914 29 49 51; info line 902 10 00 07; www.comadrid.es/turismo). M: Banco de España. Brochures, transportation info, and maps for the Comunidad. Extremely helpful; make this your first stop. **Municipal Office,** Pl. Mayor, 3 (☎913 66 54 77 or 58 816 36). M: Sol. Hands out indispensable city and transportation maps and a complete guide to accommodations, as well as *In Madrid* and *Enjoy Madrid,* monthly activities and information guides. In 2004, it will expand and move across the plaza. Open M-Sa 10am-8pm, Su 10am-3pm. **Branch** at Mercado Pta. de Toledo, Ronda de Toledo, 1, stand #3134 (☎913 64 18 75). M: Pta. de Toledo. In a gallery with large banners on a plaza across from the Metro station. Open M-Sa 9am-7pm, Su 9am-3pm. **Branches** at Estación Chamartín (see p. 97) and the airport (see p. 96). **El Corte Inglés** also offers **free maps** and information (see p. 103).

▓ **General Info Line:** ☎901 30 06 00. Run by the Ayuntamiento. They'll tell you anything about Madrid, from police locations to zoo hours. Ask for *inglés* to speak with an English-speaking operator.

Websites: www.comadrid.es/turismo; www.tourspain.es; www.cronicamadrid.com; www.guiadelocio.com; www.madridman.com; www.red2000.com/spain/madrid.

Tours: Tours can be pricy but informative. Read the fine print before signing on. The Ayuntamiento offers various **walking tours** through the city; call or pick up more info at the municipal tourist office. (☎915 88 29 06; advance tickets ☎902 22 16 22. €3.10, students, children, and seniors €2.50. Tours in English and Spanish.). **Madrid Vision** (☎917 79 18 88 or 915 41 63 21; www.madridvision.es) offers tours of the city on double decker buses. A great option for those with limited time. There are 3 routes (Madrid Histórico, Moderno, and Monumental) each of which makes 15-20 key stops around the city. Get off and on the bus as you please. Weekdays adults €9.62, children and seniors €4.81; weekends €10.82/5.41. Two-day tickets also available. **Juliá Tours,** Gran Vía, 65 (☎915 59 96 05; www.juliatours.com). M: Pl. de España. Offers pricey tours of Andalucía, Portugal, and Morocco. Open daily 9am-8;30pm.

Budget Travel:

Viajes TIVE, C. Fernando el Católico, 88 (☎915 43 74 12; fax 44 00 62). M: Moncloa. Walk straight down C. Arcipreste de Hita and turn left on C. Fernando el Católico. A great resource for long-term visitors. ISIC €6; HI card €5, over 30 €11, non-Spaniards €18.06. Organizes group excursions and language classes. Lodging and student residence info. English sometimes spoken. Open M-F 9am-2pm, information only. Arrive early to avoid lines.

Comunidad de Madrid, Dirección General de Juventud, Gran Vía, 10 (☎901 51 06 10 or 917 20 11 82; www.madrid.org/inforjoven). M: Banco de España. It offers services similar to TIVE, but doesn't sell tickets. Open Sept.-July M-F 9am-2pm and 5-8pm; Aug. 9am-2pm.

ASATEJ Group, C. San Jerónimo, 18, 1st fl. (☎915 22 96 93; www.asatej.com). M: Sol or Sevilla. Backpackers sell student airfares, tours, car rental, bus passes, ISIC cards, and other travel needs. Open M-F 10:30am-7:30pm, Sa 10:30am-1:30pm.

Viajes Barceló, C. de la Princesa, 3 (☎915 59 18 19, customer service 902 11 62 26; www.barceloviajes.com), M: Ventura Rodríguez or Pl. de España. Student travel. Open daily 10am-7pm.

Currency Exchange: Banco Santander Central Hispano charges no commission on travelers checks up to €600. Also offers the best rates on AmEx travelers checks. **Main branch,** Pl. Canalejas, 1 (☎915 58 11 11). M: Sol. Follow C. San Jerónimo to Pl. Canalejas. Open Apr.-Sept. M-F 8:30am-2pm; Oct.-Mar. M-Th 8:30am-4:30pm, F 8:30am-2pm, Sa 8:30am-1pm. **Banks** usually charge 1-2% commission (minimum charge €3). Booths in Sol and Gran Vía, open as late as midnight and on weekends, have poor rates and are not a good deal. **ATMs** are everywhere and can be operated in English. **Servi Red, Servi Caixa,** and **Telebanco** machines accept bank cards with one or more of the Cirrus, PLUS, EuroCard, or NYCE logos. See **ATM Cards,** p. 18.

American Express: Pl. de las Cortes, 2 (Traveler services: ☎917 43 77 40; currency exchange: ☎43 77 55), entrance on C. del Marqués de Cubas. M: Banco de España. Offers **currency exchange** (no commission on cash or AmEx travelers checks; small set fee for non-AmEx travelers checks), will hold mail for 30 days, and can help send and receive wired money. Traveler services open M-F 9am-7:30pm, Sa 10am-2pm; currency exchange open M-F 9am-7:30pm, Sa 9am-2pm. 24hr. Express Cash machine outside. Also airport office (☎913 93 82 22 or 93 82 15). To report or cancel lost travelers checks, call toll free ☎900 81 00 29.

Lost or stolen credit cards: American Express (☎917 43 70 00); VISA (☎915 19 21 00); MasterCard (☎915 19 21 00); any credit card (☎915 81 18 11).

LOCAL SERVICES

Luggage Storage: Available at the airport and bus and train stations.

El Corte Inglés: Calle de Preciados, 3 (☎913 79 80 00). M: Sol; **Calle Goya, 76** (☎914 32 93 00). M: Goya; **Calle de la Princesa, 56** (☎914 54 60 00). M: Argüelles; **Calle Raimundo Fernández Villaverde, 79** (☎914 18 88 00). M: Nuevos Ministerios. Other locations in Madrid and throughout Spain. *La mama grande* of department stores, the chain's official motto is: "A place to shop. A place to dream." No matter what you need, from groceries or train tickets, you can find it here. Currency exchange with no commission but mediocre rates. Open M-Sa 10am-10pm, first Su of each month 11am-9pm.

English-Language Periodicals: International edition dailies and weeklies available at kiosks everywhere, especially on Gran Vía, Paseos del Prado, Recoletos, and Castellana, and around Pta. del Sol. If you're dying for the *New York Times,* try one of the **VIPS** restaurants (see **Red-Eye Establishments,** p. 109).

Language Service: Forocio, C. San Jerónimo, 18, 1st fl. (☎902 36 36 33 or 915 22 56 77; www.forocio.com). M: Sol. An organization dedicated to bringing foreigners and natives together to share languages and good times. Sponsors weekly international parties. Open M-F 10am-10pm.

Libraries: The municipal tourist office has a comprehensive list of *bibliotecas* around the city. These include **Bibliotecas Municipales Especializadas,** numerous branches of the **Bibliotecas Públicas Municipales por Distritos** (22 locations), and **Bibliotecas Populares** (18 locations). Large branch at M: Puerta de Toledo with English-language periodicals. (☎913 66 54 07. Open M-F 8:30am-8:45pm, Sa 9am-1:45pm.)

Religious Services: Our Lady of Mercy, C. Alfonso XIII, 165 (☎917 73 98 29), at Pl. Habana. Sunday Mass in English 11am, followed by coffee and doughnuts. **Immanuel Baptist Church,** C. Hernández de Tejada, 4 (☎914 07 43 47). English services Su 11am and 7pm. **Community Church of Madrid,** C. Bravo Murillo, 85. M: Cuatro Caminos. . Multi-denominational Protestant services in English Su 10am. **British Embassy Church of St. George,** C. Núñez de Balboa, 43 (☎915 76 51 09). M: Velázquez. Services Su 8:30, 10, and 11:15am. **Sinagoga Beth Yaacov,** C. Balmes, 3 (☎915 91 31 31). M: Iglesia. Services F 8pm, Sa 9:15am. Kosher restaurant can be reserved. Passport sometimes required. Spanish only. **Centro Islámico,** C. Alonso Cano, 3 (☎914 48 05 54). M: Iglesia. Services and language classes. Open M-F 10:45am-2pm.

Women's Services: For general information on women's services in Spain or to report an incident, call **Instituto de la Mujer** (☎900 19 10 10). For literature concerning women's issues, try the **Librería de Mujeres,** C. San Cristóbal, 17 (☎915 21 70 43; www.unapalabraotra.org/libreriamujeres.html), near Pl. Mayor. M: Sol. From Sol, C. San Cristóbal is the 2nd left off C. Mayor. The shop's motto is *"Los libros no muerden, el feminismo tampoco."* (Books don't bite; neither does feminism.) Books and gifts, but more of a resource for Spanish speakers. Helpful with finding local support and discussion groups. Open M-F 10am-2pm and 5-8pm, Oct.-May also Sa 10am-2pm.

Gay and Lesbian Services: Most establishments in Chueca carry a free guide to gay nightlife in Spain called **Shanguide.** If you can't find one right away, just ask someone in a store near Pl. Chueca and they will tell you where to get one. This guide book offers detailed listings and maps of the many gay bars, clubs, cafes, restaurants, bookstores, shops, and associations in and around Madrid. Alternatively, you can purchase **Zero** (€3.60) at any kiosk. The magazine includes a small pull-out guide to nightlife and gay activities. These listings are often more up to date than the **Spartacus International Gay Guide,** sold at almost any newsstand or bookstore. Support groups and associations: **Colectivo de Gais y Lesbianas de Madrid (COGAM),** C. de Fuencarral, 37 (☎915 22 45 17; fax 24 02 00; www.cogam.org). M: Gran Vía. Provides a wide range of services and activities of interest to gays, lesbians, and bisexuals. English usually spoken. Free screenings of gay-interest movies, COGAM youth group (25 and under), and HIV-positive support group (M-F 6-10pm). Reception daily M-Sa 5:30-9pm. Free counseling M-Th 7-9pm. Library open daily 7-9pm. Once every 2 months, COGAM publishes **Entiendes...?,** a magazine in Spanish about gay issues that also lists activities and nightspots for every town in Spain. **Berkana Librería Gay y Lesbiana,** C. Hortaleza, 64 (☎915 22 55 99; www.libreriaberkana.com) has guidebooks, contact information, and listings (see **Books,** p. 114). Most entertainment guides list gay and lesbian clubs. **GAY-INFORM,** a gay info line (☎915 23 00 70), provides information in Spanish (and sometimes French and English) about gay associations, leisure activities, and health issues. The same number has info on sports, workshops in French and English, dinners, and **Brujulai,** COGAM's weekend excursion group. Open daily 5-9pm.

Laundromat: Lavandería Ondablu, C. de León, 3 (☎913 69 50 71). M: Antón Martín, Sol, or Sevilla. Open daily 9am-10:30pm. Also at C. de la Hortaleza, 84 (☎915 31 28 73), next to Piazziolo. M: Chueca. Same hours and prices. Just up the street is **Lavandería Cervantes,** C. de León, 6. Wash €2, dry €1. Open daily 9am-9pm.

EMERGENCY & COMMUNICATIONS

Emergency: ☎112 (for all emergencies). ☎091 or 092 (national and local police).

Police: C. de los Madrazos, 9 (☎915 41 71 60). M: Sevilla. English forms available. To report crimes in the **Metro,** go to the office in the Sol station. Open daily 8am-11pm. **Guardia Civil** (☎062 or 915 34 02 00). **Protección Civil** (☎915 37 31 00).

Crisis Lines: Poison Control (24hr. ☎915 62 04 20). **Rape Hotline** (☎915 74 01 10). Open M-F 10am-2pm and 4-7pm (at other times, machine-recorded instructions).

Help Lines: AIDS Info Hotline (☎900 11 10 00). Open M-F 10am-10pm. **Detox** (☎900 16 15 15). Open daily 9am-9pm. **Alcoholics Anonymous,** C. Juan Bravo, 40, 2nd fl. (English ☎913 09 19 47; Spanish ☎913 41 82 82). M: Núñez de Balboa.

Late-Night Pharmacy: Dial ☎098, the general Madrid info line, to find the nearest one. One located at **Calle Mayor, 13** (☎913 66 46 16), off Puerta del Sol, and another at **Calle Mayor, 59** (☎915 48 00 14), closer to M: Ópera.

First Aid Stations: Scattered about the city, all open 24hr. Ask for *primeros auxilios.* One at **Calle de Navas de Tolosa** (☎915 21 00 25), M: Callao.

Hospitals: Prompt appointments are hard to obtain, but public hospitals don't require advance payment. Emergency rooms are the best option for immediate attention. US insurance is not accepted, but get a receipt, and your insurance may pick up the tab when you get home. General emergency exam runs €150. For non-emergency concerns, **Anglo-American Medical Unit,** C. del Conde de Aranda, 1, 1st fl. (☎914 35 18 23), is quick and friendly. M: Serrano or Retiro. Doctors, dentists, and optometrists. Run partly by British and Americans. Regular personnel on duty 9am-8pm. Not an emergency clinic. Initial visit €66 for students, €100 for non-students. AmEx/MC/V. Embassies and consulates keep lists of English-speaking doctors in private practice. **Hospital Clínico San Carlos** (☎913 30 30 00), on Pl. Cristo Rey. M: Islas Filipinas or Moncloa.

Emergency Clinics: In a **medical emergency,** dial ☎061 or 112. **Hospital de Madrid,** Pl. del Conde del Valle Suchil, 16 (☎914 47 66 00; www.hospitaldemadrid.com). **Equipo Quirúrgico Municipal No. 1,** C. Montesa, 22 (☎915 88 51 00). M: Manuel Becerra. **Hospital Ramón y Cajal** (☎913 36 80 00), Ctra. Colmenar Viejo, km9100. Bus #135 from Pl. de Castilla. **Red Cross** (☎915 22 22 22; info 902 22 22 92).

Telephones: Information ☎1003. No English spoken. (For further information, see **Keeping in Touch,** p. 34.)

Internet Access: Hundreds of Internet cafes are spread across the city. The rates are generally consistent (roughly €0.80-1.50 per 30min., €1.30-2.50 per hr.).

  ■ **Easy Everything,** C. de la Montera, 10 (☎915 21 18 65; www.easyeverything.com). M: Sol. Lots of computers, unbeatably fast connections, good music, a cafe, and cheap rates. You are not obligated to use all of your purchased time at once, making quick email checks easy and cost-efficient. Rates fluctuate based on the number of computers in use. Open daily 8am-1am.

  Conéctate, C. Isaac Peral, 4 (☎915 44 54 65; www.conectate.es). M: Moncloa. A computer zone for students with over 300 flat-screens and some of the lowest rates in Madrid. Open 24hr. Also has stations in several VIPS restaurants (C. Serrano, Alcalá, Parque, Velázquez).

  Yazzgo Internet, Puerta del Sol, 6; Gran Vía, 60; Gran Vía, 69; Gran Vía, 84; Estación Chamartín; Estación Méndez Álvaro. (☎915 22 11 20; www.yazzgo.com). Trendy work center with locations throughout Madrid. Open daily 8:30am-10:30pm, except Gran Vía, 69, open 8:30am-1am.

  Oficina13, C. Mayor, 1, 4th fl., office 13 (☎915 23 20 88). M: Sol. Take the elevator up and buzz the office. Friendly service and U2 songs abound. Open M-Sa 10am-10pm, Su 11am-10:30pm.

Post Office: Palacio de Comunicaciones, C. de Alcalá, 51, on Pl. de la Cibeles (☎902 19 71 97). M: Banco de España. Enormous, ornate palace on the far side of the plaza from the Metro. Info (main vestibule) open M-Sa 8am-9:30pm. Windows open M-Sa 8:30am-9:30pm, Su 9am-2pm for stamp purchases. Receive **Lista de Correos** (Poste Restante) at windows 80-82; passport required. For **certified mail, telex, fax** service, and the information booth, enter main door. Send packages at windows marked "Todos Los Productos" behind the main info counter or through door N (enter from C. Montalbán); cash only. Postal Express is at door K (off Po. del Prado). **Postal Code:** 28080.

🔓 ACCOMMODATIONS

The demand for rooms in Madrid is always high and increases dramatically in summer. Though the city is filled with hostels, good quality at good prices can be hard to find. Prices range from €17 to €50 per person, depending on location, amenities, and season. Don't be deceived; higher prices do not necessarily translate into nicer accommodations. Reservations are strongly recommended at the top listings in the sections below. Try negotiating the price if you plan on staying awhile.

Because there are so many reasonably priced hostels (*hostales*) in Madrid, the listings here focus on them almost exclusively. Be aware that there are other accommodation options in Madrid, including hotels and *pensiones*. In Madrid, the difference between a one-star *hostal* and a *pensión* is often minimal. A room in a one- or two-star *hostal* has at least the basics: bed, closet space, desk with chair, sink and towel, window, light fixture, fake flowers, a lock on the door, and the occasional religious icon. Winter heating is standard; air-conditioning is not. Unless otherwise noted, communal bathrooms (toilet and shower) are the norm. Most places accept reservations, but none require them. Still, reservations are recommended in summer and on weekends year-round, especially in the Puerta del Sol area and at the first place *Let's Go* lists in each district. Hostels in Madrid are generally well-kept and comfortable; some are simply spectacular. Owners are usually accustomed to opening the doors, albeit groggily, at all hours or providing keys for guests, but ask before club-hopping into the wee hours; late-night lockouts and confrontations with irate owners are never fun. *Pensiones* are like boarding houses: they sometimes have curfews and often host guests staying for longer periods of time. Good deals can often be found outside central locations, and Madrid's stellar public transportation makes virtually any place central.

Budget lodgings are rare near the **Chamartín** train station, as is the case in most of the residential districts located away from the city center. There are a handful of hostels near the **Atocha** train station, the closest of which are down Po. de Santa María de la Cabeza. Be aware that this neighborhood is not as safe as those that are more central. The tourist office in Pl. Mayor has a full list of lodgings.

ACCOMMODATIONS BY PRICE

UNDER €15(❶)
🔲 Hostal-Residencia Luz — EC
Albergue Juvenil Santa Cruz de Marcenado — A

€15-25 (❷)
🔲 Hostal-Residencia Domínguez — MC
🔲 Hostal Paz — EC
Hostal Abril — MC
Hostal Alicante — EC
Hostal Los Arcos — EC
Hostal-Residencia Carreras — H
Hostal Esparteros — EC
Hostal-Residencia Lido — H
Hostal Medieval — MC
Hostal Palacios/Ribadavia — MC
Hostal Portugal — EC
Hostal-Residencia Ríos — A
Hostal-Residencia Sud-Americana — H
Hostal Villar — H
Los Amigos Backpackers' Hostel — H

€26-35 (❸)
Hostal A. Nebrija — GV
Hostal Aguilar — H
Hostal Cantábrico — EC

Hostal Chelo — MC
Hostal Internacional — H
Hostal Lauria — GV
Hostal Margarita — GV
Hostal Oriente — EC
Hostal R. Rodriguez — H
Hostal-Residencia Rober — EC
Hostal Santillan — GV
Hostal Triana — GV

€36-55 (❹)
🔲 Hostal Gonzalo — H
Hostal-Residencia Alibel — GV
Hostal Armesto — H
Hostal-Residencia Cruz-Sol — EC
Hostal-Residencia Lamalonga — GV
Hostal Lorenzo — MC
Hotel Monaco — MC
Hostal Sardinero — H
Hostal Valencia — EC
Hispa Domus — GV

OVER €55 (❺)
Hostal Madrid — EC

A Argüelles **EC** El Centro, Ópera, Sol, & Plaza Mayor **GV** Gran Vía **H** Huertas **M** Malasaña & Chueca **L** Lavapiés, La Latina, & Atocha

CAMPING

Tourist offices provide info about the 13 campsites within 50km of Madrid. Similar info can be found in the *Guía Oficial de Campings* (official camping guide), available at most bookstores and on reserve at tourist offices. The *Mapa de*

Campings shows the location of every official campsite in Spain. Also ask for the brochure *Hoteles, Campings, Apartamentos*, which lists hotels, campsites, and apartments in and around Madrid. For further camping info, contact the *Consejería de Educación de Juventud* (☎915 22 29 41).

Camping Alpha (☎916 95 80 69), on a tree-lined site 12.4km down Ctra. de Andalucía in Getafe. M: Legazpi. From the Metro station take bus #447, which stops next to the Nissan dealership (10min., every 30min. until 10pm, €1.25). Ask to off at the pedestrian overpass for the campsite. Cross the bridge and walk 1.5km back toward Madrid along a busy highway; camping signs lead the way. Pool, showers, and laundry. €5 per person, €5.23 per tent, €5.19 per car. ❶

Camping Osuna (☎917 41 05 10), on Av. Logroño. M: Canillejas. From the Metro, cross the pedestrian overpass, walk through the parking lot, and turn right along the freeway. Pass under a freeway and an arch and look for campground signs. Or grab the #101 bus from the Metro toward Barajas and ask for the campsite. Closer than Alpha, but not as nice. Showers, laundromat, supermarket, and restaurant/bar. Reception open daily 8:30am-10pm. €5 per person, per tent, and per car. €4.20 for electricity. ❶.

🖸 FOOD

In Madrid, it's easy to eat without emptying your wallet. You can't walk a block without tripping over at least five *cafeterías*, where a sandwich, coffee, and dessert go for €3.60. Vegetarians should check out the *Guía del Ocio* (€1), which has a complete listing of Madrid's vegetarian havens under the section *Otras Cocinas*. Check out www.mundovegetariano.com. Even carnivores may appreciate a veggie meal, given Madrid's indulgence in fatty meats and fried preparation.

Expect to spend at least €7 for a full meal at a *restaurante*, one step up from the typical *cafetería*. Most restaurants offer a *menú del día*, which includes bread, one drink, and a choice from the day's selections for appetizers, main courses, and desserts. For €6.75-9, it's a fantastic way to fill up. Keep the following buzz words in mind for quicker, cheaper *madrileño* fare: *bocadillo* (a sandwich on a long, hard roll, €2-2.75); *sandwich* (on sliced bread; ask for it *a la plancha* if you want it grilled, €2.25); *croissant* (with ham and cheese, €1.50); *ración* (a large *tapa*, served with bread €1.85-3.75); and *empanada* (a puff pastry with meat filling, €1.25-1.85). See the **Glossary,** p. 815, for additional translations.

In general, *restaurantes* are open 1-4pm and 8pm-midnight or 1am; in the following listings, this is the case unless otherwise noted. More casual establishments such as *mesones, cafeterías, bares, cafés, terrazas,* and *tabernas* serve drinks and foodstuffs all day until midnight, though some are closed on Sundays.

FOOD SHOPPING

In general, groceries get cheaper the farther you get from the center. Specialty items may require a visit to a pricey store in the center, but for daily fare, slipping into any corner store will reward you with an inexpensive selection of standards at drastically lower prices than would be found in a major chain.

Groceries: %Dia and **Champion** are the cheapest city-wide supermarket chains, though their locations tend to be a bit far from the city center. To satisfy grocery needs near El Centro, try the numerous *alimentaciones* (food marts) on side streets that sell drinks, candy, ice cream, and some basics. The *supermercado* in the basement of **El Corte Inglés** near Puerta del Sol (see p. 103) is somewhat pricier but über-convenient. Other more upscale options are **Mantequerías Leonesas, Expreso,** and **Jumbo.**

FOOD BY TYPE

TAPAS	
▨ Casa Alberto ❷	H
▨ Los Gabrieles ❶	
La Toscana ❷	EC
Casa Amadeo ❷	L
La Trucha ❸	EC
Taberna del Alabarder ❶	EC
La Princesita ❶	AM
El Encinar de el Bierzo ❷	L

CAFES ❶	
▨ Café-Botillería Manuela	
▨ Café de Oriente	EC
Café Gijón	
Café Comercial	B
La Botillería del Café de Oriente	EC
Eucalipto	L
Café del Real	EC

TRADITIONAL SPANISH	
▨ Ananias ❸	AM
▨ Restaurante Casa Botín	EC
▨ Arrocería Gala ❸	H
El Carabinero ❷	B
Cáscaras ❷	AM
La Finca de Susana ❷	GV
Lhardy Restaurante ❺	EC
Museo del Jamón	EC
Museo Chicote	GV
Parilla Matador ❹	EC
La Sacristía ❹	MC
La Sanabresa ❷	H
Gula Gula ❹	H

PASTRIES	
Horno La Santiagüesa ❶	EC
Horno San Onofre ❶	MC

OUTSIDE ESPAÑA	
▨ Al-Jaima, Cocina del Desierto ❷	MC
▨ Inshala ❸	EC
Arepas con Todo ❸	B
Bar Samara ❸	B
Bósforos ❶	EC
Chez Pomme ❶	MC
Collage ❸	B
La Carreta ❸	MC
La Crêperie ❶	AM
El Cuchi ❸	EC
El Rey del Barrio ❸	MC
La Farfalla ❷	H
La Gata Flora ❷	MC
Osteria Il Regno de Napoli ❷	B
Pizzaiolo ❷	MC
Pizzeria Cervantes ❷	EC
Pizzeria Vesuvio ❶	MC
La Vaca Argentina ❹	AM

VEGETARIAN	
▨ La Granja Restaurante ❷	MC
Al Natural ❸	H
Chez Pomme ❶	MC
El Estragón Vegetariano ❸	L
El Granero de Lavapiés ❷	L
Restaurante Integral Artemisa ❷	EC
Vegaviana ❷	MC

🍎 **AM** Argüelles & Moncloa **B** Bilbao **EC** El Centro, Sol, & Plaza Mayor **GV** Gran Vía **H** Huertas **L** Lavapiés, La Latina, & Atocha **MC** Malasaña & Chueca

Markets: Mercado de San Miguel, a covered market on Pl. de San Miguel, off the northwest corner of Pl. Mayor, sells the finest seafood and produce in the city at high prices. A wide selection of tourists can be found on display between the *bacalao* and the tuna. Open M-F 9:30am-2:30pm and 5:15-8:15pm, Sa 9am-2:30pm. **Mercado de la Cebada,** at the intersection of C. Toledo and C. San Francisco, is larger and less expensive and caters to many more locals. Open M-Sa 8am-2pm and 5:30-8pm.

Pastry Shops: These are everywhere. The sublime **Horno La Santiagüesa,** C. Mayor, 73, sells everything from *roscones de reyes* (sweet bread for the Feast of the Epiphany) to *empanadas* and pastries doused in rich chocolate. Don't pass through without trying the *tarta de santiago* (almond sweet bread). Open M-Sa 8am-9pm, Su 8am-9pm. **Horno San Onofre,** C. San Onofre, 4 (☎915 32 90 60), off C. de Fuencarral, serves sumptuous fruit tarts and *suspiros de modistilla* (seamstress's sighs), a *madrileño* specialty. Open M-Sa 9am-9pm, Su 9am-8pm.

Red-Eye Establishments: *Guía del Ocio* lists late-night eateries under *Cenar a última hora*. **VIPS**, at Gran Vía, 43 (☎915 42 15 78; M: Callao); C. Serrano, 41 (M: Serrano); C. de la Princesa, 5 (M: Ventura Rodríguez); C. de Fuencarral 101 (M: Tribunal); and other locations is a standard late-night option. An American-style diner with cushioned booths, average service, and overpriced burgers with cheese fries, VIPS also carries English books and magazines, records, and canned food. Open daily 9am-3am. **7-Eleven** stores are scattered in Ópera, Alonso Martínez (C. Mejía Lequerida), and Av. de América. **Hot & Cool**, C. de Gaztambide in Moncloa-Argüelles, serves fresh *bocadillos* until 3am on weekends. **Street vendors** sell cheap *bocadillos* and Chinese food to hungry clubbers until late. *Cervecerías* open until 2am aren't hard to find in this area.

TAPAS

Not so long ago, bartenders in Andalucía used to cover (*tapar*) drinks with saucers to keep out flies. Later, servers began putting little sandwiches on the saucers, and there you have it: *tapas*. Hopping from bar to bar gobbling *tapas* is an active alternative to a full sit-down meal and a fun way to sample food you might never even dream of trying. Most *tapas* bars (*tascas* or *tabernas*) are open noon-4pm and 8pm-midnight or later. Some, like **Museo del Jamón** (see **p. 118**), double as restaurants, and many cluster around **Plaza Santa Ana** and **Plaza Mayor** (beware the tourist traps!). Authentic bars pack **Calle Cuchilleros** and **Calle de la Cruz.**

Casa Alberto, C. de las Huertas, 18 (☎914 29 93 56). M: Antón Martín. Patrons spill out into the night air to wait for a spot at the bar. Cervantes wrote the second part of *El Quijote* here. All *tapas* are original house recipes. Sample the *gambas al ajillo* (shrimp in garlic and hot peppers; €7.50) or the filled *canapés* (€2-2.20). Sit-down dinner is a bit pricy. Open Tu-Sa noon-5:30pm and 8pm-1:30am. AmEx/MC/V. ❷

Los Gabrieles, C. de Echegaray, 17 (☎914 29 62 61). The tiled mural at the back depicts famous artists—from Velázquez to Goya—as stumble-drunks. Serves *tapas* by afternoon and drinks by night. Flamenco night Tu. Open daily 1pm-late. ❶

La Toscana, C. Manuel Fernández González, 10-12 (☎914 29 60 31). M: Sol or Sevilla. A local crowd hangs out over *tapas* of *morcilla asado* (€8). Despite the antique lettering and wrought iron, the range of dishes is anything but medieval. Spacious bar jam-packed on weekends. Open Tu-Sa 1-4pm and 8pm-midnight. ❷

Casa Amadeo, Pl. de Cascorro, 18 (☎913 65 94 39). M: La Latina. The jovial owner of 60 years supervises the making of house specialty *caracoles* (snails; *tapas* €4.80, *ración* €12) and *chorizo* made with snails (€4.80). Eat them on checkered tablecloths or at the bar. Other *raciones* €2-5.50. Open Tu-Su 10:30am-4pm and 7-10:30pm. ❷

La Trucha, C. Núñez de Arce, 6 (☎915 32 08 90). M: Sol. Another location, with terrace, C. Manuel Fernández González, 3 (☎914 29 58 33). Impressive selection of seasonal veggies (€5-9) and daily specials. Grab the *rabo de toro* (stewed bull's tail; €9.30). Entrees €12-15. Open M-Sa 12:30-4pm and 7:30pm-midnight. AmEx/MC/V. ❸

Taberna del Alabarder, C. de Felipe V, 6 (☎915 47 25 77 or 41 46 70), just off Pl. del Oriente. M: Ópera. Overlooking the glorious Palacio Real, try the nationally-famous *patatas al pobre* (potatoes with garlic) or *tigres unidad* (fried mussels). *Tapas* €1.30-7.70, *raciones* €3.70-21.20. Open M-Sa 1-4pm and 8:45pm-midnight. AmEx/MC/V. ❶

La Princesita, C. de la Princesa, 80 (☎915 43 70 71). M: Argüelles. Students crowd this ordinary-looking bar late in the day to enjoy *tapas* like *queso de cabrales* (goat cheese; €1). Open M-W 10am-11:30pm, Th-Su 10am-midnight. ❶

Cafetería-Restaurante El Encinar de el Bierzo, C. de Toledo, 82 (☎913 66 23 89). M: La Latina. A neighborhood landmark loaded with locals. House specialties *conejo al ajillo* (rabbit with garlic; €12) and *gambas a la plancha* (grilled shrimp; €10). *Menú* €7, €10 on Su. Open daily 1-4:30pm and 9-11:30pm. MC/V. ❷

CAFES

Madrid's cafes offer ambience as well as caffeine, allowing contemplative coffee drinkers to lose themselves in atmosphere, history, and image. Marvel at the scenery, reflect, and linger for an hour or two in these historic cafes—an economical way to soak up a little of Madrid's culture and finally write those postcards you bought a few days ago. You won't be bothered with the check until you ask.

■ **Café-Botillería Manuela,** C. de San Vicente Ferrer, 29 (☎915 31 70 37). M: Tribunal. Upbeat music and occasional impromptu piano playing add to Manuela's inviting atmosphere. Contemporary artwork lining the walls contrasts with late 19th-century decor and a gorgeous older bar. Specialty international cocktails (€3-5), coffees (€3.50-4.50), fruit shakes and juices, as well as a traditional *tapas* menu (€2-8). Story-telling, literature reviews, live music (Sa 9:30pm), and poetry nights are highlights. Open July-Aug. Tu-Su 6pm-2:30am; Sept.-June daily 4pm-2am.

■ **Café de Oriente,** Pl. del Oriente, 2 (☎915 47 15 64). M: Ópera. An old-fashioned cafe catering to a ritzy, older crowd. Spectacular view of the Palacio Real from the *terraza*, especially at night when floodlights illuminate the facade. Specialty coffees (€1.80-5.55) live up to their price. Open Su-Th 8:30am-1:30am, F-Sa 8:30am-12:30am.

Café Gijón, Po. de Recoletos, 21 (☎915 21 54 25). M: Colón. Enjoy thought-provoking conversation and good coffee in this historic landmark, popular with intellectuals who frequent the place for *tertulias* (get-togethers) with their peers. Café Gijón makes the perfect stop during your walking tour of the *paseos*. Coffees from €2.60. Open M-Th and Su 7am-1:30am, F-Sa 7am-2am. AmEx/MC/V.

Café Comercial, Glorieta de Bilbao, 7 (☎915 21 56 55). M: Bilbao. Founded in 1887, Madrid's oldest cafe boasts high ceilings, cushioned chairs, and huge mirrors perfect for people-watching. Frequented by artists and Republican aviators alike, Comercial saw the first anti-Franco protests take place. Coffee €1.10 at the bar, €1.80 at a table. Open M-Th 7:30am-1:30am, F-Sa 8am-2am, Su 10am-1am.

La Botillería del Café de Oriente, Pl. del Oriente, 4 (☎915 48 46 20). M: Ópera. Yet another gorgeous cafe situated at the entrance to Pl. del Oriente with views of the gardens, the Palacio Real, and the plaza. Both a cafe and a restaurant, with a variety of coffees (€2.50), teas (€2.25), and wines (€1.90-5.70). Open daily 12:30pm-1:30am.

Eucalipto, C. de Argumosa, 4. M: Lavapiés. Take a break from normal coffee fare and head for refreshing *zumos tropicales* (fresh fruit drinks; €2.60-3.50). Spike up the night with a *daiquiri* (€4.50-4.80), or enjoy a fantastic fruit salad big enough to share (€7). Lively sidewalk seating. Open daily M-Th 6pm-2am, F-Sa 6pm-3am, Su 2pm-midnight.

Café del Real, Pl. de Isabel II, 2 (☎915 47 21 24). M: Ópera. Hang out at the cafe upstairs, lined with tables surrounded by theatrical pictures on burgundy and gold walls, or go downstairs to the pizzeria for a quick bite. Coffee €1.30 at the bar, €1.90 at the table. Open M-Th 9am-1am, F-Sa 10am-3pm, Su 10am-midnight.

◎ SIGHTS

Madrid, large as it may seem, is a walker's city. Its fantastic public transportation system should only be used for longer distances, or between the day's starting and ending points. Although the word *paseo* refers to a major avenue (such as *Paseo de la Castellana* or *Paseo del Prado*) it literally means "a stroll." Do just that from Sol to Cibeles and from Plaza Mayor to the Palacio Real—sights will kindly introduce themselves. The city's art and architecture and its culture and atmosphere convince wide-eyed walkers that it was once the capital of the world's greatest empire. While Madrid is perfect for walking, it also offers some of the world's best places to relax. Whether soothing tired feet after perusing the *triángulo de arte* or seeking shelter from the summer's sweltering heat, there's nothing better than a shaded sidewalk cafe or a romantic park.

For hardcore visitors with a checklist of destinations, the municipal tourist office's *Plano de Transportes* map, which marks monuments as well as bus and Metro lines, is indispensable. In the following pages, sights are arranged by neighborhood. Each section has a designated center from which all directions are given. If you are trying to design a walking tour of the entire city, it is best to begin in El Centro, the self-evident nucleus of Madrid. The neighborhoods naturally fall in geographical order from there; a good day of sightseeing might move from historic Madrid, to the cafes of Huertas, to the celebrated *paseos*, to a stroll through El Retiro (see the **Walking Tour,** p. 140). El Pardo falls last as a separate trip.

🎵 ENTERTAINMENT

Anyone interested in the latest on live entertainment—from music to dance to theater—should stop by the **Círculo de Bellas Artes,** C. Marqués de Casa Riera, 2 (☎913 60 54 00; fax 915 23 28 12) at M: Sevilla or Banco de España. The six-floor building not only houses performance venues and art exhibits, but also serves as an organizing center for events throughout Madrid; it has virtually all current information on performances. Their monthly magazine, *Minerva*, is indispensable.

MUSIC

In summer, Madrid sponsors free concerts, ranging from classical and jazz to bolero and salsa, at Pl. Mayor, Lavapiés, Oriente, and Villa de París; check the *Guía del Ocio* for the current schedule. Many nightspots also have live music.

The **Auditorio Nacional,** C. Príncipe de Vergara, 146, home to the National Orchestra, features Madrid's best classical performances. (☎913 37 01 00. M: Cruz del Rayo. €5-25.) **Fundació Joan March,** C. Castelló, 77, hosts summer cultural activities such as lecture series (usually Tu and Th 7:30pm) and sponsors free concerts. (☎914 35 42 40. M: Núñez de Balboa. Concerts M, W, and Sa; call ahead for details.) **Teatro Monumental,** C. de Atocha, 65, is home to Madrid's Symphonic Orchestra. Reinforced concrete—a Spanish invention—was first used in its construction in the 1920s, so be prepared for unusual acoustics. (☎914 29 81 19. M: Antón Martín.) For opera and *zarzuela* (light opera specific to Madrid), head for the ornate **Teatro de la Zarzuela,** C. Jovellanos, 4, modeled on Milan's La Scala. (☎915 24 54 10. M: Sevilla or Banco de España.) The city's principal performance venue is the prestigious **Teatro Real,** Pl. de Isabel II, featuring the city's best ballet and opera. (☎915 16 06 06. M: Ópera.) The grand 19th-century **Teatro de la Ópera** is the city's principal venue for classical ballet. Most theaters close in July and August.

FLAMENCO

Flamenco in Madrid is tourist-oriented and expensive. A few nightlife spots are authentic (see **Cardamomo,** p. 129), but pricy. **Casa Patas,** C. Cañizares, 10, offers excellent quality for a bit less than usual. Summer courses are taught in flamenco dance and song. (☎913 69 04 96; www.casapatas.com. M: Antón Martín. Call for prices and reservations.) **Café de Chinitas,** C. Torija, 7, is as overstated as they come. Shows start at 10:30pm and midnight, but memories last forever—or at least they should, given the price. (☎915 47 15 02 or 59 51 35. M:

Santo Domingo. Cover €24 and up.) At **Corral de la Morería,** C. Morería, 17, by the Viaducto on C. Bailén, shows start at 9:45pm and last until 2am. (☎913 65 84 46. M: Ópera or La Latina. Cover €30.) **Teatro Albéniz,** C. de la Paz, 11, hosts an annual *Certamen de Coreografía de Danza Española y Flamenco* that features original music and extraordinary flamenco. (☎915 31 83 11. M: Sol.)

FILM

In summer, the city sponsors free movies and plays, all listed in the *Guía del Ocio* and the entertainment supplements of Friday newspapers. In July, watch for the **Fescinal,** a film festival at the Parque de la Florida. Most cinemas show three films per day, at around 4:30, 7:30, and 10:30pm. Tickets cost €2.40-5.40. Some cinemas offer weekday-only matinée student discounts for €3.65. Wednesday (sometimes Monday instead) is *día del espectador,* when tickets cost around €3—show up early. Check the *versión original (V.O. subtitulada)* listings in the *Guía del Ocio* for English movies subtitled in Spanish. Three excellent movie theaters cluster near M: Ventura Rodríguez, between Pl. de España and Argüelles. **Princesa,** C. de la Princesa, 3 (☎915 41 41 00), shows mainstream Spanish films and subtitled foreign films. The theater/bar **Alphaville,** C. Martín de los Héroes, 14 (☎915 59 38 36), behind Princesa and underneath the patio, shows current alternative and mainstream Spanish titles. **Renoir,** C. Raimundo Fernández Villaverde, 10 (☎915 41 41 00), shows highly acclaimed recent films, many foreign and subtitled. Check the *Guía del Ocio* for other cinema megaplexes in and around the city.

THEATER

Huertas, east of Sol, is Madrid's theater district. In July and August, Pl. Mayor, Lavapiés, and Villa de París frequently host outdoor performances . For a complete list of theaters and shows, consult the *Guía del Ocio.* Seeing a play in Madrid is an entertaining way to participate in traditional culture and to practice your Spanish. Tickets to shows start around €24, but special deals for as low as €12 are not uncommon. Theater-goers should consult the magazines published by state-sponsored theaters, such as **Teatro Español,** C. del Príncipe, 25, in Pl. de Santa Ana (☎913 60 14 80; M: Sol or Sevilla), **Teatro Infanta Isabel,** Barquillo, 24 (☎915 21 02 12; M: Banco de España), and the superb **Teatro María Guerrero,** C. Tamayo y Baus, 4 (☎913 10 15 00; M: Colón). Tickets can be purchased at theater box offices or at ticket agencies. (**El Corte Inglés** ☎ 902 40 02 22. **FNAC** ☎915 95 62 00. **Crisol** ☎902 11 83 12. **TelEntrada** ☎902 10 12 12.)

FÚTBOL

Spaniards obsess over *fútbol* (soccer). The festivities start hours before matches as fans congregate in the streets, headphones and radio in one hand and *cerveza* in the other, listening to pregame commentary and discussing it with other diehards. If either **Real Madrid** (in all white) or **Atlético de Madrid** (in red and white stripes) wins a match, count on streets clogged with honking cars. Every Sunday and some Saturdays between September and June, one of these two teams plays at home. Real Madrid plays at **Estadio Santiago Bernabéu,** Po. de la Castellana, 104. (☎914 57 11 12. M: Santiago Bernabéu.) Atlético de Madrid plays at **Estadio Vicente Calderón,** C. Virgen del Puerto, 67. (☎913 66 47 07. M: Pirámides or Marqués de Vadillos.) Tickets cost €18-42 and sell out quickly.

RECREATIONAL SPORTS

Madrid's swimming pools provide the perfect solution to summertime heat and land-locked shortcomings. Gawkers be warned; most women go topless. (☎915 40 39 39 for pool information. Municipal tourist office offers a comprehensive list of the 25 pools in and around Madrid. All pools have same timetable and prices.) Swimmers splash in the outdoor pools at **Lago/Casa de Campo,** on C. del Ángel. The Lago pools are yet another one of Madrid's social meccas, with several pools and sunbathing areas, including Madrid's equivalent of a "gay beach." Lots of kids, ice cream stands, and fun. Watch your valuables. (☎914 63 00 50. M: Lago. Open 10:30am-8pm. €3.40.) Other cooling relief includes-the pool at **Peñuelas,** on C. Arganda. (☎914 74 28 08. M: Acacias, Pirámides, or Embajadores; or bus #18.)

Call the **Oficina de Información Deportiva** (☎914 63 55 63) for more information on outdoor recreation in Madrid. The tourist office's *Plano de las Instalaciones Deportivas Municipales* lists areas open to the public. For **cycling info** and bicycle repair, cruise over to **Calmera Bicicletas,** C. de Atocha, 98. (☎915 27 75 74; www.calmera.net. M: Anton Martín.)

BULLFIGHTS

Bullfighters are either loved or loathed. So, too, are the bullfights themselves. Nevertheless, bullfights are a Spanish tradition, and locals joke that they are the only things in Spain ever to start on time. Hemingway-toting Americans and true fans of a contorted struggle between man and nature clog Pl. de las Ventas for the heart-pounding, albeit gruesome events.

From May 15 to May 22 every year, the **Fiestas de San Isidro** provide a daily *corrida* (bullfight) with top *matadores* and the fiercest bulls. The fights are nationally televised; those without tickets crowd into bars. There are also bullfights every Sunday in summer from March to October and less frequently throughout the rest of the year. Look for posters in bars and cafes for upcoming *corridas* (especially on C. Victoria, off C. San Jerónimo). **Plaza de las Ventas,** C. de Alcalá, 237, is the biggest ring in Spain. (☎913 56 22 00; www.las-ventas.com. M: Ventas.) A seat costs €5-92, depending on its location in the *sol* (sun) or *sombra* (shade); shade is more expensive. Tickets are available the Friday and Saturday before and the Sunday of the bullfight. **Plaza de Toros Palacio de Vista Alegre** also hosts bullfights and cultural events. (☎914 22 07 80. M: Vista Alegre. Call ahead for schedule and prices.) To watch amateurs, head to the **bullfighting school,** which has its own *corridas*. (☎914 70 19 90. M: Batán. Open Sa 7:30pm. Tickets €7, children €3.50.)

⌐ SHOPPING

For upscale shopping, sashay down swanky **Calle Serrano** and **Calle Velázquez** in the famous **Salamanca** district (near Pl. de Colón), where fine boutiques and specialty stores line the streets. Stores like Gucci, Prada, and Calvin Klein provide fabulous shopping bags to showcase your purchases. Most major department stores can be found between Puerta del Sol and Callao, with smaller clothing stores scattered along Gran Vía. **El Cortes Inglés,** Spain's unavoidable all-in-one store, sports over 10 locations throughout the city. Countless clothing boutiques in **Chueca** specialize in hot clubwear, tight jeans, and sexy day-wear. **Mercado Fuencarral,** C. de Fuencarral, 42, specializes in funky attire and tattoo/piercing parlors. Most stores in Madrid are open 10am-2pm and 5-8pm. Some stay open on Saturday afternoon and during *siesta*. By law, *grandes almacenes* (department stores) may open only the first Sunday of every month, a vestige of the country's Roman Catholic heritage. Many boutiques close in August, when almost everyone flees to the coast. Non-EU residents can shop tax-free at major stores, as long as they remember to ask for their VAT return form (☎900 43 54 82 for more info). **Inal** publishes a yearly *Guía esencial para vivir en Madrid,* which includes descriptions of most stores.

MADRID

MALLS

Mallrats may go through a bit of withdrawal in Madrid, since smaller, scattered stores are the norm. **La Vaguada** (M: Barrio del Pilar; bus #132 from Moncloa), in the northern neighborhood of **Madrid-2,** is Madrid's first experiment in super-malls. It offers everything the homesick Anglophone could want: 350 shops, including The Body Shop, Burberry's, a food court with a trusty McDonald's, multi-cinemas, and a bowling alley. (Open daily 10am-10pm.) **ABC,** C. Serrano, 61, in the old ABC newspaper headquarters, has a modern complex of food courts and Spanish clothing chains from Mango to Zara. (M: Castellano. Open daily 10am-9:30pm.) Madrid's outlet mall is **Las Rozas,** C. Juan Ramón Jiménez, a 20min. drive from the center, with up to 60% off favorite brands. (☎916 40 49 08; www.valueretail.com.) By far the poshest shopping mall is the **Galería del Prado,** Pl. de las Cortes, located beneath the Hotel Palace and across Po. de la Castellana from the Ritz. (M: Banco de España. Open M-Sa 10am-9pm.)

■ EL RASTRO (FLEA MARKET)

For hundreds of years, *El Rastro* has been a Sunday morning tradition in Madrid. The market begins in La Latina at Pl. Cascorro off C. de Toledo and ends at the bottom of C. Ribera de Curtidores. Get lost in the insanity and the excitement as your senses become overwhelmed with sights, sounds, and smells from every direction. Seek out that souvenir you've been dying for since your first day in Madrid and haggle for it until you're blue in the face. At *El Rastro* you can find anything, from pots to jeans to antique tools to pet birds. As crazy as the market seems, it is actually thematically organized. The main street is a labyrinth of cheap jewelry, incense, and sunglasses, branching out into side streets, each with its own concert of vendors and wares. Antique-sellers contribute their peculiar mustiness to C. del Prado. *Tapas* bars and small restaurants line the streets and provide an air-conditioned respite for market-weary bargain hunters. The flea market is a pickpocket's paradise, so leave your camera in your room, bust out the money belt, or turn that backpack into a frontpack. Police are everywhere if you have any problems. El Rastro is open Sundays and holidays from 9am to 2pm.

BOOKS

If you plan to take Spanish language classes when you return to your home country, get the reading list ahead of time and buy books here. The pain you'll suffer lugging them around on your trip is nothing compared to the pain you'll suffer when you have to pay higher prices purchasing them outside Spain.

Altair, C. Gaztambide, 31 (☎915 43 53 00). M: Moncloa or Argüelles. Comprehensive travel bookstore, with the world's best travel guides and others. Knowledgeable staff. Open M-Sa 10:30am-2:30pm and 4:30-8:30pm.

Berkana Librería Gay y Lesbiana, C. Hortaleza, 64 (☎/fax 915 22 55 99). M: Chueca. Gay and lesbian bookstore with loads of contact info for foreigners and a free map of gay Madrid. Open M-F 10:30am-2pm and 5-8:30pm, Sa noon-2pm and 5-8:30pm.

Booksellers, C. José Abascal, 48 (☎914 42 79 59, 42 81 04, or 913 99 33 87). M: Gregorio Marañón. A vast array of books, videos, magazines, and children's literature in English. Open M-F 9:30am-2pm and 5-8pm, Sa 10am-2pm.

Casa del Libro, Gran Vía, 29 (☎915 22 66 57; www.casadelibro.com). M: Callao. Madrid's largest and most comprehensive bookstore. **Branch** at C. del Maestro Victoria.

FNAC, C. Preciados, 28 (☎915 95 62 00; www.fnac.es). M: Callao. Best music and book selection. English books on 3rd fl. Open M-Sa 10am-9:30pm, Su noon-9:30pm.

◪ NIGHTLIFE

Madrid offers some of the greatest nightlife in the world. As the sun sets, the streets and plazas begin to exude a frenetic energy, an intoxicating mixture of excitement and alcohol. Partying in Madrid is a celebration of life and a denial of the necessity of sleep—why go to bed when the party rages until 7am? Undeterred by occasional spells of bad weather, traffic jams on small streets, and shady characters that always seem to appear in Madrid's plazas, party-goers in Madrid have only one goal for the night: fun. Both gay and straight bar- and club-hoppers will be overwhelmed by the countless ways to spend a single evening. Proud of their nocturnal offerings—*madrileños* will tell you with a straight face that they were bored in Paris or New York—they insist that no one goes to bed until they've "killed the night" and, in most cases, a good part of the following morning.

An average successful night involves several neighborhoods and countless venues; half the party is the in-between. A typical evening might start in the *tapas* bars of Huertas, move to a first-session disco in Malasaña, and then crash the wild parties of Chueca. Some clubs don't even bother opening until 4 or 5am; the only (relatively) quiet nights of the week are Monday and Tuesday. For clubs and discos, life begins around 2am. Many discos have "afternoon" sessions for teens (7pm-midnight; cover €1.50-6), but the "night" sessions (lasting until dawn) are when people really let their hair down. The *entrada* (cover) often includes a drink and can be as high as €15; men may be charged up to €3 more than women, if women are charged at all. Venues often change their prices depending on the night, with Saturdays being the most expensive. Keep an eye out for *invitaciones* and *oferta* cards—in stores, restaurants, tourist publications, tourist offices, and on the street—that offer discounts or free admission. For the most up-to-date info on what's going on, scan Madrid's entertainment guides (see **Read This,** p. 100).

◪ FESTIVALS

The city bursts with street fiestas, dancing, and processions during **Carnaval** in February, culminating on Ash Wednesday with the beginning of Lent and the *Entierro de la Sardina* (Burial of the Sardine) procession in the Casa de Campo. In late April, the city bubbles with the renowned **International Theater Festival.** The Comunidad de Madrid celebrates its struggle against the French invasion of 1808 during the **Fiestas del 2 de Mayo** with bullfights and concerts. Starting May 15, the week-long **Fiestas de San Isidro** honor Madrid's patron saint with a pilgrimage to the saint's meadow, various concerts and parades, and Spain's best bullfights. At the end of June, Madrid goes mad with **Orgullo Gay** (Gay Pride). Outrageous floats filled with drag queens, muscle boys, and politically active lesbians shut down traffic between El Retiro and Puerta del Sol on the Saturday of pride weekend. The weekend is filled with free concerts in Pl. Chueca and Pl. de Vázquez de Mella and bar crawls among the congested streets of Chueca. Throughout the summer, the city sponsors the **Veranos de la Villa,** an outstanding and varied set of cultural activities, including concerts (some free) by internationally-renowned artists of all styles, open-air movies, plays, art exhibits, an international film festival, opera, *zarzuela* (light Spanish opera), ballet, and sports. The **Festivales de Otoño** (Autumn Festivals), from September to November, also bring an impressive array of music, theater, and film. On November 1, an **International Jazz Festival** entices great musicians to Madrid. On New Year's Eve, **El Fin del Año,** crowds gather at Puerta del Sol to countdown to the new year and eat 12 *uvas* (grapes), one by one, as the clock strikes midnight. The brochure *Las Fiestas de España*, available at tourist offices and bigger hotels, contains comprehensive details on Spain's festivals.

EL CENTRO: SOL, ÓPERA & PLAZA MAYOR

Puerta del Sol is the center of the city in the center of the country. All roads converge here (it's Spain's km0) and most visitors ramble through at least once. Signs indicating *hostales* and *pensiones* stick out from flower-potted balconies and decaying facades on narrow, sloping streets. For better deals in quieter spots, stray several blocks from Sol. Don't be afraid to climb that extra flight of dusty stairs to find a good deal. The following listings fall in the area between the Sol and Ópera Metro stops. Price and location in El Centro are as good as they get, especially if you are planning to brave the legendary nightlife. Buses #3, 25, 39, and 500 serve Ópera; buses #3, 5 (from Atocha), 15, 20, 50, 51, 52, 53, and 150 serve Sol.

▌ ACCOMMODATIONS

▓ **Hostal Paz,** C. Flora, 4, 1st and 4th fl. (☎915 47 30 47). M: Ópera. Unbeatable hospitality from wonderful owners. Peaceful, secure, and spotless rooms with large windows, satellite TV, and A/C. Reservations advised. Laundry €9. Singles €20; doubles €30-36; triples €45. Monthly rentals available but must be arranged far in advance. MC/V. ❷

▓ **Hostal-Residencia Luz,** C. Fuentes, 10, 3rd fl. (☎915 42 07 59 or 59 74 18; fax 42 07 59). M: Ópera. Twelve sunny, newly redecorated rooms exude comfort: hardwood floors, elegant furniture, beautiful curtains and bedspreads. Satellite TV, A/C, fax, and public phone. Laundry €6. Singles €15; doubles €33.50-39; triples €39-45. Discounts for longer stays. Reservations advised. ❶

Hostal-Residencia Rober, C. de Arenal, 26, 5th fl. (☎915 41 91 75). M: Ópera. Quiet *hostal* with brilliant balcony views down C. de Arenal. Smoking strictly prohibited. All 14 spartan but pristine sound-proof rooms have their own tiny TVs and A/C. Singles with double bed and shower €24 for one person, €26 for 2 people, with bath €34; doubles with bath €39; triples with bath €59. Good discounts for longer stays. MC/V. ❸

Hostal Valencia, Pl. del Oriente, 2, 3rd fl. (☎915 59 84 50). M: Ópera. Narrow glass elevator lifts you to elegant rooms, each uniquely decorated, overlooking the gorgeous Pl. del Oriente and Palacio Real. All rooms have TV. Interior singles €42; doubles €72; master suite €92. Reservations advised. ❹

Hostal Oriente, C. de Arenal, 23 , 1st fl. (☎915 48 03 14; fax 47 84 53; www.hostalo-riente.com). M: Ópera. Classy, newly-renovated hostel with friendly owners and inviting reception area. Fourteen squeaky-clean rooms have TV, phone, A/C, safe, and private bath. Singles €33; doubles €50; triples €66. ❸

Hostal Esparteros, C. de Esparteros, 12, 4th fl. (☎/fax 915 21 09 03). M: Sol. Sparkling rooms with balcony or large windows vary in size; some have private bath (no fans or A/C). English-speaking owner ensures a terrific stay. Laundry €7. Singles €25; doubles €35; triples €42. 10% discount for longer stays. Family also owns **Hostal Los Arcos,** C. Marqués Viudo de Ponteojs, 3, 2nd fl. (☎915 22 59 76; fax 32 78 96). ❷

Hostal-Residencia Cruz-Sol, Pl. Santa Cruz, 6, 3rd fl. (☎915 32 71 97). M: Sol. Clean and comfy hostel boasts modern rooms with parquet floors, double-paned windows, safes, heat, phones, Internet jacks, A/C, and baths. Vending machines slake late-night thirst. Laundry €11. Singles €36; doubles €48; triples €60; quads €72. MC/V. ❹

Hostal Madrid, C. de Esparteros, 6, 2nd fl. (☎915 22 00 60; fax 32 35 10; www.hostal-madrid.info), off C. Mayor. M: Sol. Larger hostel with rooms containing TV, phone, safe, A/C, and new bathrooms. Also rents 7 well-furnished apartments available on nightly (€90-115 for 2 people), weekly, or monthly basis; big discounts for longer stays. English spoken. Reservations 4 days ahead advised. Singles €50-58; doubles €70; triple with balcony €88. MC/V. ❺

Hostal Cantábrico, C. de la Cruz, 5 (☎915 31 01 30 or 21 33 03). M: Sol. Welcoming reception leads to rooms with complete bath, some with nice balcony views. Over 100 years in operation. Singles €31; doubles €46; triples €61. ❸

Hostal Portugal, C. Flora, 4, 1st fl. (☎915 59 40 14). M: Ópera. Old rooms with saggy beds, TV, bath, and high prices, but a great location, especially if Paz is full and you're tired of hauling your luggage. Singles €24; doubles €38; triples €45; quads €60. ❷

Hostal Alicante, C. de Arenal, 16, 2nd fl. (☎915 31 51 78). M: Ópera or Sol. Clean rooms with TV and heat, some with fans. Singles €23; doubles €38, with bath €42; triples with bath €60. MC/V. ❷

🍴 FOOD

Flooded with tourists looking for "traditional" fare, this area abounds with overpriced mediocre food. A little sifting, however, can lead to some amazing restaurants at decent prices. Streets off M: Ópera teem with crowded cafes, markets, and restaurants. Side streets off Puerta del Sol offer international cuisine. Places with menus in several different languages tend to be tourist traps; avoid them like green *gambas*. Cruise to nearby Pl. de Santa Ana for better deals. The surrounding streets, especially through Arco de los Cuchilleros in the southwest corner of Pl. Mayor, house specialty shops and renowned *mesones*. Head here for garlicky *tapas* and pitchers of sangría in a festive, albeit touristy, atmosphere.

Lavapiés and La Latina, the neighborhoods south of Sol bounded by C. de Atocha and C. de Toledo, are generally residential and working class. No caviar or champagne here, but you'll find plenty of *menús* for around €6.50. Grab some chow in a funky outdoor eatery on **Calle de Argumosa,** or head up the hill toward Huertas for more tasty options.

🏆 **El Estragón Vegetariano,** Pl. de la Paja, 10 (☎913 65 89 82; www.guiadelocio.com/estragonvegetariano); on the far side of the plaza. M: La Latina. Perhaps the best medium-priced restaurant—of any kind—in Madrid, with vegetarian food that could convince even the most die-hard carnivores to switch teams. Treat yourself to *crêpes a la Museliño,* the house specialty, or try the delicious and creative *menú* (M-F €9; Sa-Su and evenings €18). Open daily 1:30-4:30pm and 8pm-1am. AmEx/MC/V. ❸

🏆 **Inshala,** C. Amnistía, 10 (☎915 48 26 32). M: Ópera. Eclectic menu filled with delicious Spanish, Mexican, Japanese, Italian, and Moroccan dishes. Weekday lunch *menú* €8. Dinner €8-15. Reservations strongly recommended for both lunch and dinner. Open M-Th noon-2am, F-Sa noon-3am. ❸

NO WORK, ALL PLAY

OPEN-AIR, AMONG STARS

During Madrid's *Veranos de la Villa,* the Centro Cultural Conde Duque draws *madrileños* and visitors alike for an open-air music festival loaded with international stars. In 2003, artists included Brazilian crooner Caetano Veloso, Cape Verdean Cesaria Èvoara, American Bonnie Raitt, recent Grammy-winning Cuban Ibrahim Ferrer, and a host of jazz, rock, and flamenco artists. Take a break from sightseeing and take advantage of this festival in THE cultural center of Madrid.

This is also an opportune time to experience one of Spain's oldest and most traditional types of performace—*Zarzuela.* This is Spain's very own breed of opera, which really seems more a cross between opera, show tunes, and comedic musical. These performances are often bordering on amusing as they blatantly portray the more patronistic gender roles of turn-of-the-century Spain.

Centro Cultural Conde Duque, C. Conde Duque, 9-11. ☎915 88 58 61 or 88 59 28; www.muni-madrid.es/condeduque. M: Noviciado or Ventura Rodriguez. Concerts run from late June-July. Free-€30. Contact Caixa Catalunya for tickets ☎902 10 12 12.

Bósforos, C. de la Cruz, 10 (☎917 96 91 41). M: Sol. One of the many Turkish restaurants in Madrid. Serves succulent *Doner Kebap* (chicken or lamb gyro sandwich). Probably the most delicious and least expensive lunch in Madrid. *Tavuk Kebap* with all the trimmings €3. Entrees €2.40-5.50. Open Su-Th noon-1am, F-Sa noon-2:30am. ❶

Restaurante Casa Botín, C. de Cuchilleros, 17 (☎913 66 42 17 or 66 30 26), off Pl. Mayor. According to the *Guinness Book of World Records,* Casa Botín is the oldest restaurant in the world (founded 1725). Chow down on a variety of simple but filling Spanish dishes (€7-24.25; *menú* €29.50). A favorite among tourists. Lunch served daily 1-4pm, dinner 8pm-midnight. ❸

El Granero de Lavapiés, C. de Argumosa, 10 (☎914 67 76 11). M: Lavapiés. For 16 years, frescoes and inventive specials have kept this hideaway packed with locals. Vegetarian *menú* M-Sa €7.70. Open Su-Th 1-4pm, F-Sa 1-4pm and 8:30-11pm. MC/V. ❷

Museo del Jamón, C. San Jerónimo, 6 (☎915 21 03 46). M: Sol. 5 other locations in Madrid, including C. Mayor, 7 (☎915 31 45 50). A vegetarian's nightmare and pork lover's dream. Dodge hooves and shanks at the metallic bar or head to the upstairs dining room (open at 1pm) for the chef's specialties (€3.75-7). *Menús* €6.90-13. Generous plates €4-6. Open M-Th 9am-12:30pm, F-Sa 9am-1am, Su 10am-12:30pm. ❶

El Cuchi, C. de Cuchilleros, 3 (☎913 66 44 24). Outside Pl. Mayor, but better and cheaper than the restaurants inside. Delicious Mexican food in a festive setting. Entrees €5.70-18.90. Open M-Sa 1pm-midnight, Su 1-4pm and 8pm-midnight. AmEx/MC/V. ❸

Lhardy Restaurante, C. San Jerónimo, 8 (☎915 21 33 85), at C. Victoria. M: Sol. Get slicked up and bring an overstuffed wallet for an expensive, delicious meal. This gorgeous 160-year-old restaurant is replete with original wallpaper and woodwork. The house specialty, *cocido de garbanzos* (chickpea stew; €27.50), has won deserved fame as a *madrileño* specialty. Open M-Sa 1-3:30pm and 8:30-11:30pm, Su 1-3:30pm. AmEx/MC/V. ❺

Parilla Matador, C. de La Cruz, 13 (☎915 22 35 95), off C. San Jerónimo. Wander into this pleasant and casual *parilla* for a scrumptious meal. Cooks grill a variety of meats and vegetables à la carte (€9-17) or as part of a 7-course meal (€29-38). Open daily 1-4:30pm, Su-Th 8pm-midnight, F-Sa 8pm-1am. ❹

🇬 SIGHTS

The area known as El Centro, spreading out from Puerta del Sol ("Gate of the Sun"), is the gateway to the history and spirit of Madrid. Although several rulers carved the winding streets, the Habsburg and Bourbon families left El Centro's most celebrated monuments. As a result, El Centro is divided into two major sections: Madrid de los Habsburgos and Madrid de los Borbones. Most Habsburg directions are given from Puerta del Sol and Bourbon directions from Ópera. The sights are easily accessible by Metro and by foot, and the neighborhood itself is quite easy to navigate. All of El Centro can be conquered in a single day, but take more time to leisurely enjoy the sights and marvel at their beauty.

PUERTA DEL SOL

Kilómetro 0—the origin of six national highways fanning out to the rest of Spain—marks the country's physical center in the most chaotic of Madrid's numerous plazas, Puerta del Sol. Sol bustles day and night with taxis, street performers, and countless locals trying to evade the tourists. A web of pedestrian-only tributaries originating at Gran Vía leads a rush of consumers down a gallery of stores, funneling them into Sol.

Named for the actual Puerta del Sol that stood here in the 16th century, Sol is today dominated by government buildings, stores, and restaurants. Spaniards and tourists alike converge upon *El oso y el madroño*, a bronze statue of a bear and a strawberry tree, now a symbol of Madrid. On New Year's Eve, citizens congregate in Sol to gobble one grape per chime as the clock strikes midnight.

HABSBURG MADRID

"Old Madrid," the city's central neighborhood, is the most densely packed with both monuments and tourists. In the 16th century, the Habsburgs funded the construction of **Plaza Mayor** and the **Catedral de San Isidro.** Many of Old Madrid's buildings, however, date from much earlier, some from as far back as the Moorish empire. When Felipe II moved the seat of Castilla from Toledo to Madrid (then only a town of 20,000) in 1561, he and his descendants commissioned the court architects (including Juan de Herrera, master behind the austere El Escorial) to update many of Madrid's buildings to the latest styles. Another Juan, Juan de Villanueva, added his architectural flavor to the mix under Carlos III, designing the Prado. After only a century of development and expansion, Madrid more than doubled in population. Today, central Madrid, from the celebrated street of Alcalá to the iron verandas of Plaza Mayor, still reflects the power of the Habsburgs and the architecture of Juan de Herrera and Juan de Villanueva.

PLAZA MAYOR. In 1620, Pl. Mayor was completed for Felipe III; his statue, installed in 1847, graces the plaza's center. Though designed by Juan de Herrera, Pl. Mayor is much softer in style than stolid El Escorial. Its elegant arcades, spindly towers, and pleasant verandas are defining elements of the "Madrid style," which inspired architects across the city and throughout the country. With lances of exaggerated length, 17th-century nobles on horseback spent Sunday afternoons chasing bulls in the plaza. The nobility had such a jolly time that eventually everyone joined in the fun. Citizens, on foot and armed with sticks, also began running after those pesky bulls. The tradition came to be known as a *corrida*, from the verb *correr* (to run). Later, Carlos II (the Bewitched) sanctioned chasing heretics as well, generously offering Pl. Mayor as the site of a grand auto-da-fé during the Inquisition. Thankfully, that tradition burned out.

Toward evening, Pl. Mayor awakens as *madrileños* resurface, tourists multiply, and cafe tables fill with lively patrons. Live performances of flamenco and music are a common treat. While the cafes are a nice spot for a drink, food is overpriced; save dinner for elsewhere. On Sunday mornings, the plaza holds a rare coin and stamp sale, marking the starting point of **El Rastro** (see p. 114). During the annual **Fiesta de San Isidro** (May 15-22, see p. 113), the plaza explodes with celebration. *(From Pta. del Sol, walk down C. Mayor. M: Sol.)*

CATEDRAL DE SAN ISIDRO. This cathedral, which commemorates San Isidro, protector of crops and patron saint of Madrid, has had a turbulent history. It was designed in the Jesuit Baroque style at the beginning of the 17th century before San Isidro's remains were brought here in 1769. During the Civil War, rioting workers burned the exterior—only the primary nave and a few Baroque decorations remain from the original. The cathedral, which has since been restored, reigned as *the* cathedral of Madrid from the late 19th century until the Catedral de la Almudena (see p. 121) was consecrated in 1993. *(From Pta. del Sol, take C. Mayor to Pl. Mayor, cross the plaza, and exit onto C. de Toledo. The cathedral is located at the intersection of C. de Toledo and C. de Sacramento. M: Latina. Open for Mass only.)*

PLAZA DE LA VILLA. When Felipe II made Madrid the capital of his empire in 1561, most of the town huddled between Pl. Mayor and the Palacio Real; Pl. de la Villa marks the heart of what was once Old Madrid. Though only a handful of medieval buildings remain, the plaza still features a stunning courtyard (surrounding the statue of Don Álvaro de Bazán), beautiful tilework, and eclectic architecture. The horseshoe-shaped door on C. Codo is one of the few examples of the Gothic-Mudéjar style left in Madrid, and the 15th-century Torre de los Lujanes (on the left when looking from C. Mayor) is the sole remnant of the once-lavish residence of the Lujanes family. Across the plaza is the 17th-century Ayuntamiento (Casa de la Villa), designed in 1640 by Juan Gómez de Mora as both the mayor's home and the city jail. Inside is Goya's *Allegory of the City of Madrid* (1819). The neighboring Casa de Cisneros, a 16th-century Plateresque house, also served as a government building when Habsburg officials annexed it for the city's growing bureaucracy. *(From Pta. del Sol, go down C. Mayor and past Pl. Mayor. M: Sol.)*

CONVENTO DE LAS DESCALZAS REALES. In 1559, Juana of Austria, Felipe II's sister, converted the former royal palace into a convent; today it is home to 26 Franciscan nuns who watch over Juana's tomb. The **Salón de Tápices** contains 10 renowned tapestries based on cartoons by Rubens, as well as Santa Ursula's jewel-encrusted bones in *El viaje de Santa Úrsula y las once mil vírgenes (The Journey of Santa Úrsula and the Eleven Thousand Virgins)*. Claudio Coello's magnificent 17th-century frescoes line the staircase. Lines are long in the summer; arrive early. *(Pl. las Descalzas, between Pl. de Callao and Pta. de Sol. ☎915 47 53 50. M: Callao or Sol. Open Tu-Th and Sa 10:30am-12:45pm and 4-5:45pm, F 10:30am-12:45pm, Su 11am-1:45pm. €4.10, students €2.40. W free for EU citizens.)*

CONVENTO DE LA ENCARNACIÓN. Designed by Juan de Herrera's disciple Juan de Gómez, the monastery is an oasis in the middle of Madrid's bustle, housing more than 1500 relics of saints, including a vial of San Pantaleón's blood believed to liquify every year on July 27. According to legend, if the blood does not liquefy, disaster will strike Madrid. *(Pl. de la Encarnación. ☎915 47 53 50. M: Ópera. Open Tu-Th and Sa 10:30am-12:45pm and 4-5:45pm, F 10:30am-12:45pm, Su 11am-1:45pm. €3.46, students, under 18, and over 65 €1.80. W free for EU citizens.)*

ALONG RÍO MANZANARES. Madrid's notoriously puny river snakes its way around the city past the **Puerta de Toledo,** the triumphal arch commissioned by Joseph Bonaparte to celebrate his brother Napoleon (but completed by his enemies in honor of those who defeated the French army). The broad Baroque **Puente de Toledo** makes up for the river's inadequacies. Sandstone carvings on both sides of the bridge depict the martyrdom of San Isidro and his family. The **Puente de Segovia,** which fords the river along C. de Segovia, was conceived by Juan de Herrera. Both bridges present gorgeous views and are popular with young couples. *(To reach Puente de Toledo from Pta. del Sol take C. Mayor through the Pl. Mayor and onto C. de Toledo; follow C. de Toledo to the bridge (approx. 15min.). M: Puerta de Toledo or Ópera.)*

OTHER SIGHTS. As the legend goes, **Iglesia de San Pedro** began as a Mudéjar mosque. A 17th-century overhaul commissioned by Felipe IV infused the original structure with Baroque intricacies. *(Facing the Palacio, go left on C. de Bailén and take a right on C. de Segovia. The church will be on your right when you reach Cost. San Pedro. Open for Mass only.)* Next to Iglesia de San Pedro is the **Museo de San Isidro,** where the saint was said to have resided; his sarcophagus resides here now, in the **Capilla de San Isidro.** *(Cost. de San Andrés. M: La Latina. Open Tu-F 9:30am-8pm, Sa-Su 10am-2pm. Free.)*

BOURBON MADRID

Weakened by plagues and political losses, the Habsburg era in Spain ended with the death of Carlos II in 1700. Felipe V, the first of Spain's Bourbon monarchs, ascended the throne in 1714 after the 12-year War of the Spanish Succession. Bankruptcy, industrial stagnation, and widespread moral disillusionment compelled Felipe V to embark on a crusade of urban renewal. His successors, Fernando VI and Carlos III, fervently pursued the same ends, with astounding results. Today, the lavish palaces, churches, and parks that remain are the most touristed in Madrid; a walk around them requires planning and patience.

PALACIO REAL. The impossibly luxurious Palacio Real lounges at the western tip of central Madrid, overlooking the Río Manzanares. Felipe V commissioned Giovanni Sachetti to replace the Alcázar, which burned down in 1734, with a palace that would dwarf all others. He succeeded. When Sachetti died, Filippo Juvara took over the project, basing his new facade on Bernini's rejected designs for the Louvre. The shell took 26 years to build, and the decoration of its 2000 rooms with a vast collection of porcelain, tapestries, furniture, armor, and art dragged on for over a century. When Alfonso XIII abdicated in 1931, the Second Republic abandoned the costly construction. Today, the unfinished palace is only used by King Juan Carlos I and Queen Sofía on special occasions. Although only a fragment is complete, the palace stands as one of Europe's most grandiose residences.

The palace's most impressive rooms are decorated in the Rococo style. The **Salón de Gasparini,** site of the king's ceremonial dressing before the court, houses Goya's portrait of Carlos IV and a Mengs ceiling fresco. The **Salón del Trono** (Throne Room) also contains a ceiling fresco, painted by Tiepolo, outlining the qualities of the quintessential ruler. The **Real Oficina de Farmacia** (Royal Pharmacy) features crystal and china receptacles used to hold royal medicines, and the **Biblioteca** shelves first editions of *Don Quijote*. Also open to the public is the **Real Armería** (Armory), which displays the finest armor of the age, that of Carlos V and Felipe II, as well as other medieval weapons and artillery. *(From Pl. de Isabel II, head towards the Teatro Real. M: Ópera.* ☎ *914 54 88 00. Open Apr.-Sept. M-Sa 9am-6pm, Su 9am-3pm; Oct.-Mar. M-Sa 9:30am-5pm, Su 9am-2pm. €7, with worthwhile tour €8; students €3.30/ €8. EU citizens free W. Arrive early to avoid lines; skip M, when it is one of the only sights open.)*

CATHEDRAL DE NUESTRA SEÑORA DE LA ALMUDENA. Take a break from the cherub-filled frescoes of most cathedrals in Spain for refreshingly modern decor. Begun in 1879 and finished a century later, this cathedral is a stark contrast to the gilded Palacio Real. After a 30-year hibernation, the building received a controversial face-lift. The reasons are apparent, as the cathedral's frescoes and stained glass windows sport a discordant mix of traditional and abstract styles: gray stone walls clash with the ceiling panels of brilliant colors and sharp geometric shapes. *(Left of the Palacio Real on C. Bailén. M: Ópera. Closed during Mass. Open daily 9am-9pm. Free.)*

MUSEO DE LA REAL ACADEMIA DE BELLAS ARTES DE SAN FERNANDO. Following the example of Italy and France, Spain's Old Masters convinced Ferdinand VI to declare a royal academy in 1752 to train the country's most talented artists. The collection of Old Masters in this beautiful museum represents their legacy; it is surpassed only by the Prado. Goya's *La Tirana* and Velázquez's portrait of Felipe IV are masterpieces; the Raphael and Titian collections are also excellent. Other attractions include a room dedicated to Goya (a former academy director) and 17th-century canvases by Ribera, Murillo, Zurbarán, and Rubens. The top floor also has Picasso sketches. The **Caligrafía Real** (Royal Print and Drawing Collection) houses Goya's studio and organizes temporary exhibitions. Comprehensive guides for all collections are available at the front desk. *(C. de Alcalá, 13. ☎915 24 08 64. M: Sol or Sevilla. Open Tu-F 9am-7pm, Sa-M 9am-2:30pm. €2.50, students €1.25. W free.)*

PLAZA DEL ORIENTE. An architectural miscalculation resulted in this sculpture park. Most of its statues were designed for the palace roof, but because they were too heavy and the queen had a nightmare about the roof collapsing, they were instead placed in this leafy plaza. An equestrian statue of Felipe IV, sculpted by Pietro Tacca, dominates the plaza; other structures include the **Teatro Real,** inaugurated by Isabel II (see **Music,** p. 111). Treat yourself to a pricy coffee at one of the elegant *terrazas* fringing the plaza. *(From Pl. Isabel II, walk past Teatro Real. M: Ópera.)*

OTHER SIGHTS. The **Jardines de Sabatini,** just to the right when facing the palace, is the romantic's park of choice. Wade in the fountain and lie amongst sculpted hedges. Be sure to catch the ◙sunset from the walls above the garden. Below the Palace, the **Campo de Moro** is straight out of a fairy tale. *(Enter the Campo from the side opposite the Palace. Free.)* The **Parque de las Vistillas,** named for the tremendous *vistillas* (views) of the Palacio Real, Nuestra Señora de la Almudena, and the surrounding countryside, provides a stunning photo-op. Be cautious, as it can be dangerous at night. *(Located near Pl. Gabriel Miró. Facing the palace, turn left on C. Bailén and then right on C. Don Pedro into the plaza.)*

◙ NIGHTLIFE

In the middle of Madrid and at the heart of the action are the grandiose and spectacular clubs of El Centro. With multiple floors, swinging lights, cages, and disco balls, they meet even the wildest clubber's expectations. The mainstream clubs found amid these streets are often tourist hotspots; as a result, a night of fun here is the most expensive in the city. El Centro includes more territory than Madrid's other neighborhoods, so make a plan for the night and bring a map.

▨ **Palacio Gaviria,** C. del Arenal, 9 (☎915 26 60 69; www.palaciogaviria.com). M: Sol or Ópera. A red carpet leads to 3 ballrooms-turned-club spaces, complete with dancers and blazing light shows. Different theme every night. Cover varies; Su-Th €9, F-Sa €15. Open M-W 11pm-4am, Th 10:30pm-6am, F-Sa 11pm-6am, Su 9pm-2:30am.

Suite, C. de Virgen de los Peligros, 4 (☎915 21 40 31). M: Sevilla. Classy restaurant, bar, and club boasts a lunch *menú* (€10) by day and sleek drinks by night (€5-6). Upstairs dance floor rolls with house while the crowd downstairs at the bar and terrace makes its own music. Mixed crowd. Open daily 1am-5pm and 8pm-3:30am.

Joy Madrid, C. del Arenal, 11. (☎913 66 37 33). M: Sol or Ópera. A well-dressed crowd parties the night away to disco, techno, and R&B on a 3-tiered dance floor. Cover Su-W €12, Th-Sa €15. Open daily 11:30pm-6am.

El Barbu, C. Santiago, 3 (☎915 42 56 98). M: Ópera. Chill to lounge music in a brick 3-room interior. Cover €8. Open June-Aug. M-Th 10:30pm-4am, F-Sa 10:30pm-5:30am; Sept.-May Tu-Sa 8pm-4am.

Kathmandú, C. de Señores de Luzón, 3 (☎915 41 52 53), a right off C. Mayor from Puerta del Sol, after Pl. Mayor and facing the Ayuntamiento. M: Ópera. Jammed with locals dancing to high-energy techno and acid jazz until the wee hours of the night and morning. Cover €7, includes 1 drink. Open Th midnight-5am, F-Sa midnight-6am.

Sweet Club Dance, C. de Dr. Cortezo, 1 (☎918 69 40 38). M: Tirso de Molina. Steel doors covered in steel vines lead to an outrageous scene. Cages and disco-ball dance floor get packed after 3am. Cover €9 with flyer, €12 without, includes 1 drink. Open Th-Sa 1am-6:30am.

HUERTAS

Although *madrileños* have never settled on a nickname for this neighborhood, the area between C. San Jerónimo and C. de las Huertas is generally referred to as Huertas. Once a seedy area and a Hemingway hangout, Huertas has shaped up to be a cultural hotbed of food and drink. Though quieter than El Centro, Malasaña, and Chueca, **Plaza Santa Ana, Calle del Príncipe,** and **Calle de Echegaray** offer some of the best bars in Madrid, and **Calle de Ventura de la Vega** some of the best restaurants. Sol, Pl. Mayor, *el triángulo del arte,* and Estación Atocha are all within walking distance. Sol-bound buses stop near accommodations on C. del Príncipe, C. Núñez de Arce, and C. San Jerónimo; buses #14, 27, 37, and 45 run along Po. del Prado. The most convenient Metro stops are Sol, Sevilla, and Antón Martín.

ACCOMMODATIONS

Hostal Gonzalo, C. de Cervantes, 34, 3rd fl. (☎914 29 27 14; fax 20 20 07), off C. de León. M: Antón Martín. A budget traveler's dream. The friendly staff welcomes you to this lively *hostal* with newly renovated rooms, pristine baths, firm beds, TVs, and fans in summer. Leather-plush lounge. Singles €38; doubles €47; triples €60. AmEx/MC/V. ❹

Hostal Internacional, C. de Echegaray, 5, 2nd fl. (☎914 29 62 09). M: Sol. With extensive renovations completed 2 years ago, Internacional's rooms are new and crisp, all with A/C, safe, and shower. Also boasts a nice common room. Singles €25-30; doubles €40. Cash only. ❸

Hostal-Residencia Lido, C. de Echegaray, 5, 2nd fl. (☎914 29 62 07). M: Sol or Sevilla. Across the hall from Internacional, Lido also recently finished a makeover, showcasing new rooms with comfy beds, TV, refrigerator, fans, and full bath. Singles €22-25, with bath €25-30; doubles €35-40. ❷

Hostal Villar, C. del Príncipe, 18 (☎915 31 66 00; www.arrakis.es/~h-villar). M: Sol or Sevilla. The 1970s stormed through this building, leaving behind 46 decidedly brown, unintentionally retro rooms with TV and phone, some with A/C. Big lounge for socializing. Singles €22, with bath €25; doubles €30/€40; triples €42/€56. MC/V. ❷

Hostal Aguilar, C. San Jerónimo, 32, 2nd fl. (☎914 29 59 26 or 29 36 61; www.hostalaguilar.com). M: Sol or Sevilla. Clean, expansive, modern rooms with vast bathrooms, telephones, A/C, safe boxes, and TVs. Hemingway purportedly spent many nights in room 107. Elegantly spare lounge with deep couches serves as a meeting ground for clubbers. Singles €33; doubles €45; triples €60; quads €73. MC/V. ❸

Hostal Sardinero, C. del Prado, 16, 3rd fl. (☎914 29 41 12). An upscale hostel with all the creature comforts of a hotel, Sardinero offers sparkling and elegant accommodations with A/C, TV, phone, safe, and private baths. Gorgeous balconies are an added perk. 24hr. reception. Doubles only. One person €50, otherwise €60. MC/V. ❹

Hostal Armesto, C. de San Agustín, 6, 1st fl. (☎/fax 914 29 90 31 or 29 09 40), in front of Pl. Cortés. M: Antón Martín. This small hostel offers exceptional hospitality and a quiet night's sleep for an older crowd. Some rooms have garden view, all have private baths, TV, and fan. Singles €45; doubles €50; triples €65. AmEx/MC/V. ❹

Hostal-Residencia Carreras, C. del Príncipe, 18, 3rd fl. (☎/fax 915 22 00 36), off C. San Jerónimo. M: Antón Martín, Sol, or Sevilla. Request a room with a balcony—they tend to be larger. Most rooms have been renovated recently. All have TV, fan, and safe. Small, central lounge. Singles €21, with bath €48; doubles €36, with shower €42-48; triples €54/€60. AmEx/MC/V. ❷

Hostal R. Rodríguez, C. Núñez de Arce, 9, 3rd fl. (☎915 22 44 31). M: Sol or Sevilla. Clean shared baths and spacious rooms. 24hr. reception. English spoken. Singles €25; doubles €42, with bath €47; triples with bath €65. AmEx/MC/V. ❸

ON THE MENU

TAPAS

So you've finally found a hostel, only been lost twice, and are ready to experience the *madrileño* lifestyle. Clearly, it's time for drinks and *tapas*. These tasty little dishes are Spain's answer to *hors d'oeuvres*, with more taste and less pretension. The only problem is, what are you going to order?

To the untrained reader, *tapas* menus are often cryptic and undecipherable—if the bar has even bothered to print any. To make sure you don't end up eating the stewed parts of the ox you rode in on, keep the following words in mind. Servings come in three sizes: *pincho* (normally eaten with toothpicks between sips of beer), *tapa* (small plate), or *ración* (sizable, meal portion). *Aceitunas* (olives), *albóndigas* (meatballs), *anchoas* (anchovies), *callos* (tripe), *chorizo* (sausage), *croquetas* (croquettes), *gambas* (shrimp), *jamón* (ham), *patatas bravas* (fried potatoes with spicy sauce), *pimientos* (peppers), *pulpo* (octopus), and *tortillla española* (onion and potato omelette) comprise any basic menu. More adventurous travelers should try *morcilla* (blood sausage) or *sesos* (cow's brains). Bartenders will often offer tastes of *tapas* with your drink and strike up a conversation in the spirit of Madrid's generosity and charm. To ensure full treatment and local respect, the house *cerveza* is always a good choice.

Los Amigos Backpackers' Hostel, C. de Campomanes, 6, 4th fl. (☎915 47 17 07). M: Ópera. Just over a year old, Los Amigos offers bright and clean dorm-style accommodations (rooms with 4, 6, or 8 beds) with common baths. Amenities include a kitchen, a festive common room with bar and occasional parties, laundry (€5) and Internet (€2 per hr.). 24hr. reception. €5 sheet deposit. Dorms €15, breakfast included. MC/V. ❷

Hostal-Residencia Sud-Americana, Po. del Prado, 12, 6th fl. (☎914 29 25 64), across from the Prado. M: Antón Martín or Atocha. Airy doubles facing the Prado with views of the Paseo. Great location, simple rooms. Singles €18; doubles €35; triples €50. ❷

◖ FOOD

A popular place among locals, Pl. de Santa Ana is perfect for killing some time with a drink and snack. Straying slightly from its center, **Calles de Echegaray, Ventura de la Vega,** and **Manuel Fernández González** offer the best food options; quality is high and prices are low. As the evening grows and wine flows, these streets become the first stop of a night out in Madrid.

🖾 **Arrocería Gala,** C. de Moratín, 22 (☎914 29 25 62; www.paellas-gala.com). M: Antón Martín. The *paella* buck stops here, with decor as colorful and varied as its specialty. *Menú* (€14) offers choice of *paella*, along with salad, bread, wine, and dessert. Excellent sangría. Enjoy a romantic meal under the high, lit roof of the vine-covered interior garden. Reserve on weekends. Open daily 1:30-5pm and 9pm-11pm. Cash only. ❸

La Sanabresa, C. de Amor de Dios, 9 (☎914 29 03 38). M: Antón Martín. Incredibly popular with locals, La Sanabresa's plastic tablecloths are always covered with great food that costs next to nothing. Menus offer many delicious options (€6.90-7.50). Open daily 1-4pm and 8:30-11pm. MC/V. ❷

Al Natural, C. de Zorrilla, 11 (☎913 69 47 09; www.alnatural.biz). M: Sevilla. From the Metro, a left off C. de Cedaceros. A unique and creative offering of vegetarian Mediterranean dishes (€8-12) served in a lively, candle-lit atmosphere. Try a salad with wheat rolls. Open M-Sa 1-4pm and 9pm-midnight, Su 1-4pm. ❸

La Farfalla, C. de Santa María, 17 (☎913 69 46 91). M: Antón Martín. One block from the Metro along C. de las Huertas; look for the butterfly. This intimate restaurant's specialty is Argentine-style grilled meat *(parilla),* but don't miss the thin-crust pizzas (€5.30). Open for dinner Su-Th 9:30pm-3am, F-Sa 9:30pm-4am. AmEx/MC/V. ❷

Gula Gula, C. Infante 5 (☎914 20 29 19; www.gulagula.net), off C. de Echegaray near C. de las Huertas. M: Antón Martín. New location at Gran Vía, 1 (☎915 22 87 64). You better work! Outrageous drag and cabaret shows complement the all-you-can-eat buffet (lunch €9; dinner €18.75, includes cold buffet plus an ordered hot dish). Reserve for weekend dinner 1 week ahead. Open daily 1-5pm and 9pm-3am. AmEx/MC/V. ❹

Pizzería Cervantes, C. de León, 8 (☎914 20 12 98), off C. del Prado. Hands down one of the best cheap lunch *menús* in the area (€7; served M-F), offering much more than pizza and including a selection of exquisite desserts. Most entrees €6. Open Su-M and W-Th 1-4:30pm and 8:30-12:15pm, Tu 7pm-12:15am, F-Sa 1-4:30pm and 8:30pm-1:30am. AmEx/MC/V. ❷

Restaurante Integral Artemisa, C. de Ventura de la Vega, 4 (☎914 29 50 92), off C. San Jerónimo (D4). M: Sol. 2nd location in Pl. del Carmen, at Tres Cruces, 4 (☎915 21 87 21). Elegant vegetarian food served in a long, mellow dining area. Veggie *menú* €9. No smoking. Open daily 1:30-4pm and 9pm-midnight. AmEx/MC/V. ❷

🔘 SIGHTS

The area east of Sol is a wedge bordered by C. de Alcalá to the north, C. de Atocha to the south, and Po. del Prado to the east. Off C. San Jerónimo a myriad of streets slope downward, outward, and eastward toward various points along Po. del Prado and Pl. Cánovas de Castillo. **Plaza de Santa Ana** and its *terrazas* are the center of this old literary neighborhood; all directions in this section start from there. Huertas's sights, from authors' houses to famous cafes, reflect its artistic past. Home to Cervantes, Góngora, Quevedo, Calderón de la Barca, and Moratín during its *Siglo de Oro* heyday (see **Literature,** p. 78), Huertas enjoyed a fleeting return to literary prominence when Hemingway dropped by to drink in the 1920s.

CASA DE LOPE DE VEGA. Golden Age authors Lope de Vega and Miguel de Cervantes were bitter rivals, but Lope de Vega's 17th-century home is ironically located on C. de Cervantes. (Logically, Cervantes is buried on C. de Lope de Vega.) A prolific playwright and poet, Lope de Vega spent the last 25 years of his life writing over two-thirds of his plays in this house. *(C. de Cervantes, 11. With your back to Pl. de Santa Ana, turn left on C. del Prado, right on C. de León, and left on C. de Cervantes. ☎914 29 92 16. Open Th-F 9:30am-2pm, Sa 10am-2pm. Call ahead for definite schedules and prices.)*

CÍRCULO DE BELLAS ARTES. Designed by Antonio Palacios, this building encloses two stages and several studios for lectures and workshops run by prominent artists. The Círculo is the energetic hub of much of Madrid's art, sponsoring and organizing performances and shows around the city. Pick up their free monthly magazine, *Minerva*, at the entrance. Many facilities are for *socios* (members) only, but exhibition galleries are open to the public. A cafe with terrace seating is in front of the center. *(C. de Alcalá, 42. From Pl. de Santa Ana, go up C. del Príncipe, cross C. San Jerónimo, and continue toward C. de Alcalá. Turn right on C. de Alcalá. ☎913 60 54 00. Hours and admission vary with exhibitions. Cafe open daily 10am-1am.)*

FACADES. Juan de Villanueva's simple **Real Academia de la Historia** houses an old library and exemplifies Madrid-style architecture. *(At the C. de León and C. de las Huertas intersection. From Pl. de Santa Ana, take C. del Príncipe; turn left on C. de las Huertas. Library access for researchers only.)* Eighteenth-century architect Pedro de Ribera designed the impressive facades of the **Palacios de Miraflores** and **del Marqués de Ugena.** *(Palacio de Miraflores, C. San Jerónimo, 15. Palacio de Marqués de Ugena, Pl. de Canalejas, 3.)*

MADRID

🏛 MUSEUMS

Madrid's great museums need no introduction. If you're not a student and plan on visiting the big three, your best bet is the **Paseo del Arte** ticket (€7.66), which grants admission to the Museo del Prado, Museo Nacional Centro de Arte Reina Sofía, and Museo Thyssen-Bornemisza. The pass is available at all three museums.

MUSEO DEL PRADO

Po. del Prado at Pl. Cánovas del Castillo. M: Banco de España or Atocha. ☎/fax 913 30 28 00; http://museoprado.mcu.es. Open Tu-Su 9am-7pm. €3, students €1.50, under 18 and over 65 free. Su free.

The Prado is Spain's most prestigious museum, as well as one of Europe's finest centers for art from the 12th through 17th centuries. In 1785, architect **Juan de Villanueva** began construction of the Neoclassical building, following Carlos III's order for a museum of natural history and sciences. In 1819 Fernando VII transformed it into the royal painting archive; the museum's 7000 pieces are the result of hundreds of years of Bourbon art collecting. The walls are filled with Spanish and foreign masterpieces, including a comprehensive selection from the Flemish and Venetian schools. The museum is well-organized: each room is numbered and described in the museum's free guide. The sheer quantity of paintings means you'll have to be selective—walk past the rooms of imitation Rubens and Rococo cherubs and into the groves of the masters. The ground floor houses Spanish painting from the 12th through 16th centuries and 15th through 16th century Flemish, German, and Italian paintings. The first floor contains 17th-century works, and 18th-century paintings are located on the second floor. In addition to the free, indispensable floorplan you receive upon entry, the museum's guidebooks help you sift through the floors and offer extensive art history and criticism (€0.60-18).

DIEGO VELÁZQUEZ. The first floor houses Spanish, Flemish, French, Dutch, and Italian works from the 16th and 17th centuries. The most notable of these are an unparalleled collection of works by Diego Velázquez (1599-1660), court painter and interior decorator for Felipe IV (portraits of the foppish monarch abound). Because of their unforgiving realism and use of light, Velázquez's works resonate even in the 21st century. Several of his most famous paintings are here, including *Las hilanderas (The Weavers)*, *Los borrachos (The Drunkards)*, and *La fragua de Vulcano (Vulcan's Forge)*. With *Las lanzas (The Spears or The Surrender of Breda)*, Velázquez began to experiment with spatial perspective, developing the technique to imply continuous movement. Smoke from a recent battle clears in the background as an anxious horse dominates the foreground. Velázquez's technique, called illusionism, climaxed in his magnum opus *Las meninas (The Maids of Honor)*, dubbed an "encounter" rather than a painting. The snapshot quality of the figures transformed painting in the 17th century.

FRANCISCO DE GOYA. In 1785, Francisco de Goya y Lucientes (1746-1828) became the court portraitist. Perhaps the most interesting aspect of his works is that he managed to depict the royal family so unflatteringly and satirically without being expelled from court. Some suggest that he manipulated light and shadow to focus the viewer's gaze on the figure of the queen (rather than the centrally located king) in *La familia de Carlos IV*—a discreet way of supporting popular contemporary opinion about the true power behind the monarchy. The stark *Dos de Mayo* and *Fusilamientos de Tres de Mayo*, which depict the terrors of the Revolution of 1808, may be Goya's most recognized works. Also notable is the expressionless woman in *La maja vestida* and *La maja desnuda*. Perhaps the most evocative pieces in the Goya collection are the *Pinturas Negras (Black*

Paintings). These paintings were aptly named for the darkness of both the colors and the subject matter—Goya painted them in the house where he lived at the end of his life, deaf and alone. *Saturno devorando a su hijo (Saturn Devouring His Son)* stands out, a reminder from an ailing artist that time eventually destroys its creations. Goya violently captures the moment when Saturn eats his children upon hearing a prophesy that one of them would overthrow him.

ITALIAN, FLEMISH & OTHER SPANISH ARTISTS. The ground floor of the Prado displays many of **El Greco's** (Doménikos Theotokópoulos, 1541-1614) religious paintings. *La Trinidad (The Trinity)* and *La adoración de los pastores (The Adoration of the Shepherds)* are characterized by El Greco's luminous colors, elongated figures, and mystical subjects. On the second floor are other works by Spanish artists, including **Bartolomeo Murillo's** *Familia con pájaro pequeño (Family with Small Bird)*, **José de Ribera's** *El martirio de San Bartolomeo (Martyrdom of Saint Bartholomew)*, and **Francisco de Zurbarán's** *La inmaculada.*

The collection of **Italian** works is formidable, including **Titian's** portraits of Carlos I and Felipe II and **Raphael's** *El cardenal desconocido (The Unknown Cardinal).* **Tintoretto's** rendition of the homicidal seductress Judith and her hapless victim Holofernes, as well as his *Washing of the Feet* are here as well. Some minor **Botticellis** and a slew of his imitators are also on display. Among the works by **Rubens,** *The Adoration of the Magi* bests reflect his voluptuous style.

As a result of the Spanish Habsburgs' control of the Netherlands, the **Flemish** holdings are also top-notch. **Van Dyck's** *Marquesa de Legunes* is here, as well as works by **Albrecht Dürer.** Especially harrowing is **Peter Breughel the Elder's** *The Triumph of Death,* in which Death drives a carriage of skulls on a decaying horse. **Hieronymus Bosch's** moralistic *The Garden of Earthly Delights* is a favorite, with detailed depictions of hedonism and the destiny that awaits its practitioners.

CASÓN DEL BUEN RETIRO. Three minutes from the Prado Museum is the Casón del Buen Retiro, which, while closed for renovations, is still worth a peek. Once part of Felipe IV's Palacio del Buen Retiro, the Casón was destroyed in the Napoleonic wars. The rebuilt version normally houses the Prado's 19th- and 20th-century works, currently on loan to the Museo Nacional Centro de Arte Reina Sofía. *(C. Alfonso XII, 28. ☎ 913 30 28 60. Closed for renovations.)*

▧ MUSEO NACIONAL CENTRO DE ARTE REINA SOFÍA

C. Santa Isabel, 52. M: Atocha. ☎ 914 67 50 62 or 68 30 02; http://museoreinaso-fia.mcu.es. Open M and W-Sa 10am-9pm, Su 10am-2:30pm. €3, students €1.50. Sa after 2:30pm, Su, and holidays free.

Since King Juan Carlos I decreed this renovated hospital a national museum in 1988, the Reina Sofía's collection of **20th-century art** has grown steadily. Entrance through the soaring glass elevators adds to the mystique and character of the museum. The second and fourth floors are mazes of permanent exhibits charting the Spanish avant-garde and contemporary movements. Rooms dedicated to Juan Gris, Joan Miró, and Salvador Dalí display Spain's vital contributions to the Surrealist movement. Miró's works show a spare, colorful abstraction, while Dalí's paintings, including *Monumental imperial a la mujer niña* and *El enigma sin fin,* portray the artist's Freudian nightmares and sexual fantasies.

Picasso's masterpiece **Guernica** is the highlight of the Reina Sofía's permanent collection. Now freed from its restrictive glass cover, it depicts the Basque town bombed by the Germans at Franco's request during the Spanish Civil War (see **The Tragedy of Guernica,** p. 526). Picasso denounced the bloodshed in a huge, colorless work of contorted, agonized figures. While many have attempted to explain the allegory behind this work and its components, Picasso himself refused even the idea of explicit symbolism; nonetheless, most critics insist that the screaming horse represents war and the twisted bull represents Spain. Picasso loaned the canvas to the Museum of Modern Art in New York on the condition that it be returned to Spain when democracy was restored. In 1981, six years after Franco's death, *Guernica* was delivered to Madrid's Casón del Buen Retiro. The subsequent move to the Reina Sofía sparked an international controversy—Picasso's other stipulation had been that the painting hang only in the Prado, to affirm his equivalent status with artists like Titian and Velázquez. Basques want the painting relocated to the Guggenheim in Bilbao, but Madrid officials declare it too delicate to move. Preliminary sketches and a myriad of other Picasso paintings surround *Guernica*, testimony to his breadth of talent. Two other Picasso works of note are *Woman in Blue* and *Painter with Model*.

▧ MUSEO THYSSEN-BORNEMISZA

On the corner of Po. del Prado and C. San Jerónimo. M: Banco de España. Bus #6, 14, 27, 37, or 45. ☎913 69 01 51; www.museothyssen.org. Open Tu-Su 10am-7pm. Last entrance 6:30pm. €4.80, students with ISIC and seniors €3, under 12 free.

Unlike the Prado and the Reina Sofía, the Thyssen-Bornemisza covers a wide range of periods and media; exhibits range from 14th-century canvases to 20th-century sculptures. The museum is housed in the 18th-century **Palacio de Villahermosa** and contains the former collection of Baron Heinrich Thyssen-Bornemisza. The baron donated his collection in 1993, and today the museum is the world's most extensive private showcase. To view the collection in chronological order and observe an evolution of styles, begin on the top floor and work down.

The top floor is dedicated to the **Old Masters,** including such notables as Hans Holbein's austere *Portrait of Henry VIII* and El Greco's *Annunciation*. The organization of the Thyssen-Bornemisza provokes natural comparisons across centuries—note how the representation of the body evolves from Lucas Cranach's *The Nymph of the Spring* to Titian's *Saint Jerome in the Desert* to Anthony van Dyck's *Portrait of Jacques Le Roy*. In both variety and quality, the Thyssen-Bornemisza's **Baroque** collection, including pieces by Caravaggio, José de Ribera, and Claude Lorraine, overshadows that of the Prado.

The movement from the dark canvases of the top floor to the vibrant ones below reflects the revolutionary command of light and the arbitrary use of color that became popular in the 17th century. During this period, Dutch works, such as Frans Hals's *Family Group in a Landscape*, began to display a mastery of natural light. The **Impressionist** and **Post-Impressionist** collections explode with texture and color—look for works by Renoir, Manet, Degas, Monet, van Gogh, Cézanne, and Matisse. Though less well-known, the **Expressionist** artists are well-represented, with noteworthy works by Nolde, Marc, and Beckmann. The museum is also home to Europe's only collection of North American 19th-century painting.

The highlight of the tour is the museum's **20th-century** collection. Modern artists represented include Picasso, Léger, Mondrian, Miró, Kandinsky, Gorky, Pollack, Rothko, Dalí, Hopper, Chagall, Ernst, Klee, and O'Keefe, among others.

▧ NIGHTLIFE

Plaza de Santa Ana, the pulsing heart of Huertas, brims with *terrazas*, bars, and live street music. Many bars convert to clubs as the night unfolds, spinning house and techno on intimate dance floors. With its variety of styles, Huertas is one of the best places to party. **Calle del Príncipe** is lined with smaller spots, but check out the larger *discotecas* on **Calle de Atocha.** Most locals begin their evenings here and emerge, slightly worn out and more than slightly later, from El Centro and Chueca.

DISCOTECAS

Kapital, C. de Atocha, 125 (☎914 20 29 06). M: Atocha. *Tumba la casa* (bring down the house) on 7 floors of *discoteca* insanity. From hip-hop to house, open *terrazas* to cinemas, lose yourself (and maybe your friends) in the madness. Dress to impress (the bouncer). Drinks €9. Cover €12, includes 1 drink. Open Th-Su midnight-6am and afternoons F-Su (5:30-11pm). **Sundance** (an unthemed excuse to party) draws crowds on Su. Gets going around 2am.

Ananda, Estación Atocha, 2, Esq. Av. Ciudad de Barcelona. Descend the stairs into a mass of partygoers. Large outdoor *terraza* equipped with multiple bars and a 20-something crowd. Dance in the white room indoors. W and Su transform Ananda into a Sundance party packed with crowds to rival weekend nights. Cover €10, might include a drink. Drinks €8. Open daily 11pm-dawn.

No Se Lo Digas a Nadie, C. de Ventura de la Vega, 7 (☎913 69 17 27), next to Pl. de Santa Ana. M: Sevilla. Head through the garage doors onto the packed dance floor and squeeze in some dancing along your bar crawl, or play a game of pool upstairs. Drinks €3-5. Open Tu-W until 3:30am, Th-Sa until 6am.

Villa Rosa, Pl. de Santa Ana, 15 (☎925 21 36 89). M: Sol or Sevilla. American pop meets Moorish architecture in this Alhambra-inspired disco, which sports 4 bars and a raised dance floor. Frescoed and tiled walls compete with flat-screen TVs for attention. Cover F-Sa €7. Drinks €7. Open M-Sa 11pm-6am.

BARRES-MUSICALES

Cardamomo, C. de Echegaray, 15 (☎913 69 07 57). M: Sevilla. Flamenco music spins all night. A local crowd dances flamenco occasionally, but come W nights to see professionals do it. Mondays bump with Brazilian and other exotic beats. Open 9pm-4am.

La Comedia, C. del Príncipe, 16 (☎915 21 51 64). M: Sevilla. Americans feel at home in a crowd dancing to hip-hop, R&B, and reggae. Hit up the DJ with requests; he spins to please. Beer €4.20, drinks €6. Open daily 9pm-4am.

Café Jazz Populart, C. de las Huertas, 22 (☎914 29 84 07; www.populart.es). M: Sevilla or Antón Martín. This intimate, smoke-filled scene hosts local and foreign talent. Live jazz, blues, and reggae. Shows daily 11pm-2am. Open daily 6pm-3am.

Café Central, Pl. de Ángel, 10 (☎913 69 41 43), off Pl. de Santa Ana. M: Antón Martín or Sol. Art Deco meets old-world cafe in one of Europe's top jazz venues. Mesmerized listeners recline in each others' arms. An older audience. Shows nightly. Beer €2. Cover €8-25, depending on who's playing. Open daily 1:30pm-2:30am, F and Sa until 3am.

La Boca del Lobo, C. de Echegaray, 11 (☎914 29 70 13). M: Sevilla. Live shows of reggae, funk, blues, and rock bands hit this 2-story joint, drawing a varied crowd. Waterfall mirrors in the bathrooms may drench you. Shows W-Th 10:30pm. Cover €6. Open daily 10pm-3:30am.

BARS

El Café de Sheherezade, C. Santa María, 18 (☎913 69 24 74), a block from C. de las Huertas. M: Antón Martín. Recline on opulent pillows while sipping exotic infusions in a bohemian atmosphere. Surrounded by Middle Eastern music and decor, groups cluster around *pipas* (€7-10) that filter sweet, incense-like smoke through whiskey or water. Late nights sometimes end with belly dancing. Open in summer Su-Th 6pm-2:30am, F-Sa 6pm-3:30am; in winter Su-Th 5pm-2am, F-Sa 5pm-3am.

Trocha, C. de las Huertas, 55 (☎914 29 78 61). M: Antón Martín or Sol. Come here for Brazilian *capirinhas* (lime, ice, rum, and sugar drinks; €4.80). The delicious and potent drinks (ask for *flor de caña*) are served in a chill setting with jazz tunes and cushioned wicker couches. Open Su-Th 6pm-3am, F-Sa 6pm-4am.

Mauna Loa, Pl. de Santa Ana, 13 (☎914 29 70 62). M: Sevilla or Sol. Feels like Hawaii—birds fly freely between low chairs and the scantily clad dance to upbeat tunes. Sip on a *fuerte volcano* (€6-10) through an enormous straw at this crowded pre-party destination. Open Su-Th 6pm-2am, F-Sa 6pm-3am.

Viva Madrid, C. Manuel Fernández González, 7 (☎914 29 36 40), off C. de Echegaray. M: Sol or Sevilla. *"Lo mejor del mundo"* is the humble motto of this daytime cafe/nighttime foray. A local favorite for a romantic evening. Cocktails €7. Open daily 1pm-2am.

Naturbier, Pl. de Santa Ana, 9 (☎914 29 39 18). M: Sol or Sevilla. Join the locals who pour in for the excellent locally-brewed *bier*, inspired by their motto "beer is important to human nutrition." Superior lager €1.80-4.20; it gets cheaper as you progress to the innermost of the 3 bars. Open Su-Th 11am-1:30am, F-Sa 11am-2:30am.

El Parnaso, C. de Moratín, 25 (☎686 62 67 53). Off the beaten path, this *dadista* bar is packed with eclectic sculptures and an equally eclectic late-night crowd. Come here for a drink (€5-7) and some tasty Moroccan sweets. Open Tu-Su 8pm-3am.

GRAN VÍA

The neon lights of Broadway and the Champs-Élysées have met their match on Gran Vía. The massive avenue glows and pulsates with the sharp lights of sex shops, McDonald's, and five-star hotels in a 24-hour parade of flashing cars, swishing skirts, and stack-heeled shoes. *Hostal* signs pepper the horizon, but accommodations tend to be pricier and less comfortable than in other areas. Have your wits about you when returning late at night. El Centro and Huertas provide safer bargains. Buses #1, 2, 44, 46, 74, 75, 133, 146, 147, and 148 reach Pl. Callao; buses #1, 2, 3, 40, 46, 74, 146, and 149 service both Pl. de España and Pl. Callao. The closest Metro stops are Gran Vía, Callao, Santo Domingo, and Banco de España.

▐ ACCOMMODATIONS

Hostal A. Nebrija, Gran Vía, 67, 8th fl., elevator A (☎915 47 73 19). M: Pl. de España. A grandson continues his grandparents' tradition with pleasant, spacious rooms offering magnificent views of the city. A very tidy building, and heavily furnished in classic style. All rooms have TVs and fans. Singles €26; doubles €36; triples €49. AmEx/MC/V. ❸

Hostal Santillan, Gran Vía, 64, 8th fl. (☎/fax 915 48 23 28). M: Pl. de España. Take the glass elevator to the top floor of this gorgeous building; the friendly management, the Beatles, and little dwarfs. Simple rooms all have showers, sinks, TVs, fans, and safes. Vending machine. Singles €30; doubles €45; triples €60. MC/V. ❸

Hostal Margarita, Gran Vía, 50, 5th fl. (☎/fax 915 47 35 49). M: Callao. Warm and inviting family offers simple rooms with large windows, TV, and telephone, most with street views. Family shares TV lounge and big kitchen. Laundry €10. Reservations recommended. Singles €25; doubles €36, with bath €38; triples with bath €48. MC/V. ❸

Hostal Triana, C. de la Salud, 13, 1st fl. (☎915 32 68 12; www.hostaltriana.com). M: Callao or Gran Vía. The sign is quite visible. With its white walls, soothing environment, and attentive receptionists, Hostal Triana feels like the spa of the hostel world. All rooms have TV, fan, and private bath. Reserve at least 2 weeks ahead. Singles €30; doubles €42, with A/C €45; triples €57. ❸

Hostal-Residencia Alibel, Gran Vía, 44, 8th fl. (☎915 21 00 51). M: Callao. Well-lit, spacious rooms with great views show off Alibel's recent face-lift. All have private baths, TVs, fans, and balconies. Doubles €35; triples €42. ❹

Hostal Lauria, Gran Vía, 50, 4th fl. (☎/fax 915 41 91 82; www.geocities.com/hostal lauria). M: Callao. Spotless sleeping quarters are well endowed with large beds, baths, phones, fans, and TVs. Lounge with couches, TV, and stereo. English and French spoken. Singles €33; doubles €42; triples €57. MC/V. ❸

Hostal-Residencia Lamalonga, Gran Vía, 56, 2nd fl. (☎915 47 26 31 or 47 68 94). M: Santo Domingo. Rooms with views, A/C, TV, full bath, and phone. Singles €36; doubles €48; triples €58. 10% discount for stays over 5 days. MC/V. ❹

🔾 FOOD

Tourist and locals alike battle their love/hate relationships for the Golden Arches, KFC, and Burger King under the shimmering lights of Gran Vía. Long lines at fast-food joints demonstrate that convenience and time often outweigh fine dining. Fear not—there are still some culinary diamonds hidden in the fast-food rough.

La Finca de Susana, C. de Arlabán, 4 (☎913 69 35 57). M: Sevilla. Probably the most popular lunch eatery in all of Madrid, where delicious fine dining and swanky surroundings come at an extremely low price (*menú* €6.95). Be prepared to wait in line. Open daily 1-3:45pm, 8:30-11:45pm. AmEx/MC/V. ❷

Museo Chicote, C. Gran Vía, 12 (☎915 32 97 80). M: Gran Vía. Lose yourself in green leather booths amidst pictures of stars from Ava Gardner and John Wayne to Lola Flores and Luis Buñuel. Throw back a cocktail with Madrid's socialites after 11pm. Lunchtime *menú* €8.50-9. Lunch served 1-4pm. Open M-Sa 8am-3am. ❷

🔾 SIGHTS

Urban planners paved Gran Vía in 1910 to link C. de la Princesa with Pl. de la Cibeles, creating the cosmopolitan center of life in the city. After Madrid gained wealth as a neutral supplier during WWI, the city funneled much of its earnings into making Gran Vía one of the world's great thoroughfares. Today, movie theaters and fast-food joints line the most commercialized street in Madrid. To see it, just throw yourself in among the throngs on the sidewalk and keep up the pace.

Sol's shopping streets converge at Gran Vía's highest elevation in **Plaza de Callao** (M: Callao). C. Postigo San Martín splits off southward, where you'll find the famed **Convento de las Descalzas Reales** (see p. 120). Westward from Pl. de Callao (left when facing the conspicuous sex shop), Gran Vía descends toward **Plaza de España** (M: Pl. de España), where a statue commemorates Spain's most prized fictional duo: Cervantes's Don Quijote and Sancho Panza (riding horseback and muleback, respectively). Next to Pl. de España are two of Madrid's tallest skyscrapers, the **Telefónica building** (1929) and the **Edificio de España** (1953). Louis S. Weeks of the Chicago School designed the Telefónica building, the tallest concrete building in existence at the time (81m), and Franco's architect designed the Edificio de España. Tucked between the two skyscrapers on C. San Leonardo is the small **Iglesia de San Marcos,** a Neoclassical church composed of five intersecting ellipses—this Euclidean dream of a church doesn't have a straight line.

NIGHTLIFE

The deepest drum and bass pounds in the boisterous landmark clubs on the side streets of Gran Vía well into the early morning. Subtlety has never been a strong suit for this area, nor is it known for its safety; a mix of sketchy tourists and sketchier locals makes Gran Vía less than ideal for late-night wandering.

■ **Pasapoga,** Gran Vía, 37 (☎915 47 57 11 or 32 16 44), around the corner from Pl. de Callao. M: Callao. Gay nightlife explodes here on weekends, especially Saturdays. Strut down the ivory-banistered staircase and feel like the princess or *reina que tú eres*. Circular dance floor and spectacular chandelier. Pumping techno, pop, and house. Beautiful interior, beautiful people. Cover €15. Disco F and Sa. Open Tu-Su 6pm-dawn.

Cool, C. de Isabel la Católica, 6 (☎915 42 34 39). M: Santo Domingo. Heavenly drag performances and the occasional underworldly goth party for a wild, mixed crowd. Mesmerizing video projections give this club the production value of international venues, which fits the mix of locals, Brits, and Americans yelling to be heard over the latest house. Special **Shangay Tea Dance** for primarily gay crowd on Sundays. Drinks €5-8. Cover varies, usually includes 1 drink. F-Sa midnight-late, Sunday opens at 9pm; free with flyer before 9:30pm.

Soul Kitchen, C. de Mesonero Romanos, 13 (☎915 32 15 24), off Gran Vía. M: Callao or Gran Vía. Get your freak on at the only real hip-hop club in town. Those in the know arrive around 3am to a packed dance floor. Open W-Sa 1pm-5am.

MALASAÑA & CHUECA

Split down the middle by C. de Fuencarral, Malasaña and Chueca are two of Madrid's best hard-core party pits. Beyond outrageous nightlife and numerous drinking outlets, the area offers a wide range of excellent restaurants, great shopping, and charming plazas. Chueca is hip, fun, funky, and wild. While the pleasure dome of Madrid's gay population, it offers something for everyone.

ACCOMMODATIONS

Hostales and *pensiones* in Malasaña and Chueca are usually located on the upper floors of older buildings, and accommodations can be a bit pricier here than in other areas. Buses #3, 40, and 149 run along C. de Fuencarral and C. Hortaleza. Metro stops Chueca, Gran Vía, and Tribunal service the area.

■ **Hostal-Residencia Domínguez,** C. Santa Brígida, 1, 1st fl. (☎/fax 915 32 15 47). M: Tribunal. The doubles on the 2nd and 3rd fl. are immaculate and brand new. Hospitable young owner is ready with tips on local nightlife. English spoken. Singles €22, with bath €29.45; doubles with bath and A/C €40. ❷

Hostal Chelo, C. Hortaleza, 17, 3rd fl. (☎915 32 70 33; www.chelo.com). M: Gran Vía. In addition to its great location, the biggest draw of this *hostal* is the helpful staff, educated on everything and anything about Madrid. Rooms are clean and spacious, with TV, fan, and full bath. English spoken. Singles €30; doubles €38. ❸

Hostal Lorenzo, C. Clavel, 8 (☎915 21 30 57; fax 32 79 78). M: Gran Vía. In the process of converting from a *hostal* to a hotel, Lorenzo has renovated 2 floors to produce elegant and affordable accommodations equipped with crisp, new furniture, modern baths, and sound-proof windows. Older rooms on the 3rd fl. are cheaper. Reservations recommended. Singles €45; doubles €65-80. IVA not included. AmEx/MC/V. ❹

Hostal Palacios/Hostal Ribadavia, C. de Fuencarral, 25, 1st-3rd fl. (☎915 31 10 58 or 31 48 47). M: Gran Vía. Both *hostales* run by the same cheerful family. Palacio (1st- 2nd fl.) offers large, tiled rooms with elegant modern furniture. Older Ribadavia (3rd fl.) has comfortable rooms with TVs. Spotless rooms all have fans. Singles €20, with bath €30; doubles €30/€36; triples €45/€51; quads with bath €60. AmEx/MC/V. ❷

Hotel Lorenzo, C. Clavel, 8 (☎915 21 30 57; fax 32 79 78; www.hotel/sanlorenzo.com). M: Gran Vía. A former hostel, Hotel Lorenzo has renovated 3 floors to produce elegant accommodations equipped with crisp, new furniture, modern baths, A/C, TV, phone, and sound-proof windows. Other amenities include a lounge, coffee bar, room service, laundry, and parking. Reservations recommended. Singles €50; doubles €75-85. IVA not included. AmEx/MC/V. ❹

Hispa Domus, C. San Bartolomé, 4, 2nd fl. (☎915 23 81 27; www.hispadomus.com). M: Chueca or Gran Vía. Small, welcoming hostel catering to a gay clientele. Gregarious staff and colorful rooms, complete with A/C, bath, satellite TV, and postmodern decor. English and Italian spoken. Reservations required. Singles €42; doubles €59. MC/V. ❹

Hostal Medieval, C. de Fuencarral, 46, 2nd fl. (☎915 22 25 49). M: Tribunal. Central location, hospitable owners, and large, clean older rooms with shower and sink. TV lounge honors Real Madrid. Singles €22; doubles €30, with bath €36; triples €44. ❷

Hostal Abril, C. de Fuencarral, 39, 4th fl. (☎915 31 53 38). M: Tribunal or Gran Vía. Rooms reminiscent of your college dorm, but cleaner and cozier. Those with balconies are surprisingly tranquil for the spicy location. Singles €18, with shower €20; doubles with bath €36; triples with bath €46. ❷

Hotel Mónaco, C. Barbieri, 5 (☎915 52 46 30; fax 21 16 01). M: Chueca or Gran Vía. In the 1900s a brothel catering to Madrid's high society, Hotel Mónaco still encourages naughtiness. Frescoes of Eve-like temptresses excite the imagination while hundreds of mirrors and *palacio*-sized beds fulfill the reality. Green-lit lounge and a lively bar/cafeteria area. Adventurous older crowd. Simple singles €48; doubles €66; triples €86; quads €105. AmEx/MC/V. ❹

◖ FOOD

Before the nightime insanity begins, Malasaña and Chueca offer some of the best dining options in all of Madrid. The area showcases exceptional vegetarian, Middle Eastern, and Italian restaurants. Most eateries are small and intimate, with high quality and low prices.

■ **La Granja Restaurante Vegetariano,** C. de San Andrés, 11 (☎915 32 87 93). M: Tribunal or Bilbao. Dimmed yellow lights glow above intricately tiled walls in this Arabicthemed restaurant. Youthful crowd, friendly owner, and big portions. *Menú* €7.50. Open daily 1:30-4:15pm and 8:30pm-midnight. MC/V. ❷

■ **Al-Jaima, Cocina del Desierto,** C. Barbieri, 1 (☎915 23 11 42). M: Gran Vía or Chueca. Lebanese, Moroccan, and Egyptian food transport you to North Africa. Specialties include the *pastela*, couscous, shish kebabs, and *tajine* (€4-8). Open daily 1:30-4pm and 9pm-midnight. Dinner reservations highly recommended, sometimes required. ❷

Pizzeria Vesuvio, C. de Hortaleza, 4 (☎915 21 51 71). M: Gran Vía. Mix and match pasta and sauce or try the 30+ varieties of personal pizzas. Fresh, delicious food and fast service. Try the *pasta fresca*. Fight the crowd for a counter seat or order to go. Meals €3.30-5. Open M-Th 1-4pm and 8pm-midnight, F-Sa 1-4pm and 8pm-1am. ❶

MADRID

El Rey del Barrio, C. de Hernán Cortés, 19 (☎915 32 97 01). M: Chueca. A bright, festive, authentic Mexican restaurant offering delicious food and desserts. Try the homemade fruit-infused tequila. Tacos and enchiladas €7.50-10; 2-person *menús* €12-25; desserts €5. IVA not included. Open M 8pm-2am, Tu-Sa 1:30-4pm and 8pm-2am. ❸

Chez Pomme, C. de Pelayo, 4 (☎915 32 16 46). M: Chueca. Quiet, artsy spot that serves filling portions of French vegetarian (and non-veggie) cuisine. Try the *berenjenas al horno* (baked eggplant), one of the many tofu dishes, or a creative salad (€5-8.50). *Menú* €6, dinner *menú* €12. Open M-Th 2-4:30pm and 9-midnight, F-Sa until 2-4:30pm and 9pm-12:30am. ❶

Pizzaiolo, C. de Hortaleza, 84 (☎913 19 29 64). M: Chueca. Authentic Italian pizzas made with fresh ingredients. Friendly staff and casual atmosphere. Has a host of maps and pamphlets on gay Madrid. Open M-F noon-5pm and 7pm-1am, Sa-Su 7pm-2am. ❷

Vegaviana, C. de Pelayo, 35 (☎913 08 03 81). M: Chueca. Wholesome vegetarian cuisine. Very popular with locals and tourists. Lunch *menú* €7.25, meals €7.20-7.80. Pizzas €6.50. Open Tu-Sa 1:30-4pm and 9pm-midnight. No smoking. ❷

La Carreta, C. Barbieri, 10 (☎915 32 70 42 or 21 60 97). M: Gran Vía or Chueca. Small, friendly spot specializing in Argentinian, Uruguayan, and Chilean meals. Beef specialties. Lunch *menú* €10.50. Entrees €5.95-15. Occasional tango performances on weekend evenings (usually F-Sa 10:30pm; call for schedule). Reservations recommended. Open Su-M and W-Sa 1:30-5pm and 9pm-4am. ❸

La Sacristía, C. de las Infantas, 28 (☎915 22 09 45). M: Gran Vía or Chueca. Creative Spanish cuisine, including 60 types of *bacalao* (€16). Choose the more casual bar seating for a shorter menu and a cheaper meal. Lunch and dinner only. Open M-Sa 8am-2am. AmEx/MC/V. ❹

La Gata Flora, C. de San Vicente Ferrer, 33 (☎ 915 21 27 92 or 21 20 20). M: Noviciado or Tribunal. Pizza (€5.70-7.50), pasta (€6.20-7.30), drinks, and desserts in a festive setting. Pitcher of sangría €6.40. Open daily Su-Th 2-4pm and 8:30pm-midnight, F-Sa 2-4pm and 8:30pm-1am. ❷

👁 SIGHTS

Devoid of the numerous historic monuments and palaces that characterize most of Madrid, the labyrinthine streets of Malasaña and Chueca house countless undocumented "sights," from platform shoe stores to spontaneous street performers. These streets are an ultra-modern, funkified relief for travelers weary of crucifixes and brushstrokes. Chueca, in particular, remains the ideal area for people-watching and boutique shopping. By night, both of these districts bristle with Madrid's alternative scene. Overall, most of the scenery lies in the people, though the region between **Calle de Fuencarral** and **Calle de San Bernardo** contains some of Madrid's most avant-garde architecture and current art exhibitions.

IGLESIA DE LAS SALESAS REALES. Bourbon King Fernando VI commissioned this church in 1758 at the request of his wife, Doña Bárbara. The Baroque-Neoclassical domed church is clad in granite, with facade sculptures by Alfonso Vergaza and a dome painting by the brothers González Velázquez. The church's ostentatious facade and interior prompted critics to pun on the queen's name: "Barbaric queen, barbaric tastes, barbaric building, barbarous expense," they said, giving rise to the expression *"¡qué bárbaro!"* Today, the expression refers to absurdity, extravagance, or just plain craziness. (*C. de Bárbara de Braganza, 1. M: Colón. From Pl. Colón, go down Po. de Recoletos and make a right on C. de Bárbara de Braganza. ☎913 19 48 11. Open for Mass only; consult tourist office for details.*)

MUSEO MUNICIPAL. An Isabelline facade masks a collection of documents and art detailing the history of Madrid, including the first complete 16th-century map of the city. *(C. de Fuencarral, 78. ☎915 88 86 72. M: Tribunal. Open Tu-Sa 9:30am-8pm. Free.)*

MUSEO ROMÁNTICO. Housed in a 19th-century mansion, this museum is a time capsule of the Romantic period's decorative arts. *(C. San Mateo, 13. ☎914 48 10 45; www.mcu.es/nmuseos/romantico. M: Alonso Martínez. Open Tu-Sa 9:30am-3pm, Su 10am-3pm. Closed Aug. €2.40, students €1.20. Su free. Closed for renovations until 2004.)*

🄽 NIGHTLIFE

Chueca and Malasaña come to life in the early evening, especially in **Plaza Chueca** and **Plaza Dos de Mayo.** By sunset, these plazas are social meccas—places to hang out, meet your friends, and get drunk. Bar-filled streets radiate from the plazas; though people eventually migrate away from the plazas, they still remain busy with activity well into *la madrugada* (dawn). The alcoholic circus known as Chueca nightlife guarantees entertainment from locals, tourists, and random, questionable characters who tend to pass out on plaza benches. Beyond the plazas, most nightlife tends toward classy cafes, cruisy bars, and shady clubs. Though Chueca is largely gay, most of the establishments in the area are quite mixed. The area is ideal for bar-hopping until 2 or 3am, when it's time to hit the clubs near Sol, El Centro, and Gran Vía.

🄼 Acuarela, C. de Gravina, 10 (☎915 22 21 43). M: Chueca. A welcome alternative to the club scene. Buddhas and candles surround cushy antique furniture, providing inspiration for good conversation and a nice buzz. Coffees and teas €1.75-5.40. Liquor €3.50-4.50. Open daily 3pm-3am.

Why Not?, C. San Bartolomé, 7. M: Chueca. When in doubt at 1-3am, people flock to Why Not? Small downstairs bar packed almost every night of the week with a wild, mixed crowd. Open daily 10pm-6am. The same owners manage **Polana,** C. Barbieri, 8-10 (☎915 32 33 05), which gets going around 2:30am, blasting campy Spanish pop music for a mainly gay crowd. Open M-Th and Su 11pm-4am, F-Sa 11pm-8am.

El Clandestino, C. del Barquillo, 34 (☎915 21 55 63). M: Chueca. A chill twenty-something crowd drinks at the bar upstairs, then heads down to the caves to nod and dance along with the DJ's acid jazz, fusion, and funk selections. Live music most Th-Sa at 11 or 11:30pm. Open M-Sa 6:30pm-3am.

Mama Ines, C. de Hortaleza, 22 (☎915 23 23 33; www.mamaines.com). M: Chueca. Chic cafe/bar with perfect diva lighting. Great for drinks and conversation. Good desserts, light meals, and teas. Open Su-Th 10am-2am, F-Sa 10am-3am.

Star's Café Dance, C. Marqués de Valdeiglesias, 5 (☎915 22 27 12). M: Chueca. A stylish cafe during the week complements a vivacious dance club downstairs on the weekends. Come well dressed. Open M-Th 1pm-2am, F-Sa 1pm-4am.

Liquid, C. del Barquillo, 8 (☎915 32 74 28). M: Chueca or Banco de España. Water bubbling through glass near the front door leads to a video bar playing English songs. Clientele is quite refined and mostly gay. Open Tu-Su 9pm-3am, F-Sa until 3:30am.

Vía Láctea, C. de Velarde, 18 (☎914 66 75 81). M: Tribunal. Dive into the Brit underground scene nightly from 9-11pm when soft drinks and beer on tap are €2-3.50 each. After midnight, a late 20s crowd gets groovy between the pink walls. The loudspeakers can be deafening. Pool tables. Th funk and *afrodisia.* Open daily 7:30pm-3am.

Café la Palma, C. de la Palma, 62 (☎915 22 50 31). M: San Bernardo or Noviciado. Slip back into the comfy pillows of this decadent venue for live music and late-night whispering. Beer €2.10. Mixed drinks €5. Open daily 4pm-3:30am.

El Truco, C. de Gravina, 10 (☎915 32 89 21). M: Chueca. Watch the smoky windows from Pl. Chueca to see shadows of people dancing inside. Bar features local artists' works and pop artists' hits. Outdoor seating in Pl. Chueca is a welcome alternative to the noisy interior. Lesbian-friendly. Open Su-Th 8pm-2am, F-Sa 9pm-4am. Same owners run **Escape,** also on the plaza. Open F-Sa midnight-7am.

ARGÜELLES & MONCLOA

The 19th century witnessed the growth of several neighborhoods around the core of the city north and northwest of the Palacio Real. Today, the area known as Argüelles and the zone around **Calle San Bernardo** form a cluttered mixture of middle-class homes, student apartments, and bohemian hangouts, all brimming with cultural activity. Heavily bombarded during the Spanish Civil War, Argüelles inspired Chilean poet Pablo Neruda to write *España en el corazón*.

High-schoolers dominate Moncloa's streets. Unless you're Lolita, or looking for one, the only reason to leave Madrid's better nighttime areas for Moncloa is **Los Bajos,** a concrete megaplex of diminutive bars serving incredibly **cheap drinks.** The bars tend to be slightly grimy, the dance floors small, and the crowd pre-pubescent, but at €1 each, the *chupitos* (shots) are hard to turn down. (Bars are usually only open F-Sa and close 1-2am. From M: Moncloa, cross C. Isaac Peral in front of Pl. Moncloa, passing under the gate onto C. Gatzambide, 35.)

◤ ACCOMMODATIONS

Albergue Juvenil Santa Cruz de Marcenado (HI), C. de Santa Cruz de Marcenado, 28 (☎915 47 45 32; fax 48 11 96). M: Argüelles. From the Metro, walk 1 block down C. Alberto Aguilera away from C. de la Princesa, turn right on C. de Serrano Jóver, then left on C. Santa Cruz de Marcenado. Lounge is great for mingling and late-night card playing. The 72 beds fill quickly, even in winter. Separate floors for men and women. English sometimes spoken. Rooms have cubbies, but use the lockers outside the rooms (€2 extra). Breakfast included. Sheets provided. Laundry €3. 3-day max. stay. Quiet hours after midnight. Reception daily 9am-10pm. 1:30am curfew. Reserve in advance by mail, fax, or in person, or arrive early and pray. Closed Christmas and New Year's. €3.50 extra per night without HI card (€21). Dorms €7.80, over 26 €11.56. ❶

Hostal-Residencia Rios, C. Juan Álvarez Mendizabal, 44, 4th fl. (☎915 59 51 56). M: Ventura Rodríguez or Argüelles. Face the shrubbery, walk 3 blocks left up C. de la Princesa to C. Rey Francisco, go 3 blocks to C. Juan Álvarez Mendizabal, and turn left again. Nothing fancy; just clean, cheap, comfortable rooms close to the park, some with A/C (€6). Singles €17; doubles with shower €32; triples €45. ❷

◖ FOOD

Argüelles is a middle-class neighborhood near the Ciudad Universitaria. It's geared toward locals rather than tourists and is therefore full of inexpensive markets, moderately priced restaurants, and informal neighborhood bars. Check out the *terrazas* on Po. del Pintor Rosales overlooking the park.

▨ **Ananias,** C. Galileo, 9 (☎914 48 68 01). M: Argüelles, a left off C. Alberto Aguilera. Swirling waiters serve Castilian dishes with a flourish. *Torero* paraphernalia covers the walls in the front room, while regulars enjoy the elegance of the back room. Entrees €7.40-15. Open Su 1-4pm, M-Tu and Th-Sa 1-4pm and 9pm-midnight. AmEx/MC/V. ❸

Cáscaras, C. Ventura Rodríguez, 7 (☎ 915 42 83 36). M: Ventura Rodríguez. Sleek interior enhances the dining experience. Popular for *tapas, pinchos,* and ice-cold Mahou beer in the early afternoon and evening. Exotic vegetarian entrees €5.50-6.65. Open M-Th 7am-1am, F-Sa 10am-2am, Su 10am-1am. AmEx/MC/V. ❷

La Crêperie, Po. del Pintor Rosales, 28 (☎915 48 23 58). M: Ventura Rodríguez. The cherub decorations are almost as sweet as the dessert crêpes (€2.60-4.55). Eat lunch and dinner crêpes (€3.75-6.30) on the chic Po. del Pintor Rosales *terraza.* Open Su-Th 1:30-4:15pm and 8pm-1am, F-Sa 1:30-4:15pm and 8pm-1:15am. ❶

La Vaca Argentina, Po. del Pintor Rosales, 52 (☎915 59 66 05). M: Moncloa or Argüelles. Follow C. Marqués de Urquijo downhill, then take a left on Po. del Pintor Rosales. One of 10 of its kind in Madrid, this restaurant is famous for its steak specialties (€7-27) and infamous for the cowhide wallpaper. Salads €4.50-5.70. Open daily 1-5pm and 9pm-midnight. AmEx/MC/V. ❹

◎ SIGHTS

▨ **MUSEO DE AMÉRICA.** This under-appreciated museum reopened after painstaking renovations; it is now a must-see. It documents the cultures of America's pre-Columbian civilizations and the legacy of Spanish conquest with detail and insight. The wealth of Pre-Columbian artifacts include tools, pottery, codices, ceremonial and daily dress, funereal shrouds, and mummies. Colonial accounts and artwork provide insight into the conquistadors' perspectives on the peoples encountered. Especially fascinating are instructional paintings depicting mixed families and the various ethnic identities assigned their offspring. To fully appreciate the museum's offerings, visitors should set aside an entire morning or afternoon for all the exhibits. A reading knowledge of Spanish is helpful for detailed understanding, although the English brochure provides a solid overview. *(Av. de los Reyes Católicos, 6, next to the Faro de Moncloa. ☎915 49 26 41. M: Moncloa. Open Tu-Su 9:30am-3pm. €3, students €1.50, under 18 and over 65 free. Su free.)*

TEMPLO DE DEBOD. Built by Pharaoh Zakheramon in the 4th century BC, it's the only Egyptian temple in Spain. The Egyptian government shipped the temple stone by stone to Spain in appreciation of Spanish archaeologists who helped rescue the Abu Simbel temples from the floods of the Aswan dam. The **Parque de la Montaña** is home to the temple and two of its three original gateways and provides a peaceful haven with beautiful views. At ▧sunset, marvel at the landscape from the lookout points. *(M: Ventura Rodríguez. From the Metro, walk down C. Ventura Rodríguez to Parque de la Montaña; the temple is on the left. ☎917 65 10 08. Open Apr. 1-Sept. 31 Tu-F 10am-2pm and 4-8pm; Sa-Su 10am-2pm. Oct. 1-Mar. 1 Tu-F 9:45am-1:15pm and 4:15-5:45pm, Sa-Su 9:45am-1:45pm. Free. Parque free and open daily year-round.)*

ERMITA DE SAN ANTONIO DE LA FLORIDA. Although out of the way, the Ermita is worth the trouble. It contains Goya's pantheon—a frescoed dome arches above his buried corpse. Goya's skull, apparently stolen by a phrenologist, was missing when the corpse arrived from France. Every 12th of June, single *madrileñas* pay homage to San Antonio's statue to beg his help in the husband-hunt. *(M: Príncipe Pío. From the Metro, go left on C. de Buen Altamirano, walk through the park, and turn left on Po. de la Florida; the Ermita is at the end of the street. ☎915 42 07 22. Open Tu-F 10am-2pm and 4-8pm, Sa-Su 10am-2pm. Free.)*

CASA DEL CAMPO. Take the **Teleférico** from Rosales into the city's largest park. Shaded by pines, oaks, and cypresses, large numbers of families, joggers, and walkers roam the grounds by day. Early morning reveals evidence of questionable nighttime activities; it's wise to stay away after dark. Inside the amusement park, **Parque de Atracciones,** relive your childhood on the roller coaster. One of Madrid's

MADRID

largest pools is in the corner of the park, next to M: Lago. *(Take bus #33 or M: Batán. Walk up the main street away from the lake.* ☎914 63 29 00; www.parquedeatracciones.es. *Open Su-F noon-11pm, Sa noon-midnight.)* The **Zoo/Aquarium** is 5min. away. *(*☎915 12 37 70. *Open M-F 10:30am-8pm, Sa-Su 10:30am-9:30pm. €12.75, children under 8 €10.30.)*

MUSEO CERRALBO. This unusual palatial museum displays an eclectic collection of furniture and ornamentation, including a Louis XVI-style French piano. El Greco's *The Ecstasy of Saint Francis* adorns the chapel. *(C. Ventura Rodríguez, 17.* ☎915 47 36 46. *M: Ventura Rodríguez or Pl. de España. Open Tu-Sa 9:30am-3pm, Su 10am-3pm. €2.40, students €1.20, under 18 and over 65 free. W and Su free.)*

OTHER SIGHTS. The **Parque del Oeste** is a large, sloping park known for the **Rosaleda** (rose garden) at its bottom. A yearly competition determines which award-winning rose will be added to the permanent collection. *(M: Moncloa. From the Metro, take C. de la Princesa. Garden open daily 10am-8pm.)* A prime example of Fascist Neoclassicism, the arcaded **Cuartel General del Aire (Ejército del Aire)** commands the view on the other side of the Arco de la Victoria (by the Moncloa Metro station). The renovation of Felipe V's soldiers' barracks has produced one of Madrid's finest cultural centers, the **Centro Cultural Conde Duque,** which hosts travelling exhibitions. *(C. Conde Duque, 11.* ☎915 88 58 34. *M: Noviciado.)* The fabulous **Museo de América** (see p. 137) is a bit farther down the avenue, past the **Arco de Moncloa.** The **Faro de Moncloa** is a 92m high metal tower near the museum that offers views of the city. On a clear day, you can see El Escorial. *(Av. Arco de la Victoria.* ☎915 44 81 04. *Open Tu-Su 10am-2pm, 5-8pm. To ascend the Faro de Moncloa €1, over 65 and under 10 €0.50)*

BILBAO

The area north of Glorieta de Bilbao (M: Bilbao), in the "V" formed by C. de Fuencarral and C. de Luchana including Pl. de Olavide, is the ethnic food nexus of Madrid; it overflows with bars, clubs, cafes, and restaurants of all nationalities. **Calle Hartzenbusch** and **Calle Cisneros** present endless options for cheap *tapas* to the youthful crowd that swarms the area at night. In the student-filled streets radiating from **Glorieta de Bilbao,** it's easy to find a cheap drink. Although discos are plentiful, revelers don't come here to dance; it's the *terrazas* that are packed late into the night with lively customers sipping icy Mahou on Pl. de Olavide, C. de Fuencarral, and C. de Luchana.

◻ FOOD

▦ **Osteria Il Regno de Napoli,** C. San Andrés, 21 (☎914 45 63 00). From Gl. de Bilbao, head 1 block down C. Carranza. Delicious Italian cuisine in an understatedly hip environment. Lunch *menú* €10; dinner entrees €7.85-12. Reserve ahead on weekends. Open M-F 2-4pm and 9pm-midnight, Sa 9pm-midnight, Su 2-4pm. AmEx/MC/V. ❷

El Carabinero, C. Cardenal Cisneros, 33 (☎914 47 68 28). Don't worry if you can't get a table at this festive local right away: pass the time at the bar with sangría and some *tapas. Raciones* €4.50-18; *menú* €7.50. Open M-Sa 1-5pm and 8pm-1am. ❷

Arepas con Todo, C. Hartzenbusch, 19 (☎914 48 75 45), off C. Cardenal Cisneros from C. de Luchana. Hanging gourds and waitresses in festive dress fill this classic Colombian restaurant. A rotating *menú* (€10-12), plus 60 fixed dishes (€11-14.50). Only the live music repeats itself. For dinner, make reservations. Open daily 2pm-1am. MC/V. ❸

Collage, C. de Olid, 6 (☎914 48 45 62), 3rd street on the right off C. de Fuencarral. M: Bilbao. A group of Swedish chefs mix and match in style. Entrees €10.95-17.45. *Menú* €7.50. Open M 1:30-4pm, Tu-F 1:30-4pm and 8:30pm-midnight, Sa 8:30pm-midnight. AmEx/MC/V. ❸

Bar Samara, C. Cardenal Cisneros, 13 (☎914 48 80 56). From M: Bilbao, walk up C. de Luchana and take a quick left. Bills itself as Egyptian. Middle Eastern staples. Kebabs and other entrees €11-15. Open Tu-Th 2-4pm and 8:30pm-midnight, F-Su 2-4pm and 8:30pm-1am. ❸

☕ NIGHTLIFE

Barnon, C. de Santa Engracia, 17 (☎914 47 38 87). M: Alonso Martínez or Tribunal. Barnon actually bars many from its hip-hop scene if you're not as cool as the owner, Real Madrid's stud *fútbol* forward. Dress well. Tu is salsa night, free lessons 11pm-midnight. Drinks €10. Open Su and W-Sa 9pm-6am.

Clamores Jazz Club, C. Albuquerque, 14 (☎914 45 79 38), off C. Cardenal Cisneros. M: Bilbao. Swanky, neon setting and Madrid's more interesting jazz. The cover (€3-9) gets slipped into the bill if you're there for the jazz, starting around 10pm Tu-Su. Check posters outside and arrive early for a seat. Open M-Th and Su 6:30pm-3am, F-Sa 6pm-4am.

Big Bamboo, C. del Barquillo, 42 (☎915 62 88 38). M: Alonso Martínez. Infiltrate the Rasta scene at this international club that grooves to smooth reggae. W and Th theater shows. Drinks €2.40-3. Open M-Th 10:30pm-6am, F-Sa 10:30pm-7am.

PARQUE DEL BUEN RETIRO

With the construction of the 300-acre Parque del Buen Retiro, Felipe IV intended to transform the former hunting grounds into a personal retreat, *un buen retiro.* Today, the magnificent park and its accompanying gardens are filled with palm-readers, sunbathers, young couples, soccer players, reflective students, and occasional drug pushers (just ignore them and they should leave you alone). The northeast corner of the park enchants with medieval monastic ruins and waterfalls. The park also houses the spectacular Palacio de Cristal and Estanque Grande. On weekends, the promenades fill with musicians, families, and young lovers; on summer nights (when only the north gate remains open), the lively bars and cafes scattered around the park become quite active. The park is easily accessible from the Retiro Metro stop. There are four park entrances: C. Alfonso XII, C. de Alcalá, Pl. de la Independencia, and Av. Menéndez y Pelayo. Avoid venturing alone after dark.

ESTANQUE GRANDE. Overlooked by Alfonso XII's mausoleum, rowers crowd the rectangular lake in the middle of the park, the Estanque Grande. The lake has been the social center of El Retiro ever since aspiring caricaturists, fortune-tellers, and sunflower-seed vendors first parked their goods along its marble shores. The colonnaded monument is the perfect spot for late afternoon relaxation and people-watching. *(The Pl. de la Independencia entrance leads to Av. de Méjico, the path to the lake.)*

PALACIO DE VELÁZQUEZ. This Velázquez creation has billowing ceilings, marble floors, and ideal lighting. The Palacio de Velázquez exhibits works in conjunction with the Museo Nacional Centro de Arte Reina Sofía (see p. 127). Exhibits change quite frequently. *(From the Estanque, walk straight to Pl. de Honduras and turn left on Po. Venezuela. The palace will be on your right. ☎915 73 62 45. Open M and W-Sa Apr.- Sept. 11am-8pm, Su 11am-6pm; Oct.-Mar. 10am-6pm, also Su 10am-4pm. Free.)*

PALACIO DE CRISTAL. Built by Ricardo Velázquez to exhibit flowers from the Philippines in 1887, this exquisite steel-and-glass structure hosts a variety of art shows and exhibits, with subjects ranging from Bugs Bunny to Spanish portraiture to vocal recognition of bird calls. *(From Palacio de Velázquez, head out the main door until you reach the lake and the palace. ☎915 74 66 14. Open M and W-Sa Apr.- Sept. 11am-8pm, Su 11am-6pm; Oct.-Mar. 10am-6pm, also Su 10am-4pm. Free.)*

MADRID

OTHER SIGHTS. Bullets from the 1921 assassination of prime minister Eduardo Dato permanently scarred the eastern face of the Puerta de Alcalá (1778), outside El Retiro's Puerta de la Independencia. To the south, the Casón del Buen Retiro faces the park (see p. 127); behind it sits the Museo del Ejército. In this stately fragment of the Casón del Buen Retiro stands a vast collection of over 27,000 artifacts tracing the history of the Spanish military. Each room is dedicated to a different period or conquest; the most famous contains the *Tizona* sword of El Cid Campeador and a fragment of the cross Columbus was wearing when he arrived in the New World. The two buildings are remnants of Felipe IV's palace, which burned down in 1764. *(C. Méndez Núñez, 1. ☎915 22 89 77. M: Retiro or Banco de España. Open Tu-Su 10am-2pm. €0.60, students €0.30, under 18 and over 65 free. Sa free.)*

EL PARDO

Built as a hunting lodge for Carlos I in 1547, El Pardo was enlarged by generations of Habsburgs and Bourbons. Though Spain's growing capital eventually engulfed El Pardo, it still stands as one of Spain's greatest country palaces. El Pardo gained attention in 1940 when Franco decided to make it his home; he resided here until his death in 1975. Although politics have changed, the palace is still the official reception site for distinguished foreign visitors. Renowned for its collection of **tapestries**—several of which were designed by Goya—the palace also holds a Velázquez painting and Ribera's *Techo de los hombres ilustres (Ceiling of the Illustrious Men)*. You can also see the bedroom cabinet in which Franco kept Santa Teresa's silver-encrusted hand. Entrance to the palace's **capilla** and the nearby **Casita del Príncipe,** created by Juan de Villanueva of Museo del Prado fame, is free. *(Take bus #601 from the stop in front of the Ejército del Aire building above M: Moncloa (every 15min., €0.95). ☎913 76 15 00. Palace open Apr.-Sept. M-Sa 10:30am-6pm, Su 9:25am-1:40pm; Oct.-Mar. M-Sa 10:30am-5pm, Su 9:55am-1:40pm. Compulsory 45min. guided tour in Spanish. €3, students €1.50. W free for EU citizens.)*

◪ THE PASEOS: A WALKING TOUR

Madrid's thoroughfare *paseos* connect the city through three fused segments, **Paseo del Prado, Paseo de Recoletos,** and **Paseo de la Castellana,** running from Madrid-Atocha in the south to Madrid-Chamartín in the north. The *paseos* are a great starting point for walking tours, since most major sights branch out from these main avenues. Plants, gardens, and cafes separate traffic in pleasant median oases along your stroll. A walking tour could last several hours, an entire day, or even several days, depending on how much time you want to spend at the various sights and how far you stray from the main *paseo* paths. You may be tempted to head to El Retiro after the Museo del Prado, or venture to Puerta del Sol once you have reached Pl. de la Cibeles. Regardless of the path chosen, the *paseos* are a simple way to acquaint yourself with the city and organize a daily itinerary.

The Paseo del Prado connects Atocha to Pl. de la Cibeles, passing the **Museo del Prado** (p. 126), the **Museo Thyssen-Bornemisza** (p. 128), and the Ritz Hotel. Along the Paseo de Recoletos, extending from Pl. de la Cibeles to Pl. de Colón, the *nouveaux riche* congregate at luxuriously shaded *terrazas*. Contemporary Madrid stretches farther north along Po. de la Castellana (lined with bank buildings from the 1970s and 80s) to Pl. de Castilla's *Puerta de Europa* (leaning twin towers).

PASEO DEL PRADO

Modeled after the Piazza Navona in Rome, Paseo del Prado is the center of Madrid's art district. Virtually every major museum is in the vicinity of this museum mile, known as the *triángulo de arte*. Directly across from Estación Atocha, the **Museo Nacional Centro de Arte Reina Sofía** (p. 127), home of Picasso's *Guernica*, presides over Pl. del Emperador Carlos V. Its innovative glass elevators and outdoor sculptures hint at the impressive collection of modern art within.

Walking up Po. del Prado, you'll pass the **Real Jardín Botánico** on the right. Opened during Carlos III's reign, the garden showcases over 30,000 species of plants, ranging from traditional roses to medicinal herbs. Just about anyone will appreciate the garden's vast collection of imported trees, bushes, and flowers. *(Pl. de Murillo, 2, next to the Prado.* ☎ *914 20 30 17; www.rjb.csic.es. Open in summer daily 10am-9pm; winter 10am-6pm; spring and fall 10am-7pm.* €*1.50, students* €*0.75.)* Next to the garden is the world-renowned **Museo del Prado** (p. 126) and behind it, on C. Ruiz de Alarcón, stands the **Iglesia de San Jerónimo**, Madrid's royal church. Built by Hieronymite monks and re-endowed by *los Reyes Catolicos,* the church has witnessed a few joyous milestones, including the coronation of Fernando and Isabel and the marriage of King Alfonso XIII. These days, only the highest of high-society weddings are held in the church. *(Open daily 8am-1:30pm and 5-8:30pm.)* Back on Po. del Prado, to the north in Pl. de la Lealtad, stands the **Obelisco a los Mártires del 2 de Mayo,** filled with the ashes of those who died in the 1808 uprising against Napoleon. Its four statues represent Constancy, Virtue, Valor, and Patriotism, and the flame burns continuously in honor of the patriots. Behind the memorial sits the colonnaded Greco-Roman-style **Bolsa de Madrid** (Stock Exchange), designed by Repullés. Ventura Rodríguez's **Fuente de Neptuno,** in Pl. Cánovas de Castillo, is one of three aquatic masterpieces along the avenue. Crossing the plaza will bring you to another of Madrid's great museums, the **Museo Thyssen-Bornemisza** (p. 128).

The arts of the Po. del Prado meld into the Po. de Recoletos at the tulip-encircled **Plaza de la Cibeles** (see **Sex in the Cibeles,** below). *Madrileños* protected this emblem of their city (best viewed at dusk) during Franco's bomb raids by covering it with a pyramid of sandbags. From the plaza, the small **Museo Naval** is to the right. *(Entrance at Po. del Prado, 5.* ☎ *913 79 52 99; www.armada.mde.es. Open Tu-Su 10am-1:30pm. Closed Aug. Free.)* In the southeast corner of the plaza sits the spectacular neo-Baroque **Palacio de Comunicaciones** (p. 105), designed by Antonio Palacios and Julián Otamendi of Otto Wagner's Vienna School in 1920. Looking to your right up C. de Alcalá from the Palacio de Comunicaciones is Sabatini's **Puerta de Alcalá,** the 18th-century emblematic gateway and court symbol. On the northeastern corner of the plaza roundabout (behind black gates) is the former **Palacio de Linares,** a 19th-century townhouse built for Madrid nobility. Proven by a team of "scientists" to be inhabited by ghosts, it was transformed into the **Casa de América,** with a library and lecture halls for the study of Latin American culture and politics. It sponsors art exhibitions, tours of the palace, and guest lectures. *(Po. de Recoletos, 2. M: Banco de España.* ☎ *915 95 48 00. Open Tu-Sa 11am-2pm and 5-8pm, Su 11am-2pm.)*

SEX IN THE CIBELES

The Plaza de la Cibeles, with its infamous marble fountain, has been Madrid's spiritual center since its construction in 1781. Depicting the fertility goddess's triumph over the emblematic Castilian lions, the fountain's image of Cybele has long captivated citizens. Legend has it that the fleet-footed Atlanta, one of Cybele's maids, would take as her lover only the man who could outrun her. No man was up to the challenge until one cunning suitor instructed his cohorts to scatter golden apples (as distractions) in Atlanta's path. The goddess Cybele, watching the prank, was overcome with rage at men's evil ways. After punishing the plotters by turning them into lions, she hitched them to her own carriage. This assertion of power and sexuality charmed Madrid, resulting in the proverb *"más popular que Cibeles."*

PASEO DE RECOLETOS

Continuing north toward the brown Torres de Colón (Towers of Columbus), you'll pass the Biblioteca Nacional (National Library), where the sleek Museo del Libro displays treasures from the monarchy's collection, including a first edition copy of *Don Quijote. (Entrance at #20. Open Tu-Sa 10am-9pm, Su 10am-2pm. Free.)* Behind the library lies the massive **Museo Arqueológico Nacional.** After countless moves,

Madrid's display of the history of the Western world settled in this huge museum in 1895. Founded by a decree of Isabel II, the museum houses an astounding collection of items from Spain's past, including the country's most famous archaeological find, *Dama de Elche*, a 4th-century funerary urn, Felipe II's astrolabe, and a 16th-century porcelain clock belonging to Lady Baza. Outside stands a replica of the Altamira caves and their Paleolithic paintings. *(C. Serrano 13.* ☎ *915 77 79 12; www.man.es. M: Serrano. Open Tu-Sa 9:30am-8:30pm; summer 9:30am-6:30pm, Su 9:30am-2:30pm; winter 9:30am-2pm. €3. Sa after 2:30pm and Su free.)* The museum entrance is on C. Serrano, an avenue lined with pricy boutiques in the posh **Barrio de Salamanca.** The museum and library huddle just beyond the modern **Plaza de Colón** (M: Colón) and the adjoining **Jardines del Descubrimiento** (Gardens of Discovery). At one side loom huge clay boulders, inscribed with trivia about the New World, including Seneca's prediction of its discovery, the names of the mariners on board the caravels, and passages from Columbus's diary. From a thundering fountain in the center of the plaza rises a neo-Gothic spire honoring Columbus. A huge inlaid map detailing Columbus's journey covers the wall behind the waterfall. Concerts, lectures, ballets, and plays are held in the **Centro Cultural de la Villa** (☎ 914 80 03 00), the municipal art center beneath the statue and waterfall.

PASEO DE LA CASTELLANA

Nineteenth- and early 20th-century aristocrats dislodged themselves from Old Madrid to settle along Po. de la Castellana. During the Spanish Civil War, Republican forces used the mansions as barracks. Most were torn down in the 1960s when banks and insurance companies commissioned new, more innovative structures. Competition begat architectural excellence, offering the lowly pedestrian a rich man's spectacle of architecture and fashion. Some notables include: Rafael Moneo's **Bankinter,** #29, the first to integrate rather than demolish a townhouse; **Banco Urquijo,** known as "the coffeepot;" the Sevillian-tiled **Edificio ABC,** #34, former office of the conservative, monarchical newspaper and now a shopping center; the pink **Edificio Bankunion,** #46; **Banca Catalana Occidente,** #50, which looks like an ice cube on a cracker; and the famous **Edificio La Caixa,** #61.

Just south of the American Embassy, between Pl. de Colón and Glorieta de Emilio Castelar, is an **open-air sculpture museum** displaying works by Joan Miró, González, and Eduardo Chillida. Look up—works also hang from the bridge. Intimate, private museums, including the **Museo Lázaro Galdiano** (p. 142), are just off Po. de la Castellana. At **Plaza de Lima** is the 110,000-seat **Estadio Santiago Bernabéu** (M: Lima), home to the beloved **Real Madrid** soccer club, winner of its 9th European Championship in 2002 and its 29th Spanish La Liga Championship in 2003. Farther north, the **Puerta de Europa,** with its two 27-story leaning towers connected by a tunnel, dominates Pl. de Castilla (M: Pl. de Castilla). They were designed by American John Bergee as a doorway to the city.

MUSEO LÁZARO GALDIANO. This small palace, once owned by 19th-century financier Lázaro Galdiano, displays a private collection of Italian Renaissance bronzes and Celtic and Visigoth brasses. Paintings include Leonardo da Vinci's *The Savior* and Hieronymus Bosch's *Ecce Homo*, as well as works by the Spanish trifecta: El Greco, Velázquez, and Goya. *(C. Serrano, 122. Turn right off Po. de la Castellana onto C. María de Molina.* ☎ *915 61 60 84. M: Rubén Darío or Núñez de Balboa. Closed for renovations until at least 2004.)*

MUSEO SOROLLA. The former residence and studio of the Valencian painter displays his own priceless paintings and sculptures, accompanied by works of other painters of his time. Sorolla's charming house and garden are as captivating as his work, including *Trata de Blancas* and *Clotilde con traje de noche*. *(Po. General Martínez Campos, 37.* ☎ *913 10 15 84. M: Iglesia or Rubén Darío. Open Tu-Sa 9:30am-3pm, Su 10am-3pm. €2.40, students €1.20. Su Free.)*

THE RIGHT TO PARTY After 40 years of Franco-imposed repression, Madrid was a cultural explosion waiting to happen. Franco's death in 1975 served as a catalyst for change; not a day passed before every newspaper printed a pornographic photo on its front page. *El Destapeo* ("the uncorking" or "uncovering" that followed Franco's regime) and *La Movida* ("the Movement," which took place a few years later) exploded in Madrid, inspiring political diversity, apolitical revelry, and eccentricity of all kinds. Filmmaker Pedro Almodóvar became a reflection of the movement and its most famous member, creating farcical films about loony grandmothers, outgoing young women, unapologetic homosexuals, and troubled students. Gradually, *La Movida* became too much for the city. Artists and club-rats were forced to give up their favorite pastimes for practical jobs—no one could afford to keep up the careless and eccentric lifestyle that *La Movida* represented. Remnants of *La Movida* are still visible, however, in today's outrageous clubs, ambitious bars, and in the excitement of young *madrileños* planning to *ir de marcha* ("to party," literally "to go marching"). Madrid is one of the hardest-working and hardest-partying cities in the world.

▣ DAYTRIP FROM MADRID

SAN LORENZO DE EL ESCORIAL ☎918

San Lorenzo's El Escorial—half monastery and half mausoleum—is the most popular daytrip from Madrid. Although Felipe II constructed El Escorial primarily for himself and God, the complex, with its magnificent library, palaces, and art, seems as if it were made for tourists. Visits are popular during the *Fiestas de San Lorenzo* (August 10-20), when parades of giant figures line the streets and fireworks fill the sky, and on *Romería a la Ermita de la Virgen de Grácia*, the second Sunday in September, when folk dancing contests fill the forests. The whole town shuts down on Mondays.

▣▣ TRANSPORTATION & PRACTICAL INFORMATION. Autocares Herranz buses (☎918 96 90 28) travel from Madrid's **Moncloa Metro station** to El Escorial (50min.; every 15min. M-F 6:55am-11:30pm, Sa 9am-10:15pm, Su 9am-11pm; €2.85) and back (every 15min. M-F 6am-10:30pm, Sa 7:45am-9pm, Su 7:45am-10pm; €2.85). El Escorial's **train station** (☎918 90 00 15, RENFE info 902 24 02 02), on Ctra. Estación, is 2km outside of town. Trains run to **Atocha** and **Chamartín** stations in **Madrid** (1hr.; M-F 9 per day, Sa-Su 5 per day 10:15am-9:26pm; round-trip €2.65). The **tourist office** is beneath an archway near the monastery at C. Grimaldi, 2. (☎/fax 918 90 53 13; www.sanlorenzodeelescorial.org. Open M-Th 11am-6pm, F-Su 10am-7pm.) With your back to the **bus station,** turn right down C. Juan de Toledo, then make a right onto C. Floridablanca. Follow C. Floridablanca until the first archway on your left. From the **train station,** take the shuttle to the bus station (M-F every 15-20min. 7:23am-10:38pm, Sa-Su every 20-60min. 9:44am-10:38pm; €0.90) or exit the train station, walk straight ahead, and follow the signs (25min. walk uphill). For a more peaceful walk, exit the train station and enter the Casita del Príncipe main entrance straight ahead. Start walking uphill and take the C. de los Tilos path, which leaves you by the monastery (25min.). In an **emergency** call ☎112 or the **police,** Pl. de la Constitución, 1 (☎918 90 52 23).

▣▣ ACCOMMODATIONS & FOOD. Because of its proximity to Madrid, El Escorial is usually done as a daytrip. However, for those wishing to stay, **Hostal Cristina ❸,** C. Calvario, 45, fits the bill with private baths, TVs, and phones. (☎918 90 19 61; fax 90 12 04. July-Aug. doubles €45; rest of year €43. MC/V.) To reach **Residencia Juvenil El Escorial (HI) ❶,** C. Residencia, 14, from C. del Rey, turn right on

C. Tozas, left onto C. Claudio Coello, left again onto Po. Unamuno, then right onto C. Residencia. (☎918 90 59 24; fax 90 06 20. HI card required. Closed Sept. Laundry €2. Dorms €7.80, with dinner €10.60, with lunch and dinner €12.70; over 26 €10.80/€14/€16.80. IVA not included. MC/V.) **Restaurante El Trillo ❷**, C. Cervantes, 6, a straight shot uphill from the tourist office, serves a traditional *menú* indoors for €7, outside for €8. (☎680 18 90 34. Open daily 1:30-4:30pm and 8pm-midnight. MC/V.) Self-caterers head to **Mercado San Lorenzo**, C. del Rey, 7, just off the central plaza. (Open M-Sa 9am-2pm and 6-9pm.)

EL ESCORIAL

☎918 90 59 03 or 90 59 04. Complex open Tu-Su Apr.-Sept. 10am-6pm; Oct.-Mar. 10am-5pm. Last admission to palaces, pantheons, and museums 1hr. before closing. Complete visit takes 2hr. Spanish tours leave every 15min.; ask at the desk for the next English tour. Monastery €7, students and seniors €3.50, guided tour €8. W free for EU citizens. A joint admission ticket is available for both El Escorial and El Valle de los Caídos. €9.50 with guide, €8.50 without guide, students €5.)

MONASTERIO. Felipe II built the **Monasterio de San Lorenzo del Escorial** as a gift to God, his people, and himself to commemorate his victory over the French at the battle of San Quintín in 1557. He commissioned Juan Bautista de Toledo to design the monastery-mausoleum complex four years later; Juan de Herrera inherited the job when Toledo died in 1567. Except for the Panteón Real and minor additions, the monastery was completed in just 21 years. Felipe oversaw much of the work from a chair-shaped rock, **Silla de Felipe II** (Felipe's Chair), 7km from the site.

Considering the resources Felipe II commanded, the building is noteworthy for its symmetry and simplicity; Felipe himself described it as "majesty without ostentation." Honoring the *desornamentado* style, the monastery is pieced together with granite hewn from surrounding quarries. The entire structure is built around a gridiron pattern: four massive towers pin the corners, and a great dome surmounts the towers of the central basilica, giving the ensemble a pyramidal shape. At Felipe II's behest, steep slate roofs—the first of their kind in Spain—were introduced from Flanders. Slate spires lend grace to the grim structure, further mellowed by the glowing *Colmenar* stone.

GALLERIES & LIVING QUARTERS. To avoid the worst of the crowds, enter El Escorial through the traditional gateway on C. Floridablanca, where you'll find a collection of Flemish tapestries and paintings. The collection exudes much of the same severity as the monastery, with somber works like El Greco's *Martirio de San Mauricio y la Legión* and Roger van der Weyden's glowing *Calvary*. The adjacent **Museo de Arquitectura and Pintura** has an exhibition comparing El Escorial's construction to that of other related structures and displays wooden models of 16th-century machinery. Though masterpieces by Bosch, Durer, El Greco, Tintoretto, Titian, Van Dyck, and Zurbarán still adorn the walls, most of the collection is now housed in Madrid's Museo del Prado.

Azulejos (tiles) from Toledo line the **Palacio Real,** which includes the **Salón del Trono** (Throne Room) and two dwellings: Felipe II's spartan 16th-century apartments and the more luxurious 18th-century rooms of Carlos III and Carlos IV. Pastoral images inundate the **Puertas de Marguetería,** German doors painstakingly carved from 18 species of wood. The **Sala de Batallas** (Battle Room) links the two parts of the palace with frescoes by Italian artists Grabelo and Castello. The walls and ceiling trumpet first Castile's and then united Spain's greatest victories— including Juan II's 1431 triumph over the Muslims at Higueruela, Felipe's II's successful expeditions in the Azores, and the Battle of San Quintín. Maps line the walls; the last one on the right portrays the world as (mis)understood by 16th-century Europeans. Downstairs in the royal chambers, Felipe II's miniscule bed attests to his asceticism.

LIBRARY. The **biblioteca** on the second floor holds numerous priceless books and manuscripts, though several fires have reduced the collection. Alfonso X's *Cantigas de Santa María*, the Book of Hours of the Catholic monarchs, Saint Teresa's manuscripts and diary, the gold-scrolled *Aureus Codex* (by German Emperor Conrad III, 1039), and an 11th-century *Commentary on the Apocalypse* by Beato de Liébana are just a sampling of the manuscripts. Allegorical frescoes of the quadrivium and trivium (seven fields of knowledge) grace the ceiling.

BASILICA. The lower cloister leads to the basilica. Marble steps arrive at an altar adorned by two groups of sculptures. The figures on the left represent assorted relatives of Felipe II, including his parents Carlos I and Isabel, his daughter María, and his sisters María (Queen of Hungary) and Leonor (Queen of France). Those on the right depict Felipe II with his three successive wives and his son Carlos. The **Coro Alto** (High Choir) has a magnificent ceiling fresco of an angel-filled heaven. The **cloister** shines under Titian's fresco of the martyrdom of San Lorenzo.

PANTHEONS. The nearby **Panteón Real**, filled with tombs of past monarchs, glistens with intricate gold and marble designs completed in 1654. Felipe II ordered that its design allow for Mass to be conducted over his father's tomb. The connecting **Pudreria**, where bodies dried before interment, is thankfully out of commission. Two centuries later, the **Panteón de los Infantes** was built for the youngest of the royals and has space for over 50 infants. It is rumored that many of the royalty's illegitimate children, including a son of Charles V, lie within the crypts.

CASITAS. Commissioned by the Prince of Asturias, later to become Carlos IV, the **Casita del Príncipe** displays a collection of ornaments, including chandeliers, lamps, rugs, furniture, clocks, tapestries, china, and engraved oranges. Though the French roughed up the *casita* during the Napoleonic invasions, Fernando VII later redecorated many rooms in the then-popular Empire style. *(Approx. 1km from the monastery on the way to Madrid. Call ahead for reservations ☎918 90 59 03 weekdays, 90 04 21 weekends. Open Sa-Su 10am-1pm and 4-6:30pm. Visitors may enter only with a guided tour (every 30min.); 10-person max.; €3.60 per person, students and seniors €1.80.)* The simpler **Casita del Infante,** commissioned as a retreat in the mid-16th century by Carlos's brother, Gabriel de Borbón, was meant to entertain guests with stunning views and musical performances. *(Open Semana Santa and July-Sept. Tu-Su 10am-7pm; final entrance 30min. before closing. €3.40)*

NEAR EL ESCORIAL: EL VALLE DE LOS CAÍDOS

El Valle de los Caídos is accessible only via El Escorial. Autocares Herranz runs one bus to the monument. (☎918 90 41 25 or 96 90 28. 20min., leaves El Escorial from C. Juan de Toledo Tu-Su 3:15pm and returns 5:30pm, round-trip plus admission €7.70, funicular not included. Mass M-Sa 11am; Su 11am, 12:30, 1, and 5:30pm. Entrance gate open Tu-Su 10am-6pm. €5, seniors and students €2.50. W free for EU citizens. Funicular to the cross €2.50. A joint admission ticket is availble for both El Escorial and El Valle de los Caídos. €9.50 with guide, €8.50 without guide, students €5.)

In a once-untouched valley 8km north of El Escorial, General Franco forced Republican prisoners to build the overpowering monument of Santa Cruz del Valle de los Caídos (Holy Cross of the Valley of the Fallen) as a memorial to those who gave their lives in the Spanish Civil War. Although ostensibly a monument to both sides, the massive granite cross (150m tall and 46m wide) implicitly honors only those who died "serving Dios and España" (i.e. the Fascist Nationalists)—many who worked on the monument also died under the grueling conditions of its construction. To climb to the base of the cross, use the stairs adjacent to the automatic lift or follow the paved road up to the trailhead just past the monastery on the right. Apocalyptic tapestries line the cave-like **basilica,** where lies the ghost of Fascist architecture; death-angels carry swords and angry light fixtures. Behind the chapel walls lie 40,000 dead. Beside the high altar, located directly underneath the mammoth cross with its mammoth statues, rest **José Antonio Primo de Rivera** (founder of the Fascist Falange party) and General Franco himself.

COMUNIDAD DE MADRID

The Comunidad de Madrid is an autonomous administrative region smack in the middle of Spain, bordered by Castilla y León to the north and west and Castilla La Mancha to the south and east. Beyond Madrid proper, the Comunidad offers travelers a variety of daytrips to exquisite cultural landscapes and small town serenity.

ALCALÁ DE HENARES

Alcalá de Henares (pop. 165,000) draws intellectuals desiring to continue the tradition of the city's distinguished offspring, including Golden Age authors Miguel de Cervantes, Francisco de Quevedo, and Lope de Vega. Alcalá's history and exceptional Renaissance architecture make the city well worth a peek.

TRANSPORTATION & PRACTICAL INFORMATION. The **train station** is on Po. de la Estación (☎915 63 02 02). **Cercanías** trains run to Estación Atocha in **Madrid** (50min., daily every 10min. 6:30am-9:16pm, €2.10). **Continental Auto,** Av. Guadalajara, 5 (☎918 88 16 22), runs buses between Alcalá and **Madrid** (45min.; M-Sa every 15min. 6:15am-10:45pm, Su every 30min. 7-9am and every 20min. 9am-11pm; €1.83). To reach the city center from the bus station, turn right on Av. Guadalajara and continue as it turns into C. de Libreros. The **tourist office,** Callejón de Santa María, 1, at Pl. de Cervantes, has a map and a list of accommodations and restaurants. (☎918 89 26 94. Open June and Sept. daily 10am-2pm and 5-7:30pm; July-Aug. Tu-Sa 10am-2pm and 5-7:30pm; Oct.-May 10am-2pm and 4-6:30pm.) **ATMs** line C. de Libreros, and **Banco Santander Central Hispano** is at C. de Libreros, 19. Important phone numbers include **emergency** ☎112; **ambulance** ☎061; and **police** ☎918 81 92 63. **Existen,** C. Mayor, 73, offers cheap and speedy **Internet access.** (☎918 83 06 70. €0.80 per 30min., €1.50 per hr. Open M-Sa 10am-midnight, Su noon-midnight.) The **post office** is at Pl. de Cervantes, 5. (☎918 89 23 34. Open M-F 8:30am-8:30pm, Sa 9:30am-1pm.) The **postal code** ranges from 28801 to 28807.

ACCOMMODATIONS & FOOD. Some of the least expensive rooms are at **Hostal Jacinto ❷,** Po. de la Estación, 2, 2nd staircase, 1-D. Pleasant tiled rooms all have sinks, TVs, and winter heat. (☎/fax 918 89 14 32. Singles with shower €22; doubles €34, with bath €37; triples €40.) Or, try **Hostal El Torero ❷,** Av. de Madrid, 14, past Pl. de los Santos Niños. (☎918 89 03 73. Singles €19; doubles with bath €34.40.) Alcalá's famed *almendras garrapiñadas* (honey- and sugar-coated almonds) beg to be sampled. For fantastically cheap *menús*, take C. Mayor from Pl. de Cervantes and check out the restaurants on the right side of the street. Try **El Gringo Viejo ❸,** C. Ramón y Cajal, 8, for great Mexican entrees (€6-17) and burgers. (☎918 78 89 01. Open M-Th 8:30am-midnight, F 8:30am-1am, Sa 10:30am-1am, Su 11am-midnight. MC/V.) For groceries, stop at the gigantic **Champion** behind the bus station on Vía Complutense. From the train station, take a left at the traffic circle. (☎918 89 36 37. Open June 15-Sept. 15 M-Sa 9am-10pm; Sept. 16-June 14 M-Sa 9:15am-9:15pm. MC/V.) **El Ruedo ❶,** C. de Libreros, 38, through the archway on the left side of the street if walking toward Pl. de Cervantes, offers a welcome break from heavy *comida típica* with a menu full of delicious crêpes and desserts. Vegetarian options abound. (☎918 80 69 19. Crêpes €4.50-12. Pitas and pastas €4.50-6.50. Lunch *menú* €6.60. Open M-F 8:30am-midnight, Sa-Su 8:30am-1am.)

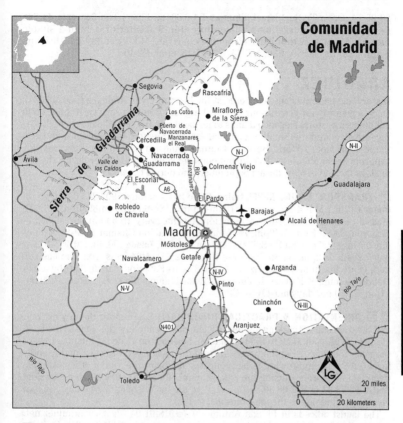

Comunidad
de Madrid

Segovia
Rascafría
Los Cotos
Miraflores
de la Sierra
Puerto de
Navacerrada
Cercedilla
Manzanares
el Real
N-I
Navacerrada
Guadarrama
Colmenar Viejo
Valle de
los Caídos
Ávila
El Escorial
A6
Río Manzanares
El Pardo
Barajas
Guadalajara
N-II
Robledo
de Chavela
Alcalá de Henares
Madrid
Móstoles
Navalcarnero
Getafe
Arganda
N-IV
Río Tajo
N-V
Pinto
Chinchón
N-III
N401
Aranjuez
Río Tajo
Toledo
Sierra de Guadarrama
0   20 miles
0   20 kilometers

MADRID

◙ **SIGHTS. Plaza de Cervantes,** filled with cafes, rose bushes, and a statue of its namesake, bursts with color in the summertime. At the end of the plaza opposite C. de Libreros lie the **ruinas de Santa María,** the remains of a 16th-century church destroyed during the Spanish Civil War. In the surviving **Capilla del Oidor,** rotating art exhibits surround the fountain where Cervantes was christened. (Open June-Sept. Tu-Su noon-2pm and 5-8pm; Oct.-May Tu-Su noon-2pm and 6-9pm. Free.) Just before Pl. de Cervantes in Pl. de San Diego, take a left off C. de Libreros onto C. Bedel to see the **Colegio Mayor de San Ildefonso** (☎918 85 40 00). In the **paraninfo,** where doctorates were once awarded, the king now presents the Premio Cervantes, Spain's most prestigious literary award. The *paraninfo* and **Capilla de San Ildefonso** both have spectacular Mudéjar ceilings. (By tour only. Consult tourist office for up-to-date schedules. €2.50.) The town's **Catedral Magistral,** at the end of C. Mayor in Pl. de los Santos Niños, is one of only two in the world with this title (the other is in Lovaina, Belgium). To be so named, each priest must also be a university professor. (Open M-Sa 9-11:30am and 6:30-8:30pm, Su 9am-12:45pm and 6:30-9pm. Free.) Down C. Mayor from Pl. de Cervantes is the **Casa de Cervantes,** the reconstructed house where the author was born in 1547. The house displays a variety of period furniture and editions of *Don Quijote* in languages Cervantes never knew. (☎918

89 96 54. Open Tu-Su 10am-1:30pm and 4-6:30pm. Free.) The **Convento de San Bernardo** hides a gorgeous 17th-century elliptical interior behind a simple facade. (Mandatory tour leaves from the courtyard M-F 2 per day 1:45, 6:30pm; Sa-Su 7 per day 12:30, 1:30, 5, 5:45, 6:30, 7:15, 8pm; €2.10.)

ARANJUEZ

History and natural beauty converge at the heart of green Aranjuez (pop. 43,000). Once a getaway for generations of Habsburg and Bourbon royalty, Aranjuez still maintains a pastoral elegance thanks to its dazzling gardens and palaces. UNESCO recently declared this small city, famed for its strawberries, asparagus, and aesthetic landscape, a World Heritage Cultural Landscape. Aranjuez is an easy day trip from either Madrid or Toledo, but consider staying a bit longer during the festivals at the end of May, during September, and during *Carnaval*.

TRANSPORTATION. RENFE trains, C. de la Estación (☎902 24 00 42), go to: **Cuenca** (2hr.; M-F 4-5 per day 6:10am-8:14pm, Sa-Su 9:23am-8:14pm; €6.55); **Madrid** (45min.; *cercanías* to Estación Atocha every 15-30min. M-F 5:30am-11:30pm, Sa-Su 6am-11:30pm; *regionales* to Estación Chamartín M-F 8-10 per day 6:57am-9:27pm, Sa-Su 8:57am-9:27pm; €2.65); **Toledo** (30min.; M-F 7-10 per day 7:20am-9:12pm, Sa-Su 9:17am-9:12pm; €2.45). **AISA** runs from the **bus station,** C. de las Infantas, 16 (☎918 91 01 83), to Estación Sur de Autobuses in **Madrid** (45min.; M-F every 15-30min. 6:30am-11:30pm, Sa every 45min. 7:30am-11pm, Su 10 per day 8am-11pm; €3).

ORIENTATION & PRACTICAL INFORMATION. To enter the city by foot, exit the train station parking lot, take a right, and then follow the signs to the Palacio Real. With your back to the bus station, head left on C. de las Infantas toward the main fountain. Orienting yourself from the palace is fairly easy, and friendly locals can point you toward either your destination or the tourist office. Alternatively, on the corner outside the palace, climb aboard the **Chiquitren de Aranjuez** (☎918 92 93 92 or 902 08 80 89) to catch all the major sights in one day (€5, not including admission to the museums and sights).

The **tourist office** is in Pl. San Antonio, 9. (☎918 91 04 27; www.aranjuez.net. Open daily 10am-7:30pm.) Local services include: **emergency** ☎112; **police,** C. de las Infantas, 36 (☎918 09 09 80); **pharmacy,** on the corner of C. del Capitán Angosto Gómez Castrillón and C. Real. (Open M-F 9:30am-1:45pm and 5:30-8:30pm, Sa 10am-1:45pm. MC/V.) For **Internet access,** head to **Arancyb,** up the street from the tourist office through the plaza arches. From Ctra. de Andalucía, take a left on C. del Gobernador, 67. (☎918 91 28 62. €0.60 for 15min., €2.40 per hr. Open M-Sa 11am-3am, Su 4-11pm.) The **post office** is on C. Peñarredonda, 3, off C. del Capitán Angosto Gómez Castrillón. (☎918 91 11 32. Open M-F 8:30am-2:30pm, Sa 9:30am-1pm.) **Postal Code:** 28300.

ACCOMMODATIONS & FOOD. Aranjuez has a wide variety of choices for accommodations and food, especially for a city its size. **Hostal Infantas ❶,** C. de las Infantas, 4-6, is on the left with your back to the bus station. All rooms have sinks, TV, and phones; doubles with shower or bath have A/C. (☎918 91 13 41; fax 91 66 43. Singles €15, with shower €23.50; doubles €25/€41.50, with bath €44. MC/V.) The rooms at **Hostal Castilla ❸,** Ctra. de Andalucía, 98, face a garden terrace. All have TV, A/C, telephone, and bath. (☎918 91 26 27; fax 91 61 33. Breakfast €3. Singles €35; doubles €45.) The same owners run **Hostal Rusiñol ❷** on C. de San Antonio with fewer amenities for fewer euros, though rooms still have TV. (☎918 91 01 55. Doubles €29, with shower €35, with bath €39.) **Camping Soto del Castillo ❶,**

across the Río Tajo and off the highway to the right, sits amid lush fields and offers a restaurant, supermarket, and swimming pool. (☎918 91 13 95. €3.85-4.15 per person, €4.15-4.50 per tent, €3.20-3.50 per car. Open year-round. MC/V.) For groceries or a quick meal, try the **Mercado de Abastos** on Ctra. de Andalucía. With your back to the tourist office, go left through the arch; the market is on the left. (Open M-F 9am-2pm and 6-9pm, Sa 9am-2pm.) Be sure to grab some delicious ▤*fresas con nata* (strawberries and cream) from the vendors just over the small river bridge near the main fountain (in front of the palace gardens). For some savory asparagus specialties and typical Spanish entrees, head to **El Rana Verde ❸**, C. de la Reina, 1 (☎918 01 15 71) or **La Alegría de la Huerta ❸**, Ctra. de Madrid, 4. (☎918 91 29 38. Dinner €12-16. Open daily 9am-4pm and 9pm-midnight.)

🅖 **SIGHTS.** Juan de Herrera, chief architect of gloomy El Escorial, designed the resplendent white brick of the stately **Palacio Real** under the direction of Felipe II. In subsequent years, Felipe V, Fernando VI, and Carlos III all had the palace enlarged and embellished to suit their own tastes. Particularly remarkable are the Oriental **porcelain room,** with hand-tooled and painted three-dimensional ceramic Rococo walls, and the Mozárabe **smoking room,** which bears a striking resemblance to rooms of the Alhambra. On your way out, take note of the last room of the **Museo de la Vida en Palacio,** which contains the toys and other diversionary objects of the royal children. (☎918 91 07 40. Open Tu-Sa Apr.-Sept. 10am-6:15pm; Oct.-Mar. 10am-5:15pm. Compulsory 30min. tours in Spanish, English, or Italian leave about every 15min. €3, students €1.50. EU citizens free W.) Just outside the palace begins a labyrinth of river walkways, freshly trimmed hedges, and mythological statues. The garden motif continues farther away from the palace on C. de la Reina with the **Jardín del Príncipe,** built for the amusement of Carlos IV. (Open daily Apr.-Sept. 8am-6:30pm; Oct.-Mar. 8am-8:30pm. Free.) A 30min. stroll through the park leads to the **Casa del Labrador,** a mock cottage full of Neoclassical decorative arts. (Located 3km down C. de la Reina from the Palacio Real. ☎918 91 03 05. Reserve ahead; small groups only. Open daily 10am-sunset. €3, students and children under 16 €1.50.)

The **Falúas Museum,** once home to the Tajo's sailing squad, stores royal gondolas. (Open Tu-Su June-Aug. 10am-6:15pm; Sept.-May 10am-5:15pm. €3.40, students and under 16 €1.70. EU citizens free W.) **Aranjuez, Una Gran Fiesta,** has exhibits that take you through the history of the bullfight. (Pl. de Toros, all the way up Ctra. de Andalucía from the tourist office. ☎918 92 16 43. Open Tu-Su Apr.-Sept. 11am-7:30pm; Oct.-Mar. 11am-5:30pm. €3; students, seniors, and under 16 €1.20.)

SIERRA DE GUADARRAMA

The Sierra de Guadarrama is a pine-covered mountain range halfway between Madrid and Segovia. With *La Mujer Muerta* (The Dead Woman) to the west, the *Sierra de la Maliciosa* (Mountain of the Evil Woman) to the east, and the less-imaginatively-named *Siete Picos* (Seven Peaks) between the two, the Sierra draws both summer and winter visitors to hike and ski.

CERCEDILLA   ☎918

A picturesque chalet town blessed with great weather, Cercedilla is the ideal base for venturing into the Sierras. In the summer, cooler temperatures and a relaxed pace lure sweltering city-dwellers; in the winter, skiers enjoy the nearby resorts. For those weary of Madrid's sights, Cercedilla has no monuments, churches, or museums. Instead, it offers great day hikes that provide an escape from the city.

MADRID

⚡🏠 TRANSPORTATION & PRACTICAL INFORMATION. Cercedilla makes an easy daytrip from Madrid. Camping is not allowed in the area, so pack for a day hike or reserve a hostel in advance for extended stays. The **train station** (☎918 52 00 57), at the base of the hill on C. Emilio Serrano, sends trains to: **El Escorial** via **Villalba** (1hr.; 20 per day Su-F 7:11am-9:26pm, Sa 9:32am-9:26pm; €1.15); **Los Cotos** via **Puerto de Navacerrada** (45min.; Su-F every hr. 9:35am-7:35pm, Sa every 2hr. 10:35am-6:35pm; €3.40); **Atocha** or **Chamartín station (Madrid)** via **Villalba** (1½hr.; over 20 per day Su-F 6:07am-10:35pm, Sa 6:37am-9:35pm; €3.40); **Segovia** (45min., 8-9 per day 7:27am-9:23pm, €2.10); **Villalba** (30min.; M-F 6:37am-9:35pm, Sa-Su 9:35am-9:35pm; €1.65). The **bus station,** Av. José Antonio, 2 (☎918 52 02 39), sends buses to **Madrid** (M-F 29 per day 6am-8:45pm, Sa 15-17 per day 6:20am-8:45pm, Su 17 per day 8:30am-9:30pm; €2.50).

Upon arrival in Cercedilla, first-timers should proceed to the **Consejería de Medio Ambiente** to pick up **tourist information** and great hiking maps, some even in English. This is the starting point for several hikes (see **Hiking,** below). To get there from the train or bus station, you might want to call a **taxi** (☎918 52 03 24) or just wait for one, though this can take a while. The Consejería is roughly 3km from the train station on **Carretera las Dehesas,** km 2. By foot (40min., a hike in itself), go straight uphill and stay left at the fork. Services include: **emergency** (☎112), **police** (☎639 35 17 91), and the **Centro de Salud** (☎918 52 30 31).

🏠🍴 ACCOMMODATIONS & FOOD. Many of the youth hostels in Cercedilla are booked during the summer by camp groups and other organizations. For most *albergues* and *hostales,* reservations should be made more than 15 days in advance. The closest to the train station is **Hostal Longinos "El Aribel" ❷,** right across the street from the train station. Longinos has spacious rooms, with TV and a retro feel. (☎918 52 15 11 or 52 06 86. Singles €25; doubles with bath €40.) For cheaper, more rustic accommodations, try **Villa Castora (HI) ❶,** about 1km up Ctra. Las Dehesas on the left. (☎918 52 03 34; fax 52 24 11. All rooms with private bath. Reservations strongly recommended. Reception open 8am-10pm. Room and 3 meals €12.60, with 2 meals €10.60, only breakfast €7.80; over 26 €16.80/€14/€10.80.) **Hostal La Maya ❹,** C. Carrera del Señor, 2, has rooms with TVs, sofas, and modern private baths. (☎918 52 22 52. Doubles €40. MC/V.) Camping is strictly controlled throughout the Sierra de Guadarrama and is prohibited throughout the area surrounding Cercedilla. The Consejería can provide a list of Cercedilla's restaurant choices. For groceries, **Supermarket Gigante,** C. Doctor Cañados, 2, is in the town center off Av. del Generalísimo. (☎918 52 23 19. Open M-Sa 9:30am-2pm and 5:30-9pm, Su 9:30am-2pm.) Convenience stores outside the bus and train stations sell all the essentials.

🥾 HIKING. The **Consejería de Medio Ambiente** functions as a **tourist office** and offers hiking information. (☎/fax 918 52 22 13. Open daily 10am-6pm. Some English spoken.) The Consejería provides detailed maps of six trails and day hikes through the surrounding Sierra region, ranging from the challenging 14.3km (5-6hr.) **El GR-10** to the more relaxed 4km (1½hr.) **Camino Puricelli.** Some of the hiking around Cercedilla begins up **Carretera las Dehesas,** near the Consejería. Atop the *carretera,* the **Calzada Romana** (about 1.5km from the Consejería) offers hiking along a Roman road that once connected Madrid to Segovia (1½hr. trail). Those who prefer wheels over heels should check out the bicycle trails.

PUERTO DE NAVACERRADA & LOS COTOS

A year-round magnet for nature lovers, **Puerto de Navacerrada** offers **skiing** in the winter (late December-early April) and beautiful **hiking** in the summer. Visitors should arrange such activities in advance by contacting relevant organizations or visiting available websites. Backpackers in search of challenging hikes often take the popular **Camino Schmid,** a 7km trail from Navacerrada to Pradera de los Corralillos; from there it is another 3km to the Consejería in Cercedilla.

Deporte y Montaña, 1.5km from the train station, offers info on many outdoor activities. (Madrid office ☎918 52 14 35, Navacerrada office ☎918 52 33 02; www.puertonavacerrada.com.) More details can be found at the **Asociación Turística de Estaciones de Esquí y Montaña** (☎913 50 20 20) in Madrid. To head straight for the trails, exit the train station, turn left at the highway, then left again (off the road) at the large intersection marking the pass. The dirt path leads uphill to several trailpaths through the pine forests. For budget accommodations in Navacerrada, try **Albergue Álvaro Iglesias ①.** Four-person rooms have shared baths and a TV lounge. (☎918 52 38 87. Room and breakfast €7.80, room and 2 meals €10.60, *pensión completa* (room and 3 meals) €12.66; guests over 26 €10.80/€14/€16.80.)

CASTILLA LA MANCHA

Cervantes chose to set Don Quijote's adventures in La Mancha to evoke a cultural and material backwater. While Castilla La Mancha (*manxa* means parched earth in Arabic, and *mancha* is Spanish for stain) is one of Spain's least developed regions, this battered, windswept plateau possesses an austere beauty. Its tumultuous history, gloomy medieval fortresses, and brooding cliffs evoke both melancholy and reverence. Long ago, this region was the epicenter of conflict between Christians and Muslims. After Christian forces arrived in Muslim Spain, La Mancha became the domain of the military orders Santiago, Calatrava, Montesa, and San Juan, which were modeled after such crusading institutions as the Knights Templar, a society of powerful warrior-monks. In the 14th and 15th centuries, the region saw fearsome struggles between the kingdoms of Castilla and Aragón until they united in 1492 under Fernando and Isabel.

Castilla La Mancha is Spain's largest wine-producing region (*Valdepeñas* and *Manzanares* are popular table wines), and its abundant olive groves and hunting influence many local recipes, including Toledo's famed partridge dish. Stews, roast meats, and game are all *manchego* staples. *Gazpacho manchego* (a hearty stew of rabbit, lamb, chicken, and pork) and *queso manchego* (Castile's beloved cheese) are local specialties.

TOLEDO ☎925

For Cervantes, Toledo was the "glory of Spain and light of her cities." Cossío called it "the most brilliant and evocative summary of Spain's history." Toledo holds a special mystique and charm, opening a page of history against a spectacular backdrop. Modern-day Toledo (pop. 66,000) may be marred by swarms of tourists and caravans of kitsch, but it remains a treasure trove of Spanish culture. The city's numerous churches, synagogues, and mosques share twisting alleyways, emblematic of a time when Spain's three religions coexisted peacefully. Visitors pay monetary homage to Toledo's Damascene swords and knives, colorful pottery, and almond-paste marzipan. In June, Toledo comes alive with costumed processions during its renowned Corpus Cristi celebration.

◖ TRANSPORTATION

Trains: Po. de la Rosa, 2 (RENFE Info ☎902 24 02 02), in an exquisite neo-Mudéjar station just over Puente de Azarquiel. One line to either **Atocha** or **Chamartín** station in **Madrid** (1-1½hr.; 9-10 per day M-F 6:30am-8:58pm, Sa-Su 8:25am-8:58pm; €4.90-€5.45), usually via **Aranjuez** (35min.; 8-9 per day M-F 6:30am-8:58pm, Sa-Su 8:25am-8:58pm; €2.45).

Buses: Av. Castilla La Mancha (☎925 21 58 50), 5min. from Puerta de Bisagra, the city gate. Information booth open daily 7am-11pm. **Alsina Graells** (☎925 21 58 50 in Toledo and 963 49 72 30 in Valencia) goes to **Valencia** (5½hr.,1 per day M-F 3pm, €17; buy ticket on board). **Continental Auto** (☎925 22 36 41 in Toledo and 915 27 29 61 in Madrid) runs to Estación Sur de Autobuses in **Madrid** (1½hr.; every 30min. M-F 6am-10pm, Sa 6:30am-10pm, Su 8:30am-11:30pm; €3.89).

Public Transportation: Buses #5 and 6 service several city points, mainly the bus and train stations and the very central **Plaza de Zocodóver.** Buses stop to the right of the train station, underneath and across the street from the bus station (€0.80).

Taxis: Radio Taxi and **Gruas de Toledo** (☎925 25 50 50 or 22 70 70.)

Castilla La Mancha

Zaragoza

Salamanca

Segovia

Sigüenza

N-VI

N-II

Ávila

E90

El Escorial

Guadalajara

Madrid

Talavera de la Reina

E90

Esquivias

N-V

Tarancón

Cuenca

Río Tajo

Toledo

N-III

E901

Río Júcar

San Martín de Montalbán

Orgaz

Mora

N320

El Toboso

Belmonte

Alarcón

Consuegra

A31

Río Guadiana

Alcázar de San Juan

Daimiel

Argamasilla de Alba

Ciudad Real

Manzanares

Albacete

Almagro

N430

Puertollano

N-IV

Valdepeñas

E5

40 miles

40 kilometers

Hellín

Córdoba

Murcia

Car Rental: Avis, C. Venancio González, 9 (☎925 21 45 35 or 21 57 94). From €60 per day. 23+. Open M-F 9:30am-1:30pm and 4:30-8pm. **Hertz** (☎925 25 38 90), at the train station. From €69 per day (includes IVA and insurance). Open M-F 9am-1:30pm and 4:30-7pm, Sa 9am-1pm.

✦ 🛈 ORIENTATION & PRACTICAL INFORMATION

Toledo is an almost unconquerable maze of narrow streets where pedestrians and cars battle for sovereignty. To get to **Plaza de Zocodóver** in the town center by bus, take bus #5 or 6 (€0.80) from the stop on the right after you exit the train or bus station. On foot from the train station, turn right and follow the left fork uphill to a smaller bridge, **Puente de Alcántara.** Cross the bridge to the stone staircase (through a set of arches); after climbing the stairs, turn left and continue upward, veering right at C. Cervantes, which leads to Pl. de Zocodóver. From the bus station, exit the restaurant, head straight toward the traffic circle, and take the first right on the steep highway that surrounds the city. Despite well-labeled streets, visitors are likely to lose their way; luckily, wandering is the best way to discover Toledo's tangled beauty. The **Zocotren,** a miniature tourist train, provides a 50min. tour of Toledo and its sights—including an incredible view of the city from across the Tajo. (☎925 23 22 10. Trains leave from Pl. de Zocodóver in summer every 30min., in winter every hr. Tour narration in English and Spanish. Buy tickets at the shop next to the pharmacy in Pl. de Zocodóver. €3.60, children €2.15.)

Tourist Office: Regional office, Puerta de Bisagra, s/n (☎925 22 08 43). From the train station, turn right and take the busy right-hand fork across the bridge (Puente de Azarquiel), following the city walls until you reach the second traffic circle; the office is across the road, outside the walls. English-speaking staff offers handy maps. Open July-Sept. M-Sa 9am-7pm, Su 9am-3pm; Oct.-June M-F 9am-6pm, Sa 9am-7pm, Su 9am-3pm. **Municipal office,** Pl. del Ayuntamiento, s/n (☎925 25 40 30). Multilingual staff. Open Tu-Su 10:30am-2:30pm and 4:30-7pm. **Zococentro,** another information office, is just off Pl. de Zocodóver. Open in summer 10:30am-7pm, in winter 10:30am-6pm.

Currency Exchange: Banco Santander Central Hispano, C. del Comercio, 47 (☎925 22 98 00). No commission and a 24hr. **ATM.** Open Apr.-Sept. M-F 8:30am-2pm; Oct.-Mar. M-F 8:30am-2pm, Sa 8:30am-1pm.

Luggage Storage: At the **bus station** (€0.80-1.20). Open daily 7am-11pm. At the **train station** (€3). Open daily 7am-9:30pm.

Emergency: ☎112. **Local police:** ☎092, at the intersection of Av. de la Reconquista and Av. de Carlos III.

Late-Night Pharmacy: (☎925 22 17 68), Pl. de Zocodóver.

Hospital: Hospital Virgen de la Salud (☎925 26 92 00), Av. de Barber, outside the city walls. With your back to Puerta de Bisagra, take a left until you reach Glorieta de la Reconquista. Take Av. de la Reconquista to Pl. de Colón; Av. de Barber is to the left.

Internet Access: Options are extremely limited, but access is available at **Zococentro** (see **tourist office,** above) and at the sporadically open **La Repro,** C. Unión, s/n.

Post Office: C. de la Plata, 1 (☎925 22 36 11; fax 21 57 64). **Lista de Correos.** Open M-F 8:30am-8:30pm, Sa 9am-2pm. **Postal Code:** 45070.

ACCOMMODATIONS

Toledo is chock-full of accommodations, but finding a bed during the summer can be a hassle, especially on weekends. Reservations are strongly recommended. Last-minute planners, try the tourist office if you run into trouble. There are several camping grounds around Toledo. Out-of-town sites bring quiet and shade; those in town trade convenience for noise.

Residencia Juvenil San Servando (HI), Castillo de San Servando (☎925 22 45 54). Cross the street from the train station, turn left, then immediately right up Subida del Hospital. When the steps reach a road, turn right, then right again, following the signs to Hospital Provincial. The steep walk uphill past the hospital leads to the *hostal,* housed in a 14th-century castle. From the bus station, exit the restaurant, go toward the traffic circle, and continue straight uphill; cross the footbridge to the left and head up to the castle. Attractive, monumental building has 38 rooms, each with 2-4 bunk beds and private bath, some with views. Pool in summer. TV room. Sheets included. Dorms €8.41, breakfast €1.59; over 26 €11/€2. HI card required. ❶

Hostal Centro, C. Nueva, 13 (☎925 25 70 91; www.hostalcentro.com), toward C. del Comercio on Pl. de Zocodóver. Centrally located for discovering the city. Clean, spacious rooms with TV, bath, A/C, phone. New rooftop terrace affords sunbathing and a view of the plaza. Friendly staff. Singles €30; doubles €42; triples €60. MC/V. ❸

Hostal Descalzos, C. de los Descalzos, 30 (☎925 22 28 88; www.hostaldescalzos.com), down the steps off Po. del Tránsito. Recently refurbished hostel with stunning views. Modern rooms with TV, A/C, full bath, and phone, some with balconies. Rooms

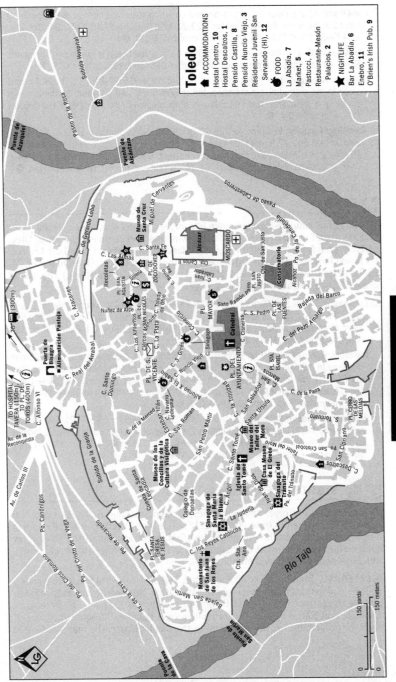

Toledo

ACCOMMODATIONS
Hostal Centro, **10**
Hostal Descalzos, **1**
Pensión Castilla, **8**
Pensión Nuncio Viejo, **3**
Residencia Juvenil San
Servando (HI), **12**

FOOD
La Abadía, **7**
Market, **5**
Pastucci, **4**
Restaurante-Mesón
Palacios, **2**

NIGHTLIFE
Bar La Abadía, **6**
Enebro, **11**
O'Brien's Irish Pub, **9**

#41 and 42 are favorites; prices depend on which room you choose. Small pool/big jacuzzi in backyard. Apr.-Oct. singles €29.21-41.87; doubles €46.73-52.34. Oct.-Mar. €24.54-35.89/€39.25-44.86. IVA not included. MC/V. ❸

Pensión Castilla, C. Recoletos, 6 (☎925 25 63 18). The hostel is upstairs in the corner. Basic, clean rooms at a great location. Singles €15; doubles with bath €25. ❷

Pensión Nuncio Viejo, C. Nuncio Viejo, 19, 3rd fl. (☎925 22 81 78). These 7 rooms close to the cathedral are cramped, but they're bright and polished. Motherly owner cooks up a great breakfast (€1.50) and other meals (€7.50). Singles €19; doubles €30, with bath €34. ❷

Camping: Camping El Greco (☎925 22 00 90), 1.5km from town on Ctra. CM-4000, km0.7. Take bus #7 from Pl. de Zocodóver. Shady, wooded site between the river and an olive grove. Restaurant, bar, and supermarket. Swimming pool during the summer. Open year-round. €4.40 per person, €4.24 per tent and per car. IVA not included. ❶

▐ FOOD

Toledo grinds almonds into marzipan of every shape and size, from colorful fruity nuggets to half-moon cookies; *pastelería* windows beckon on every corner. Alternatively, grab fresh fruit and the basics at **Alimentación Pantoja,** C. Real del Arrabal, 30, inside Puerta de Bisagra and across from the tourist office. (Open June-Aug. M-Sa 9am-11pm, Su 9am-3pm; Sept.-May M-Sa 9am-10pm, Su 9am-3pm.) The **market** is in Pl. Mayor, behind the cathedral. (Open M-Sa 9am-8pm.)

▨ **La Abadía,** Pl. de San Nicolás, 3 (☎925 25 11 40). Bear left when C. de la Sillería splits; Pl. de San Nicolás is to the right. Dine on the delicious lunch *menú* (€8.50) in a maze of cave-like underground rooms. Open M-Th 8am-12:30am, F 8am-1:30am, Sa noon-1:30am. AmEx/MC/V. ❷

Pastucci, C. Sinagoga, 10 (☎925 25 77 42). From Pl. de Zocodóver take C. del Comercio; keep to the right through the underpass just past Rodier. Cheerful atmosphere. Pastas €5.45-7.85. Small pizza €6-8.45. 10% discount with your *Let's Go* guide (cash only). Open in summer M-Th 12:15pm-midnight, F-Su noon-4pm and 8pm-midnight; in winter noon-4pm and 7pm-midnight. MC/V. ❶

Restaurante-Mesón Palacios, C. Alfonso X El Sabio, 3 (☎925 21 59 72). Two palatial *menús* (€6-10.21) loaded with meat, fish, and egg dishes—including Toledo's famous partridge dish—let you dine with class. Entrees €4-12. Open M-Sa 1-4pm and 7-11pm, Su noon-4pm. Closed Su in Aug. AmEx/MC/V. ❷

◉ ▥ SIGHTS & MUSEUMS

Toledo's excellent museums, churches, synagogues, and mosques make the city almost impossible to see thoroughly in one day. Toledo's attractions form a belt around its middle within the fortified walls, attributed to 7th-century King Wamba. An east-west tour beginning in Pl. de Zocodóver is largely downhill. Most sights are closed Mondays.

▨ **CATEDRAL.** Built between 1226 and 1498, Toledo's cathedral boasts five naves, delicate stained glass, and unapologetic ostentation. Noteworthy art and sculpture include the 14th-century Gothic *Virgen Blanca* by the entrance, El Greco's *El Espolio,* and Narciso Tomés's *Transparente,* a Spanish-Baroque whirlpool of architecture, sculpture, and painting. In the **Capilla Mayor,** the massive Gothic

EL GRECO'S THREE MISTAKES

Upon a visit to the sacristy of Toledo's cathedral, the eye is quickly drawn to the large El Greco painting at the end of the room. El Greco painted *El Espolio*—his first painting—specifically for the cathedral, although neither party had thought to negotiate costs before the completion of the work. The cathedral's clergy were unhappy with the painting due to three mistakes El Greco had inadvertently made. The first is an anachronism: the scene depicts the point in the Bible at which the Roman soldiers are about to remove Jesus's gown, but the soldier standing to his left is wearing distinctly 16th-century armor. El Greco's second mistake was painting three women in the bottom left corner; according to the New Testament, no women were present at that moment. The clergy's final complaint was that the artist painted ordinary men's heads higher than the head of Jesus; even in art, Christ is more holy than humans. The two parties went to court over the matter, eventually working out a compromise. In the end, El Greco won something more valuable than money—the court battle threw him into the spotlight, earning him a slew of new commissions and spreading his reputation.

altarpiece stretches to the ceiling. The tomb of Cardinal Mendoza, founder of the Spanish Inquisition, lies to the left. Beneath the dome is the **Capilla Mozárabe**, the only place in the world where the ancient Visigoth Mass (in Mozarabic) is still held. The **treasury** flaunts interesting ornamentation, including a replica of one of Columbus's ships and a 400-pound, 16th-century gold monstrosity lugged through the streets during the annual Corpus Cristi procession. The **sacristía** holds 18 El Grecos and 2 Van Dycks, along with a portrait of every archbishop of Toledo. The red hats hanging from the ceiling mark the cardinals' tombs. (☎ 925 22 22 41. *Open daily June-Aug. 10am-noon and 4-6pm; Sept.-July 10am-noon and 4-6pm. The cathedral is free, but it's worth the €4.95 to see the sacristía and capillas. Open June-Aug. M-Sa 10:30am-6:30pm, Su 2-6pm; Sept.-May M-Sa 10:30am-6pm, Su 2-6pm. €4.95. Audio guide in English, French, and Italian; €2.70 . Tickets sold at the store opposite the entrance. Modest dress required.*)

■ **ALCÁZAR.** Toledo's most formidable landmark, the Alcázar served as a military stronghold for the Romans, Visigoths, Moors, and Spaniards. Much of the building was reduced to rubble during the Civil War, when Fascist troops used the Alcázar as their refuge. Don't miss the room detailing Colonel Moscardó's refusal to surrender the Alcázar, even at the cost of his son's life. Visit the dark, windowless basement refuge where over 500 civilians hid during the siege. The rooms above ground have been turned into a national military museum complete with armor, swords, guns, knives, and comparatively benign dried plants. (*Cuesta de Carlos V, 2, a block down from Pl. de Zocodóver.* ☎ 925 22 16 73. *Open Tu-Su 9:30am-2pm. €2. Free W.*)

EL GRECO. Greek painter Doménikos Theotokópoulos, known better as El Greco, spent most of his life in Toledo. Many works are displayed throughout town, but the majority of his masterpieces have been carted off to the Prado and other big-name museums. The **Iglesia de Santo Tomé** houses his famous *El entierro del Conde de Orgaz (The Burial of Count Orgaz)*. The stark figure staring out from the back is El Greco himself, and the boy is his son, Jorge Manuel, architect of Toledo's city hall. (*Pl. del Conde, 1.* ☎ 925 25 60 98. *Open daily Mar.-Oct. 15 10am-6:45pm; Oct.16-Feb. 10am-5:45pm. €1.50.*) Downhill and to the left lies the **Casa Museo del Greco**, containing 19 of his works, including a copy of the detailed *Vista y plano de Toledo*. (*C. Samuel Leví, 2.* ☎ 925 22 40 46. *Open Tu-Sa 10am-2pm and 4-6pm, Su 10am-2pm. €2.40; students, under 18, and over 65 free. Sa-Su afternoons free.*)

CASTILLA
LA MANCHA

Outside handsome Puerta de Bisagra, the 16th-century **Hospital de Tavera** displays 5 El Grecos and several works by his mentor, Titian. *(C. del Duque de Lerma, 2. ☎ 925 22 04 51. Near the tourist office. Open daily 10:30am-1:30pm and 3:30-6pm. €3.)*

SINAGOGUES. Only two of the many sinagogues original to Toledo's *judería* (Jewish quarter) have been preserved. Samuel Ha Leví, diplomat and treasurer to Pedro el Cruel, built the **Sinagoga del Tránsito** in 1366. Its simple exterior hides an ornate sanctuary with Mudéjar plasterwork and an *artesonado* (coffered) wood ceiling. The Hebrew-inscribed walls are taken mostly from the Psalter. Inside, the **Museo Sefardí** is packed with artifacts, including a Torah (parts of which are over 400 years old) and a beautiful set of Sephardic wedding costumes. *(C. Samuel Leví, s/n. ☎ 925 22 36 65. Closed for renovations at time of publication; call ahead for hours. €2.40, students and under 18 €1.20. Free Sa after 4pm and Su.)* **Sinagoga de Santa María la Blanca,** down the street to the right, is a monument to the intersection of Christian, Jewish, and Islamic culture in Toledo. It was originally built as a mosque; however, the Jews purchased it to serve as the city's principal synagogue before it was converted into a church around 1550. Now secular, its Moorish arches and tranquil garden make for a pleasant retreat. *(C. de los Reyes Católicos, 2. ☎ 925 22 72 57. Open daily June-Aug. 10am-2pm and 3:30-7pm; Sept.-May 10am-2pm and 3:30-6pm. €1.50.)*

MONASTERIO DE SAN JUAN DE LOS REYES. At the far western edge of the city stands this Franciscan monastery commissioned by Fernando and Isabel to commemorate their victory over the Portuguese in the Battle of Toro (1476). The cloister, covered with the initials of *los Reyes Católicos*, melds Gothic and Mudéjar architecture. The Catholic monarchs planned to use the church as their burial place, but changed their minds after their 1492 victory over the Moorish kingdom of Granada. *(☎ 925 22 38 02. Open daily Apr.-Sept. 10am-1:45pm and 3:30-6:45pm; Oct.-Mar. 10am-2pm and 3:30-6pm. €1.50.)*

MUSEUMS. Toledo was the seat of Visigoth rule and culture for three centuries prior to the Muslim invasion in 711. The **Museo del Taller del Moro,** on C. Bulas up from Iglesia de Santo Tomé, features outstanding woodwork, plasterwork, and tiles. *(C. Taller del Moro, 3. Head through Pl. de San Antonio and down C. San Bernardo. ☎ 925 22 71 15. Open Tu-Sa 10am-2pm and 4-6:30pm, Su 10am-2pm. €0.60.)* The exhibits at the **Museo de los Concilios y de la Cultura Visigótica** pale in comparison to their beautiful setting: a 13th-century Mudéjar church. *(C. San Clemente, 4. ☎ 925 22 78 72. Open Tu-Sa 10am-2pm and 4-6:30pm, Su 10am-2pm. €0.60, students €0.30.)* The impressive and under-touristed **Museo de Santa Cruz** (1504) exhibits a handful of El Grecos in its eclectic art collection, which also includes remains from archaeological digs throughout the province. *(C. Miguel de Cervantes, 3. ☎ 925 22 10 36. Open Tu-Sa 10am-6:30pm, Su 10am-2pm. €1.20.)*

🎬 NIGHTLIFE

For nightlife, head through the arch and to the left from Pl. de Zocodóver to **Calle Santa Fé,** brimming with beer and local youth. **Enebro,** tucked away on small Pl. Santiago de los Caballeros off C. Miguel de Cervantes, lures in customers with free evening *tapas*. *(☎ 925 22 21 11. Beer €1.20. No cover. Open daily 11am-4pm and 7pm-1:30am.)* **Calle de la Sillería** and **Calle de los Alfileritos** host a few upscale bars and clubs, including **Bar La Abadía.** *(☎ 925 25 11 40. For directions, see p. 156.)* **O'Brien's Irish Pub,** C. Las Armas, 12, fills with 20-somethings later in the evening and has live music on Thursdays at 11pm. *(☎ 925 21 26 65. Guinness €3.80. Open Su-Th noon-2:30am, F-Sa noon-4am. MC/V.)*

⚡ DAYTRIP FROM TOLEDO

CONSUEGRA

Samar buses (☎925 22 39 15) depart for Consuegra from the Toledo bus station (1¼hr.; M-F 10 per day 9:15am-8:45pm, Sa 5 per day 9:15am-11pm, Su 3 per day 10:30am-7:30pm; €3.30) and return from C. Castilla de la Mancha (1¼hr.; M-F 5 per day 6:10am-3:25pm, Sa-Su 4 per day 6:55am-5:55pm). In Toledo, buy tickets at the office; upon return, buy tickets from the driver. Plan around bus departure times so you don't have to spend the night.

Of all Manchegan villages, tiny Consuegra, replete with windmills, vast landscapes, and medieval charm, provides the most raw material for summoning Don Quixote's world. The village **castle,** called *crestería manchega* by locals, was a Roman, then Arab, then Castilian fortress. (Call for ever-changing hours.) **El Cid's** only son, Diego, died in the stable; you can visit a lavish monument in his honor near the Ayuntamiento. Though small, Consuegra is home to a palace, a Franciscan convent, and a Carmelite monastery. The **tourist office,** located halfway up the road to the castle on the left, will gladly provide more information. (☎925 47 57 31. Open June-Sept. M-F 9:30am-2pm and 4:30-7pm, Sa-Su 10:30am-2pm and 4:30-7pm; Oct.-May daily 9:30am-2pm and 3:30-6pm.)

ALMAGRO ☎926

Most of the year, sleepy Almagro, with its narrow cobblestone streets and endless rows of whitewashed and half-timbered houses, evokes the image of the quintessential, relaxed Spanish town. But for three weeks every July, all the world's a stage in Almagro, when the world-renowned classical theater festival swells the town with local and international visitors. Even if the play's not your thing, Almagro makes a pleasant stop on your way to Andalucía.

📧 **TRANSPORTATION.** The **train station is** at Po. de la Estación (☎926 86 02 76), outside the city center, at the end of the pedestrian street. To get from the station to Pl. Mayor, walk down Po. de la Estación and turn left onto C. Rondo de Calatrava; turn right onto C. Madre de Dios (a sign points to Centro Urbano), which becomes C. Feria and leads to the plaza. To **Ciudad Real** (15min., 5 per day 8:40am-10:20pm, €1.65-1.95) and **Madrid** (2¾hr., 3 and 6:05pm, €11.65-€14.59). Change at Ciudad Real for **Córdoba, Sevilla, Granada,** and **Valencia.** Buses (☎926 86 02 50) stop at a brick building at the far end of Ejido de Calatrava, left of the Hospedería Municipal de Almagro. **AISA** (926 21 13 42) buses go to **Ciudad Real,** the connection point for most other cities (30min.; M-F 7 per day 8am-6:15pm, Sa 9:15am and 3pm; €1.46) and **Madrid** (2¼hr.; M-F 3 per day 7, 9:40am, 4pm; €10.40).

🖥🔌 **ORIENTATION & PRACTICAL INFORMATION.** The center of Almagro is the long, arcaded Pl. Mayor. From the bus station, walk down C. Rondo de Calatrava, turn left on C. Madre de Dios, and follow it straight to the plaza. The **tourist office,** Pl. Mayor, 1, is located on the ground floor of the Ayuntamiento, directly beneath the clocktower. (☎926 86 07 17. Open Apr.-June and Sept. Tu-F 10am-2pm and 5-8pm, Sa 10am-2pm and 5-7pm, Su 11am-2pm and 5-7pm; July-Aug. Tu-Sa 10am-2pm and 6-9pm, Su 11am-2pm and 6-8pm; Oct.-Mar. Tu-F 10am-2pm and 4-7pm, Sa-Su 10am-2pm and 4-6pm. All sights have coordinated their hours with the tourist office.) **Banks** and **ATMs** line C. Mayor de Carnicerías. Services include: **emergency** ☎926 86 00 33; **police,** C. Mercado, 1 (☎609 01 41 36), adjacent to the Pl. Mayor; **Centro de Salud,** C. Mayor de Carnicerías, 11 (☎926 86 10 26); **Internet access, Cybernet,** C. Ronda de Calatrava, 8, across the park from the Hospedería (Tu-Su 5-11pm; €2 per hr.); **post office,** C. Mayor de Carnicerías, 16 (☎926 86 00 52; open M-F 8:30am-2:30pm, Sa 9:30am-1pm.). **Postal Code:** 13270.

ACCOMMODATIONS & FOOD. Finding a place to sleep during the theater festival, from the first Thursday to the last Sunday of July, can be a drama in and of itself. Reserve as early as April, particularly at the **Hospedería de Almagro ❷**, Ejido de Calatrava, s/n. The rooms are bright and spacious, and many overlook a pleasant courtyard, echoing the austere decor of the adjacent monastery. Clean baths, phones, and TVs provide for a comfortable stay. (☎926 88 20 87; fax 88 21 22. Aug.-June singles with bath €19.75; doubles with shower €27, with bath €33. July €22.50/€33/€39. MC/V.) To the right of the Hospedería is the more expensive **Hotel Don Diego ❸**, C. Bolaños, 1, which has brightly lit hallways and equally clean and comfortable rooms, all complete with bath, shower, TV, and phone. (☎926 86 12 87; fax 86 05 74. Aug.-June singles €31.50; doubles €44; triples €59. July €49/ €67/€82.) Closer to Pl. Mayor is **La Posada de Almagro ❹**, C. Gran Maestre, 5. From the tourist office, head towards the opposite end of the Pl. Mayor, passing the small park and **statue** of Diego de Almagro on the left. Make an immediate right on C. Gran Maestre. Inside the large wooden gate is a beautiful courtyard with hanging vines and potted flowers. Rooms are charming and rustic, with colorfully tiled bathrooms. (☎/fax 926 24 12 01. Aug.-June singles €36; doubles €55; triples €67. July €48/€75/€90.) Outdoor **restaurants** crowd Pl. Mayor, offering some of the best (and most expensive) food in town. Inside the **Hospedería de Almagro** is the cozy dining hall of **Restaurante Dos Toreadores ❷**, which has an extensive selection of seafood, meat, poultry, and vegetable entrees (€5-11). Especially good is the *pisto manchego*, a regional green pepper and tomato stew. (Open daily July-Aug. 1:30-4pm and 9-11:30pm. Sept.-June 1:30-4pm and 8:30-11pm.) Fresh fruits and veggies are sold at the outdoor **market**. From Pl. Mayor, walk down C. Mayor de Carnicerías for one block, then turn left on Rastro de San Juan. (Open W 8am-3pm.)

SIGHTS & ENTERTAINMENT. Plaza Mayor is square one for cultural sites in Almagro. Here you can find the **Corral de Comedias,** an open-air multilevel theater resembling Shakespeare's Globe. This theater is the only one left intact from the Golden Age of Spanish drama, and its stage was home to the works of such literary masters as Cervantes and Lope de Vega. (☎926 86 15 39. Same hours as tourist office. €2, children and groups of 15 or more €1.50.) Directly across the plaza from the *corral* and through a few arches, the **Museo Nacional del Teatro** displays the history of Spanish drama. Ticket includes entrance to the museum's temporary exhibits on different aspects of Spanish theater, such as costumes and stage design, which are housed in the Iglesia de San Agustín, on the corner of C. San Agustín and C. Feria. (☎/fax 926 26 10 14. Same hours as tourist office. €1.20; under 18, Sa afternoon, and Su morning free.) The closing act of the theater tour is the **Teatro Municipal,** C. San Agustín, 20. Follow C. San Agustín out of Pl. Mayor and look for a crimson and white building on the right. Inside is a renovated theater and a small collection of elaborate costumes. (☎926 86 13 61. Same hours as tourist office.) Teatro Municipal hosts modern Spanish plays weekends in September, October, and November. Contact the *teatro* for programs and details in August.

FESTIVALS. Every year, prestigious theater companies and players from around the world descend on the town for the **Festival Internacional de Teatro Clásico de Almagro** from the first Thursday to the last Sunday in July. Daily performances of Spanish and international classics take place in the Corral de Comedias, Teatro Hospital de San Juan de Dios, Teatro Municipal, Claustro de los Domínicos, Teatro Infantil, Teatro en la Calle, Patio de Fucares, and Seminarios. The **box office** is in the Palacio de los Medrano, C. San Agustín, 7. (☎902 10 12 12; www.festivaldealmagro.com. Open May-June Th 11:30am-1:30pm; July daily 11:30am-2pm and 7:30-10:30pm. MC/V.) There are daily productions in July at 10:45pm at most venues, but some theaters have earlier showtimes. Look online or inquire at the tourist office for specific times. Tickets are €11-16 (Tu half-price) and should be purchased in May before the festival begins, as they tend to sell out very quickly. The festival also has an office in Madrid at C. del Príncipe, 14 (☎915 21 07 20), and the 2004 program is listed online. From Sept.-June, there are **classical theater** performances nearly every weekend at the Corral. (☎926 88 24 58; www.corraldecomedias.com. Performances at 7, 7:30, or 9pm, depending on the date. Programs available online and at the tourist office.)

CUENCA ☎969

Cuenca (pop. 50,000) owes its fame to its location. Perched atop a hill, the city is flanked by two rivers and the stunning rock formations they have created. These natural boundaries have served the city well; Muslims and then Christians settled in Cuenca because it was a nearly impenetrable natural fortress. The city now strains against its boundaries as modern commercial life spills downhill into New Cuenca. The enchanting old city still safeguards most of Cuenca's treasures, including the famed *casas colgadas* (hanging houses) dangling high above the Río Huécar and the Plaza Mayor's magnificent cathedral.

▐ TRANSPORTATION

Trains: C. Mariano Catalina, 10 (☎902 24 02 02). To: **Aranjuez** (2hr., 3-4 per day 7:05am-6:55pm, €6.55); **Madrid** (2½-3hr., 5-6 per day 7:05am-6:55pm, €8.95); **Valencia** (3-4hr.; 3-4 per day M-F 7:45am-7pm, Sa-Su 11:19am-7pm; €9.85).

Buses: C. Fermín Caballero, 20 (☎969 22 70 87). Info open daily 7am-9pm. **AutoRes** (☎969 22 11 84) to **Madrid** (2½hr.; 8-9 per day M-Sa 7:30am-8pm, Su 8am-10pm; €8.20-10.15). **Ciudad Directo** to **Toledo** (2½hr.; M-Sa 3 per day 6:30am, 4, 5pm; €10). **SIAL** (☎969 22 27 51) to **Barcelona** (9hr.; M-Sa 1 per day 9:30am, Su 2 per day 9:30am, 2pm; €29.47).

Taxis: Radio Taxi (☎969 23 33 43). From the train station to Pl. Mayor €3.60.

◄◄ ▐ ORIENTATION & PRACTICAL INFORMATION

Upon exiting the train station, the back of the bus station (a large brick building) will be directly in front of you; head up the steps to C. Fermín Caballero and turn right to enter the bus station. To reach **Plaza Mayor** in the old city from either station, take a left onto C. Fermín Caballero, following it as it becomes C. Cervantes, C. José Cobo, and finally, bearing slightly left through Pl. de la Hispanidad, **Calle Carretería.** Large street signs should show you the way. Alternately, take the #1 bus (every 20min., €0.60) to the last stop in the old city. From the bus stop on C. Carretería, head towards the river and turn right on C. Fray Luis de León; it's a grueling uphill walk to Pl. Mayor and the old city (20-25min.).

Tourist Office: Pl. Mayor (☎969 23 21 19; www.aytocuenca.org). C. Alfonso VIII broadens into Pl. Mayor. Some English spoken. Open July-Sept. M-Sa 9am-9pm, Su 9am-2pm; Oct.-June M-Sa 9am-2pm and 4-6pm, Su 9am-2pm.

Currency Exchange: Banco Santander Central Hispano, C. Carretería, 23 (☎969 21 17 26). Open Apr.-Sept. M-F 8:30am-2pm; Oct.-Mar. M-F 8:30am-2pm, Sa 8:30am-1pm.

Luggage Storage: At the **train station** (€3 per day; open daily 7:30am-9:30pm) and the **bus station** (€1.50 minimum per day; open daily 6am-9pm).

Emergency: ☎112. **Police:** C. Martínez Kleyser, 4 (☎091 or 092).

Pharmacy: Farmacia Castellanos, C. Cervantes, 12 (☎969 21 23 37), at the corner of C. Alférez Rubianes. Open Apr.-Oct. M-F 9:30am-2pm and 5-8pm, Sa 10am-2pm; Nov.-Mar. M-F 9:30am-2pm and 4:30-7:30pm, Sa 10am-2pm.

Internet Access: La Repro, C. Jorge Torner, 39 (☎ 969 24 01 36). From the bus station, take C. Fermín Caballero toward the city center; turn right at the first stop light and walk up C. Julio Larrañaga 1 block. Primarily a copy shop, though there is ample internet access upstairs and to the right. €1.20 per hr. Open M-F 10am-2pm and 5-8:30pm, Sa 10am-2pm. **Cyber Viajero**, Av. de la República Argentina, 3 (☎969 22 65 62). €2 per hr. or €6 for 4 hr. Open M-Sa 10:30am-2pm and 5-11pm.

Post Office: Parque de San Julián, 16 (☎969 22 90 16). Open M-F 8:30am-8:30pm, Sa 9:30am-2pm. Smaller **branch** with fewer services right next to the train station. Open M-F 8:30am-2:30pm, Sa 9:30am-1pm. **Postal Code: 16004.**

ACCOMMODATIONS

The dearth of cheap lodging in the old city may convince you to stay in the new city's less luxurious hostels. Rooms on the hill charge for their spectacular views.

■ **Posada de San José**, C. Julián Romero, 4 (☎ 969 21 13 00; fax 23 03 65). Cushy beds and gorgeous views. Some rooms with balconies, all with modern full baths. Reservations recommended July-Nov. and F-Sa year-round. Singles €20, with bath €41; doubles €31, with bath €61; triples with sink €42; quads with bath €97. *Semana Santa* prices higher; weeknight and low season prices lower. AmEx/MC/V. ❷

■ **Hostal Cánovas**, C. Fray Luis de León, 38, 1st fl. (☎969 21 39 73; www.servinet.net/canovas). Newly-refurbished rooms feel both elegant and comfortable. Shining hard-wood floors, balconies in all doubles, and private baths justify the price. Convenient access to both new and old Cuenca. Weekdays doubles €40; triples €52. Weekends and holidays €45/€57. Singles available some weekdays and in winter. MC/V. ❹

Pensión Tabanqueta, C. del Trabuco, 13 (☎969 21 12 90), up C. San Pedro from the cathedral past Pl. del Trabuco. Quite a hike from New Cuenca, but if you're after a room with a view, it may be worth the trip. Popular terrace bar shouldn't be missed. Singles €15; doubles €30; triples €45. ❷

Pensión Central, C. Alonso Chirino, 7, 2nd fl. (☎969 21 15 11). Clean, old-fashioned rooms with big windows, high ceilings, and sinks. Balconies to the street and courtyard views. Two common bathrooms. Breakfast, lunch, and dinner at a reasonable rate. July-Sept. singles €13; doubles €21.50; triples €29. Oct.-June €11.50/€19/€25.50. ❶

Hostelería Mota, Pl. de la Constitución, 6, 1st fl. (☎969 22 55 67). Marble floors, polished wooden walls, and A/C. Cheerful modern rooms have sinks and TVs. Singles occasionally available in winter. Doubles €28, with bath €37. ❸

FOOD

The area around Pl. Mayor is filled with mid- to high-priced restaurants, but side-streets near the plaza yield cheaper alternatives. Budget eateries line **Calle Cervantes** and **Avenida de la República Argentina**; the cafes off **Calle Fray Luis de León** are even cheaper. Area specialties *Resoli*, a liqueur of coffee, sugar, orange peel, and eau-de-vie, and *alajú*, a nougat of honey, almonds, and figs, are a heavenly match. For fresh fruit, vegetables, meat, and cheese, hit the **market** on C. Fray Luis de León. (Open M-Sa 8:30am-2pm.) Grab **groceries** at %**Día** on Av. Castilla La Mancha. (Open M-Th 9:30am-2pm and 5:30-8:30pm, F-Sa 9am-2:30pm and 5:30-9pm.)

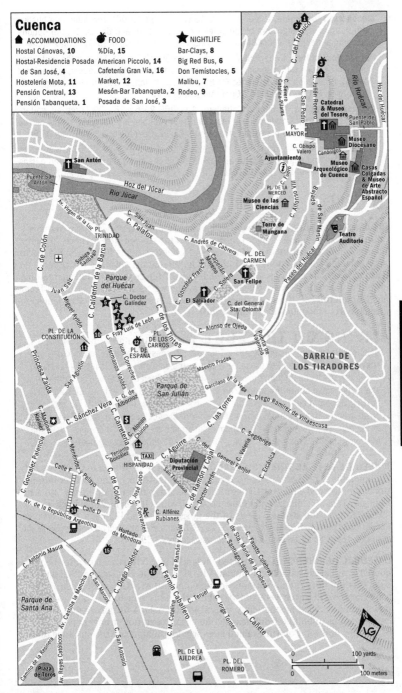

Cuenca

ACCOMMODATIONS
Hostal Cánovas, **10**
Hostal-Residencia Posada de San José, **4**
Hostelería Mota, **11**
Pensión Central, **13**
Pensión Tabanqueta, **1**

FOOD
%Día, **15**
American Piccolo, **14**
Cafetería Gran Vía, **16**
Market, **12**
Mesón-Bar Tabanqueta, **2**
Posada de San José, **3**

NIGHTLIFE
Bar-Clays, **8**
Big Red Bus, **6**
Don Temístocles, **5**
Malibu, **7**
Rodeo, **9**

Mesón-Bar Tabanqueta, C. del Trabuco, 13 (☎ 969 21 12 90). This little cafe bustles with patrons enjoying views of the gorge over cheap food and drinks. Several options including a *menú del día* (€8) and sandwiches (€2.40-5). Open Tu-Su noon-2am. ❶

Posada de San José, C. de Julián Romero, 4 (☎969 21 13 00). Soak in the ambience and terrace views with a serving of *pisto* (stew made of tomatoes, peppers, and onions; €3.45). *Bocadillos* and omelettes €1.80-3.60. Lamb, tenderloin, and fried trout €5-9. Open Tu-Su 8-11am and 6-10:30pm. AmEx/MC/V. ❶

Cafetería Gran Vía, C. Fermín Caballero, 4 (☎969 23 62 26). Well-dressed waiters attend the elegant wooden dining room and scurry among the people-watchers on the outdoor patio. Combo plates of fish and pork €7-11. Open daily 7:30pm-1am. V. ❷

American Piccolo, Av. de la República Argentina, 14 (☎969 21 28 55). Ignore the cheesy sign and enjoy the photos and prints at this cheerful *trattoria*. Pizzas and pastas €5-8. Lunch *menú* €9. Open M-Tu and Th-Su 1:30-4pm and 8-11:30pm. MC/V. ❷

👁 SIGHTS

🏠**CASAS COLGADAS.** Cuenca draws its fame from the gravity-defying *casas colgadas* that have dangled over the riverbanks for six centuries. These "hanging houses," built precariously on the edges of Cuenca's high cliffs, are believed to have been the summer homes of 14th-century monarchs. A walk across Puente de San Pablo at sunset offers a spectacular view of the *casas* and the surrounding cliffs. For fantastic views of Cuenca, stroll along two trails that flank Hoz del Júcar and Hoz del Huécar (the steep river gorges on either side of the old city). Maps are available from the municipal tourist office.

LIVING ON THE EDGE Very little is known about Cuenca's unique 14th-century *casas colgadas*. They were supposedly built to house kings; one is even named Casa del Rey. Casa de la Sirena, the only other remaining original hanging house, got its name from the siren-like screams emitted by a Cuenca *señorita* when she flung herself out of the window after her son was killed by her lover. Despite their striking appearance, the *casas* did not become famous until recently. In fact, the *casas* were completely run down when the city of Cuenca decided to rehabilitate them in the early twentieth century, transforming them into magnificent museums. Now one of central Spain's greatest attractions, the houses draw thousands of visitors annually.

MUSEO DE ARTE ABSTRACTO ESPAÑOL. Inside one of the *casas*, the award-winning Museo de Arte Abstracto Español exhibits works by the odd yet internationally renowned Abstract Generation of Spanish painters. All pieces, most by Canogar, Tápies, Chillida, and Fernando Zóbel, were chosen by Zóbel himself. The "White Room" and striking views of the gorge are added bonuses. *(Pl. Ciudad de Ronda; follow signs from Pl. Mayor. ☎969 21 29 83. Open Tu-F 11am-2pm and 4-6pm, Sa 11am-2pm and 4-8pm, Su 11am-2pm. €3, students and seniors €1.50.)*

CATEDRAL DE CUENCA. Constructed under Alfonso VIII six years after he conquered Castilla, the cathedral dominates Pl. Mayor. A perfect square, 25m on each side, it is the only Anglo-Norman Gothic cathedral in Spain. A Spanish Renaissance facade and tower were added in the 16th and 17th centuries, only to be torn down when deemed aesthetically inappropriate. A 1724 fire prevented a subsequent attempt to build a front, leaving the current exterior strangely reminiscent of a Hollywood set. Colorful stained glass windows illuminate the entrance to the

Museo del Tesoro, which houses late medieval psalters and gold jewelry. More impressive is the **Sala Capitular** with its delightful ceiling. *(Pl. Mayor. Cathedral open daily 9am-2pm and 4-6pm; museum open Tu-Sa 11am-2pm and 4-6pm, Su 11am-2pm. Cathedral free, museum €1.50.)*

OTHER SIGHTS. Perhaps the most beautiful of the museums along C. de Julián Romero is the **Museo Diocesano,** whose exhibits include Juan de Borgoña's altarpiece from the local Convento de San Pablo, colossal Flemish tapestries, splendid rugs, and two El Grecos—*Oración del huerto* and *Cristo con la cruz.* *(☎969 22 42 10. Open Apr.-Sept. Tu-Sa 11am-2pm and 5-8pm, Su 11am-2pm; Oct.-Mar. Tu-Sa 11am-2pm and 4-7pm. €2.)* Down C. Obispo Valero, the **Museo Arqueológico de Cuenca** is a treasure trove of Roman mosaics, ceramics, and coins and Visigoth jewelry. *(☎969 21 30 69. Open June-Sept. Tu-Sa 10am-2pm and 5-7pm, Su 11am-2pm; Oct.-June Tu-Sa 10am-2pm and 4-7pm, Su and holidays 11am-2pm. €1.20, students €0.60. Sa afternoon and Su free.)*

■ NIGHTLIFE

Cuenca's nightlife scene extends into the wee hours of the morning. The older crowd stays near Pl. Mayor, while teens and twenty-somethings flock to the newer city. Several bars with young, well-dressed crowds line **Calle Doctor Galíndez,** off C. Fray Luis de León. It's a hot spot in the new city, but a long, dark walk down the hill from Old Cuenca; a taxi costs about €3.60. **Bar-Clays** (opens at 7pm), **Malibu** (opens at 11:30pm), **Rodeo** (opens Tu, Th-Su, and "sometimes" M and W at 11pm), and **Don Temístocles** (opens at 11pm) along C. Doctor Galíndez are nearly identical, with fun-loving bartenders, darts, and a plethora of mixed drinks. Closing hours are generally between 2 and 4:30 am. For two floors of dance and drink, catch the **Big Red Bus** on C. Doctor Galíndez. The spacious dance floors fill quickly after midnight as partiers from nearby bars suddenly and simultaneously feel the urge to groove to techno, pop, and hip-hop. (Drinks €2-4. Open daily 11:30pm-4am.)

SIGÜENZA ☎949

Peaceful and lovely Sigüenza (pop. 5000) is somewhat humdrum for any longer than a day. Its rosy stone buildings and red-roofed houses surround a storybook Gothic cathedral and castle, both of which deserve a peek. During the Spanish Civil War, the Republicans seized the cathedral and the Nationalists took the castle, providing more action than this small town has seen since. Sigüenza's medieval architecture has been painstakingly restored, and a walk through the streets—from the 12th-century medieval city to the 18th-century Baroque neighborhoods—makes an enjoyable escape from Madrid.

■ TRANSPORTATION & PRACTICAL INFORMATION. The **train station** (☎949 39 14 94) is at the end of Av. de Alfonso VI. Trains run to Estación Chamartín in **Madrid** (1½-2hr., 6-7 per day 6:52am-8:17pm, €7.20-8.25) and **Soria** (1½hr.; daily 2 per day 9:45am, 8:48pm; F 3 per day 9:45am, 5:20, 8:48pm; €5). For a **taxi** call ☎949 39 14 11. **Luggage storage** is at the train station (€1.80 per locker). To get to the **tourist office,** follow Av. de Alfonso VI to the first intersection after the Parque de la Alameda (on the left). The office is just around the corner in the restored Ermita. (☎949 34 70 07. Open M-F 10am-2:30pm and 4-6:30pm, Sa 9:30am-3pm and 3:30-7pm, Su 9:30am-3:30pm. Closed M Oct.-Apr.) Across the intersection **Banco Santander Hispano Central,** Av. Calvo Siteco, 9, has a 24hr. **ATM.** (☎949 39 01 50; open M-F 8:30am-2pm.) **Internet** is available at a coin-operated machine in **Don**

Rodrigo Pizzeria, C. del Cardenal Mendoza, 16, on the corner of C. del Humilladero. (☎949 39 16 19. €1 per 15min. Open 8am-midnight.) Services include: **emergency** (☎949 30 00 19); **Red Cross,** Ctra. Madrid (☎949 39 13 33); **police,** Ctra. de Atienzo (☎949 39 01 95). **Post office:** C. de Villaviciosa, 10, off Pl. Hilario Yabén. (☎949 39 08 44. Open M-F 8:30am-2:30pm, Sa 9:30am-1pm.) **Postal Code:** 19250.

ri ACCOMMODATIONS. Although you can do Sigüenza in a few hours, train schedules might force you to spend the night. The **Pensión Venancio ❶,** C. San Roque, 3, is old but charming. Rooms have heating in winter. From the station, follow Av. de Alfonso VI and turn left at the first intersection onto Av. Pío XII. (☎949 39 03 47. Singles €14; doubles €26; triples €37.) Small places to eat offering delicious *menús* for under €8 can be found everywhere.

◙ SIGHTS. The tourist office leads guided **city tours,** including entrance to all parts of the cathedral, for €6. From the bottom of the hill, two buildings jut out from Sigüenza's low skyline: the cathedral and the fortified **castle,** a 12th-century castle-turned-*parador* (luxury hotel). Restored in the 1970s, the castle merits an uphill stroll through the cobblestone streets, even just for a peek into the luxuriously decorated *parador* and its marvelous view. To get to the ◙**cathedral,** follow Av. de Alfonso VI uphill (it changes to C. del Humilladero), then take a left onto C. del Cardenal Mendoza. Work on the cathedral began in the mid-12th century and continued until the 16th century; it combines Romanesque, Mudéjar, Plateresque, and Gothic styles. One of the structure's most renowned features is the 15th-century **Tumba del Doncel,** a tomb commissioned by Queen Isabel in memory of a page who died fighting the Muslims in Granada. The sacristry's Renaissance ceiling boasts 304 stone portraits carved by Alanso de Covarrubias. The adjoining chapel houses El Greco's *Anunciación*. (☎619 36 27 15. Cathedral open daily 9am-1:30pm and 4:30-8pm. Free. Tours in Spanish, required for entry to sacristy and chapel. Tours year-round Tu-Sa 11am, noon, 12:45, 4:30, 5:30pm; June-Nov. 12 also Su noon, 5:30pm; Nov. 13-May also Su noon, 1, 5:30pm. €3.) Opposite the cathedral, the small **Museo de Arte Antiguo** (Museo Diocesano) houses standard medieval and early modern religious works, including a Ribera and Zurbarán's *La Inmaculada Niña*. (☎949 39 10 23. Call ahead, as it is currently undergoing extensive restoration work. Open Tu-Su 11am-2pm and 4-7pm. €2.)

CASTILLA Y LEÓN

The aqueduct of Segovia, the Gothic cathedrals of Burgos and León, the Romanesque belfries along Camino de Santiago, the sandstone of Salamanca, and the city walls of Ávila: these images, ingrained in the collective memory of the Spanish consciousness, all belong to Castilla y León. Age-old traditions are preserved particularly vehemently here: in the public slaughter of pigs in Medina de Rioseco, in the fire bull at Coca, and in the *cabezadas* (bowling) in León. Well before Castilla's famous 1469 confederation with Aragón, when Fernando of Aragón and Isabel of Castilla were united in world-shaking matrimony, it was clear that Castilla had its act together. During the High Middle Ages, the region emerged from obscurity to lead the Christian charge against Islam. Castilian nobles, sanguine from the spoils of combat, introduced the concept of a unified Spain (under Castilian command, of course), and *castellano* ("Spanish") became the dominant language throughout the nation. Castilla's comrade in arms, imperious León, though chagrined to be lumped with Castilla in a 1970s provincial reorganization, has much in common with its more famous co-province.

HIGHLIGHTS OF CASTILLA Y LEÓN

BASK in the sunlight streaming through the stained-glass windows of **León's** Gothic cathedral (see p. 194).

GO BLIND trying to find the little frog on the facade of the **Universidad de Salamanca** (see p. 182). If you do, you'll have good luck.

REDEFINE obsession with St. Teresa in medieval **Ávila** (see p. 174).

GORGE yourself on chocolate in **Astorga,** home to one of the few Gaudí structures outside Barcelona (see p. 195).

EXPLORE the streets of **Valladolid** in the steps of Columbus, Cervantes, and Magellan (see p. 196).

BAA-GAIN for sheep at the market in **Medina del Campo** (see p. 199).

SEGOVIA ☎ 921

Segovia (pop. 56,000) is immersed in legend. The history that surrounds each monument in the "Stone Ship" that is Segovia—so named because of the prow-shaped profile of the city's Alcázar, its cathedral's mast-like tower, and the world-famous aqueduct that comprises the ship's helm—are told and retold. Legend has it that the devil constructed the aqueduct in one night in a failed effort to win the soul of a Segovian water-seller named Juanilla. Devil or not, Segovia's attractions and winding alleyways draw their share of Spanish and international tourists, as well as students looking for language practice. Such old-town charm comes at a price; food and accommodations are more expensive here than in Madrid.

◪ TRANSPORTATION

Trains: Po. Obispo Quesada, (☎921 42 07 74). To **Madrid** (2hr.; 7-9 per day M-F 5:55am-8:55pm, Sa-Su 8:55am-8:55pm; €5) and **Villalba** (1hr., 7-9 per day M-F 7am-8:57pm, €3.25), the transfer for **Ávila, El Escorial, León,** and **Salamanca.**

CASTILLA Y LEÓN

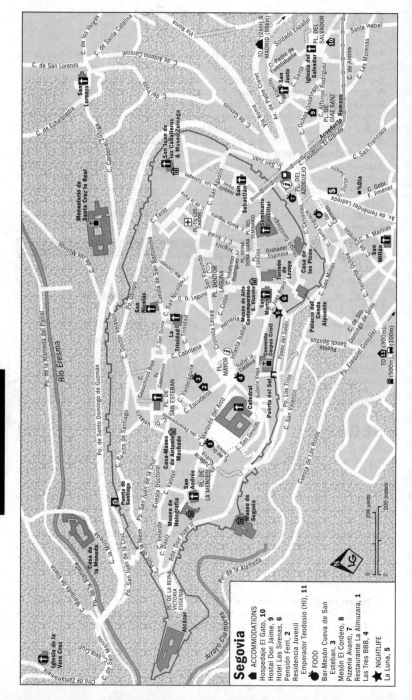

Segovia

♦ ACCOMMODATIONS
Hospedaje El Gato, **10**
Hostal Don Jaime, **9**
Hotel Las Sirenas, **6**
Pensión Ferri, **2**
Residencia Juvenil
Emperador Teodosio (HI), **11**

♦ FOOD
Bar-Mesón Cueva de San
Esteban, **3**
Mesón El Cordero, **8**
Pizzeria Avanti, **7**
Restaurante La Almuzara, **1**
Las Tres BBB, **4**

★ NIGHTLIFE
La Luna, **5**

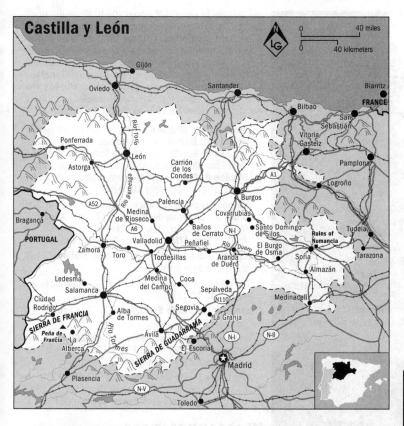

Castilla y León

Buses: Estación Municipal de Autobuses, Po. Ezequiel González, 12 (☎921 42 77 07). **Linecar** (☎921 42 77 06) to: **Salamanca** (3hr.; 4 per day M-F 8:50am-5:45pm, Sa 3 per day 8:50am, 1:30, 5:45pm; Su 1 per day 5:45pm; €8.50); **Valladolid** (2hr.; M-F 12 per day and Sa 8 per day 6:45am-9pm, Su 6 per day 9am-9pm; €6). **La Sepulvedana** (☎921 42 77 07) to: **Ávila** (1hr.; M-F 4 per day 7:45, 10:30am, 2:30, 7:30pm; Sa also at 8pm; €3.65); **La Granja** (20min.; 9-15 per day M-Sa 7:40am-9:30pm, Su 10:30am-10:30pm; round-trip €1.50); **Madrid** (1½hr.; M-F every 30min. 6am-9:30pm, Sa 7:30am-9:30pm, Su 8:30am-10:30pm; €5.51).

Public Transportation: Transportes Urbanos de Segovia, Pl. Mayor, 8 (☎921 46 03 29). €0.65; 10-trip **Bono-Bus** pass €4.13, sold at the office.

Taxis: Radio Taxi (24hr. ☎921 44 50 00). Taxis pull up by the train and bus stations.

✦ 🔢 ORIENTATION & PRACTICAL INFORMATION

Take any bus from the train station (€0.65) to **Plaza Mayor,** the city's historic center, or **Plaza del Azoguejo,** just downhill from Pl. Mayor. The **Paseo del Salón** bus (M-F every 30min. 7:45am-10:15pm) runs directly to the steps of **Puerta del Sol.** The Pl.

THE LOCAL LEGEND

A MOTHER'S SACRIFICE

The majestic, snow-covered mountain framing Segovia's cathedral and Alcázar is known as *La Mujer Muerta* (The Dead Woman) and commemorates a bloody but moving turn of events. According to local folklore, *la mujer*, the wife of a chief, was widowed when her twin sons were but young boys. As only one of the two could inherit his father's rule, the mother grew fearful of impending fratricide once the children came of age. She offered her life to God as a sacrifice, hoping this act would save both her sons. Unfortunately, it settled nothing. On a summer's day years later, as the two young men prepared to fight each other for supremacy, it suddenly began to snow. By the time the storm dissipated, a snow-capped mountain had materialized upon the scene of the proposed battleground. As all soon acknowledged, it was the resting body of the twins' mother. *Segovianos* insist that two small clouds float closer to the mountain every day at dusk—the two sons kissing their mother goodnight.

del Azoguejo bus (M-F every 30min. 7:30am-10pm, Sa-Su 7:45am-10:15pm) goes to the **aqueduct** and **municipal tourist office**. On foot from the **train station** (20min.), turn right, cross the street, and walk toward town along Po. Obispo Quesada, becoming Av. Conde de Sepúlveda, then Po. Ezequiel González, before coming to the bus station. From the **bus station** (15min.), cross Po. Ezequiel González and follow Av. de Fernández Ladreda to Pl. del Azoguejo.

Tourist Office: Regional office, Pl. Mayor, 10 (☎921 46 03 34). Map almost as good as ours. Open June-Aug. Su-Th 9am-8pm, F-Sa 9am-9pm; Sept.-May M-F 9am-2pm and 5-7pm, Sa-Su 9am-2pm and 5-8pm. **Municipal office,** Pl. del Azoguejo, 1 (☎921 46 29 06 or 46 29 14). Open daily 10am-8pm.

Currency Exchange: Banco Santander Central Hispano, Av. de Fernández Ladreda, 17. Open Apr.-Sept. M-F 8:30am-2pm; Oct.-Mar. M-F 8:30am-2pm, Sa 8:30am-1pm. **ATMs** line Av. de Fernández Ladreda.

Luggage Storage: Lockers at the **train station** €3 per day. Open daily 6am-10pm.

Emergency: Municipal Police, C. Guadarrama, 26 (☎921 43 12 12).

Hospital: Policlínico San Agustín, C. San Agustín, 13 (☎921 41 92 75).

Internet Access: Locutorio Mundo 2000, Pl. del Azoguejo, 4 (☎921 44 52 93). €0.90 per 30min., €1 per hr. Open daily 11am-11pm.

Post Office: Pl. Doctor Laguna, 5 (☎921 46 16 16), up C. Cronista Lecea from Pl. Mayor. Open M-F 8:30am-8:30pm, Sa 9:30am-2pm. **Postal Code:** 40001.

🛏 ACCOMMODATIONS

Segovia's numerous sights and proximity to Madrid and La Granja make rooms scarce during the summer. Reservations are a must for any of the hotels, especially those in or around major plazas. *Pensiones* are significantly cheaper, but rooms tend to be on the less comfortable side of "basic."

Hospedaje El Gato, Pl. del Salvador, 10 (☎921 42 32 44; fax 43 80 47). Beautiful patchwork and pine rooms made even more so with A/C, satellite TV, and private baths. Doubles €35; triples €48.50. ❸

Hotel Las Sirenas, C. Juan Bravo, 30 (☎921 46 26 63; fax 46 26 57), down C. Cervantes. Luxurious rooms with TV, shower, telephone, and A/C. Reservations encouraged. Singles €36-45, with bath €42-50; doubles with bath €56. AmEx/MC/V. ❹

Hostal Don Jaime, C. Ochoa Ondategui, 8 (☎921 44 47 87). Wood paneling and white walls in rooms with TV, phone, and large mirrors. Breakfast €3. Singles €22, with bath €30; doubles €30/€40; triples with bath €50. MC/V. ❷

Pensión Ferri, C. Escuderos, 10 (☎921 46 09 57), off Pl. Mayor. A fortifying experience: rustic but tidy rooms with stone walls, some with windows, overlooking a bountiful garden. Central location. Showers €2. Singles €13; doubles €19. ❶

Residencia Juvenil Emperador Teodosio (HI), Av. Conde de Sepúlveda, 4 (☎921 44 11 11 or 44 10 47). Look for a bright red fire escape in front. From the train station, turn right down Po. Obispo Quesada, continuing as it becomes Av. Conde de Sepúlveda (10min.). From the bus station, turn right on Po. Ezequiel González, continuing as it becomes Av. Conde de Sepúlveda (10min.). Private baths. HI card required. Max. 3-night stay. Lockout 2am. Breakfast €1. Open July 1-Sept. 15. Dorms €6.61, with full meals €13.82; over 26 €9.32/€18.63. ❶

Camping: Camping Acueducto, C. Borbón, 49/Highway CN-601, km112 (☎921 42 50 00), 2km toward La Granja. Take the AutoBus Urbano (€0.65) from Pl. del Azoguejo to Nueva Segovia. Restaurant, supermarket, hot showers, pool, and laundry. Open *Semana Santa*-Sept. €4 per person, tent, and car. ❶

🍴 FOOD

To avoid tourist traps, steer clear of Pl. Mayor, Pl. del Azoguejo, and any menus posted on worn "medieval" parchment. *Sopa castellana* (soup with bread, eggs, and garlic), *cochinillo asado* (roast suckling pig), and lamb are all regional specialities. Segovia's many sights and steps are ideal for picnics. A **market** (9am-2:30pm) comes to Pl. Mayor every Thursday and next to Av. de la Constitución every Saturday. Buy **groceries** at **%Día,** C. Gobernador Fernández Jiménez, 3, off Av. de Fernández Ladreda. (Open M-Th 9:30am-8:30pm, F-Sa 9am-9pm.)

▨ **Bar-Mesón Cueva de San Esteban,** C. Valdeláguila, 15 (☎921 46 09 82). The owner knows his wines (he won the 2002 "nose of gold" trophy) and his food. Attentive and friendly service in both the entrance room and the 600 year-old cave-turned-*comedor*. Casual yet classy, this *cueva* could make anyone feel like a connoisseur. Lunch *menú* M-F €8, Sa-Su €10. Entrees €7-14. Wines €1-3. IVA not included. Open daily 10am-midnight. MC/V. ❸

Mesón El Cordero, C. del Carmen, 4-6 (☎921 46 33 45). A superb fine-dining establishment. Spreads of wine, meats, and other specials are a feast for the eyes and the stomach. Selection of *menús*, including vegetarian fare, €9 and up. Meat entrees €9-15. Open M-Sa 12:30-4:30pm and 8pm-midnight, Su 12-6pm. MC/V. ❸

Restaurante La Almuzara, C. Marqués del Arco, 3 (☎921 46 06 22), past the cathedral. Vegetarian cuisine. Large salads €3.60-9. Luncheon *menú* €9. Meat entrees also offered €6-10. Open W-Su 12:45-4pm and 8pm-midnight, Tu 8pm-midnight. MC/V. ❷

Las Tres BBB, Pl. Mayor, 13 (☎921 46 21 25). Follow locals here for cheap eats. Specializing in seafood (€2.40-8.40), Las Tres BBB offers all the basics, including simple *bocadillos* (€1.80-2.70). Open daily 8am-midnight. ❶

Pizzeria Avanti Restaurante, C. Santa Columba, 5 (☎921 46 60 22), up the steps to the right of the regional tourist office. Cheap pizzas (€6.95), hamburgers (€3.10), and typical Spanish fare provide a much-needed respite from the inflated prices of nearby restaurants. Open daily 12:30-4pm and 7:30-midnight. ❶

◎ SIGHTS

Segovia rewards the wanderer. Its picturesque museums, palaces, churches, and streets beg you to put aside your tourist brochure and just explore. Often overlooked by tourists are Segovia's peaceful northern regions, outside the walls and away from the Alcázar. For a long, relaxing walk, tour the monasteries and churches along the Río Eresma.

AQUEDUCT. The ever-engineering Romans built Segovia's aqueduct around 50 BC to pipe in water from the Río Frío, 18km away. Today, *segovianos* use it to pipe tourists into the old city. The two tiers of 163 arches supported by 128 pillars span 813m and reach a height of 29m near Pl. del Azoguejo. Some 20,000 blocks of granite were used in the construction—without a drop of mortar. This spectacular feat of engineering, restored by the monarchy in the 15th century, can transport 30L of water per second and was used until the late 1940s. (*Near Pl. del Azoguejo. Free.*)

ALCÁZAR. From afar, Segovia's Alcázar looks strangely familiar, but fear not; Disneyworld's Magic Kingdom palace is thousands of miles away. Of classic late-medieval design, it dominates the far northern end of the old quarter and provides astounding views of Queen Victoria Eugenia's gardens and the surrounding countryside. Fortifications have occupied this site since the time of the Celts due to its strategic location at the confluence of two rivers. Alfonso X, who allegedly believed he was God, took the original 11th-century fortress and beautified it. Successive monarchs added to the Alcázar's grandeur, and the final touches were added for the coronation of Isabel I as queen of Castilla in 1474. The walls of the **Sala de Reyes** (Room of Kings) are adorned with wood- and gold-inlaid friezes of monarchs. In the **Sala de Solio** (throne room), the inscription above the throne reads: *"tanto monta, monta tanto"* (she mounts, as does he). Get your mind out of the gutter—it means that Fernando and Isabel had equal authority as sovereigns. The **Museo Real Colegio de Artillería** commemorates the period during which the Alcázar was used as a artillery school (1764-1862). Cannon, charts, and models abound. For a great view (and workout), climb the seemingly endless spiral staircase that begins in the gift shop to stand atop the "prow" of the stone ship Segovia. (*Pl. de la Reina Victoria Eugenia. ☎921 46 07 59. Open Apr.-Sept. daily 10am-7pm; Nov.-Mar. daily 10am-6pm; Oct. M-F 10am-6pm, Sa-Su 10am-7pm. €3.10, seniors and students €2.20. Audio guides available in English, €3.*)

CATHEDRAL. In 1525, Charles V commissioned the construction of a cathedral to replace the 12th-century edifice destroyed in the *Revuelta de las Comunidades*. The new one, he hoped, would tower over Pl. Mayor. When it was finished 200 years later, with 23 chapels and a gilt treasury, the cathedral earned the nickname "The Lady of All Cathedrals." The **Sala Capitular,** hung with 17th-century tapestries, displays an ornate silver-and-gold chariot. Off the cloister is the **Capilla de Santa Catalina,** filled with incredible crucifixes, chalices, and candelabras. (*☎921 46 22 05. Open daily Apr.-Oct. 9am-6:30pm; Nov.-Mar. 9:30am-6pm; final entrance 30min. before closing. Mass M-Sa 10, 11am; Su 11am, 12:30, 2pm. €2, under 14 and Su until 2:30pm free.*)

▥ MUSEUMS

▧ **CASA-MUSEO DE ANTONIO MACHADO.** Antonio Machado (1875-1939)—literature professor, playwright, and, above all, author of love poems and melancholic verse—never made much money. The poet rented this small *pensión*-turned-museum from 1919 to 1932 for 3 pesetas per day. A short, informative tour details major influences on Machado's poetry, including the 1909 death of his first wife and a subsequent affair with a married Segovian woman he called "Guiomar" in his writings. The poet's modest room has been left untouched, filled with original manuscripts and portraits (including a Picasso) on its walls. Of his room Machado once wrote (upside down) *"Blanca Hospedería, Celda de Viajero, ¡Con la Sombra Mi!"* (Modest and clean lodging, traveler's cell, alone with my shadow!). Though significantly more humble than the Alcázar, this museum holds its own among Segovia's treasures. *(C. des Desamparados, 5. ☎921 46 03 77. Open W-Su 11am-2pm and 4:30-7:30pm. Guided Spanish tour required. €1.50, W free.)*

MUSEO DE ARTE CONTEMPORÁNEO ESTEBAN VICENTE. This elegant museum holds a permanent collection of native Segovian Esteban Vicente's works and a prestigious exhibition of contemporary art. *(Pl. de las Bellas Artes, just above Pl. de San Martín, off C. de Cervantes. ☎921 46 20 10. Open Tu-Sa 11am-2pm and 4-7pm, Su and festivals 11am-2pm. €2.40, students and seniors €1.20. Th free.)*

MUSEO ZULOAGA. Ceramics fans, head here first. A former church and palace in Pl. Colmenares was the home and workshop of Daniel Zuloaga, an early 20th-century artist whose tile murals grace many walls in Madrid. It now showcases his paintings, tilework, and ceramics. *(☎921 46 33 48. Open Tu-Sa 10am-2pm and 4-7pm, Su 10am-2pm. €1.20, students and seniors free.)*

OUTSIDE THE WALLS. A walk away from the city beyond the meandering Río Eresma offers a welcome change of pace. Be prepared, however, for a grueling uphill trek back to the city. Nearby is the **Monasterio de Santa Cruz la Real,** a mysterious dodecagonal basilica built by the mystical Knights Templar in 1208. *(Follow C. Pozo de la Nieve, on the left leaving the Alcázar, down the 2nd stone staircase to Po. San Juan de la Cruz. 20min. walk. ☎921 43 14 75. Open Tu-Su Apr.-Sept. 10:30am-1:30pm and 3:30-7pm; Oct. and Dec.-Mar. 10:30am-1:30pm and 3:30-6pm. €1.50; W free for Spanish citizens.)*

🟥🟦 NIGHTLIFE & FESTIVALS

Though the city isn't known for its sleepless nights, when it comes to nightlife, *segovianos* (and their visitors) go all out. Packed with bars and cafes, Pl. Mayor is the center of Segovian nightlife. Specifically, head for **Calle Infanta Isabel** (creatively nicknamed "calle de los barres" by the locals) and follow the crowd to find the hopping place of the evening. The **bars** filling Pl. del Azoguejo and C. Carmen, near the aqueduct, are frequented by the high school set. **Club** headquarters are C. Ruíz de Alda, off Pl. del Azoguejo. You can count on a party every night of the week at **La Luna,** C. Pta. de la Luna, 8. From Pl. Mayor, head down C. Isabel la Católica onto C. Juan Bravo and take your second right. A young local and international crowd mixes it up in this popular discopub, downing cheap shots and Heineken. *(☎921 46 26 51. Shots €1. Beer €1.50. Open daily 4:30pm-4am.)*

From June 24 to 29, Segovia holds a **fiesta** in honor of San Juan and San Pedro. During the festival there are free open-air concerts on Pl. del Azoguejo, as well as dances and fireworks on June 29. **Zamarramala,** 3km northwest of Segovia, hosts the **Fiestas de Santa Águeda** on the weekend following February 5. Women take over the town's administration for a day, dress in period costumes, and parade through the streets to commemorate a sneak attack on the Alcázar in which the townswomen distracted the castle guards with wine and song. And maybe something else. The all-female local council takes advantage of its authority to ridicule men and, at the festival's end, burn a male effigy.

CASTILLA Y LEÓN

◪ DAYTRIP FROM SEGOVIA

◪LA GRANJA DE SAN ILDEFONSO

La Sepulvedana buses (☎921 42 77 07) run from Segovia to La Granja (20min.; 9-12 per day M-Sa 7:40am-9:30pm, Su 10:30am-10:30pm; return M-Sa 7:20am-9pm, Su 11am-10pm; €1.50 round-trip). From the bus stop, walk uphill through the ornate gates and watch for signs. ☎921 47 00 19. Open daily Apr.-Sept. 10am-6pm; Oct.-Mar. 10am-1:30pm and 3-5pm, Su 10am-2pm. Mandatory guided tours in Spanish depart every 15min. €5; students, under 16, and EU seniors €2.50; children under 5 free. EU citizens free W.

A must-see for any visitor to Segovia, the **royal palace** of La Granja, 9km southeast of the city, is the most extravagant of Spain's four royal summer retreats (the others being El Pardo, El Escorial, and Aranjuez). Felipe V, the first Bourbon King of Spain and grandson of Louis XIV, detested the Habsburgs' austere El Escorial. Nostalgic for Versailles, where he spent his childhood, he commissioned La Granja in the early 18th century, choosing the site based on its hunting and gardening potential. A fire destroyed the living quarters in 1918, but the structure was rebuilt in 1932 to house one of the world's finest collections of Flemish tapestries. The highlight of the collection is the nine-tapestry series entitled *The Honours* by Pierre van Aelst; it was said to be an allegory of Emperor Charles's moral development. Don't miss the floor below, however, which hosts four tapestries by Goya as well as the 16th-century "Triumphs of Petrarch" and 17th-century "History of Venus" series. Frenchman René Carlier designed the **gardens** surrounding the palace. Carefully manicured hedges form labyrinthine pathways around impressive flowerbeds, but even those are no match for the decadent ◪**Cascadas Nuevas,** an ensemble of illuminated fountains, pools, and pavilions that represents the continents and seasons. (Fountains usually run W and Sa-Su at 5:30pm; consult with the tourist office. Gardens open daily Nov.-Feb. 10am-6pm, Mar. and Oct. 10am-6:30pm, Apr. 10am-7pm, May-June 16 and Sept. 10am-8pm, June 17-Aug. 10am-9pm. W, Sa, Su €3.40; students €1.70. M-Tu and Th-F free.)

ÁVILA   ☎920

Ávila (pop. 50,000) has two main attractions: an impressive set of restored 12th-century stone city walls and the isolated abode of Santa Teresa de Jesús. Museums and monuments welcome outsiders to learn about Santa Teresa, depicting her divine visitations and ecstatic visions in exhaustive detail; the celebration of her day (Oct. 15) lasts a full week. The popular and plentiful *yemas de Ávila*, gooey pastry balls made with honey and egg, lure hungry visitors inside the city's walls, a place untouched by pollution, advertisements, or the blare of tourist traffic. Ávila is well worth a daytrip from Segovia, Salamanca, or Madrid.

▐ TRANSPORTATION

Trains: Av. de la Estación, 40 (☎902 24 02 02). Info open daily 7am-2pm and 3-8:30pm. To: **El Escorial** (1hr.; 9 per day M-F 5:30am-8:37pm, Sa 9:15am-8:37pm, Su 9:15am-8:37pm; €3.25); **Madrid** (1½-2hr.; 15-19 per day M-F 5:30am-10:13pm, Sa-Su 7:10am-10:15pm; €6); **Salamanca** (1¾hr., 5-6 per day 7:10am-10:49pm, €7); **Valladolid** (1½hr.; 5-9 per day M-F and Su 9:53am-9:53pm, Sa 9:53am-8pm; €6.35); **Villalba,** for transfer to **Segovia** (1hr., 16 per day, €5.40).

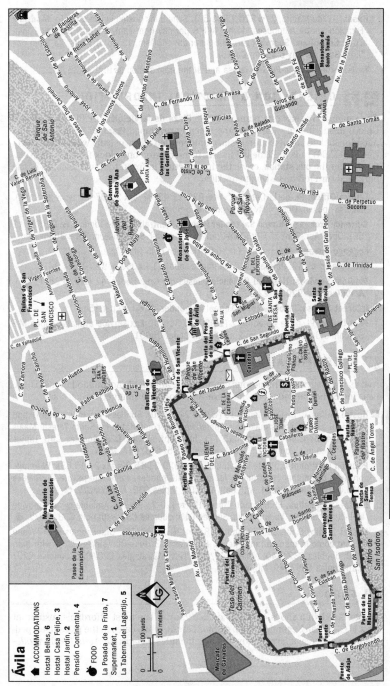

Buses: Av. de Madrid, 2 (☎920 22 01 54). Schedules posted in windows. To: **Madrid's** Estación Sur de Autobuses (1½hr.; M-F 8 per day 6am-7pm, Sa-Su 4 per day 10am-7pm; €6.26) and **Segovia** (1hr.; M-F 3 per day 9:30am, 12:45, 6:30pm; Sa 1 per day 9am, Su 1 per day 6:45pm; €3.65).

Taxis: Radio Taxis in Pl. Sta. Teresa and at the train station (☎920 35 35 45).

✦🛈 ORIENTATION & PRACTICAL INFORMATION

The tangled city has two main squares: **Plaza de la Victoria** (or Pl. del Mercado Chico) inside the city walls and the recently revamped **Plaza de Santa Teresa** just outside. Stick to labeled streets, since unidentified alleys usually wind out of town. Bus #1 (€0.60) runs to Pl. de la Victoria from the stop one block from the train station. From the **bus station,** cross the intersection in front, follow the length of the park, and turn left on C. Duque de Alba.

Tourist Office: Pl. de la Catedral, 4 (☎920 21 13 87; fax 25 37 17; www.avila.net). English spoken. Open daily 9am-2pm and 5-8pm.

Currency Exchange: Banco Santander Hispano Central, Pl. José Tomé, 2 (☎920 21 11 50). Open Apr.-Sept. M-F 8:30am-2pm; Oct.-May M-F 8:30am-2pm, Sa 8:30am-1pm.

Luggage storage: Bus station. €0.30-0.70. Open daily 9am-7pm.

Emergency: ☎ 112. **Police:** Av. de la Inmaculada, 11 (☎092 or 920 35 24 24).

Medical Services: Hospital Provincial, Jesús del Gran Poder, 42 (☎920 35 72 00). **Ambulance:** ☎920 22 22 22.

Internet Access: Arroba@25, C. Ferreal Hernández, 1. €0.60 per 15min.

Post Office: Pl. de la Catedral, 2 (☎920 35 31 06). **Fax service** available. Open M-F 8:30am-8:30pm, Sa 9:30am-2pm. **Postal Code:** 05001.

⌂ ACCOMMODATIONS

Ávila's walls surround numerous comfortable, affordable accommodations. Those near the cathedral and Pl. de Sta. Teresa fill up in the summer, so call early.

▨ **Hostal Bellas,** C. de Caballeros, 19 (☎920 21 29 10). Spotless, airy rooms with TV and luxurious private baths make this *hostal* way too comfortable for Santa Teresa. Meals available (*pensión completa* €15.17). July-Sept. singles €28; doubles €40; triples (added bed in a double) €53. Oct.-June €23.75/€33/€44. MC/V. ❸

Pensión Continental, Pl. de la Catedral, 6 (☎920 21 15 02; fax 21 15 63). TV lounge provides communal atmosphere. All rooms with phones, some with private TV. Singles €15.05; doubles €25.84, with bath €33.06; triples €39. AmEx/MC/V. ❷

Hostal Casa Felipe, Pl. Mercado Chico, 12 (☎920 21 39 24). Amiable owners provide well-lit rooms with TVs and sinks. Singles €19; doubles €32, with bath €38. MC/V. ❷

Hostal Jardín, C. de San Segundo, 38 (☎920 21 10 74). Older rooms with TV and phone come in many arrangements. Breakfast €3. June-Oct. singles €24, with bath €30; doubles €32/€40; triples €43/€54. Nov.-May singles €20/€26; doubles €29/€36; triples €39/€49. MC/V. ❷

◖ FOOD

Budget sandwich shops circle Pl. de la Victoria. The most affordable restaurant area is C. de San Segundo, off Pl. de Sta. Teresa, while cafes in the plaza itself peddle more expensive fare. Renowned fare includes *ternera de Ávila* (veal), *molle-*

jas (sweetbread), and *yemas de Santa Teresa* or *yemas de Ávila.* Every Friday, the **mercado** in Pl. de la Victoria sells produce from 10am to 2pm. The **supermarket,** C. Juan José Martín, 6, stocks all the basics. Open M-Sa 9:45am-2pm and 5-8pm.

> **La Taberna del Lagartijo,** C. Martín Carramolino, 4 (☎920 22 88 25), just behind Iglesia de San Juan in Pl. de la Victoria. An impressive collection of autographed bullfight photos hangs from the walls, or avoid the *toro* scene by eating outdoors. *Menú* €10. Open M-Th 1:30-4pm and 8-midnight. MC/V. ❷

> **Restaurante La Posada de la Fruta,** Pl. Pedro Dávila, 8 (☎920 25 47 02). Airy indoor terrace creates a serene dining experience. *Menú* €12. Sandwiches and a less expensive *menú* (up to €7.90-9). Open daily 1-4pm and 8:30-11:30pm. ❸

🧭 SIGHTS

🏯**LAS MURALLAS.** Each summer, shutter-happy hordes attack Ávila's **city walls,** the first stop on the way into its inner city. Modern research has placed construction of the 2500 battlements, 88 towers, and six gates in the 12th century, though legend holds that they are the oldest in Spain, dating back to 1090. **Cimorro,** the most imposing of the towers, doubles as the cathedral's apse. On the inside, in the corner to the right of the cathedral, is all that remains of a former **Alcázar:** mere outlines of two windows and two balconies. If you wish to walk along the 2½km of walls, start from Puerta del Alcázar. *(Walk straight ahead with your back to Pl. de Sta. Teresa. Open Semana Santa-Oct. 15 daily 10am-8pm; rest of the year Tu-Su 11am-6pm. €3.50, student groups and under 8 €2.)* The best view of the walls and of Ávila itself is from the **Cuatro Postes,** a four-pillared structure past the Río Adaja, 1½km along the highway to Salamanca. It was here that Santa Teresa was caught by her uncle as she and her brother tried to flee the Islamic south. *(From Pl. de Sta. Teresa, walk through the inner city and out the Puerta del Puente. Cross the bridge and follow the road to your right for about 1km. Total walk 25min.)*

CATEDRAL. Some believe that the profile of the cathedral looming over the watchtowers inspired Santa Teresa's famous metaphor of the soul as a diamond castle. Begun in the late 12th century, Ávila's is the oldest Spanish cathedral in the transitional style between the Romanesque and Gothic; whistling wind makes the gloomy interior even more so. Look for the **Altar de La Virgen de la Caridad,** where 12-year-old Santa Teresa prostrated herself after the death of her mother. Behind the main altar is the alabaster **tomb** of Cardinal Alonso de Madrigal, a bishop of Ávila and prolific writer whose dark complexion won him the title "El Tostado" (The Swarthy, or "Toasted"). The nickname spread, and during the Golden Age, it became popular to call an aspiring author *un tostado.* The **museum** displays an El Greco portrait, enormous *libros de canti* (hymnals) that make you feel like Alice in Wonderland, and Juan de Arfe's silver, six-leveled **Custodia del Corpus,** complete with swiveling bells. *(Pl. de la Catedral. ☎920 21 16 41. Open Apr.-May M-F 10am-6pm, Sa 10am-7pm, Su noon-6pm; Nov.-Mar. M-F 10am-5pm, Sa 10am-6pm, Su noon-6pm. Last entrance 45min. before closing. Cathedral free; museum €2.50.)*

OTHER SIGHTS. Santa Teresa's admirers built the 17th-century **Convento de Santa Teresa** on the site of her birth. *(Inside the city walls, near Puerta de Sta. Teresa. Open daily 9:30am-1:30pm and 3:30-7pm.)* The **Sala de Reliquías,** a small building near the convent, is a small scrapbook of Santa Teresa relics, including her right ring finger, the sole of her sandal, and the cord she used to flagellate herself. *(Open daily Apr.-Oct. 9:30am-1:30pm and 3:30-7:30pm; Nov.-Mar. Tu-Su 10am-1:30pm and 3:30-5:30pm. Last entrance 30min. before closing. Free.)* For a larger collection of items that Santa Teresa may have touched, looked at, or lived among, visit the **Museo de Santa Teresa,** built into the convent's crypt around the corner to the left of the entrance. *(☎920 22 07 08. Open daily Apr.-Oct. 10am-2pm and 4-7pm; Nov.-Mar. Tu-Su 10am-1:30pm and 3:30-5:30pm. Last entrance 30min. before closing. €2.)*

MONASTERIO DE LA ENCARNACIÓN. Santa Teresa must have found comfort in Christ; it definitely wasn't provided in her 30-year residence, now known as the Monasterio de la Encarnación. Among its interesting relics is a wooden log she used as her pillow. The mandatory guided tour visits Santa Teresa's tiny cell and the small rooms where nuns observed their guests through barred windows. Santa Teresa had her mystical encounter with the child Jesus on the **main staircase.** Upstairs from the cloister, a **museum** features a collection of personal effects given to the convent by wealthier nuns as bribes to procure entrance. *(Po. de la Encarnación. ☎920 21 12 12. Museum open daily M-F 9:30am-1:30pm and 3:30-6pm, Sa-Su 10am-1:30pm and 3:30-6pm.)*

MONASTERIO DE SANTO TOMÁS. Fernando and Isabel used this monastery as a summer refuge and as a seat of the Inquisition. Inside the church, in front of the *retablo*, is the tomb of Prince Don Juan, Fernando and Isabel's only son, who died in 1497 at age 19. To the right of the altar is the **Capilla del Santo Cristo,** where Santa Teresa came to pray and confess. Also here are three contrasting cloisters: the Tuscan **Claustro del Noviciado** (Cloister of the Noviciate), the Gothic **Claustro del Silencio** (Cloister of Silence), and the Renaissance-Transition **Claustro de los Reyes** (Cloister of the Kings). *(Pl. Granada, 1. ☎920 22 04 00. Monastery open daily in summer 10am-12:45pm and 4-7:45pm, winter 10am-1pm and 4-8pm. Free. Cloisters open Nov.-Mar. Tu-Su 10am-1:30pm and 3:30-5:30pm. Last entrance 30min. before closing. €1.)*

SALAMANCA ☎923

Salamanca la blanca, city of scholars, saints, royals, and rogues, showcases the best examples of Spanish Plateresque by day and a vivacious club scene that contends with Barcelona and Madrid by night. Exquisite filigree-like work on golden sandstone adorns the arches and graceful towers that command Salamanca's skyline from the tiny Río Tormes to the colossal cathedral. Look closely: Salamanca has many hidden architectural surprises that reward the diligent visitor, from modern interpretations of cathedral iconography to a mythological calendar near the Plaza Mayor. If the architecture is not attraction enough, the prestigious Universidad de Salamanca, grouped in medieval times with Bologna, Paris, and Oxford as one of the "four leading lights of the world," continues to add the energy of its thousands of students to the already well-touristed city—an explosive mix that provides what locals claim to be Spain's best nightlife.

▐ TRANSPORTATION

Trains: Po. de la Estación (☎ 923 12 02 02). To: **Ávila** (1½hr., 6-7 per day 6:05am-7:55pm, €5.50-7); **Lisboa** (6hr., 1 per day 4:51am, €35); **Madrid** (2½hr., 5-6 per day 6:05am-7:53pm, €13.60); **Palencia** (2hr.; daily at 1:55pm, Th, F, Sa, and Su at 7:50pm; €8.10-14); **Valladolid** (2hr., 8-12 per day 12:05am-8:05pm, €5.50-12).

Buses: Av. Filiberto Villalobos, 71-85 (☎923 23 67 17). Take C. Ramón y Cajal to Po. de San Vicente. Cross this avenue, and C. Ramón y Cajal becomes Av. Filiberto Villalobos. Open M-F 8am-8:30pm, Sa 9am-2:30pm and 4:30-6:30pm, Su 10am-2pm and 4-7:30pm. To: **Ávila** (1½hr.; M-F 4 per day 6:30am-8:30pm, Sa 4 per day 9am-8:30pm,

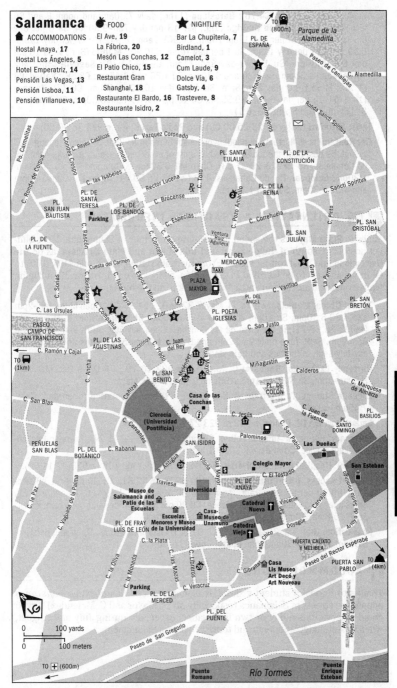

Salamanca

🏠 ACCOMMODATIONS

Hostal Anaya, **17**
Hostal Los Ángeles, **5**
Hotel Emperatriz, **14**
Pensión Las Vegas, **13**
Pensión Lisboa, **11**
Pensión Villanueva, **10**

🍎 FOOD

El Ave, **19**
La Fábrica, **20**
Mesón Las Conchas, **12**
El Patio Chico, **15**
Restaurant Gran
 Shanghai, **18**
Restaurante El Bardo, **16**
Restaurante Isidro, **2**

⭐ NIGHTLIFE

Bar La Chupitería, **7**
Birdland, **1**
Camelot, **3**
Cum Laude, **9**
Dolce Vía, **6**
Gatsby, **4**
Trastevere, **8**

CASTILLA Y LEÓN

Su 3:30 and 8:30pm; €4.76); **Barcelona** (11hr.; daily 7:30am and noon, F and Su also 4pm; €39); **Ciudad Rodrigo** (1hr.; M-F 13 per day 7am-9:30pm, Sa 6 per day 8:30am-6pm, Su 4 per day 11am-10pm; €4.90); **León** (2½hr.; M-F 3 per day 11am-6:30pm, Sa 1 per day 11am, Su 1 per day 10pm; €10.90); **Madrid** (3hr.; M-Sa 16 per day 6am-9:30pm, Su 16 per day 8am-11pm; €9.89-14.70); **Segovia** (3hr.; M-F 7:30am and 1:30pm, Sa 7:30 and 9:30am, Su 1:30 and 8:45pm; €8.58); **Valladolid** (1½hr.; M-Sa 6 per day 8am-8pm, Su 4 per day 10:30am-10pm; €6.35); **Zamora** (1hr.; M-F 15 per day 6:40am-9:35pm, Sa 10 per day 7:45am-8:30pm, Su 7 per day 8:45am-10:15pm; €3.65).

Taxis: Auto-Taxi (24hr. ☎923 25 00 09) and **Radio Taxi** (24hr. ☎923 25 00 00).

Car Rental: Prices fluctuate depending on length of rental and age of person renting. Call to find the best deal; the tourist office has a list of every rental agency in town. **Avis,** Po. de Canalejas, 49 (☎923 26 97 53). Open M-F 9:30am-1:30pm and 4-7pm, Sa 9am-1:30pm. **Europcar,** Po. de Canalejas, 123 (☎923 26 90 41). Open M-F 9am-1:30pm and 4:30-7:30pm, Sa 9am-1:30pm.

■ 🛈 ORIENTATION & PRACTICAL INFORMATION

Majestic **Plaza Mayor** is the social and geographic center of Salamanca. Most budget hostels lie south of the plaza around Rúa Mayor and **Plaza de Anaya,** as do the **Universidad** and most tourist sights. From the **train station,** catch bus #1 (€0.60) to Gran Vía and ask to be let off at Pl. San Julián, a block from Pl. Mayor. It's a 20min. walk from the train station and a 15min. walk from the bus station.

Tourist Office: Municipal office, Pl. Mayor, 32 (☎923 21 83 42). Open M-Sa 9am-2pm and 4:30-6:30pm, Su 10am-2pm and 4:30-6:30pm. **Regional office,** R. Mayor, s/n (☎923 26 58 71), in the Casa de las Conchas. Open July-Aug. Su-Th 9am-8pm, F-Sa 9am-9pm. Sept.-June daily 9am-2pm and 5-8pm. **Information booths** open occasionally July-Sept. in the bus and train stations.

Currency Exchange: Banesto: C. Toro, 13 (☎902 30 70 30). Open Oct.-Mar. M-F 8:30am-2pm, Sa 8:30am-1pm. **ATMs** on C. Toro and R. Mayor.

Luggage Storage: At the **train station** (24hr., €3) and **bus station** (open daily 7am-7:45pm. €0.60).

Emergency: ☎112. **Police:** ☎092 or 923 27 91 38.

Pharmacy: Farmacia Amador Felipe, C. Toro, 25 (☎923 21 41 24). Friendly, English-speaking service. Open daily 9:30am-10pm.

Hospital: Hospital Clínico Universitario, Po. de San Vicente, 108 (☎923 29 11 00).

Internet Access: CiberPlaza, Pl. Mayor, 10 (☎923 26 42 81). €1.20 per hr. 10:30am-9pm; €0.90 per hr. 9pm-2am. Open daily 10:30am-2am. **Yazgo,** C. Palominos, 21, offers a less crowded surfing experience. €0.90 per hr. 9am-5pm and 8pm-1am; €1.80 per hr. 5-8pm. 30min. minimum. Open daily 9am-1am.

Post Office: Gran Vía, 25-29 (☎923 28 09 02). **Lista de Correos.** Open M-F 8:30am-8:30pm and Sa 9:30am-2pm. **Postal Code:** 37080.

🛏 ACCOMMODATIONS

Thanks to floods of student visitors, reasonably priced *hostales* and *pensiones* pepper the streets of Salamanca (especially off Pl. Mayor and C. Meléndez). Try to make reservations a day or two in advance, especially during July and August, when hostel-hungry students and tourists overrun Salamanca.

Pensión Las Vegas, C. Meléndez, 13, 1st fl. (☎923 21 87 49). Hospitality from friendly owners, flowered terraces, TVs, and towels make this *pensión* a great deal. Singles with small shower €18; doubles €24, with bath €30-36; triples with bath €45. MC/V. ❷

Pensión Villanueva, C. San Justo, 8, 1st fl. (☎923 26 88 33). Let talkative Sra. Manuela share her local lore. Decent-sized rooms with simple beds. Reservations for F-Su only. Singles €13; doubles €26. Extra beds €13 per person. ❶

Pensión Los Ángeles, Pl. Mayor, 10, 2nd-3rd floors (☎923 21 81 66). Unbeatable location for *muy poco dinero*. Rooms with balconies opening onto the stunning Pl. Mayor need to be reserved far in advance. English spoken. Singles €15-16; doubles €28-30, with bath €30-32; triples and above €15 per person. ❷

Pensión Lisboa, C. Meléndez, 1 (☎923 21 43 33). Stare at the pink walls from the comfort of your soft pink bed as you bask in the heat emanating from your charming pink radiator. Rooms are small but clean; most have sinks and some have rooftop city views. Singles €16; doubles €32. ❷

Hostal Emperatriz, R. Mayor, 16 (☎/fax 923 21 87 83). This hostel operates out of the hotel next door. To register, go to the hotel lobby. Don't let the dark, creaky staircase deter you—the spacious rooms above include full bathroom and telephone. Try to get a room facing R. Mayor for a great view, though they can be noisy. Breakfast €2.10. Singles €24; doubles €33; triples €44. ❷ Next door, the pricier **Hotel Emperatriz,** R. Mayor, 18 (☎923 21 91 56) offers brightly-lit rooms oozing with medieval charm: wooden, old-style beds and hand-carved drawers. Singles €36; doubles €51. ❹

Hostal Anaya, C. Jesús, 18 (☎923 27 17 73). Steps away from the Pl. Mayor and most historical sights, Hostal Anaya offers clean rooms, heating, and service that will make you feel at home. Singles €24; doubles with shared bath €36, with private bath €42; triples €54; quads €72. ❷

Camping: Camping Regio on Ctra. Salamanca (☎923 13 88 88), 4km toward Madrid. Albertur buses leave from Gran Vía every 30min. near Pl. San Julián. First-class sites with hot showers. Tennis courts and restaurants in a tourist complex next door. €3 per person, €5.50 per tent, and €2.90 per car. MC/V. ❶

FOOD

Salamanca sports a cornucopia of restaurants offering everything from *salmantino* dishes like *chanfaina* (a type of beef stew) and *tostón asado* (roasted baby pork) to cheeseburgers. Cafes and restaurants surrounding Pl. Mayor provide great views of the plaza and excellent food; you can get a three-course meal for a little over €8. **Champion,** C. Toro, 64. (Open M-Sa 9:15am-9:15pm.)

El Patio Chico, C. Meléndez, 13 (☎923 26 51 03). *Salmantinos* crowd this place at lunch and dinner, but the hefty and delicious portions are worth the wait. If all the outdoor tables have been voraciously snapped up, take a chance with the throng inside. Try the *morcilla picante* (spicy blood sausage). *Bocadillos* €2-3. Entrees €4-8. *Menús* €11. Open daily 1-4pm and 8pm-midnight. ❷

La Fábrica, C. Libreros, 47-49 (☎923 26 85 69). Students head straight for La Fábrica's wooden floors and 80s music after a night in the University library. Two central green tables make it look more like a hangout than a restaurant, but good, cheap food keeps the students coming. *Bocadillos* €3-6. *Menú* €8.50. Open daily 9am until the last customer leaves—usually 2am, weekends 4am. ❶

Mesón Las Conchas, R. Mayor, 16 (☎923 21 21 67). Sit outdoors on R. Mayor to enjoy the storks atop Iglesia de San Martín by summer and stunning views of the catedral nueva year-round. Great for intimate conversations or unabashed people-watching. *Menú* €10.50. *Raciones* €6-14. Open daily 1-4pm and 8pm-midnight. MC/V. ❷

Restaurant Gran Shanghai, R. Mayor, 35-37 (☎923 21 18 10). Delicious and supremely affordable Chinese food located near Pl. de Anaya. Serving up soups (€2-3), rice (€2-4), and other entrees (€3-9) in a pleasant, quiet setting. ❶

Restaurante El Bardo, C. Compañía, 8 (☎923 21 90 89), between the Casa de las Conchas and the Clerecía. Traditional Spanish food and low prices keep the tiled tables full. *Menú* €9. Entrees €6-13. Open daily 1:30-4pm and 9-11:30pm. MC/V. ❷

Restaurante Isidro, C. Pozo Amarillo, 19 (☎923 26 28 48), a block from Pl. Mayor. Don't let the fake roses fool you—this is a quality place. Prompt courteous service and large portions. Numerous vegetable, egg, seafood, and meat entrees €3-9. *Menú* €8.40. Open daily 1-4pm and 8pm-midnight. MC/V. ❷

El Ave, C. Libreros, 24 (☎923 26 45 11). A beautiful dining hall decorated with Native American-themed stained glass and paintings. Besides the typical *menús* (€9.60) and entrees (starting at €5.40), El Ave offers a selection of pastries and ice cream right near the Universidad. Open daily 8am-2am. ❷

SIGHTS & MUSEUMS

■ LA UNIVERSIDAD DE SALAMANCA

From Pl. Mayor follow R. Mayor, veer right onto R. Antigua, then left onto C. Libreros; the university is on the left. University ☎923 29 44 00. Museum ☎923 29 12 25. Open M-F 9:30am-1:30pm and 4-7:30pm, Sa 9:30am-1:30pm and 4-7pm, Su 10am-1:30pm. University and museum €2.40, students and seniors €1.20.

The great university, established in 1218, is *the* focal point of Salamanca. Though next to the cathedrals on R. Mayor, it is best approached from C. Libreros. The university's entrance is one of the best examples of Spanish Plateresque, a style named after the work of *plateros* (silversmiths). Iron oxide-rich sandstone quarried in this region is pliable and easy to work with when new, but hardens and weathers like marble or granite when old, thus creating the illusion of silver filigree-like work on hard stone. Experts still offer dozens of explanations for the hermeneutic symbols that grace this spectacular entrance, but some facets are easier to read. The central medallion depicts Fernando and Isabel, *los Reyes Católicos.* Sculpted into the facade is a tiny frog perched atop a skull; according to legend, those who can spot the frog without assistance will be blessed with good luck, and even marriage. Try standing away from finger-pointing tourist groups if you actually want to accomplish this feat. If you fail, don't despair: you'll find millions of frog-themed trinkets along R. Mayor.

The old lecture halls inside the Universidad are open to the public. Entering the cool stone foyer feels like stepping into another era; a cough echoes through the building and outdoor noise disappears. The 15th-century classroom **Aula Fray Luis de León** has been left in more or less its original state; medieval students considered the hard benches luxurious, as most students then sat on the floor. A plaque bears Unamuno's famous love poem to the students of Salamanca. The **Paraninfo** (auditorium) contains Baroque tapestries and a portrait of Carlos IV attributed to Goya. The 18th-century **chapel,** almost gaudy with red curtains on the walls, red

UNDER PRESSURE Look closely at the walls of the university and cathedral and you'll see faded red scrawlings on the sandstone; this is not graffiti. Eight hundred years ago, students of the University of Salamanca attended classes in the Old Cathedral. They would come to the church the night before their final exam to pray for success; the rigorous oral test (in logic and rhetoric) was administered the next day in front of *La Capilla de Santa Bárbara,* now known as *La Capilla del Estudiante.* Those fortunate enough to pass left the cathedral through the main entrance to shouts of congratulations from the throng of anxious *salmantinos* waiting outside. Later that evening, the town would host a bullfight in honor of the new graduates; the fresh blood of the bull was then mixed with a flour paste and used to paint the names of the new doctors on the university and cathedral walls.

velvet chairs, and a red altar, contains the tomb of Fray Luis. The **Biblioteca Antigua,** one of Europe's oldest libraries on the second floor, is the most spectacular room of all, located atop a magnificent Plateresque staircase. The staircase itself is another famous case of contending symbols and interpretations, but it is generally considered to represent the ascent of the scholar through careless youth, love, and adventure on the perilous path to the true love of knowledge.

The university entrance faces the **Patio de las Escuelas,** home to a statue of Fray Luis de León, a university professor and one of the most respected literati of the Golden Age. A Hebrew scholar and classical Spanish stylist, Fray Luis was arrested by the Inquisition for translating Solomon's *Song of Songs* into Castilian and for preferring the Hebrew version of the Bible to the Latin one. After five years of imprisonment, he returned to the university and began his first lecture, *"Como decíamos ayer..."* ("As we were saying yesterday..."). The patio is surrounded by the **Escuelas Menores,** with a smaller version of the main entryway's Plateresque facade. Don't miss the **University Museum.** Walk through the hall on the left corner of the patio; the museum is on your left. The reconstructed **Cielo de Salamanca,** the library's famous 15th-century ceiling fresco of the zodiac by the celebrated Fernando Gallego, is preserved here in all its splendor. Take a peek at the intricate strongbox with its many locks. *(Below Pl. San Isidro, off R. Mayor. University ☎ 923 29 44 00. Museum ☎ 923 29 12 25. Open M-F 9:30am-1:30pm and 4-7:30pm, Sa 9:30am-1:30pm and 4-7pm, Su 10am-1:30pm. Both €2.40, students and seniors €1.20.)*

OTHER SIGHTS & MUSEUMS

▨ **PLAZA MAYOR.** Salamanca's Plaza Mayor, considered one of the most beautiful squares in Spain, is the people-watching site *par excellence.* Hundreds of tables border the colonnade, while in the center street performers and musicians entertain and couples stroll hand in hand. Cut from the same majestic sandstone that pervades *salmantino* architecture, the plaza appears golden in the afternoon sun and when the evening lights come up to collective gasps of admiration. Designed and built by Alberto Churriguera (see **Architecture,** p. 76) between 1729 and 1755, the plaza contains 88 towering arches, the **Ayuntamiento,** and three pavilions dedicated to historical figures. The **Pabellón Real,** to the right of the Ayuntamiento, honors the Spanish monarchy (and, quite controversially, 20th-century dictator Francisco Franco, behind the blue tarpaulin); the **Pabellón del Sur,** in front of the Ayuntamiento, is dedicated to famous Spanish conquistadors; and the **Pabellón del Oeste,** to the left of the Ayuntamiento, pays homage to important *salmantinos* like San Juan de Sahagún, Santa Teresa, and Miguel de Unamuno. Before the pavilions were built, the square served as the town bullring. Locals probably wouldn't mind a premature release of some of those bulls during the summer, when wide-eyed tourist groups flood the plaza.

CATEDRAL NUEVA. It took 220 years to build this holy example of the Spanish Gothic (1513-1733). While several architects decided to retain the original late Gothic style, they could not resist adding touches from later periods, most notably to its Baroque tower, one of Spain's tallest. Inside, the cathedral is separated into many small chapels dedicated to various saints or important locals. These surround a center chapel and an enormous organ, whose pipes rise toward the ceiling. Architects of modern renovations left their marks also: look for an astronaut and a dragon eating an ice cream cone on the left side of the main door. *(Pl. de Anaya. Open daily Apr.-Sept. 9am-2pm and 4-8pm; Oct.-Mar. 9am-1pm and 4-6pm. Free.)*

CATEDRAL VIEJA. The smaller Catedral Vieja (1140) was built in the Romanesque style. Its cupola is one of the most detailed in Spain and is assembled from many intricately-carved miniature pieces. Above the high altar, apocalyptic angels separate the sinners from the saved. The oldest original part of the cathedral is the **Capilla de San Martín,** with brilliant frescoes dating from 1242. Look for the image of the Virgen de la Vega, Salamanca's patron saint. Students used to face the **Capilla de Santa Bárbara,** or the Capilla del Título, as they took their final exams. Other points of interest include a document signed by **El Cid Campeador** and the crucifix he held at his death. The **museum** features a paneled ceiling by Fernando Gallego and the Mudéjar Salinas organ, one of the oldest in Europe. Be sure to check out the famed **Patio Chico** behind the cathedral, where students congregate to chat and play music and tourists head for a splendid view of both cathedrals. *(Enter through the Catedral Nueva. Museum ☎923 21 74 76. Cathedral open Apr.-Sept. daily 10am-1:30pm and 4-7:30pm. €3, students €2.25, children €1.50.)*

CASA LIS MUSEO ART NOUVEAU Y ART DECO. Cross the threshold of this odd-looking building and enter the bizarre. Salamancan industrialist Miguel de Lis collaborated with modernist architect Joaquín Vargas to design the building, which now showcases Lis's eclectic art collection. Exhibits range from elegant fans signed by such noteworthies as Salvador Dalí, to odd porcelain dolls with two faces, to racy small sculptures of animals and people in compromising positions. *(C. Gibraltar, 14, behind the cathedrals. ☎923 12 14 25. Open Apr.-Oct.15 Tu-F 11am-2pm and 5-9pm, Sa-Su 11am-9pm; Oct. 16-Mar. Tu-F 11am-2pm and 4-7pm, Sa-Su 11am-8pm. €2.10, students €1.50, children and Tu mornings free.)*

CONVENTO DE SAN ESTEBAN. While on a fundraising endeavor, Columbus spent time in one of Salamanca's most dramatic monasteries, the Convento de San Esteban. When illuminated by the afternoon sun, the stoning of St. Stephen and the crucifixion of Christ seem to come alive on its facade. The beautiful **Claustro de los Reyes** (Kings' Cloister), with its Gothic interior and Plateresque exterior, is visibly the product of two different eras. José Churriguera's central altarpiece (1693) is a masterpiece of Spanish Baroque. Also worth seeing is the **Panteón de los Teólogos,** home to the remains of the most decorated Dominican theologians of the university. *(Off C. San Pablo and C. Palominos. ☎923 21 50 00. Open Tu-Su Apr.-Sept. 9am-1pm and 4-8pm; Oct.-Mar. 9am-1pm and 4-6pm. €1.20, free W mornings.)*

CASA DE LAS CONCHAS. Follow R. Mayor until you reach a plaza with an organ pipe fountain. Take a right and look up at the face of the building on your right. Yup, those are sandstone shells. The 15th-century Casa de las Conchas (House of Shells), with over 300 large scallop halves, is one of Salamanca's most famous landmarks. Pilgrims who journeyed to Santiago de Compostela (see p. 565) traditionally wore shells to commemorate their visit to the tomb of St. James. The owner of the *casa* allegedly created this monument either to honor the renowned pilgrimage or to honor his wife, whose family shield was decorated with scallops. Legend has it that the Jesuits bought and leveled every house in the area to build the college—*except* the Casa de las Conchas, despite their shady offer of one gold coin for every sandstone shell. The building now hosts the public library and provincial tourist office. *(C. Compañía, 39. Library ☎923 26 93 17. Open M-F 9am-9pm, Sa-Su 9am-2pm and 4-7pm. Free.)*

LA CLERECÍA. Directly across from the Casa de las Conchas is La Clerecía (Royal College of the Holy Spirit), the main building of La Universidad Pontificia de Salamanca, a private educational institution unaffiliated with the Universidad de Salamanca. When Saint Ignatius of Loyola, founder of the Jesuits, arrived in Salamanca in the early 16th century, he was imprisoned for 20 days for heresy. Once the Jesuits were finally recognized by the Church, Loyola decided to claim recompense for his mistreatment by creating an enormous church and college of the Jesuit Order. Founded in 1611 with the financial aid of Margarita of Austria (Felipe III's wife), the college actually owes its name to King Carlos III, who expelled the Jesuits from Spain and made the institute property of the Real Clerecía in the 18th century. The building has a unique U-shaped groundplan, allowing visitors to peer over the Cloister of Studies into the lower gallery and courtyard. *(☎923 26 46 60. Open for Mass M-Sa 1:15 and 7pm, Su noon. Free.)*

MUSEO DE SALAMANCA. Across from the university in the Patio de las Escuelas, the Museum of Salamanca occupies an astounding 15th-century building that was once home to Álvarez Albarca, physician to Fernando and Isabel. Along with the Casa de las Conchas, this structure is among Spain's most important examples of 15th-century architecture. The museum has an intriguing collection of painting and sculpture as well as some temporary archaeology and ethnology exhibits. Its most important canvases are Juan de Flandes's portrait of St. Andrew and Luis de Morales's *Llanto por Cristo muerto*. *(Patio de las Escuelas, 2. ☎923 21 22 35. Open Tu-Sa 8am-2pm and 4:30-8pm, Su 9:30am-2:30pm. €1.20, students free.)*

FISHING FOR LOVE
In Spain, young women rather than dolphins are threatened by the tuna industry. According to legend, the unwary might have their hearts captured by a charming bard. *Las tunas* are university student music bands dating back to 1215, during the reign of King Alfonso X the Wise. Originally founded by students who needed to earn money for their studies, *tunas* have become a form of social competition in modern universities, as well as paid entertainment for private parties and high-class restaurants. To become a *tuna*, *pardillos* (candidates) must prove their wit and artistic ability in a series of tests, culminating with the consumption of a bowl of The Soup of Charity, a painfully fiery concoction mixed by veteran *tunas*. The chosen ones take an oath over a tambourine, the symbol of the *tuna*, and are given a *tuna* sash and nickname for life.

CASA MUSEO DE UNAMUNO. Miguel de Unamuno, rector of the university during the early 20th century, is revered as one of the founding figures of the Spanish literary phenomenon known as the "Generation of '98." Unamuno passionately opposed dictatorship and encouraged his students to do so as well. His stand against General Miguel Primo de Rivera's 1923 coup led to his dismissal, though he was triumphantly reinstated some years later. Unamuno lived here while rector, and his original furniture has been preserved, along with many photographs and letters. (*To the right of the university's main entrance. Ring bell if house appears closed.* ☎923 29 44 00, ext. 1196. Open July-Sept. Tu-F 9:30am-1:30pm, Sa-Su 10am-1:30pm; Oct.-June Tu-F 9:30am-1:30pm and 4-6pm, Sa-Su 10am-2pm. Research room open M-F 9am-2pm. Mandatory tour in Spanish every 30min., €1.80.)

PUENTE ROMANO. A 2000-year-old Roman bridge over storied waters spans the scenic Río Tormes at the edge of the city. It was once part of the *Camino de la Plata* (Silver Way), an ancient Roman trade route running from Mérida in Extremadura to Astorga in Castilla y León. In medieval times, the *Camino de la Plata* was the route most Andalusian and Castilian Christians took to complete their pilgrimage to Santiago de Compostela. A headless granite bull called the **Toro Ibérico** guards one end of the bridge. Though it dates to pre-Roman times, the bull gained fame in the 16th century when it appeared in *Lazarillo de Tormes*, the prototype of the picaresque novel and a predecessor of *Don Quijote;* in one episode, Lazarillo gets his head slammed into the bull's ear after cheating his blind employer.

NIGHTLIFE

Salmantinos claim Salamanca to be the best place in Spain *para ir de marcha* (to go out). It is said that there is one bar for every hundred people that live here. *Chupiterías* (bars mostly selling shots), *barres*, and *discotecas* line nearly every street, and when some close at 4am, others are just opening. *La marcha* starts in Pl. Mayor, where members of local college or graduate-school **tunas** (medieval-style student troubadour groups) finish their rounds. Dressed in traditional black capes, they strut around the plaza with guitars, mandolins, *bandurrías*, and tambourines, serenading women while students start hit the many bars and *mesones* in the area. Student nightlife spreads out to **Gran Vía, Calle Bordadores,** and side streets. Spacious disco/bars blast music into the wee hours of the morning. **Calle Prior** and **Rúa Mayor** are full of bars; **Plaza de San Juan Bautista** fills with university students kicking off their evening—partner in one hand, infamous *litro* of beer in the other. Intense late-night drunken revelry occurs off **Calle Varillas** until dawn.

Bar La Chupitería, Pl. Monterrey, s/n. Unusually low prices have built La Chupitería's reputation among students as a premier pre-gaming establishment. Make your way through the crowds to order from the changing list of speciality shots, *Los Exóticos.* Shots €0.90, *chupitos* (slightly larger than shots) €1.

Duende Bar, Pl. de San Juan Bautista, 7. A typical *bar de copas* where *salmantino* students begin their night of partying. Drink *litros* of beer or sangría for €3, or just buy a bottle of wine (starting at €4) and talk in the teeming plaza til you feel like dancing.

Birdland, C. Azafranal, 57 (☎923 60 05 25). Drink to modern funk jazz. Thirty-somethings take a break from the club scene to enjoy a lower-decibel conversation after passing the obscene graffiti on the staircase. Beer €1.50-2.40. Mixed drinks €3-6. Open Su-Th 4pm-3am, F-Sa 4pm-4:30am; opens 6:30pm in summer.

Gatsby, C. Bordadores, 6 (☎923 26 75 77). Find your disco Daisy among the African masks and macabre decor. Beer €1.80. Sangría €2.10. Mixed drinks €4.25. Specials nearly every night. Open Su-Th 10pm-4am, F-Sa 7pm-6:30am.

Cum Laude, C. Prior, 5. On this bar's dance floor, a replica of the Pl. Mayor, partying starts at 11pm and doesn't stop until 4:30am. Mixed drinks €5-8. Bouncers can be particular about dressing well on weekend nights. No sneakers.

Trastavere, Pl. Monterrey, 8 (☎923 26 13 00). The inebriated local crowd from La Chupitería spills onto Trastavere's Greek-themed dance floor late into the night. Disco lights and streamers galore. Beer €4. *Copas* €5 and up. Open M-W 8pm-4am, Th 8am-5am, F-Su 8pm-7am.

Camelot, C. Bordadores, 3. Holy ruins shake to the techno beat—this club was built in the remains of an old church purchased from a nearby convent. Flags of medieval English houses fluttering in the background provide a noble backdrop for the intense drinking and dancing taking place on both floors. Mixed drinks from €3.

La Dolce Vita, Gran Vía, 48. Groove on Gran Vía to salsa and pop in a totally kitsch Hollywood-themed disco. Beer €3. Mixed drinks €5 and up. Open daily 10pm-4:30am.

🎵 🎭 ENTERTAINMENT & FESTIVALS

Ocio, a free pamphlet distributed at the tourist office and at some bars, lists everything from movies and special events to bus schedules. Posters at the **Colegio Mayor** (in Pl. de Anaya) advertise university events, free films, and student theater. The city hosts many events and festivals during the summer. On June 12, in honor of San Juan de Sahagún, there is a **corrida de toros** charity event in the **Plaza de Toros.** Take C. Zamora to Po. Dr. Torres Villarroel; the bullring lies just beyond Pl. de la Glorieta. Parades and craft fairs grace Pl. de Anaya until June 15. September 8-15, Salamanca indulges in exhibitions, most honoring the tradition of bullfighting that has made the region's *ganaderías* (bull farms) the best in all of Spain. Salamanca goes all out during *Semana Santa,* with local traditions like **Lunes de Aguas,** celebrated the Monday after Easter, when locals take off from work and head for the provinces to picnic with their families and feast on *hornazo* (a meat pie, usually made of ham and eggs). This feast

THE BIG SPLURGE

THE FOURTEENTH CENTURY'S FINEST

Seated in the 14th-century fortress of Enrique II of Trastámara, the tranquil *Parador de Ciudad Rodrigo* offers a unique taste of medieval life in luxury. With its monumental ramparts serving as the symbol of Ciudad Rodrigo and overlooking the beautiful Río Águeda and Roman bridge, the parador is a splendid location to unwind and enjoy the rugged countryside of Castilla y León. Only 27km from the Portuguese border, the castle is the starting point of the fortified walls which run around the city, making it a focal defense point during the numerous border wars with Portugal. Today, the chambers of the castle have been converted to luxurious rooms decorated with armor and period furniture, recreating an atmosphere of 14th-century Spain. The dining hall with its original stone arches serves carefully prepared local delicacies like *tostón* (suckling pig) and *huevos con farinato* (eggs with local sausage). Relaxing amidst the ivy covered walls of this parador is extremely popular; reservations are expected months ahead of time, especially during weekends and holidays. The entire province of Salamanca is also accessible from this location, permitting quick countryside excursions.

Parador de Ciudad Rodrigo, Pl. Castillo, 1 (☎923 46 01 50; fax 46 04 04). Singles €71-81; doubles €89-101; suites for 2 €123.

remembers the tradition of banishing local prostitutes across the river during the 40 days of Lent; they used to return triumphantly on *Lunes de Quasimodo*, when eager (male) *salmantinos* would picnic along the bridge to await their arrival. Those were the days.

🔎 DAYTRIP FROM SALAMANCA

CIUDAD RODRIGO

Buses arrive from the Salamanca station, Av. Filiberto Villalobos, 71-85 (1hr.; M-F 13 per day 7am-9:30pm, Sa 6 per day 8:30am-6pm, Su 4 per day 11am-10pm; €4.57). Buy tickets from El Pilar, windows 23 and 24. Last buses return to Salamanca M-F 7:30pm, Sa 5:45pm, and Su 8pm.

The hushed, labyrinthine streets and 18th-century ramparts of Ciudad Rodrigo, a sleepy town just 27km from Portugal, harbor myriad sandstone cathedrals, Roman ruins, and medieval masonry. Although the town was originally a Roman outpost, today it is known for its namesake, Conde Rodrigo González Girón, the count who brought the site back to life in 1100 after destructive Moorish invasions. Fortified during the numerous border wars between Spain and Portugal, the walled city of Ciudad Rodrigo soon grew into a prominent outpost for the Spanish military. Now, in peacetime, the city has applied its history to the tourist industry, prompting excursions by travelers unsated by Salamanca's masterpieces.

The **cathedral** is the town's crowning glory. Originally a Romanesque church commissioned by Fernando II of León, it was later modified in the 16th-century Gothic style. Rodrigo Alemán worked on the **coro** (choir) from 1498 to 1504. Look for the sculptor's signature—a carving of his head hidden among the rest of the carvings. The two 16th-century organs star in a series of concerts every August. The cathedral's **claustro** (cloister) is the highlight of a trip to Ciudad Rodrigo. The capitals of the ruined columns are covered with figures doing everything from making love to playing peek-a-boo to flirting with cannibalism. The cathedral's **museum** is filled with unique pieces, including an ancient clavichord, the cathedral's "ballot box," richly embroidered robes and slippers worn by bishops and priors, and Velázquez's *Llanto de Adán y Eva por Abel muerto*. (Cathedral open daily 10am-1pm and Su 4-7pm. Free. Cloister and museum open daily 10am-1pm and 3:30-7pm; Su 4-7pm. Free. €2, W free 3:30-7pm. Fee includes tour in Spanish.) From the bus station entrance, take a left onto Campo de Toledo (with the station behind you) and then the second right onto Av. Yurramendi (uphill). Pass through the stone arch and keep going straight into town, taking your first right onto Pl. de San Salvador. The cathedral is to your right.

The **bus station** (☎923 46 10 09) is on Campo de Toledo, 3-25. From the bus station, follow the directions to the cathedral (see above) until you pass the stone arch. The **tourist office**, Pl. de Amayuelas, 5, is immediately to the left, across the street and before the cathedral. (☎923 46 05 61. Open M-F 9am-2pm and 5-7pm, Sa-Su 10am-2pm and 5-8pm. French spoken.) To get to Pl. Mayor from the tourist office, continue straight on Pl. de Amayuelas into town, then turn left onto C. del Cardenal Pacheco just before Pl. de San Salvador and make a left again in C. Julián Sánchez; Pl. Mayor is at the end of this street. Most **restaurants, bars, and cafes** in town cluster on Pl. Mayor and on the streets around it. If you are looking for traditional Spanish cuisine, try **Cafetería Arcos ❷**, Pl. Mayor, 17, where a three-course *menú* is €8.50. (☎ 923 46 06 64. Open 8:30am-12:30am.) Near Pl. Mayor is **Pizzaria Tussilago ❶**, C. Julián Sánchez, 7, offering pizzas and other Italian delights starting at €4. (☎923 48 22 26. Open 11:30am-4pm and 7pm-2am.)

NEAR SALAMANCA

ZAMORA

Atop a cliff over the Río Duero, Zamora (pop. 70,000) is a beguiling mix of modern and medieval: 11th-century churches rub shoulders with Mango and Zara, 15th-century palaces harbor Internet cafes and luxury hotels, tangled and narrow streets empty onto grand *avenidas*, and the magnificent 12th-century cathedral overlooks modern subdivisions and steel bridges in the distance. While locals enjoy the town's modern conveniences, it is Zamora's history as one of the most powerful cities in medieval Castile that continually lures Spanish tourists. Monuments in nearly every plaza and street venerate Zamora's infamous figures, including the fierce Roman warrior Viriato, who was born here, El Cid, the Spanish hero who fled here, and Sancho II, who died here during an attempt to overthrow his sister and claim the House of Castile as his own. Zamora is only a short bus ride from Salamanca, making it an easy—and worthwhile—trip.

■▪ TRANSPORTATION & PRACTICAL INFORMATION. The best way to reach Zamora is by **bus.** Buses leave from the station on Av. Alfonso Peña (☎980 52 12 81; open 24hr.; lockers €1-2) and travel to: **Madrid** (3½hr.; M-Sa 3 per day 10:30am-5:30pm, Su 6 per day 10:30am-9:30pm; €11.46); **Salamanca** (1hr.; M-F 15 per day 6:40am-9:35pm, Sa 10 per day 7:45am-8:30pm, Su 6 per day 10am-9pm; €3.60); **Valladolid** (1½hr.; M-F 7 per day 7am-6:30pm, Sa 5 per day 8am-5:30pm, Su 3 per day 10:30am, noon, 10pm; €5.55). **Trains** leave from C. de la Estación (24hr. ☎980 52 11 10) at the end of Av. Alfonso Peña and go to **Madrid** (3hr.; daily 3 per day 3:50am, 2:23, 6:20pm; €21.08) and **Valladolid** (1½hr.; daily 2 per day 8:32am and 7:40pm; €6.30). The train and bus stations are both a 15min. walk from Pl. Mayor. The **tourist office** is at Pl. Arias Gonzalo, 6. From the bus station, exit the bus arrival platform and turn left onto Av. Alfonso Peña. Walk straight for several blocks, through the Pl. Mayor, until you hit R. de los Francos. At Pl. los Ciento, take a left onto C. Magistral Erro, and turn right at the end. (☎/fax 987 53 36 94; www.ayto-zamora.org. Open M-Sa Apr.-Sept. 10am-2pm and 4-7pm, Oct.-Mar. 10am-2pm and 5-8pm.) If you decide to stay for the night, good **accommodations** can be found at **Hostal La Reina ❷,** C. Reina, 1, in Pl. Mayor. The hostal features TV, A/C, and private baths. (☎980 53 39 39. Singles €18; doubles €30.) Pl. Mayor also hosts several restaurants and is a pleasant place to sit down and have some **food.**

◙ SIGHTS. Zamora's foremost monument is its Romanesque **cathedral,** built from the 12th to 15th centuries. Its Byzantine cupola is notable for its **Bishop's Door,** an entrance in the side of the dome that can be reached only by a vertigo-inducing flight of stairs. Inside, the cathedral's highlights are its intricately carved choir stalls (complete with seated apostles laughing and singing) and the main altar, an ornate marble and gold structure. Golden angels keep watch from a blue sky above. In the cloister, the **Museo de la Catedral** features the priceless 15th-century **Black Tapestries,** which tell the story of the Trojan War and Achilles's defeat. From Pl. Mayor, with the Ayuntamiento on your left and the church on your right, continue straight onto C. de Ramón Carrión. This turns into R. de los Francos and then R. de los Notarios. At Pl. Pío XII, turn left onto Puerta del Obispo. The cathedral is on the right. (☎980 53 06 44. Cathedral and museum open Tu-Su 10am-2pm and 5-8pm; Mass daily at 10am, also Sa 6pm and Su 1pm. Cathedral free; museum €2.) The **Parque del Castillo,** behind the cathedral, is a great spot for a picnic.

Twelve striking **Romanesque churches** remain within the walls of the old city, gleaming in the wake of recent restoration. Almost all were built in the 11th and 12th centuries, though their ornate altars were not added until the 15th-16th centuries. Visitors can follow the **Romanesque Route,** a self-guided tour of all of the churches available from the tourist office. With their gray stone, dark interiors, and sculptures of Christ in the sepulcher, all twelve churches tend to blend together. There are, however, a few standouts. In Pl. Mayor, the **Iglesia San Juan** is notable for its luminescent, marble-veined windows. **La Magdalena,** straight up C. de Ramón Carrión from Pl. Mayor, features an intricately carved south door; it also houses a Mary Magdalene icon, one of the most revered religious works of art in Zamora. Across the street from La Magdalena on C. de Ramón Carrión is the **Convento del Tránsito,** a convent of Carmelite nuns who watch over *La Virgen del Tránsito,* the patron saint of Zamora; she is credited with miracles ranging from bringing rain during a drought to protecting El Cid. Finally, **Iglesia Santa María la Nueva** was the site of one of Zamora's most significant historical events, *El Motín de la Trucha;* in 1158 villagers set the church on fire (with the nobles inside) to protest a law giving noblemen priority over plebeians in buying trout. While it may sound silly, the event was one of the first in a series that led to the rise of the Spanish middle class. To get to the church from Pl. Mayor, walk up C. Sacramento and turn right onto C. Barandales; the church is in Pl. Santa María la Nueva. (All open Mar.-Sept. Tu-Sa 10am-1pm and 5-8pm. Free.)

The ◪**Museo de Semana Santa,** Pl. Santa María la Nueva, 9, is a rare find. Hooded mannequins guard elaborately sculpted floats that depict the stations of the Vía Crucis. These mannequins were used during *romerías,* processions during *Semana Santa;* Zamora has one of the most decorated Easter celebrations in all of Spain. From Pl. Mayor, take C. Sacramento and turn right on C. Barandales. (☎980 53 22 95. Open M-Sa 10am-2pm and 5-8pm, Su 10am-2pm. €2.70.)

LEÓN   ☎987

The residents of León (pop. 145,000) are proud of their riverside oasis. From the tangled streets of the *barrio gótico* to the stunning cathedral, locals boast that their city is the best in all of Castile, if not in all of Spain. It's fitting that the city's unofficial mascot is the oh-so-proud lion—images of lions are everywhere, and the local moniker for residents of the area is *leones.* Strangely enough, the city's name has nothing to do with lions. Instead, it stems from *legio,* a name that the Roman Legion gave the town in AD 68. During the Middle Ages, the city was an important stop on the pilgrim route to Santiago de Compostela—and it continues to be, as gold shells marking the *camino's* path through the city center attest. León was also an essential defense point against Moorish invaders during *la Reconquista.* Today, the city is best known for its cathedral, whose spectacular blue stained-glass windows have earned León the nickname *La Ciudad Azul.* While history provides León with its local prominence, it is the city's serene parks and vibrant outdoor life that make it worth exploring.

▐ **TRANSPORTATION**

Trains: RENFE, Av. de Astorga, 2 (☎902 24 02 02). Open 24hr. To: **Barcelona** (9½hr.; M-F and Su 3 per day 12:25am, 1:21, 9:47pm; Sa 2 per day 12:25am, 1:21pm; €30-50); **Bilbao** (5½hr., daily 1 per day 3:16pm, €13.20-16); **Burgos** (2-3hr., daily 9-12 per day 1:42am-7pm, F and Su also 9:30pm; €14.50); **La Coruña** (7hr., express 4½hr.; M, W, F 2 per day 4:34am, 2:07pm; Tu, Th, Su 3 per day 4:34am, 2:07, 4:59pm; Sa 3 per day 4:34am, 2:07, 5:19pm; €22.50); **Gijón** (3hr.; M-F 7 per day 4:45am-7:40pm, Sa 7 per day 4:45pm-7pm, Su 6 per day 8:30am-7:40pm; €7-16) via **Oviedo** (2hr.; €6-14.50); **Madrid** (4½hr.; M-Sa 6 per day 1:12am-6:12pm, Su 2 per day 5:45pm and 7:05pm; €21.70-32); **Valladolid** (2½hr., daily 13-15 per day

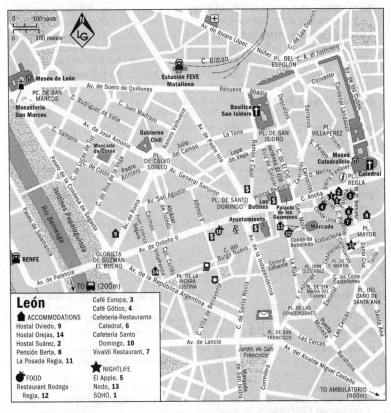

León	
▲ ACCOMMODATIONS	Café Europa, 3
Hostal Oviedo, 9	Café Gótico, 4
Hostal Orejas, 14	Cafetería-Restaurante
Hostal Suárez, 2	Catedral, 6
Pensión Berta, 8	Cafetería Santo
La Posada Regia, 11	Domingo, 10
	Vivaldi Restaurant, 7
● FOOD	
Restaurant Bodega	★ NIGHTLIFE
Regia, 12	El Apple, 5
	Nodo, 13
	SOHO, 1

CASTILLA Y LEÓN

1:25am-8:35pm, €9.25-17). **FEVE,** Av. del Padre Isla, 48 (☎987 22 59 19), for local destinations. Train and bus schedules are printed daily in *Diario de León* (€0.65).

Buses: Estación de Autobuses, Po. del Ingeniero Sáenz de Miera (☎987 21 00 00). Info open daily 7:30am-9pm. To: **Madrid** (4½hr.; M-F 12 per day 2:30am-10:30pm, Sa-Su 8 per day 2:30am-7:30pm; €17.95-29.74); **Salamanca** (2½hr.; M-F 4 per day 8am-3:15pm, Su 4 per day 10:15am-7pm, Sa 1 per day 8am; €8.14); **Santander** (5hr., M-Sa 1 per day 4pm, €10.37); **Valladolid** (2hr., daily 8 per day 2:30am-10:30pm, €7.27); **Zamora** (2½hr.; M-F 9 per day 8am-9:15pm, Sa 6 per day 8am-5pm, Su 4 per day 10:15am-7pm; €7.12).

Taxis: Radio Taxi (☎987 24 24 51 or 24 12 11). 24hr. service.

Car Rental: Hertz, C. Sampiro, 20 (☎987 23 19 99). 25+ and must have had license for 1yr. Open M-F 9am-2pm and 4-7pm, Sa 9am-1pm.

ORIENTATION & PRACTICAL INFORMATION

Most of León, including the old city *(León Gótico)* and modern commercial district, lies on the east side of the **Río Bernesga.** The bus and train stations are across the river in the west end. Av. de Palencia leads across the river to **Glorieta de Guzmán el Bueno,** where, after the rotary, it becomes **Avenida de Ordoño II,** which bisects the new city. At Pl. de Santo Domingo, Av. de Ordoño II becomes **Calle Ancha,** which splits the old town in two and leads to the cathedral.

Tourist Office: Pl. Regla, 3 (☎987 23 70 82). Free city maps, regional brochures, and accommodations guide. Open M-F 9am-2pm and 5-7pm, Sa-Su 10am-2pm and 5-7pm.

Currency Exchange: ATMs and **banks** line Pl. de Santo Domingo. **Banco Santander Central Hispano,** Pl. de Santo Domingo (☎902 24 24 24). Open M-F 8:30am-2:30pm. **Citibank,** on Av. de la Independencia at C. Legión VII. Open M-F 8:30am-2pm.

Luggage Storage: At the **train station** (€3). Open 24hr. At the **bus station** (€2). Buy tokens M-F 7:30am-9pm, Sa 8am-1pm and 2:15-8:30pm, Su 3:30-8:30pm.

English-Language Bookstore: Librería Galatea, C. Sierra Pambley, 1 (☎987 27 26 52). Open M-F 10am-2pm and 5-8:30pm, Sa 10am-2pm.

Emergency: ☎112. **Police:** C. Villa de Benavente, 6 (☎987 20 73 12).

Medical Services: Hospital Virgen Blanca (☎987 23 74 00), off C. San Antonio. **Medical emergency:** ☎987 22 22 22.

Late-Night Pharmacy: Farmacia Mata Espeso, Av. de Ordoño II, 3, is open all night. Open M-F 9:30am-2pm, 4:30-8pm, and 10pm-9:30am; Sa-Su 10pm-9:30am.

Internet Access: NavegaWeb, C. del Burgo Nuevo, 15, in the Telefónica store. €1.80 per hr. Open daily 10am-2pm and 5-10pm.

Post Office: Jardín de San Francisco (☎987 23 90 79; fax 87 60 78). **Lista de Correos** (windows #12-13) and **fax** available. Open M-F 8:30am-8:30pm, Sa 9:30am-2pm. **Postal Code:** 24004.

☰ ACCOMMODATIONS

Budget beds are fairly easy to come by in León, thanks to the yearly influx of pilgrims on their way to Santiago, but *pensiones* tend to fill during the June fiestas. Rooms cluster on **Avenida de Roma, Avenida de Ordoño II,** and **Avenida de la República Argentina,** which lead into the old town from Pl. Glorieta de Guzmán el Bueno.

Hostal Orejas, C. Villafranca, 6, 2nd fl. (☎987 25 29 09). Sparkling new rooms, complete with bath, shower, and cable TV. Free Internet access. Singles €30; doubles €39-49; triples €62; extra bed €10. MC/V. ❸

Hostal Oviedo, Av. de Roma, 26, 2nd fl. (☎987 22 22 36). Street-side rooms have terraces. Shared bathrooms are kept impeccably clean and have great lighting. Singles €15; doubles €25; triples €36. ❷

Pensión Berta, Pl. Mayor, 8, 2nd fl. (☎987 25 70 39). Caring owner maintains average-sized rooms accented by cheerful decor and their central location in the *barrio húmedo*, with all-night bars just steps away. Singles €12; doubles €22. ❶

Hostal Suárez, C. Ancha, 7 (☎987 25 42 88). Prime location, seconds away from the cathedral. Rooms are spacious with high ceilings and soft beds. No heat. Open Apr.-Nov. Doubles €20; triples €25. ❷

La Posada Regia, C. General Mola, 9-11 (☎987 21 30 31). A three-star hotel with handsome, uniquely shaped rooms with individualized decor. In the heart of the old city. Breakfast buffet included. Singles €54.66; doubles €90. IVA not included. ❺

☰ FOOD

Inexpensive eateries fill the area near the cathedral and on the small streets off C. Ancha; also check Pl. de San Martín, near Pl. Mayor. Meat-lovers will rejoice, as many variations of pork top the local menus. Fresh produce as well as bread, cheese, and milk are available at the **Mercado Municipal del Conde,** Pl. del Conde, off C. General Mola. (Open M-Sa 9am-3:30pm.)

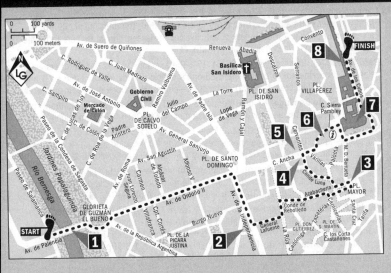

You've seen the cathedral, walked through the old city, and visited the basilica. What are you going to do now? Well, it's not Disney World, but León has a few more surprises in store for the over-churched, over-monumented visitor.

1. Hop, skip, and play along the **Río Bernesga,** crossing it either via the stepping stones in front of the bus station or on the Roman bridge, Puente San Marcos, at the end of Gran Vía de San Marcos. A stroll down Av. de Palencia to the bridge guarded by two **lions** yields an awe-inspiring view of some of the Picos de Europa mountains only a few miles away. Beware: two lions guard this bridge, which leads into Glorieta Guzmán el Bueno.

2. Watch a movie from your own red-velvet-interior private balcony at the **Teatro Emperador,** Av. de la Independencia, 14 (☎987 25 09 20). Built in 1951 complete with a grand staircase crowned with crystal chandeliers, the theater showcases the summer's latest movies and hosts winter's best live performances.

3. Jumpstart your sense at the **mercado** in Pl. Mayor. Colorful tents shelter vibrantly colored fresh fruits, vegetables, and olives, making for a uniquely enchanting market scene. (The market sets up in the plaza Monday through Thursday, 8am-3pm.)

4. Find your remedy among hundreds of antique medicinal vessels in the **Farmacia Dr. Alonson Núñez,** C. Ancha, 23, dating from 1827. The vintage serpentine door handles provde the cure for the common doorknob.

5. Right across the street is **El Capitán,** where you can pick your favorite vintage poster from among the hundreds plastered to the ceiling. Mind the burning candlesticks. (At the corner of C. Ancha and C. Cervantes, s/n.)

6. Sneak a peek into the **Edificio Zuloaga,** whose *azulejo* (tile) interior often goes unseen. Afterwards, drink up in the pleasant courtyard. (C. Sierra Pambley, 3.)

7. Visit the beautiful **Gothic cathedral** just one more time, to make your trip to León complete. Go at a different time of day to catch the full radiance of the morning and afternoon sun pouring in through its two-story stained glass windows. Better yet, go on a Sunday, right after Mass, when the organ is playing and the smell of incense lingers in the air.

8. Walk around the city's impressive **medieval walls** and *cubos* lining Av. de los Cubos and the Hospital de San Isidoro.

▨ **Café Gótico,** C. Varillas, 5 (☎987 08 49 56). Delicious, fresh, and carefully prepared food with pleasant outdoor seating close to the cathedral. The daily *menú* (€9.50) has a vegetarian option. A wide variety of enticing coffee dessert drinks. Be sure to try the incredible *BonBon*. Open daily 9am-very late. ❷

Café Europa, Pl. Regla, 9 (☎987 25 61 17). The spacious, sunny terrace offers great views of the cathedral to complement Europa's delicious varieties of coffee (€2) and pastries. Also offers breakfast (€3) and tasty ice cream (€1). Open daily 9am-11pm. ❶

Cafetería Santo Domingo, Av. de Ordoño II, 3 (☎987 26 13 84). Family restaurant specializing in ice creams and pastries. 3-course *menús* €9. Open daily 8am-midnight. ❷

Restaurant Bodega Regia, C. General Mola, 9 (☎987 21 31 73). Part of the hotel of the same name, Bodega Regia specializes in *cocina leonesa* and has an excellent reputation. Full *menú* with wine €15. Open daily 1:30pm-late. AmEx/MC/V. ❸

Cafetería-Restaurante Catedral, C. Mariano Domínguez Berrueta, 17 (☎987 21 59 18). Huge portions, garlic-laden trout, and homemade desserts. *Menú del día* €8. Open M and Th-Sa 10am-midnight; Tu-W and Su 10am-4pm. AmEx/MC/V. ❷

Vivaldi Restaurant, C. Cardiles Platerías, 4 (☎987 26 07 60). A wide selection of meats (€16.30-18.40) and vegetables prepared with creative recipes. Also serves a variety of cheeses (€7-10) in a spacious, breezy setting. *Menú* €30-40 for one person, but cheaper for more (€60 for 4). Open July-Aug. M-Sa 1-3:30pm and 9-11:30pm; Sept.-June Tu-Su 1-3:30pm and 9-11:30pm. MC/V. ❺

👁 SIGHTS

León has several worthwhile sights, crowned by its magnificent cathedral. The city still retains some of a small-town feel and has many attractive parks where weary travelers can sit and laze away the day.

▨ **IGLESIA CATEDRAL DE SANTA MARÍA.** The 13th-century Gothic cathedral, *La Pulchra Leonina*, is arguably the most beautiful cathedral in Spain. It is also one of country's best examples of Gothic architecture. The exceptional facade depicts smiling saints amidst bug-eyed monsters munching on the damned. But the real attractions are its stained-glass windows, which feature angelic saints and brilliant flowers, and the elaborate altar painting of the stations of the Vía Crucis. *(On Pl. Regla. ☎987 87 57 70. Open daily in summer 8:30am-2:30pm and 5-7pm; in winter 8:30am-1:30pm and 4-7pm. Free. Museum open in summer daily 9:30am-1:30pm and 4-6:30pm; in winter M-F 9:30am-1pm and 4-6pm, Sa 9:30am-1:30pm. Cathedral €3.50, cloisters €0.60.)*

BASÍLICA SAN ISIDORO. The Romanesque Basílica San Isidoro was dedicated in the 11th century to San Isidoro of Sevilla. After his death, his remains were brought from Muslim-dominated Andalucía to the Christian stronghold of León. The corpses of countless royals rest in the **Panteón Real,** where the ceilings are covered by vibrant 12th-century frescoes. The unusual Annunciation and Roman agricultural calendar are noteworthy. Admission to the pantheon includes entrance to the library, which houses a 10th-century handwritten Bible, and to the treasury, home of the agate chalices of Doña Urraca, King Fernando I's daughter. *(On Pl. San Isidoro. Open M-Sa 9am-1:30pm and 4-6:30pm, Su 9am-1:30pm. €3.)*

OTHER SIGHTS. The **Museo de León** displays an extensive archaeological collection with pieces dating from the Paleolithic era; particularly stunning are the 4th-century Roman mosaics. *(Pl. de San Marcos. ☎987 24 50 61. Open July-Sept. Tu-Sa 10am-2pm and 5-8pm, Su 10am-4pm; Oct.-June Tu-Sa 10am-2pm and 4-7pm, Su 10am-4pm. €1.20, free for students Sa-Su.)* **Casa de los Botines** is one of the few buildings outside Catalunya designed by modernist architect Antoni Gaudí, the most famous member of the *Modernisme* movement in Spain. The relatively restrained structure contains hints of his later style in its turrets and windows (see **Barcelona**, p. 392). It now contains bank offices and is not open to the public. Some of León's most enjoyable attractions are its parks and promenades, where locals spend their evenings picnicking and exchanging *besos*. Two of the most peaceful are the **Jardines El Cid**, directly behind Casa de los Botines on Pilotos Reguera between El Cid and Ruiz de Salazar, and the **Jardines Papalaguinda**, running along the river from Pl. de San Marcos in the north to the Pl. de Toros in the south.

■ ■ NIGHTLIFE & FESTIVALS

For nearby bars, discos, and techno music, head to the *barrio húmedo* (drinker's neighborhood) around **Plaza de San Martín** and **Plaza Mayor**. Walk up C. Ancha toward the cathedral and take a right on C. Varillas (which becomes C. Cardiles Platerías). To reach Pl. de San Martín, take a right where the street ends at C. Carnicerías; to reach Pl. Mayor, take a left onto C. Plegaria at the end of C. Cardiles Platerías. All bars here are open Monday-Thursday until 2am and Friday-Sunday until 5-6am. **Nodo**, with entrances at C. Ramiro II, 1, and C. Matasiete, 7, attracts a young crowd with a mix of popular Spanish beats. For a club with funkier decor but similar crowds and music head to **SOHO**, C. Varillas, 4. Around the corner is the sleek **El Apple**, C. la Paloma, 1, playing fewer mainstream songs to a slightly dressier crowd. After 2am, the crowds weave to the many discos and bars of **Avenida de Lancia** and **Calle Conde de Guillén**.

In June, León's 3500km of trout-fishable streams draw the **International Trout Festival**. Festivals commemorating **San Juan** and **San Pedro** occur June 21-30. Highlights include a *corrida de torros* (bullfight) and the feast days of San Juan on June 23 and San Pedro on June 30. King Juan Carlos I and Queen Sofía sometimes attend the fiestas and the cathedral's **International Organ Festival** on October 5.

■ DAYTRIP FROM LEÓN

ASTORGA

Astorga is most easily reached by bus from León, Po. del Ingeniero Sáenz de Miera (45min.; M-F 16 per day 6am-9:30pm, Sa-Su 6-7 per day 8:30am-8:30pm; €3). RENFE runs trains to Astorga from León (45min.; M-Tu and Th-F 5 per day 2:04am-8:29pm, W 6 per day 2:04am-8:29pm, Sa 4 per day 2:04am-8:29pm, Su 3 per day 2:15am-8:29pm; €3), but the station is a 15min. walk uphill from the main sights.

For the rich and pious, there was really no way to avoid Astorga in the 15th century, since it was an important stop on both *La Ruta de la Plata*, the Roman silver route, and *El Camino de Santiago*, the pilgrim's path to Santiago de Compostela that begins in the French Pyrenees. In the early 17th century it became one of the world's main chocolate-making centers; a few die-hards still produce bars of authentic *chocolate de Astorga*.

Today Astorga is perhaps most distinguished by the ◼**Palacio Episcopal**, designed in the late 19th century by Antoni Gaudí. The palace's turrets, main entryway, and beveled stone exterior are characteristic of Gaudí's style. Gaudí built the palace to replace the one which burned down in 1886, but no bishop has ever actually lived there. Now the fascinating palace houses the **Museo de los Caminos**, dedicated to the various paths toward Santiago de Compostela that converge in 2000-year-old Astorga. (☎987 61 88 82. Open July-Sept. Tu-Sa 10am-2pm and 4-8pm, Su 10am-2pm; Oct.-June Tu-Sa 11am-2pm and 4-6pm, Su 11am-2pm. €2.50.) The **cathedral**, directly to the left when facing the Palacio Episcopal, is definitely worth a quick visit. While it is neither as well-preserved nor as opulent as León's cathedral, its emptiness—there are no pews, chapel gates, or candle tables—affords a rare opportunity to experience the immensity of Gothic architecture. The cathedral's **museum** has 10 rooms filled with religious relics and a series of paintings depicting the temptations of St. Anthony—including several panels of his gruesome attack by demons. (Both open daily 10am-2pm and 4-8pm. Cathedral free; museum €2.50; €4 for a joint ticket with the Museo de los Caminos.) The sweet-toothed must stop by the **Museo de Chocolate,** C. José María Goy, 5. From the Palacio Episcopal, walk up C. los Sitios to Pl. Obispo Alcolea; veer to the right onto C. Lorenzo Segura and C. José María Goy is on the right. Learn everything you ever wanted to know about chocolate. The museum sells old advertisement reproductions and Astorga-made chocolate bars, pieces of which you can try for free. (Open Tu-Sa 10:30am-2pm and 4:30-8pm, Su 10:30am-2pm. €0.90.) You can purchase chocolate and other sugary delights next door at the **Confitería la Mallorquina,** C. Lorenzo Segura, 7. (Open daily 10am-2pm and 4-7pm.) Visiting Astorga without buying a box of *milagritos* or *hojaldres* pastries would be a sin.

The **bus station,** Av. las Murallas, 54 (☎987 61 93 51), faces the back of the Palacio Episcopal. To get to the town center from the RENFE **train station** (☎987 84 21 22), on Pl. de la Estación, cross the parking lot in front of the station and follow C. Pedro de Castro until it crosses C. Puerta de Rey. A large building (Casa Granell) is on the right. Walk through the city wall onto C. Enfermas and turn right onto C. los Sitios, which will bring you to the palace. With your back to the palace, the **tourist office,** Glorieta Eduardo de Castro, 5, is directly in front of you across the plaza. (☎987 61 82 22. Open Sa-M 9am-8:30pm, Tu-F 10am-2pm and 4-8:30pm.)

VALLADOLID
☎983

For nearly 300 years, Valladolid was the most important town in Castile; when Fernando and Isabel married here in 1469, it stood at the forefront of Spanish politics, finance, and culture. Explorers Fernão Magelhães (Ferdinand Magellan) and Juan Sebastián El Cano came to Valladolid to discuss their plans to circumnavigate the globe, newly discovered to be round. Miguel de Cervantes, creator of the hero Don Quijote, lived here; in 1506, Christopher Columbus died here. Close to a century later, shady dealings by minister Conde Duque de Lerma brought the city's glory days to an end. In return for a whopping bribe, Lerma took Valladolid (then capital of Castile) out of the running for capital of Spain. Today, the city has little to offer visitors beyond its sculpture museum and relics of a Renaissance past. It does, however, offer a glimpse of the unaffected Spanish urban life.

▣ TRANSPORTATION

Flights: Villanubla Airport, CN-601, km13 (☎983 41 54 00). Daily flights to **Barcelona** and **Paris.** June-Oct. service to the **Balearic Islands.** Info open daily 8am-8pm. **Iberia** (☎983 56 01 62). Open daily 8am-8pm. Taxi to airport €11-12.

Trains: Estación del Norte, C. Recondo, s/n (☎902 24 02 02), south of the Parque del Campo Grande. Info open daily 7am-8pm. Trains to: **Barcelona** (9¾-11hr.; M-F and Su 2 per day 9:18am, 9:30pm; Sa 1 per day 8:10pm; €35.50); **Bilbao** (4hr.; M, W, F 1 per day 6:27pm; €18.50); **Burgos** (1¾-2½hr.; M-F 11 per day 1:42am-11:30pm, Sa-Su 7 per day noon-11:45pm; €5.85); **León** (2-3hr.; M-Sa 8 per day 1:12am-8:35pm, Su 7 per day 10:26am-5:25pm; €7.90); **Lisboa, PT** (7¾hr., daily 1 per day 3:20am, €40); **Madrid** (3-3¾hr.; M-F 13 per day 4am-8:41pm, Sa 12 per day 4am-8:41pm, Su 11 per day 7am-9pm; €11.40-22); **Oviedo** (4-5½hr.; M-Sa 3 per day 1:42, 10:26am, 5:25pm; Su 2 per day 10:26am, 5:25pm; €26.23); **Paris, FR** (11hr., daily 1 per day

9:20pm, €83.50); **Salamanca** (1¾-2¾hr.; M-F 7 per day 7:15am-8:45pm, Sa 7 per day 9:45am-8:15pm, Su 6 per day 7:05am-10:02pm; €5.35-11.50); **Santander** (3-6hr.; M-F 7 per day 9:35am-1:42am, Sa 8 per day 7:15am-1:42am, Su 7 per day 7:15am-6:40pm; €11.40-24); **San Sebastián** (5hr.; daily 3 per day 3:41, 11:47am, 12:25pm; €21.50-28); **Zamora** (2hr., daily 1 per day 8:36am, €6.45-12).

Buses: C. de Puente Colgante, 2 (☎983 23 63 08). Info open daily 8am-10pm. **ALSA** to: **Barcelona** (10hr.; daily 2 per day 12:35, 7:50pm; €35.88); **Bilbao** (5hr.; M-Th and Sa 2 per day 1:35, 5:30pm; F 3 per day 1:35, 3:30, 5:30pm; Su 2 per day 5:30, 7:15pm; €18.50-24); **Burgos** (1¾-2¾hr., M-Th and Su 5 per day 9:45am-9:45pm, €6.20); **León** (2hr.; M-F 10 per day 2:45am-12:45am, Sa 7 per day 2:45am-12:45am, Su 6 per day 2:45am-9:45pm; €9.25); **Madrid** (2¼hr.; M-Sa 18 per day 4:15am-12:30am, Su 19 per day 10:15am-10pm; €11.40); **Oviedo** (3¼-4¼hr., 4 per day 2:15am-7pm, €12.25); **Santander** (4hr.; 2 per day M-Th and Sa 9:45am, 4:45pm; F and Su 4:45, 8pm; €11.40). **La Regional** to **Palencia** (45min.; M-F every hr. 7am-9pm, Sa 5 per day 8am-8:15pm, Su 3 per day 10am-10pm; €3) and **Zamora** (1½hr.; M-F 7 per day 7am-6:30pm; Sa 5 per day 8am-5:30pm; Su 3 per day 10:30am, 5, 10pm; €6.45).

Taxis: Agrupación de Taxistas de Valladolid 24hr. ☎983 20 77 55.

◀▮ 🛈 ORIENTATION & PRACTICAL INFORMATION

The bus and train stations sit on the southern edge of town, beneath the Parque del Campo Grande. To get from the **bus station** to the **tourist office** (15min.), exit at the corner of Po. del Arco de Ladrillo and C. San José. (Do not exit onto the corner of Po. del Arco de Ladrillo and C. de Puente Colgante.) Turn left onto Po. del Arco de Ladrillo and keep right onto C. Ladrillo at the rotary. Follow C. Ladrillo to Po. de Los Filipinos. At the edge of Parque del Campo Grande, take the pedestrian path through the park. When you reach Pl. de Zorrilla at the end of the park, C. Santiago—the street the tourist office is on—will be directly across the rotary. From the front entrance of the **train station** (10min.), walk up the street perpendicular to the station, C. Estación del Norte, following it to Pl. de Colón. Follow the rotary to the right; Av. Acera de Recoletos will be the third street on your right, running alongside the park, and will take you directly to Pl. de Zorrilla. C. Santiago is the second street to the right from this rotary. **Plaza Mayor** is straight up C. Santiago from the tourist office; the **cathedral** and **sculpture museum** are 10min. to the north.

Tourist Office: C. Santiago, 19 (☎983 34 40 13). Open daily 9am-10pm.

Currency Exchange: Banco Santander Central Hispano, C. Perú, 6 (☎902 24 24 24), on the corner of Av. Acera de Recoletos. Open M-F 8:30am-2:30pm. **Citibank,** C. Miguel Iscar, 7, off Pl. de Zorrilla. Open M-F 8am-2pm.

Luggage Storage: At the **train station.** Lockers €2.50. 24hr. At the **bus station.** €0.60 per bag. Open M-Sa 8am-10pm.

Emergency: ☎091 or 092. **Local Police:** In the Ayuntamiento (☎983 42 61 07).

Medical Services: Ambulance/Emergencies: ☎061. **Residencia Sanitaria Pío del Río Hortega,** Av. de Santa Teresa, s/n (☎983 42 04 00). **Red Cross** (☎983 22 22 22).

Late-Night Pharmacy: Pharmacies line C. Santiago. **Licenciada López,** Po. de Zorrilla, 85, is the only night pharmacy. Open M-Th and Sa-Su 10pm-9:30am, F 10pm-10am.

Internet Access: Ciberc@fé Segafredo, Po. de Zorrilla, 46 (☎983 33 80 63). From Pl. de Zorrilla, walk down Po. de Zorrilla alongside park; cafe is on right before Av. García Morato. Exact change for machines. €0.60 per 15min. Open daily 8am-midnight.

CASTILLA Y LEÓN

Post Office: Pl. Rinconada, s/n (☎983 33 02 31), near the Ayuntamiento. **Faxes** and **Lista de Correos.** Open M-Sa 8:30am-8:30pm, Su 8:30am-2pm. **Postal Code:** 47001.

ACCOMMODATIONS

Cheap lodgings with winter heat are easy to come by. The streets off Av. Acera de Recoletos near the train station are packed with *pensiones*, as are those near the cathedral and behind Pl. Mayor at Pl. del Val.

Pensión Dani, C. Perú, 11, 1st fl. (☎983 30 02 49), near Parque del Campo Grande. Has large, comfortable, well-maintained rooms. Hardwood floors and new, clean, sheets. Singles €11; doubles €19. ❶

Pensión Dos Rosas, C. Perú, 11, 2nd fl. (☎983 20 74 39). The rooms at Dos Rosas are just as spacious and well-kept as those at Dani. Not surprisingly, the prices are similar. Portable heaters in winter. Singles €11; doubles €20; triple €30. ❶

Hostal Residencia Val II, Pl. del Val, 6, 1st fl. (☎983 37 57 52), a few blocks from Pl. Mayor. TV common area and quiet lounge. Huge rooms with eclectic quilts open onto private terraces. Singles €15, with bath €27; doubles €24/€33. ❷

Hotel Olid Meliá, Pl. San Miguel, 10 (☎983 35 72 00; fax 33 68 28). A huge 7-story building with conference rooms, bars, a nice restaurant, and comfortable, fully-equipped rooms. Singles €78; doubles €85. IVA not included. AmEx/MC/V. ❺

FOOD

Eateries abound between Pl. Mayor and Pl. del Val and near the cathedral. **Mercado del Val,** in Pl. del Val just off Pl. Mayor, has fresh food. (Open M-Sa 6am-3pm.)

Cantina La Puñeta, C. Santa María, 19 (☎983 20 71 36). With a wooden bar, pastel-colored walls, and delicious burritos, La Puñeta is a great place for Tex-Mex fanatics. Salads €5-6, entrees €5-8. Open daily 1-5pm and 8pm-midnight. ❷

Casa San Pedro Regalad, Pl. Ochavo, 1 (☎983 34 45 06), near the Pl. Mayor. Descend into the pleasantly isolated cavernous depths of this 16th-century *bodega* to enjoy elegant dining. *Menú* €7.50. Open daily 1:30-3:30pm and 8-11:30pm. AmEx/MC/V. ❷

Restaurante Chino Gran Muralla, C. Santa María, 1 (☎983 34 23 07), off C. Santiago, north of Pl. de Zorrilla. Neon dragons greet patrons at this Spanish pagoda. 4-course *menú del día* €4.25. Open daily 11:30am-5pm and 7pm-12:30am. ❶

SIGHTS

Valladolid is surrounded by churches, bridges, and picturesque pastures. Unfortunately, the city itself is not quite as blessed. Other than the few sights listed below, Valladolid simply doesn't have that much to offer.

CATEDRAL METROPOLITANA. This Romanesque cathedral was partly designed by Juan de Herrera, creator of El Escorial (see p. 149). Despite the fact that other architects felt the need to ornament—gargoyles leer down at parishioners—the cathedral is still an excellent example of Herrera's *desornamentado* style of plain masonry. The extensive **Museo Diocesano,** in the cathedral's Gothic addition, houses the remains of the original 11th- to 13th-century structure as well as Herrera's model of the basilica. *(C. Arribas, 1, in Pl. de la Universidad. From Pl. Mayor, walk up*

C. Ferrari. After 2 blocks, veer left onto Bajada de la Libertad. At Pl. de la Libertad, turn right. ☎983 30 43 62. Cathedral and museum open Tu-Sa 10am-1:30pm and 4:30-7pm, Su 10am-2pm. Cathedral free. Museum €2.50.)

CASA DE CERVANTES. The supposed home in which Cervantes penned his epic *Don Quijote* from 1603-1606, the *casa* houses an amusing collection of old books and furniture; the medieval bed-warmer is its only unique highlight. *(C. Rastro. From Pl. de Zorrilla, walk up C. Miguel Iscar; C. Rastro will be 2 blocks up on your right. ☎983 33 88 10. Open Tu-Sa 9:30am-3:30pm, Su 10am-3pm. €2.50, students with ID €1.25, under 18 and over 65 free; Su free.)*

🎭 ENTERTAINMENT

Valladolid's cafes and bars are lively, though nothing to write home about. A student crowd fills the countless bars on **Calle Paraíso,** just beyond the cathedral. From Pl. de la Universidad at the cathedral, turn left onto C. Duque de Lerma, then right onto C. Marqués del Duero; C. Paraíso will be on the right. For pubs, try **Plaza San Miguel** (from Pl. Mayor, walk up Pl. Corrillo, turn left onto C. Val; after the plaza, continue onto C. Zapico; at Pl. los Arces, turn left onto C. San Antonio de Padua, which brings you to Pl. San Miguel) and **Calle Santa María,** off C. Santiago. Cafes on **Calle Vicente Moliner** draw an older crowd; from Pl. Mayor, walk up C. Ferrari, and at Pl. Fuente Dorada, C. Vicente Moliner is on the left. The neighborhood around **Plaza Martí Monsó,** however, is the most central nightlife in Valladolid. In addition to its numerous all-night *tapas* bars such as **El Concho,** C. Correos, 2 (open daily 8:30pm-2:30am), and chic wine bars like **Vino Tinto,** C. Calixto Fernández de la Torre, 4 (open M-Sa 7pm-4am), this neighborhood also houses Valladolid's two best dance clubs. **TinTin,** C. Campanas, 12, is deservedly the most popular bar in Valladolid (open Tu-Sa 10pm-sunrise).

International Cinema Week (Oct. 21-31) features indie European films. **Fiesta Mayor** begins September 21, featuring bullfights, carnivals, and parades.

🏛 DAYTRIPS FROM VALLADOLID

MEDINA DEL CAMPO

Medina del Campo is a 30min. bus ride from Valladolid. La Regional V.S.A. runs buses back to Valladolid from the bus stop at the Pl. de San Agustín (30min.; M-F 16 per day 7am-7:30pm, Sa 10 per day 8am-7:30pm; around €3). Tickets and information are available at the neighboring Bar Punto Rojo (☎983 80 05 35).

Medina del Campo was once *the* destination of wealthy medieval traders and money lenders. At its peak, the town was world-famous for its banking business and sheep industry and drew tens of thousands of visitors a year. Nowadays, Medina del Campo is an untouristed oasis free of the visiting hordes of years past, a pleasant daytrip away from the bustle of Valladolid. An informative and well-kept collection of artifacts from Medina del Campo's more prosperous times is housed in **El Fundación Museo de las Ferias,** C. San Martín, 9. To get to the museum from the bus stop, cross the street with the statue of the two dogs on your right, and veer left onto C. San Martín. The museum, located in the former church of San Martín, features first-rate examples of market objects from the wool, textile, art, and silver industries as well as the weights and scales used for trading. (☎983 83 75 27. Open Tu-Sa 10am-1:30pm and 4-7pm, Su 11am-2pm. €1.50, students €1.) For another glimpse of the town's bygone glory days, visit the **sheep market,** down

Av. de Portugal just beyond the Pl. de Toros. (Su 7am-noon.) Medina del Campo's most impressive sight is perhaps the robust, red-brick 15th century **Castillo de la Mota**. Queen Isabel and Juana la Loca, her daughter, once lived in the castle. To get there from the museum, continue down C. San Martín and turn right on C. Almirante, which leads to Pl. Mayor. Exit Pl. Mayor from the corner opposite the tourist office on C. Maldonado. At the street end, turn left onto C. Claudio Moyano, crossing the river and walking underneath the highway. Turn right and walk uphill onto Av. de la Estación. (☎983 80 10 24. Open M-Sa 11am-2pm and 4-7pm, Su 11am-2pm. To visit the underground defensive tunnels, call the tourist office and set up an appointment. Free.)

The town center is Pl. Mayor de la Hispanidad, where restaurants, benches, and stores abound. From the bus stop, take C. San Martín and continue past the museum. Go right on C. Almirante until you reach the plazaand the **tourist office.** (☎983 81 13 57. Open M-F 8am-3pm and 5-8pm. Su 10am-2pm.)

TORDESILLAS

Tordesillas is a quick 30min. bus ride from Valladolid. To get back, go to the bus station on C. de Valdehuertos, 1 (☎983 77 00 72). La Regional V.S.A. runs buses to Valladolid (30min.; M-F 14 per day 7am-7:30pm, Sa 8 per day 7:45am-6:30pm, Su 5 per day 11:30am-11pm; €1.80) and Zamora (1hr.; M-F 7 per day 9am-8:30pm, Sa 5 per day 9am-6:30pm, Su 9am, 3:30, 8:30pm; €3.85).

A playing field and building ground for several Catholic kings and queens, Tordesillas (pop. 8190) is best known as the site of the signing of the 1494 treaty which divided the New World between Spain and Portugal. The walls of the old city prevent unwanted modern tastes and tempos from spoiling the town's precious monasteries, churches, and easy-going hospitality.

One of the town's most unique artistic sights is the ■**Museo y Centro Didáctico del Encaje de Castilla y León,** C. Carnicerías, 4. This internationally-recognized sewing museum and research center conserves historical designs and creates modern ones. In the free guided tour, prepare to be awed by the exquisite, seemingly flawless pieces. (☎983 79 60 35; www.museoencaje.com. Open M-F 5-8pm, Sa noon-2pm and 5-8pm, Su 2-4pm. Free.) Another sight of artistic interest is the **Real Monasterio de Santa Clara,** on C. Santa Clara. Construction for this palace-gone-monastery was completed under Pedro I, who dedicated it to his mistress, María de Padilla. The palace's Moorish influence can be traced to María's wish to import elements of her native Andalucía. Queen Juana la Loca was confined here until her death in 1555. The guided tour, included with admission, takes you through several impressive rooms, the most spectacular of which is the main chapel. Covered with a shimmering coffered ceiling emblazoned in gold, it is as remarkable as many rooms of the Alhambra. (Open Oct.-Mar. Tu-Sa 10am-1:30pm and 4-5:45pm, Su 10:30am-1:30pm; Apr.-Sept. Tu-Sa 10am-1:30pm and 3:30-5:30pm, Su 10:30am-1:30pm and 3:30-5:30pm. €3.60, with ISIC card €2, W free for EU citizens.) For history buffs, the **Museo del Tratado,** on C. Tratado, contains all you need to know—and more—about the Treaty of Tordesillas. The displays include replicas of 15th century maps and models of the Niña, Pinta, and Santa María. (Open Tu-Sa 10:30am-1:30pm and 5-7pm, Su 10:30am-1:30pm. Free.)

The center of the town and the old district is the Pl. Mayor, a 10min. walk from the bus station. All major sights are within a few blocks of it. Standing with your back to the station platform, turn right onto C. Valdehuertos, which quickly merges with Av. Madrid Coruña. Continue straight until you reach the statue of a bull. Take the road to its left, C. del Empedrado, which turns into C. San Antolín, and continue straight until you reach the Pl. Mayor. Several sights stem off of C. Antolín, which leads you to the medieval bridge over the Río Duero. The **tourist office,** C. Tratado, shares the same entrance as the museum. (☎983 77 10 67;

www.tordesillas.net. Open Tu-Sa 10am-1:30pm and 5-7:30pm, Su 10am-2pm.) Restaurants crowd the Pl. Mayor. **Mesón Antolín ❹**, C. San Antolín, 8, off of the Pl. Mayor, serves Castilian fare prepared with fresh ingredients. (☎983 79 67 71. Entrees €18-30. Open daily 1-4pm and 8-11pm. MC/V.) If you are planning on staying the night, the adjoining ⬛**Hostal San Antolín ❸** is an excellent choice. Its elegant, spotless rooms with shining hardwood floors are the closest accommodations to the Pl. Mayor. Private baths, TV, A/C, towels, and toiletries are all included. (☎/fax 983 79 67 71; www.iespana.es/tordesillas_es/sanantolin. Singles €28; doubles €46.) Cheaper lodgings can be found at **Puerta de la Villa ❶**, Av. Valladolid, 54, a 10min. walk from the Pl. Mayor. The rooms are simple, clean, and have soft sheets. (☎983 77 19 90. Singles €12, with bath €18; doubles €24/€26.)

BURGOS
☎947

Travelers remember two things about Burgos (pop. 346,000): the church and the cheese. When entering the city, the traveler's first view is of the magnificent Gothic spires of Burgos's cathedral towering over even the most remote streets and plazas. While this architectural and religious landmark is the city's claim to fame, there is much more to the town than transepts and altars. Food connoisseurs will appreciate the delectable *queso de Burgos* and *morcilla*, a blood sausage with rice and tripe, all washed down with a glass of Burgos's famous Ribera del Duero wine. From quiet strollers along the Río Arlanzón to college kids out on the town, Burgos conveys an aura of vivacity, prosperity, and elegance. This aura is quite possibly due to Burgos's 500-year stint as Castile's capital. Every street seems to mark some historical legacy, particularly those involving El Cid Campeador, the region's hero. Each plaza and *paseo* is graced with marvels like the Puente de Santa María and the Monasterio de Las Huelgas Reales. Perhaps the heroes and kings of yore just knew a good thing when they saw it; what with its debauched nightlife and unique cuisine, Burgos is a city fit for both kings and commoners.

▐ TRANSPORTATION

Trains: Av. Conde de Guadalhorce, s/n (☎947 20 35 60). 10min. walk or €3 taxi ride to the city center. Info open daily 7am-10pm. To: **Barcelona** (9-14hr., 4 per day 2:17am-11:40pm, €32); **Bilbao** (2½-4hr.; M-F 5 per day 3:17am-6:44pm, Sa 4 per day 3:17am-6:44pm, Su 3 per day 12:57-6:44pm; €14); **La Coruña** (6-9hr., 3 per day 12pm-2:38am, €30.50-38); **Lisboa** (8-10hr., 2am, €34.50); **Madrid** (3-5½hr.; M-F 7 per day 2:20am-7:09pm, Sa-Su 6 per day 2:20am-7:09pm; €22-28); **Palencia** (45min.; M-F 8 per day 2:38am-8:20pm, Sa-Su 6 per day 2:38am-8:20pm; €3.40-12); **Valladolid** (1-2hr., 12 per day 1:44am-11:07pm, €5.85-11.50).

Buses: C. Miranda, 4 (☎947 28 88 55). To: **Barcelona** (7½hr.; M-Sa 6 per day, Su 5 per day noon-12:35am; €29.19); **Bilbao** (2-3hr., M-F 4 per day 8:30am-7pm, €9); **La Coruña/Santiago de Compostela** (7hr., 1 per day 10am, €33.18); **León** (3½hr., M-Sa 1 per day 10:45am, €19.82); **Madrid** (2¾hr., M-F 12 per day 7:30am-3:45am, €12.80); **Oviedo** (4-5hr., 4 per day 4:45am-9:15pm, €11); **Salamanca** (4hr., M-Sa 1 per day 10:45am, €12.59); **San Sebastián** (4-5hr., 7 per day 7:15am-3:15am, €12.61); **Santander** (3hr., 4 per day 10:30am-3:15am, €8.85); **Valladolid/Zamora** (2hr., M-Sa 4 per day 5:15am-6:30pm, €6.50); **Vitoria-Gasteiz** (2hr., 9 per day 7:15am-3:15am, €6.03).

Car Rental: Hertz, C. Progreso, 5 (☎947 20 16 75, reservations 902 40 24 05). 25+. Credit card in driver's name required for deposit. Small cars with unlimited mileage from €66 per day. Open M-F 9am-1pm and 4-7pm, Sa 9am-1pm. AmEx/MC/V.

Taxis: Abutaxi (☎947 27 77 77) or **Radio Taxi** (☎947 48 10 10). 24hr. service.

✦ 🛈 ORIENTATION & PRACTICAL INFORMATION

The Río Arlanzón splits Burgos north-south. While the **train** and **bus stations** are on the south side, the **Catedral Santa Iglesia** and most other sights of interest are in the north. Turning left from **Puente de Santa María** brings you to the cathedral, while a right on **Paseo del Espolón** leads to **Plaza Mayor** and **Plaza de la Libertad**.

Tourist Office: Pl. de San Fernando, 2 (☎947 20 31 25; fax 27 65 29). Open M-F 10am-2pm and 4:30-7:30pm, Sa-Su and holidays 10am-1:30pm and 4-7:30pm.

Currency Exchange: Banco Santander Central Hispano, Pl. de España, 6 (☎904 24 24 24). Open M-F 8:30am-2pm.

Emergency: ☎091 or 092. **Guardia Civil,** Av. Cantabria, 87-95 (☎062 or 947 22 22 63). **Police,** Av. Cantabria, 54 (☎947 28 88 39).

Pharmacy: Farmacia Natividad Combarro Rodríguez, C. San Juan, 25 (☎947 20 12 89). Open M-F 9:45am-2pm and 5-8pm, Sa 10:15am-2pm. All pharmacies post a list of late-night and Su pharmacies in their windows.

Medical Services: Ambulance ☎947 23 22 22. **Hospital General Yagüe,** Av. del Cid Campeador, 96 (☎947 28 18 00). **Hospital de San Juan de Dios,** Po. de la Isla, 41 (☎947 25 77 30).

Internet Access: Café Cabaret Ciber-Café, C. la Puebla, 21. €1.20 per 15min. Printing €0.10 per page. Open M-Th 4pm-2am, F 4pm-4am, Sa 5pm-4am, Su 5pm-2am.

Post Office: Pl. del Conde de Castro, s/n (☎947 26 27 50, info 902 19 71 97; fax 947 26 57 11). **Lista de Correos** and **fax** services (€11 1st page, €3 each additional page). Open M-F 8:30am-8:30pm, Sa 9:30am-2pm. **Postal Code:** 09070.

▌ ACCOMMODATIONS

Inexpensive *pensiones* line the streets near **Plaza Alonso Martínez.** The C. San Juan area is also dotted with reasonably priced hostels. Otherwise, the tourist office distributes a complete list of accommodations. Reservations are crucial on summer weekends, for the festivals in June and July, and throughout August.

Hostal Joma, C. San Juan, 26, 2nd fl. (☎947 20 33 50). Spotless rooms in a large, modern building. Singles €15; doubles €20. ❷

Hotel Norte y Londres, Pl. Alonso Martínez, 10 (☎947 26 41 25 or 26 12 68; fax 27 73 75; www.hotelnorteylondres.com). Enormous rooms with bath, TV, and great views of the city. Singles €43; doubles €65. ❹

Camping: Fuentes Blancas, Pl. de la Vega, 6, 1st fl. (☎947 20 54 57). The "Fuentes Blancas" bus leaves from Pl. de España (July-Sept. 15 9:30am, 12:30, 4:15, 7:15pm; €0.50). Swimming pool, showers, restaurant, and currency exchange on site. €3.50 per person, €3 per tent and per car. Open Apr.-Sept. MC/V. ❶

◖ FOOD

Burgaleses take pride in their delicious *queso de Burgos*, a cheese usually served with honey or in a *tarta* as dessert, and their *morcilla* sausage. The area around **Plaza Alonso Martínez** is laden with restaurants serving these staples, while C. San Lorenzo is *tapas* heaven. **Mercado Municipal de Abastos (Sur)** on C. Miranda sells fresh meat and bread. (Open M-Sa 7am-3pm, or until the vendors sell out.)

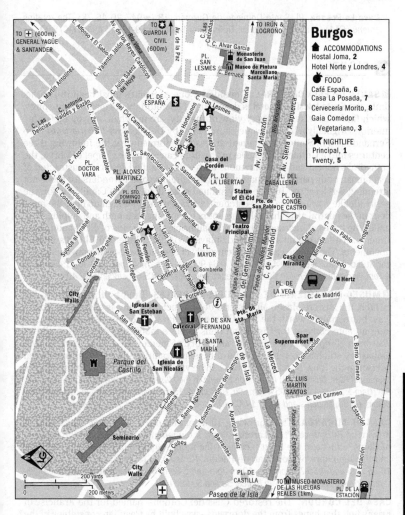

Burgos

🏠 ACCOMMODATIONS
Hostal Joma, **2**
Hotel Norte y Londres, **4**

🍎 FOOD
Café España, **6**
Casa La Posada, **7**
Cervecería Morito, **8**
Gaia Comedor
  Vegetariano, **3**

⭐ NIGHTLIFE
Principal, **1**
Twenty, **5**

🍽 **Gaia Comedor Vegetariano,** C. San Francisco, 31 (☎947 23 76 45). This counter-cultural luncheonette features a rotating international menu that would make Mother Earth proud. Four-course *menú* €7. Open M-Sa 1:30-4pm. ❷

Cervecería Morito, C. Sombrerería, 27 (☎947 26 75 55). Good food and great service make Morito a hit with the locals. Try the *tarta al whisky* (€3.50). *Raciones* €1.50-7. Open M-Sa 7pm-2am. Cash only. ❶

Café España, C. Laín Calvo, 12 (☎947 20 53 37; www.cafeespana.com). A traditional cafe founded in 1921 with a wide variety of coffees, teas, and infusions (€1-3). Its bright terrace is a great place to spend a quiet afternoon. Open daily 10am-midnight. ❶

Casa La Posada, Pl. Santo Domingo de Guzmán, 18 (☎947 20 45 78). The rotating *menú* (€11) features a local dish. Open daily 1-4pm and 9-11pm. AmEx/MC/V. ❸

🄖 SIGHTS

🖾 **SANTA IGLESIA CATEDRAL.** Considered one of Spain's most beautiful cathedrals, the **Santa Iglesia Catedral** is deserving of its notoriety. Its magnificent spires, which find their way into every view of the city, are matched only by its Gothic interior. Originally a Romanesque church built by 13th-century *Reconquista* hero Fernando III (El Santo), the cathedral was transformed over the following three centuries into a Gothic marvel. Devout visitors can enter the Chapel of Christ, the cathedral's holiest and most infamous arch—the crucified Jesus is constructed of real human body parts. Fortunately, the cathedral has other wonders for those not attending services: the 16th-century stained glass dome of the Capilla Mayor; the eerily lifelike *papamoscas* (fly-catcher), a strange creature high up near the main door in the central aisle that tolls the hours by opening its mouth and gulping; and, under the transept, marked only by a small brick, the remains of El Cid and Doña Jiménez. The cathedral's **museum** displays a Visigoth Bible and El Cid's nuptial documents. Though the cathedral is currently undergoing long-term renovations, you can still drop in. (☎ 947 20 47 12. Open M-Sa 9:30am-1pm and 4-7pm, Su 9:30-11:45am and 4-7pm. Audioguide in English €0.50. Cathedral free. Museum €3.60, students €2.40.)

🖾 **MUSEO-MONASTERIO DE LAS HUELGAS REALES.** Built by King Alfonso VIII in 1188, the austere Museo-Monasterio de las Huelgas Reales is slightly out of the way, but certainly worth the trip. Once a summer palace for Castilian kings and later an elite convent for Cistercian nuns, today's monastery-as-museum allows visitors a glimpse of the austerity and glory of medieval Castilian royalty. The monastery still has powerful ties; its abbess has traditionally served as a personal advisor to the king. Burial wardrobes can be viewed in the **Museo de Telas**. (*Take the "Barrio del Pilar" bus (€0.50) from Pl. de España to the Museo stop. ☎947 20 16 30. Open Tu-Sa 10am-1:15pm and 3:45-5:45pm, Su 10:30am-2:15pm. Mandatory tours in Spanish every 30min. €4.80, students and under 14 €2.40, under 5 and EU citizens free. W free.)*

CASA DE MIRANDA. This sprawling 16th-century mansion houses four floors of provincial Burgalese art and archaeology. Included in the exhibits are the remains of Cluny, a piece of the front facade of the monastery at Santo Domingo de Silos, and the sepulchre of Don Juan de Padilla. (*C. Miranda, 13. ☎947 26 58 75. Open Tu-F 10am-2pm and 4:30-7:30pm, Sa 10am-2pm and 5-8pm, Su 10am-2pm. €1.20; under 18, senior citizens, and students with ID free. Sa and Su free.)*

CASA DEL CORDÓN. The restored Casa del Cordón—named for the Franciscan Friar's belt that hangs from the doorway—was built by Castilian constables in the 15th century. On April 23, 1497, Columbus met with Fernando and Isabel here after his second trip to America, and here Felipe el Hermoso breathed his last ragged breath after an exhausting game of *jai alai*. Upon his death, his wife Juana dragged his corpse through the streets, earning the nickname Juana la Loca (the Mad). (*C. Santander, on the other side of the statue of El Cid, on the right. Hours vary.)*

PARQUE DEL CASTILLO. Atop a hill high above the cathedral, the ruins of a medieval castle and a sprawling, tangled park preside over Burgos. Sections of the walls and building demolished by Napoleonic troops are still undergoing reconstruction. The bleached castle rocks offer astounding views of the red roofs of Burgos and the surrounding countryside. (*From the front entrance of Iglesia San Esteban, climb the 200 steps directly across the street. Free.)*

🎵 🍷 NIGHTLIFE & FESTIVALS

In Burgos, as in most Spanish towns, nightlife starts late. By midnight, C. Avellanos (across from Pl. Alonso Martínez) fills with night owls migrating onto nearby **Calle Huerto del Rey.** If you have to hit the sack early on a Saturday night, wake up Sunday to join the crowds still dancing at *discotecas* along C. San Juan and C. la Puebla and in the disco complex on Pl. San Lesmes. Nightlife shifts into overdrive during the last week in June, when Burgos honors its patron saints with concerts, parades, fireworks, bullfights, and dances. The day after **Corpus Christi** (June 11 in 2004), citizens parade through town with the *pendón de las Navas*, a banner captured from the Moors during the 1212 battle of Las Navas de Tolosa.

La Mansión, C. la Puebla, 10. This little bar-that-could has more CDs than bottles behind the bar. The owner and his bartenders are none-too-quietly waging war against the pop music that dominates the late-night scene, serving up a mix of rock, funk, and blues that goes well with any *cerveza* (€2). Open M-W 6pm-1am, Th-Sa 8pm-5am.

Twenty, C. Huerto del Rey, 20 (☎947 26 46 92). Easily the most popular and crowded stop on the Huerto del Rey club-hopping route. Techno predominates on the multi-level dance floor. Beer €2. Open M-Sa 7pm-5am, Su 7pm-midnight.

La Cuca, C. la Puebla, 17 (☎947 27 88 97). Burgos's trendsetters enjoy evenings packed tightly between La Cuca's bright orange walls. Entertain yourself interpreting the caveman-like abstract drawings. Open daily from 6pm until the last person leaves.

Principal, C. la Puebla, 40, at the corner of C. San Juan and C. San Lesmes. The sleek limestone-and-glass bar attracts an older, low-key crowd. Open daily 4pm-4am.

🏞 DAYTRIP FROM BURGOS

SANTO DOMINGO DE SILOS

Arcoredillo runs a bus to Santo Domingo from Burgos, C. Miranda, 4 (1½hr.; departs Burgos M-F 5:30pm, departs Santo Domingo M-F 8:30am; €4.50). Because buses depart Santo Domingo only in the morning, visitors without cars may have to stay a night. To get from Burgos to Santo Domingo de Silos (50km) by car, take N-234 toward Salas de los Infantes to Hortigüela. From there, C-110, which borders the Arlanza River, will pass the monastery of San Pedro de Arlanza before arriving at Covarrubias; it's only 17km farther.

Since 1993, the Benedictine monks of Santo Domingo de Silos (pop. 380) have sold five million recordings, including the Gregorian chant album that reached #1 on global charts. In the **Abadía de Santo Domingo de Silos,** listeners are transported back in time as black-cloaked monks chant along with the organ and the soothing echoes of their own voices. Sit in at morning song at high Mass at 9am (Su at noon), vespers at 7pm (in summer Th 8pm), and compline at 9:40pm. The **museum** and **cloister** next door highlight an ancient pharmacy of 300-year-old chemicals, skulls, and preserved animal parts. (☎947 39 00 68. Museum and cloister open Tu-Sa 10am-1pm and 4:30-6pm, Su-M 4:30-6pm. €1.50.) The real attraction of Santo Domingo, however, is the town itself; the view from the hill behind the abbey is a miracle all its own. Rooms are easy to find in this friendly little town—a good thing since visitors without cars are almost obligated to stay the night. Near the bus stop, **Hostal Santo Domingo ❷,** C. Santo Domingo, 14-16, has well-kept, air-conditioned rooms with full baths, phones, and TVs. (☎947 39 00 53; www.hostal-santodomingodesilos.com. Singles €22; doubles €33-48.) Just up the street is **Hostal Cruces ❷,** Pl. Mayor, 20, offering clean, sunny rooms with baths. Los señores Cruces speak proficient English, French, and a little German. (☎947 39 00 64. Singles €21; doubles €33. V.) Both *hostales* feature **restaurants ❷** downstairs (€5-12).

PALENCIA ☎979

Although Palencia (pop. 80,000) lacks the attractions and pizzazz of its fellow Castilian capitals, it is, of course, rich in history and religious monuments. After being catapulted to Spanish fame for fending off the Duke of Lancaster's 14th-century attack, Palencia underwent a surge of construction. As a result, its historic center is riddled with 14th- to 16th-century churches. While not as well-known as the cathedrals in León or Burgos, many are better-preserved and provide a worthwhile glimpse into the development of Romanesque and Gothic architecture. Modern arts focus on handicrafts, especially pure wool blankets and pottery. Most travelers should skip Palencia, but those with time to spare can explore its compact city center peppered with a series of modern sculptures, or join the locals in an afternoon of sunbathing in the riverside Parque Islas dos Aguas.

■ **TRANSPORTATION. RENFE trains** depart from Parque Jardinillos de la Estación, s/n (☎979 74 30 19 or 902 24 02 02) to: **Barcelona** (8½-9hr., 3 per day 1:30am-11pm, €36.50); **Bilbao** and **San Sebastián** (4hr., 1 per day 4:19pm, €16.50); **Burgos** (1hr.; M-F 2 per day 7:45am and 3:45pm; Sa-Su 8 per day 11:38am-1:30am; €3.75); **La Coruña** (8hr.; 3 per day 3:25am, 1, 4pm; €35); **León** (1¼hr., M-Sa 5 per day 8:08am-9:42pm, €6.95); **Madrid** (3-5hr.; M-Sa 9 per day 4:34am-8:10pm, Su 9 per day 8:15am-8:25pm; €15.40); **Oviedo** (4-5hr., 6 per day, €28); **Salamanca** (2½hr., daily 1:20pm, €8.10); **Santander** (3-3¾hr., 6 per day, €9.85); **Valladolid** (45min., 10 per day 7:33am-11:08pm, €3.05); **Zamora** (2hr., M-Sa 1 per day 8am, €18). **Buses** depart from Jardinillos de la Estación, s/n (☎979 74 32 22). Info booth open M-F 8am-10:30pm, Sa-Su 8am-1:30pm and 5-10:30pm. To **Burgos** (1½hr., 3 per day 9am-7:30pm, €3.85) and **Valladolid** (45min.; M-F every hr. 7am-10pm, Sa 6 per day 8am-7:30pm, Su 3 per day 11am, 4, 9pm; €3).

■ **ORIENTATION & PRACTICAL INFORMATION.** Palencian life is centered around **Calle Mayor,** a broad pedestrian avenue. From the bus or train station, head past the Jardinillos de la Estación to Pl. León; from there you can see the foot traffic on C. Mayor. The **tourist office,** C. Mayor, 105, is a 15min. walk down C. Mayor from Pl. León. (☎979 74 00 68. Open M-F 9am-2pm and 5-7pm, Sa-Su 11am-2pm and 5-8pm.) Services include: **BBVA bank,** C. Mayor, 64 (☎902 22 44 66; open M-F 8:30am-2pm); **emergency** ☎091 or 092; **local police,** C. Ortega y Gasset, s/n (☎979 71 82 00); **medical emergency,** ☎979 70 21 00 or 71 29 00; **Clínica Virgen de la Salud,** Av. Simón Nieto, 31 (☎ 979 74 77 00); and **Internet access,** at Zon@virtual, C. Estrada, 7 (open M-F 11am-3pm and 4:30-11pm; €1.80 per hour). Of the two **post offices,** the one at Pl. León, 2 (☎979 74 21 80; fax 74 22 60), sends and receives **faxes.** The office next to the train station (☎979 74 21 77) provides **Lista de Correos.** (Both open M-F 8:30am-8:30pm, Sa 9:30am-2pm.) **Postal Code:** 34001.

■ **ACCOMMODATIONS & FOOD.** Palencia caters less to tourists than many of its neighbors, so its hotels and hostels are less abundant and more expensive. Hostels can be found on the many side streets branching off C. Mayor. One of the best is **Tres de noviembre** ❷, C. Mancornador, 18, just off C. Mayor across from the tourist office, at the end of C. Los Manteros. TVs and radios in every room make for a media-rich evening. (☎ 979 70 30 42. Singles with showers €16, with full bath €21; doubles €40). Located in the trendy *zona vieja* district, **Hostal Ávila** ❸, C. Conde de Vallellano, 5, has telephones, TVs, radios, a common room, a parking garage, and a cafeteria (€3-9). (From Pl. León on C. Mayor, turn left on C. San Bernardo, which becomes C. Empedrada. ☎979 71 19 10. Singles €30; doubles €40.) Dining options are equally limited in Palencia, but by no means nonexistent. For good food at reasonable prices, head to **Cervecería Gambrinus** ❶, C. Patio Castaño,

1 (☎979 75 08 28), off C. Mayor from Pl. León. Their *solomillo al roquefort* (€2) is basically a Philly cheesesteak minus the Philly. *Raciones* €2-8. If all else fails, there's always **El Árbol supermarket,** C. Mayor, 99.

◨ **SIGHTS.** Palencia's biggest attraction is its Gothic cathedral, **Santa Iglesia de San Pedro,** where 14 year-old Catherine of Lancaster married 10 year-old Enrique III in 1388. Ahh, young love. Built between the 14th and 16th centuries with predominantly Gothic features, the cathedral has a sandstone and pastel interior. During the Spanish tour, guides illuminate the various altars and then lead visitors down a stone staircase to the spooky **Cripta de San Antolín,** a 7th-century sepulchre. The cathedral's **museum** houses El Greco's famed *San Sebastián* and some spectacular 16th-century Flemish tapestries—not to mention a tiny caricature of Carlos V. From Pl. León, walk down C. Eduardo Dato, and at Pl. Carmelitas turn left onto C. Santa Teresa de Jesús; the cathedral is at the end of this street in Pl. de la Inmaculada Concepción. (☎979 70 13 47. Open M-Sa 9am-1:30pm and 4:30-7:30pm, Su 9am-1:30pm. Tours in Spanish M-Sa 10:30am, 1:30, 4:30, 5:30, and 11:15pm. Cathedral free, museum €3.) Of the other churches in town, the favorite of El Cid fans is **Iglesia de San Miguel.** According to legend, it was here that El Cid Campeador wed Doña Jimena. Its most notable feature is the 13th-century Gothic tower graced with tall openwork windows. Check at the tourist office to see if renovations are complete. To reach the church from the cathedral, walk down C. San Pedro from Pl. de la Inmaculada Concepción, and turn left onto C. General Mola, which takes you directly to San Miguel. (☎979 70 08 84. Open M-Sa 9:30am-1:30pm and 6-7:30pm, Su 9:30am-2pm and 6-8pm. Free.)

◨◨ **NIGHTLIFE & FESTIVALS.** When you tire of hanging out with dead *palentinos* at the Cripta de San Antolín, go meet some live ones in the *zona vieja*, Palencia's most happening neighborhood, bordered by C. Colón, Po. del Salón, Av. Casado del Alisal, and C. Becerro de Bengoa. Palencia claims to be the birthplace of the university, and you'll certainly find the college crowd at **Merlin,** C. Conde de Vallellano, 4, where they serve up drinks and dancing dungeons-and-dragons style. (Across from Hostal Ávila. Open daily 7pm-5:30am.) Next door is the oh-so-sophisticated **La Oficina,** C. Empedrada, 3. Other hotspots include **Friends** and the basketball-themed **Barsket,** both on C. Estrada. The **Fiesta de San Antolín** (Sept. 2) celebrates Palencia's patron saint and hosts the biggest party of the year.

SORIA ☎975

Though museums and surrounding archaeological sites are the city's biggest attractions, Soria (pop. 37,000) also claims the lush Parque Alameda de Cervantes, a lively city center, and, on its outskirts, the intriguing Monasterio de San Juan de Duero and Ermita de San Saturio. Though built as a fortress against invasions from neighboring Aragón, the city proper is idyllic and peaceful.

▐ **TRANSPORTATION**

Trains: Estación El Cañuelo (☎975 23 02 02), Ctra. de Madrid. Buses (€0.45) run from Pl. Mariano Granados to the station 20min. before each train departs and return with new arrivals. To: **Madrid** (3hr.; M-F 2 per day 7:40am, 5:40pm; Sa 1 per day 8:45am; Su 2 per day 8:45am, 6:25pm; €11.65) via **Alcalá de Henares** (2¾hr., €9.66).

Buses: Av. de Valladolid (☎975 22 51 60). Info open daily 9am-7pm and 8-10pm. **Continental Auto** (☎975 22 44 01) to: **Logroño** (1½hr.; 4-7 per day M-Sa 11am-7:45pm, Su 11am-12:15am; €5.45); **Madrid** (2½hr.; 6-9 per day M-Th and Sa 9:15am-8:45pm,

F and Su 9:15am-11:45pm; €11.68); **Pamplona** (2hr.; 4-7 per day M-Th and Sa 10:45am-10:15pm, F and Su 10:45am-12:15am; €10.51). **La Serrana** (☎975 22 20 60) to **Burgos** (2½hr.; 1-3 per day M-F 7am-6:30pm, Sa 1 per day 1:45pm; €8.65). **Therpasa** (☎975 22 20 60) to **Zaragoza** (2¼hr.; 3-6 per day M-Sa 7:30am-8pm, Su noon-9pm; €8.10) via **Tarazona** (1hr., €4.06). **Linecar** (☎975 22 15 55) to **Valladolid** (3hr.; 3 per day M-Sa 9:45am-6:45pm, Su 11:15am-6:45pm; €10.90).

Car Rental: Europcar, C. Ángel Terrel, 3-5 (☎975 22 05 05), off Av. San Benito. 21+. Open M-F 9:30am-1:30pm and 4:30-8pm, Sa 10:30am-1pm. AmEx/MC/V.

Taxis: ☎975 21 30 34. Stands at Pl. Mariano Granados and bus station.

ORIENTATION & PRACTICAL INFORMATION

The city center is about a 15min. walk from the **bus station.** From the traffic circle outside the station, **Avenida de Valladolid** runs downhill to the *centro ciudad.* Keep walking for five blocks and bear right at the fork onto Po. del Espolón, which borders the **Parque Alameda de Cervantes.** When the park ends, **Plaza Mariano Granados** will be directly in front of you. To reach the center from the **train station,** either take the shuttle or turn left onto **Calle Madrid** and follow the signs to *centro ciudad.* Continue on C. Almazán as it bears left and becomes Av. de Mariano Vicén, follow the road for six blocks, and keep left at the fork onto Av. Alfonso VIII until you reach Pl. Mariano Granados. From the side of the plaza opposite the park, C. Marqués de Vadillo leads to C. El Collado, the shopping street cutting through the old quarter to **Plaza Mayor.**

Tourist Office: C. Medinaceli, 2 (☎975 21 20 52; www.turismodesoria.com). From Pl. Mariano Granados, walk one block up Av. Alfonso VIII. English-speaking staff. Open July-Aug. Su-Th 9am-8pm, F-Sa 9am-9pm; Sept.-June 9am-2pm and 5-8pm.

Currency Exchange: Banco Santander Central Hispano, C. El Collado, 56 (☎975 22 02 25). Open Apr.-Sept. M-F 8:30am-2pm; Oct.-May M-F 8:30am-2pm, Sa 8:30am-1pm.

Luggage Storage: At the **bus station.** 1st day €0.60, €0.30 each additional day. Open daily 9am-7pm and 8-10pm.

Emergency: ☎112. **Guardia Civil:** C. Eduardo Saavedra, 6 (☎062). **Municipal Police:** C. Obispo Agustín, 1 (☎092 or 975 21 18 62).

Medical Services: Urgencias Capital (☎975 22 15 50), Po. del Espolón.

Internet Access: Cyber Centro, Pje. Tejera, 16 (☎975 23 90 85). Down the small tunnel between C. las Casas and C. Caro on Po. Tejera. €2.40 per 30min.; €3.60 per hr. Free soft drink every hour. Open M-F 10:30am-2pm and 5-9pm, Sa 10:30am-2:30pm.

Post Office: Po. del Espolón, 6 (☎975 22 13 99, info hotline 902 19 71 97; fax 975 23 35 61). Open M-F 8:30am-8:30pm, Sa 9:30am-2pm. **Postal Code:** 42070.

ACCOMMODATIONS

■ **Solar de Tejada,** C. Claustrilla, 1 (☎/fax 975 23 00 54; http://perso.wanadoo.es/solardetejada), on the corner of C. El Collado, off Pl. Mariano Granados. Look for a blue sign with a moon. Fully equipped rooms with balconies, each one whimsically decorated with cast-iron flower bedposts, stained-glass lamps, and the like. Singles €47; doubles €52; triples €61. IVA not included. ❹

Hostal Residencia Alvi, C. Alberca, 2 (☎975 22 81 12; fax 22 81 40). Across the street from Solar de Tejada. Big rooms with TVs, A/C, full baths, and big beds. Minus all the bells and whistles of Solar, but at nearly half the price, you really won't miss the flower bedposts. Breakfast €2.41. Singles €26; doubles €46. ❸

Residencia Juvenil Juan Antonio Gaya Nuñoz (HI), Po. San Francisco (☎975 22 14 66). With your back to the tourist office, take C. Nicolás Rabal along the park from Pl. Mariano Granados. Take your 2nd left onto C. Santa Luisa de Marillac and look for yellowish dorms ahead. Spacious dorm-style rooms with large bathrooms. Extremely convenient location and great price. Check-in before 8pm. Curfew at midnight. Open July 1-Sept. 15. 3-night max. stay when full. HI members only. Breakfast €1. Doubles have private bath. Dorms €6.51, over 26 €8.71. ❶

Pension Ersogo, C. Alberca, 4 (☎975 21 35 08). Next to Hostal Residencia Alvi. Seven sunny 4th fl. rooms with 2 squeaky-clean common baths. Large single beds and tiny TVs next to wide windows. Singles €15; doubles €22; triples €30. ❷

Casa Diocesana Pío XII, C. San Juan, 5 (☎975 21 21 76; fax 24 02 78). From Pl. Mariano Granados, go up C. El Collado and right on C. San Juan after Pl. San Blas y el Rosel; in the tall building with the huge cross. Hide away in monasterial rooms. Public telephone and laundry. Breakfast €2.68. July-Aug. singles €16.05, with bath €24.03; doubles €25.68/€33. Sept.-June €13.84/€19/€21.04/€28. MC/V. ❷

Camping: Camping Fuente la Teja (☎975 22 29 67), 2km from town on Ctra. de Madrid (km233). Huge new cafeteria. Swimming pool open July-Aug. Camping open *Semana Santa*-Sept. €3.30 per person and per car, €4 per tent (IVA not included). MC/V. ❶

◗ FOOD

Savor *chorizo* and *migas* at the bars and inexpensive restaurants peppering C. Manuel Vicente Tutot. Buy fresh foods at the small **market** in Pl. Bernardo Robles on C. los Estudios, left off C. El Collado. (Open M-Sa 8:30am-2pm.) **SPAR supermarket** is at Av. de Mariano Vicén, 10, four blocks from Pl. Mariano Granados toward the train station. (Open M-Sa 9am-2pm and 5:30-8:30pm. MC/V.)

La Parrilla, Po. Tejera, 20 (☎975 21 44 32). From Pl. Mariano Granados, take C. Ferial and continue 3 blocks up the hill to Po. Tejera. Traditional dining in a friendly atmosphere. Popular *menú* available at every meal except Sa dinner (€8.65). Entrees €7-13, but the appetizers (€4-8) are big enough to make meals. Open M-F and Su 1-4pm and 9-11pm, Sa 1-4pm and 9pm-midnight. MC/V. ❷

Nuevo Siglo, C. Almazán, 9 (☎975 22 13 32). Good Chinese food in an attractive dining room at obscenely cheap prices. Entrees €3-6. *Menú* €5.38. ❶

Callado 58, C. Callado, 58 (☎975 24 00 53). Large meals; larger frozen desserts. Unique ice cream concoctions (€4.25-5.35), shakes (€3.50), and heaping banana splits (€4.25). Combo plates €8.25-12.45. Open daily 8am-11pm. ❸

◗ SIGHTS

The great 20th-century poet Antonio Machado once likened the **Río Duero** to a drawn bow arching around Soria. To find the river from Pl. Mariano Granados, walk past the sign for Restaurante Nueva York and straight down C. Zapatería, which changes to C. Real. Follow this road to Pl. San Pedro; the bridge lies ahead.

◗ ERMITA DE SAN SATURIO. Soria's biggest draw is well worth the 1.5km trek downstream. The 17th-century Ermita de San Saturio, built into the side of a cliff, is a heavenly retreat where light seeps into the caves through stained-glass windows. San Saturio himself keeps vigil over the upstairs chapel, every inch of which is covered by frescos. To get there by car, cross the bridge onto Ctra. de Ágreda, turning right with the road. On foot, take the shorter, cooler, more scenic route through the lush **Soto Playa.** Turn right just before the main bridge and cross the red and green footbridge. Keeping the river to your left, walk along the small island, meandering across small footpaths and boardwalks until you see the hermitage. *(Open Su year-round 10:30am-2pm; July-Aug. Tu-Sa 10am-2pm and 5-9pm; May 11-31 and Sept.-Oct. 13 Tu-Sa 10:30am-2pm and 4:30-7:30pm; Oct. 14-May 10 Tu-Sa 10:30am-2pm and 4:30-6:30pm. Free.)*

MONASTERIO DE SAN JUAN DE DUERO. The Monasterio San Juan de Duero sits quietly by the river amid cottonwoods and grass. The church, dating from the 12th century, is quite simple. Its graceful arches blend Romanesque and Islamic styles and are all that remain of the 13th-century cloister. Inside, an annex to the Museo Numantino displays medieval artifacts. *(Turn left after crossing the bridge. Open Tu-Sa July-Sept. 10am-2pm and 5-8pm; Oct.-June 10am-2pm and 4-7pm; Su year-round 10am-2pm. €0.60; under 18, over 65, and students free. Sa-Su free.)*

MUSEO NUMANTINO. The museum exhibits an impressive collection of Celto-Iberian and Roman artifacts excavated from nearby Numancia. *(Po. del Espolón, 8. ☎975 22 13 97. Same hours as the Monasterio de San Juan de Duero. €1.20; under 18, over 65, and students free. Sa-Su free.)*

🎵 🎭 ENTERTAINMENT & NIGHTLIFE

In the first week of August, Soria hosts a festival of concerts and street theater, as well as other events throughout the summer. Pick up the free *Actividades Culturales* in the tourist office for specific dates. As the moon rises, revelers of all ages crowd **Plaza Ramón Benito Aceña** and the adjacent **Plaza San Clemente,** off C. El Collado. At the dim and narrow **La Ventana de la Apolonia,** Pl. Ramón Benito Aceña, 8 (☎975 23 02 43), you can crowd yourself in with the locals or take it out to the even more crowded plaza and have a peek through the window display, which features the latest in local art. Late-night disco-bars center around the intersection of **Rota de Calatañazor** and **Calle Cardenal Frías,** near Pl. de Toros. On weekends, youths convene in **Parque Alameda de Cervantes** with store-bought spirits. A few small clubs lie near **Calle Zapatería.** Spend a night out with the younger, hipper *sorianos* crowded around the intimate tables of **Bar Ogham,** C. Nicolás Rabal, 3. (☎975 22 57 71. Open daily noon-3am.) **Kavanagh's,** C. del Campo, 14, offers a friendly setting with great deals on large quantities of alcohol. Tired of the traditional wine and beer? A *calimocho* or lemon- or orange-flavored *orgasmo* (€3.50 per L) should do the trick. (☎975 22 47 01. Open M-Sa noon-midnight.)

🏛 DAYTRIP FROM SORIA

NUMANCIA

*With a **car,** take N-111 toward Logroño for 6km and look for the signs. Without a car, good luck. The **bus** to Garray comes within 1km of the ruins (15min.; in summer M-F 2 per day 2, 5:45pm, Sa 1 per day 5:45pm; in winter 1 per day M-F 2pm, F and Sa also 6pm; €1), but the return buses run only in summer (summer M-F 2 per day 8:50am, 2:20pm; Su and holidays 1 per day 2:20pm). A **taxi** costs €20 round-trip, plus wait. Ruins ☎975 18 07 12. Open June-Aug. Tu-Sa 10am-2pm and 5-9pm, Su 10am-2pm; Sept.-Oct. and Apr.-May Tu-Sa 10am-2pm and 4-7pm, Su 10am-2pm; Nov.-Mar. Tu-Sa 10am-2pm and 3:30-6pm, Su 10am-2pm. €1; under 18, over 65, and students free. Sa-Su free.*

Archaeology fans will enjoy the ruins of Numancia, a hilltop settlement 7km north of Soria that dates back more than 4000 years. The Celto-Iberians settled here by the 2nd century BC and resisted Roman conquest. It took 10 years of war and the leadership of Scipio Africanus to dislodge them. Scipio encircled the town in a system of thick walls in order to starve its residents. After his victory, he kept 50 survivors as trophies, sold the rest into slavery, burned the city, and divided its lands among his allies. Numancia lived on as a metaphor for patriotic heroism in Golden Age and Neoclassical tragedies, and the ruins, though battered, are worth a visit.

In Garray, the **Aula Arqueológica "El Cerco de Numancia"** features exhibits about ancient Numancia and the surrounding area, as well as a gift shop. From the ruins, turn left on Garray's main road back toward Soria; it will be on your right. (☎975 25 20 01. Open year-round Su 10am-2pm; Tu-Sa June-Aug. 10am-2pm and 5-9pm; Apr.-May and Sept.-Oct. 10am-2pm and 4-7pm; Nov.-Mar. 10am-2pm and 3:30-6pm. €0.60, under 15 free.)

EXTREMADURA

The aptly named Extremadura is a land of harsh beauty and cruel extremes. Arid plains bake under the intense summer sun, relieved only by scattered patches of sunflowers. Yet the traveler who braves the Extremaduran plains is rewarded with stunning ruins and peaceful towns. Compared to the hectic pace of nearby Madrid, life in Extremadura is unhurried and far less modern, as though the region's history still dominates its present character. Though these are the lands that hardened New World *conquistadores* like Hernán Cortés and Francisco Pizarro, Extremadura itself has remained unexplored even by most Spaniards. Mérida's Roman ruins and the hushed ancient beauty of Trujillo and Cáceres are only beginning to draw flocks of admirers looking for the traditional Spanish countryside. Beyond the region's rugged landscape, its hearty pastoral cuisine is especially appealing; local specialties include rabbit, partridge, lizard with green sauce, wild pigeon with herbs, and *migas* (fried bread crumbs) with hot chocolate. Thick *cocido* (chick pea stew) warms *extremeños* in winter, while endless varieties of *gazpacho* (including an unusual white variation) cool them in summer.

CÁCERES ☎927

Stepping into Cáceres's *barrio antiguo* is an immediate time warp. The bustle of the modern city is silenced and the purely medieval takes over. Unlike many other Golden Age cities, Cáceres lacks the clichéd mix of old and new. Built between the 14th and 16th centuries by rival noble families vying for socio-political control, the old quarter remains frozen in that era's architecture, culture, and decor, each building a miniature palace demonstrating power and wealth. Stop by and wander the town's wonderful maze of palaces and mansions inhabited by the town's fine-feathered storks. Although Cáceres's newer areas are less interesting, the *Parque del Príncipe* and healthy nightlife provide ample amusement for a short stay.

▐▀ TRANSPORTATION

Trains: RENFE (☎902 24 02 02), on Av. de Alemania, 3km from the old city. Across the highway from the bus station. Info window open daily 9am-9pm. To: **Badajoz** (2hr.; 11:55am, 1:44, 7pm; €6.55-14.50); **Lisboa, PT** (6hr., 1 per day 3am, €32); **Madrid** (4hr., 5-6 per day 4:10am-7pm, €4.50-21); **Mérida** (1hr., 5 per day 8:19am-7pm, €3.25-11.50); **Sevilla** (4hr., 1 per day 8:19am, €14.35).

Buses: (☎902 42 22 42), on Ctra. Sevilla. Info open M-Th 7:30am-7:30pm, Sa 8:30am-9pm, Su 8:30am-11:30pm. Buses to: **Badajoz** (1½hr.; M-F 6-8 per day 7:30am-7:30pm; Sa 2 per day 8am, 4:30 pm; Su 4 per day 3:30-9pm; €6.70); **Madrid** (4-5hr.; 7-8 per day M-F 1:45am-6pm, Sa 1:45am-3:30pm, Su 1:45am-7pm; €16.17); **Mérida** (1hr.; M-Th 4 per day 6:30am-7:30pm; F 5 per day 6:30am-8:30pm; Sa 2 per day 1, 5pm; Su 3 per day 10am-8:30pm; €4.08); **Salamanca** (4hr.; 3-6 per day M-F 7am-6pm, Sa 7am-2pm, Su 5-7pm; €11.40); **Sevilla** (4hr., M-F 6 per day 4:10am-8:45pm, €14.16); **Trujillo** (45min.; M-F 3 per day 1-5:30pm, Sa 1 per day 1pm, Su 1 per day 7:30pm; €2.58); **Valladolid** (5½hr.; daily 2 per day 12:30, 5:30pm; €17.04).

Taxis: Radio Taxi (☎927 21 21 21). Stands at Pl. Mayor and bus and train stations.

Car Rental: Avis (☎689 84 90 18), in the bus station. 1-day rental from €72. 23+. Open in summer M-F 9:30am-1pm and 5-8pm (in winter 5-8pm only), Sa 9:30am-1pm.

ORIENTATION

The **ciudad monumental** (*barrio antiguo*) and the commercial **Avenida de España** flank **Plaza Mayor**. The plaza is 3km from the **bus** and **train stations**, which face each other across the rotary intersection of Av. de la Hispanidad and Av. de Alemania. From the bus or train station, the best way to get to the center of town is via the #1 bus (€0.60), which currently stops at the far end of Av. de Alemania across from the train station; however, this stop is subject to change, so verify at the info window or with locals if a bus stop is not visible. Hop off at Pl. Obispo Galarza. Facing the bus stop, start right and take your first left down the steps near the "Pl. Mayor 60m" sign. At the first intersection, turn right, then left to continue downhill and past the next intersection. When you reach the arches, Pl. Mayor will be to your left. Bus #2 stops on Av. de la Hispanidad, around the corner to the right as you emerge from the bus station, and runs to **Plaza de América,** hub of the new downtown area. From there, *ciudad monumental* signs point up tree-lined **Avenida de España (Paseo de Cánovas)** toward Pl. Mayor.

EXTREMADURA

🛈 PRACTICAL INFORMATION

Tourist Office: Pl. Mayor, s/n (☎927 01 08 34). Open July-Sept. M-F 9am-2pm and 5-7pm, Sa-Su 9:45am-2pm; Oct.-June M-F 9am-2pm and 4-6pm, Sa-Su 9:45am-2pm. The **Patronato de Turismo** (☎927 25 55 97), C. Amargura, in the Palacio de Carvajal, provides quality maps of the monuments and hosts a modern art museum. Open M-F 8am-8pm, Sa-Su 10am-2pm. **Branch** office with an excellent map operates at C. Ancha, 7 (☎927 24 71 72). Open M-Sa 10am-2pm and 5-8pm, Su 10am-2pm.

Currency Exchange: Banks line Av. de España and the streets leading to Pl. Mayor.

Luggage Storage: At the train station (€3 per day) and bus station (€0.60 per day).

Emergency: ☎091. **Police: Municipal** (☎927 24 84 24), C. Diego María Crehuet.

Late-Night Pharmacies: Farmacia Castel, Pl. Mayor, 28A (☎927 24 50 87); **Farmacia Jiménez Rebolledo,** C. los Pintores, 23 (☎927 24 55 18); and **Farmacia Acedo,** C. los Pintores, 31 (☎927 24 55 26) post the list of 24hr. pharmacies.

Hospital: Hospital Provincial (☎927 25 68 00), on Av. de España.

Internet Access: Ciberjust, C. Diego María Crehuet, 7 (☎927 21 46 77). €2 per hr. Open M-Sa 10am-2:30pm and 4:30pm-midnight, Su 5pm-2:30am.

Post Office: Av. Miguel Primo de Rivera (☎927 62 66 81). Open for stamps and **Lista de Correos** M-F 8:30am-8:30pm, Sa 9:30am-2pm. **Postal Code:** 10071.

🛏 ACCOMMODATIONS

Hostales are scattered throughout the new city and line Pl. Mayor in the old town. Prices rise during festivals, and advance reservations are recommended on summer weekends, especially for *pensiones* near Pl. Mayor. Late-night arrivals, never fear—24hr. reception is the norm.

Pensión Carretero, Pl. Mayor, 22 (☎927 24 74 82). Some rooms have balconies overlooking the plaza. Spacious TV lounge. The staff is warm and friendly. Singles €13; doubles €22; triples €30. MC/V. ❶

Hostal Residencia Almonte, C. Gil Cordero, 6 (☎927 24 09 25; fax 24 86 02). A bit of a hike from Pl. Mayor, it has a parking garage for 3 lucky cars (€3). A/C €2.40 extra. Singles €21; doubles €32; triples €38; quads €44. MC/V. ❷

Pension Márquez, C. Gabriel y Galán, 2 (☎927 24 49 60), off Pl. Mayor. The friendly owner makes Márquez feel like home, even if the Ayuntamiento across the street is not the most picturesque view. Hall baths. Doubles €20; triples €30. ❷

Hotel Iberia, C. los Pintores, 2 (☎927 24 76 34). Iberia is decked out with 16th-century paintings and furniture. Excellent rooms with TV, private bathrooms, and A/C for relatively low prices. Breakfast €3.30. Singles €40; doubles €50; triples €60. MC/V. ❹

🍴 FOOD

Pl. Mayor overflows with restaurants and cafes serving up *bocadillos, raciones,* and *menús.* Side streets offer less touristed local bars and pastry shops. **Hiper Tambo,** C. Alfonso IX, 25 (☎927 21 17 71; open M-Sa 9:30am-9pm) sells groceries.

El Toro, C. General Ezponda, 2 (☎927 21 15 48). Serves yuppified Spanish cuisine in a terra cotta and marble setting. For a quicker meal, try the co-owned and contiguous **Cafetería El Patio** on Pl. Mayor. Entrees €6.60-15. *Menú* €9-12. Open Tu-Sa 11am-5pm and 8pm-1am. MC/V. ❸

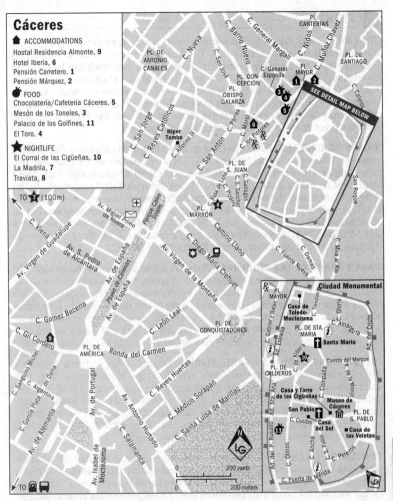

Cáceres

🏠 **ACCOMMODATIONS**
Hostal Residencia Almonte, **9**
Hotel Iberia, **6**
Pensión Carretero, **1**
Pensión Márquez, **2**

🍎 **FOOD**
Chocolatería/Cafetería Cáceres, **5**
Mesón de los Toneles, **3**
Palacio de los Golfines, **11**
El Toro, **4**

⭐ **NIGHTLIFE**
El Corral de las Cigüeñas, **10**
La Madrila, **7**
Traviata, **8**

Mesón de los Toneles, C. General Ezponda, 8 (☎927 21 61 70). Traditional *cocina extremeña* in a dim but folkloric setting. Don't leave without trying the delicious *migas extremeñas* (€5). Entrees €5-13. *Menú* €10; *menú del día* €7.80. Open daily 11am-5pm and 7pm-2:30am. ❷

Chocolatería/Cafetería Cáceres, Pl. Mayor, 16 (☎927 24 97 63). A convenient restaurant with a spacious terrace and quick service. Standard Iberian fare in *extremeño* style. Breakfast €5. Entrees €6-12. *Menú* €7-9. ❷

Restaurante Palacio de los Golfines, Ad. del Padre Rosalío, 2 (☎927 24 24 14). Dine like a nobleman in an unbeatable location. Situated in a gorgeous 15th-century palace in the old city, Golfines has received numerous awards for its exquisite Spanish cuisine. Appetizers €3.50-10. Entrees €11-25. *Menú* €25. Open Tu-Sa 1-4pm and 8pm-midnight; Su mornings only. MC/V. ❹

EXTREMADURA

👁 SIGHTS

The golden, stork-filled *ciudad monumental* is a melting pot of architectural ensembles: Roman, Arabic, Gothic, Renaissance, and even Incan influences (brought back by the *conquistadores* along with all that gold) can be detected throughout. The main attraction is the neighborhood as a whole, since most buildings don't open their doors to tourists. Turn off that internal compass and just wander along the narrow, winding streets. Though the area is small, a tourist office map will come in handy. *(From Pl. Mayor, take the stairs from the left of the tourist office to the Arco de la Estrella, the entrance to the walled old city.)*

MUSEO DE CÁCERES. Inside the Casa de los Caballos, the Museo de Cáceres is a must-see, housing a tiny but brilliant *Who's Who* of Spanish art. The museum features originals by El Greco, Picasso, Miró, and recent abstractionist stars, along with rotating exhibits. Also called the Museo Provincial de Arqueología, Bellas Artes y Costumbres, the neighboring **Casa de las Veletas** (House of Weathervanes) displays Celtiberian stone animals, Roman and Visigothic tombstones, and an astonishing ▇ Muslim cistern. *(☎927 24 72 34. Open Apr. 14-Sept. Tu-Sa 9am-2:30pm and 5-8:30pm, Su 10:15am-2:30pm; Oct.-Apr. 13 Tu-Sa 9am-2:30pm and 4-7:15pm, Su 10:15am-2:30pm. €1.20; students, seniors, EU citizens free. Su free.)*

CASA Y TORRE DE LAS CIGÜEÑAS. Cáceres's aristocracy was a war-like lot. The city's monarchs removed all battlements and spires from local lords' houses to punish their violent quarreling. Due to his loyalty to the ruling family, Don Golfín's Casa y Torre de las Cigüeñas (House and Tower of the Storks) was the lone estate allowed to keep its battlements. The storks are still grateful. *(From Arco de la Estrella, take a right up the hill, a left onto Adarve de Sta. Ana, another right, then a quick left onto C. de los Condes. Pass through Pl. de San Mateo to Pl. de Conde Canilleros; La Casa is on your left.)*

IGLESIA CONCATEDRAL DE SANTA MARÍA. A statue of San Pedro de Alcántara, one of Extremadura's two patron saints, eyes Pl. de Sta. María from a corner pedestal outside the cathedral. His shiny toes are the result of years of good-luck toe-rubbing. Built between 1229 and 1547, the Gothic cathedral has a remarkable ceiling and an intricate, 16th-century carved altar. An audio guide (€1) on the history of the church is available inside. (Pl. de Sta. María, s/n. ☎927 21 53 13. Open M-Sa 10am-2pm and 5-8pm, Su 9:30am-2pm and 5-7:30pm. Free.)

CONVENTO DE SAN PABLO. The convent is late-Gothic eye candy for architecture addicts. Cloistered nuns sell delicious pastries through a peculiar door that prevents customers from seeing them. Have your pastry selection ready from the list on the wall and ask politely at open hours, even if the door does not seem to be open. *(To the left of Casa y Torre de las Cigüeñas. Open M-Sa 9am-1pm and 5-8pm. Pastries €3-9.)*

OTHER SIGHTS. Most *palacios* and *casas* in the *ciudad monumental* are still inhabited and closed to visitors. The 16th-century **Casa Del Sol** is the most famous of Cáceres's numerous mansions; its crest is the city's emblem. The **Casa de Toledo-Moctezuma** was built by the grandson of the Aztec princess Isabel Moctezuma to represent a unification of the old and new worlds. *(On Pl. del Conde de Canilleros, to the left as you enter Arco de la Estrella. ☎927 24 92 94.)* On October 26, 1936, in the **Palacio de los Golfines de Arriba,** yet another Golfín family palace, Francisco Franco was proclaimed head of the Spanish state and general of its armies. *(Sandwiched by C. Olmos and Adarve de Sta. Ana.)*

NIGHTLIFE

Just follow the flock for a tipsy evening in Cáceres—the nobles never partied this good. Revelry starts in Pl. Mayor and along C. Pizarro, lined with live-music bars. For live jazz music, poetry festivals, and tarot reading, head to **El Corral de las Cigüeñas,** Cuesta de Aldana, 6, in the old city. Friday night concerts (tickets €3-8) echo throughout the *ciudad monumental.* (☎927 21 58 36. Open M and W-Su 7pm until the last customer leaves. Beer €2; mixed drinks €4 and up.) **Traviata,** Donoso Cortés, 10, is a hip musical cafe blasting both techno and pop. (☎927 21 13 74; drinks €3, no cover.) Later, the party migrates to **La Madrila,** a club-filled area near Pl. del Albatros in the new city. From Pl. Mayor, take Av. de España, make a right onto Av. Miguel Primo de Rivera, and cross the intersection onto C. Dr. Fleming.

DAYTRIP FROM CÁCERES

GUADALUPE

Transportation to and from Guadalupe can be somewhat tricky; most visitors arrive via tour bus or in their own cars. Empresa Mirat (☎927 23 48 63) sends buses from Cáceres to Guadalupe via Trujillo (2½hr., M-Sa 2 per day 1:30 and 5:30pm, €7.50) and back (M-Sa 2 per day 5:30 and 7:30am).

Guadalupe rests on a mountainside in the Sierra de Guadalupe two hours east of Trujillo and four hours southwest of Madrid. The **Real Monasterio de Santa María de Guadalupe,** with its eclectic history and decadent architecture, is a worthy daytrip, particularly for pilgrims and backpackers. The fairy-tale monastery has even been nicknamed "the Spanish Sistine Chapel." At the Battle of Salado in 1340, Alfonso XI, believed to have been aided by the Virgin Mary, defeated a much superior Muslim army. As a token of his gratitude, he commissioned the lavish Real Monasterio. Years later, it became customary to grant licenses for foreign expeditions on the premises; in fact, Columbus finalized his contract with Fernando and Isabel here. To pay homage to the city, he named one of the islands he discovered Guadalupe (now known as Turugueira). The most prominent object in the basilica is the **Icon of the Virgin,** carved of wood, blackened with age, and cloaked in robes of silver and gold. (Monastery open daily 9:30am-1pm and 3:30-6:30pm. €3.)

The **tourist office** in **Plaza Mayor** posts information on the door; follow signs from the bus station. (☎927 15 41 28. Open June-Aug. Tu-F 10am-2pm and 5-7pm, Sa-Su 10am-2pm; Sept.-May Tu-F 10am-2pm and 4-6pm, Sa-Su 10am-2pm.) Travelers looking for food or beds should head to Pl. Mayor.

TRUJILLO ☎927

The gem of Extremadura, hill-top Trujillo (pop. 9800) is an enchanting old-world town. Often called the "Cradle of Conquistadors," Trujillo furnished history with over 600 explorers of the New World, including Peru's conqueror Francisco Pizarro and the Amazon's first European explorer, Francisco de Orellana. Scattered with medieval palaces, Roman ruins, Arabic fortresses, and churches of every era, Trujillo is a hodgepodge of histories and cultures. Its most impressive monument is also its highest: the 10th-century Moorish castle commands a stunning panoramic view of the surrounding plains. The pace of life today is slow and tranquil, and locals and visitors alike spend evenings sipping *cafe con leche* at the plaza's many cafes while relishing the beauty of this well-preserved city.

⊑ TRANSPORTATION. The **bus station** (☎927 32 18 22 or 32 06 61) is at the corner of C. de las Cruces and C. del M. de Albayada; look for the **AutoRes** sign. As most buses stop only en route to larger destinations, there are not always seats available—check ahead. Buses run to: **Badajoz** (2hr.; 9-10 per day 4:15am-11:40pm; €8.11); **Cáceres** (45min.; 6-8 per day M-Th and Sa 11:15am-10:30pm, F and Su 11:15am-1:15am; €2.58); **Madrid** (2½hr.; 14-16 per day Su-F 2:15am-8:30pm, Sa 2:15am-6:15pm; €13.59); **Salamanca** (5hr.; M-Sa 10:30am, Su 6pm; €13.82).

⚶ PRACTICAL INFORMATION. The English-speaking **tourist office** is in Pl. Mayor, on the left when facing Pizarro's statue. Info is posted in the windows when it's closed. (☎927 32 26 77. Open June-Sept. 9:30am-2pm and 4:30-7:30pm; Oct.-May 9:30am-2pm and 4-8pm.) Guided tours leave from Pl. Mayor at 11:30am and 5pm (€6.50). **Currency exchange** and an **ATM** are at **Banco Santander Central Hispano,** Pl. Mayor, 25. (☎927 24 24 24. Open Oct.-Mar. M-F 8:30am-2:30pm and Sa 8:30am-1pm; Apr.-Sept. M-F 8:30am-2:30pm.) In a medical **emergency** call ☎112 or the **centro de salud** (☎927 32 20 16). The **police** are at C. Carnicería, 2 (☎927 32 01 08 or 608 70 65 17), just off Pl. Mayor. Get your **Internet** fix at **Ciberalia,** C. Tiendas, 18, off Pl. Mayor. (☎927 65 90 89. €2 per hr. Open daily 10am-2am.)The **post office,** Po. Ruíz de Mendoza, 28, is on the way from the station to Pl. Mayor. (☎927 32 05 33. Open M-F 9am-2:30pm, Sa 9:30am-1pm.) **Postal Code:** 10200.

⚶⚳ ACCOMMODATIONS & FOOD. Get medieval at ▨**Hostal Trujillo ②,** C. de Francisco Pizarro, 4-6. From the bus station, turn left on C. de las Cruces, right on C. de la Encarnación, then right again onto C. de Francisco Pizarro. The armor, lance, and shield-bedecked halls of this renovated 15th-century hospital lead to classy rooms with full bath, A/C, and satellite TV. The only downside is the 10min. uphill walk to Pl. Mayor and all the sights. (☎/fax 927 32 22 74; www.hostaltrujillo.com. Singles €24; doubles €39.23.) The pleasant **Camas Boni ①,** C. Domingo Ramos, 11, recently bought by a friendly German and Spanish couple, is off Pl. Mayor, on the street directly across from the church. With comfortable and clean rooms, a TV lounge, and a location only steps from all the major sites, you can't go wrong here. (☎927 32 16 04. Call from the bus station and the owners will pick you up for free. Singles €14; doubles €25, with bath €30-35; extra bed €10.) **Posada Dos Orillas ⑤,** C. Cambreras, 6, offers top notch rooms in Trujillo's historic center. The decor of Dos Orillas' seven exclusive rooms are inspired by the seven cities in Latin America named Trujillo, giving this 16th-century building and its beautiful garden an eclectic feel. (☎927 65 90 79; www.dosorillas.com. Rooms all with private bath, Internet jacks, cable TV, and A/C. Huge breakfast buffet €9. Doubles €84.14 plus tax; extra bed €30. MC/V.)

Meals in Trujillo are unfortunately overpriced. The best spot for a meal in Trujillo is a shaded table in the garden of **Meson Alberca ③,** C. Victoria, 8, which serves a great three-course *menú* (€14-19) with regional favorites in this tourist-free sanctum. (☎927 32 22 09. Open Su-Tu, Th-Sa 11am-5pm and 8:30pm-1am. AmEx/MC/V.) For something substantially cheaper, try **La Tahona ①,** C. Afueras, 2, which serves pizzas (€3.25-5.50), sandwiches (€2.25-2.75), and pastas (€3.75-5) to a local crowd. (Exit Pl. Mayor by the church and walk down the street for 4 blocks. ☎927 32 18 49. Open M 7:30pm-midnight, Tu-Su 1-4pm and 7:30pm-midnight.) Enjoy glorious views of the plaza along with delectable coffees, hot chocolates, and snacks at the trendy **Que Arte! ①,** Pl. Mayor, 7. (☎927 32 29 96. Drinks €1.40-2.75; sandwiches €1.80-2.50; *tapas* €1.50-2. Open Tu-Su 5pm-2am.) If all else fails, head to **Consum Supermarket,** Av. Monfrague. (Open M-Sa 9:30am-10pm. MC/V.)

◙ **SIGHTS.** An afternoon stroll through Trujillo's *barrio* may be the best in Extremadura. Sights run €1.25-1.50 and are open daily June-Sept. 10am-2pm and 5-8:30pm, Oct.-May 9:30am-2pm and 4:30-8pm, except where otherwise indicated. A *bono* ticket (€4), available at the tourist office, allows entrance to the Casa-Museo de Pizarro, the Arab castle, and Iglesia de Santiago, and includes a guide book. The tourist office offers tours of the old city, including the Museo del Traje.

Trujillo's **Plaza Mayor** was the inspiration for the Plaza de Armas in Cuzco, Perú, constructed after Francisco Pizarro defeated the Incas. Palaces, arched corridors, and cafes surround the central fountain and the Estatua de Pizarro. The gift of an American admirer of Pizarro, the bronze statue was erected in 1929 and, like the plaza, has a twin in Lima, Perú. Festooned with stork nests, **Iglesia de San Martín** dominates the plaza's northeastern corner. The church has several historic tombs, but contrary to local lore, Francisco de Orellana does not rest here. (Open M-Sa 10am-2pm and 4:30-7:30pm, Su 10am-2pm and 4:30-7pm. €1.25. Mass M-Sa 7:30pm, Su 1 and 7:30pm. Free.) Across the street, the seven chimneys of the **Palacio de los Duques de San Carlos** symbolize the religions compromised in the New World. (Open daily 9:30am-1pm and 4:30-6:30pm. €1.25.)

At the entrance to the *zona monumental*, the 13th-century **Puerta de Santiago** is connected to the **Iglesia de Santiago.** The tower is the oldest part of the church, and served as a defensive structure. The Gothic **Iglesia de Santa María la Mayor** is still farther up the hill. According to legend, the giant soldier Diego García de Paredes picked up the fountain (now located next to the rear door) at age 11 and carried it to his mother. After a fatal fall from a horse, the giant was buried here. Commonly known as the "Extremaduran Samson," the giant is referenced in chapter 32 of Cervantes's *Don Quijote*. The church's 25-panel Gothic altar-piece was painted by master Fernando Gallego in 1480. Climbing the tiny steps of the Romanesque church tower is exhausting, but the view of Trujillo from the top is breathtaking. (Open May-Oct. 10am-2pm and 4:30-8pm, Nov.-Apr. 10am-2pm and 4-7pm. €1.25. Mass Su 11am.) To the left of the church is the restored **Museo de la Coria,** which explores the relationship between Extremadura and Latin America during *la Conquista* and the later independence of the new continent. (Open Sa-Su 11:30am-2pm. Free.) To the right of the church, inside a restored convent, is the **Museo del Traje,** exhibiting the spectacular evening gowns worn by royalty and famous actresses from the 17th century on. (Open 10am-2pm and 5-8:30pm. €1.50.) To get to the **Casa-Museo de Pizarro,** walk uphill on the stone road to the right of the Iglesia de Santa María. The bottom floor of the house is a reproduction of a 15th-century nobleman's living quarters, while the top floor is dedicated to the life and times of Francisco Pizarro. Crowning the hill are the ruins of a 10th-century ■**Arab castle.** Pacing the battlements and ramparts are like playing in your best Lego creation. Enjoy a view of unspoiled landscape, with Trujillo on one side and fields scattered with ancient battlements on the other.

MÉRIDA ☎924

For quality of Roman ruins per square foot, it doesn't get better than Mérida (pop. 60,000). In 26 BC, as a reward for services rendered to the Roman Empire, Augustus Caesar granted a heroic group of veteran legionnaires a new city in Lusitania, a province comprised of Portugal and part of Spain. The veterans chose a lovely spot surrounded by hills on the banks of the Río Guadiana to found their new home, which they named Augusta Emerita. Not content to rest on their laurels and itching to gossip with fellow patricians in Sevilla and Salamanca, the soldiers built the largest bridge in Lusitania, the Puente Romano. The nostalgic crew adorned their "little Rome" with baths, aqueducts, a hippodrome, an arena, and a famous amphitheater. Modern Mérida has complemented the Roman buildings with walk-

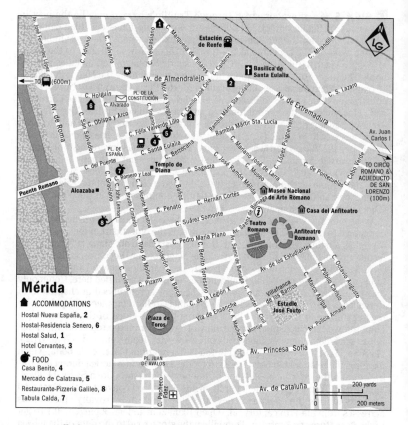

Mérida

🏠 ACCOMMODATIONS
Hostal Nueva España, **2**
Hostal-Residencia Senero, **6**
Hostal Salud, **1**
Hotel Cervantes, **3**

🍎 FOOD
Casa Benito, **4**
Mercado de Calatrava, **5**
Restaurante-Pizzeria Galileo, **8**
Tabula Calda, **7**

ways, small plazas, and the world-class Museo Romano. In July and August, the spectacular *Festival de Teatro Clásico* presents some of Europe's finest classical and modern theater and dance, performed among the ruins.

🔲 TRANSPORTATION

Trains: C. Carderos, s/n (☎902 24 02 02). Info window open daily 7am-10pm. To: **Badajoz** (1hr.; M-Sa 7:12am-10:16pm, Su 2:18-10:16pm; €2.65-9.85); **Cáceres** (1hr., 3-4 per day 8:05am-9pm, €3.25-10.52); **Lisboa, PT** (transfer in Cáceres); **Madrid** (4hr.; Su-F 2 per day 1:26, 9pm; Sa 1 per day 1:26pm; €19-27); **Sevilla** (4½hr., 1 per day 9:25am, €10.75); **Zafra** (1hr., 1 per day 9:25am, €3.25).

Buses: Av. de la Libertad, s/n (☎924 37 14 04). Info booth open M-F 7am-11pm, Sa-Su 7am-1pm and 3:15-11pm. **ALSA** (☎902 42 22 42) goes to **Salamanca** (5hr.; 4-5 per day M-Sa 9:15am-1:30am, Su 9:15am-12:10am; €14) and **Sevilla** (3hr., 6-8 per day 5:05am-10:45pm, €10.51). **AutoRes** (☎924 37 19 55) goes to **Madrid** (5½hr.; 7-8 per day M-F 8:45am-7:15pm, Sa 8:45am-4:45pm, Su 9:45am-7:15pm; €17-20). **LEDA** (☎924 37 14 03) sends buses to: **Badajoz** (1hr.; 4-9 per day M-F 8am-10:50pm, Sa 8:45am-10:50pm, Su 11:40am-10:50pm; €3.67); **Cáceres** (1hr.; 2-4

per day M-Th 9:10am-9:15pm, F-Sa 9:10am-3:50pm, Su 5:50-8:30pm; €4.08);
Sevilla (3hr.; 7-9 per day M-F 7am-8:30pm, Sa 7am-6pm, Su 9am-8:30pm; €10.51).

Taxis: Teletaxi (☎924 31 57 56). 24hr.

Car Rental: Avis (☎924 37 33 11), at the bus station. From €48 per day plus IVA. Insurance included. 23+. Open M-F 9am-1pm and 5-8pm, Sa 9:30am-1pm.

✳🛈 ORIENTATION & PRACTICAL INFORMATION

Plaza de España, the town center, is two blocks up from the Puente Romano and easily accessible from the **Teatro Romano.** Walking outward from the center, cafes and shops around the plaza quickly transform into quiet residential neighborhoods, and streets often lose their signs. From the **bus station** to Pl. de España, cross the suspension bridge and turn right on Av. de Roma. Continue along the river until you reach the Puente Romano, then turn left on C. del Puente. From the **train station,** take C. Carderos and its continuation, C. Camilo José Cela; bear right onto C. Félix Valverde Lillo and follow it to Pl. de España (5-10min.).

Tourist Office: Av. J. Álvarez Saenz de Buruaga, s/n (☎924 00 97 30; fax 00 97 30). English-speaking staff. Ask for anything from information on the *Festival de Teatro Clásico* to a full-color guide to *extremeño* ecotourism in Dutch. Open in summer M-F 9am-1:45pm and 5-7:15pm, Sa-Su 9:30am-1:45pm; in winter M-F 9am-1:45pm and 4-6:15pm, Sa-Su 9:30am-1:45pm.

Emergency: ☎112. **Police:** ☎092. **Medical Assistance:** ☎924 38 10 18.

Hospital: Residencia Sanitaria de la Seguridad Social Centralita (☎924 38 10 00).

Internet Access: Escuela de Idiomas Santa Eulalia, C. Santa Eulalia, 19, 2nd fl. (☎924 31 19 60). 30min. minimum. €1 per 30min., €1.50 per hr. Open M-F July-Sept. 10am-2pm and 7-10pm; Oct.-June 10am-3pm and 5-10pm.

Post Office: Pl. de la Constitución (☎924 31 24 58; fax 30 24 56). Open July 15-Sept. 15 M-F 8:30am-2:30pm, Sa 9:30am-1pm; Sept. 16-July 14 M-F 8:30am-8:30pm, Sa 9:30am-1pm. **Postal Code:** 06800.

🏠 ACCOMMODATIONS

Despite the flocks of visor-sporting tourists, finding a reasonably-priced room in Mérida won't leave you in ruins. Check the tourist office for complete listings.

Hostal-Residencia Senero, C. Holguín, 12 (☎924 31 72 07). Lively, charming owners make Mérida feel like home. Simple, large, and clean rooms, some with a balcony facing the street. A/C €4.20 extra. Apr.-Oct. and Dec. 22-31 singles €17, with bath €21; doubles with bath €32. Nov.-Dec. 21 and Jan.-Apr. €15.50/€19/€29. MC/V. ❷

Hostal Nueva España, Av. de Extremadura, 6 (☎924 31 33 56 or 31 32 11). Standard rooms come with private baths. Apr.-Sept. singles €23; doubles €35; triples €45. Oct.-Mar. €18/€31/€41. MC/V. ❷

Hostal Salud, C. Vespasiano, 41 (☎626 32 41 67; fax 924 31 22 59). Though the reception area could be better maintained, rooms are large and well-furnished with TV and private bath. Singles €18; doubles €30, with A/C €36. MC/V. ❷

Hotel Cervantes, C. Camilo José Cela, 8 (☎924 31 49 01 or 31 13 42). Centrally located, modern building with comfortable facilities. Bright rooms with large screen TV and great baths. Breakfast €3.90. Singles €40; doubles €60. AmEx/MC/V. ❹

🍴 FOOD

Plaza de España is filled with overpriced outdoor cafes. Buy fresh foods at the **market** in Pl. Mercado de Calatrava. (Open M-Sa 8am-2pm.) Buy groceries at **El Árbol,** C. Félix Valverde Lillo, 8 (☎924 30 13 56. Open M-Sa 9:30am-2pm and 6-9pm; MC/ V), or at its **branch** closer to the train station on C. Marquesa de Pinares.

🍴 **Restaurante-Pizzeria Galileo,** C. John Lennon, 28 (☎924 31 55 05). A glass-floored dining room reveals the Roman ruins below. Fresh salads, pastas, and 34 creative varieties of pizza. Entrees €4-6. Open Th-Su 1:30pm-midnight. MC/V. ❶

Casa Benito, C. San Francisco, 3 (☎924 31 55 00). The ivy-walled terrace is the perfect place for a beer. Tapas €0.60-3. Bocadillos €2-6. Open M-Sa 9am-midnight. ❶

Tabula Calda, C. Romero y Leal, 11 (☎924 30 49 50; www.tabulacalda.com). The house special Sephardi-Jewish salad with orange, sugar, and olive oil is a good start to any meal. Tables in an interior garden make Tabula the perfect setting for an intimate meal. Entrees start at €10 and 3-course menús at €15. Open daily June-Sept. 1-4:30pm and 8pm-12:30am; Oct.-May 1-4:30pm and 7:30pm-midnight. V. ❸

👁 SIGHTS

From the **Puente Romano** to astrological mosaics, Mérida offers Spain's best view of Roman civilization in Iberia. A **combined ticket,** valid for all the listings below—except the Museo Nacional de Arte Romano—can be purchased at any of the sights. (€7.20, EU students €3.60. Valid for several days and includes a guide book to the ruins.) The **ruins** are all open June-Sept. daily 9:30am-1:45pm and 5-7:15pm; Oct.-May 9:30am-1:45pm and 4-6:15pm.

MUSEO NACIONAL DE ARTE ROMANO. Enormous, elegant galleries under brick arches house all the Roman memorabilia you could ask for: statues, dioramas, coins, and other relics. The reconstruction of the interior decor in a Roman house is particularly stunning. The **cripta** displays parts of an ancient Augusta Emerita street found at the time of the museum's construction. Budget anywhere from 40 minutes to several hours here. (C. José Ramón Mélida, 2. ☎924 31 16 90. Open June-Sept. Tu-Sa 10am-2pm and 5-7pm, Su and holidays 10am-2pm; Oct.-May Tu-Sa 10am-2pm and 4-6pm, Su and holidays 10am-2pm. €2.40, EU students €1.20. Sa afternoon and Su free.)

TEATRO ROMANO & ANFITEATRO ROMANO. The spectacular teatro was a gift from Agrippa, a Roman administrator, in 16 BC. Its 6000 seats face a scaenaefrons, an incredible marble colonnade built upstage. Today the stage features performances of Spanish classical theater during the popular **Festival de Teatro Clásico de Mérida** every July and August. (Performances on alternate days July-Aug. 10:45pm. Info at the Oficina del Festival, C. Santa Eulalia, 4, or ☎924 00 49 30; www.festivaldemerida.com. Tickets €9-36. Combined ticket for all performances €100-250. Consult tourist office for more info Sept.-June.) Inaugurated in 8 BC, the anfiteatro was used for contests between any combination of animals and men, so long as blood was shed. (In the park across from the Museo Nacional; also accessible by tunnel from the cripta. €5.10, including Teatro.)

CASA DEL MITREO & CASA DEL ANFITEATRO. These ruins of Roman homes showcase some of the world's finest Roman mosaics. Casa del Mitreo's **Mosaico Cosmológico** is world-famous among Roman historians and depicts the Romans' conception of the world and forces of nature. Casa del Anfiteatro can be seen from the street, but enter for a closer look at foundations and arrangements of residential quarters in Roman Iberia. (Casa del Anfiteatro is between the Anfiteatro Romano and the Museo de Arte Romano. Casa del Mitreo is on Vía Ensanche opposite Pl. de Toros. Each €2.55.)

BULLBOARDS Staring glassy-eyed out the window of your preferred mode of transportation, you may notice rather unusual monuments along the highway: massive, black paper cut-outs of solitary bulls. Once upon a time (in the 1980s) these cut-outs were advertisements for Osborne Sherry. In the early 1990s, however, billboards were prohibited on national roads. A plan was drafted to take the bulls down, but Spaniards protested, as the lone bull towering along the roadside had become an important national symbol. After considerable clamoring and hoofing, the bulls were painted black and left to loom proudly against the horizon. The familiar shape now decorates t-shirts and pins in souvenir shops, but the real thing is still impressive. Keep your eyes peeled as you ride through the countryside.

OTHER RUINS. At the end of Rbla. Mártir Santa Eulalia stand the **Museo, Basílica,** and **Iglesia de Santa Eulalia,** all commemorating the child martyr. In 1990, in the midst of repairs to the 6th-century church, layers of previous construction were uncovered to reveal the ruins of Roman houses dating from the 3rd to 1st centuries BC, a 4th-century necropolis, and a basilica dedicated to Santa Eulalia. (*Museum and basilica €2.55. Church open daily during services at 8:30am and 8pm. Free.*) Near the theater complex is the **Circo Romano,** or hippodrome. Diocles, the most famous Lusitanian racer, had his start here; he ended his career with a whopping 1462 victories. Once filled with spectators, the arena (capacity 30,000) is currently under excavation and is closed to the public—though the view from the outside is still worth the trip. Next to the Circo stand the remains of the **Acueducto de San Lázaro.** (*From C. Cabo Verde take the pedestrian walkway underneath the train tracks.*) The **Templo de Diana** is the only surviving Roman temple of worship, and its impressive colonnaded facade is worth a visit. (*C. Sagasta. Free.*) Built from materials discarded by the Visigoths, the **Alcazaba** was designed by the Moors to guard the Roman bridge. Today, only the walls and interior ruins remain. (*Near the Puente Romano. €2.55.*)

BADAJOZ
☎924

Badajoz (pop. 120,000) is not a stop on most travel itineraries, for good reason. Known mostly as a transportation hub on the way into Portugal, Badajoz has only recently refreshed its ruins, cleared up much of the industrial pollution that once plagued it, and added a tourist office—making forced layovers en route to or from Portugal a bit more pleasant. Three happening *zonas de pubs* and a contemporary art museum provide for an afternoon's distraction while waiting for the long ride to Lisboa. Nightlife here can be pretty hot; parties erupt in the evening in Plaza de España and along the river, enticing jealous Portuguese neighbors to cross the border and partake in the fun.

▐ TRANSPORTATION

From Badajoz, buses to Portugal are faster and more convenient than trains.

Trains: Av. Carolina Coronado (☎924 27 11 70). From the train station to Pl. de la Libertad, take bus #1 (€0.60). Info booth open daily 9am-10pm. Trains to: **Cáceres** (2½hr.; M-F and Su 2 per day 8:15am, 2:30pm; Sa 1 per day 8:15am; €8.70-13); **Madrid** (5hr.; M-F and Su 3 per day 8:15am-2:30pm; Sa 2 per day 8:15am, 12:30pm; €27-30.50); **Mérida** (1½hr., 7 per day 6:40am-7:40pm, €2.65-11).

Buses: Central Station, C. José Rebollo López, 2 (☎924 25 86 61). Info booth open daily 7:45am-1am. Buses #3, 6a, 6b, and 9 run between the station and Pl. de la Libertad (€0.60). Schedules are particularly flexible; call ahead.

ALSA to: **Cáceres** (1½hr.; M 3 per day 8am-4:30pm, Tu-Sa 9:30am and 4:30pm, Su 4:30pm; €7) on its way to **Salamanca** (5hr., €18.39); **Lisboa** (3½hr., daily at 3:45am and 4pm, €17).

AutoRes (☎924 23 85 15 or 902 02 09 99) to: **Lisboa** (2½hr.; daily 5pm and 2am, F also at 8:30pm; €14); **Madrid** (4hr., 9-10 per day 12:30am-4pm, €21.70-25.50); **Trujillo** (2hr.; M-Th and Sa 6 per day 8am-4pm, F 8am-6:30pm, Su 9am-6:30pm; €8.11-10).

Caballero (☎924 25 57 56) to **Cáceres** (1½hr.; M-F 6 per day 7:30am-7:30pm; Sa 2 per day 8am, 2:30pm; Su 4 per day 2:30-9pm; €5.60). **Damas** to **Sevilla** (4½hr.; M-F 7 per day 6:45am-8pm, Sa-Su 3-4 per day 9am-8pm; €11.83).

LEDA (☎924 23 34 78) to **Mérida** (1½hr.; M-F 8 per day 8:30am-9pm, Sa 4 per day 9:30am-9pm, Su 3 per day 3, 7:30, 9:30pm; €3.67).

Taxis: At bus and train stations and Pl. de España. **Radio-Taxi** (24hr. ☎924 24 31 01).

✚ 🛈 ORIENTATION & PRACTICAL INFORMATION

Across the Río Guadiana from the **train station** and home to the municipal tourist office, **Plaza de España** is the heart of Badajoz. From the plaza, C. Juan de Ribera and C. Pedro de Valdivia lead to Pl. Dragones Hernán Cortés; one block to the right is **Plaza de la Libertad** (5min.) and the regional **tourist office**. Between Pl. de España and Pl. de la Libertad is **Paseo de San Francisco,** home to the **post office** and **supermarket.** From the **train station,** follow Av. Carolina Coronado straight to Puente de las Palmas, cross the bridge, then continue straight on C. Prim. Turn left onto C. Juan de Ribera at Pl. Minayo to get to Pl. de España, or right to Pl. de la Libertad (35min.). Bus #1 runs from the train station to Pl. de la Libertad, directly across from the regional tourist office. From the **bus station,** turn left, take a quick right, and then turn left onto C. Damián Téllez la Fuente. Pass straight through Pl. de la Constitución and Pl. Dragones Hernán Cortés to Pl. de España (20min.).

Tourist Office: Municipal Office, Pje. San Juan (☎924 22 49 81). Facing the Ayuntamiento from Pl. de España, take C. San Juan to its left. English spoken. Open M-F 10am-2pm and 5-7pm, Sa 10am-1:30pm. **Regional Office,** Pl. de la Libertad, 3 (☎924 01 36 59). Open M-F 9am-2pm and 5-7pm, Sa-Su 10am-2pm. **Juventud/Oficina de Información Juvenil,** Ronda de Pilar, 20 (☎924 22 44 49), has info on nightlife. Open June-Sept. M-F 9am-2pm and 5:30-7:30pm; Oct.-May 8am-3pm and 6:30-8:30pm.

Luggage Storage: In the bus station (€0.60) and train station (€3).

Emergency: ☎092. **Police:** Av. de Ramón y Cajal (☎091 or 924 21 00 72).

Hospital: Hospital Perpetual Socorro, Ctra. de Valverde, s/n (☎924 23 04 00).

Internet Access: HD Zone, C. Antonio Montero Moreno, 6A (☎924 24 86 16). €1.50 per hr. until 2pm, €2 per hr. after. Open daily 8am-2am.

Post Office: Po. de San Francisco, 4 (☎924 22 25 48). **Lista de Correos.** M-F 8am-9pm, Sa 9am-2pm. **Postal Code:** 06001.

🛏 ACCOMMODATIONS

Hostales line streets radiating from Pl. de España.

Hostal Niza II, C. Arco Agüero, 45 (☎924 22 38 81 or 22 31 73). From Pl. de España take C. San Blas downhill, then take your first right onto C. Arco Agüero. Sturdy brown rooms with A/C, TV, and private bath. Owner eagerly provides maps, brochures, and history. Singles €23; doubles €38; triples €47. ❷

Pensión Pintor, C. Arco Agüero, 26 (☎924 22 42 28). You may need to ring the bell across the street at #33. Simple but comfortable rooms make for a pleasant layover. One single with bath €20; doubles €23, with bath, TV, and A/C €35. ❷

Hotel Condedú, C. Muñoz Torrero, 27 (☎924 20 72 47). Off one of the busiest side streets from Pl. de España. Offers luxurious, quiet rooms equipped with TV, bathroom, A/C, telephone, and those irresistible minibars. Singles €36.40; doubles €53.50. ❹

🍴 FOOD

For **groceries,** head to **Consum,** next to the post office. (Open M-Sa 9am-9pm. MC/V.) Beyond Pl. de España, cafes and eateries crowd **Paseo de San Francisco.**

Cocina Portuguesa, C. Muñoz Torrero, 7 (☎924 26 34 97). Try traditional Portuguese food without crossing the nearby border. Portuguese specialties (€4.80-15), fish and meats (€5.50-8). Open daily 2-4:30pm and 9pm-12:30am. ❶

Bar-Restaurante La Ria, Pl. de España, s/n. Behind the glitzy bar and fast food decor lie yummy *raciones* and traditional Spanish foods, setting your pocketbook back only €2.50-4. Three-course *menú del día* €7.50. Open 10am-midnight. ❷

Restaurant Simbo, Av. José María Alcaraz y Alenda, 33 (☎924 25 24 74). From Av. de María Auxiliadora, take a right onto Av. Sinforiano Madroñero; it's the 3rd street on the right. Aromas of eastern spices greet travelers looking for large portions of delicious Cantonese food. Entrees €3. Open M-Th and Su 11:30am-2:30pm and 8pm-midnight, F-Sa 11:30am-2:30pm and 7:30pm-12:30am. ❶

👁 SIGHTS

In 1995, Badajoz renovated its high-security prison to make way for the **Museo Extremeño e Iberoamericano de Arte Contemporáneo.** Five floors exhibit recent works from Spain, Portugal, and Latin America. The permanent collection includes Marta María Pérez Bravo's photo of a woman's breasts as a communion offering. From Pl. de España, head down C. Juan de Ribera, continuing as it turns into Av. de Europa; the museum is on the left after Pl. de la Constitución. (☎924 26 03 84. Open Tu-Sa 10am-1:30pm and 5-8pm, Sun 10am-1:30pm. Free.) Badajoz's old quarter, including **Plaza de España** and **Paseo de San Francisco,** is rich with history. With one Renaissance, one Gothic, and one Plateresque window, the 13th-century **cathedral** (a converted mosque) in Pl. de España is an artistic timeline. (Open daily 11am-1pm. Free.) The ruins of the **Alcazaba,** a Moorish citadel, stand at the top of the hill. (Ruins and archaeological museum open Tu-Su 10am-3pm. Free.)

🍸 NIGHTLIFE

Locals rave about Badajoz's **nightlife** and **pub culture**—the only redeeming aspect of an overnight stay in this town. City maps proudly display three *zonas de pubs.* The largest and, according to some locals, best of the three is in the old quarter, where every street off Pl. de España has at least three bars. Though usually home to a more elderly local crowd than the other two, Badajoz mainstay bars such as **Mercantil,** C. Zurbarán, 10, populate this area. With live music every Thursday and Friday starting at 11pm and a large floor to groove on, Mercantil spins a mix of Spanish hip-hop, jazz, and pop on non-current days to packed crowds late into the night. (Beer €2. Mixed drinks €4 and up. Open daily June-Aug. after 4pm, Sept.-May after 8pm. Closing hours depend on the crowd and can vary from 2-5am.)

University students crowd the area around the intersection of Av. José María Alcaraz y Alenda and Av. de Sinforiano Madroñero. (Walking downhill from Pl. de la Constitución on Av. Fernando Calzadilla Maestre, turn right onto Av. Juan Pereda Pila, left at Av. de María Auxiliadora, and right again onto Av. de Sinforiano

Madroñero. The *zona de pubs* is up two intersections straight ahead, a 30min. walk from Pl. de España. Ask directions to **Cinema Puerta Real** near Cta. de la Granadilla, a movie theater converted into a student hangout by night, with free Internet access and locals chilling at the bar. (Open Th-Sa 10pm-2am.) The final and newest *zona de pubs* is located across the river. A mix of young, old, tourist, local, and Portuguese revelers are attracted to this parkside bar zone packed on weekend evenings. Crossing Puente de Palmas en route to the train station, turn left on Av. Adolfo Díaz Ambrona and pass by the Puente de la Universidad on your left. Happening pubs such as **C.K., Flydays,** and **Robinson** are located on your right. One caveat: Badajoz nightlife can be quite tame Monday-Wednesday, and the long walks may be unrewarding. Stick to Pl. de España if stuck in Badajoz during the week; the nightclubs are 5km away from town on Av. Luis Movilla Montero and require wheels to reach.

ANDALUCÍA

Andalucía is, without a doubt, Spain at its best. Many of the quintessential images of Spain—from bullfighting to *flamenco*, from Moorish architecture to grandiose churches, from glorious castles to Roman ruins, and from sun-drenched beaches to expanses of olive groves—can all be found in this region. The intoxicating mix of cultures that helped make southern Spain what it is today can be seen both in the area's largest metropolises and in some of its tiniest towns.

The ancient kingdom of Tartessus—what some say is the same Tarshish mentioned in the Bible for its fabulous troves of silver—grew wealthy off the Sierra Nevada's rich ore deposits. The Greeks and Phoenicians established colonies here and traded up and down the coast, and the Romans later cultivated wheat, olive oil, and wine from the fertile soil watered by the Guadalquivir. In the 5th century AD, the Vandals flitted through the region on their way to North Africa, leaving little more than a name—Vandalusia (House of the Vandals). The Moors provided a more enduring influence. Arriving in 711 and establishing a yet-unbroken link to Africa and the Islamic world, they endowed the region with far more than the *flamenco* music and gypsy ballads proverbially associated with southern Spain.

Moorish rule lasted until 1492, and under it Sevilla and Granada reached the pinnacle of Islamic arts, while Córdoba matured into the most culturally and intellectually influential city in Islam. The Moors preserved and perfected Roman architecture, blending it with their own to create a style that became distinctively and uniquely Andalusian—patios, garden oases with fountains and ponds, and alternating red brick and white stone bands are its hallmarks. Two descendent peoples, the Mozárabes (Christians of Muslim Spain), and later the Mudéjares (Moors who remained in Spain after *la Reconquista*), made further architectural impacts, the former with horseshoe arches and the latter with intricate wooden ceilings. The mingling of Roman and Moorish influences sparked the European Renaissance, merging Classical wisdom and science with that of the Arab world.

HIGHLIGHTS OF ANDALUCÍA

FIND OUT what all the **flamenco** fuss is about (see p. 237).

SAMPLE enough **sherry** to get yourself sufficiently silly (see p. 266).

GET CLEAN —sultan style—in **Córdoba's** Arab baths (see p. 253).

WONDER why your neck is sore after gazing at Sevilla's **Catedral** ceiling (see p. 275).

EXULT in **Semana Santa** madness, and never party the same way again (see p. 321).

DISCOVER what happens when the **Costa del Sol** meets James Bond (see p. 291).

SEVILLA ☎ 954

Sevilla (pop. 700,000) is arguably the most charming and romantic of Spain's great cities. Narrow, tangled streets unfold from the center leading to an awe-inspiring cathedral, the third largest in the world, and to the city's world-class Alcázar, a great Moorish and Catholic palace and the official residence of the king and queen of Spain. Tourists, locals, students, history buffs, *flamenco* lovers, and partiers alike infuse Sevilla with an energy and vibrancy hard to match. The budget traveler's experience here, although varied, can be one of the best in Spain—it's not uncommon to strike up a conversation with the traveler or student next to you at a *flamenco* bar, and with so many students packed in during the academic year,

ANDALUCÍA

the opportunities for things to do and see on a tight budget are truly overwhelming. Contemporary Sevilla is the product of an ancient and impressive history. Once the site of a Roman acropolis founded by Julius Caesar, it later became the capital of the Moorish empire and a focal point of the Spanish Renaissance. Sevilla is now the guardian of traditional Andalusian culture: *flamenco, tapas*, and bullfighting. For a taste of Sevilla gone *really* wild, visit during its most prominent festivals—*Semana Santa* and *Feria de Abril* are among the most lavish celebrations in all of Europe, and are yet another reason to visit.

HOW TO USE THIS SECTION. Sevilla is divided into several neighborhoods. We have grouped together all of each area's accommodations, food, sights, museums, and nightlife listings. General information on these aspects of Sevilla, as well as shopping and specific listings for camping and entertainment (including sports, theater, concerts, and film) appears after the practical information.

■ INTERCITY TRANSPORTATION

BY PLANE

All flights arrive at **Aeropuerto San Pablo**, Ctra. de Madrid (☎954 44 90 00), 12km outside town. A taxi from the town center costs approx. €13. **Los Amarillos** (☎954 98 91 84) runs a bus from outside Hotel Alfonso XIII at Pta. de Jerez (M-F every 30-45min., Sa-Su every hr. 6:15am-11pm; €2.40). **Iberia**, C. Guadaira, 8 (☎954 22 89 01, nationwide 902 40 05 00; open M-F 9am-1:30pm) books 6 flights per day to **Barcelona** (55min.) and **Madrid** (45min.). For student fares to destinations within Spain and around the world, head to **Barceló Viajes** (see **Local Services**, p. 234).

BY TRAIN

Estación Santa Justa, Av. de Kansas City (☎954 41 41 11. Info and reservations open daily 4:30am-12:30am, ticket sales daily 6am-10:30pm). Services include **luggage storage, car rental,** and **ATM**. In town, international bookings must be made at the **RENFE** office, C. Zaragoza, 29. (☎954 54 02 02. Open M-F 9am-1:15pm and 4-7pm.)

Altaria and **Talgo** trains run to: **Barcelona** (10½-13hr.; 3 per day 8am, 9:45am, 10:20pm; €48.50-66.50); **Córdoba** (1hr.; 2 per day 9:44am, 6:15pm; €23.50); **Madrid** (3½hr.; 2 per day 9:44am, 6:15pm; €50); **Valencia** (9hr., 1 per day 8am, €41.50); **Zaragoza** (7½hr., 1 per day 9:43am, €58).

AVE trains run to **Córdoba** (45min., 18-20 per day 6:30am-9:05pm, €17-19) and **Madrid** (2½hr., 18-20 per day 6:30am-9:05pm, €57-64).

Regionales trains run to: **Almería** (5½hr., 4 per day 7am-5:40pm, €27.20); **Antequera** (2hr., 3 per day 7am-5:40pm, €10.20); **Cáceres** (5½hr., 1 per day 4:15pm, €14.35); **Cádiz** (2hr.; 7-12 per day M-F 6:53am-9:35pm, Sa-Su 9am-9:35pm; €8.25); **Córdoba** (1½hr., 8 per day 7:50am-9:55pm, €6.95); **Granada** (3hr., 4 per day 7am-5:40pm, €17); **Huelva** (1½hr., 2-3 per day 9:10am-8:45pm, €6.35); **Jaén** (2-3hr., 1 per day 6:46pm, €14.40); **Málaga** (2½hr., 4-6 per day 7:40am-8:10pm, €13.60); **Osuna** (1hr., 6 per day 7:40am-6:35pm, €6.35).

BY BUS

Estación Prado de San Sebastián, C. Manuel Vázquez Sagastizabal, serves most of Andalucía. (☎954 41 71 11. Open daily 5:30am-1am.) Look carefully; the station is in a yellow building next to a restaurant and is not marked on the street. **Estación Plaza de Armas** (☎954 90 80 40) primarily serves areas outside of Andalucía.

ANDALUCÍA

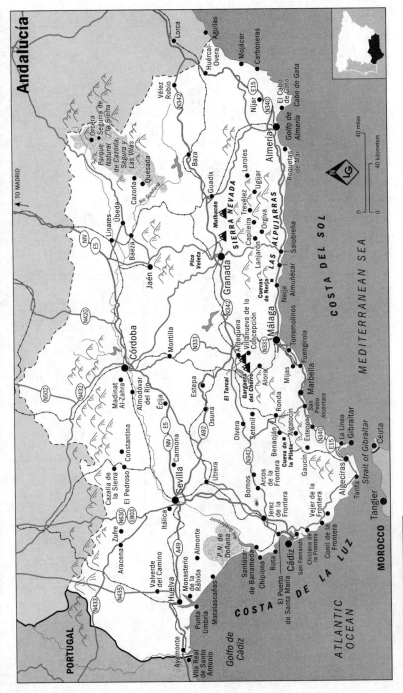

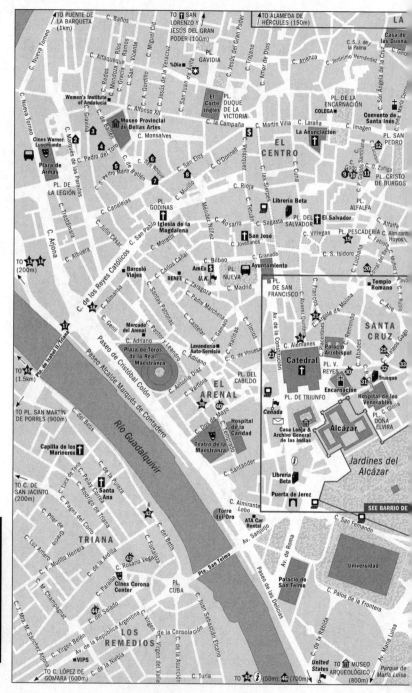

Sevilla

🏠 ACCOMMODATIONS

Espiau, **11**
Hostal Arizona, **4**
Hostal Atenas, **14**
Hostal Bienvenido, **29**
Hostal Buen Dormir, **27**
Hostal Dulces-Sueños, **36**
Hostal Goya, **25**
Hostal La Gloria, **7**
Hostal Lis, **12**
Hostal Lis II, **8**
Hostal Paris, **5**
Hostal Río Sol, **2**
Hostal Romero, **3**
Hostal Sierpes, **20**
Hostal-Residencia Córdoba, **26**
Hostal-Residencia Monreal, **31**
Hotel Zaida, **6**
Pensión Vergara, **33**
Sevilla Youth Hostal (HI), **46**

🍴 FOOD

Acropolis Taberna Griega, **43**
Café-Bar Campanario, **30**
Café-Bar Jerusalém, **44**
Café Cáceres, **28**
Habanita Bar Restaurant, **9**

Histórico Horno, S.A., **23**
La Mia Tana, **10**
Restaurante Coello, **35**
Restaurante-Bar El Barratillo/
Casa Chari, **40**
El Rinconcillo, **13**
San Marco, **32**

⭐ NIGHTLIFE

Antigüedades, **21**
El Arenal, **39**
El Capote, **17**
La Carbonería, **22**
Casa de la Memoria de
Al-Andalus, **34**
Catedral, **19**
Coliseum, **18**
Flaherty's, **24**
Fundición, **42**
Los Gallos, **38**
Isbiliyya, **18**
El Palacio Andaluz, **1**
Palenque, **41**
El Tamboril, **37**
Terraza Chile, **45**
Tribal, **15**

ANDALUCÍA

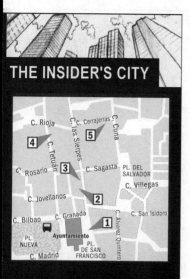

THE INSIDER'S CITY

THE BARGAINS OF SEVILLA

Sevilla is a city full of wonderful *artesanía* and plenty of people selling it. Avoid the overpriced tourist shops by the cathedral and head to specialty stores for high-quality, authentic merchandise. After dropping a few euros on authentic trappings, you can dress in *flamenco* fashion, bat your eyes at that handsome Don Juan from behind a hand-made fan, and wrap yourself in a luxurious silk shawl like a true *sevillana*.

1. Abanicos de Sevilla, Pl. San Francisco, 7 (☎954 21 38 18). Large selection of hand-painted fans, from dirt cheap to outrageously expensive. Open June-Aug. M-F 9:30am-1:30pm and 5-8:30pm, Sa 9:30am-2pm; Sept.-May M-Sa 9:30am-1:30pm and 5-8:30pm. MC/V.

2. Martian Cerámica Sevillana, C. las Sierpes, 74 (☎954 21 34 13). Colorful hand-painted ceramics, all made in Sevilla. Tiny trays and vases start at €3, larger ones run €20-30. Open M-Sa 10am-2pm and 5-8:30pm. MC/V.

ESTACIÓN PRADO DE SAN SEBASTIÁN

Alsina Graells (☎954 41 88 11). Open daily 6:30am-11pm. MC/V. To: **Almería** (7hr., 1 per day 4pm, €26.19); **Córdoba** (2hr., 10-12 per day 7:30am-9:30pm, €8.55); **Granada** (3hr., 10 per day 8am-11pm, €16); **Jaén** (4hr., 3-5 per day 7:30am-6pm, €15.35); **Málaga** (2½hr., 10-12 per day 7am-midnight, €13.03); **Murcia** (8hr.; 2 per day 8, 11am; €31.16); **Nerja** (4hr., 1 per day 6pm, €16).

Los Amarillos (☎954 98 91 84). Open M-F 7:30am-2pm and 2:30-8pm, Sa-Su 7:30am-2pm and 2:30-9pm. To: **Arcos de la Frontera** (2hr.; 2 per day 8am, 4:30pm; €6.33); **Marbella** (3hr.; 3 per day 8am, 4, 8pm; €13.26); **Ronda** (2½hr., 3-5 per day 7am-5pm, €9); **Sanlúcar de Barrameda** and **Chipiona** (2hr., 10 per day 7am-9pm, €6.23-6.83).

Transportes Comes (☎954 41 68 58). Open M-Sa 6:30am-10pm. To: **Algeciras** (3½hr., 4 per day 9am-8pm, €14.23); **Cádiz** (1½hr., 14 per day 7am-10pm, €9.32); **Jerez de la Frontera** (1½hr., 9-10 per day 9am-10pm, €5.62); **Tarifa** (3hr., 4 per day 9am-8pm, €14.01).

ESTACIÓN PLAZA DE ARMAS

ALSA (☎954 90 78 00 or 902 42 22 42). Open M-F and Su 5:45am-11pm, Sa 8am-10:45pm. To: **Cáceres** (4¼hr., 7 per day 6am-10:30pm, €14.16); **León** (11hr.; 3 per day 6, 11am, 9pm; €35.59); **Salamanca** (8hr., 5 per day 6am-10:30pm, €24.45); **Valencia** (9-11hr.; 3 per day 9:30am, 5:30, 9:30pm; €41-49). Under 26 and seniors 10% discount, under 12 50% discount.

Autocares Anibal (☎902 36 00 73). To **Lisboa** (6½hr.; 1 per day M-Th 11:45pm, F 11:30am; €28). 10% student discount.

Damas (☎954 90 80 40). Open M-F 6:30am-9:30pm, Sa-Su 7am-9pm. To **Badajoz** (3½hr., 5 per day 6:45am-8pm, €10.86) and **Huelva** (1¼hr., 21-24 per day 6am-9pm, €6.11).

Socibus (☎954 90 11 60 or 902 22 92 92; fax 954 90 16 92). Open daily 7:30-10am and 10:30am-12:45am. To **Madrid** (6hr., 14 per day 8am-1am, €15.95).

■ ORIENTATION

The **Río Guadalquivir** flows roughly north to south through the city, bordered by the busy Paseo de Cristobal, which becomes Paseo de las Delicias by the municipal tourist office. Most of the touristed areas of Sevilla, including **Santa Cruz** and **El Arenal,** are on the east bank. The historic and proud *barrios* of **Triana, Santa Cecilia,** and **Los Remedios** and the **Expo '92 fairgrounds** occupy the western bank. The cathedral, next to Santa Cruz, is

Sevilla's centerpiece. If you're disoriented, look for conspicuous **La Giralda** (the minaret-turned-bell tower). **Avenida de la Constitución,** home of the tourist office, runs alongside the cathedral. **El Centro,** a busy commercial pedestrian zone, lies north of the cathedral, starting where Av. de la Constitución hits **Plaza Nueva,** site of the Ayuntamiento. **Calle Tetuán,** a popular street for shopping, takes off from Pl. Nueva and runs northward through El Centro.

To get to Santa Cruz from the **train station,** take bus C-2 and transfer to C-3 at the Jardines del Valle; it will drop you off at the **Jardines de Murillo.** Walk right one block past the gardens; C. Santa María la Blanca is on the left. Otherwise, it's a 15-20min. walk. To reach El Centro from the **train station,** catch bus #32 to **Plaza de la Encarnación,** several blocks north of the cathedral. Bus C-4 connects the bus station at **Plaza de Armas** to Prado de San Sebastián.

▐ LOCAL TRANSPORTATION

Public Transportation: TUSSAM (☎900 71 01 71; www.tussam.es). Most bus lines run every 10min. daily 6am-11:15pm and converge in Pl. Nueva, Pl. de la Encarnación, and in front of the cathedral. **Night service** departs from Pl. Nueva (every hr. midnight-2am; F-Sa all night). C-3 and C-4 circle the center, and #34 hits the youth hostel, university, cathedral, and Pl. Nueva. €0.90, *bonobús* (10 rides) €4.50, 30-day pass €26.

Taxis: TeleTaxi (☎954 62 22 22); **Radio Taxi** (☎954 58 00 00). Base rate €1, €0.40 per km, Su 25% surcharge. Extra charge for luggage and night taxis.

Car Rental: Hertz, at the airport (☎954 25 42 98) and train station (☎954 53 39 14). General information and reservations (☎902 40 24 05.) 21+. From €52.50 per day. Open daily 8am-midnight. AmEx/MC/V. **ATA,** C. Almirante Lobo, 2 (☎954 22 09 58). 21+. Manual shift only. From €36 per day plus tax. Open M-F 9am-2pm and 4:30-8:30pm, Sa 9am-2pm. MC/V.

Moped Rental: Alkimoto, C. Fernando Tirado, 5 (☎954 58 49 27). €21 per day. Open M-F 9am-1:30pm and 5-8pm.

▐ PRACTICAL INFORMATION

TOURIST & FINANCIAL SERVICES

Tourist Offices: Centro de Información de Sevilla, Po. de las Delicias, 9 (☎954 23 44 65; www.turismo.sevilla.org). English spoken. Maps, info on flamenco, hostels, etc. Open M-F 8am-7pm. **Turismo Andaluz,** Av. de la Constitución, 21B (☎954 22 14 04; fax 22 97 53). Info on all of Andalucía. English spoken. Open M-F 9am-7pm, Sa 10am-2pm and 3-7pm, Su 10am-2pm.

3. Artesanía Textil, C. las Sierpes, 70 (☎954 56 28 40). Authentic, hand-sewn, silk shawls. Prices start at €56. Open June-Aug. M-F 10am-1:30pm and 5:15-8:15pm, Sa 10am-1:30pm; Sept.-May M-Sa 10am-1:30pm and 5:15-8:15pm. MC/V.

4. Diza, C. Tetuán, 5 (☎954 21 41 54). Lots of *abanicos* (fans), some dating back to the 19th-century. Hand-painted fans €3.75 and up. June-Aug. M-F 9:30am-1:30pm and 5-8:30pm, Sa 9:30am-2pm; Sept.-May M-Sa 9:30am-1:30pm and 5-8:30pm. MC/V.

5. Trajes Sevillanos, Modas Muñoz, C. Cerrajería, 5 (☎954 22 85 96). The real deal when it comes to traditional *flamenco* outfits. Very colorful, high-quality costumes, with equally high price tags (€120 and up). Also sells *flamenco* accessories (fans, flowers, etc.). Open M-F 10am-1:30pm and 5-8:30pm, Sa 10am-1:30pm. MC/V.

Currency Exchange: Banco Santander Central Hispano, C. la Campaña, 19 (☎902 24 24 24). Open M-F 8:30am-2pm, Sa 8:30am-1pm. **Exchanges** are scattered around the cathedral and are useful when banks are closed; most are open daily until 8pm. While they claim to be "commission-free," the exchange rate will be better at a bank.

Banks and **ATMs:** Along Av. de la Constitución and near Pl. Nueva.

American Express: Pl. Nueva, 7 (☎954 21 16 17). Open M-F 9:30am-1:30pm and 4:30-7:30pm, Sa 10am-1pm.

LOCAL SERVICES

Luggage Storage: Estación Prado de San Sebastián (€0.90 per bag per day; open 6:30am-10pm); **Estación Plaza de Armas** (€3 per day); **train station** (€3 per day).

English-Language Bookstore: Librería Beta, C. Sagasta, 16 (☎954 22 84 95). Good selection of books and travel guides, including ▇ *Let's Go.* **Branch,** Av. de la Constitución, 27 (☎954 56 07 03). Both open June-Aug. M-F 10am-2pm and 5:30-9pm, Sa 10am-2pm; Sept.-May M-F 10am-2pm and 5-8:30pm, Sa 10am-2pm. MC/V. **Trueque,** C. Pasaje de Vila, 2 (☎954 56 32 66). Great used bookstore with plenty of books in English (paperback novels €1-5; hardcovers up to €20). Open M-Sa 10:30am-1:30pm.

VIPS: Av. de la República Argentina, 25 (☎954 27 93 97). International newspapers, books, liquor, non-perishable groceries, and an American-style restaurant. Open Su-Th 8am-1:30am, F 8am-3:30am, Sa 9am-3am. MC/V.

El Corte Inglés: Pl. Duque de la Victoria (☎954 27 93 97). Huge department store with English-language books. Supermarket on ground floor. Open M-Sa 10am-10pm and first Su of each month. MC/V.

Budget Travel Agency: Barceló Viajes, C. de los Reyes Católicos, 11 (☎954 22 61 31). An STA Travel affiliate. Open June-Sept. M-F 9:30am-1:30pm and 5-8pm, Sa 10am-1pm; Oct.-May M-F 9:30am-1:30pm and 4:30-7:30pm, Sa 10am-1pm. MC/V.

Women's Services: Women's Institute of Andalucía, C. Alfonso XII, 52 (24hr. toll-free hotline ☎900 20 09 99, office 954 03 49 53; www.iam.juntadeandalucia.es). Info on feminist and lesbian organizations, plus legal and psychological services for rape victims. Office open to public Th-Tu 10am-1pm.

Gay and Lesbian Services: COLEGA (Colectiva de Lesbianas y Gays de Andalucía), Pl. de la Encarnación, 23, 2nd fl. (☎954 50 13 77; fax 56 33 66; www.colegaweb.net). Look for the sign in the window; the door is not marked. Open M-F 10am-2pm.

Laundromat: Lavandería Auto-Servicio, C. Castelar, 2 (☎954 21 05 35). Wash and dry €6 per 5kg. Open M-Sa 9:30am-1:30pm and 5-8:30pm.

Alternatives to Tourism: Sevilla is full of language schools; ask at the tourist office . All schools can arrange student accommodations and offer excursions for an additional fee. **CLIC** and **Don Quijote** come highly recommended (see **Language Schools,** p. 61).

EMERGENCY & COMMUNICATIONS

Emergency: Medical: ☎061. **Police:** Po. Concordia (Local ☎092, national 091).

24hr. Pharmacy: Check list posted at any pharmacy for those open 24hr.

Medical Assistance: Red Cross: (☎913 35 45 45). **Ambulatorio Esperanza Macarena** (☎954 42 01 05). **Hospital Universitario Virgen Macarena,** Av. Dr. Fedriani (☎954 24 81 81). English spoken.

Internet Access:

Sevilla Internet Center, C. Almirantazgo, 2, 2nd fl. (☎954 50 02 75). €3 per hr.; €1.80 per hr. with pre-paid cards. Open M-F 9am-10pm, Sa-Su 10am-10pm.

CiberBoston, C. San Fernando, 23 (☎954 21 94 49). €2 per hr.; Sa special €1 per hr. Open June-Sept. M-F 10am-1am, Sa noon-midnight; Oct.-May M-F 10am-1pm, Sa-Su noon-midnight. Closed Aug. 1-17.

The Email Place, C. las Sierpes, 54 (☎954 21 85 92). €2.20 per hr.; min. 10min. (€0.70). Open Oct.-May M-F 10am-11pm, Sa-Su noon-9pm; June-Sept. M-F 10am-10pm, Sa-Su noon-9pm.

WORKcenter, C. San Fernando, 1 (☎954 21 20 74; www.workcenter.es). An office center providing Internet access (€0.50 for 10min.; €3 per hr.). Fax, photocopy, and other services. Sells office supplies and film. Open 24hr. MC/V.

@DS Macarena, C. de San Luis, 108 (☎954 38 06 13), in La Macarena. €1.50 per hr. Open daily June-Aug. 11am-11:30pm, Sept.-May 11am-midnight.

Post Office: Av. de la Constitución, 32 (☎954 21 64 76). **Lista de Correos** and fax. Open M-F 10am-8:30pm, Sa 8:30am-2pm. **Postal Code:** 41080.

ACCOMMODATIONS

The *Semana Santa* processions in Sevilla are the largest in Spain and without doubt the most internationally acclaimed. During **Semana Santa** and **Feria de Abril,** vacant rooms vanish and prices soar. It is absolutely imperative to reserve several months in advance. The tourist office has lists of *casas particulares* (private residences) that open for visitors on special occasions. In general, you should reserve at least two weeks in advance throughout Spain.

ACCOMMODATIONS BY PRICE

UNDER €15 ❶		€26-35 ❸	
Sevilla Youth Hostel	ON	Hostal Río Sol	ON
Camping Sevilla	ON	Hostal Romero	ON
Club de Campo	ON	Hostal-Residencia Montreal	SC
		Pensión Cruces El Patio	SC
€15-25 ❷		€26-35 ❸	
🎫 Pensión Vergara	SC	Hostal Arizona	ON
🎫 Espiau	EC	Hostal Atenas	SC
🎫 Hostal Macarena	M	Hostal Paris	ON
Hostal Alameda	M	Hostal-Residencia Córdoba	SC
Hostal Bienvenido	SC	€36-55 ❹	
Hostal Buen Dormir	SC	Hostal Goya	SC
Hostal Dulces-Sueños	SC	Hostal Sierpes	SC
Hostal La Gloria	EC	Hostal Zaida	EC
Hostal Lis	EC	Hostal-Residencia Córdoba	SC
Hostal Lis II	EC		

EC El Centro **M** La Macarena **ON** Outer Neighborhoods **SC** Santa Cruz

SIGHTS

Sevilla has many beautiful sights, from Roman ruins and Gothic cathedrals to modern parks and riverside esplanades. While most visits tend to center around the amazing **Catedral** and **Alcázar,** there is much more to Sevilla than this clash of ideological architecture. The streets surrounding these central icons themselves are a narrow, winding wonderland, where *tapas* and *artesanía* dominate. The **Plaza de Toros de la Real Maestranza** is nestled along the riverbank, and serves as an ideal place to begin a scenic tour along the Guadalquivir. Heading south toward the **Torre del Oro,** you are just blocks from the garden oases that offer respite from the intensity of activity and heat that claims the central areas of the city. The **Jardines** behind the Alcázar are flanked by the **Jardines de Murillo,** and from there, it is a short jaunt to the stately **Plaza de España** and nearby **Parque de María Luisa.** Ventures inland yield encounters of the commercial kind in **El Centro,** and of the virginal kind in **La Macarena,** just northwest of El Centro.

ANDALUCÍA

🍴 FOOD

Sevilla is a city of *tapas;* locals spend their evenings relaxing and socializing over plates of *caracoles*, *cocido andaluz* (thick chickpea soup), *pisto* (tomato and eggplant hash), *espinacas con garbanzos*, and fresh seafood. The local favorite, *salmorejo* (a thicker, gazpacho-like soup, eaten with bread), is especially good. For those on a tighter budget, markets such as **Mercado del Arenal**, near the bullring on C. Pastor y Leandro, have fresh meat and produce (open M-Sa 9am-2pm). For a supermarket, try the mammoth one in the basement of **El Corte Inglés**, Pl. Duque de la Victoria (open M-Sa and first Su of each month 10am-10pm), or head to any one of the myriad smaller markets around the city such as **%Día** and **Super Sol**.

FOOD BY TYPE

TRADITIONAL SPANISH		**CUBAN**	
Restaurante El Baratillo/Casa Chari ❶	AT	🍴 Habanita Bar Restaurante ❷	EC
Café-Bar Campanario ❷	SC		
Restaurante Coello ❸	SC	**MIDDLE EASTERN**	
El Rinconcillo ❷	EC	Café-Bar Jerusalém ❶	AT
Ancha de la Feria ❶	M		
		PIZZA/ITALIAN	
DESSERT		San Marco ❷	SC
Histórico Horno, SA ❷	AT	La Mia Tana ❶	EC
GREEK		**BREAKFAST**	
Acropolis Taberna Griega ❶	AT	Café Cáceres ❶	SC

AT El Arenal & Triana **EC** El Centro **M** Macarena **SC** Santa Cruz

🎵 NIGHTLIFE

Sevilla's reputation for partying is tried and true. A typical night of *la marcha* (going out) begins with visits to several bars for *tapas* and *copas*, continues with dancing at *discotecas*, and culminates with an early morning breakfast of *churros con chocolate*. Most clubs don't get crowded until well after midnight; the real fun often starts after 3am. Popular bars can be found around **Calle Mateos Gago** near the cathedral, **Calle Adriano** by the bullring, and **Calle del Betis** across the river in Triana; several popular summertime clubs lie along the river near **Puente de la Barqueta**. Sevilla is also famous for its *botellón*, the (mostly student) tradition of getting drunk in massive crowds in plazas or at bars along the river to start the night. In the winter, the most popular places for *botellón* are in Pl. Alfalfa and Pl. del Salvador. In summer, the crowds sweep toward the river in hopes of a breeze, and even on "slow" nights, most *terrazas* stay open until 4am. During the school year, bars and clubs get packed regardless of the night; during the emptier summer months, it takes a bit more searching to find crowds on weeknights.

🎭 ENTERTAINMENT

The tourist office distributes *El Giraldillo*, a free monthly magazine with complete listings on music, art exhibits, theater, dance, fairs, and film.

THEATERS

Sevilla is a haven for the performing arts. The venerable **Teatro Lope de Vega** (☎954 59 08 53), near Parque de María Luisa, has long been the city's leading stage. Ask about scheduled events at the tourist office or check the bulletin board in the university lobby on C. San Fernando. **Sala la Herrería** and **Sala la Imperdible** put on avant-garde productions in Pl. San Antonio de Padua. (Both ☎954 38 82 19.) **Teatro de la Maestranza**, on the river between the Torre del Oro and the bullring, is a splendid concert hall accommodating orchestral performances, opera, and dance. (☎954 22 65 73. Box office open M-F 10am-2pm and 6-9pm.) On spring and summer evenings, neighborhood fairs are often accompanied by free **open-air concerts** in Santa Cruz and Triana; inquire at the tourist office for specific schedules and locations. **Cine Avenida**, C. Marqués de las Paradas, 15 (☎954 29 30 25), and **Corona Center**, (☎954 27 80 64), in the mall between C. Salado and C. Paraíso in Triana, screen original-language films, subtitled in Spanish. **Cines Warner Lusomundo**, Co. Comercial Plaza de Armas (☎902 23 33 43) shows American films dubbed in Spanish. **Cines Corona Center**, in the mall between C. Salado and C. Paraíso, screens subtitled films, often in English. (☎954 27 80 64. M-F €3, Sa-Su €3.50.) For more, look under "Cinema" in *El Giraldillo* or any local newspaper.

FLAMENCO

Flamenco, originally brought to Spain by the *gitanos* (Roma people), is at its best in Sevilla. Traditionally consisting of dance, guitar, and song, it expresses the passion and soul of the region. Rhythmic clapping, intricate fretwork on the guitar, throaty wailing, and rapid foot-tapping form a mesmerizing backdrop for the swirling dancers. *Flamenco* can be seen in either a *tablao*, where skilled professional dancers perform, or in *tabernas*, bars where locals merrily dance *sevillanas*. Both have merit, but for those on a budget the *tabernas* tend to be free. The tourist office provides a complete list of both *tablaos* and *tabernas*. Be sure to ask about student discounts when buying tickets for shows.

TABLAOS

Small and intimate **Los Gallos**, Pl. de Santa Cruz, 11, is probably the best tourist show in Sevilla. Buy tickets in advance at hostels or stores in Santa Cruz and arrive early. (☎954 21 69 81. Shows nightly 9 and 11:30pm. Cover €27.05, includes 1 drink.) Less expensive alternatives are the impressive 1hr. shows at the cultural center **⬛Casa de la Memoria Al-Andalus**, C. Ximénez de Enciso, 28. Ask at the tourist office or swing by their ticket office for a schedule of different themed performances. (☎/fax 954 56 06 70. *Flamenco* shows nightly at 9pm; very limited seating so buy tickets in advance. €11, students €9.) **El Arenal** is also a *tablao-restaurante*, so you can eat a meal while watching. (Shows nightly 9 and 11pm. Cover €29, includes 1 drink. Avoid the expensive dinner option.) **El Patio Sevillano**, Po. de Cristóbal Colón, 11, offers nightly performances at 7:30

THE LOCAL STORY

OF MOSQUITOES AND MOSQUES

Travelers have often been confused by the similarity of the words "mosquito" and "mosque" in Spanish. It only gets worse for the Andalusian tourist, with the terms *mezquita* and *moscuito* sounding almost identical. Legends have it that the word *mezquita* came from a phrase coined during *la Reconquista*: "We shall find the Moors where they gather (a mosque) and swat them like mosquitoes." Legends aside, linguists have ever been careful to point out the different roots of these similar words. *Mosque* comes from the French *mosquée*, which is in turn a borrowing from the Spanish *mezquita*, which comes from the Arab *mesgid* (literally, place of prostration or worship). *Mosquito*, however, is simply the addition of the Spanish diminutive "*ita*" to the Spanish word for fly—*mosca*, giving *mosquita*, or "little fly."

Perhaps you were among the lucky travelers who were blissfully unaware of the striking similarity of these words, and the potentially dangerous pitfalls of the language. But now that we mention it, it is rather confusing, isn't it? Aren't you glad we mentioned it?

and 10pm. (☎954 21 41 20. €27, includes 1 drink). **El Palacio Andaluz**, C. María Auxiliadora, 18, has a mixed *flamenco* and classical dance show. (☎954 53 47 20. Shows nightly at 10pm. Advance reservation or ticket purchase required. €27.50, includes 1 drink.) **Sol Café Cantante**, C. del Sol, 5, has 90min. shows of dancing, music, and singing. (☎954 22 51 65. Shows W-Sa 9pm. €18, students €11; includes 1 drink.) Though somewhat farther afield in Puerta Osario, **Las Brujas**, C. Gonzalo Bilbao, 10, is certainly worth the trek. (☎954 41 36 51. Shows daily 9:15 and 11:30pm. Cover €23, includes 1 drink; buy tickets in advance.)

TABERNAS

El Tamboril, Pl. de Santa Cruz, hosts a primarily middle-aged tourist crowd for midnight *canciones* and dancing. (☎954 56 15 90. Open daily June-Sept. 5pm-3am; Oct.-May noon-3am.) **La Carbonería**, C. Levies, 18, is a large bar complex with a courtyard popular with backpackers. Bar-filled **Calle del Betis**, across the river, hosts several other *tabernas:* **Lo Nuestro, El Rejoneo**, and **Taberna Flamenca Triana**.

FÚTBOL

Sevilla has two wildly popular pro teams that play at **Estadio Sánchez Pizjuán** (☎954 53 53 53) on Av. de Eduardo Dato. Buy tickets at the stadium; price and availability depend on the quality of the match-up. Even if you can't make it, the jerseyed crowds in the streets make the whole city feel like a stadium: **Real Betis** wears green and white, **Sevilla** white and red. Both teams struggle against the competitive Barcelona and Real Madrid clubs; over the last few years Real Betis has underachieved, but locals are optimistic for the coming years, particularly with 2002 World Cup star and Spanish national team member Joaquín on the field.

BULLFIGHTING

Sevilla's bullring, one of the most beautiful in Spain, hosts bullfights from *Semana Santa* through October. The cheapest place to buy tickets is at the ring on Po. Alcalde Marqués de Contadero. However, when there's a good *cartel* (line-up), the booths on C. las Sierpes, C. Velázquez, and Pl. de Toros might be the only source of advance tickets. Ticket prices, depending on the quality of both seat and matador, can run from €18 for a *grada de sol* (nosebleed seat in the sun) to €75 for a *barrera de sombra* (front-row seat in the shade). Scalpers usually add 20% to the ticket price. *Corridas de toros* (bullfights) and *novilladas* (apprentice bullfighters with younger bulls) are held on the 13 days around the *Feria de Abril* and into May, every Sunday April-June and September-October, more often during *Corpus Cristi* in June and early July, and during the *Feria de San Miguel* near the end of September. During July and August, *corridas* occur on occasional Thursdays at 9pm; check posters around town. Some of the most popular *sevillano* bullfighters include **El Juli, Joselito**, and **José Tomás**. (For current info and **ticket sales**, call ☎954 50 13 82. For more info on **bullfighting**, see p. 81.)

SHOPPING

Sevilla is a great place to find Andalusian crafts such as hand-embroidered silk and lace shawls and traditional *flamenco* wear, albeit often at somewhat inflated tourist prices. C. las Sierpes is in the center of the main shopping area. Its environs, including C. San Eloy, C. Velázquez, and C. Francos, offer a wide array of crafts, as well as modern clothing, shoe stores, and jewelry. In January and June, all the stores hold huge 🖊*rebajas* (sales), where everything is marked down 30-70%. A large, eclectic **flea market** is held Thursday 9am-2pm, extending from C. Feria to C. Regina in La Macarena.

◘ FESTIVALS

Sevilla swells with tourists during its *fiestas*, and with good reason: they are insanely fun. If you're in Spain during any of the major festivals, head straight to Sevilla—you won't regret it. If you can remember it, that is. Reserve a room weeks or months in advance, and expect to pay up to twice what you'd normally pay.

SEMANA SANTA. Sevilla's world-famous *Semana Santa* lasts from Palm Sunday to Easter Sunday (Apr. 13-20 in 2004). In each neighborhood of the city, thousands of penitents in hooded cassocks guide *pasos* (stunning, extravagant floats) through the streets, illuminated by hundreds of candles. The climax is Good Friday, when the entire city turns out for the procession along the bridges and through the oldest neighborhoods. Book rooms well in advance and expect to pay triple the usual price. The tourist office has a helpful booklet on where to eat and sleep during the week's festivities.

FERIA DE ABRIL. Two or three weeks after *Semana Santa* (Apr. 27-May 2 in 2004), the city rewards itself for its Lenten piety with the *Feria de Abril*. Begun as part of a 19th-century revolt against foreign influence, the *Feria* has grown into a massive celebration of all things Andalusian. Circuses, bullfights, and *flamenco* shows roar into the night in a showcase of local customs and camaraderie. A spectacular array of flowers and lanterns decorates over 1000 kiosks, tents, and pavilions, collectively called *casetas*. Each has the elements necessary for a rollicking time: small kitchen, bar, and dance floor. Locals stroll from one to the next, sharing drinks and food amid the lively music and dance. Most *casetas* are privately owned, and the only way to get invited is by making friends with the locals. There are a few large public *casetas* with drink and dancing though. Either way, people-watching from the sidelines can be almost as exciting, as costumed girls dance *sevillanas* and men parade on horseback through the streets. The city holds bullfights daily during the festival; buy tickets in advance. *(The fairgrounds are on the southern end of Los Remedios.)*

SANTA CRUZ

The area claims some of Sevilla's most well-known sights, and something amazing will distract you around every corner. Even if you forget exactly where you are, you'll remember every vivid inch of the neighborhood's streets and gardens.

◤ ACCOMMODATIONS

The narrow streets east of the cathedral around C. Santa María la Blanca are full of cheap hostels with virtually identical rooms. The neighborhood is overwhelmingly touristed, but its disorienting streets and shady plazas are all within a few minutes' walk of the cathedral, the Alcázar, and El Centro.

Pensión Vergara, C. Ximénez de Enciso, 11, 2nd fl. (☎954 21 56 68). Beautiful rooms of varying size with lace bedspreads, antique-style furniture, and a sitting room with a small book swap. All rooms have fans. Towels provided on request. Singles, doubles, triples, and quads €18 per person. ❷

Hostal Buen Dormir, C. Farnesio, 8 (☎954 21 06 82). Quilted bedspreads, tiled walls, and sunny rooms—all with A/C—make *hostal* "Good Sleep" one of the best deals in town. Rooftop terrace. Laundry €6. Singles €18; doubles €30, with shower €35, with bath €40; triples with shower €50, with bath €55. ❷

Hostal Dulces-Sueños, C. Puerta de la Carne, 21 (☎954 41 93 93). Brightly painted, comfortable rooms, some with A/C. Clean common baths. Rooftop terrace. Prices with *Let's Go:* singles €20; doubles €40, with bath €50; triple with bath €65. MC/V. ❷

Hostal Atenas, C. Caballerizas, 1 (☎954 21 80 47; fax 22 76 90). Slightly pricier than other options, but with good reason—all sunny, orange-painted rooms come with private baths and A/C. Singles €28.89; doubles €54.57; triples €69.55. MC/V. ❸

Hostal Bienvenido, C. Archeros, 14 (☎954 41 36 55). Simple but cheap. Five rooftop rooms surround a social patio; downstairs rooms overlook an inner atrium. Backpacker crowd. Singles €20; doubles €30-37; triples and quads €15-16 per person. ❷

Hostal-Residencia Córdoba, C. Farnesio, 12 (☎954 22 74 98). Immaculate and spacious air-conditioned rooms are worth the extra euros. A/C functions from 4pm-4am, 3pm-5am when the summer meltdown strikes. 3am curfew. Singles €27, with bath €33; doubles €41/€50. *Semana Santa* and *Feria* €36/€48/€56/€65. ❸

Hostal Goya, C. Mateos Gago, 31 (☎954 21 11 70). Hotel-like, but worth the splurge only if you get an outside-facing room; inner ones are dim. Spacious and sparkling clean rooms have A/C and private baths. June-Mar. singles €40; doubles €65; triples €91; quads €107. Apr.-May and *Semana Santa* €45/€75/€105/€123. MC/V. ❹

Hostal Sierpes, C. Corral del Rey, 22 (☎954 22 49 48; fax 21 21 07). Lace-canopied lobby and beautiful common spaces belie boring but clean rooms. All rooms with baths, many with A/C. Parking €12. Mar.-June and Aug.-Dec. singles €40; doubles €59; triples €77; quads €96. Holidays and festivals €65/€85/€111/€141. Jan.-Feb. and July €31/€43/€55/€67. ❹

Hostal-Residencia Monreal, C. Rodrigo Caro, 8 (☎954 21 41 66). Rooms with bath are spacious and beautiful; those without are basic. Ask for one overlooking the plaza. The downstairs cafe caters to backpackers (breakfast €2.50-4). Singles €20; doubles €40, with bath €60. MC/V. ❷

Pensión Cruces El Patio, C. Cruces, 10 (☎954 22 96 33 or 22 60 41). Cool, leafy courtyard, but disappointingly bare rooms. Singles €20; doubles €30, with bath €40; triples €45; quads €60. ❷

⬛ FOOD

Restaurants near the cathedral cater almost exclusively to tourists. Beware the unexceptional, omnipresent *menús* featuring *gazpacho* and *paella* for €7. Food quality and prices improve in the backstreet establishments between the cathedral and the river in El Arenal and along side streets in Santa Cruz.

San Marco, C. Mesón del Moro, 6 (☎954 21 43 90), several blocks from the cathedral. Amazing pizzas, pastas, and Italian desserts in an even more amazing setting—an 18th-century house with 17th-century Arab baths. Surprisingly affordable, and highly recommended by locals. Entrees €4.90-7.50. Open Tu-Su 1:15-4:30pm and 8:15pm-12:30am. MC/V. Other locations in equally impressive settings at C. Betis, 68 (☎28 03 10), and at C. Santo Domingo de la Calzada, 5 (☎58 33 43). ❷

Café-Bar Campanario, C. Mateos Gago, 8 (☎954 56 41 89). Mixes the best (and strongest) jugs of sangría around (half-liter €7.25, liter €9.65). *Tapas* €1.50-2, *raciones* €6-8.40. Open daily 11am-midnight. ❷

Café Cáceres, C. San José, 24 (☎954 21 51 31). The closest thing to a buffet-style breakfast in Sevilla. Choose from a spread of cheeses, jams, and countless condiments, fresh orange juice, and numerous omelets. *Desayuno de la casa* (orange juice, coffee, ham, eggs, and toast) €4.50. Open M-Sa 7:30am-8pm, Su 7:30am-4pm. ❶

Restaurante Coello, C. Doncella, 8 (☎954 42 10 82), on a tiny street off C. Santa María la Blanca. Dine in tablecloth style in the bright yellow interior or outside on the narrow cobblestone street. Although they have a relatively cheap *menú* (€8), you're better off splurging on their delicately prepared *a la carte* meat and fish entrees (€10-15). Appetizers €4-10. Open daily noon-midnight. MC/V. ❸

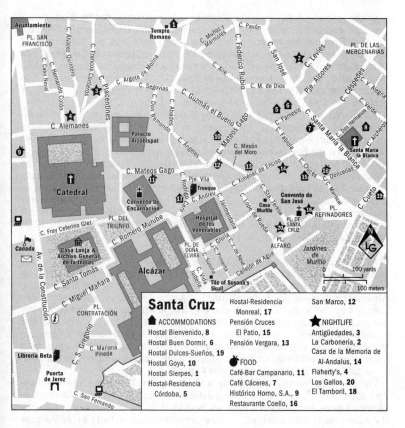

Santa Cruz

ACCOMMODATIONS
Hostal Bienvenido, **8**
Hostal Buen Dormir, **6**
Hostal Dulces-Sueños, **19**
Hostal Goya, **10**
Hostal Sierpes, **1**
Hostal-Residencia
  Córdoba, **5**
Hostal-Residencia
  Monreal, **17**
Pensión Cruces
  El Patio, **15**
Pensión Vergara, **13**

FOOD
Café-Bar Campanario, **11**
Café Cáceres, **7**
Histórico Horno, S.A., **9**
Restaurante Coello, **16**
San Marco, **12**

NIGHTLIFE
Antigüedades, **3**
La Carbonería, **2**
Casa de la Memoria de
  Al-Andalus, **14**
Flaherty's, **4**
Los Gallos, **20**
El Tamboril, **18**

🕲 SIGHTS

The tourist office has a detailed map of the winding alleys, wrought-iron gates, and courtyards of Santa Cruz. Its monuments form the most vivid images in the mosaic that is Sevilla and harken back to its history as the one-time *judería*.

▨ CATEDRAL. Legend has it that in 1401 the *reconquistadores* wished to demonstrate their religious fervor by constructing a church so great, they said, that "those who come after us will take us for madmen." With 44 individual chapels, the cathedral of Sevilla is the third largest in the world, after St. Peter's Basilica in Rome and St. Paul's Cathedral in London, and the biggest Gothic edifice ever constructed. Not surprisingly, it took more than a century to build.

In 1401, a 12th-century Almohad mosque was destroyed to clear space for the massive cathedral. All that remains is the **Patio de Los Naranjos,** where the faithful washed before prayer, the Puerta del Perdón entryway from C. Alemanes, and the famed **La Giralda** minaret, built in 1198. The tower and its twins in Marrakesh and Rabat are the oldest and longest-surviving Almohad minarets. There are 35 ramps inside leading to the tower's top that once allowed the *muezzin* to climb up on his horse for the call to prayer; today they enable tourists to take pictures.

In the center of the cathedral, the Renaissance-style **Capilla Real** stands opposite **choirstalls** made of mahogany recycled from a 19th-century Austrian railway. The **Retablo mayor,** one of the largest in the world, is a golden wall of intricately wrought saints and disciples. Nearby, the **Sepulcro de Cristóbal Colón** (Columbus's tomb) supposedly holds the explorer's remains, brought back to Sevilla after Cuba's independence in 1902 (the tomb had been located in Havana's cathedral). The black-and-gold pallbearers represent the eternally grateful monarchs of Castilla, León, Aragón, and Navarra.

Farther on and to the right stands the **Sacristía Mayor** (treasury), which holds gilded panels of Alfonso X el Sabio by Juan de Arefe, works by Ribera and Murillo, and a glittering *Corpus Cristi* icon, **La Custodia Processional.** A small, disembodied head of John the Baptist eyes visitors who enter the gift shop. It overlooks keys presented to the city of Sevilla by Jewish leaders after Fernando III ousted the Muslims in 1248. In the northwest corner of the cathedral lies the architecturally stunning **Sala de las Columnas.** Each year, restoration and maintenance expenses on the cathedral total over €3.8 million. *(☎ 954 21 49 71. Entrance by Pl. de la Virgen de los Reyes. Open M-Sa 11am-5pm, Su 2:30-6pm. Last entrance 1hr. before closing. €6, seniors and students €1.50, under 12 free; Su free. Mass held in the Capilla Real M-Sa 8:30, 10am, noon; Su 8:30, 10, 11am, noon, 1pm.)*

■**ALCÁZAR.** The oldest European palace still used as a private residence for royals, Sevilla's Alcázar is nothing short of magnificent. Like the Alhambra in Granada, the Alcázar has Moorish architecture and gardens, and although the Alhambra gets more press, the Alcázar is equally, if not more, impressive. Constructed by the Moors in the 7th century, the palace was embellished greatly during the 15th century and now displays an interesting mix of Moorish and Christian architecture, seen most prominently in the *mudéjar* style of many of the arches, tiles, and ceilings. Fernando and Isabel are the palace's most well-known former residents; Carlos V also lived here, marrying his cousin Isabel of Portugal in the incestuous **Salón Techo Carlos V.**

Visitors enter through the **Patio de la Montería,** directly across from the intricate Almohad facade of the Moorish palace. Through the archway lie the Arabic residences, including the **Patio del Yeso** used by Moorish governors before the palace itself was even built, and the exquisitely carved **Patio de las Muñecas** (Patio of the Dolls), so named because of miniature faces carved into the bottom of one of the room's pillars. Originally a courtyard, the Patio de las Muñecas served as a private area for Moorish kings, with an escape path (no longer in existence) so that in case of an attack the king would not have to cross the open space. Of the Christian additions, the most notable is the **Patio de las Doncellas** (Patio of the Maids). Court life in the Alcázar revolved around this colonnaded quadrangle, which is encircled by archways adorned with glistening tilework. The golden-domed **Salón de los Embajadores** (Ambassadors' Room) is allegedly the site where Fernando and Isabel welcomed Columbus back from the New World. Several beautiful silk tapestries adorn the walls of the appropriately named **Sala de Tapices.** The son of Fernando and Isabel, Prince Juan, was born in the red-and-blue tiled **Cuarto del Príncipe;** the room was named for him after his untimely death, supposedly of a broken heart.

The **private residences** upstairs, the official home of the king and queen of Spain, and where they stay when they visit Sevilla, have been renovated and redecorated throughout the centuries; most of the furniture today dates from the 18th and 19th centuries. These residences are accessible only by 25min. guided tours (see info below). Peaceful **gardens** stretch from the residential quarters in all directions. *(Pl. del Triunfo, 7. ☎ 954 50 23 23. Open Tu-Sa 9:30am-7pm, Su 9:30am-5pm. €5; students, handicapped, residents, over 65, and under 16 free. Tours of the upper palace living quarters every*

30min. June-July 10am-1:30pm, Aug.-May 10am-1:30pm and 3:30-5:30pm; €3. Fifteen people max. per tour, so buy tickets in advance. Worthwhile audioguides give anecdotes, historical info, and a clearly marked route through the complex; €3.)

CASA LONJA. Between the cathedral and the Alcázar stands the 16th-century Casa Lonja, built by Felipe II as a *casa de contratación* (commercial exchange) for trade with the Americas. In 1785, Carlos III converted the building into the **Archivo General de las Índias.** Today it contains a collection of over 44,000 documents relating to the discovery and conquest of the New World. Among its books is Juan Bautista Muñoz's "definitive" history of the conquest, commissioned by Carlos III. Other highlights include Juan de la Costa's wildly inaccurate *Mapa Mundi* (map of the world), letters from Columbus to Fernando and Isabel, and a 1590 letter from Cervantes (pre-*Don Quijote*) requesting employment in America. At the time of publication, the building was closed for a 30-month, €7.3 million renovation, but the facade itself is worth a look. (☎954 21 12 34. *Full access to documents is limited to scholars.)*

TEMPLO ROMANO. A few blocks southeast of Pl. del Salvador on C. Mármoles stand the excavated ruins of a Roman temple. The remaining columns rise 15m from below street level and offer a glimpse of the literal depth of Sevilla's history; river sediment that accumulated after the construction of the temple caused the ground level to rise.

OTHER SIGHTS. Fernando III forced Jews in flight from the Toledo Inquisition to live here, and it thrived as a lively Jewish quarter. On **Calle Susona,** the ceramic tile of a skull rests above a door, evoking the tale of beautiful Susona, a Jewish girl who fell in love with a Christian knight. When Susona learned that her father and friends planned to kill several inquisitors, including the knight, she warned her lover. A bloody reprisal was unleashed on the Jewish ghetto, during which Susona's entire family was slaughtered. She requested that her skull be placed above the doorway in atonement for her betrayal, and there it supposedly remained until the 18th century. C. Susona leads to **Plaza Doña Elvira,** where *sevillano* Lope de Rueda's works, precursors to the dramas of Spain's Golden Age, were staged. A turn down C. Gloria leads to the 17th-century **Hospital de los Venerables,** a hospital-church adorned with art from the *Sevillana* School. (☎954 56 26 96. *Open daily for guided visits 10am-2pm and 4-8pm. €3.60, students and over 65 €1.80.)*

    Calle Lope de Rueda, off C. Ximénez de Enciso, is graced with two noble mansions, beyond which lies the charming and fragrant **Plaza de Santa Cruz,** built on the former site of the neighborhood's main synagogue. South of the plaza are the **Jardines de Murillo,** a shady expanse of shrubbery and benches. The **Convento de San José** cherishes a cloak and portrait of Santa Teresa de Ávila. (*C. Santa Teresa, off Pl. de Santa Cruz. Open daily 9-11am. Free.*) The church in Pl. de Santa Cruz houses the grave of artist Bartoloméo Murillo, who died in what is now known as the **Casa Murillo** after falling from a scaffold while painting frescoes in Cádiz's Iglesia de los Capuchinos. The house has information on Murillo's life and work. (*C. Santa Teresa, 8.* ☎954 22 12 72. *Open M-F 8am-3pm and 4-8pm. Free.*) **Iglesia de Santa María la Blanca** was built in 1391 on the foundation of a synagogue. It features red marble columns, Baroque plasterwork, and Murillo's *Last Supper.* (*C. Santa María la Blanca. Open M-Sa 10-11am and 6:30-8pm, Su 9:30am-2pm and 6:30-8pm. Free.)*

◪ NIGHTLIFE

▨ **La Carbonería,** C. Levies, 18 (☎954 21 44 60). Don't let the drab entrance hall deter you—beyond lies a gigantic, popular bar with free live *flamenco* and an outdoor patio replete with banana trees and picnic tables. *Fla*menco nightly at midnight and occasional theatrical performances earlier. Live blues Sa 11pm. *Tapas* (€1.50-2) served until late. Beer €1.50. Mixed drinks €4.50. Sangría pitchers €8. Open July-Aug. M-Sa 8pm-4am, Su 8pm-2:30am; Sept.-May M-Sa 8pm-4am, Su 7pm-3am.

Terraza Chile, Po. de las Delicias. A calm, peaceful *terraza* by day, Chile morphs into a packed dance club and bar by night, with loud salsa and pop to keep this small breezy dance club packed and pounding throughout the early morning hours. Young *sevillano* professionals mingle with Euro-chic American exchange students. Beer €1.50. Mixed drinks €5. Open June-Sept. daily 8am-5am; Oct.-May Th-Sa 8pm-5am.

Flaherty's, C. Alemanes, 7 (☎954 21 04 51). Gigantic, sprawling Irish pub, and the most popular bar in the city center among tourists, expats, and students foreign and local. Friendly atmosphere for travelers on their own. 4 beers on tap, including Guinness. Serves international food daily until 11:30pm (entrees and sandwiches €5-10). Beer €2. Mixed drinks €4.60. Open daily 11am-3am.

Antigüedades, C. Argote de Molina, 40. This mellow bar with small tables plays jazzy soul for a mid-20s and up crowd. Creative redecorating every few months. Beer €1.50. Mixed drinks €4. Open Su-Th 8pm-3am, F-Sa 9pm-4am.

EL CENTRO

El Centro, a mess of narrow streets radiating from Pl. de la Encarnación and Pl. Duque de la Victoria, is a bustling shopping district during the day, but most streets are deserted at night. The area near Pl. Alfalfa, a prime *tapas* bar location packed day and night, is a bit more lively.

ACCOMMODATIONS

Espiau, C. Pérez Galdós, 1A (☎954 21 06 82). A friendly Spanish and British couple keep the most beautiful *hostal* in town. Rooms with high ceilings, full-length tiled mirrors, and unique decorations surround a huge, sunny living room. Singles €22; doubles €42, with bath €48; triples €54. Discounts for longer stays. ❷

Hostal Lis, C. Escarpín, 10 (☎954 21 30 88). Cozy, blue-and-yellow tiled rooms in a traditional *sevillana* house. Owner is currently adding A/C to all rooms and a rooftop terrace "specifically for sunbathing." Free Internet access. Laundry €5 for 5kg. All rooms have fans. Singles with shower €21; doubles with bath used as singles €30; doubles with bath €42; triples with bath €63. MC/V. ❷

Hostal La Gloria, C. San Eloy, 58, 2nd fl. (☎954 22 26 73), at the end of a lively shopping street. Faded white rooms, but one of the best deals in town. Singles €18; doubles €30, with bath €36; limited triples €45. ❷

Hostal Lis II, C. Clavide, 5 (☎954 56 02 28). Smack in the middle of the main shopping zone, but marginally pricy for what you get. Pleasant but simple rooms all have fans. Internet €1.20 per 30min., €1.80 per hr. Singles €24.10; doubles €37.85, with bath €44.70; triples €58.50; quads €72.25. ❷

Hotel Zaida, C. San Roque, 26 (☎954 21 36 12; fax 21 88 10; www.ahsevilla.com). Hotel-sized lobby with wicker furniture disguises simple rooms with bath, TV, and A/C. Singles €36.50; doubles €55. *Semana Santa* and *Feria* €51.50/€109.50. ❹

FOOD

Packed with shoppers by day and young people by night, this area is full of unassuming restaurants and *tapas* bars. Streets surrounding **Plaza Alfalfa** are home to endless local restaurants serving *comida típica;* it's also a great place to look for the best international cuisine this side of the river.

■ **Habanita Bar Restaurante,** C. Golfo, 3 (☎606 71 64 56; www.andalunet.com/habanita). Popular cafe serving Cuban fare, pastas, salads, and Caribbean drinks. Warm orange walls and Cuban jazz grace the indoor dining room, while outdoor seating provides cool breezes. Vegetarian and vegan options. Meals €4.80-9.95. Open daily 12:30-4:30pm and 8pm-12:30am; closed Su night. MC/V. ❷

La Mia Tana, C. Pérez Galdós, 24 (☎954 22 68 97). So good you can smell the pizza from two blocks away. Checkered tablecloths and rustic interior. Unbelievably affordable. Huge variety of pizzas (€3.60-4.95 for a small; €8.50-11.75 large), pastas (€4), and other assorted non-Italian specialties like *empanadas* and *kebabs* (€3.50-4.50). Open daily 1-4:30pm and 8pm-2am. ❶

El Rinconcillo, C. Gerona, 40 (☎954 22 31 83). Founded in 1670 and among the oldest in town, this *bodega* is the epitome of local hangouts, teeming with gray-haired men deep in conversation. Sip *cerveza* and savor *olivas* on top of discarded Tío Pepe barrels. *Tapas* €1.25-2. *Raciones* €4-10. Open daily 1pm-2am. AmEx/MC/V. ❷

🇬 SIGHTS

■ **MUSEO PROVINCIAL DE BELLAS ARTES.** Cobbled together from decommissioned convents in the mid-1800s, this museum contains Spain's finest collection of works by painters of the *Sevillana* School, most notably Murillo, Valdés Leal, and Zurbarán, as well as El Greco and Dutch master Jan Breughel. Although the art (displayed more or less chronologically as well as thematically) is heavily biased toward religious themes, later works include some landscape paintings and portraits depicting Sevilla, its environs, and residents. The actual building itself, as well as its many tiny courtyards, is as impressive as the art inside. *(Pl. del Museo, 9.* ☎ *954 22 07 90. Open Tu 3-8pm, W-Sa 9am-8pm, Su 9am-2pm. €1.50, EU citizens free.)*

CONVENTO DE SANTA INÉS. The founder of Convento de Santa Inés, as legend has it, was pursued so insistently by King Pedro the Cruel that she disfigured her face with boiling oil so he would leave her alone. Cooking liquids are used more positively today—the cloistered nuns sell puff pastries and coffee cakes through the courtyard's revolving window. *(C. María Coronel. Sweets €2.50-3.60, sold M-Sa 9am-1pm and 4-7pm.)*

LAS SIERPES & THE ARISTOCRATIC QUARTER. Originating from Pl. San Francisco, **Calle las Sierpes** cuts through the Aristocratic Quarter. At the beginning of this pedestrian street lined with shoe stores, fan shops, and chic boutiques, a plaque marks the spot where the royal prison once loomed. Some scholars believe Cervantes began writing *Don Quijote* here.

CASA DE PILATOS. Inhabited continuously by Spanish aristocrats since the 15th century, this private residence has only recently been opened to the bourgeois public, although sections are still used as a private home. On the ground floor, Roman artifacts and tropical gardens coexist in Mudéjar patios. The second floor, features rooms decorated over the centuries with oil portraits, sculptures, painted ceilings, and tapestries. *(Pl. Pilatos, 1.* ☎ *954 22 52 98. Open daily 9am-7pm. Guided tours every 30min. 10am-6:30pm. €5 ground level only, €8 ground level and upper chambers.)*

IGLESIA DEL SALVADOR. Fronted by a Montañés sculpture, this 17th-century church was built on the foundations of the city's main mosque. The courtyard and the belfry's base are remnants of the old building. As grandiose as a cathedral, the church is adorned with exceptional Baroque *retablos*, sculptures, and paintings, including Montañés's *Jesús de la pasión*. As of publication, the church was closed for renovations; check the sign on the door to see if it has reopened. *(Pl. del Salvador, 1 block from C. las Sierpes.)*

ANDALUCÍA

OTHER SIGHTS. The **Ayuntamiento** has 16th-century Gothic and Renaissance interior halls, a richly decorated domed ceiling, and a Plateresque facade. Impressive artwork graces many of the walls, and art exhibitions take place frequently; check with the tourist office for information. *(Pl. San Francisco, enter from Pl. Nueva. ☎954 59 01 01. Open Sept.-June Tu-Th 5:30-6:30pm. Free. Passport or other official documentation required.)* The **Iglesia de la Anunciación** features a pantheon honoring illustrious *sevillanos*, including poet Gustavo Adolfo Bécquer. *(Pl. de la Encarnación, enter on C. Laraña. Open daily 9am-1pm. Mass M-Sa noon, Su 12:30pm; Th, Su also 8:30pm. Free.)*

🎭 NIGHTLIFE

🏳️ **Isbiliyya,** Po. de Cristóbal Colón, 2 (☎954 21 04 60). Popular riverfront gay, lesbian, and straight bar with outdoor seating and an ample dance floor. Plays percussion-filled dance music and hosts drag performances Tu, Th, and Su (approx. 1:30am). Beer €2-2.50. Mixed drinks €5. Open daily 8pm-6am.

El Capote, C. Arjona and C. de los Reyes Católicos. A popular outdoor bar full of tables overlooking the river. Live music performances in summer. Experience *botellón* as you head toward the river past young *sevillanos* swigging *cuba libres.* Open June-Sept. 15 daily noon-4am.

LA MACARENA

The area north of El Centro is quiet, residential, and much less touristed than the rest of the city. Some of Sevilla's best deals lie amidst the centuries-old churches that grace the neighborhood, all within a 20min. walk of El Centro (the cathedral is at least a 30min. walk).

🏨 🍴 ACCOMMODATIONS & FOOD

🏨 **Hostal Macarena,** C. de San Luis, 91 (☎954 37 01 41). Curtains, tiles, wooden furniture, and quilted bedspreads make Macarena's rooms homey and welcoming. All rooms with A/C. Singles €20; doubles €30, with bath €40; triples €51. MC/V. ❷

Hostal Alameda, Alameda de Hércules, 31 (☎954 90 01 91; fax 90 22 48). Sterile, hotel-like rooms all have bath and A/C. Singles €20; doubles €40. MC/V. ❷

Ancha de la Feria, C. Feria, 61 (☎954 90 97 45). Snack on delicious homemade *tapas* (€1.50-2; *raciones* €4 and up) in this bright and airy local bar/restaurant. Old sherry barrels line the walls and ceiling. Great *menú del día* (€5.80), served afternoons only. Open Tu-Sa 9am-4pm and 9pm-1am, Su 9am-4pm. ❶

👁 SIGHTS

La Macarena is the virgin of the city and namesake of an enchanting church and neighborhood northwest of El Centro.

CONVENTO DE SANTA PAULA. Convento de Santa Paula includes a church with Gothic, Mudéjar, and Renaissance elements, a magnificent ceiling, and Montañés sculptures. *(Pl. Santa Paula. ☎954 53 63 30. Open Tu-Su 10:30am-12:30pm and 4:30-6:30pm.)* The **museum** has religious sculptures and paintings including Ribera's *St. Jerome.* Nuns peddle scrumptious 🍯homemade marmalade and angel hair pastries. Knock if the door is closed. *(Pl. Santa Paula, 11. Open Tu-Su 10am-1pm and 4:30-6:30pm. Museum €2; marmalades €2.70 for 300g.)*

La Macarena

▲ ACCOMMODATIONS
Hostal Alameda, **5**
Hostal Macarena, **4**

◗ FOOD
Ancha de la Feria, **6**

★ NIGHTLIFE
Coliseum, **1**
Palenque, **2**
Tribal, **3**

CHURCHES. A stretch of **murallas** created in the 12th century runs between Pta. Macarena and Pta. Córdoba on Ronda de Capuchinos. Flanking the west end of the walls, the **Basílica Macarena** houses the venerated image of *La Virgen de la Macarena*, who is borne through the streets at the climax of the *Semana Santa* processions. A **treasury** glitters with the virgin's jewels and other finery. *(C. Béquer, 1. ☎ 954 90 18 00. Basilica open M-Sa 9am-2pm and 5-9pm, Su 9:30am-2pm and 5-9pm. Free. Mass M-F 9, 11:30am, 8, 8:30pm; Sa 9am and 8pm; Su 10:30am, 12:30, 8pm. Treasury open daily 9:30am-2pm and 5-8pm. €3, students and over 65 €1.50; Sa free.)* Opposite the belfry of the Iglesia de San Marcos rises **Iglesia de Santa Isabel,** featuring an altarpiece by Montañés. Nearby stands the exuberantly Baroque **Iglesia de San Luis,** crowned by octagonal glazed-tile domes. The site of the church was the endpoint of a 12-step prayer route based on the ascent to Golgotha. *(C. San Luis. ☎ 954 55 02 07. Open Tu-Th 9am-2pm, F-Sa 9am-2pm and 5-8pm.)* Toward the river is **Iglesia de San Lorenzo y Jesús del Gran Poder,** with Montañés's remarkably lifelike sculpture *El Cristo del gran poder.* Worshipers kiss Jesus's ankle. *(Pl. San Lorenzo. ☎ 954 91 56 86. Open M-Th 8am-1:30pm and 6-9pm, F 7:30am-10pm, Sa-Su 8am-2pm and 6-9pm. Free.)*

OTHER SIGHTS. A large garden beyond the *murallas* and the basilica leads to the **Hospital de las Cinco Llagas,** a spectacular Renaissance building recently renovated to host the Andalusian parliament. Thursday mornings from 9am to 2pm a large **flea market** is held along C. la Feria.

◐ NIGHTLIFE

The area near Pte. de la Barqueta is *the* place to go dancing during summer, as all *sevillanos* in the know can attest. The near side of the river features several combination *terraza*/discos, while the far side hosts the more rowdy all-out clubbing scene. From La Macarena, follow C. Resolana to C. Nueva Torneo, which runs by Pte. de la Barqueta. (The A2 night bus runs at midnight, 1, and 2am from Pl. Nueva; ask to be let off near Pte. de la Barqueta. Taxi from Pl. Nueva should cost around €5.)

■ **Palenque,** Av. Blas Pascal, on the grounds of Cartuja '93. Cross Pte. de la Barqueta, turn left and follow C. Materatico Rey Pastor to the intersection. Turn left again and look for the entrance on the right. Gigantic dance club, complete with two dance floors, two musical choices, and a small ice skating rink (€3, including skate rental). More casual "funky" hip-hop night Th, popular with foreigners. F-Sa dress to impress or you'll be turned away at the door. Mainly *sevillano* university crowd. Beer €3. Mixed drinks €5. Fa-Sa cover €7, Th free. Open in summer June-Sept. Th-Sa midnight-7am.

Tribal, next to Pte. de la Barqueta. Popular *discoteca* playing American hip-hop and Latin favorites. Outdoor patio overlooking the river. W hip-hop nights are the most popular with backpacker crowd. Beer €3.50. Mixed drinks €5.50. No cover before 1am. After 1am cover €6-10, includes 1 drink. Open W-Sa 10pm-6am.

Coliseum, across from Tribal. A trendy, chill cross between a summer *terraza* and a disco. Upscale 20-somethings sip drinks at tables overlooking the river or crowd the small dance floor. Beer €3. Mixed drinks €5.50. Cover €7, includes 1 drink; look for free admission coupons from promoters in town. Open May-Sept. W-Su 10pm-late.

EL ARENAL & TRIANA

Immortalized by *Siglo de Oro* writers Lope de Vega, Francisco de Quevedo, and Miguel de Cervantes, Triana was Sevilla's chaotic 16th- and 17th-century mariners' district. Today, this neighborhood on the far side of the river is home to many of Sevilla's best ethnic restaurants. Sushi bars and Mexican food are as common as *tapas*. Avoid overpriced C. del Betis and plunge down less expensive side streets. *Tapas* bars cluster around **Plaza San Martín** and along **Calle San Jacinto,** the neighborhood's northern border. El Arenal was once a stretch of sand by the harbor on the opposite bank, exposed when the river was diverted to its present course.

◖ FOOD

■ **Restaurante-Bar El Baratillo/Casa Chari,** C. Pavía, 12 (☎954 22 96 51). A backpacker and local favorite; the hospitable owner will help you practice your Spanish. Ask 1hr. in advance for the tour-de-force: homemade *paella* (vegetarian options available) with a jar of wine, beer, or sangría (€18 for 2 people). *Menú* €4-9. Open M-F 10am-10pm, Sa 10am-5pm; open later when busy. ❶

Histórico Horno, SA, Av. de la Constitución, 16 (☎954 22 18 19). Heavenly pastries, cookies, ice cream, and cakes will satisfy any sugar craving. Great prepared foods by the kg. Enjoy your delicacy in air-conditioned bliss at one of the small tables or have it *para llevar* (to go). Open M-Sa 7:30am-11pm, Su 9am-11pm. MC/V. ❷

Acropolis Taberna Griega, C. Rosario Vega, 10 (☎954 28 46 85). This small restaurant serves delicious Greek food, and vegetarian options sprout up all over the menu. Very popular with foreign students and locals, so reserve ahead for the busy weekends. Entrees and appetizers €2.50-4. Open M 8:30-11:30pm, Tu-Th 1:30-3:30pm and 8:30-11:30pm, F-Sa 1:30-3:30pm and 8:30-midnight. Closed Aug. MC/V. ❶

Café-Bar Jerusalém, C. Salado, 6. Neighborhood *kebab* bar with chicken, lamb, pork, and cheese *schwarmas* (€3-4.50). Open Su-Th 8pm-2am, F-Sa 8pm-3am. AmEx/V. ●

☉ SIGHTS

The inviting riverside esplanade Po. Alcalde Marqués de Contadero stretches along the banks of the Guadalquivir from the base of the Torre del Oro. Bridge-heavy **boat tours** of Sevilla leave from in front of the tower (1hr., €4.20).

PLAZA DE TOROS DE LA REAL MAESTRANZA. Bullfighting has for centuries been a central aspect of life in Sevilla, evidenced by the city's beautiful and world-renowned Plaza de Toros. Construction began in 1761 and took over 120 years to finish. Home to one of the two great bullfighting schools (the other is in **Ronda,** see p. 303), the plaza fills to capacity (13,800) for the 13 *corridas* of the *Feria de Abril* as well as for weekly fights. Multilingual tours take visitors through a small but informative museum, as well as behind the ring to the chapel where *matadores* pray before fights, and the medical emergency room used when their prayers go unanswered. (☎ 954 22 45 77. Open on non-bullfight days 9:30am-7pm; on bullfight days 9:30am-3pm. Tours in English and Spanish every 20min. €4. See **bullfights,** p. 238, for tickets.)

HOSPITAL DE LA CARIDAD. A 17th-century complex of arcaded courtyards, this hospital was founded by Don Miguel de Mañara, believed to be the model for legendary *sevillano* Don Juan. This notorious playboy converted to a life of piety and charity after allegedly stumbling out of an orgy into his own funeral cortège. Don Miguel's body rests inside the crypt of the **Iglesia de San Jorge,** part of the hospital. The church's walls display paintings and frescos by Valdés Leal and Murillo, who couldn't refrain from holding his nose when he saw Leal's morbid *Finis Gloria Mundi,* which depicts corpses of a peasant, a bishop, and a king beneath an apocalyptic rendition of Justice and the Seven Deadly Sins. (C. Temprado. ☎ 954 22 32 32. Open M-Sa 9am-1:30pm and 3:30-7:30pm, Su 9am-1pm. €3.)

TORRE DEL ORO. The 12-sided Torre del Oro (Gold Tower), built by the Almohads in the early 13th century, overlooks the river from Po. de Cristóbal Colón. Today, a tiny yellow dome is all that remains of the glistening golden tiles that once covered the entire tower. Inside is the **Museo Náutico,** a storehouse of naval relics with illustrations of Sevilla as a bustling 17th-century port. (☎ 954 22 24 19. Open Sept.-July Tu-F 10am-2pm, Sa-Su 11am-2pm. €1, Tu free.) On the far bank of the river, the **Torre de la Plata** (Silver Tower) used to be connected to the Torre de Oro by underwater chains designed to protect the city from river-borne trespassers. With old-fashioned piracy no longer a concern, the Torre de la Plata has since been absorbed by the modern version: a bank building.

OTHER SIGHTS. The **Capilla de los Marineros** in Triana was constructed in the 18th century to worship the Esperanza de Triana, who, along with the Virgin Mary and the Macarena, is one of the most adored figures of Sevilla. (C. de la Pureza, 53. ☎ 954 33 26 45. Open M-Sa 9am-1pm and 5:30-9pm. Free.) One block farther inland, midway between Puente de Isabel II and Puente de San Telmo, stands the **Iglesia de Santa Ana,** Sevilla's oldest church and the focal point of the exuberant *fiestas* that take over the area in July. (C. Pelay Correa. Open M and W 7:30-8:30pm.) The terraced riverside promenade **Calle del Betis** is an ideal spot from which to view Sevilla's skyline.

ANDALUCÍA

■ **NIGHTLIFE**

Fundición, C. del Betis, 49-50. The most popular bar among American exchange students; packed during the school year, empty in summer. American music and decor fill the huge interior. Beer €2.50. Mixed drinks €5. Open Sept.-July 14 M-Sa 10pm-5am.

Catedral, Cuesta del Rosario, 12 (☎630 61 55 02). Underground disco with a metal, stone, and wood decor. No cover for women and those with coupons (available in stores, restaurants, and hostels). Cover for men €6, includes 1 mixed drink or 2 beers. Open Sept.-June W-Sa midnight-6am.

OUTER NEIGHBORHOODS

NEAR ESTACIÓN PLAZA DE ARMAS

Several hostels line C. Gravina, parallel to C. Marqués de las Paradas two blocks from the station. Hostels here tend to be cheaper than those in other neighborhoods and are convenient for exploring El Centro (10min.) and C. del Betis and Triana on the west bank of the river (10-15min.). Be prepared to schlep at least 20-30min. to the cathedral and the sight-filled Santa Cruz neighborhood.

Hostal Arizona, C. Pedro del Toro, 14 (☎954 21 60 42). Deals on balconied rooms. Mar.-Oct. singles €20; doubles €30, with bath €36. Nov.-Apr. €15/€30/€36. ❷

Hostal Río Sol, C. Marqués de las Paradas, 25 (☎954 22 90 38). Circular staircase leads to clean rooms within your budget. Singles €15, with bath €21; doubles with bath, TV, and A/C €42. MC/V. ❷

Hostal Paris, C. San Pedro Mártir, 14 (☎954 22 98 61 or 21 96 45; fax 21 96 45). Comfortable rooms have baths, A/C, phone, and TV. Mar.-Oct. singles €38.50; doubles €53.50. Nov.-Feb. €32.10/€48.40. AmEx/MC/V. ❸

Hostal Romero, C. Gravina, 34 (☎954 21 13 53). Friendly owners run an eclectic and homey *hostal* with simple, clean, and cheap rooms. Singles €20; doubles €30, with bath €40; triples €60. ❷

Sevilla Youth Hostel (HI), C. Isaac Peral, 2 (☎954 61 31 50; fax 61 31 58; reservas@inturjoven.junta-andalucia.es). Take bus #34 across from the tourist office near the cathedral; the 5th stop is behind the hostel. Isolated and difficult to find. Taxi from the cathedral approx. €5. A/C. Many private baths. Breakfast included. Doubles, triples, and quads. Dorms Mar.-Oct. €12.90, 26+ €17.25; Nov.-Feb. €10.90/€15.20. Non-members can pay an additional €3 a night for 6 nights to become members. ❶

Camping: Camping Sevilla, Ctra. Madrid-Cádiz, km 534 (☎954 51 43 79), near the airport. Take bus #70 (stops 800m away at Parque Alcosa) from Prado de San Sebastián. Hot showers, supermarket, and pool. €3 per person; €3 per car; €2.50 per tent. ❶

Club de Campo, C. de la Libertad, 13, Ctra. Sevilla-Dos Hermanas (☎954 72 02 50), 8km out of town. Los Amarillos buses leave from C. Infante Carlos de Borbón, at the back of Prado San Sebastián, to Dos Hermanas (every 45min., €0.75). Lots of grass and a pool. €3.40 per person; €3 per child; €3.40 per car; €3.40 per tent. ❶

PLAZA DE ESPAÑA

The twin spires of Plaza de España tower above the city skyline. Designed by Aníbal González, one of Sevilla's most prominent 20th-century architects, the building spans more than 200m. Horse-drawn carriages clatter in front of the plaza and rowboats can be rented to navigate its narrow moat. Mosaics depicting every provincial capital in Spain line the crumbling colonnade, and above them balconies offer a beautiful view of the surrounding gardens. The nearby **Parque de María Luisa** is a reminder of Sevilla's 1929 plans for an Ibero-American world fair. *(Adjacent to Pl. de España. Open daily 8am-10pm.)*

☒ DAYTRIPS FROM SEVILLA

OSUNA

Trains from Sevilla (1hr., 6 per day 7:30am-6:35pm, €6.35). Empresa Dipasa/Linesur (☎954 98 82 22) runs buses to and from Sevilla's Estación Prado de San Sebastián (1½hr., 5-11 per day 6:15am-7:40pm, €5.66).

Julius Caesar founded Osuna (pop. 17,500), naming it after the *osos* (bears) that once lumbered about its hills. Visitors today come for its myriad churches and convents and tranquil, intimate feel. Most sights are found on the hill which rises above town; the tourist office has good maps with highlighted walking tours. The **Colegiata de Santa María de la Asunción,** C. Callejón de las Descalzas, was commissioned by the Dukes of Osuna in the Renaissance style and now houses the **Museo de Arte Sacro Panteón Ducal.** The Colegiata contains a spectacular array of paintings, including religious artifacts and five Riberas. (From Pl. Mayor, walk to the adjacent Pl. Duquesa Osuna and then uphill to Pl. de la Encarnación; knock to enter. ☎954 81 04 44. Mandatory guided tours. Open May-Sept. Tu-Su 10am-1:30pm and 4-6pm; Oct.-Apr. Tu-Su 10am-1:30pm and 3:30-6:30pm. €2.) On the right side of the church sits the university and ☒**Convento de la Encarnación,** Pl. de la Encarnación, 2, a Baroque church founded by the Duke of Osuna in 1626 and lavishly decorated in the 18th century. A resident nun will show you room upon room of polychromed wooden sculptures, silver crucifixes, painted tiles, and handmade Christ-doll clothes. Make sure to knock and wait until the previous tour group finishes. (☎954 81 11 21. Open May-Sept. Tu-Sa 10:30am-1:30pm and 4-7pm, Su 10:30am-1:30pm; Oct.-Apr. Tu-Su 10:30am-1:30pm. €2. Mass daily 8:30am. Free.)

To reach Pl. Mayor from the **train station** (☎/fax 954 81 03 08; open 7am-8pm), walk up Av. de la Estación, curving right on C. Mancilla. At Pl. Salitre, turn left on C. Carmen and then right on C. Sevilla, which leads into the plaza. The **bus station** is on Av. de la Constitución. (Ticket office open M-F 6:30-9am, 10am-2:30pm, 3:15-6pm, and 7-8pm; Sa 7:30-9am and 10:30am-2pm; Su 3-4pm and 7-8pm.) To get to Pl. Mayor from the bus station, exit right and walk downhill on C. Santa Ana past Pl. Santa Rita; continue on Av. Arjona until the plaza. The **tourist office** is in Pl. Mayor. (☎954 81 57 32. Open M-Sa 9am-2pm.)

ITÁLICA

Take the Empresa Casal bus (☎954 41 06 58) toward Santiponce from the Pl. de Armas bus station, platform 34. Get off at the last stop (30min.; M-Sa every 30min. 6:30am-midnight, Su every hr., on the ½hr. 7:30am-midnight; €0.94). Pay onboard. The entrance to the ruins is located next to the gas station where the bus drops you. When returning to Sevilla, wait at the bus sign in front of the entrance to Itálica; the bus will turn around in the neighboring gas station.

Just 9km northwest of Sevilla and right outside the village of **Santiponce** (pop. 7000) lie the excavated ruins of Itálica, the first important Roman settlement in Iberia. The birthplace of emperors Trajan (AD 53) and Hadrian (AD 76), Itálica was founded in 206 BC as a settlement for soldiers wounded in the Battle of Illipa, and was later utilized as a strategic military outpost. During the 4th and 5th centuries AD, the city burgeoned into a cosmopolitan trading center, but by the early 500s, Sevilla had become the regional seat of power. Archaeological excavations began in the 18th century and continue today, although the oldest neighborhoods in Itálica are still buried under downtown Santiponce and may never be recovered. The **Casa del Planetario** (The House of Planets) has intricate **mosaic floors** depicting the seven gods that represent planets, whose names are given to the days of the week; other nearby houses, such as the **Casa de Neptuno,** also have equally detailed floors. There are also reconstructed patios and a bakery depicting life as it was during the decline of the city. The amazingly well-preserved **anfiteatro,** among Spain's largest, at one time seated 25,000. It was used to stage fights between gladiators and lions. Today, visitors can wander the grounds and the curving hallways that circle the structure at the center of the city. Although there is plenty of grass and shade, the ruins themselves are in direct sunlight, so bring lots of water. (☎955 99 73 76. Open Apr.-Sept. Tu-Sa 8:30am-8:30pm, Su 9am-3pm; Oct.-Mar. Tu-Sa 9am-5:30pm, Su 10am-4pm. €1.50, EU citizens free.)

CARMONA

Empresa Casal buses to Carmona depart Sevilla from the Pr. de San Sebastián station, platform 25. (1hr.; M-F 16 per day 7am-10pm, Sa 10 per day 7:45am-9pm, Su 8 per day 9am-10pm; €2; pay on the bus.) In Carmona, buses return to Sevilla from the main square, along Av. Jorge Bonsor (8-20 per day 6:15am-9pm).

Thirty-three kilometers east of Sevilla, ancient Carmona (pop. 25,300) dominates a hill overlooking the countryside. Founded by the Carthaginians, it became an important trade city during Roman occupation in later centuries, and a Moorish stronghold thereafter. Moorish palaces mingle with Renaissance mansions in a network of streets partially enclosed by fortified walls. The **Puerta de Sevilla,** a horseshoe-shaped passageway with both Roman and Arab architectural elements, and the Baroque **Puerta de Córdoba,** on the opposite end of town, once linked Carmona to the east and west. From the bus stop, walk from the back of the bus onto C. San Pedro. On the right is the **Iglesia de San Pedro,** whose Mudéjar tower is a scaled-down copy of Sevilla's Giralda. (☎954 14 12 77. Open Th-M 11am-2pm; closed July. €1.20. Mass Sa-Su 8:30pm. Free.) Enter the **Alcázar de la Puerta Sevilla,** across the roundabout, through the tourist office on the right. Although some remains on the site date as far back as the 14th to 12th centuries BC, the fortress reached its heyday between the 3rd to 1st centuries BC as a key defensive structure. The Alcázar originally served as a Carthaginian fortification against Roman attack, and later was expanded and used by the Romans themselves. During the reign of Augustus, the structure was expanded to its current size. (☎954 19 09 55. Open M-Sa 10am-6pm, Su 10am-3pm. €2; students, seniors, and children under 12 €1; M free.) From the Alcázar, take C. Prim and then C. Martín to find Pl. Marqués de las Torres, where the late-Gothic **Iglesia de Santa María** was built over an old mosque. The splendid **Patio de los Naranjos** remains from Moorish days. An even older Visigothic liturgical calendar graces one of the columns. (☎954 14 13 30. M-Sa 10am-2pm and 5:30-7:30pm, Su 9am-2pm. Free. Mass daily 8pm.) The **Alcázar del Rey Don Pedro,** an old Almohad fortress and now a ritzy hotel, guards the eastern edge of town. In the opposite direction from the bus stop, along C. Enmedio, lie the ruins of the **Necrópolis Romana,** Av. de Jorge Bonsor, 9 (☎954 14 08 11). Highlights include the **Tumba de Servilia** and **Tumba del Elefante,** where depictions of Mother Nature and Eastern divinities are overshadowed by the presence of a giant stone elephant. The **Museo Arqueológico** has remains from over a thousand tombs unearthed at the necropolis. (Both open June-Aug. Tu-F 8:30am-2pm, Sa 10am-2pm; Sept.-May Tu-F 9am-5pm, Sa-Su 10am-2pm. €1.50, EU citizens free.) The **tourist office,** at the entrance to the Alcázar , is located down C. San Pedro from the bus stop. (☎954 19 09 55; fax 19 00 80. English spoken. Open M-Sa 10am-6pm, Su 10am-3pm.) The **police** (☎954 14 00 08) are on C. Carmen Llorca.

ANDALUCÍA

HUELVA ☎ 959

While many Spaniards vacation on the beaches of the Huelva province (the Costa de la Luz), its capital city offers little more than an industrial port; not much is appealing about Huelva (pop. 140,000) other than its proximity to the towns from which Columbus mustered men. Nevertheless, it is often a necessary stop en route to some of the region's more beautiful beaches, as well as for those on the backpacker pilgrimage to Lagos. Spending a night in Huelva can be relaxing.

TRANSPORTATION. RENFE trains on Av. de Italia (info: ☎ 902 24 02 02; station: ☎ 959 24 56 14) run to: **Córdoba** (2¼hr., 1 per day 4:50pm, €28.50); **Madrid** (4¼hr., 1 per day 4:50pm, €54); **Sevilla** (1½hr., 3 per day 7:15am-7pm, €6.35). **Buses** depart from Av. Dr. Rubio (☎ 959 25 69 00) to: **Cádiz** (5hr., 1 per day 9:30am, €15.41); **Faro, Portugal** (2½hr.; 2 per day 9am, 6pm; €5); **Lagos, Portugal** (5hr.; 2 per day 9am, 6pm; €10); **Madrid** (7hr., 4 per day 9:45am-11:15pm, €18.70); **Málaga** (8am, €19.44); **Sevilla** (1hr., 9-20 per day 7am-9pm, €6.11).

ORIENTATION & PRACTICAL INFORMATION. The central axis of the city is **Avenida Martín Alonso Pinzón** (Gran Vía). To reach it from the train station, go out the front door, cross the street, and go straight down the street in front of you, C. Alonso XII. From the bus station, exit across Av. Alemania. Take C. Gravina, turn left onto C. M. Núñez, then right onto C. Concepción. Follow C. Concepción for three blocks, then turn left. Av. Martín Alonso Pinzón is one block over. The **Junta de Andalucía tourist office,** Av. de Alemania, 12, across from the bus station and half a block to the right, has endless information and maps on regional beaches and excursions. (☎ 959 25 74 03. English spoken Open M 9am-3pm, T-F 9am-7pm, Sa 10am-2pm.) The bus station has lockers for **luggage storage** (€3 per day). **Police** are on Av. Tomás Domínguez de Ortiz, 2 (national ☎ 091; local ☎ 959 24 93 50). For **Internet access,** try **Cybercafe Interpool,** C. Vázquez Limón, 9. (☎ 959 80 24 78. Open M-F 10am-1am, Sa-Su 6pm-1am. €1 per 30min.) **Santander Central Hispano** is at C. Palacios, 10. (☎ 902 24 24 24. Open M-F 8:30am-2pm, Sa 8:30am-1pm.) The **post office** (☎ 959 24 91 84) is at Av. Tomás Domínguez de Ortiz, 1.

ACCOMMODATIONS & FOOD. Unless you're stuck waiting overnight for a bus or train, there's really no reason to spend the night in Huelva. If you do need somewhere to crash, look for cheap *hostals* clustered between the train station and Av. Martín Alonso Pinzón. A decent option is the somewhat out-of-the-way **Albergue Juvenil Huelva ❶,** on Av. Marchena Colombo, 14, a good base for daytrips to nearby beaches. (Take city bus #6 from the central bus station, €0.95. ☎ 959 25 37 93. Up to 4 people per room. Breakfast included. Some wheelchair-accessible rooms. July-Aug. €13.35 per person, 26+ €17.85. Sept.-June €11.30/€15.75. €3.50 extra per day for non-members. AmEx/MC/V.) **Mercado de Carmen,** the town's market, is at the intersection of C. Barcelona, C. Carmen, and C. Duque de la Victoria; it sells fresh fish and produce daily 8am-2pm. Look for inexpensive restaurants and cafeterias in the center of town on the pedestrian streets, such as C. Concepción, C. Palacios, and C. Arq. Carasca.

CÓRDOBA ☎ 957

Abundant courtyards, flowers dripping from balconies, and narrow, winding streets make Córdoba (pop. 310,000) a captivating and unhurried city. Perched on the south bank of the Río Guadalquivir, it was once the largest city in western Europe and for three centuries the hub of the Moorish Empire, capital of the mighty Ummayad Caliphate and rivaled only by Baghdad and Cairo. Córdoba

ANDALUCÍA

remembers that heyday with amazingly well-preserved monuments of Roman, Jewish, Islamic, and Catholic origin, each accentuating the other in their baffling proximity. Only in Toledo are the remnants of Spain's colorful heritage as visibly intermixed. The *judería* is one of Spain's oldest Jewish quarters, containing one of the few synagogues in the Iberian peninsula, and the 14th-century Palacio del Marqués de Viana anticipates Spain's Golden Age by three centuries. Spectacular scenery, hearty locals, and refreshing fountains charm visitors with the grace of a Córdoban *flamenco* dancer.

▐ TRANSPORTATION

Trains: Pl. de las Tres Culturas (RENFE info ☎957 24 02 02; www.renfe.es), off Av. de América. To: **Algeciras** (5 per day 4:55am-4:39pm, €16.20-26.50); **Barcelona** (10-11hr., 4 per day 9:45am-11:34pm, €47-64.50); **Cádiz** (2½-3hr., 5 per day 6am-8pm, €15.40-31.50); **Madrid** (2-4hr., 22-31 per day 2:16am-11:42pm, €25-47); **Málaga** (2-3hr., 10-12 per day 6:40am-10:10pm, €13-19); **Sevilla** (45min.-1hr., 20-29 per day 8:40am-11:40pm, €6.95-23.50). For international tickets, contact **RENFE,** Ronda de los Tejares, 10.

Buses: Estación de Autobuses (☎957 40 40 40; fax 40 44 15), on Av. de América across from the train station.

Alsina Graells Sur (☎957 27 81 00) to: **Algeciras** (5hr., 2 per day, €19.49); **Almería** (5hr., 8am, €19.50); **Antequera** (2½hr., 9am and 4pm, €7.50); **Cádiz** via Sevilla (4-5hr.; M-F 10am, daily 6pm; €17.89); **Granada** (3hr., 8-9 per day 8am-8:30pm, €10.35); **Málaga** (3-3½hr., 5 per day 8am-7pm, €10.45); **Sevilla** (2hr., 10-13 per day 5:30am-9:30pm, €8.57).

Bacoma (☎957 45 65 14) goes to: **Barcelona** (10hr., 3 per day 12:35am-7:15pm, €68.05), as well as **Baeza** and **Valencia**. **Secorbus** (☎902 22 92 92) provides cheap service to **Madrid** (4½hr., 6-7 per day 1am-7:30pm, €10.55).

Transportes Ureña (☎957 40 45 58) runs to **Jaén** (2hr., 6-8 per day 7:30am-8pm, €6.68). **Autocares Priego** (☎957 40 44 79), **Empresa Carrera** (☎957 40 44 14), and **Empresa Rafael Ramírez** (☎957 42 21 77) run buses to surrounding towns and camping sites.

Local Transportation: Twelve bus lines (☎957 25 57 00) cover the city, running from the wee hours until 11pm. **Bus #3** makes a loop from the bus and train stations through Pl. de las Tendillas, up to the Santuario, then back along the river and up C. Doctor Fleming. **Bus #10** runs from the train station to Barrio Brillante. Purchase tickets on board. €0.80.

Taxis: Radio Taxi (☎957 76 44 44) has stands at most busy intersections throughout the city. Be sure that the meter is turned on before you leave. From the *judería* to the bus and train stations €3-5; to Barrio Brillante €3.60-6.

Car Rental: Hertz (☎957 49 29 61; fax 40 20 60), in the train station. Charges €61.39 per day for a compact car, discounts for longer time periods. 25+. Open M-F 8:30am-10pm, Sa 9am-7pm, Su 9am-2pm.

✦ ORIENTATION

Córdoba is split between two parts: the old city and the new. The modern and commercial northern half extends from the train station on Av. de América down to **Plaza de las Tendillas**, the center of the city. The old section in the south is a medieval maze known as the **judería** (Jewish quarter). This tangle of beautiful and disorienting streets extends from Pl. de las Tendillas to the banks of the Río Guadalquivir, winding past the **Mezquita** and **Alcázar**. The easiest way to reach the old city from the train station or the bus station is to take city bus #3 to **Plaza Campo Santo de los Mártires** (€0.80). Overly concerned locals may encourage you to get off near Pl. Potro since the bus seemingly heads in the opposite direction, but hang on to your backpack and your seat—the #3 will make a loop and return along the river to the old city. Alternatively, the walk is about 20min. From the train station,

Córdoba

⌂ ACCOMMODATIONS

Hostal Almanzor, **18**
Hostal Deanes, **12**
Hostal El Triunfo, **25**
Hostal La Calleja, **19**
Hostal La Fuente, **20**
Hostal Los Omeyas, **16**
Hostal Maestre, **22**
Hostal Rey Heredia, **17**
Hostal-Residencia
  Séneca, **13**
Hotel-Residencia
  Boston, **6**
Residencia Juvenil
  Córdoba (HI), **23**

🍴 FOOD

Caroche Centro Cafetería, **8**
El Caballo Rojo, **15**
El Picantón, **11**
Mesón Cespedes, **14**
Mesón San Basilio, **26**
Sociedad de Plateros, **21**
Taberna Casa Salinas, **10**

★ NIGHTLIFE

La Bulería, **9**
Club Don Luis, **3**
Club Kachamba, **4**
La Comuna, **5**
La Moncloa, **2**
Soul, **7**
Tablao Cardenal, **24**
La Torre, **1**

ANDALUCÍA

with your back to the platforms, exit left, cross the parking plaza, and make a right onto Av. de los Mozárabes. When you reach the Roman columns, turn left and cross Gta. Sargentos Provisionales. Make a right on Po. de la Victoria and veer toward the left until you reach Puerto Almodóvar; you are now in the old city.

⑦ PRACTICAL INFORMATION

Tourist Offices: Oficina Municipal de Turismo y Congresos, Pl. Judá Levi (☎957 20 05 22). Open M-F 8:30am-2:30pm. Call first, as the office may be under construction. **Tourist Office of Andalucía,** C. Torrijos, 10 (☎957 47 12 35). From the train station, take bus #3 along the river until a stone arch appears on the right. English-speaking staff distributes free map of the monument section. Open May-Sept. M-F 9:30am-8pm, Sa 10am-7pm, Su 10am-2pm; Oct.-Apr. M-F 9:30am-6pm, Su 10am-2pm.

Tours: Córdoba Vision, Av. Doctor Marañón, 1 (☎957 76 02 41). Offers excellent 4-hr. long guided tours in English, French, or Spanish. Walking tour of Córdoba's monuments Tu-Su 10:30am, €25. Tour of **Madinat al-Zahra:** summer Tu-F 6pm, Su and holidays 10:30am; winter Tu-F 4pm, Sa 10:30am and 4pm; Su and holidays 10:30am; €18.

Currency Exchange: Banco Santander Central Hispano, Pl. de las Tendillas, 5 (☎957 49 70 00). No commission up to €600. Open M-F 8:30am-2:30pm. **Banks** and **ATMs** can be found on the streets surrounding La Mezquita and Pl. de las Tendillas.

Luggage Storage: Lockers at the train and bus stations open 24hr. (€2.40-4.50).

El Corte Inglés: Av. Ronda de los Tejares, 30 (☎957 22 28 81), on the corner of Av. del Gran Capitán. Sells an excellent street map (€3.10). Open M-Sa 10am-10pm.

Laundry: Teleseco, Ronda de Isasa, 10 (☎957 48 33 56), 1 block from La Mezquita near the river. Coin service or dry cleaning. Washers €4.80, dryers €3.

Emergency: ☎092. **Police:** Av. Doctor Fleming, 2 (☎957 59 45 80).

Late-Night Pharmacy: On a rotating basis. List posted outside the pharmacy in Pl. de las Tendillas and in the local newspaper.

Medical Assistance: Emergencies ☎061. **Red Cross Hospital,** Po. de la Victoria (emergency ☎957 22 22 22, main line 42 06 66). English spoken. Open M-F 9am-1:30pm, 4:30-5:30pm. **Ambulance:** ☎902 50 50 61 (urgent), or 76 73 59.

Internet Access: In the old city, surf at **NavegaWeb,** Pl. Judá Levi. Enter through the HI youth hostel (☎957 29 30 89). Slick new machines, A/C, and a youth hostel crowd make this a popular pick. €1.20 per hour. Open daily 10am-10pm. **e-Net,** C. García Lovera, 10 (☎957 48 14 62). €1.20 per hr., €8 per 10 hr., and €15 per 20 hr. Printing €0.15 per page, color €0.30. Fax €1 per page. Open daily 9am-2pm and 5-10pm.

Post Office: C. Cruz Conde, 15 (☎957 47 97 96). **Lista de Correos.** Open M-F 8:30am-8:30pm, Sa-Su 9:30am-2pm. **Postal Code:** 14070.

⚑ ACCOMMODATIONS

Hostels cluster between the **Mezquita** and **C. de San Fernando.** Córdoba is especially crowded during *Semana Santa* and from May-Sept.—you may have to call two to three months in advance for reservations. Prices are higher in summer.

IN & AROUND THE JUDERÍA

The *judería's* whitewashed walls, twisting streets, and proximity to sights make it a great place to stay. During the day, souvenir booths and cafes keep the streets lively, but the area feels desolate at night. Take bus #3 from the train station to Pl. Campo Santo de los Mártires and go up C. Manríques to reach the neighborhood.

■ **Residencia Juvenil Córdoba (HI)**, Pl. Judá Leví (☎957 29 01 66). A former mental asylum converted into a backpacker's paradise with large, sterile doubles, triples, and quads, with bath and A/C. Public phones and a conveniently-located Internet cafe (see Navegaweb). Wheelchair accessible. Breakfast included, lunch and dinner €4.70. Communal storage available. Towels €1.10. Laundry €2.50 per washer, €1.50 per dryer. 24hr. reception. Reservations recommended. €13.35 per person; over 26 €17.85; €3.50 extra per day for nonmembers. Private rooms with per-bed surcharge. MC/V. ❶

Hostal El Triunfo, C. Corregidor Luis de la Cerda, 79 (☎957 49 84 84 or 902 15 83 92; www.htriunfo.com). Luxurious at reasonable prices, all rooms boast A/C, phone, TV, bath, and safe. The third floor terrace offers a picturesque view of the Río Guadalquivir and the Torre de la Calahorra. Cafe open 8am-11pm. Parking €12 per day. Wheelchair accessible. Singles €26.12-39.19; doubles €45.72-58.79; triples available. ❸

Hostal-Residencia Séneca, C. Conde y Luque, 7 (☎/fax 957 47 32 34). A beautiful courtyard greets you as you enter this home-like hostel. All rooms have fans, most have A/C. Breakfast included. Reservations recommended. Singles with sink €21-22, with bath €31-34; doubles €32-36/€41-43; triples €40-48/€54-58. ❷

Hostal Deanes, C. Deanes, 6 (☎957 29 37 44). In a 16th-century building, 5 rooms with cavernous baths surround a busy courtyard cafe (open daily 9am-10:30pm, raciones €5-9). Check out the autographed pictures of famous matadors in the adjacent bar. Reserve in Dec. and during Semana Santa. Doubles €31, extra bed €10. ❷

BETWEEN LA MEZQUITA & CALLE DE SAN FERNANDO

Hostal Rey Heredia, C. del Rey Heredia, 26 (☎957 47 41 82). A great deal for budget travelers. Pencil sketches of Córdoban monuments and Andalusian decor provide conversation pieces. Many rooms have sink and/or shower. Singles €12; doubles €24. ❶

Hostal Maestre, C. Romero Barros, 4-5 (☎/fax 957 47 53 95), off C. de San Fernando. Immaculate rooms with windows overlooking the street or one of two courtyards. All with private bath, most with TV. First floor rooms have fans, other floors A/C. English spoken. Parking €6 per day. Breakfast €2.50. Singles €22; doubles €33; triples €42. ❷

Hostal La Fuente, C. de San Fernando, 51 (☎957 48 78 27 or 48 14 78). Large rooms with bath, TV, and doubles with A/C. A terrace overlooks the Iglesia de San Francisco. Cafe serves beer and coffee. Security boxes at reception for valuables. Breakfast €2.40. Parking €8. Singles €20-24; doubles €36-40; triples €48-55. AmEx/MC/V. ❷

Hostal Almanzor, C. Cardenal González, 10 (☎/fax 957 48 54 00). All singles have king-sized beds. Spotless rooms with balcony-like windows, TVs, bath, and A/C. Parking included. 24hr. reception. Singles €9-12; doubles €18-30. AmEx/MC/V. ❶

Hostal La Calleja, Calleja de Rufino Blanco y Sánchez, 6 (☎/fax 957 48 66 06). Pleasant staff and comfortable rooms keep you cool with A/C. 24hr. reception. Singles €17, with bath and TV €19.23; doubles €30/€35. MC/V. ❷

Hostal Los Omeyas, C. de la Encarnación, 17 (☎957 49 22 67 or 49 21 99; fax 49 16 59). Named after the Moorish dynasty that ruled from Córdoba, Los Omeyas offers marble rooms and Moorish decor, all with A/C, TV, phone, and bath. Breakfast served 8-11am (€3.50). Parking €12 per day. Singles €34-40; doubles €52-64. V. ❹

ELSEWHERE

Hotel Residencia Boston, C. Málaga, 2 (☎957 47 41 76; fax 47 85 23). All rooms equipped with A/C, TV, phone, safe, and bath. Breakfast €3. Laundry service. Parking nearby. Singles €27-30; doubles €42-49; triples €51-55. AmEx/MC/V. ❸

Camping Municipal, Av. del Brillante, 50 (☎957 40 38 36). From the train station, turn left on Av. de América, left on Av. del Brillante, and walk uphill for 20min. Bus #10 and 11 from Av. Cervantes stop across the street. Pool, supermarket, restaurant, free hot showers, and laundry (€3). Some English and French spoken. Very close to Córdoba's

ANDALUCÍA

THE HIDDEN DEAL

ZESTFULLY CLEAN

Under the caliphate, Arab culture flowered in Córdoba, and along with the marketplaces (souks) and public fountains, came the Arab baths (baños árabes or hammam in Arabic). Most of these were abandoned and either destroyed or left to ruin after la Reconquista, since Catholics did not have a tradition of public bathing. Nevertheless, many around the country have been restored and opened for public usage. Escape temporarily to 11th century Andalucía. The rich Arabic decor, combined with gracious service, make the Córdoban baths a fine spot to relax and wash away your travels. Like any traditional Arab bath, there is a dressing room, cold room, temperate room, and two hot rooms. You can process in ceremonial order, or choose your own sudsy adventure. If your indulgent side has not yet been adequately doused, massages and a tea-drinking room with music, Moorish pastries, and even belly dancing await you for a few extra clam shells. *Baños Árabes, Hammam, Medin Caliphal. C. Corredor Luis de la Cerda, 51, 14003. ☎957 48 47 46, fax 47 99 17; medinacaliphal@grupoandalus.com. Open daily, inc. festivals. Baths every other hour from 10am-midnight. One bath €12; four baths €34; bath, massage, aromatherapy, and tea €21; bath and message with student ID €16. Reservations needed.*

nightlife. Wheelchair accessible. IVA not included. One person and tent €8; two people and tent €12; two people, car, and tent €16; two people and camper €17. ❶

☕ FOOD

The Mezquita area falls flat with many hyper-touristed restaurants, but a 5min. walk in any direction yields local specialties at reasonable prices. In the evenings, locals converge at the outdoor *terrazas* between **C. Severo Ochoa** and **C. Dr. Jiménez Díaz** for drinks and *tapas*. Cheap eateries cluster farther away from the *judería* in **Barrio Cruz Conde** and around **Avenida Menéndez Pidal** and **Plaza de las Tendillas.** Regional specialties include *salmorejo* (a gazpacho-like cream soup topped with hard-boiled eggs and pieces of ham) and *rabo de toro* (bull's tail simmered in tomato sauce). **El Corte Inglés,** Av. Ronda de los Tejares, 30 (open M-Sa 10am-10pm) has a grocery store.

⊠ El Picantón, C. Fernández Ruano, 19. Great for budget travelers; take ordinary *tapas*, pour on *salsa picante*, stick it in a roll, and *voilà*: a cheap, hearty meal. No seats. *Bocadillos* €1-3, *tapas* €1-3, beer €1. Open daily 10am-3:30pm and 8pm-midnight. ❶

Taberna Casa Salinas, Puerto de Almodóvar (☎957 29 08 46). Pepe Salinas has been running this place for over 38 years. Eschew the jam-packed bar and enjoy the mellow A/C dining room, or if the weather is right, request a table on the romantic outdoor patio. *Media raciones* €4.80-8.40. Entrees €3.61-6. Open M-Sa 11:30am-4:30pm and 8:30pm-12:30am, Su 11:30am-4:30pm. Closed Aug. ❷

Sociedad de Plateros, C. de San Francisco, 6 (☎957 47 00 42). White-haired men play dominoes; tourists relax on the shaded patio. A Córdoba mainstay since 1872. *Media raciones* and *raciones* €2.60-6.20. Bar open Tu-Su 8am-4:30pm and 8pm-midnight. Restaurant open 1-4pm and 8pm-midnight June-Aug. M-Sa, Sept.-May Tu-Su. MC/V. ❶

Mesón San Basilio, C. San Basilio, 19 (☎957 29 70 07). Two floors surround a breezy patio. *Menú* M-F €6.50, Sa-Su €10. *Raciones* €2.70. Entrees €6.50-14. Open daily 1-4pm and 8pm-midnight. ❷

Caroche Centro Cafetería, C. García Lovera, 7 (☎957 49 25 71). Don't let the address fool you. Caroche Centro sits on C. Claudio Marcelo *across* from C. García Lovera. The large-screen TV and blustery A/C combine with affordable food to make this a great refuge from the heat. *Menú* €6. Entrees €4-9. Open daily 7:30am-4am. ❷

Meson Céspedes, C. Céspedes, 12. (☎957 48 32 29). If you must eat in the super-touristed Mezquita area, head here for decent and reasonably priced food in this simple restaurant. Fish and meat entrees €3-10, two-course *menú* €5. ❶

El Caballo Rojo Restaurante, C. Cardenal Herrero, 28 (☎957 47 53 75). Advertises traditional favorites and "constant experiments with the spices and virgin olive oil of Mozárabe cuisine." Eat *tapas* in the bar (€2-15), or enjoy a meal in the restaurant. Fish and vegetarian options (€10-18). Open daily 1pm-4:30pm and 8:30pm-2am. MC/V. ❸

🅖 SIGHTS

📛 LA MEZQUITA

☎957 47 05 12. Open Apr.-June M-Sa 10am-7:30pm, Su and holidays 2-7:30pm; July-Oct. daily 10am-7pm; Nov.-Mar. daily 10am-6pm. €6.50, children under 10 free. Wheelchair accessible. Last ticket sold 30min. before closing. Opens M-Sa 8:30am for Mass starting at 9:30am; Su Mass 11am, noon, and 1pm. Take advantage of the free hours of admission M-Sa from 8:30-10am during Mass. Strict silence is enforced; no groups.

Built in 784 on the site of a Visigoth basilica, this architectural masterpiece is considered the most important Islamic monument in the Western world. Over the course of the following two centuries, La Mezquita was enlarged to cover an area the size of several city blocks with more than 850 columns, making it the largest mosque in the Islamic world at the time of its completion. Visitors enter through the **Patio de los Naranjos,** an arcaded courtyard featuring carefully spaced orange trees, palm trees, and fountains, where the dutiful performed their ablutions before prayer. The **Torre del Alminar** encloses remains of the minaret from which the *muezzin* called for prayer.

The grand, multiple entrances to the mosque were closed during its conversion to a Gothic cathedral, and entrance today is through the right corner of the facade. Entering into the oldest part of the mosque, built under Abd Al-Rahman I, the multiple pillars carved from granite and marble are capped by characteristically banded Moorish arches of different heights.

La Mezquita's most elaborate additions—the dazzling **mihrab** (prayer niche) and the triple **maksourah** (caliph's niche)—were created in the 10th century. Historians to this day are stumped as to why the *mihrab* does not face Mecca. Muslim architects had highly precise methods of calculation, and such a "mistake" is highly unlikely. One theory holds that it symbolized separation from Baghdad, ruled by the rival Abbasid dynasty. Nevertheless, prayers continue in the traditional direction. The *mihrab* formerly housed a gilt copy of the Qur'an and remains covered in Kufic inscriptions reciting the 99 names of *Allah*. Holy Roman Emperor Constantine VII gave the caliphs the nearly 35 tons of intricate gold, pink, and blue marble Byzantine mosaics shimmering across the arches of the *mihrab*. To its left and right, panels glorify the new caliph of the Muslim world.

At the far end of the Mezquita lies the **Capilla Villaviciosa,** where caliphal vaulting appeared for the first time. Completed in 1371, it was the first Christian chapel to be built in the mosque, thus beginning the transition of La Mezquita into a place of Christian worship. In 1523, Bishop Alonso Manrique, an ally of Carlos V, proposed the construction of a cathedral in the center of the mosque. The town rallied violently against the idea, promising painful death to any worker who helped tear down La Mezquita. Nevertheless, a towering **crucero** (transept) and **coro** (choir stall) were eventually erected, incongruously planting a richly adorned Baroque cathedral amidst far more austere environs. Constructed over 200 years, it is possible to see the stylistic progression from Gothic to Renaissance to Early Baroque in the ceiling and walls of the cathedral. The townspeople were less than pleased, and even Carlos V regretted the changes to La Mezquita, lamenting, "You have destroyed something unique to create something commonplace." What remains, though, is far from commonplace, for the juxtaposition of the two architectural styles and programs accentuates the individual qualities of each.

IN & AROUND THE JUDERÍA

A combined ticket for the Alcázar, Museo Taurino y de Arte Cordobés, and Museo Julio Romero is available at all three locations. €7.05, students €3.60; free on Friday.

■ **ALCÁZAR.** Along the river on the left side of La Mezquita lies the Alcázar, whose walls enclose a garden with terraced flower beds, ponds, palm trees, and fountains. Built in 1328 during *la Reconquista*, the building was both a fortress and a residence for Alfonso XI. Fernando and Isabel bade Columbus farewell here, and from 1490 to 1821, it served as a headquarters for the Inquisition. The museum displays 1st-century Roman mosaics and a 3rd-century Roman marble sarcophagus. Don't miss the Arab bath turned Counter-Reformation interrogation chamber in the basement. *Cordobeses* come to take a break from the heat in the splendid gardens, open June-Sept. from 8pm-midnight. (☎957 42 01 51. *Open July-Aug. 8:30am-2:30pm; May-June and Sept. Tu-Sa 10am-2pm and 5:30-7:30pm, Su and holidays 9:30am-2:30pm; Oct.-Apr. Tu-Sa 10am-2pm and 4:30-6:30pm, Su and holidays 9:30am-2:30pm. Closed M. F free. €2, students €1.)*

SINAGOGA. Built in 1315, the synagogue is a hollow remnant of Córdoba's once vibrant Jewish community. Adorned with Mozárabe patterns and Hebrew inscriptions, the walls of the small temple have been restored to much of their original intricacy, although little else has been preserved. The only other synagogues to survive the 1492 expulsion of the Jews from Spain are both in Toledo. *(C. Judíos, 20, just past the statue of Maimónides. ☎957 20 29 28. Open M-Sa 10am-2pm and 2:30-5:30pm, Su 10am-1:30pm. €0.50, EU citizens free.)*

MUSEO TAURINO Y DE ARTE CORDOBÉS. Get ready for a lot of bull. Dedicated to the history and lore of the bullfight, rooms contain uniforms, posters, and artifacts from decades of bullfighting in Spain. The main exhibit includes a replica of the tomb of Spain's most famous matador, the dashing Manolete, and the hide of the bull that killed him. *(Pl. Maimónides. ☎957 20 10 56. Open July-Aug. Tu-Sa 8:30am-2:30pm, Su 9:30am-2:30pm; Sept.-June Tu-Sa 10am-2pm and 5:30-7:30pm, Su 9:30am-2:30pm. Last entrance 15min. before closing. €2.91, students €1.48, seniors free. F free.)*

MUSEO DIOCESANO DE BELLAS ARTES. Once the home of Córdoba's bishops while the Inquisition raged within the Alcázar, this 17th-century ecclesiastical palace houses a modest collection of Renaissance and Baroque religious art. *(C. Torrijos, 12, across from the Mezquita in the Palacio de Congresos. ☎957 49 60 85. Open July-Aug. M-Sa 9:30am-3pm; Sept.-June M-F 9:30am-1:30pm and 2-6pm, Sa 9:30am-1:30pm. €1.20, under 12 free. Free with admission to La Mezquita.)*

OTHER SIGHTS. Townspeople take great pride in their traditional **patios,** many dating from Roman times. These open-air courtyards, tranquil havens of orange and lemon trees, flowers, and fountains, flourish in the old quarter. Among the streets of exceptional beauty are **Calleja del Indiano,** off C. Fernández Ruano at Pl. Ángel Torres, and the aptly named **Calleja de Flores,** off C. Blanco Belmonte, where lustrous geraniums in full bloom crowd along the white walls of the alley. In Pl. Tiberiades, rub the toes of the statue of **Maimónides** to gain the knowledge of this 12th-century Jewish philosopher and religious rationalist. The statue was used as the model for the face of the New Israeli Shekel. Further past the statue is **Casa Andalusí,** a house restored to its 12th-century state. The tranquil home features mosaic floors, fountains, old Arabic texts and coins, a replication of a paper factory, and an ancient well in the basement. (C. Judíos, 12, between the Sinagoga and the Puerta de Almodóvar. Open M-Sa 10:30am-8:30pm. €2.50.)

OUTSIDE THE JUDERÍA

MUSEO JULIO ROMERO DE TORRES. Spice up your life with Romero's sensual portraits of Córdoban women, exhibited in the artist's former home. Only the Andalusian sun gets hotter. (Pl. Potro, 5-10min. from La Mezquita. ☎957 49 19 09. Open May-Sept. Tu-Sa 10am-2pm and 5:30-7:30pm, Su and holidays 9:30am-2:30pm. Last entrance 30min. before closing. €2.95, students €1.48. F free.

MUSEO DE BELLAS ARTES. Across the courtyard from Museo Julio Romero de Torres, this museum now occupies a building that served as a hospital during the reign of Fernando and Isabel. Its small revolving collection displays Renaissance sketches and works by modern Córdoban artists. Don't miss the sculptures by Mateo Inurria and Juan de Mesa on the ground floor. (Pl. Potro, 5-10 min. from La Mezquita. ☎957 47 33 45. Open Tu 3-10pm, W-Sa 9am-8pm, Su and holidays 9am-3pm. Last entrance 15min. before closing. €1.50, EU citizens free.)

PALACIO DEL MARQUÉS DE VIANA. An elegant 14th-century mansion, the palace displays 12 Córdoban patios complete with sprawling gardens, majestic fountains, tapestries, furniture, and porcelain. (Pl. Don Gome, 2. A 20min. walk from La Mezquita. ☎957 49 67 41. Open June 16-Sept. M-Sa 9am-2pm; Oct. 1-May M-F 10am-1pm and 4-6pm, Sa 10am-1pm. Closed June 1-16. Complete tour €6, garden and courtyards only €3.)

OTHER SIGHTS. Behind the train station, take a moment to see the **Zona Arqueológica de Cercadillas,** the ruins of a 3rd-century Roman palace discovered as the station was being built. Though signs explain the area, a free guided tour meets at the information stand in the station Sa and Su at 10am and noon. Near the Palacio del Marqués de Viana in Pl. Capuchinos (also known as Pl. de los Dolores) and next to the monastery is the **Cristo de los Faroles** (Christ of the Lanterns), one of the most famous religious icons in Spain and the site of frequent all-night vigils. The eight lanterns that are lit at night symbolize the eight provinces of Andalucía. Facing the Museo de Bellas Artes and the Museo Julio Romero de Torres is the **Posada del Potro,** a 14th-century inn mentioned in *Don Quijote.* Remnants of 2nd-century **Roman water wheels** line the sides of the Río Guadalquivir. Believed to have been originally used by Romans as mills, they were later used to bring water to the caliph's palace. The mills continued to function until Isabel la Católica demanded they be shut down: they disturbed her sleep. Spanning the river near the Mezquita is the pedestrian **Puente Romano,** a restored Roman bridge. The bridge passes through a natural bird sanctuary on its way to the **Torre de la Calahorra,** a Muslim military tower built in 1369 to protect the Roman bridge. The tower now houses a museum highlighting Córdoba's medieval cultures. (Open daily 10am-2pm and 4:30-8:30pm; Audio tour €3.40. €3.60, students €2.40.)

🎧 NIGHTLIFE

Nightlife in Córdoba thrives in the city center and the chic **Barrio Brillante,** uphill from Av. de América. Throngs of well-dressed young people clog the streets, hopping from one packed outdoor bar to another until reaching a dance club. Bus #10 goes to Brillante from the train station until about 11pm, but the bars do not wake up until at least 1am (most stay open until 4am). A taxi should cost €3-6. If you're walking, head up Av. del Brillante (45min. from the bottom of the old city), passing **Pub BSO** along the way at C. Llanos de Pretorio. Right around the corner is **Brujas Bar,** where every Tuesday and Thursday, witches can tell your

ANDALUCÍA

fortune. During the cooler months of winter, nightlife tends to center in the neighborhood where the Universidad de Córdoba used to be, especially in pubs on **Calle Los Alderetes** and **Calle Julio Pellicer,** and near the **Plaza de la Corredera.** From there, the crowds move on to Av. del Gran Capitán and C. Cruz Conde. While *cordobeses* and tourists groove together every weekend even until the rising sun, the nightlife Sunday to Wednesday can be quite non-existent, as bars and clubs shut down around midnight. However, a stroll after 10pm along the **walk-through fountains** and falling sheets of water that line Av. de América between Pl. de Colón and the train station is a rewarding way to cool off from the heat, meet locals, or simply people-watch.

■ **Soul,** C. Alfonso XIII, 3 (☎957 49 15 80). A hip, relaxed bar where you can chat with friends at cozy tables or mingle with locals, international students, and dread-locked bartenders. Offers reggae, drum and bass, deep house, DJ, and jazz music. Beer €1.20. Mixed drinks €4.50. Try the delectable Honey Rum. Open Sept.-June 9pm-3am. MC/V.

La Comuna, C. del Caño, 1 (☎610 71 55 63; www.lacomuna.es.fm). Alternative music, bartenders' wild stories, and an energetic crowd make La Comuna popular with exchange students. Beer €2. Mixed drinks €4. Open Sept.-June noon-4am.

La Torre, C. Poeta Emilio Prados. An outdoor nightclub with a slightly younger crowd that plays a mix of well-known Latin music and Spanish pop. Beer €1.50. Mixed drinks around €4. Open 11pm-4:30am. Across the street is **Cafetería Terra,** where locals converge before hitting Brillante's bars and clubs.

La Moncloa, Av. del Brillante s/n (☎957 27 23 11). A hut-like enterprise taking its name from Madrid's presidential palace, Monloa draws a university crowd with dancing and Spanish pop. Beer €2-2.50. Mixed drinks €3-5.

Club Don Luis, Av. del Brillante. Much like its neighbor La Moncloa, with less dance. The party doesn't start until 1am. Young crowd, cheap beer (€2). Open midnight-4am.

Club Kachamba, Av. del Brillante. The friendly staff at Kachamba makes it another entertaining stop on a tour of Av. del Brillante's popular nightclubs. With the same owners as Club Kachamba, **Cachao** and **La Toscana** offer late-night dancing starting at 3am. You'll need to take a cab to these hip *discotecas,* located at Ctra. de Trasierra.

ENTERTAINMENT

For the latest cultural events, pick up a free copy of the *Guía del Ocio* at the tourist office. Though *flamenco* is not cheap in Córdoba, the shows are high-quality and worth a visit for those not heading to Sevilla. Prize-winning dancers perform *flamenco puro* at **Tablao Cardenal,** C. Torrijos, 10, facing La Mezquita. Reserve seats at the *Tablao* or your hostel. (☎957 48 33 20. Shows M-Sa 10:30pm. €18, includes 1 drink.) A cheaper but equally viable option is **La Bulería,** C. Pedro López, 3, with nightly shows also at 10:30pm. (☎957 48 38 39. €11, includes 1 drink).

DAYTRIP FROM CÓRDOBA

MADINAT AL-ZAHRA

Madinat al-Zahra can be hard to reach. The O-8 bus (☎957 25 57 00) leaves from Av. de la República Argentina in Córdoba for Cruce Madinat al-Zahra, 3km from the site (10min. past every hr., €0.80) and from Puerta del Puente (every hr., €0.80). From the bus stop, it's a 45min. walk, mostly uphill. The return bus stops along the highway at the cross, on the opposite side of the street from the gas station. A taxi from Córdoba to the site costs about €24. Córdoba Vision also offers transportation and tours (see p. 256).

Legend has it that Abd al-Rahman III built the city of Madinat al-Zahra for his favorite concubine, Zahra. Since Zahra pined for the snow-capped peaks of her hometown in Granada, the thoughtful Abd al-Rahman planted white-blossoming almond groves to substitute for the snowcaps of the Sierra Nevada. Historians, on the other hand, tend to believe that Madinat al-Zahra (literally, the prosperous city) was built to demonstrate Abd al-Rahman III's power as the new caliph in al-Andalus. If so, he must have been effective, for this 10th-century medina was considered one of the greatest cities of its time before it was abandoned by Al-Mansur, sacked by Berbers, vandalized by locals, and buried by mountain silt. Construction began in 940, and the city was constructed rapidly out of the world's best materials; 10,000 people worked day and night to complete it within fifty years. The city built so quickly had a short but exciting life; between 940 and 1010, it served as the seat of the Córdoban caliphate, receiving ambassadors from Byzantium and Germany. It was constructed in three terraces (one for the nobility, another for servants, and a third for an enclosed garden and almond grove), and included roads, bridges, and aqueducts. Today, Madinat al-Zahra rests in ruins, but with the help of reconstructions one can still get a sense of its past. Amazingly, only 10% of this impressive city has been unearthed so far. English/Spanish placards and an accompanying color pamphlet explain the history and major sites within the ruins. Don't miss the (mostly) reconstructed throne room or the world's largest archaeological jigsaw puzzle: millions of fragments from the intricate wall waiting to be reassembled by scholars. A complete tour of the ruins takes 20-45min. (☎957 32 91 30. Open May-mid-Sept. Tu-Sa 10am-8:30pm, Su and holidays 10am-2pm; mid-Sept-Apr. Tu-Su and holidays 10am-2pm. €1.50, EU citizens free.)

JEREZ DE LA FRONTERA
☎956

Jerez de la Frontera (pop. 200,000) is the cradle of three staples of Andalusian culture: *flamenco*, Carthusian horses, and, of course, *jerez* (sherry). It is the sheer quantity and quality of this third staple that draws in the tourists, most of whom are older, well-to-do Europeans. The city also makes a good departure point for the *ruta de los pueblos blancos*, but those not particularly interested in *bodega* tours or horse shows would be better off spending their time elsewhere.

█ TRANSPORTATION

Flights: Airport, Ctra. Jerez-Sevilla (☎956 15 00 00), 7km from town. Taxi to the airport €12. **Iberia** (☎956 18 43 94) has an office at the terminal.

Trains: Pl. de la Estación (☎956 34 23 19). **RENFE,** C. Larga, 34 (☎902 24 02 02). To: **Barcelona** (12hr.; 2 per day 8:36am, 9pm; €61.50-67.50); **Cádiz** (45min., every 30min. 6:45am-10:15pm, €3.05); **Madrid** (4½hr.; 2 per day 8:36am, 5pm; €53.50); **Sevilla** (1¼hr., 12 per day 6:34am-9:40pm, €5.75).

Buses: C. Cartuja (☎956 34 52 07), at the corner of C. Madre de Dios.

Transportes Los Amarillos (☎956 32 93 47) runs to **Arcos de la Frontera** (30min., 8-17 per day 7am-9pm, €2) and **Córdoba** (3hr., 1 per day 5pm, €13.19).

Transportes Generales Comes (☎956 34 21 74) runs to: **Cádiz** (1hr., 20 per day 7am-11:15pm, €2.45); **Granada** (5hr., 1 per day 12:45pm, €21.80); **Puerto Santa María** (30min., 14-24 per day 7am-11:15pm, €1.03); **Ronda** (2¾hr., 4 per day 7:45am-3:30pm, €8.89); **Sevilla** (1½hr., 8-10 per day 9am-11pm, €5.82).

Linesur (☎956 34 10 63) runs to: **Algeciras** (2hr., 7-8 per day 8am-10:30pm, €7.34); **Chipiona** (1hr., 7 per day 9:30am-9:30pm, €2); **Sanlúcar** (30min.; M-F every hr. 7am-10pm, Sa-Su every 2hr.; €1.43); **Sevilla** (1½hr., 7-8 per day 8:30am-7:45pm, €4.81).

Secorbus (☎902 22 92 92) goes to **Madrid** (7hr., 6 per day 8:50am-11:50pm, €20.30).

Local Transportation: Each of the 12 **bus** lines runs every 15min. (less frequently at night). Most pass through Pl. del Arenal or next to Pl. Romero Martínez. €0.70. **Info office** (☎956 34 34 46) in Pl. del Arenal.

ANDALUCÍA

THE LOCAL STORY

LIQUOR FOR LINGUISTS

The Islamic prohibition against consumption of alcohol did not prevent Jerez's Moorish merchants from exporting wine to the infidel English in the 12th-century. "Sherry," an anglicization of Shir-az, the Arabic name for Jerez, is a legacy of this early commerce.

Today, only wines produced in Jerez, Sanlúcar de Barrameda, and Puerto de Santa María are considered sherries. There is no vintage sherry; wines from various years are continuously combined in what is known as the *solera* process. A different process—placing burnt distilled wine in old sherry casks—eventually results in cognac. Unable to use the term for the same reason that wineries in other regions cannot call their products sherry, Jerez's merchants have settled with "brandy," another English bastardization, this time of the Dutch word "brandewyn," meaning "burnt wine."

Impress your friends at dinner parties by knowing the trinity of major sherry types: **Fino:** A dry, light colored sherry served chilled and sipped with *tapas* popular in Andalucía. Manzanilla, a type of *fino* from Sanlúcar de Barrameda, is slightly salty. **Amontillado:** Somewhat sweeter and amber in color. Excellent with white meat and cheese. **Oloroso dulce:** A dessert wine, dark in color, with a raisin-like taste. Go ahead, be pretentious. You know you want to.

Car Rental: Niza, Ctra. N-IV Madrid-Cádiz, km634 (☎956 30 28 60). Take Av. Alcalde Álvaro Domecq to highway N-IV towards Sevilla. From €58 per day. 21+ and must have had license for at least 1yr. Open daily 8:30am-1 pm and 4:30-8pm.

⬛ 🛈 ORIENTATION & PRACTICAL INFORMATION

The labyrinthine streets of Jerez are difficult to navigate without a map. Get one free from the tourist office at Pl. del Arenal or buy one at any bookstore or newsstand (€2.60). C. Medina, which leads into **Plaza Romero Martínez** (the city's commercial center). From here, walk left on C. Cerrón to reach C. Santa María and C. Lancería, heading into **Plaza del Arenal** and the **tourist office. Calle Lancería** and **Calle Larga** make up the main pedestrian thoroughfare in the center of the city.

Tourist Office: Pl. del Arenal (☎956 35 96 54). English-speaking staff has free maps and info on sherry production, *bodega* tours, and horse shows. Open June-Sept. M-F 10am-3pm and 5-7pm, Sa-Su 9:30am-2pm; Oct.-May M-F 9am-2:30pm and 4:30-6:30pm, Sa-Su 9am-2pm.

Currency Exchange: Banco Santander Central Hispano, C. Larga, 11 (☎902 24 24 24). Open M-F 8:30am-1:30pm.

Emergency: ☎061. **Police:** ☎091 or 956 33 03 46.

Medical Assistance: Ambulatorio de la Seguridad Social, C. José Luis Díez (☎956 32 32 02).

Internet Access: Locutorio Jerez, C. San Agustín, 15. €1.60 per hr. Open M-Sa 11am-11pm, Su 4-11pm. **The Big Orange,** C. Antonia de Jesús Tirado (☎956 35 01 01), near the bus station. €1.80 per hr. Open Su-Th 11am-1am, F-Sa 11am-3am.

Post Office: C. Cerrón, 2 (☎956 34 22 95). Open M-F 8:30am-8:30pm, Sa 9am-2pm. **Lista de Correos** open M-Sa 9am-2pm. **Postal Code:** 11480.

🏠 ACCOMMODATIONS

Finding a place to crash in Jerez is as easy as finding a cork to sniff, though few accommodations are cheap. Look along C. Medina, near the bus station, and on C. Arcos, which intersects C. Medina at Pl. Romero Martínez. Prices increase during Jerez's festivals during September and October.

Hostal San Miguel, Pl. San Miguel, 4 (☎/fax 956 34 85 62). Rooms are adorned with crimson bedspreads and huge double doors. Ask for a room with a balcony for views of the church; others face the inside. All rooms have TV and A/C. Older building still feels elegant. Singles €15, with bath €20; doubles €35/€40; triples €50/€55. ❷

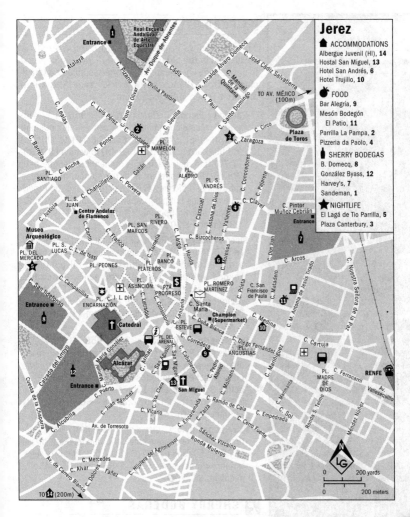

Jerez

🏠 ACCOMMODATIONS
Albergue Juvenil (HI), **14**
Hostal San Miguel, **13**
Hotel San Andrés, **6**
Hotel Trujillo, **10**

🍎 FOOD
Bar Alegría, **9**
Mesón Bodegón
El Patio, **11**
Parrilla La Pampa, **2**
Pizzeria da Paolo, **4**

🍶 SHERRY BODEGAS
B. Domecq, **8**
González Byass, **12**
Harvey's, **7**
Sandeman, **1**

⭐ NIGHTLIFE
El Lagá de Tío Parrilla, **5**
Plaza Canterbury, **3**

Hotel San Andrés, C. Morenos, 12 (☎956 34 09 83; fax 34 31 96). Hallways adorned with vines and Andalusian tile enclose two plant-filled patios. Singles €20, with bath and TV €24; doubles €24/€38. ❷

Hotel Trujillo, C. Medina, 38 (☎956 34 24 38). Rooms have marble floors, bath, phone, and TV; most have A/C. Parking €6 per day. Aug. singles €25; doubles €48. Sept.-July €20/€40. MC/V. ❷

Albergue Juvenil (HI), Av. Carrero Blanco, 30 (☎956 14 39 01; fax 14 32 63), a 25min. walk or 10min. bus ride from downtown; 35min. from the bus and train stations. Bus #1 goes to Pl. del Arenal, while #9 goes to the bus station. Clean rooms, a pool (open July-Aug.), tennis and basketball courts, a small soccer field, a TV/VCR room, and a rooftop terrace. Laundry service €2.40. Reservations required. June-Sept. dorms €11, over 26 €15.75. Oct.-May €8.80/ €11.90. HI member card €5, over 26 €11. ❶

ANDALUCÍA

THE LOCAL STORY

TOO MUCH SHERRY TO CARRY

I'll start by saying that I don't even really like the stuff. But Jerez is a funny place—it's so easy to get wrapped up in all the hulabaloo of the *bodegas* and believe that sherry is the BEST DRINK EVER. Or something very close.

Over the past few days, I've been on more *bodega* tours than I ever thought possible and sampled more than my fair share of sherry. Now, despite the fact that I would never otherwise drink sherry as my beverage of choice, these tours are oh-so-conveniently planned for you to end up in—guess what—a gift shop brimming with elegant bottles of sherry in every possible variety. I couldn't resist. Maybe all the sherry went to my head, but as I finished my first tour, I couldn't possibly leave without bringing home a bottle (or two, or three). Then it was on to the next *bodega*, and I just HAD to have some of Harvey's Cream. After 2 days, my backpack looked like a liquor cabinet, and I looked quite the lush.

By the time I arrived in Sevilla several days later, I realized several important things. 1) Liquor is heavy. 2) Everything you see in the gift shops can be purchased at any supermarket, often for less. 3) Any smart person waits until the trip is nearly through before stocking up. And 4) I still don't like sherry that much, but, that's what fellow travelers are for.

—*Marla Kaplan, 2004*

◘ FOOD

Tapas-hoppers bounce around Pl. del Arenal, C. Larga, and in the old town around Pl. del Banco; food in Jerez is rarely cheap. For groceries, head to **Champion**, C. Doña Blanca, a few blocks from Pl. Romero Martínez (open M-Sa 9am-10pm).

Parilla La Pampa, C. Guadalete, 24 (☎956 34 17 49), near Pl. Mamelón. Although you can get all kinds and cuts of meat, from pork (€5.50-8.70) to chicken (€5.90-6.90) to veal (€3.40-9.40) to ostrich (€16.20-17.70), the real specialty is authentic Argentine beef (€8.75-19.70), straight from the source. Argentinian soft rock and pictures of the *pampas* make the experience anything but plain. Open June-Sept. M-Sa 12:30-4:30pm and 8:30pm-midnight; Oct.-May Th-Tu 12:30-4:30pm and 8:30-midnight. ❹

Mesón Bodegon El Patio, C. San Francisco de Paula, 7 (☎956 34 07 36). Savor sumptuous traditional fare in a dining room with brightly-colored oil paintings. Loaded with eggs, sausage, and garlic, the sizzling *sopa de ajo* (€4.25) is a meal in itself. Stick to *raciones* €4.81-9; skip the overpriced €20 *menú*. Open M-Sa 11:30am-4:30pm and 8pm-12:30am. MC/V. ❷

Bar Alegría, C. Corredera, 30 (☎956 33 80 70), 3 blocks from Pl. del Arenal. One of the truly great, local, untouristy bars in the city center. Great *croquettas de pollo* (chicken croquettes; *tapas* size €1.50). Arrive before 8:30pm or after 10:30pm, or expect to wait for a table. *Tapas* €1.50, *raciones* €6. Open daily 7:30am-midnight. ❶

Pizzeria da Paolo, C. Clavel at C. Valientes. Like a semi-fancy Italian restaurant, only affordable. Great pizzas (€4.80-7.50) and pastas (€4.50-7.50). Plenty of vegetarian options. Open Tu-Su 1:15-4pm and 8:45pm-midnight. MC/V. ❶

⚔ SHERRY BODEGAS

People come to Jerez for the *jerez*. Multilingual tour guides distill the sherry-making process for you, then give you (lots of) free samples . The best time to visit is early September during the harvest; the worst is August when many *bodegas* close down. Group reservations for tours must be made at least one week in advance; reservations for individuals are usually unnecessary. Call ahead for exact times. Looking for a job? Many *bodegas* hire and train English-speaking tour guides for as few as two or three months (even if you're not a wino), depending on need. Call to inquire; a summer of sherry could be in your future.

B. Domecq, C. San Idelfonso, 3 (☎956 15 15 00; www.domecq.es). Founded in 1730, Domecq is the oldest and largest *bodega* in town. 1½hr. tours include an informative 15min. video followed by a stroll through some of the warehouses and gardens of the sprawling complex. Very generous unlimited sampling of 3 sherries and 2 brandies. Tours every hr. M-F 10am-1pm, €5. Guides available. Reservations required. Group visits available on weekends. AmEx/MC/V.

González Byass, C. Manuel María González, 12 (☎956 35 70 16; www.gonzalezbyass.es). The makers of the popular Tío Pepe brand seen all over the city. The Disneyworld of *bodegas*: uncomfortably commercial and definitely overblown, but worth visiting; very kid-friendly as well. Trolleys whisk visitors past the world's largest weathervane and a storage room designed by Gustave Eiffel. At the end of the tour, a trained mouse climbs a miniature ladder to sip a glass of *oloroso*. Check out the rows upon rows of celebrity- and politician-autographed wine barrels—Steven Spielberg, Margaret Thatcher, and Orson Welles, among others. June-Sept. tours in English M-Sa every hr. 11:30am-1:30pm and 4:30-6:30pm; in Spanish M-Sa every hr. 11am-2pm and 5-7pm, Su 11am-1pm. Oct.-May tours in English M-Sa every hr. 11:30am-5:30pm, Su 11:30am-1:30pm; in Spanish M-Sa every hr. 11am-6pm, Su 11am-1pm. €7, 2pm tour with light *tapas* €11.50. AmEx/MC/V.

Sandeman, C. Pizarro, 10 (☎956 31 29 95; www.sandeman.com). Although most associated with port, Sandeman (est. 1790) is also a leading sherry producer. Their labels sport a stylish black-caped *Don*. Immaculate grounds and *bodegas*. 1hr. tours M-F every hr. 10:30am-4:30pm, Sa 11:30am-1:30pm, Su for groups only. €4.50. MC/V.

Harvey's, C. Arcos, 57 (☎956 34 60 04; www.jerezharveys.es). Makers of Harvey's Cream, the best selling sherry in the world. Visit includes a video of the production process and a tour featuring peacocks, countless oak barrels, and a crocodile. 1½hr. tours M-F 10am and noon (€4.50), Sa noon (€7). Reservations required for groups. MC/V.

🧭 SIGHTS

ALCÁZAR. Seized by Christian knights under Alfonso X during *la Reconquista* of Jerez in 1255, the Alcázar has slowly changed over the centuries. During the 1300s, the Moorish governor's private mosque was transformed into a chapel to commemorate the intercession of the Virgin Mary on behalf of Christian raids into the Kingdom of Granada. Later, in the 17th century, the neighboring Arab baths became servants' quarters for the Palacio de Villavicencio, where the **Cámara Oscura** resides today. Designed along a model by Leonardo Da Vinci, it uses reflective lenses to project panoramas of the city. (☎956 31 97 98. Open May-Sept. 15 M-Sa 10am-8pm, Su 10am-3pm; Sept. 16-Apr. daily 10am-6pm. Alcázar only €1.30, students €0.65; Alcázar and Cámara Oscura €3.30, students €2.60.)

REAL ESCUELA ANDALUZA DE ARTE EQUESTRE. Jerez's love for wine is almost matched by its passion for horses. During the first or second week of May, the Royal Andalusian School of Equestrian Art) sponsors the **Feria del Caballo**—a horse fair with shows, carriage competitions, and races of Jerez-bred Carthusian horses. During the rest of the year, weekly shows feature a troupe of horses dancing in choreographed sequences. The training sessions are almost as impressive. The new, interactive **Museo del Enganche** (Harness Museum), on the school grounds, displays old-fashioned carriages led by specially trained horses. (Av. Duque de Abrantes. ☎956 31 96 35; www.realescuela.org. Training sessions year-round M and W, during July-Sept. also F; 10am-1pm. €6. Shows year-round Th noon, March-Oct. Tu noon, Aug. also F noon; €13-21, children and over 65 40% off. Museum and training session €7; museum only €3. MC/V.)

ANDALUCÍA

THE BIG SPLURGE

FINE FEATHERED FRIENDS

Bust out your binoculars—the 60,000 acre **Parque Nacional Coto de Doñana** on the Río Guadalquivir delta is home to flamingos, vultures, mongeese, wild boars, and lynx. If ornithological delights don't entice you, the salt marshes, sand dunes, wooded areas, and beach might. Nature purists beware, though, lest you stumble upon the lair of the dreaded species *turgrupus touristicus*—the park borders Matalascañas, with a concrete shopping center and hotel complex.

(Access to most of the park is restricted, and back-country hiking and camping are prohibited. The park can be visited only on a guided tour. Call the Visitor's Center ☎ 956 38 16 35. Open daily June-Aug. 9am-8pm; Sept.-May 9am-2:30pm and 4-7pm. 4hr. guided tours daily 8:30am and 5pm, €9.50.

The western end of the park is accessible from Huelva and Matalascañas. Boat tours on the **S.S. Real Fernando** depart from **Sanlúcar**. ☎ 956 36 38 13. 4hr.; daily June.-Sept. 10am and 5pm; Apr., May, and Oct. 10am and 4pm; Nov.-Mar. 10am; €14.64. Call or visit the office in the old ice factory by the dock on Av. Bajo de Guía. Those more interested in sand than life on the wild side can take the launch across the bay (8am-8pm, leaves when full, €3) to one of the few non-touristed beaches in Spain.)

🎵 📻 ENTERTAINMENT & NIGHTLIFE

FLAMENCO. Rare footage of Spain's most highly regarded *flamenco* singers, dancers, and guitarists is available for viewing at the **Centro Andaluz de Flamenco,** in Palacio Pemartín, on Pl. San Juan. The library upstairs has lots of information on *flamenco* in the city and region. (☎ 956 34 92 65; www.caf.cica.es. Open M-F 9am-2pm. Videos every hr. 10am-2pm. Free.) Most *peñas* and *tablaos* (clubs and bars that host *flamenco*) hide in the old town and host special performances during July and August. Ask for details in the tourist office or look for posters along the main streets; occasionally there are free performances in evenings in some plazas. For more frequent (and touristy) shows, make the trek to **El Lagá de Tío Parrilla,** Pl. del Mercado, which hosts some of Jerez's best *flamenco*. (☎/fax 956 33 83 34. Shows M-Sa 10:30pm and 12:30am. Reservations requested. Cover €12, includes 1 drink.)

NIGHTLIFE. Visitors to Jerez tend to be on the older side, and nightlife in the city center caters directly to them—there are plenty of *tapas* bars where you can knock back a few glasses of sherry, but to get to the more lively, younger scene, it's necessary to head to the outskirts of the city. Although certainly not authentically Spanish, the Irish-themed bar and disco complex **Plaza Canterbury,** C. Paul at C. Zaragoza, is definitely a hot spot for tourists and students alike, with two bars (one serving tapas), an outdoor patio, and a popular club. (Beer at bars €1.50, mixed drinks €4; at club €2.50/€5. Cover at disco €8. Bars open daily 4pm-4am, disco open Sept.-June F-Sa 1:30-7am.) A slew of bars and clubs lines the well-lit **Avenida Méjico** between C. Santo Domingo and C. Salvatierra and some of the side streets (a 25min. walk from Pl. del Arenal).

FESTIVALS. Autumn, in addition to being grape harvest season, is festival season, when Jerez showcases its best equine and *flamenco* traditions. These festivals are collectively known as the **Fiestas de Otoño,** occurring from early September until the end of October. In September, the **Fiesta de la Bulería** celebrates *flamenco*, as does the **Festival de Teatro, Música, y Baile.** The largest **horse parade** in the world, with races in Pl. del Arenal, is the highlight of the final week. Check at the tourist office for details; schedules are available in September for the upcoming year.

SANLÚCAR DE BARRAMEDA ☎956

Sanlúcar de Barrameda (pop. 62,000), at the mouth of the Río Guadalquivir, borders both the Parque Nacional Coto de Doñana and a variety of relatively uncrowded beaches. Visitors come to Sanlúcar mostly to get a taste of southern Spain's sherry *bodegas*, fine sands, and *cascos antiguos* without all the tourists of nearby Jerez and Cádiz. This seaside corner of the illustrious "sherry triangle," along with Jerez and El Puerto de Santa María, makes for a good weekend getaway, but there's not enough to entertain visitors for much longer.

█ TRANSPORTATION. The bus station is on Av. de la Estación, 1 block from the main Calzada del Ejército. **Transportes Los Amarillos** (☎956 38 50 60) runs **buses** to: **Cádiz** (1hr., 5-11 per day 6:15am-7:20pm, €2.64); **Chipiona** (30min., 8-15 per day 8:15am-10:40pm, €0.73); **Sevilla** (2hr., 6-12 per day 6:45am-8:15pm, €6.23). **Linesur** (☎956 34 10 63) goes to **Jerez** (45min.; M-F every hr. 7:20am-10:20pm, Sa-Su every 2 hr.; €1.43). Buy tickets on the bus. For **taxis,** call ☎956 36 11 02 or 36 00 04.

█ █ ORIENTATION & PRACTICAL INFORMATION. The **tourist office** is in a Moorish-looking building on Calzada del Ejército, which runs perpendicular to the beach. English-speaking staff has info on the **Parque Nacional Coto de Doñana.** (☎ 956 36 61 10. Open daily June-Aug. 10am-2pm and 6-8pm; Sept.-May 10am-2pm and 4-6pm.) To hit the beach from the bus station, exit right and turn left at the intersection; for the historic center and tourist office, turn right at the intersection. Services include: **emergency** ☎061; **Ambulatorio de la S.S.** on Calzada del Ejército (☎956 36 71 65); **police,** Av. de la Constitución (☎956 38 80 11); **Internet access** at **Cyber Guadalquivir,** C. Infante Beatriz, 11 (€1.80 per hr.; open daily 10am-2am); **post office,** C. Correos and Av. Cerro Falcón, toward the beach from the tourist office (☎956 36 09 37; open M-F 8:30am-2:30pm, Sa 9am-1pm). **Postal Code:** 11540.

█ █ ACCOMMODATIONS & FOOD. Few true bargains exist in Sanlúcar; it may be worth it to inquire at doorway signs reading *"se alquilan habitaciones"* (rooms for rent). **Hostal La Blanca Paloma ❷,** Pl. San Roque, 15, keeps clean rooms of varying sizes, a few with balconies. (☎956 36 36 44. Singles €15; doubles €27; triples €39.) Sanlúcar is famous for its *langostinos*. For a sit-down meal, head for the side streets off C. San Juan or uphill into the *casco antiguo. Terrazas* fill Pl. San Roque and Pl. del Cabildo, this tree-lined neighbor. Satisfy that sweet tooth at **Helados Artesanos Toni ❶,** Pl. del Cabildo, 2. Established in 1896, Toni has the best ice cream in town hands down. (Small cone €1; large €2. Open daily 11am-2am.)

█ █ SIGHTS & ENTERTAINMENT. Two impressive palaces compete with the enormous 14th-century **Iglesia de Nuestra Señora de la O,** Pl. de la Paz, for the attention of sun-struck tourists. (☎956 36 05 55. Mass M-F 8pm; Su 9am, noon, 8pm. Open 30min. before and after Mass. Free.) Sanlúcar has put its historic buildings to good use; most are still inhabited or have been transformed into offices. The **Palacio Medina Sidonia,** Pl. Condes de Niebla, is still inhabited by the Duque de Medina Sidonia. (☎956 36 01 61. Open Su 10:30am-1:30pm. Free.) The 19th-century **Palacio de Orleáns y Borbón** now houses the Ayuntamiento. (☎956 38 80 00. Open M-F 10am-1:30pm. Free.) Sanlúcar's sandy **beaches** stretch for 6km from the mouth of the Río Guadalquivir toward the open Atlantic. At low tide, sandbars make it possible to walk halfway out into the river. Several **bodegas** tower over Sanlúcar's small streets; check at the tourist office for their schedules. (Tours M-Sa. Call for exact times. €1.80-3.) Locals celebrate their sherry during the **Feria de la Manza-**

nilla (late May or early June). In August, ▨**Carreras de Caballos** (horse races) thunder along the beach, and the **Festival de la Exaltación del Río Guadalquivir** brings poetry readings, a *flamenco* competition, dancing, and bullfights.

ARCOS DE LA FRONTERA ☎956

"Imagine a long, narrow ridge, undulating; place on it little white houses, clustered among others more ancient; imagine that both sides of the mountain have been cut away, dropping downward sheer and straight; and at the foot of this wall a slow, silent river, its murky waters licking the yellowish stone, then going on its destructive course throughout the fields. . . and when you have imagined all this, you will have but a pale image of Arcos." Though Spanish novelist Azorín was waxing poetic here, he's not far off. The most popular of Spain's *pueblos blancos*, Arcos (pop. 33,000) is a historic and romantic gem. Emanating like gossamer strings from the Plaza del Cabildo, the convoluted medieval streets lead visitors past geranium-lined balconies and tranquil farmers' markets lying unperturbed in the sun.

▙ TRANSPORTATION

Buses: Station, C. Corregidores. **Los Amarillos buses** (☎956 70 49 77) go to **Jerez** (30min.; M-F 8-18 per day 6:30am-8:15pm, Sa-Su 8am-6:30pm; €2) and **Sevilla** (2hr.; 2 per day 7am, 5pm; €6.12). **Transportes Generales Comes** to: **Cádiz** (1½hr., 6 per day 7:20am-7:15pm, €4.60); **Costa del Sol** (3-4hr., 1 per day 4pm, €9.21-12.36); **Ronda** (1¾hr., 4 per day 8:15am-2pm, €6).

Taxis: Radio Taxi (24hr. ☎956 70 13 55). Taxis cluster around C. Debajo del Corral.

▟ ▛ ORIENTATION & PRACTICAL INFORMATION

To reach the town center from the bus station, exit left, follow the road, and turn left again. Continue uphill for two blocks on C. Josefa Moreno Seguro, taking a right on C. Muñoz Vázquez. From there it's a 20min. walk uphill. Continue straight until reaching Pl. de España, then veer left onto C. Debajo del Coral, which quickly changes into C. Corredera; the old quarter is 500m ahead. Mini-buses run every 30min. from the bus station to C. Corredera (€0.81). A taxi costs €3.

Tourist Office: Pl. del Cabildo (☎956 70 22 64). Open Mar. 15-Oct. 15 M-Sa 10am-2pm and 4-8pm; Oct. 16-Mar. 14 M-Sa 10am-2pm and 3:30-7:30pm. **Tours** of the old city M-F 10:30am, 5pm; Sa 10:30am. €3, children free. Also gives patio tours M-F noon, 6:30pm; Sa noon. €3.

Bank: Banco Santander Central Hispano, C. Corredera, 62 (☎902 24 24 24). Open M-F 8:30am-2pm, Sa 8:30am-1pm.

Emergency: ☎091. **Police:** C. Nueva (☎956 70 16 52).

Medical Emergency: ☎061 or 956 51 15 53. **Hospital: Centro de Salud,** C. Rafael Benat Rubio (☎956 70 0787), in the Barrio Bajo.

Pharmacy: Ldo. Ildefonso Guerrero Seijo, C. Corredera, 11 (☎956 70 02 13). Open Apr.-Sept. M-F 9:30am-1:30pm and 5-9pm; Oct.-Mar. M-F 9:30am-1:30pm and 4:30-8pm, Sa 9:30am-1:30pm.

Post Office: C. Murete, 24 (☎956 70 15 60), overlooking the cliffs and the river. Open M-F 8:30am-2:30pm, Sa 9:30am-1pm. **Postal Code:** 11630.

ACCOMMODATIONS

Arcos has only a few budget hostels, although for only a few euros more, you can often get a room at one of the classier hotels in town. Call ahead during *Semana Santa* and in the summer to be safe.

Pensión Callejon de las Monjas, C. Deán Espinosa, 4 (☎956 70 23 02), shaded by the buttresses of Iglesia de Sta. María. Entrepreneurial owner runs a hostel in addition to a restaurant and barbershop on the ground floor. Spotless rooms, some with TV, bath, and A/C. Singles €18, with bath €22; doubles €27/€33, with large terrace €39; suite for 4 people €66. MC/V. ❷

Hotel La Fonda, C. Corredera, 83 (☎956 70 00 57; fax 70 36 61). Originally a 19th-century inn, La Fonda still retains its oldtime charm. Wide, plushly-carpeted hallways lead to large rooms with balconies, some with terraces. Breakfast included. Mar.-Oct. 15 singles €29; doubles €51.50. Oct.-Feb. €19/€32. AmEx/MC/V. ❸

Hostal San Marcos, C. Marqués de Torresoto, 6 (☎956 70 07 21), past C. Deán Espinosa and Pl. del Cabildo. Ascend the steep, tiled stairs to quiet rooms, all with large private baths. Restaurant below serves one of the cheapest *menús* in town (€6). Prices depend on room and season. Singles €20-25; doubles €30-36. MC/V. ❷

FOOD

Cheap cafes and restaurants huddle at the bottom end of C. Corredera, while *tapas* nirvana can be reached uphill in the old quarter.

Mesón Los Murales, Pl. Boticas, 1 (☎956 70 06 07). Enjoy delicious *comida típica* in the blue-and-white decorated interior, or on the peaceful plaza outside. Great homemade flan (€2.40). Entrees €4.80-8.40. *Menú* €7.50. Open daily 9am-11pm. ❷

Los Faraones, C. Debajo del Corral, 8 (☎956 70 06 12), downhill from C. Corredera. Arab cuisine and hearty Spanish staples prepared by a friendly Egyptian-Spanish couple. Extensive vegetarian *menú* €11, regular meaty *menú* €9, *platos combinados* €6. Open Tu-Su 9am-5:30pm and 8pm-midnight. ❷

Restaurante El Convento, C. Marqués de Torresoto, 7 (☎956 70 41 28), across from Hostal San Marcos. Slightly exotic Andalusian fare—rabbit, partridge, duck, deer, etc.— served in a 17th-century setting. Appetizers €4-9, entrees €7-15. Open daily 1-4pm and 7:30-10pm. Closed the 1st or 2nd week of July. MC/V. ❸

SIGHTS & FESTIVALS

The most beautiful sights in Arcos are the winding white alleys, Roman ruins, and hanging flowers of the old quarter, combined with the view from ◪**Plaza del Cabildo.** The balcony, overlooking the entire region, earned the nickname *Balcón de Coño* because the view is so startling that people often exclaim ¡*coño!* (expletive) in disbelief. In this square stands the **Basílica de Santa María de la Asunción,** a blend of Baroque, Renaissance, and Gothic styles built between the 15th and 18th centuries. A symbol of the Inquisition—a circular design within which exorcisms were once performed—is still etched into the ground on the church's left side. (Open M-F 10am-1pm and 4-7pm, Sa 10am-2pm. €1.50.) The late Gothic **Iglesia de San Pedro** stands on the site of an Arab fortress in the old quarter. A collection of religious paintings by Murillo, Zurbarán, and Ribera decorates the interior. (Open Sa 10am-1pm and 4-7pm, Su 10am-1:30pm. €1.50. Mass 11:30am. Free.) An artificial **lake** built in 1960 laps at Arcos's feet; although you can't swim in the lake itself, the scenic beach, **Mesón de la Molinera,** is a pretty change of scenery and a popular spot for a *paseo.* Buses run from Arcos (M-Sa 5 per day 9:15am-8:15pm, Su 2-4 per day 12:15-8:15pm; €0.81). **Festivals** in Arcos are highly spirited and quite popular; book accommodations far in advance. A favorite is the **Toro de Aleluya,** held on Easter Sunday: two bulls run rampant through the steep, cobbled streets amidst *flamenco,* drinking, and general merriment.

CÁDIZ   ☎956

Located on a peninsula, Cádiz (pop. 155,000) has a powerful ocean on one side and a placid bay on the other. Despite this, one can wander through the narrow streets of the old town, strolling from plaza to plaza between soaring cathedrals and outdoor cafes without realizing the city is surrounded by water. Cádiz is both a thriving metropolis and a touristed beach town. Founded by the Phoenicians in 1100 BC, Cádiz is thought to be the oldest inhabited city in Europe. From the 16th to the 18th century, the Spanish colonial shipping industry transformed the port into one of the wealthiest in Europe. The city is renowned for its extravagant *Carnaval,* the only festival of its size and kind not suppressed during the Franco regime. Perhaps Spain's most dazzling party, *Carnaval* makes Cádiz an essential stop on February itineraries. During the rest of the year, Cádiz offers a little of everything to visitors—a thoroughly Spanish city trimmed by golden sand beaches.

▌ TRANSPORTATION

Trains: RENFE, Pl. de Sevilla (☎956 25 43 01). To: **Barcelona** (12hr.; 2 per day 8am, 8:25pm; €61.50); **Córdoba** (3hr., 4 per day 8am-8:25pm, €15.40-30.50); **Jerez** (40min., 15-21 per day 6:36am-10:06pm, €3.05); **Madrid** (5hr.; 2 per day 8am, 4:25pm; €55-85); **Sevilla** (2hr., 12 per day 5:55am-7:57pm, €8.25-18).

Buses: Several private companies operate out of small stations in Cádiz.

Secorbus (☎902 22 92 92) runs to **Madrid** (8hr., 6 per day 8:10am-11:10pm, €21.05). Buses depart from near Estadio Ramón de Carranza, past Glorieta Ingeniero La Cierva in new Cádiz.

Transportes Los Amarillos (☎956 28 58 52) depart from beside the port in front of Paseo de Canalejas. Purchase tickets on the bus or at the Viajes Socialtur office on nearby Av. Ramón de Carranza, 31 (open M-F 9:30am-1:30pm and 5-8:30pm, alternate Sa 10am-1pm). To: **Arcos de la Frontera** (1hr., 7 per day 12:30-7:15pm, €3.77); **Chipiona** (1½hr., 5-11 per day 7:15am-7:30pm, €3.24); **Sanlúcar** (1hr., 5-11 per day 7:15am-7:30pm, €2.64).

Transportes Generales Comes, Pl. de la Hispanidad, 1 (☎956 22 78 11). To: **Algeciras** (3hr., 10 per day 6:45am-8pm, €8.51); **Córdoba** (5hr.; M-F 7am, daily 1 per day 4pm; €17.89); **Arcos de la Frontera** (1½hr., 4-6 per day 7am-6:30pm, €4.60); **Granada** (5hr., 4 per day 9am-9pm, €25.30); **Jerez de la Frontera** (45min., 8-22 per day 6am-9pm, €2.45); **La Línea** (3hr.; 3 per day 11:30am, 2, 5pm; €10.06); **Málaga** (4hr., 6 per day 6:45am-8pm, €17.84); **Ronda** (3hr.; 3 per day 7, 10:30am, 2:30pm; €11.46); **Sevilla** (2hr., 11-14 per day 7am-10pm, €9.32); **Vejer de la Frontera** (1½hr., 6-9 per day 9am-9:15pm, €4).

Ferry: El Vaporcito (☎956 87 02 70) departs from a dock behind the Estación Marítima near the Transportes Generales Comes station and runs to **Puerto de Santa María** (30-45min., 4-6 per day 10am-8:30pm, return 9am-7:30pm; €2.50, bikes €1).

Municipal Buses: (☎956 26 28 06). Pick up a map/schedule and *bonobus* (discount packet of 10 tickets for €6) at the kiosk across from the Transportes Generales Comes bus station. Most lines run through Pl. de España. Beach bums' favorite bus #1 (Cortadura) runs along the shore to new Cádiz (every 10min. 6:40am-1:10am, €0.80). Bus #7 runs the same route, leaving from **Playa de la Caleta.**

Taxis: ☎956 21 21 21.

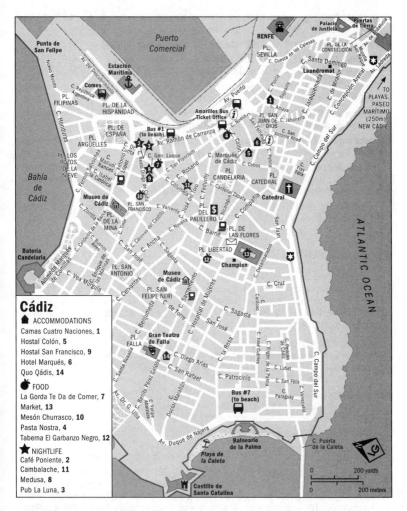

Cádiz

♠ ACCOMMODATIONS
Camas Cuatro Naciones, **1**
Hostal Colón, **5**
Hostal San Francisco, **9**
Hotel Marqués, **6**
Quo Qádis, **14**

● FOOD
La Gorda Te Da de Comer, **7**
Market, **13**
Mesón Churrasco, **10**
Pasta Nostra, **4**
Taberna El Garbanzo Negro, **12**

★ NIGHTLIFE
Café Poniente, **2**
Cambalache, **11**
Medusa, **8**
Pub La Luna, **3**

ORIENTATION & PRACTICAL INFORMATION

Cádiz's old town was built on the end of the peninsula, and the new town grew up behind it farther inland. The old town hosts most of the cheap hostels and historic sights (not to mention the bus and train stations), while the new town is home to high-rise hotels, numerous bars and restaurants, and kilometers of lovely sand. When you take the bus into new Cádiz (down the main avenue), hop off at **Glorieta Ingeniero La Cierva.** The beach lies directly behind it.

> **Tourist Office: Municipal,** Pl. San Juan de Dios, 11 (☎956 24 10 01). Useful free map. English spoken. Open M-F 9am-2pm and 5-8pm. On weekends, a kiosk opens in front of the main office (open Sa-Su and holidays June-Sept. 10am-1pm and 5-7:30pm; Oct.-May 10am-1:30pm and 4-6pm). **Junta de Andalucía,** Av. Ramón de Carranza (☎956 25 86 46). Large selection of regional maps. Open M and Sa 9am-2pm, Tu-F 9am-7pm.

Currency Exchange: Banco Santander Central Hispano, C. Columela, 13 (☎902 24 24 24). Open M-F 8:30am-2pm, Sa 8:30am-1pm.

Luggage Storage: Lockers at train station (€3 per day). Open daily 8am-11pm.

Student Travel Agency: Barceló Viajes, C. San Francisco, 15 (☎956 21 22 23; www.barceloviajes.com). Open M-F 9:30am-1:30pm and 5-9pm, Sa 9:30am-1:30pm.

Emergency: ☎061. **Municipal police:** ☎092, C. Campo del Sur in the new city. **National police:** Av. de Andalucía, 28 (☎091), in the new city.

Medical Assistance: Ambulatorio Vargas Ponce (☎062 or 956 28 38 55). **Hospital: Centro de Salud,** Av. Ana de Viya, 21 (☎956 24 21 00).

Laundromat: Lavandería Europa, C. Santo Domingo, 17 (☎956 25 73 98). €3 per kg. Open M-F 9am-1pm and 3-7pm, Sa 9am-1pm.

Internet Access: Enred@dos, C. Sacramento, 36 (☎956 80 81 81) and **Enred@dos 2,** C. Isabel la Católica. Both €2.40 per hr. Open M-Sa 11am-11pm. **Salon Columela,** C. Columela. Coin-operated. €0.50 per 15min. Open daily 9am-10:30pm.

Post Office: Pl. de las Flores (☎956 21 39 45). Open M-F 8:30am-8:30pm, Sa 9:30am-2pm. **Postal Code:** 11070.

ACCOMMODATIONS

Most hostels huddle around the harbor, in and around Pl. San Juan de Dios. Others are scattered throughout the old town. Singles and private bathrooms are scarce. Call months in advance to find a room during February's *Carnaval;* calling a few days ahead during the summer should be fine. Many owners are willing to bargain a bit on rates, except during the busiest times of the year.

Hostal San Francisco, C. San Francisco, 12 (☎956 22 18 42). Spacious rooms surround a Spanish patio with Japanese decor. Large communal baths. July-Sept. singles €20; €27, with bath €42. May-June €18/€28/€38. Oct.-Apr. €16/€27/€35. AmEx/MC/V. ❷

Hotel Marqués, C. Marqués de Cádiz, 1 (☎956 28 58 54). Spacious, clean rooms with new, firm mattresses surround enclosed inner courtyard. All rooms with balcony. Singles €18; doubles €25, with bath €35; triples €35. ❷

Hostal Colón, C. Marqués de Cádiz, 6 (☎956 28 53 51). Spotless, very sunny white rooms with sinks, colorful tiles, and balconies. Has a great rooftop terrace. July-Sept. and *Semana Santa* doubles €32; triples €48. Oct.-June €28/€40. ❸

Quo Qádis, C. Diego Arias, 1 (☎/fax 956 22 19 39). Old but clean rooms, roof terrace, laundry facilities (€4.80), and a social atmosphere. Vegetarian dinners (€3.50). Bike rental €6 per day. Self-serve breakfast included. Sheets €1.20. Dorm rooms sleep 10; women's dorm is windowless. Regular rooms are mediocre for the price. Lockout 11am-5pm for dorms. Dorms €6; doubles €24, with shower €30; triples €36. 10% discount if you arrive by bike. ❶

Camas Cuatro Naciones, C. Plocia, 3 (☎956 25 55 39). Very bare, very tiny rooms with industrial-looking metal beds, but one of the cheapest places to stay in Cádiz. Some inner rooms have windows only onto the hallway. June-Sept. singles €12, with balcony €15; doubles €25. Oct.-May €11/€12/€21. ❶

FOOD

Once you leave Pl. San Juan de Dios, finding eateries can be a trying experience. Opt for cafes and *heladerías* in any of Cádiz's many plazas, or try the streets off C. San Francisco for local *tapas* bars and restaurants. To stock up on food for the beach, head to **Supermarket Champion,** next to the market off Pl. de las Flores (open M-Sa 9am-10pm), or try the market behind the plaza.

Taberna El Garbanzo Negro, C. Sacramento, 18 (☎956 22 10 90). Extensive menu features delicious variations on traditional Spanish staples such as meat croquettes and squid and potatoes stew (½ *raciones* €2-3.60, *raciones* €4-7). Wooden tables, stools, and art deco posters make this a cross between a traditional restaurant and a trendy *tapas* bar. Great *tinto del verano* (€1.20). *Menú del día* €6.50, served afternoons only. Open M 1-4:30pm, Tu-Th and Sa-Su 1-4:30pm and 8:30pm-12:30am. ❶

Pasta Nostra, C. Cristóbal Colón (☎956 25 27 23). Hidden away on a tiny side street with only a few tables, Pasta Nostra has a surprisingly local feel to it. Mouth-watering ravioli, lasagna, salads, and crêpes served up *con gusto* by the owner himself. *Tapas*-sized pasta portions €2.60. Entrees €5.20-6.50. Pizzas €5.20. Open June-Sept. M-Sa 12:30-4pm and 8pm-midnight; Oct.-May Tu-Su 12:30-4pm and 8pm-midnight. ❶

La Gorda Te Da de Comer, C. General Luque, 1. Brand spanking new, boldly painted, and kid-friendly, this new *tapas* bar puts a 21st-century spin on ages-old culinary practices. *Tapas* (€1.20-1.50). Open M 9pm-12:30am, Tu-Sa 1-5pm and 9pm-12:30am. ❶

Mesón Churrasco, C. San Francisco, 3 (☎956 22 03 73). Traditional *bodega* packed with locals and legs of ham (their specialty). *Tapas* €1.20-3; *raciones* €3 and up. Open daily 9am-4pm and 8pm-midnight. ❶

⬢ SIGHTS

■**CATEDRAL.** This gold-domed 18th-century masterpiece is considered the last great cathedral financed by colonial riches. It took 116 years to build, resulting in a mix of Baroque and Neoclassical styles. The treasury bulges with valuables—the *Custodia del Millón* is said to be set with a million precious stones. Visit the nearby **museum** for all sorts of treasures and art. *(Pl. de la Catedral. ☎956 28 61 54. Mass W and F 7:30pm, Su noon. Open Tu-F 10am-1:30pm and 4:30-7:30pm, Sa 10am-1:30pm. Last entrance 30min. before close. Admission includes cathedral and museum. €3, children €2.)*

PASEO. Cádiz's seaside *paseo* runs around the old city and along the Atlantic; walking the path is a good way to get a feel for the layout of the city. Stupendous views of ships leaving the harbor recall Spain's golden age. Exotic trees, fanciful hedges, and a few chattering monkeys enliven the adjacent **Parque Genovés.** On the beachside of the city, the *paseo* stretches all the way to the new city. *(Paseo accessible via Pl. Argüelles or C. Fermín Salvochea, off Pl. de España.)*

MUSEO DE CÁDIZ. Due to a fusion of the Fine Arts and Provincial Archaeological Museums, Murillo, Rubens, and Zurbarán live here in unholy union with Phoenician sarcophagi, ancient jewelry, blown glass, and pottery. The first floor displays archaeological exhibits; the second houses mostly religious, 17th- to 19th-century paintings; the third holds an impressive collection of modern art. *(Pl. Mina. ☎956 21 22 81. Handicapped accessible. Open for guided tours Tu 9am-2:30pm by appt. only; for public Tu 2:30-8pm, W-Sa 9am-8pm, Su 9:30am-2:30pm. €1.50, EU citizens and students with ID free.)*

⬢ BEACHES

As Cádiz was built on a peninsula, the exhaust-spewing ships on one coast don't pollute the pristine beaches on the other. **Playa de la Caleta** is the most convenient beach to the old city, at the far tip of Cádiz. Better sand and more space can be found in the new city, serviced by bus #1, leaving from Pl. de España (€0.80), or reached by walking along the *paseo* by the water (20-30min. from behind the cathedral). The first beach beyond the rocks is the unremarkable **Playa de Santa María del Mar.** Next to it, ■**Playa de la Victoria** has earned a *bandera azul*. Get off bus #1 at Glorieta Ingeniero La Cierva in front of McDonald's. A more natural landscape with fewer hotels belongs to **Playa de Cortadura,** where another *bandera azul* flaps proudly. Take bus #1 until it almost reaches the highway, where the bus turns around. The boardwalk ends here, and the sunbather density falls steadily.

ANDALUCÍA

▓▓ NIGHTLIFE & FESTIVALS

Cádiz's nightlife migrates depending on the season; in winter the scene is situated primarily in the old city, while summer takes the party closer to the beach in the new city. In the old city, look for bars on the side streets off C. Columela and C. San Francisco. The popular bar **Cambalache,** C. José del Toro, 20, on the left after the intersection with C. Columela, gets packed Thursday nights when there's live jazz. (☎607 86 58 01. Beer generally runs €1.50, while mixed drinks will set you back €4. Open daily 8:30pm-late.) For a more alternative scene, head to nearby **Medusa,** C. General Luque, 8, where university students mingle to the tunes of Cold Play and Radiohead, among others. Wednesdays are international night, with €1 beers. (Beer €1.50. Mixed drinks €4. Dancing on weekends. Open Su and Tu-Th 10pm-3:30am; F-Sa 10pm-4:30am.) Nearby **Pub La Luna,** on C. Dr. Zurita, hosts a mixed gay and lesbian scene with Friday night drag queen performances at midnight. (Open Tu-Su 11pm-4am.) **Café Poniente,** C. Beato Diego de Cádiz, 18, attracts a mostly gay, male crowd. (Open Su-Th 11pm-3am, F-Sa 11pm-4:30am.)

In the new city, C. General Muñoz Arenillas, off Glorieta Ingeniero La Cierva, and **Paseo Marítimo,** the main drag along Playa Victoria, have some of Cádiz's best bars. Especially popular in summer are the numerous *chiringuitos* (beach bars). **Barabass,** on C. General Muñoz Arenillas, is one of the most popular disco-bars, featuring sparkling lights, a dance floor, and pop music. (Open daily 4pm-6am.) Club-rats will prefer **Punto de San Felipe,** a strip of 10 bars and clubs reached by walking north along the sea from Pl. de España (take a right before the tunnel); these spots don't get going until 4 or 5am.

Carnaval insanity is legendary. The gray of winter gives way to dazzling color as the city hosts one of the most raucous *carnavales* in the world (February 19-29 in 2004). Costumed dancers, street singers, ebullient residents, and spectators from the world over take to the streets in a week-long frenzy that makes New Orleans's Mardi Gras look like Thursday night bingo at the old folks' home.

VEJER DE LA FRONTERA ☎956

Glistening white above the turquoise sea and rolling hills and valleys, beautiful Vejer (pop. 20,000) is one of Andalucía's most enchanting *pueblos blancos.* Fourteenth-century homes line cobblestoned alleys, and gray-haired men discuss politics on street corners. A mere village, Vejer is a great place to unwind for a few hours. Although formal sights are far between, the chance to wander the town's enchanting streets alone merits a visit. For the more restless, it is best explored as a daytrip from Cádiz or a stop en route to or from Tarifa.

▐ TRANSPORTATION. While some buses stop at the end of **Avenida de Los Remedios,** which leads uphill into **La Plazuela** (10min.), many leave you by the highway at **La Barca de Vejer,** a small town at the base of the hill. Take one of the numerous taxis waiting by the bus stop (€5). The alternative, an arduous 20min. uphill climb, is extremely difficult with a backpack. If you do make the trek, climb the cobbled track to the left of the restaurant. When you reach the top, follow the road to the left to reach quiet **Plaza de España;** the road on the right leads uphill to smaller La Plazuela, a tiny intersection where Av. de Los Remedios and C. Juan Bueno meet.

For **bus** info and tickets, stop by the small **Transportes Generales Comes** office, La Plazuela, 2b. (☎956 44 71 46. Open M-F 9am-2:30pm and 6-11pm, Sa-Su 11am-2:30pm and 6-11pm. When the office is closed, buy tickets on the bus.) From the stop on Av. de Los Remedios, buses leave for **Cádiz** (1½hr., 8 per day 7:15am-8pm, €4). For other destinations, descend the hill (1½km) to **La Barca de Vejer.** (Buses leave for La Barca de Vejer every 15min. 10:15am-10:15pm, €0.95.) Service to: **Algeciras** (2hr., 11 per day 7:45am-10:45pm, €4.73); **Málaga** (4hr.; 2 per day 7:45am, 5pm; €13.77); **Sevilla** (3½hr., 4 per day 8:30am-5:40pm, €10.50); **Tarifa** (1hr., 11 per day 7:45am-10:45pm, €3.18). For a **taxi,** call ☎956 45 04 08.

⁊ PRACTICAL INFORMATION. The staff at the **tourist office,** C. Marqués de Tamarón, 10, speaks English. (☎956 45 17 36. Open June-Aug. M-F 9am-2pm and 6:30-8pm, in Aug. also Sa 10:30am-2pm; Sept.-May call for hours.) Services include: **Banco Santander Central Hispano,** C. Juan Bueno, 5 (☎902 24 24 24; open M-F 8:30am-2pm, Sa 8:30am-1pm); **Centro de Salud,** Av. de Andalucía (☎956 44 76 25); **police,** Av. de Andalucía, 9 (☎956 45 04 00); **post office** at C. Juan Bueno, 10 (☎956 45 02 38; open M-F 8:30am-2:30pm, Sa 9:30am-1pm). **Postal Code:** 11150.

⌂⌂ ACCOMMODATIONS & FOOD. The most affordable places to stay in Vejer are *casas particulares* (private houses); the tourist office has an extensive list of *hostales* and *casas* if the places below are full. Several options line C. San Filmo; to get there, follow C. Juan Relinque from La Plazuela, go right through small Pl. del Mercado, and head left uphill. Each of the seven rooms at the beautiful and tranquil *casa rural* ▩**El Cobijo de Vejer ❺,** C. San Filmo, 7, is uniquely decorated, with views of the ocean or surrounding valley. Alcoves, mini-kitchens, laundry, terraces, and sitting rooms are just some of the perks available, depending on the room. All rooms are wired for Internet and have A/C, satellite TV, and a refrigerator. (☎956 45 50 23; www.elcobijo.com. Reserve in advance. Breakfast included. June-Sept. and *Semana Santa* doubles €51-60; Oct.-May €45-54.) Certainly not as charming, but convenient and with more rooms, is the sterile **Hostal La Posada ❷,** Av. de Los Remedios, 21. (☎956 45 02 58. Singles €18; doubles with bath €36.) Friendly Sra. Rosa Romero owns **Casa Los Cántaros ❷,** C. San Filmo, 14, a beautifully restored Andalusian home with a grape-vined patio. The spotless rooms boast antique furniture, private bathrooms, and kitchen access. (☎956 44 75 92. Doubles June-Sept. €24; Oct.-May €23.)

The cheapest eats are *tapas* or *raciones* at the bars around La Plazuela; full-service restaurants are more expensive. The to-die-for food at French-owned creperie **La Chozita ❷,** Pl. de España, 28, is well worth the splurge. Sweet and savory crepes (€2.50) are made of only the freshest ingredients, and some have a fusion of French and Caribbean influences. (☎956 44 75 29. Live jazz and salsa some nights. Open daily noon-late.) Renowned for its *jamón ibérico*, family-run **Mesón Pepe Julián ❷,** C. Juan Relinque, 7, prepares the best *tapas* in town (€1-1.50) and serves reasonably priced entrees (€4.20-8) to a largely local crowd. (Open daily 11:30am-4pm and 7:30pm-midnight; Oct.-June closed W. MC/V.)

◉ SIGHTS. The best way to enjoy Vejer is by wandering along the labyrinthine streets and cliffside *paseos,* as those are more interesting than Vejer's actual monuments. The 9th-century **Castillo Moro,** down C. Ramón y Cajal from the church, almost blends in with the surrounding scenery. (Erratic schedule; inquire at tourist office for updated hours.) **Iglesia del Divino Salvador,** behind the tourist office, is a choice blend of Romanesque, Mudéjar, and Gothic styles. (Mass daily 8:30pm). Ten kilometers from Vejer on the road to Los Caños lies **El Palmar,** 7km of fine white sand and clear waters easily accessible by car or bus (June-Aug. 4 per day 11:45am-8:45pm, €0.80). Catch the Cádiz-bound bus to **Conil de la Frontera** and walk southeast along the beach for 3-4km. For information on the town and outdoor activities, consult **Discover Andalucía,** Av. de los Remedios, 45b, across from the bus stop. (☎956 44 75 75. Bicycles €12-15 per day. Surfboards from €6 per day. Open M-F 9am-2pm and 6-9pm, Sa 9am-2pm. AmEx/MC/V.)

ANDALUCÍA

◨ **FESTIVALS.** Vejer throws brilliant *fiestas*. Soon after the **Corpus Cristi** revelry in June comes the **Candelas de San Juan** (June 23), climaxing with the midnight release of the *toro de fuego* (bull of fire). A local (obviously, one with a death wish) dressed in an iron bull costume charges the crowd as the firecrackers attached to his body fly off in all directions. The town demonstrates its creativity again during the delirious **Semana Santa** celebrations, when a *toro embolao* (sheathed bull) with wooden balls affixed to the tips of his horns is set loose through the narrow streets of Vejer on Easter Sunday. The good-natured **Feria de Primavera** (2 weeks after *Semana Santa*) is a bit tamer, with people dancing *sevillanas* and downing cups of *fino* until sunrise.

TARIFA
☎956

When the wind picks up in Tarifa (pop. 15,000), the southernmost city in continental Europe, visitors can easily understand why it is known, even to locals, as the Hawaii of Spain. World-renowned winds combined with kilometers of empty, white, sandy beaches bring some of the best wind and kite surfers from around the world, while the tropical, relaxed environment beckons to those a little less adventurous who come for the beautiful beaches and hip lifestyle. Expect to see more Reefs, board shorts, and Quicksilver attire than you ever thought existed in Spain; in fact, everything about Tarifa defies all expectations. Locationwise, it doesn't get much better than this. Directly across the Strait of Gibraltar from Tangier, Tarifa boasts incomparable views of Morocco to the south, the Atlantic to the east, and the Mediterranean to the west from numerous outlooks—from few, if any, other places in the world can you see two continents and two wide open seas at once.

◧ **TRANSPORTATION. Transportes Generales Comes** buses roll in from C. Batalla del Salado, 19. (☎956 67 57 55. Open M-F 7:30-11am and 2-6:30pm, Sa-Su 3-8pm. The bus schedule is posted on the window; when the office is closed, buy your tickets from the driver.) **Buses** run to: **Algeciras** (30min., 10 per day 6:30am-8:15pm, €1.49); **Cádiz** (2¼hr., 7 per day 7:25am-8:55pm, €6.96); **La Línea** (1hr., 7 per day 10:30am-10:50pm, €3.14); **Sevilla** (3hr., 4 per day 8am-5:10pm, €14.01). **FRS ferries** (☎956 68 18 30; www.frs.com) leave from the port at the end of Po. de la Alameda for **Tangier** (35min.; daily 2 per day 11:30am and 7:30pm, return daily 2 per day 8:30am and 4pm Morocco time; €24, round-trip €45, children €12/22.50, small car €72, motorcycle €22.50).

◪◨ **ORIENTATION & PRACTICAL INFORMATION.** The small **bus station** is on C. Batalla del Salado. With your back to the station turn right and walk a short distance to the intersection with Av. de Andalucía. To reach the center of the old town, cross Av. de Andalucía and pass under the arch. To the left is C. Nuestra Señora de la Luz; follow this street to its end and you will be on C. Sancho IV el Bravo, the location of many cafes and restaurants. To reach the **tourist office,** turn right on Av. de Andalucía. The pedestrian thoroughfare Po. de la Alameda will be about one block ahead on the left; the tourist office is in the center. Ask at the tourist office for adventure sports information. (☎956 68 09 93. Open June-Sept. M-F 10am-9pm, Sa-Su 10am-2pm and 6-8pm; Oct.-May M-F 10am-2pm and 5-7pm, Sa 10am-2pm.) Exchange currency at **Banco Santander Central Hispano,** C. Batalla del Salado, 17. (☎902 24 24 24. Open M-F 8:30am-2pm, Sa 8:30am-1pm; May-Sept. M-F 8:30am-2pm,) Services include: **emergency** ☎112; **police,** Pl. Santa María, 3 (☎956 68 41 86); **Hospital de Tarifa** (☎956 68 15 15). **Internet** access is available at **Tarifa Diving,** Av. de la Constitución, near the tourist office (€2.50 per hr.; open Tu-Sa 10:30am-2pm and 5:30-9pm) and **Ciber-Papelería Pandor@'s,** C. Sancho IV el Bravo, 5 (€3 per hr.; open June-Aug. daily 10am-1am; Sept.-May M-F 10am-2pm and 4-11pm, Sa-Su 10am-2pm and 5pm-midnight). **Exchange books** at **Café Zumo,** C. Sancho IV el Bravo. (☎956 62 72 51. Books €2 with an exchange, €4 without. Open daily 9am-2:30pm and 5:30-9pm.) The **post office,** C. Coronel Moscardó, 9, is near Pl. San Mateo. (☎956 68 42 37. Open M-F 8:30am-2:30pm, Sa 9:30am-1pm.) **Postal Code:** 11380.

⬛⬛ ACCOMMODATIONS & FOOD. Affordable rooms line main C. Batalla del Salado and its side streets. Prices rise significantly in summer; those visiting in August and on weekends from June to September should call ahead and arrive early. Comfortable **Hostal Villanueva ❷,** Av. de Andalucía, 11, features a rooftop terrace with an ocean view and spotless rooms, all with bath. (☎956 68 41 49. Singles €20; doubles €35-42.) For slightly posher accommodations, try **Hotel La Mirada ❸,** C. San Sebastián, 1, only 3min. from the beach. The gigantic third floor patio has amazing ocean views, as do some rooms. From C. Batalla del Salado, walk away from the old town, turn left on C. Callao, and take the second right. (☎956 68 44 27. All rooms with bath. Singles €30-42; doubles €54-66.) Truly hard-core windsurfers often stay at one of the several **campgrounds** along the beach several kilometers from town; all have full bath and shower facilities, bars, and mini-supermarkets. Guests must bring their own tent. Although Cádiz-bound buses will drop you off if you ask, flagging one down to get back to town is next to impossible; call for a taxi or befriend a fellow surfer with a car. Try **Camping Río Jara ❶,** 4km from town (☎956 68 05 70; €11 per person and tent) or **Camping Tarifa ❶,** 6km from town (☎958 68 47 78; €8.50 per person and tent, €5.50 per additional person), both along highway CN-340. Other campgrounds are farther afield.

For cheap and varied sandwiches, try any one of the many *bagueterías* lining C. Sancho IV el Bravo and the side streets nearby (€1.50-3). **◼Misiana ❷,** C. San Joaquín, 2, on the corner of C. Sancho IV el Bravo, serves gourmet crêpes, pastas, salads, and sandwiches. Munch along and sip endless varieties of tea on the outdoor patio or the uniquely decorated, lounge-like dining room. (☎956 62 70 83. Lots of veggie options. Entrees €4-7. Turns into a popular bar at night. Open daily 9am-2am; kitchen open 9am-5pm and 7-11pm.) **Restaurante La Estrella ❶,** C. Nuestra Señora de la Luz, 20, specializes in fish and *paella,* and has a great *menú* for €6. (☎619 53 94 60. Open in summer daily 11am-4pm and 7:30pm-midnight; in winter M-W and F-Su 11am-4pm and 7:30pm-midnight.)

◖◗ SIGHTS & ENTERTAINMENT. Next to the port and just outside the old town stand the ruins of the **Castillo de Guzmán el Bueno.** In the 13th century, the Moors kidnapped Guzmán's son and threatened his life if Guzmán didn't relinquish the castle. Surprisingly, the father didn't surrender, even after his son's throat was slashed before his eyes. (Open Tu-Su 11am-2pm and 6-8pm. Oct.-Apr. 11am-2pm and 4-6pm. €1.80.) Those with something less historic in mind can head 200m south to **Playa de los Lances** for 5km of the finest white sand on the Atlantic coast. Bathers should be aware of the occasional high winds and strong undertow. Adjacent to Playa de los Lances is **Playa Chica,** which is tiny but more sheltered from the winds. **Tarifa Spin Out Surfbase,** 9km up the road toward Cádiz (ask the bus driver on the Cádiz route to stop, or take a taxi for about €6), rents **windsurfing** and **kite surfing** boards and instructs all levels. (☎956 23 63 52; www.tarifaspinout.com. Windsurf rental €24 per hr., €48 per day; 2hr. lesson including all equipment €48. Kite and board rental €28 per hr., €58 per day; 2hr. lesson including all equipment €68. Book in advance.) Many campgrounds and hotels along CN-340 between km 70 and km 80 provide instruction and gear for outdoor sports; ask at the tourist office for their extensive list of kite and windsurfing schools and rental places.

ANDALUCÍA

At night, sunburnt travelers mellow out in the old town's many bars, which range from jazz to psychedelic to Irish. People start migrating to the clubs around 1 or 2am. The *terrazas* on C. Sancho IV el Bravo fill at night with locals and windsurfers chatting over beer or coffee. **Moskito**, C. San Francisco, 11, is a combination bar-club, with great music, a large dance floor, and delicious tropical cocktails. (Free salsa lessons W 10pm. Beer €2. Mixed drinks €4; cocktails €6. No cover. Open in summer daily 11pm-4:30am; in winter Th-Sa 11pm-4:30am.) **La Tribu**, C. Nuestra Señora de la Luz, 7, makes some of the best and most creative cocktails in town, while trance and techno pump energy into the otherwise chill nightspot. (Beer €2-3. Shots €1.50. Mixed drinks €4-6. Open daily 8pm-2 or 3am.)

ALGECIRAS ☎956

Franco dreamed of transforming Algeciras into a burgeoning southern metropolis that would eclipse Gibraltar as the commercial center of the southwestern Mediterranean and force the Royal Army out of Iberia. Innumerable concrete wharfs and slapdash highrises remain, but so do the British. And, unfortunately, despite a peaceful and nicer old neighborhood set back from the port, Algeciras remains a somewhat dingy city. You'd be best off just passing through.

▉ TRANSPORTATION. Trains: RENFE, Ctra. a Cádiz (☎902 24 02 02), down C. San Bernardo. To **Granada** (4hr., 3 per day 7:40am-3:55pm, €15.40) and **Ronda** (1½hr., 4 per day 7:40am-6:25pm, €5.75). Also to **Bobadilla** (€9.25), with connections to: **Córdoba** (5hr., 6 per day 6:10am-9:35pm, €26.50); **Málaga** (3½hr., 7 per day 8:43am-9:39pm, €13.75); **Sevilla** (6hr., 4 per day 8:31am-8:50pm, €19.35).

Buses: Buses depart from the separate addresses as indicated.

Empresa Portillo, Av. Virgen del Carmen, 15 (☎956 65 43 04). To: **Córdoba** (6hr., 2 per day 8am and 3:15pm, €19.49); **Granada** (4hr., 4 per day 8am-5:45pm, €17.37); **Málaga** (3hr., 8-9 per day 8:15am-10pm, €9.33); **Marbella** (1hr., 8-9 per day 8:15am-10pm, €5.18).

La Línea to: **Gibraltar** (45min., daily every 30min. 7am-9:45pm, €1.55); **Madrid** (8hr., 4 per day 8:10am-9:45pm, €22.85); **Sevilla** (4hr., 5 per day 7:30am-4:45pm, €14.25); **Tarifa** (40min., 7-10 per day 7:05am-9pm, €1.49).

Transportes Generales Comes, C. San Bernardo, 1 (☎956 65 34 56), by Hotel Octavio and across from the train station. To: **Cádiz** (2½hr., 10 per day 7am-10:30pm, €8.51).

Ferries: From the bus and train stations, follow C. San Bernardo to C. Juan de la Cierva, and turn left at its end; the port entrance will be on your right. Tickets are overpriced at the train station; book at a travel agency in town or at the port. Only **Trasmediterránea** (☎902 45 46 45 or 956 58 34 00), at the entrance to the port, offers Eurail discounts. Open daily 9am-7pm. MC/V. All ferry companies sell tickets for all departures at the same price, regardless of whose boat it is. *Embarcaciones rápidas (*fast ferries) depart for **Ceuta** (see p. 777), a Spanish enclave in North Africa; normal and fast ferries leave for the Moroccan port of **Tangier** (see p. 771). Allow 30min. to clear customs and board, 90min. with a car. Summer ferries to **Ceuta** (35min.; depart 14 per day 6am-9:45pm, return 7:30am-11pm Moroccan time; €21.05, under 12 €10.52, small car €60.70, motorcycle €19.60) and **Tangier** (2½hr.; depart every hr. 7am-10pm, return 6am-9pm Moroccan time; €23.30, with Eurail pass €18.70, under 12 €11.65, small car €71.90, motorcycle €22.20. Fast ferries also go to **Tangier** (1hr., 5 per day 7:30am-7:30pm, €25). Limited service in winter. MC/V.

▉▉ ORIENTATION & PRACTICAL INFORMATION

Lined with travel agencies, banks, and hotels, **Avenida de la Marina** runs along the coast, turning into Av. Virgen del Carmen north of the port. **Calle Juan de la Cierva** runs perpendicular to the coast from the port, becoming **Calle San Bernardo** as it nears the **train** and **bus stations.** The train station is directly across the street from the Comes Bus Station; the Portillo bus station is near the port. To reach the **tourist office** from the train station, follow C. San Bernardo along the abandoned tracks toward the port, past a parking lot on the left. From the **port**, take a left onto Av. Virgen del Carmen, then a quick right onto C. Juan de la Cierva; the office is on the left. To get to the old center of town and its outdoor cafes and stores, walk past the port on Av. de la Marina and after 5min. take a left on C. Trafalgar, which intersects C. Alfonso XI and later C. Regino Martínez, the main pedestrian thoroughfare. All services necessary for transit to Morocco cluster near the port, accessible by a single gate and driveway. Be wary of imposters peddling ferry tickets.

Tourist Office: C. Juan de la Cierva (☎956 57 26 36; fax 57 04 75). Provides maps (free for Algeciras, €0.60 for other cities). Some English spoken. Open M-F 9am-2pm.

Currency Exchange: Banco Santander Central Hispano, Av. Virgen del Carmen, 9-11. Open M-F 8:30am-2pm, Sa 8:30am-1pm. Other banks line Av. de la Marina and continue past the port. For a daytrip to Tangier, buying **dirham** may not be necessary; many places accept euros and you will not be able to convert your dirham back once you return. For longer trips, change money in Morocco. For more info, see p. 771.

Luggage Storage: At the **train station,** €3 per day. Open daily 5:30am-10:30pm. At the **port,** lockers €2.40; behind the counter €1.20-1.80 per item. Open daily 7am-9:30pm.

Emergency: ☎061. **Police: Local,** C. Ruiz Zorrilla (☎092 or 956 66 01 55).

Medical Assistance: Ambulatorio Central, Pl. Menéndez Tolosa (☎956 66 19 56).

Internet Access: Travel agencies along Av. de la Marina offer Internet access for €2-3 per hr.; look for signs in windows.

Post Office: C. Ruiz Zorrilla, 42 (☎956 66 36 48). **Lista de Correos.** Open M-F 8:30am-2:30pm, Sa 9:30am-1pm. **Postal Code:** 11203.

ACCOMMODATIONS

Hostels line **Calle José Santacana,** parallel to the seafront along Av. de la Marina and about a 10min. walk from the bus and train stations. From either station, follow C. San Bernardo, turning left before the bush-lined median; take a right onto Av. Segismundo Moret and then take the 3rd left, C. José Santacana. Women traveling alone, however, might not feel safe there after dark; it's worth the extra few euros for a better neighborhood.

Hostal Residencia Versailles, C. Montero Ríos, 12 (☎/fax 956 65 42 11). If the Sun King had stayed here, he would have been close to the bus station. Clean, well-sized rooms, all with phones, TV, and bathrooms. Singles with shower €18; doubles with shower €30, with bath €35. ❷

Hotel Reina Cristina, Po. de la Conferencia (☎956 60 26 22), a 10min. walk down Av. de la Marina when facing the port. Spend your days in Morocco and your nights in luxury at this 4-star hotel. An oasis of tranquility and beauty amidst the hubbub of the city. Well-manicured grounds, pool, and restaurant. All rooms have bath, safe, A/C, TV, and phone. Singles €48.35-65.85, doubles €62.22-97.19. AmEx/MC/V. ❺

Hostal Nuestra Sra. de la Palma, Pl. Nuestra Señora de la Palma, 12 (☎956 63 24 81), right next to the market. Some of the cheaper, more decent rooms in town, close to the port. Marginally better neighborhood than hostels down the street on C. José Santacana. All rooms with bath and TV. Doubles €28; triples €42. ❸

FOOD

Outdoor cafes line C. Regino Martínez, Algeciras's main drag. Authentic Moroccan specialties are served in small restaurants all around. The **supermarket** is on the corner of C. José Santacana and C. Maroto. (Open daily 9am-2pm and 5-8pm.) The outdoor **market** at Pl. Nuestra Señora de la Palma is at the end of C. José Santacana. (Open M-Sa 8:30am-2pm.) **Montes Restaurante ❷**, C. Castellar, 36 (☎956 65 69 05), is packed day and night with foreigners in transit. Montes boasts an extensive menu of *comida típica* with more than 29 varieties of *tapas*, as well as filling meat, fish, and seafood entrees (€6-12). Open daily 8am-midnight. MC/V. For Moroccan fare with flair, swing by **La Alegría ❶**, C. José Santacana, 6. This menuless restaurant dishes out huge portions of chicken, lamb, and vegetarian entrees from their glass display case (€5-6). Open daily 7am-1am.

GIBRALTAR

Emerging from the morning mist, the Rock of Gibraltar's craggy face menaces those who pass by its shores. Ancient seafarers referred to the rock as one of the Pillars of Hercules, believing that it marked the end of the world. Today, it is known affectionately to locals as "Gib" and is home to more fish 'n' chips plates and pints of bitter per capita than anywhere in the Mediterranean. Though Gibraltar is officially a self-governing British colony, Spain continues to campaign for sovereignty. When a 1969 vote showed that Gibraltar's populace favored its colonial ties to Britain (a near-tie: 12,138 to 44), Franco sealed off the border. After 16 years of isolation and a decade of negotiations, the border re-opened on February 4, 1985. Tourists and residents now cross with ease, but Gibraltar has a culture all its own, one that remains detached from Spain. While the peculiar mix of wild roaming primates (the only to be found in Europe) and a curious enclave of not-quite-British-definitely-not-Spanish culture definitely make Gibraltar worth visiting, it is in many ways a tourist trap. Cross the border, spend a day exploring the Rock and stocking up on duty-free liquor and tobacco, then scurry back to Spain.

▮ TRANSPORTATION

Flights: Airport (☎730 26). **British Airways** (☎793 00) flies to **London** (2½hr., 2 per day, £168/€233) for those scared to set foot back in Spain.

Buses: From **La Línea**, on the Spanish border, to: **Algeciras** (40min., daily every 30min. 7:45am-10:15pm, €1.55); **Cádiz** (3hr., 4 per day 6:30am-8pm, €10.06); **Granada** (5hr.; 2 per day 7:15am, 2:15pm; €16.58); **Madrid** (7hr.; 2 per day 1:10, 10:15pm; €2.23); **Málaga** (3¼hr., 4 per day 7:30am-5:30pm, €8.54); **Marbella** (1¾hr., 4 per day 7:15am-5:30pm, €4.65); **Sevilla** (6hr.; 3 per day 7am, 3, 4:15pm; €17.85); **Tarifa** (1hr., 6 per day 6:30am-9pm, €3.14).

Ferries: Turner & Co., 65/67 Irish Town St. (☎783 05; fax 720 06). To: **Tangier** (1¼hr.; F 6pm, return Sa 5:30pm Moroccan time; £18/€32, under 12 £9/€16.20).

Public Transport: Most bus lines run from one end of the Rock to the other. Buses #9 and 10 go between the border and the Rock for £0.45/€0.70. Unlimited day pass €2.

Taxis: Gibraltar Taxi Association ☎700 27.

❗ POUNDS OR EUROS. Although **euros** are accepted almost everywhere (except in pay phones and public establishments), the **pound sterling (£)** is the preferred method of payment in Gibraltar. Merchants sometimes charge a higher price in euros than in the pound's exchange equivalent. Unless stated otherwise, assume an establishment will accept euros. Change is often given in British currency rather than euros. As of press date, **1£ = €1.56.**

Gibraltar

🏠 ACCOMMODATIONS
Emile Youth Hostel
Gibraltar, **1**
Queen's Hotel, **4**

🍎 FOOD
The Viceroy of India, **3**
Uncle Sam's, **2**

✈🚌 ORIENTATION & PRACTICAL INFORMATION

Buses from Spain terminate in the nearby town of **La Línea**. From the bus station, walk directly toward the Rock; the border is 5min. away. Once through Spanish customs and Gibraltar's passport control, catch bus #9 or 10 or walk across the airport tarmac (look both ways and hold hands) into town (20min.). Cars take longer to enter and exit Gibraltar; the queue often takes an hour or more. If walking, stay left on Av. Winston Churchill when the road forks with Corral Ln.

Tourist Office: Duke of Kent House, Cathedral Sq. (☎450 00). Open M-F 9am-5:30pm. **Branch,** Watergate House, Casemates Sq. (☎749 82). Open M-F 9am-5:30pm, Sa-Su 10am-3pm. **Info booth** at Spanish border. Open daily 7am-10pm.

Luggage Storage: Bus station in La Línea. €4 per day. Open daily 7am-10pm.

Bookstore: Gibraltar Bookshop, 300 Main St. (☎718 94). Tons of paperbacks, including 📖 Let's Go. Open M-F 10am-6:30pm. AmEx/MC/V.

Emergency: ☎199. **Police:** 120 Irish Town St. (☎725 00).

Hospital: St. Bernard's Hospital on Hospital Hill (☎797 00).

ANDALUCÍA

Telephone Code: From Britain (00) 350. From the US (011) 350. From Spain 9567.

Internet Access: Café Cyberworld, Ocean Heights Gallery, Queensway Rd. (☎514 16) £4.50/€7.50 per hr. Open daily noon-midnight. **John McIntosh Hall Library,** 308 Main St., 2nd fl. £0.75 per 30min., but a slower connection. Open M-F 9:30am-7:30pm.

Post Office: 104 Main St. (☎756 62). **Poste Restante** address: LAST NAME, First Name. Poste Restante, Gibraltar (Main Post Office). Open June-mid-Sept. M-F 9am-2:15pm, Sa 10am-1pm. Mid-Sept.-May M-F 9am-4:30pm, Sa 10am-1pm. Pounds only.

ACCOMMODATIONS & FOOD

Gibraltar is best done as a daytrip. The few accommodations in the area are pricy and often full, especially in the summer, and camping is illegal. At worst, you can crash across the border in La Línea. Back on the Rock, ⬛**Emile Youth Hostel Gibraltar ❷, on** Montague Bastian, has bunkbeds in cheerfully-painted rooms with clean communal bathrooms. (☎511 06. Breakfast included. Lockout 10:30am-4:30pm. Dorms and singles £15/€25; doubles £30/€50.) Located near the base of the cable cars, the older **Queen's Hotel ❷,** 1 Boyd St., has rooms with terraces and TV. (☎740 00. English breakfast included. Free parking. Singles £26, with bath £40; doubles £40/£60-70. 20% student discount with cash payment, 15% with credit card. MC/V.) International restaurants are easy to find, but you may choke on the prices. Sample the tasty results of Gibraltar's large, thriving Jewish community at **Uncle Sam's ❶,** 62 Irish Town St., a Kosher deli and grocer. The bagel sandwiches are especially good, as is the matzah ball soup. (☎512 36. Sandwiches £2.95; soup £3.45, entrees like *schnitzel* £5.95. Open summer Su-F 9am-11pm, low season 9am-7pm; closes at dusk on F.) Another good option is **The Viceroy of India ❸,** serving fabulous Indian food. (Entrees £3.75-4.75 for vegetarian dishes; meat and seafood £5.95-9.75. Open M-F noon-3pm and 7-11pm, Sa 7-11pm. MC/V.) As a back-up, there's the **Checkout** supermarket on Main St. next to Marks & Spencer. (Open M-F 8:30am-8pm, Sa 10am-6pm, Su 1am-3pm. MC/V.)

SIGHTS

⬛THE ROCK OF GIBRALTAR

*Top of the Rock Nature Reserve is accessible by car or cable car, or for the truly adventurous and athletic, by foot. **Cable cars** (☎778 26) depart daily every 10min. 9:30am-5:15pm; last return 5:45pm. Tickets sold until 5:15pm. It's possible to buy a ticket for only the cable car (round-trip £6.50/€11, one-way £5/€8.50), but if you plan on visiting any of the sights highlighted below, it's better to buy a **combined admittance ticket** (they don't offer individual sight tickets), including one-way cable car ride, for £7.50/€12.50. The walk down takes 2-3hr, including stops at the sights. **Tour** operators offer van or taxi tours that take visitors to all attractions in about 1½hr.; these are only a good choice if you really want to see all the sights, but don't want to walk at all. If you **drive** individually, there is a €7 per person entrance fee, including all sights, plus €1.50 per car. The truly budget-savvy walk both ways. To walk up, take Library St. to Library Ramp from Main St., follow it uphill to the end and turn right. At the next intersection there will be a sign for the footpath to the Rock. Follow the footpath uphill for 20min. until you hit a road mid-rock, and turn left.*

No visit to Gibraltar is complete without a visit to the legendary Rock. About halfway up the Rock (at the first cable car stop, or a 25min. walk from the top stop) is the infamous **Apes' Den,** where a colony of **Barbary apes** cavorts on the sides of rocks, the tops of taxis, and tourists' heads. These disturbingly tailless apes have inhabited Gibraltar since the 18th century. When the ape population nearly went extinct in 1944, Churchill ordered reinforcements from North Africa; now they are proliferating at such at rate that population control has become an issue. The apes are very tourist-friendly and have been known to steal food and other items from visitors; keep all food hidden and bags closed to avoid unwanted confrontations with the animals. At the northern tip of the Rock, facing Spain, are the **Great Siege Tunnels.** Originally used to fend off a combined Franco-Spanish siege at the end of the American Revolution, the tunnels were later expanded during WWII to span 33 miles underground. Near the tunnels, on the way back to town, is the old **Moorish castle,** rebuilt several times, the last being 1333. Although the castle is currently under renovation, the exterior still merits a quick look when already on the Rock. Thousands of years of water erosion carved the eerie chambers of **St. Michael's Cave,** located 500m opposite the siege tunnels. Ask at the entrance about getting a guided tour to the lower caves, with an underground lake and dramatic stalagmites. At the southern tip of Gibraltar, guarded by three machine guns and a lighthouse, **Europa Point** commands a view of the straits; the lighthouse can be seen from 37km away at sea. Nearby the **Ibrahim-Al-Ibrahim Mosque,** Europe's largest, and the **Shrine of Our Lady of Europe** face each other in pluralistic harmony. (Take bus #3 or 1B from Line Wall Rd., just off Main St., all the way to the end. Departs every 15min., £0.45/€0.70.)

COSTA DEL SOL

The coast has sold its soul to the Devil, and now he's starting to collect. Artifice covers the once-natural charms as chic promenades, swanky hotels, and apartment buildings burgeon between small towns and the shoreline. The Costa del Sol officially extends from Tarifa in the southwest to Cabo de Gata, east of Almería; post-industrial Málaga lies smack in the middle. To the northeast, coastal hills dip straight into the ocean, where rocky beaches help preserve some of the shore's natural beauty. To the southwest, however, waves seem to wash up onto more concrete than sand. That said, nothing can take away from the coast's major attraction: eight months of spring and four months of summer. News of Costa del Sol's fantastic weather has spread far and wide, and July and August bring swarms of pale-skinned northern Europeans; along much of the coast English is heard as commonly as Spanish. Reservations are almost essential in the summer anywhere along the coast, especially at sparse budget hostels. June is the best time to visit, when summer has already hit the beach but tourists haven't. Private bus lines offer connections along the coast itself—trains go only as far as Málaga and Fuengirola.

MÁLAGA ☎952

Celebrated by the likes of Hans Christian Andersen, Málaga (pop. 550,000) is the largest Andalusian city on the coast and the birthplace of Pablo Picasso. While Málaga's beaches are better known for bars than sand, the city has much to offer. You'll find locals mixed with foreign exchange students strolling and meeting in sidewalk cafes for beer and *tapas*, exuberant nightlife, and all the requisite historical monuments—fortress, cathedral, and bullring. The city's charming *casco antiguo* is the cultural, historical, and culinary heart of the city and should not be missed. Because it is a critical transportation hub, many see Málaga en route to other coastal stops, but it is well worth a day or two in its own right. Neighboring Torremolinos attracts package tourists with its mediocre beaches and questionable nightlife, but Málaga and nearby Fuengirola and Nerja are more worthwhile.

ANDALUCÍA

▐ TRANSPORTATION

Flights: (☎952 04 88 04). From the airport, bus #19 (every 30min. 6:30am-11:35pm, €1.20) runs from the "City Bus" sign, stopping at the bus station and at the corner of C. Molina Lario and Postigo de los Abades behind the cathedral. RENFE trains connect the city and the airport (12min., €0.81). **Iberia,** C. Molina Lario, 13 (☎952 13 61 66; 24hr. reservations 902 40 05 00), has numerous daily international flights.

Trains: Estación de Málaga, Explanada de la Estación (☎952 36 02 02). Take bus #3 at Po. del Parque or #4 at Pl. de la Marina to the station. **RENFE** office, C. Strachan, 4 (☎902 24 02 02). To: **Barcelona** (13hr., 2 per day 7:05am and 9pm, €49.50); **Córdoba** (2hr., 12 per day 6:45am-9pm, €13); **Fuengirola** (30min., every 30min. 7:15am-10:30pm, €1.20); **Madrid** (5hr., 7 per day 6:45am-7:45pm, €53); **Sevilla** (3hr., 5 per day 7:45am-8pm, €13.60); **Torremolinos** (20min., every 30min. 5:45am-10:13pm, €1.10). Reservations on long-distance trains are highly recommended.

Buses: Po. de los Tilos (☎952 35 00 61; **ALSA** 902 42 22 42; **Alsina Graells Sur** 952 31 82 95; **Casado** 952 31 59 08; **Daibus** 952 31 52 47; **Portillo** 952 36 01 91), 1 block from the RENFE station along C. Roger de Flor. To: **Algeciras** (3hr., 16 per day 5am-9:45pm, €8.95); **Almería** (8 per day 7am-7am, €13.16); **Antequera** (1hr., 9-12 per day 7am-10pm, €3.24); **Cádiz** (5hr., 5 per day 6:45am-8pm, €17.82); **Córdoba** (3hr., 5 per day 9am-6pm, €10.45); **Fuengirola** (30min., every 30min., €2.07); **Granada** (2hr., 17 per day 7am-9pm, €8.04); **Madrid** (7hr., 12per day 8:30am-1am, €17.94); **Marbella** (1½hr., approx. every hr. 7am-8pm, €4.14); **Murcia** (6hr., 5 per day 8:30am-9:45pm, €26); **Nerja** (1hr., approx. every 45 min. 7am-11pm, €3.05); **Ronda** (3hr., 4 per day 8:15am-4:30pm, €8.04); **Sevilla** (3hr., 11-12 per day 7am-3am, €13.03); **Torremolinos** (20min., every 15min. 6:15am-1am, €0.95).

Taxis: Radio Taxi (☎952 32 00 00 or 33 33 33). From town center to the waterfront €6; to the airport €10.

▐ ▐ ORIENTATION & PRACTICAL INFORMATION

The bus and train stations lie a block away from each other along C. Roger de Flor, on the other side of the Río Guadalmedina from the historical center and the majority of other sights. To get to the town center from the **bus station** (20min.), exit right onto Callejones del Perchel, walk straight through the big intersection with Av. de la Aurora, take a right on Av. de Andalucía, and cross Puente de Tetuán. From here, **Alameda Principal** leads into **Plaza de la Marina.** Or, take bus #4 or 21 along the same route (€0.81). From Pl. de la Marina, C. Molina Lario leads to the **cathedral** and the old town. C. Marqués de Larios, the main shopping and pedestrian street, connects Pl. de la Marina to **Plaza de la Constitución.** Behind the plaza, C. Granada leads to many good *tapas* bars and **Plaza de la Merced,** renowned for its nightlife. Av. Cánovas del Castillo leads to **Playa de la Malagueta** (20min. walk), Málaga's closest beach worth visiting. After dark, be wary of the neighborhoods of **Cruz del Molinillo** (near the market), as well as desolate beaches.

Tourist Offices: Municipal, Av. de Cervantes, 1 (☎/fax 952 60 44 10). Open M-F 8:15am-2pm and 4:30-7pm, Sa-Su 9:30am-1:30pm. More convenient office on Pl. de la Marina (☎952 12 20 20; open M-F 9am-7pm). **Junta de Andalucía,** Pje. de Chinitas, 4 (☎952 21 34 45). Open M-F 8:30am-8:30pm, Sa-Su 10am-2pm.

Currency Exchange: Banks (and **ATMs**) line most major roads and cluster around the intersection of Alameda Principal and C. Marqués de Larios. Most open M-F 8:30am-2pm; some open Sa mornings as well.

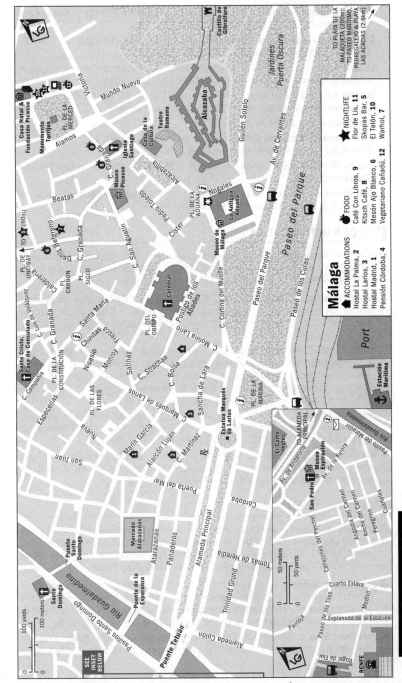

Málaga

▲ ACCOMMODATIONS
Hostal La Palma, 2
Hostal Larios, 3
Hostal Madrid, 1
Pensión Córdoba, 4

● FOOD
Café Con Libros, 9
Kitsch Café, 8
Mesón Ajo Blanco, 6
Vegetariano Cañadú, 12

★ NIGHTLIFE
Flor de Lis, 11
Skopas Bar, 5
El Telón, 10
Warhol, 7

ANDALUCÍA

Luggage Storage: Lockers at the **train station** (open daily 7am-10:45pm) and **bus station** (open daily 6:30am-11pm). Both €2.40-4.50 for 24hr.

English-Language Bookstore: Rayuela Idiomas, Pl. de la Merced, 17 (☎952 22 48 10). Open M-F 9:45am-1:30pm and 5-8:30pm, Sa 10am-2pm.

El Corte Inglés: Av. de Andalucía, 4-6 (☎952 07 65 00). Department store with a supermarket downstairs; sells a street map of Málaga. Open M-Sa 10am-10pm. AmEx/MC/V.

Internet Access: Internet Meeting Point, Pl. de la Merced, 14. Internet €1 per hr. Also has a pool table, video games, and a coffee and liquor bar. Open daily 10am-1:30am.

Emergency: ☎112. **Police:** ☎952 12 65 00.

24hr. Pharmacy: Farmacia Caffarena, Alameda Principal, 2 (☎952 21 28 58), at the intersection with C. Marqués de Larios. Open 24 hr.

Medical Services: ☎952 30 30 34 (urgent), ☎952 39 04 00 (non-urgent). **Medical Emergency:** ☎061.

Post Office: Av. de Andalucía, 1 (☎902 19 71 97). **Lista de Correos.** Open M-F 8:30am-8:30pm, Sa 9:30am-2pm. **Postal Code:** 29080.

ACCOMMODATIONS

"Budget" accommodations in Málaga aren't exactly budget—expect to pay at least €18-22 for a single, and more if you want a private bath. Most *hostales* are in the old town, between Pl. de la Marina and Pl. de la Constitución.

Hostal La Palma, C. Martínez, 7 (☎952 22 67 72). Spotless, with a great family atmosphere. Cheaper rooms are simple but clean, with common baths; pricier ones are brand new with A/C, mini-terraces, and private baths. Call ahead. Singles €21-25; doubles and triples also available. ❷

Hostal Larios, C. Marqués de Larios, 9, 3rd fl. (☎952 22 54 90). It's worth the mini-splurge for Larios's sparkling, brightly-painted rooms, and its unbeatable location on the premiere pedestrian thoroughfare. No need to pay for a room with a private bath; the common ones couldn't be cleaner or newer. All rooms with TV and A/C. Singles €27, with bath €35; doubles €37/45; triples with bath €63. V. ❸

Pensión Córdoba, C. Bolsa, 11 (☎952 21 44 69). Decent-sized rooms with sinks and antique furniture; some rooms have balconies. Spotless common baths. Reserve 1-2 days in advance. Singles €15; doubles €25-28; triples €42. ❶

Hostal Madrid, C. Marín García, 4, 2nd fl. (☎952 22 45 92). About as cheap as it gets in the city, Madrid offers basic but clean rooms with private balconies and showers. No reservations accepted. Singles €15-20; doubles €25-40. ❷

FOOD

Beachfront restaurants specialize in fresh seafood; for anything else, stick to the restaurants and *tapas* bars hiding in the streets around C. Granada, Pl. de la Constitución, and Pl. de la Merced. Fresh produce fills the **market** on C. Ataranzas (open daily 8am-2pm), and you can buy groceries at **El Corte Inglés.**

■ **Vegetariano Cañadú,** Pl. de la Merced, 21 (☎952 22 90 56; www.cuidate.com/canadu). Feast on hearty meatless entrees, salads, soups, and smoothies in this airy and bright gem of a restaurant. Occasional live music. Open Su-Th 1:30-4pm and 8-11pm, F-Sa 1:30-4pm and 8pm-midnight. Closed Tu evening. AmEx/MC/V. ❶

■ **Café Con Libros,** C. Granada, 73. Curl up with a book (€5 deposit) in this cozy cafe, or chat with friends and locals outside on the highly-coveted swing seats. A wide array of coffees, teas, and smoothies (€1-3); they also sell beer and liquor, as well as baked goods and other sundry food items. Open M-Th 4pm-midnight, F-Sa 4pm-1am. ❶

Kitsch Cafe, C. Granada, 44 (☎952 60 83 78). Artsy, colorful, and eclectic, it certainly lives up to its name. While they serve full meals, come here instead for their great breakfasts (€2) or to enjoy a cup of coffee, tea, or alcoholic drink while people watching from their outdoor tables. Comfy couches by the windows are great for chilly winter days. Open M-W 9am-1am, Th 9am-midnight, F 9am-3am, Sa noon-3am. ❶

Mesón Ajo Blanco, Pl. de Uncibay, 2 (☎952 21 29 35). Sample traditional Spanish cuisine one notch above the norm. Popular with both locals and tourists, Ajo Blanco is a cross between a neighborhood bar and a full-fledged restaurant, featuring meat-heavy baguettes (€3) and tapas (€2-8). Wash it all down with a pitcher of sangría or a drink from the full bar. Open Su-Th noon-1am, F-Sa noon-2am. ❷

🎦 SIGHTS

ALCAZABA. Towering high above the city, the Alcazaba is Málaga's most imposing sight, offering great views of the harbor, and capturing a medieval tranquility within its brick and stone walls. Guarding the east end of Po. del Parque, this 11th-century structure was originally built and used as both a military fortress and royal palace for Moorish kings. (*Open June-Aug. Tu-Su 9:30am-8pm; Sept.-May Tu-Sa 8:30am-7pm. €1.80, students and senior citizens €0.60, children under 7 free.*)

SANTA IGLESIA CATEDRAL DE MÁLAGA. Málaga's breathtaking cathedral blends Gothic, Renaissance, and Baroque styles. The incredibly intricate structure, complete with detailed columns, beautiful stained glass windows, and more than 15 side chapels, was built on the site of a former mosque; the courtyard outside is all that remains of the mosque. Although work on the cathedral began in 1527 and continued for centuries thanks to a hefty harbor tax, the cathedral's second tower, under construction from the 16th to 19th century, was never completed—hence the cathedral's nickname *La Manquita* (One-Armed Lady). The small museum upstairs displays religious art, and is certainly worth a peek. (*C. Molina Lario, 4. ☎952 22 03 45. Open M-F 10am-6:45pm, Sa 10am-5:45. €3. Mass M-Sa 9am, Su all day. Admission free; informative audio guide included.*)

CASTILLO DE GIBRALFARO. An Arab lighthouse was built in this Phoenician castle, which offers sweeping views of Málaga and the Mediterranean. The grounds are relatively untouristed, so it can feel somewhat desolate; avoid exploring the grounds alone. (*Bus #35 to the castle leaves every 20min. from Pl. de la Aduana, €1.80; otherwise it's a steep uphill hike. Open daily Apr.-Oct. 9am-7:45pm; Nov.-Mar. 9am-5:45pm.*)

CASA NATAL Y FUNDACIÓN PICASSO. Picasso may have high-tailed it out of Málaga when he was young, but according to local officials, he always "felt himself to be a true *malagueño*." The artist's birthplace now houses the Picasso Foundation, which organizes a series of exhibitions, concerts, and lectures. The first floor has been converted into a gift shop and exhibits on gallery; upstairs is a permanent collection of photographs, drawings, and letters of correspondence by and about Picasso himself. One room in the front of the house is decorated to look as it did when Picasso lived here; glass cases display his christening gown. (*Pl. de la Merced. ☎952 06 02 15. Open M-Sa 10am-2pm and 5-8pm, Su 10am-2pm. Free.*)

MUSEO PICASSO. A new museum dedicated to the life and works of Pablo Picasso will reside at the corner of C. San Agustín and C. Granada. Expected to be completed in October 2003.

NIGHTLIFE

Malagueños like to party in zones, the most popular of which is smack in the middle of old Málaga. In general, the night doesn't get going until nearly 1am on weekends, earlier during the week. Many of the city's restaurants morph into popular bars late at night as well. On weekends, crowds invade the bars and pubs closer to Málaga's center, particularly in the area between C. Comedias and C. Granada, near Pl. de la Constitución and Pl. de la Merced. More bars surround Pl. de la Merced, such as **Flor de Lis,** a primarily gay bar with great ambience and live DJs spinning house music. (Open Su-Th 11am-2am, F-Sa 11am-3am.) Right next door is ■**El Telón,** which entertains a mixed crowd with hip-hop Latino dance music and deliciously tropical drinks like *mojitos* and *caipirinhas.* (Beer €1.50-2.40. Mixed drinks €3.60 and up. Open daily 10:30-2:30am.) Chill in the crowded bar area or let loose on the adjacent dance floor at **Skopas Bar,** C. Casablanca, 2, one block from Pl. de Uncibay. Arrive early on weekends to avoid a line. (Beer €2-2.50. Mixed drinks €4-4.50. 21+. Open Th-Sa 10:30pm-4am.) To seriously get your dance on, head to **Warhol,** C. Denis Belgrano, 8, where an international crowd pulsates to jazz-infused house spun by excellent DJs in a chrome-covered interior. (Beer €2-2.50. Mixed drinks €5. No cover. Open Tu-Sa midnight-7am.) For a change in scenery, head to **Playa de la Malagueta,** a 30min. walk but quick bus ride on #3, 4, 12, 16, 19, or 25, where young locals party at beachfront bars and *chiringuitos.*

DAYTRIP FROM MÁLAGA

TORREMOLINOS

Trains (☎902 24 02 02) connect Málaga and Torremolinos (30min.; every 30min. 5:45am-10:30pm, return 6:52am-11:34pm; €1.10). Portillo buses (☎952 38 24 19) also make the trip (30min., every 20-30min., €1.05)

Thirty minutes of public transportation from Málaga can get you to some of the best beaches in the area. Tons of t-shirt shops and beachfront restaurants specializing in fresh fish dot the waterfront, while throngs of *malagueños* and tourists crowd the kilometers of soft sand in search of sun. To get to the **beach** from the train station, exit the station, turn left, and take a right on C. San Miguel, a pedestrian street that winds down to the beach, changing names along the way. Get maps of the city at the beachfront **tourist office,** in Pl. de las Comunidades Autónomas. (☎952 81 78. Open M-F 9:30am-2:30pm.) Rent **bikes** and **scooters** at **Moto Mercado,** Pl. de las Comunidades Autónomas, along Po. Marítimo. (☎952 05 26 71. Must have valid drivers licence. 16+ for scooters and motorcycles. Bicycles €50 deposit, €10 per day; scooters €100 deposit, €24-30 per day; motorcycles credit card deposit, €42-120 per day. Open M-Sa 9:30am-7:30pm, Su 9am-2pm.)

What cheap accommodations there are lie on the other side of town from the beach. If you decide to spend the night, **Hostal Micaela ❷,** C. Bajondillo, 4, a continuation of C. San Miguel, is about as cheap as you'll get within a few minutes of the beach. (☎952 38 33 10. All rooms with bath and fan. Singles €25; doubles €35; triples €45. €5 discount in winter.) Although there are more restaurants and bars lining the waterfront than meals to be had, **Restaurante Bananas ❶,** at the far end of the beach by La Roca Chica, is a peaceful, more secluded alternative to other places on the strip. Straw tables and chairs, a huge drink menu, and a beautiful porch overlooking the Mediterranean make Bananas almost tropical. (Full breakfast €3-6. Seafood entrees €4-9; meat entrees €3-7. Open daily 9am-2am.)

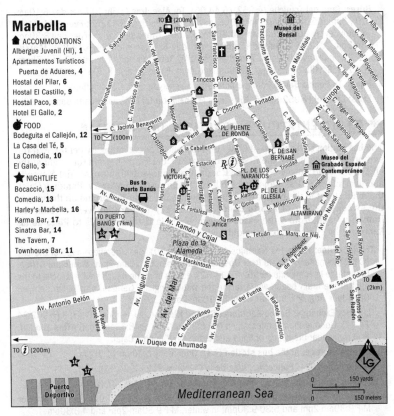

Marbella

🏠 ACCOMMODATIONS
Albergue Juvenil (HI), **1**
Apartamentos Turísticos
  Puerta de Aduares, **4**
Hostal del Pilar, **6**
Hostal El Castillo, **9**
Hostal Paco, **8**
Hotel El Gallo, **2**

🍴 FOOD
Bodeguita el Callejón, **12**
La Casa del Té, **5**
La Comedia, **10**
El Gallo, **3**

⭐ NIGHTLIFE
Bocaccio, **15**
Comedia, **13**
Harley's Marbella, **16**
Karma Bar, **17**
Sinatra Bar, **14**
The Tavern, **7**
Townhouse Bar, **11**

MARBELLA

☎ 952

Like your vacation spots shaken, not "shtirred?" Scottish smoothie Sean Connery and a host of other jet-setters choose Marbella (pop. 116,000; and 500,000+ in summer) as their vacation home. With gorgeous beaches that stretch for kilometers and a decidedly more sophisticated atmosphere than much of the Costa del Sol, it's no wonder that Marbella and the cosmopolitan enclave seven kilometers away at Puerto Banús attract the rich and famous. Marbella's center, however, retains a very Spanish feel, despite rampant tourism. The city has a long history as an important merchant town occupied by the Phoenicians, Greeks, Romans, and Arabs. Remnants of this history can be felt in the well-preserved architecture and streets of the *casco antiguo*. Today Marbella serves primarily as an elegant beachside retreat for a wealthy international crowd, and there are more yachts than hostels. Because of the mountains nearby, Marbella's winter temperatures tend to be 5-8°F warmer than Málaga's, and beach season lasts at least 10 months, so don't even think about leaving your tan at home.

🚌 TRANSPORTATION

Marbella, 56km south of Málaga, can be reached only by bus.

ANDALUCÍA

Buses: Ctra. del Trapiche (☎952 76 44 00). To: **Algeciras** (1½hr., 17 per day 6:10am-10:35pm, €5.18); **Cádiz** (4hr., 6 per day 7:30am-8:45pm, €13.69); **Fuengirola** (1hr., approx. every 35min. 6:45am-10:30pm, €2.05); **Granada** (3½hr., 7per day 8:30am-6:55pm, €12.18); **Madrid** (7½hr., 7 per day 8:30am-midnight, €19.82); **Málaga** (1½hr., daily every 30min. 7am-8pm, €4.14); **Ronda** (1½hr., 7 per day 9am-8:55pm, €4.27); **Sevilla** (4hr.; 2 per day 9am and 4pm, F and Su also 8:30pm; €13.26).

Boats: To **Puerto Banús** from the port (30min.; every hr.; €5, €8 roundtrip).

Taxis: Taxi Sol (☎952 82 35 35) serves Marbella center (€4) and Puerto Banús (€12).

■ ♂ ORIENTATION & PRACTICAL INFORMATION

The **bus station** is at the top of Ctra. del Trapiche. To reach the city center, exit the station, walk left, make the first right onto Ctra. del Trapiche, and turn right at the end of the road onto C. Salvador Rueda. Continue downhill on Av. del Mercado and turn left on C. Castillejos, which leads to the perpendicular Av. Ramón y Cajal, the main street in the new town—this becomes Av. Ricardo Soriano on the way to the swanky harbor of **Puerto Banús** (7km away). C. Peral curves up from Av. Ramón y Cajal around the **casco antiguo**. C. de la Estación leads to **Plaza de los Naranjos,** the central hub of the old town.

Tourist Office: Pl. de los Naranjos (☎952 82 35 50). Sells detailed maps of the city (€0.60); smaller ones are free. Open M-F 9am-9pm, Sa 10am-2pm. **Municipal Office,** Glorieta de la Fontanilla (☎952 77 14 42), across from the beach several blocks to the right of the main beach when facing the water. English, German, and Dutch spoken. Open June-Aug. M-F 9:30am-9pm, Sa 10am-2pm.

Currency Exchange: Banco Santander Central Hispano, Av. Ramón y Cajal, 9 (☎902 24 24 24). Good exchange rates. Open M-F 8:30am-2pm, Sa 8:30am-1pm. **ATMs** abound, especially near the *casco antiguo* and along Av. Ramón y Cajal.

Luggage Storage: At the **bus station** (€3). Open daily 6:30am-11:30pm.

Emergency: ☎091. **Police:** Av. Juan de la Cierva (☎952 82 24 94).

Medical Emergency: ☎061. **Hospital: Comarcal,** CN-340, km187 (☎952 86 27 48).

Pharmacy: Farmacia Espejo, Pl. de los Naranjos, 4 (☎952 77 12 91). Open in summer M-F 9:30am-2pm and 5:30-9:30pm; in winter, M-F 9:30am-2pm and 4-8:30pm.

Internet Access: Neotel Locutorios, Pl. Puente de Ronda, 6 (☎655 54 73 11). €2.60 per hr. Open daily 10am-2pm and 4pm-midnight. MC/V. **Sky Techno,** C. Sierra Blanca, 3. €2 per hr. Open daily 10am-2am.

Post Office: C. Jacinto Benavente, 26 (☎952 77 28 98), uphill from C. Ricardo Soriano. Open M-F 8:30am-8:30pm, Sa 9:30am-1pm. **Postal Code:** 29600.

♠ ACCOMMODATIONS & CAMPING

If you are reservationless, especially from June to September, arrive early and pray for a miracle; swing by the youth hostel first; it's most likely to have beds.

Hostal del Pilar, C. Mesoncillo, 4 (☎952 82 99 36). Run by two accommodating Scots, this 17th-century inn was originally run by monks as a home for pilgrims. Now it's a haven for backpackers, with clean and comfortable if sparse rooms, shared bathrooms, and a pool table. Crackling fires warm the downstairs bar during winter. Hearty English breakfast €5. Roof mattresses available when rooms are full. Ask about weekly winter rates. July-Aug. €20, Sept.-June €15 per person. ❷

Albergue Juvenil (HI), Ctra. del Trapiche, 2 (☎952 77 14 91; fax 86 32 27). Exit left from the bus station, turn right and follow Ctra. del Trapiche almost until the end. Very social, fun atmosphere. International backpackers gather around the huge ■ pool.

Other facilities include a garden, TV room, pool table, basketball court, and self-service laundry (€5). Doubles, triples, and quads, many with private bathrooms. June 15-Sept. 15 €13.35 per person, over 26 €17.85. Apr.-June 14 and Sept. 16-Oct. €11.30/ €15.75. Nov.-Mar. €9.05/€11.95. €3 fee for non HI-members. MC/V. ❶

Apartamentos Turísticos Puerta de Aduares, C. Aduar, 18 (☎/fax 952 82 13 12). Stunningly beautiful, fully-equipped apartments make for a worthwhile splurge. Two-person, studio-like apartments; 4-person suites with 2 bedrooms, a living room, and a bathroom. All suites have brand-new kitchens and A/C; some have balconies. June-Aug. doubles €76, quads €142; Sept.-May €56/€112. Extra bed €20. MC/V. ❺

El Castillo, Pl. San Bernabé, 2 (☎952 77 17 39; fax 82 11 98). Sunny rooms with high ceilings, fans, and spacious baths. July-Sept. singles €24; doubles €39. Mar.-June and Oct. €22/€36. Nov.-Feb. €19/€29.50. MC/V. ❷

Hostal Paco, C. Peral, 16 (☎952 77 12 00; fax 82 22 65). Large cheerful rooms all with bath, down the street from several nightlife spots. Phone and TV in lobby. July-Oct. 15 and *Semana Santa* singles €33; doubles €48. Oct. 16-June €30/€42. MC/V. ❸

Hotel El Gallo, C. Lobatos, 44 (☎952 82 79 89). The restaurant has been a success for years; the same family decided to try their luck with a hostel, and so far it looks good. All rooms have private bath, TV, and A/C. Singles €25-35; doubles €35-54, depending on the season. Discounts for extended stays. MC/V. ❸

🍴 FOOD

Terrazas filling Pl. de los Naranjos are not particularly budget-friendly—the multilingual menus spell tourist trap. Restaurants farther uphill are less picturesque, but easier on the wallet. The waterfront has similar eateries, but a livelier, younger atmosphere. Locals retreat to Av. Nabeul for cheap eats. The municipal **market** is on Av. del Mercado, uphill from C. Peral. (Open M-Sa 8am-2pm.)

▨ **El Gallo,** C. Lobatas, 44 (☎952 82 79 98). One of the few truly local restaurants in the area; ironically a perennial favorite with backpackers as well. Huge portions and cheap, flavorful meals. *Tapas* from €1. Entrees (such as rabbit in garlic sauce, pork fillet, or chicken €2.50-8). Open M and W-Su 1-4pm and 7-11:30pm. MC/V. ❶

▨ **La Casa del Té,** C. Ancha, 7 (☎639 16 79 18). Mellow, candlelit rooms filled with cushions, paintings, and incense. Chill background music. Vegetarian sandwiches and crêpes (€2-2.25), *batidos* (€2.25), and an array of teas and coffees. Limited dinner menu M-Sa 8:30-10:30pm. Open M and W-F 10am-1:30pm and 5-11:30pm; Sa-Su 5-11:30pm. ❶

Bodeguita el Callejón, C. Alamo, 5 (☎649 715 314). Hidden in an alley, this small restaurant is a welcome respite from the city's pricey tourist restaurants. Wine casks and hanging hams create an authentic feel, while the stellar specialties—*jamón ibérico*, cheeses, and regional wines—seal the deal. *Tapas* €1.30-2.50. *Raciones* €3.50-10. Sangría €8.50 per pitcher. Open Th-Tu 12:30-3pm and 8pm-midnight. ❶

La Comedia, Pl. Victoria (☎/fax 952 77 64 78). Creative modern cuisine in a trendy, airy atmosphere overlooking a small plaza. Entrees €11.80-18.70. Vegetarian options available. Open Tu-Su 7pm-1am. AmEx/MC/V. ❸

🔎 SIGHTS

Although most visitors come to Marbella for the 320 days of sunshine a year, no visit would be complete without a stroll through the ▨ **casco antiguo,** a maze of cobbled streets and white-washed facades trimmed with wild roses, topped off with expensive tourist restaurants. The **Museo del Grabado Español Contemporáneo,** C. Hospital Bazán, in a restored hospital for the poor, contains a smattering of

ANDALUCÍA

engravings by Miró, Picasso, Dalí, Goya, and contemporary artists. (☎952 82 50 35. Open Tu-Sa 10am-2pm and 5:30-8:30pm. €2.50.) To the northeast is the **Parque Arroyo de la Represa** and the **Museo del Bonsai**, home to four rooms of bonsai trees, including a 500-year-old Chinese ficus. (Av. de Maiz Viñals. ☎952 86 29 26. Open daily 10:30am-1:30pm and 4-7pm. €3, under 12 €1.50.)

■ NIGHTLIFE

Nightlife in Marbella begins and ends late and is very much scattered throughout town. Except for the busiest weeks of the summer, bars in the *casco antiguo* and along the waterfront only get packed on weekend nights; the expensive bars and clubs in Puerto Banús are busy all the time. Mellow but fun ▧ **Townhouse Bar,** C. Alamo, serves a variety of pre-made, secret-recipe shots to a 20 and 30-something crowd; their specialty is Apple Pie—it ain't mama's. (Beer €1.50. Mixed drinks €4.50. Shots €1.50. Open daily 10pm-3am.) A few blocks away, travelers and resident Brits mingle and down pints at **The Tavern,** C. Peral, 7. (Beer €1.50. Mixed drinks €4. Open daily 8pm-late.) **Bocaccio,** C. Puerta del Mar, 16, is one of the more popular gay bars. (Beer €3. Mixed drinks €5. Open daily 11pm-3 or 4am.)

Much of Marbella's nightlife clusters at the **Puerto Deportivo.** The brand-new **Karma Bar,** attracts young Brits who come to get a few drinks before heading to Puerto Banús. (Half-price beer and wine during happy hour, daily 9-11pm. Mixed drinks €4.80. Open Su-Th 2pm-2am, F-Sa 2pm-3am.) A distinctively non-motorcycle crowd gathers across the port at **Harley's Marbella,** where 1950s-70s American decor almost turns the place into a museum. (Su karaoke. Limited food during the day. Beer €1.50. Mixed drinks €4.60. Open daily 9:30am-3am.)

The bars and clubs lining the yacht port and C. Ribera are hard to miss. Buses run on the hour all night from Av. Ricardo Soriano (destination San Pedro, €0.95). Taxis from Marbella center (€10-12) stop near the port's popular celebrity-sighting hangout, **Sinatra Bar.** (Mixed drinks €5-8. Open daily 11pm.) An equally trendy crowd can be found sipping expensive but mouth-watering Cuban cocktails and frozen drinks at **La Habana de Hemingway,** on the port near the entrance to town. (Beer €3.50. Cocktails a whopping €10. Open daily 9pm-3am.) **Flicks,** in Pl. del Puerto near the end of C. Ribera, offers a less pretentious, younger scene. A pool table, blasting English music, and a casual atmosphere are a nice change from the uppity places on the strip. (Beer €3. Mixed drinks €6. Open daily 8pm-3 or 4am.)

Around 4am, the action shifts to the clubs. **Comedia,** (terrace-level, C. Ribera) draws in the dancing crowd with a glam ambience and high energy techno, hip-hop, and house music. (Cover €20. Mixed drinks €7. Open June-Oct. daily 11pm-5am; Nov.-May Th-Sa 11pm-5am.) Arrive "early" (before 2:30am) to avoid the long lines at the hugely popular after-hours club, **Scream,** in Pl. del Puerto. (Mixed drinks €9. Cover €20. Open daily 1-7am.)

◪ BEACHES

If you like to walk, the 7km stroll from Marbella center to **Puerto Banús,** almost entirely along a boardwalk, is one of the most beautiful ways to spend an hour and a half; stop in the middle at one of many secluded beaches to cool off. If you prefer to sit back and enjoy the ride, city buses along Av. Richard Soriano (destination San Pedro or Hipercor, €0.95) bring you to chic and trendy Puerto Banús, where brilliant beaches are buffered by imposing, white yachts and row upon row of boutiques and restaurants. On exceptionally clear days, the Moroccan coast is barely visible. The port has been frequented by the likes of Sean Connery, King Fahd of Saudi Arabia (who built a palace modeled on the White House), Antonio Banderas, and even the late Princess Diana. Throngs of well-dressed Euro-chicks and *chicos* mill about the marina in search of well-banked spouses. With 22km of beach, Marbella offers a variety of settings despite its homogenous facade. Shores to the east of the port are popular with British backpackers; those to the west attract a more posh crowd. **Funny Beach,** popular with families, is a 10min. bus ride (take the bus to Fuengirola and ask the driver to stop, €1), or walk 2km east along the beach. You'll find a paradise of beach games, including jet-skiing and volleyball. The myriad beaches between Marbella and Puerto Banús are especially picturesque.

NERJA   ☎952

Renowned for its beaches, caves, and extremely picturesque Balcón de Europa overlooking the Mediterranean, Nerja (pop. 15,000) offers all the comforts and clutter of a coastal resort town. Bikini-clad tourists and flip-flopped anglophones crowd the spectacular beaches, but even despite the rampant tourism, this white-washed town remains one of the most charming on the eastern end of the Costa del Sol. To top it off, Nerja offers one of the coast's most enticing yet unpretentious nightlife scenes, catering to locals and tourists of all ages and tastes. If we could give an entire town a thumbpick, Nerja would be at the top of the list.

🚺 PRACTICAL INFORMATION. The **bus stop,** Av. de Pescia, (☎952 52 15 04), sends buses to: **Almería** (3½hr., 6 per day 8am-7:50pm, €9.69); **Almuñécar** (30min., 9 per day 6:30am-8:30pm, €2.07); **Granada** (2¼hr.; 3 per day 6:30am, 4:45, 7:15pm; €7.34); **Málaga** (1½hr., 12-18 per day 6:30am-9:45pm, €3.15); **Sevilla** (4hr.; 3 per day 7:30am, 4:30pm, 2am; €15.31). For a good map of Nerja and information on the caves and beaches head to the multilingual **tourist office,** Pta. del Mar, 2. From the bus ticket counter, cross Av. de Pescia, walk through the small plaza, and continue downhill on C. Pintada to the end; the tourist office is on the left beside the Balcón de Europa. (☎952 52 15 31. Open June-Aug. M-F 10am-2pm and 5-8pm, Sa 10am-1pm; reduced low-season hours.) Services include: **pharmacy,** C. Pintada, 48, (☎958 63 06 98); **medical emergency** ☎112; **police** C. Virgen del Pilar, 1 (☎952 52 02 96); **Internet,** Med Web Café, Av. Castilla Pérez, 21, at the bottom on the right, open daily 10am-midnight, with a helpful multi-lingual staff, printing, coffee, snacks, and smoothies (Internet €3 per hr.); and the **post office,** C. Almirante Ferrandiz, 6 (☎952 52 17 49; open M-F 8:30am-2:30pm, Sa 9:30am-1pm). **Postal Code:** 29780.

🚹🛏 ACCOMMODATIONS & FOOD. 🏠Hostal Estrella del Mar ❸, C. Bellavista, 5, may be a bit of a hike from the bus stop, but the homey atmosphere, bright and airy rooms, and incredible views from some balconies are well worth the schlepp. From the bus station, cross the street, but stay on Av. de Pescia past the traffic circle and take your fourth right on C. de Andalucía. Make another right on C. Asensio Cabanillas and then a left on C. Bellavista; the *hostal* is on your left, only minutes from the beach. (☎952 52 04 61. Breakfast €2.90. July-Sept. 15 singles €28, doubles €37; Sept. 16-June €20/€29; €7 charge per extra person. Closed Nov.-Mar.) Alternatively, **Pensión Residencia Mena ❷,** C. El Barrio, 15, conveniently located off the Balcón de Europa, has comfortable and clean rooms, complete with tiled floors and private baths. (☎952 52 05 41; fax 52 83 45. Apr.-Oct. 15 singles €19.50; doubles €30; Aug., *Semana Santa,* and holidays €23/€36.50, Oct.-Mar. €17/€24, €3.50 extra for a room with a view.) Conveniently located only two blocks from the bus stop and a 5-10min. walk to the Balcón de Europa, **Hostal Plaza Cantarero ❷,** C. Pintada, 117, gives you more for your budget dollar with fresh rooms, new private baths, TVs, and fans upon request. Although far from major nightlife areas, the street is well-lit at night. (☎952 52 87 28; www.hostalplazacantarero.com. Breakfast €2.90. June 16-Sept. singles €26; doubles €46; Apr.-June €22/€36; Oct.-Mar. €18/€28; Extra bed €9. MC/V.)

Overpriced restaurants near and along the Balcón de Europa tempt passersby with views. If you're craving British food, beer, or accents, you're in the right place; finding authentic Spanish cuisine for anything less than a fortune, on the other hand, is a bit harder. To splurge on some excellent food in a less touristy atmosphere than by the Balcón, head to one of the several restaurants on C. Gloria, off C. Pintada, halfway down the hill. A cheaper option is the excellent menu at **Café-Bar Los Mariscos ❷**, C. Cristo, 17. Eat at the bar itself in the adjacent dining room or on one of the two patios out back. (☎952 52 27 14. *Tapas* start at €3; entrees at €4.75. Open Tu-Su 12:30-3pm and 7pm-midnight.) Grab some sandwiches (€2-3) for the beach or stay for a coffee drink at ◙**La Vaca Loca ❶**, C. Diputación, 25, where brightly-colored walls and cozy tables make for a fun and casual atmosphere. (☎952 52 27 63. Open M-Sa 10am-10pm, Su noon-8pm.) A **supermarket** can be found on C. Antonio Ferrandiz. (Open M-Sa 9:30am-9:30pm.)

◙ **SIGHTS.** To get to the ◙**Balcón de Europa**, a promenade overlooking the Playa de la Caletilla that was once part of a 9th-century castle, cross Av. de Pescia from the bus station and turn right on C. Pintada, which leads downhill. The **Nerja caves** attract herds of visitors and are reputed to be one of the most frequently-visited monuments in Spain. Approximately 3 kilometers outside of town, they are best reached by taxi or bus (15 per day, €0.70). The caves are open daily in summer 10am-2pm and 4-8pm; in winter 10am-2pm and 4-6:30pm (€5.) A set of stairs to the right of the tourist office leads down to a walkway along the shore, heading east from the *Balcón*, past **Playa de Calahonda** and **Playa Carabeo** to **Playa Burriana,** which earned an EU blue flag for cleanliness. Burriana is the most crowded, but longest, beach with lots of tourists and restaurants. To reach the sprawling and less crowded **Playa de la Torrecilla** (also a blue flag beach) from the *Balcón*, cut through town towards the Playa de la Torrecilla apartments and follow the shoreline (15min.). Closer and popular with locals, but more crowded, is **Playa del Salón**, accessible through an alley off the *Balcón*, to the right of Restaurante Marisal.

◙ **NIGHTLIFE.** For a relatively small town, Nerja has a surprisingly lively nightlife, with a little bit (or a lot) of something for everyone. A youthful crowd of both locals and sunburnt tourists heads to the unfortunately-named ◙**Plaza Tutti Frutti,** where more than 10 bars compete for attention. Of these, **Bar Vertigo** is one of the most popular, with colorful lights, an immense outdoor seating area, and a dance floor and bar seating inside. (Beer €2. Mixed drinks €4.50. Open daily 10pm-3am.) For something a bit different, **Blanco y Negro**, C. Pintada, 35, on the opposite side of town, attracts visitors of all ages with a trendy atmosphere, popular nightly karaoke, and familiar British and American music. (Mixed drinks €4, beer €1-2. Open Su-Th 10pm-3am, F-Sa 10pm-4am; reduced low-season hours.) Middle-aged couples tend to congregate at any one of Nerja's many cookie-cutter British pubs; look for the beer logo sign hanging from a door and there's sure to be a crowd.

ALMUÑÉCAR   ☎958

In the 4th century BC, a booming fish-salting industry brought prosperity to this Phoenician port town known as **Sexi**. The Romans seized control a century later, constructing temples and a massive aqueduct. Though not quite as exciting as its Phoenician name suggests, Almuñécar might merit a visit by those in search of the comforts of city life alongside expansive boardwalks and beaches, minus the throngs of tourists. However, for something a bit more charming than somewhat unappealing 1970s-style architecture and tall apartment buildings towering over the beach, it may be better to look elsewhere.

■ PRACTICAL INFORMATION. The **bus station** (☎958 63 01 40) is at the corner of Av. Fenicia and Av. Juan Carlos I, in the huge round building. Buses run to: **Almería** (3hr., 6 per day 4:15-6:30pm, €8.38); **Granada** (1½hr., 7 per day 6:30am-8pm, €5.95); **Madrid** (7hr.; 2 per day 8:15am, 4:15pm; €16.33); **Málaga** (1½hr., 7 per day 7am-9:15pm, €5.22); **Nerja** (20min., 8 per day 7:15am-9:15pm, €2.07); **Sevilla** (5hr.; 2 per day 1:30, 4:15pm; €18.19). The **tourist office** is in the mauve mansion at the bottom of Av. de Europa. From the bus station, exit right, go straight around the rotary, follow C. de la Concepción around the turn, and take a left on Av. de Europa. (☎958 63 11 25. Open daily 10am-2pm and 5-8pm.) **Luggage storage** at lockers in the bus station. (€2. Open daily 6:30am-9:30pm.) Services include: **medical emergency** ☎061 or 112; **police** at the Ayuntamiento in Pl. de la Constitución (emergency ☎092 or non-emergency 958 63 94 30); **medical care** (☎958 63 20 63).

■ ACCOMMODATIONS & FOOD. Several reasonably priced hostels lie on Av. de Europa; other budget options lie on the outskirts of the city. Follow directions above to the tourist office to get to Av. de Europa's hostels. The posh **Hotel Casablanca ❸**, Pl. San Cristóbal, 4, in a beautiful pink-and-white building across from the beach, is surprisingly affordable. (☎958 63 55 75. June-Aug. doubles €60; Sept.-May €50.) Situated across from the tourist office, **Hotel Goya ❷**, Av. de Europa, 31, has comfortable rooms with dark wood furniture, baths, and phones. (☎958 63 05 50 or 63 11 92. July-Sept. and *Semana Santa* singles €30; doubles €53, with breakfast €73. Low-season prices substantially lower. AmEx/MC/V.) Plenty of beach-front *terrazas* line Po. Puerta del Mar and Po. San Cristóbal, providing a place to savor the catch of the day. **Oasis Café-Bar ❷**, Pl. de la Constitución, 10, serves a cross between British and Spanish food—if that's possible—and is happy to cook your order to your liking. (☎958 88 03 31. Entrees €7-8. Open daily 10am-late.) **%Dia,** behind the bus station, sells groceries.

■ SIGHTS & BEACHES. Almuñécar's historical protagonists, the Phoenicians, Romans, and Moors, all fought over this subtropical paradise, and each left a distinct mark. The Moorish **Castillo de San Miguel,** converted to a Christian fortress and renamed in 1489, rests atop a massive hill at the front of Pl. Puerta del Mar. Bombarded by the British during the Napoleonic Wars, it was cleared of rubble and converted to a cemetery before its most recent incarnation as a museum. Check out the fantastic coastal views from the top. (Open Tu-Sa 10:30am-1:30pm and 5-7:30pm, Su 10:30am-2pm. €2, children €1.40.) Almuñécar is also home to nearly 100 different species of birds, which nest in the **Parque Ornitológico Loro Sexi** beside El Castillo de San Miguel, 100m from the beach. (Open daily 11am-2pm and 4:30-6:30pm. €2, under 12 €1.40.) Uphill from the tourist office, **Parque El Majuelo** has 400 varieties of imported plants amidst cement walkways and the ruins of a Roman-Punic fishing factory. (Open daily dawn-dusk. Free.)

Located on the **Costa Tropical,** Almuñécar's main draw is its crowded beaches. Jutting into the sea, **Peñón del Santo,** a point of land crowned by a giant cross, separates the two main beaches. Both **Playa San Cristóbal** and **Playa del Mar** feature gray sands and lots of sunbathing Spaniards and Brits. To reach either beach, follow Av. de Europa to the sea; San Cristóbal is on the right, del Mar is on the left. Beyond Puerta del Mar lies the beautiful and less frequented **Playa de Velilla.** Buses to Málaga go through **La Herradura** (15min., 10 per day 7am-9:15pm, €0.70), a suburb/beach frequented by windsurfers and scuba divers. The largest **nude beach** on the Costa Tropical is **Playa Cantarriján,** accessible by car or taxi en route to Nerja.

ANDALUCÍA

ALMERÍA
☎ 590

Exciting nightlife, flowery promenades, and an extensive coastline have turned the once-poor city of Almería into a choice spot for weekend getaways. The cranes, bulldozers, and other construction equipment that frame the city are a testament to its growing popularity. Despite the ugly urban sprawl of the city's outskirts, the beautiful plazas, streets, and port make the city center a desirable destination. A huge Moorish fortress, the Alcazaba, presides over the city, but the best parts of Almería are the kilometers of sand stretching along the sea toward Cabo de Gata, at the eastern edge of the Costa del Sol.

🖳 TRANSPORTATION. The **airport** (☎950 21 37 00), 9km outside town, has daily flights to Madrid and Barcelona. **Trains,** Pl. de la Estación (☎902 24 02 02), run to: **Barcelona** (14hr.; W, F, Su 1 per day 7:30am; €48.50); **Granada** (2hr., 4 per day 6am-6:10pm, €11.35); **Madrid** (7hr.; 2 per day 7:15am, 3:45pm; €34.25-43.25); **Sevilla** (6hr., 4 per day 6am-6pm, €27.20); **Valencia** (8hr.; W, F, Su 1 per day 7:30am; €35). **Buses** (☎902 42 22 42) leave from Pl. de la Estación. **ALSA/Enatcar** goes to: **Barcelona** (14hr., 6 per day 8:30am-10:30pm, €51.29); **Mojácar** (1½hr., 4-5 per day 5:15am-7:45pm, €5.50); **Murcia** (3hr., 3 per day 10am-5pm, €14.22-16.90); **Valencia** (8hr., 4 per day 8:30am-9:30pm, €29.29). **Alsina Graells** sends buses to: **Córdoba** (6hr., 1 per day 3:30pm, €19.45); **Granada** (2hr., 10 per day 7am-7pm, €9.10); **Málaga** (3½hr., 10 per day 6:30am-11pm, €26.19); **Sevilla** (5½-9hr., 3 per day 9:30am-11pm, €26.19). **Almeraya** goes to **Madrid** (8hr., 6 per day 9:30am-1:30am, €20.43).

🖳🛈 ORIENTATION & PRACTICAL INFORMATION. The city revolves around **Puerta de Purchena,** a six-way intersection just down C. Tiendas from the old town. To reach Pta. de Purchena from the **bus station** or the connected **train station** on Pl. Estación, walk straight out the front door and take a left onto Av. de la Estación after one block, turn right onto Av. Federico García Lorca, then left onto Rbla. Obispo Orbera. Po. de Almería runs out of Pta. de Purchena to the port—any services, including banks with **ATMs,** can be found on Po. de Almería or just off it. The **tourist office** is in Mirador de la Rambla, a small building in the middle of pedestrian Av. Federico García Lorca, one block toward the port from the intersection with Av. de la Estación. (☎950 28 07 48. Open M-F 10am-1pm and 5:30-7:30pm, Sa 10am-12pm.) The commercial **port** lies directly in front of the Parque de Salmerón. Services include: **emergency** (☎112); **police,** C. Santos Zarate (☎92); **Hospital Torre Cardenas** (☎950 01 60 00); **post office,** Pl. Juan Cassinello, down Po. de Almería. (☎950 23 72 07; open M-F 8:30am-8:30pm, Sa 9:30am-2pm.) **Postal Code:** 04080.

🛏 ACCOMMODATIONS. Rooms in Almería tend to be rather uninspiring. The tourist office provides a list of accommodations, most of which surround Pta. de Purchena. Those seeking quiet rooms with private bath, TV, and A/C should check out **Hostal Residencia Nixar ❷,** C. Antonio Vico, 24, a few blocks up from Pl. del Carmen. The hostal has a funky tropical atmosphere downstairs with wicker chairs and potted palms, and simple rooms with cheerful bedspreads and modern baths. (☎950 23 72 55. July-Aug. €25 singles; doubles €42.30; triples €50. Sept.-June €20.35/€35.30/€41.) Less than a block down the street is **Hotel La Perla ❹,** Pl. del Carmen, 7, which has recently-refurbished rooms with bath, TV, and A/C that are popular with an older crowd. Long hallways with plush carpets and bronze chandeliers give a feeling of elegance and comfort in a simple setting. (☎950 23 88 77. Singles €35-46.28; doubles €40-57.10. IVA not included.) **Hostal Americano ❷,** Av. de la Estación, on the corner of C. Federico García Lorca, is one of the simpler hostels in town, with small but comfortable rooms and long, marble halls. (☎950 28 10 15. Singles €20, with bath €21-26; doubles €32-36/€35-42.)

🔲 **FOOD.** Cafes line Po. de Almería. Eat a traditional Andalusian meal on barrels of olive oil amidst photos of famous *matadores* and hanging hams at **Bodega Las Botas ❷**, C. Fructuoso Pérez, 3, a side-street off Po. de Almería one block before Pta. de Purchena. The *bodega* offers good cold cut platters (€5.45-9) and fresh fish entrees for €10-14. (☎950 26 22 72. Open daily noon-4pm and 8pm-2am.) If you're looking for a break from Spanish food, head to **Pizzeria-Ristorante Nello ❷**, Av. de la Estación, 26, one block down from Hostal Americano towards the bus station. Nello serves excellent pizza (€7.50-9.50) and pasta (€9.75) in a traditional Italian setting—bottles of wine and old photographs adorn a wooden trellis. (☎950 26 77 39. Open daily noon-4pm and 8pm-midnight.) With ham chandeliers and over 70 types of *tapas* (all €0.65), **Casa Puga ❶**, C. Jovellanos, 7, in the old quarter, attracts a lively crowd. (☎950 23 15 30. Open M-Sa 11am-4pm and 8pm-midnight.) Across the street and down one block is the **Museo del Aceite**, C. Real, 15, which offers visitors a free tour through the history of olive oil and a small restaurant in which to experience its present state, with *tapas* for €1-3. (Open M-F 11am-3pm and 6:30-10pm, Sa 11am-3pm.) The local supermarket is **Champion,** on Po. de Almería. (☎950 23 28 00. Open M-Sa 9:15am-9:15pm.)

🔲 **SIGHTS.** Built in 995 by order of Abderramán III of Córdoba, the ▨**Alcazaba,** a magnificent 14-acre Moorish fortress, spans two ridges overlooking the city and the sea. Time your visit so you can make the short trek up to the fortress for stunning views of the city at sunset. Also, the small museum contains Moorish artifacts recovered from archaeological digs in the area. *(From Pl. del Carmen next to Pta. de Purchena, follow C. Antonio Vico. ☎950 27 16 17. Open Tu-Sa 9am-8:30pm. €1.50, EU citizens free.)* The **cathedral,** in the old town, resembles a fortress; its design was intended to prevent raids by Berber pirates. Though spartan and blockish on the outside, the inside is all Renaissance with a touch of Baroque on the altar. *(☎609 57 58 02. Open M-F 10am-4:30pm, Sa 10am-1pm, and during Mass. €1.80.)*

🔲 **NIGHTLIFE.** Pubs, bars, and discos fill the small streets behind the post office, known as *cuatro calles,* where throngs of students and adults can be seen partaking in *la marcha* as early as 11pm. By far the most popular hot spot is the disco ▨**Dolce Vita,** Po. de Almería, where several cavernous dance floors, numerous bars, and pulsating music keep the tight-bodied crowd going until nearly 6am. (M-F no cover, Sa cover €6, Su cover €5. Cover includes one drink. Beer €2.50. Mixed drinks €5. Open nightly 11pm-6:30am.) The next stop for the younger crowd is **Enebro,** C. San Pedro, 13, a lively pub that features loud Spanish pop. (Beer €2.50. Mixed drinks €4. Open nightly until 4am.) **Chupitería Dalia,** C. Dalia, 3, serves up a variety of not-so-subtly-named shooters like *orgasmo de manga.* (☎950 26 25 84. Cocktail shots €8, shots €2, *copas* €4. Open daily 10pm-3am.) Those too old to giggle at a buttery nipple gather at the outdoor tables and by the bar at **The Irish Tavern,** C. Antonio González Eges, 4 (beer €2-3, mixed drinks €4.50; open daily 3pm-4:30am), then head over to dance at **Parrot's Café,** C. Trajana at the corner of C. San Pedro (mixed drinks €3.50; open Th-Sa 11pm-4am). When the weekend partying is done, locals head to **Vertice Pub,** C. Eduardo Pérez, 4, for beer (€2.50) and chill jazz music. (☎652 95 09 32. Open daily 10:30pm-4am.)

🔲 **BEACHES.** Almería's beaches offer relief from stifling heat in the city. From the port, walk past La Rambla Belén along Po. Marítimo. To your right you'll find Playa Almadravillas, whose waters are often churned up by the traffic of private yachts motoring in and out of the nearby marina. Farther down Po. Marítimo, well past the marina, are Playa Ciudad Luminosa and Playa del Zapillo, which offer swimmers calmer waters flanked by numerous stone jetties. The beaches generally improve north of the city towards the protected coast of Cabo de Gata.

ANDALUCÍA

THE LOCAL STORY

ONCE UPON A TIME

One of Mojácar's claims to fame involves Walt Disney and is, appropriately enough, a fairy tale. One version of the legend has it that a beautiful but poor washerwoman named Isabel Zamora fell in love with a (married) member of the town's high society. She gave birth to an illegitimate son on December 5, 1901, naming him José. A young miner named Guirao married Isabel to save her honor and help care for the child, but he soon died. Isabel, penniless and determined to change her luck, brought José to America and left him in the care of a farmer couple—Elias and Flora Disney who later adopted him and named him Walt. Years later, in 1940, two men clad in gray suits arrived in Mojacar, asking to see the birth registry. A town official later noticed that the record for José Guirao had been ripped out, presumably stolen by the two mystery men. Who were they? Envoys of the Disney Corporation protecting their boss? FBI agents looking for blackmail material? Regardless, they had managed to bury the secret Spanish heritage of an American cultural icon. The rest is history.

Or really only legend. Among the story's many inconsistencies, no adoption or naturalization papers exist for this supposedly adopted child, and biographical evidence shows that no opportunity existed for the Disneys to come into contact with Isabel Zamora. Despite the rags-to-riches appeal of the story of Isabel Zamora's son, these facts support the conclusion that Walt Disney was, in fact, born in Chicago the legitimate, biological son of Elias and Flora Disney.

⟩ DAYTRIP FROM ALMERÍA

CABO DE GATA

Alsina Graells (☎ 950 23 51 68) sends buses to San Miguel de Cabo de Gata (1hr.; M-F 6 per day 8am-9pm, Sa-Su 4 per day 8am-8pm; return M-F 7 per day 7am-10pm, Sa-Su 4 per day 9am-9pm; €1.94). Autocares Bernardo (☎ 950 25 04 22) runs to San José (45min.; M-F 2 per day 1:15, 6:30pm; Sa 3 per day 10am, 2:15, 6:30pm; Su 2 per day 10am, 6:30pm; return M-F 4 per day 7, 11am, 3:15, 7:30pm; Sa 4 per day 8, 11am, 3:15, 7:30pm; Su 2 per day 11am, 7:30pm; €3).

For a quieter, more relaxed beach experience than in Almería, long stretches of pleasant beaches await in the fishing town of **San Miguel de Cabo de Gata** (or simply Cabo de Gata). Farther south, the little resort of **San José** boasts an even more unspoiled beach and serves as a base for exploring the park (see below). Contact the **tourist office** in San José for information on water sports, bike and car rentals, and maps for visiting the secluded **calas** (coves) along the coast. (☎ 950 38 02 99. Open daily 10am-2pm and 4-8pm, Su 10am-2pm. Some English spoken.)

The pristine ⧉**Parque Natural de Cabo de Gata-Níjar,** a 60km stretch of protected coast and inland environs, lies 30km east of urban Almería. The near-desolate peninsula juxtaposes tropical and barren climates; flamingos flock to the area's salt marshes, while the desert and mountains farther inland entice hikers. Many come to Cabo de Gata to dive at **Mermaid's Reef** or windsurf off **Playa de San Miguel.** Both **Grupo J. 126** (☎ 950 38 02 99) and **Ocio y Mar** (☎ 608 05 64 77) provide info and tours of the park; contact them a day or two in advance for tours and equipment rental.

MOJÁCAR   ☎ 950

Mojácar is the kind of vacation spot one might see on a postcard: a white-stoned, picture-perfect, hilltop village with 17km of smooth coastline. During the day, the village clears out as tourists head downhill to the turquoise Mediterranean to escape the heat. Later, stunning sunsets find tourists and residents relaxing on the numerous outdoor terraces, sipping tropical drinks in the shade of beachfront bars, or strolling along the boardwalk. The beachfront resorts fill up quickly in July and August when hordes of international visitors join the large contingent of German, British, and American expats who have made Mojácar their home—don't be surprised to hear more English than Spanish from visitors and residents alike.

⌐ TRANSPORTATION. The main bus stop (there is no station) is in front of the shopping plaza near the beach. Most buses also stop just below town. Ask for "Mojácar playa" for the beach or "Mojácar pueblo" for the town. **ALSA/Enatcar** buses (☎902 42 22 42) leave for: **Almería** (1½hr.; M-Sa 7 per day, Su 2 per day 7:50am-11:10pm; €5.10); **Barcelona** (12hr., 2 per day, €39.65); **Madrid** (8hr., 1-2 per day, €26.10); **Murcia** (2½hr.; M-F 8 per day, Sa-Su 4-5 per day 7:05am-9:35pm; €8.72). For a **taxi** call ☎608 33 93 42 or 659 93 69 08, or wait at the Pl. Nueva stop in town. The tourist office has a list of nearly a dozen **car rental** agencies. **Indal-futur,** Po. del Mediterráneo, 293, rents **scooters.** (☎609 02 65 26. €27 per day. Driver's license and €35 deposit required. Open M-F 10am-2pm and 5-8pm.)

▊▊ ORIENTATION & PRACTICAL INFORMATION. Mojácar is split into two parts: the beach, lined with pricy hotels, tourist-oriented restaurants, and the best nightlife spots along Po. del Mediterráneo, and the *pueblo*, where everyday life centers around Pl. Nueva. The town rests atop a hill and is connected to the beach by a winding road. Most buses stop both at the "official" stop in front of the shopping plaza by the beach and at the lowest point of the village itself; since most budget lodging is in town, get off at the latter stop. The 30min. hike up the hill from the beach or the main bus stop to Pl. Nueva is not for the faint of heart, but yellow **Transportes Urbanos** buses run to and from town and the beachfront bus stop. (Daily 2 per hr. 9:30am-1:30pm and 5pm-midnight, 1 per hr. 1:30-5pm; €0.60.) This same bus line also services the various beaches along the coast. Lines A and B both run in a continuous loop between the two ends of the beach and the town, starting at Hotel Indalo at the far end of the beach to the right from town (Playa de las Ventanicas), then going up to town, then to Marina de las Torres at the other end of the beach, then back along Po. del Mediterráneo to Hotel Indalo. The point where the road to town meets Po. del Mediterráneo is the main bus stop, called the *cruce* (crossing). Check the main bus stop or the tourist office for schedules.

The main **tourist office** (☎950 61 50 25; www.mojacarviva.com; open M-F 10am-2pm and 5-8pm, Sa 10:30am-1:30pm), **police** (☎950 47 20 00), and **post office** (open M-F 12:30-2:30pm, Sa 10am-noon) are all in the indoor arcade a few steps below Pl. Nueva. There is also a **tourist office branch** on Po. del Mediterráneo on the beach across the street from the large shopping center (same hours as the main office). **Bish's Lavandería,** Po. del Mediterráneo, will fluff and fold your grimy garments for €2.60 per kilo. (☎950 47 80 11. Self-serve washers €4.40-5.40; dryers €1.50 per 15 min. Open M-Sa 9am-5pm. Last wash 4pm.) **Postal Code:** 04638.

▐ ACCOMMODATIONS. Finding a bed in Mojácar at the last minute can be difficult, especially in high season (July and August) when the city is taken over by partying tourists. The simple but pleasant accommodations at **Casa Justa ❷,** C. Morote, 5, give you the most for your money. From Pl. Nueva, take a right on C. Alcalde Jacinto, a left on C. Estación Nueva, a right on C. Esteve, a sharp right again on C. Ruíz and go down the hill to C. Morote. (☎950 47 83 72. Singles €15; doubles €30-42, some with A/C and private bath.) Those wishing to stay on the beachfront have several options along Po. del Mediterráneo. **Hostal Flamenco ❸,** Po. del Mediterráneo, s/n, has simple and airy rooms with bath, TV, and A/C. All doubles have terraces overlooking the sea, and guests can use the swimming pool across the road for relief after a day in saltwater. (☎950 47 82 27. June-Aug. singles €30, with terrace €35; doubles €60. Sept.-May €24/€30/€36.) The five elegant bedrooms at **Pensión Torreón ❹,** C. Jazmín, 4, are decorated with a resort aesthetic appropriate for their fantastic oceanfront views. From Pl. Nueva, follow C. Indalo and take the second right on C. Enmedio, then take a left downhill along C. Unión, and a right at the end of the hill onto C. Jazmín. (☎950 47 52 59. Call early to reserve a room. Doubles with shared bath €36.)

⬤ FOOD. You'll find more variety and better value in town than at the beach, although the fresh seafood restaurants with their feet in the sand are occasionally worth the splurge. Po. del Mediterráneo seeks to please the beachgoer wth ice cream shops, pizzerias, and, occasionally, Spanish cuisine. For dinner, head to **◪La Cantina ❷**, Po. del Mediterráneo, 2, in Tito's Beach complex, for quite possibly the most authentic tacos and quesadillas (€5-7) in southern Spain. Never mind the Dutch cook. (☎950 47 88 41. Reservations suggested on weekends. Open daily 7:30pm-midnight.) **Pizzeria Pulcinella ❷**, C. Puntica, 5, caters to the tourist but still prepares some of the best Italian cuisine in town. Follow C. Indalo from Pl. Nueva, take a left on C. Enmedia and a right at the end onto C. Puntica. (☎950 47 84 01. Pizzas €5-8, pasta €6-8. Open Tu-Su 8pm-midnight. MC/V.) If you wish to dine close to the beach, or are just too lazy to schlep uphill, try **Bar Restaurante Estrella del Mar ❶**, Po. del Mediterráneo, 311, a couple of blocks past Indal-futur scooter rentals from the main bus stop. Grab lunch on the cheery patio out front, or savor a longer dinner (classic Spanish cuisine with specialty seafood plates; €4-12) in the tile-floored room behind the bar. (☎950 47 23 50. Open daily 10am-11pm.)

◪BEACHES. Tourists come to Mojácar for the beaches. Buses run twice an hour between the town and beach and along the shore (see **Practical Information,** above). In town, buses leave from the stop below Pl. Nueva. From the beach, get on at a stop along Po. del Mediterráneo. There are many beaches to choose from, from the crowded **Playa del Cantal** and **Playa de la Cueva del Lobo** to the more sedate **Playa Piedra Villazar. Playa de las Ventanicas** marks the start of a gorgeous palm-lined path that stretches several kilometers to the south. The better beaches are to the right at the bottom of the hill from town, but they are also more crowded and commercialized. Those to the left are rockier, but quieter as well.

◪◪ NIGHTLIFE & ENTERTAINMENT. Mojácar pulses with nightlife. Tented *chiringuitos* (beach bars) sprawl out along the water by Po. del Mediterráneo and are the most popular places to begin (or end) a night. (Open *Semana Santa* - Oct. 31.) Go by car or scooter if you can; buses stop running at 11:30pm, and taxis disappear at sundown. Walking the poorly lit highway is a dangerous alternative. Some of the best *chiringuitos* include **◪Tito's**, Po. del Mediterráneo, 2, on Playa de las Ventanicas, which serves excellent margaritas (€3.60-4.50) in a relaxed setting and holds open-air jazz festivals every summer; call for schedules. (☎950 61 50 30. Open daily 10am-8pm.) **El Cid** and **El Patio**, both on Playa del Cantal, offer a similarly laid-back atmosphere amidst palm trees and tiki torches. (Beer €2. Both open daily 10am-1:30am.) **Lua** is an upscale *chiringuito* on Playa de las Ventanicas, about a block from Tito's. (Beer €2.10, mixed drinks €4.50. Open daily 10am-3am.) Palm trees grace the bar at **Pascha**, a popular *discoteca* on Po. del Mediterráneo. For a midnight dip to sober up before bed, the pool at **Viva Mojácar,** on the highway between the beach and the town, is open until 5am. (☎950 46 81 33.)

Back in town, expats run more laid-back watering holes. There is certainly nightlife to be had up here, though, so don't despair if you're not staying on the beach. **Plaza Nueva** encompasses pleasant bars and *terrazas*, and C. de la Estación Nueva has its own mini-scene. To get there, follow C. Indalo out of the plaza and take a right on C. Enmedio; C. de la Estación Nueva will be your first right. **La Sartén**, C. de la Estación Nueva, 19, is a comfy, funky little bar with cushions to sit on and cartoons on the wall. Catering to an international crowd, the drinks are cheap and the music is upbeat rock and pop. (Beer €1.50, mixed drinks €4. Opens at 9pm.) Next door, **La Luna** specializes in sandwiches and 22 creatively-conceived *chupitos* (shots) and drinks. Among them are the "Rusty Nail," the "Mono Caliente" (Hot Monkey), and others with racier titles. Live music is played on a "spontaneous" basis. (☎950 47 80 32. Drinks €4. Opens at 11pm.) Nestled into the corner of C. de la Estación Nueva is **Discoteca Budú**, where there's a niche for everyone amidst three dance floors, an open-air terrace, two bars, and smaller cushiony alcoves for those less inclined to bump and grind. (Beer €2.50, mixed drinks €5. Opens at 11pm.) Because Mojácar has dozens of night spots, the "in" place seems to be changing constantly; pick up the free *Mojácar Viva* leaflet at the tourist office for more detailed info.

RONDA ☎952

Flanked by rolling hills, valleys, and farms, picturesque Ronda (pop. 35,000) has all the charm of a small, medieval town but all the amenities and culture of a thriving city. Centuries-old bridges and arches span the 100m gorge, offering ample photo opportunities for the throngs of camera-toting tourists who pass through daily, while cathedrals, museums, dungeons, and plazas—not to mention the famed bull-ring—spread through the old and new cities. The old city remains from the time when Ronda was a pivotal commercial center, during the Roman era. Fortunes dwindled under Moorish rule after Al Mutadid ibn Abbad drowned the ruling lord in his bath and annexed the city for Sevilla. More recently, Ronda—the birthplace of modern bullfighting—has attracted such forlorn artists as Rainer Maria Rilke, who wrote his *Spanish Elegies* here, and Orson Welles, whose ashes are buried on a bull farm outside of town. Brimming with sights, Ronda makes an excellent base for exploring the *pueblos blancos* and the nearby Cuevas de la Pileta.

▐ TRANSPORTATION

The **train** and **bus stations** are in the new city three blocks away from each other on Av. de Andalucía. To reach the tourist office and the town center from the train station, turn right on Av. de Andalucía and follow it to Pl. Concepción García Redondo in front of the bus station. Turn left on C. la Naranja, then right four blocks up onto pedestrian Cra. Espinel, which leads to **Plaza de España.**

Trains: Av. Alférez Provisional (☎902 24 02 02). **Tickets,** C. Infantes, 20 (☎952 87 16 62). Open M-F 10am-2pm and 6-8:30pm. To: **Algeciras** (2hr., 4 per day 7:10am-8:28pm, €5.75); **Granada** (3hr.; 3 per day 9:23am, 1:40, 5:35pm; €10.30); **Madrid** (4½hr.; 2 per day 4:35, 11:27pm; €48.50); **Málaga** (2hr., 1 per day 7:50am, €7.55).

Buses: Pl. Concepción García Redondo, 2 (☎952 18 70 61 or 87 22 62). To: **Cádiz** (4hr., 4 per day 9:30am-5:30pm, €11.46); **Málaga** (2½hr.; M-F 9 per day 6am-7:30pm, fewer Sa-Su; €7.52); **Marbella** (1½hr., 5 per day 6:30am-7:45pm, €4.27); **Sevilla** (2½hr.; M-F 5 per day 7am-7pm, Sa-Su 3-4 per day 7am-7pm; €8.99).

Taxis: (☎952 87 23 16 or 670 20 74 38). From the train station to Pl. de España €4.

▚▐ ORIENTATION & PRACTICAL INFORMATION

The 18th-century **Puente Nuevo** connects Ronda's old and new sections. On the new side of the city, **Carrera Espinel** (the main street, including the pedestrian walkway known as **La Bola**) runs perpendicular to C. Virgen de la Paz. Cra. Espinel intersects C. Virgen de la Paz between the bullring and Pl. de España.

Tourist Office: Po. Blas Infante (☎952 18 71 19; www.turismoronda.es), across from the bullring. Open June-Aug. M-F 9:30am-7:30pm, Sa-Su 10am-2pm and 3:30-6:30pm; Sept.-May M-F 9:30am-6:30pm, Sa-Su 10am-2pm and 3:30-6:30pm. **Regional office,** Pl. de España, 1 (☎952 87 12 72). Open June-Aug. M-F 9am-8pm, Sa-Su 10am-2pm; Sept.-May M-F 9am-7pm, Sa-Su 10am-2pm. English spoken at both.

Currency Exchange: Banco Santander Central Hispano, Cra. Espinel, 17 (☎902 24 24 24), near C. los Remedios.Open M-F 8:30am-2pm, Sa 8:30am-1pm.

Luggage Storage: At the **bus station,** €3 per day. Open daily 9am-8pm.

Emergency: ☎092. **Police:** Pl. Duquesa de Parcent, 3 (☎952 87 13 69).

Medical Emergency: ☎952 87 17 73. **Centro de Salud** (☎952 87 56 75), on the road to El Burgo.

Pharmacy: Farmacia Homeopatia, Pl. de España, 5 (☎952 87 52 49). Open M-F 9:30am-2pm and 5-8:30pm.

Internet Access: Planet Adventure, C. Molino, 6 (☎952 87 52 49). Speedy Internet access upstairs (9am-3pm €1.80 per hr., 3-10pm €2.40 per hr.); coffee, smoothies (€1.50), and pastries (€1) downstairs. Open daily 9am-10pm.

Post Office: C. Virgen de la Paz, 20 (☎952 87 25 57), across from Pl. de Toros. **Lista de Correos.** Open M-F 8:30am-2:30pm, Sa 9:30am-1pm. **Postal Code:** 29400.

ACCOMMODATIONS

Most budget lodgings are concentrated in the new city near the bus station, along the streets perpendicular to C. Espinel—try C. la Naranja and C. Lorenzo Borrego. Expect room shortages during the *Feria de Ronda* in September.

Pensión La Purísima, C. Sevilla, 10 (☎952 87 10 50). Plant-filled hallways lead to bright rooms decorated with tasteful religious art. Some have private bath. Singles €15; doubles €28-30, with bath €30-33; triples with bath €45. ●

Hostal Ronda Sol, C. Almendra, 11 (☎952 87 44 97), and **Hostal Biarritz,** C. Almendra, 7 (☎952 87 29 10). Both are run by the same owner, have the same prices, and feature similar spotless but dark rooms. Biarritz is slightly older, but some rooms have private bath. Parking €10. Singles €11; doubles €17, with bath €25; triples €25. ●

Hotel Polo, C. Mariano Souviron, 8 (☎952 87 24 47; fax 87 24 49). Airy, sunny rooms all come with bath, A/C, heating, and satellite TV, although such comfort comes at a price. Breakfast €5. Singles €32.80-50.50; doubles €53-69. MC/V. ●

Hotel Morales, C. Sevilla, 51 (☎952 87 15 38; fax 18 70 02). With its myriad framed maps, the lobby is a cartographer's fantasy. New rooms—all with bath, some with TV— surround an enclosed inner courtyard. Singles €18-21; doubles €33-39. MC/V. ●

FOOD

Restaurants and cafes abound in Ronda, although many are geared to tourists and tend to be overpriced, especially those near Pl. de España. Rabbit and stewed bull's tail *(rabo de toro)* are local specialties.

Relax Bar and Restaurant, C. los Remedios, 27 (☎952 87 72 07; www.relaxcafe-bar.com). Crowds of English-speaking tourists and residents occupy the wooden tables and bar for vegetarian fare. *Tapas* €1, salads €4, sandwiches and open-faced "melts" €3.60-3.90. Many vegan options. Happy Hour (Tu, Th, F 10-11pm) offers half-priced beer and wine. Open daily M-F 1-4pm and 8pm-midnight. ●

La Gota de Vino 13, C. Sevilla, 13 (☎952 87 57 16). Self-proclaimed a "creative *tapas* and wine bar," La Gota serves trendy versions of *comida típica* (mostly combinations of Spanish hams and cheeses) to an equally trendy crowd of 20- and 30-something locals and tourists. Great selection of regional wines (€1.80-4.50 per glass). Some vegetarian options. *Tapas* €5-7. Open Tu-Su 7pm-2am. ●

Pizzería Ristorante Italiano Nonno Peppe, C. Nueva, 18 (☎952 87 28 50). Fabulous pizzas (€3.50-8) and pastas (€3.50-6) with many ingredients imported from Italy. Wide array of Italian desserts tempt you from a rotating glass case (€1.55-3.50). Open daily noon-4:30pm and 8pm-1am. ❶

Cafe de Ronda, C. Tenorio, 1 (☎952 87 40 91), right across the Puente Nuevo. Taking up the entire first floor of a huge mansion, this self-service cafe not only has great sandwiches (€3-3.50), salads (€3-4), breakfasts (€3.45), and specialty coffees (€1.50-3), but it also has one of the most beautiful, plant-filled patios around. Tons of airy indoor seating as well. Open M-Th 9am-9pm, F-Su 9am-midnight. ❶

🔯 SIGHTS

🖾 **PLAZA DE TOROS & MUSEO TAURINO.** Bullfighting lies at the heart of Ronda's livelihood, evident in the stunning bullring, the oldest in Spain (est. 1785) and the world-class bullfighting museum. The recently remodeled museum traces the history of the sport, focusing largely on Ronda's native matadors. Original Goya prints of fights and bullfighters, authentic costumes, weapons, and the heads of the bravest bulls grace the walls and glass cases in the narrow museum hallways, while multilingual posters describe noteworthy fights and explain the exhibits. Ronda has had its share of famous bullfighters, including the Romero dynasty—three generations of fighters from the same family. Pedro, the most famous, killed his first bull at age 17 in 1771; over the course of his career, it is said he fought more than 5600 bulls without ever being injured. The museum hallway exits into the main bullring, from which another hallway heads to walkways that encircle the bullpins used to hold bulls before a fight. In early September, the Plaza de Toros hosts *corridas goyescas* (bullfights in traditional costumes) as part of the **Feria de Ronda.** The town fills to capacity—book rooms months in advance. Aside from the *feria*, visitors must go elsewhere to see a live bullfight. *(Museum ☎952 87 15 39; www.rmcr.org. Open daily Apr. 16-Oct. 10am-8pm; Nov.-Feb 10am-6pm; Mar.-Apr. 15 10am-7pm. €5.)*

🖾 **CASA DEL REY MORO.** The name, House of the Moorish King, is misleading in many ways. Despite its name and Moorish facade, the house itself dates from the 18th century and is not the main attraction here; in fact, you can't even enter the house other than to pay your admission. Descend the steep stairs 60m into a 14th- century mine, which, over the centuries, has housed more than its share of prisoners and slaves, forced to climb up and down the stairs to gather water. At the very bottom, a small balcony brings you out at water level right above the river, looking up at the ravine walls and the city high above. The other main attraction is high atop the cliffs and house: **Forestier's Gardens,** which were designed and constructed in the 1920s by the aforementioned famous French landscape architect and boast equally impressive views as the mine, but from the completely opposite perspective. *(Cuesta de Santo Domingo, 9. Take the first left after crossing the Puente Nuevo. ☎952 18 72 00. Open daily in summer 10am-8pm; in winter 10am-7pm. €4, children €2.)*

BRIDGES. Carved by the Río Guadalquivír, Ronda's gorge extends 100m below the **Puente Nuevo,** across from Pl. de España. Arrested highwaymen were once held in a prison cell beneath the bridge's center; during the Civil War, political prisoners were thrown from the top. The view from the center is unparalleled—looking to the left with your back to Pl. de España you see the city and the other bridges, while to the right the valley and hills stretch out to the coun-

ANDALUCÍA

THE LOCAL STORY

CHASING WINDMILLS

Set in a charming old olive and flour mill in the heart of Andalucía, **Molino del Santo** is the perfect place to get away from it all. The small resort, 30min. from Ronda and a mere 5km from the incredible Cuevas de la Pileta, has accomplished the almost impossible—giving guests all the luxuries of a five-star hotel with the peacefulness usually found in country inns. Spacious, tastefully decorated rooms, all with A/C, dark wood furniture, and none with TV (in fact, there are none in the entire hotel, to maintain a sense of tranquility), give way to beautiful gardens and a large pool, where guests sunbathe and take in the incredible views of the surrounding mountains. Local chefs use only the freshest ingredients to serve at the in-house restaurant, a quaint dining room and a breathtaking terrace situated next to a pebbly, cascading stream. The bottom half of the hotel, an old mill, houses a cozy living room, where guests sit playing board games and reading in winter, often accompanied by a roaring fire.

Hotel Molino del Santo, Benaoján, two train stops from Ronda. From the train station, with your back to the tracks, head left and follow signs to the hotel. ☎952 16 71 51; fax 16 73 27; www.andalucia.com/molino. Doubles with breakfast depending on season €40-76/ day, €280-532/week; with breakfast, snack, and 3-course dinner €73-110/day, €441-770/week.

tryside. Two other bridges span the gap and can be reached by walking on C. Santo Domingo past the Casa del Rey Moro: the innovative Puente Viejo was rebuilt in 1616 over an earlier Arab bridge, with the Arco de Felipe V, built in 1742, presiding over one end of it; farther down, the Puente San Miguel (or Puente Árabe) is a prime Andalusian hybrid of a Roman base and Arabic arches.

COLEGIATA DE SANTA MARÍA LA MAYOR. Following the Christian reconquest of Ronda in 1485, this church was slowly assembled over the next two centuries and features both Gothic and Renaissance styles. Until 1485 the building was a mosque; a small arch near the entrance and a verse from the Qur'an engraved behind the sacristy are the last vestiges of the church's Moorish origins. *(Facing Pl. Duquesa de Parent in the old town. ☎952 87 22 46. Open daily high season 10am-8pm; low season 10am-6pm. €2, groups €1.50 per person.)*

PALACIO DE MONDRAGÓN. Originally inhabited by Don Fernando Valenzuela, a prominent minister under Carlos III, this 17th-century palace has since been transformed into a fascinating anthropological museum. Exhibits on ancient life in the area fill former sitting rooms and libraries. *(Two blocks behind Pl. Duquesa de Parent. ☎952 87 84 50. Open in summer M-F 10am-7pm, Sa-Su 10am-3pm; in winter M-F 10am-6pm, Sa-Su 10am-3pm. €2, students and groups €1 per person, under 12 and disabled free.)*

OTHER SIGHTS. Learn what life as a Spanish bandit was like at the tiny but informative **Museo del Bandolero,** C. Armiñán, 65, dedicated to presenting "pillage, theft, and rebellion in Spain since Roman times." *(☎952 87 77 85; www.museobandolero.com. Open daily in summer 10am-8:30pm; in winter 10am-6pm. €2.70.)* Take a trip back in time at the **Museo Lara,** which features Spanish art and antiques ranging from old clocks, telephones, and typewriters to music boxes and weapons. *(C. Armiñán, 29. ☎/fax 952 87 12 63; www.museolara.org. Open daily 11am-8pm. €2.50.)* The **Museo de Caza** displays mounted hunting trophies from four continents. With its mountains of taxidermy, it's definitely not a good place for vegetarians. *(C. Armiñán, 59. ☎952 87 78 62. Open daily 10:30am-7pm. €1.50.)*

NIGHTLIFE

Except for weekends, nightlife in Ronda is fairly low-key. At night, locals congregate in the pubs and *discotecas* along C. Jérez and the streets behind Pl. del Soxcorro. Popular with young Spaniards is **Bar Antonio,** C. San José 4, with its cheap drinks and tasty *tapas.* (Beer €0.80. Mixed drinks €3. *Tapas* €0.80. Open M-F 7am-11pm, Sa 9am-4am.) A slightly older crowd of both locals and tourists heads to **Huskies Sport Bar-Café,** C. Molino, 1, for beer and conversation. (www.huskiesbar.com. Beer €1.20. Mixed drinks €4. Open M at 8:30pm, Tu-Su at 5:30pm.)

DAYTRIP FROM RONDA

CUEVAS DE LA PILETA

*By car, take highway C-339 north (Ctra. Sevilla from the new city). The turnoff to Benaoján and the caves is about 13km out, in front of an abandoned restaurant. **Taxis** will go round-trip from Ronda for €45. A cheaper but more strenuous alternative is the **train**, via Benaoján. Trains run to Benaoján from Ronda (20min. 7:10, 9:47am, 2:34pm; return 9:01am-7:51pm. €3.50 round-trip). From the train station at Benaoján, it's a tough but scenic 1-1½hr. climb to the caves. The hike is mostly uphill and there is little shade; bring water and sturdy shoes. With your back to the train station, exit left and follow the road parallel to the tracks for 100m until the sign for Hotel Molino del Santo. Walk 15m past the sign on the narrow path next to the tracks and take your first right; continue past the hotel until you see a sign on the left for the caves. Follow the wide path for 1km up to a dilapidated farm; just before the old farm turn right onto the goat track leading uphill. There, near the summit, is a narrow highway; turn left and follow the road for 500m until you reach the cave parking lot. (☎952 16 73 43 or 16 72 02. Caves open daily 10am-1pm and 4-6pm. Mandatory 1hr. tours begin on the hour. Groups up to 8 €6.50 per person; 9 or more €6 per person.*

Twenty-two kilometers west of Ronda are the **Cuevas de la Pileta,** a dark expanse of stalactites and Paleolithic paintings, stretching for over a kilometer underground, originally formed tens of thousands of years ago by an underground river. The caves were discovered in 1906, but despite their well-preserved paintings and impressive size, have remained relatively untouristed. More than 22,000 years ago local inhabitants took refuge in these caves, painting the walls with cryptic symbols and animal imagery. The highlights are the *Yegua preñada* (pregnant mare) and the beautifully preserved *Pez* (fish). The chamber walls are darkened with soot and small human bones have been discovered in a number of locations; it's believed that the caves held special ceremonial significance during Neolithic times and were the scene of child sacrifices. Guides lead gas-lantern tours in Spanish and English. Reservations are possible in the winter, but long lines form in the summer. Wear comfortable shoes and dress warmly—even in the summer, the caves are 30°F colder than outside.

ANTEQUERA   ☎952

Few sunsets rival those seen from atop Antequera's old Moorish fortress, with views extending over the town and to the mountains. The Romans gave Antequera (pop. 42,000) its name, but older civilizations preceded them. Their mark can be seen on the outskirts of town in the pre-Roman *dólmenes* (funerary chambers built from rock slabs), some of the oldest in Europe. The alluring pancake pillars of the Sierra de Torcal, a Mars-like wasteland of eroded rock, are another nearby attraction. Smack in the middle of Andalucía, Antequera makes a good base for those wanting to see all the big cities but to stay somewhere a bit more tranquil. Wise travelers kick back here for a few days of inland visual splendor among Antequera's rolling hills and rich history.

ANDALUCÍA

⌐ TRANSPORTATION

Trains: Av. de la Estación (☎902 24 02 02). To: **Algeciras** (4hr., 3 per day 8:23am-7:25pm, €10.30); **Granada** (2hr., 6 per day 8:37am-7:22pm, €5.75); **Ronda** (1hr.; 3 per day 8:36am, 3, 7:19pm; €4.90); **Sevilla** (2½hr., 4 per day 9:38am-10:04pm, €10.20).

Buses: Po. García del Olmo (☎952 84 13 65). To: **Córdoba** (2¼hr.; 2 per day 9:45am, 4:45pm; €7.46); **Granada** (2hr., 5 per day 6:30am-1am, €6.19); **Málaga** (45min., 9-12 per day 8:15am-10pm, €3.24); **Murcia** (5½hr.; 2 per day 1, 9:45am; €20.10); **Sevilla** (2¼hr., 5 per day 4am-6:45pm, €9.91).

Taxis: Taxi Radio Antequera (☎952 84 55 30) services Antequera and will go to Sierra de Torcal. Fare to town center approx. €4, but the walk is manageable.

■✦ ⑦ ORIENTATION & PRACTICAL INFORMATION

From the train station, it's a 10min. hike up a shadeless hill along Av. de la Estación to reach **Plaza de San Sebastián**, the town center. At the top, continue straight past the market, turn right on C. de la Encarnación, and pass the Museo Municipal to reach the plaza. Alternatively, from the bus station it is just under a 15min. walk *down* a shadeless hill. Exit the station and turn right on Ctra. del Albergue, then left onto Alameda de Andalucía which, keeping to the right, becomes C. Infante Don Fernando and leads to the tourist office and Pl. de San Sebastián.

Tourist Office: Pl. de San Sebastián, 7 (☎/fax 952 70 25 05). Open June 15-Sept. 15 M-Sa 11am-2pm and 5-8pm, Su 11am-2pm; Sept. 16-June 14 M-Sa 10:30am-1:30pm and 4-7pm, Su 11am-2pm.

Bank: Banco Santander Central Hispano, C. Infante Don Fernando, 51 (☎902 24 24 24). Open M-F 8:30am-2pm, Sa 8:30am-1pm.

Emergency: ☎112. **Medical Emergency:** ☎952 84 19 66. **Municipal Police:** Av. de la Legión (☎952 70 81 04).

Pharmacy: Pl. de San Francisco. Open M-F 9am-1:30pm and 5-8:30pm, Sa 10:30am-1:30pm.

Hospital: Hospital Comarcal, C. Polígono Industrial, 67 (☎952 84 62 63, urgent care 951 06 11 50).

Internet Access: Sala Ozono, C. Merecillas, 14 (☎952 84 10 84). €1.50 per hr. Open daily 11am-midnight.

Post Office: C. Nájera (☎952 84 20 83). Open M-F 8am-2pm, Sa 9:30am-1pm. **Postal Code:** 29200.

�🏠 ACCOMMODATIONS

▨ **Pensión Toril,** C. Toril, 3-5 (☎/fax 952 84 31 84), off Pl. de San Francisco. Accommodating owner lets bright, clean rooms with fans and TV. Locals gather on the patio to chat over dominoes. The restaurant downstairs serves a filling *menú* complete with wine for €6. Meals served daily 1-4pm. Breakfast €1.50. Parking included. Singles €10, with bath €15; doubles €20/24. ❶

Hotel Plaza San Sebastián, Pl. San Sebastián, 4 (☎952 84 42 39; www.hotelplaza-sansebastian.com). Luxury for a fraction of what you would pay in a big city. Read in the sun on the beautifully tiled terrace, watch TV from the comfy leather sofas in the lounge, enjoy a delicious and filling *menú* (€7) at the downstairs restaurant, then relax in your newly renovated, air-conditioned room. All rooms with bath and TV. Singles €25; doubles €39; prices slightly higher during *Semana Santa.* ❷

Hotel Residencia Colón, C. Infante Don Fernando, 29 (☎952 84 00 10; www.castelcolon.com). Eclectic, sprawling, and mazelike, this 2-star hotel has large, surprisingly inexpensive—albeit slightly dark—rooms. Great location. Handicapped-accessible. Rooms with private bath have A/C. Singles €10, with bath €20; doubles €20/€35; triples with bath €52; quads with bath €65. ❶

🍴 FOOD

Restaurant options in Antequera are surprisingly limited. The restaurants at the hostels and hotels listed above are a good bet for an authentic *menú*, as are the restaurants lining C. Calzada. Get fresh produce, fish, and meats at the **market** in Pl. San Francisco. (Open M-Sa 8am-3pm.) **Mercadona,** C. Calzada, 18, and C. Infante Don Fernando, 17, has all the basics. (Open M-Sa 9am-9pm. MC/V.)

Manolo Bar, C. Calzada, 14 (☎952 84 10 15). This cavernous bar is filled with cowboy paraphernalia and good-humored patrons. Eat inside or on the outdoor patio. Ultra-cheap *tapas* €1; *raciones* €5-6; sangría €2. Open W-Th 5pm-1am, F-Sa 5pm-3am. ❶

La Espuela, C. San Agustín, 1 (☎952 70 30 31). An elegant Italian restaurant serving pizza and pasta, as well as fish, meat, and veggie options (entrees €8-16). *Menú* €13.50. Open daily noon-midnight. MC/V. ❸

Cafetería Florida, C. Lucena, 44 (☎952 70 10 14). A safe bet for breakfast and lunch; closed for dinner. Although they have great *tapas* (try the stuffed artichokes), you can't beat the cheap, filling *menú* (€6). Open M-Th and Sa 7am-8pm, F 7am-midnight. V. ❶

🎯 SIGHTS

LOS DÓLMENES. Antequera's three ancient caves are some of the oldest in Europe. Once burial chambers with storerooms for the riches of the dead, they were long ago looted but remain highly worthy of spelunking. The 200-ton roof of the **Cueva de Menga** (2500 BC) was hauled five miles to its present location. Carved millennia ago, the four figures engraved on the chamber walls typify Mediterranean Stone Age art (look closely to be able to decipher the art). The **Cueva de Viera** (2000 BC), uncovered in 1905, begins with a narrow passageway leading deep into the darkness of the earth. Somewhat farther afield, **Cueva del Romeral** (1800 BC) consists of a long corridor leading to two round chambers; the second was used for funerary offerings. *(1km walk to reach the Cuevas de Menga and Viera; follow signs toward Granada from the town center (20min.) and watch for a small sign past the gas station. To reach Cueva del Romeral from the other caves, continue on the highway to Granada for another 3km. After the 4th rotary, across from Mercadona, a gravel road leads to a narrow path bordered by cyprus trees. Take this path across the tracks to reach the cave. Ask the guard to let you in if the gate is locked. All 3 caves open Tu 10am-2pm, W-Sa 9am-3pm, Su 9:30am-2pm. Free.)*

OTHER SIGHTS. Back in town, all that remains of the **Alcazaba** are its two towers, the wall between them, and some well-trimmed hedges. From the top, visitors get unparalleled views of the city and surrounding countryside; it's especially magnificent at dusk. *(Always open, although it's best to go during daylight hours. Free.)* Next door, the towering **Real Colegiata de Santa María la Mayor** was the first church in Andalucía to incorporate Renaissance style. *(Open July-Sept. 15 Tu-F 10:30am-2pm and 8-10pm; Sa 10:30am-2pm, Su 11:30am-2pm; Sept. 15-June Tu-F 10:30am-2pm and 4:30-7:30pm, Sa 10:30am-2pm, Su 11:30am-2pm. Free.)* To the left of the church when facing it are the ruins of **Las Termas de Santa María.** The Roman thermal baths, excavated in 1988, feature mosaic tiles, although they're almost impossible to see from the church plaza. Downhill one block from the tourist office in the Palacio de Nájera, the **Museo Municipal** exhibits avant-garde 1970s paintings by native son Cristóbal

THE LOCAL STORY

"I'LL HAVE MINE MINUS MEAT!"

"You're in the wrong country, my friend!" remarked a friendly bartender in Granada when I declined his offer of free *chorizo tapas* with my drink. Seeking to allay further generous, yet still carnivorous, overtures with the statement "Soy vegeteriano" only brought weird looks followed by attempts to feed me some form of fish or poultry. Indeed, in a country tempting travelers with local delights such as omelettes with, among other things, bull's brains and testicles, asking for a *bocadilla de queso* does seem pretty lame. When every *sandwich vegetal* includes anchovies, how does a herbivore survive?

The vegetarian adventurer quickly learns. Beyond the obvious *tortilla española* and the *ensalada mixta*, waiters are often happy to prepare *paella verdura sin carne*, or any dish *sin pescados* or *pollo*. While a majority of Spanish cuisine will still rely on a base of ham or fish, a detailed explanation of dietary concerns along the lines of "without anything that moves," usually elicits chuckles and acquiescence, even though strange looks are not compeltely avoided. Soon enough those partial to plants will navigate fluently among *patatas a los pobres* and *gazpacho andaluz*. "Switch my *chorizo* for *patatas bravas*, please."

Toral alongside dozens of Roman artifacts, including the graceful **Efebo**, a rare bronze statue of a Roman page. (☎ 952 70 40 21. Open Tu-F 9am-2:30pm, Sa 10am-1:30pm, Su 11am-1:30pm, mandatory guided tours leave from entrance every 30min. €3.)

▶ DAYTRIP FROM ANTEQUERA

EL TORCAL DE ANTEQUERA

Two-thirds of the 13km to the Sierra de Torcal can be covered by bus. Ask the driver to let you off at the turnoff for El Torcal; from there it's a 5km walk. Casado buses (☎ 952 84 19 57) leave from Antequera (M-F 1pm, €2); the return bus leaves from the turnoff (M-F 4:15pm). You can also take a taxi (have the tourist office call one for you, or the fare may be higher) to the refugio (round-trip €21); the driver will wait for 1hr.

A garden of wind-sculpted boulders, the Sierra de Torcal glows like the surface of a barren and distant planet. The central peak, **El Torcal** (1369m), takes up most of the horizon, but the surrounding clumps of eroded rocks are even more extraordinary. Declared a natural park in 1978, the Sierra stretches for 11.7km. Several trails circle the summit. The well-traveled green arrow path (1½km) takes about 45min.; the red arrow path (4½km) takes over 2hr. All but the green path require a guided tour; call the **Centro de Información** for more details. (☎ 952 03 13 89. Open daily 10am-8pm.) Each path begins and ends at the *refugio* (lodge) at the mountain base. Try to catch the sunset and the spectacular mountain view from the striking ▧**Mirador de las Ventanillas.**

GRANADA ☎ 958

The splendors of the Alhambra, the magnificent palace which crowns the highest point of the city, have fascinated both prince and pauper for centuries. To this day, visitors are still captivated by the charm, the mystery, and the indescribable romance that emanates from the very stones of its ancient and winding streets.

Conquered by invading Muslim armies in 711, Granada blossomed into one of Europe's wealthiest, most refined cities. As Christian armies turned back the tide of Moorish conquest in the 13th century, the city became the last Muslim outpost on the peninsula, surrounded by a unified Christian kingdom. Due to the relentless Christian onslaught and growing disputes and corruption within the ruling dynasty, Moorish domination over Granada began to wane by the end of the 15th century. Fernando and Isabel cap-

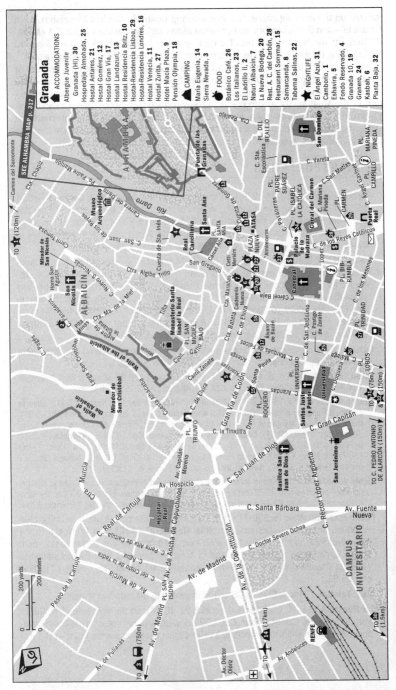

Granada

ACCOMMODATIONS
Albergue Juvenile
Granada (HI), 30
Hospedaje Almohada, 25
Hostal Antares, 21
Hostal Gomérez, 12
Hostal Gran Vía, 17
Hostal Landazuri, 13
Hostal Residencia Britz, 10
Hostal-Residencia Lisboa, 29
Hostal-Residencia Londres, 16
Hostal Venecia, 11
Hostal Zurita, 27
Hotel Macia Plaza, 9
Pensión Olympia, 18

CAMPING
María Eugenia, 14
Sierra Nevada, 3

FOOD
Botánico Café, 26
Los Italianos, 23
El Ladrillo II, 2
Naturi Albaicín, 7
La Nueva Bodega, 20
Rest. A. C. del Carbón, 28
Restaurant Sonymar, 15
Samarcanda, 8
Taberna Salinas, 22

★ NIGHTLIFE
El Ángel Azul, 31
Cambrio, 1
Eslvaira, 5
Fondo Reservado, 4
Granada 10, 19
Granero, 24
Kasbah, 6
Planta Baja, 32

ANDALUCÍA

italized on the ensuing chaos, finally capturing Boabdil—the last Moorish ruler of Granada—and the Alhambra on the momentous night of January 1, 1492. As Boabdil fled, his mother berated him for casting a longing look back at the Alhambra saying, "You do well to weep as a woman for what you could not defend as a man." Although the Christians torched all the mosques and the lower city, embers of Granada's Arab past still linger. The Albaicín, an enchanting maze of Moorish houses and twisting alleys, is Spain's best-preserved Arab quarter and the only part of the Muslim city to survive *la Reconquista* intact. Since then, Granada has grown into a university town, surrendering to thronging crowds of international students, backpackers, and Andalusian youth. Spend a day or two discovering the history of Moorish Spain and experiencing the energetic local nightlife.

▐ TRANSPORTATION

Flights: Airport (☎958 24 52 37), 17km west of the city. **Autocares J. Gonzales** (☎958 13 13 09) runs a bus from Gran Vía, in front of the cathedral, to the airport. (5 per day 8am-7pm, €3.) A **taxi** to the airport costs €15. **Iberia** (☎902 40 05 00), at the corner of Pl. Isabel la Católica and C. Pavaneras (open M-F 9am-1:45pm and 4-7pm), flies to **Barcelona** (1hr., 3 per day, €135) and **Madrid** (30min., 4 per day, €85).

Trains: RENFE Station Av. Andaluces (☎902 24 02 02). Take bus #3-6, 9, or 11 from Gran Vía to the stop marked Constitución 3 and turn left on Av. Andaluces. To: **Algeciras** (5-7hr., 3 per day 7:10am-5:50pm, €15.40); **Almería** (3hr., 4 per day 10am-8:47pm, €11.35); **Antequera** (2hr., 3 per day 7:10am-5:50pm, €6.35); **Barcelona** (12-13hr.; daily 10:10pm, M, Th, Sa also 8:30am; €47.50-49); **Madrid** (5-6hr.; 2 per day 7:55am, 4:40pm; €28-44); **Ronda** (3-4hr., 3 per day 7:10am-5:50pm, €10.30); **Sevilla** (4-5hr., 4 per day 8:18am-8:43pm, €17).

Buses: All major intercity bus routes originate from the **bus station** on the outskirts of Granada on Ctra. de Madrid, near C. Arzobispo Pedro de Castro.

ALSA (☎902 42 22 42) to: **Alicante** (6hr., 8 per day, €22.82); **Barcelona** (14hr., 7 per day, €56.40); **Valencia** (10hr., 7 per day, €34.41). All buses run 2:15am-11:30pm.

Alsina Graells (☎958 18 54 80) to: **Algeciras** (5hr., 6 per day 9am-8pm, €17.37); **Almería** (2¼hr., 12 per day 6:45am-8pm, €9.10); **Almuñecar** (1½hr., 7 per day 7:30am-8pm, €5.95); the villages in **Las Alpujarras** (3 per day 10:30am, noon, 5:15pm; €6.69-12); **Antequera** (2hr., 3-5 per day 3-7pm, €6.09); **Cádiz** (4hr., 4 per day 3am-6:30pm, €25.30); **Córdoba** (3hr., 10 per day 7:30am-8pm, €10.35); (4½hr., 2 per day 8am and 3pm, €15.48); **Jaén** (1½hr., 17 per day 7am-9:30pm, €6.24); **Madrid** (5hr., 14 per day 7am-1:30am, €12.45); **Málaga** (2hr., 17 per day 7am-9pm, €8.04); **Sevilla** (3hr., 10 per day 3am-8pm, €15.98).

Junta de Andalucía, the regional government, charters buses to **Veleta** from the Granada bus station. Call ahead (☎630 95 97 39) for reservations and information. (45 min.; 5-7 per day 9am-6:40pm; €3 one-way, €4.80 round-trip, 50% discount for seniors and children 4-9, under 3 free.

Public Transportation: (☎900 71 09 00). Pick up the cute pocket bus map at the tourist office. Important buses include: **"Bus Alhambra" (#30)** from Pl. Nueva to the Alhambra; **#31** from Pl. Nueva to the Albaicín; **#10** from the bus station to the youth hostel, C. de Ronda, C. Recogidas, and C. Acera de Darro; **#3** from the bus station to Av. de la Constitución, Gran Vía, and Pl. Isabel la Católica. €0.85, *bonobus* (10 tickets) €5.02.

Taxis: Teletaxi, (24hr. ☎958 28 06 54), with service to Granada and environs.

Car Rental: Atasa, Pl. Cuchilleros, 1 (☎958 22 40 04), on the right side of Pl. Nueva from Pl. Isabel la Católica. From €283.39 per week with unlimited mileage and insurance. Prices rise with shorter rentals. 21+ and must have had license for at least 1yr.

▚ 🛈 ORIENTATION & PRACTICAL INFORMATION

The geographic center of Granada is small **Plaza Isabel la Católica,** at the intersection of the city's two main arteries, **Calle de los Reyes Católicos** and **Gran Vía de Colón.** On Gran Vía, you'll find the **cathedral.** Two short blocks uphill on C. de los Reyes Católicos sits Pl. Nueva. Downhill, also along C. de los Reyes Católicos, lie **Plaza Carmen** and **Puerta Real,** the six-way intersection of C. de los Reyes Católicos, C. de Recogidos, C. de los Mesones, Acera de Darro, C. Ángel Ganivet, and Acera del Casino. The **Alhambra** commands the steep hill up from Pl. Nueva.

Tourist Office: Oficina Provincial, Pl. Mariana Pineda, 10 (☎958 24 71 28). English spoken. Open M-F 9am-8pm, Sa 10am-7pm, Su 10am-4pm. **Junta de Andalucía,** C. Mariana Pineda (☎958 22 59 90). Open M-Sa 9am-7pm, Su 10am-2pm.

Currency Exchange: Banco Santander Central Hispano, Gran Vía, 3 (☎958 21 73 00). Exchanges money and AmEx traveler's checks commission free. Open May-Sept. M-F 9am-2pm; Oct.-Apr. M-Sa 9am-2pm.

American Express: C. de los Reyes Católicos, 31 (☎958 22 45 12). Open M-F 9am-1:30pm and 2-9pm, Sa 10am-2pm.

Luggage Storage: 24hr. storage at the **train station** (€3).

El Corte Inglés: C. Genil, 20-22 (☎958 22 32 40). Follow Acera del Casino from Pta. Real to C. Genil. Good map for €2.85. Open M-Sa 10am-10pm.

English-Language Bookstore: Metro, C. Gracia, 31 (☎958 26 15 65). Vast foreign language section. Open M-F 10am-2pm and 5-8:30pm, Sa 11am-2pm.

Gay and Lesbian Services: Juvenós, C. Lavadero de las Tablas, 15, organizes weekly activities for gay youth. **Información Homosexual Hotline** ☎958 20 06 02.

Laundromat: C. de la Paz, 19. Wash €5; dry €1 per 15min. Detergent, softener, and bleach available. Open M-F 10am-2pm and 5-8pm.

Emergency: ☎112. **Police:** C. Duquesa, 21 (☎958 24 81 00). English spoken.

Pharmacy: Farmacia Gran Vía, Gran Vía, 6 (☎958 22 29 90). Open M-F 9:30am-2pm and 5-8:30pm.

Medical Assistance: Clínica de San Cecilio, C. Dr. Olóriz, 16 (☎958 28 02 00 or 27 20 00), on the road to Jaén. **Ambulance:** ☎958 28 44 50.

Internet Access: NavegaWeb, C. de los Reyes Católicos , 55. English spoken. €1.50 per hr., students €1. Open 10am-11pm. **Net** (☎958 22 69 19) has 2 locations: Pl. de los Girones, 3, up C. Pavaneras from Pl. Isabel la Católica (€1 per hr.) and C. Buensuceso, 22, 1 block from Pl. Trinidad. English spoken. €0.75 per hr. Both open M-F 9am-11pm, Sa-Su 10am-11pm.

Post Office: Pta. Real (☎958 22 48 35). **Lista de Correos** and **fax** service. Open M-F 8am-9pm, Sa 9:30am-2pm. Wires money M-F 8:30am-2:30pm. **Postal Code:** 18009.

▐▜ ACCOMMODATIONS & CAMPING

NEAR PLAZA NUEVA

Hostels line Cuesta de Gomérez, the street leading uphill to the Alhambra, to the right of Pl. Nueva. Crashing in this area is wise for those planning to spend serious time at the Alhambra complex, but these spots tend to fill up quickest.

■ **Hostal Venecia,** Cuesta de Gomérez, 2, 3rd fl. (☎958 22 39 87). A hint of incense, homey rooms, and attentive service with morning tea make Sergio and María del Carmen's small *hostal* the best bargain in town. Reserve early, especially in summer, since the secret is out. Singles €15; doubles €26; triples and quads €13 per person. ❶

Hostal Residencia Britz, Cuesta de Gomérez, 1 (☎/fax 958 22 36 52). Laundry €4 (no dryer). 24hr. reception. English spoken. Singles €18; doubles €27.50, with bath €38. 6% discount if you show your copy of *Let's Go* and pay in cash. MC/V. ❷

Hostal Gomérez, Cuesta de Gomérez, 10 (☎958 22 44 37). Simple rooms with hall baths. Multilingual owner will assist guests planning longer stays. Laundry €6 per load. Singles €15; doubles €24; triples €30. ❷

Hostal Landazuri, Cuesta de Gomérez, 24 (☎/fax 958 22 36 52). Plain hallways open into large, colorful rooms. A rooftop terrace with potted flowers and ivy provides guests with splendid views of the Alhambra and Sierra Nevada. Front door locked after 1am. English spoken. Singles €20, with bath €28; doubles €24/€36; suite €40. ❷

Hotel Macia Plaza, Pl. Nueva, 4 (☎958 22 75 36; fax 22 75 33). A modern, comfortable hotel centrally located on the plaza. All rooms are carpeted and have marble baths, TV, phone, and A/C. Singles €47; doubles €70; triples €90. ❹

NEAR THE CATHEDRAL/UNIVERSITY

Hostels surround Pl. Trinidad, at the end of C. de los Mesones when coming from Pta. Real. Many *pensiones* around C. de los Mesones cater to students during the academic year but free up during the summer, offering excellent deals to the diligent stair-climber. The ones listed below are open year-round.

■ **Hospedaje Almohada,** C. Postigo de Zarate, 4 (☎958 20 74 46. If Mercedes, the hip proprietress, isn't in, call her cell phone ☎627 47 25 53). A successful experiment in communal living: guests cook for themselves and each other, gathering at the end of the day to fraternize over Cruzcampo and olives in the cozy den. Rooms are small but personable, decorated with handicrafts made by the owner. Laundry €3. Dorms €14 per person; singles €16; doubles €30; triples €40. Negotiate for longer stays. ❶

Hostal Zurita, Pl. Trinidad, 7 (☎958 27 50 20). Bright rooms with floral sheets and sound-proof balcony doors conceal high quality beds and A/C. Singles €17; doubles €29, with bath €36; triples €40/€50. ❷

Hostal-Residencia Lisboa, Pl. Carmen, 29 (☎958 22 14 13 or 22 14 14; fax 22 14 87). Singles €18, with bath €30; doubles €27/€40; triples €33/€50. MC/V. ❷

ALONG GRAN VÍA DE COLÓN

Hostels are sprinkled along Gran Vía. In all cases, rooms with balconies over the street are much noisier than those that open onto an inner patio.

Hostal Antares, C. Cetti Meriém, 10 (☎958 22 83 13). Sparkling tiled floors, large and well-lit rooms, and good service make this a choice place to crash. Rooms with A/C and TV available. English spoken. Luggage storage €2 per day. Singles €18; doubles €28, with bath €36. ❷

Hostal-Residencia Londres, Gran Vía, 29, 6th fl. (☎958 27 80 34), perched atop a fin-de-siècle edifice with multiple patios. Great views of the Alhambra and the cathedral from most rooms. One large bath for every 2 bedrooms. English spoken. Singles €18; doubles €27, with bath €35; €10 each additional person. ❷

Pensión Olympia, C. Álvaro de Bazán, 6 (☎958 27 82 38). A standard *pensión* with simple rooms. Singles €15; doubles €20, with shower €25, with bath €30. MC/V. ❶

Hostal Gran Vía, Gran Vía, 17 (☎958 27 92 12). Singles with shower €17; doubles with shower €25, with bath €33; triples €35/€45. ❷

ELSEWHERE

Albergue Juvenil Granada (HI), C. de Ramón y Cajal, 2 (☎958 00 29 00 or 00 29 01). From the bus station, take bus #10; from the train station #11; ask the driver to stop at "El Estadio de la Juventud." Across the field on the left. Towels €1.50. 24hr. reception. Dorms €10-12; over 26 €14-16. Non-HI guests can join for an extra €3.50 per night for 6 nights. ❶

CAMPING

Buses serve five campgrounds within 5km of Granada. Check the departure schedules at the tourist office, sit up front, and ask bus drivers to alert you to your stop.

Sierra Nevada, Av. de Madrid, 107 (☎958 15 00 62; fax 15 09 54). Take bus #3 or 10. Shady trees, modern facilities, a large outdoor pool, and free hot showers. If you arrive when the town fair is here, stay elsewhere—you'll have clown nightmares. Open Mar.-Oct. €3.78 per person, children under 10 €3.15. ❶

María Eugenia, Ctra. Nacional, 342 (☎958 20 06 06; fax 20 94 10), at km436 on the road to Málaga. Take the Santa Fé or Chauchina bus from the train station (every 30min.). Open year-round. €3 per person, children €2.40. ❶

🍴 FOOD

Granada offers a variety of ethnic restaurants to relieve those who have had a bit too much fish. North African cuisine can be found around the **Albaicín,** while more typical *menú* fare awaits in Pl. Nueva and Pl. Trinidad. The adventurous eat well in Granada—*tortilla sacromonte* (omelette with calf's brains, bull testicles, ham, shrimp, and veggies), *sesos a la romana* (batter-fried calf's brains), and *rabo de toro* (bull's tail) are common. Picnickers can gather fresh fruit and vegetables at the **market** on C. San Agustín. Get groceries at **Supermercado T. Mariscal,** C. Genil, next to El Corte Inglés. (Open M-F 9:30am-2pm and 5-9pm, Sa 9:30am-2pm.)

NEAR PLAZA NUEVA

Plaza Nueva abounds with large, generic indoor/outdoor cafes located right on the square itself. Those seeking more authentic fare (and not the kind whose menus are translated into five different languages) would do better to comb the small side streets which lead from the plaza. The bars around Pl. Nueva, like most everywhere in Granada, offer *tapas* for **free** (with a drink).

Restaurant Sonymar, Pl. Boquero, 6 (☎958 27 10 63). Relish the amazing service and delicious food of this secluded neighborhood eatery. *Menú* €5.86. Four-course *menús* €11.70-13, entrees €7.20-12.60. Open daily 1-4pm and 8-11:30pm. AmEx/V. ❷

Taberna Salinas, C. de Elvira, 13 (☎958 22 14 11). Rustic tavern serving generous portions. Share a *tabla salinas surtida* (plate of cheeses, pâté, and cold cuts; €13.65) with friends, and choose from a wide selection of grilled meats and seafood for your main course (€7-18). Open daily 12:30pm-2am. V. ❸

La Nueva Bodega, C. Cetti Meriém, 9 (☎958 22 59 34). Locals stake out the bar as tourists dine on hearty traditional cuisine. *Menús* €4.20-8.95. *Tapas* €3.95. Open daily noon-midnight. ❶

ALBAICÍN

Wander the romantic, winding streets of the Albaicín and you'll discover a number of budget bars and restaurants on the slopes above Pl. Nueva. This is a veritable paradise for connoisseurs of Middle Eastern cuisine. Stop anywhere for a cheap schwarma or falafel sandwich. C. Calderería Nueva, off C. de Elvira leading from the plaza, is crammed with teahouses and cafes.

🔲 **Naturi Albaicín,** C. Calderería Nueva, 10 (☎958 22 06 27). Excellent vegetarian restaurant with a serene Moroccan ambience. Tasty options include *berenjenas rellenas* (stuffed eggplant), quiche, and *kefir* (a yogurt drink). No alcohol served. *Menús* €6.90-8.30. Open M-Th and Sa 1-4pm and 7-11pm, F 7-11pm. ❷

El Ladrillo II, C. Panaderos, 13 (☎958 29 26 51). Feast on seafood under the stars while listening to the romantic strains of *sevillanas*. The *menú* claims—with some credibility—to offer "the biggest portions in Spain." Entrees €6.60-12. Open daily 12:30pm-1:30am. MC/V. ❷

Samarcanda, C. Calderería Vieja, 3 (☎958 21 00 04). Lebanese cuisine at its finest. Excellent hummus (€5), couscous (€6.30-9), and shish kebab (€10) can be ordered á la carte, or for €38, order a *Mesa Libanesa* platter to share: it comes with a bottle of Lebanese wine. Open Th-Tu 1-4:30pm and 7:30pm-midnight. ❷

GRAN VÍA & ELSEWHERE

Restaurante Asador Corrala del Carbón, C. Mariana Pineda, 8 (☎958 22 38 10). Savor traditional Andalusian grilled meat in an indoor recreation of an old neighborhood courtyard in Granada. Entrees €8-17. Open daily 1-4pm and 8:30pm-midnight. ❸

Botánico Café, C. Málaga, 3 (☎958 27 15 98). This hip cafe is a major student hangout where a fusion of cultural food traditions brings new life to Spanish favorites. Entrees €4.80-9. Open Su-Th noon-1am, F-Sa noon-2am. ❷

Los Italianos, Gran Vía, 4 (☎958 22 40 34). Popular gelato parlor with 26 heavenly flavors draws nightly crowds from the discos in the area after the parties have ended. Two scoops €1, ice cream sundaes €1.20-2.50. Cold drinks (lemonade, *leche fría*) €1.20. Open daily 9am-3am. ❶

👁 SIGHTS

*Caja General de Ahorros de Granada, Pl. Isabel la Católica, 6, and the tourist office sell a **"bono turístico" pass** (€18.03) good for 1 week, which provides direct access to the Alhambra and several other sights throughout Granada. Also includes 10 free trips on any local bus line to destinations within the city. (☎902 10 00 95. Open M-F 8:30am-2:15pm all year and Nov.1-Mar. 30 also on Th 5:15-7:30pm.)*

▨ THE ALHAMBRA

*To reach the Alhambra, take Cuesta de Gomérez off Pl. Nueva and be prepared to pant (20min.; no unauthorized cars 9am-9pm), or take the quick **Alhambra-Neptuno microbus** from Pl. Nueva (every 5min., €0.85). ☎958 22 15 03; Reservations ☎902 22 44 60, www.alhambratickets.com. Open Apr.-Sept. daily 8:30am-8pm; Oct.-Mar. M-Sa 9am-5:45pm. **Moonlight tours** (€8) are romantic and unforgettable. June-Sept. Tu, Th, Sa 10-11:30pm; Oct.-May Sa 8-10pm; enquire for details at the Alhambra information desk. Audioguides available, narrated by "Washington Irving" in Spanish, English, French, German, and Italian (€3). €8, children under 8 and disabled free. Limited to 8000 visitors per day June-Sept., 6300 Oct.-May, so get there very early or reserve online. Enter the Palace of the Nasrids (Alcázar) during the time specified on your ticket, but stay as long as desired. It is possible to reserve tickets a few days in advance at banks for a €0.75 charge; this is recommended especially July-Aug. and Semana Santa. BBVA branches across the country will also book tickets.*

From the streets of Granada, the Alhambra, meaning "the red one" in Arabic, appears simple, blocky, faded—a child's toy castle planted in the foothills of the Sierra Nevada. Once inside, however, you will discover an elaborate and detailed world, one that magically unites water, light, wood, stucco, and ceramics to create a fortress-palace of rich aesthetic and symbolic grandeur. Celebrated by poets and artists throughout the ages, the Alhambra continues to inspire all who visit with its timeless beauty. The age-old saying holds true: *"Si mueres sin ver la Alhambra, no has vivido"* (If you die without seeing the Alhambra, you have not lived).

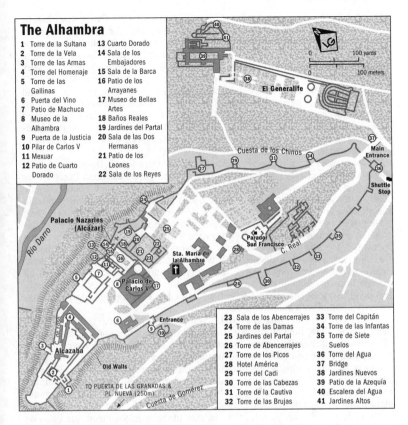

The Alhambra

1 Torre de la Sultana
2 Torre de la Vela
3 Torre de las Armas
4 Torre del Homenaje
5 Torre de las Gallinas
6 Puerta del Vino
7 Patio de Machuca
8 Museo de la Alhambra
9 Puerta de la Justicia
10 Pilar de Carlos V
11 Mexuar
12 Patio de Cuarto Dorado
13 Cuarto Dorado
14 Sala de los Embajadores
15 Sala de la Barca
16 Patio de los Arrayanes
17 Museo de Bellas Artes
18 Baños Reales
19 Jardínes del Partal
20 Sala de las Dos Hermanas
21 Patio de los Leones
22 Sala de los Reyes

23 Sala de los Abencerrajes
24 Torre de las Damas
25 Jardines del Partal
26 Torre de Abencerrajes
27 Torre de los Picos
28 Hotel América
29 Torre del Cadi
30 Torre de las Cabezas
31 Torre de la Cautiva
32 Torre de las Brujas
33 Torre del Capitán
34 Torre de las Infantas
35 Torre de Siete Suelos
36 Torre del Agua
37 Bridge
38 Jardines Nuevos
39 Patio de la Azequía
40 Escalera del Agua
41 Jardines Altos

ALCAZABA. The Christians drove the first Nasrid King Alhamar from the Albaicín to this more strategic hill, where he built the series of rust-colored brick towers which form the Alcazaba, or fortress. A dark, spiraling staircase leads to the **Torre de la Vela** (watchtower), where visitors get a great 360° view of Granada and the surrounding mountains. The tower's bells were rung to warn of impending danger and to coordinate the Moorish irrigation system. Every January 1st, during the annual commemoration of the Christian conquest of Granada, an old legend holds that any local girl who scrambles up the tower and rings the bell by hand before the first day of the actual new year will receive a wedding proposal within 365 days. Exit through the **Puerta del Vino,** the original entrance to the medina, where inhabitants of the Alhambra once bought tax-free wine (alas, no more).

ALCÁZAR. Follow signs to the *Palacio Nazaries* to see the Alcázar, a royal palace built for Moorish rulers Yusuf I (1333-1354) and Muhammed V (1354-1391). Yusuf I was murdered in an isolated basement of the Alcázar, leaving his son Muhammed V to complete the palace. The entrance leads into the **Mexuar,** a great, pillared council chamber. Note the glazed tile arrangements that reiterate the Nasrid mantra: "There is no victor but God." Attached to the Mexuar is a small paryer hall, with an intricately decorated *Mihrab*, marking the direction of prayer to Mecca. The Mexuar adjoins the **Patio del Cuarto Dorado** (Patio of the Gilded Hall). The magnificently carved walls are topped by the shielded windows of the harem, such that the women could see out but no one could see in. The *hammams*, or Arab baths of the Nasrid palace, are behind an iron-grilled door, but have been permanently closed for preservation. Off the far side of the patio, foliated horseshoe archways of diminishing width open onto the **Cuarto Dorado** (Gilded Hall), decorated by Muhammed V. Its painstakingly carved wooden ceiling, inlaid with ivory and mother-of-pearl, displays polygonal figures and colorful ceramic *dados*.

Next is the **Patio de los Arrayanes** (Courtyard of Myrtles), an expanse of emerald water filled with goldfish and bubbling fountains. Stand at the top of the patio for a glimpse of the 14th-century **Fachada de Serallo**, the palace's elaborately carved facade. The long and slender **Sala de la Barca** (Boat Gallery), with an inverted boat-hull ceiling, flanks the courtyard. The walls are covered with the 99 names of Allah, as well as the familiar Nasrid slogan.

Granada was formally surrendered to *los Reyes Católicos* in the elaborate **Sala de los Embajadores** (Hall of Ambassadors), adjoining the Sala de la Barca to the north, and here Fernando and Columbus discussed finding a new route to India. Every surface of this magnificent square hall is intricately wrought with symbolic inscriptions and ornamental patterns. The Mozárabe dome, carved of more than 8000 pieces of wood and inlaid cedar, is by far the most impressive part of the room. A section of the original floor remains in the center. From the Patio de los Arrayanes, the Sala de los Mozárabes leads to the **Patio de los Leones** (Courtyard of the Lions), the grandest display of Nasrid art in the palace, where a rhythmic arcade of marble columns borders the courtyard, and a fountain supported by 12 marble lions babbles in the middle. Some believe that this fountain originally belonged to one of the sultan's Jewish advisors, but was transferred to this patio and redecorated with Muslim motifs.

Moving counter-clockwise around the courtyard, the next room is the **Sala de los Abencerrajes.** Here, Boabdil had the throats of 16 sons of the Abencerrajes family slit after one of them had allegedly had amorous encounters with his concubine Zorahayda. The rust-colored stains in the basin are said to mark the indelible traces of the butchering; evidently none of this bothered Holy Roman Emperor Charles V, who dined here during the construction of his neighboring *palazzo*. Light bleeds into the room through the intricate domed ceiling, which features an eight-pointed star, a design said to represent terrestrial and heavenly harmony.

Through stalactite archways, at the far end of the courtyard from the Patio de los Leones, lies the **Sala de los Reyes** (Hall of Kings). The only human representations in the entire palace—the 21 sultans who ruled from the Alhambra, important assemblies, and hunting parties—are depicted on detailed sheepskin paintings fixed to the walls with bamboo pins. On the remaining side of the courtyard, the resplendent **Sala de las Dos Hermanas** (Chamber of the Two Sisters) has a *muqarnas* (honeycombed) dome comprised of thousands of tiny cells. This stalactite-like structure is typical of Islamic architecture and represents an ascencion and the opening doors of heaven. From here, the secluded **Mirador de Daraxa** overlooks the Jardines de Daraxa (Gardens of the Sultana).

Passing the room where American author Washington Irving resided in 1829 and wrote the famous *Tales of the Alhambra* (1832), a courtyard leads to the **Baños Reales,** an unimpressive 14th-century addition, towards the royal gardens and the exit. Do not leave the Nasrid Palace unless you are satisfied with your visit, as you will not be permitted reentry.

TOWERS & GARDENS. Just outside the eastern wall of the Alcázar in the **Jardines del Partal**, lily-studded pools stand beside rose-laden terraces. The **Torre de las Damas** (Ladies' Tower) soars above it all. A series of six additional towers traverses the area between the Alcazaba and El Generalife.

EL GENERALIFE. Over a bridge, across the **Callejón de los Cipreses** and the shady **Callejón de las Adelfas,** are the vibrant blossoms, towering cypresses, and streaming waterways of El Generalife, the sultan's vacation retreat. In 1313 Arab engineers changed the Darro's flow by 18km and employed dams and channels to prepare the soil for Aben Walid Ismail's design of El Generalife. Over the centuries, the estate passed through private hands until it was finally repatriated in 1931. The two buildings of El Generalife, the **Palacio** and the **Sala Regia,** connect across the **Patio de la Acequia** (Courtyard of the Irrigation Channel), embellished with a narrow pool fed by fountains that form an aquatic archway. Honeysuckle vines scale the back wall, and shady benches invite long rests. An old oak tree stands here at the place where the sultana Zorahayda apparently had several amorous encounters with a nobleman from the Abencerrajes tribe. Although currently a mere shadow of its past glory, El Generalife still merits a visit.

PALACIO DE CARLOS V. After *la Reconquista* drove the Moors from Spain, Fernando and Isabel restored the Alcázar. Little did they know that two generations later, Emperor Charles V would demolish part of it to make way for his *palazzo,* a Renaissance masterpiece by Michelangelo disciple Pedro Machuca. A square building with a circular inner courtyard wrapped in two stories of Doric colonnades, it is Machuca's only surviving design. Although the palace is incongruous with the surrounding Moorish splendor, scholars concede that it is one of the most beautiful Renaissance buildings in Spain. Inside, the small but impressive **Museo de la Alhambra** contains the only original furnishings remaining from the Alhambra. (☎958 22 62 79. Open Tu-Sa 9am-2:30pm. Free.) Upstairs, the **Museo de Bellas Artes** displays religious sculptures and paintings of the Granada School dating from the 16th century. (☎958 22 48 43. Open Apr.-Sept. Tu 2:30-6pm, W-Sa 9am-6pm, Su 9am-2:30pm; Oct.-Mar. Tu 2:30-7:45pm, W-Sa 9am-7:45pm, Su 9am-2:30pm. €1.50.)

■ ALBAICÍN

Although generally safe, the Albaicín is disorienting and should be approached with caution at night. Bus #12 runs from beside the cathedral to C. Pagés at the top of the Albaicín.

A labyrinth of steep streets and narrow alleys, the Albaicín was the only Moorish neighborhood to escape the torches of *la Reconquista* and remains a key stop in Granada. After the fall of the Alhambra, a small Muslim population remained here until being expelled in the 17th century. Today, with its abundance of North African cuisine, outdoor bazaars blasting Arabic music, teahouses, and the presence of a mosque near Pl. San Nicolás, the Albaicín attests to the persistence of Islamic influence in Andalucía. Spectacular sunsets over the surrounding mountains can be seen from C. Cruz de Quirós, above C. de Elvira.

The best way to explore this maze is to proceed along Carrera del Darro off Pl. Santa Ana, climb the Cuesta del Chapiz on the left, then wander through Muslim ramparts, cisterns, and gates. On Pl. Santa Ana, the 16th-century **Real Cancillería** (or *Audiencia*), with its beautiful arcaded patio and stalactite ceiling, was the Christians' Ayuntamiento. Farther uphill are the 11th-century **Arab baths.** (Carrera del Darro, 31. ☎958 02 78 00. Open Tu-Sa 10am-2pm. Free.) The **Museo Arqueológico** showcases funerary urns, classical sculpture, Carthaginian vases, Muslim lamps, and ceramics. (Carrera del Darro, 41. ☎958 22 56 40. Open Tu 3-8pm, W-Sa 9am-8pm, Su 9am-2:30pm. €1.50, EU citizens free.) The ■**mirador** adjacent to **Iglesia de San Nicolás** affords the city's best view of the Alhambra, especially in winter when snow adorns the Sierra Nevada behind it. From C. de Elvira, go up C. Calderería Nueva to C. San Gregorio and continue uphill on this street past Pl.

Algibe de Trillo, where it becomes Cta. Algibe de Trillo. At Pl. Camino, make a left on Cta. Tomasa and another left on Atarazana Cta. Cabras. The mirador will be on your right.

IN THE CATHEDRAL QUARTER

■ **CAPILLA REAL.** Downhill from the Alhambra's Arabic splendor, through the Puerta Real off Gran Vía de Colón, on C. Oficios, the Capilla Real (Royal Chapel), Fernando and Isabel's private chapel, exemplifies Christian Granada. During their prosperous reign, the Catholic Monarchs funneled almost a quarter of the royal income into the chapel's construction (1504-1521) to build a proper burial place. Their efforts did not go unrewarded; intricate Gothic masonry and meticulously rendered figurines, as well as **La Reja,** the gilded iron grille of Master Bartolomé, grace the couple's resting place. Behind La Reja lie the almost lifelike marble figures of the royals themselves. Fernando and Isabel are on the right, when facing the altar; beside them sleeps their daughter Juana la Loca (the Mad) and her husband Felipe el Hermoso (the Fair). Much to the horror of the rest of the royal family, Juana insisted on keeping the body of her husband with her for an unpleasantly long time after he died. The lead caskets, where all four monarchs were laid to rest, lie directly below the marble sarcophagi in a crypt down a small stairway on the left. The smaller, fifth coffin belongs to the hastily buried child-king of Portugal, Miguel, whose death allowed Carlos V to ascend to the throne.

SACRISTÍA. Next door in the sacristy, Isabel's private **art collection,** the highlight of the chapel, favors Flemish and German artists of the 15th century. The glittering **royal jewels**—the queen's golden crown and scepter and the king's sword—shine in the middle of the sacristy. Nearby are the Christian banners which first fluttered in triumph over the Alhambra. (☎ *958 22 92 39. Capilla Real and Sacristía both open M-Sa 10:30am-1pm and 4-7pm, Su 11am-1pm and 4-5pm. €2.50.*)

CATEDRAL. Behind the Capilla Real and the Sacristía is Granada's cathedral. Construction of the cathedral began upon the smoldering embers of Granada's largest mosque after *la Reconquista* and was not completed until 1704. The first purely Renaissance cathedral in Spain, its massive Corinthian pillars support a 45m vaulted nave. (☎ *958 22 29 59. Open Apr.-Sept. M-Sa 10:45am-1:30pm and 4-7pm, Su 4-7pm; Oct.-Mar. M-Sa 10:30am-1:30pm and 3:30-6:30pm, Su 11am-1:30pm. €2.50.*)

OTHER SIGHTS. The 16th-century **Hospital Real** is divided into four tiled courtyards. Above the main staircase, the Mudéjar coffered ceiling echoes those of the Alhambra. (*Av. Hospicio. Open M-F 9am-2pm. Free.*) The 14th-century **Monasterio de San Jerónimo** is around the corner. Though badly damaged by Napoleon's troops, it has since been restored. (☎ *958 27 93 37. Open Apr.-Sept. M-Sa 10am-1:30pm and 4-7pm, Su 11am-1:30pm; Oct.-Mar. M-Sa 10am-1pm and 3-6:30pm, Su 11am-1:30pm. €2.10.*)

ⓒ NIGHTLIFE

Granada's "free *tapas* with a drink" tradition lures students and tourists out to the many pubs and bars spread across several neighborhoods, genres, and energy levels. Some great *tapas* bars are found off the side streets near Pl. Nueva. The most boisterous crowds hang out on C. Pedro Antonio de Alarcón, running from Pl. Albert Einstein to Ancha de Gracia, while hip new bars and clubs line C. de Elvira from Cárcel to C. Cedrán. A few gay bars cluster around Carrera del Darro, while a more openly gay scene can be found at Parque del Triunfo and Po. del Salón.

■ **Camborio,** Camino del Sacromonte, 48 (☎958 22 12 15), a 20min. walk uphill from Pl. Nueva. Gypsies and highwaymen once roamed the caves of Sacromonte, now the domain of scantily-clad clubbers. Pop music echoes through labyrinthine dance floors to the rooftop terraces above. Striking view of the Alhambra at sunrise. €4.50 cover on F and Sa. Beer €1.80-3. Open Tu-Sa 11pm-dawn.

■ **Granero,** Pl. Luis Rosales (☎958 22 89 79). A New Age bar bulging with Spanish yuppies. Still groovin' early in the week. Low on tourists, high on local style. Salsa and Spanish pop pervade. Beer €2.40. Mixed drinks €3-4.20. Open daily 10pm-dawn.

Planta Baja, C. Horno de Abad, 11 (☎958 25 35 09). Live bands play regularly within the concrete confines of this techno dance club. Full listing of all bands and performances on front window. Wildly popular with students. Beer €1.80. Cover €3. Open from fall until early July Th-Sa 10pm-6am.

Kasbah, C. Calderería Nueva, 4 (☎958 22 79 36). Relax amidst the Middle Eastern comforts of this candlelit cafe. Silky embroidered pillows and romantic nooks abound. Busy in the evening; crowds empty late at night. Arab pastries and an exhaustive selection of Moroccan teas (€1.80). Open daily 3pm-3am.

Granada 10, C. Cárcel Baja, 3 (☎958 22 40 01). Movie theater by evening, raging dance club by night. Perhaps the most flashy and opulent disco you'll ever see (at least in Granada). €6 cover Th-Sa includes one drink. Open daily.

Fondo Reservado, Cuesta de Sta. Inés, off Carrera del Darro. A gay-friendly bar with a mixed crowd that parties hard. Beer €2.60. Mixed drinks €3.60. Opens daily at 11pm.

El Angel Azul, C. Lavadero de las Tablas, 15. Well-established gay bar with a basement dance floor and curtained booths. Monthly drag shows and striptease contests. Shares building with Juvenós. Beer €2.40. Open daily midnight-5am.

🎵 ENTERTAINMENT

The daily paper, *Ideal*, lists entertainment venues in the back under *Cine y Espectáculos;* the Friday supplement highlights bars and special events. The *Guía del Ocio* (€0.85), sold at newsstands, lists clubs, pubs, and cafes.

FLAMENCO & JAZZ
The most "authentic" *flamenco* performances, which change monthly, are advertised on posters around town. The tourist office provides a list of nightly *tablaos*. A smoky, intimate setting awaits at **Eshavira,** C. Postigo de la Cuna, in a very secluded alley off C. Azacayas, between C. de Elvira and Gran Vía. This joint is *the* place to go for *flamenco,* jazz, or a fusion of the two. Photos of Nat King Cole and other jazz greats plaster the walls. Those with musical talent who wish to stage their own impromptu concerts can pick up the guitar or sit down at the piano which the owner has provided specifically for this purpose. (☎958 29 08 29. Call for schedule. Minimum 1 drink, €2.60 and up.)

FESTIVALS
Parties sweep Granada in the summer. The **Corpus Cristi** celebrations, processions, and bullfights in May are world famous. That same month, avant-garde theater groups from around the world make a pilgrimage to Granada for the **International Theater Festival** (☎958 22 93 44). The **Festival Internacional de Música y Danza** (mid-

June to early July) sponsors open-air performances of classical music, ballet, and *flamenco* in the Palacio de Carlos V and other outdoor venues. (☎958 22 18 44; www.granadafestival.org. Tickets €6-36, senior and youth discounts available.)

🖪 DAYTRIP FROM GRANADA

GUADIX

From the station on C. Santa Rosa, Maestra buses (☎958 66 06 57) depart for: Almería (1½hr., 3 per day 8am-6pm, €6.60); Granada (1hr.; M-Sa 11 per day 6:45am-6:45pm, Su 6 per day 9:45am-8:30pm; €3.95); and Jaén (1½hr.; 2 per day 11am, 6pm; €7.08). Coming in from Granada, ask to be let off at Pl. de las Américas, near Guadix's cathedral, to avoid a 15min. walk from the bus station. The tourist office, on Av. Mariana Pineda, is several blocks to the left when your back is to the cathedral. (☎958 66 26 65. Open regularly M-F 8am-3pm, though sometimes later at the staff's discretion.)

Dug (literally) into the rock basin of what was once a prehistoric lake, Guadix (pop. 20,000) has been populated for thousands of years. But what distinguishes Guadix from other cities in Spain and the rest of the world is that almost half of its residents live in *casas cueva* (cave houses). The **barriada de cuevas** is a 10min. walk uphill from the cathedral; signs point the way up winding streets. One well-preserved cave serves as the **Cueva-Museo de Alfarería,** C. San Miguel, 47. Duck in to see earthenware artifacts and a water well dating to 1650, as well as a large collection of decorative and domestic pottery from the Moorish and modern ages of Guadix. (☎958 66 47 67. Open M-Sa 10am-2pm and 4-8pm, Su 11am-2pm. €2, groups €1.50 per person, children €1.) A diverting stop along the route to the *barriada de cuevas* is the **Cueva-Museo de Costumbres Populares,** on the right off C. Canada de las Perales, which showcases an intact cave house, albeit over-furnished with anachronistic artifacts. (Open M-Sa 10am-2pm and 5-7pm, Su 10am-2pm. €1.30, groups €0.80 per person, children €0.65.) The ◪**Mirador Cerro de la Bala** affords a magnificent 360° view of the snow-capped Sierra Nevadas in the distance, and the *barriada de cuevas*, the Alcazaba Árabe, and the cathedral below. Back in town, the *casco antiguo* begins at the impressive **cathedral.** Up any of the slanting side streets to the left, you'll find the **Alcazaba Árabe,** a series of 11th-century turrets that commands an amazing view. (Tu-Sa 11am-2pm and 4-6:30pm, Su 11am-2pm. €1.20, groups €0.60 per person.)

Despite Guadix's impressive attractions, the city remains relatively untouristed; accommodations are scarce, but prices are reasonable. Experience cave living at **Chez Jean & Julia** ❺/❻, Ermita Nueva, 67, run by an amiable French couple in the *barriada de cuevas.* Groups of 2-6 can rent cool mini-cave apartments complete with kitchen and bath. Reserve months ahead. (☎958 66 91 91. Cave apartment June-Sept., Christmas, Easter, and Semana Santa €61; Oct.-May €48; Caveless doubles and triples €33, breakfast included.) Those who prefer more modern comforts should check out **Hotel Mulhacen** ❸, Av. Buenos Aires, 43, on the highway towards Murcia. Most rooms are handicapped-accessible. (☎958 66 07 50. June-Aug. singles €31.10; doubles €39.67. Sept.-May €25.54/€32.76.) Another caveless option is **Pensión El Retiro** ❶, Av. Mariana Pineda, 40, near the tourist office. El Retiro offers simple double beds. (☎958 665 166. €12 per person.) **Mesón Granadul** ❷, on the corner of C. San Miguel and Av. Mariana Pineda, is popular with locals and serves good tapas and *raciones.* (☎958 66 61 28. Entrees €4-9.)

LAS ALPUJARRAS

Buses leave Granada at 10:30am, noon, and 5:15pm for the villages, and return from the farthest town, Alcutar, at 5am and 5pm. Get a schedule at the bus station in Granada or see those pasted on shop windows near the bus stops. Discovery Walking Guides, Ltd. publishes a superb guidebook with blow-by-blow accounts of every trail in Las Alpujarras. (www.walking.demon.co.uk; €15.)

The *pueblos blancos* (white villages) of Las Alpujarras blanket the southern slopes of the Sierra Nevada in an area known as *la Falda* (the skirt). Although busloads of European tourists have recently discovered the rustic beauty of these settlements and their neighboring hiking trails, Las Alpujarras remain one of Spain's poorest areas. The villages' slow-paced lifestyle, well-preserved beauty, and cultural traditions make for a refreshing change from the more bustling cities of Andalucía. Staying a day or two in any village will treat the traveler to the region's hospitality and a taste of Spain's natural beauty. For the more active tourist, the mountains offer plenty of climbing and hiking opportunities, with some backpackers spending months amidst the streams, trails, and wild boars.

Although the roads are now paved and the towns well-traveled, a medieval Berber influence is still evident in the region's architecture; the low-slung houses rendered from earth and slate quite closely resemble those in Morocco's Atlas Mountains. With the fall of Granada in 1492, the Berbers relocated to the Alpujarras, and Christian-Muslim conflict continued until 1610, when John of Austria finally ousted the Moors. The legacy of Moorish defiance lives on every June during Trevélez's *Fiestas de Moros y Cristianos*. Galician settlers made the Alpujarras their home after the Moors were expelled, introducing Celtic and Visigothic traditions found nowhere else in Andalucía.

Las Alpujarras can best be appreciated by car, but for those without wheels, Alsina Graells buses travel from Granada to many of the high-altitude towns. The buses trace switchback after unnerving switchback, hugging the scenic road. Bus drivers often stop to let travelers off at intermediate points. Some hard-core visitors hike from place to place, and locals, well aware of transportation problems, often sympathize with hitchhikers. *Let's Go* does not recommend hitchhiking.

Those interested in exploring the wilderness of the Sierra Nevada will find more than their fill of treks leading out from each town, particularly Capileira and Trevélez. Though there are splendid treks at every level of difficulty, serious hikers must be well-prepared to face the climatic changes of the high Sierra range. A good map, compass, warm clothes, cooking and camping equipment, and possibly even a GPS system for GPS-waymarked maps and trails are necessary for long stays and treks in the mountains. The short-term hiker need not despair, however; plenty of challenging treks can be completed with sturdy boots and water, by setting out from one village and arriving at another before the late summer sundown.

PAMPANEIRA

As the road winds in serpentine curves up to the high Alpujarran villages, the landscape quickly becomes harsh. A sign at the entrance to Pampaniera (pop. 360) nevertheless encourages visitors: *Quédate a vivir con nosotros*—"stay and live with us." Pampaneira (1059m) is the first in a trio of hamlets overlooking the **Poqueira Gorge,** a massive ravine cut by the Río Poqueira; the town makes a great springboard for climbing to **Bubión** (about 1hr.) and **Capileira** (2hr.). The trail to both begins from behind the church at the very top of town; a sign points the way. If you lose the trail or start at the wrong point, look towards the church of Bubión and head uphill. Through abandoned terrace farms and steep bush, you will rejoin the trail quickly. **Nevadensis** offers hiking tours of the Sierra Nevada, organizes horseback riding, and even arranges rural accommodations. Located in the small main square, they also serve as the town's **tourist office**. (☎958 76 31 27; fax 76 33 01; www.nevadensis.com. Open Tu-Sa 10am-2pm and 5-7pm, Su-M 10am-3pm.)

Hostal Pampaneira ❷, C. José Antonio Primo de Rivera, 1, just off the highway in front of the bus stop, has large rooms with private baths and extremely comfortable beds. (☎958 76 30 02. Singles €20; doubles €30; triples €40. MC/V.) The hostal's **restaurant ❷** is usually buzzing with activity in the evenings, with local men playing card games and families out to dine. The food is simple, hearty, no-nonsense fare, and the charming old patron will pepper your dinnertime with information on the local scene. (Entrees €3.90-7.20. Open for lunch and dinner. MC/V.) Local taverns offer pool tables and music, and the locals joke, "Madrid is peaceful. It's all happening in Pampaneira!"

BUBIÓN

Bubión, a steep 3km (1hr.) hike on a dirt trail from Pampaneira, is resplendent with Berber architecture, village charm, and enough *artesanía* (typical arts and crafts) to make your head spin. If you are hiking with the sunrise, however, carry some water and snacks with you since everything in this sleepy town opens late. Those not up for the steep hike can catch the "early" bus from Pampaneira at 12:35pm. For tourist info, stop by **Rustic Blue,** Barrio La Ermita, where the intrepid Australian staff has been organizing excursions, rural lodging, guided hikes, and horseback rides into the mountains for seven years. (☎958 76 33 81; fax 76 31 34. English and French spoken. Open M-F 10am-2pm and 5-8pm, Sa 11am-2pm.) If a night stay is on the itinerary in this small, charming town, ◪**Las Terrazas ❷**, Pta. del Sol, has several flower-filled terraces and cozy rooms that overlook the valley. (☎958 76 30 34. Singles €20; doubles €27.) **Ciber Monfi Café Morisco ❸** offers Moorish-flavored food in an Arabesque setting, along with internet access. Follow signs pointing to Ciber Monfi from anywhere in town. (Closed Tu. Usually open late afternoons, but hours vary.) The **Teide ❷** offers large, filling portions of traditional food. (Entrees €4-9. Open daily 9-11am, 1:30-4pm, and 8-10:30pm. MC.)

CAPILEIRA

Capileira (1436m), perched atop the Poqueira Gorge (2½hr. from Granada and a 1hr. hike on the trail or a 20min. walk on the road from Bubión), makes a good base for exploring the neighboring villages and the back side of *la Falda*. A tedious ascent to Mulhacén (3479) mitigated only by spectacular gorges and views is possible from Capileira via the *refugio* (shelter); however, softcore climbers might prefer to start from the more commonly-used base town Trevélez. Looming peaks tower over cobblestone alleys, with the distant valley below. Enjoy small luxuries in the tiled **Hostal Paco López ❷**, Ctra. de la Sierra, 5, with balconies, TVs, and bathrooms in every room. (☎958 76 30 11. Singles €18; doubles €30.) A filling *menú* (€6-9) is served at **Restaurant Poqueira ❷**, C. Dr. Castillo, 6. (Open Su and Tu-Sa for lunch and dinner.)

TREVÉLEZ

Jamón serrano, and lots of it, distinguishes Trevélez, continental Spain's highest community (1476m). The town is known all over Andalucía for its cured pork, whose special qualities will probably elude all but the true connoisseur. Trevélez's cold is the cure for the common ham, providing the "ideal microclimate." Nearly everything in this tiny town revolves around the ham industry, but it still has its share of history and charm. Steep roads weave through three *barrios*, and water rushes through Moorish irrigation systems still intact from 1000 years ago.

Trevélez is a logical base for the ascent to **Mulhacén** (3479m), one of the highest peaks of the Sierra Nevada. Every August, throngs of locals climb to pay homage to the **Virgen de las Nieves** (Virgin of the Snows). Summit-bound travelers should prepare with proper cold equipment and head north on the trail leaving the upper village from behind the church; avoid the trail that follows the swampy Río Trevélez. Continue past the Cresta de los Postreros for a good 4-5hr. until you reach the **Cañada de Siete Lagunas** (the largest lake, Laguna Hondera, should be directly in front of you); go right to see the **Cueva del Cura**, a famous cave refuge. To reach Mulhacén, go up the ridge south of the refuge (3-4hr. further). Since both itineraries take a considerable amount of time, it is not advisable to hike Mulhacén the same day you visit the lake. Regardless of which trail you choose, you should purchase a **map** and hiking guide of the Sierra Nevada, such as the one by **Alpina** (€5.48), available in any souvenir shop.

Budget beds aren't hard to find in Trevélez. **Hostal González ❷**, Pl. Francisco Abellán, behind the tavern of the same name, has perfectly comfortable, clean rooms waiting beyond the grungy exterior. (☎958 85 85 31. Singles €15; doubles €25. MC.) If you like ham, you're in luck—nearly every **restaurant** in town either advertises ham specials or has the meat hanging from the ceiling. Any one of the restaurants in the main plaza by the bus station serves up a variety of tasty local dishes, most often made of pork products. Non-pork entrees exist as well (though less abundantly), and the *menú* options (approx. €6.60) tend to include tm.-

JAÉN ☎953

More than a stop on the road to Baeza, Spain's olive oil capital is a destination well worth exploring. Its winding hillside streets, mountaintop castle, and fascinating museums make the bustling transportation hub great for an afternoon stroll.

█ TRANSPORTATION. Trains (☎902 24 02 02) depart from Po. de la Estación at the bottom of the slope and run to: **Córdoba** (1½hr., 1 per day 8am, €7.55); **Madrid** (4-5hr.; 2 per day 9:20am, 3:50pm; €19.55); **Sevilla** (3hr., 1 per day 8am, €14.50). Alsina Graells **buses**, Pl. Coca de la Piñera (☎953 25 50 14), serve the most common destinations (counter #14): to **Baeza** (1hr., 16 per day 8:30am-9:15pm, €3.12); **Cazorla** (2hr.; 2 per day noon, 4:30pm; €6.47); **Granada** (1½hr., 15 per day 7:30am-9pm, €6.24); **Málaga** (3hr., 4 per day 7:30am-4:30pm, €13.91).

█ █ ORIENTATION & PRACTICAL INFORMATION. Jaén centers around **Plaza de la Constitución**. From the plaza, **Calle Bernabé Soriano** leads uphill to the cathedral and the old section of town. **Calle Maestra,** home to the tourist office, is up several blocks to the right. To reach the town center from the bus station, exit from the depot and follow Av. de Madrid uphill to Pl. de la Constitución (5min.). From the train station, turn right on Po. de la Estación, which becomes C. Roldán y Marín. If you're not up for the 25min. walk, take the #1 bus along Po. de la Estación (€0.70) or take a taxi (€3). The **tourist office**, C. Maestra, 13, is near the cathedral and has an excellent English-speaking staff. (☎/fax 953 24 26 24. Open July-Aug. M-F 10am-8pm, Sa-Su 10am-1pm. Sept.-June M-F 10am-7pm, Sa-Su 10am-1pm.) Other services include: **Banco Santander Central Hispano**, Pl. de la Constitución (☎902 24 24 24; open June-Sept. M-F 8:30am-2pm, Sa 8:30am-1pm; Oct.-May M-F 8:30am-2pm); **luggage storage** at the bus station (€1.80 for

ANDALUCÍA

326 ■ LAS ALPUJARRAS

24hr.) or the train station (€3 for 24 hr.); **emergency** ☎112; **police** ☎953 21 91 05. **Internet access** is available at **Cu@k Internet,** C. Adarves Bajos, 24. From Pl. de la Constitución, turn left onto C. Ignacio Figueroa and continue downhill past the church of San Ildefonso until it becomes C. Vicente Montuno. Make a left onto C. Adarves Bajos; it's on your right. (☎953 19 06 16. €2 per hr. Open M-F 11am-2:30pm and 5:30pm-3am, Sa 11am-3pm and 6pm-12:30am, Su 12-3pm and 6pm-midnight.) Alternatively, try **Cyberam,** Fuente Don Diego, Bajo, C. Adarves Bajos. (☎ 953 08 87 62. €2 per hr. Open 9am-2pm and 5-10pm.) The **post office,** Pl. de Jardinillos, s/n, is next to the pedestrian street Miguel de Priego, which becomes Jardinillos when it hits the plaza. From Pl. de la Constitución, turn right on C. San Clemente until you reach Pl. de Jardinillos. (☎953 24 78 00. Open M-F 8:30am-8:30pm, Sa 9:30am-1pm.) **Postal Code:** 23004.

⌐⌐ ACCOMMODATIONS & FOOD. Most of Jaén's accommodations lie close to the cathedral and along Av. de Madrid. The central location of **Hostal Carlos V ❷,** Av. de Madrid, 4, 2nd fl., downhill from Pl. de la Constitución, compensates for its tiny rooms. All six rooms share a single hallway and bathroom with shower. (☎953 22 20 91. Singles €16.25; doubles €28.25; triples €38.25.) Nearby is the comfortable **Hostal Martín ❷,** C. Cuatro Torres, 5, with clean, medium-sized rooms with private baths. Turn right and up on C. Cuatro Torres from Pl. de la Constitución. (☎953 24 36 78; Singles €20; doubles €30.) Those seeking more modern rooms—some even have body-massaging showerheads—with TV, phone, bath, and elevator should head to **Hotel Europa ❸,** Pl. de Belén, 1. Walking downhill on Av. de Madrid from Pl. de la Constitución, turn right on Av. de Granada and then left on Cuesta de Belén. Walk halfway up the hill; the hotel is on your left. Europa might be closed for renovations July-Sept 2004; call ahead to check. (☎953 22 27 00. Singles €34.24; doubles €58.85; triples €67.41.) The extensive menu at ◙**Colón Cafetería ❶,** C. Navas de Tolosa, 7, along the main pedestrian walkway, includes everything from *churros* (€0.55-0.75) to *batidos helados* (frappes; €1.50-3), and a wide variety of other dishes. (☎953 22 77 35. Open 8am-10pm.) Delicious Andalusian fare can be found at **Restaurante La Abadía ❸,** C. Melchor Cobo Medina, 19, where hearty portions (€9-18) are served in a cozy, rustic setting. Heading toward Pl. de la Constitución on Av. de Madrid, turn left on C. Dr. Sagaz Zubelzu and veer to the right. (☎953 24 50 38. Open daily 1-6pm and 8:30pm-1am.)

◙♫ SIGHTS & ENTERTAINMENT. Andrés de Vandelvira designed Jaén's trademark **Catedral de Santa María,** on C. Bernabé Soriano uphill from Pl. de la Constitución. (☎953 23 42 33. Open Apr.-June and Sept. daily 8:30am-1pm and 5-8pm; July and Aug. M-Sa 8:30am-1pm and 5-8pm; Oct.-Mar. M-Sa 8:30am-1pm and 4-7pm, Su 8:30am-1pm and 5-7pm. Free.) The attached **Museo de la Catedral** displays sundry objects of interest, among them candlesticks by Maestro Bartolomé. (☎953 22 46 75. Open Tu-Su 10am-1pm and afternoons when the cathedral is open. €1.20.) Jaén's most imposing and least accessible sight is the 13th-century stone **Castillo de Santa Catalina,** a 5km hike from the center of town. Built by the Moors, expanded by Fernando III, and reinforced by the French during the occupation of Spain (1810-1812), the recently renovated castle provides a grand look into Jaén's rich and varied past. Don't miss the spectacular view of the city and its surrounding olive groves from the promontory. (☎953 12 07 33. Open Sept.-Apr. Tu-Su 10am-2pm and 3:30-7:30pm; May-Aug. 5-9pm. €3; youth card and groups of 15 or more €2 per person. Those preferring to avoid a sweaty walk can take a taxi (€5.40) from the bus station.) The Renaissance ◙**Palacio de Villardompardo,** in Pl. Santa Luisa Marillac at the far end of C. Maestra, contains incredibly well preserved 11th-century Moorish baths—Spain's largest—and an art museum which houses the second-largest collection of *Narif* artwork in the world. (Follow C. Maestra from the cathedral to C. Martínez Molina. ☎953 23 62 92. Open Tu-F 9am-8pm, Sa-Su 9:30am-2:30pm. Free.)

Uphill from the cathedral and right next to the tourist office, **Peña Flamenca Jaén,** C. Maestra, 11, serves up drinks and *flamenco*. Try the *manzanillo*, Andalucía's specialty apple liqueur. (☎953 23 17 10. €1.50 for a beer, which includes a *tapa* of your choice. Mixed drinks €3 and up. Open M-F noon-4pm and 8pm-1am, Sa-Su noon-1am.) For a break from *el tapeo*, hire a taxi to **Moët** (like the champagne), Av. de Andalucía, 10, near the train station. This ultra-hip bar attracts an effervescent crowd of local students and professionals in their 20s. On the weekends, it turns into a disco, with a DJ spinning the latest in Spanish pop. (☎953 27 30 94. Beer €1.80, mixed drinks €4 and up. Open M-W 4pm-4:30am and Th-Sa 4pm until the last customer stumbles out the door.)

BAEZA   ☎953

With its beautiful plazas and amazingly well-preserved monuments, Baeza (pop. 17,000) is frozen in its 15th-century architectural heyday, unspoiled by modern life. Nearby Úbeda may have similar architecture and attractions, but Baeza's overall small-town feel makes it the more desirable destination. Even though a half-day stroll can exhaust the intimate *barrio monumental*, Baeza's alluring charm will make it difficult to leave.

⌨ TRANSPORTATION. Trains leave **Estación Linares-Baeza** (☎902 24 02 02), 13km out of town on the road to Madrid (reached from the bus station in Baeza, 15 min., 8 per day 7:45am-9pm, €0.85), for **Madrid** (3hr., 5 per day 7am-6pm, €17) and **Málaga** (4hr.; 2 per day 2:45, 5pm; €19). At the top of Av. Alcalde Puche Pardo, as it becomes C. Julio Burell, the **bus station** (☎953 74 04 68) offers service to: **Cazorla** (1½hr.; 3 per day 1, 5:30, 7:30pm; €3.41); **Granada** (2-3hr., 9 per day 7:55am-6:45pm, €9.11); **Jaén** (1hr., 14 per day 7:10am-8:15pm, €3.12).

⌨⌨ ORIENTATION & PRACTICAL INFORMATION. Marking the center of town, **Plaza de España** leads downhill to **Paseo de la Constitución.** To get to Pl. de España from the bus station, follow C. Julio Burell to C. San Pablo and continue to the plaza. The **tourist office,** in Pl. del Pópulo, offers guided tours of the town. (☎953 74 04 44. Open July-Sept. M-F 9am-2:30pm and 5-7pm, Sa 10am-1pm and 4-7pm, Su 10am-1pm; Oct.-June M-F 9am-2:30pm and 4-6pm, Sa 10am-1pm and 4-6pm, Su 10am-1pm.) Services include: **emergency** ☎112; **police,** C. Cardenal Benavides, 5 (☎953 74 06 59); **Centro de Salud Comarcal,** Av. Alcalde Puche Pardo, s/n, past the bus station (☎953 74 29 00). For **Internet access** try **Microware,** Po. Tundidores, 13, in Pl. de la Constitución. (☎953 74 70 10. €1.80 per hr. Open M-W and Th-Su 10:30am-2pm and 5-10pm.) The **post office** is on C. Julio Burell, 19. (☎953 74 08 39. Open M-F 8:30am-2:30pm, Sa 9am-1pm.) **Postal Code:** 23440.

⌨⌨ ACCOMMODATIONS & FOOD. Baeza's hostels are hidden throughout the city. **Hostal El Patio ❶,** C. Conde de Romanones, 13, has the cheapest rooms in town and a location in the middle of the *barrio monumental* that's hard to beat. (☎953 74 02 00. Singles €10, with shower €13; doubles €19, with bath €25; triples with bath €34.) Directly uphill from Pl. de España, **Hostal Comercio ❷,** C. San Pablo, 21, has cozy rooms, all with private bathrooms. (☎953 74 01 00. Singles €15; doubles €27.) Several bars and restaurants line Po. de la Constitución, and almost all serve *comida típica*. Of these, **Mesón Restaurante La Góndola ❸,** Portales Carbonería, 13, offers an extensive menu, with a fine selection of meat, seafood, and *perdiz* (partridge), the tasty local specialty cooked in a garlic-based vegetable stew. (☎ 953 74 29 84. Entrees €10-15. Open daily 9am-1am.) Locals themselves choose bar **Guadalquivir ❶**, C. San Pablo, 42. (☎ 953 74 15 29. *Bocadillos* €1.65-2.10, *raciones* €4.80-6. Open daily noon-4pm and 8:30pm-midnight.)

◘ **SIGHTS.** Most major sights in Baeza's intimate and well-preserved **barrio monumental** are free. With your back to the tourist office, walk up the stairs to your right, then take a left on C. Conde de Romanones; at the street's end stands the **Antigua Universidad** (founded in 1595), whose courtyard served as an outdoor classroom where 20th-century poet Antonio Machado taught French. (Open M-Tu and Th-Su 10am-1:30pm and 4-6:30pm. Free.) Farther down C. Conde de Romanones stands the 13th-century **Iglesia de Santa Cruz,** Baeza's oldest church and one of the only Romanesque structures in Andalucía, which contains frescoes of La Virgen, Santa Catalina, and San Sebastián. (Open M-Sa 11am-1pm and Su noon-2pm. Free.) Next door to the church is a small ◙**museum** which houses ornate icons, artifacts, and carriages gilt with gold and silver. Especially exciting are the macabre costumes and old church documents from the annual procession of the religious brotherhood of Santa Vera Cruz, held during *Semana Santa.* (Open daily 11am-1:30pm and 4:30-7pm. Free.) On the other side of Pl. de la Santa Cruz, adjacent to the imposing 15th-century **Palacio Jabalquinto** (currently closed for restoration), the **seminario's** facade bears the names of some egotistical graduates and a caricature of an unpopular professor, rumored to be painted in bull's blood. Across Pl. Santa María from the seminary towers, the **Santa Iglesia Catedral** houses *La Custodia de Baeza,* the second most important Corpus Christi icon in Spain, trumped only by Toledo's. (Open daily Jun.-Aug. 10:30am-1pm and 4:30-6:30pm; Sept.-May 10:30am-1pm and 4:15-6pm. Free.) Fabulous ◙**views** of the olive tree-carpeted Guadalquivir Valley unfold from the park atop the old city wall, reached by walking along Po. de las Murallas.

CAZORLA ☎ 953

Guarded by the lofty peaks of the Sierra Nevada, irrigated by swift rapids, dramatic cascades, and tranquil lakes, and peppered with fantastic mountaintop villages, the ◙**Parque Natural de las Sierras de Cazorla, Segura, y las Villas** is a heavenly escape from the urban milieu of Andalucía. With over 210,000 densely forested hectares of protected mountains and waterways, the national park offers some of the best hiking, mountain biking, and horseback riding in Spain, and abundant wildlife makes it a veritable paradise for animal lovers.

The park is best reached from the town of **Cazorla** (pop. 9000), which serves as a base for most trails and transportation into the park. Arrive in Cazorla a day before exploring the park, both to plan your routes and to enjoy this quaint town nestled between foreboding cliffs and two ancient castles.

◪ ⊞ **ORIENTATION & PRACTICAL INFORMATION.** The center of Cazorla clusters around two plazas—**Plaza de Corredera** and **Plaza de la Constitución.** To reach **Pl. de Corredera** from the bus stop, face the peaks and walk down narrow C. Dr. Muñoz to the right. Farther downhill past Pl. de Corredera are Pl. de Santa María and the **barrio antiguo. Alsina Graells buses** (☎ 953 75 21 57) depart from Pl. de la Constitución for: **Granada** (4hr.; M-F 7am, noon, 5:30pm; Sa 7am, 5:30pm; Su 8am, 5:30pm; €12.60) and **Jaén** (2hr., 5 per day 7am-5:30pm, €3.74-€6.85). Buy tickets in the tiny office across from the plaza bus depot (open daily 6:30am-5:30pm). The **tourist office,** Po. Santo Cristo, 17, is up a garden-lined walkway from Pl. de la Constitución. (☎ 953 71 01 02; fax 72 00 60. Open M-F 10am-2pm and 5-

9pm.) Services include: **emergency** ☎112; **police** on Pl. de Corredera (☎953 72 01 81); **Centro de Salud,** Av. Ximénez de Rada, 1 (☎953 72 10 61); and the **post office,** C. Mariano Extremera, 2, uphill from Pl. de Corredera. (☎953 72 02 61. Open M-F 8:30am-2:30pm, Sa 9am-1pm.) **Postal Code:** 23470.

⌐⌐ ACCOMMODATIONS & FOOD. From the far end of Pl. de Corredera, walk uphill on C. Carmen to reach the ◪**Albergue Juvenil Cazorla (HI) ❶,** Pl. Mauricio Martínez, 6. This hostel has a TV lounge, basketball/soccer court, and a heaven-sent pool, although it's only open for swimming mid-June through mid-September. (☎953 72 03 29. Breakfast and sheets provided. HI members June-Sept. €10.90, over 26 €15.20; Oct.-May €8.50/€11.50.) **Hostal Betis ❶,** Pl. de Corredera, 19, has incredible views of the valley from most rooms. (☎953 72 05 40. Singles with bath €12; doubles €24, with bath €26.) To the left of Pl. de Corredera if you are heading down C. Doctor Muñoz is the impeccable **Hotel Guadalquivir ❸,** C. Nueva, 6. Spacious and airy rooms with marble floors and private bathrooms plus an attentive staff make this a very comfortable place to crash after a long day of hiking. (☎953 72 02 68. Singles €27-28; doubles €37-39; triples €52-54.)

Open-air bar/restaurants serving traditional platters such as *rin-ran* (a cold soup of potatoes, red peppers, olives, and fish) line Pl. de Corredera and Pl. de Sta. María. Perhaps the best bargain in town is **La Taberna ❶,** C. Nueva, s/n, on a side street off Pl. de Corredera (across from Hotel Guadalquivir), where brightly tiled walls and a casual environment attract a range of patrons. (☎953 71 01 22. *Tapas/raciones* €4.81-7.21. Open M and W-Su noon-4:30pm and 7:30pm-midnight.) For a romantic, candlelit dinner at the foot of the **Castillo de la Yedra,** and in front of the enchanting ruins of the 13th-century **Iglesia de Santa María,** head to **Cueva de Juan Pedro ❷,** C. La Hoz, 2 in the Pl. de Sta. María. House specialties include *patata a lo pobre* (potato sautéed with onion, green pepper, and egg; €6) and *jabali al horno* (roast wild boar; €9). The restaurant's rustic mountain decor gives it a very cozy feel, but if the weather is nice, get a table outside beside the ruins. (☎953 72 12 25. Open daily noon-4:30pm and 6-11pm.) The **market** is at Pl. Mercado, downstairs from C. Dr. Muñoz (open M-F 9am-noon), and a larger **supermarket** is in Pl. de Corredera. (Open M-F 9am-noon and 6-9pm, Sa 9am-noon.)

◪ SIGHTS. The medieval **Castillo de la Yedra** rises majestically above the town. Begun by Roman builders, the castle provides a lovely view of town from its solitary turrets. (☎953 71 00 39. Open Tu 3-8pm, W-Sa 9am-8pm, Su 9am-3pm. €1.50, EU citizens free.) A 25min. hike up C. Carmen and Camino de Iruela leads to the charming village of **La Iruela,** lined with white houses and flowering balconies. Continue for another 20min. to the three **Miradores de los Merendores,** skirting the edges of the natural park and affording magnificent views of the moutains, the *castillo,* and the olive-laden vistas of the Guadalquivir valley. Inquire at the tourist office about the short and easy trails that lead from the miradores into the park and back to Cazorla. The majority of visitors to Cazorla come for the **Parque Natural de las Sierras de Cazorla, Segura, y las Villas.** The truly adventurous can take a 9hr. round-trip hike from Cazorla to the park; stop by the tourist office for a map.

⚐ OUTDOOR ACTIVITIES

To start out, drive to or ask to be let off the morning bus from Cazorla at the **Torre del Vinage** visitors center. The visitors center sits at the trailhead of the popular Cerrada de Elias hike along the enchanting Río Borosa. Since the center does not open till 10am, make sure you bring a map, sack lunch, bottled water, sunscreen, sturdy hiking shoes, and a windbreaker. The hike is not very strenuous and can be completed at a leisurely pace.

▶ **HIKING.** Carcesa Buses run from Pl. de la Constitución in Cazorla to the park's visitors' center (1hr.; July-Sept. M-Sa 6:30am and 2:30pm, return at 8am and 4:15pm; Oct.-June M-F 6am and 2:45pm, return at 7am and 4:15pm, Sa 6:30am and 2:30pm, return at 8am and 4:15pm; €3; buy tickets on the bus. Service subject to change.) Many trailheads and excursions begin at the Torre del Vinagre Visitors' Center. (☎953 71 30 40. Open M-Sa 10am-2pm and 4-7pm, hours vary slightly Sept.-May. Call ahead to make sure the center is open.)

The popular **Sendero Cerrada de Elias/Río Borosa trailhead** offers 4km and 12km hikes up the river canyon. From the visitor's center, cross the road and bear left, heading downhill according to the "Central Eléctrica" sign. At the bottom of the hill, cross the Río Guadalquivir, which at this point is nothing more than a stream. Continue down this road for about 2km, passing the *piscifactoria* (trout hatchery) on the left, until you come to a parking lot beside the swift and cold Río Borosa. Pass the lot and head toward the unpaved road where the marked trail begins. Walk along the trail—which follows the Borosa—for about 30min. If the weather is warm, stop for a dip in the refreshingly cool **river pools** designated *sitio de baño*. At the fork in the trail, take the path that goes in the direction of Laguna de Valdeazores. With the Borosa to your left, continue for another 30min. towards a gorge, a favorite watering hole for park wildlife, including ibex, *jabali* (wild boar), and *mouflon* (a variety of sheep). At the next fork, take the right side of the trail marked **Cerrada de Elias.** Shortly you will enter a narrow part of the gorge—the *cerrada* itself. This beautiful 30min. section along catwalks attached to the limestone cliff climbs above inviting pools and dramatic cascades along what is perhaps the most memorable part of Borosa's course. After passing this point, continue for another hour to reach the artificial **Laguna de Aguas Negras** (a reservoir) and the **Laguna de Valdeazores** (a natural lake). Or, you can head back towards Torre del Vinagre, stopping along the way for another dip or a refreshing drink from one of the many fountains which dot the trail. Allow 3½hr. to get to Cerrada de Elias and back (10km) and 6hr. to get to the lakes and back (24km).

◨ **GUIDED TOURS.** Five hundred meters down the road from Torre del Vinagre is the Picadero "El Cortijo" stable, which rents horses. (☎649 32 40 38. €12 per hr.) Cazorla Cars, C. Hilario Marco, s/n, at the junction of the autoroute heading to Santo Tome-Villacarillo, rents good 4x4 vehicles. Cazorla Cars also has a branch inside the park at Arroyo Frío, 8km from Torre del Vinagre. (☎953 72 19 92; www.cazorlacars.com. €65 per day.) For guided excursions by 4x4 vehicle through the park, stop by Quercus, C. Juan Domingo, 2. Tours can be arranged with an English-speaking guide. (☎953 72 01 15. Map €2.70. Half-day tours €17-36. Jeep rental prices and availability subject to change. Open daily 9am-2pm and 5-9pm, holidays 10am-2pm and 6-9pm.)

◪ **MOTORING.** If you have come by car, the most interesting areas of the park are wide open. A drive along autoroute A-319 towards Cazorla will take you to the source of the Río Guadalquivir, where breathtaking waterfalls and scenic trails wind alongside the river. Heading in the opposite direction reveals the magnificent **Embalse de Tranco de Beas,** providing heavenly views of mountains and the lake towards the northern side of the park. Here, the mountaintop villages of **Segura de la Sierra** and **Hornos** with commanding Moorish forts will enchant even the most unromantic traveler. The view in Hornos from the ramparts of the Arab fort of Segura de la Sierra, near the old church, commands the Embalse de Tranco de Beas and the entire northern edge of the park. Allow 5-6hr. to enjoy the towns on your winding drive to the north side. If you decide to forgo a night in one of the park's campgrounds (ask at the visitors center for variable hours and prices), exit the park from the north side via **La Puerta de Segura** onto autoroute N-322 towards Úbeda, connecting to C-323 from Villacarillo to Mogon and Santo Tome, and finally JV 7101 to Cazorla. Driving on unlit winding mountain roads after dark, when they are plagued with speeding locals, is not advisable.

VALENCIA & MURCIA

VALENCIA

With a coastline of popular beaches and a rolling interior, Valencia is something of a natural wonder. The farmlands are a patchwork of orange orchards and vegetable fields, all fed by Moorish irrigation systems. Bordering the lush heart of Valencia, the 466km of Mediterranean shoreline alternate between soft dunes and jagged promontories. Valencia's natural beauty has found a place even in its cities, where carefully landscaped gardens display ornate fountains and exotic plants.

Valencia's past is a tangle of power struggles between the whole cast of usual suspects: Phoenicians, Carthaginians, Greeks, Romans, and Moors. The region first fell under Castilian control when El Cid expelled the Moors in 1094; he ruled it in the name of Alfonso VI until his death in 1099. Without El Cid's powerful influence, the region again fell to the Moors, remaining an Arab stronghold until 1238. In the 1930s, Valencia was again besieged, this time by Franco's troops. *Valencianos* resisted with characteristic strength; Valencia was the last region incorporated into Franco's Spain. In 1977, the region finally regained autonomy.

Valencià, the regional language spoken sparingly in the north and inland, is a dialect of Catalán. Although Valencia's regionalism is not as intense as Catalunya's, the Generalitat's recent mandate that all students enroll in one course of *valencià* reflects a resurgence of regional pride. Valencia's festivals are some of the wildest in Spain, and its culinary heritage has had a pronounced impact on Spanish cuisine: *paella*, now considered a quintessentially Spanish dish, was first concocted somewhere in the region's fields, and Valencian oranges are widely accepted as the best in the nation, if not the world.

HIGHLIGHTS OF VALENCIA & MURCIA

GET FIRED UP during **Valencia**'s hottest party, *Las Fallas* (see p. 355).

RETURN to nature in the **Parc Natural de L'Albufera** (see p. 340).

ROCK ON atop Calpe's high-flying **Peñón d'Ifach** (see p. 352).

DELVE into Spain's Roman past at **Cartagena** (see p. 360**).**

VALENCIA ☎963

Though Valencia's population (750,000) makes it the third largest city in Spain, it has very little of the ugly urban sprawl which characterizes many Spanish cities. An architectural wonder, Valencia is among the few places in Europe where ultra-modern styles are successfully blended with the traditional. It is a city of great contrasts, from the white-sand beaches of its coast to the multitude of parks which lie in the dried-up bed of the Río Turia to its palm tree-lined avenues and thoroughfares. Valencia seems to possess all the best of its sister cities: the bustling energy of Madrid, the vibrance of Alicante, the off-beat sophistication of Barcelona, and the friendly warmth of Sevilla. Despite its cosmopolitan modernity, Valencia still manages to retain a certain small-town charm that enchants all those who visit.

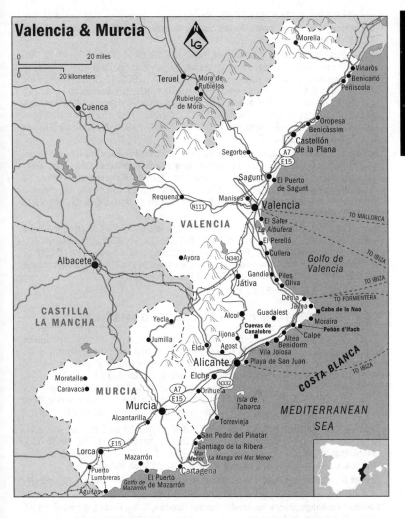

Valencia & Murcia

0   20 miles
0   20 kilometers

TO MALLORCA

TO IBIZA

TO IBIZA

TO FORMENTERA

TO IBIZA

Morella
Vinaròs
Benicarló
Peñiscola
Teruel
Mora de Rubielos
Rubielos de Móra
Cuenca
Oropesa
Benicàssim
Castellón de la Plana
Segorbe
Sagunt
El Puerto de Sagunt
Requena
Manises
Valencia
El Saler
La Albufera
VALENCIA
El Perelló
Ayora
Cullera
Albacete
Golfo de Valencia
Gandía
Piles
Oliva
Játiva
CASTILLA LA MANCHA
Denia
Jávea
Cabo de la Nao
Alcoi
Guadalest
Moraira
Peñón d'Ifach
Yecla
Cuevas de Canalobre
Calpe
Altea
Jijona
Benidorm
Jumilla
Vila Joiosa
Elda
Agost
Playa de San Juan
Alicante
Moratalla
Elche
Caravaca
N332
COSTA BLANCA
MURCIA
Orihuela
Isla de Tabarca
Murcia
Alcantarilla
MEDITERRANEAN SEA
Torrevieja
San Pedro del Pinatar
Lorca
Santiago de la Ribera
Mazarrón
Mar Menor
La Manga del Mar Menor
Puerto Lumbreras
El Puerto de Mazarrón
Cartagena
Águilas
Golfo de Mazarrón

TRANSPORTATION

Flights: Airport (☎961 59 85 00), 8km from the city. **Cercanías** trains run between the airport and train station (30min.; M-F every 30min., Sa-Su every hr. 7:03am-10:03pm; €1.10). Many flights to the Islas Baleares. **Iberia,** C. La Paz, 14 (☎963 52 75 52, 24hr. info and reservations 902 40 05 00). Open M-F 9am-2pm and 4-7pm.

Trains: Estació del Nord, C. Xátiva, 24 (☎963 52 02 02). Ticket windows open 7:30am-9:30pm. **RENFE** (24hr. ☎902 24 02 02) to: **Alicante** (2-3hr., 9 per day 7am-10:35pm, €10-25); **Barcelona** (3hr., 12 per day 5:45am-8:45pm, €33.50); **Madrid** (3½hr., 9 per day 6:45am-9:15pm, €18-36.50); **Sevilla** (8½hr., 1 per day 11:30am, €41.50). **Cercanías** trains run at least twice an hour to: **Gandía** (1hr., €3.35); **Játiva** (45min., €2.55); **Sagunto** (30min., €2.15).

Buses: Estación Terminal d'Autobuses, Av. Menéndez Pidal, 13 (☎963 49 72 22), across the riverbed, a 25min. walk from the city center. Municipal bus #8 runs between Pl. del Ajuntament and the bus station (€0.90). **ALSA** (☎902 42 22 42) to: **Alicante** via the **Costa Blanca** (4½hr., 13 per day 6:30am-6pm, €13-15); **Barcelona** (4½hr., 15 per day 1am-10pm, €21); **Granada** (8hr., 11 per day 6am-4:45am, €34.41); **Málaga** (11hr., 9 per day 4:15am-2:30am, €42.29); **Sevilla** (11hr.; 3per day 10:30am, 10:30pm, 3am; €41-48). **Auto Res** (☎963 49 22 30) goes to **Madrid** (4hr., 13 per day 7am-3am, €19.23-23.20).

Ferries: Trasmediterránea, Estació Marítima (☎902 45 46 45). Take bus #4 from Pl. del Ajuntament or #1 or 2 from the bus station. To **Mallorca** and **Ibiza** (1-2 per day, €30-69, depending on speed and class). One 15hr. ferry to **Menorca** each week (Sa 11:30pm, prices vary). Buy tickets at a travel agency or at the port on the day of departure. **Trasmapi-Balearia** (☎902 16 01 80) runs ferries from Dénia in Alicante to Eivissa. See **By Boat,** p. 363.

Public Transportation: EMT Office, Pl. Correu Vell, 5 (☎963 15 85 15). Open M-F 8am-2pm. Bus #8 runs to the bus station. Buses #10, 21, 22, and 23 go to Las Arenas and Malvarrosa along Pg. Marítim. Buy tickets (€0.90) on board; 10-ride ticket (€4.70) or 1-day pass (€3) available at newsstands. Service stops at 10:30pm. **Late-night buses** go through Pl. Ayuntamento (every 45min. 11pm-1:38am).

Taxis: ☎963 70 33 33 or 57 13 13.

■✱ 🛈 ORIENTATION & PRACTICAL INFORMATION

Since **Estació del Nord** lies very close to the center of the city, it is most convenient to enter Valencia by train. **Avenida Marqués de Sotelo** runs from the train station to **Plaça del Ajuntament,** the center of town. Just about everything of interest, except for the university and beaches, is in the **casco antiguo,** nestled in a bend of the now-diverted Río Turia, whose dry riverbed loops around the center of the city. Because of Valencia's size, it's best to take advantage of the extensive bus system to see more than just the small area within walking distance of the center.

Tourist Office: Regional office, C. de la Paz, 46-48 (☎963 98 64 22). Open M-F 9am-7pm, Sa 10am-7pm. **Branch,** Estació del Nord, C. Xátiva, 24 (☎963 52 85 73). **Municipal office,** Pl. del Ajuntament, 1 (☎963 51 04 17). Open M-F 9am-2pm. **Branch,** C. Poeta Querol, s/n (☎963 51 49 07). Open M-Sa 9am-3pm.

Budget Travel: Barceló Viajes: C. de la Paz, 38 (☎963 51 47 84). ISIC €4.20. Open M-F 9:30am-1:30pm and 4:30-8:30pm, Sa 9:30am-1pm.

Currency Exchange: Banco Santander Central Hispano, C. las Barcas, 8 (☎963 53 81 00), offers decent exchange rates and no commission on traveler's checks.

American Express: Duna Viajes, C. Cirilo Amorós, 88 (☎963 74 15 62; fax 34 57 00). From C. Don Juan de Austria, follow C. Sorní to Pl. América. C. Cirilo Amorós is on the right. Open M-F 9:30am-2pm and 5-8pm, Sa 10am-1pm.

Luggage Storage: 24hr. storage at the bus station (€1-3.50) and train station (€2.40-4.50). Open 7:30am-9:30pm.

El Corte Inglés, C. Colón and C. Pintor Sorolla (☎963 51 24 44). Open M-Sa 10am-10pm. Sells groceries and anything else you could possibly consume or carry.

Laundromat: Lavandería El Mercat, Pl. del Mercat, 12 (☎963 91 20 10). Full-service wash and dry in 2-3hr. for €9. Open M-F 10am-2pm and 5-9pm, Sa 10am-2pm.

Emergency: ☎112. **Ambulance:** ☎085.

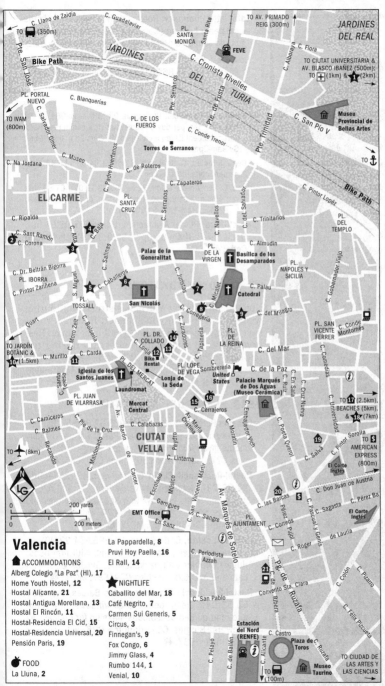

Valencia

ACCOMMODATIONS
Alberg Colegio "La Paz" (HI), 17
Home Youth Hostel, 12
Hostal Alicante, 21
Hostal Antigua Morellana, 13
Hostal El Rincón, 11
Hostal-Residencia El Cid, 15
Hostal-Residencia Universal, 20
Pensión Paris, 19

FOOD
La Lluna, 2
La Pappardella, 8
Pruvi Hoy Paella, 16
El Rall, 14

NIGHTLIFE
Caballito del Mar, 18
Café Negrito, 7
Carmen Sui Generis, 5
Circus, 3
Finnegan's, 9
Fox Congo, 6
Jimmy Glass, 4
Rumbo 144, 1
Venial, 10

ON THE MENU

RICE IS NICE

Paella is known throughout the world as a quintessentially Spanish dish, but any *valenciano* can tell you where it started—here. From the region's rice fields to the factories where it is carefully processed to the tables of the best restaurants, rice is the spice of life in Valencia. The techniques of preparation have been perfected for years by rice cultivators, processors, and *paelleros* (traditionally male). And don't call it all *paella;* there are hundreds of different rice dishes, each different in ingredients and preparation.

Paella, for example, is the Valenciano word for the typical pan in which the rice *paella* dish (originally called *arroz en paella*) is cooked. *Arroz a banda,* similar to *paella,* is traditionally a more humble dish enjoyed by fishermen, where the fish is cooked separately (*a banda*) from the rice, saffron, garlic, and tomato.

If you prefer your rice baked, try *arroz al horno,* very popular in la Ribera and la Huerta for its mixes of meats and vegetables and slightly less complicated recipe. If you don't prefer rice at all, try *fideuá,* the cousin of *paella,* made with noodles instead of rice. Whichever you choose, you are certain not to be disappointed, so long as you go for the authentic version. Avoid the more touristy restaurants bearing pictures of pre-made *paellas* on sandwich boards; what you see is what you get, and it's not the real thing.

Late-Night Pharmacy: Rotates daily. Check listing in the local paper *Levante* (€0.80) or check the *farmacias de guardia* schedule posted outside any pharmacy.

Hospital: Hospital Clínico Universitario, Av. Blasco Ibáñez, 17 (☎963 86 26 00), at the corner of C. Dr. Ferrer. Take bus #41, 71, or 81 from Pl. del Ajuntament.

Internet Access:

Fundación Bancaixa, Pl. Tetuán, 23, 5th fl. (☎963 87 58 64). Free 1hr. per day on somewhat slow computers. Passport or student ID required. Open M-F 9am-2pm and 4-9pm, Sa 9am-2pm.

Confederación, C. de Ribera, 8 (☎963 94 03 11). 46 ultramodern computers. €3 per hr.

Ono, C. San Vicente Mártir, 22 (☎963 28 19 02). €1.80 buys you 45min. 9am-2pm. 30min. 2-10pm, or 1hr. 10pm-1am. Open M-Sa 9am-1am, Su 10am-1am.

Post Office: Pl. del Ajuntament, 24 (☎963 51 67 50). Open M-F 8:30am-8:30pm, Sa 9:30am-2pm. **Postal Code:** 46080.

ACCOMMODATIONS

Hostels may clutter Valencia's streets, but during weekends, especially in summer, finding a room isn't always easy—it's best to call in advance. Reservations are especially necessary during the *papier-mâché* orgy of *Las Fallas* (Mar. 12-19). The best deals cluster around **Plaça del Ajuntament** and **Plaça del Mercat.**

NEAR PLAÇA DEL AJUNTAMENT

Pensión Paris, C. Salvá, 12 (☎963 52 67 66). Thirteen spotless rooms with balconies. Pastel walls and sunny rooms give an inviting, homey feel. Singles €18; doubles €27, with shower €30; triples €39/€43. ❷

Hostal-Residencia El Cid, C. Cerrajeros, 13 (☎/fax 963 92 23 23). Room quality varies from TVs and A/C to just a fan. Pretty hallways with Spanish floral tiles and windows. Singles €12; doubles €24, with shower €32, with bath €34-36. AmEx/MC/V. ❶

Hostal Alicante, C. de Ribera, 8 (☎963 51 22 96). As central as it gets, clean and well-lit, with firm beds. Hugely popular with backpackers. Singles €20, with bath and A/C €28; doubles €29/€37. MC/V. ❷

Hostal-Residencia Universal, C. las Barcas, 5 (☎963 51 53 84). Clean rooms, large windows, new furniture, and quilted bedspreads make up for the hallway showers. Singles €17; doubles €26, with shower €29; triples €37. ❷

NEAR PLAÇA DEL MERCAT

■ **Home Youth Hostel,** C. Lonja, 4 (☎963 91 62 29). Comfy lounge with multicolored walls and hanging mobiles is a hopping social center. The perks: beer in the vending machine, free kitchen use, large collection of DVDs. The flaw: rooms sizzle in summer. Coed hall baths with showers. Internet €0.50 for 15min. Laundry service €5.50 for wash and dry. Bike rental €8 per day; €30 deposit. Dorms €14; singles €21; doubles €32; triples €48; quads €64. **Second location,** C. Cadirers, 11 (☎963 92 40 63; www.likeathome.net), a block away. Rooms €120-150 per month. ❷/❶

Hostal Antigua Morellana, C. En Bou, 2 (☎/fax 963 91 57 73). Brightly lit, quiet, and comfortable rooms with bath, A/C, TV, and phone. Shining wood furniture and classic, crimson bed linens and drapes. Caters to an older crowd. Singles €30; doubles €45. ❸

Hostal El Rincón, C. Carda, 11 (☎963 91 79 98). Bright hallways lead to bare-walled but clean rooms. Singles €10, with bath €13; doubles €18/€24. MC/V. ❶

NEAR THE BEACH

Alberg Colegio "La Paz" (HI), Av. del Port, 69 (☎963 69 01 52), nearly halfway between the city and the port. Take bus #19 from Pl. del Ajuntament (next to Citibank) and get off at the 8th stop on Av. del Porto. 2-4 people and a bathroom in every room. Breakfast included. Sheets €3. Curfew 3am. Reception 3pm-2am. Open July-Sept. 15. Dorms €10, over 26 €12. ❶

🍴 FOOD

Paella may be the most famous, but it is actually just one of 200 Valencian rice dishes. Other specialties include *arroz a banda* (rice and fish with garlic, onion, tomatoes, and saffron), *all i pebre* (eels fried in oil, paprika, and garlic), *fideua* (*paella* with noodles instead of rice), and *sepia con salsa verd* (cuttlefish with garlic and parsley). Valencia's restaurants are generally cheap and perfect for people on the run. Bushels of fresh fish, meat, and fruit are sold at the **Mercat Central,** on Pl. del Mercat (open M-Sa 7am-3pm). For **groceries,** stop by **El Corte Inglés.**

■ **El Rall,** C. Tundidores, 2 (☎963 92 20 90), between the Lonja and Pl. Negrito. Excellent *paella* (€7.50-10 per person, 2 person minimum) and other seafood dishes served outdoors in a small, pleasant square. Open daily 1-4pm and 8-11pm. ❷

La Lluna (☎963 92 21 46), C. Sant Ramón. A veggie restaurant to moon over. Funky setting created by hanging lampshades, tiled walls, and homestyle tablecloths. Serves a 4-course *menú* (€5.75) weekday afternoons. Entrees €3.50-4. Open M-Sa 1:30-3:30pm and 9-11:30pm. ❶

La Pappardella, C. Bordadores, 5 (☎963 91 89 15). Two floors of pasta bliss. Vast selection of dishes ranging from basic spaghetti, oil, and garlic to exotic pastas complemented by fresh vegetables, meats, and seafood (€5-8). *Menú* €8. Open daily 2-4pm and 9pm-midnight. ❶

Restaurante Pruvi Hoy Paella, C. Cerrajeros, 3. Good, homestyle *paella* served in a no-frills setting. *Menu del día* €8. Open daily 1:30-4pm and 8-11pm. ❷

👁 SIGHTS

Touring Valencia on foot is a good test of stamina. Most of the sights line the Turia riverbed or cluster near Pl. de la Reina, which is linked to Pl. Ayuntamento by C. Sant Vicente Mártir. EMT bus #5, dubbed the **Bus Turístic** (☎963 52 83 99), makes a loop around the old town sights (€1).

■ **CIUDAD DE LAS ARTES Y LAS CIENCIAS.** Modern, airy, and thoroughly fascinating, Valencia's latest urban creation dedicated to the arts and sciences has raised quite a stir. Built on the dried-up bed of the Río Turia, this mini-city has already become the fourth biggest tourist destination in Spain. The complex is divided into four large attractions, all surrounding a vast reflecting pool. Designed by renowned Spanish architect Santiago Calatrava, the complex is nothing short of stunning. Even the parking garage is a work of art, with a garden terrace, **L'Umbracle**, on the roof. **L'Hemisfèric**, a sleek glass and steel capsule, wows the eyes with its IMAX theater, laser shows, and planetarium, while **L'Oceanogràfic** recreates diverse aquatic environments in an underground water-world. The enormous **Palau de les Arts**, which is scheduled to be completed by 2004, will house stages for opera, theater, and dance. The **Museu de Les Ciencies Príncipe Felipe,** the gleaming centerpiece, is packed with students and tourists learning through hands-on exhibits on science and technology. Visitors come as much for the building's extraordinary design as for the museum itself. *(Bus #35 runs from Pl. Ayuntamento.* ☎ *902 10 00 31; www.cac.es. Daily IMAX shows €6.60; M-F children and students €4.80. Museum open June 15-Sept. 15 daily 10am-9pm; Sept. 16-June 14 M-F and Su 10am-8pm, Sa 10am-9pm. €6, M-F children and students €4.21. L'Oceanogràfic open June 21-Sept. 7 daily 10am-midnight; Mar 15-June 20 and Sept. 8-Oct. 12 M-F 10am-8pm, Sa and Su 10am-10pm; Jan. 1-Mar. 14 and Oct. 13-Dec. 31 M-F 10am-6pm, Sa-Su 10am-8pm.)*

■ **CATEDRAL.** Begun in the 13th century and completed in 1482, this magnificent cathedral is the region's most impressive building. The three different entrances display a melange of Romanesque, Gothic, and Baroque architectural styles. Incredible views of Valencia's skyline can be seen from atop the **Miguelete** (the cathedral tower). French novelist Victor Hugo once counted 300 bell towers in the city from this vantage point. The interior is lined with altars, each with its own design and character. The **Museu de la Catedral** squeezes a great many treasures into three tiny rooms—one for the Gothic period, one for the Renaissance, and one Mannerist. Check out the overwrought tabernacle made from 1200kg of gold, silver, platinum, emeralds, and sapphires, plus a Holy Grail, two Goyas, and the Crucifijo de Marfil statues, which depict "man's passions." *(Pl. de la Reina. Cathedral* ☎ *963 91 01 89. Open daily 7:30am-1pm and 4:30-8:30pm. Closes earlier in winter. Free. Tower open daily 10am-1pm and 4:30-7pm. €1.20. Museum* ☎ *963 91 81 27. Open year-round daily 10am-1pm, Mar.-Nov. M-Sa 10am-1pm and 4:30-6pm. €1.20.)*

MUSEU PROVINCIAL DE BELLES ARTES. One of Valencia's finer attractions, this museum features a wide array of paintings. One floor is dedicated to 14th- to 16th-century Valencian art and another to more recent works. The museum has been named one of Spain's premier art galleries. The collection features El Greco's *San Juan Bautista*, Velázquez's self-portrait, Ribera's *Santa Teresa*, and a slew of Goyas. Check out the sculpture pavilion. *(C. Sant Pío V, near the Jardines del Real.* ☎ *963 60 57 93. Open Tu-Sa 10am-8pm. Free.)*

INSTITUT VALENCIÀ D'ART MODERN (IVAM). See everything from classic avant-garde to 1970s clash. IVAM is also home to a collection of abstract works by 20th-century sculptor Julio González, among others. The rotating temporary exhibits are extremely popular. *(C. Guillém de Castro, 118, west across the riverbed. Take bus #5.* ☎ *963 86 30 00. Open Tu-Su 10am-10pm. €2.10, students €1.05; Su free.)*

PARKS. Manicured parks surround the city center. Horticulturists will marvel at the **Jardín Botànic**, a university-maintained garden that cultivates 43,000 plants of 300 international species. *(C. Quart, 80, on the western end of Río Turia near Gran Vía Fernando el Católico.* ☎ *963 91 16 57. Open Tu-Su 10am-9pm, closes earlier in winter. €0.30.)*

One block farther, a series of well-kept recreation areas lines the banks and bed of the Río Turia. Next to the Museu Provincial de Belles Artes, off C. Sant Pío V, is the popular **Jardines del Real,** home to ponds, caged birds, fountains, and greenhouses.

OTHER SIGHTS. The elliptical **Basílica Virgen dels Desamparats** houses a resplendent golden altar. *(Open for Mass M-F 7am-2pm and 5-9pm, Su 7:30am-2:30pm and 5-9:30pm. Free.)* The old **Lonja de la Seda (Silk Exchange)** is one of the foremost examples of Valencian Gothic architecture and a testament to Valencia's prominence in the medieval silk trade. *(Pl. del Mercat. ☎ 963 52 54 78. Open Tu-Sa 9:15am-2pm and 5:30-9pm, Su 9am-1:30pm. Free.)*

FESTIVALS

Valencia's most famous festival is **Las Fallas,** March 12-19. During **Semana Santa** a few weeks later, monks clog the streets enacting Biblical scenes, and children perform the miracle plays of St. Vicent Ferrer. **Corpus Cristi** follows soon after with its display of *rocas* (huge carriages symbolizing Biblical mysteries). The **Festiu de Juliol** (Festival of July) brings fireworks, riverside concerts, bullfights, and a *batalla dels flors*—a violet skirmish in which flowers are tossed between parade-goers and girls on passing floats.

NIGHTLIFE

Use your *siesta* wisely—Valencia's nightlife requires drinking and dancing until sunrise. Bars and pubs in **El Carme,** just beyond the market, start up at 11:30pm. Follow Pl. del Mercat and C. Bolsería (bearing right) to Pl. Tossal, where outdoor terraces, upbeat music, and *agua de Valencia* (orange juice, champagne, and vodka) energize the masses. Many bars can also be found along **Calle Caballeros** in El Carme. One of the most popular establishments here is **Carmen Sui Generis,** C. Caballeros, 38, an upscale lounge with eclectic decor and chic clientele set in an 18th-century palace. (☎ 963 92 52 73. Cocktails €5-6. Open W-Sa 11pm-3am.) Popular with locals is **Café Negrito,** Pl. del Negrito, 1, off C. Caballeros, a loud bar and cafe which prides itself on its *agua de Valencia* (€6; large €21) and outdoor tables. (☎ 963 91 42 33. Open daily 10pm-3am.) Fans of house music flock to **Circus,** C. Alta, 11, a hip bar with brightly painted walls and disco balls. (☎ 963 91 38 16. Beer €2.50-4.50. Open daily 8pm-3am.) An older crowd fills the dark, spacious bar **Fox Congo,** C. Caballeros, 35, but later in the evening the crowd is more mixed and favors dancing. (☎ 963 92 55 27. Beer €3.60; mixed drinks €5.40. Open daily 7pm-3:30am.) Sip martinis (€4-6) to the soothing sounds of classic jazz at **Jimmy Glass,** an ultra-cool bar on C. Baja, 28, not far from Circus. American students frequent **Finnegan's,** at Pl. de la Reina, 19, an Irish pub in front of the cathedral. (☎ 963 91 05 03. Beer €3.10. Open M-Th 12:30pm-1am, F-Su 12:30pm-3am.)

Discos, which normally don't draw a crowd until at least 3am, dominate the university area, particularly on **Avinguda Blasco Ibáñez. Rumbo 144,** Av. Blasco Ibáñez, 144, spins Spanish pop and house and is popular among local students and foreigners alike. (☎ 963 71 00 25. Cover €9. Open Th-Sa midnight-7am.) There are a few smaller discos in El Carme, most of which are popular with both gay and straight patrons. A lively and popular gay club is **Venial,** C. Quart, 34 (☎ 963 91 73 56), by the Jardín Botànic. In summer, some of the best places to be seen are the outdoor discos at Platja de Malvarrosa. (Open daily 6pm-7:30am. Cover Th €6, F-Sa €10.) **Caballito de Mar,** C. Eugenio Viñes, 22 (☎ 963 71 07 63), is the most popular and heats up with a psychedelic tunnel and huge outdoor deck. For more info, consult the *Qué y Dónde* weekly magazine (€1) or the weekly entertainment supplement, *La Cartelera* (€0.75), both available at newsstands.

◪ BEACHES

Sand-seekers can join the topless by bouncing down to the expansive and packed beaches on Valencia's coast. The sand and water quality are less than spectacular, but the blistering heat converts everyone into sea-lovers. The most popular beaches are **Las Arenas** and **Malvarrosa,** connected by a bustling boardwalk. Buses #20, 21, 22, and 23 all pass by the sands. Equally crowded but more attractive is **Salér,** a pine-bordered strand 14km from the city that divides a lagoon from the sea. Cafeterias and snack bars line the shore. **Autobuses Buñol** (☎963 49 14 25) go to Salér (on the way to El Perello) from the intersection of Gran Vía de Germanías and C. Sueca. To get to the bus stop, exit the train station and take the street to the right (between the station and the bullring) to Gran Vía de Germanías. The bus stop is one block down (25min., every 30min. 7am-10pm, €0.90).

◪ DAYTRIPS FROM VALENCIA

SAGUNTO (SAGUNT)

Cercanías trains (☎962 66 07 28) from Valencia (C-6 line) stop in Sagunto (30min.; M-F 37 per day 6:10am-10:30pm, Sa-Su 15 per day 7:20am-10:30pm; €2.10), as do ALSA buses (☎964 66 18 50; 45min., daily every 30min. 7am-10:30pm, €2).

The residents of Sagunto are thought to be the most courageous in Spain. This reputation dates back to the 3rd century BC, when the citizens of Phoenician-controlled Sagunto (then called Saguntum) held out for an eight-month siege by Hannibal's Carthaginians. Some sources say that on the brink of annihilation, Sagunto's women, children, and elderly threw themselves into a burning furnace; others insist that the residents chose starvation over defeat.

The architectural medley of Sagunto's monuments reflects a long list of conquering forces. The highlight of the old town is its refurbished **medieval castle,** declared a national monument in 1931. (Open June-Sept. Tu-Sa 10am-8pm, Su 10am-2pm; Oct.-May Tu-Sa 10am-2pm and 4-6pm, Su 10am-2pm. Free.) Along the way into town is the **Teatro Romano,** which has survived a controversial restoration process to become an impressive modern performance stage. It is built entirely on the skeleton of the original Roman structure. Ask at the **tourist office** in Pl. Cronisto Chabret, at the far end from the Ayuntamiento, for a list of performances. (☎962 66 22 13; www.sagunt.com/turismo. Open M 10am-2pm and 5-8pm, Tu-Th 9am-2pm and 4-8pm, F 9am-2pm and 4-6:30pm, Sa 8:45am-1:45pm, Su 10am-2pm.) By the port (4km from the town center), Sagunto's **beaches** attract summer travelers. **Puerto de Sagunto** bears the EU's *bandera azul.* **Buses** to the beaches leave from Av. Santos Patronos next to the tourist office (every 30min. 7am-9:30pm, €0.60).

L'ALBUFERA

The park is a 40min. bus ride (15km) from Valencia. To catch the return bus, walk with your back to the lagoon and cross the bridge on your right.

Spain's largest lagoon, L'Albufera, and the surrounding **Parc Natural de L'Albufera** are a nature lover's paradise. Trails for biking and hiking ring the lake (6km in diameter) while small fishing boats hide amid tall wetland reeds. L'Albufera, one of the wettest regions on the Iberian peninsula, is a prime spot for bird watching—over 250 migrant species make temporary camp along its shores. Ask at a Valencia tourist office (see p. 334) for information on boat tours and cultural excursions.

JÁTIVA (XÀTIVA)

Trains are the best way to get in and out of Játiva. RENFE (☎963 52 02 02) runs from Valencia to Játiva (1hr., every 30min. 6am-10pm, €2.55). From Játiva, trains run to Valencia (6am-10pm) and Alicante (1½hr., 3 per day, €17). To reach the old village from the train station, walk straight up Baixada de l'Estació and turn left at its end.

Once the second most populous city in Valencia, Játiva, a mecca of palaces and churches, was burned to the ground by Felipe V in the 18th century. Today it is simply a quiet town with little to offer other than its impressive castle and its annual festival. Held since 1250, Játiva's **Fira festival** storms the city August 15-20 with live music, bullfights, and pulling (tug-of-war) contests. **Alameda de Jaume I** divides the town into the new and the old villages, starting from the foot of a hill topped by an awe-inspiring castle. The ■**castle** above has two sections: the **castell machor**, on the right as you enter, and the pre-Roman **castell chicotet.** The former, used from the 13th through the 16th century, bears the scars of siege and earthquake. Its vaulted **prison** has held some famous wrongdoers, including Fernando el Católico and the Comte d'Urgell, would-be usurper of the Aragonese throne. The Comte is now buried in its chapel. To get there, it's a 30min. walk uphill. A tourist train chugs up to the castle at 12:30 and 4:30pm. (Open in summer Tu-Su 10am-7pm; in winter Tu-Su 10am-6pm. €1.50, students and seniors €0.75.) The **tourist office,** Alameda Jaume I, 50, is across from the Ayuntamiento. (☎962 27 33 46. English spoken. Open June 15-Sept. 15 Tu-F 10am-2:30pm and 5-7pm, Sa-Su 10am-2pm; Sept. 16-June 14 Tu-F 9am-2pm and 4-6pm, Sa-Su 10am-2pm.)

MORELLA   ☎964

Rising majestically above the fertile valley below, the medieval fortress town of Morella (pop. 2000), located in the northernmost extremes of the Comunitat Valenciana, is an isolated gem for the traveler. With picturesque cobblestone streets, impressive medieval walls, and a castle crowning its highest point, the town offers soothing vistas for those who wish to get away from the hustle and bustle of Barcelona or the Costa Blanca. Tourists are only the latest in a long line of people who have been drawn to Morella, as the town has also hosted Celts, Romans, and Moors at various times throughout its history.

▐▋ TRANSPORTATION & PRACTICAL INFORMATION. Morella is hard to reach. Most visitors arrive via Valencia, though the city is also accessible from Barcelona. Travelers must make a connection at **Castelló,** on the **Cercanías train** line from Valencia (1hr.; M-F 36 per day 6:10am-10:30pm, €3.15; Sa-Su 15 per day 7:20am-10:30pm, €3.30). From Barcelona, the **RENFE** Mediterranean goes to Castelló (2½hr., 17 per day 8am-9pm, €14-23). **Autos Mediterráneo** (☎964 22 00 54 or 22 05 36) departs from the bus stop outside of Castelló's train station for **Morella** (2½hr.; M-F 2 per day 7:30am and 3:45pm, Sa 1 per day 3:45pm; returns M-F 2 per day 7:30am, 4pm, Sa 1 per day 4pm; €7.20). The bus from Castelló doesn't originate at the bus stop, however, and stops there only briefly, so keep an eye out for it. The return bus makes only one stop in Morella. Morella's **tourist office,** Pl. San Miguel, s/n, is right by Pta. de San Miguel, the enormous arched entrance to the city. (☎964 17 30 32; www.morella.net. Open July-Aug. M-Sa 10am-2pm and 4-7pm, Su 10am-2pm; Sept.-June Tu-Sa 10am-2pm and 4-6pm.) In an **emergency,** dial ☎112. For **medical assistance,** call ☎964 16 09 62.

▐▋ ACCOMMODATIONS & FOOD. Once you pass through the Gothic archways of Morella, you may never want to leave. ■**Hostal La Muralla ❷,** C. Muralla, 12, has rooms with TV and private bath. (☎964 16 02 43. Breakfast €2.50. Singles €21.50; doubles €31. MC/V.) Live royally (on budget) at **Hostal El Cid ❸,** Portal Sant Mateu, 3, 1 block to the right of the bus stop when facing the city wall. Gigantic rooms come with colorful plaid bedspreads, TV, phone, and bathtub; some have balconies. (☎964 16 01 25. Singles €29-37; doubles €38-69. V.) Those seeking a touch of elegance will find it in the comfortable rooms of **Hotel Cardenal Ram ❸,** Cuesta Suner, 1, built in a 15th-century palace at the end of the colonnade on C. Don Blasco de Alagón. All rooms have large bath, TV, phone, and heat. (☎964 17 30 85. Singles €35; doubles €55.)

BONFIRE OF THE EFFIGIES

Everyone knows that Spain loves a party. But during the rollicking *Festival de Sant Joan* (June 20-29), Alicante takes it to the next level. Only Pamplona's running of the bulls even comes close. For 75 years, the city has ushered in the summer with over a week of parades, parties, and papiér-maché. The festival arose from an old tradition of burning unusable materials on the summer solstice; starting in 1928 the festivities were expanded to encompass the feast day of Saint John the Baptist, and the burning of unusable materials became the burning of satiric effigies (*fogueres* or *hogueras*, depending on the dialect), and all-around merrymaking.

The first 5 days of the festival are without a doubt the core of the celebration. On the evening of the 19th, streets are blocked off and about 180 huge, colorful *fogueres* are erected throughout the city. Strings of lights in intricate patterns are hung from lampposts and tented *racós* and *barracas* (dancing areas and street bars) fill the streets. During the fiesta, the city is more packed at 5am than 5pm as young and old gather from midnight until dawn, dancing and drinking in unrestrained outdoor revelry—for one week straight.

But daylight brings no rest: fireworks explode daily at 2pm, children set off their own, locals and visitors watch spectacular street

The town's gourmet cuisine is filled with *trufas* dug up from under the local turf. Specialties include *paté de trufas* and *cordero relleno trufado*. Eating out is somewhat pricy, and options are limited—most eateries are located on shop-lined C. Don Blasco de Alagón, Morella's main street. **Restaurante Cardenal Ram ❷,** Cuesta Suner, 1, in the hotel, serves delicious local favorites, including hen, quail, rabbit, and truffle-stuffed lamb (€8-13), in a beautiful dining room with views of the countryside. (☎964 17 30 85. *Menú* €12-25. Open Tu-Sa 1:30-4pm and 8:30-10:15pm. MC/V.) Those looking to escape the truffle madness run to **Restaurante Lola ❶,** C. Blasco de Alagón, 21, for the best Italian cuisine in town. (☎964 16 03 87. Entrees €4.80-9.20. *Menú* €10. Open M-Sa noon-4:30pm and 8:30pm-2am.)

◙ **SIGHTS.** Perched atop a massive rock, the ▨**Castell de Morella** dazzles even the most seasoned of castle-goers. Celts, Romans, and Moors have all defended Morella's walls as their own. El Cid stormed the summit in 1084, and Don Blasco de Alagón took the town in the name of Jaume I in 1232. Civil wars in the 19th century and an internal explosion have damaged the castle, but the resulting craters only add to the intrigue. Artillery walls surround the exterior, with openings just wide enough for the sights of battling archers or the lens of a camera. Inspect the **Cadro guardhouse** and the **Catxo dungeon,** where the prince of Viana was imprisoned in the 15th century. (☎964 17 31 28. Entrance on C. Hospital, uphill from the basilica and through the Convento de San Francisco. Open June-Sept. 9:30am-7:30pm; Oct.-May 10am-6:30pm. €1.80, students €1.20.) In Pl. Arciprestal, on the way to the castle, the ceiling of Gothic **Basílica Santa María la Mayor** hovers over a winding stairwell, a large organ, and the ghostly statue of Nuestra Señora de la Asunción. Bracketed by golden chandeliers, the altar is almost as breathtaking as the basilica's original 14th-century stained glass windows. (Open June-Aug. Tu-Su 11am-2pm and 4-7pm; Sept.-May noon-2pm and 4-6pm. Mass M-F 7pm; Sa 8:15pm; Su 10am, 5, 6:30pm. Basilica free. Museum €0.90.) Exit the city from Pta. de San Miguel, turn left, and walk 5min. to the remnants of the Gothic **aqueduct.** Knights, jesters, minstrels, and tourists flock to the town on the first weekend in July for the **Medieval Fair.** Activities include concerts, medieval banquets, and craft shows. Ask the tourist office for more information.

COSTA BLANCA

You could spend a lifetime touring the charming resort towns of the Costa Blanca. The "white coast" that extends from Dénia through Calpe to Alicante takes its name from the fine white sand of its shores. A varied terrain of hills blanketed with cherry blossoms, jagged mountains, lush pine-covered slopes, and natural lagoons surrounds densely populated coastal towns. Altea, Calpe, Dénia, and especially Jávea offer relief from the disco droves that energize Alicante and Benidorm, although even these towns are not tourist-free.

COASTAL TRANSPORTATION

TRAINS. Ferrocarrils de la Generalitat Valenciana (☎965 92 02 02, in Alicante 26 27 31) hits almost every town and beach along the coast with its Alicante-Dénia line. Trains run from Alicante to: **Altea** (1½hr., every hr. 6am-9pm except noon, €3.80); **Benidorm** (1hr., every hr. 6am-9pm, €3.10); **Calpe** (1¾hr., 8 per day 6am-9pm, €4.75); **Dénia** (2¼hr., 8 per day 6am-9pm, €6.85). From Dénia and Calpe, trains return to **Alicante** every 2hr. (6:25am-7:25pm), while from Altea and Benidorm trains depart every hr. (6:24am-10:24pm). **Trensnochador** (☎965 26 22 33), the night train from Alicante, runs July-Sept. (Su-Th 4 per night to Altea and Benidorm, 3 per night to Calpe and Dénia; 10:20pm-6am; F-Sa every hr. to Altea and Benidorm, 3 per night to Calpe and Dénia) to **Altea, Benidorm, Calpe,** and **Dénia.**

BUSES. Buses are the easiest and most cost-efficient way to get around the Costa Blanca. **ALSA** (☎902 42 22 42) runs between Alicante and Valencia, stopping in towns along the Costa Blanca. From **Valencia** buses run to: **Alicante** (2-4hr., 12-15 per day 4:45am-10:45pm, €13-15); **Benidorm** (4hr., 15-18 per day 4:45am-9:45pm, €11.55); **Calpe/Altea** (3-4½hr., 8-10 per day 6am-5pm, €9.35-10.55); **Dénia** (1hr., 11-12 per day 5:15am-10:45pm, €4.75); **Gandía** (1hr., 9-11 per day 4:45am-9:45pm, €5.05); **Jávea** (2-3hr., 6 per day 6:30am-9:45pm, €8.30). From **Alicante** buses run to: **Altea** (1½hr., 11 per day 6:30am-8pm, €3.80); **Benidorm** (1hr., 20 per day 6am-10pm, €3.15); **Calpe** (1½hr., 11 per day 6:30am-8pm, €5.95); **Dénia** (2½hr., 10 per day 6am-8pm, €7.90); **Jávea** (2½hr., 6 per day 8am-9pm, €7.05); **Valencia** (4-4½ hr., 10 per day 6:30am-6pm, €13-15).

processions, and traditional music fills the air all afternoon. In the early evening, visitors are treated to the Bellesa del Foc (Beauty Queen of Fire) competion.

And yet it continues. The festival reaches a fever pitch on the evening of Sant Joan's feast day (June 24). At midnight, during an extensive fireworks display, the effigies are set ablaze in a ceremony known as *la Cremá* (the burning). Firefighters then proceed to soak everyone nearby during *la Banyá* (the bath) and the party continues until dawn—wet.

Just when you thought *valencianos* couldn't party a minute longer, fireworks competitions break out on the beach from the 25th-29th and a medieval market is set up in the city center. While there's certainly a fair amount of *fiesta* to be had in the later days, the first half of the week is an unparalleled, unforgettable spectacle not to be missed. Make reservations well in advance, as the city swells with visitors starting as early as the week before the festival.

On March 12-19, Valencia goes at it again when *Las Fallas* grips the city. The city explodes with festivity, including parades, bullfights, fireworks, and street dancing. Neighborhoods compete to build the most elaborate satirical *papier-mâché* effigy; over 300 such enormous *ninots* spring up in the streets. On the final day—*la nit del foc* (fire night)—Valencians burn all the *ninots* simultaneously in one last, clamorous inferno meant to bring luck for the agricultural season and exorcize the social ills satirized by the *papier-mâché* giants.

ALICANTE (ALACANT)   ☎965

A mural in Alicante's bus station proclaims "Bienvenido seas, viajero: Alicante te ofrece sosiego y luz radiante" (May you be welcome, traveler: Alicante offers you peace and radiant light). Peace might not always be found in the vibrant streets of Alicante (pop. 285,000), as ETA set off a bomb in a hotel here in summer 2003, but radiance is never lacking. While undoubtedly a firmly Spanish city, Alicante has an extra sparkle to it that rivals any other locale and possesses an energy uniquely its own. The residents are friendlier, the nightlife is livelier (particularly during the explosive festival de Sant Joan), and even the beaches seem sunnier. A manageable city in size and scope, Alicante feels unlike its comrades in every way and is a city no traveler should miss.

⌐ TRANSPORTATION

Flights: Aeroport Internacional El Altet (☎966 91 90 00), 11km from town. **Iberia** (24hr. ☎902 40 05 00) and **Air Europa** (☎902 24 00 42) have daily flights to Madrid, Barcelona, and the Balearic Islands, among other destinations. **Alcoyana** (☎965 16 79 11) bus C-6 runs to the airport from Pl. Luceros (every 40min., €0.85).

Trains: RENFE, Estación Término (☎902 24 02 02), on Av. de Salamanca. Info open daily 7am-midnight. To: **Barcelona** (4½-6hr., 9 per day 6:55am-6:30pm, €43-67); **Elche** (30min., every hr. 6:05am-10:05pm, €1.60); **Madrid** (4hr., 9 per day 7am-8pm, €35.54); **Murcia** (1½hr., every hr. 6:05am-10:05pm, €3.65); **Valencia** (1½hr., 10 per day 6:55am-8:20pm, €8.58-31.80). **Ferrocarriles de la Generalitat Valenciana,** Estació Marina, Av. Villajoyosa, 2 (☎965 26 27 31). Service along the **Costa Blanca.** In summer the **Trensnochador** (night trains; ☎965 26 27 31) runs to **beaches** near Alicante, including **Altea** and **Benidorm,** with some continuing to **Dénia** (July-Aug. F-Sa every hr. 9pm-5am, Su-Th 4 per night 9pm-5am; €0.90-4.20).

Buses: C. Portugal, 17 (☎965 13 07 00). Any right turn runs directly to the waterfront. **ALSA** (☎902 42 22 42) to: **Altea** (1hr., 9 per day 7am-8pm, €3.80); **Barcelona** (7hr., 13 per day 1am-10:30pm, €33.58); **Calpe** (1½hr., 6-10 per day 6:30am-7:30pm, €5.50); **Dénia** (2½hr., 10 per day 12am-8pm, €7.90); **Granada** (6hr., 9 per day 2:20am-11:59pm, €22.82); **Jávea** (2hr., 5 per day 9am-8pm, €7.05); **Madrid** (5hr., 9 per day 8am-midnight, €22.44); **Málaga** (8hr., 7 per day 2:20am-11:59pm, €28); **Sevilla** (10hr., 3 per day 10:45am-11:45pm, €39.76); **Valencia** (2½hr., 8-10 per day 7am-9pm, €14.85). **Mollá** (☎965 13 08 51) to **Elche** (30min.; M-F 2 per hr. 7am-10pm, Sa every hr. 8am-10pm, Su 8 per day 9am-9:30pm; €1.55).

Ferries: Balearia Eurolines Maritimes (☎902 16 01 80) departs from nearby **Dénia.**

Taxis: Teletaxi ☎965 25 25 11.

Public Transportation: TAM (☎965 14 09 36). Buses #21 and 22 run from the train station in Alicante to Playa San Juan. €0.80.

◢▊ 🛈 ORIENTATION & PRACTICAL INFORMATION

Originating at the train station, **Avenida de la Estación** becomes **Avenida Alfonso X El Sabio** after passing through Pl. Luceros. **Explanada d'Espanya** stretches along the waterfront between Rbla. Méndez Nuñez and Av. Federico Soto; the two reach back up to Av. Alfonso X El Sabio.

Tourist Office: Municipal office, C. Portugal, 17 (☎965 92 98 02). English spoken. Open M-Sa 9am-2pm and 4-8pm. **Regional office,** Rbla. de Méndez Núñez, 23 (☎965 20 00 00). English spoken. Open June-Aug. M-F 10am-8pm; Sept.-May M-F 10am-7pm, Sa 10am-2pm and 3-7pm. **Airport branch** open Tu-Sa 10am-2pm and 5-8pm.

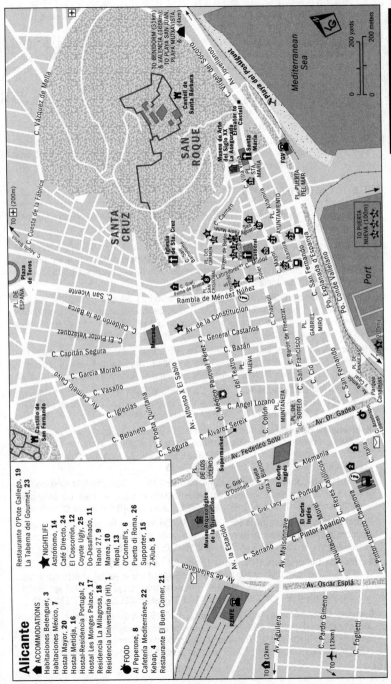

VALENCIA &
MURCIA

Alicante

▲ ACCOMMODATIONS
Habitaciones Belenguer, **3**
Habitaciones México, **7**
Hostal Mayor, **20**
Hostal Metídja, **16**
Hostal-Residencia Portugal, **2**
Hostal Les Monges Palace, **17**
Residencia La Milagrosa, **18**
Residencia Universitaria (HI), **1**

🍽 FOOD
Al Peperone, **8**
Cafetería Mediterráneo, **22**
Kebap, **4**
Restaurante El Buen Comer, **21**
Restaurante O'Pote Gallego, **19**
La Taberna del Gourmet, **23**

★ NIGHTLIFE
Astrónomo, **14**
Café Directo, **24**
El Coscorrón, **12**
Coyote Ugly, **25**
Do-Desafinado, **11**
Hanoi 27, **9**
Marea, **10**
Nepal, **13**
O'Connell's, **6**
Puerto di Roma, **26**
Supporter, **15**
Z-Klub, **5**

Budget Travel: TIVE, Pl. San Cristóbal, 8 (☎965 21 16 86). ISIC €4.20. HI card €10.80. Open M-F 9am-1:30pm and 5-8pm.

Luggage Storage: Bus station (€2-3.80 per bag; open M-Sa 8am-9:30pm, Su 10am-1pm and 3:45-7pm) and **train station** (€2.40 per bag; open daily 7am-midnight).

Emergency: ☎112. **Police:** Comisaría, C. Médico Pascual Pérez, 27 (☎965 10 72 00).

Hospital: Hospital General, C. Maestro Alonzo, 109 (☎965 93 83 00).

Internet Access: Fundación BanCaja, Rbla. de Méndez Núñez, 4, 2nd fl. 1hr. free with ISIC. Open M-F 10am-2pm and 5-9pm, Sa 9am-2pm. **Yazzgo,** Explanada d'Espanya, 3. €2.40 per hr., 5hr. for €6. Open M-Sa 8am-11pm, Su 9am-11pm.

Post Office: Corner of C. Arzobispo Loaces and C. Alemania (☎965 21 99 84). Open M-F 8:30am-8:30pm, Sa 9:30am-2pm. **Branch,** Bono Guarner, 2 (☎965 22 78 71), next to the train station. Open M-F 8:30am-8:30pm, Sa 9:30am-1pm. **Postal Code:** 03070.

ACCOMMODATIONS

Although hostels seem to be everywhere, good accommodations require an early arrival or a reservation, especially during the *Festival de Sant Joan*

Habitaciones México, C. General Primo de Rivera, 10 (☎965 20 93 07), offers small but cozy rooms. Wonderful owners and backpacker clientele make for a lively, comfortable stay. Free Internet access and kitchen use. Laundry €6. Singles €12-15; doubles €27, with bath €33; triples €33/€36. ❶

Hostal Les Monges Palace, C. San Agustín, 4 (☎965 21 50 46). Excellent rooms with TVs, baths, and paintings. Some have A/C/, jacuzzis, and saunas, but you'll pay more. Internet access available in rooms or at reception (€3 per hr.). Reception 24hr. Parking €8 per day. Singles €24-35; doubles €27-39; triples €44-60. MC/V. ❷

Residencia La Milagrosa, C. Villa Vieja (☎965 21 69 18). Thirty simple, sparkling rooms blocks from the beach. Huge rooftop garden terrace with a view of the castle makes it even sweeter. Hallway baths. Free kitchen use. Rooms €15-18 per person. ❷

Hostal-Residencia Portugal, C. Portugal, 26 (☎965 92 92 44). Clean, modern rooms in a central location. Ask to face the street with a balcony. In-room TV €3. Singles €18-20; doubles €27-29, with bath €32-34; triples negotiable. ❷

Habitaciones Belenguer, C. Alemania, 15 (☎965 92 79 47). Simple, clean rooms with tile floors, sinks, and TV. Most have hallway baths. Very convenient to the bus station, beach, and center of town. Free Internet and kitchen use. Laundry €6. Singles €12-15; doubles €27, with bath €33; triples €33/€36. ❶

Hostal Metidja, Rbla. de Méndez Núñez, 26 (☎965 14 36 17), right next door to Havana Café. Ultra clean accommodations with hallway baths scented like baby powder. All rooms with TV and A/C. Singles €24-27; doubles €40-45; triples €55-58. ❷

Hostal Mayor, C. Mayor, 5 (☎965 20 13 83). Centrally-located with simple, brightly painted rooms and clean hallway baths. Proximity to the beach and the bars of the *casco antiguo* ensures noise at night. Singles €20; doubles €30; triple €45. ❷

Residencia Universitaria (HI), Av. Orihuela, 59 (☎965 11 30 44). Take bus #03 (€0.80). Dorms with bath and A/C. Travelers mingle at the snack bar, by the big-screen TV, doing free laundry, or over foosball. Three-day max. stay. Open July-Sept. Dorms €7.20, with breakfast €8, with 3 meals €14.60; over 26 €10.20/€11/€17.60. ❶

Camping: Camping Playa Mutxavista (☎965 65 45 26), on the beach a few km north of the city center (bus #21, €0.80). Take C. Doctor Ochoa away from the beach and turn at Torre Edinso apartments. Restaurant and supermarket on site. Washing machines €5. Free showers. June-Sept. €3.65 per person, €11.90 per tent; Oct.-May €2/€8. ❶

⬥ FOOD

Most visitors refuel along the main pedestrian streets; prices are reasonable despite the crowds of tourists. The numerous Turkish and Lebanese *kebap* restaurants are the best bargains in the city. Smaller, cheaper, family-run *bar-restaurantes* in the old city have fewer visitors, but also less variety. The **market** is on Av. Alfonso X el Sabio (open M-Sa 8am-2pm. Buy basics at **Supermarket Mercadona**, C. Álvarez Sereix, 5 (☎965 21 58 94. Open M-Sa 9am-9pm.)

Kebap, Av. Dr. Gadea, 5 (☎965 22 92 35), near the corner of C. Italia. Mouth-watering Middle Eastern cuisine. *Rollos* (pitas with meat or veggies; €2.40) are the most popular dish. Heaping entrees €5.70-7. Open daily 1-4pm and 8pm-midnight. ❶

La Taberna del Gourmet, C. San Fernando, 10 (☎965 20 42 33). Traditional restaurant which specializes in a *menú* for 2, which includes a wide selection of *paella*, fish, and meat dishes (€16.53-19.53). Other entrees €6-19. Open daily 8pm-midnight. ❸

Restaurante El Buen Comer, C. Mayor, 8 (☎965 21 31 03). Fabulous *menú* options— the weekday lunch at €8.75 is the best budget option. Open daily 10am-midnight. ❷

Al Peperone, Pl. San Cristóbal, 2-B (☎965 14 65 21). In the plaza, off Rbla. Méndez Núñez. Rich, thin crust pizzas (€5-14) and daily pasta specials (€5-6.50) served in a fun, eclectically modern setting. Open daily 2-4pm and 9pm-midnight. ❶

Cafetería Mediterráneo, C. Altamira, 8 (☎965 14 08 40), 2 blocks from the Explanada. A cafe bursting with locals at all hours of the day. Chrome bar displays an array of raw fish. Four-course *menú* €6. Open M-Sa 7am-10pm. ❶

Restaurante O'Pote Gallego, Pl. Santísima Faz, 6 (☎965 20 80 84), in the square behind the Ayuntamiento. Galician and Valencian specialties served in a pleasant outdoor setting. Meat and fish entrees €7-12.95. Open daily 1-4pm and 5-11pm. ❷

⬤ ⬥ SIGHTS & BEACHES

With drawbridges, dark passageways, and hidden tunnels, the **Castell de Santa Bárbara** keeps silent guard over Alicante's beach. The 200m high fortress built by the Carthaginians boasts a dry moat, dungeon, and ammunition storeroom. The *Albacar Vell*, constructed during the Middle Ages, holds a vast sculpture garden with exhibits of Spanish greats. A paved road from the old section of Alicante leads to the top, although most people opt for the **elevator** rising from a hidden entrance on Av. Jovellanos, just across the street from Playa Postiguet, near the white pedestrian overpass. (☎965 26 31 31. Castle open Apr.-Sept. 10am-7:30pm; Oct.-Mar. 9am-6:30pm. Free. Elevator €2.40.) The **Museu de Arte del Siglo XX La Asegurada,** Pl. Santa María, 3, showcases modern art, including several works by Picasso and Dalí. The museum offers free guided tours if reserved in advance. (☎965 14 07 68. Open May 15-Sept. 14 Tu-F 10am-2pm and 5-9pm, Sa-Su 10:30am-2:30pm; Sept. 15-May 14 Tu-F 10am-2pm and 4-8pm, Sa-Su 10:30am-2:30pm. Free.)

Alicante's **Playa del Postiguet,** just meters to the left of the new port, is perpetually packed with sunbathers, volleyball players, and children on the loose. For more peaceful shores, the 6km of **Playa de San Juan** and **Playa del Mutxavista** are the nearest options. Both **Playa del Postiguet** and **Playa de San Juan** wave the EU *bandera azul* for great waters and beautiful sands. The **Costa Blanca's** gorgeous shores extend to the north along the Alicante-Dénia train line. (To San Juan, take TAM bus #21, 22, or 31. For Mutxavista, take #21. Each departs every 15min., €0.80. The Alicante-Dénia train leaves from the main station every hr. and stops at Playa del Muxtavista and Playa de San Juan, €0.75.)

VALENCIA & MURCIA

🎵 NIGHTLIFE

The discos and port-side pubs of Alicante make for vibrant and varied nightlife. For yet wilder nightlife, **Benidorm**, 45min. away, rocks out with several huge *discotecas*, all accessible from July to August by FGV's special **Trensnochador** (see **Trains**, p. 344). Other bars and disco-pubs nearby include the surf-themed, hole-in-the-wall **Marea**, C. Padre Maltés at the corner of C. Virgen del Belén. Across the street are: upscale **Astrónomo**, featuring mean bouncers and a large, outdoor terrace; and **Nepal**, attracting well-dressed Spanish yuppies.

CASCO VIEJO

Most night owls kick off the evening with bar-hopping in the *casco antiguo*, though there are enough watering-holes in this area to keep even the most alcohol-tolerant of partygoers busy until morning. **Plaza San Cristóbal** offers several popular bars; others line the streets behind the cathedral and down toward the water.

🍹 **Coscorrón**, C. Tarifa, 3. For a famous *mojito* (lemon, rum, mint, and sugar; €2.10), head to Coscorrón, so named for the bump on the head you might receive on the 4-foot high door. Open since 1936, it claims to be the oldest bar in Alicante. Stay downstairs and admire decades of political stickers, or climb upstairs for more breathing room and writing on the walls. Open Su-Th 10:30pm-2:30am, F-Sa 11pm-4:30am.

Supporter, C. San Nicolás 14. Take a break from Spanish pop. A mix of modern and classic rock in a funky bar with concert tickets from the last 20 years adorning the walls. Beer €1.50-3. Mixed drinks €3-4. (Open Th-Sa 10:30pm-4:30am.)

Hanoi 27, Pl. Quijano, 13-14. Those escaping the bar madness head to the peaceful rooftop terrace, despite the raucous dance floor below. Mixed drinks from €4.50.

Do-Desafinado, C. Santo Tomás, 6. (☎670 40 82 36). A self-consciously sophisticated crowd sips martinis (€7) and discusses art to the sounds of St. Germain at this eclectically decorated cafe-bar. Open Th-Sa 9pm-4:30am, Su 6:30pm-3am.

NEAR THE PORT

Alicante's **main port** houses a complex of bars overlooking the water. These tend to fill up a bit later than the bars in town. A dance-happy crowd fills the discos on the **Puerto Nuevo**, to the left when facing the water. None of these charge cover, though there is sometimes a drink minimum. The most lively spots are **Puerto Di Roma**, with a well-dressed, mixed-age crowd, and **Café Directo**. If English is your language of choice, **Coyote Ugly** is right next door. Like in the movie, the bartenders here are hot, but the crowd is uninspiring (and mostly British).

🍹 **O'Connell's**, Av. de la Constitución, 14 (☎965 14 05 84). Away from the *casco antiguo*, American and British exchange students hang out and hook up at this lively Irish pub. Beer €1.50-3. Open M-F 4pm-4am, Sa-Su 5pm-5am.

Z-Klub, coming off Rbla. de Méndez Núñez, make a right on Po. de la Explanada and walk for 2 blocks; the club is on your right on a small side-street. The truly elite clubbers in Alicante head to the ultra-modern, where top quality DJs spin house all night long for a mixed gay-straight crowd. Cover €12-15, includes 1 drink. Open Th-Sa 12-6am.

🎭 🎵 FESTIVALS & ENTERTAINMENT

From June 20-29, hedonism rules during the 🎆**Festival de Sant Joan**, culminating on the 24th. The **Verge del Remei** procession begins in Alicante on August 3rd; pilgrims then trek to the monastery of Santa Faz the following Thursday. Alicante honors *La Virgen del Remedio* all summer during the **Fiestas del Verano**, when numerous concerts and theatrical performances are held in the new open-air theater on the port. During July and August, Playa de San Juan becomes a stage for **ballet** and **musical performances,** part of the *Plataforma Cultural* series. (Open nightly until 9pm. Events on Playa de San Juan free, in port cover from €9.)

 DAYTRIPS FROM ALICANTE

ELCHE (ELX)

RENFE trains run from Alicante every hr. 6:05am-10:05pm, €1.50-1.80. Mollá buses (☎965 13 08 51) leave Alicante M-F 2 per hr. 7am-10pm, Sa every hr. 8am-10pm, Su 8 per day 9am-9:30pm; €1.55.

A lush oasis of a city 23km from Alicante and surrounded by one of Europe's only palm forests, Elche is a refreshing change from the monochromatic cities lining the rest of the *Costa Blanca.* Elche's parks make for a great daytrip; heading to nearby beaches is also an option, although better beaches lie farther north. Of Elche's parks and public gardens, by far the most beautiful is **Hort del Cura** (Priest's Orchard), where magnificent trees shade colorful flower beds. (Open June-Aug. 9am-9pm; Sept.-May 9am-6pm. €4, includes audioguide.) At the corner of Av. Ferrocarril and Po. de la Estación begins the **Parque Municipal,** where palm trees, grassy promenades, and playgrounds make for a cheerful, family-oriented park. (Open daily June-Aug. 7am-midnight; Sept.-May 7am-9pm.) Both the **train station** (Estación Parque; ☎902 24 02 02) and the **bus station** (☎965 45 58 58) are located along Av. de la Libertat. To get to the town center, bear left on Po. de la Estación. The **tourist office** is on Pl. Parc, at the end of Po. de la Estación. (☎965 45 27 47. English spoken. Open M-F 10am-7pm, Sa 10am-2:30pm, Su 10am-2pm.)

ISLA TABARCA

Cruceros Kon Tiki (☎965 21 63 96) departs daily from the dock on Explanada d'Espanya in Alicante to Tabarca. (High-speed 30min., regular 1hr; July-Aug. 3 per day 11am, 12:30, 2:30pm; Sept.-June. 1 per day 11am. Ferries return July-Aug. 4 per day 2, 5:30, 6:30, 7:30pm; Sept.-June 1 per day 5pm. Extra service sometimes added in low season, departing Sa-Su 11am, 12:30pm, 3:40pm; returning at 2, 5, 6:30pm. Round-trip €14.)

Still a quiet fishing village, this tiny island 15km south of Alicante offers an old fort, several fresh seafood restaurants, a rocky beach with beautiful turquoise water, and several coves with tide pools perfect for a refreshing dip in the sea. Despite its petite proportions, tourists have begun to make the island a choice daytrip destination. The only **beach** is straight ahead when you come off the dock; rent beach chairs and umbrellas from an attendant (chairs €5 per day, 2 chairs and umbrella €10). To the left, the remnants of the tiny **fort,** once a jail for Spanish exiles, overlooks the Mediterranean on three sides. To find the **tide pools,** head to the right past the beach when you come off the dock and proceed down the main street through town until you reach a large stone gate. Walk through the gate to find several tide pools and small, rocky coves. Seafood **restaurants** line the narrow strip between the fort and the beach—all serve delicious *comida típica* with *menús* ranging from €8-11. For **tourist info** and the **police** call ☎965 96 00 58.

BENIDORM ☎965

A carnival-like beach culture abounds in Benidorm, from the countless rows of sandal and sunglass shops along Playa del Levante to the heart of the *casco antiguo,* where hordes of sunburnt tourists crowd the streets 24 hours a day. Thousands of visitors from the British Isles, the Netherlands, and Belgium come to Benidorm every summer, some merely to sunbathe on the city's 5km of white-sand beaches. Those wishing to own a piece of the madness settle down in the numerous apartment buildings that dot the skyline. If it's the quintessential tranquility of the Costa Blanca that you seek, bypass Benidorm and head north toward the calmer towns of Altea and Jávea. But if you want to party, Benidorm's unbelievable nightlife will keep you going from dusk till dawn, every day of the week.

■ 🛈 ORIENTATION & PRACTICAL INFORMATION. The **train station** (☎965 85 18 95) is located on C. de l'Estació, at the top of a small hill above the city. Local bus #7 departs from the train station for the city center. (☎965 85 43 22. Every 30min. 6:30am-9:50pm. €0.80.) For **taxis** call ☎965 86 26 26. A ride from the train station to the city center will set you back €3-5. The **bus stop** (there's no real bus station) is on Av. de Europa, about 4 blocks inland from the beach, close to the city center. The *casco antiguo*, which forms the center of the city, divides Benidorm into two sections. To the north, along boardwalk **Avenida d'Alcoi,** is the main beach, **Playa de Levante,** as well as larger streets where most big hotels and apartment buildings are located. To the south is the seaside **Parque de Elche** and a more secluded beach, **Playa de Poniente.**

To get to the **tourist office,** Av. de Martínez Alejos, 16, from the bus stop, continue down Av. de Europa toward the beach, make a right at Av. del Mediterráneo, and continue until you hit **Plaza de la Hispanidad.** Veer left onto C. Dr. Pérez Llorca, and make a left on Av. de Martínez Alejos. (☎965 85 32 24. Open July-Sept. M-Sa 9am-9pm; Oct.-June M-F 9:30am-1:30pm and 4:30-7:30pm, Sa 10am-1:30pm and 4:30-7:30pm.) **Banks** and **ATMs** line C. Dr. Pérez Llorca and the pedestrian street that leads to the boardwalk, Av. de Martínez Alejos. **Internet access** is at **Cybercat Café,** on the bottom floor of the arcade/cafeteria complex **El Otro Mundo de Jaime,** Av. Ruzafa, 2, near the *casco antiguo*. (☎965 86 79 04. €1 for 20min. Open daily 10am-2am.) In an **emergency,** call ☎112. The **post office** is located at Pl. Dr. Fleming, 1. (☎965 85 34 34. Open M-F 8:30am-2:30pm, Sa 9:30am-1pm.) **Postal Code:** 03500.

🛏 ACCOMMODATIONS. Though Benidorm has abundant upscale hotels and resorts, it has little to offer in terms of affordable lodging for the budget traveler. The most reasonably priced accommodations are found in the *casco antiguo*. A few blocks up the street from the tourist office is **Hostal Tabarca ❷,** Av. Ruzafa, 9, with speckled tile floors, narrow, spartan rooms and clean hallway baths. (☎965 85 77 08. June-Sept. singles €25; doubles €30; Oct.-May €15/€18.) If you continue on Av. Ruzafa, more spacious rooms with balconies and bath can be found at **Pensión La Orozca ❸,** Av. Ruzafa, 37. (☎965 85 05 25. All rooms have private bath. Singles €25-30; doubles €35-50.) Those seeking peace and quiet will find it in the cheerful, modern rooms of **Hotel La Santa Faç ❹,** C. La Santa Faç, 18. (☎965 85 40 63. All rooms with bath, A/C, TV, and phone. Singles €42; doubles €61-72.)

🍴 FOOD. The main **produce market** is on Vía de Emilio Ortuño, just outside the *casco antiguo*. (Open M-Sa 8am-3pm.) The main supermarket, **Mercadona,** is one block up C. Mirador, off Vía de Emilio Ortuño. (Open M-Sa 9am-9:30pm.) Restaurants are found every few meters along **Calle Esperanto** and **Calle Gerona,** and consist mainly of pizzerias, a couple of Indian and Turkish restaurants, and eateries whose neon signs and huge, illuminated outdoor menus offer "international cuisine"—more varieties of pizza. For pub grub, head to C. Mayor and the many side streets in the *casco antiguo*, but if you seek *comida típica*, **Restaurante Albufera ❷,** on the corner of C. Gerona and Av. del Dr. Orts Llorca, has a huge menu and hearty portions of Spanish fare at reasonable prices. (☎965 86 56 61. Most entrees €8-12. Open daily 1-4pm and 8pm-midnight.) Look for the giant *paella* on the sign outside the **Restaurante Aitona ❷,** Av. Ruzafa, for excellent *paella* dishes (€8-10). Vegetarians shouldn't miss the heaping grilled vegetable platter (€9.50). Call ahead for reservations; you wouldn't want to miss the vegetables and meat hanging from the ceiling and deer heads staring from the walls. (☎965 85 30 10. Open daily 1pm-midnight.) For a filling meal with the locals, try **La Tasca del Pueblo ❷**, Marqués de Comillas, 5, with wooden chairs and tiled walls, offering a huge selection of meat and fish dishes for €7-10. (☎966 80 63 12. Open daily noon-1am.)

⑤◻ SIGHTS & FESTIVALS. It's difficult to find many remnants of Benidorm's historic past, since most of what was once the old city is now enveloped by modern high-rises and wide roadways. Tucked within the narrow streets of the *casco antiguo*, however, are the ruins of the **Castillo-Mirador de Benidorm**, Pl. del Castell, at the end of **El Carrer dels Gats**, the old main street. Built in the 14th century to protect the city from attacks by Berber pirates, the castle now affords excellent views of Playa del Levante to the north and Playa de Poniente to the south, as well as **Benidorm Island**, the enormous slanted rock formation in the water directly in front of the main beach. Spectacular sunsets can be seen from the castle's famous **mirador**, known as "The Balcony of the Mediterranean." Any visit to Benidorm is not complete without a stroll along the 2080m long **Paseo Marítimo de la Playa de Levante**. Dotted with hip cafes and bars, this expansive boardwalk is the place to see and be seen, as the beautiful (and the not so beautiful) traverse its length at all hours of the day and night. Benidorm has a small **Moros y Cristianos Festival** the first weekend in October, but the city is best known for its international music festival, **Festival de la Canción de Benidorm,** held every year in early to mid-June.

◪ NIGHTLIFE. Nightlife in Benidorm usually follows an expensive, exhaustive, but hedonistically fulfilling pattern, every night in July and August and weekends the rest of the year. Locals and tourists alike begin their party trek through the city around midnight in the various bars and taverns in the *casco antiguo*. Close to the Ayuntamiento is ◪**La Sal,** C. Costera del Barco, 5. Located in an old, half-timbered house, this small establishment is packed on the weekends with an ultra-hip crowd of mainly Spanish and German patrons. (☎966 87 34 94. Beer €4.80. Open daily 10:30pm-4am.) Wildly popular among locals is **Ándale Ándale,** C. Alameda, 24, which serves mixed drinks (€4 and up) to well-dressed Spanish yuppies who like to rock out to the latest in Spanish pop.

When most bars close or start winding down (generally around 3am), partygoers head toward the beach, since some of the craziest disco-pubs in Benidorm line the Po. Marítimo de la Playa de Levante, all near the corner of Av. Bilbao. If all you want to do is dance (particularly on top of bars and pool tables), head to ◪**Penelope**, whose multiple bars and packed dance floor make it one of the hippest venues on the beach. Most disco-pubs are open nightly in summer and on weekends during the rest of the year 11pm-5am. None charge cover, but drinks can get expensive (beer €5-6). A mixed gay-straight crowd grooves to house at **Ku,** while young and old party to a variety of music at **KM** and **Richard's New Look.** Keep an eye out for club promoters standing outside entrances, as they often give out coupons for free shots at the bars or free admission to discos.

Around 4am, the party shifts from the beach to the huge disco gardens on **Avenida de la Comunitat Valenciana.** You may not be in a state to walk, so it is best to take a **taxi** (€3.20). If you do walk, bring a burly friend, as the road becomes a dark highway a few blocks before the clubs. Once there, numerous discos line both sides of the street. ◪**Racha** is a cavernous locale specializing in Spanish pop. **Pachá,** Spain's largest disco chain, has a venue here that is hugely popular with tourists. Palatial **Radical** plays hardcore house for a sophisticated crowd. Most head to **Space** around 6 or 7am to watch the sunrise over the city. The majority of these clubs are open every night in the summer midnight-6am, and on the weekends throughout the rest of the year. Covers run €6-7. Mixed drinks start at €6.

ALTEA

Unlike the majority of towns lining the Costa Blanca, Altea's coastline betrays little of its growing tourism industry. Restaurants remain modest (but not necessarily cheap), daily life appears uninterrupted, and huge hotels have yet to spring up. A long jetty with a charming walkway protects Altea's calm stretch of shoreline from waves, and serene, pebbly beaches fan out from one end of town to the other. From the beach, narrow cobblestone streets wind up to **Plaza de la Iglesia**. Shaded by the cobalt dome of the church of the **Virgen del Consuelo**, the square commands breathtaking views of the Mediterranean. The main thoroughfare, **Comte d'Altea**, (in which C. La Mar becomes Pl. del Convent), is filled with snack shops and beachware. During the last week of September the city erupts with music, gunpowder, and dance for the **Fiestas de Moros y Cristianos.**

Both **trains** and **buses** stop at the foot of the hill on C. La Mar (head left to go toward the center). If you're arriving by bus from Alicante, get off at the first stop; if arriving from Valencia, get off at the second stop. **Maps** are available at the train station. The **tourist office** is on C. Sant Pere, 9, parallel to C. La Mar, right by the water. From the train station or the bus stop, walk toward the sea. (☎965 84 41 14; fax 84 42 13. Open June-Aug. M-F 10am-2pm and 5-7:30pm; Sept.-May M-Sa 10am-2pm and 5-7:30pm.) Services include: **emergency** ☎112; **police,** C. La Mar, 91, ☎965 84 55 11; **ambulance** ☎965 84 35 32. **Internet access** is available at **Red Attack,** C. Garganes, 9. (☎966 88 12 91. €1.20 per 30min. Open June-Aug. M-F 11am-2pm and 6pm-2am, Sa-Su 6pm-2am; Sept.-May M-F 10am-2am, Sa-Su noon-2am). The **post office** is at C. Llavador, 4, behind Av. del Rei Jaume I. Cross the train tracks by way of the pedestrian overpass and take a left. (☎965 84 01 74. Open M-F 8:30am-2:30pm, Sa 9:30am-1pm.) **Postal Code:** 03590.

Don't plan on making up for lost euros in Altea, as the vacation vibe here is partnered with vacation prices. Among the cheapest options available is **Habitaciones La Mar, 82 ❷**, C. La Mar, 82, close to the train station. The rooms are small and clean with hallway baths, but those overlooking the street can be noisy. (☎965 84 30 16. Doubles €24-30.) **Hostal Paco ❸**, Av del Rei Jaume I, 7-A, just off Comte d'Altea, provides A/C, full baths, TVs, and wide windows. (☎965 84 05 41. Singles €24-34; doubles €45-57.) For breakfast Altea has many pastry shops and bakeries along Comte d'Altea, near the Pl. del Ayuntamiento. For lunch or dinner, head to Av. del Rei Jaume I, parallel to the water, and its sidestreets—here you'll find seafood restaurants, pizzerias, and even some Chinese restaurants with entrees ranging €7-10. Try **La Liebre ❷**, Po. Mediterráneo, 39, which specializes in typical Spanish fare and untypically delicious gazpacho. Don't miss the banana split €2.40. (☎965 84 57 79. *Menú* €9. Open daily 1pm-midnight.) There are a number of bars on the waterfront that cater to an older crowd and close early; local and foreign partygoers head to Benidorm and Alicante for nightlife and entertainment.

CALPE (CALP)

With t-shirt stores lining the streets and beaches packed with foreigners, Calpe seems the classic tourist trap—yet the flocks of visitors descend for good reason. The **⬛Peñón d'Ifach** (327m), a massive, flat-topped rock formation whose precipitous face edges right on the sea, towers above the beach and town. To hike to the Peñón d'Ifach (2½hr. round-trip), walk past the tourist office, then turn right on Av. del Port, and left on Av. Isla de Formentera, following the signs. On a clear day, one can see Ibiza from the cliffs and caves above Calpe. The beaches are the town's main draw and lure visitors with kilometers of white sand.

Calpe's main avenue, **Avenida Gabriel Miró**, descends to the blue-flagged (EU-praised) **Playa Arenal-Bol.** Beyond the Peñón, both **Playa La Fossa-Levante** and the cove of **⬛Calalga** bear the same *bandera azul*. **ALSA buses** (☎965 83 90 29) stop

2km from the beach at C. Capitán Pérez Jordá (see **Coastal Transportation,** p. 343). From the station, set out straight down Av. Masnou (toward the rotary), which curves around to the left before turning into C. Goleta and leading ultimately into Pl. de la Constitución. From the plaza to the water, turn right down **Avenida de Gabriel Miró** and follow the smell of the sea. Taking the **Autobuses Ifach bus** past the bus station to the beach is a less strenuous option (1 per hr., €0.80). The **train station** is about a 15min. uphill walk from the bus stop on some roads without sidewalks; it's better to hop on an Ifach bus, which runs in a circuit between the station, beach, and town. If all else fails, call a **taxi** (☎965 83 78 78).

With your back to the bus station, turning right will bring you downhill to a neighborhood of gorgeous Mediterranean architecture. A 20min. beach walk along the street running from the old town leads to the main **tourist office,** Av. Ejércitos Españoles, 44. (Open June-Aug. M-Sa 9am-9pm, Su 10:30am-2pm; Sept.-May M-F 9am-2pm and 4-8pm, Sa 10am-2pm.) The **police,** Av. Ejércitos Españoles (☎965 08 90 00), are several doors down. **DIP Internet Center,** C. Benidorm, 1, is right off Av. de Gabriel Miró, three blocks from the beach. (☎965 83 93 83. Coin-operated computers €1 for 20min. Open daily 10am-11pm.) For a comfortable bed, try the tiny, bright **Pensión Céntrica ❶,** Pl. Ifach. All rooms have sinks, but the toilets are relegated to hallway bathrooms. Food and drinks available in a cozy bar-restaurant, where breakfast (€2) is offered. (☎965 83 55 28. €11 per person; mostly doubles, two singles.) Other affordable lodging options are located in the narrow streets of the *casco antiguo,* above **Plaza de la Constitución** off Av. de Gabriel Miró. Among these is **Hostal El Parque ❶,** C. Portalet, 4, with simple, clean rooms with bath. (☎965 83 07 70. Doubles €45.) The most reasonably priced restaurants in Calpe can also be found in the *casco antiguo.* **Casa Florencia ❷,** C. del Mar, 21, serves delicious seafood *paellas* and other rice dishes for two or more people for €12. Dine al fresco on the sunny terrace with colorful tiling. (☎965 83 35 84. Call ahead for reservations. Open daily 1-11pm.) A number of small bars can be found behind Pl. de la Constitución and along the beach headed toward the Peñón de Ifach, but for a wilder scene, your best bet is to go to Benidorm or Alicante.

DÉNIA ☎966

Set halfway between Valencia and Alicante along the Golfo de Valencia, Dénia (named by the Greeks for Diana, goddess of the hunt, the moon, and purity) is an upscale family resort cached in a relatively quiet Spanish city. Though the town has little to offer budget travelers in the way of bargains, its beautiful beaches, water sports, and tasty restaurants are enough to tempt even the most thrifty to splurge. Dénia's harbor serves as an important ferry connection to the Balearic Islands. Come summertime, the town erupts in celebration with several wild festivals, abandoning Diana's purity for the hunt.

🛈 ☷ ORIENTATION & PRACTICAL INFORMATION. The **train station** (☎965 78 04 45) is on C. Calderón de la Barca, just off C. Patricio Ferrándiz. The **bus station** is on Pl. Arxiduc Carles. For train and bus schedules, see **Coastal Transportation,** p. 343. **Local buses** (☎966 42 14 08) depart from the tourist office for nearby beaches. Take the bus marked "Marina" or "Calma" for the best beaches; the bus marked "Rotas" heads in the opposite direction. (Marinas depart every hour on the hour, 8am-8pm; Rotas on the half hour 8:30am-9:30pm, no bus at 2:30pm; Calmas on the half hour 8:30am-9:30pm, no bus at 2:30, 3:30, 5:30, or 7:30pm; €0.80.) To reach the Balearics by sea, consult **Balearia Eurolinies Marítimes,** in Pl. Oculista Buigues, between the tourist office and the water. (☎902 16 01 80; www.balearia.com.) Ferries run from Dénia to **Palma** and **Ibiza** (€46.50-58). For full ferry info, see **By Boat,** p. 363. For **taxis,** call ☎965 78 65 65.

Local services, including local **buses, trains, ferries,** and the **post office,** are located on **Calle Patricio Ferrándiz,** which runs straight to the port. The **tourist office** sits on Pl. Oculista Buígues, 9, 30m inland from Estació Marítima, at the end of C. Patricio Ferrándiz. To get to the tourist office from the bus station, turn left out of the plaza onto C. Patricio Ferrándiz; from the train station, go straight ahead, then veer right. (☎966 42 23 67; www.denia.net. Open Sept.-June M-Sa 9:30am-1:30pm and 4:30-7:30pm, Su 9:30am-1:30pm; July-Aug. M-Su 9:30am-2pm and 4:30-8pm.) Three blocks from C. Patricio Ferrándiz, shop-and restaurant-lined **Calle Marqués de Campo** is the main tourist strip. In an emergency, contact the **police** at ☎092. **Internet access** is available at **Cyber Mon,** on C. Carlos Sentí in the Mon Blau complex. This is the large blue building next to the market, on the block between C. de la Mar and C. Magallanes; head upstairs through the arcade. (Open daily 10am-11pm. Coin-operated computers €1.50 per hr.)

▮▮ ACCOMMODATIONS & FOOD. Dénia certainly doesn't cater to budget travelers, especially in the lodging department. Be prepared to shell out €30 or more for a single room in the summer. **Hostal L'Anfora ❷,** Explanada de Cervantes, 8, has some of the most inexpensive rooms in town. (☎966 43 01 01. Deposit required. July-Sept. singles €30; doubles €50; Oct.-June €24/€38. MC/V.) With A/ C, TVs, and private baths, **Hostal Comercio ❸,** C. de la Vía, 43, may appear more of a hotel than a hostel. Colorful sheets complement bright, airy rooms. (☎965 78 00 71; fax 78 23 00. July-Sept. singles €32; doubles €52; May-June €30/€47; Oct.-Apr. €24/€32. MC/V.) Other relatively inexpensive accommodations can be found along **Avenida del Cid** at the foot of the hill leading to the *castillo.* **Hostal Cristina ❷,** Av. del Cid, 5, has small, cozy rooms with wood furniture, floral tiling, and the curtains to match. All with bath, most with A/C and TV. (☎966 42 31 58. Singles €20-24; doubles €24-36.) **Camping Las Marinas ❶,** C. Les Bovetes Nord, 4, is a 3km bus ride (€0.80) from Platja Jorge Joan. Take the buses marked *"Racón."* Hot water, supermarket, restaurant, and beach-side locale are all added bonuses. (☎966 47 41 85 or 75 51 88. Open year-round. €4.80 per person and per tent.) **Restaurants** line C. Marqués de Campo and the Explanada de Cervantes, though most cater to the hyper-tourist. Cheaper eateries sit merely a block or two off the main streets. Despite its portside location, **Khyber I ❶,** Pl. Fontanella, 4, serves up reasonably priced and authentic curries and other Indian cuisine. (☎965 78 56 04. Entrees €4.60-6. Open daily 1-4pm and 9-11pm.) Right next door is **Clima ❷,** Pl. Drassanes, 5. With a huge menu consisting of everything from *paellas* (€7-9) to pizza (€7-10) to sandwiches (€4-6), this restaurant caters to a wide array of culinary tastes, with a pleasant terrace right on the boardwalk. (☎965 78 10 54. Open daily 1pm-midnight.) Vegetarian delights are to be found at **Caña de Azúcar ❶,** C. Extremaduras, 3, right off C. de la Mar near C. Fora Mur. Meat-free fare abounds, ranging from soy burgers to salads to couscous. Most entrees €4-7, a 3-course lunch *menú* (which changes daily) €9.50. Smoothies and fresh juices €2-4. (☎677 09 83 50. Open Tu-Su 11am-5pm and 7pm-midnight.) The **market** is on C. Carlos Sentí, 6, in a large orange building (open M-Sa 7am-2pm), and there is a **Másymás** supermarket at the bus station in Pl. Arxiduc Carles (open M-Sa 9am-9pm).

◎▮ SIGHTS & BEACHES. An 18th-century **castle** sprawls across the hill overlooking the marina. Centuries earlier, Jaime II enforced the 1304 separation between the town below and the castle above by displacing all of Dénia's inhabitants to the *villa vella,* or old town, beyond the castle walls. (☎966 42 06 56. Open daily June 10am-1:30pm and 4-7:30pm; July-Aug. 10:30am-1:30pm and 5-8:30pm; Sept. 10:30am-1:30pm and 5-8pm; Oct. 10am-1pm and 3-6:30pm Nov.-Mar. 10am-1pm and 3-6pm; Apr.-May 10am-1:30pm and 3:30-7pm. €1.80.) A **tourist train** chugs to the castle from the tourist office (M-Su 4:15 and 5:45, except Tu. €3.60 includes entrance to the castle), or you can walk by way of the stairs next to the town hall.

Dénia's biggest attraction, however, is its 14km of pristine **beaches.** Windsurfers skip over the waves off **Platja Els Molins** (north of the port on the "Marina" bus), while scuba divers explore the depths off **Las Platjas Area de Las Rotes** (south of the port on the "Rotas" bus). Those who want a beach merely to sit and relax on have plenty of options—among them, **Platja Les Marines, Platja Les Bovetes,** and **Platja Punta Raset,** all close to the center of town. The tourist office provides a pamphlet detailing the services available on each beach, as well as the trails available to hike in nearby **Montgó Natural Park** (☎966 42 32 05).

■ **FESTIVALS.** Dénia holds a miniature **Fallas Festival** March 16 to 20, burning effigies on the final midnight. During **Festa Major** (early July), locals prove they're just as gutsy as their fellow countrymen in Pamplona—bulls and fans dive as one into a pool of water, a feat known as **bous a la mar.** In mid-July, the **Fiestas de la Santísima Sangre** feature street dances, concerts, mock battles, and fireworks over the harbor. The parades and religious plays of the **Fiesta de Moros y Cristianos** celebration also take place between August 14 and 17. Book accomodations in advance for summer festivals.

JÁVEA (XÀBIA)

Jávea's harbors shelter tranquil waters free from tourists—while British families venture here in summer, backpackers head to younger, more popular destinations.

Inconvenient transportation has spared the town from heavy tourist loads. **ALSA buses** stop at C. Príncipe de Asturias, but arrive only six times per day (see **Coastal Transportation,** p. 343). To get to the port, take the **municipal bus.** (☎966 42 14 08. June-Sept. every 30min., Oct.-May every hr., 8am-2pm and 4-10pm. €0.80.) If you don't feel like waiting, continue on Av. Alicante, which runs to the port (20min.). **Autocarres Carrió** (☎965 58 10 36) run between Dénia and Jávea (30min., 7 per day 8am-7pm, €1.40). Although the municipal bus runs from the port along a long stretch of pebbled bathing spots, Jávea's real beauties—its pristine beaches, coves, and cliffs—are not well served by public transportation. Jávea has three **tourist offices**—most convenient are those near the port, Pl. Almirante Bastarreche, 24 (☎965 79 07 39), and by the Ayuntamiento, Pl. de la Iglesia, 6. (☎965 79 43 56; all are open M-F 9am-1pm and 5-8pm, Sa 10am-1pm and 5-8pm, Su 10am-1pm.) Jávea's location may necessitate an overnight stay. **Pensión La Favorita ❷,** C. Magallanes, 4, is as good as it gets—bright, colorful rooms with a cheerful atmosphere, two blocks from the beach. Follow signs to the *pensión* from the tourist office in the port. (☎965 79 04 77. Singles €18-24; doubles €24-37, with bath €30-42.) **Restaurants** line C. Andrés Lambert and consist mainly of pizzerias and seafood *freidurías* (for the finest in fried fish).

A number of secluded coves line the coast south of the port. Jávea's most popular beaches, **Playa La Granadella, Playa de Ambolo,** and **Playa La Barraca,** about 5km south of the port along Ctra. del Cabo de la Nao, can best be reached by car. Ask the tourist office for a map and driving directions. The **Fiesta de Moros y Cristianos** erupts during the second half of July; fireworks jolt wide-eyed tourists roaming among costumed Moors and Christians, as parades, bands, and contests provide a welcome distraction from the heat of summer.

GANDÍA

Five centuries before the EU began blue-flagging beaches, the powerful Borjas family of Valencia had already discovered Gandía and transformed it into a center of noble beach bumming. Today, Gandía still gets most of its income from visitors seeking the peace of a seaside retreat. Fine sands stretch for kilometers, so not

THIS LITTLE RESEARCHER WENT TO MARKET

It could be a 16th-century abbey, in the open air, or a movie theatre. Regardless of outward appearances, I know exactly what to expect as I walk in: an overwhelming and exciting mixture of smells, sounds, accents, and faces. This is one of my favorite places in Spain: the market.

From Mojácar to Murcia , the market became one of the first places I would go in a new town. On my fast-paced itinerary, the market provided a sense of routine and stability—it was a familiar place and comfortable environment where, after a bit of practice, I knew my way around, what to expect, and how to behave.

But the allure of the market isn't merely its familiarity—far from it. I grew to love going for the possibilities of the unexpected. More than beaches or bars, the market gives you a glimpse into lives of locals in their daily routines. Sometimes I would strike up a conversation; other days I would simply watch and learn just as much. While I didn't always blend in, I enjoyed being part of a community, if only for a few minutes.

Market-hopping can be satisfying for those looking for local culture, bargains, and good food. Even thousands of miles from home, it doesn't take more than bread and fresh fruit to make you happy.

surprisingly, the most popular activity here is sunbathing.

RENFE trains (☎902 24 02 02) run from **Valencia** (1hr., every 30min. 6am-10pm, €3.35). **ALSA,** C. Magistrado Catalán, 3 (☎962 96 50 66), runs **buses to Alicante** (3-4hr., 11 per day 6:30am-10pm, €9.25) and **Valencia** (1-1½hr., 9-11 per day 7:55am-8pm, €5.05). Buses to Alicante stop in **Altea** (€5.40), **Calpe** (€4.20), and **Dénia** (€2.50). Departing from the tourist office, **La Marina buses,** Marqués de Campo, 14, run to the **beach** along Pg. Marítim (every 15min.; last bus 1am in summer, 11:30pm in winter; €0.90).The majority of services in Gandía are located near the **train station** on Marqués de Campo; everything else is by the beach. The **tourist office,** Marqués de Campo, is across from the train station. (☎962 87 77 88. English spoken. Open June-Aug. M-F 9:30am-1:30pm and 4:30-7:30pm, Sa 10am-1:30pm; Sept.-May M-F 9:30am-1:30pm and 4-7pm, Sa 10am-1pm.) Services include **emergency** ☎112 and **police** ☎962 87 88 00. The **post office,** Pl. Jaume I, 7, is a few blocks behind the Ayuntamiento. (☎962 87 10 91. Open M-F 8:30am-2:30pm.) **Postal Code:** 46700.

Gandía is full of expensive hotels; those who want to stay cheaply here should make reservations. **Habitaciones Rosmar ❷,** C. Cullera, 8, has the cheapest rooms and is a 3min. walk from the beach, with hallway baths shared among three tasteful rooms. (☎962 84 31 96. Open Apr.-Sept., but be sure to call ahead. Singles €17-21; doubles €30-36.) **El Nido ❸,** C. Alcoy, 22, is right off the beach but pricier. Ask for an ocean view. (☎962 84 46 40. Sept.-June doubles €40, July €45, Aug. €54.) Most restaurants are located along the beach and in the pedestrian streets near the train station. Among these is **Tasca Mediterráneo ❷,** Parc de l'Estació, 21, near the bus station, which serves hearty grilled fish dishes and *paellas* from €7.50-10. (☎962 87 35 07. Open M-Tu and Th-Su 1pm-midnight.) Stock up on groceries at **Supermarket Mercadona,** C. Perú, across the street from the bus station behind the train station. (Open M-Sa 9am-9pm.)

PLATJA DE PILES

Just 10km south of Gandía, Platja de Piles offers seemingly endless stretches of tranquil, white-sand beaches. From Gandía, **La Amistad buses,** Av. Marqués de Campo, 9 (☎962 87 44 10), run to and from Platja de Piles (June-Aug. M-Sa 9 per day 8:30am-8pm, Sept.-May 4-5 per day; €0.75). Buses depart from behind the train station, across from the supermarket. While in Piles, spend the night at 🏠**Alberg Mar i Vent (HI) ❶,** C. Dr. Fleming. The beach is out the back door. The owner organizes **bike** (€6 per day) and **kayak rental,** as well as **windsurfing** lessons. The hostel will be closed for renovations until March of 2004. (☎962 83 17 48 or 83 16 25. 3-day max. stay, flexible if uncrowded. Curfew weeknights 2am, Sa 4am. Closed Dec. and Jan. Meals €4.85-5.10. Sheets €1.80. Dorms €6-9, over 26 €9-10.20.) Reasonably priced **restaurants** and **bars** serving everything from *paella* to pizza are found below the apartment buildings in the *urbanizaciones* surrounding the hostel—most are usually open daily from noon until midnight.

MURCIA

The tiny province of Murcia, bordered by Valencia to the north, the Mediterranean to the east, and Andalucía to the west, may be in the shadow of more touristed regions, but its sunny, warm climate, tiny beach resort towns, and thriving capital city give it more than its share of character. Four centuries ago, a bizarre wave of plagues, floods, and earthquakes wreaked havoc throughout Murcia. Along with utterly destroying some areas, the earthquakes uncovered a rich supply of minerals and natural springs. Today, thermal spas, pottery factories, and paprika mills pepper the lively coastal towns, and orange and apricot orchards convince visitors of Murcia's reputation as the *Huerta de Europa* (Europe's Orchard).

MURCIA   ☎968

Murcianos will tell you that their city is a pleasant place to visit from fall until spring, when the city thrives off the energy of its university. However, from mid-July to mid-September, Murcia becomes a ghost town; even the most loyal residents flee the oppressive heat of the city for the nearby Mediterranean. Though modern Murcia boasts parks, cafes, and tree-lined avenues, the winding lanes of its old quarter reveal the Moorish heart of the historic city of *Mursiya*, as Abderramán II named it upon its founding in 825 AD.

▐ TRANSPORTATION. Aeropuerto de San Javier (☎968 17 20 00), about 30km to the southeast, has flights to Barcelona, Madrid, and London. **RENFE trains** (☎902 24 02 02), at Pl. Industria, head for: **Alicante** (2hr., 9-17 per day, €3.75); **Barcelona** (7-10hr., 2 per day, €41.50); **Lorca** (1hr., every hr., €3.75); **Madrid** (5-6hr., 5 per day, €34); **Valencia** (3½hr., 3 per day, €25.50). **Buses** (☎968 29 22 11) leave from C. San Andrés, behind the Museo Salzillo, to: **Alicante** (1½hr., 7 per day 8:15am-8:15pm, €4.50); **Almería** (4hr., 9 per day 5:30am-8:30pm, €14); **Barcelona** (8½hr., 8 per day, €38.50); **Dénia** (3½hr., 4 per day 2am-9:10pm, €10.50); **Granada** (4-5hr., 5 per day 8:30am-10pm, €16.50); **La Manga del Mar Menor** (1hr.; Sept.-June 2 per day, July-Aug. every hr.; €5); **Lorca** (1½hr., 12 per day 7am-9pm, €3.50); **Madrid** (5-6hr., 12 per day 7am-midnight, €21-34); **Málaga** (7hr., 6 per day 2:20am-11:45pm, €24); **Sevilla** (7-9hr., 3 per day 10:30am-9pm, €31.50); **Valencia** (3¾hr., 4-12 per day 8am-9:30pm, €11.50). **Municipal buses** (€0.70) cover the city and outskirts; bus #9 runs past the train and bus stations.

▐▐ ORIENTATION & PRACTICAL INFORMATION. The **Río Segura** divides the city, with sights and services to the north and the train station to the south (take bus #9, 17, or 39 between the two). The **tourist office** is in Plaza Cardenal Belluga, at the end of C. Trapería across from the cathedral. (☎968 35 87 49; www.murciaciudad.com. Open June-Sept. M-Sa 5:30-9:30pm, Su 10am-2pm; Oct.-May M-Sa 10am-2pm and 4-8pm.). The **regional tourist office** is in Palacio González Campuzano—the red building in Pl. Julián Romea (☎968 27 76 76. Open M-F 9am-2pm and 5-7pm, Sa 10:30am-1pm.) The bus station provides **luggage storage** (€2.40 per day). Local services include: **emergency** (☎112); **police,** Av. San Juan de la Cruz (☎968 26 66 00);

Hospital Morales Meseguer, Av. Marqués de Vélez, 22 (☎968 36 09 00). For **Internet** access, visit **Cyber Ocio,** C. Albudeiteros, 3. Take a right off C. Serrano Alcázar, off Pl. Julián Romea. (☎968 93 05 96. €1 per 30min., €1.50 per hr. 11am-2pm and after 9pm; €1.20/€2.40 from 4:30-9pm. Open daily 11am-2pm and 4:30pm-late.) The **post office,** Pl. Circular, 8a, is near the intersection with Av. Primo de Rivera. (☎968 24 10 37. Open M-F 8:30am-8pm, Sa 9:30am-2pm.) **Postal Code:** 30008.

▮▮ ACCOMMODATIONS & FOOD. When Murcia steams up and empties out in summer, finding a room is the only breeze in town; it is a considerably more difficult task in winter. One of the few decent budget options is **Hostal-Residencia Murcia ❷,** C. Vinader, 6, off Pl. Sta. Isabel; take bus #11 from the train station. Rooms have TVs, phones, and A/C. (☎968 21 99 63. Singles €18, with bath €30; doubles €36/€43.) Another reasonable option is centrally-located **Pensión Hispano I ❷,** C. Trapería, 8. (☎968 21 61 52. Singles €17, with shower €24, with bath €27; doubles with shower €32, with bath €36; triples with bath €45.)

Although ice cream shops and outdoor cafes seem to be everywhere, finding a decent meal is a bit harder. The area around **Plaza de San Juan,** near the river, is home to a number of popular restaurants and *tapas* bars; local favorites include **La Alegría de la Huerta,** Pl. de San Juan, s/n, and **La Parranda,** Pl. de San Juan, 7. For the usual selection of Spanish cuisine served by good-humored *camareros,* head to **Mesón-Restaurante Hermanos Rubio ❶,** Pl. Sta. Isabel, 3. Be sure to try the *gazpacho murciano,* which adds a savory new twist to the Andalucian favorite—bacon. (☎968 21 20 40. *Menú* €9. Open daily 8am-midnight, closed Su afternoons. AmEx/MC/V.) Sample the Murcian harvest at the **market** on C. de Verónicas (open M-Sa 9am-1pm) and C. Sierra del la Pila, near the bus station (open M-Sa 8:30am-3pm).

◪ SIGHTS. The palatial **Casino de Murcia** (Casino Cultural), C. Trapería, 18, began as a gentlemen's club for the city's 19th- and 20th-century bourgeoisie. Current members have use of the entire building, from its lounges to its libraries. The rooms were each designed thematically, including the Versailles ballroom, English billiard room, Arabic patio, and Oxford library. Many of these magnificent rooms are open to the public. (☎968 21 22 55. Open daily 10am-9pm. €1.20.) Several blocks toward the university, Murcia's **Museo de Bellas Artes,** C. Obispo Frutos, 12, is the region's largest art museum, with over 1000 works and an extensive collection of local art. (☎968 23 93 46. Open July-Aug. M-Sa 10am-2:30pm; Sept.-June M-F 9:30am-2pm and 4-8:30pm, Sa 10am-2pm. €1.20.) From the museum, continue on C. Obispo Frutos toward the river. The **Museo Taurino,** Jardín El Salitre, off C. Acisclo Díaz, displays bullfighting memorabilia, matador costumes, and mounted bulls' heads that pay homage to particularly valorous beasts. Of particular importance is the shrine to José Manuel Calvo Benichon's shredded, bloody shirt, worn the day he was gored to death in Sevilla by his 598kg opponent. (☎968 28 59 76. Open June-Aug. M-F 10am-2pm and 5-8pm; Sept.-May M-F 10am-2pm and 5-8pm, Su 11am-2pm. Free.)

Just outside Murcia, the Río España courses through the mountains, pines, and sagebrush of the **Parque Natural Sierra España.** The flowers explode into dazzling color in springtime, the best season to visit the park. The park is best accessed from **Lorca** (see **Daytrips from Murcia,** below), but the lack of public transportation to the park necessitates renting a car. Stop by the tourist office for bike routes, hiking trail maps, and logistical information.

▮▮ NIGHTLIFE & ENTERTAINMENT. Much of Murcia's nightlife centers around the city's numerous plazas. The *tapas* bars in Pl. de San Juan, two blocks from the river by Pl. Cruz Roja, are great places for starting the night. **Café-Pub Pura Vida,** Pl. Periodista Jaime Campmany, a left off C. Isidoro de la Cierva, is one of the more popular spots. (Mixed drinks €3-3.60. Open W-Sa 9pm-2:30am.) Most clubs are clustered around **Parque Atalayas,** the large park off Ronda Levante, a main thoroughfare in the city. Others lie near the university, along C. Doctor Fleming and Pl. Universidad, where students liven things up Th-Sa nights. If you're up for sensory overload, hit **Zig Zag,** a terraced complex of restaurants, movie theaters, clubs, 10 bars, and even a bowling alley. Take Av. Juan Carlos I from Pl. Circular and follow it for about 15 min. The building is on your left past a large sports stadium. After 11pm, the streets around the complex grow darker and emptier, and you may want to take a cab home. (Bowling €3.30 per person, beer €2.10. No cover. Open daily 10pm-4am.) On Holy Saturday, the **Fiesta de Primavera** starts a week-long celebration that brings jazz and theater performances to the city.

⚡ DAYTRIPS FROM MURCIA

ÁGUILAS

RENFE Cercanías trains (☎ 902 24 02 02) leave from Lorca (5 per day, €0.95) and from Murcia (€4.75). There are also buses from Murcia via Lorca (9 per day, €5.10).

EU blue-flagged beaches line the shores of Águilas, the easternmost town along *la Costa Cálida* (the hot coast), and frequent buses and trains make it the most accessible beach getaway from Murcia. Águilas's beaches and turquoise waters are the main draw, though the **Torre de Cope** and **Castillo de San Juan de las Águilas,** featuring incredible views of the coast, are popular stops in the city's *casco antiguo*. To reach them, take C. Isaac Peral out of Pl. de España, then follow C. Sánchez Fortuna out of Pl. Asunción Balaguer. **Playa de Levante Puerto,** the closest *bandera azul* beach to town, is to the left of the port when facing the water. At the next cove over, **Playa las Delicias** is cleaner and more popular.

Plaza de España, the center of town, is about a 10min. walk from the adjoining bus and train stations. From the station, head toward the beach, take a right by the water, and another right at the pier onto C. Coronel Pareja. The **tourist office,** C. Coronel Pareja, is a block toward the water from the plaza. (☎ 968 49 32 85 or 49 31 73. Open July-Aug. M-F 9am-2pm and 5-10pm, Sa 10am-2pm; Sept.-June M-F 9am-2pm and 5-9pm, Sa 10am-2pm.) *Paella* is the beachfront favorite, and any number of cafes and restaurants along the water serve steaming platters of it. Head back to Murcia for the night, as accommodations here are limited and expensive.

LORCA

RENFE Cercanías trains (☎ 902 24 02 02) run to Lorca's Satullena Station, Ex. de la Estación (1hr., every hr. 6:45am-9:45pm, €3.65). The bus station (☎ 968 46 92 70) sends buses to Murcia (every hr., €3.33) and Águilas (30min.; M-F 9 per day, Sa-Su 2-3 per day; €1.75).

A stroll through Lorca, from the modern train station to the crumbling medieval castle, leads you through centuries of architectural variety. Medieval ghettos, Renaissance artistry, post-Franco urban expansion, and contemporary elitism all flavor the town's neighborhoods. Ancient and medieval battles left Lorca without the orchards that extend through the rest of the region. Yet each conquering force left its own peculiar imprint on the **castillo** atop Lorca's central hill, a 20min. walk from Pl. de España. The castle itself is being converted into a pricy hotel, but the facade is the real attraction. Moors built the **Torre Espolón** shortly before the city fell to Alfonso X el Sabio of Castilla, who in a fit of self-adulation ordered the construction of the **Torre Alfonsín.** Today, the ruins of the **Ermita de San Clemente** deteriorate at the castle's eastern edge.

When Granada fell in 1492, inhabitants moved to the bottom of the slope, leaving in their wake three idyllic churches—**Santa María, San Juan,** and **San Pedro.** Starting anew, Lorcans erected six monasteries and the **Colegiata de San Patricio.** One of many well-preserved private residences, the **Casa de los Guevara** features a pre-19th-century pharmacy. (Open M-F 11am-1pm and 5-7pm. Free.) The **tourist office** is near Casa de los Guevara on C. Lope Gisbert. (☎968 46 61 57. Open M-F 9am-2pm and 5-7:30pm, Sa 11am-2pm.) **Luggage storage** is available in the bus station (€1.80 per day). Enjoy lunch at **Don Jamón ❶**, C. Musso Valiente, 2, off Av. Juan Carlos I. (☎968 47 07 89. *Tapas* €2. Open M-Sa noon-4pm and 8pm-1am, Su 8pm-1am.) Other restaurants serving *comida típica* can be found near Pl. de España.

LA MANGA DEL MAR MENOR

Autobuses Hermanos Gimenez/Lycar (☎ 968 29 22 11) run to and from Murcia (3-6 per day, €4.66) and make several stops along the strip. Autocares Costa Azul (☎ 968 50 15 43) go to Alicante (2½hr., 1 per day 6:30am, €6.20).

A geological fluke created the popular vacation spot known as La Manga del Mar Menor. Centuries of marine deposits settled over a small volcanic ridge and then solidified into a 19km strip of land separating the Mar Menor (Lesser Sea) from the Mediterranean. Windsurfers take advantage of the waveless sea, while beach-lovers relax in the white sands and crystal waters of the Mediterranean.

La Manga has one main road, **Gran Vía,** that runs its length. Addresses are indicated by km point (km 0 is at the mainland pole), plazas, and *urbanizaciones* (commercial complexes). Local **buses** zip back and forth along La Manga (every 20-30min., after 4am every hr., €0.70-1.80). **Bike Service** rents bikes at rates ranging from €6 for 2hr. to €55 per week. Special rates for families and groups. (☎619 99 21 14. Open M-Sa 10am-2pm and 4-9pm.) **Escuela de Vela Pedruchillo**, km 8-9, sells **water sports** equipment. (☎ 968 14 04 12. Open daily 10am-2pm and 4-8pm.) The **tourist office,** Gran Vía, Salida 2, km 0, has a map and accommodations list. (☎968 56 49 58. Open M-F 10am-2pm and 5-7pm, Sa 10:30am-1:30pm.) **Centro Comercial Manga del Mar,** Salida 6, km 1, harbors a taxi stand, an **El Árbol** supermarket (open M-Sa 9:30am-10pm, Su 9:30am-3pm), and various rental agencies. **Iber Car** rents cars for 1 day (€51-90), 3 days (€115-271), or 1 week (€180-481). You must be at least 25 years old and have current driver's license. (☎968 56 35 54. Open M-F 10am-1:30pm and 5-8pm, Sa 10am-1:30pm. AmEx/V.)

For budget accommodations, try **Pensión Mikaela ❶**, C. Amoladeras, 13, in Cabo de Palos, a town away from the strip. From the office, head down the street away from the beach, take a left off C. Subida al Faro and another left off C. Amoladeras. You'll find simple, airy rooms a little removed from the beach, but easily accessible by bus. (Meal plans available in the adjoining restaurant. July-Sept. singles €12.50; doubles €21, with bath €36. Oct.-June €11.62/€16.82/€30.)

CARTAGENA

For those burnt out by the beaches and hungering for a little history, a day in Cartagena might just do the trick. As the current tourism campaign contends, Cartagena certainly is a "Port of Cultures." Founded in 227 BC by the Carthagenian general Asdrubal, the city of Qart Hadast ("New City") was modeled after Carthage itself and served as the main Punic metropolis in Iberia, rich in natural resources and privileged by its protected interior port. Little changed when the Romans took over 20 years later after crushing Carthage in the Punic Wars—not even their name for the city, Carthago Nova. Today, Cartagena remains a bustling port city with much to offer. From fresh seafood restaurants to lush gardens, modern cultural festivals to Roman ruins (and, of course, beaches aplenty), any traveler can see why Cartagena has stood fast through the centuries.

◨◪ TRANSPORTATION & PRACTICAL INFORMATION. The **train station** is in Pl. de México. To get to the city center and tourist office, walk straight ahead on Av. de América to reach Pl. Bastarreche. **RENFE trains** (☎902 24 02 02) head to and from **Murcia** (1hr., 4-7 per day 7:30am-10pm, €3) and **Barcelona** (8-10hr., 1 per day 8:40am) via **Alicante.** Luggage storage €2.40 per day. Ticket office open 5am-9:30pm, customer service open 5am-11pm. The **bus station** is next to Pl. Bastarreche; head out and to the right; the plaza is on the left. **Autocares Costa Azul** (☎968 50 15 43) runs buses to **Alicante** (2hr., 8 per day 8am-5pm, €6). **Alsina Graells** buses go to **Cádiz** (2 per day 10:30am, 9pm; €43.36); **Granada** (4 per day 8:30am-9pm, €19.29); **Málaga** (2 per day 8:30am, 5pm; €27.18); **Sevilla** (3 per day 10:30am, 3, 9pm; €34.04). **ALSA/Enatcar** heads to **Madrid** (5-6hr., M-F and Su 2 per day 6:15am, 4pm; Sa 4pm); €23.93 and **Barcelona** (10hr., 1 per day, €39.50) via **Valencia.**

The **tourist office** (☎968 50 64 83) in Pl. Bastarreche provides architectural walking tours of the city and has a map and accommodations list.

■ ▯ ACCOMMODATIONS & FOOD. There are some luxury hotels, but more affordable accommodations are few and far between; probably best to head to Murcia for the night. If you want to stay, **Pensión Liarte ❶,** C. Muralla de la Tierra, 26, has simple rooms at great rates, though in a slightly run-down part of town. The 24hr. watchman ensures a pleasant stay. To get there, follow C. San Diego out of Pl. Bastarreche, take a right after the plaza on C. Sor Francisca Armendáriz, and then a left up the hill. (☎968 50 58 73. Singles €12; doubles €17, with bath €22; triples €25.) Those hungry for more than history should head to the numerous *tapas* bars in town, particularly on C. Puertas de Murcia. For seafood and rices, the port is the place to be. Follow C. Trovero and then C. Cuesta del Batel from Pl. Bastarreche. **Techos Bajos ❷,** at the bottom of the hill on the left, is a good budget option with a lively picnic atmosphere and seafood specialties, and its neighbors can easily accommodate deeper pockets. (Appetizers €4-8. Entrees €8-15).

◙ SIGHTS. Little remains of Qart Hadast today (the Romans quite successfully planted their own city on top of it) except parts of the original defensive wall, discovered in the late 1980s during excavation for a parking garage. They are now on display at the informative **Centro de Interpretación de la Muralla Púnica (CIMP),** which provides detailed information about the Punic history of the city. (Pl. Bastarreche. Open Tu-Su 10am-4pm and 5-9pm. €3.50.) Roman artifacts abound, though they are sadly far from complete. Remnants of the **Augusteum,** a site dedicated to the cult worship of the emperor Augustus, and the **Decumanum,** a Roman road, shed light on life in Carthago Nova, as does the **Interpretation Center** located in the **Castillo de la Concepción.** The castle perches high above the port in beautiful, lush gardens that make it well worth the climb. A panoramic elevator is in the works. There is also a semi-preserved Roman theater on the edge of town; ask at the tourist office for information. (Augusteum: C. Caballero, 2. Open Tu-Sa 10am-2pm and 6-9pm, Su 10am-2pm. €2. Decumanum: Pl. de los Tres Reyes. Open Tu-Sa 10am-2pm and 6-9pm, €2, but also visible through windows the plaza as well. Castillo de la Concepción: open Tu-Su 10am-2pm and 5-9pm. €3.50. A discount pass to all three sights can be purchased at any sight for €8, students €6.) Cartagena's history didn't stop with the fall of the Roman empire, however; the tourist office also provides "Baroque and Neoclassical" and "Modernist and Eclectic" architectural **walking tours.**

LAS ISLAS BALEARES

Dreaming of the vast fortunes to be made in the 21st-century tourist industry, throughout history nearly every culture with boats and colonists to spare has scrambled to conquer the Balearic Islands. Spain won the race centuries ago, and today the foreign invasion continues, as 2 million tourists flood the islands' discos and beaches annually.

While all four islands—Mallorca, Menorca, Ibiza, and Formentera—share fame for their gorgeous beaches and landscapes, each has its own special character. Mallorca, home to the capital city of Palma, absorbs the bulk of high-class, package-tour invaders. With its museums and nightlife, Palma competes with Ibiza City as the Balearics' cultural hub. Mallorca also harbors natural beauty, though all too often finding it requires wading through the urban jungle. Ibiza, a counter-cultural haven since the 1960s, is the style center of the islands. With monstrous discos and a stronghold of crazy, beautiful party-goers, Ibiza affords the best nightlife in Europe. Formentera, the smallest and most distant island, is more peaceful with unspoiled sands and unpaved roads. Menorca, wrapped in green fields and stone walls, leads a private life of empty white beaches, hidden coves, and mysterious Bronze Age megaliths.

Summers are hot, dry, crowded, and fun; winters are chilly and slow. Spring and autumn can be sumptuous, but the beaches remain cool; nightlife doesn't heat up until early July. Most hours, schedules, and prices listed are for summer only. Low-season prices at hotels can drop by up to half, and hours are often cut back.

HIGHLIGHTS OF LAS ISLAS BALEARES

PARTY with German tourists at Palma's **El Arenal** beach (see p. 341).

PARTY with Brits in **Sant Antoni** (see p. 389).

REDEFINE THE PARTY in **Ibiza** (see p. 383).

◼ GETTING THERE

Flying to the islands is cheap and faster than a ferry. Those under 26 can receive discounts from **Iberia/Aviaco Airlines** (☎902 40 05 00 in Barcelona). **SOM** (Servicios de Ocio Marítimo; ☎971 31 03 99) lines up bus companies, ferry lines, and *discotecas* for packages to Ibiza designed for disco fiends who seek transportation and an all-night party but have no use for lodging. Book tickets through a travel agency in Barcelona, Valencia, or on any of the islands.

BY PLANE

Scheduled flights are the easiest to book, and flights from Spain to any of the islands won't break the bank. Frequent flights soar from cities throughout Spain and Europe (including Frankfurt, London, and Paris). Many daily **Iberia** flights (☎902 40 05 00) connect Palma and Ibiza to Barcelona, Madrid, and Valencia. Service from Alicante and Bilbao also exists, but is less frequent.

Iberia offers **student fares** (with an ISIC) on flights from Barcelona (40min., €60-120) and Madrid (1hr., €150-180). **Air Europa** (☎902 24 00 42) and **Spanair** (☎902 13 14 15) also offer inexpensive flights to the islands. Schedules and prices are subject to change. Another option is **charter flights,** which can be the cheapest and quickest means of travel. Most deals entail a stay in a hotel, but some companies (called *mayoristas*) sell unoccupied seats on package-tour flights. The leftover spots ("seat only" deals) can be found in newspaper ads or through travel agencies

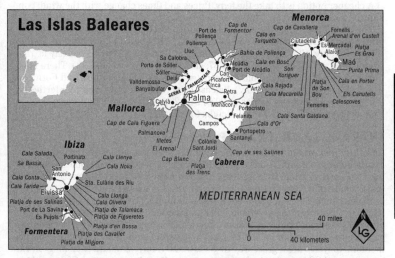

Las Islas Baleares

(check **TIVE** and other budget travel havens in any Spanish city). Prices during summer and *Semana Santa* are higher than in low season (Oct.-May). During low season, tickets are easy to get a week or so before departure. Those traveling in July or August should reserve several weeks in advance.

BY BOAT

Ferry service is considerably less expensive than flights, but longer in duration. On-board discos and small swimming pools on some boats ease the longer ride. Ferries run from Barcelona and Valencia to Palma (Mallorca) and Ibiza City (Eivissa); ferries also run from Dénia (in Alicante) to Ibiza. Seats may be available up to an hour before departure, but reserve tickets a few days in advance.

Balearia (☎902 16 01 80; www.balearia.com) ferries run from **Dénia's** Estació Marítima to **Ibiza** (2-4½hr., 3 per day, from €46), continuing on to **Palma** (€46+).

Buquebus (☎902 41 42 42 or 934 81 73 60) has super-fast catamaran service between **Barcelona** and **Palma** (4hr., 2 per day, €49; cars €112).

Trasmediterránea (☎902 45 46 45; www.trasmediterranea.com) boats depart daily from **Barcelona's** Estació Marítima Moll and **Valencia's** Estació Marítima to **Mallorca, Menorca,** and **Ibiza**. Fares from the mainland to the islands are €43 slowpoke, €58 fast boat. Fares between the islands range from €23 slow to €37 fast.

Umafisa Lines (☎902 19 10 68 or 971 31 02 01) has service between **Barcelona** and **Ibiza** 3 times per week. €47.10, some economy tickets available for €38.

⌁ GETTING AROUND

INTER-ISLAND TRANSPORT

Iberia flies between Palma and Ibiza (45min., 5 per day, €54-80) and between Palma and Mahón, Menorca (35min., 4 per day, from €54). **Air Europa** (☎902 24 00 42) and **Spanair** (☎902 13 14 15) connect the islands at similar prices. Student discounts are often available. However, flying isn't necessarily the best way to go.

A cheaper option is to take the **ferry**. Prices and times change with the wind; consult the tourist office or a travel agent. Ferries to and from Mahón are lengthy (6½hr.), but "fast ferries" now make the journey between the other three islands in under 3hr. **Trasmediterránea** (☎902 45 46 45) sails between Palma and Mahón (6½hr., Su only, €23) and between Palma and Ibiza (fast 2½hr., 1 per day at 7am from Palma, or 7:45am from Ibiza, €37; slow 4½hr., 3 per week, €23). There is no direct Mahón-Ibiza connection. **Trasmapi** (☎971 31 20 71) links Ibiza and Formentera (fast ferry 25min., 12 per day). **Umafisa Lines** (☎971 31 45 13) runs car ferries on the same route. **Iscomar Ferries** (☎902 11 91 28) run between Menorca's Port de Ciutadella and Mallorca's Port d'Alcúdia for daytrips.

INTRA-ISLAND TRANSPORT

The three major islands have extensive **bus** systems, although transportation nearly comes to a halt Sundays in most locations, so check schedules. Mallorca has two narrow-gauge **train** systems that are more of a tourist attraction than a major mode of transportation. Intra-island travel is reasonably priced—bus fares between cities range €1.20-6 each way. While it's possible to visit any of the islands without renting a vehicle, cars and mopeds are a great way (if you can afford it) to explore remote areas not accessible by bus. In Mallorca and Menorca, cars are the best option, while in Ibiza, a moped is more than adequate. On Formentera, bicycles are a great way to get around. A tiny, standard transmission **car** costs around €36 per day including insurance. **Mopeds** are around €18, and **bicycles** a mere €6-10. Prices drop in low season and for long-term rentals.

MALLORCA

Mallorca has long attracted the rich and famous. The site of the scandalous honeymoon of Polish pianist Frédéric Chopin and French novelist George Sand, Mallorca is also a choice vacation spot for Spain's royal family. European package tourists converge on the island in summer, often suffocating the coastline.

Nevertheless, there are legitimate reasons for such Mallorca lust. To the northwest, white beaches and olive trees adorn the jagged Sierra de Tramontana. To the east, expansive beaches sink into calm bays, while to the southeast, caves mask underground treasure. Inland, towns retain their unique culture, where windmills drawing water for almond groves power a thriving agricultural economy. Although the coastline has been sacrificed to developers, even the most jaded travelers sigh at the expanses of sea, sand, and rock that sprawl across much of the island.

PALMA ☎971

A stroll along Palma's (pop. 323,000) streets can be a dizzying, yet thoroughly satisfying, experience. Wander through the expansive maze of twisting lanes in the old quarter and you forget that you are on an island. After a visit to the various department and designer stores near Plaça d'Espanya, it becomes hard to imagine that the city was once a devotional retreat for Fernando and Isabel. Head to the beach, and you suddenly feel as though you're no longer in Spain, given the abundance of German and British tourists sunbathing on the white sands. Nevertheless, despite the fairly recent foreign invasion and growth as a major urban center, Palma still retains a genuinely local flavor. In its many cafes and traditional *tapas* bars, where the native dialect of *mallorquí* is the only language heard, it becomes clear why Palma reigns as the undisputed cultural capital of the Balearics.

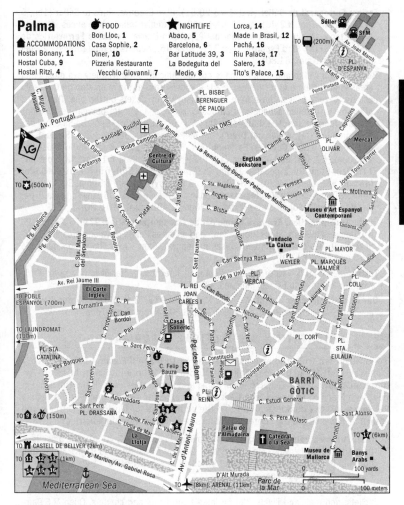

Palma

🍎 FOOD
Bon Lloc, **1**
Casa Sophie, **2**
Diner, **10**
Pizzeria Restaurante
Vecchio Giovanni, **7**

★ NIGHTLIFE
Abaco, **5**
Barcelona, **6**
Bar Latitude 39, **3**
La Bodeguita del
Medio, **8**

Lorca, **14**
Made in Brasil, **12**
Pachá, **16**
Riu Palace, **17**
Salero, **13**
Tito's Palace, **15**

🏠 ACCOMMODATIONS
Hostal Bonany, **11**
Hostal Cuba, **9**
Hostal Ritzi, **4**

ISLAS BALEARES

TRANSPORTATION

Flights: Aeroport Son San Juan (☎971 78 90 00), 8km from downtown Palma. Bus #1 runs between the airport and the port, stopping along the way in Pl. d'Espanya (every 15min. 6am-2:30am, €1.80). **Iberia** (☎902 40 05 00), **Air Europa** (☎902 24 00 42), foreign carriers, and a host of charter operators all offer service to Palma. See **By Plane,** p. 362, or **Inter-Island Transport,** p. 363.

Ferries: Trasmediterránea, Estació Marítima, 2 (☎902 45 46 45). Ferries dock at Moll Pelaires south of the city. Bus #1 goes along Pg. Marítim/Av. Gabriel Roca. Tickets sold M-F 9am-1pm and 5-7pm, Sa 9am-noon. Tickets and info also available at travel agencies. Daily ferries to Barcelona, Ibiza, and Valencia. **Balearia** (☎902 16 01 80) sends ferries to Dénia. See **By Boat,** p. 363, or **Transportation,** p. 363.

Trains: Ferrocarril de Sóller (☎971 75 20 51), Pl. d'Espanya. Runs to **Sóller** (1hr., 5 per day 8am-7pm, €2.40). Avoid the 10:40am "tourist train" when prices inflate to €4.80 for a 10min. stop in Mirador del Pujol d'en Banya. **Servicios Ferroviarios de Mallorca (SFM)**, Pl. d'Espanya, 6 (☎971 75 22 45), departs to **Inca** (35min., 22 per day 5:45am-10pm, €1.80).

Buses: Bus travel to and from Palma is not too difficult, but travel between most other areas is inefficient and restrictive. Nearly all buses stop at the main stop on C. Eusebi Estada, several blocks down from Pl. d'Espanya; buy tickets on the bus. The tourist office has a detailed schedule of all buses. Some of the more popular destinations include: **Alcúdia** and **Port d'Alcúdia** (1hr.; M-F 16 per day 8am-9pm, Sa-Su 5 per day 9:30am-9pm; €4); **Coves del Drac** (1hr., M-F 4 per day 10am-1:30pm, Sa-Su 1 per day 10am; €6.35); **Covetes/Es Trenc** (M-F 3 per day 10am-5pm, Sa-Su 1 per day 10:30am; €3.84); **Port Pollenca** (1hr.; M-F 5 per day 9am-7:15pm, Sa 3 per day 11:30am-6pm, Su 2 per day 10am, 8:30pm; €4.60); **Sóller** and **Port de Sóller** (45min.; M-F every hr. 8:30am-8:30pm, Sa 3 per day 10:30am-7:30pm, Su 3 per day 9am-5:30pm; €2.20); **Valldemossa** (30min.; M-F every 2hr. 7:30am-7pm; Sa 2 per day 11:30am, 3:30pm; Su 2 per day 10:30am, 12:30pm; €1.10-2.20).

Public Transportation: Empresa Municipal de Transportes (EMT; ☎971 75 22 45). Pl. d'Espanya is the hub. Stops around town and as far as Palma Nova and Arenal. €1, 10 tickets €9. Buy tickets onboard. Buses run approx. 6am-10pm. The airport bus (#1) runs until 2am (€1.80).

Taxis: (☎971 75 54 40 or 40 14 14). Airport fare from center of town approx. €15. From the old town to Estació Marítima, €8-10.

Car Rental: Mascaro Crespi, Av. Joan Miró, 9 (☎971 73 61 03). €30 per day with insurance. Open M-Sa 8am-1pm and 3-7pm, Su 9am-1pm and 5-7pm.

✠ ⍰ ORIENTATION & PRACTICAL INFORMATION

To get to town from the airport, take bus #1 to **Plaça d'Espanya** (15min., every 20min., €1.80). From the dock, take Pg. Marítim/Av. Gabriel Roca, or bus #1 to Av. d'Antoni Maura, which leads to **Plaça Reina** and **Passeig des Born**. From the sea, Pg. des Born leads to **Plaça Rei Joan Carles I,** the center of the old town, and **Avinguda Rei Jaume III,** the business artery. To the right, C. de la Unió leads (after some stairs) to **Plaça Major,** the center of Palma's pedestrian shopping district.

Tourist Offices: Palma branch, C. Sant Dominic, 11 (☎971 72 40 90). The office is at the bottom of a stairway, below street level. Open M-F 9am-8pm, Sa 9am-1:30pm. **Info booth** in Pl. d'Espanya. **Island tourist office,** Pl. Reina, 2 (☎971 71 22 16). Open M-F 9am-8pm, Sa 10am-2pm.

Budget Travel: TIVE, C. Jeróni Antic, 5 (☎971 71 17 85). ISIC cards, HI cards, Interrail tickets, and mainland flights. Not for inter-island travel and charters. Open M-F 9am-2pm and 5-7:30pm.

Currency Exchange: Santander Central Hispano, Pg. des Born, 17 (☎971 72 51 46). Open May-Sept. M-F 8:30am-2:30pm; Oct.-Apr. M-F 8:30am-2:30pm, Sa 8:30am-1pm.

El Corte Inglés: Av. Rei Jaume III, 15 (☎971 77 01 77) and Av. Alexandre Roselló, 12-16. Both open M-Sa 9:30am-9:30pm.

English Bookstore: Book Inn, C. Horts, 20 (☎971 71 38 98). Open M-F 10am-1:30pm and 4:30-8pm.

Women's Center: Centro de Derechos Mujeres, C. Galería, 4 (☎971 77 49 74, 24hr. hotline 900 19 10 10). Rape crisis assistance available. Open M-F 9am-2pm.

Laundromat: Coronet Lavandería, a block from Hostal Cuba. €9 for 5kg. Open M-Sa 8am-1pm.

Bike Rental: Rent a Bike Palma, C. del Mar, 10 (☎971 71 81 58). Bicycles €3 for first hr., €1.10 per subsequent hr., €9 per day. Inline skates €2.50/€1/€8. Open M-Sa 10am-10:30pm, Sa 10am-10pm, Su noon-10pm.

Emergency: ☎112. **Police:** Av. Sant Ferrà (☎091 or 092).

Late-Night Pharmacy: Rotates daily; see listings in the local paper, *Diario de Mallorca*.

Medical Services: Clínica Juaneda, C. Son Espanyolet, 55 (☎971 73 16 47), and **Femenía,** Av. Camilo José Cela, 20 (☎971 45 23 23). **Clínica Rotger,** C. Santiago Rusiñol, 9 (☎971 44 85 00), is more centrally located. All open 24hr.

Internet Access: Xpace, C. Sant Gaieta, 4D (☎971 72 92 19). €2.50 per hr., €6 for 4hr. Sign up a friend and get 1hr. free. Open M-Sa 9am-1am, Su 2pm-1am. **Cyber Central,** C. Soletat, 4 (☎971 71 29 27). €2.50 per hr., €1 for 20min. Open M-F 9:30am-10:30pm, Sa 10am-10pm, Su noon-10pm.

Post Office: C. de la Constitució, 5 (☎902 19 71 97). Parcels upstairs. **Fax** service. Open M-F 8:30am-8:30pm, Sa 9:30am-2pm. **Postal Code:** 07080.

ACCOMMODATIONS

This resort town has few *hostals* and few bargains. Call ahead in summer.

Hostal Cuba, C. Sant Magí, 1 (☎971 73 81 59), at C. Argentina. From Pl. Rei Joan Carles I, turn left and walk down Av. Jaume III, cross the river, and turn left on C. Argentina. Spotless rooms with high ceilings, modern baths, and pretty wood furniture. Second-floor rooms are cushier than first-floor rooms. Singles €20; doubles €36. ❷

Hostal Ritzi, C. Apuntadors, 6 (☎971 71 46 10), conveniently situated above "Big Byte" cybercafe. Centrally located *hostal* with rooms overlooking an interior patio that can get noisy at night. Rooms have a funky, old-fashioned feel with nifty metal light fixtures and lace curtains. Laundry €7. Singles €25; doubles €35, with bath €38-49. ❷

Alberg Platja de Palma (HI), C. Costa Brava, 13 (☎971 26 08 92), in El Arenal. Take bus #15 from Pl. d'Espanya or Pl. Reina (every 8min., €1) and get off at C. Costa Brava, about 45min. from city center. Four-person dorms with shower. HI card required. Breakfast included. Sheets €2.50. Laundry €6. 24hr. reception. Dorms €9-12, 27+ €10.20-14. ❶

Hostal Bonany, C. Almirante Cervera, 5 (☎971 73 79 24), in a wealthy residential area 3km from the town center. Take bus #3, 20, 21, or 22 from Pl. d'Espanya

THE LOCAL STORY

PRELUDE TO A BREAKUP

Mallorca's most famous vacationers are the Polish composer Frédéric Chopin and his lover, French novelist George Sand (Aurore Dupin), who spent the winter of 1838-39 here. Though it was intended to be a honeymoon of sorts for the two lovers, the vacation was doomed from the outset. Chopin suffered from tuberculosis at the time, constantly in pain and prone to black moods. Sand, a passionate free-thinker, felt trapped on the island, as is evident in her writings. The couple's presence, along with Sand's two children from a previous marriage, caused a stir among the townsfolk, who tormented the couple through the windows of cells #2 and 4 of the Cartoixa Real, which they occupied during their stay. Sand documents these incidents in her book *Un Hiver a Majorque* (A Winter in Mallorca) and refers to the local villagers as "barbarians and monkeys." Despite these less than ideal circumstances, Chopin produced some of his greatest pieces while on the island. Sadly, Chopin and Sand's love affair ended on a sour note when the two realized their personalities were too divergent and that nothing could eliminate their differences. Thus, in February of 1839, they boarded the same ship which had taken them to Mallorca less than four months before and, after reaching the Spanish mainland, parted forever.

to Av. Joan Miró and walk up C. Camilo José Cela. Take the first right, then the first left. Feels more like a hotel than a *hostal:* large swimming pool, comfy sitting room, and clean, spacious rooms with bath and balcony. Breakfast €3. Singles €26; doubles €40. ❸

🍴 FOOD

Palma's many ethnic restaurants are paradise for those sick of *tapas.* Pricy but popular outdoor restaurants fill **Plaça Mayor** and **Plaça Llotja,** but budget eaters head to the side streets off **Passeig del Born,** to the cheap digs along **Avinguda Joan Miró,** or to the pizzerias along **Passeig Marítim.** Make sure to try the *ensaimadas* (pastries smothered in powdered sugar) and the *sopa mallorquina* (a pizza-like snack of stewed vegetables over brown bread). Two **markets** vie for customers: one, Mercat de l'Olivar, is in Pl. Olivar off C. Padre Atanasio, and the other, Mercat Santa Catalina, is across town at the corner of C. Pou and C. Dameto. For **groceries,** try **Servicio y Precios** on C. Felip Bauza, near C. Apuntadors and Pl. Reina (☎ 900 70 30 70; open M-F 8:30am-8:30pm, Sa 9am-2pm), or the supermarket downstairs in either **El Corte Inglés** (see **Orientation & Practical Information**).

Diner, C. Sant Magí, 23 (☎ 971 73 62 20). American-style favorites served in a kitschy, classic diner setting. Delicious, affordable menu includes burgers (€3-5), hot dogs and grilled cheese (€3.50), tuna melt (€5), ribs (€6.50), and more. Open 24hr. ❶

Bon Lloc, C. Sant Feliu, 7 (☎ 971 71 86 17). Ultra hip vegetarian restaurant. Menu features salads (€5.70), falafel (€7.20), and dishes like basmati rice with Chinese-style sauteed vegetables (€9.60). Midday *menú* €10. Open M-Th 1-4pm, F-Sa 1-4pm and 8:30-11:30pm. MC/V. ❷

Casa Sophie, C. Apuntadors, 24 (☎ 971 21 40 11). Cheap, scrumptious fare in a simple, bohemian venue. Homestyle menu features many vegetarian options like vegetable couscous, pasta, and polenta. Entrees €4-7. Open Tu-Sa 1-3pm and 9pm-1am. ❶

Pizzeria Restaurante Vecchio Giovanni, C. Sant Joan, 3 (☎ 971 72 28 79). Lively family restaurant with excellent pizzas (€7-9) and pastas (€6-12). Don't be fooled by the touristy facade; the food is great. Gets crowded for dinner, especially on weekends. Open daily noon-3:30pm and 6:30pm-midnight. ❷

👁 🏛 SIGHTS & MUSEUMS

Palma's architecture melds Arabic, Christian, and Modernist styles into a reflection of the island's multicultural past and present. Many of its landmarks are nestled amidst the narrow streets of the *Barri Gòtic* (Gothic quarter).

CATEDRAL (LA SEU). This Gothic giant towers over Palma and the bay. The cathedral, dedicated to Palma's patron saint San Sebastián, was begun in the 1300s, finished in 1601, and then modified by Gaudí in *modernista* fashion in 1909. Now the interior and the ceiling ornamentation blend smoothly with the stately exterior. Its southern facade, perhaps the most impressive, overlooks a reflective pool and the ocean. (*C. Palau Reial, 29.* ☎ *971 72 31 30. Cathedral and museum open Apr.-Oct. M-F 10am-6pm, Sa 10am-2pm; Nov.-Mar. M-F 10am-3pm. €3.50.*)

PALAU DE L'ALMUDAINA. Built by the Moors, this imposing austere palace was at one point a stronghold of Fernando and Isabel. Guided tours, which pass through the museum, are given in numerous languages. The pleasant garden off Pl. Reina directly in front of the palace also merits a visit. (*C. Palau Reial.* ☎ *971 21 41 34. Open Apr.-Sept. M-F 10am-6:30pm; Oct.-Mar. M-F 10am-2pm and 4-6pm, Sa 10am-2pm. Guided visits €4, unguided €3.20. Students and children €2.25. EU citizens free on W.*)

CASTELL DE BELLVER. Overlooking the city and bay, Castell de Bellver was a summer residence for 14th-century royalty; it also housed Mallorca's most distinguished prisoners. The castle contains a municipal museum and models of archaeological sites. *(Bus #3, 21, or 22 from Pl. d'Espanya. ☎971 73 06 57. Open Apr.-Sept. M-Sa 8am-8:30pm, Su 10am-5pm; Oct.-Mar. M-Sa 8am-7:15pm, Su 10am-5pm. €1.73.)*

MUSEU D'ART ESPANYOL CONTEMPORANI. Now part of the Fundació Joan March, this mansion-turned-museum displays works of the 20th century's most iconic Spanish artists—Picasso, Dalí, Miró, Juan Gris, and Antoni Tápies. *(C. Sant Miquel, 11. ☎971 71 35 15. Open M-F 10am-6:30pm, Sa 10am-1:30pm. €3.)*

OTHER MUSEUMS. Inaugurated in December 1992, the **Fundació Pilar i Joan Miró** displays the works from Miró's Palma studio at the time of his death. *(C. Saridakis, 29. From Pl. d'Espanya, take bus #3, 21, or 22 to Av. Joan Miró. ☎971 70 14 20. Open May 16-Sept. 14 Tu-Sa 10am-7pm, Su 10am-3pm; Sept. 15-May 15 Tu-Sa 10am-6pm, Su 10am-3pm. €4.40.)* **Fundació "la Caixa"** hosts a collection of Modernist paintings in Doménech i Muntaner's Modernist Gran Hotel. *(Pl. Weyler, 3. ☎971 17 85 00. Open Tu-Sa 10am-9pm, Su 10am-2pm. Free.)* The **Casal Solleric** houses modern art. *(Pg. del Born, 27. ☎971 72 20 92. Open Tu-Sa 10:30am-1:45pm, Su 10am-1:45pm. Free.)* **Centre de Cultura "Sa Nostra"** features rotating exhibits and cultural events such as lectures, concerts, and movies. Swing by for a schedule of upcoming events. *(C. de la Concepció, 12. ☎971 72 52 10. Open Tu-F 10:30am-9pm, Sa 10am-1:30pm.)* The **Museu de Mallorca** is ideal for travelers interested in archaeology or medieval painting. *(C. Portella, 5. ☎971 71 75 40. Open Tu-Sa 10am-7pm, Su 10am-2pm. €2.40.)*

◖ BEACHES

Mallorca is a huge island, and many of the best beaches are a haul from Palma. Still, several picturesque (though touristy) stretches of sand are accessible by city bus. The beach at **El Arenal** (Platja de Palma, bus #15), 11km to the southeast (toward the airport), is the prime stomping ground of Mallorca's most sunburnt German tourists. The waterfront area is full of German signs for restaurants, bars, and hotels—think *Frankfurt am Mediterranean*. The beach is one of the longest and most crowded in the area, but with white sands and turquoise water, it's enough to make even the Germans smile. Other beaches close to Palma include **Palma Nova** (bus #21), 15km southwest, and **Illetes** (bus #3), 9km southwest, which are smaller than El Arenal, but equally popular. The tourist office distributes a list of 40 nearby beaches—take your pick and remember to say *danke*.

◖ ♫ NIGHTLIFE & ENTERTAINMENT

BARS

In the past, Pl. Reina and Pl. Llotja were the place for bar-hoppers, but a recent law requiring downtown bars to close by 3am has shifted the action to the waterfront. Nevertheless, many partiers still start in the *casco viejo*.

La Bodeguita del Medio, C. Vallseca, 18, plays Cuban rhythms and serves tasty *mojitos*. Mixed drinks €5. Open Th-Sa 8pm-3am, Su-W 8pm-1am.

Bar Latitude 39, C. Felip Bauza, 8. Follow the Aussies to this yachtie bar. Beer €1.50. "Twofer nights"—2 for the price of 1—Tu, Th, and Sa 9-10pm. Open M-Sa 7pm-3am.

Barcelona, C. Apuntadors, 5, a small, dark bar with lots of atmosphere, jams with live music from midnight to 3am. Cover €1.80 for live concerts. Open Su-Th 8:30pm-1am, F-Sa 8:30pm-3am.

Abaco, C. Sant Joan, 1. For pure decadence (and €15 drinks), head here. Fresh fruit, flowers, and candies fill this former mansion, while the upper rooms offer tapestries, velvet couches, and oil paintings. Open daily 10am-3pm.

DISCOS

Palma's clubbers start the night in the *bares-musicales* on the **Passeig Marítim/ Avinguda Gabriel Roca** strip which runs along the water from Av. d'Antoni Maura to the ferry station. Each mini-disco boasts different tunes, but Spanish pop dominates. These bars are about a 20min. walk from Pl. Reina, or you can hop on bus #1 from Pl. d'Espanya. (Bus service stops at 2:30am.) Nearby, several clubs and bars are centered on Pl. Gomilia and along Av. Joan Miró—but exercise caution here at night, as there have been a number of reported instances of petty crime occurring here in recent years. The bars and clubs around **El Arenal** (a.k.a., Berlin) are German-owned, German-filled, and German-centric. When the bar scene fades at 3am, partiers migrate to Palma's *discotecas*, which attract more locals than tourists.

▓ **Riu Palace,** one block in from the beach. If you don't mind partying with Deutschland, quite possibly the best deal for entertainment in Palma is here at the palace. Two huge rooms, one playing techno and the other spinning hip-hop, fill nightly with hip, young, fashion-conscious German disco fiends. All guests receive free t-shirts, "Rapper caps," necklaces, and coupons for free food at a nearby beer garden. Themed parties every weekend. Cover €15; open bar, all you can drink. Open daily 10pm-6:30am.

Made in Brasil, Pg. Marítim, 27 (open daily 8pm-4am) and dance-crazy **Salero,** Pg. Marítim, 31 (open daily 8pm-6am) explode into salsa come 2am. Mixed drinks €3-5.

Lorca, C. Federico García Lorca, 21. Great spot for gay nightlife. Blue and yellow walls pay homage to the Andalusian poet himself while the mostly gay crowd moves to a mix of pop, rock, and flamenco. Mixed drinks €4. Open daily 11am-3am.

Tito's Palace, Pg. Marítim. Palma's hippest disco, with two floors of house in an indoor colosseum of mirrors and lights. Cover €15-18. Open daily 11pm-6am.

Pachá, a couple of blocks farther down Av. Gabriel Roca. A toned-down version of the Ibiza landmark, but this little sibling has a massive dance floor, tropical terrace, and enthusiastic patrons. Cover €12-18. Open daily 11pm-6:30am.

Entertainment *à la Mallorca* has a Spanish flavor often missing in the other isles. The tourist office keeps a list of sporting activities, concerts, and exhibits. Every Friday, *El Día del Mundo* (€0.75) publishes an entertainment supplement with listings of bars and discos, and *La Calle* offers a monthly review of hotspots.

Mallorcans use any and every occasion as an excuse to party. One of the more colorful bashes, **Día de Sant Joan** (June 24), brings singing, dancing, and drinking to Parc de la Mar. The celebration begins the night before with a fireworks display.

WESTERN MALLORCA

Ten minutes beyond the modern roads and white highrises of Palma, the road enters a ravine where the island's first cave dwellers lived and rises in tight, narrow curves. On the north road beyond Valldemossa, olive groves pitch steeply toward the sea. This is western Mallorca, one of the most beautiful landscapes in the Mediterranean. It has inspired a range of creative minds, from lovers Chopin and George Sand to writer Robert Graves and actor Michael Douglas. These villages and beaches will enchant you even if you've never tickled the ivories, spilled any ink, or robbed the cradle.

VALLDEMOSSA

Nord Balear buses (☎ 971 49 06 80) to Valldemossa leave Palma at C. Arxiduc Salvador, 1 (30min., 7 per day 7:30am-7:30pm, €1.20).

Valldemossa's tiny, shaded streets huddle beneath the slopes of the Sierra de Tramontana. Little in this quaint, peaceful village hints at the passion that scandalized townsfolk during the winter of 1838 when Frédéric Chopin and George Sand stayed in the 14th-century monastery **Cartoixa Reial** (see **Prelude to a Breakup,** p. 28). Chopin memorabilia includes the piano which he carried up the mountain in several pieces. Piano recitals try to recapture the magic in summer. (☎971 61 21 06. Recitals every hr. on the ½hr. Open M-Sa 9:30am-6pm, Su 10am-1pm. €9. Includes entrance to the **Museu Municipal** and the **Palau del Rei Sancho,** where folk dances take place M and Th 11am-1:30pm.) Cafes around the main square serve simple fare—linger over your meal because once the few stores and sights close, there's nothing else to do.

SÓLLER

The old-fashioned Palma-Sóller train, run by Ferrocarril de Sóller, C. Castanyer, 7, is a highlight. The brave-hearted ride between cars as they pass through orchards and tunnels. (☎ 971 63 03 01, Palma 971 75 20 51. 5 per day 8am-7pm, €2.40.)

Sóller basks in a fertile valley 30km up the coast from Valldemossa. Oranges and tomatoes are the principal crops, and every plot of land is lined with either citrus groves or sunburnt tourists. The town's backdrop of spectacular mountains and quaint squares makes for a pleasant change from Palma's touristy beaches. In mid to late July, the Ajuntament hosts a **Folk Dancing Festival.** Sóller's **tourist office,** in an old trolley car in Pl. d'Espanya downstairs from the train station, has accommodations listings and maps. (☎971 63 02 00. Open M-F 9:30am-1:30pm and 3-5pm, Sa-Su 10am-1pm. Info posted in front of the church in Pl. de la Constitució if the office is closed.) Restaurants fill Pl. de la Constitució, but if you don't need a full meal, try the *coca mallorquina,* a cold pizza-like snack (about €1.80) in local bakeries.

PORT DE SÓLLER

Nord Balear "tunnel express" buses link Port de Sóller to Palma (1hr., every hr. 7am-9pm, €2.10). Trolleys also connect Sóller and Port de Sóller (every 30min. 7am-8:15pm, €1).

From Sóller it's a 30min. walk (or a short ride on the Nord Balear bus) to Port de Sóller, where a pebbly beach lines the bay. The **tourist office,** C. Canonge Oliver, 10, has quality maps and a list of accommodations and car rental agencies. (☎/fax 971 63 30 42. Open M-F 9am-12:45pm and 2:40-4:45pm, Sa 10:10am-12:45pm.) Two **grocery stores** are on C. Jaume Torrens, and **restaurants** line the beach. The surrounding area's famous **coves** are most easily explored by **boat.**

SA CALOBRA

Tramontana and Barcos Azules sail to Sa Calobra from the port near the last trolley stop in Port de Sóller. (Call ☎ 971 63 31 09 or 63 01 70 for information and schedules. May-Oct. 15 3-5 per day 10am-3pm, return 4 per day 10:45am-5pm; €9.) Buy tickets across the street from the last tram stop.

Like a serpent, the road to the dramatic cove of Sa Calobra writhes over 10 nail-biting kilometers while dropping 1000m to the sea. The boat from Port de Sóller is easier on the nerves. **Torrent de Pareis,** a spectacular cove which leads into a ravine with freshwater pools, is a 15min. hike from the bottom of the road and a popular photo opportunity (look for a landing packed with tourists). Sa Calobra itself is a smooth pebble beach bordered by cliffs. Like the rest of the island, its beauty is scarred by a plague of tourist restaurants, tourist gift shops, and touring tourists.

NORTHERN MALLORCA

Known for their long beaches and rocky coves, the northern gulfs of Mallorca are popular among the older, package-tour crowd; much of the coast is swamped beyond belief. The drive can be stunning, and though the region's coves and beaches are far from secluded, they are among the most beautiful on the island.

PORT D'ALCÚDIA (PUERTO DE ALCÚDIA)

Port d'Alcúdia is far from undiscovered. The beaches along the shallow bay are packed with hotels, bars, and pizzerias. The excessive number of arcades and ice cream stands testify to Port d'Alcúdia's popularity among families with children of the little-and-screaming variety. Despite its tourist infestation, Port d'Alcúdia makes a nice base for exploring the stunning beaches of the northeastern coast. If you have a car, take the road towards **Artà** and then **Capdepera** from town. About 20km from Port d'Alcúdia, you will see signs leading to **Cala Torta** along a bumpy dirt road. Cala Torta itself is the most touristed of the three arid coves which make up the northeastern corner of the island. If you hike from this beach over the cliffs to the west, you come to **Cala Mitjana,** a beautiful cove with crashing waves and tide pools filled with seaweed. (Beach chairs and umbrellas €2.) Past Cala Mitjana is **Es Matzoc,** a pleasant white-sanded beach that is not entirely overrun by tourists. If you're looking for more than a beach, visit Alcúdia's old town with 14th-century ramparts, **Roman remains** dating from 2 BC, and town walls that have experienced a series of medieval razings and re-buildings. (15min. walk from the beach; buses depart every 15min. from C. dels Mariners.) The **Museu Pollentia** documents archaeological discoveries on Mallorca. (☎971 54 70 04. Open T-F 10am-1:30pm and 3:30-5:30pm, Sa-Su 10:30am-1pm. €1.20.) **Parc de s'Albufera des Grau,** within walking distance of the beach, is filled with marshes, flowers, and dunes. (Open daily in summer 10am-7pm, in winter 10am-5pm. Free.) The tourist office has a brochure of 10 hiking/biking excursions.

Buses (☎971 54 56 96), run to Alcúdia (€3.90) and Port d'Alcúdia (€4) from Pl. d'Espanya in **Palma** (1hr.; M-Sa 16 per day 8am-9pm, Su 5 per day 9:30am-9pm). The bus to Port Pollença and Cap de Formentor leaves from the corner of C. del Coral and Pg. Marítim. The **tourist office** is on Pg. Marítim in a small plaza at the far end of the beach, on the left as you face the water. (☎971 54 72 57. Schedule constantly changes; call for hours.) In an emergency call the **police** at ☎971 54 50 66.

In the port, **Hostal Calma ❷,** C. de Teodor Canet, 25, offers pleasant, whitewalled rooms with private bath. (☎971 54 85 85. Singles €20.50; doubles €36.) **Alberg Victoria (HI) ❶,** C. Cap del Pinar, 4, lies 100m from a beach on the Bahía de Pollença. From the town center, signs lead 4km to Malpas and point to the hostel. (1hr. walk or €7 taxi ride. Reserve in advance. ☎971 54 53 95. Breakfast included. HI members only. €12.50, over 27 €15.60.) For food, hit up one of the **restaurants** along the port, or head to **Supermercats Aprop,** C. dels Mariners, 14, to get groceries (open M-Sa 9:30am-9:30pm, Su 9am-2pm).

PORT POLLENÇA (PUERTO POLLENSA)

Autocares Mallorca buses connect Alcúdia and Pollença (20min., M-Sa every 15min. 8:30am-1:30pm and 2:30-8:15pm, €0.90). Autocares Villalonga, C. San Isidro, 4 (☎971 53 00 57) go to Palma (1hr., 5 per day 7:15am-5pm, €4.30). Buses stop at the rotary at the end of Pg. Saralegui.

Popular among British and northern Europeans, calmer and classier than its neighboring beach towns, Port Pollença features a beautiful man-made beach along a crescent-shaped bay. Cafes, restaurants, and pubs cater to a more refined crowd of middle-aged tourists, though the town isn't particularly expensive. You can't walk more than a few feet without stumbling upon a car rental agency, Internet cafe, or restaurant. The **tourist office,** C. Monges, is one block from the bus stop. (☎971 86 54 67. Open M-F 8am-3pm and 5-7pm, Sa 9am-2pm.) **Rent March,** C. Joan XXIII, 89, rents bikes and mopeds. (☎971 86 47 84. Open Mar.-Nov. M-Sa 9am-1pm and 3-8pm, Su 9am-12:30pm. Bikes €5-11 per day; mopeds €21-55 per day.) In an emergency, dial ☎112 or the **police** (☎971 53 04 37). **Hostal Corro ❸,** C. Joan XXIII, 68, offers clean, colorful rooms blocks from the beach. Expect hall baths. (☎971 86 50 05. Doubles €36, for one person €30; triples €42, with private bath €48.) The area hosts a **music festival** in July and August, with concerts every Wednesday and Saturday night. A complete schedule of events and list of ticket vendors is available at the tourist office (tickets €16-36).

CAP DE FORMENTOR

Buses stop 6km away from the end of Cap de Formentor. Autocares Villalonga, C. San Isidro, 4 (☎971 53 00 57), sends one bus daily from Palma (10:15am, returns 3:30pm; €4.80). Autocares Mallorca (☎971 54 56 96) leave from Port Pollença (2 per day 9am-2:15pm, €2.40). A boat (☎971 86 40 14) goes to Platja Formentor from Port Pollença's Estació Marítima (every hr. 10am-3pm, no boat at 2pm; returns every hr. 11:30am-5:30pm, no boat at 2:30 and 4:30pm; round-trip €7.30).

A trek to Cap de Formentor, 15km northeast of Port Pollença, leads to dramatic seaside cliffs, a lighthouse, and a spectacular view—all enjoyed by dozens of tourist families. Before the final kilometer, the road drops to **Platja Formentor,** where a canopy of evergreens seems to sink into the water. If you have your own transportation, head downhill from the lighthouse to the bottom of the road for two of the most beautiful coves in Mallorca. On the right is the small dirt parking lot for **Cala Figuera,** a cove surrounded by jagged cliffs popular with private yachts. Across the road to your right is a small wooden sign pointing in the direction of ◪**Cala Murta,** perhaps the only secluded cove on the island. From the road, follow the dirt path indicated by the sign until you come to a small electrical station. Bear right and you will see the cove's tiny pebbly beach and turquoise water.

SOUTHEASTERN MALLORCA

Signs along the highway of Mallorca's southeast coast might as well read "Welcome Tourist Hordes," as much of the area has been built up by developers. The scalloped bays on the coast east of Cap de Salinas, Mallorca's southernmost point, are their most recent discovery. Still, the breathtaking scenery and intriguing caves remain relatively unspoiled.

◪**COVES DEL DRAC.** The Coves del Drac (Dragon's Caves), near Porto Cristo, are among the island's most dramatic natural wonders, with red and pink stalagtites. A 30min. walk into the depths of the caves is one of the largest underground lakes in the world. The performances given by classical musicians boating across the lake are classified somewhere between absurd and bizarre, though certainly unique and somehow beautiful; audience members can take free boat rides after the concert. *(A bus to the caves runs from the main station by Pl. d'Espanya in Palma. 1hr.; M-Sa 4 per day 10am-1:30pm, Su 1 per day 10am; €6.35.)*

PLATJA DES TRENC. West of Cap de Salinas and east of Cap Blanc sprawls one of Mallorca's best beaches, Platja des Trenc. In most cases, a 1-2km walk is usually enough to put plenty of sand between you and the thickest crowds. *(Buses run to Platja des Trenc in the summer from Pl. d'Espanya in Palma. M-Sa 3 per day 10am-5pm, Su 1 per day 10:30am; €3.84.)*

MENORCA

Menorca's beaches, rustic landscapes, and picturesque towns draw ecologists, sun worshippers, and photographers. In 1993, UNESCO declared the island a biosphere reserve; since then, administrators have emphasized preservation of Menorca's natural harbors, pristine beaches, rocky northern coast, and network of farmlands. The act has also encouraged protection, excavation, and study of Menorca's stone burial chambers and homestead complexes, remnants of a mysterious Talayotic stone-age culture dating from 1400 BC. Since its incorporation into the Catalan kingdom in 1287, Menorca (pop. 71,617) has endured a succession of foreign invaders—Arab, Turkish, French, and British. Quieter and more upscale than the other Balearics, Menorca attracts wealthy young families in search of a peaceful beach vacation and has less to offer budget travelers than its larger neighbors. Most families that come here tend to stay in resorts and apartments along the beaches; the towns themselves sometimes offer reasonable prices. Students make their appearance here before the real tourist season starts, usually in the spring, while everyone else arrives full-force come August. Menorca's main cities, Mahón and Ciutadella, serve as gateways to the island's real attractions.

MAHÓN (MAÓ) ☎971

Atop a steep bluff, Mahón's (pop. 25,000) whitewashed houses overlook a well-trafficked harbor, bustling during the day and tranquil at sunset. The British occupied the city for most of the 18th century, leaving Georgian doors, brass knockers, and wooden shutters in their wake. Two centuries later, the predominance of British tourists testifies to Britain's continuing influence. Most people clear out during the day, using the town as a jumping off point for the numerous beaches nearby; public buses go to some of the more popular stretches of sand. Others spend their hours window-shopping along Mahón's pedestrian streets. The city comes alive in early evening when sunburnt visitors return from the beaches and sea breezes cool the city down. Despite the presence of bars and clubs, Mahón's nightlife is centered more around lingering over dinner than all-night partying.

▶ TRANSPORTATION

Flights: Airport (☎971 15 70 00), 7km out of town. **Iberia/Aviaco** (☎971 36 90 15); **Air Europa** (☎971 24 00 42 or 15 70 31); **SpanAir** (☎971 15 70 98). In summer advance booking is essential. See **By Plane,** p. 362, and **Inter-Island Transport,** p. 363. City center accessible only by taxi.

Ferries: Estació Marítima, Moll de Ponent (☎971 36 60 50). Open M-F 8am-1pm and 5-7pm, Sa 8am-noon, Su 8-10:30am and 3:30-5:15pm. **Trasmediterránea** (☎971 36 29 50) sends ferries daily to **Barcelona** and weekly to **Palma** and **Valencia. Balearia** sends ferries to **Alcúdia, Mallorca.** For more info, see **By Boat,** p. 363, and **Inter-Island Transport,** p. 363.

Buses: Check the tourist office or the newspapers *Menorca Diario Insular* and *Menorca* for schedules. There is no central bus station; buses stop around Pl. de s'Esplanada. **Transportes Menorca** (TMSA☎971 36 03 61), a right on Av. J.A. Clavé, off Pl. de s'Esplanada. To: **Ciutadella** via **Ferreries** and **Es Mercadal** (1hr., 6 per day 8am-7pm, €3.51); **Es Castell** (20min., every 30min. 7:45am-8:45pm, €1); **Platja Punta Prima** (20min., 9 per day 8:30am-7:30pm, €1.10); **Son Bou** (30min., 6 per day 8:30am-7pm, €1.75). All depart from the depot near Pl. de s'Esplanada, up Av. J.A. Clavé and

ISLAS BALEARES

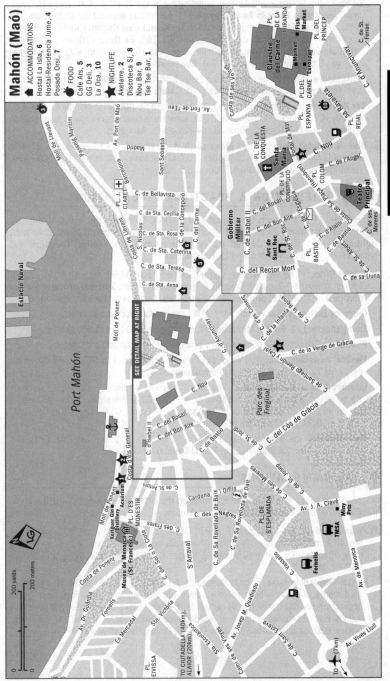

Mahón (Maó)

ACCOMMODATIONS
Hostal La Isla, **6**
Hostal-Residencia Jume, **4**
Posada Orsi, **7**

FOOD
Cafe Ars, **5**
GG Deli, **3**
La Oca, **10**

NIGHTLIFE
Akelarre, **2**
Discoteca Sí, **8**
Nou Bar, **9**
Tse Tse Bar, **1**

Port Mahón

Estació Naval

SEE DETAIL MAP AT RIGHT

Museu de Menorca (St. Francesc)
Xoriguer Gin Distillery
Aquarium
PL. D'ES MONESTIR
PL. FRANCESC
Moll de Ponent
Costa d'ets General

Moll de Llevant
Passeig Marítim
Av. Port de Maó
Madrid
Sant Sebastià
PL. J. CLARET
C. de Bellavista
Costa de Llevant
S. Nicolau
C. de Sta. Cecilia
C. de Sta. Rosa
C. de la Concepció
C. del Carme
C. de Sta. Caterina
C. de Sta. Teresa
C. de Sta. Anna
Av. Fort de l'Eau

Cardona
C. de Sa Rovellada de Baix
C. des Frares
C. des Negres
C. de Sa Rovellada de Dalt
S'Arraval
C. de Sant Antoni
C. Nou
C. del Rosari
C. del Bon Aire
C. de Bastió
C. d'Isabel II
C. d'Alfonso XIII

Parc des Freginal
C. de la Infanta
C. de la Verge de Gràcia
C. de Santiago Ramón y Cajal
C. de St. Jordi
C. del Cós de Gràcia
C. de Ses Moreres
C. de St. Josep
C. Vassallo
PL. DE S'ESPLANADA
Av. J. A. Clavé
Miny Prix
TMSA
Fornells

TO CIUTADELLA (40km), ALAIOR (20km)
Fornells
Av. Dr. Guàrdia
Costa de Ponent
C. de Solo o La Clote
Es Mercadal
Sta. Victòria
PL. EIVISSA
Camí de ses Vinyes
Sta. Escolástica
C. de Josep M. Quadrado
C. de Sant Esteve
Av. de Menorca
Av. Vives Llull
TO (7km)

Detail map (right):
Claustre del Carme
Market
Eurospar
Fish Market
PL. DE LA MIRANDA
PL. DEL PRÍNCEP
C. de St. Ferran
Costa de ses Voltes
PL. DEL CARME
PL. ESPANYA
PL. REIAL
C. de sa Ravaleta
PL. DE LA CONQUESTA
Santa Maria
Portal de Mar
C. Nou
C. de l'Angel
PL. (Hannover)
PL. COLOM
PL. DE LA CONSTITUCIÓ
Gobierno Militar
C. de Isabel II
C. del Rosari
C. del Bon Aire
C. de l'Església
Costa d'es Pont des Castell
Teatre Principal
C. d'Alaior
C. de St. Roc
Arc de Sant Roc
PL. BASTIÓ
C. de s'Albert
C. de sa Lluna
C. del Rector Mort
C. de ses Moreres

200 yards
200 metres

on your right. Tickets available when boarding the bus or at office on Av. Josep M. Quadrado. **Autobuses Fornells Roca Triay** (☎971 37 66 21) depart from C. Vassallo, the same depot as TMSA, but around a corner. To: **Arenal d'en Castell** (30min., 5 per day 10:40am-7pm, Su 3 per day 11am-7pm, €1.70); **Es Grau** (20min., 3 per day 10:30am-6pm, €1.10); **Fornells** (40min., 5 per day 10:40am-7pm, €2.50); **Son Parc** (30min., 5 per day 11am-7pm, €1.70). Buy tickets on board.

Taxis: Main stand at Pl. de s'Esplanada (☎971 36 12 83), or **Radio Taxi** (☎971 36 71 11). To: **airport** (€8); **Cala Mesquida** (€8); **Cala'n Porter** (€11.75); **Es Castell** (€5).

Car Rental: Autos Menorsur, C. Luna, 23 (☎971 36 56 66), off C. Hannóver. Aug. €40 per day, €210 per week; July €36/€180; substantial discounts in low season. English spoken. Open M-F 10am-1:30pm and 5-8pm, Sa-Su 9am-2pm.

Bike & Scooter Rental: Autos Menorca, Moll de Llevant, 35-36 (☎971 35 47 86), Puerto de Mahón. Bicycles €10 per day, €37-42 per week. Scooters €21-27/€93-150. Open Apr.-Sept. daily 9:30am-1:30pm and 5-7:30pm.

✴ 🔢 ORIENTATION & PRACTICAL INFORMATION

Take a taxi (€8) between the **airport** and Mahón. To get to the heart of the city from the **ferry station,** go left (with your back to the water) about 150m, then turn right at the steps that cut through the serpentine **Costa de ses Voltes.** The steps end between Pl. de la Conquesta and Pl. d'Espanya.

Tourist Office: C. de Sa Rovellada de Dalt, 24 (☎971 36 37 90; fax 36 74 15). English spoken. Open M-F 9am-1:30pm and 5-7pm, Sa 9am-1pm. **Summer office** at the airport (☎971 15 71 15) provides similar materials. Open daily Mar.-Oct. 8am-11pm.

Currency Exchange: Banks with 24hr. **ATMs** line C. Hannóver and C. Nou.

Emergency: ☎112. **Police: Municipal,** Pl. de la Constitució (☎971 36 39 61).

Pharmacy: Check the list outside of any pharmacy for the *farmacia de guardia.*

Medical Assistance: Hospital Verge del Toro, C. Barcelona, 3 (☎971 15 77 00; emergency 36 77 26). English spoken. **Ambulance:** ☎061.

Internet Access: Comunicate, C. Vassallo, 22 (☎971 36 55 11). €3 per hr., students €1.50 per hr. Open M-Sa 10am-11pm, Su 6-11pm. **Ciber Principal,** C. Nou, 25 (☎971 36 26 89). €1.20 up to 20min., €2.40 for up to 40min., €3.50 up to 1hr. Open M-F 9:30am-10pm, Sa 11am-2pm and 6-10pm.

Post Office: C. del Bon Aire, 11-13 (☎971 35 66 34), at C. de l'Església. Open M-F 8:30am-8:30pm, Sa 9:30am-2pm. **Postal Code:** 07703.

🏠 ACCOMMODATIONS

It's easier to find a room in Menorca than on the other islands, but it's still a good idea to call ahead, especially in July and August.

▨ **Posada Orsi,** C. de la Infanta, 19 (☎971 36 47 51). Renovated in 2003, rooms are beautiful, modern, and fun. Brightly colored walls and linens. Comfy TV room and sitting room. Breakfast €5. Call before arriving. Singles €15-21; doubles €26-35, with shower €30-42. MC/V. ❷

Hostal-Residencia Jume, C. de la Concepció, 6 (☎971 36 32 66; fax 36 48 78). Standard rooms, all with full bath. Large windows and efficient fans cool things down nicely in summer. Breakfast included by default for €4 extra; make sure to specify if you don't want it. Lots of services available at reception—car rental, books, snacks, etc. June-Aug. singles €20; doubles €40. Sept.-May €18-36. Closed Dec. 15-Jan. 5. ❷

Hostal La Isla, C. de Santa Catalina, 4 (☎/fax 971 36 64 92). Immaculate rooms all come with private bath. Restaurant downstairs serves a typical *menú*. Singles €24.50; doubles €40. MC/V. ❷

▐ FOOD

Café-bars around Pl. de la Constitució, Reial, and s'Esplanada serve *platos combinados* (€2.70-5.10) to sidewalk throngs of hungry customers, though the majority of tourists head to the scenic restaurants on the port, where prices match the upscale atmosphere. Seafood is a specialty among chefs here, but restaurants serve a myriad of other favorites. Regional specialties include *sobrassada* (soft sausage spread), *crespells* (biscuits), and *rubiols* (turnovers filled with fish or vegetables). *Mahónesa* (mayonnaise), which was invented on the island, is popular in many of the more exotic dishes. There is a produce **market** in the large Claustre del Carme, which extends from Pl. d'Espanya to Pl. de la Miranda, with entrances at all four corners. (Open M-Sa 9am-2pm.) **Groceries** are sold below the produce market at **Eurospar** (☎971 36 93 80; open M-Sa 8am-8pm) and at **Miny Prix,** on the corner of Av. J.A. Clavé and Av. de Menorca (open M-Sa 8am-2pm and 5-8:30pm). **Grand General Delicatessen ❶,** Moll de Llevant, 319, has fresh vegetarian dishes, fish and meat entrees, Italian sandwiches, and an excellent variety of salads. The 20min. walk from the port is well worth it. (Sandwiches €1.50-2.10, entrees €3.90-6. Open M-Sa noon-midnight. ☎971 35 28 05.) In town, **La Oca ❷,** C. s'Arravaleta, 27, off Pl. del Carme, serves reasonably priced pizzas (€6.45-8.10) and pastas for €7.50-10. (☎971 35 37 45. Open daily noon-4pm and 7:30-11pm.) For lighter fare in a bohemian setting, try **Cafe Ars ❷,** C. del Carme, 13 . Salads (€5-9), pastas (€5-7), and sandwiches (€2.50-3.50) are tasty and affordable. Dim lights and jazz are a nice way to relax, and large windows frame the outside world. (☎971 36 80 41. Three-course *menú* €11. Open M-Sa 10am-midnight.)

▐ SIGHTS

The most awe-inspiring sights in Menorca lie outside of its cities, although Mahón does have a few attractions. The **Museo de Menorca,** Av. Dr. Guàrdia, an old Franciscan monastery closed in 1835, displays excavated items and exhibits on Menorcan history dating back to Talayotic times. (☎971 35 09 55. Open Tu-Su 10am-2pm and 6-8:30pm. €2.) Founded in 1287 and rebuilt in 1772, the **Església de Santa María La Major,** in Pl. de la Constitución, trembles from the 51 stops, four keyboards, and 3210 pipes of its über-organ, built by the Swiss Juan Kilburz in 1810. (Free organ concerts M-Sa 11am. Open for visits 8am-1pm and 6-8:30pm.) The **Arc de Sant Roc,** up C. Sant Roc from Pl. de la Constitució, straddles the streets of Mahón. It is the last fragment of the medieval wall built to defend the city from Catalan pirates. Get sauced off free liquor samples at the **Xoriguer Gin Distillery** on the port. Through glass windows at the back of the store, visitors watch their drinks bubble and froth in large copper vats. (☎971 36 21 97. Open M-F 8am-7pm, Sa 9am-1pm.) Mahón is close to numerous **archaeological sites,** including prehistoric caves, settlements, and monuments, but they are accessible only by car; see the tourist office for info on a self-guided driving tour. Perhaps the most famous of these monuments is **Torre d'en Galmes,** off the road to Platges de Son Bou from Alaior. Atop a hill overlooking the island's interior, this Talayotic city dates from 1400 BC and served as both a religious and commercial center for Menorca's original inhabitants. Though many of the monuments have yet to be fully excavated and seem to be nothing more than piles of disorganized rubble, of special interest is the eerie **Sala Hipostila,** a prehistoric house whose roof is suspended by columns which are narrower at their bases than at their crowns. (Open daily 10am-8pm. €1.80.)

ISLAS BALEARES

🔊 🎵 NIGHTLIFE & FESTIVALS

Mahón is not known for its nightlife. Weekdays are quiet except in August, and weekends are relatively tame. A string of *bares-musicales* line the **Costa d'els General,** near the water. The colorful, lively **Tse Tse Bar,** Moll de Ponent, 14, fills nightly with energetic 18- to 20-year-olds eager to take advantage of the ample dance floor. An upstairs *terraza* has an unbeatable view of the harbor. (Beer €2.40; mixed drinks €5. Open daily 10pm-4am, in winter Th-Sa 10pm-4am.) One of the more fashionable places on the strip is **Akelarre,** Moll de Ponent, 41-43, a spacious, trendy bar and dance club. Occasional free jazz concerts start earlier. A mixed straight-gay crowd fills the dance floors upstairs around midnight. (☎971 36 85 20. Open daily June-Oct. 8am-5am; Nov.-May 7:30pm-4am.) Away from the port, **Discoteca Sí,** C. Verge de Grácia, 16, turns on the strobe light after midnight, while **Nou Bar,** C. Nou, 1, 2nd fl., serves drinks (€4-6) to a calm, older crowd. (Both open daily noon-3pm and 7:30pm-3am.)

Film lovers should check out **cine a la fresca,** held every night except Friday in the Claustre del Carme at 10pm. A different film is shown each week in the outdoor courtyard of the cloister. Look for the posters around town advertising the current movie. (Enter from Pl. de la Miranda. €5.)

From May to September, merchants sell shoes, clothes, and souvenirs in **mercadillos** held daily in various town squares (Es Castell M and W; Ferrerias Tu and F; Mahón Tu and Sa; Alaior Th; Ciutadella F-Sa; Mercadal Su). In mid-July, Mahón's **Verge del Carme** celebration brings a colorfully trimmed armada into the harbor. Mahón's **Festival de Música de Maó** in July and August showcases Santa María's Swiss organ. (Pl. de la Constitució. Festival concerts start at 9:30pm; see tourist office for upcoming events. Seat "donation" €3.)

NEAR MAHÓN

The coves and beaches near Mahón are best explored with a rental car and the *Let's Go to the Beach* brochure (not an official *Let's Go* guide) and map available at the tourist office. The highway from Mahón to Ciutadella is straight and well-maintained; local roads are curvy, pot-holed, and often unpaved. Be careful when driving at night. The beaches below are listed from closest to farthest from Mahón.

NORTH SHORE

ALBUFERA ES GRAU. A large natural reserve, Albufera Es Grau entices visitors with lagoons, pine woods, and farmland, as well as diverse flora and fauna. Recreational activities include hiking to the coves across the bay. Some of the best swimming areas are across from the main lagoon and uphill from town, along a series of bluffs that form secluded coves; here, only the sound of the clear water lapping at the rocks can be heard. **Viajes Isla Colom** sends boats from the marina on the lagoon in Es Grau to **Illa d'en Colom,** a tiny island with more beaches. (☎971 35 98 67; 4 boats per day 10:30am-5pm, last boat returns at 7pm. Autocares Fornells leave from C. Vassallo in Mahón. 20min., 3 per day 10:30am-6pm, €1.10.)

ARENAL D'EN CASTELL. Breathtaking views, calm water, and packed sands make this tiny cove a popular destination for daytrippers from Mahón and the vacationing families who populate the upscale resorts and condos dotting the slope above the beach. A tourist train, "Arenal Na Macaret Express," makes the short trip from the bus stop in Arenal across a narrow strip of land to **Macaret,** a tiny fishing village with an even tinier beach. (Autocares Fornells leave from C. Vassallo in Mahón. 30min.; M-Sa 5 per day 10:40am-7pm, Su 3 per day 11am, 1:30, 7pm; €1.70.)

FORNELLS. A small fishing village known for its lobster farms, Fornells has only recently begun to attract tourists. However, more and more tourist-oriented venues are opening; restaurants, gift shops, and diving and boat rental agencies dot the main port road. Windsurfers zip around Fornells's long, shallow port, while beach gurus make excursions to **Cala Tirant** and **Binimella,** both only a few kilometers to the west. Fornells also serves as a calm base from which to explore coves and jagged cliffs by car or bike, as bus service is very limited. (*Autobuses Roca Triay run to Fornells from C. Vassallo in Mahón. 30min., 5 per day 10am-7pm, €2.50.*)

CAP DE CAVALLERIA. Off the main road to Fornells, along a lonely, windswept highway that is more frequently used by goats than tourists, is the breathtaking landscape of Cap de Cavalleria. Bearing a striking resemblance to parts of the British Isles, the green hills dotted with medieval ruins that characterize this cape lead to a series of white limestone cliffs crowned by a beautiful lighthouse overlooking the deep blue water below. Though there are several beaches along the cape, it is best to come here for a relaxing picnic on the seaside bluffs.

SOUTH SHORE

PUNTA PRIMA. While this beach may not be as secluded or expansive as some, it draws a crowd with its proximity to Mahón. A lighthouse on a strip of land across from the beach overlooks the coastline. (*TMSA buses run to and from Pl. de s'Esplanada in Mahón. 20min., 8 per day 8:30am-7:30pm, €1.10.*)

ELS CANUTELLS. Situated off the road from Mahón to Cala'n Porter (a 15min. drive from Mahón), Els Canutells is a pleasant and secluded cove with calm, turquoise waters good for swimming and snorkeling. A couple of bars and restaurants lie on the road above the cove. (*TMSA buses run to and from Av. Josep M. Quadrado in Mahón. 20 min., 4 per day 8:45am-7pm, €1.10.*)

CALESCOVES. Past Els Canutells and off the road from Mahón to Cala'n Porter (a 20min. drive from Mahón) is this pristine serpentine cove with rocky cliffs and a small beach perfect for a refreshing swim. Equally refreshing is this area's lack of tourists. Since Calescoves cannot be reached by public transportation, you'll need to drive. Park at the top of the hill and continue down the dirt path for about 20min. until you reach the rocky part of the cove.

CALA'N PORTER. Expansive and touristy, Cala'n Porter greets thousands of visitors each summer with its whitewashed houses, orange stucco roofs, and red sidewalks. Its small but well-used beach lies at the bottom of a steep, bouldered hillside, but pedestrian access is easy via the main road and a marked staircase. (*TMSA buses run to and from Av. Josep M. Quadrado in Mahón. 7 per day 9:30am-7:30pm, €1.10.*) A 10min. walk away, at the end of Av. Central, the ■ **Covas d'en Xoroi** dominate cliffs high above the sea. The caves are inhabited by a network of bars by day and a popular disco (which attracts a largely young British crowd) by night. (*☎971 37 72 36. Bars open Apr.-Oct. daily 10:30am-9pm. Disco open nightly at 11pm. Foam parties every Th. Cover for bars €4.90, includes 1 drink. Cover for disco €15.*)

PLATGES DE SON BOU. The longest beach on the island, Son Bou offers 4km of sand on the southern shore, covered with throngs of sunburned tourists. As the most popular of Menorca's beaches, it's also the most visitor-friendly, with frequent bus service to and from Mahón and Ciutadella, endless beach chairs, umbrellas for rent, and cafes. There are even *discotecas* only two blocks from the sand. Be aware, though, that part of the beach is also for nudists, and the farther away from the commercial center you walk, the more naked it gets. (*TMSA buses to the beachesleave from Av. Josep M. Quadrado in Mahón. 30min., 7 per day 8:45am-7pm,*

€1.65.) For those who choose to stay late, **Disco/Bar Copacabana,** in the Nuevo Centro Comercial, on the left when heading away from the water, is the best place to rock your evening, all the while with a great view of the water. *(Open May-Oct. daily 11pm-3:30am.)* If you're just in the mood for a relaxing frozen drink, head across the street to the big rattan chairs and couches of **Bou Hai Hawaiian Bar,** serving margaritas and daiquiris for €5.50. *(Open daily noon-3am.)* If you do choose to stay late, make sure you have a rental car or a place to stay—there is no public transportation back to Mahón until the morning, and the last bus back is at 7:35pm.

CALA MITJANA & ■CALA MITJANETA. On the main highway from Mahón to Ciutadella, head toward Ferreries, and then take the road to Santa Galdana. Directly on your left before reaching the roundabout above the town is the dirt road that leads to **Cala Mitjana** (a 30min. drive from Mahón). Park your car in the small dirt lot and continue on foot to the small beach overlooking a dramatic cove bordered by white limestone cliffs that plunge into the turquoise sea. Though this beach is not totally secluded, if you climb the staircase on your right upon entering the cove and head down the dirt path for about 5min., you get to **Cala Mitjaneta,** a smaller cove affording even more dramatic views of limestone cliffs and the wide expanse of the Mediterranean beyond the inlet. While some visitors wade into the water here, others prove their bravery (or recklessness) by diving from the rocks.

CIUTADELLA (CIUDADELA)   ☎971

Ciutadella's (pop. 15,000) narrow, cobblestoned paths weave between neighborhoods nearly undisturbed by tourists, while only blocks away, restaurants, shops, and postcard vendors compete for attention in the crowded plazas. There is a seductive charm to the city's ancient streets, broad *plaças*, and winding port, and the rugged beauty of the surrounding countryside and nearby beaches provides an easy, exciting escape from city congestion.

▢ TRANSPORTATION

Buses: Transportes Menorca (TMSA) buses leave from C. Barcelona, 8 (☎971 38 03 93), and go to **Mahón** (1 hr., 6 per day 8am-7pm, €3.70). **Autocares Torres** (☎971 38 64 61) offers daily service from the front of the ticket booth in Pl. de s'Explanada to surrounding beaches, all of which are 15-30min. away. To: **Cala Blanca** and **Santandria** (15min., 15 per day 7am-11:15pm, €1.05); **Cala Blanes, Los Delfines,** and **Cala Forçat** (10-20min., 23 per day 7am-11:35pm, €1.05); **Cala Bosch** and **Son Xoriguer** (25-30min., 24 per day 7am-midnight, €1.05); **Sa Caleta** and **Son Blanc** (10-15 min., 18 per day 9am-midnight, €1.05).

Ferries: Iscomar de Ferrys (☎902 11 91 28) runs between Ciutadella and **Alcúdia, Mallorca** (2½hr.; M-F 2 per day 11:30am, 8pm, Sa-Su 1 per day 8pm; €31). **Cape Balear** (☎902 10 04 44) links Ciutadella to **Cala Ratjada, Menorca** (55min.; May-Oct. 2 per day 7:30am, 7:30pm; €45).

Taxis: (☎971 38 28 96 or 38 11 97). Pl. de s'Explanada is a prime hailing spot.

Car Rental: Europcar, Av. de Jaume I, 59 (☎971 38 29 98). 21+. From €39 per day and from €210 per week. Open daily 9am-8pm.

Bike and Scooter Rental: Velos Joan, C. de Sant Isidre, 32-34 (☎971 38 15 76). Bike rental €6 per day, €20-26 per week. Scooters €41-72 for 2 days, €127-236 per week. 2-day min. scooter rental. Open M-F 8:30am-1:30pm, Sa 9am-1:30pm.

✳ 🛈 ORIENTATION & PRACTICAL INFORMATION

To get from the **bus station** to **Plaça de la Catedral** and the tourist office, head left half a block, take a left on Camí de Maó, go straight through Pl. d'Alfons III, and continue along C. de Maó as it turns into C. Josep M. Quadrado (ses Voltes) after crossing Pl. Nova. To get from Pl. de la Catedral to **Plaça de s'Explanada** (also called Pl. dels Pins), exit the plaza on C. Major del Born with the cathedral behind you and to the right, cross Pl. d'es Born on its right side, and bear diagonally across to the left. The **port** and its accompanying street, C. Marina, lie below the rest of the city and can be reached via a stone stairway just off the corner of Pl. d'es Born.

Tourist Office: Pl. de la Catedral, 3 (☎971 38 26 93). Excellent maps available. English and German spoken. Open M-F 9am-9pm, Sa 9am-1pm, Su 5-8pm.

Banks: BBVA, Pl. d'es Born, 14 (☎971 48 40 04). Open M-F 8:30am-2pm.

Emergency: ☎ 112 or 092. **Police:** Pl. d'es Born (☎971 38 07 87).

Medical Emergencies: Clínica Menorca, C. Canonge Moll (☎971 48 05 05). 24hr.

Internet Access: Accesso Directo, Pl. de s'Esplanada, 37 (☎971 38 42 15). €2 for 50 min. Open M-Sa 9am-midnight.

Post Office: Pl. d'es Born (☎971 38 00 81). Open May-Oct. M-F 8:30am-8:30pm, Sa 9:30am-1pm; Nov.-Apr. M-F 8:30am-2:30pm, Sa 9:30am-1pm. **Postal Code:** 07760.

🛏 ACCOMMODATIONS

Hostels are packed and pricy during peak season (June 15-early Sept.)—double rooms usually run over €30. Always call ahead in the summer.

Hostal Residencia Oasis, C. de Sant Isidre, 33 (☎971 38 21 97). From Pl. de s'Explanada, take Av. del Capità Negrete to Pl. d'Artrutx and C. de Sant Isidre. A centrally located floral paradise. Gorgeous garden patio and dining area. Rooms are clean and bright. Breakfast included. Doubles with bath €44-48. ❹

Casa de Huespedes Sa Posada, C. Ibiza, 14 (☎971 38 58 96 or 38 57 78), off Pl. de s'Explanada. Look carefully for the small CH sign above the door. If you're lucky enough to score 1 of the 7 double rooms at this *hostal,* you'll be rewarded with some of the cheapest and comfiest accommodations in Ciutadella. Smallish rooms all have private baths and refrigerators. Aug. doubles €36; July and Sept. €30; Oct.-May €26. ❸

Hotel Geminis, C. Josepa Rossinyol, 4 (☎971 38 58 96; fax 38 36 83). Take C. del Sud off Av. del Capità Negrete from Pl. de s'Explanada; turn left onto C. Josepa Rossinyol. Rooms with pretty wood furniture, phones, baths, A/C, and TVs. Outdoor terrace has small pool. Restaurant and plush sitting room. Breakfast included. Mid-June to Sept. singles €42; doubles €75. Oct.-Mar. €22.50/€36. Apr. to mid-June €27/45. ❸

🍴 FOOD

Most of Ciutadella's options are touristy. Nicer restaurants surround the port, while more generic spots near Pl. de s'Explanada and along C. de Josep M. Quadrado offer cheaper fare. Shop at the **market** on Pl. de la Libertat, or try **Supermarket Super Avui,** C. Sant Onofre, 12. (☎971 38 27 28. Open M-Sa 10am-2pm and 5-8pm.)

La Guitarra, C. Nuestra Sra. dels Dolors, 1 (☎971 38 13 55). Take C. Major del Born off Pl. d'es Born and turn right on C. del Roser, which leads to C. Nuestra Sra. dels Dolors. For traditional island cuisine, descend to this stone cave-turned-restaurant and sample

NO WORK, ALL PLAY

HOLD YOUR HORSES!

On the last Thursday in June, Ciutadella celebrates *La Fiesta de San Juan*, a wild festival that rivals the infamous *San Fermines*. It coincides with the shortest night of the year, the summer solstice, and in its pagan origins, is thought to mark the triumph of light over dark. One of the most important features of the festivities is fire, and the ashes of the numerous bonfires are thought to cure skin diseases. One is advised (by legend, not by *Let's Go*) to jump through the fire a minimum of three times in order to insure a good year.

The party formally begins with the arrival of the *fabioler* (herald of the ceremony) on a white horse. Playing a drum and flute, he gallops through town for four hours with crowds of drunken Menorcans following close behind. At 6pm, village men ride 250 wild horses through town on their hind legs. Successfully bipedal horses are rewarded with cheers of *"Olé!"* and the rest charge into the crowd, often knocking over bystanders. In 1999, one horse crashed down on the mayor of Menorca, ending his term for good. Note bene for future office-holders: some PR opportunities just aren't worth it.

the mysterious *sopa mallorquina,* a traditional meat and veggie soup (€4.95). *Menú* €10. Entrees €6.60-18. Open June-Sept. M-Sa 12:30-3:15pm and 7-11pm. MC/V. ❸

Bar-Restaurante Can Tomás, C. Sant Joan Baptista, 8 (☎971 38 44 98), around the corner from La Guitarra. Typical Spanish fare served in *platos combinados* (€4-7). Local feel and no-frills setting. Open M-Sa 10am-midnight. ❷

Pizzeria Restaurant Raco d'es Palau, C. del Palau, 3 (☎971 38 54 02), in an alley off C. Major del Born. Pleasant indoor and outdoor seating complements great pizza (€5.15-6.35) and seafood dishes (€6.25-16). Open daily 4pm-midnight. MC/V. ❷

SIGHTS & ENTERTAINMENT

An interesting complement to Menorca's beaches are the remnants of its various archaeological sites. Dating from the Bronze Age, the ⬛**Naveta des Tudons,** one of the oldest structures in Europe, sits 4km from the city. These ruins of community tombs are the island's best preserved. **Torretrencada** and **Torrellafuda** were rounded towers that overlooked the countryside. Both protect Stonehenge-like *taulas,* formations that have stood for over 3000 years. Buses don't come near these sights, so consider **hiking** (about 5km) along C. Camí Vell de Maó. The descriptive *Archaeological Guide to Menorca* is available at the tourist office.

The Ciutadella community is one of early-to-bedders. **Asere,** C. de Curniola, 23, one block off Pl. Nova, spices things up a bit with a Cuban theme and frozen drinks (open F-Sa 8pm-midnight). From the first week in July to the beginning of September, Ciutadella hosts the **Festival de Música d'Estiu,** featuring some of the world's top classical musicians. Tickets (€9.60-21) are sold at **Foto Born,** C. Seminari, 14 (☎971 38 17 54), and at the box office (open daily 9:30am-1:30pm and 5-8pm). Concerts take place in the cloisters of the seminary. On June 22, even veteran partiers from Palma and Ibiza join locals as they burn gallons of midnight oil during **La Fiesta de San Juan,** Menorca's biggest *fiesta.* A week before the festivities, which include jousting and equestrian displays, a man clad in a sheepskin carries a decorated lamb on his shoulders through the city.

BEACHES

The more popular Menorcan beaches (accessible by bus from Mahón and Ciutadella) are located in somewhat touristy areas and are overrun by resort hotels, bars, restaurants, and postcard shops. Many beaches are located in small coves. While these are more secluded, the more accessible beaches can get fairly packed during the day. Never fear: Menorca has over 80 beaches. With a car, moped, or a little legwork, endless stretches of less-crowded sands are easily accessible. The northern beaches are rocky. Finer sands, however, are hidden under hundreds of tourists on the southern coast. Most of the beaches listed below are accessible by bus; for a complete list of beaches accessible by car, request the *Let's Go to the Beach* brochure (not an official *Let's Go* guide) at the tourist office.

NEAR CIUTADELLA

■ **NORTH SHORE.** The stretch east of Cala Morell is home to the most outstanding beaches on the island. The **Platges d'Algaiarens** may be the superstars of the series, including Cala en Carabó, Penyal de l'Anticrist, Sa Falconera, and Cala Pilar Ets Alocs. Secluded beaches surrounded by pine forests in a lush valley allow you to forget the outside world for a few hours. *(A taxi from Ciutadella costs €12, but arrange the return trip in advance; there are no pay phones and cell phones may lose coverage.)*

CALA'N BOSCH & SON XORIGUER. Five-star resorts provide the backdrop for Cala'n Bosch, a popular cove situated between jagged cliffs. Because of its proximity to Ciutadella, this is one of the more crowded beaches, but with fruit sellers and restaurants, it's worth visiting. Just down the road from Cala'n Bosch, the beach at Son Xoriguer isn't quite as hectic as its neighbor, but is equally beautiful. *(Both accessible by Torres bus from Ciutadella. 24 per day 7am-midnight, €1.10.)*

EIVISSA (IBIZA)

Nowhere on Earth does style rule over substance (or do substances rule over style) more than on Ibiza (pop. 84,000). Once a 1960s hippie enclave, Ibiza has forgotten her roots in favor of a new age of decadence. Disco fiends, high-fashion gurus, movie stars, and party-hungry backpackers arrive in droves to debauch in the island's outrageous, sex- and substance-driven culture. However, not every night on the island has to be filled with such hedonism and glam; much of Ibiza's wild see-and-be-seen disco culture is at only a few megaclubs. It's not uncommon to see people arriving at discos in jeans or shorts, or to spend a night just chilling at a waterfront bar. A thriving gay community lends credence to Ibiza's image as a center of tolerance, but the island's high price tags preclude true diversity.

Surprisingly, there is more to Ibiza than spectacular nightlife; its beaches and mountains are some of the most spectacular in all the Balearics. The island's rich history has left its mark in the form of several ancient castles—the most prominent in Eivissa (Ibiza City). Since the Carthaginians retreated to Ibiza from the mainland in 656 BC, the island's list of conquerors reads like a "Who's Who of Ancient Western Civilization." Perhaps the most famous was the 1235 invasion by the Catalans, who brought Christianity and built the walls that still fortify Eivissa.

EIVISSA (IBIZA CITY)

Eivissa (pop. 35,000) is the world's biggest 24hr. party. The town itself is like Dr. Jekyll and Mr. Hyde. During the day, families meander and sightsee through the walled D'alt Vila, and the city streets remain tranquil while the majority of visitors sleep off hangovers, tanning at nearby beaches. Eivissa could easily be mistaken for any other seaside village in Spain. At night, however, there's no mistaking this town for any other. Flashy bars appear seemingly out of nowhere, filling street after street with neon lights, blasting music, and fast-talking club promoters; grab a front-row seat at the outdoor tables to enjoy the prime people-watching action. Come 3am, the scene migrates to the clubs, where parties last until dawn (and often well into the next day)—then it all begins again.

▐ TRANSPORTATION

Flights: Airport (☎971 80 90 00), 7km south of the city. Bus #10 runs between the airport and Av. d'Isidor Macabich, 20, in town (30min., every hr. 7am-11.10pm, €1). Info booth open 24hr. **Iberia,** Pg. Vara de Rey, 15 (☎902 40 05 00 or 971 30 03 00), flies to Alicante, Barcelona, Madrid, Palma, and Valencia. **Air Europa** and **Spanair** offer similar options. See **By Plane,** p. 362, or **Inter-Island Transport,** p. 363.

Ferries: Estació Marítima. Trasmediterránea (☎971 31 51 00 or 902 45 46 45) sells tickets at Estació Marítima and sends ferries to **Barcelona, Palma,** and **Valencia.** Office open M-F 9am-1pm, 4:30-7:30pm, and 2hr. before ferry departures. **Trasmapi-Balearia** (☎971 31 40 05 or 902 16 01 80) runs daily to and from **Dénia,** near Alicante; a connection in Eivissa continues to and from **Palma.** Office open M-F 9am-2:15pm, 4:30-8pm, and midnight-1:15am; Sa 9am-2:15pm and 6-8pm; Su 9am-2:15pm and midnight-1:15am. **Umafisa Lines** (☎971 21 02 01) sends ferries to and from **Barcelona** 3-4 times per week. For rates, fares, and schedules, see **By Boat,** p. 363, or **Inter-Island Transport,** p.363.

Buses: Ibiza has a fairly extensive bus system, although some buses to more remote beaches and villages run only a few times per day; plan accordingly. The main bus stop is on Av. d'Isidor Macabich, past Pl. d'Enric Fajarnés i Tur when walking away from the port. For an exact schedule, check the tourist office or *El Diario.* Intercity buses (€1.80) leave from Av. d'Isidor Macabich, 42 (☎971 31 21 17) to **Sant Antoni** (M-Sa every 15min., Su every 30min. 7am-11:30pm) and **Santa Eulària des Riu** (M-F every 30min., Sa-Su every hr. 7:30am-11:30pm). Buses (☎971 34 03 82) to the beaches cost €1.15 and leave from Av. d'Isidor Macabich, 20, and Av. d'Espanya to: **Cala Tarida** (5 per day 10:10am-6:45pm); **Cap Martinet** (M-Sa 11 per day 8:15am-8pm); **Platja d'en Bossa** (every 30min. 8:30am-11pm); **Salinas** (every hr. 9:30am-7:30pm).

Taxis: ☎971 30 70 00 or 30 66 02.

Car and Moped Rental: Casa Valentín, Av. B.V. Ramón, 19 (☎971 31 08 22). Mopeds €25-30 per day. Cars from €39. Open daily 9am-1pm and 3:30-8:30pm.

✴▐ ORIENTATION & PRACTICAL INFORMATION

Three distinct sections make up the city. **Sa Penya,** in front of Estació Marítima, is crammed with bars and boutiques. Atop the hill behind Sa Penya, high walls circle **Dalt Vila,** the old city. **La Marina** and the commercial district occupy the gridded streets to the far right of the Estació (with your back to the water). **Avinguda d'Espanya,** continuing from Pg. Vara de Rey, heads toward the airport and local beaches. The local paper *Diario de Ibiza* (€1; www.diariodeibiza.es) has an *Agenda* page that lists essential information, including the bus schedule for the entire island, the ferry schedule, the schedule of all domestic flights to and from Ibiza, water and weather forecasts, info on the island's 24hr. pharmacies, a list of 24hr. gas stations, and important phone numbers.

Tourist Office: Pl. d'Antoni Riquer, 2 (☎971 30 19 00). Open M-F 9:30am-1:30pm and 5-7:30pm, Sa 10:30am-1pm. **Booth** at the airport (☎971 80 91 18). Open May-Oct. M-Sa 9am-2pm and 3-8pm, Su 9am-2pm.

Currency Exchange: Exchanges are all over town; banks and ATMs offer better rates. **La Caixa,** Av. d'Isidor Macabich, has good exchange rates for cash and travelers checks.

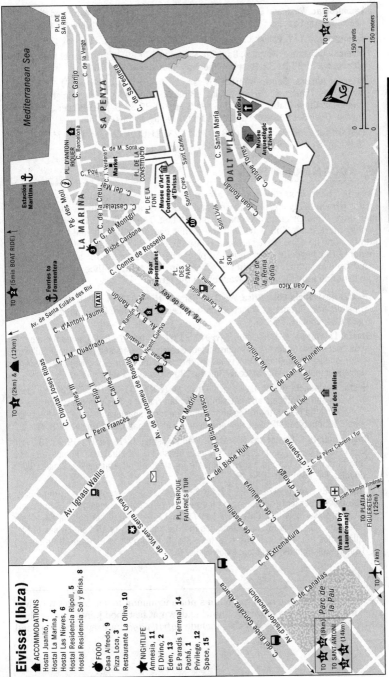

ISLAS BALEARES

Laundromat: Wash and Dry, Av. d'Espanya, 53 (☎971 39 48 22). Wash and dry €4.20 each. **Internet** access €5.40 per hr. Open M-F 10am-3pm and 5-10pm, Sa 10am-5pm.

Emergency: ☎112. **Police:** C. de Vicent Serra i Orvay, 25 (☎971 31 58 61).

Medical Assistance: Hospital, Barri Can Misses (☎971 39 70 00), west of town. **Ambulance:** ☎971 39 32 32. **Hospital Nuestra Señora** (☎971 39 70 21).

Internet Access: Centro Internet Eivissa, Av. Ignasi Wallis, 39 (☎971 31 81 61). €1.20 per 15min., €1.50 per 30min., €3 per hr. Open M-Sa 10am-midnight, Su 5pm-midnight. **Ciber Matic,** C. Cayetà Soler, 3 (☎971 30 33 82). €1.80 per 30min., €3 per hr. Open Sept.-June M-Sa 10am-11pm, July-Aug. M-Sa 1pm-2am.

Post Office: C. de Madrid, s/n (☎971 31 43 23). **Lista de Correos.** Open M-F 8:30am-8:30pm, Sa 9:30am-2pm. **Postal Code:** 07800.

ACCOMMODATIONS

Decent, cheap *hostales* in town are rare, especially in the summer—but then again, who actually *sleeps* here anyway? Call several weeks in advance for summer stays, when prices climb and hostels fill fast. The letters "CH" (*casa de huéspedes*) mark many doorways, but the owner can often be reached by the phone number on the door. Eivissa has a relatively safe and up-all-night lifestyle, and owners offer keys for 24hr. entry. All prices listed below are for high season and can drop by as much as €12 in the off-season. The tourist office offers an extensive list of all lodging options available in the city.

Hostal Residencia Sol y Brisa, Av. B. V. Ramón, 15 (☎971 31 08 18; fax 30 30 32). Upstairs from Pizzeria da Franco. Clean and centrally located. Social atmosphere. Singles €24; doubles €42. ❷

Hostal La Marina, C. Barcelona, 7 (☎971 31 01 72; fax 31 48 94), amid the the raucous bar scene. Rooms have sophisticated, vaguely ocean-related decor. Four buildings offer lodging ranging from stark to lavish. The best (and most expensive) have TV, A/C, private bath, carpet, and balcony. Singles €30-62; doubles €41-150. ❸

Hostal Residencia Ripoll, C. Vicent Cuervo, 14 (☎971 31 42 75). Fastidiously clean hallways and bathrooms and unusually large, fan-cooled rooms with pretty bedspreads are among the best in town. The apartments are more spacious and fun. July-Sept. singles €30; doubles €42; 3-person apartments with TV, patio, and kitchen €78. ❸

Hostal Juanito & Hostal Las Nieves, C. Joan d'Austria, 17-18 (☎971 19 03 19). Run by the same owner, both hostels offer cheap housing in a central area. Rooms are basic and bare-walled, but more than adequate for sleeping off a hangover. Singles €21; doubles €42, with bath €50. ❷

Camping: Es Cana (☎971 33 21 17; fax 33 99 71). €5.95 per person, €1.80 per site, €5.60-9.95 per tent (depending on the number of people). Bungalow €45-65, cabin €15-25. Reserve via fax. **Cala Nova** (☎971 33 17 74). €4.70 per person, €4.10 per tent. Both sites close to Sta. Eulària des Riu. Take bus #13 or 15 from Eivissa to Sta. Eulària des Riu, and then bus #18 from Sta. Eulària d'alt to Es Cana. Both sites a 10min. walk from the bus stop; follow signs. ❶

FOOD

Inexpensive cuisine is hard to find; it's not uncommon to see budget travelers stocking up at grocery stores or chowing down at fast food joints to save their euros for the discos. Ibizan dishes include *sofrit pagès*, a deep-fried lamb and chicken dish; *flao*, a lush lemon- and mint-tinged cheesecake; and *graxonera*, cinnamon-dusted pudding made from eggs and bits of *ensaimada* (candied bread). The **Mercat Vell** sells meat, fruit, and vegetables (open M-Sa 7am-1pm). For **groceries**, try **Spar**. (Open M-Sa 9am-9pm.)

> **Pizza Loca,** C. de Lluís Tur i Palau, 15 (☎971 31 45 68). Rectangular pizzas with a variety of toppings including vegetables, tuna, and salami. Eat outside at wooden tables or get it to go and chow down on the beach. Slices €2-3. Open daily noon-5am. ❶
>
> **Restaurante La Oliva,** C. Santa Creu, 2 (☎971 30 57 52). Pricy but scrumptious Italian fare. Get a candlelit outdoor table and people-watch. Pasta €8-11; meat and fish entrees €9-18. Open daily 8pm-1am. ❸
>
> **Casa Alfredo,** Pg. Vara de Rey, 16. Fish, meat, and heavenly desserts fill the *menú* (€6-9) that locals deem the best in town. Open M-Sa 1-4pm and 8pm-midnight. ❷

🅢 SIGHTS

Wrapped in 16th-century walls, **Dalt Vila** (High Town) rises above the town. Its twisting streets lead to the 14th-century **cathedral,** built in several phases and styles. (Open daily 10:30am-1pm.) Next to the cathedral is the **Museu Arqueològic d'Eivissa,** home to a variety of regional artifacts. (Open Tu-Sa 10am-2pm and 6-8pm, Su 10am-2pm. €2, students €1.) Amid stone walls, the small **Museu d'Art Contemporani d'Eivissa** displays a range of art exhibitions. (C. Sa Carrossa, on the left when entering from Pl. de sa Font. ☎971 30 27 23. Open M-F 10am-1pm and 6:30-10pm, Sa 10am-1:30pm. €1.20, students free.) The archaeological museum, **Puig des Molins,** Vía Romana, displays Punic, Roman, and Iberian artifacts. (☎971 30 17 71. Open M-Sa 10am-2pm and 5-8pm, Su 10am-2pm. €1.20.)

🅒 BEACHES

The power of the rising sun draws thousands of topless solar zombies to nearby tanning grounds. **Platja Figueretes,** a thin stretch of sand in the shadow of large hotels, is the best foot-accessible beach from Eivissa. To get there, walk down Av. d'Espanya and take a left on C. Juan Ramón Jiménez. Farther down, **Platja d'en Bossa** is the liveliest of Ibiza's beaches, home to numerous beach bars, as well as throngs of sun-seeking tourists. **Platja des Duros** is tucked across the bay from Sa Penya and Sa Marina, just before the lighthouse. At **Platja de Talamanca,** the water—more an enclosed bay than open sea—is accessible on foot by following the road to the new port and continuing on to the beach (20min.). 🖾**Platja de ses Salinas** is one of Ibiza's most popular and famous beaches, although others are actually more scenic. Bask among the beautiful people and groove to chilled-out house pulsating from **Sa Trincha** bar at the end of the beach. Neighboring **Platja des Cavallet** is decidedly clothing-optional and attracts a beautiful, largely gay crowd. To get to both, take the bus from Eivissa to Salinas; for Es Cavallet, get off at the stop before Salinas (look for the T-intersection to the left or just ask the bus driver) and walk to the beach (10min.) or walk from Salinas (20min.).

More private coastal stretches lie in the northern part of the island and are accessible by car or moped. Among these, the German enclave at **Cala de Sant Vicent** (past Santa Eulària des Riu on the road to St. Carles de Peralta) offers white sands and breathtaking views that are far from secluded, but peaceful nonetheless. The small coves in the rocky northernmost point of the island (between Portinatx and St. Agnes de Corona) are worth visiting if you seek serenity or the company of modern-day flower children. **Cala Xarraca** is a beautiful EU *bandera azul* cove popular with families, who fight for spots on its small beach. The views from **Cap de Rubió** are among the most dramatic on the island. On the road from Sant Miquel to Sant Mateu, take the left fork up a semi-paved road; the road rises and then drops suddenly to a rocky path, which leads to impressive limestone cliffs. Hike down to any of the coves at the bottom of the paths next to the abandoned mine shafts, and you'll be rewarded with your own private swimming hole.

◪ NIGHTLIFE

The crowds return from the beaches by nightfall, when even the stores dazzle with throbbing techno and flashing lights. Herds of men and women representing each club parade through the streets, advertising their disco and trying to outdo others. Meanwhile, seaport bars crawl with aggressive promoters. **Bars** in Eivissa are crowded midnight-3am and are everyone's first stop before hitting the discos. The scene centers around **Carrer de Barcelona** and spins outward into the sidestreets. **Carrer de la Verge** is the center of gay nightlife and outrageous fashion. Cocktails cost as much as €10 and beer rings in at around €6, so if you plan on drinking a lot, either pre-game on your own or head to the cheaper bar scene in Sant Antoni.

The island's ◪**discos** (virtually all have a mixed gay/straight crowd) are world-famous—veterans claim that you will never experience anything half as wild or fun. The best sources of information are disco-goers and the zillions of posters that plaster the stores and restaurants of La Marina and Sa Penya. There is something different each day of the week, and each club is known for a particular theme party—be sure to hit up a club on a popular night, or you'll end up shelling out a lot of money for a not-so-happening party. For listings, check out *Ministry in Ibiza* or *DJ* magazines, free at many hostels, bars, and restaurants. Drinks at Ibiza's clubs cost about €10 and covers start at €30. If you know where you're going ahead of time, buy your disco tickets from a promoter at or in front of the bars in town; you'll pay €6-18 less than what you would pay at the door, and it's completely legit—some tickets even include transportation and admission afterwards to **Space,** the beachfront after-hours club, although these deals are more commonly found in Sant Antoni. Generally, disco-goers bar-hop in Eivissa or Sant Antoni and jet off to clubs via bus or taxi around 3am. The **Discobus** runs to all the major hotspots (leaves Eivissa from Av. d'Isidor Macabich every hr. 12:30am-6:30am, schedule for other stops available at tourist office and hotels, €1.50).

◪ **Privilege** (☎971 19 80 86; www.privilege-ibiza.com), on the Discobus to Sant Antoni or a €9 taxi. The world's largest club, according to the *Guinness Book of World Records.* This enormous complex packs in up to 10,000 with bars in the double digits and a pool. *The* place to be on Monday for its infamous "Manumission" parties. Dance the night away in the huge main room or explore the smaller bars and terraces. Cover €40 and up. Open June-Sept. daily midnight-7am. V.

Pachá (☎971 31 36 00; www.pacha.com), 15min. walk from the port, 2min. in a taxi. The most famous club chain in Spain, and the most elegant of Ibiza's discos. Locals and tourists get their groove on in a dim, beautiful setting. "Ministry of Sound" on Th brings a big crowd, and "Made in Italy" on F is, not surprisingly, popular with Italian clubbers. Only club open year-round in Ibiza. Cover €50. Open daily midnight-7:30am.

Amnesia (☎971 19 80 41; www.amnesiaibiza.com), on the road to Sant Antoni; take the Discobus. Converted warehouse with psychedelic lights and movie screens has 2 gigantic rooms; a largely gay crowd congregates in the one to the left. Foam parties Su and W. Best known for "Cream" on Th, when London DJs play hard house or trance. Cover €40 and up. Open daily midnight-7am.

Space, Platja d'en Bossa (☎971 39 67 93; www.space-ibiza.com). Starts hopping around 8am, peaks mid-afternoon, and doesn't wind down until after 5pm. The metallic get-up and techno music are almost as hardcore as the dancers. An outdoor dance terrace has a more low-key atmosphere. Known for its Su morning show; Sa, M, and Tu mornings are popular too. Hosts the official after-parties for "Ministry of Sound" at Pachá, "Manumission" at Privilege, and "La Troya Asesina" (the infamous drag queen party) at Amnesia. Cover €30-40.

Eden, C. Salvador Espíritu (☎971 34 25 51), across from the beach in Sant Antoni. Gaining in popularity, Eden pulls out all the stops for "Judgement Sunday," when DJ Judge Jules attracts huge crowds. Popular among British visitors. Retro nights on Tu feature house from the past decade. More manageable than some of the larger clubs—the dance floor is big enough for a night of dancing, but you won't get lost in the crowd. Cover €37-45. Open daily midnight-7am.

El Divino, Puerto Ibiza Nueva (☎971 19 01 76 or 31 83 38; www.eldivino-ibiza.com). Small, energetic club on the water—worth coming just for the view, although exotic dancers, thumping house, and lively crowd aren't too shabby either. Head to the waterfront terrace for a break from the techno insanity. El Divino fliers serve as free passes for the disco shuttle boat—otherwise, it costs €1.50 each way. Cover €40. Open mid-June to mid-Sept. daily midnight-6am.

Es Paradis Terrenal, C. Salvador Espíritu, 20 (☎971 34 66 00; www.esparadis.com), in Sant Antoni. Looks are deceiving: a classy environment hosts some not-so-classy behavior at water parties on Tu and F. Other nights provide a more basic club experience, with decent crowds and good dancing. Cover €36 and up. Open midnight-6am.

SANT ANTONI (SAN ANTONTIO DE PORTMANY)

Every summer, masses of young Brits migrate to Sant Antoni. The rowdy nightlife and down-to-earth atmosphere combined with proximity to some of the island's best beaches turn the town into a twenty-something enclave. With two clubs, plenty of bars, and cheaper food and accommodations than Eivissa, Sant Antoni is the perfect budget alternative to its sister city's high prices and lifestyle. While the rowdy, largely British scene dominates some streets (especially C. de Santa Agnés, or "the West End), Sant Antoni's quieter streets and squares provide a relaxing alternative to the loud, up-all-night atmosphere that prevails on much of the island.

TRANSPORTATION & PRACTICAL INFORMATION. Buses run from from Pg. de la Mar in Sant Antoni to: **Cala Bassa** (20min., 8 per day 9:30am-6:30pm, €1.15); **Cala Conta** (15min., 7 per day 9:10am-6pm, €1.15); **Cala Tarida** (10min., 8 per day 9:30am-7:05pm, €1.15); **Eivissa** (25min.; every 30min. M-Sa 7-9:30am and 10-11:30pm, every 15min. 9:45am-9:30pm, Su every 30min. 7:30am-10:30pm; €1.45); **Santa Eulária** (35min., M-Sa 4 per day 9:30am-6pm; €1.05). **Ferries** leave Sant Antoni for **Dénia** (see **Transportation,** p. 364). Smaller companies run daily **boats** to nearby beaches. Signs posted daily along the port have schedules. For a **taxi,** call ☎971 34 07 79. Sant Antoni is easy to get around, as major streets lie on something of a grid.

For **car** and **moped rental,** try **Motos Luis,** Av. Portmany, 5. (☎971 34 05 21. Mopeds €22 and up. Cars €39 and up. Open M-Sa 9am-2pm and 4-8pm, Su 9am-2pm.) The **tourist office** is a stone building in the middle of the pedestrian thoroughfare by Pg. de ses Fonts. (☎971 34 33 63. Open M-F 9:30am-2:30pm and 3-8:30pm, Sa 9am-1pm, Su 9:30am-1:30pm.) In an **emergency,** call ☎112 or the **police,** Av. Portmany, km14 (☎971 34 08 30). The **Centro de Salud** is on C. d'Alacant (☎ 971 34 51 21).

⌂▢ ACCOMMODATIONS & FOOD. *Hostales* in Sant Antoni are numerous, cheap, and full of Brits. Call well in advance for any summer stay; in the low season, prices drop. ▨**Hostal Residencia Roig ❸,** C. del Progrés, 44, has gorgeous, clean rooms all with private bath, comfortable couches in the lobby, and access to a nearby hotel's pool. (☎971 34 04 83. Singles €27; doubles €48.) The large bedrooms, huge TV lounge, and great location make **Hostal Salada ❷,** C. de la Soledat, 34, one of the best bargains in town. Walk up C. B.V. Ramón from the port and turn left on to C. de la Soledat. (☎971 34 11 30. Singles €18.50; doubles €30.50-33.50; triples €36.50.) Another option is clean, spacious **Hostal Rita ❷,** C. B. V. Ramón, 17B. Doubles and triples have private baths; singles share common baths. (☎971 34 63 32. Singles €18; doubles €32; triples €45.) **Restaurants** are everywhere in Sant Antoni. A variety of choices are available at the outdoor cafes along Pg. de la Mar or on its sidestreets leading uphill. Of the more trendy beachfront establishments, ▨**The Orange Corner ❶,** Av. Doctor Fleming, 2-4, stands out. The orange building right on the water serves cheap sandwiches, salads, fruit drinks, milkshakes, and alcoholic favorites. (Entrees €5-8. Alcoholic milkshakes €6, non-alcoholic shakes and smoothies €4. Open daily 10am-4am.) For cheap eats with an ocean view in a slightly less hectic setting, try **Manilla ❶,** C. del General Balanzat, 19, just down the beach from Café de la Mar. Pastas (€4-5), Mexican entrees (€8-12), and crêpes (€6-8.50) are served by candlelight on an ample terrace with a bubbling fountain. (☎971 34 55 24. Open daily noon-midnight.)

▨▢ BEACHES & NIGHTLIFE. The town itself is situated on a long, narrow strip of sand, but better beaches are only a stone's throw away. Check out **Cala Bassa,** one of the more popular tanning spots, for a gorgeous (and sometimes nude) beach that's accessible by bus. **Cala Gració,** 1.5km from Sant Antoni, is easily reached by foot. **Santa Eulària des Riu** is more built up and substantially larger than some of the other beaches nearby. Hoof it or bike to the small coves of **Es Povet** and **Caló d'es Moro.** If you have a car or moped, head to **Cala Salada,** just a few kilometers north of town, for calm, beautiful waters and a picturesque hippie community. Sant Antoni's **nightlife** revolves largely around three main areas. The area on the far end of town, near the littered beach of Es Ganguil, has several waterfront bars. Crowds gather on the small beach to watch the ▨**sunset** and chill to mellow house. **Café de la Mar,** "the original sunset bar," serves overpriced drinks, chic **Café Mambo** is a popular pre-party bar, and, much farther down toward Caló d'es Moro, **Kanya** offers a lively scene. The crowded streets of town are packed with low-key watering holes and drunk pre-partiers. The clubs **Eden** and **Es Paradis Terrenal,** beach bars (including the popular and upscale **M Bar**), and mini-discos facing the main beach round out the options. Compared to the competitive club scene of Eivissa, the nightlife options in Sant Antoni can be much more casual and relaxed.

FORMENTERA

The tiny island of Formentera provides a quiet getaway from more hectic Ibiza. Despite the recent invasions by bourgeois, beach-hungry Germans and Italians, the island's stunning beaches maintain a sense of hypnotic calm. Join Formentera's "save our island" spirit by hiking or renting a bike—the tourist office offers a comprehensive list of Green Tours for hikers and cyclists, and bike paths are plentiful. The island itself is pricy, and is often visited simply as an expensive daytrip from Eivissa. While Formentera provides tranquility and natural beauty, with a little effort the same can be found more cheaply on Ibiza. For transportation to Formentera, see **Inter-Island Transportation,** p. 363.

BARCELONA

Barcelona loves to indulge in the fantastic. From the urban carnival that is Las Ramblas to buildings with no straight lines, the city pushes the limits of style in everything it does, and gets away with it. As the center of the whimsical and daring *Modernisme* architectural movement, Barcelona holds fairy-tale creations that are like no others in the world; as home to three of the most well-known Surrealist painters—Salvador Dalí, Pablo Picasso, and Joan Miró—even the most famous art of Barcelona is grounded in a reality alternative to the one that the rest of us know.

The time is now for Barcelona. In the quarter-century since the end of Franco's oppressive regime, Spain has blossomed, with Barcelona at the forefront. It has led the autonomous region of Catalunya in an esoteric and unique resurgence of culture. The city's major makeover during the late 1980s and early 1990s, intended as preparation for the 1992 Olympics, was so successful that *barceloneses* have continued to reinvent their home. The result is a vanguard city squeezed between the mesmerizing blue waters of the Mediterranean and the green Tibidabo hills, flashing with such vibrant colors and intense energy that you'll see Barcelona long after you have closed your eyes. Take a short siesta, and then stay up as late as you can; you will need every hour available to fully explore this city. Barcelona is a gateway, not only to Catalunya but also to the Mediterranean and the Pyrenees. Pack your swimsuit and your skis, your art history book and your clubbing shoes, and don't worry if you don't speak Spanish—neither does Barcelona.

HIGHLIGHTS OF BARCELONA

SCREAM your lungs out while cheering for Barça in electric, 120,000-seat **Camp Nou,** Europe's largest *fútbol* ground (see p. 404).

AMUSE yourself in front of the giant phallus at the **Museu de l'Erotica** (see p. 410).

INDULGE in sweet, sweet sin at the **Museu de la Xocolat,** where you can sample scrumptious treats and even learn to prepare some yourself (see p. 414).

EXPAND your cultural horizons while taking in Barcelona's art scene. Be sure to check out **La Sagrada Família,** Gaudí's unfinished masterpiece and tomb (see p. 418), and **Museu Picasso,** one of the best collections of Picasso's works in the world (see p. 414).

HOW TO USE THIS CHAPTER. Barcelona is divided into several neighborhoods *(barris),* four of which are covered here. We have grouped together all of each *barri's* accommodations, food, sights, museums, and nightlife listings. General information on these aspects of Barcelona, as well as shopping and specific listings for camping and entertainment (including sports, theater, concerts, and film) appears after the practical information.

✈ INTERCITY TRANSPORTATION

Flights: Aeroport El Prat de Llobregat (BCN; ☎932 98 38 38), 12km southwest of Barcelona. To get to Pl. Catalunya, take the **Aerobus** (approx. 40min.; daily every 15min.; to Pl. Catalunya M-F 6am-midnight, Sa-Su 6:30am-midnight; to the airport M-F 5:30am-11:15pm, Sa-Su 6am-11:20pm; €3.30) or a RENFE **train** (40min.; daily every 30min.; from airport 6:10am-11:15pm, from Estació Barcelona-Sants 5:30am-11:20pm; €2.20).

Trains: Barcelona has 2 main train stations. For general info about trains and train stations, call ☎902 24 02 02. **Estació Barcelona-Sants,** in Pl. Països Catalans (M: Sants-Estació) is the main terminal for domestic and international traffic. **Estació França,** on Av. Marquès de l'Argentera (M: Barceloneta), services regional destinations, including Girona, Tarragona, Zaragoza, and some international arrivals. **RENFE** (☎902 24 02 02, international ☎934 90 11 22; www.renfe.es) to: **Bilbao** (8-9hr., daily 5 per day, €30-32); **Madrid** (7-8hr., daily 7 per day, €31-42); **San Sebastián** (8-9hr., daily 5 per day, €31); **Sevilla** (11-12hr., daily 6 per day, €47-51); **Valencia** (3-5hr., daily 15 per day, €28-32). International destinations include **Milan, IT** (via Figueres and Nice) and **Montpellier, FR** with connections to Geneva, Paris, and various stops along the French Riviera. 20% discount on round-trip tickets.

Buses: Most buses arrive at the **Barcelona Estació Nord d'Autobusos,** C. Alí Bei, 80 (☎932 65 61 32). M: Arc de Triomf. **Sarfa** (☎902 30 20 25; www.sarfa.com) goes to: **Cadaqués** (2½hr.; daily 2 per day 11:15am, 8:25pm; €16); **Palafrugell** (2hr., daily 13 per day, €12); **Tossa del Mar** (1½hr., daily 10 per day, €8). **Linebús** (☎932 65 07 00) goes to **Paris, FR** (13hr., M-Sa 1 per day 8pm, €80), southern France, and Morocco. Under 26 and over 60 discounted. **ALSA/Enatcar** (☎902 42 22 42; www.alsa.es) goes to: **Alicante** (9hr., daily 3 per day, €33); **Madrid** (8hr., daily 13 per day, €22); **Naples, IT** (24hr., daily 1 per day 5:15pm, €113); **Valencia** (4hr., daily 16 per day, €21); **Zaragoza** (3½-4½hr., daily 20 per day, €18).

Ferries: Trasmediterránea (☎902 45 46 45), in Estació Marítima-Moll Barcelona, Moll Sant Bertran. In summer only to: **Ibiza** (10-11hr., daily 1 per day M-Sa, €46); **Mahón** (10½hr., daily 1 per day starting mid-June, €46); **Palma** (3½hr., daily 1 per day, €65).

✚ ORIENTATION

Barcelona's layout is simple. Imagine yourself perched on Columbus's head at the **Monument a Colom** (on Pg. de Colom, along the shore), viewing the city with the sea at your back. From the harbor, the city slopes upward to the mountains. From the Columbus monument, **Las Ramblas,** the main thoroughfare, runs from the harbor up to **Plaça de Catalunya** (M: Catalunya), the city's center. **Ciutat Vella** is the heavily touristed historic neighborhood, which centers around Las Ramblas and includes the Barri Gòtic, La Ribera, and El Raval. The **Barri Gòtic** is east of Las Ramblas (to the right, with your back to the sea), enclosed on the other side by **Vía Laietana.** East of Vía Laietana lies the maze-like neighborhood of **La Ribera,** which borders Parc de la Ciutadella and Estació de França (train station). To the west of Las Ramblas (to the left, with your back to the sea) is **El Raval.** Beyond La Ribera—farther east, outside Ciutat Vella—are **Poble Nou** and **Port Olímpic,** with its twin towers (the tallest buildings in Barcelona) and an assortment of discos and restaurants. Beyond El Raval (to the west) rises **Montjuic,** crammed with gardens, museums, the 1992 Olympic grounds, and a stunning castle. Directly behind your perch on the Monument a Colom is the **Port Vell** (Old Port) development, where a wavy bridge leads across to the ultra-modern shopping and entertainment complexes **Moll d'Espanya** and **Maremàgnum.** Beyond Ciutat Vella is **l'Eixample,** the gridded neighborhood created during the expansion of the 1860s, which runs from Pl. de Catalunya toward the mountains. **Gran Via de les Corts Catalanes** defines its lower edge, and the **Passeig de Gràcia,** l'Eixample's main street, bisects the neighborhood. **Avinguda Diagonal** marks the border between l'Eixample and the **Zona Alta** ("Uptown"), which includes Pedralbes, Gràcia, and other older neighborhoods in the foothills. The peak of **Tibidabo,** the northwest border of the city, offers the most comprehensive view of Barcelona.

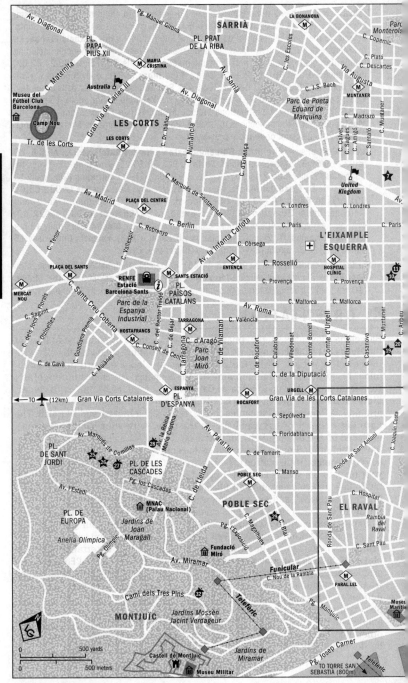

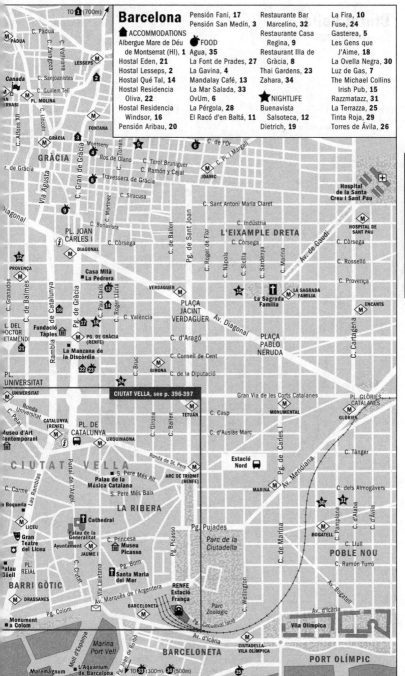

Barcelona

🏠 ACCOMMODATIONS
Albergue Mare de Déu de Montserrat (HI), 1
Hostal Eden, 21
Hostal Lesseps, 2
Hostal Qué Tal, 14
Hostal Residencia Oliva, 22
Hostal Residencia Windsor, 16
Pensión Aribau, 20
Pensión Fani, 17
Pensión San Medín, 3

🍴 FOOD
Agua, 35
La Font de Prades, 27
La Gavina, 4
Mandalay Café, 13
La Mar Salada, 33
OvUm, 6
La Pérgola, 28
El Racó d'en Baltá, 11
Restaurante Bar Marcelino, 32
Restaurante Casa Regina, 9
Restaurant Illa de Gràcia, 8
Thai Gardens, 23
Zahara, 34

⭐ NIGHTLIFE
Buenavista Salsoteca, 12
Dietrich, 19
La Fira, 10
Fuse, 24
Gasterea, 5
Les Gens que J'Aime, 18
La Ovella Negra, 30
Luz de Gas, 7
The Michael Collins Irish Pub, 15
Razzmatazz, 31
La Terrazza, 25
Tinta Roja, 29
Torres de Ávila, 26

CIUTAT VELLA, see p. 396-397

BARCELONA

Ciutat Vella
see legend p. 398

Universitat de Barcelona
PL. DE LA
UNIVERSITAT Ⓜ
UNIVERSITAT
Via de les Corts Catalanes

C. Sepulveda
C. Muntaner
R. de Sant Antoni
C. Torres i Amat
PL. CASTELLA
❷
C. Gravina
C. Pelai
Ronda Universitat
Rambla de Catalunya

C. Villarroel
C. Casanova
C. Tallers
C. Bergara
Triangle Shopping Center

C. Comte D'Urgel
C. Floridablanca
C. Valldonzella
Centro de Cultura Contemporania
C. Montalegre

BARCELONA

C. Tigre ✦❺
C. Paloma
C. Ferlandina ❾
Museu d'Art Contemporani 🏛 ❿
PL. DELS ANGELS

Tamarit
Ronda de Sant Antoni
Nou de Dulce
C. Sant Gil
C. Sant Vicentç
C. de la Lluna
C. Joaquim Costa
C. Elisabets
❶❶
❶❷
C. Santa

SANT ANTONI Ⓜ
C. Princep de Biarn
Bisbe Laguarda
C. La Riera Alta
C. d'Erasme de Janer
C. Alta
C. Peu de la Creu
C. Angels
C. Dr. Dou
C. Xuclà
❶❹
C. Las Ramblas
❶❺
❶❻
PL. VILA DE MADRID

C. Sant Antoni Abat
C. la Cendra
EL RAVAL
C. Carme
❷❷
C. d'en Bot
C. Portaferrissa
❷❹

C. la Cera ❷⓿
C. de Vistalegre
C. L'Hospital
C. de la Riera Baixa
C. d'en Roig
C. Egipciaques
C. Florists de la Rambla
❷❸
Palau de la Virreina
La Boqueria
C. d'En Roca
C. Petritxol
❷❺
C. d'En Roca
❷❼
❷❽

C. la Reina Amalia
Ronda de Sant Pau
C. de L'Aurora
C. les Carretes
C. S. Pacia
C. Sant Jeroni
C. la Cadena
C. L'Hospital
Museu de l'Eròtica 🏛
❷❻ PL. DEL PI
EL CALL
C. Casañas
C. Banys Nous

C. Lelaltat
PL. J. Mª FOLCH I TORRES
C. la Riereta
C. Sant Rafael
C. d'en Robador
C. Junta de Comerç
LICEU Ⓜ
C. la Boqueria
❸❼
❸❽ ❸❾ ❹⓿
❹❶
C. Ferran
C. d'Avinyó
❺❶

C. Sta. Elena
C. Sant Josep Oriol
PL. SALVADOR SEGUÍ
❸❸
C. de Sant Pau
Gran Teatre del Liceu ❸❹ ❸❺
❸❻
C. de la Unió
❹❸

C. les Flors
Rambla del Raval
C. C. d'Espalter
❸❶
❸❷
C. S. Ramón
C. Marqués del Barbera
C. de les Penedides
PL. REIAL ❹❾
C. la Lleona

PARAL.LEL (FUNICULAR) Ⓜ
C. Abat Safont
C. de l'Hort de Sant Pau
C. S. Oleguer
❹❻
C. Nou de la Rambla
Palau Güell
❹❼
❹❽ ❺⓿
C. d'n'Agla
PL. GEORGE ORWELL (PL. TRIPPY)

C. les Tapies
C. Cabanes
C. de Santa Madrona
C. L'Est
C. Arc del Teatre
C. Guardia
C. Lancaster
❻❹
❻❺
C. Escudellers ❻❻ ❻❼
C. Rull
C. Códols
C. Serra

Av. del Paral.lel
C. Via i Vila
C. de Puigxuriguer
Jardins de les Tres Xemeneies
C. l-t Om
Av. de les Drassanes
Centre D'Art de Santa Mònica 🏛
Santa Mònica
PL. DEL TEATRE
Ptge. dels Escudellers
C. Nou Sant Francesc
C. Ample

TO MONTJUÏC (100m)
C. Piquer
Pg. de Montjuïc
C. Palaudaries
C. Cid
C. Peracamps
C. Cervelló
C. Montserrat
C. Portal Santa Madrona
Museu de Cera 🏛
❼❶
Las Ramblas
PL. DUC DE MEDINACELI
❼❷

C. Carrera
C. Alsabreda
Museu Marítim 🏛
DRASSANES Ⓜ
C. Josep Anselm Clavé
Pg. de Colom
Ronda del Litoral

PL. PORTAL DE LA PAU
■ Monument a Colom

TO MAREMAGNUM (80m) ↓

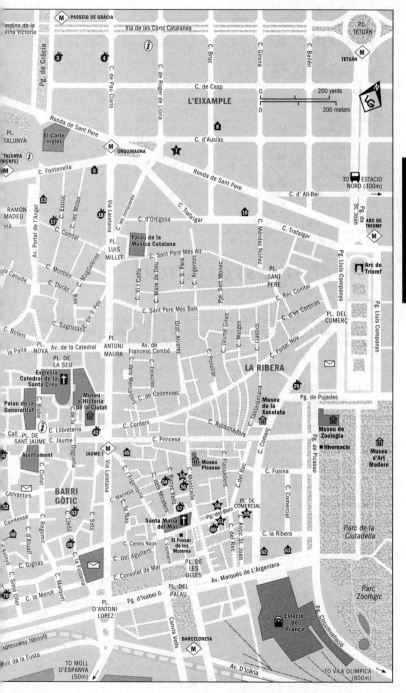

Ciutat Vella

see map p. 396-397

🏠 **ACCOMMODATIONS**
Albergue de Juventud
    Kabul, **48**
Barcelona Mar Youth
    Hostel, **30**
California Hotel, **43**
Casa de Huéspedes
    Mari-Luz, **52**
Gothic Point Youth
    Hostal, **45**
Hostal Avinyó, **68**
Hostal Benidorm, **64**
Hostal Campi, **15**
Hostal de Ribagorza, **19**
Hostal Levante, **51**
Hostal Malda, **27**
Hostal Nuevo Colón, **63**
Hostal Opera, **34**
Hostal Parisien, **25**

Hostal Plaza, **6**
Hostal Residencia
    Lausanne, **13**
Hostal Residencia
    Rembrandt, **24**
Hostal San Remo, **8**
Hotel Lloret, **11**
Hotel Peninsular, **33**
Hotel Toledano/Hostal
    Residencia Capitol, **12**
Ideal Youth Hostel, **36**
Mare Nostrum, **35**
Pensión Ciutadella, **62**
Pensión Fernando, **40**
Pensión L'Isard, **2**

🍎 **FOOD**
L'Antic Bocoi del Gòtic, **53**
Arc Café, **70**
The Bagel Shop, **16**
Bar Ra, **23**
Bodega la Tinaja, **60**
Buenas Migas, **14**

Café de l'Ópera, **37**
Los Caracoles, **66**
La Colmena, **42**
Comme-Bio, **1**
Dos Trece, **22**
Irati, **26**
Laie Llibreria Café, **4**
Mi Burrito y Yo, **44**
El Pebre Blau, **57**
Pla dels Angels, **10**
Els Quatre Gats, **17**
Les Quinze Nits, **49**
Restaurante Can Lluís, **20**
El Salón, **69**
Taira, **29**
Terrablava, **18**
Txapela, **3**
Va de Vi, **54**
Xaloc, **28**
Xampanyet, **56**

⭐**NIGHTLIFE**
El Born, **61**
El Bosq de les Fades, **71**
Casa Almirall, **9**
El Copetin, **58**
Fonfone, **67**
Glaciar Bar, **50**
Jamboree, **47**
London Bar, **46**
Margarita Blue, **72**
Marsella Bar, **32**
Molly's Fair City, **38**
Muebles Navarro
    (El Café que Pone), **21**
New York, **65**
Palau Dalmases, **55**
La Paloma, **5**
Pitin Bar, **59**
Salvation, **7**
Sant Pau 68, **31**
Schilling, **39**
Vildsvin, **41**

🚆 LOCAL TRANSPORTATION

MAPS

El Corte Inglés distributes a good free map (see p. 400). The Barcelona **tourist office** (Pl. de Catalunya and Pl. Sant Jaume) has maps with a good enlarged inset of the *Barri Gòtic.* The *Guia d'Autobusos Urbans de Barcelona,* free at tourist offices and Metro stations, maps out the city's bus Metro lines; the *Guia Fàcil del Bus per Mour't per Barcelona,* also free, describes the routes in more detail.

METRO & BUS

Barcelona's public transportation (info ☎010) is quick and cheap. If you plan to use public transportation extensively, there are several *abonos* (passes) available, all of which work interchangeably for the Metro, bus, urban lines of the FGC commuter trains, and the Nitbus. The **T-1 pass** (€5.80) is valid for 10 rides and saves you nearly 50% off the cost of single tickets. The **T-Día pass** (€4.40) is good for a full day of unlimited travel, the **3 Dies** (€11.30) gets you three days of unlimited travel, and the **5 Dies** (€17.30) is good for five days. These three save you money if you use the Metro more than three times per day.

Metro: (☎934 86 07 52; www.tmb.net). Vending machines and ticket windows sell passes. Red diamonds with the letter "M" mark stations. Hold on to your ticket until you exit—riding without one carries a fine of €40. Trains run M-Th 5am-midnight, F-Sa 5am-2am, Su and holidays 6am-midnight. €1.05 per *sencillo* (single ride).

Ferrocarrils de la Generalitat de Catalunya (FGC): (☎932 05 15 15; www.fgc.es). Commuter trains to local destinations with main stations at Pl. de Catalunya and Pl. d'Espanya. Blue symbols resembling 2 interlocking Vs mark Metro connections. The commuter line charges the same as the Metro (€1.05) until Tibidabo. After that, rates go up by zone: zone 2 destinations €1.55, zone 3 destinations €2.20. Metro passes are valid on FGC trains. Info office at the Pl. de Catalunya station open M-F 7am-9pm.

Nitbus: (☎901 511 151). 16 different lines run every 20-30min. 10:30pm-4:30am, depending on the line; a few run until 5:30am. All buses depart from Pl. de Catalunya; a Metro pass is valid on the Nitbus. The buses stop in front of most of the club complexes and work their way through Ciutat Vella and the Zona Alta. Maps are available at *estancos* (tobacco shops) and marked by signs in Metro stations.

Buses: Go just about anywhere, usually from 5am-10pm. €1.05.

Bus Turístic: Hop-on, hop-off tours of the city. See p. 403.

TAXIS

On weekend nights, you may wait up to 30min. in some locations; long lines form at popular club spots like the Port Olímpic. A *lliure* or *libre* sign or a green light on the roof means vacant; yellow means occupied. To call a cab, try **RadioTaxi** (☎932 25 00 00) or **Servi Taxi** (☎933 30 03 00). **Disabled travelers** should call ☎934 20 80 88.

CAR RENTAL

Avis/Auto Europe, C. de Casanova, 209 (☎932 09 95 33).

Budget, Av. de Josep Tarradellas, 35 (☎934 10 25 08). 25+. **Branch** in El Prat de Llobregat airport (see p. 392).

Docar, C. Montnegre, 18 (24hr. ☎934 39 81 19). M: Les Corts. Open M-F 8:30am-2pm and 3:30-8pm, Sa 9am-2pm.

Hertz, C. Tuset, 10 (☎932 17 80 76; www.hertz.es). M: Diagonal or FCG: Gràcia. Open M-F 9am-2pm and 4-7pm, Sa 9am-2pm. **Branch** office at airport (☎932 98 36 37).

Vanguard Rent a Car, C. Viladomat, 297 (☎934 39 38 80). 19+. Rents mopeds from €38 per day. More expensive 2-person *motos* also available. Includes insurance and helmet. Open M-F 8am-1:30pm and 4-7:30pm, Sa-Su 9am-1pm.

PRACTICAL INFORMATION

TOURIST & FINANCIAL SERVICES

Tourist Offices: Plaça de Catalunya, Pl. de Catalunya, 17S (☎907 30 12 82). M: Catalunya. Open daily 9am-9pm. **Plaça de Sant Jaume,** Pl. de Sant Jaume, 1. M: Jaume I. Open M-Sa 10am-8pm, Su 10am-2pm. **Oficina de Turisme de Catalunya,** Pg. de Gràcia, 107 (☎932 38 40 00; www.gencat.es/probert). M: Diagonal. Open M-Sa 10am-7pm, Su 10am-2pm. **Estació Barcelona-Sants,** Pl. Països Catalans. M: Sants-Estació. Station open M-F 4:30am-midnight, Sa-Su 5am-midnight. **Aeroport El Prat de Llobregat** (☎934 78 05 65), international terminal. Open daily 9am-9pm. **Tourist Office Representatives** dot the city in the summer. Open July-Sept. daily 10am-8pm.

Tours: In addition to the Bus Turístic (see p. 403), the Pl. de Catalunya tourist office offers walking tours of the *Barri Gòtic* Sa-Su at 10am (English) and noon (Catalan and Spanish). Group size limited; buy tickets in advance. (☎906 301 282 for info. €6.60, age 4-12 €3.)

Budget Travel: usit UNLIMITED, Ronda Universitat, 16 (☎934 12 01 04; fax 934 12 39 84; www.unlimited.es). Open M-F 10am-8:30pm and Sa 10am-1:30pm.

Currency Exchange: As always, **ATMs** give the best rates. The next best rates are available at banks. General banking hours M-F 8:30am-2pm.

American Express: Pg. de Gràcia, 101 (☎933 01 11 66). M: Diagonal. Open M-F 9:30am-6pm, Sa 10am-noon. Also at Las Ramblas, 74 (☎933 01 11 66). Open daily 9am-8pm.

LOCAL SERVICES

Luggage Storage: Estació Barcelona-Sants. M: Sants-Estació. Lockers €4.50 per 24hr. Open daily 5:30am-11pm. **Estació de França.** M: Barceloneta. Open daily 7am-10pm.

Libraries: Biblioteca Sant Pau, C. de l'Hospital, 56 (☎933 02 07 97). M: Liceu. Walk to the far end of the courtyard; the library is on the left. Do not confuse it with the Catalan library you'll see first, which requires permission to enter. Open M, W, F 3:30-8:30pm; Tu, Th, Sa 10am-2pm and 3:30-8:30pm. **Institut d'Estudis Nordamericans,** Via Augusta, 123 (☎932 40 51 10). Open Sept.-July M-F 9am-2pm and 4-7pm.

El Corte Inglés, Pl. de Catalunya, 14. M: Catalunya. Supermarket in basement. Open M-Sa and 1st Su of month 10am-10pm.

Religious Services: Comunidad Israelita de Barcelona (Jewish services), C. Avenir, 29 (☎932 00 61 48). **Comunidad Musulmana** (Muslim services), Mosque Toarek Ben Ziad, C. de l'Hospital, 91 (☎934 41 91 49). Services daily at prayer times. **Església Catedral de la Santa Creu** (Catholic services), in Pl. de la Seu. M: Jaume I. Cloister open 9am-1:15pm and 4-7pm.

Gay & Lesbian Services: Antinous, C. Josep Anselm Clavé, 6 (☎933 01 90 70; www.antinouslibros.com). M: Drassanes. A large bookstore and cafe specializing in gay and lesbian books, including several guide books. Decent selection of books in English. Open M-F 11am-2pm and 5-9pm, Sa noon-2pm and 5-9pm. **Cómplices,** C. Cervantes, 2 (☎934 12 72 83). M: Liceu. A bookstore with publications in English and Spanish and a decent selection of gay films. Also provides a **map** of Barcelona's gay bars and discos. Open M-F 10:30am-8:30pm, Sa noon-8:30pm.

Laundromats: Tintoreria Ferrán, C. Ferrán, 11. M: Liceu. Open M-F 9am-8pm. **Tintoreria San Pablo,** C. San Pau 105 (☎933 29 42 49). M: Paral·lel. Wash, dry, and fold €10; do-it-yourself €7.25. Open July-Sept. M-F 9am-2pm; Oct.-June M-F 9am-2pm and 4-8pm.

EMERGENCY & COMMUNICATIONS

Emergency: ☎112. **Local police:** ☎092. **National police:** ☎091. **Medical:** ☎061.

Police: Las Ramblas, 43 (☎933 44 13 00). M: Liceu. Multilingual officers. Open 24hr.

Late-Night Pharmacy: Rotates; check any pharmacy window for the nearest on duty.

Hospital: Hospital Clínic, C. de Villarroel, 170 (☎932 27 54 00). M: Hospital Clínic. Main entrance at the intersection of C. Roselló and C. Casanova. **Hospital de la Santa Creu i Sant Pau** (☎932 91 90 00, emergency 91 91 91). M: Hospital de Sant Pau. **Hospital Vall d' Hebron** (☎932 74 60 00). M: Vall d'Hebron.

Internet Access:

▓**EasyEverything,** Las Ramblas, 31. M: Liceu. About €1.20 per 40min. Open 24hr. **Branch** at Ronda Universitat, 35. M: Catalunya.

Bcnet (Internet Gallery Café), C. Barra de Ferro, 3, down the street from the Museu Picasso. M: Jaume I. €3 per hr.; 10hr. ticket €20. Open daily 10am-1am.

Cybermundo Internet Centre, C. Bergara, 3 and C. de Balmes, 8. M: Catalunya. Just off Pl. de Catalunya, behind the Triangle shopping mall. Disks allowed. €1 per hr. Open daily 9am-1am.

Workcenter, Av. Diagonal, 441. M: Hospital Clínic or Diagonal. **Branch** at C. Roger de Llúria, 2. M: Urquinaona. €0.52 per 10min. Open 24hr.

CiberOpción, Gran Via, 602. M: Universitat. €0.60 per 30min. Open M-F 9am-1am, Sa-Su 11am-1am.

Telephones: Buy phone cards at tobacco stores, tourist offices, and newsstands. **Private phone service** (☎/fax 934 90 76 50) at Estació Barcelona-Sants. M: Sants-Estació. Open M-Sa 8am-9:45pm. **Directory Assistance:** ☎1003 for numbers within Spain, 1008 for numbers within Europe, 1005 for numbers outside Europe.

Post Office: Pl. d'Antoni López (☎902 19 71 97). M: Jaume I or Barceloneta. Fax and **Lista de Correos.** Open M-F 8:30am-9:30pm. **Postal Code:** 08003.

⌐ ACCOMMODATIONS

While accommodations in Barcelona are easy to spot, finding a room in one can be more difficult. If it is one of the busier travel months (June-September or December), just wandering up and down Las Ramblas looking for a place to stay can quickly turn into a frustrating experience. If you want to stay in the touristy areas—Barri Gòtic or Las Ramblas—make reservations weeks or even months ahead. Consider staying outside heavily-trafficked Ciutat Vella; there are plenty of hostels in the Zona Alta, particularly in Gràcia, that will have more vacancies. Accommodations are listed by neighborhood and ranked by decreasing value.

CAMPING

Although no campsites lie within the city, intercity buses (€1.50) run to the following locations in 20-45min. The **Associació de Càmpings de Barcelona,** Gran Via de les Corts Catalanes, 608 (☎93 412 59 55; www.campingsbcn.com) has more info.

El Toro Bravo, Autovía de Castelldefells, km11 (☎936 37 34 62; www.eltorobravo.com). Take bus L95 (€1.50) from Pl. de Catalunya to the campsite, 11km south. Offers beach access, laundry facilities, currency exchange, 3 pools, 2 bars, a restaurant, and a supermarket. Possibility for long-term stays. Reception 8am-7pm. June 15-Aug. €5.20 per person, €5.50 per site, €5.20 per car, €4 electricity charge; Sept.-June 14 €5 per person, €5 per site, €5 per car, €4 electricity charge. AmEx/MC/V. ●

Filipinas, Autovía de Castelldefells, km12 (☎936 58 28 95), 1km down the road from El Toro Bravo (see above), accessible by bus L95. Same prices and services as El Toro Bravo. AmEx/MC/V. ●

ACCOMMODATIONS BY PRICE

UNDER €15 ●		Hostal Levante	BG
Ideal Youth Hostel	ER	Hostal Residencia Oliva	EIX
Albergue Mare de Déu de Mont. (HI)	G	Pensión Ciutadella	RB
		Hostal Nuevo Colón	RB
€15-25 ❷		Hostal Ópera	ER
Hostal Campi	BG	Hostal Parisien	BG
Pensión Fernando	BG	Hotel Peninsular	ER
Pensión L'Isard	ER	Pensión San Medín	G
Hostal-Residencia Rembrandt	BG	Hostal San Remo	EIX
Hostal de Ribagorza	RB	Hotel Toledano/Hostal Res. Cap.	BG
Hostal Avinyó	BG	Hostal Residencia Windsor	EIX
Barcelona Mar Youth Hostel	ER		
Hostal Benidorm	BG	**€36-55 ❹**	
Pensión Fani	EIX	Hostal Lesseps	G
Gothic Point Youth Hostel	RB	Pensión Aribau	EIX
Albergue de Juventud Kabul	BG	California Hotel	BG
Hostal Malda	BG	Hotel Lloret	BG
Casa de Huéspedes Mari-Luz	BG		
		ABOVE €55 ❺	
€26-35 ❸		Hostal Plaza	BG
Hostal Eden	EIX		

BG Barri Gòtic **RB** La Ribera **ER** El Raval **EIX** l'Eixample **G** Gràcia

FOOD

Barcelona offers every kind of food you could possibly desire. Whether it be Basque, Chinese, Indian, or American, chances are you'll find an establishment that will meet and exceed your culinary expectations. While it's tempting to stick to familiar foods, be sure to sample the local flavors. Catalan cuisine is definitely worthwhile. If you want to live cheap and do as *barceloneses* do, buy your food fresh at a *mercat* (marketplace) and hit up a grocery store for other essentials.

Markets: La Boquería (Mercat de Sant Josep), off Las Ramblas. M: Liceu. Wholesale prices for fruit, cheese, and wine. **Mercat de la Concepi,** on C. València between C. Bruc and C. Girona. M: Girona. Smaller version of La Boquería.

Supermarkets: Champion, Las Ramblas, 113. M: Liceu. Open M-Sa 9am-9pm. **El Corte Inglés,** Pl. de Catalunya, 14. M: Catalunya. Supermarket in basement. Open M-Sa and 1st Su of each month 10am-10pm.

TAPAS

Hopping from one *tapas* bar to another is a fun and cheap way to pass the evening. When you arrive, don't wait to be seated and don't look for a waiter to serve you; most *tapas* bars are self-serve and standing (or crowding) room only. Ask for a *plato* (plate) and help yourself to the toothpick-skewered goodies that line the bars. Keep your toothpicks—they'll be tallied up on your way out to determine your bill. If you're tired of standing at the bar, most places offer more expensive sit-down menus as well. Barcelona's many *tapas* (sometimes called *pintxos*) bars, concentrated in La Ribera and Gràcia, often serve *montaditos*, thick slices of bread topped with all sorts of delectables from sausage to tortillas to anchovies. Vegetarian *tapas* are rare—be forewarned, for example, that slender white strands on some *montaditos* are actually eels masquerading as noodles. Generally served around lunchtime and dinnertime, *montaditos* are presented on platters at the bar. *Montaditos* go well with a glass of *cava*—Catalan champagne—or a cup of *sidra*, a Basque alcoholic cider generally poured from several feet above the glass.

FOOD BY TYPE

TAPAS		**OUTSIDE ESPAÑA**	
▨ Café de l'Ópera	BG ❷	The Bagel Shop	BG ❶
Txapela (Euskal Taberna)	EIX ❷	La Gavina	G ❸
Va de Vi	RB ❷	Mandalay Café	EIX ❷
Xampanyet	RB ❶	La Mar Salada	W ❸
		Pla dels Angels	ER ❷
CATALAN & SPANISH		El Racó d'en Baltá	EIX ❸
▨ Agua	W ❸	El Salón	BG ❷
▨ Laie Llibreria Café	EIX ❷	Taira	LR ❹
▨ Mi Burrito y Yo	BG ❹	Thai Gardens	EIX ❸
▨ OvUm	G ❸		
▨ Les Quinze Nits	BG ❶	**VEGETARIAN**	
Bodega La Tinaja	RB ❷	▨ Agua	W ❸
Buenas Migas	ER ❶	▨ Bar Ra	ER ❷
Los Caracoles	BG ❸	▨ Comme-Bio	EIX ❷
La Colmena	BG ❶	▨ OvUm	G ❸
DosTrece	ER ❸	La Buena Tierra	G ❷
La Flauta	EIX ❷	Restaurante Casa Regina	G ❸
Irati	BG ❷	Restaurante Illa de Gràcia	G ❶
L'Antic Bocoi del Gòtic	BG ❷	Terrablava	BG ❷
El Pebre Blau	BG ❷		
Els Quatre Gats	BG ❸	**CAFES**	
Restaurante Can Lluís	ER ❸	Arc Café	BG ❷
Txapela (Euskal Taberna)	EIX ❷	Buenas Migas	ER ❶
Xaloc	BG ❶	Laie Llibreria Café	EIX ❷
		Zahara	W ❷

BG Barri Gòtic **RB** La Ribera **ER** El Raval **EIX** l'Eixample **W** Waterfront **G** Gràcia

👁 🏛 SIGHTS & MUSEUMS

Barcelona has always been on the cutting edge of defining what can be included in the category of "art"; the city's museums range from Surrealist and classical masterpieces to historical exhibits and one-of-a-kind curiosities. Architecturally, Barcelona is defined by its unique Modernista treasures. Las Ramblas—a bustling avenue smack in the city center—and the Barri Gòtic, Barcelona's "old city," are the traditional tourist areas. But don't neglect vibrant La Ribera and El Raval, the upscale avenues of l'Eixample, the panoramic city views from Montjuïc and Tibidabo, Gaudí's Park Güell, or the harbor-side Port Olímpic.

RUTA DEL MODERNISME

For those with a few days in the city and an interest in seeing some of the most popular sights, the Ruta del Modernisme is the cheapest and most flexible option. The Ruta del Modernisme is not a tour precisely, in the sense that it doesn't offer a guide or organized transportation; it's a ticket which provides discount admission to dozens of Modernist buildings throughout the city. Passes (€3.60; students, over 65, and groups over 10 people €2.60) are good for 30 days and give holders a 25-30% discount on entrance to the Palau de la Música Catalana, Fundació Antoni Tàpies, the Museu d'Art Modern, Museu de Zoologia, tours of l'Hospital de la Santa Creu i Sant Pau and the facades of La Manzana de la Discòrdia (Casas Amatller, Lleó i Morera, and Batlló), and map tours of Gaudí, Domènech i Montaner, and Puig i Cadafalch buildings, among other attractions. The pass comes with a map and a pamphlet that gives a history of the different sites that is helpful in prioritizing visits. Purchase passes at **Casa Amatller**, Pg. de Gràcia, 41 (M: Pg. de Gràcia, L2/ 3/4; ☎934 88 01 39; www.rutamodernisme.com) near the intersection with C. Aragó. Many of these sights have tour time and length restrictions; visiting all of them on the same day is virtually impossible.

BUS TURÍSTIC

Sit back and let the sights come to you. The Bus Turístic stops at 26 points of interest along two different elliptical routes (red for north-bound buses, blue for southbound). Tickets come with a comprehensive eight-language brochure with information about each sight. A full ride on both routes takes 3-3½ hours depending on traffic, but feel free to get on and off as often as you want. You can buy tickets once on board, or ahead of time at **Turisme de Catalunya**, 17 Pl. de Catalunya (☎906 30 12 82), in front of El Corte Inglés. Many of the museums and sights covered by the bus offer discounts with the bus ticket; keep in mind that some are closed on Mondays. Overall, the bus is a good idea if you want to see the whole city quickly, as it cuts transportation time. (Buses run daily except Dec. 25 and Jan. 1, every 10-30min. 9am-9:30pm; 1-day pass €15, ages 4-12 €9; 2-day pass €19.)

▣ ENTERTAINMENT

MUSIC, THEATER & DANCE

Barcelona offers many options for theater aficionados, though most performances are in Catalan (*Guía del Ocio* lists the language of the performance). Reserve tickets through **Tel Entrada** (24hr. ☎902 10 12 12; www. telentrada.com) or any branch of **Caixa Catalunya** bank (open M-F 8am-2:30pm). The **Grec** summer festival turns Barcelona into an international theater, music, and dance extravaganza from late June to the end of July (www.grec.bcn.com). For info about the festival, which takes place in venues across the city, ask at the tourist office, stop by the booth at the bottom of Pl. de Catalunya for the duration of the festival, or swing by the **Institut de Cultura de Barcelona (ICUB)**, Palau de la Virreina, Las Ramblas, 99. (☎933 01 77 75. Open Tu-Sa 11am-8:30pm, Su 11am-3pm. Grec ticket sales M-Sa 10am-9pm. Most performances €24.) Another resource is www.travelhaven.com/ activities/barcelona/barcelona.html, providing 10% discounts for performances at the Palau de la Música Catalana, Gran Teatre del Liceu, and l'Auditori.

BARCELONA

Palau de la Música Catalana, C. Sant Francesc de Paula, 2 (☎932 95 72 00; www.palaumusica.org). M: Jaume I. Off Via Laietana near Pl. Urquinaona. Box office open M-Sa 9:45am-3pm, Su from 1hr. prior to the concert. No concerts in Aug.; check the *Guía del Ocio* for listings. Concert tickets €6-150. MC/V.

Centre Artesà Tradicionàrius, Tv. de Sant Antoni, 6-8 (☎932 18 44 85), in Gràcia. M: Fontana. Catalan folk music concerts Sept.-June F 10pm. Tickets €10. Open M-F 11am-2pm and 5-9pm. Closed Aug.

Gran Teatre del Liceu, Las Ramblas, 51-59 (☎934 85 99 13, 24hr. ticket sales ☎902 33 22 11; www.liceubarcelona.com), on Las Ramblas. M: Liceu. Founded in 1847, destroyed by fire in 1994, and recently reopened, Liceu has regained its status as the city's finest venue. Tickets start at €7 and rise fast. Reserve tickets well in advance.

L'Auditori, C. Lepanto, 150 (☎932 47 93 00; www.auditori.com), in l'Eixample between M: Marina and Glòries. The Auditori is home to the city orchestra. Concerts from late Sept. to mid-July, with performances F at 7pm, Sa at 9pm, and Su at 11am. Tickets €10-43 (Su is cheapest). Available by phone, through ServiCaixa, or at ticket windows (open M-Sa noon-9pm, Su 1hr. before show starts and 1hr. after it has begun).

El Tablao de Carmen (☎933 25 68 95; www.tablaodecarmen.com), on Av. Marqués de Comillas, inside Poble Espanyol. M: Espanya. Restaurant with flamenco shows. Dinner and show €53, drink and show €28. Open Tu-Su from 8pm; shows Tu-Th and Su 9:30pm and 11:30pm, F-Sa 9:30pm and midnight. Call ahead for reservations. MC/V.

FILM

Most screens show the latest Hollywood features, some in the original English. The *Cine* section in the *Guía del Ocio* denotes subtitled films with *V.O. subtitulada (versión original);* other foreign films are dubbed *(doblado),* usually in Catalan. Many theaters have a discount day (usually Monday). **Cine Malda,** C. del Pi, 5, is the only theater in the city which lets you see two movies with one ticket. (M: Liceu. ☎933 17 85 29. M €4.20, Tu-F €5.30, Sa-Su €5.50. Cash only.) **Filmoteca,** Av. Sarrià, 33, screens classic, cult, and otherwise exceptional films. (M: Hospital Clínic. ☎934 10 75 90. €3.) **Méliès Cinemas,** C. de Villarroel, 102, shows classics. (M: Urgell. ☎934 51 00 51. M €2.70, Tu-Su €4.) **Icària-Yelmo,** C. Salvador Espriu, 61, in the Olympic Village, boasts 15 screens and *V.O.* (☎932 21 75 85. M matinees €4.30, Tu-Su €5.75.) The new **IMAX Port Vell** on the Moll d'Espanya next to the aquarium and Maremàgnum, has an IMAX screen, an Omnimax 30m in diameter, and 3-D projection. Get tickets at the door, through **ServiCaixa** machines, or by phone. (☎932 25 11 11. €10, matinees €7. Showtimes 10:30am-12:30am.)

FÚTBOL

For the record, the lunatics covered head to toe in red and blue didn't just escape from an asylum—they are **F.C. Barcelona (Barça)** fans. Grab some face paint and head to the 120,000-seat **Camp Nou,** Europe's largest *fútbol* ground. On game days, the stadium is packed with thousands of screaming, rabid fans cheering on their favorite team, one of the world's most popular. The box office is on C. Arístedes Maillol, 12-18. Get tickets early. (From €30-60.) After firing coach Luis Van Gaal in 2003, Barça's all set for a redemptive 2003-2004 season. **R.C. Deportivo Espanyol,** a.k.a. *los periquitos* (parakeets), Barcelona's second professional soccer team, spreads its wings at **Estadi Olímpic,** Pg. Olímpic, 17-19. This team isn't as renowned as Barça, but the games are fun and **free.** Get tickets from Banca Catalana or call Tel Entrada (24hr. ☎902 10 12 12).

RECREATIONAL SPORTS

The tourist offices can provide info about swimming, cycling, tennis, squash, sailing, hiking, scuba diving, white-water rafting, kayaking, and most other sports.

Piscines Bernat Picornell, Av. Estadi, 30-40 (☎934 23 40 41), to the right when facing the stadium. Test your swimming in the Olympic pools—2 gorgeous facilities nestled in stadium seating. €4.40 for outdoor pool; €8 for workout facilities including sauna, massage parlor, and gym. Outdoor pool open M-Sa 9am-9pm, Su 9am-8pm. Workout facilities open M-F 7am-midnight, Sa 7am-9pm, Su 7:30am-8pm.

Club Sant Jordi, C. París, 114 (☎934 10 92 61). M: Sants. Passes available for other facilities including sauna, weights, and stairmaster. Bring your passport. Pool use €3.60. Open M-F 7am-9:45pm, Sa 8am-6pm, Su and holidays 9am-2pm. Closed 1st week in Aug.

Beaches: The entire strip between Vila Olímpica and Barceloneta is a long public beach accessible from M: Ciutadella or Barceloneta. The closest and most popular is **Platja Barceloneta,** off Pg. Marítim. Beware (or be aware) of nudity on **Platja San Sebastià.** The southernmost section of the beach is primarily gay.

BULLFIGHTS

Although the best *matadors* rarely venture out of Madrid, Sevilla, and Málaga, Barcelona's **Plaça de Toros Monumental,** Gran Vía de les Corts Catalans, 743, is an excellent facility, complete with Moorish influences. (☎932 45 58 04. M: Monumental.) Bullfights take place during the summer tourist season, since tourists are about the only people who go (June-Oct. Su at 7pm; doors open at 5:30pm). Tickets are available at travel agencies or ServiCaixa ("la Caixa" banks; ☎902 33 22 11; €18-95). The box office also sells tickets before the start of the fight.

☐ SHOPPING

Barcelona is cosmopolitan, trendy, and trashy; shopping options reflect all these personalities. The **Barri Gòtic** bursts with both trendy and alternative clothing and accessories. If you're on the prowl for typical European women's clothing, check out C. Portaferrisa and Av. Portal de l'Angel. If you're more into the alternative scene, take a stroll down C. Avinyó and its smaller side streets. You can find all sorts of less expensive jewelry, accessories, and other cool knick-knacks perfect for gift-giving on C. Boquería. If you're looking for more legitimate jewelry, meander into one of the gems on C. Call. If you have extra cash or just want to go drool on the windows of European designers, check out Pg. de Gràcia in **l'Eixample.** One place to try for bargains is **Calle Girona,** between C. Casp and Gran Via, in **l'Eixample,** where you'll find a small line of discount shops offering girls' and women's clothing, and men's dress clothes, shoes, bags, and accessories. (M: Tetuán, L2. Walk two blocks down Gran Via and take a left on C. Girona.) **Calle Bruc,** one street over, offers more retail delights for bargain-hunters. Be aware that stores marked "Venta al Mejor" are wholesale sellers who aren't happy with only windowshopping. Another area to try for discounts is the **Mercat Alternatiu (Alternative Market)** on C. Riera Baixa in **El Raval.** (M: Liceu. Take C. de l'Hospital—a right off Las Ramblas if you're facing the ocean—and follow it to C. Riera Baixa, the 7th right, shortly after the stone hospital building.) This street is crammed with secondhand and thrift stores covering everything from music to clothes.

MALLS

Spain has a series of laws against franchises in order to protect the economic prosperity of small businesses. The theory is that if franchises are allowed to be open all the time, small business, whose limited staff must take off Sundays and for *siesta*, will have no way to compete. These monstrous department stores are open only six days a week; commercial law prevents them from being open on Sundays, except for the first Sunday of each month.

El Corte Inglés, Pl. de Catalunya, 14 (☎933 06 38 00; www.elcorteingles.es). M: Catalunya, L1/3. **Free map** of Barcelona. Also has English books, hair salon, rooftop cafeteria, supermarket, the *oportunidades* discount department, currency exchange, and telephones. Open M-Sa and first Su of every month 10am-10pm. **Branches:** across the street from the tourist office, Portal de l'Àngel, 19-20 (M: Catalunya, L1/3); Av. Diagonal, 471-473 (M: Hospital Clínic, L5); Av. Diagonal, 617 (M: Maria Cristina, L3).

Triangle, Pl. de Catalunya, 4 (☎933 18 01 08; www.triangle.es). M: Catalunya, L1/3. Since its opening in 1999, architecture buffs have bemoaned this shopping center's utter lack of imagination and style. Shopaholics, however, are more enthusiastic. The upper floor **FNAC** electronics store/bookstore and the first floor of clothing and sunglasses shops are favorites. Triangle's branch of **Sephora** is the largest cosmetics store in the world in square footage. Open M-Sa 10am-10pm.

Maremàgnum, Moll d'Espanya (☎932 25 81 00; www.maremagnum.es), in Port Vell. M: Drassanes, L3. Small stores fill the first 2 floors of this mall and all-around leisure super-stop that dominates the waterfront skyline. A must-see for *fútbol* (soccer) fans is the **Botiga del Barça,** a smaller version of the official F.C. Barcelona souvenir shop at Camp Nou stadium (see p. 404), featuring posters, jerseys, and all varieties of memorabilia pertaining to the beloved Catalan team. Stores open daily, most 11am-11pm. (At night, bars and clubs open as Maremàgnum transforms into a nightlife playground.)

BOOKS

Llibreria del Raval, C. Elisabets, 6 (☎933 17 02 93), off Las Ramblas in El Raval. M: Catalunya. Literature and nonfiction in 4 languages (Catalan, Spanish, English, and French) fill the shelves of this spacious bookstore, born in 1693 as the Gothic-style Church of la Misericòrdia. Pocket Catalan/Spanish and Catalan/English dictionaries (€11) are useful for travelers. Open M-Sa 10am-9pm.

Bell Books, C. Sant Salvador, 41 (☎678 89 15 81), in Gràcia. M: Lesseps. Follow Trav. del Dalt and make a right on C. Verdi and a left on Sant Salvador. Best used bookstore around, run by an eccentric British expat and her cat, Arnold Schwarzenegger. Trade-ins accepted. Video club includes English films. Open M-F 1-8pm, Sa 10am-8pm.

Crisol Libros y Más, La Rambla de Catalunya, 81 (☎932 15 27 20; www.crisol.es), in l'Eixample. M: Pg. de Gràcia. This Madrid transplant stocks a wide range of music (lots of international titles), books (fiction, plays, self-help, cooking, travel guides, road maps), magazines, videos, DVDs, small gifts, and stationery. There is also a large children's section, some English novels, and original English-version videos. Open M-Sa 9am-10pm. Wheelchair accessible. AmEx/MC/V.

▨ NIGHTLIFE

The nightlife in Barcelona needs no introduction: whether you're looking for psychedelic absinthe shots, a great place for grunge rock, a sunrise foam party, or just someplace quiet to sit back and enjoy a drink (surrounded by fake gnomes), this city has it all. Things don't get going until late (don't bother showing up at a club before 1am) and keep going for as long as you can handle it. Check the *Guía del Ocio*, available at newsstands, for even more up-to-date listings of nighttime fun.

▨ FESTIVALS

While Barcelona is quite different from the rest of Spain, the city shares at least one thing in common with the rest of the country—it knows how to have fun. Festivals abound in this happening city; the trick is to know what will be going on during your visit. For information on all festivals, call the tourist office ☎933 01 77 75 (open M-F 10am-2pm and 4-8pm). Remember to double check sight and museum hours during festival times as well as during the Christmas season and during *Semana Santa*. The **Festa de Sant Jordi** (St. George; Apr. 24) celebrates Catalunya's patron saint with a feast. Men give women roses, and women give men books. On August 15-21, city folk jam at Gràcia's **Festa Mayor;** lights blaze in *plaças* and music plays all night. The **Sónar** music festival comes to town in mid-June, attracting renowned DJs and electronic enthusiasts from all over the world for three days of concerts and partying. The **Festa de Música** (July 1), a city-wide celebration of music, comes soon afterward, during which free concerts are held all over Barcelona. During July and August, the **Grec Festival** hosts dance and concert performances, as well as film screenings, in different concert venues. On September 11, the **Festa Nacional de Catalunya** brings traditional costumes, dancing, and Catalan flags hanging from balconies.

BARRI GÒTIC & LAS RAMBLAS

As the oldest sections of Barcelona, the Barri Gòtic and Las Ramblas are the tourist centers of the city. Originally settled by the Romans in the 3rd century BC, the Barri Gòtic is built on top of the original Roman city, Barcino. Subsequent layers of medieval Catholic rule cover Barcino in a maze of narrow, cobbled streets dense with historic and artistic landmarks. The modern tourist industry has added shops, hostels, and bars to the churches and other monuments left over from the Middle Ages. Take a stroll down **Carrer Avinyó** and you'll see some of Barcelona's most treasured architectural landmarks, just meters away from the area's most popular bars and restaurants. Whether you are drawn in by the new or the old, there is something for everyone in this labyrinth.

⚑ ACCOMMODATIONS

LOWER BARRI GÒTIC

The following hostels are between C. Ferran and the water. Backpackers flock here to be close to hip Las Ramblas.

▣ **Hostal Levante,** Baixada de San Miquel, 2 (☎933 17 95 65; www.hostallevante.com). M: Liceu. The best deal in Barri Gòtic. 50 large, tastefully decorated rooms with light wood interiors and balconies or fans, and a relaxing TV lounge. Ask for one of the newly renovated rooms. Six very chic apartments also available; each has room for 4 to 8 people and includes kitchen, living room, wood floor, and laundry machine. Singles €30; doubles €50-60; apartments €30 per person per night. MC/V. ❸

▣ **Pensión Fernando,** C. Ferran, 31 (☎/fax 933 01 79 93; www.barcelona-on-line.es/fernando). M: Liceu. This clean hostel is so well located it fills its 20 rooms almost entirely from walk-in requests. Beds come with free lockers in the spacious dorms. Fans in every room. Common TV/dining room. In summer dorms €19, with bath €20; doubles €45/58; triples with bath €68. MC/V. ❷

Hostal Benidorm, Las Ramblas, 37 (☎933 02 20 54). M: Drassanes. The best value on Las Ramblas, with phones and complete baths in each of the very clean rooms, balconies overlooking Las Ramblas, and excellent prices. Singles €30; doubles €45-53; triples €65; quads €75; quints €85-90. ❸

Casa de Huéspedes Mari-Luz, C. Palau, 4 (☎/fax 933 17 34 63). M: Liceu. Tidy 4- to 6-person dorm rooms and a few comfortable doubles. Reservations require a credit card. In summer dorms €16; doubles €41. Off-season prices lower. MC/V. ❷

Hostal Avinyó, C. Avinyó, 42 (☎933 18 79 45; www.hostalavinyo.com). M: Drassanes. Rooms with couches, high ceilings, fans, safes, and stained-glass windows. Singles €22; doubles €34, with bath €47; triples €48/€66. ❷

Albergue de Juventud Kabul, Pl. Reial, 17 (☎933 18 51 90; www.kabul-hostel.com). M: Liceu. Legendary among backpackers; squeezes in up to 200 frat boys at a time. Key deposit €10. Laundry €2.50. No reservations. Dorms €20. ❷

Hotel Toledano/Hostal Residencia Capitol, Las Ramblas, 138 (☎933 01 08 72; www.hoteltoledano.com). M: Catalunya. Rooms come with cable TV and phones. 4th-floor hotel, with bath: singles €35; doubles €57; triples €72; quads €81. 5th-floor hostal: singles €28; doubles €39; triples €51; quads €58. AmEx/MC/V. ❸

California Hotel, C. Rauric, 14 (☎933 17 77 66). M: Liceu. Enjoy one of the 31 clean, sparkling rooms, all with TV, phone, full bath, and A/C. Convenient location. Singles €52; doubles €82; triples €102. AmEx/MC/V. ❹

Hostal Parisien, Las Ramblas, 114 (☎933 01 62 83). M: Liceu. Well-kept rooms keep young guests happy. Quiet hours after midnight. Prices vary, but generally singles €30; doubles with bath €54; triples with bath €57. ❸

UPPER BARRI GÒTIC

This section of the Barri Gòtic is between C. Fontanella and C. Ferran. **Portal de l'Àngel,** a pedestrian avenue, runs through the middle. Rooms are pricier than in the lower Barri Gòtic but more serene. Early reservations are essential in summer.

▧ **Hostal-Residencia Rembrandt,** C. Portaferrissa, 23 (☎/fax 933 18 10 11). M: Liceu. This fantastic hostel has 28 rooms that are much nicer than those of any other hostel in the area; all *habitaciones* are unique in their own way, some with large baths, patios, TVs, and/or sitting areas. Be sure to take advantage of the restaurant-quality dining area for breakfast (served 9:30-10:30am, €5). Fans €2 per night. Singles €25, with bath €35; doubles €42/€50; triples €60/€65. MC/V. ❸

▧ **Hostal Plaza,** C. Fontanella, 18 (☎/fax 933 01 01 39; www.plazahostal.com). Savvy, super-friendly Texan owners; fun, brightly painted rooms with wicker furniture; great location. Laundry €9. Internet access €1 per 15min. Singles €60, with bath €75; doubles €65/€75; triples €86/€96. 10% discount Nov. and Feb. AmEx/MC/V. ❺

Hostal Campi, C. Canuda, 4 (☎/fax 933 01 35 45; hcampi@terra.es). A great bargain with large balconies. Call ahead to reserve 9am-8pm. Prices vary, but generally doubles €42, with bath €49; triples €58/€68. ❷

Hotel Lloret, Las Ramblas, 125 (☎933 17 33 66). M: Catalunya. New rooms include large bathrooms, tasteful furniture, A/C, heat, TV, and phone. Worth the cost. Singles €45-48; doubles €75-81; triples €89-95; quads €105. AmEx/MC/V. ❹

Hostal Malda, C. Pi, 5 (☎933 17 30 02), inside a shopping center. M: Liceu. Keeps rooms occupied year round by offering quality rooms at unbeatable prices. Reservations recommended. Singles €13; doubles €26; triples with shower €36. Cash only. ❶

Hostal Residencia Lausanne, Av. Portal de l'Angel, 24 (☎933 02 11 39). M: Catalunya. Small hostel includes a posh lounge with TV and vending machines. Doubles €48, with bath €65. Cash only. ❷

Mare Nostrum, Las Ramblas, 67 (☎933 18 53 40; fax 934 12 30 69). M: Liceu. The swankiest hostel on the strip. Rooms have A/C and satellite TV. Breakfast included. Singles €57, with bath €72; doubles €66/€76; triples €88/€100; quads €99/€114. ❺

⚑ FOOD

LOWER BARRI GÒTIC

☒ **Café de l'Ópera,** Las Ramblas, 74 (☎933 17 75 85). M: Liceu. A drink here used to be a post-opera bourgeois tradition. Hot chocolate €1.70. *Churros* €1.20. *Tapas* €2-4. Salads €2-8. Open M-Th 9am-2:30am, F-Sa 9am-2:45am, Su 10am-2:30am. ❶

☒ **Mi Burrito y Yo,** C. del Pas de l'Ensenyança, 2 (☎933 18 27 42). M: Jaume I. Not a Mexican joint (*burrito* here means "little donkey"), but rather inviting and lively. Live music 9:30pm. Entrees €12-20. Open daily 1pm-midnight. AmEx/MC/V. ❹

L'Antic Bocoi del Gòtic, Baixada de Viladecols, 3 (☎933 10 50 67). M: Jaume I. Formed in part by an ancient first-century Roman wall. Tiny and romantic. Excellent salads (€4.25-7.60), pâtés (€8-12), and cheeses (€10-12). Reservations recommended. Open M-Sa 8:30pm-midnight. AmEx/MC/V. ❷

Les Quinze Nits, Pl. Reial, 6 (☎933 17 30 75). M: Liceu. One of the most popular restaurants in Barcelona, with nightly lines. Delicious Catalan entrees at unbeatable prices (€3-7). No reservations. Open daily 1-3:45pm and 8:30-11:30pm. AmEx/MC/V. ❶

Los Caracoles, C. Escudellers, 14 (☎933 01 20 41). M: Drassanes. What started as a snail shop has evolved into a delicious Catalan restaurant. Specialties include *caracoles* (snails; €8) and rabbit (€11). Open daily 1pm-midnight. AmEx/MC/V. ❸

Irati, C. Cardenal Casañas, 17 (☎933 02 30 84). M: Liceu. An excellent Basque *tapas* bar. Keep your toothpicks to figure out your bill. Bartenders pour *sidra* (cider) behind their backs. Entrees €13-20. Open daily noon-1am. AmEx/MC/V. ❹

El Salón, C. l'Hostal d'en Sol, 6-8 (☎93 315 21 59). M: Jaume I. A mellow bar-bistro serving *gnocchi*, chicken, pork, and fish (€8-15). *Menú* €9.50. Wine €2-6. Cocktails €4.50. Open M-Sa 1:30pm-2:30am. AmEx/MC/V. ❷

Arc Café, C. Carabassa, 19 (☎93 302 52 04). M: Drassanes. Away from the crowds, this gay-friendly cafe serves creative soups and salads. Entrees €5-8. Lunch *menú* €7.50. Open M-Th 9am-1am, F 9am-3am, Sa 11am-3am, Su 11am-1am. ❷

UPPER BARRI GÒTIC

Els Quatre Gats, C. Montsió, 3 (☎933 02 41 40). M: Catalunya. An old Modernist hangout of Picasso's with lots of Bohemian character; he loved it so much he designed a personalized menu. Entrees €12-18. Live piano and violin 9pm-1am. Open daily 1pm-1am. Closed Aug. AmEx/MC/V. ❸

Terrablava, Via Laietana, 55 (☎933 22 15 85). An all-you-can-eat buffet of veggies, pasta, pizza, meat dishes, fruit, coffee, and one of the most extensive salad bars in the area. Buffet €8.40. Open daily 12:30pm-1am. Cash only. ❷

The Bagel Shop, C. Canuda, 25 (☎933 02 41 61). M: Catalunya. Barcelona meets New York City. Diverse bagel selection (€0.60 each), bagel sandwiches (€3-5), and varied spreads, from cream cheese to caramel (€3-6). Open M-Sa 9:30am-9:30pm, Su (Sept.-June only) 11am-4pm. ❶

La Colmena, Pl. de l'Àngel, 12 (☎933 15 13 56). M: Jaume I. This divine pastry and candy shop tempts all; don't walk in unless you're prepared to buy, because you *will*— no one's strong enough to resist. Pastries €1-4. Open daily 9am-9pm. AmEx/MC/V. ❶

Xaloc, C. de la Palla, 13-17 (☎933 01 19 90). M: Liceu. This classy delicatessen is centered around a butcher counter with pig legs hanging from the high ceiling. Meat and poultry sandwiches on tasty baguettes €3-7. Open daily 9am-midnight. AmEx/MC/V. ❶

BARCELONA

 **SIGHTS & MUSEUMS**

LAS RAMBLAS

Las Ramblas, a pedestrian-only median strip roughly 1km long, is a cosmopolitan cornucopia of street performers, fortune-tellers, human statues, vendors, and artists, all for the benefit of the visiting droves of tourists. A stroll along this bustling avenue can be an adventure at almost any hour, day or night. The wide, tree-lined thoroughfare dubbed Las Ramblas is actually composed of five (six if you count the small Rambla de Mar) distinct *ramblas* (promenades) that together form one boulevard starting at the Pl. de Catalunya and the **Font de Canaletes** (more a pump than a fountain)—visitors who wish to eventually return to Barcelona are supposed to sample the water. Halfway down Las Ramblas, **Joan Miró's** pavement mosaic brightens up the street. Pass the **Monument a Colom** on your way out to the Rambla de Mar and a beautiful view of the Mediterranean.

GRAN TEATRE DEL LICEU. Once one of Europe's leading stages, the Liceu has been ravaged by anarchists, bombs, and fires. It is adorned with palatial ornamentation, gold facades, sculptures, and grand rooms—including a fantastic Spanish hall of mirrors. (*Las Ramblas, 51-59, by C. Sant Pau. M: Liceu, L3.* ☎ *934 85 99 13. Office open M-F 2-8:30pm and 1hr. before performances. Tours M-F 10am, by reservation only. €5.*)

CENTRE D'ART DE SANTA MÓNICA. One can only imagine what the nuns of this former convent would have thought of the edgy art installations (recently "How Difficult it is to Sleep Alone" and "Transsexual Express") that rotate through this gallery, which is definitely worth a visit for modern art fans. (*Las Ramblas, 7. M: Drassanes.* ☎ *933 16 27 27. Open M-F 11am–2pm and 5-8pm. Call for info on exhibitions. Free.*)

MONUMENT A COLOM. Ruis i Taulet's Monument a Colom towers at the port end of Las Ramblas. Nineteenth-century *Renaixença* enthusiasts convinced themselves that Columbus was Catalán, from a town near Girona. The fact that Columbus points proudly toward Libya, not the Americas, doesn't help the claim; historians agree that Columbus was from Italy. Take the elevator to the top to enjoy a stunning view. (*Portal de la Pau. M: Drassanes. Elevator open June-Sept. daily 9am-8:30pm; Apr.-May 10am-2pm and 3:30-7:30pm, Sa-Su 10am-7:30pm; Oct.-Mar. M-F 10am-1:30pm and 3:30-6:30pm, Sa-Su 10am-6:30pm. €1.80, children and over 65 €1.20.*)

LA BOQUERÍA (MERCAT DE SANT JOSEP). Besides being one of the cheapest and best places to get food in the city, La Boquería is a sight in itself: a traditional Catalan market located in a giant, all-steel Modernist structure. Specialized vendors sell delicious produce, fish, and meat from one of a seemingly infinite number of independent stands inside. (*Las Ramblas, 95. M: Liceu. Open M-Sa 8am-8pm.*)

MUSEU DE L'ERÒTICA. As Spain's only erotica museum, the exhibits attract many of Barcelona's most intrepid tourists. The random assortment spans human history (somewhat unevenly) and depicts a variety of seemingly impossible sexual acrobatics that push the limits of human flexibility. The seven-foot wooden phallus is an irresistible photo op. (*Las Ramblas, 96. M: Catalunya, L1/3.* ☎ *933 18 98 65. Open June-Sept. 10am-midnight; Oct.-May 11am-9pm. €7.50, students €6.50.*)

PALAU DE LA VIRREINA. Once the residence of a Peruvian viceroy, today this 18th-century palace houses contemporary photography, music, and graphics exhibits. Also on display are the latest incarnations of the 3-5m tall dolls which have taken part in the city's Carnival celebrations since 1399. Be sure to check out the famous rainbow stained-glass facade of the **Casa Beethoven** next door at Las Ramblas, 97, now a well-stocked music store. (*Las Ramblas, 99. M: Liceu.* ☎ *93 316 10 00. Open Tu-Sa 11am-8:30pm; Su 11am-3pm. Free.*)

MUSEU DE CERA (WAX MUSEUM). Some 300 wax figures form an endless parade of celebrities, fictional characters, and European historical figures you've probably never heard of; the most recognizable are generally ones with distinctive facial hair, like Fidel Castro and Chewbacca from Star Wars. *(Las Ramblas, 4. M: Drassanes. ☎ 933 17 26 49. Open July-Sept. daily 10am-8pm; Oct.-June M-F 10am-1:30pm and 4-7:30pm, Sa-Su and holidays 11am-2pm and 4:30-8:30pm. €6.70, ages 5-11 €3.80.)*

BARRI GÒTIC

While the ancient cathedrals and palaces gives the impression that this neighborhood's time has passed, the area is still very much alive, as evident in the ever-crowded streets. As the oldest part of Barcelona, the Barri Gòtic came into existence well before the inception of the grid layout (found in l'Eixample), taking form during Roman times and continuing to develop during the medieval period.

ESGLÉSIA CATEDRAL DE LA SANTA CREU. This cathedral is one of Barcelona's most popular monuments. Beyond the choir are the altar with the bronze cross designed by Frederic Marès in 1976 and the sunken Crypt of Santa Eulalia, one of Barcelona's patron saints. The cathedral museum holds Bartolomé Bermejo's *Pietà*. Catch a performance of the *sardana* in front of the cathedral on Sunday after mass; services begin at noon and 6:30pm. *(M: Jaume I. In Pl. Seu, up C. Bisbe from Pl. St. Jaume. Cathedral open daily 8am-1:30pm and 4-7:30pm. Cloister open 9am-1:15pm and 4-7pm. Elevator to the roof open M-Sa 10:30am-12:30pm and 4:30-6pm; €1.40. Choir area open M-F 9am-1pm and 4-7pm, Sa-Su 9am-1pm; €1. English audioguide €1.)*

PLAÇA DE SANT JAUME. Plaça de Sant Jaume has been Barcelona's political center since Roman times. Two of Cataluña's most important buildings have dominated the square since 1823: the **Palau de la Generalitat,** the headquarters of Cataluña's government, and the **Ajuntament,** the city hall. *(Generalitat open Su 10:30am-1:30pm. Closed Aug. Mandatory tours in Catalán, Spanish, or English every 30min. starting at 10:30am. Free. Ajuntament open Su 10am-1:45pm. Free.)*

MUSEU D'HISTÒRIA DE LA CIUTAT. There are two components to the Museu d'Història de la Ciutat (Museum of the History of Barcelona): the Palau Reial Major and the subterranean excavations of the Roman city Barcino. Built on top of the fourth-century city walls, the **Palau Reial Major** served as the residence of the Catalan-Aragonese monarchs. When restoration on the building began, the **Saló de Tinell** (Throne Room) was discovered wholly intact under a baroque chapel. The huge Gothic room is believed to be the place where Fernando and Isabel received Columbus after his journey to America. Today, it houses year-long temporary exhibitions. The second part of the museum lies underground; this 4000 sq. meter ⚑**archaeological exhibit** was excavated from 1930 to 1960 and displays incredibly intact 1st- to 6th-century remains of the Roman city of Barcino. *(Pl. del Rei. M: Jaume I. ☎ 933 15 11 11. Open June-Sept. Su 10am-3pm, Tu-Sa 10am-8pm; Oct.-May Su 10am-3pm, Tu-Sa 10am-2pm and 4-8pm. Museum €4, students €2.50. Exhibition €3.50, students €2. Combined museum and exhibition €6, students €4. Pamphlets available in English.)*

EL CALL (JEWISH QUARTER). Although today there is little indicating the Jewish heritage of this area, for centuries El Call was the most vibrant center of intellectual and financial activity in all of Barcelona. One Jewish synagogue was turned into a church, the **Església de Sant Jaume** (C. Ferran, 28). However, the only remaining tangible evidence of Jewish inhabitants in El Call is the ancient **Hebrew plaque** on tiny C. Marlet. *(M: Liceu.)*

PLAÇA REIAL. This is the most crowded, happening *plaça* in the entire Barri Gòtic, where tourists and locals congregate to eat and drink at night, and to buy and sell at the Sunday morning flea market. Francesc Daniel Milona designed the *plaça*, replacing decrepit Barri Gòtic streets with this large, architecturally cohesive *plaça* in the 1850s. Near the fountain in the center of the square there are two street lamps designed by Antoni Gaudí. *(M: Liceu or Drassanes.)*

📻 NIGHTLIFE

Here, cookie-cutter *cervecerías* and *bar-restaurantes* can be found every five steps. The Barri Gòtic is perfect for chit-chatting your night away, sipping *sangría*, or scoping out your next dance partner.

Fonfone, C. Escudellers, 24. M: Liceu or Drassanes. Atmospheric lighting and cool sounds draw 1-3am crowds. Different DJs every night from all over the world. Beer €3.20. Mixed drinks €6. Open Su-Th 9:30pm-2:30am, F-Sa 9:30pm-3am.

Molly's Fair City, C. Ferran, 7. M: Liceu. The place to go if you're looking to meet English-speaking tourists in the Barri Gòtic, guzzling pricy but strong mixed drinks. Guinness on tap €5. Bottled beer €4. Mixed drinks €7. Open Su-Th 8pm-2:30am, F-Sa 7pm-3am.

Jamboree, Pl. Reial, 17. M: Liceu. In the corner immediately to your right coming from Las Ramblas. What was once a convent now serves as one of the city's most popular live music venues. Daily jazz or blues performances. Cover M-F €6, Sa-Su €9-12; includes one drink. Open daily 11pm-1am. Upstairs, the attached club **Tarantos** hosts flamenco shows (€25). Open M-Sa 9:30pm-midnight.

Schilling, C. Ferran, 23. M: Liceu, L3. One of the more chill and spacious bars in the area. Mixed gay and straight crowd. Excellent *sangría* (pitcher €14). Mixed drinks €5. Wine and beer €2. Open daily 10am-2:30am.

Vildsvin, C. Ferran, 38. M: Liceu. Oysters and international beers (€4-8) are the specialties at this Norwegian bar. *Tapas* €3-5. Desserts €3.50-5. *Entrees* €8-14. Open M-Th 9am-2am, F-Sa 9am-3am. AmEx/MC/V.

El Bosq de les Fades, (☎933 17 26 49). M: Drassanes, near the Wax Museum. This bar comes complete with gnarly trees and gnomes. A good place to hang before hitting up a club. Open M-Th 10am-1:30am, F-Sa 10am-2:30am.

Glaciar Bar, Pl. Reial, 3. M: Liceu. A hidden treasure in a sea of indistinguishable tourist bars. Plenty of outside tables. Beer €1.50-2. Mixed drinks €4. Liter of *sangría* €10. Open M-Sa 4pm-2:30am, Su 8am-2:30am. Cash only.

New York, C. Escudellers, 5. M: Drassanes. Once a strip joint, New York is now the biggest club in the Barri Gòtic. Crowds don't arrive until after 3am; music includes reggae and British pop. Cover 11:30pm-2am €6 (includes 1 beer); 2-5am €13 (includes any drink). Open Th-Sa midnight-5am. Cash only.

Margarita Blue, C. Josep Anselm Clavé, 6. M: Drassanes. This Mexican-themed bar draws a 20- and 30-something crowd. Blue margaritas €3. W night drag queen performances. Open Su-W 7pm-2am, Th 7pm-2:30am, F-Sa 7pm-3am.

LA RIBERA

As the stomping ground of Barcelona's many fishermen and merchants, La Ribera has always had a working-class feel. However, its confines were witness to two of the most major events to shape Barcelona's history. In the 18th century, Felipe V demolished much of La Ribera, then the city's commercial hub, to make space for the impressive Ciutadella, then the seat of Madrid's oppressive control and now a park. Angry that Barcelona had sought his opponent, the Archduke Carlos, as its leader, Felipe V stuffed the wealthy, and therefore powerful, citizens of Barcelona into the Ciutadella's chambers. Luckily, his successors were more lenient on their subjects, most victims were freed, and La Ribera was subsequently rejuvenated. Then, when in 1888 the former site of Ciutadella became home to the Universal Exposition, La Ribera served as its launching point, displaying the new flare of Modernisme and the simplicity of old Spanish architecture and values. In recent years, the neighborhood has evolved into Barcelona's bohemian nucleus, attracting a young, artsy crowd of locals and a few expats and tourists in the know.

ACCOMMODATIONS

Hostal de Ribagorza, C. Trafalgar, 39 (☎/fax 933 19 19 68). M: Urquinaona. Rooms in a Modernist building complete with marble staircase and tile floors. TVs, fans, and homey decorations. Doubles only €38-50. Prices decrease a bit the rest of the year. ❷

Pensión Ciutadella, C. Comerç, 33. M: Barceloneta (☎933 19 62 03). Small hostel with spacious rooms, each with fan, TV, and balcony. Family feel. Doubles only. June-Sept. €36-40, with bath €50; Nov.-Feb. €36/€40. ❸

Hostal Nuevo Colón, Av. Marqués de l'Argentera, 19 (☎933 19 50 77; www.hostalnuevocolon.com). M: Barceloneta. Modern rooms and a common area with TV. Singles €35; doubles €48, with bath €62. 6-person apartments with kitchens €150 per day. ❸

Gothic Point Youth Hostel, C. Vigatans, 5 (☎932 68 78 08). M: Jaume I. Lobby area with free Internet access and large TV. 150 beds in dorm-style rooms with A/C. Breakfast included. In high season dorms €20; off-season €17. AmEx/MC/V. ❷

FOOD

El Pebre Blau, C. Banys Vells, 21 (☎933 19 13 08). M: Jaume I. This gourmet restaurant serves delicate dishes that creatively fuse Mediterranean, Oriental, and Sephardic flavors. The specialties—foie gras with apricots and honeyed sauce, and seared duck with forest berries—are to die for. Dessert will never be the same after trying the balsamic vinegar ice cream. Kitchen open daily 8:30pm-midnight; reservations recommended on weekends. Wheelchair-accessible. MC/V. ❹

Bodega La Tinaja, C. Esparteria, 9 (☎933 10 22 50). M: Jaume I. The wine selection is excellent (€1.50-5 per glass). The cheese, pate, fish, and meat accompaniments for bread are mouth-watering. Mix and match new tastes in this wood-beamed restaurant. Open Su and Tu-Sa 6pm-2am. MC/V. ❷

Taira, C. Comerç, 7 (☎933 10 24 97). From M: Jaume I, follow C. Princesa, then turn left on C. Comerç. Chill on floor-level futons and funky chairs at this swank sushi hot spot. Splurge on the *moriawase* (€17), and finish up with a *sorbete de sake* (€4). *Menú* €8. Cafeteria open M-F 8am-4pm, restaurant open Tu-Sa 1-4pm and 9pm-midnight, Su 8:30pm-1am. Wheelchair-accessible. AmEx/MC/V. ❹

Xampanyet, C. Montcada, 22 (☎933 19 70 03). M: Jaume. Next to the Museu Picasso and packed with people. The house special—*cava* (choose from 17 varieties)—is served with anchovies and, of course, bread with tomato (€1.10). Bottles €6.50 and up. Open Tu-Sa noon-4pm and 7-11:30pm, Su noon-4pm. Closed Aug. ❶

Va de Vi, C. Banys Vells, 16 (☎933 19 29 00). M: Jaume I. Possibly the most romantic restaurant in La Ribera. Choose from over 170 varieties of wine and cava (glasses €1.60-4), a wide selection of cheeses (€4-15.50) and *tapas* (€1.80-13). Open Su-W 6pm-1am, Th 6pm-2am, F-Sa 6pm-3am. Wheelchair-accessible. ❷

◉ 🏛 SIGHTS & MUSEUMS

■ **MUSEU PICASSO.** The most-visited museum in Barcelona traces the development of Picasso as an artist, with the world's best collection of work from his formative Barcelona period. *(C. Montcada, 15-19. M: Jaume I. Open Tu-Sa 10am-8pm, Su 10am-3pm. €5, students and seniors €2.50. Under 16 free. First Su of each month free.)*

■ **PALAU DE LA MÚSICA CATALANA.** In 1891, the Orfeo Catalán choir society commissioned Modernist Luis Domènech i Montaner to design this must-see concert venue. The music hall glows with tall stained-glass windows, an ornate chandelier, marble reliefs, intricate woodwork, and ceramic mosaics. Concerts given at the Palau include symphonic and choral music in addition to more modern pop, rock, and jazz. *(C. Sant Francese de Paula, 2. ☎932 95 72 00; www.palaumusica.org. M: Jaume I. Mandatory tours in English every hr. Reserve 1 day in advance. Open daily Aug. 10am-6pm; Sept.-July 10am-3:30pm. €5, students and seniors €4. Check the Guía del Ocio for concert listings. Concert tickets €6-150. MC/V.)*

■ **MUSEU DE LA XOCOLAT.** Arguably the most delectable museum in Spain. If you can halt the inevitable salivation for a few moments, the museum presents gobs of information about the history, production, and ingestion of this sensuous treat. Perhaps more interesting are the exquisite chocolate sculptures, particularly the edible La Sagrada Família. The small cafe offers workshops on cake baking and chocolate tasting. *(Pl. Pons i Clerch. M: Jaume I. Open M and W-Sa 10am-7pm, Su 10am-3pm. Workshops from €6; reservations required. €3.80, students and seniors €3.30.)*

PARC DE LA CIUTADELLA. Host of the 1888 Universal Exposition, the park harbors several museums, well-labeled horticulture, the wacky Cascada fountains, a pond, and a zoo. Buildings of note include Domènech i Montaner's Modernista **Castell dels Tres Dracs** (now the Museu de Zoología), the geological museum, and Josep Amergós's **Hivernacle.** In the **Parc Zoològic,** ■**Floquet de Neu** (a.k.a. *Copito de Nieve;* Little Snowflake), the world's only known albino gorilla, lounges in the sun. *(M: Ciutadella. Open daily May-Aug. 9:30am-7:30pm; Apr. and Sept. 10am-7pm; Mar. and Oct. 10am-6pm; Nov.-Feb. 10am-5pm. €12.)* The nearby **Museu d'Art Modern** houses a potpourri of works by 19th-century Catalán artists. *(Pl. d'Armes. Open Tu-Sa 10am-7pm, Su 10am-2:30pm. €3, students €2. First Th of every month free.)*

SANTA MARIA DEL MAR. This architectural wonder was built in the 14th century in a quick 55 years. At a distance of 13m apart, the supporting columns span a width greater than any other medieval building in the world. It's a fascinating example of the limits of Gothic architecture—were it 2ft. taller, the roof would collapsed from structural instability. *(Pl. Santa Maria, 1. M: Jaume I. Open M-Sa 9am-1:30pm and 4:30-8pm, Su 9am-2pm and 5-8:30pm. Free.)*

EL FOSSAR DE LES MORERES. The Catalans who resisted Felipe V's conquering troops in 1714 lie here in a mass grave, commemorated by mulberry trees *(moreres)* and a plaque with a verse by poet Serafi Pitarra: "In the Mulberry Cemetery no traitors are buried. Even though we lose our flags, this will be the urn of honor." Demonstrators and patriots converge here on *La Diada* (Catalan National Day, September 11), to commemorate the siege of Barcelona and the subsequent ban on displays of Catalan nationalism. *(Off C. de Santa Maria behind the church.)*

◖ NIGHTLIFE

El Copetin, Pg. del Born, 19. M: Jaume I. Cuban rhythm infuses everything in this casual nightspot. *Mojitos* €5. Open Su-Th 7pm-2:30am, F-Sa 7pm-3am.

El Born, Pg. del Born, 26. M: Jaume I. Sit at the marble counter over the basins where fish were once sold or follow spiral staircase upstairs for a meal. Fondues €12-15. Excellent cocktails €4-6. Open Su-Th 6pm-2am, F-Sa 6pm-3am.

Palau Dalmases, C. Montcada, 20. M: Jaume I. A self-labeled "Baroque space" in a 17th-century palace. Live opera performances Th at 11pm (€18, includes one drink). Drinks €6-10. Open Tu-Sa 10pm-2am, Su 6-10pm.

Pitin Bar, Pg. del Born, 34. M: Barceloneta. Trippy lounge music will put you in the mood for absinthe (€2.70). Mixed drinks €4.50-8. Open daily 6pm-3am.

EL RAVAL

Located next to Las Ramblas and the Barri Gòtic, El Raval tends to be a favorite of Barcelona's natives rather than its tourists. This diverse and culturally rich working-class neighborhood has a special charm, with small, quirky shops and eateries, welcoming bars, and hidden historical attractions. Beginning as a small rural area outside of the city walls, El Raval was enveloped by the new city boundaries in the 14th century and has been squeezing people in ever since. The situation became critical in the late 19th and early 20th centuries, when over-crowding led to an urban nightmare of rampant crime, prostitution, and drug use. Revitalization efforts, especially since the '92 Olympic games, have worked wonders, however; new museums and cultural centers have paved the way for trendy restaurants and bars, and today El Raval is emerging as one of Barcelona's most dynamic areas.

ACCOMMODATIONS

Be careful in the areas nearer to the port and farther from Las Ramblas.

Pensión L'Isard, C. Tallers, 82 (☎/fax 933 02 51 83). M: Universitat. A clean find with enough closet space for even the worst over-packer. Singles €20; doubles €36, with bath €52; triples €52. ❷

Ideal Youth Hostel, C. la Unió, 12 (☎933 42 61 77; www.idealhostel.com). M: Liceu. One of the best deals in the city. Breakfast included. Free Internet access in the swanky lobby area. Sheets €2.50. Laundry €4. Dorms €16. ❷

Hostal Opera, C. de Sant Pau, 20 (☎933 18 82 01; info@hostalopera.com). M: Liceu. Recently renovated rooms feel like new. Bath, telephone, and A/C in every room. Internet access in the common room. Singles €35; doubles €55; triples €80. MC/V. ❸

Hotel Peninsular, C. de Sant Pau, 34 (☎933 02 31 38). M: Liceu. This building is now one of the sights on the Ruta del Modernisme. Rooms come with telephones and A/C. Breakfast included. Singles €30, with bath €50; doubles €50/70. MC/V. ❸

Barcelona Mar Youth Hostel, C. de Sant Pau, 80 (☎933 24 85 30; www.youthostel.com). M: Paral·lel. This new hostel crams 120 dorm-style beds rooms with A/C. All beds come with a safe for personal belongings. Laundry service. Internet €1 per 30min. Breakfast included. In summer dorms €21-23; in winter €14-18. ❷

FOOD

Pla dels Angels, C. Ferlandina, 23 (☎934 43 31 03). M: Universitat. The funky decor of this colorful, inexpensive eatery is fitting for its proximity to the contemporary art museum. Indulge in *gnocchi* with curry sauce and raisins (€3.20). Entrees €5-6. Open M-Th 1-4pm and 9-11:30pm, F-Sa 9pm-midnight. Cash only. ❷

Bar Ra, Pl. de la Garduña (☎933 01 41 63, reservations 615 95 98 72). M: Liceu. Everything about Ra exudes cool. Try the excellent vegetarian lasagna (€7.50) or duck magret with mango sauce (€9.50). Entrees €6.50-13. Open M-Sa 9am-midnight. Su brunch noon-6pm. Dinner by reservation only. AmEx/MC/V. ❷

BARCELONA

Buenas Migas, Pl. Bonsuccés, 6 (☎933 18 37 08). M: Catalunya. Enjoy coffee or tea (€1-1.30) at one of the shaded outside tables, or stay in the rustic-feeling interior with your *foccacia* (€2-4) topped with everything from vegetables to bacon and brie. Open Su-W 10am-10pm, Th-Sa 10am-midnight. Cash only. ❶

DosTrece, C. Carme 40, (☎93 301 73 06; www.dostrece.net). M: Catalunya. Crowds of young locals dine in the fine decor of stained glass and candles, while listening to live music (jazz Tu, flamenco W, hip-hop Th, soul F, and house Sa). Lunch *menú* €9. Entrees €7-15. Open M-Sa 1:30-4pm and 9-midnight. Terrace open until 3am. AmEx/MC/V. ❸

Restaurante Can Lluís, C. Cera, 49 (☎934 41 11 87). M: Sant Antoni. From the Metro, head down Ronda S. Pau and take the 2nd left on C. Cera. Eschewing trendiness, the menu is filled with traditional Catalan favorites including lamb ribs (€10) and fresh-grilled asparagus (€5.40). Lunch *menú* €7. Dinner *menús* (€20-35) include wine. Open M-Sa 1:30-4pm and 8:30-11:30pm. V. ❸

👁 🏛 SIGHTS & MUSEUMS

▓PALAU GÜELL. Gaudí's 1886 Palau Güell—the Modernist residence built for patron Eusebi Güell (of Park Güell fame)—has one of Barcelona's most spectacular interiors. Güell spared no expense on this house, considered to be the first where Gaudí's unique style truly showed. *(C. Nou de La Rambla, 3-5. M: Liceu. Mandatory tour every 15min. Open Mar.-Oct. Su 10am-2pm, M-Sa 10am-8pm, last tour at 6:15pm; Nov.-Dec. M-Sa 10am-6pm. €3, students €1.50.)*

MUSEU D'ART CONTEMPORANI (MACBA). This monstrosity of a building was constructed with the idea that sparse decor would allow the art to speak for itself. The MACBA has received worldwide acclaim for its focus on avant-garde art between the two world wars, as well as Surrealist and contemporary art. *(Pl. dels Àngels, 1. M: Catalunya. Open July-Sept. M, W, F 11am-8pm, Th 11am-9:30pm, Sa 10am-8pm, Su 10am-3pm; Oct.-June M and W-F 11am-7:30pm, Sa 10am-8pm, Su 10am-3pm. €7, students €3., under 17 free.)*

CENTRE DE CULTURA CONTEMPORÀNIA DE BARCELONA (CCCB). The center stands out for its mixture of architectural styles, consisting of an early 20th-century theater and its 1994 addition, a sleek wing of black glass. The institute shows a variety of temporary exhibits, including film screenings and music performances; check the *Guia del Ocio* for scheduled events. *(Casa de Caritat. C. Montalegre, 5. M: Catalunya or Universitat. ☎933 06 41 00. Open Tu, Th, and F 11am-2pm and 4-8pm; W and Sa 11am-8pm; Su and holidays 11am-7pm. €4, students €3, W €3 for all, children free.)*

🎷 NIGHTLIFE

If glamorous clubs and all-night dancing are your scene, El Raval is not for you. The streets are densely packed with a bar for every variety of bar-hopper—Irish pubbers, American backpackers, absinthe abusers, social drinkers, lounge lizards, and foosball maniacs will find themselves at home in El Raval.

▓Casa Almirall, C. Joaquim Costa, 33. M: Universitat. Barcelona's oldest bar, founded in 1860. Cavernous space with weathered couches. The staff will walk you through your first glass of *absenta* (absinthe; €4.50)—and cut you off after your second. Beer €2. Mixed drinks €5. Open Su-Th 6:30pm-2:30am, F-Sa 6:30pm-3am.

Muebles Navarro (El Café que Pone), C. la Riera Alta, 4-6. Enjoy the mellow ambience and watch friends get friendlier as they sink into the comfy couches together. Beer and wine €2-3. Mixed drinks €5-7. Open Tu-Th 6pm-2am, F-Sa 6pm-3am.

London Bar, C. Nou de la Rambla, 34. M: Liceu. Rub shoulders with unruly, fun-loving expats at this Modernist tavern. Live music nightly. Beer, wine, and absinthe €2-3. Open Su and Tu-Th 7:30pm-4:30am, F-Sa 7:30pm-5am. AmEx/MC/V.

Sant Pau 68, C. de Sant Pau, 68. M: Liceu. One of the hippest bars in El Raval. Drinks €2-5. Open Tu-Th 8pm-2:30am, F-Sa 8pm-3am. Cash only.

La Paloma, C. Tigre, 27. M: Universitat. One would never guess that this dance hall, with its theater-like interior, was a factory until 1903. Live salsa and popular Spanish music keep a mature clientele dancing through the night. Mixed drinks €7. Cover €7. Open Su and Th 6-9:30pm, F 6-9:30pm and 11:30pm-4am, Sa 6-9:30pm and 11:30pm-5am.

Marsella Bar, C. de Sant Pau, 65. M: Liceu. Religious figurines grace the walls; perhaps they're praying for the absinthe drinkers (€3.40) who frequent the place. Mixed drinks €2-6. Open M-Th 10pm-2:30am, F-Sa 10pm-3:30am.

L'EIXAMPLE

Barcelona's l'Eixample (Enlargement; luh-SHOMP-luh) is remarkable for the unusual circumstances leading to its development. Right around the time when the oppressive Bourbon walls around the old city were finally demolished in 1854, the Catalan cultural Renaixença was picking up. As the number of wealthy benefactors of industrialization grew, utopian socialist theories spread like wildfire through philosophical circles, including those of l'Eixample designer **Ildefons Cerdà i Sunyer.** The gridded streets are filled with relatively wealthy residents, designer shops, corporate buildings, and eateries from around the world. Most tourists only see the Pg. de Gràcia and La Sagrada Família areas, but if you have the energy to explore the whole neighborhood, you'll get a great lesson in Modernisme, and a better feel for the Barcelona beyond the tourist attractions.

⌂ ACCOMMODATIONS

▒ Hostal Residencia Oliva, Pg. de Gràcia, 32, 4th fl. (☎934 88 01 62 or 88 17 89; www.lasguias.com/hostaloliva). M: Pg. de Gràcia. Elegant wood-worked bureaus, mirrors, ceilings, and a light marble floor give this hostel a classy ambience. Singles €26; doubles €48, with bath €55; triple with bath €78. ❸

▒ Pensión Fani, C. València, 278 (☎932 15 36 45). M: Catalunya. Oozes quirky charm. Rooms rented by month; single nights also available. Singles €280 per month; doubles €500 per month; triples €780 per month. One-night stay €20 per person. ❷

Hostal Eden, C. Balmes, 55 (☎934 52 66 20; http://hostaleden.net). M: Pg. de Gràcia. Modern rooms are equipped with TVs and fans; most have big, new bathrooms. May-Oct. singles €29, with bath €39; doubles €39/€60. Nov.-Apr. singles €23/€32; doubles €29/€45. AmEx/MC/V. ❸

Hostal Qué Tal, C. Mallorca, 290 (☎/fax 934 59 23 66; www.quetalbarcelona.com), near C. Bruc. M: Pg. de Gràcia or Verdaguer. This high-quality gay- and lesbian-friendly hostel has one of the best interiors of all the hostels in the city. Singles €39; doubles €58, with bath €78. ❹

Hostal San Remo, C. Bruc, 20 (☎933 02 19 89; www.hostalsanremo.com). M: Urquinaona. All rooms have TV, A/C, and soundproof windows. Reserve early. Singles €30; doubles €42, with bath €55. Nov. and Jan.-Feb. reduced prices. MC/V. ❸

Pensión Aribau, C. Aribau, 37 (☎/fax 934 53 11 06). M: Pg. de Gràcia. All rooms with TVs, most with A/C. Reservations recommended. Singles €36; doubles €45, with bath €60; triples with bath €70. Prices decrease in low season. AmEx/MC/V. ❹

Hostal Residencia Windsor, Rambla de Catalunya, 84 (☎932 15 11 98). M: Pg. de Gràcia. Rooms come equipped with comfy sleep sofas and heat in winter. Singles €25, with bath €42; doubles €52/€60; extra beds €10. ❷

🍴 FOOD

🍴 **El Racó d'en Baltá,** C. Aribau, 125 (☎934 53 10 44). M: Hospital Clínic. Offers creative Mediterranean dishes. Fish and meat entrees €12-17. Open Tu-Th 1-3:30pm and 9-10:45pm, F-Sa 1-3:30pm and 9-11pm, Su 9-10:45pm. AmEx/MC/V. ❸

🍴 **Comme-Bio,** Av. Gran Via, 603 (☎933 01 03 760). The antithesis of traditional Catalan food, this place has hummus, tofu, and yogurt. Restaurant and small grocery store. Pasta, rice, and veggie pizzas €9. Salads €6-8. Open daily 9am-11:30pm. ❷

Thai Gardens, C. Diputació, 273 (☎934 87 98 98). M: Catalunya. Extravagant decor. Weekday lunch *menú* €11; dinner *menú* €11. Pad thai €6. Entrees €9-14. Open Su-Th 1-4pm and 8pm-midnight, F-Sa 1:30-4pm and 8pm-1am. ❸

Laie Llibreria Café, C. Pau Claris, 85 (☎933 02 63 10; www.laie.es). M: Urquinaona. This urban oasis offers a fresh, plentiful all-you-can-eat buffet (€8.30). Internet €1 per 15min. Open M-F 9am-1am, Sa 10am-1am. AmEx/MC/V. ❷

Mandalay Café, C. Provença, 330 (☎934 58 60 17; www.mandalaycafe.net). Exotic pan-Asian cuisine, including gourmet dim sum and elegant salads. F-Sa night trapeze artist around 11pm. Entrees €9-13. Open Tu-Sa 8:30pm-midnight. AmEx/MC/V. ❸

Txapela (Euskal Taberna), Pg. de Gràcia, 8-10 (☎934 12 02 89). M: Catalunya. This Basque restaurant is a godsend for the *tapas*-clueless traveler who wants to learn. *Tapas* €1.05. Open M-Th 8am-1:30am, F-Su 10am-2am. Wheelchair-accessible. ❷

📷 🏛 SIGHTS & MUSEUMS

The Catalan *Renaixença* and the growth of Barcelona during the 19th century pushed the city past its medieval walls and into modernity. Ildefons Cerdà drew up a plan for a new neighborhood where people of all social classes could live side by side; however, l'Eixample did not thrive as a utopian community but rather as a playground for the bourgeois. But despite the gentrification, the original Modernist architecture that draws visitors remains intact.

🏛 **LA SAGRADA FAMÍLIA.** Although Antoni Gaudí's unfinished masterpiece is barely a shell of the intended finished product, La Sagrada Família is without a doubt the world's most visited construction site. Despite the fact that only eight of the eighteen planned towers have been completed (and those the shortest, at that) and the church still doesn't have an "interior," millions of people make the touristic pilgrimage to witness its work-in-progress majesty. Of the three proposed facades, only the Nativity Facade was finished under Gaudí. A furor has arisen over recent additions, especially sculptor Josep Subirachs's Cubist Passion Facade, which is criticized for being inconsistent with Gaudí's plans. *(C. Mallorca, 401. M: Sagrada Família. Open daily Apr.-Sept. 9am-8pm, elevator open 9:30am-7:45pm; Oct.-Mar. 9am-6pm, elevator open 9:30am-5:45pm. Excellent guided tours Apr.-Sept. daily every hour 11am-5pm; Oct. 11am,-3pm; Nov.-Mar. Su-M and F-Sa 11am-1pm. €3. Entrance €8, students €5. Cash only.)*

🏛 **LA MANZANA DE LA DISCÒRDIA.** A short walk from Pl. de Catalunya, the odd-numbered side of Pg. de Gràcia between C. Aragó and Consell de Cent is popularly known as *la manzana de la discòrdia* (block of discord). Its name comes from the stylistic clashing of three buildings. Regrettably, the bottom two floors of **Casa Lleó i Morera,** by Domènech i Montaner, were destroyed to make room for a fancy store, but you can buy the **Ruta del Modernisme pass** there and take a short tour of the upstairs, where sprouting flowers, stained glass, and legendary doorway sculptures adorn the interior. Puig i Cadafalch opted for a geometric, Moorish-influenced pattern on the facade of **Casa Amatller** at #41. Gaudí's balconies ripple like water, and tiles sparkle in blue-purple glory on **Casa Batlló**, #43. The most popular interpretation of Casa Batlló is that the building represents Catalunya's patron Sant Jordi (St. George) slaying a dragon; the chimney plays the lance, the scaly roof is the dragon's back, and the bony balconies are the remains of his victims. The ChupaChups lollipop candy now owns the Casa Batlló, and it is closed to the public except for tours. (*Open M-Sa 9am-2pm, Su 9am-8pm. €8, students €6.*)

CASA MILÀ (LA PEDRERA). Modernism buffs argue that the spectacular Casa Milà apartment building, an undulating mass of granite popularly known as *La Pedrera* (the Stone Quarry), is Gaudí's most refined work. Note the intricate ironwork around the balconies and the irregularity of the front gate's egg-shaped window panes. The roof sprouts chimneys that resemble armored soldiers, one of which is decorated with broken champagne bottles. Rooftop tours provide a closer look at these Prussian helmets. The winding brick attic has been transformed into the **Espai Gaudí**, a multimedia presentation of Gaudí's life and works. (*Pg. de Gràcia, 92. Open daily 10am-8pm. €7; students and over 65 €3.50. Free guided tours in English M-F 4pm, Sa-Su 11am.*)

HOSPITAL DE LA SANTA CREU I SANT PAU. Designated a UNESCO monument in 1997, the brilliant Modernist Hospital de la Santa Creu i Sant Pau was Domènech i Montaner's lifetime masterpiece. The entire complex covers nine full l'Eixample blocks (320 acres) and the pavilions are whimsically decorated, resembling gingerbread houses. The outdoor spaces are an oasis in the desert of urban gridding; they once included a small forest and still boast more than 300 different types of plants, as well as plenty shaded paths. (*Sant Antoni M. Claret, 167. M: Hospital de St. Pau, L5. ☎ 934 88 20 78. Hospital grounds open 24hr. 50min. guided tours Sa-Su 10am-2pm every 30min. Last tour leaves 1:30pm. €4.30, students and over-65 €3.*)

FUNDACIÓ ANTONI TÀPIES. Antoni Tàpies is one of Catalunya's best-known artists; his works often defy definition, springing from Surrealism and Magicism. Tàpies's massive and bizarre wire sculpture (*Cloud with Chair*) atop Domènech i Montaner's red brick building announces this collection of contemporary abstract art. The top floor of the foundation is dedicated to famous Catalans, particularly Tàpies, while the other two floors feature temporary exhibits of other modern artists' work. (*C. Aragó, 255. M: Pg. de Gràcia. ☎ 934 87 03 15. Museum open Su and Tu-Sa 10am-8pm. €4.20, students and seniors €2.10.*)

⚡ NIGHTLIFE

L'Eixample has upscale bars and some of the best gay nightlife in Europe, as evident in the area's nickname, "Gaixample."

Buenavista Salsoteca, C. Rosselló, 217. FGC: Provença. This over-the-top club manages to attract a chill mixed crowd. Free salsa and merengue lessons W-Th 10:30pm. F-Sa cover €9, includes 1 drink. Open W-Th 11pm-4am, F-Sa 11pm-5am, Su 8pm-2am.

Dietrich, C. Consell de Cent, 255. M: Pg. de Gràcia. An unflattering painting of Marlene Dietrich in the semi-nude greets a mostly gay crowd. Nightly drag/strip/dance shows. Beer €3.50. Mixed drinks €5-8. Open Su-Th 10:30pm-2:30am, F-Sa 10:30pm-3am.

La Fira, C. Provença, 171. M: Hospital Clínic or FGC: Provença. Bartenders serve a hip crowd dangling from carousel swings and surrounded by creepy fun-house mirrors. DJs spin funk, disco, and oldies. Open M-Th 10pm-3am, F-Sa 10pm-4:30am, Su 6pm-1am.

Fuse, C. Roger de Llúria, 40. M: Tetuán or Pg. de Gràcia. A hip Japanese-Mediterranean restaurant, cocktail bar, and dance club. Mixed gay and straight crowd. Beer €3, mixed drinks €6. Restaurant open M-Sa 8:30pm-1am. Bar open Th-Sa 1-3am. MC/V.

Les Gens que J'Aime, C. València, 286. M: Pg. de Gràcia. Travel back to Gaudí's time in this intimate bar. Background soul, funk, and jazz soothes patrons. Beer €3. Half-bottles of wine €9. Open daily June-Aug. 7-pm-3am, Sept.-May 6pm-3am.

Luz de Gas, C. Muntaner, 246. M: Diagonal. Chandeliers and deep red walls set the mood in this hip club. Live music every night. Beer €6. Mixed drinks €9. Concerts €15; check *Guia del Ocio* for listings and times. Open daily 11pm-5am; July-Aug. closed Su.

Salvation, Ronda de St. Pere, 19-21. M: Urquinaona. The place to come if you've sinned and want to keep on sinning. A popular gay club. Beer €5. Mixed drinks €8. Cover €11, includes 1 drink. Open F-Su midnight-6am.

The Michael Collins Irish Pub, Pl. Sagrada Família, 4. M: Sagrada Família. 100% Irish, from the waitstaff to the smoky, wooden decor. American and European sports on the TV. Draft beer €4. Mixed drinks €5. Open daily 2pm-3am.

MONTJUÏC

Montjuïc (mon-joo-EEK), the hill at the southwest end of the city, is one of the oldest sections of Barcelona; throughout Barcelona's history, whoever controlled Montjuïc's peak controlled the city. The Laietani collected oysters on Montjuïc before they were subdued by the Romans, who erected a temple to Jupiter on its slopes. Since then, dozens of despotic rulers have constructed and modified the **Castell de Montjuïc,** built atop the ancient Jewish cemetery (hence the name Montjuïc, Hill of the Jews). In the 20th century, Franco made the Castell de Montjuïc one of his "interrogation" headquarters; somewhere deep in the recesses of the structure, his *beneméritos* ("honorable ones," a.k.a. the militia) are believed to have shot Catalunya's former president, Lluís Companys, in 1941. The fort was not re-dedicated to the city until 1960. Since re-acquiring the mountain, Barcelona has given Montjuïc a new identity, transforming it from a military stronghold into a vast park by day and a playground by night. Today the park is one of the city's most visited attractions, with a little bit of something for everyone—world-famous art museums and theater, Olympic history and facilities, walking and biking trails, a healthy/unhealthy dose of nightlife, and an awe-inspiring historical cemetery.

🔾 FOOD

Food options are not as plentiful in Montjuïc as in the rest of the city. The Fundació Miró, MNAC, Castell de Montjuïc, and Teatre Grec all have pleasant cafes, but to find more than drinks and sandwiches, enter the depths of Poble Espanyol. *Menús* of all sorts run €10-15; otherwise, try one of the listings below. Some restaurants, bars, and grocery stores also line **Avinguda ParaHel** in Poble Sec.

La Font de Prades, (☎934 26 75 19) at the Plaça de la Font in Poble Espanyol. M: Espanya, L1/3. Set back in a quiet, less-trafficked area of Poble Espanyol, is this surprisingly elegant restaurant. Slightly more tranquil than neighboring restaurants. *Menú* €13. Open Tu-Sa 1-4pm. ❸

La Pérgola, (☎933 25 20 08) at the corner of Av. Reina María Cristina and Av. del Marqués de Comillas. M: Espanya, L1/3. 2 different restaurants at the same location. One offers a tasty buffet-style menú (€10) popular with both international businessmen and tourists. Open daily 9:30am-9pm. After 4pm, drinks only. Closed M-Tu the first 2 weeks of Aug. The other offers a classic full-service dining room in which the tuxedoed staff will serve you such carefully prepared favorites as Perigord duck marinated in ginger (€13). Menú €42. Open daily 1-4pm. Closed Aug. ❸

Restaurante Bar Marcelino, (☎934 41 10 79), Av. Miramar outside the funicular station. Refresh yourself at the bar or enjoy a selection of combination plates, sandwiches, and pizzas (around €6) on the outdoor patio. Open M-W and F-Su 8am-9:30pm. ❷

◉ 🏛 SIGHTS & MUSEUMS

▨ **FUNDACIÓ MIRÓ.** Designed by Miró's friend Josep Lluís Sert and tucked into the side of Montjuïc, the Fundació links interior and exterior spaces with massive windows and outdoor patios. Skylights illuminate an extensive collection of statues and paintings from Miró's career. His best-known pieces in the museum include *El Carnival de Arlequin, La Masia,* and *L'or de L'azuz.* Room 13 displays experimental work by young artists. The Fundació also sponsors music and film festivals. *(Av. Miramar, 71-75. Take the funicular from M: ParaHel. Open July-Aug. Tu-W and F-Sa 10am-8pm, Th 10am-9:30pm, Su 10am-2:30pm; Oct.-June Tu-W and F-Sa 10am-7pm, Th 10am-9:30pm, Su 10am-2:30pm. €7.20, students and seniors €4.)*

▨ **MUSEU NACIONAL D'ART DE CATALUNYA (PALAU NACIONAL).** Designed by Enric Catá and Pedro Cendoya for the 1929 International Exposition, the beautiful Palau Nacional has housed the Museu Nacional d'Art de Catalunya (MNAC) since 1934. Its main hall is a public event space, while the wings are home to the world's finest collection of Catalan Romanesque art and a wide variety of Gothic pieces. The Romanesque frescoes, now integrated as murals into dummy chapels, were salvaged in the 1920s from their original, less protected locations in northern Catalunya's churches. The museum's Gothic art corridor displays paintings on wood, the medium of choice during that period. The chronological tour of the galleries underlines the growing influence of Italy over Catalunya's artistic development, and ends with a breathtaking series of paintings by Gothic master Bernat Martorell. Behind the building the **Fonts Luminoses** (the Illuminated Fountains) are dominated by the central **Font Mágica,** which are employed in weekend laser shows during the summer. *(From M: Espanya, walk up Av. Reina María Cristina, away from the twin brick towers, and take the escalators to the top. Open Tu–Sa 10am-7pm, Su 10am-2:30pm. €4.80, with temporary exhibits €6, temporary exhibit only €4.20; 30% discount for students and seniors.)*

▨ **CASTELL DE MONTJUÏC.** A visit to this historic fortress and its **Museum Militar** is a great way to get an overview of the city's layout and history. From the castle's exterior *mirador,* gaze over the city. Enjoy coffee at the cafe while cannons stare you down. *(From M: ParaHel, take the funicular to Av. Miramar and then the Teleféric de Montjuïc cable car to the castle. Teleféric open M-Sa 11:15am-9pm. One-way €3.20, round-trip €4.50. Or, walk up the steep slope on C. Foc, next to the funicular station. Open daily Mar. 15-Nov. 15 9:30am-8pm; Nov. 16-Mar. 14 9:30am-5pm. Castle and mirador €1.)*

🎶 NIGHTLIFE

Lower Montjuïc is home to Barcelona's epic "disco theme park," **Poble Espanyol,** Av. Marqués de Comillas (☎933 22 03 26). Fall in love with the craziest disco experience in all of Barcelona at some of the most popular (and surreal) discos: **La Terrazza** (an outdoor madhouse; open Sept.-June Su and Th-Sa midnight-6am; July-Aug. Su only), **Torres de Ávila** (with speedy glass elevators; open Th-Sa midnight-6:30am), and ▨**Tinta Roja** (for tango lovers; open July-Aug. Tu-Th 7pm-1:30am, F-Sa 8pm-3am; Sept.-June also Tu-Th). Dancing starts at 1am and ends after 8am.

THE WATERFRONT

In addition to the piers of **Barceloneta** and **Port Vell, Poble Nou** and **Port Olímpic** are also part of Barcelona's coastline. Barceloneta, or "Little Barcelona," was born out of necessity. In 1718, La Ribera was butchered to make room for the enormous

Ciutadella fortress; the destruction of this historic neighborhood left thousands homeless, and it was not until 30 years later that the city created Barceloneta to house the displaced refugees. This area follows a carefully planned grid pattern, which would later influence the design of l'Eixample. Because of its seaside location, Barceloneta became home to the city's sailors, fishermen, and their families. Barcelona's drive to refurbish its waterfront resulted in the expansion of Port Vell. After moving a congested coastal road underground, the city opened Moll de la Fusta, a wide pedestrian zone that leads to the beaches of Barceloneta and connects the bright **Maremàgnum** and the **Moll d'Espanya.** Today, the rejuvenated Port Vell—the "Old Port"—is as hedonistic and touristy as Barcelona gets.

Until the last few decades, Poble Nou consisted mainly of factories, warehouses, and low-income housing. Auto shops and commercial supply stores still abound, but the major factories were all removed for the **1992 Olympics.** When Barcelona was granted its Olympic bid in 1986, this privilege presented a two-sided problem: comfortably housing 15,000 athletes while beautifying the city's long-ignored coastline. Oriol Bohigas, Josep Martorell, David Mackay, and Albert Puig Domènech designed the solution: the **Vila Olímpica,** a residential area with wide streets, symmetrical apartment buildings, pristine parks, and open-air art. Most social activity in the area takes place in the L-shaped **Port Olímpic,** home to docked sailboats, over 20 restaurants, a large casino, and a long strip of brash nightclubs.

◨ FOOD

◪ **Agua,** Pg. Marítim de la Barceloneta, 30 (☎ 932 25 12 72; www.grupotragaluz.com), the farthest establishment to the right of the copper fish. This upscale restaurant attracts large numbers of tourists, trendy *barceloneses,* and GQ-business-types. Stare at the Picasso wannabes that dot the walls as you enjoy Agua's specialties: delicate seafood and rice dishes. Vegetarian options. Entrees €5.50-27. Wheelchair-accessible. Open daily 1:30-4pm and 8:30pm-midnight. Reservations recommended. AmEx/MC/V. ❸

◪ **Zahara,** Pg. Joan de Borbó, 69 (☎ 932 21 37 65; www.zahara.com). This hip cocktail bar is a diamond in the rough of mainstream Barceloneta cafes. The extensive drink menu makes use of color-codes and icons to inform on the content and the potency of each cocktail. Tasty salads €8-9, sandwiches €4-5, cocktails €6-9, beer €2.50. Open daily 10am-3am. MC/V. ❷

La Mar Salada, Pg. Joan de Borbó, 58 (☎ 932 21 21 27). M: Barceloneta. Penny pinchers should try the mussels (€7.50), while bigger spenders can opt for the huge 2-person shellfish platter, which includes crab, oysters, clams, small Norwegian lobsters, and large prawns (€46). Seating for large groups available upstairs. *Menú* €8. Open Su-M and W-Sa 1-4pm and 8pm-midnight. AmEx/MC/V. ❸

◉ 🏛 SIGHTS & MUSEUMS

◪ **MUSEU MARÍTIM.** The *Drassanes Reiales de Barcelona* (Royal Shipyards of Barcelona) are considered the world's greatest standing example of civil (i.e. non-religious) Gothic architecture and are currently awaiting nomination as a UNESCO World Heritage Site. The complex consists of a series of huge indoor bays with slender pillars, in which entire ships could be constructed and stored over the winter. Since 1941, the building has housed the Maritime Museum, which traces the evolution of shipbuilding and life on the high seas. *(Av. Drassanes, off the rotary around the Monument a Colom. M: Drassanes, L3. ☎933 42 99 20. Open daily 10am-7pm. €5.40; under-16, students, and seniors €2.70.)*

■ **L'AQUÀRIUM DE BARCELONA.** Barcelona's aquarium—the largest in Europe—is an aquatic wonder, featuring a large number of octopi and penguins. The highlight is a 75m glass tunnel through an ocean tank of sharks, sting rays, and a two-dimensional fish. *(Moll d'Espanya, next to Maremàgnum. M: Drassanes. Open July-Aug. daily 9:30am-11pm; Sept.-June 9:30am-9pm. €13, students €12, under 12 and seniors €9.)*

■ **TORRE SAN SEBASTIÀ.** One of the easiest and best ways to view the city is on these cable cars, which span the entire Port Vell, connecting beachy Barceloneta with mountainous Montjuïc. The full ride, which takes about 10min. each way and makes an intermediate stop at the Jaume I tower near Colom, gives an aerial perspective of the entire city. *(Pg. Joan de Borbó. M: Barceloneta. In Port Vell, as you walk down Joan de Borbó and see the beaches to the left, stay right and look for the high tower. To Jaume I round-trip €7.50; to Montjuïc one-way €7.50, round-trip €9.50. Open daily 11am-8pm).*

VILA OLÍMPICA. The Vila Olímpica, beyond the east side of the zoo, was built to house 15,000 athletes and entertain millions of tourists for the 1992 Summer Olympics. It's home to several public parks, a shopping center, and business offices. In **Barceloneta,** beaches stretch out from the port. *(M: Ciutadella/Vila Olímpica. Walk along the waterfront on Ronda Litoral toward the two towers.)*

■ NIGHTLIFE

POBLE NOU & PORT OLÍMPIC

L'Ovella Negra (Megataverna del Poble Nou), C. Zamora, 78. *The* place to come for the first few beers of the night. Foosball games on the 2nd floor are nearly as intense as the real-life Barça/Real Madrid rivalry. Large beers €2. Cocktails from €2. Open F-Sa 5pm-3am, Su 5-10:30pm; kitchen open until 12:30am.

Club Danzatoria, C. Ramón Trias Fargas, 24. The sleek interior make this one of the hottest places in town, if not to get a date then at least to people-watch. All house music all the time. Cover €15, includes one drink. Open Th-Su midnight until late.

Razzmatazz, C. Pamplona, 88. M: Marina. A huge warehouse-turned-entertainment complex, with strobe-lit dance floors and concert space for indie-rock. Cover €9, includes 1 drink. Concert prices vary; call ahead for listings. Beer €3. Cocktails from €5. Open F-Sa and holidays midnight-4am. MC/V.

MAREMÀGNUM

Like Dr. Jekyll, Barcelona's biggest mall (see p. 406) has another personality. At night, the complex turns into a tri-level maze of clubs, each playing its own music for a throng of tourists and the occasional Spaniard. This is not the most authentic experience in Barcelona, but it is an experience. No one charges cover; clubs make their money from exorbitant drink prices. Good luck catching a cab home.

ZONA ALTA: GRÀCIA & OUTER *BARRIS*

Zona Alta ("Uptown") is the section of Barcelona that lies at the top of most maps: past l'Eixample, in and around the Collserola mountains, and away from the low-lying waterfront districts. The Zona Alta is made of several formerly independent towns. Although all of these have now been incorporated into Barcelona's city limits as residential areas, each neighborhood retains its own character.

The most visited part of Zona Alta is Gràcia, which was incorporated into Barcelona in 1897, much to the protest of its residents. Calls for Gràcian independence continue even today, albeit with less frequency. The area has always had a political streak—a theme that appears in the names of Mercat de Llibertat, Pl. de la Revolució, and others. After incorporation, the area continued to be a center of left-wing activism and resistance, even throughout the oppressive Franco regime. Gràcia packs a surprising number of Modernist buildings and parks, international cuisine, and chic shops into a relatively small area, making it a good choice for exploring. And because it is relatively untouched by tourism, Gràcia retains a local charm that has been sapped from some of Barcelona's more popular sections.

♜ ACCOMMODATIONS

Gràcia is Barcelona's "undiscovered" quarter, so last-minute arrivals may find vacancies here.

▨ Hostal Lesseps, C. Gran de Gràcia, 239 (☎932 18 44 34). M: Lesseps. Spacious, classy rooms sport red velvet wallpaper. All 16 rooms have a TV and bath; 4 have A/C (€5.60 extra). Singles €38; doubles €60; triples €75; quads €90. MC/V. ❹

Pensión San Medín, C. Gran de Gràcia, 125 (☎932 17 30 68; www.sanmedin.com). M: Fontana. Embroidered curtains and ornate tiling adorn this family-run pension. Common room with TV. Singles €30, with bath €39; doubles €48/60. MC/V. ❸

Albergue Mare de Déu de Montserrat (HI), Pg. Mare de Déu del Coll, 41-51 (☎932 10 51 51; www.tujuca.com). This gorgeous 220-bed hostel is a great way to meet other backpackers. Breakfast included. Flexible 3-day max. stay. Dorms €18, under 26 €14. Members only. AmEx/MC/V. ❶

◖ FOOD

▨ OvUm, C. Encarnació, 56. M: Joanic. Follow C. Escorial for 2 blocks and turn left on C. Encarnació. True to its name, this charming low-lit restaurant features egg specialties and vegetarian options with a Catalan twist. Meat lovers won't be disappointed by the Nius (€5), round bread filled with ham, pork, and egg and cooked in an oven. Open Tu-Su noon-1pm and 8:30-midnight. Closed 1st week of Aug. AmEx/MC/V. ❷

La Buena Tierra, C. Encarnació, 56 (☎932 19 82 13). M: Joanic. Follow C. Escorial for 2 blocks, turn left on C. Encarnació. Vegetarian dishes and a terrace. Entrees €4.50-7. Open Tu-F 1-4pm and 8-11pm, F 1-4pm and 8pm-midnight, Su 1-4pm. D. ❷

La Gavina, C. Ros de Olano, 17 (☎934 15 74 50), at the corner of C. St. Joaquím. Funky Italian pizzeria complete with a life-size patron saint. Pizzas €7.50-16. Open Tu-Su 2pm-1am, F-Sa 2pm-2am. Wheelchair-accessible. ❸

Restaurant Illa de Gràcia, C. Sant Domenec, 19 (☎932 38 02 29). M: Diagonal. Follow Gran de Gràcia for 5 blocks and make a right onto C. Sant Domenec. Huge vegetarian menu with tons of well-balanced options. Entrees €3-5. Open Tu-Su 2-4pm and 9pm-midnight. Closed last two weeks in Aug. D/MC/V. ❶

Restaurante Casa Regina (El 19 De La Riera), C. Riera De Sant Miquel, 19 (☎932 37 86 01). M: Diagonal. Serves only organic food, including grilled meats and vegetarian options. *Menú* €9.50, entrees €5-42. Open M-Sa 1-4pm and 9-11:30pm. MC/V. ❸

☉ 🏛 SIGHTS & MUSEUMS

▨ PARK GÜELL. This fantastic park was designed entirely by Gaudí but—in typical Gaudí fashion—was not completed until after his death. Gaudí intended Park Güell to be a garden city, and its dwarfish buildings and sparkling ceramic-mosaic stairways were designed to house the city's elite. Two mosaic staircases flank the park, leading to a towering Modernist pavilion that Gaudí originally designed as an open-air market. The longest park bench in the world, a multicolored serpentine wonder made of tile shards, decorates the top of the pavilion. In the midst of the park is the **Casa-Museu Gaudí.** *(Bus #24 from Pl. Catalunya stops at the upper entrance. Park free. Open May-Sept. daily 10am-9pm; Mar.-Apr. and Oct. 10am-7pm; Nov.-Feb. 10am-6pm. Museum open daily Apr.-Sept. 10am-8pm; Oct.-Mar. 10am-6pm. €4, students €3.)*

▨ MUSEU DEL FÚTBOL CLUB BARCELONA. A close second to the Picasso Museum as Barcelona's most-visited museum, the FCB museum merits all the attention it gets. Sports fans will appreciate the storied history of the team. The high point is the chance to enter the stadium and take in the enormity of Camp Nou. *(C. Arístides Maillol, next to the stadium. M: Collblanc. Enter through access gates 7 or 9. Open M-Sa 10am-6:30pm, Su 10am-2pm. €5, under-13 €3.50.)*

🎵 NIGHTLIFE

The area around C. de Marià Cubí has great nightlife, unpoisoned by tourists, but you'll have to take a taxi. For more accessible fun in Gràcia, head to Pl. Sol.

▨ Otto Zutz, C. Lincoln, 15 (www.ottozutz.com). FGC: Pl. Molina. Groove to house, hip-hop, and funk while Japanimation lights up the top floor. Beer €5. Cover €15, includes 1 drink; email ahead for a discount. Open Tu-Sa midnight-6:30am.

▨ D Mer, C. Plató, 13. FCG: Muntaner. A blue-hued heaven for lesbians of all ages. A touch of class, a dash of whimsy, and a ton of fun. Cover €6, includes 1 drink. Beer €3.50. Mixed drinks €6. Open Th-Sa 11pm-3:30am.

Gasterea, C. Verdi, 39. M: Fontana. Yellow walls cast a warm glow in this table-less bar. Mixed drinks €5. Su-Tu and Th 7pm-1am, F-Sa 7pm-2am. Cash only.

Bar Marcel, C. Santaló, 42. When midnight strikes, locals pack the place in search of cheap booze. Certainly not the fanciest bar in the neighborhood, but possibly the most loved. Beer €1.60. Mixed drinks €5. Prices vary. Open daily 8pm-3am.

🏛 DAYTRIP FROM BARCELONA

MONTSERRAT   ☎938

A 1235m peak protruding from the Río Llobregat Valley with a colorful interplay of limestone, quartz, and slate stone, Montserrat (Sawed Mountain) inspires poets, artists, and travelers. A millennium ago, a wandering mountaineer had a vision of the Virgin Mary; as story spread, pilgrims flocked to the mountain. The monastery to the Virgin, founded in 1025 by the opportunistic Bishop Oliba, is today tended by 80 Benedictine monks. During the Catalan *Renaixença* (renaissance) of the 19th century, politicians and artists like poets Joan Maragall and Jacint Verdaguer turned to Montserrat as a source of Catalan legend and tradition. Under Franco, it became a center for Catalan resistance. Today, the site attracts devout worshipers and tourists who come to see the Virgin of Montserrat, her ornate basilica, the art museum, and the panoramic views of the mountain's stunning rocks.

TRANSPORTATION. FGC (☎932 05 15 15) line R5 runs to Montserrat from M: Espanya in Barcelona (1hr.; every hr. 8:36am-5:36pm; round-trip including cable car €11.30); get off at Aeri de Montserrat, not Olesa de Montserrat. From there, catch the **Aeri cable car** to the monastery. (Daily July-Aug. every 15min. 9:25am-6:35pm, Mar. and Oct. 9:25am-1:45pm and 2:20-6:45pm; price included in FCG fare or €6 by itself. Schedules change frequently; call ☎938 77 77 01 to check.) **Autocars Julià** buses run to the monastery, from near Estació Sants. (Leaves Barcelona daily at 9am and returns at 5pm. Call ☎933 17 64 54 for reservations. €10. MC/V.) If you plan to use the funiculars to hike, consider the **Tot Montserrat** available at tourist offices or in M: Espanya; it includes tickets for the FGC, cable car, mountain funiculars, Museu de Montserrat (see below), and a meal, all for €34 (€20 if you buy it at Montserrat without the FCG fare). Call ☎938 35 03 84 for a **taxi.**

PRACTICAL INFORMATION. Montserrat is not a town, but a monastery with adjacent lodging and food for religious and camera-toting pilgrims. Visitor services are in Pl. Creu, the area straight ahead from the top of the Aeri cable car steps. The **info booth** in Pl. Creu provides free maps, schedules of religious services, and advice on mountain navigation. (☎938 77 77 77. Open July-Sept. daily 9am-7pm; Oct.-June M-F 9am-5pm, Sa-Su 9am-7pm.) For more detailed information, buy the *Official Guide to Montserrat* (€6.40) or the guide to the museum (€6.30). Services include: **ambulance** or the **mountain rescue team** (☎904 10 55 55); **ATMs;** and a **post office** (open daily 10am-1pm).

FOOD. Pick up some food for your hike at **Queviures supermarket** in Pl. Creu. For a quick meal, **Bar de la Plaça ❶** is next to the supermarket (*bocadillos* and hamburgers €2.60-3.60; open M-F 9:30am-5pm, Sa 9:30am-4:40pm). The **self-service cafetería ❷** for *Tot Montserrat* card-holders is up the hill to the right from the cable car steps (open Feb.-Dec. daily noon-4pm), as is **Restaurant de Montserrat ❸**. (*Menú* €12, kids €5.40. Open Mar. 15-Nov. 15 daily noon-4:30pm. MC/V.) The **Restaurant Hotel Abat Cisneros ❺** offers an expensive *menú* (€23.30) in a nice setting. (Open daily 1-4pm and 8-10pm. AmEx/MC/V.)

SIGHTS. Above Pl. Creu, the **basilica** looks onto Pl. Santa Noría. Next to the main chapel, a route through side chapels leads to the 12th-century Romanesque **La Moreneta** (the black Virgin), an icon of Mary. (Walkway open Nov.-June M-F 8-10:30am and noon-6:30pm, Sa-Su 8-10:30am and noon-6:30pm; July-Sept. daily 8-10:30am and noon-6:30pm.) Legend has it that St. Peter hid the figure, carved by St. Luke, in Montserrat's caves. The solemn little statue is now showcased in a silver case. For luck, rub the orb in Mary's hand. If you can, catch a performance of the renowned **Escalonia boys' choir** in the basilica. (Daily at 1pm and 7:30pm, except late June and July.) Also in Pl. Santa María, the **Museo de Montserrat** has a variety of art, from a mummified Egyptian to Picasso's *Sardana of Peace*, painted for Montserrat. The Impressionist paintings are its highlights; Ramon Casas's *Madeline Absinthe* is one of the evocative portraits. (Open July-Sept. M-F 10am-7pm, Sa-Su 9:30am-7pm; Nov.-June M-F 10am-6pm, Sa-Su 9:30am-6:30pm. €4.50, students and over 65 €3.50, children ages 10-14 €3, under 10 free.)

☒ WALKS. Some of the most beautiful areas of the mountain are accessible only on foot. The **Santa Cova funicular** descends from Pl. Creu to paths which wind to ancient hermitages. (Apr.-Oct. daily every 20min. 10am-6pm; Nov.-Mar. Sa-Su only 10am-5pm. Round-trip €2.50.) Take the **St. Joan funicular** for inspirational views of Montserrat. (Apr.-Oct. daily every 20min. 10am-6pm; Nov.-Mar. M-F 11am-5pm, Sa-Su 10am-5pm. Round-trip €6.10; joint round-trip ticket with the Sta. Cova funicular €6.90, over 65 €6.20, ages 10-14 €3.50.) The dilapidated **St. Joan monastery** and **shrine** are only a 20min. tromp from the highest station. The real prize is **Sant Jerónim** (the area's highest peak at 1235m), with its views of Montserrat's mystical rocks. The serrated outcroppings are named for human forms, including "The Bewitched Friars" and "The Mummy." The hike is about 2½hr. from Pl. Creu or a one-hour trek from the terminus of the St. Joan funicular. The paths are long and winding but not difficult—after all, they were made for guys wearing long robes. En route, take a sharp left after about 45min.; you'll come to a little old chapel. Otherwise, you're headed straight for a helicopter pad. On a clear day, the hike offers views of Barcelona and surrounding areas. For **guided visits** and hikes, call ☎938 77 77 01 two weeks in advance. (Hiking tour in English €6.50, museum tour €5, joint tour €14. In Spanish, hiking and museum tour €4 each, joint tour €7.) For rock climbing and athletic hiking in the area, call Marcel Millet at ☎938 35 02 51 or stop by his hiking/climbing office next to the Montserrat campsite.

NEAR BARCELONA

SITGES   ☎938

Forty kilometers south of Barcelona, the beach town of Sitges deserves its self-ordained title, "jewel of the Mediterranean," with its prime tanning grounds baked by 300 sunny days a year. First prominent in the late 19th century as one of the principal centers of the *Modernisme* art movement, today Sitges is swarmed by tourists from around the world who have heard the tales of its thriving gay community and vibrant nightlife. Whereas this flood of daytripping Spaniards, tourist families, and twenty-something partiers tends to drown many towns in the banalities of commercial tourism, in Sitges it only seems to supply exhilarating flavor. So close it's in the same area code as Barcelona, Sitges is the ideal daytrip and well worth a couple of nights' stay.

▣ TRANSPORTATION

Cercanías Trains (RENFE; ☎934 90 02 02) run from Estació Barcelona-Sants to Sitges (40min., every 15-30min. 5:27am-11:52pm, €2.20) and continue on to **Vilanova** (7min.; every 15-30min., last train from Sitges at 12:44am; €1.05). To get to the beaches between the two cities, rent a car in Barcelona or in Sitges at **Europcar** (☎938 11 19 96), on the first floor of the Mercat next to the train station. For a **taxi,** call ☎938 94 13 29. A taxi between Barcelona and Sitges costs €45-50.

▣ ▨ ORIENTATION & PRACTICAL INFORMATION

Most everyone coming into Sitges starts out at the RENFE train station, on **Carrer Carbonell,** in the northern section of town. From here, the town center is 5min. by foot, the beach about 10min. To get to either, take a right as you leave the station, and then your third left onto **Carrer Sant Francesc.** This will lead straight to the old town, and intersect with **Carrer Parellades,** the main path of stores and restaurants, which runs parallel to the ocean. Any street off Parellades will lead you to the waterfront. **Passeig Ribera** runs along the central and most crowded beaches.

For a good free map and info on accommodations, stop by the **tourist office,** Sínia Morera, 1. From the station, turn right onto C. Carbonell and take a right a block later. The office is across the street, a block to the left—look for the sign with the big "i". (☎938 94 50 04. Open July-Aug. daily 9am-9pm; Sept.-June Su-M and W-Sa 9am-3pm and 4-6:30pm.) In summer, a smaller branch opens by the museums on C. Fonollar. (☎938 94 42 51. Open Su 11am-2pm, W-F 10:30am-1:30pm, Sa 11am-2pm and 4-7pm.) **Super Avui,** C. Carbonell, 24, is a **supermarket** across from the train station. (Open M-Sa 9am-9pm.) Other town services include **medical assistance** (☎938 94 64 26) and **emergency assistance** (☎938 94 39 49). The local **police** (☎904 10 10 92) are in the Pl. Ajuntament. To get there from C. Parellades, take C. Major south; the station is on the right. **Internet access** and **fax** services are available at **Café Art,** C. Sant Frances, 42 (☎938 11 00 52; €1 per 30min., €1.50 per hr.; open daily 11am-1am) and **Sitges Internet Access,** C. Espanya, 7. (☎938 11 40 03; non-members pay €4.50 per hr., €1.20 per 15min.; open daily 11am-1am). The **post office** is in Pl. d'Espanya. (☎938 94 12 47. Open M-F 8:30am-2:30pm, Sa 9:30am-1pm. No packages Sa.) **Postal Code:** 08870.

ACCOMMODATIONS

Accommodations are expensive and difficult to find on summer weekends, so consider daytripping to Sitges from Barcelona and reserve early if you plan to stay. Sitges nightlife is crazy and you may not actually end up needing a bed of your own, anyway. In the listings below, price range includes both low season and high season, with lower prices corresponding to low season.

Hostal Parellades, C. Parellades, 11 (☎938 94 08 01), one block from the beach. Offers clean rooms and an airy terrace. Dirt cheap for Sitges. Singles €24; doubles €40, with bath €45; triples with bath €50. Cash only. ❷

Hotel El Cid, C. Sant Josep, 39 (☎938 94 18 42; fax 94 63 35). From the train station, take the 4th left off C. Carbonell. One of the best deals in town. All 77 of the colorful and comfortable rooms come with bathrooms, safety deposit box, and A/C. Small pool, bar and garden in back. Breakfast included. Doubles €37-63. MC/V. ❸

Hostal Internacional, C. Sant Francesc, 52 (☎938 94 26 90; www.sitges.tv). Bright rooms not far from the train station. Doubles €31-37, with bath €37-43. MC/V. ❷

FOOD

Izarra, C. Mayor 24 (☎938 94 73 70), behind the museum area. This Basque *tapas* bar can be either a quick food fix before a long night of club-hopping or a more substantial and leisurely meal before a short night with the family. Ask for a *plato* and grab whatever *tapas* look tastiest, from Basque fish *tapas* to more traditional Spanish *croquetas* to chicken wings (€0.75 each). Big entrees (€5-11.50) and Basque *sidra* (cider; €2) are also available. Open daily 1:30-4pm and 8:30-11pm. MC/V. ❷

Restaurante La Oca, C. Parellades, 41 (☎938 94 79 36). Chickens roasting on an open fire attract long lines of hungry tourists. Try the succulent *pollastre* (roasted chicken) for €5.10 or cover one with sauce for €5.75. The chicken *croquetas* (€2.60) are outstanding. Open Su-F 1pm-midnight, Sa 1pm-1am. MC/V. ❷

SITGES ■ 429

Restaurante El Pozo, C. Sant Pau, 3 (☎938 94 11 04), off C. Parellades, is a throwback to the town's days as a quiet fishing village. Paintings depicting rustic Spanish landscapes dot the walls inside this tiny tavern. Fresh fish tastes as if someone caught it just for you. Seafood-heavy menu, with plenty of wine and beer to fill your stomach to the brim. Entrees (€7-13) include lobster soup, sole, shrimp, and squid. Open M-W and F-Su 1:30-4pm and 7-11pm. MC/V. ❷

SIGHTS

The pedestrian walkway **Carrer Parellades,** which features shopping, eating, and drinking galore, is the central attraction. Cultural activities may seem as undesirable as rain to some beachgoers, but Sitges has some can't-miss sights, including Morell's whimsical **Modernist clock tower,** Pl. Cap de la Vila, 2, above Optica at the intersection of Parellades and Sant Francesc. Behind it, on C. Fonollar, the **Museu Cau Ferrat** (☎938 94 03 64) hangs over the water's edge. Once home to Catalan Modernist Santiago Rusinyol and a meeting point for young Catalan artists Pablo Picasso and Ramón Casas, the building is a shrine to Modernist iron work, glass work, and painting. The extensive collection of wrought iron was amassed by Rusinyol in an effort to symbolize the various traditions of the 18th century lost in exchange for the progress of the 19th and 20th centuries. Next door, the **Museu Maricel del Mar** (☎938 94 03 64) has a select collection of Romanesque and Gothic painting and sculptures, as well as an interesting marine collection showcasing models of the Catalan navy and the Catalan fishing fleet. Farther into town, the **Museu Romàntic,** C. Sant Gaudenci, 1, off C. Parellades, is a 19th-century bourgeois house filled with period pieces like music boxes and over 400 17th- to 19th-century dolls from all over the world. (☎938 94 29 69; m.sitges@diba.es. All 3 museums open in summer Tu-Su 10am-2pm and 5-9pm; rest of the year Su 10am-3pm, Tu-F 10am-1:30pm and 3-6:30pm, Sa 10am-7pm. Combo entrance good for 30 days €5.40, students €3; otherwise €3 per museum, students and seniors €1.50.) Across the street from the museums, the stately **Palau Maricel,** on C. Fonollar, built in 1910 for American millionaire Charles Deering, wows visitors with its sumptuous halls and rich gardens. Guided tours are available on summer nights and include a glass of *cava* (champagne); on Friday, Saturday, and Sunday nights, a piano and soprano concert complete the evening. Call ahead for reservations. (☎938 11 33 11. Tours €6; F-Su concert and tour €8.)

BEACHES

Sitges's proximity to Barcelona and its beautiful beaches make it a viable alternative to the crowded sands of Barceloneta or Port Olímpic. Plenty of soothing sand accommodates hordes of sun worshipers on hot summer days. At **Platja de la Fragata,** the beach farthest to the left as you face the sea, sand sculptors create new masterpieces every summer day. By midday, the beaches closest to downtown can become almost unbearably crowded. The best beaches, with calmer water and more open space, are one or two kilometers walk farther down, at **Platja de la Barra** and **Platja de Terramar.** Rocks shield the beaches from waves, creating a shallow ocean swimming pool that extends far into the water and is ideal for children. Showers and Red Cross stations abound. In an **emergency,** call ☎938 11 76 25.

BARCELONA

🖼️ 🎵 NIGHTLIFE & ENTERTAINMENT

While Sitges is an easy daytrip, it's almost better to go for a night-trip. The wild clubs are the perfect escape from the confines of the decidedly more cosmopolitan night scene of Barcelona. The place to be at sundown is **Carrer Primer de Maig** (which runs directly from the beach and Pg. Ribera) and its continuation, **Carrer Marqués Montroig,** off C. Parellades. Bars and clubs line both sides of the small street, blasting pop and house from 10pm until 3am. The clubs here are wide-open and accepting, with a vibrant mixed crowd of gay people, straight people, the occasional drag queen, and families. There's no cover anywhere, making for great bar- and club-hopping. Beers at most places go for about €3, mixed drinks €6. Even crazier is the "disco-beach" **Atlàntida,** in Sector Terramar (☎938 94 26 77; foam parties on Th and Su nights), and the legendary **Pachá,** on Pg. Sant Didac in nearby Vallpineda (☎938 94 22 98). Buses run all night on weekends to the two discos from C. Primer de Maig. Other popular nightspots can be found on C. Bonaire and C. Sant Pau, but most open only on weekends.

Sitges celebrates holidays by sparing no extravagance and pushing the boundaries of style. During the **Festa de Corpus Christi** in June, townspeople collaborate to create intricate fresh-flower carpets. For papier-mâché dragons, devils, and giants dancing in the streets, visit during the **Festa Major,** held August 22-27 in honor of the town's patron saint Bartolomé. Nothing compares to the **Carnaval,** a preparation for Catholic fasting during the first week of Lent (Feb. 27-Mar. 5). Spaniards crash the town for a frenzy of parades, dancing, outrageous costumes, and vats of alcohol. The last night is the wildest, as hundreds of drag queens parade through the streets. On the first Sunday in March, a pistol shot starts the Rally de **Coches de Epoca,** an antique car race from Barcelona to Sitges. June brings the **International Theater Festival** (€10-22 per show), and July and August the International Jazz Festival (€10.50 per concert). From September 12-14, competitors trod on fresh grapes on the beach for the annual **Grape Harvest.** October 1-12 brings the famous **Festival Internacional de Cinema de Catalunya.**

NEAR SITGES: VILANOVA I LA GELTRÙ

One of Catalunya's most important ports, **Vilanova i la Geltrù,** actually turns out to be two cities in one: an industrial hub and a well-groomed beach town. There is little in the dusty uptown area, save old churches and stone facades; most visitors spend the day on the beach (10min. from the train station). To get to the **beaches,** exit the station, turn left on C. Forn de Vidre, and take the third left onto Rambla de la Pau. You'll know you're going the right way on Rambla de la Pau when you head under a pedestrian overpass; after that, follow the *rambla* all the way to the port and onto **Passeig del Carme.** The **tourist office,** about 100m to the right off Pg. del Carme in a small park called **Parc de Ribes Roges,** offers excellent **maps.** (☎938 15 45 17. Open July-Aug. M-Sa 10am-8pm, Su 10am-2pm; Sept.-June M-Sa 10am-2pm.) The wide **Platja de Ribes Roges** is past the tourist office; to the left is the smaller **Platja del Far.** Expect fine sand, sun, and a bit of company. The beaches are refreshingly calm, like giant kiddie-pools but with the added bonus of topless women. If you decide to stay in town, the popular **Can Gatell ❸,** C. Puigcerdà 6-16, has clean rooms and full baths. With your back to the station, head down C. Victor Balaguer and at the end, turn right onto La Rambla and then take the first left. (☎938 93 01 17. Singles €30; doubles €47, with A/C €53. Extra bed €10.) The hostel's *menú* (€8, served M-F, includes wine) is popular with locals. (Open daily 7-

10:30am, 1-5pm, and 8:30-10pm.) Numerous pricy restaurants serve fresh seafood along Pg. del Carme. An inexpensive alternative is **Supermarket Orangutan,** Rambla de la Pau, 36, on the way to the beach. (Open M-Sa 9:30am-2pm and 5:30-9pm.)

Cercanías **trains** (RENFE) run from Vilanova to Sitges (7min., every 15-30min., €1.05) and continue to Barcelona (50min., €2.65). **Mon Bus** (☎938 93 70 60) connects Vilanova to Sitges (€1.25), Vilafranca (€1.60), and Barcelona (€3). The bus station is in the plaza in front of the train station. A **taxi** (☎938 93 32 41) from Vilanova to Sitges costs about €9-12.

CATALUÑA (CATALUNYA)

From rocky Costa Brava to smooth Costa Dorada, the lush Pyrenees to chic Barcelona, Cataluña is a vacation in itself. It has been graced with many of the nation's richest resources, making it the most prosperous region in Iberia. *Catalanes* are famous for their resourcefulness and work ethic. As the saying goes, *"El Català de les pedres fa pa"* (the Catalan makes bread out of stones).

Colonized first by the Greeks and the Carthaginians, Cataluña was later one of Rome's favored provinces. Only briefly subdued by the Moors, Cataluña's counts achieved independence in AD 987. Cataluña grew powerful as she joined the throne of Aragón in 1137; while this union empowered Cataluña to pursue her own empire for a time, it ultimately doomed her to be subjugated to subsequent Spanish rule. King Felipe V was finally able to fully suppress Cataluña in the early 18th century when the Catalans sided against him in the War of Spanish Succession (1702-1714). In the late 18th century, the region's fortunes revived when it developed into one of Europe's premier textile manufacturers, opening trade with the Americas. Nineteenth-century industrial expansion nourished arts and sciences, ushering in an age known as the Catalan Renaixença (Renaissance). The 20th century gave birth to the Modernist movement and an all-star list of artists and architects, including Picasso, Miró, Dalí, Antoni Gaudí i Comet, Lluís Domènech i Montaner, and Josep Puig i Cadafalch. Home to staunch opponents of the Fascists during Spain's Civil War, Cataluña lost its autonomy in 1939. During his regime, Franco suppressed Catalan language instruction (except in universities) and limited Catalan publications.

Since Cataluña regained regional autonomy in 1977, Catalan media and arts have flourished; Catalan is once again the official language. While some worry that the use of the regional dialect will discourage talented Spaniards from working or studying in Cataluña, effectively isolating the region, others argue that extensive regional autonomy has generally led to progressive ends. Many *catalanes* will answer inquiring visitors in Catalan even if asked in Castilian. Lauded throughout Spain, Catalan cuisine boasts *pa amb tomaquet* (bread smeared with olive oil, tomato, and garlic), and *alioli* (a garlic and olive oil sauce). Cataluña offers visitors the chance to experience a different side of Spain's multifaceted persona.

COSTA DORADA

TARRAGONA ☎977

Tarragona's strategic position made the city a provincial Roman capital under Augustus; today an amphitheater and other ruins pay homage to the city's imperial days. These vestiges of Tarragona's august past are the city's most compelling attractions, but plenty of visitors are satisfied with a sightseeing-light and beach-heavy stay in Cataluña's second most important port city.

▐ TRANSPORTATION

Trains: ☎902 24 02 02. On Pl. Pedrera by the water. Info open daily 6am-9pm. The best transportation option. To: **Alicante** (4hr., 10 per day, €34.50); **Barcelona** (1¼hr., 30 per day 5:15am-11:04pm, €4.25); **Madrid** (6½-8hr., 4 per day, €40.50); **Sitges** (45min., 20 per day, €2.60); **Valencia** (2-3hr., 15 per day 4:34am-9:49pm, €13.50); **Zaragoza** (4hr., 10 per day, €14.40).

Buses: ☎977 22 91 26. Pl. Imperial Tarraco. **ALSA/Enatcar** (☎902 42 22 42). To **Barcelona** (1½hr., 8 per day, €8), **Valencia** (4hr., 6 per day, €15.20), and elsewhere.

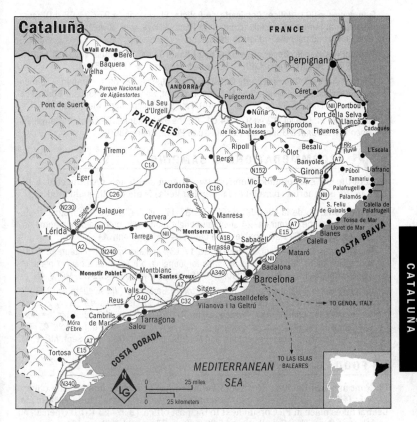

Cataluña

FRANCE

■ Vall d'Aran
Beret
Perpignan
Báquera
Vielha
Parque Nacional
de Aigüestortes
ANDORRA
Céret
Pont de Suert
La Seu
d'Urgell
Puigcerdà
PYRENEES
(NII) Portbou
Port de la Selva
Llançà
Cadaqués
Sant Joan
de les Abadesses
Camprodon
Figueres
L'Escala
Tremp
Ripoll
Olot
Besalú
Río
Fluvià
A7
Púbol
Llafranc
(C14)
Berga
Banyoles
Tamariu
Éger
(N152)
Girona
Palafrugell
Cardona
(C16)
Vic
Río Ter
Palamós
(C26)
NII
S. Feliu
de Guíxols
Calella de
Palafrugell
(N230)
Balaguer
Cervera
Río Cardener
Manresa
A7
Tossa de Mar
Lloret de Mar
Lérida
Río Segre
NII
Tàrrega
NII
Montserrat
(A18)
Sabadell
E15
Blanes
Calella
COSTA BRAVA
(A2)
(N240)
Terrassa
Mataró
Monestir Poblet ■
Montblanc
■ Santes Creus
(A340)
NII
Badalona
Valls
(A7)
Sitges
Barcelona
Reus
(240)
(C32)
Castelldefels
Vilanova i la Geltrú
TO GENOA, ITALY
Móra
d'Ebre
Cambrils
de Mar
Tarragona
Salou
COSTA DORADA
Tortosa
(A7)
(E15)
MEDITERRANEAN
SEA
TO LAS ISLAS
BALEARES
(N340)
LG
0   25 miles
0   25 kilometers

CATALUÑA

Public Transportation: EMT Buses (☎977 54 94 80) run daily 6am-11pm. €1, 10-ride *abono* ticket €4.40.

Taxi: Radio Taxi (☎977 22 14 14).

✈ 🛈 ORIENTATION & PRACTICAL INFORMATION

Most sights are clustered on a hill, surrounded by remnants of Roman walls. At the foot of the hill, **La Rambla Vella** and **La Rambla Nova** (parallel to one another and perpendicular to the sea) are the main thoroughfares of the new city. La Rambla Nova runs from **Passeig de les Palmeres** (which overlooks the sea) to **Plaça Imperial Tarraco,** the monstrous rotunda and home of the bus station. To reach the old quarter from the train station, turn right and walk 150m to the stairs parallel to the shore.

Tourist Office: C. Major, 39 (☎977 25 07 95; www.tarragonaturisme.com), below the cathedral steps. Crucial **free map** and a guide to Tarragona's Roman ruins. Open M-F 9am-9pm, Sa 9am-2pm and 4-9pm, Su and holidays 10am-2pm.

Tourist Information Booths: Pl. Imperial Tarraco, at the bottom of La Rambla Vella outside the bus station; branch where Av. de Catalunya meets Vía de l'Impera Romi. Both open July-Sept. daily 10am-1:30pm and 4:30-8pm; Nov.-June Sa-Su 10am-2pm.

Luggage Storage: At the train station 4:30am-midnight; €4.50.

Emergency: ☎091. **Police: Comisaria de Policía,** Pl. Orleans (☎977 24 98 44). From Pl. Imperial Tarraco on the inland end of La Rambla Nova, walk down Av. President Lluís Companys and take the 3rd left to the station.

Medical Assistance: Hospital de Sant Pau i Santa Tecla, La Rambla Vella, 14 (☎977 25 15 70). **Hospital Joan XXIII,** C. Dr. Mallafré Guasch (☎977 29 58 00).

Internet Access: Ciberspai.net, C. Estanislao Figueras, 58, off the Imperial Tarraco rotunda. €0.75 per 15min. Open M-F 9am-midnight, Sa-Su 10am-midnight. **Biblioteca Pública,** C. Fortuny, 30 (☎977 24 05 44). Free use of computers with passport.

Post Office: Pl. Corsini, 12 (☎977 24 01 49), below La Rambla Nova off C. Canyelles. Open M-F 8:30am-8:30pm, Sa 9:30am-1pm. **Postal Code:** 43001.

🏠 ACCOMMODATIONS & CAMPING

Most of the city's accommodations are two- to four-star hotels near the center. Pl. Font in the old quarter (parallel to La Rambla Vella) is filled with quality lodging.

Hostal Noria, Pl. de la Font, 53 (☎977 23 87 17), in the heart of the historic town. Enter through the restaurant. 24 clean and bright rooms with pretty-in-pink bathrooms. Singles with bath €21-28, doubles with bath €34-45. Cash only. ❷

Hostal Forum, Pl. de la Font, 37 (☎977 23 17 18), upstairs from the restaurant. Clean rooms and baths don't leave much space for lounging, but Forum is a decent place to sleep for the night. Singles with bath €16-19; doubles with bath €32-38. MC/V. ❷

Camping: Several campsites line the road toward Barcelona (Via Augusta or CN-340) along the northern beaches, especially around km 1.17. Take bus #9 (every 20min., €1) from Pl. Imperial Tarraco. **Tarraco** (☎/fax 977 29 02 89 and 22 48 59) is the closest campsite, at Platja de l'Arrabassada. Well-kept facilities near the beach. €2.75-3.75 per person, per car, or per tent, and €2-2.50 per child. Open Apr.-Sept. MC/V. ❶

🍴 FOOD

Pl. Font and Las Ramblas Nova and Vella are full of restaurants serving cheap *menús* (€5-7.50) and greasy *platos combinados*. Tarragona's indoor **Mercado Central** takes place in Pl. Corsini next to the post office. (☎977 23 15 51. Open M-W and Sa 8am-2pm, Th-F 7am-2pm and 5:30-8:30pm. Flea market Tu and Th.) For **groceries,** head to **Champión,** C. Augusta at Comte de Rius, between Las Ramblas Nova and Vella. (Open M-Sa 9am-9:15pm.) **El Serrallo,** the fishermen's quarter right next to the harbor, has the best seafood. Try your food with Tarragona's typical **romesco sauce,** simmered from red peppers, toasted almonds, and hazelnuts.

Restaurant Les Coques, Nou Patriarca, 2 (☎977 22 83 00), off Pl. La Seu near the cathedral. Roman walls, chandeliers, paintings, antiques, and wine bottles create an eclectic interior. The ambience is relaxing, and waiters provide first class service. Try the cod filet with garlic sauce (€17.20), grilled baby goat (€12), or fresh Tarragonan *cigalitas* (a native shellfish related to shrimp) sauteed in a garlic sauce (€16). Entrees €10-32. Open M-Sa 1:15-3:45pm and 9-10:45pm. AmEx/MC/V. ❹

La Teula, C. Mercería, 16 (☎977 23 99 89), in the old city near Pl. del Fórum. Great for salads (€4-6) and toasted sandwiches with interesting Catalan veggie and meat combos (€7-12). Lunch *menú* €7.90. Open daily noon-4pm and 8pm-midnight. MC/V. ❷

Restaurant El Caserón, C. Ces del Bou, 9 (☎977 23 93 28), parallel to La Rambla Vella. Popular local diner serving homestyle food. Entrees €4.25-13. *Menú* €7.50. Open M and Sa-Su 8:30-11pm, Tu-F 1-4pm and 8:30-10:30pm. MC/V. ❷

🔲 🌀 SIGHTS & BEACHES

Tarragona's status as provincial capital transformed the small military enclosure into a glorious imperial port. Countless Roman ruins stand silently amid 20th-century hustle and bustle, all just minutes from the beach.

🔲 ROMAN RUINS. Below Pg. Palmeres and set amid gardens above Platja del Miracle beach is the **Roman Amphitheater** (☎ 977 44 25 79), where gladiators once killed wild animals and each other. In AD 259, the Christian bishop Fructuosus and his two deacons were burned alive here; in the sixth century, these martyrs were honored with a basilica built in the arena.

Next to the Museu Nacional Arqueològic in Pl. Rei is the entrance to the **Pretori I Circ Romans** (☎ 977 24 19 52), which houses the **Praetorium Tower,** the former administrative center of the region, and the **Roman Circus,** the site of chariot races and other spectacles. Visitors descend into the long, dark tunnels that led fans to their seats, and see a model reconstruction of what the complex looked like. The Praetorium was the governor's palace in the first century BC. Rumor has it that the infamous hand-washer Pontius Pilate was born here.

The scattered **Fòrum Romà,** with reconstructed Corinthian columns, lies near the post office on C. Lleida. Once the center of the town, its distance clearly demonstrates how far the walls of the ancient city extended. To see what remains of the second-century BC walls, stroll through the **Passeig Arqueològic.** The walls originally stretched to the sea and fortified the entire city. *(All ruins open May-Sept. Su 9am-3pm, Tu-Sa 9am-9pm; Oct.-Apr. Tu-Su 9am-7pm. Admission to each €2, students €0.65.)*

MUSEUMS. The **Museu Nacional Arqueològic,** across Pl. Rei from the Praetorium, displays ancient architecture, utensils, statues, and mosaics, and offers descriptions of daily life in the Roman Empire. *(☎ 977 23 62 09. Open June-Sept. Tu-Su 10am-8pm; Oct.-May Tu-Su 10am-1:30pm and 4-7pm. €2.40, students €1.20; includes the necropolis.)* The early Christian burial site at the **Museu i Necròpolis Paleocristians,** Av. Ramón y Cajal, 78, has yielded a rich variety of urns, tombs, and s phagi, the best of which are in the small museum. *(☎ 977 21 11 75. Open June-Sept. Tu-Sa 10am-8pm, Su 10am-2pm; Oct.-May Su 10am-2pm, Tu-Sa 10am-1:30pm and 4-7pm. €2.40, students €1.20; Tu free.)* If you've had too much Roman roamin', descend the steps in front of the cathedral and take the third right onto C. Cavellares to the **Casa-Museu Castellarnau.** It housed the Viscounts of Castellarnau in the 18th century. *(☎ 977 24 22 20. Open May-Sept. Tu-Sa 9am-9pm, Su 9am-3pm; Oct.-Apr. Tu-Su 9am-7pm. €2, students €0.65.)*

BEACHES. The hidden access to **Platja del Miracle,** the town's main beach, is along Baixada del Miracle, starting off Pl. Arce Ochotorena, beyond the Roman theater. Walk away from the theater until you reach the underpass, under the train tracks, to the beach. Though not on par with the region's other beaches, it's not bad for a few hours of relaxation. A bit farther away are the larger beaches, **Platja l'Arrabassada** and **Platja Llarga.** *(Take bus #1 or 9 from Pl. Imperial Tarraco or any of the other stops.)*

OTHER SIGHTS. The **Pont del Diable** (Devil's Bridge), a Roman aqueduct 10min. outside of the city, is visible on the way in and out of town by bus. Take municipal bus #5 (every 20min., €1) from the corner of C. Christòfer Colom and Av. Prat de la Riba or from Pl. Imperial Tarraco. Lit by octagonal rose windows flanking the transept is the gigantic Romanesque-Gothic 🔲**cathedral,** which dates from 1331 and is one of the most magnificent cathedrals in Cataluña. The stunning interior holds the tomb of Joan d'Aragó. The adjoining **Diocesan Museum** showcases religious relics from the last 700 years. *(Entrance to both on C. Claustre, near Pl. La Seu. Open mid-Mar. to May M-Sa 10am-1pm and 4-7pm; mid-June to Oct. M-Sa 10am-7pm; mid-Oct. to mid-Nov. M-Sa 10am-5pm; mid-Nov. to mid-Mar. M-Sa 10am-2pm. €2.40, students €1.50.)*

🅟 🅠 NIGHTLIFE & FESTIVALS

Weekend nightlife in Tarragona is on a much smaller scale than that of Sitges and Barcelona. Between 5 and 9pm, Las Ramblas Nova and Vella (and the area in between) are packed with strolling families. After 9pm, the bars liven up; around 10pm on Saturdays in summer, fireworks brighten the skies. The place to be is **Port Esportiu,** a portside plaza full of restaurant-bars and mini-discos. Heading up La Rambla Nova away from the beach, take a left onto C. Unió; bear left at Pl. General Prim and follow C. Apodaca to its end. Cross the tracks; the fun will be to the left.

The end of July ushers in the **Fiesta de Tarragona,** which goes through the first week of August (☎977 24 47 95, tickets 24hr. 902 33 22 11). Pyromaniacs shouldn't miss the first week of July when fireworks light up the beach in **El Concurso Internacional de Fuegos Artificiales.** On even-numbered years, the first Sunday in October brings the **Concurs de Castells,** a competition of tall human towers, as high as seven to nine "stories," called *castells. Castells* also appear amid beasts and fireworks during the annual **Fiesta de Santa Tecla** (Sept. 23). If you're unable to catch the *castellers* in person, don't miss the monument to the *castellers* on La Rambla Nova.

COSTA BRAVA   ☎972

Skirting the Mediterranean Sea from Barcelona to the French border, the Costa Brava's jagged cliffs and pristine beaches draw throngs of European visitors, especially in July and August. Early June and late September can be remarkably peaceful; the water is already warm and the beaches much less crowded. In the winter Costa Brava lives up to its name, as fierce winds sweep the coast, leaving behind tranquil, near-empty beach towns. The rocky shores have traditionally attracted romantics and artists, like Marc Chagall and Salvador Dalí, a Costa Brava native. Dalí's house in Cadaqués and his museum in Figueres display the largest collections of his work in Europe.

TOSSA DE MAR   ☎972

Falling in love in (or with) Tossa de Mar is easy. In 1934, French artist Marc Chagall commenced a 40-year love affair with this seaside village, deeming it "Blue Paradise." When *The Flying Dutchman* was filmed here in 1951, Ava Gardner fell hard for Spanish bullfighter-turned-actor Mario Cabrera, much to the chagrin of Frank Sinatra, her husband at the time. (A statue of the actress in Tossa's old city commemorates her visit.) Like many coastal cities, Tossa (pop. 4000) suffers from the usual tourist industry blemishes: souvenir shops, inflated prices, and crowded beaches. That said, it resists a generic beach town ambiance, drawing from its historical legacy and cliff-studded landscape to preserve a unique small-town feel.

▐ TRANSPORTATION

Buses: (☎972 34 09 03) on Av. Pelegrí at Pl. de les Nacions Sense Estat. Ticket booth open daily 7am-12:40pm and 2:20-8:10pm. **Pujol i Pujol** (☎610 50 58 84) goes to **Lloret del Mar** (20min.; June-Aug. every 30min., Sept.-May every hr. 8am-8:10pm; €1.10). **Sarfa** (☎97 234 09 03) goes to **Barcelona** (2hr.; 18 per day 7:40am-noon and 3-7:40pm; €7.80) and **Girona** (1hr.; 1 per day at 7:30am; €4).

Boats go to towns along the coast, including Lloret and St. Feliu. **Viajes Marítimos,** (☎616 90 91 00 or 972 36 90 95; www.viajesmaritimos.com) depart 9:25am-6:45pm; tickets €5-16. Buy tickets on Pg. de Mar in front of the First Aid/Emergency stand.

Car Rental: Viajes Tramontana, Av. Costa Brava, 23 (☎972 34 28 29 or 972 34 27 53). **Avis** (☎902 13 55 31) and their affiliates **Olimpia** (☎972 34 02 41) and **SACAR** (☎972 34 10 73) operate from the same storefront. 21+; if under 25, Avis charges an additional €6 per day. Major credit card, driver's license (international driver's license required for longer rentals), and passport required. One-day rentals €39-60. Open daily July-Aug. 9am-9pm; Apr.-June and Sept.-Nov. 9am-3pm and 4-8pm.

Boat rentals: Kayaks Nicolau (☎972 34 26 46), on the beach at Mar Menuda, offers 1½hr. trips to Cala Bona (10am, noon, and 4pm; €10.30), but deals vary—check at the beach. Kayak and paddle boat rental €6 per hr. Open Apr.15-Oct.15 daily 9am-7pm.

Bike & Moped Rentals: Jimbo Bikes, La Rambla Pau Casals, 12 (☎972 34 30 44; jimbotossa@logicontrol.es). Staff gives bike route information; bring license for moped rental. Mountain bikes €3.50-4.50 per hr., €17-21 per day. Open M-Sa 10am-8pm, Su 9:30am-2pm and 4-8pm. AmEx/MC/V.

Taxis: ☎972 34 05 49. Stand outside the bus station.

■✦ 🛈 ORIENTATION & PRACTICAL INFORMATION

Buses arrive at **Plaça de les Nacions Sense Estat** where **Avinguda del Pelegrí** and **Avinguda Ferrán Agulló** meet; the town slopes down to the waterfront. Walk away from the station down Av. Ferrán Agulló and turn right on Av. Costa Brava; as it turns into Pou de la Vila, take a right on any of the side streets and continue until your feet get wet (10min. total). **Passeig del Mar,** to the right at the end of Av. Costa Brava, curves along **Platja Gran** (Tossa's main beach) to the old quarter, **Vila Vella.**

Tourist Office: Av. Pelegrí, 25 (☎972 34 01 08; www.infotossa.com), in the bus terminal at Av. Ferrán Agulló and Av. Pelegrí. Grab a handy, thoroughly indexed map. English, French, and Spanish spoken. Advice on hiking trails and sights and a posted schedule of upcoming events. Leads weekend guided hikes and walks in the mountains June-Aug. (€6-9). Maps have marked paths if you ditch the guide. Open June 15-Sept. 15 Su 10am-2pm and 5-8pm, M-Sa 9am-9pm; Apr.-June 15 and Oct. Su 10:30am-1:30pm, M-Sa 10am-2pm and 4-8pm; Nov.-Mar. M-Sa 10am-1pm and 4-7pm.

Currency Exchange: Banco Santander Central Hispano, Av. Ferrán Agulló, 2 (☎972 34 10 65). Open M-F 8:30am-2pm. MC/V.

Police: Municipal Police, Av. Pelegrí, 14 (☎972 34 01 35). English spoken. They'll escort you to a **24hr. pharmacy** at night if necessary.

Pharmacy: Farmàcia Castelló, Av. Ferrán Agulló, 12. Open daily 9:30am-1:30pm and 4:30pm-9pm; 8pm close in winter.

Medical Services: Casa del Mar (☎972 34 18 28 or 34 01 54), Av. de Catalunya. Primary care and immediate attention. The nearest hospital is in Blanes, 30min. south.

Internet Access: Tossa Bar Playa, C. Socors, 6, off the main beach; €1 per 15min., €2 per 30min. Open May-Oct. daily 10am-10pm. **Tossa Locutorio,** C. Sant Telm, 20 (☎660 12 60 29). Internet (€0.75 per 15min.) and long-distance phone calls. Open daily Apr.-Sept. 10:30am-midnight; Oct.-Nov. and Mar. daily 10:30am-11pm;. Dec.-Feb. open Sa-Su 4-9:30pm.

Post Office: C. Maria Auxiliadora, 4 (☎972 34 04 57), down Av. Pelegrí from the tourist office. Open M-F 8:30am-2:30pm, Sa 9:30am-1pm. **Postal Code:** 17320.

🛏 ACCOMMODATIONS

Tossa is a seasonal town; many hostels, restaurants, and bars are open only from May to October. During July, August, and festivals, Tossa fills quickly; make reservations in advance. The **old quarter** hotels are the only ones really worth considering. The tourist office website (www.infotossa.com) also lists rooms.

▨ **Fonda/Can Luna,** C. Roqueta, 20 (☎972 34 03 65). From Pg. del Mar, turn right onto C. Peixeteras, veer left onto C. Estalt, walk uphill until the dead end, go left, and head straight. Delightful family offers immaculate singles, doubles, and triples with private baths. Breakfast included—eat on the rooftop terrace and enjoy a breathtaking view. Washing machine €6. A popular choice with Spanish tourists; rooms are booked months in advance in summer. Sept.-June €15 per person; July-Aug. €17. Cash only. ❶

Pensión Carmen Pepi, C. Sant Miguel, 10 (☎972 34 05 26). Turn left off Av. de Pelegrí onto Maria Auxiliadora and veer right through Pl. de l'Antic Hospital and onto C. Sant Miguel. This old, traditional house with its small, greenery-covered courtyard has an authentic feel and good location. The high-ceilinged rooms, each with bath, are somewhat beyond their prime, but are spacious and comfy. Breakfast €3. July-Aug. singles €20; doubles €40. May-June €17/€30; Sept.-Apr. €15/€30. Cash only. ❷

L'Hostalet de Tossa, Pl. de l'Església, 3 (☎972 34 18 53; www.hostelettossa.com), in front of the Sant Vicenç church. Clean and annually renovated with hotel-quality rooms. Many of L'Hostalet's 32 double rooms with baths overlook its orange tree terrace and face the church. Common areas boast foosball, pool table, and TV. In-room TV or balcony extra €4 per day. Doubles Apr.-May and Oct. €18; June-July 14 and Sept. €21; *Semana Santa* (week before Easter) and July-Aug. €28. MC/V. ❷

Pensión Moré, C. Sant Telmo, 9 (☎972 34 03 39). Downstairs sits a dim, cozy sitting room with TV. Upstairs are large doubles and triples with views of the old quarter. Common bath. July-Aug. doubles €24; triples €36, Sept.-June €20/€30. Cash only. ❶

Camping: Can Martí (☎972 34 08 51), at the end of La Rambla Pau Casals, off Av. Ferrán Agulló, 15min. from the bus station. Popular, tree-lined campsite on fringes of a wildlife reserve. Hot-water showers, telephones, swimming pool, and restaurant. Near the municipal sports area. June 20–Aug. €5.50 per person, €6 per tent, €3.50 per car; May 12-June 19 and Sept. 1-16 €4.50/ €5/€2.70. Travelers checks or cash. ❶

🍴 FOOD

The old quarter has the best cuisine and ambiance in Tossa. Restaurants catering to tourists serve up *menús* at reasonable prices; most specialize in local seafood. If you need groceries, head to **Magatzems Palau,** C. Enric Granados 4. (☎972 34 08 58. Open daily June-Sept. 8am-9pm.)

Restaurant Santa Marta, C. Francesc Aromi, 2 (☎972 34 04 72), just inside entrance to the old fortress off C. Portal. Housed in one of the medieval dwellings long ago inhabited by the city's elite, log-cut tables and chairs spill out of the stone-walled, romantically dimmed interior and onto an elegant patio covered by soft, shady leaves. The contemporary cuisine proves a delectable contrast to the historic building, with such winners as salmon with raspberry and kiwi sauce (€12.95). Entrees €9.85-27.95. Open *Semana Santa* to Oct. 15 daily 12:30-4pm and 7:30-11pm. AmEx/MC/V. ❸

La Taberna de Tossa, C. Sant Telm, 26 (☎972 34 19 39). In the heart of the old quarter, right off La Guardia. Serves up inexpensive house wine (€3.60 per L), traditional *tapas* (€1.75-4.30), and provincial specialities in a large Old-World style dining room. Popular among Spanish tourists. Entrees €4.10-10.95. Open Apr.-Sept. daily 1-4pm and 7pm-1am; Oct.-Mar. F-Su 1-4pm and 7pm-1am. V. ❷

Restaurant Marina, C. Tarull, 6 (☎972 34 07 57). Faces the Eglésia de Sant Vincenç and has outdoor seating for prime people-watching. A nice family restaurant with benches bedecked with green checkered tablecloths. Multilingual menu features pizza, meat, fish dishes, and lots of *paella,* including a vegetarian option. Entrees €3.50-12.30. *Menús* €8.50 and €10.50. Open daily 10am-midnight. MC/V. ❷

Pizzeria Anna, Pont Vell, 13 (☎972 34 28 51). Turn right on Pont Vell from Pg. Mar; it's the small restaurant on the left-hand corner with C. Portal. Though homesick Italians might be a bit disappointed, the seafood-sick traveler will be in heaven. Pasta €4.25-5.50; pizza €5.25-7. Open Mar.-Nov. daily noon-4pm and 7-midnight. AmEx/MC/V. ❶

Dino's, Sant Telm, 28 (☎972 34 07 30). Italian fare with German flare. Open for late afternoon dining when others are closed. Pizzas €5.50-7. Open daily 1pm-midnight. ❷

👁 SIGHTS & BEACHES

Inside the walled fortress of the Vila Vella, a spiral of medieval alleys leads to tiny Pl. Pintor J. Roig y Soler, where the ■**Museu Municipal** has a collection of 1920s and 1930s art, including one of the few Chagall paintings still in Spain. Tossa's Roman mosaics (dating from the 4th to the 1st century BC), and other artifacts from the nearby Vila Romana are displayed in a 12th-century palace-turned-museum. (☎972 34 07 09. Open June 1-15 and Sept. 16-30 M-F 11am-1pm and 3-5pm, Sa-Su 11am-6pm; June 16-Sept. 15 daily 10am-8pm; Oct. M-F 11am-1pm and 3-5pm, Sa-Su 11am-5pm. €3, students and seniors €1.80.)

Tossa's main beach, **La Platja Gran,** is surrounded by cliffs and the dreamy Vila Vella, and draws the majority of beach-goers. To escape the crowds, visit some of the neighboring *calas* (small coves), accessible by foot. The tiny ■**Es Codolar** sits just under the tower of the Vila Vella palace, hugged by precipices cloaked in foliage. To get there, follow C. Portal to the end. Snorkeling and diving are popular sports; pick up gear at **Andrea's Diving Center,** C. San Raimon de Penyafort, 11 (☎972 34 20 26). Well-marked hiking and mountain-biking paths also crisscross the **Massif of Cadiretes** wildlife reserve and offer impressive views of the coastline. For less strenuous activity, several companies, like **Fonda Cristal,** send glass-bottomed boats to nearby beaches and caves, where you can sometimes jump in for a swim. Tickets are available at booths on the Platja Gran. (☎972 34 22 29. 1hr.; 17 per day; €7.50 per person, children €5.) **Club Aire Libre,** on the highway to Lloret, organizes various excursions and rents equipment for water sports. (☎972 34 12 77. Canoeing and kayaking €13, water skiing €26 for 2 lessons, scuba diving €264 for 5-day certification course, sailing €11 per hr., windsurfing €10.30 per hr.)

NIGHTLIFE

Bars line the streets of the old quarter and occasionally offer live music. At ■**Bar Trinquet,** C. Sant Josep, 9, flirt over dripping candles under romantic chandeliers or enjoy the stars in the ivy-covered interior courtyard. **Bar El Pirat,** C. Portal, 32, and its companion bar **Piratin,** C. Portal, 30, have outdoor tables overlooking the sea at Es Codolar. (☎972 34 14 43. Open Apr.-Oct. daily 11pm-3am.) For live music try **Don Pepe,** C. Estalt, 6, a small bar which hosts a flamenco guitarist every night. (☎972 34 22 66. Open Apr.-Oct. daily 9:45pm-4:30am.)

PALAFRUGELL ☎972

In 988, inhabitants of the beach town of Llafranc founded inland Palafrugell, seeking refuge from the constant plundering of Mediterranean pirates. Today, budget travelers come here to flee the wallet plundering of seaside hotels and restaurants.

Forty kilometers east of Girona, Palafrugell serves as a base for trips to the nearby beach towns Calella, Llafranc, and Tamariu, which cater to wealthy Europeans whose idea of budget accommodation is any hotel that doesn't leave mints on the pillow. To save some euros, stay in bland and beachless Palafrugell and daytrip to the beaches, connected by the Camino de Ronda footpaths.

▐ TRANSPORTATION

Buses: Sarfa, C. Torres Jonama, 73-79 (☎972 30 06 23). Prices rise on weekends. To: **Barcelona** (2hr.; 12 per day, last bus 7:30pm; €11.40); **Calella** and **Llafranc** (15-20min.; in summer 12-24 per day, in winter 4-5 per day; €1.05); **Figueres** (1½hr., 3-4 per day, €5.65); **Girona** (1hr., 18 per day, €3.75).

Taxis: Radio Taxi (☎972 61 00 00). 24hr. service throughout the area. **Taxi Costa Brava,** C. Lluís Companys, 4 (☎972 61 22 22 daytime, 659 30 61 57 nighttime.) Stands in Palafrugell located on the corner of C. Torres Jonama and C. de Girona, and on the corner of C. de la Lluna and C. Sant Sebastià, by the Pl. Camp d'en Prats.

▐ ▐ ORIENTATION & PRACTICAL INFORMATION

To get from the bus station to the center of town, turn right and walk down C. Torres Jonama to C. de Pi i Maragall. Then turn right and walk past the Guardia Civil and the market until you hit **Plaça Nova,** the main square, from which C. San Sebastià and C. Cavallers branch. On your way you'll pass **Plaça l'Església** on the right. To get to the nearby beach towns of Calella, Llafranc, and Tamariu, take a bus (see **Transportation,** above), spin away on a moped or mountain bike, or take a pleasant, if lengthy, walk through the countryside (about 1hr. to each town).

Tourist Office: Can Rosés, Pl. l'Església (☎972 61 18 20; www.palafrugell.net). First right off C. Cavallers walking away from Pl. Nova. Ask for the indispensable *Guía Municipal,* updated monthly, with relevant nightlife information. **Branch** at C. Carrilet, 2 (☎972 30 02 28; fax 61 12 61). From the bus station, go left on C. Torres Jonama, left again at the traffic circle, and walk about 200m. Both open May-Sept. M-Sa 10am-1pm and 5-8pm, Su 10am-1pm; Oct.-Apr. M-Sa 10am-1pm and 4-7pm, Su 10am-1pm; Carrilet branch also open July-Aug. M-Sa 9am-9pm, Su 10am-1pm.

Currency Exchange: Banesto, C. Torres Jonama, 43 (☎972 30 18 22), at the corner of C. l'Estrella. **ATM.** Open M-F 8:30am-2pm, Sa 8:30am-1pm. **Caja Madrid,** C. Torres Jonama, 45 (☎972 30 60 22), across from Banesto, cashes **travelers checks. ATM.** Open daily 8:15am-2pm.

Money Transfer: Western Union, C. Torres Jonama, 2 (☎922 30 11 03). Open daily 10am-10pm.

Luggage Storage: Sarfa **bus station;** the attendant will hold your bag for €1.30 per day.

Roadside Emergency: ☎112. **Police:** ☎092. **Municipal police:** ☎972 61 31 01, at Av. Josep Pla and C. Cervantes. Call them for **24hr. pharmacy** info.

Medical Services: Centro de Atención Primaria (CAP), C. d'Angel Guimerà, 6 (clinic and non-emergencies ☎972 61 06 07, emergencies and ambulance 972 30 00 23). Open 24hr. **Red Cross,** C. Ample, 130 (☎972 30 09 92).

Internet Access: Internet Papereria Palé, C. Cavallers, 16 (☎972 30 12 48). €1 per 30min. Open July-Sept. Su 10am-1:30pm, M-F 9am-1pm and 4:30-8:30pm, Sa 9am-1pm and 5-9pm.

Post Office: C. Barris i Buixó, 23 (☎972 30 06 07). **Lista de Correos.** Open M-F 8:30am-2:30pm, Sa 9:30am-1pm. **Postal Code:** 17200.

ACCOMMODATIONS

Though options are few, accommodation prices are reasonable and room quality high in Palafrugell. Be sure to call ahead on summer weekends.

Fonda l'Estrella, C. Quatre Cases, 13-17 (☎/fax 972 30 00 05), at the corner of C. la Caritat, a right off C. Torres Jonama. This building, from the turn of the 17th century, has high-ceilinged, well-lit rooms with sinks off a Moorish courtyard bursting with plant life. Common baths, but even the bathrooms of this carefully preserved 1605 historic building are gorgeous. Renovations are scheduled; 5 rooms will have private baths. Breakfast served in high season, €4. June-Sept. singles €26; doubles €35; July-Aug. doubles €39; triples and quads available. Call ahead for dates and prices in Apr. and May. ❸

Hostal Plaja, C. Sant Sebastià, 34 (☎972 30 05 26; www.hostalplaja.com), off Pl. Nova. Frescoed foyer gives way to a courtyard surrounded by spotless rooms, all with balconies, bathrooms, TVs, bottled water, clotheslines, and new beds. Singles €26; doubles €46. ❷

Camping: Moby Dick, Av. Costa Verda, 16-28 (☎972 61 43 07). Take the Sarfa bus to Calella and ask the driver to let you off. No white whale in sight, but it is close to the water. Open May-Sept. €4.35 per adult, €2.50 per child, €4.35 per tent, €4.35 per car July-Aug.; prices decrease Apr.-June and Sept. ❶

FOOD

Restaurants near the beach are predictably expensive, making meals in Palafrugell proper a wiser option. For some reason, the town has a disproportionately high number of pizzerias and Italian restaurants. Shrugs one local, "We just really like pizza." **L'Arcobaleno** ❷, C. Mayor, 3, brings a touch of Tuscany to Catalan classics. The delicious all-inclusive lunchtime *menú* (€7.50) has everything from *gnocci* to roast chicken. (☎97 261 06 95. Open Apr.-Sept. 14 daily 1-4pm and 6:30pm-midnight; Sept. 15-Mar. closed M. AmEx/MC/V.) **Pizzeria Vapor** ❷, C. de les Botines, 21, is a popular restaurant with, in addition to the requisite pizza (€4.50-5.50), a fresh *menú* for €7. (☎97 230 57 03. Entrees €4.50-10. Open June-Aug. daily noon-4:30pm and 7pm-midnight; Sept.-May Su, Tu-Sa noon-4:30pm and 7pm-midnight.) For a respite from pizza and a return to Catalan classics, **Restaurant La Taverna** ❷, C. Giralt i Subiros, 3 (☎97 230 04 30), across from the Església de Sant Marti, serves the traditional fare; the rotisserie chicken is delicious. (Entrees €5-11. Lunch menu €9. Open daily 1-4pm and 7:30-11:30pm.)

SIGHTS & ENTERTAINMENT

In addition to its nearby beaches, Palafrugell boasts one of the world's few cork museums. The **Museu del Suro,** C. Tarongeta, 31, has everything you ever (never?) wanted to know about cork. (☎97 230 78 25. English explanations available. Open June 15-Sept. 15 daily 10am-2pm and 4-9pm; Sept.16-June 14 Su 10:30am-1:30pm, Tu-Sa 5-8pm. €1.20, students and seniors €0.60.) The **Teatre Municipal (TMP),** C. de Sta. Margarida, 1 (☎97 261 11 72), has weekly film showings and theater productions as well as occasional dance and music.

A Palafrugell Friday evening stroll ends up at **Plaza Nova,** where young and old often dance the traditional Catalan *sardana* around 10:30pm in July and August; some nights also offer live music. The tourist office prints a monthly bulletin of upcoming events; also check the *Guía Municipal*. The town's biggest party takes place July 19-21, when the dance-intensive **Festa Major** bursts into the streets. Calella honors **Sant Pere** on June 29 with lots of *sardana* danc-

CATALUÑA

ing, and Tamariu celebrates on August 15, coinciding with the Assumption of the Blessed Mother. The **Festivals of the Hanaveras** (Spanish-Cuban sea songs) come to town the first Saturday of every July.

GIRONA   ☎972

Girona (pop. 70,000) is a world-class city that the world has yet to notice. A Roman settlement and then an important medieval center, Girona was one of the few Spanish cities where Christians, Arabs, and Jews were able to peacefully coexist—for a time. Girona was the founding place of the renowned *cabalistas de Girona*, a group of 12th-century rabbis who created an oral tradition called the *Kabbala* based on numerological readings of the Torah. The city is divided by the Riu Onyar, which separates the medieval alleys and Romanesque buildings of the old quarter from the Spanish dwellings of the new.

▐ TRANSPORTATION

Flights: Aeropuerto de Girona-Costa Brava, Termino Municipal de Vilobi d'Onyar (☎972 18 66 00), is small and services few regular flights on **Iberia** (☎972 47 41 92; www.iberia.com) and **Ryanair** (www.ryanair.com). Airport tourist office (☎972 18 67 08) has more complete information. €15 from the airport to the Old City by taxi (12km).

Trains: RENFE (☎972 24 02 02; www.renfe.es), in Pl. d'Espanya. Info open daily 5:45am-10pm. To: **Barcelona** (1½hr.; M-F 24 per day 6am-9:30pm, Sa-Su starting 9:48am-9:30pm; €5); **Figueres** (30-40min., 23 per day 6:15am-10:44pm, €2.10); **Flaca** (30min., 11-15 per day 7:45am-10:30pm, €1.35); **Madrid** (10½hr., 1 per day, €35); **Paris, FR** (11hr.; 1 per day at 10:17pm; €109, under 26 €85); **Portbou** (1hr., 10 per day 6:15am-10:44pm, €3.25).

Buses: Next to the train station. **Sarfa** (☎972 20 17 96; open daily 7:30am-8:30pm) runs to: **Cadaques** (€6.85); **Celra** (€1.10); **Palafrugell** (1hr., 17 per day, €5), for connections to Begur, Llafranc, Calella, and Tamariu; **Tossa de Mar** (40min.; July-Aug. 2 per day, Sept.-June 1 per day). **Teisa** (☎972 20 02 75; open M-F 9am-1pm and 3:30-7:15pm, Sa-Su 9am-1pm, Su 4:30-5:30pm; cash only) runs to: **Lérida** (3½hr.; 2 per day; €15.80, students €14.20); **Olot** (1hr., 9 per day, €4.30); **Ripoll** (2hr.; M-F 3 per day, Sa-Su 2 per day; €9.35); **St. Feliu** (1hr.; 9-14 per day M-F €3.25, Sa-Su; €3.70). **Barcelona Bus** (☎972 20 24 32; www.barcelonabus.com; open M-F 6:30-10:10am, 10:40am-2:25pm, and 4:30-7:10pm; MC/V) sends express buses to **Barcelona** (1¼hr.; M-F 5 per day, Sa-Su 3 per day; €11.45) and **Figueres** (50min.; M-F 6 per day, Sa 2 per day, Su 3 per day; €4.55). International travel by bus is also available through **Eurolines** buses to destinations throughout Europe and Morocco.

Public transportation: City buses (☎972 20 1540) cover the city, although most everything is within walking distance. Schedules and route maps available at the tourist office. All service stops when the University of Girona closes (mid-June to mid-Sept.).

Car Rental: Europcar (☎650 45 31 46; www.europcar.es), in the train station. Open M-F 9am-1:30pm and 4:30-7pm, Sa 9am-2pm. Must be 21+ and have had a license for 1 year. MC/V. **Avis** (☎972 22 46 64, reservations 902 13 55 31; www.avis.es) is across from Europcar inside the train station. Must be 23+ and have had a valid licence for at least 1 year. From €17 per day. Extra charge of €10 per day for those under 25. Open M-F 9am-1pm and 4-7pm, Sa 9am-1pm. AmEx/MC/V.

Bike Rental: Bicicletes TRAFACH (☎972 23 49 43) in Salt, 2km from Girona. Open Th-F 1:30-8:30pm. €14 per day. **Centre BTT** (☎972 46 82 42), in Quart, 3km from Girona, open Sa-Su 8am-3pm.

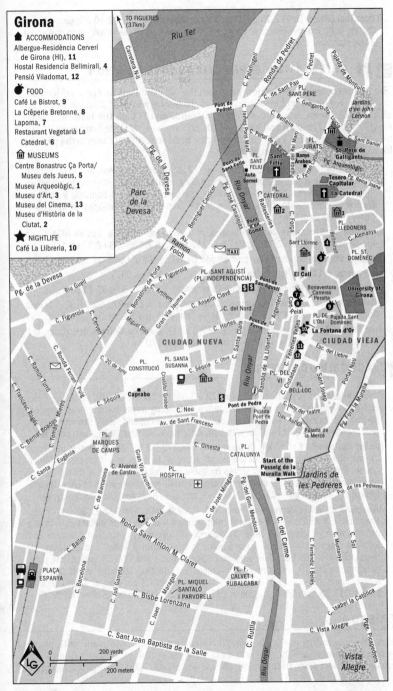

Girona

↑ ACCOMMODATIONS
Albergue-Residència Cerverí
  de Girona (HI), **11**
Hostal Residencia Bellmirall, **4**
Pensió Viladomat, **12**

● FOOD
Café Le Bistrot, **9**
La Crêperie Bretonne, **8**
Lapoma, **7**
Restaurant Vegetarià La
  Catedral, **6**

🏛 MUSEUMS
Centre Bonastruc Ça Porta/
  Museu dels Jueus, **5**
Museu Arqueològic, **1**
Museu d'Art, **3**
Museu del Cinema, **13**
Museu d'Història de la
  Ciutat, **2**

★ NIGHTLIFE
Café La Llibreria, **10**

CATALUÑA

Taxis: Taxi Girona (☎972 20 33 77; 24hr.) or **Girotaxi** (☎972 22 10 20; 6am-11pm). Stands at Pl. Independència or Pont de Pedra. Taxis cannot be hailed; go to one of the 2 taxi stands or call.

✦ 🛈 ORIENTATION & PRACTICAL INFORMATION

The **Riu Onyar** separates the new city from the old. The **Pont de Pedra** bridge connects the two banks and leads into the old quarter by way of C. Ciutadans, C. Peralta, and C. Força, which lead to the cathedral and **El Call,** the historic Jewish neighborhood. The **train** and **bus terminals** are situated off C. de Barcelona, in the modern neighborhood. To get to the old city, head straight out through the parking lot and turn left on C. de Barcelona.

Tourist Office: Rambla de la Llibertat, 1 (☎972 22 65 75), near Pont de Pedra. English spoken. Pick up a map and the bi-weekly *La Guía*, in Catalan but with easy-to-follow listings of local events. Open M-F 8am-8pm, Sa 8am-2pm and 4-8pm, Su 9am-2pm. **Branch** in Plaça del Vi. Open in summer M-F 9am-3pm, Sa 9am-2pm; in winter M-F 9am-7pm, Sa 9am-2pm.

Bank: Banco Santander Central Hispano, at C. Nou and Gran Vía, has an **ATM.** Open Apr.-Sept. M-F 8:30am-2:30pm; Oct.-Mar. M-F 8:30am-2:30pm, Sa 8:30am-1pm.

Luggage Storage: Lockers in the train station €4.50 per 24hr. Open M-F 6:30am-10pm.

Emergency: ☎112. **Police: Policía Municipal,** C. Bacià, 4 (☎092).

Hospital: Hospital Municipal de Santa Caterina, Pl. Hospital, 5 (☎97 218 26 00).

Internet Access: Corado Telephone, C. de Barcelona, 31 (☎972 22 28 75), across from the train station. €2 per hr. Open M-Sa 9am-2pm and 5-9pm.

Post Office: Av. Ramón Folch, 2 (☎972 22 21 11). **Lista de Correos** only. Open M-F 8:30am-8:30pm and Sa 9:30am-2pm. **Postal Code:** 17070.

🛏 ACCOMMODATIONS

Pensió Viladomat, C. Ciutadans, 5 (☎972 20 31 76; fax 20 31 76). Sparkling clean and well-furnished rooms in an old apartment building in the historic neighborhood. Rooms with bath have TVs. Long-term options, apartments, and family-size rooms available. Singles €16; doubles €32, with bath €55; triple with bath €75. Cash only. ❷

Hostal Residencia Bellmirall, C. Bellmirall, 3 (☎972 20 40 09). Expensive but worth the splurge. Features delightful rooms, all with private bath, in a 14th-century stone house. Breakfast included and served by the warm hostess in the cozy dining area or plant-filled garden patio. The perfect romantic environment from which to enjoy Girona. Closed Jan.-Feb. Singles €32; doubles €56; triples €75; quads €96. Cash only. ❸

Albergue-Residència Cerverí de Girona (HI), C. Ciutadans, 9 (☎972 21 80 03, for reservations 934 83 83 63). The sterile, whitewashed walls and blue metal bunks in this college dorm building may cause flashbacks to sleep-away camp, but the price and location make it worthwhile. A good place to meet other travelers and students. 90 beds Oct.-June; 100 beds July-Sept. Sleek sitting rooms with TV/VCR, videos, and ping-pong; rooms of 2, 3, and 8 beds with lockers. Breakfast €2.70; other meals €5. Combined sheets and towel €3. Wash €2, dry €1. Internet €1 per 30min. 24hr. check-in. Dorms €13.50, over 25 €18; groups €12 per person; weekends €2 more. MC/V. ❶

🍴 FOOD

Girona's specialties are its *botifarra dolça* (sweet sausage made with pork, lemon, cinnamon, and sugar) and *xuixo* (sugar-sprinkled pastries filled with cream). The best place to find good, cheap food is on C. Cort Reial, at the top of C.

Argenteria. La Rambla is home to tourist cafes with ubiquitous terrace seating. In summer, an open **market** can be found near the Polideportivo in Parc de la Deversa (open Tu and Sa 8am-3pm). Get your **groceries** at **Caprabo,** C. Sequia, 10, a block from C. Nou off the Gran Vía. (☎972 21 45 16. Open M-Sa 9am-9pm.)

La Crêperie Bretonne, C. Cort Reial, 14 (☎972 21 81 20). Potent proof of Girona's proximity to France, this popular crêpe joint combines a funky atmosphere with great food and cheap prices. Old French posters decorate the stone walls, and your food is cooked inside a small bus bound for "Cerbère." *Menú* €8.45. Crêpes €2.35-7. Unusual salads €6.50-7.45. Open Tu-Sa 1-4pm and 8pm-midnight, Su 8pm-midnight. MC/V. ❷

Lapoma, C. Cort Reial, 16 (☎972 21 29 09). The helpful service and delicious dishes entice many to this recently revamped restaurant. Entrees are a contemporary French twist on Catalan fare (€2.35-11.80). Wine tasting also available. Open M and W-Su 8pm-midnight; June-Sept. also noon-3:30pm. Closed Aug. AmEx/MC/V. ❷

Café Le Bistrot, Pujada Sant Domènec, 4 (☎972 21 88 03). An elegant, turn-of-the-century atmosphere, with a great view overlooking one of the old city's slanting streets. Excellent food. Fresh specialty pizzas €4.50-5.30. Crêpes €3.50-5. Lunch *menú* begins at €9.50. Terrace costs 10% extra. Open M-Th 1-4pm and 8pm-1am, F-Sa 1-4pm and 7pm-2am, Su 1-4pm and 8pm-midnight. AmEx/MC/V. ❷

Restaurant Vegetarià La Catedral, C. Clavería, 4 (☎972 21 83 88). Looking to escape the more touristed area of the city? Check out this out-of-the-way vegetarian restaurant serving creative vegetable, rice, and tofu dishes. Lunch *menú* €9.50, dinner *menú* €11.50; €1 extra for terrace. Open daily 1-4pm, F-Sa also 8:30-11pm. AmEx/MC/V. ❷

◉ SIGHTS

The narrow, winding streets of the medieval old city, interspersed with steep stairways and low arches, are ideal for wanderers. Start your self-guided historical tour at the **Pont de Pedra** and turn left at the tourist office down tree-lined **Rambla de la Llibertat.** Continue on C. Argenteria, bearing right across C. Cort Reial. Up the flight of stairs, C. Força begins on the left.

▨ EL CALL. The part of the old town around C. Força and C. Sant Llorenç was once the center of Girona's medieval Jewish community ("call" comes from *kahal,* Hebrew for "community"). The site of the last synagogue in Girona now serves as the **Centre Bonastruc Ça Porta,** named for Rabbi Moshe Ben-Nahman (Nahmanides), a scholar of Jewish mysticism (*Kabbala*) and the oral tradition. The center includes the **Museu d'Història dels Jueus Girona,** notable for its detailed wooden model of the original *call,* as well as its collection of inscribed Hebrew tombstones. *(The entrance to the Centre is off C. Força, about halfway up the hill. ☎972 21 67 61. Centre and museum open May-Oct. M-Sa 10am-8pm, Su 10am-3pm; Nov.-April M-Sa 10am-6pm, Su 10am-3pm. Museum €2, students and over 65 €1, under 16 free. The tourist office offers guided tours of El Call in July and Aug. €6 during the day, €12 at night.)*

CATHEDRAL COMPLEX. Girona's imposing Gothic **cathedral** rises 90 steps from the *plaça,* making its stairway the highest in Europe. The **Torre de Charlemany** (belltower) and **cloister** are the only structures left from the 11th and 12th centuries; the rest of the building dates from the 14th through 17th centuries. The world's widest Gothic **nave** (22m) is surpassed in sheer size only by St. Peter's in Rome. A door on the left leads to the trapezoidal cloister and the **Tesoro Capitular** (treasury), home to some of Girona's most precious possessions. The *tesoro's* (and possibly Girona's) most famous piece is the **Tapis de la Creació,** an 11th-century tapestry depicting the story of creation. *(Tesoro ☎972 21 44 26. Cathedral and tesoro open July-Sept. Tu-Sa 10am-2pm and 4-7pm; Oct.-Mar. Tu-Sa 10am-2pm and 4-6pm; Mar.-June Tu-Sa 10am-2pm and 4-7pm; open Su-M and holidays 10am-2pm year-round. €3.)*

CATALUÑA

WALKS. Girona's renowned ▒**Passeig de la Muralla**, not for the faint of heart, begins at the bottom of La Rambla in Pl. de la Marvà. Take the steps up to the guard's rampart atop the old Roman defense walls and follow them around the entire eastern side of the old town. The walk ends behind the cathedral, where the equally beautiful **Passeig Arqueològic** begins. *Passeig de la Muralla is open daily 8am-10pm.* Partly lined with cypresses and flower beds, this path skirts the northeastern medieval wall and also overlooks the city. For the less athletically inclined, a small trolley gives a 30min. guided tour of the main sights of the old town, including the town hall, cathedral, St. Feliu church, El Call, and the walls. *(In summer leaves daily every 20-25min. from the Pont de Pedra, 10am-8pm or so. In winter, it runs less frequently; check in the tourist office. Available in English. €3.)*

MUSEU DEL CINEMA. This unusual collection documents the rise of cinema from the mid-17th to the 20th centuries, with a few pieces from as early as the 11th century (Chinese shadow theater). It walks you through the chronological development of the camera obscura (9th-12th century), magic lantern (1659), panorama (1788), diorama (1822), Edison's kinetoscope (1891), and more, with several hands-on displays and a short film at the end. *(C. Sèquia, 1. ☎972 41 27 77. Open May-Sept. daily 10am-8pm; Oct.-Apr. M-F 10am-6pm, Sa 10am-8pm, Su 11am-3pm. €3, students and over 65 €1.50, under 16 free. AmEx/MC/V.)*

OTHER MUSEUMS. The remarkably well-done **Museu d'Història de la Ciutat**, C. Força 27, showcases 2000 years of Girona's history, from the first settlers in Cataluña to the present day. *(☎972 22 22 29. Open Tu-Sa 10am-2pm and 5-7pm, Su and holidays 10am-2pm. Some descriptions in English. €2, under 16 free.)* The **Banys Àrabs**, inspired by Muslim bath houses, once contained saunas and baths of varying temperatures; now the graceful 12th-century structure occasionally hosts outdoor art exhibits. *(☎972 21 32 62. Open Apr.-Sept. M-Sa 10am-7pm, Su 10am-2pm; Oct.-Mar. daily 10am-2pm. €1.50, students €0.75.)* The **Museu Arqueològic** complements its archaeological displays with detailed booklets on the area's history. *(Pl. dels Jurats. ☎972 20 26 32. Open Tu-Sa 10:30am-1:30pm and 4-7pm, Su 10am-2pm. €1.80, students €1.40, under 16 free.)* The **Museu d'Art**, next to the cathedral, holds medieval and modern art. *(☎972 20 38 34. Open Mar.-Sept. Tu-Sa 10am-7pm; Oct.-Feb. Tu-Sa 10am-6pm; Su and holidays 10am-2pm. €1.80, students or over 65 €1.40.)*

🎵 🎭 ENTERTAINMENT & NIGHTLIFE

During the latter half of May, government-sponsored **flower exhibitions** spring up all over the city; local monuments and pedestrian streets swim in blossoms, and the courtyards of Girona's fine old buildings are open to the public. Summer evenings often inspire spontaneous *sardana* dancing in the city *plaças*. Girona lights up for the **Focs de Sant Joan** on June 24, an outdoor party of fireworks and campfires.

Nightlife concentrates in **Plaça de l'Oli** (the old quarter) and in summer the expansive, impeccably designed **Parc de la Devesa**, which explodes with temporary outdoor bars. (Drinks €4.20-5.40. Open June-Sept. 15 Su-Th 10pm-3am and F-Sa 10pm-4:30am.) The bars and cafes in the old quarter are particularly mellow and relaxing, a good way to start the evening. **Platea**, on C. Fontclara, is a popular early morning dance spot on weekends. **Café la Llibreria**, C. Ciutadans, 15, serves cocktails (€4), beer (€1.50), and *tapas* (€2.10-2.70) to chic intellectual types and posers alike. (Open M-Sa 8:30am-1am, Su 8:30am-midnight. MC/V.)

FIGUERES (FIGUERAS) ☎972

In 1974, the mayor of Figueres (pop. 35,000) asked native Salvador Dalí to donate a painting to an art museum the town was planning. Dalí refused to donate a painting; he was so flattered by his hometown's recognition that he donated an entire museum. With the construction of the Teatre-Museu Dalí, Figueres was catapulted to international fame; ever since, a multilingual parade of Surrealism fans has been awed and entranced by Dalí's bizarre perspectives and erotic visions. Though it is a beachless sprawl, Figueres hides other quality museums and some pleasant cafes. If you choose to extend your visit beyond Dalí's spectacle, the town's lovely Rambla is a good place to start for food, accommodations, and further sightseeing.

TRANSPORTATION

Trains: Pl. de l'Estació. ☎902 24 02 02. To: **Barcelona** (2hr.; M-F 25 per day, Sa-Su 15 per day; €8.05); **Girona** (30min.; M-F 25 per day, Sa-Su 15 per day; €2.50); **Portbou** (30min., 11 per day, €1.85).

Buses: All buses leave from the **Estació d'Autobusos** (☎972 67 33 54), in Pl. de l'Estació. **Sarfa** (☎972 67 42 98; www.sarfa.com) runs to: **Cadaqués** (1hr.; July-Aug. 5 per day, Sept.-June 3-4 per day; €3.55); **Llançà** (25min.; July-Aug. 4 per day, Sept.-June 2 per day; €2.20); **Palafrugell** (1½hr.; M-F 4 per day, Sa-Su 3 per day; €5.80). **Barcelona Bus** (☎972 50 50 29) runs to **Barcelona** (2¼hr., 2-6 per day, €12.50) and **Girona** (1hr.; M-F 5 per day, Sa-Su 2-3 per day; €3.60). **Teisa** (☎97 250 31 75) goes to **Olot** (1hr., 3 per day, €4.35). **Eurolines** (☎972 50 63 00) ticket office is open M-F 9am-1:30pm and 3:30-9pm, Sa 10am-1pm and 6-9pm. MC/V.

Taxis: Taxis line the Rambla (☎972 50 00 08) and the train station (☎972 50 50 43).

Car Rental: Hertz, Pl. de l'Estació, 9 (☎972 67 28 01 or 902 40 24 05). All-inclusive rental from €59 per day. 23+, valid driver's license of 2 years. Open M-F 8am-1pm and 4-8pm, Sa 9am-1pm. AmEx/D/MC/V. **Avis,** Pl. de l'Estació, in the **RENFE** train station (☎972 51 31 82) rental includes taxes, insurance, unlimited kilometers. €63 per day. 23+ and credit card. Open M-Sa 9am-1pm and 4-7pm. AmEx/MC/V.

ORIENTATION & PRACTICAL INFORMATION

Trains and buses arrive at **Plaça de l'Estació** on the edge of town. Cross the plaza and bear left on C. Sant Llàtzer, walk several blocks to C. Nou, and take a right to get to Figueres's tree-filled Rambla. To reach the **tourist office,** walk up La Rambla and continue on C. Lasauca straight out from the left corner. The blue, all-knowing **"i"** beckons across the rather treacherous intersection with Ronda Frial.

Tourist Office: Main Office, Pl. Sol (☎972 50 31 55). Good map and free list of accommodations. Open July-Aug. M-Sa 9am-8pm, Su 9am-3pm; Apr.-June and Oct. M-F 9am-3pm and 4:30-8pm, Sa 9:30am-1:30pm and 3:30-6:30pm; Sept. M-Sa 9am-8pm; Nov.-Mar. M-F 9am-3pm. Two **branch offices** in summer, one at Pl. de l'Estació (open July-Sept. 15 M-Sa 10am-2pm and 4-6pm), and the other in a yellow mobile home in front of the Dalí museum (open July-Sept. 15 M-Sa 9am-8pm, Su 9am-3pm).

Currency Exchange: Banco Santander Central Hispano, La Rambla, 21. **ATM.** Open Apr.-Sept. M-F 8:30am-2pm; Oct.-Mar. M-F 8:30am-2pm, Sa 8:30am-1pm.

Luggage Storage: At the **train station,** large lockers €3; open daily 6am-11pm. At the **bus station** €2; open daily 6am-10pm.

Foreign Language Bookstore: Llibreria J. Mallart, C. Besalu, 12 (☎972 50 01 33) sells regional, Spanish, and European travel guides in English, Catalan, Spanish, and French. Open M-F 9am-1pm and 4-8pm, Sa 9:30am-1pm and 4:30-8pm.

Emergency: ☎112. **Police:** Ronda Final, 4 (☎972 51 01 11, local police emergency ☎092). **National police** (☎091) should be contacted regarding theft or loss of important document (passports), but not for emergencies.

Internet Access: Tele Haddi, C. Joan Reglá, 1 (☎972 51 30 99). €1 per 15min., €1.50 per 30min., €2.50 per 1hr. Open daily 9:30am-10pm. **Oh!net** Internet kiosk at the bus station €0.50 per 4min., €1 per 8min., €2 per 20min. **Hotel Rambla,** La Rambla, 33 (☎972 67 60 20; www.hotelrambla.net). €1 per 15min. Open 24hr.

Post Office: C. Santa Llogaia, 60-62 (☎972 50 54 31). Open M-F 8am-1pm. **Postal Code:** 17600.

ACCOMMODATIONS

Most visitors to Figueres make the journey a daytrip from Barcelona, but affordable accommodations in Figueres are easy to find. Most tend to be on the upper floors of small bars or restaurants. Some cluster on **Carrer Jonquera,** around the Dalí museum; others are located closer to **La Rambla** and **Carrer Pep Ventura.** The tourist office has an annually updated list of all pensions and hostels.

Hostal La Barretina, C. Lasauca, 13 (☎972 67 64 12 or 67 34 25). From the train station, walk up La Rambla to its end; look for C. Lasauca directly ahead. A luxury experience—each room has TV, A/C, heat, and bath. Reception in the restaurant downstairs. Reservations recommended. Singles €22; doubles €39. AmEx/MC/V. ❷

Hostal San Mar, C. Rec Arnau, 31 (☎972 50 98 13). Follow C. Girona off La Rambla and continue as it becomes C. Jonquera; take the 5th right onto C. Isabel II, then take the 2nd left. Enter through the bar. The long walk is rewarded with clean, modern rooms with bath and TV. Singles €14; doubles €28. Cash only. ❶

Pensión Mallol, C. Pep Ventura, 9 (☎972 50 22 83). Follow La Rambla toward the tourist office, turn right on Castell at its end, and take the 2nd left. Look for the "Habitaciones-Chambres" sign. Spacious and simply decorated rooms with shared bathrooms. A very good value. Singles €16; doubles €27. Cash only. ❷

FOOD

Restaurants near the Museu Dalí serve overcooked *paella* to the masses; better choices surround La Rambla on smaller side streets. The **market** is at Pl. Gra. (Open Tu, Th, and Sa 5am-2pm. Best selection on Th.) Buy groceries at **Bonpreu,** Pl. Sol, 5. (Open M-Th 9am-2pm and 5-9:30pm, F-Sa 9am-9:30pm. MC/V.)

Hotel Duran Restaurant, C. Lasauca, 5 (☎972 50 12 50). From the train station, walk up La Rambla to its end and look for C. Lasauca directly ahead. Serves traditional Catalan cuisine with a distinctive French influence. Lunch *menú* €10.25. Meat and seafood entrees €11.15-40.85. Open daily 1-3:30pm and 8:30-10:30pm. ❹

Taquería Mexicana, Restaurant Jalisco, C. Tapis, 21 (☎972 50 53 52). C. Peralada becomes C. Tapis after C. Hortes, then walk half a block more. For those looking for a change in their diet, this Jalisco-styled restaurant serves Mexican classics (entrees €4-14, mainly in the €4.50-7 range). Try the *fajitas de pollo* (€6.50). Vegetarian options. Open M-Tu and Th-Su 12:30-3:30pm and 8-11:30pm. MC/V. ❷

La Llesca, C. Mestre Falla, 15 (☎972 67 58 26), just beyond Pl. Sol. Specializes in *llesques*, toasted sandwiches topped with just about anything (€3.35-10.25). *Menú* €7.20; salads €2.70-4. Open M-Sa 8am-midnight, Su 6pm-midnight. AmEx/MC/V. ❷

SIGHTS & ENTERTAINMENT

TEATRE-MUSEU DALÍ. Welcome to the world of the Surrealist master. This building was the municipal theater for the town of Figueres before it burned down in 1939—hence the name Teatre-Museu ("theater-museum") Dalí. When Dalí decided to donate a museum to Figueres, he insisted on using the ruins of the old theater, which was where he showed his first exposition as a teenager. The resulting homage to his first gallery is the reconstructed theater, covered in sculptures of eggs and full of Dalí's painting, sculptures, other creations, and his own tomb.

In keeping with his reputation as a Fascist self-promoter, Dalí's personally designed mausoleum/museum/monument is ego-worship at its finest. Nevertheless, it should be approached as a multimedia experience—an electrifying tangle of sculpture, painting, music, and architecture. It's all here: Dalí's naughty cartoons, his dramatically low-key tomb, and many paintings of Gala, his wife and muse. The treasure trove of paintings includes, among others, the remarkable *Self Portrait with a Slice of Bacon*, *Poetry of America*, *Galarina*, and *Galatea of the Spheres*. There is also a small offering of works by other artists selected by Dalí himself, including pieces by El Greco, Marcel Duchamp, and architect Peres Piñero. (☎ 972 67 75 00; www.salvador-dali.org. From the Rambla, take C. Girona past Pl. Ajuntament as it becomes C. Jonquera. Steps by a Dalí statue to your left lead to the pink and white egg-covered museum. Open July-Sept. daily 9am-7:15pm; Oct.-June daily 10:30am-5:15pm. €9, students and seniors €6.50. Call ahead about night hours during the summer.)

OTHER SIGHTS. Delight once again in the wonders of your favorite childhood toys at the **Museu del Joguet**, winner of Spain's 1999 National Prize of Popular Culture. The colorful collection features antique dolls, board games, comics, rocking horses, toys for the blind, caganers, and more. (Sant Pere, 1, off La Rambla. ☎ 972 50 45 85; www.mjc-figueres.net. Open June-Sept. M-Sa 10am-1pm and 4-7pm, Su 11am-1:30pm and 5-7:30pm; Oct.-May Tu-Sa 10am-1pm and 4-7pm, Su 11am-1:30pm. €4.70, students and children under 12 €3.80.) Ten minutes from the Museu Dalí, the 18th-century **Castell de Sant Ferràn** commands a view of the countryside and is the largest stone fortress in Europe at 12,000 square meters. (Av. Castell de Sant Ferràn; follow Pujada del Castell from the Teatre-Museu Dalí. ☎ 972 50 60 94. Open July-Sept. 15 daily 10:30am-8pm; Mar.-July and Sept. 16-Oct. daily 10:30am-2pm and 4-6pm; Nov.-Feb. daily 10:30am-2pm. €2.10.)

FESTIVALS. In September, classical and jazz music flood Figueres during the **Festival Internacional de Música de l'Empordà**. (Tickets available at Caixa de Catalunya. Call ☎ 972 10 12 12 for info.) From September 10 through 14, the **Mostra del Vi de L'Alt Empordà**, a tribute to regional wines, brings a taste of the local vineyards to Figueres. Around May 3, the **Fires i Festes de la Santa Creu** sponsors cultural events and art exhibitions. Parties and general merrymaking can be expected at the **Festa de Sant Pere**, held June 28 to 29, which honors the town's patron saint.

CADAQUÉS & PORT LLIGAT ☎972

The whitewashed houses and small bay of Cadaqués (pop. 2000) have attracted artists, writers, and musicians ever since Dalí built his summer home in neighboring Port Lligat in the 1930s. Cadaqués is the bigger of the two overlapping towns (Port Lligat is basically just Dalí's house). The rocky beaches and dreamy landscape attract their share of tourists, but Cadaqués preserves a pleasantly laid-back atmosphere. If you're traveling to Cadaqués from September to May, it's best to make it a daytrip, as most food and entertainment options close in the low season.

⌨ TRANSPORTATION & PRACTICAL INFORMATION. Cadaqués has no train station. Sarfa **buses** (☎ 972 25 87 13) run to **Barcelona** (2½hr.; 2 per day 11:15am, 4:15pm; €16); **Figueres** (1hr., 5-7 per day, €4.50); **Girona** (2hr., 1-2 per day, €7). Bus stop to the right of the Sarfa office. With your back to the Sarfa office, walk downhill on Av. Caritat Serinyana to the waterfront **Plaça Frederic Rahola**, where a signboard map with indexed services and accommodations will orient you. The **tourist office**, C. Cotxe, 2, off Pl. Frederic Rahola, is opposite the *passeig*.

(☎972 25 83 15. Open July-Aug. M-Sa 9:30am-1:30pm and 4-8pm, Su 10:30am-1:30pm; Sept.-June M-Sa 9am-2pm and 4-7pm.) **Banco Santander Central Hispano** is at Av. Caritat Serinyana, 4. (☎972 25 83 62. Open Apr.-Sept. M-F 8:30am-2:30pm; Oct.-Mar. M-F 8:30am-2:30pm, Sa 8:30am-1pm.) Services include: **local police,** Pl. Frederic Rahola (☎972 15 93 43), by the promenade; **medical assistance** (☎972 25 88 07); the **post office,** on Av. Rierassa off Av. Caritat Serinyana. (☎972 25 87 98. Open M-F 9am-2pm, Sa 9:30am-1pm.) **Postal Code:** 17488.

■ ACCOMMODATIONS & FOOD. As Cadaqués is a beach town, many accommodations are open only during the summer. **Hostal Cristina ❸,** C. Riera, is right on the water, to the right of Av. Caritat Serinyana. Cristina offers bright, newly renovated rooms and a rooftop terrace overlooking the water. (☎972 25 81 38. Summer prices include breakfast. May-Sept. singles €26; doubles €40, with bath €52, with TV €57. Oct.-Apr. €20/€27/€38/€50. MC/V.) **Pensión Ranxo ❸,** Av. Caritat Serinyana, 13, is on the right as you walk down from the bus stop. Potted plants and whitewashed hallways lead to clean and comfortable rooms. (☎972 25 80 05. July-Sept. 15 singles €22; doubles €45. Sept. 15-June €20/€43. Travelers checks accepted. MC/V.) **Camping Cadaqués ❶,** Ctra. Port Lligat, 17, is 100m from the beach on the way to Dalí's house; follow the signs for Hotel Port Lligat. The campground is popular and crowded, but still relatively clean. (☎972 25 81 26. Open Apr.-Sept. €4 per person, €5 per tent, €4 per car.)

Cadaqués harbors the usual slew of overpriced, unexciting waterfront tourist restaurants—wander into the back streets for more interesting options. **Groceries** can be purchased at **Super Auvi,** C. Riera. (Open July 15-Aug. M-Sa 8am-2pm and 4:30-9pm, Su 8am-2pm; Sept.-July 14 M-Sa 8:30am-1:30pm and 4:30-9pm.) ◪**Can Tito ❷,** C. Vigilant, 8, is an exceptional historical and culinary experience. The stone archway at the entrance to this elegant restaurant is one of five portals dating back to AD 1100 when Cadaqués was still a fortified village at the mercy of roving pirates. Three-course lunchtime *menú* €12. (Fish and meat entrees €4.80-14. Open daily Mar.-Jan. 1:30-3pm and 8-10:30pm. MC/V.) **Restaurant Vehí ❸,** C. de l'Església, 6, serves traditional Catalan seafood. (*Menú* €11. Open Mar.-Oct.)

◙ SIGHTS & ENTERTAINMENT. Església de Santa María is a 16th-century Gothic church with a Baroque altar. Nearby, the **Museu de Cadaqués,** C. Narcis Monturiol, 15, displays rotating exhibits, often with a Dalí theme. (☎972 25 88 77. Open daily mid-June to Sept. 10:30am-1:30pm and 3-8pm. €4.50, students €3.) From the museum, it's a pleasant walk (30min.) to ◪**Casa-Museu Salvador Dalí,** in Port Lligat, the house where Dalí and his wife Gala lived until her death in 1982. With your back to the Sarfa station, take the right fork and follow the signs to Port Lligat until *Casa de Dalí* signs appear. At C. President Lluís Companys, where signs point to the house in two different directions, follow the one to the right. This modest fisherman's abode was transformed to meet the artist's eccentric needs. Though only two (unfinished) Dalí originals remain in the house, the decorating is a work in itself. (☎972 25 10 15. Open June 15-Sept. 15 daily 10:30am-9pm; Sept. 16-Nov. and Mar. 15-June 14 Tu-Su 10:30am-6pm. Tours are the only way to see the house; make reservations 1-2 days in advance. Ticket office closes 45min. before closing. €7.80; students, seniors, and children €4.80.) **Boat rides** in his *Gala* depart from the front of the house on the hour for a 55min. trip to Cap de Creus. (☎617 46 57 57. Open daily 10am-7pm. €9.) On the beach, **Escola de Vela Ones** rents kayaks, sailboats, and windsurfing gear. (☎937 53 25 12. Open daily July-Sept. 15 10am-8pm.)

CATALAN PYRENEES

While beach-goers and city-dwellers flock to Barcelona and the Costa Brava, Cataluña's portion of the Pyrenees draws a different breed of tourist. Bikinis are tossed aside for slightly better insulation as hikers and high-brow skiers, mostly from Spain and France, come for the refined ski resorts and some of Spain's wildest mountain scenery. Meanwhile, history and architecture buffs, notebooks in hand, eagerly explore the tranquil mountain towns filled with well-preserved Romanesque buildings. Early June to late September is the best time for trekking in the Pyrenees; any earlier, avalanches are a potential danger, and it can get prohibitively cold later. Tourist offices distribute pamphlets with information on scenic areas and outdoor activities. Skiers will find the *Snow in Catalonia* or *Ski España* guides most useful, and the website www.pirineo.com is a fantastic general planning resource (for skiing and hiking both) for those who can read Spanish. The Pyrenees are best explored with a car, as public transportation links are few and far between. Either way, entry from the east begins in Ripoll.

RIPOLL ☎972

Although the sleepy town of Ripoll (pop. 11,000) may seem trapped in a permanent time-warp, it continues to attract visitors in search of Spain's Romanesque architectural legacy; the elaborately carved portal of the Monasterio de Santa María is one of the most famous in all of Spain. Ripoll also serves as a convenient base for excursions to the nearby town of Sant Joan de las Abadesses.

▐▌ TRANSPORTATION. RENFE, Pl. Mova, 1 (☎972 70 06 44), runs **trains to Barcelona** (1¾hr., 9-12 per day 6:32am-6:31pm, €5) and **Puigcerdà** (1hr., 6 per day 8:56am-8:54pm, €2.51). The bus station (across a small park from the train station) sends **Teisa buses** (☎972 20 48 68) to: **Barcelona** (4hr., 12 per day, €10.80); **Girona** (2hr., 1 per day, €6.60) via **Olot**; **Sant Joan de las Abadesses** (15min., 8-10 per day, €1.10).

▐▌ PRACTICAL INFORMATION. The **tourist office**, next to the monastery on Pl. Abat Oliba, gives out free maps. (☎972 70 23 51. Open M-Sa 9:30am-1:30pm and 4-7pm, Su 10am-2pm and 4-7pm.) Connect to the **Internet** at **Xarxtel**, Pl. d'Espanya, 10. The **public library**, C. de les Vinyes, 6, offers free use of their computers. (Open M-Tu and Th-F 4-8:30pm, W 9am-1:30pm, Sa 10am-1:30pm.) Other services include: **emergency** (☎112); **police**, Pl. Ajuntament, 3 (☎972 71 44 14); the **post office**, C. d'Estació, facing the tree-lined park. (☎972 70 07 60. Open M-F 8:30am-2:30pm, Sa 9:30am-1pm.) **Postal Code:** 17500.

▐▌ ACCOMMODATIONS & FOOD. Ripoll is an ambitious daytrip; budget-friendly accommodations allow an overnight stay. The luxurious and friendly **▨Fonda La Paula ❷**, C. Berenguer, 4, on Pl. Abat Oliba, is alongside the tourist office. Cream-colored rooms combine with comfortable beds, TVs, and tiled bathrooms. (☎972 70 00 11. Singles €22; doubles €37; triples €51; quads €65. V.) Slightly more pricy is the **Hostal del Ripollès ❸**, Pl. Nova, 11. From the monastery's plaza, follow C. Sant Pere for two blocks. The hostal provides small but well-furnished rooms with TV, phone, and full bath. (☎972 70 02 15; www.elripolles.com/hostaldelripolles. Breakfast €3.65. Singles €30; doubles €48; triples €72. MC/V.)

Restaurants surround Pl. Gran. Follow C. Bisbe Morgades and take a right before the river on C. Mossen; the *plaça* is to the left. If you are looking for fancy Catalan fare, try **▨Reccapolis ❸**, Ctra. Sant Joan, 68, about a 15min. walk down Ctra. Sant Joan from Pl. Ajuntament. (☎972 70 21 06. Entrees €10-18. Open Su-Tu 1-4pm and 8:30-10:30pm, W 1-4pm, Th-Sa 1-4pm and 8:30-10:30pm. AmEx/MC/V.)

CATALUÑA

At **La Piazzetta ❷**, Pl. Nova, 11 the ambience may be Catalan, but the food is Italian. (☎972 70 02 15. Pizzas €5-9, pasta €5.50-8. Open M-Sa 1-3:15pm and 8:15-11:30pm, Su 8:15-11:30pm. MC/V.) Stock up on **groceries** at the supermarket across from the bus station, **Champion**, C. Progrés, 33-37. (☎972 70 26 32. Open M-Th 9am-9pm, F-Sa 9am-9:30pm, Su 10am-2pm. AmEx/MC/V.)

⬛ **SIGHTS.** Most visitors to Ripoll come to see the incredibly intricate 11th-century portal of the ⬛**Monasterio de Santa María.** Founded in AD 879 by Count Guifré el Pelú (Wilfred the Hairy), the Santa María monastery was once the most powerful in all of Cataluña. The curved doorway, nicknamed the "Stone Bible," depicts survival scenes from the Old and New Testaments as well as a hierarchy of the cosmos and a 12-month calendar. Panels (in Catalan) attempt to decode the doorway. Adjoining it is a beautiful two-story Romanesque and Gothic **cloister.** To reach the monastery, take a left on C. Progrés from the train and bus stations, following it until it merges with C. d'Estació. Take the first left after the colorful modern "metal dancers" onto Pont d'Olot, cross the river, then continue straight on C. Bisbe Morgades to Pl. Ajuntament and Pl. Abat Oliba. *(Church open daily 10am-1pm and 3-7pm. €2, with student card €0.50; includes entrance to the cloister.)*

PUIGCERDÀ

A challenging name for foreigners, Puigcerdà (pop. 7000; Pooch-sair-DAH) has become a popular town by virtue of its stunning location in the mountainous Cerdanya region. Puigcerdà's view of the valley is beautiful, and the town serves as a cheap base for hiking, biking, or skiing the surrounding hillsides. Puigcerdà is perhaps best known for appearing in the 1993 *Guinness Book of World Records* for the world's longest *butifarra* (sausage), a Freudian nightmare measuring 5200m.

🚆 TRANSPORTATION

RENFE trains (☎972 88 01 65) run to: **Barcelona** (3hr., 6 per day 6:33am-6:50pm, €7) and **Ripoll** (1¼hr., 6 per day 6:33am-6:50pm, €2.60). **Alsina Graells buses** (☎973 35 00 20) run to **Barcelona** (3¼hr., 2-4 per day, €12) and **La Seu d'Urgell** (1hr., 7 per day, €4). Buses depart in front of the train station and from Pl. Barcelona; purchase tickets on board. See the schedule in Bar Estació, to the right in the train station. Taxis (☎972 88 00 11) wait on Pl. Cabrinetty. For **bike rental**, try **Sports Iris**, Av. de França, 16. (☎972 88 23 98. Bikes €9 per half day, €15 per day. MC/V.)

✦ 🛈 ORIENTATION & PRACTICAL INFORMATION

Puigcerdà's center sits at the top of its own hill. Off the main plaza, **Plaça Ajuntament** is nicknamed *el balcón de Cerdanya* for its commanding view of the valley. The less picturesque **train station** is at the foot of the western slope. Buses stop at the train station and then Pl. Barcelona; get off at the second stop. To reach Pl. Ajuntament from the inconvenient train station, walk past the stairs in the station's *plaça* until you reach the first real flight of stairs (between 2 buildings). Turn right at the top, then look for the next set of stairs on your left, just before a sign for C. Hostal del Sol. Turn left at the top onto Raval de les Monges where the final set of stairs winds up to the right (make sure not to take the prior set). From the *plaça* walk one block on C. Alfons I to **Carrer Major**, the principal commercial street. Turn left on C. Major to Pl. Santa Maria. From Pl. Santa Maria with your back to the bell tower, head out diagonally to the left to Pl. Barcelona.

Tourist Office: C. Querol, 1 (☎/fax 972 88 05 42), off Pl. Ajuntament. Open M-Tu and F-Sa 9am-2pm and 3-8pm, W-Th 10am-1:30pm and 4:30-7:30pm, Su 10am-2pm.

Bank: Banco Santander Central Hispano, on Pl. Cabrinetty. Open Oct.-Mar. M-F 8:30am-2pm, Sa 8:30am-1pm; closed Sa Apr.-Sept. 24hr. **ATM** available.

Emergency: ☎091. **Municipal police,** Pl. Ajuntament, 1 (☎972 88 19 72). **Hospital: Hospital de Puigcerdá** in Pl. Santa Maria (☎972 88 01 50), behind the *campanari.*

Internet: Punt Com, C. d'Espanya, 10 (☎972 88 31 55). €1.20 per 30min. Open daily 10am-1pm and 4-8pm.

Post office: Av. Coronel Molera, 11 (☎972 88 08 14). 1½ blocks down from Pl. Barcelona. Open M-F 8:30am-2:30pm, Sa 9:30am-1pm. **Postal Code:** 17520.

ACCOMMODATIONS & FOOD

Rooms in Puigcerdà come easily, if not relatively cheaply. Most less-expensive pensiones are off Pl. Santa Maria in the old town. Try the inexpensive **Hostal Muntanya ❷,** Av. Coronel Molera, 1. Muntanya offers basic, well-kept rooms and a friendly, helpful staff. From Pl. Barcelona head down Av. Coronel Molera; it's on the left. (☎97 288 02 02. Singles €19; doubles €38; triples €57. Breakfast €3.) **Alfonso Habitaciones ❷,** C. d'Espanya, 5, offers decent, dimly-lit rooms with TVs, bathrooms, and colorful bedspreads. Heading away from the church, take a left off C. Alfons I (☎972 88 02 46. Singles €30; doubles €42. Cash only). If you're looking for something a bit nicer, try the three-star **Avet Blau Hotel ❺,** Pl. Santa Maria, 14 (right next to the bell tower) which has six spacious and comfortable doubles. You can even bring your dog, provided you don't leave it alone in the room. (☎972 88 25 52; fax 97 288 12 12. Rates vary by season, from €71 to €97. Reservations recommended.) If you're planning to ski in La Molina, try **Mare de Déu de les Neus (HI) ❶,** on Ctra. Font Canaleta, which has modern facilities and an excellent location just 500m from the La Molina RENFE station and 4km from the slopes. In winter a bus goes up to the slopes every 30min. (☎972 89 20 12; reservations ☎934 83 83 63. Breakfast included. Sheets €2. Reserve in high season. Jan.-Nov. dorms €15, over 25 €20. Dec. dorms €17/€22. Doubles and triples available, same price per person. MC/V.) **Camping Stel ❷,** 1km from Puigcerdà on the road to Llivia, offers full-service camping with the benefits of a chalet-style restaurant, bar, and lounge. (☎972 88 23 61. Site with tent and car €20, plus €5 per person. 220V electricity for €3. Open Sa-Su only June-Sept. and Oct. 27-May 1).

The neighborhood off C. Alfons I has many food options. For fresh produce, try the weekly **market** at Pl. 10 d'Abril. (Su 6am-2pm.) Get **groceries** at **Bonpreu,** Av. Colonel Molera, 12, the small supermarket diagonally across from the post office. (Open Su 10am-2pm, M-Th 9am-1:30pm and 5-9pm, F-Sa 9am-9pm. MC/V.) At **Cantina Restaurant Mexicà ❷,** Pl. Cabrinetty, 9, you can kick back with a margarita and take in some excellent and relatively authentic Mexican tacos, fajitas, and quesadillas. (☎972 88 16 58. Entrees €4-15. Open Su-W and F-Sa 1:30-3:30pm and 8:30-11:30pm.) **El Pati de la Tieta ❷,** C. Ferrers, 20, serves large portions of pasta and pizzas (€6-10) and heavenly desserts on an ivy-covered patio. (☎972 88 01 56. Fish and meat entrees €11.50-17. Open daily 1-3:30pm and 8-11:30pm. MC/V.)

SIGHTS & SLOPES

Between ski runs and cycling, dash over to the **campanario,** the octagonal bell tower in Pl. Santa Maria. This 42m high 12th-century tower is all that remains of the **Església de Santa Maria,** an eerie reminder of the destruction wreaked by the Civil War. Climb to the top for 360° views of Puigcerdà and the Pyrenees. (Open July-Aug. M-F noon-2pm and 5-8pm; Sa-Su 11am-noon and 5-8pm. Free.) The 13th-

THE BIG SPLURGE

BOÍ OH BOÍ!

You may have thought that the invigorating fresh air of the mountains and serenity of the outdoors would be enough to enliven your spirit while travelling through the Pyrenees. But maybe you have realized that hiking is just exhausting. Never fear, for just up the mountain from the tiny village of Boí, at the western edge of the Parque Nacional de Aiguestortes, lie the Caldes de Boí, natural hot springs long famous for the water which is still bottled here. Today the Hotel Caldas, newly renovated from a 17th-century hotel-and-church complex, provides the perfect place to stay while you enjoy the therapeutic properties of the Caldes' celebrated waters. The hotel complex offers several salons, decorated in the dark reds and greens of traditional hunting lodges, as well as outdoor terraces, swimming pools, and miniature golf, all at a breathtaking 1500m. The spa complex offers a variety of health treatments, but be sure not to miss the *estufas naturales:* unique in all of Europe, these natural saunas are built directly into the mountain-side, and draw their heat from deep within the mountain itself. ☎ *932 72 26 47; www.caldesdeboi.com. €56.90-€107.66 per person, and per night, with a variety of multiday package deals available. For more information contact: Caldes de Boí, Pau Claris, 162, Barcelona, 08037.*

century **Església de Sant Domènec,** on Pg. 10 d'Abril, contains several Gothic paintings considered to be among the best of their genre. (Open 9:30am-8pm. Free.) Puigcerdà's picturesque **Lake Estany,** a 2min. walk up C. Pons i Gasch from Pl. Barcelona, was created in 1380 for irrigation purposes. It now serves the town well as a lovely place to rent a boat (€2 per person per 30min.; inquire at the cafe).

Puigcerdà calls itself the "capital of snow." **Ski** in your country of choice (Spain, France, or Andorra) at one of 19 ski areas within a 50km radius. The closest and cheapest one on the Spanish side is **La Molina** (☎972 89 20 31; www.lamolina.com). Nearby **Masella** (☎972 14 40 00; www.masella.com) offers the longest run in the Pyrenees at 7km. For cross-country skiing, the closest site is **Guils** (☎972 19 70 47). A little farther out, try **Lles** (☎973 29 30 49) or **Aransa** (☎973 29 30 51). The Puigcerdà area is also popular for **biking;** the tourist office has a map with 17 routes. La Molina opens trails for biking in the summer months and provides rentals for €12.62 per day. You can also navigate the trails on horseback for €12 for an hour-long excursion. **Club Poliesportiu Puigcerdà,** on Av. del Poliesportiu, has a pool, tennis courts, basketball courts, and a skating rink. (☎972 88 02 43. Open M-F 11am-10pm, Sa 11am-9:30pm, Su 11am-8pm. €3.80 per sports facility or €6 per day.)

PARC NACIONAL D'AIGÜESTORTES I ESTANY DE SANT MAURICI

Catalunya has only one national park, but it's a big one. The **Estany de Sant Maurici,** in the east, is the park's largest lake; in the west, the wild tumbling of the Riu de Sant Nicolau through its own valley has earned it the nickname "Aigües Tortes" (Twisted Waters). Flocks of sheep roam the park's wildflower-dusted meadows as golden eagles soar above its snow-capped peaks. With more than 100 glacial lakes and over 10,000 hectares to explore, the park merits at least two days—using public transportation, it's hard to do it in fewer than three.

Free maps from the tourist offices (see below) list well-defined itineraries, but the explorer may want to drop the extra cash to buy a more detailed map (€7 in the office; available in area stores for a bit more). The red *Editorial Alpina* guides for Montardo, Vall de Boí, and Sant Maurici are particularly useful (€3).

Trail accessibility and difficulty varies by season. One particularly popular hike is the east-west traverse from Espot to Boí, an easy enough hike, but a lengthy 15km from park entrance to park entrance (see below for more on the towns themselves). **Espot** is 8km from **Estany de Sant Maurici** (2hr., Apr.-Nov., moderate difficulty due to duration). From the lake, a path climbs 2.5km to the **Portarró d'Espot**, the gateway between the park's two halves and a prime spot for viewing the scenery (June-Oct.; low difficulty, moderate if you choose to continue up to the peak of **Portarró**). Those with a car may opt for half the hike by parking in the last public access lot inside the park. From the pass it is nearly 2km to **Estany Llong** and the **Aigüestortes** themselves (about 3½hr. from Estany de Sant Maurici; June-Oct. moderate difficulty). Near the western tip of Estany Llong lies the park's first *refugio*, **Refugi d'Estany Llong ❶** (☎973 69 61 89. Open mid-June to mid-Oct. and winter weekends. In summer €6.10 per person, €6.80 in winter.) The western park entrance is a 3.5km hike from Estany Llong, and to **Boí** itself another 6.5km (May-Nov., moderate difficulty due to duration). The entire hike takes around 9hr., but can be shortened by taking a jeep from Espot (see Espot, below) to Estany de Sant Maurici or a taxi from the western entrance to Boí.

For more detailed hiking info, contact the park **tourist offices** (Espot ☎973 62 40 36, Boí 69 61 89). The park's five *refugios* (€8-10 per person) and *casas de pagés* (lodging in private homes) are good options for those planning multi-day treks.

> **!** The mountains appear calm from afar, but the region's notoriously unpredictable weather can be quite dangerous, especially in winter. Casual wandering is not recommended. Though the main trails are clearly marked, it is easy to become lost should one stray into the mountainsides.

ESPOT & ESTANY DE SANT MAURICI

The official gateway to the eastern half of the park and the best point of entrance coming from Barcelona, the tiny town of **Espot** is comprised mostly of rustic restaurants and quiet accommodations for the weary hiker. Espot is a good 4.5km from the actual entrance of the park, but the walk to it is quite scenic. Those with cars can park at the last parking lot, just outside the park entrance.

TRANSPORTATION. A four-wheel-drive **jeep service,** C. Sant Maurici, s/n (☎973 62 41 05. Dec.-Mar. 9am-5pm; July-Sept. 15 9am-8pm; Sept. 16-Nov. and Apr.-June 9am-7pm) next to the tourist office navigates the bumpy back roads from Espot to: **Amitges** (round-trip €15.50 per person), a view-blessed site near the park's biggest and best **refugio** (see below); **Estany Negre de Pegura** (€19 per person), a much less frequented area of the park; **Estany de Ratera** (€12 per person) dropping off passengers to hike down to the waterfall, then picking them up below; **Estany de Sant Maurici** (€8 round-trip per person). Unfortunately for those relying on public transportation, the **Alsina Graells bus** (☎932 65 68 66) from Barcelona (3hr., 1 per day M-Sa 1:30pm, €24)—the only mass transit in the area—only comes within 7km of Espot, on highway C-147 at the La Torrassa crossing. Ask to get off in **la Guingueta d'Aneu,** where you can call the jeep service for pickup. (☎973 62 41 05. €12 to Espot. Jeeps are operated by a driver and seat 7-8 people.)

PRACTICAL INFORMATION. The bustling **park information office** on the right as you enter Espot) provides brochures and trekking advice. (☎973 62 40 36. Open daily Apr.-Oct. 9am-1pm and 3:30-7pm; Nov.-Mar. M-Sa 9am-2pm and 3:30-6pm.) Police ☎085. In a medical **emergency,** call ☎973 62 10 05.

ACCOMMODATIONS & CAMPING. The tourist office has a list of the many local residences that take in travelers; you can often find good deals. The intrepid wanderer who happens upon one of the many shepherd's huts that dot the

CATALUÑA

park may find adequate shelter within. Be warned: safety and comfort are not assured. Cross the main bridge to **Residència Felip ❸** for comfortable rooms with a down-home touch. Follow the bridge road for two blocks and then take a left; the *residència* is just behind Hotel Roya. (☎973 62 40 93. Oct.-June doubles €24.04, with bath €30. July-Sept. and holidays €30.04/€36.) In the park proper is **Refugi d'Amitges ❶**. (☎973 25 00 07 or 25 01 09. Open Feb. 10-25, Apr. 7-16, Apr. 29-May 1, June-Sept., and holidays year round except Christmas.)

Those devoted to the ascetic life may be disappointed by the camping in Espot; all locations provide food, games, water, showers, and a selection of other amenities as well. **Casa Peret de Peretó ❶** and **Camping Solau ❶** (☎973 62 40 68) run a joint establishment, offering spacious, sunny rooms inside and 22 campsites outside on the sprawling front yard. (Doubles €36; campsites €3.85 per person, per tent, and per car.) Located 1.3km down the park entrance road on the right, **Camping Vora Parc ❶** offers the closest camping to the park, with sites along the riverbank. The stone entryway and manicured lawn are indicative of the carefully maintained sites. (☎973 25 23 24. €4.10 per person, per tent, and per car. MC/V.) **Camping de la Mola ❶** (☎973 62 40 24) and **Camping Sol i Neu ❶** (☎973 62 40 01), both on the way to Espot, provide comparatively cushy camping with laundry, market, and bar. (Open June 1-Sept. 30 and *Semana Santa*. €4.20 per person, per tent, and per car; €11.30 for all three; electricity €4.20. MC/ V.)

AIGÜESTORTES & VALL DE BOÍ

Despite the nearby ski resort in **Taüll**, Boí hasn't lost its country charm. The village's cobblestone streets wind their way through low arches and mini-plazas. Boí is the most convenient base from which to explore the western half of the park. Green RCPs (*Residencias Casa de Pagés*) indicate the many local residences offering traveler's accommodation. Although very safe, most of these private residences do not accept credit cards, have very limited space (usually only 1-2 rooms), and change hours depending on the whim of the host. Inquire at the tourist office for a comprehensive price listing of local hostels and houses.

Public transportation from the east to the medieval village is difficult but possible through **Vielha**, or through **Lleida** via Pont de Suert. If you have no other options, it's worth a try. From Lleida, catch the 9am Alsina Graells bus from Barcelona on its way to Pont de Suert. From July-Sept. 15, catch the daily 11:15am connecting bus from Pont de Suert to Boí; in winter, a school bus makes the run Wednesday and Friday at 2pm and Monday-Tuesday and Thursday at 5:30pm. From Boí's main *plaça* it's an easy taxi ride to the park. (☎973 69 63 14, in winter ☎629 20 54 89. €4 per person. €7 round trip. 8am-7pm.) Boí's **park info office** is near the bus stop on the *plaça*. (☎973 69 61 89. Open daily Apr.-Oct. 9am-1pm and 3:30-7pm, Nov.-Mar. M-Sa 9am-2pm and 3:30-6pm.) Reach the **Mossos d'Esquadra** (Catalan police) at ☎973 69 08 15. **Police** ☎088. In an **emergency** call ☎112 or 973 69 11 59.

For a more reliable option, visit one of Boí's *hostales*. **Hostal Beneria ❸**, C. Treijo, s/n (☎973 69 60 30), offers affordable prices, big, clean rooms, and a comfortable TV lounge with huge leather chairs. (Just past Hotel Pey off the main road. Dinner *menú* €10. Breakfast included. Singles €26; doubles €45.) **Hostal Fondevila ❷**, to the right of the main road through Boí, has palatial rooms with bath. (☎/fax 973 69 60 11. Reception 9am-10pm. July 18-Aug. 25 and Christmas-*Semana Santa* singles €34; doubles €48; triples €60. Rest of the year €27/€43/€55. MC/V.) At **Restaurante Pey ❸**, Pl. Treijo, 3 (☎973 69 60 36), you can sit down in the homey, sunny dining room and enjoy big servings of tasty entrees with the locals. The roasted chicken is delicious. (*Menú* €11.20. Open daily 1-4pm and 8-11pm.)

VAL D'ARAN

Some of the Catalan Pyrenees's most dazzling peaks cluster around green Val d'Aran, Catalunya's northernmost valley. Val d'Aran's main river flows into France and is hemmed in tightly by the highest peaks in the eastern range; consequently, the area's original native language is not Catalan but Aranés, a dialect close to *langue d'oc*, the medieval Romance language spoken in southern France. Today, modern transportation and the tourist industry have made substantial inroads into the valley's unique isolation, but it is still well worth exploring.

SWM SEEKING...

Tall, dark, handsome, rich, famous, powerful, and searching for life partner. Enjoys water sports (competed on the Olympic sailing team). Educated at Georgetown. Looking for that special someone—attractive, charismatic, and preferably of noble lineage—to share interests and raise a family. His name is Felipe, the Prince of Asturias and heir to the Spanish throne. With his 30th birthday just behind him and his two elder sisters recently married, all eyes are on Felipe. Whom will he choose to be his queen when he takes over one of Europe's few powerful monarchies? The competition is fierce. Lovely ladies from wealthy families are stalking the streets of Madrid and the slopes of the Val d'Aran, but so far there are no front-runners. Cross your fingers and pack something nice—you could be the next queen of Spain.

BAQUIERA-BERET & SALARDÚ

Baquiera-Beret is Spain's most chic ski resort; after all, the Spanish royal family's favorite slopes are here. Currently, about 80 alpine trails and a few cross-country ones wind down the surrounding peaks. For skiing info and reservations, contact the **Oficeria de Baquiera-Beret** (☎973 64 44 55; fax 64 44 88).

Budget accommodations have disappeared from the ski resort itself, but never fear: upstairs above the umbrella tables of Bar Montanha, the rooms of **Pensión Montanha ❷**, C. Major, 8 provide a cheap sleep. With your back to the central pizzeria, head up the front-facing side street, keeping an eye out for signs pointing to Bar Montanha. (☎973 64 41 08. Singles €18, with bath €25; doubles €25/€31.) Just up the street on Pl. Mayor, **Pensión Villa Maladetta ❷** (☎973 64 60 04) boasts big rooms with TVs and full bath. Great balcony view from the common room; ping-pong and chess in the TV lounge downstairs. (Dinner *menú* €6. July-Aug. €19 per person, May-June and Sept.-Oct. €14.76. Breakfast included. MC/V.)

Upscale restaurants abound in Baquiera-Beret and Salardú, but you haven't really eaten in style until you've hit **Eth Cabilac ❸**, C. Major, 12, next door to Pensión Montanha. Elegant food and service at reasonable prices makes Eth Cabilac a must-eat. (☎973 64 42 82. *Menú* €15. Entrees €7-15. Open daily 1-4pm and 8-11pm.) Just down the street from the church is **El Horno ❶**, C. Sant Andreu, 3, with cheap, delicious pastries you can smell a block away. (☎636 32 58 20. Pastries €0.80-€1.20. Orange juice €1. July-Aug. and Dec.-Apr. open daily 8am-2pm and 6-8pm; May-Nov. Tu-Sa 8am-2pm and 6-8pm, Su 8am-2pm.)

The town of **Salardú**, a few kilometers away, has an enormous youth hostel, the **Auberja Era Garona (HI) ❶**, Ctra. de Vielha, s/n. The hostel is accessible during high season by shuttle bus from Vielha (€0.80) and offers dorms of four and six beds, as well as bike and ski rentals through the reception desk. (☎973 64 52 71. Breakfast included. Weekend Dec.-Apr. and *Semana Santa* €16, over 25 €18.50; weekdays Dec.-Apr. and July-Sept. €13/€15.50. May-June and Sept. 16-Nov. €11/€12.) While in town, don't miss the saint-painted ceiling of Salardú's 13th-century **Església de Sant Andreu** and its incredible garden view. The town of **Vielha** is only 12km from Baquiera-Beret, and the two are

CATALUÑA

connected by a shuttle bus in July and August. Check at the tourist office for schedules. (☎973 64 51 97. July-Aug. daily 10am-1:30pm and 4-8pm, Sept.-June Tu-Su 10:30am-1:30pm and 4:30-7:30pm.

VIELHA

The biggest town in Val d'Aran, Vielha (pop. 7000) combines the warmth of its small old quarter with the bustling activity of the main commercial thoroughfare. From its prime location, Vielha welcomes hikers and skiers to its lively streets with every sort of service the outdoorsy-type might desire.

TRANSPORTATION & PRACTICAL INFORMATION. Alsina Graells (☎973 27 14 70 or 932 65 68 68) runs buses from Vielha to **Barcelona** (5½hr.; 2 per day 5:30am, 1:30pm; €23.66) and **Baquiera-Beret** (20min., 7 per day 8:20am-7:45pm, €0.80). For a Cardona **taxi** call ☎973 64 22 60. The **tourist office,** C. Sarriulèra, 10, is one block up river from Pl. dera Glèisa (look for the big wooden "i.") Staff assists hikers, skiers, and Romanesque-seekers alike. (☎973 64 01 10; fax 64 03 72. Open daily 9am-9pm.) **ATMs** pepper main Av. Castièro, which intersects the river before turning into Av. Pas d'Arró. Services include: **emergency** ☎112; **police** ☎973 64 09 72; **Internet access** at **CCV Informática,** C. Aneto, 7a. (☎973 64 12 88. Open M-F 9:30am-1:30pm and 4:30-8:30pm, Sa 9:30am-1:30pm. €4.21 per hr. MC/V.) The **post office,** C. Sarriuléra, 6, is by the tourist office. (☎973 64 09 12. Open M-F 8:30am-2:30pm, Sa 9:30am-1pm.) **Postal Code:** 25530.

ACCOMMODATIONS & FOOD. Budget travelers in need of a treat can put their feet up at the elegant yet homey █**Hotel El Ciervo** ❷, Pl. Sant Orenç, 3. Standing on the bridge with your back to the tourist office, head downhill to the left. Upon entering the plaza, turn left to face the hotel's light green, mural-bedecked exterior. (☎973 64 01 65; fax 64 20 77. Apr.-Oct. singles €20; doubles €36. Dec.-Mar and Aug. €35/€50. €9 extra for rooms with jacuzzis. Closed Nov. and the last two weeks in June.) Several other inexpensive *pensiones* also fill the end of C. Reiau, off Pg. Libertat (which intersects Av. Castièro at Pl. Sant Antoni). **Pensión Casa Vicenta** ❷, C. Reiau, 3, with its great mattresses and modern furnishings, comes highly recommended. (☎973 64 08 19. Dec.-*Semana Santa* and July 15-Sept. 15 singles €25; doubles €40. Rest of the year €18/€30. Closed Oct.-Nov.)

Quiet your rumbling stomach at the inviting **Restaurant Basteret** ❷, C. Mayor 6A, tucked into a corner facing the tourist office just across the river. Friendly staff and a well-priced daily *menú* (€8.50, including a glass of wine) make this a great spot. (☎973 64 07 14. Open daily June 1-Sept. 15 1-4pm and 8-12pm. Closed the last two weeks of Oct. and M from Sept. 16-May. MC/V.) **Eth Breç** ❶, Av. Castièro, 5, beneath Hotel d'Aran along the main road, serves incredible pastries and a selection of teas. (☎973 64 00 50. Open daily 8am-2pm and 4-9pm. MC/V.) **Era Plaça** ❶, Pl. dera Glèisa, s/n (☎973 64 02 49), serves up big pizzas (€5-7) and even bigger sandwiches (€3-4), as well as a wide selection of *raciones* for €4-8. (Just across the main road from the church. Open daily 9am-1:30am.)

SIGHTS & ENTERTAINMENT. Iglesia de San Miguel, a simple 12th-century Romanesque church, houses the intricate *Crist de Mijaran.* The church is to your left in the plaza, facing the tourist office. (Open daily 11am-8pm.) The ethnographic collection at the **Muséu de Val d'Aran,** C. Mayor, 26, sheds light on Aranese culture. (☎973 64 18 15. Open Tu-Sa 10am-1pm and 5-8pm, Su 11am-2pm. €2.) Vielha is a good base for many **outdoor activities. Camins,** Av. Pas d'Arró, 5, in the shopping gallery, is a great place to start. Staff can answer questions, organize **treks** into the Aigüestortes (from €20), lead **rafting** and **horseback trips,** and rent

mountain bikes. Ask about the popular half-day bike trip (26km one-way) to Camino Real/Vielha-Les, which promises a great workout and spectacular views. (Bikes half-day €15, full-day €21.) In conjunction with the **Escola Snowboard Val d'Aran,** Camins can also teach you how to **snowboard** (Escola ☎973 64 51 26; fax 64 41 54. Open M-F 9am-1pm and 4-8:30pm; Sa call ahead.)

When the sun goes down, the ready-to-rage of all ages run to **Eth Clót,** a self-proclaimed *bar musical.* Warm up at tables below before heading to the upstairs dance floor. (Beer €2.50. Mixed drinks €5). The bar is the perfect place to quench your grind-induced thirst and refuel for a fierce game of foosball. (Just beyond Hotel El Ciervo near Pl. Sant Orenç. Open daily 10:30pm-3am; closed Su in Oct.)

LLEIDA (LÉRIDA)   ☎973

A fair number of camera-toting visitors pass through industrious but unassuming Lérida (pop. 120,000) to see its impressive cathedral alongside the Río Segre.

⌐ TRANSPORTATION. RENFE trains (☎902 24 02 02), Pl. Berenguer IV. Trains to: **Barcelona** (2-4hr., 14 per day 5am-8:53pm, €8.10-19); **Madrid** (5hr., 3 per day 8:41am-1:25am, €34-49.50); **Tarragona** (1½-2hr., 9per day 2:48am-5:55pm, €4.25-13); and **Zaragoza** (2-4hr., 9 per day 8:41am-2:49am, €14.50-19.50). **Central Buses** (☎973 26 85 00) stop near the intersection with Av. de Catalunya. Buses to: **Andorra** (2-3hr., M-Sa 6 per day 10:15am-11pm; Su 8pm; €15.) **Barcelona** (2¼-2¾hr., 9 per day 6am-7:30pm, €14.55); **Girona** (3½hr.; Sept. 17-June 3 per day 6am-6:30 pm, July-Sept. 11 4 per day 7:30am to 5:30pm; €15.80); **Tarragona** (2hr.; M-F 6 per day 7:30am-9:15pm, Sa-Su 9:30am and 9:15pm; €4); **Zaragoza** (2¼hr., 5 per day 8am-6pm, €8-9). Yellow **city buses** (☎973 27 29 99) run throughout the city; the tourist office has a map and schedule. The most useful are the "Exterior" bus (#10) from the train station to the center, which stops along Av. de Madrid, and #15 between the train station and Seu Vella (€0.75). For a **taxi,** call **Radio Taxi** (☎973 20 30 50).

■⍰ ORIENTATION & PRACTICAL INFORMATION. Bordered by the Río Segre, Lérida sprawls up the hill toward Seu Vella. **Calle Major,** one block inland from the river, is the city's principle commercial street. Major banks and the post office line **Rambla de Ferran,** near the train station. Av. de Madrid, Av. de Catalunya, Rambla d'Aragó, and Seu Vella frame the center of the city. Pl. Sant Joan, at the end of C. Major, is for all practical purposes the tourist's center, with several hostels. Lérida has two main **tourist offices.** For info, head to the office at C. Major, 31, the street parallel to the river and one block inland. (☎973 70 03 19. Open M-F 11am-8pm, Sa 10am-8pm, Su 10am-1:30pm.) The office at Av. de Madrid, 36, around the corner from the bus station, has regional information. (☎973 27 09 97; fax 973 27 09 49. Open June-Sept. M-F 9am-2pm and 3-8pm, Sa 9am-2pm; Oct.-May M-F 9am-2pm and 3-7pm, Sa 10am-2pm.) **Banks** with 24hr. **ATMs** line Rbla. de Ferran. Other services include: **luggage storage,** at the train station (€4.50 for 24hr.), but none at the bus station; **emergency,** ☎091; **police,** Gran Passeig de Ronda, 52 (☎973 24 40 50); **Arnan de Vilanova Hospital,** Av. de l'Alcalde Rovira, 80 (☎973 24 81 00); **Cafetó Internet,** C. del Bonaire, 8. (☎973 72 51 48; €2 per hr.; open M-F 9am-2pm and 4pm-midnight, Sa 9am-2pm and 4pm-2am, Su 5pm-midnight); and the **post office,** C. Rambla de Ferran, 16, toward town from the train station. (☎973 24 70 00. M-F 8:30am-8:30pm, Sa 9:30am-2pm.) **Postal Code:** 25007.

⌂ ACCOMMODATIONS. Most budget accommodations (including those listed) double as student housing, so term-time (Oct.-June) space is limited. Sunny, freshly-painted rooms at the central **Hostal Mundial ❶,** Pl. Sant Joan, 4, provide abundant floor space, even with large beds and desks in every room. Ask for one with a balcony overlooking the plaza. (☎973 24 27 00. Singles with bath or shower €14; doubles with shower €22, with bath €26. Breakfast €3. M-F *menú* €6. Parking 9pm-9am €5.) **Alberg Sant Anastasi (HI) ❶**, Rbla. d'Aragó, 11, offers clean, 4-person rooms, free Internet, two TV lounges, and a game room. The halls can be noisy during the day, but are more subdued as bedtime approaches, thanks to the 11pm curfew. (☎973 23 60 99. €12.92; over 25 €17.43.) **Hotel Goya ❷**, C. Alcalde Costa, 9, up C. Catalunya from the river, provides comfortably-sized rooms with squeaky-clean bathrooms and framed posters. Each *habitación* comes with a desk, dresser, and small TV. (☎973 26 67 88. Singles €20; doubles €33; triples €45.)

◘ FOOD. Lérida's local specialty is *caragoles* (snails), and the city manages to consume over 12 slimy tons of them each year, most notably during their popular gastronomic festival, *Aplec del Caragol*, held the third weekend in May, F-Su night. The tourist office has a list of restaurants that serve a special *menú Xec Caragol* (€24) composed entirely of various snail dishes—some of the more popular dishes are snails cooked on a *llauna* (grill), served with *alioli* (mayonnaise and garlic), cooked with veggies on a stone tile, and *a la gormanta* (fried with seasonings). For those who would prefer to chop off one of their less important fingers than to eat snails, the area surrounding C. del Bonaire and Av. de l'Alcalde Rovira provides the majority of Lleida's restaurants, and the area around Seu Vella has a variety of tiny hole-in-the-wall establishments that serve African cuisine.

For a local favorite, head to **Iruña**, Pl. de Sant Llorenç, s/n. Inside the 17th-century farmhouse exterior, you'll find a comfortable family setting and huge courses of delicious Navarran-Basque specialties. (*Menú* €12. Open Tu-Su 1-4pm and 8-11pm.) Across from the bus station on Av. de Catalunya, the supermarket **Esclat** provides all your grocery needs. (Open 9am-9pm.) With its comfortable, attractive interior and friendly vibe, **Natural Blend**, C. Villa de Foix, 2 (in Pl. de la Catedral) is the perfect place to recharge with a coffee before heading back to C. Major for more shopping. (Open daily 8am-10pm.) To escape the afternoon heat, you can't beat **Sucs Suc**, Av. de l'Alcalde Rovira, 12, which doesn't. Though fruit smoothies are their specialty, you can also enjoy a wide variety of ice cream and crêpes (€3-4) underneath the model train zooming overhead. (☎973 22 08 56; www.turinet.net/empresa/servisucs. Entrees €5-10. Open 8am-1am. F-Sa 24hrs.)

◙ SIGHTS. High above the city, ▨**Seu Vella**, Lérida's amazing 14th-century cathedral and cloister was built upon the grounds of a Muslim mosque. When the city was conquered by Felipe V, whose plans to destroy the Seu Vella were going swimmingly until he died, both the mountaintop and Seu Vella itself were overtaken as a defensive fort. Military occupation lasted until 1948. Fine examples of architecture from the school of Lleida and 14th-century sarcophagi remain. For an excellent historical/architectural account of Seu Vella, get the audio tour for an additional €0.60. The long climb up to the **bell tower** is worth every step. Two of its seven bells are Gothic originals from the 15th century. To reach the cathedral, take the stairs or escalator up from Pl.Sant Joan; the elevator (€0.40) to your left takes you to La Seu. (☎973 23 06 53. Open daily June-Sept. 10am-1:30pm and 4-7:30pm, Oct.-May 10am-1:30pm and 3-5:30pm. Bell tower closes 30min. before rest of complex. €2.40, under 21 €1.80. under 5 and over 65 free. Tu free.)

The new **Centre d'Art de la Panera**, Pl. de la Panera, 2, houses rotating exhibitions of Catalan and Spanish art, with an emphasis on recent works. (☎973 70 03 94; cultura@paeria.es. Open Tu-Su 10am-2pm and 4-8pm. Tours Tu-Su 10am-1pm and 4-7pm, Su 10am-1pm. €3.) Lérida's Romanesque Ayuntamiento, the **Palau de la Paeria**, houses a small basement museum dedicated to the art and archaeology of the city. (C. Major. Open M-Sa 11am-2pm and 5-8pm, Sa 11am-2pm. Free.) The tiny and free **Museu d'Arte Jaume Morera** houses a rotating display of 19th- and 20th-century works; the permanent collection includes paintings by Morera himself. (C. Cavallers, 15, 2nd fl. ☎973 27 36 65. Open June 15-Sept. 15 Tu-Sa 10am-1pm and 6-9pm, Su 10am-1pm; Sept. 15-June 15. Tu-Sa 11am-2pm and 5-8pm, Su 11am-2pm.)

🔊📷 **NIGHTLIFE & ENTERTAINMENT.** The area surrounding C. del Bonaire is the best place to go bar hopping in Lleida, with **Can-Can, O'Sullivan's,** and **Maracas.**

The month of May is chock full of festivals. Besides the **Aplec del Caragol.** On May 11, the **Festa Major** is held in honor of hometown hero St. Anastasius, a Lleida native who served in the Roman army until he was martyred by order of Diocletian in 303. The festa offers colorful parades which culminate in a floral offering to the saint and the *batalla de les flors* (flower battle), as well as the ubiquitous presence of *Lo Marraco*, Lleida's resident dragon. The Sunday following the 11th witnesses a merry reenactment of the Christian victory over the Moors (arguably more merry for the Christians than the Moors), while the week of May 29 is spent celebrating the **Festivo Sant Miquel,** Lleida's patron saint.

From the end of June through September, the hillsides of Gardeny become **Gurugú,** a vast tent-city of drunken merriment, presented by a host of Lleida's bars. From Av. de Catalunya, turn left on C. Lluís Companys and follow it until Pl. dels Pagesos. Go through the plaza and turn left on C. de Saturn. Follow C. de Saturn until it ends at C. del Cardenal Cisneros, and turn left. Gurugú will be on your left. The walk isn't through the safest of neighborhoods, so try not to stray from the main streets, and travel in a group if possible. Or just take a taxi (€4). Cover €6, includes one drink.

CATALUÑA

ANDORRA

The tiny **Principat d'Andorra** (pop. 70,000) bills itself as "El País dels Pirineus," the country of the Pyrenees. Perhaps, however, Andorra is best described not as Pyre-nean, but as pyre-neon: the natural beauty of its mountain surroundings is easily matched by the artificial glitz of its flashy capital. For every nature loving visitor in search of the perfect hike or bike trail, there are a dozen bargain-hunters lured here by the sheer abundance of duty-free shopping. But Andorra is not at all embarrassed about its role as Europe's shopping mall. Far from it: Andorra embraces its unique culture, as proud of its flashy present as it is of its noble past. That past is one of rich history: according to legend, Charlemagne founded Andorra in 784 as a reward to the valley's inhabitants for having led his army against the Moors. For the next 12 centuries, the country played the rope in a game of tug-o'-war between the Spanish Counts of Urgell, the Church of Urgell, and the King of France. Not until 1990 did the country create a commission to draft a dem-ocratic constitution, adopted on March 14, 1993. For all its modern amenities, Andorra today is far less progressive than other EU nations. In the 1993 election, only the 13,000 native Andorrans (out of 65,000 total inhabitants) were granted the vote; women have had suffrage only since 1970.

Sandwiched between France and Spain, Andorra's citizens are comfortably tri-lingual, though proud of their place as the only nation where Catalan is the sole official language. Euros flow like water, as the absence of a sales tax draws con-sumers from all over Europe. Excellent skiing and biking opportunities, as well as frequent soccer matches, lure sports buffs across the border. With Andorran towns mere minutes apart thanks to the extensive local bus system, a single day can include wading through aisles of duty-free perfume, hiking through a pine-scented valley, and relaxing in a luxury spa.

⌷ TRANSPORTATION

The only way to get to Andorra is by car or bus. All traffic from Spain enters through the town of **La Seu d'Urgell;** the gateway to France is **Pas de la Casa.** Upon exiting Andorra, you must stop at customs for a brief and rubber-glove-less search.

BY BUS

Catch buses at **Estació Central d'Autobusos,** C. Bonaventura Riberaygua, in **Andorra la Vella. Andor-Inter/Samar** buses (in Madrid ☎914 68 41 90, in Toulouse 561 58 14 53, in Andorra 82 62 89) run from Andorra la Vella to **Madrid** (9hr.; Tu and F-Su 1 per day 11am; W-Th and Su 1 per day 10pm, €34.25) as does **Eurolines** (in Andorra ☎80 51 51, in Madrid 915 06 33 60; Tu-Th and Su 1 per day 11:30am, F and Su 1 per day 10pm; €33). **Alsina Graells** (Andorra ☎82 65 67) runs to **Barcelona** (4hr.; daily 5 per day 6:30, 7:30, 10:30am, 3, 6pm; €18), as does **Eurolines** (3¼hr.; daily 5 per day 6, 11am, 4, 6, 8pm; €18.50). To go anywhere in Spain other than Madrid or Barce-lona, first go to the town of La Seu d'Urgell on a **La Hispano-Andorra** bus (☎82 13 72; 30min., 5-7 buses per day, €2.50) departing from Av. Meritxell, 11. From La Seu, Alsina Graells buses continue into Spain via **Puigcerdà** (1hr.; 2 per day 8:30am, 6:15pm; €3.60) and **Lérida** (2½hr.; 2 per day 8:30am, 6:15pm; €10.10).

BY CAR

Driving in Andorra la Vella is an adventure for some, a nightmare for others. One of the Andorrans' less charming customs is their cheery refusal to put up any street signs whatsoever; navigating the cramped, crowded, twisting streets can prove a maddening chore for even the most patient driver. It's far better to ditch the car in

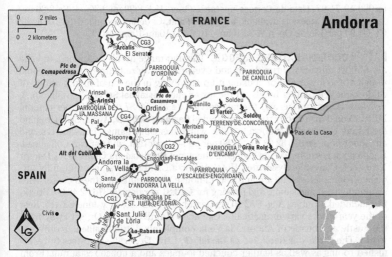

one of the many parking lots as soon as possible. Efficient intercity buses connect the villages along the three major highways that converge in Andorra la Vella. Since most towns are only 10min. apart, cities can be seen in a day via public transportation. Bus stops are easy to find, and rides are cheap, ranging from €0.70 to €1.70. All inter-city buses make every stop, so don't worry about finding the right bus—just ask the driver to alert you at your stop.

ANDORRA LA VELLA   ☎376

Andorra la Vella (pop. 20,760), the capital, is anything but *vella* (old): virtually a single cluttered road flanked by shop after duty-free shop, most of the old buildings have been upstaged by shiny new electronics and sporting goods stores. After doing a little shopping, you're best off escaping to the countryside.

■■ 7 ORIENTATION & PRACTICAL INFORMATION. Coming from Spain, visitors first pass through Sant Julià de Lòria and then tiny Santa Coloma, which runs directly into Andorra la Vella. The main thoroughfare **Avinguda Santa Coloma** becomes **Avinguda Príncep Benlloch** several blocks into the city, which in turn becomes **Avinguda Meritxell** at Pl. Príncep Benlloch before continuing on as the highway to parishes northeast of the capital. There are several **tourist offices** scattered throughout Andorra la Vella; the largest is on Pl. de la Rotonda. Multilingual staff offers free *Sports Activities* and *Hotels i Restaurants* guides. (☎376 82 71 17. Open July-Aug. M-Sa 9am-9pm, Su 9am-7pm; Sept.-June daily 9:30am-1:30pm and 3:30-7:30pm.) Exchange currency at **Banc Internacional,** Av. Meritxell, 32. (☎376 88 47 05. Open M-F 9am-1pm and 3-5pm, Sa 9am-noon.) In a **medical emergency** call ☎116 or the **police,** Prat de la Creu, 16 (☎376 87 20 00). For **weather and ski conditions,** call Ski Andorra (☎376 86 43 89). For **taxi** service, call ☎376 86 30 00.

Placing an international **telephone call** in Andorra is a chore. Many mobile plans do not service the area, and outside calling cards are just as futile; collect calls to most countries—including the US—are not possible. Buy an STA *teletarjeta* (telecard) at the tourist office or the post office (€3 min.). For directory assistance dial ☎111 or 119 (international). The **Spanish post office** is at C. Joan Maragall, 10.

(☎902 19 71 97. **Lista de Correos** upstairs. Open M-F 8:30am-2:30pm, Sa 9:30am-1pm.) **Internet access** is available at **Future@Point**, C. de la Sardana, 6. (☎376 82 82 02. €1.20 per 15min. Open M-Sa 10am-11pm, Su 10am-10pm. MC/V.)

⬛⬛ ACCOMMODATIONS & FOOD. The mid-range hotels in Andorra la Vella are almost universally run-down and overpriced; you're better off saving some dough at the lower end or sucking it up and living in the lap of luxury at one of Andorra la Vella's finer hotels. At the lower end, **Hostal del Sol ❶**, Pl. Guillemó, 3, provides decent rooms and friendly service. (☎376 82 37 01. €12.50 per person. MC/V.) You don't exactly rough it at shaded **Camping Valira ❶**, Av. de Salou, behind the Estadi Comunal d'Andorra la Vella, which has video games, hot showers, and an indoor pool. (☎376 82 23 84. €4.50 per person, per tent, and per car. Call ahead. Handicap accessible.) At the high end, check out **Hotel Andorra Center ❹**, C. Doctor Nequi, 12. Conveniently located Hotel Andorra Center offers beautiful, fully furnished rooms as well as a piano bar, in-house restaurants, a fitness center with swimming pool and sauna, and parking for €10.81 per day. (☎376 82 48 00. Breakfast included. Doubles Aug. €52.90 per person, July €26.35, May-June €22.15. Rest of the year prices vary dramatically. Call ahead. AmEx/MC/V.) Or, get away from the hustle and bustle of Andorra la Vella completely. Little **Canillo** is a different world. The three-star **Hotel Roc de Castell ❹**, Ctra. General, s/n, offers fully-furnished rooms as well as leather couched lounges and a house restaurant. From Andorra la Vella, drive straight through Canillo; the hotel will be on your left as you leave town. (☎376 85 18 25; hotelroccastell@andorra.ad. Breakfast €5. Singles €36; doubles €45.50.) **Camping Joan Ramón ❶**, Ctra. General s/n, offers extremely friendly service and the satisfaction of knowing you are as far away from Andorra la Vella as possible while still remaining in Andorra. (☎376 85 14 54. Open June 15-Sept. 20. Reception daily 9-11am and 6-9pm. If you arrive late, you can park and pay later. €2.95 per person, per tent, and per car.)

If you need proof of Andorra's cheesiness, look no further than ▣**La Casa del Formatge ❶**, C. les Canals, 4. Cheese, cheese, and more cheese await in this two-story cheese shop extravaganza. Enjoy the ample free samples while you browse the shelves of bovine statuary, or head to the wine shop upstairs. At the house restaurant you can dine on cheese entrees (€5-10) under the knowing gaze of a decidedly less-modest Mona Lisa draped in nothing but—what else?—cheesecloth. (☎376 80 75 75. Open M-F 10am-8pm, Sa 9:30am-9pm, Su 9:30am-7pm.) **Casa Teresa ❸**, C. Bonaventura Armengol, 11, has phenomenal spaghetti. If that's not enough, they also serve a variety of other delicious dishes, including large, creative pizzas, all in an elegant setting with servers who are both formal and friendly. Entrees are €7-15, pizzas run €5.25-5.85, and the *menú* costs €7.55. (☎376 82 64 76. Open daily 8am-4pm and 8-10:30pm; closed June 24-July 15.)

For shopping, check out one of the three-story supermarket monstrosities in nearby Santa Coloma, or the **Grans Magatzems Pyrénées**, Av. Meritxell, 11, the country's biggest department store, where an entire aisle is dedicated to chocolate bars. (Open Sept.-July M-F 9:30am-8pm, Sa 9:30am-9pm, Su 9:30am-7pm; Aug. and holidays M-Sa 9:30am-9pm, Su 9:30am-7pm.) Or head to **La Bauhaus**, C. Bonaventura Armengol, 11, and realize how much cooler you could actually be. A wide selection of stylish books, furniture, and other necessities of the hipster lifesyle. (☎376 86 32 36; www.labauhaus.com. Open M-F 10am-1:30pm and 3:30-8pm, Sa 10am-1:30pm and 3:30-9pm, Su 10am-2pm.)

⬛ EXCURSIONS. The best thing to do in Andorra la Vella is drop your bags in a hostel and get out. Nowhere is the contrast of old and new, or the uniquely Andorran acceptance of it, better on display than at the **Santuari de Meritxell** in

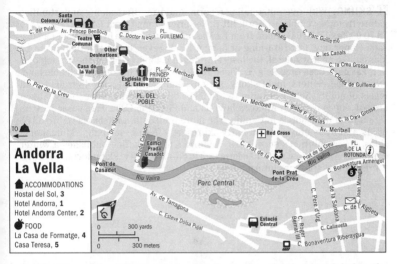

Andorra
La Vella

🏠 ACCOMMODATIONS
Hostal del Sol, 3
Hotel Andorra, 1
Hotel Andorra Center, 2
🍴 FOOD
La Casa de Formatge, 4
Casa Teresa, 5

Canillo. The original Romanesque chapel was completely remodeled in the 18th-century, which in turn burned down in 1972. The new chapel, built by Catalan architect Ricard Bofill in 1976, is an ultra-modern building which strives to incorporate elements of Andorra's disparate past: from the bell tower reminiscent of medieval moansteries to large apertures cut in an Islamic style. The Santuari houses a permanent collection dedicated to the patron saint of Andorra: the Virgin of Meritxell. (☎376 85 12 53. Open M and W-Su 9:15am-1pm and 3-6pm. Guided tours July-Oct. Free.) Have some fun in Canillo's colossal **Palau de Gel d'Andorra,** a recreational complex with swimming pool, ice-skating rink ("ice disco" by night), gym, tennis, and squash courts. Brace yourself on Fridays for the awesome power of ice-rink go-carts! (☎376 80 08 40. Open daily 10am-11:30pm; each facility has its own hours. €5.50-8 each or €12.20 for all in 1 day. Go-carts F 10:30pm-midnight. €13. Equipment rental €2.30-4.50.)

You won't believe the fantastically gaudy **Caldea-Spa,** Parc de la Mola, 10, in bordering **Escaldes-Engordany,** until you see it. It's what the Emerald City would be if the Wizard of Oz drank a lot of chablis and was really into Yanni. Enjoy an exfoliating Japanese Garden Grapefruit Bath, or some Lymphatic Facial Draining, using the Vodder method. (☎376 80 09 99. Open daily 9am-11pm. €24.50 for 3hr., plus fees for each service.) The 🖼**Microart Museum,** within the Caldea-Spa complex, houses an amazing collection of Chinese and Ukranian miniature art, including works by micromaster Nikolai Siadristy, who, using yogic breathing to steady his hand, created amazingly small, often microscopic objects, including the tiniest inscription ever made. (Open daily 9am-9pm. €3.)

🖼 🏔 **HIKING & THE OUTDOORS.** An extensive network of hiking trails traverses Andorra. The free, multilingual, and extremely helpful tourist office brochure *Sports Activities* includes 52 suggested itineraries and bike rental locations, as well as cabin and refuge locations within the principality. La Massana is home to Andorra's tallest peak, **Pic Alt de la Coma Pedrosa** (2946m). For organized hiking trips, try the **La Rabassa Sports and Nature Center** (☎32 38 68), in the parish of Sant Julià de Lòria. In addition to *refugio*-style accommodations, the center has mountain biking, guided hikes, horseback riding, archery, and field sports.

ANDORRA

⚒ SKIING. With five outstanding resorts, Andorra offers skiing opportunities galore from November to April; lift ticket prices range from €25-40. **Pal** (☎376 73 70 00; fax 83 59 04), 10km from La Massana, is accesible by bus from La Massana (5 per day, last returning at 5pm; €1.50). Seven buses run daily from La Massana to nearby **Arinsal,** the last returning at 6:45pm (€1). On the French border, **Pas de la Casa Grau Roig** (☎376 80 10 60) offers 600 hectares of skiable land, two medical centers, night skiing, lessons, and 27 lifts serving 48 trails for all levels of ability. **Soldeu-El Tarter** (☎376 89 05 00 or 89 05 01) occupies 840 hectares of slopes between Andorra la Vella and Pas de la Casa. **Free buses** pick up skiers from their hotels in Canillo. The more horizontal **La Rabassa** (☎376 32 38 68) is Andorra's only cross-country ski resort, offering sleighing, skiing, horse rides, and a children's snow park. Andorra's tourist office publishes a winter edition of *Andorra.* Call **SKI Andorra** (☎376 86 43 89; www.skiandorra.ad) or the tourist offices for more information.

ARAGÓN

A striking collage of semi-deserts and lush mountain peaks, Aragón's landscape reflects the influence of both Mediterranean and Continental climates. In the south lies a sun-baked assemblage of hardworking towns and flaxen plains, scattered with fine examples of ornate Mudéjar architecture. In the center, prosperous and industrious Zaragoza is Aragón's capital and the fifth-largest city in Spain. To the north, the stunning snow-capped peaks of the Pyrenees peer down at tiny medieval towns filled with Romanesque architecture. The Ebro, Spain's largest river, carves between these vastly different terrains.

Aragón's harsh climate, coupled with the region's strategic location, has produced a predominantly martial culture. Established as a kingdom in 1035 and united with enterprising Cataluña in 1137, Aragón forged a far-flung Mediterranean empire. But when Felipe II marched into Zaragoza in 1591, he brought the region to its knees. Economic decline followed political humiliation; as eyes turned to the New World, people (and capital) moved to the coast in search of wealth. Today, Aragón is back on its feet economically and, having gained autonomy in 1982, continues to expand its political influence. While the region's more bucolic areas continue to celebrate their traditional and popular festivals, its urban museums, parks, and historical sites have recently undergone massive restoration to improve their accessibility and attractiveness. Still, Aragón remains relatively tourist-free. Only some areas of the rural Pyrenees and the Parque Nacional Ordesa y Monte Perdido attract many visitors, and even those are mostly urban neighbors escaping the city heat during July and August.

HIGHLIGHTS OF ARAGÓN

TOAST yourself non-stop for a full week at **Teruel's** liquor fest (see p. 476).

ROUGH IT in the glorious **Parque Nacional de Ordesa** along the French border (see p. 483).

SPOT endangered Pyrenean bears in the **Valle de Ansó** (see p. 482).

ASCEND the Pyrenees' highest peak, Mt. Aneto, in **Benasque** (see p. 487).

FROLIC through the mountains, beginning in **Jaca** (see p. 478).

ZARAGOZA   ☎976

The political and cultural nexus of Aragón, beautiful Zaragoza (pop. 605,000) has found its charm in its relative international obscurity. A popular pilgrimage site ever since the Virgin Mary dropped in for a visit, it is just now making it to the top of many must-see lists. Augustus founded the city in 14 BC as a retirement colony for Roman veterans, lovingly naming it Caesaraugusta, after himself; the name was eventually blurred to Zaragoza. Though the narrow, winding streets of the *casco antiguo* remain largely intact, many of the city's major plazas and leafy *paseos* are currently torn up, to be reworked in the image of the grand Plaza del Pilar.

⌨ TRANSPORTATION

Flights: Airport☎ 976 71 23 00). **Iberia,** C. Canfranc, 9 (24hr. ☎902 40 05 00; www.iberia.com). Open M-F 9:30am-2pm and 4-7pm, Sa 9:30am-1:30pm. **Agreda Automóvil** (☎976 22 93 43 or 55 45 88) runs **buses** to the airport from Gran Vía, 4;

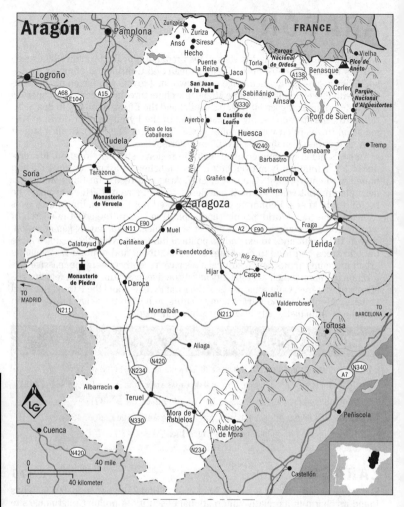

Aragón

Pl. de San Francisco; the Cámara de Comercio on Po. Isabel la Católica; and Vía Hispanidad, 100, in that order. Buses leave from Gran Vía, 4 (25min.; M-F 6, 10am, 2:45, 4:45, 6, 8, 9:15pm; Sa 6, 7, 10:15am, 2pm; Su 11:45am, 3, 7:30, 9pm; €1.50). **Taxi** to the airport approx. €14.

Trains: Estación Zaragoza-Delicias (24hr. ☎976 21 11 66), C. Rioja, 33. Taxi to Pl. de Pilar €5. Bus #51 makes several stops downtown, ending at Pl. de Basilio Paraíso (€0.65). Trains to: **Barcelona** (4hr., 14 per day 1:50am-7:00pm, €28); **Jaca** (3hr.; 2 per day 7:35am, 3:07pm; €8.90); **Lérida** (1½hr., 8 per day 2:30am-7pm, €19.50); **Logroño** (2¼hr.; 3 per day 6:30am, 5:45pm, 7:30pm; €9.25); **Madrid** (3hr., 11 per day 2:48am-11:00pm, €28); **Pamplona** (2¼hr.; 3 per day 11:30am, 2:33, 4:20pm; €9.25); **San Sebastián** (4hr., 4 per day 2:22am-5pm, €21); **Teruel** (3hr., 3 per day 8:10am, 3:45, 7:20pm; €7.45); **Valencia** (6hr.; 2 per day 8:10am, 3:45pm; €16.15).

Buses: Various bus companies dot the city, each with private terminals.

Agreda Automóvil, Po. María Agustín, 7 (☎976 43 45 10). Buses #20 and 21 stop in front. Open daily 7:30am-9pm. To: **Barcelona** (3½hr., 21 per day 1am-9:30pm, €11.20); **Madrid** (3½hr., 18-21 per day 1:15am-11pm, €11); **Soria** (2½hr.; M-Sa 3 per day 7:30am, noon, 4:30pm; Su 2 per day 9am, 2:15pm; €11.30). **Second Terminal,** Av. de Valencia, 20 (☎976 55 45 88). Enter on C. Lérida (bus #38). Buses to **Lérida** (2½hr., M-Sa 4 per day 6:45am-6:30pm, €8-9).

CONDA, Av. Navarra, 81 (☎976 33 33 72). From the station, turn right on Av. Navarra, bearing left onto Av. Madrid. Cross the pedestrian bridge. Or take bus #25 to Po. Pamplona. To **Pamplona** (2hr., 8 per day 7:15am-8:30pm, €10) and **San Sebastián** (3¼hr., 3 per day 7am-7pm, €16).

Grupo Autobús Jiménez, C. San Juan Pablo Bonet, 13 (☎976 27 61 79). To get to the station, take bus #33 from Pl. de España and watch for the road sign for C. San Juan Pablo Bonet after 2 stops on Po. de Sagasta. To **Logroño** (2½hr.; M-F and Sa 7 per day 7am-6:45pm, Sa 7am-9pm; €9.55) and **Teruel** (3hr., 4 per day 7am-6:30pm, €7.45).

La Ocense, Po. María Agustín, 7 (☎976 43 45 10). Shares a terminal with Agreda Automóvil. To **Jaca** (2¼hr., 3-4 per day 10:55am-9:40pm, €9).

Therpasa, C. General Sueiro, 22 (☎976 30 00 45). From the station, turn left and follow C. General Sueiro for 1½ blocks, then turn left again onto C. San Ignacio; turn right after 2 blocks into Pl. Basilio Paraíso. Goes to **Tarazona** (1½hr., 6 per day 10:30am-6:30pm, €5).

Public Transportation: Red TUZSA buses (☎976 59 27 27; www.tuzsa.es) cover the city (€0.65, 10-ride pass €4.08; tickets available at any kiosk). Bus #51 runs from the train station to Po. Pamplona, Pl. Basilio Paraíso, Pl. de Aragón, Pl. de España, Pl. del Pilar, and up C. San Vicente de Paul. Bus #33 is more central, passing through Po. de Sagasta, Pl. Basilio Paraíso, Po. de la Independencia, and Pl. de España.

Taxis: Radio-Taxi Aragón (☎976 38 38 38). Train station to Pl. del Pilar €4.

Car Rental: Avis, Po. Fernando el Católico, 9 (☎976 55 50 94). From Pl. Basilio Paraíso, take Gran Vía, following as it becomes Po. Fernando el Católico. €84 per day, includes insurance and 400km. 23+ with credit card and valid license. Open M-F 8am-1pm and 4-7pm, Sa 8am-12:30pm. MC/V. Other rental offices are at the train station.

■ ＊ ？ ORIENTATION & PRACTICAL INFORMATION

Bordered on the north by the Río Ebro, Zaragoza is laid out like a slightly damaged bicycle wheel. Five spokes radiate from the hub of **Plaza Basilio Paraíso.** Facing the center of the plaza with the IberCaja bank building at your back, the spokes going clockwise are: Po. de Sagasta; Po. Gran Vía, which becomes Po. Fernando el Católico; Po. Pamplona, which leads to Po. María Agustín and the **train station;** Po. de la Independencia, which ends at **Plaza de España** (the entrance to the *casco viejo*); and Po. de la Constitución, which leads to La Zona. Zaragoza is a fairly spread out city, and walking to or from the station proves to be a bit of a hike. To approach the old city from the train station, walk down C. Rioja to Av. Navarra and follow it until it becomes Av. Madrid. The *casco viejo* lies at the end of Po. de la Independencia and stretches between Pl. de España and **Plaza del Pilar.**

Tourist Office: Pl. del Pilar, s/n (☎976 20 12 00; www.turismozaragoza.com). Friendly, multilingual staff. Open daily 10am-8pm. The *Guía de servicios turísticos de Aragón,* available at any tourist office in the province, makes roaming easy, with information on accommodations and useful services. In summer, temporary **information booths** in front of many major sights offer information and free guided tours (hours vary by location).

Currency Exchange: Banks line Po. de la Independencia, with **ATMs** everywhere. **Banco Santander Central Hispano,** Pl. de Aragón, 6 (24hr. line ☎902 24 24 24) has good rates on travelers checks. Open M-F 8:30am-2:30pm, Sa 8:30am-1pm.

American Express: Viajes Turopa, Po. de Sagasta, 47 (☎976 38 39 11; fax 25 42 44). Enter around the corner, 6 blocks from Pl. Basilio Paraíso. Cannot cash travelers checks, but can give cash advances for AmEx cardholders. Bus #33 from Pl. de España stops nearby. Cardholder mail held. Open M-F 9am-1:30pm and 4-7:30pm.

El Corte Inglés: Po. de Sagasta, 3 (☎976 21 11 21); smaller store at Po. de la Independencia, 11 (☎976 23 86 44). Both open M-Sa 10am-10pm.

Luggage Storage: At the **train station** (small €2.40, large €3). Open 24hr. **Agreda Automóvil** bus station, Po. María Agustín, 7 (€1.20). Open M-F 10am-1:30pm and 4-7:30pm, Sa 10am-1:30pm. The other **Agreda Automóvil,** Av. de Valencia, 20 (€0.60 per piece per day). Open M-F 10am-2pm and 4:30-7:30pm, Sa 9am-noon. **Therpasa** bus station (€0.60). Open M-F 9am-1pm and 4:15-7:30pm, Sa 9am-12:45pm.

English-Language Bookstore: Librería General, Po. de la Independencia, 22 (☎976 22 44 83). Under the black and blue awning. 5 levels of tightly-packed shelves, with a fair English selection one floor down from the entrance. Open July-Aug. M-F 9:30am-1:30pm and 4:30-9pm, Sa 10am-2pm; Sept.-June M-F 9:30am-1:30pm and 4-8:30pm, Sa 10am-2pm and 3-9pm. AmEx/MC/V.

Laundromat: Lavandería Rossell, C. San Vicente de Paul, 27 (☎976 29 90 34). Wash and dry small load €6.30, medium €9, large €12. Open M-F 8:30am-1:15pm and 4:45-8pm, Sa 9am-1:30pm.

Emergency: ☎112. **Police:** ☎091 or 092, on C. Domingo Miral.

Medical Services: Hospital Universitario Miguel Servet, Av. Isabel la Católica, 1 (☎976 76 55 00).

Emergency: Ambulancias Cruz Roja, C. Sancho y Gil, 8 (☎976 22 48 80).

Internet Access: VIC Internet and Change Station, C. Florencio Jardiel, 3 (☎976 29 76 25). English spoken. €0.60 for 15min., €0.90 for 30min., €1.50 for 1hr. Open M-W 10am-10pm, Th-Su 10:30am-2:30pm and 5-10pm. Photo printing €0.70. **Cybercentro Zaragoza,** C. Ramón y Cajal, 45 (☎976 46 96 10). €1.50 for 1hr. Open daily 10am-2pm and 4-10:30pm.

Post Office: Po. de la Independencia, 33 (☎976 23 68 68). **Fax** and **Lista de Correos** downstairs. Open M-F 8:30am-8:30pm, Sa 9:30am-2pm. **Postal Code:** 50001.

▚ ACCOMMODATIONS

Small hostels and *pensiones* pepper the narrow streets of the central *casco viejo,* especially within the rectangle bounded by C. Alfonso I, C. Don Jaime I, Pl. de España, and Pl. del Pilar and along **Calle Madre Sacramento.** Be wary the week of October 12, when Zaragoza celebrates the *Fiesta de la Virgen del Pilar.* Make reservations as early as possible and expect to pay as much as double the rates listed below. *Ferias* (trade shows) are held from February through April (www.feriazaragoza.com), during which advance reservations are essential.

▨**Hostal Belén,** C. Predicadores, 2, 2nd fl. A and B. (☎976 28 09 13). This place is stocked: TV, A/C, heating, built-in radio, and full bathrooms in every room. F-Su doubles €50, M-Th €45. IVA included. ❹

Hostal Plaza, Pl. del Pilar, 14 (☎976 29 48 30 or 28 48 39; fax 39 94 06). Glistening modern bathrooms, TV, and phone in cozy but thin-walled rooms; interior rooms have A/C. Great location. Singles €25, with shower and sink €30; doubles €35-50. V. ❸

Albergue Juvenil Baltasar Gracián (HI), C. Franco y López, 4 (☎976 30 66 92, for reservations 71 47 97). Take bus #22 from the train station. On foot, turn right out of the station onto Av. Anselmo Clavé, take the 2nd right onto C. Burgos, following it for 6 blocks as it becomes C. Obispo Covarrubias, then turn right onto C. Franco y López. It's just past the basketball court on the corner. 50 beds in rooms of 2, 4, and 6. Quite out of the way, but a real deal. Sheets and breakfast included. Midnight curfew. Dorms €8.60-9.80, over 26 €11.56-12.84. ❶

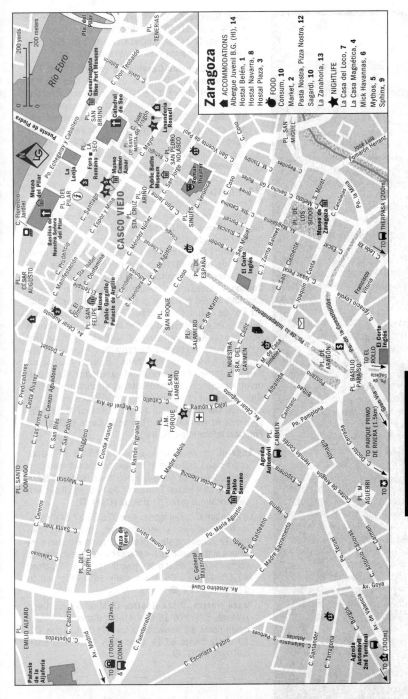

Zaragoza

■ **ACCOMMODATIONS**
Albergue Juvenil B.G. (HI), **14**
Hostal Belén, **1**
Hostal Navarra, **8**
Hostal Plaza, **3**

● **FOOD**
Consum, **10**
Market, **2**
Pasta Nostra, Pizza Nostra, **12**
Sagardi, **10**
La Zanahoria, **13**

★ **NIGHTLIFE**
La Casa del Loco, **7**
La Casa Magnética, **4**
Mick Havannas, **6**
Mythos, **5**
Sphinx, **9**

THE LOCAL LEGEND

SAINTLY SOUVENIR

Although she is frequently overshadowed by the amazing deeds of her internationally acclaimed son, the original Madonna had some adventures of her own. The blue-clad Virgin is said to have hiked from Jerusalem to Spain, arriving in the Roman city of Caesaraugustus (present-day Zaragoza) on January 2, AD 40. Mary carried with her the sacred pillar that still stands, encased in silver, in Zaragoza's awe-inspiring cathedral. The people of Aragón proudly sing that "she did not do anything like this with any other nation," reminding others that her visit was an actual "coming" rather than a mere spiritual apparition.

Zaragoza honors her divine visitor with famous shrines to the Black Virgin. A large portion of the ancient miraculous Madonnas of the world are, in fact, black; many of these resilient statues have survived centuries of war, fires, looting, and other tests of time. With regards to the origins of these shrines, many Christians simply accept that they are inexplicable mysteries of the divine feminine. The shrines are believed to have healing capabilities, and are places where brides might receive the blessing of fertility. Each manifestation of the ebony lady bears witness to an undoubtedly fantastic past.

Hostal Navarra, C. San Vicente de Paul, 30 (☎976 29 16 84 or 39 10 44). Comfortable rooms, some with balconies. TV lounge. Singles €17, with bath €21; doubles €26, with shower €29, with bath €32. ❷

Camping: Camping Casablanca (☎976 75 38 70), Barrio Valdefierro, down Ctra. de Madrid. Take bus #36 from Pl. del Pilar or Pl. de España to the suburb of Valdefierro. Ask the driver to let you off at the campsite, as it's difficult to find. Supermarket, bar, restaurant, and pool open in summer. Water and showers included. Open May-Sept. 5 and 2nd week of Oct. €4.50 per person, per tent, and per car; May-June 19 and Sept. 6-first week of Oct. €4.15 each. ❶

🍴 FOOD

Zaragoza considers itself Spain's unofficial *tapas* capital. Check out the tourist office-provided pamphlet, *Guía de Tapas.* The side streets flanking C. Don Jaime I have long been a traditional dinner area, and Pl. de Santa Marta is positively brimming with *tapas* bars, *restaurantes,* and *cervecerías* (such as **Domino, El Lino,** and **Cervecería Marpi**). More expensive and varied restaurants fill the streets branching off Po. de la Independencia. The freshest fruits and vegetables are stashed in the **market,** a long green building on Av. César Augusto off Pl. del Pilar, but you first have to get past the crowds. (Open M-F 9am-2pm and 5-8pm, Sa 9am-2pm.) Famed *frutas de Aragón,* chocolate-dipped and candied fruits in colorful wrappers, are available at almost any candy shop, souvenir store, or *carnicería.* Stock up on groceries at **Consum,** C. San Jorge, 22 (open M-Sa 9am-9pm), or at the supermarket in **El Corte Inglés** (see **Practical Information,** p. 469).

Sagardi, Pl. de España, 6 (☎976 23 16 77). Grab some *tapas* and *sidra* at the bar downstairs, and then head upstairs for copious amounts of food that looks as good as it tastes. Entrees €10-18, or go all-out with the monstrous *menú de sidrería* (€31). ❸

La Zanahoria, C. Tarragona, 4 (☎976 35 87 94). Popular with locals and college students. Spanish for "carrot," La Zanahoria stays true to its roots with excellent salads and an assortment of other veggie treats. Try the vegetable quiches, if that's your thing (€4-6.50). *Menú* €7.50. Entrees €6. Open daily 1:30-4pm and 9-11:30pm. MC/V. ❶

Pasta Nostra, Pizza Nostra, C. Marqués de Casa Jiménez, 8 (☎976 15 85 04). Big pizzas and freshly made pasta are served by a friendly staff. Pizzas €5-10. Pasta dishes €8-11. Open daily 1-4pm and 8pm-midnight. MC/V. ❷

◎ SIGHTS

PLAZA DEL PILAR

A vast square surrounded by a unique fusion of architectural styles, Plaza del Pilar alone offers enough to satisfy any traveler. The beautiful *basílica*, flanked on one side by a dignified Goya statue and a glimmering modern fountain on the other, presides over the central square. The plaza is the perfect place to begin a city tour or simply to sit and feed the pigeons all day. The city erupts for a week of unbridled craziness around October 12 in honor of **La Virgen Santa del Pilar,** one of the few remaining full-blown autumn *fiestas* in Spain; a schedule of events is available at the tourist office. City patrons San Valero and San Jorge are celebrated on January 29 and April 23, respectively.

▨ **BASÍLICA DE NUESTRA SEÑORA DEL PILAR.** This massive Baroque structure (begun in 1681, though a few of the towers weren't completed until the mid-20th century) is Zaragoza's defining landmark. The entire structure was built around the eponymous pillar, which has never moved from its original sight. The interior walls feature frescoes by Goya, González Velázquez, and Francisco Bayeau. Two bombs (now on display) were dropped on the basilica during the Spanish Civil War in 1936 but failed to explode, purportedly due to the divine intervention of the Virgin. Thank her with a kiss; there's a spot to lay lips on a pillar that was supposedly graced with her own sacred smooch. The **Museo del Pilar** exhibits the glittering *Joyero de la Virgen* (Virgin's jewels) and preliminary paintings of the ceiling frescoes. Don't miss the breathtaking panorama of Zaragoza from one of the towers. *(Pl. del Pilar. Basilica open daily 5:45am-9:30pm. Free. Museum ☎976 29 95 64. Open daily 9am-2pm and 4-6pm. €2. Elevator open June-Aug. M-Th and Sa-Su 9:30am-2pm and 4-7pm; Sept.-May M-Th and Sa-Su 9:30am-2pm and 4-6pm. €2)*

OTHER SIGHTS. On the left as you exit the *basílica* is Zaragoza's **Ayuntamiento.** Next door is the Renaissance **La Lonja,** host to occasional cultural exhibits (art, photography, etc.) and featuring the intricately vaulted ceiling of many a Zaragoza postcard. *(☎976 39 72 39. Open Tu-F 10am-2pm and 5-9pm, Su 10am-2pm. Free.)* In front of La Lonja, statues portray scenes from Goya's paintings. On the other side of C. Don Jaime I, a large marble-and-glass cube houses the entrance to the **Foro Romano,** one of three nearby museums dedicated to Zaragoza's classical past. Excavated ruins from 1 BC to AD 1 await underground. The **Museo de las Termas Públicas de Caesaraugusta,** C. San Juan y San Pedro, 3-7, and the **Caesaraugusta River Port Museum,** Pl. San Bruno, 8, display archaeological remains of baths and buildings from the same time period. *(Main office for all three at Pl. de la Seo, 2. ☎976 39 97 52. Open Tu-Sa 10am-2pm and 5-8pm, Su 10am-2pm. Guided visits begin on the hr. Prices include admission to all three museums. €3.80, students €2.50, over 65 and under 8 free.)*

BEYOND PLAZA DEL PILAR

▨ **MUSEO PABLO GARGALLO.** Dedicated to one of the most influential Aragonese sculptors of the 1920s, the Museo Pablo Gargallo houses a small collection of his works in the graceful **Palacio de los Condes de Argillo,** built in 1670. The thirty-years-in-the-making *Gran Profeta* (Great Prophet) showcases Gargallo's use of empty space as a fundamental sculptural element. These holey works are a testament to the man's immense talent as both metallurgist and artist. *(Pl. San Felipe, 3. ☎976 72 49 23. Open Tu-Sa 10am-2pm and 5-9pm, Su 10am-2pm. Free.)*

ARAGÓN

PALACIO DE LA ALJAFERÍA. The turrets, towers, and great halls of this impressive palace comprise an architectural documentary of the history of Aragón and of Spain. Following the Muslim conquest of the Iberian Peninsula in the 711, a crisis over succession smashed the kingdom into petty tributary states called *taifas*, plunging Aragón into a state of constant civil war. The palace's original defensive purposes are still on display in its thick walls and turrets, as well as the prismatic **Troubador Tower,** the palace's oldest standing structure. Sheltered within this practicality sits the decidedly ornamental **Taifal Palace,** built in the *omeya* style similar to other 8th-century Muslim palaces. When Alfonso I "El Batallador" (The Fighter) took Zaragoza from the Muslims in 1118, the Aljafería was Christianized, but the remains of the medieval Christian palace testify to the lingering influence of Islamic art and architecture. It has long served as the most important example of Mudéjar Art in Aragón. In 1492, **El Palacio de los Reyes Católicos** was erected by Ferdinand and Isabel which self-consciously replaced the Muslim traditions with the new innovations of the Renaissance. In 1593, the palace was again transformed under the orders of Felipe II. Fearing civil war, he built thick walls and an impressive moat around the palace, returning the structure to its defensive roots. *(C. Diputados. Take bus #21 or 33. ☎976 28 96 85. Open daily Apr. 15-Oct. 15 10am-2pm and 4:30-8pm; Oct. 16-April 14 M-Sa 10am-2pm and 5-8pm except Tu and F mornings, Su 10am-2pm. €1.80, students and seniors €0.90, under 12 free.)*

MUSEO DE ZARAGOZA. Archaeology buffs will love the extensive collection of Roman and other artifacts that fill the museum's ground floor. The second story exhibits Aragonese painting. The room dedicated to Goya is the most popular, though many of the others are more impressive. *(Pl. de los Sitios, 6. ☎976 22 21 81. Open Tu-Sa 10am-2pm and 5-8pm, Su 10am-2pm. Free.)*

MUSEO PABLO SERRANO. This modern building houses bronze sculptures by the fascinating Pablo Serrano (1908-1985). Look for *Gran Pan Partido* (Big Bread Sliced) and sculptural reinterpretations of works by Picasso, Velázquez, and Goya. Smaller halls feature exhibits of modern sculpture and paintings. *(Po. María Agustín, 20. ☎976 28 06 59. Open Tu-Sa 10am-2pm and 4-8pm, Su 10am-2pm. Free.)*

MUSEO CAMÓN AZNAR. If the permanent Goya exhibit isn't enough of a draw, visit for a crash course in art history; on display is an eclectic selection of works from various schools of artistry throughout the 15th to 20th centuries. The 16th-century building, typical of Aragonese Renaissance architecture, is named after its main donor. *(C. Espoz y Mina, 23. ☎976 39 73 28 or 39 73 87. Open Tu-F 9:15am-2:15pm and 6-9pm, Sa 10am-2pm and 6-9pm. €0.60. ID required for entrance.)*

🎵 NIGHTLIFE

The nightlife scene in Zaragoza is almost strictly limited to weekends; even the most popular of *tapas* bars don't see more than a trickle of visitors before Friday night. But before you condemn Zaragoza as a dead city, just wait until Saturday night, when the young and beautiful emerge from hibernation. Most locals begin their nights in **La Zona**—the streets bounded by Po. de la Constitución, C. León XIII, Po. de las Damas, and Camino de las Torres. You can gulp beer from *litros* (€2.50) in **El Rollo,** the area bounded by C. José Moncasi, C. Juan Pablo Bonet, and C. Maestro Marquina at the southern end of Po. de Sagasta. University students storm Po. de Sagasta and C. Zumalacárregui; others crowd Pl. San Felipe.

Gay bars and discos center around the west side of the *casco viejo;* mixed gay and straight crowds let loose on the small dance floor of **Sphinx,** C. Ramón y Cajal. (Cover F-Su €12. Open daily 11pm-5am.) The purely gay **Mick Havannas,** C. Ramón

Pignatelli, 7, hosts a range of guys from late teens on up with its zebra-striped wallpaper, long bar, and numerous television screens. Many start the night here before heading to Sphinx. (☎976 28 44 50. Open daily 5pm-5am.)

Partiers craving flashing lights and thumping music should head over to C. Espoz y Mina for a buffet of venues. Party like a god at ▧**Mythos,** C. Espoz y Mina, 19, where you'll dance underneath the heavens surrounded by only the hippest Greco-Roman deities. (Beer €3. Mixed drinks €5. Open Th-Sa 11pm-3:30am.) Alternatively, go to its neighbor, **La Casa Magnética,** because you haven't lived until you've danced under a huge, scary-ass veiny eye. Magnets adorn the walls, and the old-school turntable behind the bar sometimes hosts local DJs. (Beer €2. Mixed drinks €4.50. Open Tu-Th 7pm, F-Su 8pm.) The tiki-bar-meets-mom-and-pop-burger-shop eclecticism of **La Casa del Loco,** C. Mayor, 10-12, welcomes its international party crowd with frequent concerts, themed parties, and a wide range of music. (No cover. Beer €1.50. Mixed drinks €4. Open daily 10pm-5am.)

▧ DAYTRIPS FROM ZARAGOZA

Ask at the Zaragoza tourist office for info on excursions like the *Ruta del Vino* (wine route) and the *Ruta de Goya.* Students of the Romanesque should inquire about visits to the **Cinco Villas** (Five Villages).

▧ EL PARQUE DEL MONASTERIO DE PIEDRA
Aragón Tours buses, C. Almagro, 18 (☎976 21 93 20), leave from Zaragoza (2hr.; July-Oct. 15 daily 1 per day 9am, return 5pm; €14 round-trip). ☎976 84 90 11; www.monasteriopiedra.com. Open daily July-Sept. 9am-8pm, Oct.-June 9am-6pm. €9.

In the heart of semi-arid central Spain, 110km southwest of Zaragoza, El Parque del Monasterio de Piedra seems like a dream: lush greenery, cascading waterfalls, and crystalline ponds saturate the park. The monastery was founded by Cistercian monks in 1195 at the order of Alfonso II of Aragón; a second government order forced its abandonment in 1835. The monastery now serves visitors as a 3-star hotel and plays host to a wine museum of the Catalayud region, but it is the park itself which makes the trip well worth it. Don't miss the park's highlight, **La Gruta Iris** (Iris Grotto), the amazingly beautiful natural cavern behind the 53m Cascada Iris (Iris Waterfall). For a special treat, plan your visit for sunset.

TARAZONA
Buses run from the Therpasa station (☎976 30 00 45) in Zaragoza. 1hr., 4-7 per day 8am-8:30 pm, €5.20. Tarazona station (☎976 64 11 00) on Av. Navarra.

Tarazona (pop. 10,750) is known as the "Mudéjar City." Some even liken the winding streets of its medieval quarter to those in Toledo. The town makes a nice daytrip from Zaragoza, especially during *Las Fiestas de Cipotegato* (August 27-September 1). The festivities begin when the jester, clad in a psychedelic getup of red, green, and yellow, is released into the crowds at noon on the 27th. After being pelted with tomatoes, he makes his way through the city with the help of his friends. Not until he successfully completes his route is the jester's identity triumphantly revealed. The next six days are ablaze with activities, including *encierros,* bullfights, concerts, and dances honoring San Atilano, Tarazona's patron saint.

Tarazona's 13th- and 15th-century **cathedral** is closed for restorations. The towers, belfry, lantern, and plaster-work in the inner cloister are fine examples of Mudéjar work. From the cathedral, follow signs for Soria/Zaragoza down C. Laureles, then take your first right and pass through the arch to the octagonal **Plaza de Toros Vieja.** Built in the 18th century, the plaza included private residences with built-in balconies for the express purpose of watching *corridas.* Tarazona was

ARAGÓN

THE LOCAL LEGEND

KISS OF DEATH

The tombs of Diego de Marcilla and Isabel de Segura in the **Mausoleo de los Amantes** are the source of Teruel's nickname: *Ciudad de los Amantes* (City of Lovers). But far from a racy history of romantic escapades, Teruel celebrates love in a rather morbid retelling of the tragic story. It began when Diego left Teruel to make his fortune and prove his worth to Isabel's affluent family. Five years later, he returned a rich man, just in time to watch Isabel marry his childhood rival. Diego begged for one last kiss but was refused; lamentably, he immediately died of grief. At the funeral, Isabel kissed the corpse and, overcome with sorrow, died herself.

Plaques scattered about the city recall the tragic love story in moving verse. At the mausoleum, the lovers are commemorated with life-size statues, reaching out to touch each other. For a peek at the lovers' remains, duck down near their heads.

From Pl. del Torico, take the alleyway to the left of the purple Modernista house. Stairs lead directly to the mausoleum. Open M-Sa 10am-2pm and 5-7:30pm, Su 10:30am-2pm and 5-7:30pm. €0.60.

---

also the seasonal residence of Aragón's kings until the 15th century. Their Zuda (palace) has since served as the **Palacio Episcopal.** Though now the bishop's home is closed to visitors, the exterior is still worth a look. From Pl. de Toros Vieja, walk left 1 block, then up the stairs of the Recodos and Rúa Baja. Opposite the Palacio Episcopal, in the heart of **El Cinto** (the medieval quarter), rises the **Iglesia de Santa Magdalena** and its Mudéjar tower. To enter, take a left up Cuesta del Palacio from the Palacio Episcopal and then another left.

The **tourist office,** Pl. San Francisco, 1, is on the right side of the building in front of the church. (☎976 64 00 74. Open July-Aug. M-F 9am-1:30pm and 4:30-7pm, Sa-Su 10am-1:30pm and 4:30-8pm; Sept.-June M-F 9am-1:30pm and 4:30-7pm, Sa-Su 10am-1:30pm and 4:30-7pm.) **Tours** leave from the tourist office. (July-Sept. 15 Sa 12pm; rest of the year call ahead for reservations. €3.17.) **Banco Santander Central Hispano,** in Pl. San Francisco, charges no commission and has a **24-hr. ATM.** (Open Apr.-Sept. M-F 8:30am-2pm; Oct.-Mar. M-F 8:30am-2pm and Sa 8:30am-1pm.) Store **luggage** at the Therpasa station. (Open daily 6:30am-1pm and 2-10pm. €2.)

TERUEL   ☎978

Teruel (pop. 29,300), the small capital of southern Aragón, seduces visitors with its history of tragic love and rich cultural exchange. The town's lively and welcoming narrow streets and old plazas belie its cosmopolitan past. From the 12th to the 15th centuries, Muslims, Jews, and Christians lived here in cultural collusion. The resulting Mudéjar architecture blends Arab patterns with Gothic and Romanesque. The modern city, across a series of bridges on the hilltop opposite the old city, serves as a busier, more everyday counterpart to the winding streets of the *casco antiguo* and their historical gravitas. The town retains an intoxicating charm without the hordes of tourists that plague similar destinations. An easy stopover between Valencia and Zaragoza, Teruel doesn't reach its prime until July, when citizens celebrate the resilience of their *torico* (iron bull) in an 168-hour liquor fest.

╠ TRANSPORTATION. Trains depart from Camino de la Estación, 1 (☎902 24 02 02), downstairs from Pl. Ovalo, to **Valencia** (2¾hr., 3 per day 7:40am-6:37pm, €8.10) and **Zaragoza** (3½hr., 3 per day 6:45am-6:02pm, €9). **Buses** depart from the new station, Ronda de Ambeles (☎978 61 07 89), only a few blocks from the *casco antiguo.* **Abasa** (☎978 83 08 71) goes to **Barcelona** (5½-6½hr., M-Sa 1 per day 8:45am, €25). **Jiménez**

goes to **Zaragoza** (M-Sa 6 per day 7am-7pm, Su 4 per day 7am-7pm; €8). **Samar** (☎978 60 34 50) goes to: **Barcelona** (5½hr.; M-F 2 per day 8am, 12:30pm; Sa 12:30pm; Su 1 per day 4:30pm; €29.47); **Cuenca** (2hr.; M-Sa 1 per day noon, Su 9:30pm, F extra bus at 4:30am; €7.90); **Madrid** (4½-5hr.; M-Sa 4 per day 7:30am-5pm, Su 3 per day 7:30am-5pm; €15.95). To rent a car, call **BMW** (☎978 60 65 36).

■ ⚐ **ORIENTATION & PRACTICAL INFORMATION.** Teruel's somewhat non-sensical layout can be confusing. The *casco viejo* perches on a hilltop, linked to modern Teruel by bridges. The center of the *casco* is **Plaza de Carlos Castell**, affectionately known as **Plaza del Torico**. To reach Pl. del Torico from the **train station**, take the staircase from the park and follow signs to the *centro*. To get to Pl. del Torico from the new **bus station**, get on C. Judería and make the second left onto C. Hartzembusch, which zigzags to the plaza. The **tourist office** is at C. Tomás Nogues, 1. From Pl. del Torico, follow C. Ramón y Cajal (C. San Juan) and take the first left; the office is one block away on the right, at the corner. (☎ 978 60 22 79. Open M-Sa 10am-2pm and 5-8pm, Su 9am-2pm.) **Luggage storage** is available at the train station (€3 per day) and the bus station (€0.60 per piece per day; both open daily 6:30am-10:30pm). **Banco Santander Central Hispano** is at Pl. del Torico, 15. (☎978 60 11 35. Open M-F 8:30am-2:30pm; Oct.-May also Sa 8:30am-1pm.) In an **emergency,** call ☎112. The **post office,** C. Yagüe de Salas, 19, can also send **faxes.** (☎978 60 11 90 or 60 11 92. Open M-F 8:30am-8:30pm, Sa 9:30am-2pm). **Postal Code:** 44001.

⚐⚑ **ACCOMMODATIONS & FOOD.** Lodgings are scarce during August and *Semana Santa* and impossible during the *fiesta* in early July. Thought to be the oldest hostel in all of Spain, **Fonda el Tozal ❷**, C. Rincón, 5, promises the rustic charm and comfort of a *"casa rural"* with several features of typical *mudéjar* design, including stunning and spacious tiled bathrooms. Along with great beds, guests will enjoy the impressive stable-turned-bar that awaits downstairs. (☎978 61 02 07. Singles €18; doubles €42; triples €52.) To get to **Hostal Aragón ❷**, C. Santa María, 4, head in the direction the Torico faces and take the first left as you leave Pl. del Torico. Friendly owners keep airy rooms with colorful tiled floors and some with TV. (☎978 61 18 77. English spoken. Singles €16.05, with bath €21.40; doubles €24.60/€36.40; triples with bath €48.15.)

Teruel is famous for its salty, flavorful cured ham, *jamón de Teruel*, featured in *tapas* bars in Pl. del Torico. Head to the *casco viejo* to eat. **Restaurante La Parrilla ❸**, C. Esteban, 2, two blocks uphill from the tourist office, specializes in regional dishes and has a magnificent €10 *menú* with succulent meats grilled on a stone fireplace. (☎978 60 59 17. Meat entrées €8.60-19, fish €8-18. Open M-Sa 1-4:30pm and 8:30-11:30pm, Su noon-4:30pm. MC/V.) Lovers of all things Italian will appreciate the pastas and crisp specialty pizzas (€5-10) served at **Los Caprichos ❷**, C. Caracol 1, two blocks uphill from Pl. del Torico. (☎978 60 03 30. Open Tu-Su 1:30-3:30pm and 8:30-11:30pm.) There is a **market** on Pl. Domingo Gascón. (From Pl. del Torico, take C. Joaquín Costa/Tozal. Open Th 8am-1pm).

◎ **SIGHTS.** The mother of all Teruel's Mudéjar monuments is the 13th-century ▦**Catedral de Santa María de Mediavilla.** The vast difference between the chapels is noteworthy—the gilding of the *Capilla de la Inmaculada*, dating from the 19th century, is brilliant in comparison to the more subdued carvings of the 16th-century *retablo mayor*. The cathedral itself has three naves, the most recent of which wasn't finished until the late 1800s. (Open daily 11am-2pm and 4-8pm. €1.20.) Muslim artisans built the brick-and-glazed-tile **Torres Mudéjares** between the 12th and 15th centuries; after a Christian church adapted the Almohad minarets to their own purposes. The most intricately designed of the towers is the 13th-century **Torre de San Salvador,** on C. del Salvador; it is the only tower open to visitors. Climb

123 steps through several chambers to the bell tower and its panoramic views. (Open Tu-Su 11am-2pm and 4:30-7:30pm. €1.) Teruel's famous love story is kept alive at the **Mausoleo de los Amantes**. Behind the cathedral, the **Museo Provincial**, devoted mainly to archaeological and ethnographic pursuits, rests in the 16th-century **Casa de la Comunidad**, a leading example of the Aragonese Renaissance style. Don't miss the reproduction of an 18th-century chemist's shop. Rotating temporary exhibits complement the permanent collection. (Pl. Fray Anselmo Polanco. ☎978 60 01 50. Open Tu-F 10am-2pm and 4-7pm, Sa-Su 10am-2pm. Free.)

ARAGONESE PYRENEES

Aragón claims 90km of Pyrenean grandeur, bracketed by the Río Gallego in the west and the Río Nobuera in the east. Within these two frontiers, alpine meadows and 20 crystalline glaciers are tucked between gorges and jagged cliffs. Such terrain has had its use—founded in the mid-9th century upon these fortifying slopes, the Kingdom of Aragón was left unconquered by northern enemies. The most popular entry point for the Aragonese Pyrenees is Jaca, from which most head to the spectacular Parque Nacional de Ordesa. In the east, Benasque draws hardcore mountaineers with its access to the highest peaks in the Pyrenees, while the western valleys of Ansó and Hecho are ideal for less strenuous mountain rambling. Ski resorts await demanding down-hillers in Astún, Panticosa, Cerler, and Candanchú. For details on winter in Aragón, get the free tourist office pamphlets *Ski Aragón* or *El Turismo de Nieve en España*. If you're there in summer, make sure to get to the ☒**Pirineos Sur** international cultural festival during the last three weeks of July, featuring a host of concerts, markets, and foods from all over the world, focusing mainly on the Americas. Festivities rage throughout the Pyrenees, from Huesca in the south to El Portalet on the French border. For more information, head to www.pirineos-sur.com, or call ☎974 29 41 51.

JACA ☎974

Jaca (pop. 14,000) used to serve as a refuge for weary pilgrims crossing the Pyrenees to Santiago. Though the city also had a brief stint as capital of Aragón (1035-1095), for centuries it had little to offer in the way of diversion. At present, Jaca provides not only the perfect base for organizing excursions into the Pyrenees and nearby ski resorts but also holds many festivals of its own, most notably the *Fiestas de Santa Orosia y San Pedro* (June 23-29) and the biannual *Festival Internacional del Camino de Santiago* (Aug. 8-26), which showcases medieval religious themes and music. During these *fiestas*, the city is awash in various concerts and plays. Formal processions like *La Comparsa de Gigantes*—a company of characters in oversized costumes—and numerous *ad hoc* parades usually occur under the influence of many a malted beverage.

⌐ TRANSPORTATION. RENFE trains (☎974 36 13 32; ticket booth open 10am-noon and 5-7pm) to: **Madrid** (7hr.; 1 per day M-F and Su 1:45pm; €28); **Zaragoza** (3hr.; daily 2 per day 7:15am, 6:30pm; €8.95). **La Oscense buses** (☎974 35 50 60) to: **Pamplona** (2hr., 1 per day 11am, €5.82); **Sabiñánigo** (20min., 4-6 per day 8:15am-8:15pm, €1.19); **Zaragoza** (2hr., 3-4 per day, €13.80). From Sabiñánigo, **Empresa Hudebus** (☎974 21 32 77) connects to **Torla** (11am), near Ordesa and Aínsa. **Josefa Escartín buses** (☎974 36 05 08) go to **Ansó** (1½hr., M-Sa 6:30pm, €3.15) via **Hecho** (55min., €2.40) and **Siresa** (1hr., €2.65). Catch **taxis** (☎974 36 28 48) at the intersection of C. Mayor and Av. Regimento Galicia.

⊞ ⁊ ORIENTATION & PRACTICAL INFORMATION. Buses drop passengers on Av. Jacetania, at the northern edge of the city center. From the station, walk through Pl. de Biscos to C. Zocotín and continue straight ahead for two blocks to **Calle Mayor.** Take a right on C. Mayor to Pl. Cortes de Aragón, with **Avenida Regimento Galicia** on the left and **Calle Primer Viernes de Mayo** on the right. **Taxis** (☎ 620 66 07 76) stop at Pl. Cortes de Aragón. The green city bus runs from the **train station** to the center of town. To walk, take Av. Juan XXIII to its end, turn left onto Av. de Francia, continue straight as it becomes C. Primer Viernes de Mayo, and then make a left onto C. Mayor. The staff at the **tourist office,** Av. Regimiento de Galicia, 2, one block down from Pl. Cortes de Aragón, speaks English, and, if you play your cards right, they will give you more tourist literature than you can carry. (☎ 974 36 00 98; www.aytojaca.es. Open July-Aug. M-F 9am-2pm and 4:30-8pm, Sa 9am-1:30pm and 5-8pm, Su 10am-1:30pm; Sept.-June M-F 9am-1:30pm and 4:30-7pm, Sa 10am-1pm and 5-7pm.) **Alcorce,** Av. Regimiento de Galicia, 1 organizes **hiking, rock climbing, spelunking,** and **rafting** trips. (☎ 974 35 64 37; www.alcorceaventura.com. Guided hiking trips from €21 per person per day; rafting from €35; ski and snowboard rentals €15 per day. Open June-Sept. M-Sa 9:30am-1:30pm and 5:30-9pm; Oct.-May M-Sa 9:30am-1:30pm. MC/V.) Ski season is Dec.-Apr. For ski conditions, call **Teléfono Blanco** (☎ 976 20 11 12). Local services include: **Banco Santander Central Hispano,** C. Primer Viernes de Mayo (open Apr.-Sept. M-F 8:30am-2pm; Oct.-Mar. M-F 8am-2:30pm, Sa 8:30am-1pm); **police,** C. Mayor, 24 (☎ 091 or 092); **Centro de Salud,** Po. de la Constitución, 6 (☎ 974 36 07 95). For **Internet access,** try friendly **Ciber Santi,** C. Mayor, 42-44, inside La Tienda Mayor to the right. (☎ 974 35 68 69. €1.40 per 30min., €2.20 per hr. Open M-Sa 11am-2pm and 5-11pm, Su 5-11pm.) **Ciber Civa** is two stores down from the tourist office on Av. Regimiento de Galicia. (☎ 974 35 67 75. €1.90 per hr. Open M 4:45-9:15pm, Tu-Sa 11:30am-2pm and 4:45pm-1am, Su 4:15-11:15pm.) The **post office** is at C. Correos, 13. (☎ 974 35 58 86. Open M-F 8:30am-2:30pm, Sa 9:30am-1pm.) **Postal Code:** 22700.

⊓⊏ ACCOMMODATIONS & FOOD. Jaca's hostels and *pensiones* cluster around C. Mayor and the cathedral. Lodgings are scarce only during the annual *Festival Folklórico* during the week of the last Sunday in August. The generous owners of ⊠**La Casa del Arco ❷,** C. San Nicolás, 7, will welcome you into their home with incense, cool music, and delicious food in the downstairs restaurant. A common room contains a TV and library. Look for the yellow building off Pl. de Ripa, adjacent to Pl. de Biscos. (☎ 974 36 44 48. Breakfast €4. Rooms €18 per person.) To reach the large, old-fashioned rooms of **Hostal Paris ❷,** C. San Pedro, 5, from the bus station, cross the park and head right, circling around the church to the next plaza; look for the sign straight ahead. (☎ 974 36 10 20; www.jaca.com/hostalparis. July 15-Sept. 15 and *Semana Santa* singles €19; doubles €30; triples €41. Rest of year €17.60/€28/€38. **Albergue Juvenil de Escuelas Pias (HI) ❶,** Av. Perimetral, 6, offers rows of two-bunk bungalows. From C. Mayor, turn left onto Av. Regimiento de Galicia, then left again onto Av. Perimetral. (☎ 974 36 05 36. Breakfast included. Quads €12 per person.)

Bocadillos fill the menus on Av. Primer Viernes de Mayo, and locals fill the many cafes on Pl. de la Catedral. ⊠**Restaurante Vegetariano El Arco ❷,** C. San Nicolás, 74, serves an outstandingly creative, all-veggie *menú* for €10. Try the *cebolla asada con pisto y roquefort* (roasted onions with mixed vegetables in roquefort sauce) or the *plato del peregrino* (€7.80), a unique sampler prepared especially by the chef. (Open M-Sa 1-3pm and 8:30-11:30pm.) **Ulzama ❶,** Pl. de Cortes de Aragón, 8, features a wide selection of sandwiches (€2-3), tapas (€1-2), and combination plates (€4-8), as well as huge ice cream cones in a variety of flavors (€2.10). Try the vanilla whiskey milkshake (€3.45). **Supermercado ALDI,** C. Correos, 9, sells groceries. (Open M-Sa 9:30am-2pm and 5:30-8:30pm. V.)

ARAGÓN

⚡ DAYTRIPS FROM JACA

MONASTERIO DE SAN JUAN DE LA PEÑA

Taxis (☎974 36 28 48) will make the journey for €40, with a 1hr. wait before bringing you back. If you are driving, park at the lot above the monastery; a shuttle transports visitors every 30min. The adventurous can catch a bus from Jaca to Pamplona and ask to be dropped at Santa Cruz de la Seró (CN 240, km295). From there, it's a 9km hike to the monastery.

The spectacular **Monasterio de San Juan de la Peña** is purposefully difficult to reach: the Holy Grail was supposedly concealed here for three centuries. Determined hermits hid the original monastery, *monasterio viejo*, in a canyon 22km from Jaca and maintained such extreme privacy that both church and cup were kept safe from invading Moors. It's worth a visit, both for the 10th-century underground church carved directly into the rock and the 12th-century cloister wedged under a massive boulder. The carved capitals of the cloister's arcade are not to be missed. The 17th-century *monasterio alto* sits 1km uphill; it is currently undergoing massive renovations and will reopen as the **Centro de Interpretación de los Reyes de Aragón.** (☎974 35 51 19 or 35 51 45; www.monasteriosanjuan.com. Open June-Aug. daily 10am-2:30pm and 3:30-8pm; Mar. 16-May and Sept.-Oct. 15 daily 10am-2pm and 4-7pm; Oct. 16-Mar. 15 Tu-Su 11am-2pm and 4-5:30pm. €3.50 includes entrance to church in Santa Cruz de la Seró, €4.50 includes parking lot shuttle.) A **snack bar ❶** next to the parking lot sells *bocadillos* (€2-3) and other items.

CASTILLO DE LOARRE

Only serious hikers and those with cars can reach the castle. La Oscense (☎974 35 50 60) sends 1 bus from Jaca to Loarre, 5km from the castle (1hr., M-F 7:15am, €5.10); the return bus (5pm, €4.13) stops only in Ayerbe, 7km away from Loarre. Trains run only to Ayerbe (1½hr.; depart Jaca daily at 7:30am and 6:11pm, return at 8:58am and 5:18pm; €3.46). From there, take a taxi or trek 2hr. to Loarre and then another 2km uphill to the castle.

The power and magnificence of the ▓**Castillo de Loarre** are visible for kilometers in each direction. Every inch of this imposing fortress, with steep cliffs at its rear and thick walls protecting it on the hillside, is open to exploration; visitors are free to investigate on their own or go on the guided tour. Though you may want to spend your time admiring the vast countryside below, the castle's history is equally fascinating. Around 1020, Navarra's King Sancho the Elder annexed Loarre into his kingdom as a defensive bastion against the nearby Muslim stronghold of Bolea. In 1071, King Sancho Ramírez founded an Augustinian monastery here, and the castle's dual nature, military fortress and religious monastery, is still readily apparent. A crypt, which opens to the right of the steep entrance staircase, holds the remains of Demetrius, the patron saint of gladiators, who died in Loarre. Be sure to climb the Queen's Tower for a great view of the countryside below. The dark staircase leading to the crypt, as well as other dark areas of the castle, can be difficult to navigate. (Open July-Aug. daily 10am-8pm; Mar.-June and Sept. Tu-Su 10am-1:30pm and 4-7pm; Oct.-Mar. W-Su 11am-2:30pm. Free. Tours in Spanish, English, and French July-Aug. daily every 30min., Sept.-June Sa-Su only. €2)

Apart from the castle, the tiny town of **Loarre** offers a chance to really get away from it all. Spend the day relaxing in the countryside, or take advantage of one of the many nearby hiking trails. From the castle itself, you can continue up Monte Pusilibro to its 1569m peak on the **Rasal Pusilibro** trail (easy-medium difficulty, 1½hr.), or ask at the helpful tourist office at the base of the castle for more area hikes. **Camping Castillo de Loarre ❶,** down the road from the castle toward Loarre, offers friendly service, a swimming pool, a supermarket, and a brightly decorated bar and restaurant. (☎974 38 27 22. €2.70 per person and per tent; €2.40 per car.

July-Aug. and *Semana Santa* 2-person bungalows €48, 5-person €60; rest of the year €36/€48. Restaurant open 1-3pm and 8-11pm. *Menú* €11.). Loarre's only hotel, the three-star **Hospedería de Loarre ❸**, offers big well-furnished rooms and bike rental for €9 per day. (Pl. Mayor. ☎974 38 27 06. July 15-Aug. and *Semana Santa* singles €40; doubles €52. Mar.-July 14 and Sept.-Oct. €34.50/€43. Nov.-Feb. €30.50/€38.) **Casa O'Caminero ❷**, Ctra. Huesca, 8, offers delicious paellas (€10), and an €11 *menú*. (☎974 38 26 96. Open daily Apr.-Oct. 10:30am-1am.)

VALLE DE HECHO

The craggy Valle de Hecho and its picturesque hamlets 40km west of Jaca are an almost-forgotten wilderness offering some of the most undiscovered hiking opportunities in Aragón. Under the humid influence of the Atlantic, these western slopes and glacial valleys encourage dense forest growth, including the lush *Selva de Oza* filled with beech and fir trees. The valley is best visited during the summer, as it is extremely quiet during the rest of the year. A Josefa Escartín **bus** (☎974 36 05 08) leaves Jaca M-Sa at 6pm, stopping at **Hecho** (7pm) and **Siresa** (7:10pm) before continuing to **Ansó** (7:40pm). Every morning except Sunday the bus returns from **Ansó** (6:45am) via **Siresa** (7:15am) and **Hecho** (7:30am) on its way to **Jaca** (8:25am). Check out the new **El Megalitismo Pirináico**, Ctra. de Oza, km 8, a museum of the ancient stone constructions of the Pyrenees. From Hecho, take the highway to Oza and look for the sign at 8km. (Open daily 10:30am-1:30pm and 5-8pm. €2.)

HECHO (ECHO)   ☎974

Hecho (pop. 670) is the valley's geographical and administrative center, a serious title that doesn't suit the small and inviting town. The **tourist office** is in the Pallar d'Agustín, an old renovated farmhouse which also houses Hecho's **Museo de Arte Contemporáneo**. Look for the surreal paint job and the modern sculptures dotting the lawn on the main road toward Ansó. Museum and tourist office open M-Sa 10am-1:30pm and 5:30-8pm, Su 10am-2pm. Free.) The tourist office is closed Oct.-June, but the staff at the Ayuntamiento in Pl. Conde Xiquena (next to Pl. Alta, off C. Mayor) either upstairs in the office (M-F 8am-3pm) or downstairs in the library (M-F 5-7pm) are happy to answer questions during the rest of the year. The hiking experts of **Compañía de Guías Valle de Echo** on C. Lobo lead trips and rent cross-country skis. (☎974 37 52 18. Call ahead.) A **bank** with 24hr. **ATM** is on Pl. Alta, off C. Mayor. (Open Apr.-Oct. M-F 8:15am-2:30pm; Nov.-May M-W and F 8:15am-2:30pm, Th 8:15am-1:45pm and 5:15-7:30pm. MC/V.) **Supermercado Alvi** is on C. Mayor. (Open July-Sept. M-Sa 9:30am-2pm and 5-8pm, Su 10am-2pm; Oct.-June M-Sa 10am-2pm and 5-8pm.) In an **emergency**, call ☎112. The **Guardia Civil** can be reached at ☎974 37 50 04. The **post office**, Pl. Alta, is also off C. Mayor. (Open M-F 8:30am-2:30pm, Sa 9:30am-1pm.)

  Look for any of a number of *casas rurales* which provide enjoyable company in an intimate atmosphere. Follow signs toward the *centro de salud* to the tall, white **Casa Blasquico ❹**, Pl. Fuente 1. After one night, you're part of the family. Enjoy the familiarity or escape into your beautifully-decorated, flower-patterned room. All rooms have TVs, and some have a balcony. (☎974 37 50 07. Doubles €42, with living room €48. IVA not included. Closed Sept. 7-15 and Dec. 22-26. MC/V.) Downstairs, **Restaurante Gaby ❷** provides tasty, balanced meals. (Breakfast €3.50; *menú* €12.) At half the price, try the small rooms of the central but unmarked **Casa Marina ❶**, C. Medio, 12, just up the cobblestone street from the center and across from Bar Archer. (☎974 37 50 77. Doubles €21.) At the entrance to Hecho from Jaca, the well-kept sites and *albergue* bunks of **Camping Valle de Hecho ❶** are just a short walk from town. The campsite also includes a swimming pool, bar, and supermarket. (☎/fax 974 37 53 61. €3.35 per person, per tent, per car. Bunks €5.41.

IVA not included. MC/V.) For nourishment, **Serbal** ❷, C. Mayor, 6, boasts a menu with more than just predictable pork, including salad (€4.80) and chicken (€9.40). Choose between indoor dining and a romantic terrace overlooking the countryside. (☎974 37 53 35. Open daily 1:30-4pm and 8:30-11pm. MC/V.)

VALLE DE ANSÓ

Farther down the road from Jaca, the little town of Ansó rests in one of the most appealing valleys in the Pyrenees, a lush growth of oak and pine trees. You might see the very last Pyrenean bears; they reside only in this particular valley. Like Hecho, the Valle de Ansó lives for July and August, when the bulk of its visitors pour in over the mountain ridges. Visitors stop in cobblestoned Ansó before heading farther up the valley to Zuriza, the departure point for the valley's best hikes.

ANSÓ

Just east of Navarra, the cobblestone streets and matching houses of tiny Ansó (pop. 530) immediately expose its gentle warmth. The drier terrain and relatively fewer trees remind you that you have arrived in Aragón. In an old movie theater, the **nature center**, C. Santa Bárbara, 4, houses several permanent displays on the Valle de Ansó and surrounding valleys. Most interesting are the scale models of the Aragonese Pyrenees on the first floor and the entire second floor, which is devoted to the habitats, habits, history, and hopefully, the happy future of endangered Pyrenean bears. (☎974 37 02 10. Open daily June 15-Sept. 15 10am-2pm and 4-8pm; Apr.-June 14 Sa-Su 10am-2pm and 4-8pm; Sept. 16-Mar. Sa-Su 10am-2pm and 3-6pm. Reservations accepted. Free.) At the **Museo de Etnología** inside the **Iglesia de San Pedro**, antique chorus books are displayed beside mannequins modeling traditional dress. (☎974 37 00 22. Open July-Sept. 15 M-F 10:30am-1pm and 4-7pm; during the rest of the year, the priest living in the stone house across from church can open it for you. €2.) A fairly easy 4.8km roundtrip hike that begins in Ansó will take you along the paved road to a weather-sculpted rock formation called *El Fraile y la Monja* (The Monk and the Nun). Start at the town's southern edge next to the sign pointing towards Huesca and walk along the highway, heading out of town. It's then 2km downhill to the Hecho-Huesca fork. Going towards Hecho, march along the 400m traversal up the hill until you come to the first tunnel.

◪**Posada Magoria** ❸, C. Milagro, 32, offers days and nights of pure relaxation. With a backyard, covered porch, and balcony all overlooking the quiet Río Verál, Magoria is an ideal place to spend a lazy afternoon before enjoying a lengthy massage (€20) and heading down to dinner in the family-style dining room (*menú* €12; breakfast €6; home-grown vegetarian meals also offered). Once stuffed, hit the sack in one of its airy bedrooms. They might even let you play yourself a lullaby on the house guitar. (☎974 37 00 49. Singles €30; doubles with 1 bed €43, with 2 beds €50. MC/V.) The more impersonal **Hostal Aisa** ❷, just beside the post office, offers rooms with private baths. (☎974 37 00 09. Singles €22; doubles €40.) For convenience, you can't beat **Hostal Kimboa** ❹, located right on the Zuriza highway (on your right heading toward Zuriza). Enjoy its typically Aragonese *menús*, featuring such staples as *migas* and *carnes a brasa* (€10-11). All rooms have bathrooms; some have balconies. (Singles €45; doubles €50. MC/V.) The most affordable lodging is 3km out of town at *refugio*-style **Borda Changalé** ❶, Ctra. Ansó, on the way to Zuriza. Be cautious crossing the narrow bridge at the entrance. (☎974 37 00 67. English-speaking owner. Breakfast included. *Semana Santa* and July-Aug. quads with private bath €40; 8-bunk room €80. Sept.-June €10 per person.) The brand-new **Camping Valle de Ansó** ❶, Ctra. Extramuros, s/n, located below town, features gorgeous views, two swimming pools, restaurant, bar, cafeteria, as well as bike and **snowshoe** rentals and guided **hiking, rafting,** and biking tours. (Bar and cafeteria open daily 8am-midnight. Restaurant open daily 1:30-4pm and 8-11pm. *Menú* €10. €3.30 per person, per tent, per car.) The **tourist office** is on Pl. Domingo Miral. (☎974 37 02 25. Open July-Aug. daily 10am-2pm and 5-8pm.) Next door is the **post office**. (☎ 974 37 02 25. Open M-Sa 9am-2pm.)

ZURIZA & ENVIRONS

In the northern part of the Valle de Ansó (15km north of Ansó itself) lies Zuriza, which consists of little more than a single camping location, **Camping Zuriza**. Surrounding terrain alternates between the shallow hills and valleys of the campsite and the steep summit of southwestern **Ezcaurri**. Many hikers use the area as a base for the arduous trek to **Sima de San Martín**, a gorgeous trail along the French border. To get there, drive from Zuriza 12km towards Isaba until you come to the Isaba-Belagua crossroads. Take the road to Belagua, heading north along the Río Belagua. After about 12km of smooth terrain and a gentle 2km ascent, you'll near the French border and will see signs for the trail. **Camping Zuriza ❶** lies along the banks of a stream running between Ezcaurri and Hondonada. It's a great spot for fishing, hiking, and kayaking (April-May). The campground also provides a **supermarket, hostel,** and **pub/restaurant** where you can get info and maps (€4.30-6.65) of nearby trails. (☎974 37 01 96 or 37 00 77. Breakfast €2.60. Hot showers included. Campsite €3.50 per person, per tent, and per car; IVA not included. Hostel doubles €27, with bath €36. Bunks €7.50. MC/V.) From the campground, it's a mild and well-marked day hike (5hr.) to **Mesa de los Tres Reyes** (2444m), a series of peaks close to the borders of France, Navarra, and Aragón. Exhausted campers and hikers can find accommodations in nearby **Linza**.

🖿 PARQUE NACIONAL DE ORDESA

The majestic beauty of Ordesa invites you to spend a week as a vagabond. After staying the night in a crowded *refugio*, extremely well-maintained trails draw you through the park, cutting across forest, rock face, snow-covered peak, and river. No luxury living here: you sleep where you are and eat what you carry. Ordesa is located just south of the French border, and includes the canyons and valleys of Ordesa, Añisclo, Escuaín, and Pineta. Huge crowds descend into Ordesa through the village of **Torla** in July-August to traipse along the park's diverse trails.

🚆 TRANSPORTATION. All **trains** along the Zaragoza-Huesca-Jaca line stop in Sabiñánigo. **La Oscense** (☎974 35 50 60) runs a **bus** between Sabiñánigo and **Jaca** (20min., 2-3 per day 8am-5:15pm, €1.24.) From there, **Compañía Hudebus** (☎974 21 32 77) runs to **Torla** (55min.; July-Aug. daily 2 per day 11am, 6:30pm; Sept.-June M-Th 1 per day 11am, F 1 per day 6:30pm, Su 1 per day 5pm; €2.45.) During *Semana Santa* and in summer, a shuttle runs between Torla and **Ordesa** (15min.; June 28-Aug. 6am-7pm, *Semana Santa* and Sept. 6am-6pm, Oct. 7am-6:30pm; €2, round trip €3). When the shuttle is running, cars are prohibited from entering the park. The parking lot in Torla charges €0.50 per hr. from 9am-8pm; overnight parking is free. After the first 24hr., it is €0.40 per hr. It's also possible to find free roadside parking, even in high season. In low season, those without a car will have to either hike the 8km to the park entrance or catch a **Jorge Soler taxi** (☎974 48 62 43; €12), which also offers a variety of van tours for up to 8 people. To exit the park area, catch the bus as it passes through Torla at 3:30pm on its way back to Sabiñánigo.

🛈 PRACTICAL INFORMATION. Don't try to drive off the main road in any of the towns near the park, especially Torla. The narrow, steep streets were not designed with cars in mind. Just park and walk; your sanity will thank you for it. The **visitors' center** is on the left 1.8km beyond the park entrance. (Open daily 9am-1:30pm and

3-6pm.) The **park info center** in Torla, across the street from the bus stop, takes over in low season, which runs mid-Sept.-May. (Open Oct.-June M-F 8am-3pm; July-Sept. M-F 8am-3pm, Sa-Su 9am-2pm and 4:30-7pm.) You can pick up free maps and the **Senderos Sector Ordesa** trail guide from the park info center, or the indispensable *Editorial Alpina* guide (€7.50) in town. For more information, head to the **tourist office** on Pl. Nueva at the end of C. Francia (M-Sa 9am-1:30pm, 5-9pm, Su 9am-12pm). Across from the pharmacy on C. Francia, **Compañía Guías de Torla** organizes rafting, canyoning, and year-round mountaineering expeditions. (☎974 48 64 22; www.guiasdetorla.com. Open daily May-June 15 and Oct.-Nov. 5-9pm; late June-Sept. 8:30am-1:30pm and 5-10pm; Dec.-Apr. available by phone. MC/V.) In neighboring **Broto** (7km from Torla; head back down the highway and bear left at the fork), **Casteret Grupo Explora** offers year-round seasonal expeditions, as well as spelunking, rafting, and hydrospeeding (basically white-water rafting without the raft), and **Internet** access. (C. Santa Cruz, 18. ☎974 48 64 32; www.grupoexplora.com. Open daily 10am-2pm and 5-9pm. Activities €20-50; Internet €0.50 per 15min.) Local services include: **emergency** ☎112, **Guardia Civil** (☎974 48 61 60), and the **post office,** on C. Francia at Pl. de la Constitución (open M-Sa 9-11am). **Postal Code:** 22376.

⌕ ACCOMMODATIONS. Hotels and higher-end accommodations are located beside the highway before entering Torla; a few lie along the road closer to Ordesa. Torla offers the greatest number of budget accommodations, but they tend to fill up fast in July and August—reserve ahead. Don't worry about oversleeping here; the reliable town rooster sounds daily at 7:30am. Named for Ordesa's best-known celebrator, **Refugio Lucien Briet ❶**, C. Francia, s/n, has the most comfortable bunks local *refugios* have to offer. Ascend C. Francia, following the sign across the street to the left of the bus stop pointing to "Centro Población," then continue 1 block uphill. (☎974 48 62 21; www.refugiolucienbriet.com. *Menú* at **Restaurante la Brecha ❸** downstairs €11. Bunks €8. Private rooms available. MC/V.) Across the street, the funky **Refugio L'Atalaya ❶**, C. Francia, 45, is hippie-hiker heaven. The adjoining bar and restaurant, bedecked with modern art and finger paintings, are worth a visit even if you stay elsewhere. A small kitchen is available for use. (☎974 48 60 22. Open *Semana Santa*-Oct. 11. *Menú* €11-14. Loft mats €8 per person. Refugio and bar open daily 7am-2am, restaurant 1-3pm and 8-11pm. MC/V.) **Camping Ordesa ❶** and the enormous **Hotel Ordesa ❹**, just outside Torla en route to Ordesa, share a pool, restaurant, tennis courts, outdoor ping-pong, and free parking for guests, as well as a creepy logo featuring the gargantuan-eyed indigenous chamois, which looks like what would happen if aliens started mating with antelope. The hotel rooms offer great views, as well as full bathrooms and TV. (☎974 48 61 25. Camping *Semana Santa* and July-Aug. €3.50 per person, per tent, and per car; rest of the year €2.80. Hotel July 24-Aug. singles €40.12; doubles €55.64; triples €75.11; quads €89.02. July 1-23 and Sept. 1-15 €34.77/€49.75/€67.16/€79.59. Rest of the year €27.82/€39.05/€52.71/€62.47. All-you-can eat buffet €13. AmEx/MC/V.) The prettiest setting is at **Camping San Antón ❶**, the campsite closest to the park, which also rents 4-person bungalows and 4-6 person apartments. (☎974 48 60 63. Camping open *Semana Santa*-Sept., bungalows and apartments open year round. €3.50 per person, €3.30 per tent and per car. Wood bungalows *Semana Santa* and July-Aug. €80; rest of the year €72. Stone bungalows €61/€55.) Or, if you have a car and you're after supreme tranquility, head to **El Balcón del Pirineo ❺**, in tiny **Buesa,** located high up in the Valle de Broto, where the only street traffic will moo at you. El Balcón offers 4-person condominiums with full kitchens, bathrooms, dining area, washer/dryer, and sweet blessed silence. The **restaurant ❸** downstairs cooks up its *menú* (€12) on an open grill in the dining room, so the delicious smells of cooking ensure big appetites and satisfied customers. From Broto, take the Aínsa highway away from Ordesa for 8km, watch for the sign, and turn left up the mountain. (☎974 48 61 75; www.balcondelpirineo.com. *Semana Santa* and July-Aug. €80, rest of the year €55.)

🖪 **FOOD.** Most accommodations serve a very filling dinner (€13-15) and simple breakfast (included). To pick up your own food, **Supermercado Torla,** on C. Francia, is a few buildings down from Refugio L'Atalaya on the opposite side of the street. (☎974 48 63 88. Open May-Oct. daily 9am-2pm and 5-8:30pm. Nov.-Apr. closed Su. MC/V.) In Broto, the low-ceilinged stone grottoes and stone-and-thatch cottage of 🖾**Restaurante La Bóveda ❷**, Av. de Ordesa, 4, make it the perfect place to take a break from all your assorted outdoor activities. Seamlessly blending its rustic decor with simply elegant cuisine, La Bóveda offers delicious soups and appetizers (€4-9), as well as a hearty *menú* (€12). Try the house sangría (€5.75 per liter), and be sure to save room for one of the beautiful desserts (€3-6). Finish your meal off with a shot of sweet homemade *pacharán* (€1.20), a specialty of the Aragonese Pyrenees. (☎974 48 60 79; www.vallebroto.com/laboveda. Open May-Dec. 1:30-4pm and 8:30-11pm). Back in Torla, on C. Francia, **Restaurante Bar El Rebeco ❸** serves a satisfying *menú* (€12) in three dining rooms, all decorated in a delightful mish-mash of antique photos, oil paintings, country-kitchen crafts, and miniature Renaissance statuary; lower-priced entrees range from €5-12. (☎974 48 60 68. Open May-Oct. daily 1-3:30pm and 8-10:30pm. MC/V.) **Bar Restaurante Taillon ❷**, C. Francia, s/n, has sandwiches (€3) and a hearty *menú* (€10.50). Grab a beer (€1.50) and head out to the garden for an amazing view of Mt. Mondaruego. (☎974 48 63 04. Open Mar.-Nov. daily 7:30am-1am, dining room open daily 8:15-10:30pm.) In Pl. Nueva up the stairs to the right of the tourist office, **Pizzeria-Bocatería Santa Elena ❶**, C. Furquieto, s/n, offers a friendly, casual setting and cheap, hearty eats. Plus, according to the English-language menu, you can get **"Brave Potatoes with Prick Gravy"** for only €3. The pizzeria proffers a wide selection of salads (€2.50-3), *bocadillos* (€3-4), and pizzas (€5-12.50), as well as huge *jarras* of beer for €3. (☎974 48 63 59. Open daily 1:30pm-midnight.)

🖪 **HIKING.** If you can spend only one day in Ordesa, the **Soaso Circle** is the most practical hike, especially for inexperienced mountaineers. Frequent signposts along the wide trail clearly mark the 5hr. (round trip) journey up to **Refugio Góriz.** The trail passes the **Gradas de Soaso** waterfall along the way. Check weather forecasts (☎906 36 53 22 or 36 53 80) before starting out; heavy snow makes the trail impassable in winter and spring, and paths becomes dangerous in the rain. Less intrepid travelers may want to reduce the hike to 2hr. (one-way) by turning around at the *gradas*. The views from **Cascada del Cueva** (Cave Falls) and especially from **Cascada del Estrecho** (Narrow Falls) make this hike well worth it. For more experienced hikers, **Sendero 3** makes a good day hike. From the parking lot at the Pradera de Ordesa, take the trail right, which leads across the Río Arazas, and follow the signs for trail 3. The trail includes the Soaso Circle, as well as the steeper, more dangerous **Senda de los Cazadores** and the beautiful lookout point at **Calcilarruego.** Be especially careful on the descents (6-7hr. round-trip.) Try to arrive early, especially July-August, as the park is often flooded with visitors by noon.

AÍNSA (L'AINSA)

Romantic, if slightly touristy, the village of Aínsa—a 1hr. drive from Ordesa—is the ideal stop for less rugged travelers, especially families. From the friendly souvenir shops along its main intersection, Aínsa leads the visitor up a winding cobblestone staircase to its perfectly preserved medieval quarter. A thousand years ago, Aínsa was the capital of the Kingdom of Sobrarbe (incorporated into Aragón in the 11th century), and the ruins of its 11th-century **castle** on Pl. Mayor remind

ARAGÓN

visitors of its past prominence. In 1181, priests consecrated the **Iglesia de Santa María**, across the plaza from the castle, whose spiraling tower steps can be climbed for €1. An incredible view of the Parque Nacional de Ordesa's peaks awaits at its top. For those exhausted from the uphill hike to the plaza, a stairless view can be found just behind the church. The **Museo de Oficios y Artes Tradicionales**, Pl. San Salvador, 5, offers a glimpse into the Pyrenean home, with exhibits ranging from traditional ceramics to metallurgy to basket-weaving. (☎974 51 00 75; www.staragon.com/moat. Open July-Aug. daily 10:30am-2pm and 5:30-9:30pm; Apr. 20-June and Sept.-Oct. 15 Tu-Su 11am-2pm and 4:30-7:30pm. Or call ahead year-round to organize a viewing. €2.40, students €1.50. During the third week of July, Aínsa explodes with music, markets, and marching for the **Festival Celta L'Aínsa**. (Ticketed events €12 each, or €40 for the entire festival. For more information, call ☎902 19 96 16 or visit www.festivalesdearagon.net.)

⊡⊡ TRANSPORTATION & PRACTICAL INFORMATION. Compañía Hudebus (☎974 21 32 77) runs daily buses from **Sabiñánigo** to Aínsa, stopping in **Torla** along the way (2hr.; 1 per day 11am, returning at 2:30pm; €5). **Compañía Cortés** (☎974 31 15 52) runs from Aínsa to **Barbastro** (1hr., M-Sa 1 per day 7am, €4), where buses make the connection to **Benasque**. The **tourist office**, Av. Pirenáica, 1, is at the highway crossroads. (☎974 50 07 67. Open July-Aug. M-Sa 9am-9pm, Su 9am-2pm and 5-9pm; May-June and Sept. M-Sa 10am-2pm and 4-8pm, Su 10am-2pm; Oct.-Apr. Tu-Sa 10am-2pm and 4-8pm.) Although Aínsa is not as well situated for hiking as are Torla and Benasque, companies surrounding the tourist office can arrange countless outdoor activities. **Intersport** (☎974 50 09 83) and **EKM** (☎974 51 00 90) rent out bikes and lead backpacking trips; **Aguas Blancas** (☎974 51 00 80) coordinates rafting and kayaking excursions. **Internet** access is available at the **library,** C. los Murros, 2, on the top floor of the big brick building at the base of the medieval quarter (☎974 50 03 98. Open M-Tu and Th-Su 11am-1pm and 5-9pm, W 3-7pm. €1.50 per hr.) The **post office** is located on Av. Sobrarbe, down the street across from the tourist office. (☎974 50 00 71. Open M-F 9am-2pm and Sa 9am-12:30pm.)

⊡⊡ ACCOMMODATIONS & FOOD. The brand new 🏨**Hotel Villa de Aínsa ❸**, C. Santa Cruz, 20, on Pl. Santo Domingo in the medieval quarter, offers big, beautiful, fully-furnished rooms with balconies offering amazing views over the Río Cinca, as well as a terrace and downstairs lounge. (☎974 50 07 50. Apr. 20-Oct. 15 singles €29; doubles €40; triples €49. Rest of the year €21/€30/€39. Breakfast €3). **Casa Rural El Hospital ❷**, C. Santa Cruz, 3, offers equally beautiful rooms, minus the views. Only a small sign on the door marks the residence; you'll find reception in the corner boutique. (☎974 50 07 50. June 16-Sept. singles €21; doubles with bath, TV, and A/C €36. Oct.-June 15 €24/€30. MC/V.) While more luxurious establishments line the main road and aren't difficult to locate, less expensive options surround the bus stop in the new part of town. Outside of the center, **Camping Aínsa ❶**, Ctra. Aínsa-Campo, km1.8, offers a swimming pool, supermarket, bar, and restaurant. (☎974 50 02 60. €4.50 per person, per car, and per tent. Open *Semana Santa-* Oct. 15. Restaurant open daily 8am-midnight. MC/V.)

Essential groceries, and a few delicacies can be picked up at **Alimentación M. Cheliz,** Av. Ordesa. (☎974 50 00 62. Open July-Sept. daily 8:30am-9pm; Oct.-June M-Sa 8:30am-2:30pm and 4-8:30pm, Su 8:30am-2:30pm. MC/V.) **Restaurante Bodegas de Sobrarbe ❹**, Pl. Mayor, s/n, offers an elegant dining experience, whether enjoyed out on the beautiful garden terrace or deep within the dark, 11th-century interior. Order the *menú* (€18.50), or relax with a drink on the terrace (beer €1.70, wine €1.10, mixed drinks €4). Facing the castle upon entering Pl. Mayor, Bodegas de Sobrarbe is in the bottom left corner. (☎974 50 03 34. Open daily 12:30-4pm and 8:30-11pm; bar 12pm-1am.) Across from the

FAR TREK On your way to Berlin? A *Gran Recorrido* (Long Distance) trail will get you there—eventually. One of the most beautiful and rugged stretches of the pan-European *Gran Recorrido* network treks east to west just below the French-Spanish border. Strung together by old mountain roads, animal tracks, and forest paths, the Aragonese portion of **GR-3** passes by clear mountain lakes and under, over, and through snow-covered peaks (the highest being Mt. Aneto, at 3404m). Though some parts of GR-3 are pretty gentle, the full trek across Aragón requires hiking experience. The border-to-border route takes eight to ten days. For detailed info on this and other GR trails, consult tourist offices in the area and the **Federación Aragonesa de Montañismo**, C. Albareda, 7 (☎976 22 79 71) in Zaragoza, and ask for the detailed and trail-specific *Topoguía* guide. The extremely useful *Editorial Alpina* provides a good route map.

tourist office, the aptly-named **Cafetería Dos Ríos ❶**, Av. Central, 4 (☎974 50 09 61), offers a wide variety of stone-oven pizzas (€7.20) and *bocadillos* (€3.50-4) for sidewalk dining.

VALLE DE BENASQUE: BENASQUE

The Valle de Benasque is a haven for no-nonsense hikers, climbers, and skiers. Countless trails wind through the mountains, and the area teems with *refugios*, allowing for longer expeditions. With its many excursion companies and nearby trailheads, mellow **Benasque** (pop. 1100) is an excellent base for outdoor activities. Casual hikers are often scared off by the valley's reputation for serious mountaineering—the Pyrenees's highest peaks, including awe-inspiring Mt. Aneto (3404m), are here—but relaxing nature walks are within every visitor's reach.

█🛈 TRANSPORTATION & PRACTICAL INFORMATION. La Alta Aragonesa (☎974 21 07 00) runs buses to **Huesca** (3hr.; M-Sa 2 per day 6:45am, 3pm; Su 1 per day 3pm; €10). July-August, the shuttle bus **Pirineos 3000** makes frequent runs from the town to the trailhead parking lots Senarta and La Besurta. To get to the **tourist office**, C. San Pedro, s/n, face Hotel Aragüells at the main bus stop and walk one block down the alley between BBVA and the building bearing the KHURP sign. (☎/fax 974 55 12 89. Open daily 10am-2pm and 5-9pm; July-Aug. 9am-2pm and 4-9pm.) The hip **Cybercafé Surcos**, C. San Pedro, s/n, offers **Internet** access upstairs; the bar downstairs is a local favorite. (Just up C. San Pedro from the tourist office, back toward the main road. Look for the red door. Open daily 7:30pm-2:30am. €3 per hr. Coffee €1. Beer €1.50. Mixed drinks €4.) In an **emergency**, call ☎608 53 68 82. For the **Guardia Civil**, call ☎974 55 10 08. The **post office**, Pl. del Ayuntamiento, s/n, is in the Ayuntamiento across from the church. (☎974 55 20 71. Open M-F 9am-noon, Sa 10:30am-noon.) **Postal Code:** 22440.

█🛏 ACCOMMODATIONS & FOOD. Although lodgings are available within Benasque proper, you're better off staying in one of the many reasonably-priced, more-or-less modern hotels on the main road. Of these, the best are **Hotel Aneto ❷**, with its spacious wooden interiors, and the adjoining **Hostal Valero ❶**, with its smaller, less expensive rooms, both of which provide a comfortable night's rest for the travel-weary. The two share a modest pool, gym, and tennis court. (Both ☎974 55 10 61. July-Aug. and Dec.-Mar. hotel singles €31; doubles €47; triples €68. Apr.-June and Sept.-Nov. €25/€35/€52. *Hostal* singles €17; doubles €30. Apr.-June and Sept.-Nov. €12/€23. MC/V.) Better yet, head 3km up the highway toward France to **Camping Aneto ❶**, which serves as a convenient starting point for a day's hike, and offers rooms, apartments, and bungalows as well as campsites. There's also a supermarket, playground, TV lounge, bar-restaurant, and heated pool. (☎974 55 11 41. Open year-round. Rooms with shared kitchen, living room, and bathrooms €12 per person year-round. *Semana Santa*, Christmas, and July-Aug.: Camping €3.95 per person, per car, and per tent; rest of the year €3.30; 8-person condos €114.20/€102; 10-person condos €126.20/€114. 2-person bungalows weekends year-round and *Semana Santa*, Christmas, July-Aug. €66.20; rest of the year €54.10. 4-person bungalows €78.20/€66.20. IVA not included.) For an elegant treat, head to **La Parrilla ❷**, Ctra. Francia, s/n (☎97455 11 34). Award-winning chef Benito Ostarin Canals serves up creative, one-of-a-kind cuisine, perfectly balanced by the traditional Aragonese fare whipped up by La Parrilla's other chef—Benito's grandma. (Heading north on the highway, look for La Parrilla's yellow sign after Av. de Luchón. *Menú* €12. Open daily 1-4pm and 9-11pm.) Signs from C. Ministro Cornel off Pl. del Ayuntamiento will lead you to **Pub-Terraza Les Arkades ❷**, a piece of town history occupying an old stone building built in 1647. (☎974 55 12 02. *Menú* €12. Restaurant open June 22-Oct. 12 daily 1-4pm and 8-11pm; bar 5:30pm-3:30am.) Stock up at **Supermercado Aro Rojo**, C. Molino, s/n. From the highway, take Av. de los Tilos (the first left after passing the Río Esera upon entering town from the south) for a block, and then take your first left onto C. Molino, which dead ends with the supermarket. (☎974 55 28 79. Open daily *Semana Santa*, Jul.-Sept., and Oct. 12-Dec. 9am-9pm; rest of the year 9am-2pm and 5-9pm.) For fresh produce, **Fruta Albá**, C. San Pedro, is hidden in an unmarked warehouse next to Cybercafé Surcos. (Open July-Aug. daily 8:30am-1pm and 5-9pm, closed Su Sept.-June.)

⊠ **HIKING.** Experienced hikers can start out early from Benasque and hike uphill 8km on the valley road, following signs towards France. After passing the first parking area, turn onto the trail off the main road and climb up, up, and away, following the falls of the Río Cregueña. The sometimes steep but not yet technical ascent winds through glens, but never strays far from the river's edge. Four arduous hours later, you'll reach **Lago de Cregueña** (2657m), the largest and highest lake in the surrounding area. This trail is sometimes impassable in the winter months, so ask at the tourist office before putting on your hiking boots. Those wishing to scale **Mount Aneto** (3404m), the highest of the Pyrenees, can pick up some gear and head out at 5am with the experts from the **Refugio de la Reclusa ❶**. To reach the *refugio*, take the main road (follow the signs to France) north 14km until the paved road ends; from there it's a 45min. hike. (☎974 55 21 06. Open June 22-Sept. 24.) Many companies in Benasque organize trips. For less strenuous nature-wandering, head in the opposite direction down the main road and follow the signs to **Forau de Aigualluts**, a lovely pond at the base of a waterfall (40min.).

LA RIOJA & NAVARRA

From the rustic Pyrenean *pueblos* on the French border, through bustling Pamplona, to the dusty villages in the south, you can sense the immense history behind the peaceful monuments and ruins of La Rioja and Navarra. Bordered by País Vasco to the west and Aragón to the east, La Rioja and Navarra's ensconced villages greet tourists with open arms and a toast of wine.

La Rioja and great wine are literally synonymous. "Rioja" is an internationally acclaimed wine classification with an 800-year-old tradition; both the 1994 and 1995 grapes received the highest ratings possible, and since 1991 its wine has been the only in Spain to earn the coveted *Calificada* rating. The region's name derives from the Ebro tributary Río Oja, whose waters trickle through the vineyards. When ordering wine, asking for *vino* will get you the wine of the year, ordering *crianza* delivers higher-quality wine at least three years old, while a request for *gran reserva* brings the *crème de la crème* (and you'll pay for it). The best *bodegas* (wine cellars) draw from the lands in western Rioja Alta, around Haro. Try to stay sober enough to walk at least part of the Camino de Santiago, which passes through much of La Rioja. The mountainous Sierra region, with tranquil fields at the feet of towering peaks, lines La Rioja's southern border.

Lying just north of La Rioja, Navarran cities are somewhat of an oddity. Though subdued, quiet, picturesque, and religiously and politically conservative, they throw the country's wildest parties—Pamplona's outrageous *San Fermines* (July 6-14) is undoubtedly the most (in)famous. But there hasn't always been reason to celebrate. In the 13th century, the Kingdom of Navarra was divided into six districts and since then has long experienced the difficulties of Spain's on-again/off-again regionalism. The regional autonomy it gained in 1512 it lost in 1833 by supporting the losing candidate for succession during Spain's first Carlist War. To avoid another such loss, Navarra sided with the "winners" in the 20th century, allying themselves with Nationalist forces in the Spanish Civil War. They soon found that Franco's conservatism outstripped their own and had no tolerance for regional differences. Nevertheless, Navarra's spirit has remained relatively undaunted. It continues to support regionalist causes, most recently the re-establishment of provincial autonomy in 1983. Visitors, however, will find it quite difficult to separate themselves from one of Spain's most serene and storied regions.

HIGHLIGHTS OF LA RIOJA & NAVARRA

ATTACK fellow travelers at the Batalla del Vino wine fight in **Haro** (see p. 493).

RETREAT to **Roncesvalles** and blow your horn with Roland (see p. 505).

DOUBT your sanity and run with the bulls in **Pamplona** (see p. 494).

CLIMB every mountain in **Isaba**, a haven for hikers and skiers (see p. 508).

BOUNCE from *bodega* to *bodega* (free samples!) in **Logroño** (see p. 489).

LOGROÑO
☎ 941

The best entry point into the vineyard towns of La Rioja, Logroño (pop. 135,000) has always looked out for its *bodegas*: in 1635, the mayor banned carts from streets next to wineries "for fear that the vibration caused by these vehicles might affect the must." But Logroño is more than just wine. From haute couture shops to bustling avenues lined with bars serving the region's renowned *vinos* and *tapas*—not to mention the best burger in Spain—Logroño is something to write home about. Locals have claimed that Logroño feeds both the body and the soul. Although the Camino de Santiago passes through here, the soul will find little but bustling commerce for nourishment. The body, however, can feast.

⌐ TRANSPORTATION

Trains: RENFE, Pl. de Europa (☎902 24 02 02), off Av. de España on the south side of town. Info open daily 7am-11pm. To: **Barcelona** (7hr., 4 per day 4:30am-12:44am, €29-38); **Bilbao** (4hr., 3 per day 3:46pm-4am, €13.60); **Burgos** (2hr., 3 per day 2am-10:08pm, €9.25-19); **Haro** (45min., 8:17am-7:39pm, €3.05); **Madrid** (5½hr., 1 per day 10pm, €28); **Vitoria-Gasteiz** (1½hr., 6 per day 7:40am-9:40pm, €6.35; **Zaragoza** (2-2½hr., 6 per day 7:30am-10:24pm, €8.10-19).

Buses: Av. de España (☎941 23 59 83), on the corner of C. del General Vara de Rey and Av. de Pío XII. Info open M-Sa 6am-11pm, Su 7am-11pm. To: **Barcelona** (6hr., 5 per day 2:15pm-2:20am, €24); **Burgos** (2hr., 4-7 per day 8:30am-5:45pm, €6.05); **Haro** (1hr.; 7 per day 7:30am-8pm, €2.31); **Madrid** (4hr.; 5-6 per day M-Th and Sa 6:45am-7pm, F 6:45am-8pm, Su 9:30am-10pm; €16.55); **Pamplona** (2hr.; 3-5 per day M-Sa 7am-7pm, Su 10am-7pm; €6.05); **Santo Domingo de la Calzada** (1hr., 11 per day 7:15am-8pm, €2.32); **Soria** (1½hr.; M-Th and Sa 5-6 per day 6:45am-7pm, F 6:45am-10pm, Su 9:30am-10pm; €5.27); **Vitoria-Gasteiz** (2hr., 4-6 per day 7am-8pm, €7.60); **Zaragoza** (2hr., M-Sa 4-7 per day 7am-6:30pm, €8.56).

Public Transportation: All buses run to Gran Vía del Rey Juan Carlos I, 1 block from Parque del Espolón. Buses #1 and 3 pass the bus station. €0.60-0.70.

Taxis: Stands at the bus station and Parque del Espolón. **Radio Taxi** (☎941 50 50 50).

Car Rental: Europcar, C. de Chile, 1 (☎941 28 60 73), on the corner of Gran Vía. 25+. Open M-F 9am-1pm and 4-7:30pm, Sa 9:30am-1pm. AmEx/MC/V.

✳🛈 ORIENTATION & PRACTICAL INFORMATION

Gran Vía del Rey Juan Carlos I is Logroño's main thoroughfare. From the bus station, turn right onto C. del General Vara de Rey; Gran Vía will be your next left. Both the old and new towns radiate from **Parque del Espolón.** The **casco antiguo** stretches between the park and the Río Ebro on the far north side of the city. To reach the park from the **train station,** angle left on Av. de España. At the **bus station** (the next major intersection), turn right onto C. del General Vara de Rey, which leads north to the park (8min.) and the *casco antiguo.*

Tourist Office: Po. del Espolón (☎941 29 12 60). English, French, and German spoken. Open June-Oct. M-F 9am-9pm, Sa 10am-2pm and 5-8pm, Su 10am-2pm; Nov.-May M-Sa 10am-2pm and 4-8pm, Su 10am-2pm.

Currency Exchange: Banco Santander Central Hispano, on C. del General Vara de Rey at the corner of Parque del Espolón. **ATM.** Open Apr.-Sept. M-F 8:30am-2:30pm; Oct.-Mar. M-F 8:30am-2:30pm, Sa 8:30am-1pm.

Luggage Storage: At the **bus station.** €2 per locker; large bags can be left in one of the shops; ask at info desk. Open M-Sa 6am-11pm, Su 7am-11pm. At the **train station** (€3). Open daily 7am-11pm.

English-Language Bookstore: Santos Ochoa, C. de Sagasta, 3 (☎941 25 86 22). Open M-F 9:30am-1:30pm and 5-8:30pm, Sa 9:30am-1:30pm.

Emergency: ☎112. **Police:** C. Ruavieja (☎091 or 092), near Iglesia de Palacio.

Medical Services: Hospital San Millán, Av. de la Autonomía de la Rioja (☎941 29 45 00). Follow Av. de La Paz away from the *casco antiguo;* go right on Av. de la Autonomía.

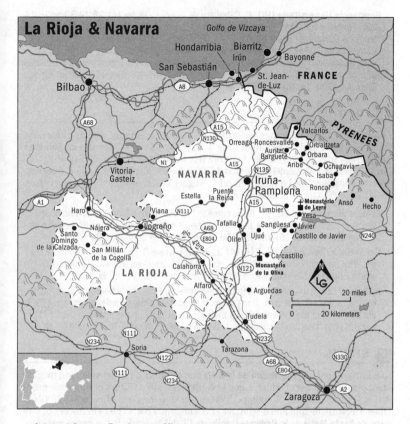

La Rioja & Navarra

Golfo de Vizcaya

FRANCE

PYRENEES

NAVARRA

LA RIOJA

Internet Access: Free Internet **Cibertecas** across the street from the bus station at Av. de Pío XII, 5, and a **Mercadoteca** on C. del Peso, between C. Capitán Eduardo Gallarza and C. de Sagasta, next to the Mercado de Abastos. Open M-Th 10am-2pm and 4-8pm, F-Sa 10am-2pm and 4pm-midnight. **Centro MAIL,** Av. Dr. Múgica, 6 (☎941 20 78 33). Video game store with a dozen computers in the back. English spoken. €0.75 per 15min. Open M-Sa 10am-2pm and 5-9pm, Su noon-2pm and 5-9pm.

Post Office: C. Pérez Galdós, 40. From the bus station, turn left and walk 5 blocks. Open M-F 8:30am-8:30pm, Sa 9:30am-2pm. **Postal Code:** 26002.

ACCOMMODATIONS

For budget accommodations, the *casco antiguo* is probably your best bet. Try C. San Juan, the second left past Parque del Espolón from the stations, or C. San Agustín and C. Laurel. Reservations are crucial for *fiesta* week near September 21.

Fonda Bilbaína, C. Capitán Eduardo Gallarza, 10, 2nd fl. (☎941 25 42 26). Take C. de Sagasta into the *casco antiguo,* turn left on C. Hermanos Moroy and then right on C. Capitán Eduardo Gallarza. Bright rooms with high ceilings, shiny floors, good beds, and sinks. Insist on a room facing the street, since the interior courtyard can be hot, noisy, and a little too intimate. Singles €21, with shower €25, with bath €28. ❷

Residencia Universitaria (HI), C. Caballero de la Rosa, 38 (☎941 26 14 30 or 26 14 22). From the train and bus stations, turn right from C. del General Vara de Rey onto Mura de Cervantes, which becomes Av. de la Paz. After 7 long blocks, turn left on C. Caballero de la Rosa and walk 3½ blocks. University dorms during the school year; used by athletic teams in summer. Public phone and 2 common rooms with TV. Doubles with bunks and private bath; rooms usually not shared. No curfew. Breakfast €1.80. Open July-Sept. 15. Bunks €8.11. ●

▐ FOOD

Logroñeses take their grapes seriously; wine is the beverage of choice with everything. C. Laurel and C. San Juan brim with bars and cafes. **Mercado de San Blas** offers fresh fruit and vegetables in a concrete building on C. Capitán Eduardo Gallarza. (Open M-F 7:30am-1:30pm and 4-7:30pm, Sa 7:30am-1:30pm.) For **groceries,** head to **Champion,** Av. La Rioja, left off C. Miguel Villanueva past the tourist office. (☎941 22 99 00. Open M-Sa 9am-9:30pm.)

El Merendero II, Gran Vía, 67. If you came to Logroño looking for the best wine in Spain, you're in luck; they also have the best burger. It may not look like much, but one bite into an *Especial* (€3.10) and you'll be convinced. Open 6pm-2am. ●

Bar Soriano, Trav. de Laurel, 2 (☎941 22 88 07), where C. Laurel turns. No indoor seating. The specialty is *champiñones con gambas* (mushrooms with shrimp; €0.75) washed down with a shot of *vino* (€0.45). Open daily 11am-3am. ●

Joshua, C. Laurel, 10, off C. Capitán Eduardo Gallarza. Find a tasty take on Middle Eastern cuisine at this informal spot. Don't worry; their special *tortuga* (turtle) pita wraps (€2-3) are only shaped like the animals. Try their succulent chicken and pistachio balls (€1) or baklava (€1). Open Th-M noon-4pm and 7pm-midnight, W noon-4pm, Tu closed. ●

◉ SIGHTS

In a Baroque palace, the **Museo de la Rioja** has a collection of art spanning the last eight centuries, most of which came from the 1835 state seizure of monastic properties. (Pl. San Agustín, 23, along C. Portales next to the post office. ☎941 29 12 59. Open Tu-Sa 10am-2pm and 4-9pm, Su 11:30am-2pm. Free.) The twin towers of **Catedral de Santa María de la Redonda** dominate Pl. del Mercado in the *casco antiguo*. (From C. del General Vara de Rey turn left on C. Portales; the cathedral is 2 blocks away. Open M-Sa 7:45am-1:30pm and 6:30-10pm, Su 8:15am-1:15pm and 6:30-9pm. Free.) The grassy knolls along the **Río Ebro** make for a nice walk; a pedestrian path runs by **Puente de Hierro** and **Puente de Piedra**.

▐◉ NIGHTLIFE & FESTIVALS

Logroño **nightlife** begins in the *casco antiguo* along C. Laurel and after midnight moves to Pl. Mayor along Pl. del Mercado, C. de Sagasta, and C. Carnicerías. Two of the best are the equally elegant **Traz Luz,** C. Portales, 71 (☎947 21 41 94) and **Noche y Día,** C. Portales, 63 (☎949 20 64 06). Or, head down to **Café Casablanca,** Av. de Portugal, 30. Warning: this classy dive may be adorned with posters and photos from the film, but that doesn't mean you should ask the bartender to play anything again. His name isn't Sam, he's heard it before, and you'll only piss him off. The **Fiestas de San Bernabé** (June 10-12) bring revelry and fireworks, but the biggest party in town begins the week of September 21 for the **Fiesta de San Mateo.** That same week, locals celebrate the grape harvest with the **Fiestas de la Vendimia,** during which they make a ceremonial offering of crushed grapes to the Virgin of Valvanera. Participants crush the grapes with their bare feet in the Parque del Espolón.

DAYTRIP FROM LOGROÑO

HARO

RENFE trains (☎941 31 15 97) connect Logroño to Haro (35min.; daily 6:40am, 6pm, also M, W, F 2:30pm; €3; additional train F 7:04pm, €8.66). Buses (☎941 31 15 43) from Logroño to Haro (1hr.; 3-6 per day M-F 7:30am-7:15pm, Sa 10:15am-7:15pm, Su 10:15am-10:30pm; €2.45).

Rubí, Paternina, Rioja Santiago, Carlos Serres: these are the names of just a few of Haro's 17 *bodegas*. Awash with the warming drink, Haro (pop. 10,000) is the heart of La Rioja's wine industry and should be a priority stop for any connoisseur or aficionado. Most wineries offer free tours of their facilities in English and Spanish between 9am and 2pm, although reservations are almost always required.

Bodegas Muga, across the Río Tirón and beyond the train tracks, can be visited without calling ahead. (☎941 31 04 98. Tours M-F 11am in English and noon in Spanish. €3.) **Bodegas Bilbaínas,** located across the river but before the train tracks, can be visited by appointment. (☎941 31 01 47. Free.) If the samples just aren't enough, hit up the **wine shops** on C. Santo Tomás. Most charge €1.35-3 per bottle, but *jarreros* (Haro locals) insist that any bottle less than €2.80 should not be consumed. The **Estación Enológica y Museo del Vino** has sleek exhibits in Spanish detailing everything you could possibly want to know about wine. (Av. Bretón de los Herreros, 4. ☎941 31 05 47. Open M-Sa 10am-2pm and 4-8pm, Su 10am-2pm. €2; W free.) Join the locals as they *ir de vinos* (go for wines) in the evening in **La Herradura,** the area around C. Santo Tomás, off Pl. de la Paz. Order *vino* and you'll get the vintage of the year (€0.35); for higher quality, order *crianza*, wine over three years old (€0.75). Haro breaks out in festivities on June 29, the day of San Pedro, when participants spray wine at innocent bystanders during the **Batalla del Vino.**

To reach **Plaza de la Paz** from the **train station,** take the road downhill, turn right and then left across the river, and follow C. Navarra uphill to the plaza (15min.). From the **bus station,** follow signs to *centro ciudad* along C. la Ventilla, continuing 2 blocks past Consum. Head diagonally left across Pl. de la Cruz onto C. Arrabal, which leads straight into Pl. de la Paz. The **tourist office,** Pl. Florentino Rodríguez, provides information on the wine routes. Take C. Virgen de la Vega from the corner of Pl. de la Paz; the office is in the plaza to the left around the bend, located in the corner of the large stone building. (☎941 30 33 66. Open July-Sept. 20 M-Sa 10am-2pm and 4:30-7:30pm, Su 10am-2pm; Sept. 21-June Tu-F and Su 10am-2pm, Sa 10am-2pm and 4-7pm.) **Luggage storage** is available in the bus station (lockers €2). **Banco Santander Central Hispano,** C. Virgen de la Vega, 20, offers **currency exchange** with no commission and a 24hr. **ATM.** (☎941 31 11 84. Open Apr.-Sept. M-F 8:30am-2pm; Oct.-Mar. M-F 8:30am-2pm, Sa 8:30am-1pm.)

CRACKING UP A visit to one of the many *bodegas* in Haro will make any visitor appreciate the art of wine-making. After the grape juice has been gathered and put into 18,000L barrels, workers must ensure that all the grape leftovers are removed from the juice. One man breaks between 1000 and 2000 eggs, separating the whites from the yolks. These egg yolks are then poured into the barrel (about 540 eggs per barrel), creating a thick film on the top. This film slowly begins to sink, and after 35 days it has removed any grape debris. The whites are then donated to neighborhood bakeries to be used in cakes.

LA RIOJA & NAVARRA

PAMPLONA (IRUÑA) ☎948

El encierro, la Fiesta del San Fermín, the Running of the Bulls, utter debauchery: call it what you will, the outrageous festival of the city's patron saint is the reason people come to Pamplona (pop. 200,000). *San Fermines* is rightly touted as the biggest and craziest festival in all Europe. Though the city's parks, museums, and monuments await exploration, it is the famous *encierro*, the focal point of the July 6-14 celebration, that draws visitors from the world over. Ever since Ernest Hemingway immortalized the *San Fermines* chaos in *The Sun Also Rises*, hordes of visitors have come to witness and experience the legendary running. At the bullring, a bust of Hemingway welcomes fans to the eight-day extravaganza of dancing, dashing, and of course, drinking—no sleeping allowed.

Although *San Fermines* may be the city's most irresistible attraction, Pamplona's lush parks, Gothic cathedral, massive citadel, and winding *casco antiguo* entertain those who show up at other times. Despite being the capital of Navarra, Pamplona's roots are truly Basque; the area was settled by the Basques long before the Roman "founders" arrived and named the city after Pompey the Great.

▐ TRANSPORTATION

Flights: Aeropuerto de Noaín (☎948 16 87 00), 6km from town. Accessible only by taxi (€8). **Iberia** (☎902 40 05 00) flies to **Barcelona** (3 per day) and **Madrid** (5 per day).

Trains: Estación RENFE, Av. de San Jorge (☎902 24 02 02). Take bus #9 from Po. Sarasate (20min., €0.70). Info open daily 6am-10pm. **Ticket office,** C. Estella, 8. (☎948 22 72 82. Open M-F 9am-1:30pm and 4:30-7:30pm, Sa 9:30am-1pm.) Pamplona's rail connections aren't the most reliable. To: **Barcelona** (6-8hr., 3-4 per day 12:28pm-12:57am, €29); **Madrid** (5hr.; 2 per day 7:15am, 6:10pm; €34); **Olite** (40min.; M-Sa 4 per day 7:25am-8:05pm; Su 2 per day 1:25, 8:05pm; €3.40); **San Sebastián** (2 per day 5:36am, 7pm; €11.50); **Vitoria-Gasteiz** (1¼hr.; M-Sa 3 per day 8:40am, 4:39, 7:35pm; Su 2 per day 4:39, 7:35pm; €4.60); **Zaragoza** (2hr.; 2 per day 12:28, 5:10pm; €13.80).

Buses: Estación de Autobuses, at the corner of C. Conde Oliveto and C. Yanguas y Miranda. **Bilman** (☎948 22 09 97) to **Barcelona** (5½hr.; 3 per day 8:35am, 4:40pm, 1:05am; €19.42). **La Burundesa (ALSA)** (☎948 22 17 66) to **Bilbao** (2hr.; M-Th and Sa 4-6 per day 7am-7pm, F 6 per day 7am-8pm, Su 4 per day 11am-8pm; €10.90) and **Vitoria-Gasteiz** (1½hr.; M-F 11 per day 7am-8:30pm, Sa 8 per day 7am-8;30pm, Su 6 per day 9am-9pm; €6). **Conda** (☎948 22 10 26) to **Madrid** (5hr.; 4-7 per day M-Th and Sa 8am-7:30pm, F and Su 8am-9:30pm; €21.55) and **Zaragoza** (2-3hr., 6-8 per day 7:15am-8:30pm, €10.92). **La Estellesa** (☎948 22 22 23) to **Logroño** (1hr.; M-F 4-5 per day 7:30am-7pm, Sa-Su 4 per day 10am-7pm; €6.20). **La Roncalesa** (☎948 22 20 79) to **Jaca** (1¾hr.; M-Sa 1 per day 8:30am, F and Su 2 per day 8:30am, 3:30pm; €5.82) and **San Sebastián** (1hr.; M-Sa 10-12 per day 7am-11pm, Su 7 per day 8:15am-11pm; €5.46). **La Tafallesa** (☎948 22 28 86) to **Olite** (50min.; M-F 8 per day 8:15am-8:30pm, Sa 6 per day 9:30am-8:30pm, Su 3 per day 1, 3:25, 8:30pm; €2.25) and **Roncal** (2hr.; M-F 1 per day 5pm, Sa 1 per day 1pm; €6.32).

Public Transportation: (☎948 42 32 42). Bus #9 runs from Po. Sarasate to the train station (20min., every 15min. 6:30am-10:15pm, €0.70). 24hr. during *San Fermines*.

Taxis: (☎948 23 23 23 or 23 23 00) at Pl. del Castillo and Parque de la Taconera.

Car Rental: Europcar, Hotel Blanca Navarra, Av. Pío XII, 43 (☎948 17 60 02). Take bus #15, 4-1 or 4-2 from Po. Sarasate and get off after the traffic circle on the way out of town. 21+. Open M-F 8:30am-1pm and 4-7:30pm, Sa 9am-1pm.

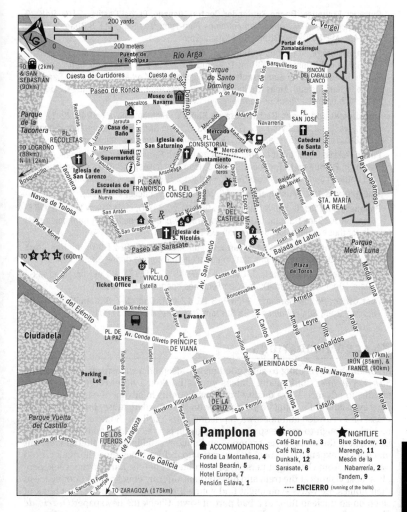

Pamplona

🏠 ACCOMMODATIONS
Fonda La Montañesa, **4**
Hostal Bearán, **5**
Hotel Europa, **7**
Pensión Eslava, **1**

🔥 FOOD
Café-Bar Iruña, **3**
Café Niza, **8**
Dunkalk, **12**
Sarasate, **6**

★ NIGHTLIFE
Blue Shadow, **10**
Marengo, **11**
Mesón de la Nabarrería, **2**
Tandem, **9**

---- **ENCIERRO** (running of the bulls)

LA RIOJA & NAVARRA

✈ 🛈 ORIENTATION & PRACTICAL INFORMATION

The **casco antiguo**, in the northeast quarter of the city, contains almost everything of interest. **Plaza del Castillo** is Pamplona's center. To reach it from the **bus station**, turn left onto Av. Conde Oliveto. From the **train station**, take bus #9 (€0.70) to the last stop; cut across Po. de Sarasate and walk diagonally left to Pl. del Castillo. North of Pl. del Castillo, the Baroque **Casa Consistorial (Ayuntamiento)** is a helpful marker in the swirl of medieval streets.

Tourist Office: C. Hilarión Eslava, 1 (☎948 20 65 40; www.cfnavarra.es). Minute-by-minute guides to the festivities are available here and at www.pamplona.net. Open during *San Fermines* daily 8am-8pm; July-Aug. M-Sa 9am-8pm, Su 10am-2pm; Sept.-June M-F 10am-2pm and 4-7pm, Sa 10am-2pm.

Currency Exchange: Banco Santander Central Hispano, Pl. del Castillo, 21 (☎948 20 86 00), has an **ATM**. Open *San Fermines* 9am-1pm; May-Sept. M-F 8:30am-2:30pm; Oct.-Apr. M-F 8:30am-2:30pm, Sa 8:30am-1pm.

Luggage Storage: At the **bus station**. Bags €2 per day, large packs €3 per day. Open M-Sa 6:15am-9:30pm, Su 6:30am-1:30pm and 2-9:30pm. Closes for *San Fermines*, when the **Escuelas de San Francisco,** the big stone building at the end of Pl. San Francisco, opens instead. Lines are long, and you must have a passport or ID. €2 per day and each time you check on your luggage. Open 24hr.

Laundromat and Public Baths: Casa de Baño, C. Hilarión Eslava (☎948 22 17 38). 4.5kg wash €3.85, dry €7.50. Open Tu-Sa 8:30am-8pm, Su 8:30am-1pm. **Showers** (€0.80). Towel €0.25, soap €0.25. Open during *San Fermines* daily 8am-9pm.

Public Toilets: Squat **toilet booths** are set up for *San Fermines,* but the permanent bathrooms in **Parque de la Taconera** (beyond Hotel Tres Reyes) and **Plaza de Sarasate** (at the bottom corner of Pl. del Castillo, toward the bus station) are more comfortable.

Emergency: ☎112. **Municipal Police:** C. Monasterio de Irache, 2 (☎092).

Pharmacy: FarPlus, C. San Nicolás, 76 (☎948 21 07 04). Open M-F 9am-1:30pm and 5-8pm, Sa 9:30am-1:30pm. **Late-night pharmacy** changes daily. All pharmacies post info for that evening's location, or call ☎948 22 21 11.

Medical Services: Hospital de Navarra, C. Irunlarrea (☎948 42 21 00). The **Red Cross** also sets up stands at the bus station and along the *corrida* during *San Fermines.*

Internet Access: Kuria.Net, C. Curia, 15 (☎948 22 30 77). €3 per hr. Open M-Sa 10am-10pm, Su 1-10pm. During *San Fermines* open daily 9am-11pm.

Post Office: Po. de Sarasate, 9 (☎948 21 12 63). Open M-F 8:30am-8:30pm, Sa 9:30am-2pm; *San Fermines* M-Sa 8:30am-2pm. **Postal Code:** 31001.

ACCOMMODATIONS

If you think you're going to get a good night's sleep on a shoestring budget during *San Fermines*, think again. Unless you've booked a hotel room at least five months in advance—or a quality hostel six months in advance—start fluffing up your sweatshirt: it's going be your pillow on the crowded, noisy, litter-laden park grass, or a crowded and not-always-pristine *pensión* floor. Some early birds may be lucky enough to secure space at campgrounds, which don't take reservations. Be warned: these can be as cramped and uncomfortable as the alternatives, but much more expensive. Expect to pay rates up to four times those normally listed (anywhere from €36-54 per person) in most budget hotels. Early in the week, people accost visitors at the train and bus stations, offering couches and floor space in their homes. Be wary—you might find yourself blowing your money for a blink of sleep on an unclean floor in a bad part of town. Check the newspaper *Diario de Navarra* for *casas particulares,* though many advertisers are hesitant to let anyone other than native Spaniards or fluent Spanish speakers into their home. Inquire at the tourist office for other listings. Many who can't find rooms (or never planned on finding them at all) sleep outside on the lawns of the Ciudadela, Pl. de los Fueros, and Pl. del Castillo, or along the banks of the river. Those who choose this risky option should store their luggage. A lucky few with cars go to nearby Estella to catch some shut-eye or snooze in their back seat—parking is free on most streets during *San Fermines.*

During the rest of the year, finding a room in Pamplona is no problem. Budget accommodations line C. San Nicolás and C. San Gregorio off Pl. del Castillo. Beware of weekends in these locations; outside rabble-rousing may make it difficult to sleep. Most hostels follow separate price schedules for *temporada alta*

(San Fermines), *temporada media* (usually only July and August, but sometimes including June and/or September), and *temporada baja* (the rest of the year). Price icons reflect *temporada media* prices.

Hotel Europa, C. Espoz y Mina, 11 (☎948 22 18 00). Offers luxurious *San Fermines* doubles at the same price as many inferior *pensiones*. Its bright rooms are away from the ruckus of C. San Nicolás. *San Fermines* singles €132; doubles €233. Rest of the year €65/€74. MC/V. ❺

Hostal Bearán, C. San Nicolás, 25 (☎948 22 34 28). Squeaky-clean rooms with phone, TV, bath, safe box, and a whopping price tag. *San Fermines* doubles €102.17; July-Sept. doubles €42.07; Oct.-June doubles €36.06. AmEx/MC/V. ❹

Fonda La Montañesa, C. San Gregorio, 2 (☎948 22 43 80), down C. San Nicolás. Older rooms, but adequate when space is tight. Pleasant, safe environment with gracious owner. Ask for a room on a higher floor during the festival. No reservations. *San Fermines* €45 per person; rest of the year €13-14. ❶

Pensión Eslava, C. Eslava, 13, 2nd fl. (☎948 22 15 58). Not as crowded as some of the other *pensiones* and relatively more quiet. Eslava has bigger, older rooms with balconies and is perfect for the last-minute traveler who hits Pamplona without reservations. San Fermines doubles only €98. Rest of the year singles €12-15; doubles €24. Discounts for longer stays. ❶

Camping Ezcaba (☎948 33 03 15), in Eusa, 7km down the road to Irún. City bus line 4-1 runs to the campground from Pl. de las Merindades (4 per day; €0.70). Hop off at the final gas station stop. Fills fast during *San Fermines*. No reservations. *San Fermines* €9 per person, per tent, and per car. Rest of the year €3.50. AmEx/MC/V. ❶

🍴 FOOD

Tiny neighborhood cafes advertise hearty *menús:* try the side streets near Pensión Santa Cecilia, C. Jarauta, C. Descalzos, near Po. de Ronda, and the area above Pl. San Francisco. C. Navarrería and Po. de Sarasate are lined with numerous *bocadillo* bars. The *barracas políticas* (bars organized by political interest groups that don't expect any interest in their platforms), next to the amusement park in the Ciudadela, offer cheap drinks. Many cafes and restaurants close for one to two weeks after *San Fermines* to recover. The **market,** C. Mercado, is to the right of the Casa Consistorial, down the stairs. (Open M-Sa 8am-2:30pm.) **Vendi Supermarket** is at the corner of C. Hilarión Eslava and C. Mayor. (Open M-F 9am-2pm and 5:30-7:30pm, Sa 9am-2pm; *San Fermines* M-Sa 9am-2pm. MC/V.)

▨ Café-Bar Iruña, Pl. del Castillo. With its ornate pillars and lush greenery, this former casino that Hemingway made famous in *The Sun Also Rises* is even more notable for its beautiful interior than for its delicious *menú* (M-F €12). Open M-Th 8am-11pm, F 8am-2am, Sa 9am-2am, Su 9am-11pm. MC/V. ❸

Restaurante Sarasate, C. San Nicolás, 19 (☎948 22 57 27), above a seafood store. Organic vegetarian dishes. Lunchtime *menú* €8. Open M-Sa 1:15-4pm, Su 9-11am. ❷

Café Niza, C. Duque de Ahumada, 2 (☎948 22 59 58). The huge, dimly-lit interior plays more like a dance club than a cafe; appreciative locals keep the place packed. *Bocadillos* €1.70. Coffee €1.10. Open M-Th 9am-11pm, F-Sa 10am-4am, Su 3-11pm. ❶

Dunkalk, C. Alhóndiga, 13, off Po. de Sarasate. This pub/eatery overflows with boomerangs, crocodile barstools, and murals of a kangaroo-filled outback. Inexpensive menu with a wide selection of beers. Large *bocadillos* €2.70-4.20. *Menú* €10.70. Chicken and other entrees €3-6. Open M-F 9am-3am, Sa-Su 11am-4am. ❶

👁 SIGHTS

CATHEDRAL & CHURCHES. Pamplona has a rich architectural legacy. Carlos III and his wife Queen Leonor are entombed in an alabaster mausoleum in the recently restored 14th-century Gothic **Catedral de Santa María.** Off the cloister is a five-chimneyed kitchen, one of four of its kind in Europe. (☎948 21 08 27. *Open M-F 10am-1:30pm and 4-7pm, Sa 10am-1:30pm. Guided tours €3.85. Group rates available.*) The 13th-century **Iglesia de San Saturnino** is near the Ayuntamiento, and Romanesque **Iglesia de San Nicolás,** in Pl. San Nicolás. (*Open daily 9am-12:30pm and 6-8:30pm. Free.*) For a peek at the legendary San Fermín and his canine comrade, head to **Iglesia de San Lorenzo,** next to the tourist office. (*C. Mayor, 74. Open daily 8am-noon and 6:30-8pm.*)

CIUDADELA. Felipe II built the pentagonal Ciudadela in an effort to secure the city from attack. Today, it's part of a grassy park that hosts an amazing *San Fermines* fireworks display and free exhibits and concerts during the summer. Its impressive **walls** scared off even clever Napoleon, who refused to launch a frontal attack and staged a trick snowball fight instead; when Spanish sentries joined in, the French entered the city through its gates. For a scenic walk to the **Ciudadela** from the old quarter, pick up C. Redín at the far end of the cathedral plaza. A left turn follows the walls past the **Portal de Zumalacárregui** and along the Río Arga. Bear left through the gardens of the **Parque de la Taconera**—where deer, swans, and peacocks roam—until reaching the Ciudadela. (*To get to the intimidating walls from Pl. del Castillo, follow Po. de Sarasate to its end, then take a right on C. Navas de Tolosa. Take your next left on C. Chinchilla; you'll see the massive entrance at the end of the street, 2 blocks down Av. del Ejército.* ☎948 22 82 37. *Open Su and Tu-Sa 7:30am-9:30pm, M 9:30am-9:30pm; closed during San Fermines. Free.*)

MUSEO DE NAVARRA. The Museo de Navarra shelters 4th-century Roman mosaics, murals from all over the region, and a collection of 14th- to 20th-century paintings, including Goya's portrait of the Marqués de San Adrián. (*Up C. Santo Domingo from Pl. Consistorial.* ☎948 42 64 92. *Open Tu-Sa 9:30am-2pm and 5-7pm, Su 11am-2pm; San Fermines Tu-Su 11am-2pm. €1.80, students €0.90. Sa afternoons and Su mornings free.*)

🎭 ENTERTAINMENT

There *is* (night)life after *San Fermines*, and it's not difficult to find. **Plaza del Castillo** is the social heart of Pamplona. High school students gather at bars in the *casco antiguo* to demonstrate their vocal abilities; singing, shouting, and any other type of loud carousing are *de rigueur*. C. San Nicolás and C. San Gregorio are nighttime favorites, as are C. Calderería, C. San Agustín, and C. Jarauta. **Mesón de la Nabarrería,** C. Navarrería, draws crowds day and night. (☎948 21 31 63. Open Su-Th 10:30am-midnight and F-Sa 11am-2:30am.) Claustrophobes and college students escape the cramped streets of the *casco antiguo* to the bars of Barrio San Juan on Av. de Bayona. **Alakarga,** Pl. Monasterio Azuelo, draws a hip, open-minded late-night crowd. (☎948 26 60 05. Beers €3. Mixed drinks €4.80. Open Su-W 10:30pm-6am; Th-Sa midnight-7am; ring the bell to enter.)

You'll find the university crowd at **Travesía de Bayona,** a small plaza of bars and *discotecas* off Av. de Bayona, just before it forks into Monasterio de Velate. The best bars are **Blue Shadow** and **Tandem,** Tr. de Bayona, 3 and 4, both of which offer good dancing, big crowds, and friendly bartenders. (Beer €3. Mixed drinks €5. Blue Shadow open Th-Sa 9pm-3:30am, Tandem open Th-Sa 6pm-6am.) Av. de Bayona also boasts the most popular and pricey of nightspots. Half a block from Pl. Juan XXIII, the enormous **Marengo,** Av. de Bayona,

2, needs five doormen to guard its threshold from sneaky fun-seekers. A ticket and clubbing gear are required. (☎948 26 55 42. Tickets €10. Beer and mixed drinks €6. O pen Th-Sa 11pm-6am.)

🔲 ▧ LOS SAN FERMINES (JULY 6-14)

> ⚠ While Pamplona is usually a very safe city, assaults and muggings skyrocket during *San Fermines*. Apparently, some characters come with shadier intentions, more interested in tourist cash than *fiesta* excitement. Do not roam alone at night, and be extremely cautious in the parks and dark streets of the *casco antiguo*. If they aren't careful, revelers in parks and along riverbanks can say *adios* to their wallets and money belts.

No limits, no lethargy, and no liability make Pamplona's **Fiestas de San Fermín**—known to most as "The Running of the Bulls"—Europe's premier party. At no other festival will you witness mayhem quite like this eight-day frenzy of parades, bullfights, parties, dancing, fireworks, concerts, wine, and more wine. *Pamploneses*, clad in white with *fajas* (red sashes) and *pañuelos* (bandanas), throw themselves into the merry-making, displaying obscene levels of physical stamina and alcohol tolerance.

Around 10am on July 6, the whole city crowds around the Ayuntamiento, in anticipation of the mayor's noon appearance. As the midday hour approaches, the mass sings and chants *"San Fermín!"* as they display their *pañuelos*, raised high above their heads. Don't commit the faux pas of wearing your *pañuelo* before the first *chupinazo* (rocket blast); tie it around your wrist to keep it safe. Also, the plaza can get unbearably packed; wear closed-toed shoes and prepare to get up close and personal with hundreds of fellow revelers. As the mayor emerges and fires the awaited *chupinazo* from the balcony, a howl explodes from the sea of expectant *sanferministas* in the plaza below. Champagne rains (as do corks) along with eggs, ketchup, wine, flour, and yellow *pimiento*. Within minutes the streets of the *casco antiguo* flood with improvised singing and dancing troupes. The *peñas*, societies more concerned with beer than bullfighting, lead the hysteria. At 5pm on the 7th and at 9 or 9:30am every other day, they are joined by the *Comparsa de Gigantes y Cabezudos*, a troupe of *gigantes* (giant wooden monarchs) and *zaldikos* (courtiers on horseback). *Kilikis* (swollen-headed buffoons) run around chasing little kids and hitting them with play clubs. These misfits, together with church and town officials, escort San Fermín on his triumphant procession through the *casco antiguo*. The saint's 15th-century statue is brought from the Iglesia de San Lorenzo at 10am on July 7, the actual day of *San Fermín*. (Virtually everything closes July 7; hours listed refer only to July 6 and 8-14.)

THE RUNNING OF THE BULLS
The *encierro* (running of the bulls), is the highlight of *San Fermines*. The ritual dates back to the 14th century, when it served the practical function of getting the bulls from their corrals to the bullring. These days, the first *encierro* of the festival is at 8am on July 7 and is repeated every day for the next seven days. Hundreds of bleary-eyed, hung-over, hyper-adrenalized runners flee from large bulls as bystanders cheer from barricades, windows, and balconies.

A rocket marks the release of the bulls into the 825m course. Six to nine animals are released from their pens as runners scurry away. If you want to participate in the bullring excitement without the risk of running with the beasts, you can line up by the Pl. de Toros well before 7:30am and run in *before* the bulls are even in sight (though such a "cowardly" act will bring booing from the locals). Three to six steers accompany the bulls—watch out, they have horns, too. Both the bulls and the mob are dangerous. Runners, all convinced the bull is right behind them, flee for dear life and act without concern for those around them. Experienced runners, many of whom view the event as an athletic art form, try to get as close to the bull as possible. The course has three sharp turns, which the bulls have difficulty cornering; when their legs slide out from under them, they falter, creating a pile of bull. Runners should avoid outside corners to prevent getting crushed under said pile, and should be especially careful at the Mercaderes-Estafeta corner.

After cascading through a perilously narrow opening (where a large proportion of injuries occur), the run pours into the bullring, amid shouts and cries from appreciative spectators. After the bulls have been safely rounded into their pens inside the Pl. de Toros, less dangerous black cows are released into the ring to "play" with the mass of 350 people. The safer alternative is to follow Hemingway's example: don't run—watch the *encierro* from the bullring instead. Music, waves, chanting, and dancing pump up spectators until the headline entertainment arrives. Bullring spectators should arrive around 6:45am. Tickets for the *Grada* section are available at 7am (M-F €3.60, Sa-Su €4.20). You can watch for free, but the free section is overcrowded, and it can be hard to see and breathe.

To watch one of the actual bullfights, you must wait in the line that forms at the bullring around 8pm every evening; earlier is always better. As one bullfight ends, tickets go on sale for the next day. (Tickets €15-70.) Cheaper, more subdued spectacles occur in the days preceding and following *San Fermines*—bargain with the scalpers outside the bullring for the best price (€4-12). Though the *sol* section can get hot, it is cheaper, closer, and generally more fun.

RUN FOR YOUR LIFE So, you're going to run with the bulls. Partaking in the *encierro* gives you a lifetime of bragging rights, but those who decide to run should seriously consider the risks involved. Some have been gored to death (the last fatality was an inexperienced American in 1995), and each day, gruesome newspaper photos of injuries are posted for all to behold. To prevent ending up on evening news programs around the world, heed a few words of *San Fermines* wisdom:

—Research the *encierro* before you run. The tourist office dispenses a pamphlet that outlines the exact route of the 3min. run and offers tips for inexperienced runners. It's a long course, and running the whole thing safely is nearly impossible. Most runners start at the Ayuntamiento, midway through the course. You should also watch it once on TV to get a glimpse of what you're in for, and then once in person, if possible.

—Do not stay up all night carousing. Not surprisingly, hung-over foreigners have the highest rate of injury. Experienced runners get a good night's sleep and arrive at the course no later than 7am. Many locals arrive at 6am. The course closes at 7:30am.

—Wear proper clothing (nothing loose or baggy) and appropriate shoes. Do not carry anything with you (especially a backpack or video camera).

—Give up on getting near the bulls and concentrate on getting to the bullring in one piece. Although some whack the bull with rolled newspapers, runners should never distract or touch the animals; anyone who does is likely to anger the bull and locals alike.

—Try not to cower in a doorway; people have been trapped and killed this way.

—Be particularly wary of isolated bulls—they seek company in the crowds.

—If you fall, **stay down.** Curl up into a fetal position, lock your hands behind your head, and **do not get up** until the clatter of hooves has passed.

THE PARTYING OF THE PARTICIPANTS

Once the running is over, the insanity spills into the streets, gathering steam until nightfall, when it explodes with singing in bars, dancing in alleys, spontaneous parades, and a no-holds-barred party in Pl. del Castillo, which quickly becomes a huge open-air dance floor. The attire for this dance-a-thon includes sturdy, closed-toed shoes (there's glass everywhere), a white t-shirt (soon to be wine-soaked), a red *pañuelo* (bandana), and a cheap bottle of champagne (to spray, of course; don't pay more than €3). English speakers often congregate where C. Estafeta hits Pl. de Toros, at an outdoor consortium of local *discotecas*. A word to the wise: avoid the fountain-jumping (you'll know it when you see it); it is stupid. It is *not* a traditional part of the festivities—it was inaugurated by Americans, Aussies, and Kiwis, and several people have died in recent years. The truly inspired partying takes place the first few days of *San Fermines*. After that, crowds thin, and the atmosphere goes from dangerously crazed to mildly insane. The party begins (or ends) each day at 6am, when bands march down the streets, waking everyone for the running. The city eases the transition with concerts, outdoor dances, and other performances. The festivities culminate at midnight on July 14 with the singing of *Pobre de mí: "Pobre de mí, pobre de mí, que se han acabado las Fiestas de San Fermín"* (Poor me, poor me, the festivals of San Fermín have ended).

Attending all eight days of the festivities is a challenge. Noisy crowds and increasingly disturbing street odors drive many away after only a few days. But if you want more, several nearby towns sponsor *encierros:* **Tudela** has its festival the week of July 24, **Tafalla** celebrates during the week of Aug. 15, and **Sangüesa** during the second week of September. Many *pamploneses* take part in a festival less touristed than their own to avoid the hordes of tourists.

■ DAYTRIPS FROM PAMPLONA

■ LUMBIER GORGES

Río Irati buses (☎948 30 35 70) run to Lumbier from Pamplona (1hr.; M-Th 3 per day 1, 3:30, 7pm; F 2 per day 1, 7pm; Sa 1 per day 1pm; return to Pamplona M-F 3 per day 7:30, 9:45am, 2:30pm; Sa 1 per day 9:45am; €2.40-3.50). From Lumbier to Iso, it's a 12km walk, drive, or taxi ride. Pedro Iso taxi ☎636 48 58 50. Parking at Foz de Lumbier is €1.50.

Two fantastic gorges cut into the mountains near Pamplona. Outside the little town of Lumbier, the **Foz de Lumbier** (Lumbier Gorge) drops 50m down to the Río Irati, and a path alongside leads through old railway tunnels. Take the path to the left at the entrance (following the N-113 signs) for an easy 5.5km nature walk that circumnavigates the gorges. Stop along the mostly flat, well-marked path at Corral de Atzuela (1.2km) to take in an astounding view, and at Puente de Diablo (Devil's Point, 4km) to examine its ruins. Just before the town of Iso, 12km down the road, the even more impressive **Foz de Arbayún** cuts a chasm through to the river below. A lookout above affords glimpses of swooping griffin vultures, while a small footpath below follows the Río Salazar toward its source.

CASTILLO DE JAVIER

La Tafallesa (☎948 22 28 86) runs a bus from Pamplona to Javier (1hr.; M-F 1 per day 5pm; Sa 1 per day 1pm; €3.63). Buses return M-Sa at 8am. A taxi (☎669 93 69 57) from Sangüesa costs approx. €9 plus the wait. Buses to Sangüesa (M-Sa 3 per day 1, 3:25, 8pm; Su 1 per day 8:15pm; €3.50) return to Pamplona (3 per day 8am, 2:40, 6:30pm; €3.50).

Near the entrance to the small village of Javier lies the majestic **Castillo de Javier,** the birthplace of San Francisco Javier (St. Francis Xavier), one of the first Jesuits and the patron saint of Navarra. This picture-perfect castle on the border between Navarra and Aragón has changed hands numerous times over the last millennium, landing finally in the Jesuits' possession. Its **Chapel of the Holy Christ** houses a 14th-century effigy that is said to have suffered a spontaneous blood-sweating fit at the moment of San Francisco Javier's death. (Open daily 9am-1pm and 4-7pm; last entrances 12:40 and 6:40pm. Occasional tours in Spanish. Donations requested.)

OLITE   ☎948

In 1347, the people of Olite (pop. 3000) extended the old town past its Roman walls into the outskirts, giving it the rounded shape it still holds today. The former home of Navarran kings, Olite is also the wine capital of Navarra. Equally proud of its past and present, Olite puts both on display: **La Fiesta de la Vendimia,** during the first two weeks of September, is a perfect occasion to celebrate the many wines of Olite, including *verjus*, the sour local specialty. Ideal for families, **Las Festivales Medievales** feature a medieval fair complete with crafts, concerts, magicians, and a royal parade during the last week of August. Olite is the perfect place to get hammered and live out your knight-in-shining-armor fantasies.

🖪🅿 **TRANSPORTATION & PRACTICAL INFORMATION. RENFE** trains (☎948 70 06 28) run to: **Pamplona** (40min., 3-5 per day, €3.60), **Tudela,** and other points on the **Vitoria-Gasteiz-Zaragoza** line. To get from the station to **Plaza de Carlos III** in the center of town, take C. de la Estación to Bar Orly, walk through the archway, and follow R. de San Francisco past **Plaza de los Teobaldos** through another arch to Plaza de Carlos III. **Buses** are cheaper and more convenient. **Conda** (☎948 22 10 26) and **La Tafallesa** (☎948 22 28 86) both run buses to **Pamplona** (35min.; M-F 7 per day 8:15am-8:30pm, Sa 6 per day 9:30am-8:30pm, Su 3 per day 1-8:30pm; €2.22). Conda also goes to **Tudela** (5-7 per day, 7:15am-9:20pm, €3). La Tafallesa arrives at Bar Orly; to reach Pl. de Carlos III, follow the directions from the train station. Conda arrives a block away. To reach Bar Orly, follow **Rúa Romana** left (past Bodega Cooperativo Olitense and Bodega Carricas). The **tourist office,** R. Mayor, 1, is off Pl. de Carlos III. (☎/fax 948 74 17 03. Open Apr.-Sept. M-F 10am-2pm and 4-7pm, Sa-Su 10am-2pm; Oct.-Mar. daily 10am-4pm.) Local services include: **banks** in Pl. de Carlos III; **emergency** ☎112; and the **post office,** R. Portillo, 3, across the plaza from the palace. (☎948 74 05 82. Open M-Sa 9-11:30am.) **Postal Code:** 31390

🛉🄲 **ACCOMMODATIONS & FOOD.** Olite's courtly airs are preserved in menu and accommodation prices everywhere. The 4 rooms of **Fonda Gambarte ❶,** R. del Seco 15, 2nd fl., off Pl. de Carlos III, share clean common baths. The in-house restaurant also serves a 2-course *menú* for €8. (☎948 74 01 39. Singles €14; doubles €23. Restaurant open July-Sept. M-F 1-3:30pm, 8:30-11:30pm. Oct.-June daily 1-3:30pm, F-Su 8:30-11:30pm. MC/V.) The pricier rooms of **Carlos III El Noble ❹,** Pl. de Carlos III, 1, all have TVs, fans, and private baths. Breakfast is included, and full and partial meal options are also available. (☎948 74 06 44; fax 71 24 67. Sept.-June singles €48.04; doubles €57.57. July-Aug. €51.25/€65.38.) The extraordinary medieval **dining room** offers a M-F *menú* for €10.50 (Open daily 1:30-4pm and 9-11pm. Cafeteria open 8am-11pm. IVA not included. MC/V.) **Camping Ciudad de Olite ❶** (☎948 74 10 14; fax 74 10 14) is 2km outside of town on Ctra. N-115 heading towards Peralta. (€3 per person and per car, €3.50 per tent. 5-person bungalows €55. MC/V.) At 🄺 **Casa Vidaurre, Obredor Artesano ❶,** C de la Estación, 3, the Vidaurre family has been making delicious pastries, cakes, and candies since 1900. You can sample all of these, as well as a wide selection of local wines and homemade meats, cheeses, and preserves at the in-house cafe, a bright, simple mix of old and new architectural styles. (☎948 74 05 79. Open daily 7:30am-3pm and 4:30-10pm. Coffee, roll, and juice €3.75.) **Supermarkets** line C. Mayor off Pl. de Carlos III, and there's an **Ali-7-Ahorro** food store at R. de San Francisco, 31.

◙ **SIGHTS.** Medieval Olite's **Palacio Real** was the 15th-century home of Carlos III and his court. Though the town's 1937 restoration was far from subtle, the palace's towers and spiral staircases are great fun to explore, entertaining many a childhood fairy tale. (☎948 74 00 35. Open daily July-Aug. 10am-2pm and 4-8pm; Apr.-June and Sept. 10am-2pm and 4-7pm; Oct.-Mar. 10am-2pm and 4-6pm; *Semana Santa* and holidays 10am-7pm. €2.70; seniors and children €1.50; under 5 free. Guided tours in Spanish every hr. on weekends.) The brand new **Centro de Exposición de la Viña y el Vino,** Pl. de los Teobaldos, 10 (☎948 74 07 54; www.centrodelvino.com) houses artful exhibits dedicated as much to the aesthetics of vines, wines, and winemaking as to wine-making's history and traditions. From Bar Orly, head up R. de San Francisco. Between the Palacio Real and the Castillo Viejo (now a *parador*) at the base of Pl. de los Teobaldos is the **Iglesia de Santa María,** noted for its 14th-century facade and belfry. (Open 30min. before mass, 9:30am daily.) The **Galerías Medievales,** down the stairs in the center of Pl. de Carlos III, houses exhibitions on Olite's medieval court. (☎948 74 18 85. Open Tu-F 11am-1pm and 5-7pm; Sa-Su 11am-2pm and 5-7pm. €1.50, including guided tour.)

ESTELLA   ☎948

Hiding between the cities of Logroño and Pamplona, charming Estella (pop. 13,000) rests in a bend of the Río Ega. What it lacks in size and glamor it makes up for in hospitality toward the faithful. With tell-tale walking sticks in hand, pilgrims traversing the Camino de Santiago have been descending on Estella since the town's founding in 1090. With an appealing plaza, mellow cafes, and a pastry shop on every corner, the town makes a perfect place to stay if you can't find Pamplona accommodations for *San Fermines.*

■◪ **ORIENTATION & PRACTICAL INFORMATION.** Two streets intersect at the heart of town. **Calle San Andrés/Baja Navarra** runs north-south from the bus station on Pl. de la Coronación to the **Plaza de los Fueros,** while **Paseo de la Inmaculada** runs east-west from C. Dr. Huarte de San Juan and **Avenida de Yerri** to the **Puente del Azucarero.** The bridge leads to the old town, where most sights and the tourist office await. Another main road, **Calle Mayor/Zapatería/Ruíz de Alda/Espoz y Mina,** runs parallel to Po. de la Inmaculada one block away. To reach the bridge from the bus station, go right and follow C. Sancho el Fuerte to Pl. San Francisco de Asis and turn right; Puente del Azucarero will be on your right.

   La Estellesa buses (☎948 55 01 27) leave from the station on Pl. de la Coronación to: **Logroño** (50min., 8-9 per day 8:30am-8:45pm, €3.57); **Pamplona** (1hr.; 4-11 per day M-Sa 7am-8pm, Su 7am-7:45pm; €3.04); **San Sebastián** (1½-2hr., 6 per day 8:45am-7:45pm, €8.63); **Zaragoza** (2½hr., M-Sa 8:30am, €11.62). Check the second page of the local newspaper, *Noticias,* for daily schedules and destinations. The **tourist office,** C. San Nicolás, 1, is straight across the bridge through Pl. de San Martín. (☎/fax 948 55 63 01. Open July-Aug. 10am-8pm; Sept.-June 10am-2pm and 4-7pm.) The local **library,** C. Ruíz de Alda 34-36, provides free **Internet** connection to patient patrons; drop by to sign up for a 30min. slot. (☎948 55 64 19. Open July-Sept. 8:30am-2:30pm; Oct.-June M-F 9am-9pm.) Local services include: **emergency** ☎112; **police,** Po. de la Inmaculada, 1 (☎092), inside the Ayuntamiento; and the **post office,** Po. de la Inmaculada, 5. (☎948 55 17 92. Open M-F 8:30am-2:30pm, Sa 9:30am-1pm.) **Postal Code:** 31200.

▞ **ACCOMMODATIONS.** With its proximity to Pamplona, Estella is a good place to catch some shut-eye during *San Fermines.* Reservations are advisable during its own *encierro* (running of the bulls) during the first week of August. From the bus station, follow C. San Andrés to C. Mayor and turn left to find **Pensión San**

Andrés ❶, C. Mayor, 1. Some rooms have TVs and refrigerators. Balconies over-looking the peaceful plaza below become exhilarating lookout points during the *encierro*. (☎948 55 41 58. July-Aug. and *Semana Santa* singles €12, with bath €23; doubles €32. MC/V.) The spacious wood-floored rooms of **Hostal Cristina ❹**, C. Baja Navarra on the corner of Pl. de los Fueros, come complete with large win-dows, private bathrooms, and TVs. (☎948 55 04 50. July-Aug. and *Semana Santa* singles €35; doubles €45. Sept.-June €35/€42. IVA not included.) **Fonda Izarra ❷**, C. Calderería, 20, off Pl. de los Fueros, offers simpler rooms with light blue walls, lace curtains, and fluffy bedding. (☎948 55 06 78. Singles €20; doubles €30. MC/V.) From the left of the tourist office, it's 1km (20min.) down-river and past the fac-tory to **Camping Lizarra ❶**, C. Ordoiz, s/n. Let the Pamplona bus driver know and he'll stop. The grounds include a supermarket, pool, 18-bed hostel, and a small res-taurant-bar. (☎948 55 17 33. €3.60 per person, children €3.20; €9.80 per *parcela* (plot with room for tent and car); hostel bunks €6.20. Open year-round. MC/V.)

🄲 FOOD. Estella is known throughout the region for its *gorrín asado* (roast pig-let, also called *gorrín de Estella*). For groceries, head to **Autoservicio Larramendi**, C. Mayor, 58. (Open M-Sa 9am-1:30pm and 5-8pm. MC/V.) Save fresh fruit and veg-etable shopping for street-side **Frutas Argandoña**, a few doors down. (Open 8:30am-1:30pm and 5-8pm.) The overwhelming portions served upstairs at **Restaurante Casanova ❷**, C. Obispo Oñate, 7, are sure to slow any pilgrim's progress. Upon entering Pl. de los Fueros from C. Baja Navarra, take a left and look for the wooden sign. (☎948 55 28 09. *Menú* M-F €8.41, Sa-Su €12.41. Fish and meat entrees €7.20-12. Open M 1-3:30pm, Tu-Su 1-3:30pm and 8:30-11pm. MC/V.) For a more economical alternative, try the *chorizo* (€1.50) at **Café-Bar Lerma ❶**, Po. de la Inmaculada, s/n, between C. San Andrés/C. Baja Navarra and C. Escultor Imberto. (*Bocadillos* €1.50; beer €1.50; fresh-squeezed orange juice, coffee, and pastry €2.50. Open daily 7am-midnight.)

🄶 🄳 SIGHTS & ENTERTAINMENT. The 12th-century **Iglesia de San Miguel** com-mands a view of Estella from the hilltop Pl. de San Miguel. Its ornately carved stone portal depicts St. Michael fighting dragons, weighing souls, and taking care of celestial business. Up the stairs and opposite the tourist office, the late Romanesque/early Gothic **Iglesia de San Pedro de la Rúa**, with its unusual half-destroyed cloister, towers above **Calle de la Rúa**. Tours of all sites (€3.65, pilgrims €3.35, children €3) can be arranged through **Cultura 5**, C. San Nicolás, 3 (☎948 55 00 70), inside the tourist office. Across from Iglesia de San Pedro and next to the tourist office, the world's oldest representation of medieval French hero Roland jousts with Farragut the Moor on the columns of the 12th-century **Palacio de los Reyes de Navarra**, now the **Museo Gustavo de Maetzu**. Inside are the impressive works of painter Gustavo de Maetzu, who spent his last years in Estella. Rotating temporary exhibits are displayed on the first floor. (☎948 54 60 37; fax 55 32 57. Open Tu-Sa 11am-1pm and 5-7pm, Su 11am-1:30pm. Free.) The week-long **Fiestas de la Virgen del Puy y San Andrés** kick off the Friday before the first Sunday in August, featuring an *encierro* of baby bulls (less ferocious than Pamplona's), kid-die entertainment, a fair, Navarrese dancing, and *gaitas* (traditional instruments of northern Spain similar to bagpipes, but without the bags).

NAVARRAN PYRENEES

The Navarran Pyrenees are not for the sedentary; only pilgrims, athletes, and wan-derlust-stricken journeyers can appreciate its well-preserved forests and topo-graphical diversity. Forbidding peaks dominate the eastern Valle de Roncal, while the mountain slopes to the west allow easy access to the area's streams, water-falls, and green meadows. Mist and fog obscure visibility at high altitudes to create a dreamy atmosphere, or nerve-racking driving conditions, depending on your point of view. While most inhabitants log or raise cattle, tourism is becoming a booming business. The French portion of El Camino de Santiago crosses the border at Roncesvalles and winds down through Pamplona on its way to Santiago de Compostela in Galicia. Many free and cheap *refugios* cater to modern-day pilgrims along the way, as well as others who don't mind sleeping beside a few scruffy travelers. Navarra's *casa rurales* (rural lodging houses) are particularly beautiful. Pick up a free copy of the *Guía de alojamientos de turismo rurales* in any of Navarra's tourist offices. As a rule, these homes are welcoming places to stay and great budget options (€21-29). For reservations, call the multilingual tourist office at ☎948 20 65 40. Pamplona is a sensible base for those dependent upon public transportation; you can head east toward Valle de Roncal, or north toward Roncesvalles. Buses are one-a-day affairs throughout most of the area.

RONCESVALLES

As the first stop in Spain on the Camino de Santiago, Roncesvalles's mist-enshrouded 10-odd buildings rest amid miles of thickly wooded mountains. The devout aren't the only ones who pass through this mountain town (pop. 31); folklore buffs come in search of the remains of Roland, Charlemagne's favorite soldier. Just up the hill from Roncesvalles in AD 778, Roland received his mortal wound, and in Puerto Ibañeta (1057m), less than 2km up the road from the monastery, he breathed his final breath. The heavily restored **Capilla de Sancti Spiritus** stands over the remains of the bone heap (courtesy of dead soldiers and pilgrims) where his tomb is thought to be. (The chapels can be visited only on guided tours.)

Inside the **Colegiata**, up the driveway from the *capilla*, the tombs of King Sancho El Fuerte (the Strong) and his bride rest in solitary splendor, lit by the huge stained-glass windows of the **Capilla de San Agustín**. (☎948 79 04 80. Chapel and cloister open *Semana Santa*-Sept. daily 10am-1:30pm and 3:30-6:30pm; Oct.-*Semana Santa* M-F 10am-5pm. €1.50.) In the decisive battle of Las Navas de Tolosa, Sancho reputedly broke the chains protecting the Arab king Miramomolin with his own hands and summarily decapitated him. The heavy iron chains hanging from the walls of the chamber are represented in Navarra's flag. The monastery's lovely French Gothic **church**, endowed by Sancho and consecrated in 1219, is its main attraction. (☎948 76 00 00. Open M-Sa 10am-8pm, Su 7am-8am. Free. **Guided visits** including all monuments and the Roncesvalles museum €3.20, students, seniors, and pilgrims with credentials €2.40.)

⁊ PRACTICAL INFORMATION. La Montañesa buses (☎948 22 15 84) run between **Pamplona** and Roncesvalles. (1¼hr.; M-F 6pm, Sa 4pm; €3.91. Return bus leaves Roncesvalles M-Sa 6:50am.) The bus stops in **Burguete** each way. A **tourist office** in the mill behind Casa Sabina Hostería offers maps and guides to the sites of Roncevalles and the Camino de Santiago. (☎948 76 03 01. Open *Semana Santa* and July-Aug. M-Sa 10am-2pm and 2:30-7pm, Su 10am-2pm; Sept.-*Semana Santa* and Apr.-June daily 10:30am-2pm.) For **Banco Santander Central Hispano** (open Apr.-Sept. M-F 8:30am-2:30pm; Oct.-Mar. M-F 8:30am-2:30pm, Sa 8:30am-1pm), **supermarkets,** and **restaurants,** head to nearby Burguete (2km south).

⍰⍰ ACCOMMODATIONS & FOOD. The monastery ❶ in Roncesvalles has free lodging for pilgrims—enter the door to the right as you face the monastery. To attain "official pilgrim" status, you'll have to make a €1 symbolic payment and obtain proper credentials: a stamped piece of paper that verifies your sacred mission. The attached **Oficina de Peregrinos** provides this service. But don't become official just to get free lodging; true pilgrims look down upon such vagrancy, and you won't be able to use the credentials until the next stop on the path anyway. (☎948 76 00 00. Reception open M-Sa 10am-1:30pm and 4-7:30pm, Su 4-6pm.) Behind the monastery is **Albergue Juvenil Roncesvalles (HI) ●**, a somber building that served as a pilgrims' hospital in the 18th century. Rec rooms are in the basement. (☎948 76 03 64. Reception 4-9pm. Internet access available. Meals available only for large groups. Members only. HI cards for sale €5, over 29 €11. Four- to 11-bed dorms €9 per pilgrim and HI members under 29; over 29 €9. Call ahead for reservations June-August.) For a more pleasant stay in Roncevalles, try **La Posada ●**, the first building on your right upon entering town. With its airy, spacious rooms and wood-beamed common room featuring couches, TV, and an exercise bike, La Posada is perfect for families. (☎948 76 00 02. *Menú* €15. *Semana Santa* and July-Aug. doubles €45, triples €50.50; quads €56; Sept.-Oct. and Dec.-June €38.50/€42.07/ €48.08/€52.89. Bar open 8:30am-10pm. Restaurant open 1-3:30pm and 8:30-10pm.) Accommodations, including several *casas rurales*, are plentiful in nearby **Burguete**. Those following the **Camino de Hemingway** can check out **Hostal Burguete ●**, C. San Nikolás, 71 (est. 1880). With its springy beds and big, old-fashioned rooms, not much has changed since Papa did some resting and writing here on his way back to Paris from *San Fermines*. (☎948 76 00 05. Breakfast €3.25. *Menú* €11.50. Aug. and *Semana Santa* singles €35.95; doubles €48.90; triples €60.90. After *Semana Santa*-July and Dec. €29.90/€39.90/ €51.90. AmEx/MC/V.)

Besides La Posada's dining room, Roncesvalles's lone restaurant is the cramped **Casa Sabina Hostería ●**, which offers an €11 *menú* and €6-11 entrees. You're better off heading to **Asador Aritza ●**, C. Kanaleburua, 6, in Burguete. The colorful dining room and pleasant country setting are perfect complements to the generous entrees (€10-17) and *menú* (€14). From Roncesvalles, Artiza is one of the first buildings on the left as you enter Burguete; look for the sign. (☎948 76 03 11. Open Su-M and W-Sa 12:30-3:15pm and 8:30-10pm. Closed M evening.)

VALLE DE SALAZAR: OCHAGAVÍA (OTSAGABIA)   ☎948

At the confluence of the Ríos Anduña, Zatoia, and Salazar sits Ochagavía (pop. 600), a picturesque mountain village typical of Navarran Pyrenees *pueblos* in appearance, if not in population. The Valle de Salazar's largest town spans both sides of the cheerful Río Anduña, 85km from Pamplona. Ochagavía's whitewashed houses and cobbled streets lead to forested mountains great for hiking, trout fishing, and cross-country skiing.

◨ ▮ TRANSPORTATION & PRACTICAL INFORMATION. Río Irati (☎948 22 14 70) runs buses to **Pamplona** (1½hr., M-Sa 1 per day 9am, €5.85) with return service to Ochagavía (1 per day M-Th 3:30pm, F 7pm, Sa 1:30pm). The **tourist office,** on the main road (Ctra. Aísaba), is in the same building as a nature center and offers a free lodging guide, *Guía de Alojamientos Turísticos.* (☎948 89 06 41; fax 89 06 79. Office open *Semana Santa*-Oct. M-Sa 10am-2pm and 4:30-7:30pm, Su 10am-2pm; Nov.-*Semana Santa* M-F and Su 10am-2pm, Sa 10am-2pm and 4-7pm.) The **nature center** (☎948 89 06 41) is open June 16-Sept. 15 M-Sa 10am-2pm and 4:30-8:30pm, Su 10am-2pm; Sept. 16-June 15 Su-Th 10am-2pm, F-Sa 10am-2pm and 4:30-7:30pm. €1.20. Several **ATMs** are located on the main road. In an **emergency,** call ☎112. The **pharmacy** is at C. Urrutia, 31 (☎948 89 05 06; open M-F 10am-2pm and 5-7:30pm, Sa 10am-2pm), and the **post office** is on C. Lavadia, near the Ayuntamiento. (☎948 89 04 52. Open M-Sa 9-10am.) **Postal Code:** 31680.

🛏️🍴 ACCOMMODATIONS & FOOD. Ask at the tourist office or look for the "CR" signs advertising one of the town's 25 *casas rurales*. A left down the street just beyond the post office will take you warm and welcoming 🏠**Casa Navarro ❷**, C. Lavadia, 6, which rents large, immaculate rooms with balconies. Look for the corner building with a wide entryway. (☎948 89 03 35. Breakfast €3. Reservations recommended. Doubles €25, with bath €30; triples €35.) Across the river from the main road, **Hostal Orialde ❸**, C. Urrutia, 6, has attractive, spacious rooms with stone floors. The dining room serves an adequate selection of entrees for €5-7. (☎948 89 00 27. *Menú* €12.80. Singles €28; doubles €37.25, with half bath €44.80; with full bath €47.65.) **Camping Osate ❶**, 500m from town (turn right at the huge painted sign), provides a campsite on the river with supermarket, bar, and paintball. Sure, you could hike, but you can also participate in glorious technicolor violence in the calm Pyrenees. (☎948 89 01 84 or 696 89 99 95. *Menú* €9. Camping €3.50 per person and per tent, €3.75 per car; 2-6 person bungalows July 15-Sept. €55-85 per day; Oct.-July 14 €40-80. MC/V.) Follow the blue "free parking" signs across the river from the main road to get to **Kixkia ❷**, C. Urrutia, s/n. With huge cider casks embedded in the far wall and long wooden tables, Kixkia is a perfect example of the *sidrerías* typical of the area. (☎948 89 05 17. Entrees €4-10. *Menú*, including all-you-can-drink cider, €22. Open daily 1:30-4pm and 8-10:30pm.)

👁️🥾 SIGHTS & HIKING. The 12th-century **Ermita de Muskilda**, housing a 15th-century Virgin, is the spiritual and cultural nexus of the town. From Ochagavía, it's a 45min. hike (4km); follow the path from behind the church, or take the road toward **Izalzu** and look for the stone cross. (☎948 89 00 38. Open July-Sept. daily 11am-2pm and 4-8pm; May-June and Oct. M-F 4-7pm, Sa-Su 11am-2pm and 4-8pm; Apr. Sa-Su 11am-2pm and 4-7pm.) Local dances featuring elaborate costumes are performed at the sanctuary on September 8, the first day of Ochagavía's annual **Festival de la Virgin de Muskilda**. Hikers will find the climb up **Pico de Orhy** (2021m) a breeze. The 1hr. trail leaving the parking lot at **Puerto de Larrau**, 9km north of Ochagavía along the highway to France, leads to panoramic views of the valley. A lengthy but smooth hike (20km; 6hr. 1-way) follows the Río Irati past the **Embalse de Irabia** lake and through the **Selva de Irati** to the town of **Orbaitzeta**; hikers should leave their cars at the **Ermita de las Nieves** 24km north of Ochagavía and head west along the river. **Cross-country skiers** can also enjoy two circuit trails originating farther down the same highway. These hikes are not accessible by bus, so those without cars must either hoof it or take a **taxi** (☎948 89 02 94 or 620 27 02 41) to the beginning of the trails. **Ekia** (☎948 89 01 84) has an office at the campground and leads guided tours for everything from rafting (€36) to spelunking (€30).

VALLE DE RONCAL

Carved by the Río Esca, Valle de Roncal is a handsome valley stretching south from the French border. Its darling towns, inviting *casas rurales*, and prime hiking trails demand that Valle de Roncal not be missed.

RONCAL   ☎948

Smack in the center of the Valle de Roncal, diminutive **Roncal** (pop. 375) prides itself on two things: its famed *queso Roncal*, a sharp, sheep's milk cheese, and its world-renowned tenor, Julián Gayarre (1844-1889). **Casa Museo Julián Gayarre**, on C. Arana, occupies the singer's birthplace, showcasing assorted memorabilia. (☎948 47 51 80. Open Apr.-Sept. Tu-Su 11:30am-1:30pm and 5-7pm; Oct.-Mar. Sa-Su 11:30am-1:30pm and 4-6pm. €1.80, seniors and students €1.60, under 12 free.) **La Tafallesa buses** (☎948 22 28 86) run to **Pamplona** (2hr., M-F 7am, €6). The **tourist**

office on Roncal's main road, Po. de Julián Gayarre, has info on hiking and *casas rurales*. (☎948 47 52 56; fax 47 53 16. Open June 15-Sept. 15 M-Sa 10am-2pm and 4:30-8:30pm, Su 10am-2pm; Sept. 16-June 14 M-F 10am-2pm, Sa 4:30-7:30pm.) Services include: **emergency** ☎112; **Guardia Civil** ☎948 47 50 05; and a **pharmacy,** next door to the tourist office (open July-Sept. M-F 10am-2pm and 5-8pm, Sa 10am-2pm; Oct.-June M-F 10am-2pm and 5-7:30pm, Sa 10am-2pm). Go to **Panadería Lus ❶,** C. Iriondoa, 3 (☎948 47 50 10), down the path next to Caja Navarra, for some wine and a taste of the lauded Roncal cheese. (Open July-Aug. 9:30am-2pm and 5:30-8:30pm, Sept.-June 9:30am-1:30pm and 5-7pm.) If you spend the night, head to wonderfully homey **Casa Villa Pepita ❶,** Po. Julián Gayarre, 4, across from the dirt playground just before the bridge. Each room has its own decoration scheme. (☎948 47 51 33. Breakfast €3.50. Meals €11. Doubles €25, with bath €33.)

ISABA & ENVIRONS   ☎948

Isaba (pop. 550) draws hikers and skiers north of Roncal to explore the surrounding mountains. A stunning hike climbs from Isaba to Zuriza in the Valle de Hecho (5-6hr.). The ascents from Collado Argibiela to Punta Abizondo (1676m) and Peña Ezkaurre (2050m) are shorter but steeper. Another recommended hike leads to neighboring Ochagavía, in the Valle de Salazar (5-6hr.). For more routes, ask at the tourist office. Ski trails run north of Isaba, at the Estación de Ski Larra-Belagna, km 18 on NA-1370, the highway towards France (call the tourist office: ☎948 89 32 51). A village festival, featuring stone-throwing contests and a local variation of polo, runs July 25-28 in honor of Santiago. Isaba breaks out in dancing and general merriment on September 16 in honor of San Cipriano, the town's patron saint.

Isaba's **tourist office,** C. Bormapea, 5, is on the right as you enter town, heading north, just before the boardwalk. (☎948 89 32 51. Open *Semana Santa*-Oct. 12 Tu-Sa 10am-2pm and 4:30-7:30pm, Su 10am-2pm; rest of year M-F 10am-2pm, Sa 4:30-7:30pm.) **Telephones** and **ATMs** can be found just uphill from the tourist office.

On the north side of town, next to the parking lot, is **Hotel Ezkaurre ❹.** Its cozy, sunny interiors and welcoming common room (complete with TV and board games) are excellently complemented by the **restaurant ❷** downstairs. Bedraggled backpackers appreciate the generous portions and down-home feel. (*Menú* €9.90, breakfast €2.85. Restaurant open 8:30-10:30am and 8:30-10:30pm. July-Sept. doubles €42; triples €56. Oct.-June €36/€48.) For a comfortable but pricy night's sleep, **Hotel Isaba ❸,** C. Bormapea, 51, below the tourist office, is less rugged than the typical *refugio*. A large, circular fireplace and two big common rooms—both filled with comfortable couches and chairs—make Isaba a great place to relax after a long day of hiking. All rooms have full bath and TV. The hotel **restaurant ❷** serves a *menú* (€13.55) and entrees (€7-11). (☎948 89 30 00. Restaurant open 7:30-10:30am, 1-3:30pm, and 8:30-10:30pm. *Semana Santa* and July 12-Aug. 28 singles €48.50; doubles €75. May-June and Sept.-Oct. €40.50/€64.25. Nov. and Jan. 7-*Semana Santa* €33/€53.50. IVA not included. MC/V.) **Albergue Oxanea ❶,** C. Bormapea, 47, offers wooden bunks and a TV lounge with VCR and board games. (☎948 89 31 53. Breakfast €2.40. Meals €9. Dorm €8, with sheets €10. Open daily Jan.-Apr. and July-Sept.; open Sa-Su only Oct.-Nov. 22 and May-June.) **Camping Asolaze ❶,** 6km up the road toward France, offers a restaurant, store, bunk-beds, and handicapped-accessible private bungalows in addition to campsites. (☎948 89 30 34. Closed Nov. 1-15. Sheets €2.80. Dorm €9. Camping €3.75 per person, per tent, per car. Bungalow doubles €30; quads €65; 6 people €80. MC/V.) The mountains open into the **Valle de Belagua,** 8km north of Isaba, where **Refugio Angel Olorón ❶** offers bunks year-round at km18 on the highway toward France. (☎/fax 948 39 40 02. Breakfast €2.50; meals €10. Dorms €8;*Federación de Montaña* and *Carnet Jovens* members €4.) Those venturing into the wilderness can hoard food for the trail at **Vendi Supermercado** on C. Mendigatxa (☎948 89 31 91).

LA RIOJA & NAVARRA

PAÍS VASCO (EUSKADI)

As the Basque saying goes, "Before God was God and the rocks were rocks, the Basques were Basque." The País Vasco is officially composed of the provinces Guipuzcoa, Alava, and Vizcaya, but the Basque homeland extends into Navarra and southwestern France, containing seven provinces in all. The varied landscape of the País Vasco resembles a nation complete unto itself, with cosmopolitan cities, verdant hills, industrial wastelands, and quaint fishing villages. The people are marked by their deep attachment to the land and immense cultural and national pride. However, it is *euskera*, a language totally unrelated to any other, that binds and quite literally defines them. Even the Basque name for themselves, *Euskaldinuak*, means "speakers of Euskera."

Though their origins are shrouded in mystery, the Basques are thought to descend from the first Europeans (some theories place Cro-Magnon main directly in their family line), whose arrival predated that of the Indo-European tribes that would go on to populate the rest of Eurasia. They might once have inhabited all of Iberia; by the time of the Romans, however, they were already confined to the Pyrenees region. Under the Romans, the Basques lived semi-autonomously until the 18th-century abolishment of the Basque *fueros* (ancient rights of self-government). The Basques enjoyed a brief return to independence under the Second Spanish Republic, but the Republican defeat in the Spanish Civil War ushered in the Fascist rule of General Francisco Franco, who heavily repressed the Basques, banning *euskera* and various cultural expressions. In 1968, in response to such indignities, the organization *Euskadi ta Askatasuna* ("Basque Country and Freedom;" ETA) began a separatist terrorist movement that has continued to this day, killing over 800 people. A short-lived 1998 cease-fire between the Spanish government and ETA did little to quell the group's violence; their most recent victim was a policeman from Sangüesa in 2003. Anti-ETA sentiment is now quite strong among País Vasco natives—posters and banners denouncing the organization line streets and hang from buildings throughout the region—but many also argue that the methods employed in the Spanish government's attempted ETA suppression/extermination undermine free speech and disregard human rights.

Most Basques share a strong desire to preserve their cultural identity. Although Castilian Spanish is the predominant language, *euskera* has enjoyed a resurgence since Franco's death. Other regional traditions like *cesta punta* or *pelota vasca* (known outside Spain as *jai-alai*) continue to thrive. Basque cuisine is some of Iberia's finest, including *bacalao a la vizcaína* (salted cod in a tomato sauce) and dishes *a la vasca* (in a parsley-steeped white wine sauce). *Tapas*, considered regional specialties, are called *pintxos* (PEEN-chos); locals wash them down with *sidra* (cider) and the local white wine, *txakoli*.

HIGHLIGHTS OF EL PAÍS VASCO

BASK in the seaside splendor of **San Sebastián (Donostia)** (p. 510).

REFLECT on disaster and renewal at the **Gernika Peace Museum** (p. 525).

GROOVE to summer tunes at **Vitoria-Gasteiz's** International Jazz Festival (p. 530).

SLUR through *pintxos* and *txakoli* as you *taberna*-hop through the region (any page.)

DISCOVER modern art, modern Spain, and a puppy made of flowers at the shiny, slippery Guggenheim in cosmopolitan **Bilbao** (p. 523).

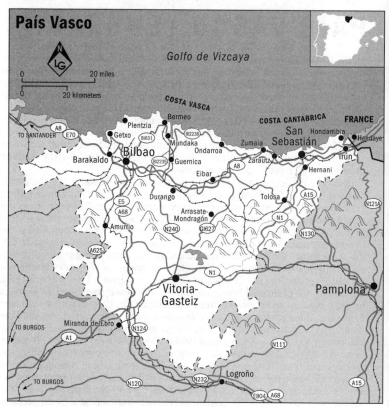

País Vasco

Golfo de Vizcaya

COSTA VASCA

Bermeo

COSTA CANTABRICA   FRANCE

Plentzia

TO SANTANDER   Getxo   Mundaka   Ondarroa   Zumaia   San Sebastián   Hondarribia   Hendaye

Bilbao   Guernica   Zárautz   Irún

Barakaldo   Eibar   Hernani

Durango   Tolosa

Amurrio   Arrasate-Mondragón

Vitoria-Gasteiz   Pamplona

Miranda de Ebro

TO BURGOS   Logroño

TO BURGOS

PAÍS VASCO

SAN SEBASTIÁN (DONOSTIA)   ☎943

San Sebastián (pop. 180,000) glitters on the shores of the Cantabrian Sea. An elaborate ivory boardwalk and wide white-sand beaches give the city an air of gentility—Queen Isabel II summered here—but belie the 21st-century edge found in its boutiques, surf-shops, and nightclubs. Such international catering doesn't interfere with the city's strong sense of regional culture. Residents and posters constantly remind you that you are not in Spain, you are in the Basque country.

In the early 19th century, San Sebastián stood as one of Spain's great ports, but much of it was destroyed during the 1813 Peninsular War. The ruined walls were finally torn down in 1863, and construction of a new city began, one whose popularity has been increasing ever since. Foreigners and land-locked Spaniards journey to San Sebastián for its world-famous beaches, bars, and scenery.

⌐ TRANSPORTATION

Flights: Airport in Hondarribia (☎943 66 85 00), 20km east of the city. **Interurbanos buses** to Hondarribia pass by the airport (45min., every 15-20min., €1.25). A **taxi** costs €25. Flights to **Madrid** (1¼hr., 3-6 per day) and **Barcelona** (1¼hr., 1-4 per day).

Trains: San Sebastián has 2 train stations; **Estación de Amara** serves local destinations. **RENFE, Estación del Norte,** Po. de Francia (☎902 24 02 02). Info open daily 7am-11pm. To: **Alicante** (10-14hr.; 1 per day F 8:10pm, Sa 9:34am; €41); **Barcelona** (9hr.; Su-F 2 per day 10:45am, 11pm; €32.50); **Burgos** (3½hr., daily 8 per day 8:32am-11pm, €18); **Madrid** (8hr.; Su-F 3 per day 8:32am-10:37pm, Sa 9:33am-10:37pm; €41); **Pamplona** (2hr.; daily 2 per day 10:45am, 11pm; €12.50); **Paris, FR via Hendaye** (8-11hr.; M-F 5 per day 7:45am-10:55pm, Sa 4 per day 7:45am-10:26pm, Su 4 per day 8:36am-10:55pm; €80); **Salamanca** (10hr.; Su-F 3 per day 8:32am, 1:37, 10:20pm; Sa 2 per day 8:32am, 10:20pm; €27); **Vigo** (12hr., daily 1 per day 9:02am, €36); **Vitoria-Gasteiz** (1¾hr.; M-F 2-6 per day 8:32am-10:37pm; Sa 3 per day 9:34am, 4:06, 10:37pm; Su 8:32am-10:37pm; €6-22); **Zaragoza** (4hr., daily 1 per day 10:45am, €19).

Buses: Stations at Av. de Sancho el Sabio, 31-33 and Po. de Vizcaya, 16.

ALSA, Po. Vizcaya, 16 (☎942 10 12 10) runs internationally to **Paris** (12hr.; daily 2 per day 12:45am, 8pmpm; €61 one-way, €108 round-trip).

Continental Auto, Av. de Sancho el Sabio, 31 (☎943 46 90 74). To: **Burgos** (3-3½hr., 6-8 per day 9am-12:30am, €12.59); **Madrid** (6hr., 10-13 per day 7am-12:30am, €25.84); **Vitoria-Gasteiz** (2hr., 7-9 per day 7:15am-12:30am, €6.35).

La Estellesa to: **Logroño** (4 per day 8am-7:15pm, €12.10).

Transportes PESA, Av. de Sancho el Sabio, 33 (☎902 10 12 10), to: **Bilbao** (1¼hr.; every 30min. M-F 6:30am-10:30pm, Sa-Su 7:30am-10:30pm; €7.50).

Interbus (☎943 64 13 02). To: **Hondarribia** (45min., every 15min. 7:25am-11:25pm, €1.25) and **Irún** (35min., every 15-30min., €1).

La Roncalesa, Po. Vizcaya, 16 (☎943 46 10 64). To **Pamplona** (1hr., 6 per day 7am-7:15pm, €5.37).

Vibasa, Po. Vizcaya, 16 (☎943 45 75 00). To **Barcelona** (7hr.; M-Th and Sa 1 per day 7am, F and Su 2 per day 3, 11:50pm; €22.15).

Public Transportation: (☎943 28 71 00). €0.80. **Bus #16** goes from Alameda del Boulevard to the campground and beaches.

Taxis: Santa Clara (☎943 36 46 46), **Vallina** (☎943 40 40 40), and **Donostia** (☎943 46 46 46). Taxis to **Pamplona** take about 45min. and cost around €83.

■ ☷ ORIENTATION & PRACTICAL INFORMATION

The **Río Urumea** splits San Sebastián. The city center, most monuments, and the two most popular beaches, **Playa de la Concha** and smaller **Playa de Ondarreta,** line the peninsula on the west side of the river; Playa de Ondarreta curves into **Monte Igueldo.** At the tip of the peninsula, separating the Río Urumea from Playa de la Concha, sits **Monte Urgull.** Just inland from Monte Urgull is the **parte vieja** (old city), San Sebastián's restaurant, nightlife, and budget accommodations nexus. **El Centro,** the city center and commercial district is just below the *parte vieja* at the base of the peninsula. On the east side of the river, **Playa de la Zurriola** attracts a younger surfing and beach crowd. The **bus station** is south of the city center on Pl. Pío XII, while the **RENFE station** and **Barrio de Gros** are to the east.

Tourist Office: Municipal Centro de Atracción y Turismo, C. Reina Regente, 3 (☎943 48 11 66). Open June-Sept. M-Sa 8am-8pm, Su 10am-2pm; Oct.-May M-Sa 9am-1:30pm and 3:30-7pm, Su 10am-2pm.

Hiking Information: Club Vasco de Camping, C. San Marcial, 19 (☎943 42 84 79). Organizes excursions. Open M-F 6-8:30pm. **Izadi,** C. Usandizaga, 18 (☎943 29 35 20), off Av. de la Libertad. Sells hiking guides and maps, some in English. Open M-F 10am-1pm and 4-8pm, Sa 10am-1:30pm and 4:30-8pm.

PAÍS VASCO

Bike Rental: Bici Rent Donosti, Po. de la Zurriola, 22 (☎943 27 92 60). 1 week min. on rentals. Provides bike trail maps. Bikes €18 per day, €12 for 4hr. Tandem bicycles €36 per day, €20 for 4hr., €6 for 1hr. For motos, call ahead.

Luggage Storage: Train station (€3 per day; buy tokens at the ticket counter). Open daily 7am-11pm.

Laundromat: Lavomatique, C. Iñigo, 14 (☎943 42 38 71). 4kg wash €3.75, 6kg wash €5.55 (cold water only), €2.70 dry. Soap €0.45. Open M-F 9:30am-2pm and 4-8pm, Sa-Su 10am-2pm.

Emergency: ☎112. **Police: Municipal,** C. Easo (☎943 45 00 00).

Medical Services: Casa de Socorro, C. Bengoetxea, 4 (☎943 44 06 33).

Internet Access: Zarr@net, C. San Lorenzo, 6 (☎943 44 68 26). Come meet Juan, the nicest man in Spain. €0.05 per min., €3 per hr. Also sells **phone cards.** Open M-Sa 10am-10pm, Su 4-10pm.

Post Office: Po. de Francia, 13 (☎943 44 68 26). Open M-F 8:30am-8:30pm, Sa 9:30am-2pm. **Postal Code:** 20012.

ACCOMMODATIONS

A bevy of small *pensiones* scatter the streets throughout *parte vieja*, but in July and August *"completo"* signs—the Spanish equivalent of "no vacancy"—begin to appear in many doorways. Particularly tight times are during *San Fermines* (July 6-14) and *Semana Grande* (starts Su the week of Aug. 15); September's film festival (starts just before the last week of Sept.) is not much better. To make matters worse, many *pensiones* don't take reservations in summer. Solo travelers should be prepared to pay for a double if unable to find a willing roommate, as single rooms are virtually impossible to come by. Late-night arrivals will have even less luck. Adept bargainers should put their skills to work as often as possible, keeping in mind that hostel owners often take pity on the more wretched-looking individuals. You haven't truly mastered the art of haggling if you think you're above begging. The tourist office has lists of accommodations, and most hostel owners know of *casas particulares* (private residences that host lodgers). Owners of these *casas* often illegally solicit guests at the RENFE station.

PARTE VIEJA

Where the younger backpackers go for a night's rest, the *parte vieja* is brimming with reasonably-priced *pensiones* and restaurants. Its proximity to Playa de la Concha and the port makes this area a prime nightspot; scores of places offer a night's sleep above loud *pintxos (tapas)* bars. Call in advance for reservations.

Pensión Amaiur, C. 31 de Agosto, 44, 2nd fl. (☎943 42 96 54). Virginia, the wonderful English-speaking owner, offers 14 beautiful rooms, each with a personal touch. Seven common baths and 2 kitchens for when you're all *pintxo*-ed out. Internet €1 per 18min. July-Sept. and *Semana Santa* €25; May-June and Oct. €22; Nov.-Apr. €18, bunk in a shared room €13. MC/V. ❷

Pensión San Lorenzo, C. San Lorenzo, 2 (☎943 42 55 16; www.infonegocio.com/pensionsanlorenzo), off C. San Juan. This sunny *hostal* features bright rooms, immaculate bathrooms, and an incredibly helpful owner. Doubles with TV, hi-fi stereo, refrigerator, kettle, and safe. All rooms with sink and shower, some with full bath. Internet with webcam €2 per hr. July-Aug. doubles €45; June and Sept.; €36; Oct.-May €24. ❹

Pensión Larrea, C. Narrica, 21, 2nd fl. (☎943 42 26 94). Spend some time with *mamá* and *papá*, the friendly owners. The rooms are plain, but comfortable and welcoming. July-Aug. singles €24; doubles €36; triples €50. Sept.-June €18/€30/€45. ❷

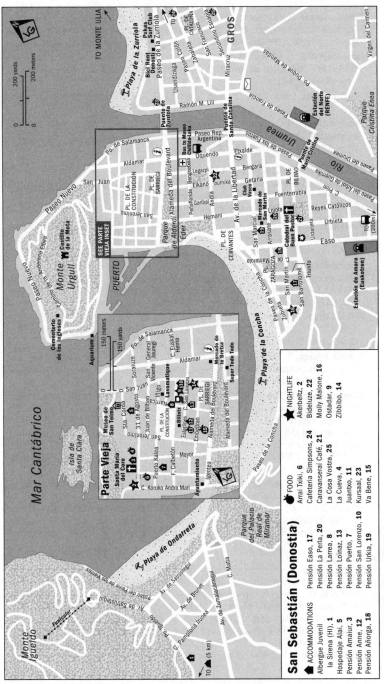

San Sebastián (Donostia)

▲ ACCOMMODATIONS

Albergue Juvenil
la Sirena (HI), **1**
Hospedaje Alai, **5**
Pensión Amaiur, **3**
Pensión Anne, **12**
Pensión Añorga, **18**
Pensión Easo, **17**
Pensión La Perla, **20**
Pensión Larrea, **8**
Pensión Loinaz, **13**
Pensión Puerto, **7**
Pensión San Lorenzo, **10**
Pensión Urkia, **19**

● FOOD

Arral Txiki, **6**
Cafetería Simpsons, **24**
Caravanserai Café, **21**
La Cosa Vostra, **25**
La Cueva, **4**
Juantxo, **11**
Kursaal, **23**
Va Bene, **15**

★ NIGHTLIFE

Akerbeltz, **2**
Bideluze, **22**
Molly Malone, **16**
Ostadar, **9**
Zibbibo, **14**

Pensión Loinaz, C. San Lorenzo, 17 (www.pensionloinaz.com). English-speaking owners. Common bathrooms. Internet €1 per 18min. Laundry €7 per load, wash and dry. July-Aug. doubles €42; triples €60. June and Sept. €36/€45. Oct.-May €27/€39. ❹

Hospedaje Alai, C. 31 de Agosto, 16, 3rd fl. (☎943 42 48 06). The Irish owner offers comfortable bunks and clean bathrooms at affordable prices. Art helps you live your mountaineering and biking dreams. July-Aug. €25; June and Sept. €12. ❷

Pensión Puerto, Puerto Kalea, 19, 2nd fl. (☎943 43 21 40). Spotless, sunny rooms with big comfy beds. July-Aug. €30. June and Sept. €20-22; Oct.-May €18. ❸

Pensión Anne, C. Esterlines, 15, 2nd fl. (☎943 42 14 38). Plain, comfortable rooms in a convenient location. €12 extra for private bath. July-Sept. singles €36; doubles €45; triples €60. Oct.-June €18/€24/€34. 10% discount with *Let's Go.* ❹

OUTSIDE THE PARTE VIEJA

Most of these places tend to be quieter than those in the *parte vieja*, yet are still close to the port, beach, bus, and train stations, no more than 5min. from the old city. This area also has some of the city's most elegant boulevards and buildings.

Pensión La Perla, C. Loiola, 10, 2nd fl. (☎943 42 81 23), on the street directly ahead of the cathedral. English spoken. Soak in your private bath, then step out onto your balcony. Heat and TV. July-Sept. singles €28-30; doubles €40. Oct.-June €24/€32. ❸

Pensión Easo, C. San Bartolomé, 24 (☎943 45 39 12; www.pensioneaso.com). Huge windows and mirrored rooms. July-Sept. 15 singles with sink €33, with shower €38, with bath €49; doubles €42/€47/€61. June and Sept. €27/€40/€33/€45. Oct.-May €25/€33/€30/€40. MC/V. ❸

Pensión Urkia, C. Urbieta, 12, 3rd fl. (☎943 42 44 36), bordering the Mercado de San Martín. Rooms with full bath and TV, all but one with balcony. July-Sept. singles €25; doubles €43; triples €60. Oct.-June €22/€30/€45. ❷

Pensión Añorga, C. Easo, 12 (☎943 46 79 45). Shares entry way with 2 other *pensiones*. Spacious rooms have shiny wood floors and comfy beds. Two quads available. July-Aug. singles €25; doubles €34, with bath €43. Sept.-June €19/€25/€32. ❷

Albergue Juvenil la Sirena (HI), Po. Igueldo, 25 (☎943 31 02 68), a light pink building 3min. from the beach. Buses #24 and 27 run from the train/bus stations to Av. de Zumalacárregui (in front of the San Sebastián Hotel). Clean rooms, multilingual staff. HI members and ISIC-carriers only. Laundry. Kitchen available 8am-10pm. Breakfast included. Sheets €2.53. Curfew Sept.-May Su-Th midnight, F-Sa 2am. July-Aug. €12.95, over 25 €14.61 (3-night max. stay if full); May 6-Jun. 7 and Apr. 8-31 €11.77/€13.80; rest of year €10.70/€12.95. MC/V. ❶

Camping: Camping Igueldo (☎943 21 45 02), 5km west of town. The 268 spots fill quickly. Beautiful views of the ocean make the drive worth it. Bus #16 ("Barrio de Igueldo-Camping") runs between the site and Alameda del Boulevard (every 30min., €0.80). *Parcelas* (spot with room for a car and tent) June-Aug. and *Semana Santa* €11, extra person €3.20. Sept.-May €9/€3. MC/V. ❶

📷 FOOD

Pintxos, chased down with *txakoli,* the fizzy regional white wine, are a religion here; bars in the *parte vieja* spread an array of enticing tidbits on toothpicks or bread. In the harbor, many places serve tangy sardines with slightly bitter *sidra.* Custom demands pouring it with arm extended to aerate the *sidra* and release its full flavor. It is also customary to pour just enough for one or two sips at a time. The streets of *parte vieja* teem with restaurants and *pintxo* bars. The clean and modern **Mercado de la Bretxa,** in an underground shopping center, sells everything from fruits and vegetables to *pintxos*. (Open M-Sa 9am-9pm, though most vendors take lunch 3-5pm.) **Mercado de San Martín** sells fresh local meats, fish, and produce. (Open M-F 7:30am-2pm and 5-7:30pm, Sa 7:30am-2pm.) For **groceries,** stop by **Super Todo Todo,** Alameda del Boulevard, 3. (☎943 42 82 59. Open M-Sa 8:30am-9pm, Su 10am-2pm. MC/V.)

PARTE VIEJA

🅢 Arrai Txiki, C. del Campanario, 3 (☎943 43 13 02; www.arraitxiki.com). The Argentinian-born, San Francisco-trained owner and chef cooks up delicious, healthy cuisine in a simple, elegant setting. Have a little fish and gaze at the vegetable-covered walls. Great vegetarian selection. Entrees €3-6. Open Su-M and W-Sa 1-4pm and 8-11pm. ❶

Juantxo, C. Esterlines. Best *bocadillos* in San Sebastián. Try the *filete* with onions, cheese, and peppers (€2.90). The bread definitely makes the sandwich. Wide selection of *bocadillos* (€2-3), *pintxos* (€1-2), and *raciones* (€2-5). Open M-Th 9am-11:30pm, F-Su 9am-1:45am. ❶

La Cueva, Pl. Trinidad (☎943 42 54 37). A cavernous restaurant serving traditional seafood cuisine prepared by an all-female staff. Quite a fancy place to eat fish. M-F *menú* €15. Grilled sea creature entrees €6-12. Open Tu-Su 1-3:30pm and 7-11pm. MC/V. ❸

Va Bene, Alameda del Boulevard, 14 (☎943 42 24 16). Frequented by tourists and locals alike, Va Bene is the place to go for high-quality, low-price American food in a retro setting with great patio seating. Cheeseburger €2.40. Open daily 11am-2am. ❶

OUTSIDE THE PARTE VIEJA

🅢 Kursaal, Po. de la Zurriola, 1 (☎943 00 31 62), in a Guggenheim-esque building across the river from the *parte vieja*. Treat yourself to an elegant lunch on their breezy patio. The chef is a legend among locals. *Menú* M-F 1-3:30pm €13, Sa-Su €15.60. MC/V. ❷

Cafeteria Simpsons, C. José Miguel Barandiaran, 20 (☎943 27 76 19). Walk all the way down Playa de la Zurriola and look for the blue building. A favorite with the local surf crowd, this cool little cafeteria is covered in tiki gods and photos of dudes on big waves. Coffee €1.10; beer €1.60. Open Su-M and W-Sa 8am-11pm. Closed Nov. ❶

La Cosa Vostra, C. Secundino Esnaola, 7, across from the movie theater. Good food, checkered tablecloths, and a slew of Italian paintings and posters await at this comfortable Italian eatery serving huge, delicious pizzas (€6). M-F *menú* €7.50. Open Su-W 1-3:30pm, Th-Sa 1-3:30pm and 8:30-11pm. ❷

Caravanserai Café, C. San Bartolomé, 1 (☎943 47 54 18), along the right side of the cathedral when facing its front doors. Chic and artsy, without the pretentious prices. Fabulous vegetarian options. Entrees €5-7. €0.60 surcharge for patio dining. Open M-Th 8am-midnight, F-Sa 8am-1am, Su 10:30am-midnight. MC/V. ❷

🜂 SIGHTS

San Sebastián's best sight is the city itself—parks, grandiose buildings, and attractive hillsides crowd San Sebastián's bay and the pleasant island of Santa Clara.

🅢 MONTE IGUELDO. Both of San Sebastián's mountains afford spectacular views, but those from Monte Igueldo win hands down. By day, the countryside meets the ocean in a line of white and blue; by night, Isla de Santa Clara seems to float in a halo of light. The sidewalk toward the mountain ends just before the base of Monte Igueldo with Eduardo Chillida's sculpture *El Peine de los Vientos* (Comb of the Winds). Though a small amusement park at the top has bumper cars, water rides, and trampolines, the magnificent view is the real entertainment. Skip the narrow, winding residential road leading to the top

PAÍS VASCO

and take the funicular instead. *(☎ 943 21 02 11. Open daily June-Sept. 10am-10pm; Oct.-Feb. Sa-Su 11am-8pm; Mar.-June Sa 11am-8pm, Su 11am-9pm. Funicular runs every 15min.; €0.85, round-trip €1.60.)*

MONTE URGULL. Across the bay from Monte Igueldo, the gravel paths on Monte Urgull wind through shady woods, monuments, and stunning vistas. The overgrown **Castillo de Santa Cruz de la Mota** tops the summit with 12 cannons, a chapel, and the statue of the *Sagrado Corazón de Jesús* blessing the city. *(Four pathways lead up to the summit from Po. Nuevo; a convenient one is located next to Museo de San Telmo. Castillo open daily May-Sept. 8am-8pm; Oct.-Apr. 8am-6pm. Free.)*

MUSEO CHILLIDA-LEKU. If Monte Igueldo's *El Peine de los Vientos* left you wanting more, the Museo Chillida-Leku is a beautiful way to satisfy your craving, housing a permanent exhibit of Eduardo Chillida's work spread throughout the garden of a restored 16th-century farmhouse. Restored by Chillida himself, the farmhouse is a work of art in its own right and boasts some of Chillida's earliest pieces. *(15min. from the town center. Bo. Jauregi, 66. ☎ 943 33 60 06. Autobuses Garayar leave from C. Okendo every 30min. By car, take N-1 out of San Sebastián south toward Vitoria-Gasteiz. Open July-Aug. and Semana Santa M and W-Sa 10:30am-7pm, Su 10:30am-3pm; Sept.-June Su-M and W-Sa 10:30am-3pm. Closed Tu, Christmas, and New Year's. Daily tours provided, as well as audio tours in 5 languages. €6, under 12 and seniors €3.)*

MUSEO DE SAN TELMO. The Museo de San Telmo resides in a Dominican monastery. The serene, overgrown cloister is strewn with Basque funerary relics, while the main museum beyond displays a fascinating array of prehistoric Basque artifacts, a few dinosaur skeletons, and a piece of contemporary art. *(Po. Nuevo. ☎ 943 42 49 70. Open Tu-Sa 10:30am-8:30pm, Su 10:30am-2pm. Free.)*

PALACES. When Queen Isabel II started vacationing here in the mid-19th century, fancy buildings sprang up like wildflowers. The **Palacio de Miramar** has passed through the hands of the Spanish court, Napoleon III, and Bismarck; it now serves as the País Vasco University, but anyone can stroll through the adjacent **Parque de Miramar** and contemplate the views of the bay. *(Between Playa de la Concha and Playa de Ondarreta. Open daily June-Aug. 9am-9pm; Sept.-May 10am-5pm. Free.)* The other royal residence, **Palacio de Ayete,** is also closed to the public, but surrounding trails aren't. *(Head up Cuesta de Aldapeta or take bus #19. Grounds open June-Aug. 10am-8:30pm; Sept.-May 10am-5pm. Free.)*

AQUARIUM. If you can't stand to eat any more of your finned friends, watch 'em. On rainy days, the aquarium, one of Europe's most modern, is worth a visit. *(Arrows point the way from the port. Po. del Muelle, 34, on Pl. de Carlos Blasco de Imaz. ☎ 943 44 00 99. Open summer daily 10am-10pm; rest of the year 10am-8pm. €6, children €4.)*

◪ BEACHES & WATER SPORTS

The gorgeous **Playa de la Concha** curves from the port to **Pico del Loro,** the promontory home of the Palacio de Miramar. The virtually flat beach disappears during high tide. Sunbathers jam onto smaller and steeper **Playa de Ondarreta,** beyond Miramar, and surfers flock to **Playa de la Zurrida,** across the river from Mt. Urgull. Picnickers head for alluring **Isla de Santa Clara** in the bay. (Motorboat ferry 5min., June-Sept. every 30min., round-trip €1.95.) The portside kiosk has more info.

Several sports-related groups offer a variety of activities and lessons. For **windsurfing** and **kayaking,** call the Real Club Náutico, C. Ijentea, 9, located on the water and shaped like a small cruise ship. (☎ 943 42 35 75. Open 10am-1pm and 4-6:30pm. Day courses €30-60.) For **parachuting,** try Urruti Sport, C. José María Soroa, 20

(☎943 27 81 96). **Surfers** can check out the Pukas Surf Club, Av. de la Zurriola, 23, for info on lessons and rentals. (☎943 42 12 05. Open M-Sa 9:30am-9pm. AmEx/MC/V.) For general information on all sports, pick up a copy of the *UDA-Actividades Deportivas* brochure at the tourist office.

🎵 NIGHTLIFE

The *parte vieja* pulls out all the stops in July and August, particularly on C. Fermín Calbetón, three blocks in from Alameda del Boulevard. During the year, when students outnumber backpackers, nightlife tends to move beyond *parte vieja*. Keep an eye out for discount coupons on the street, but be aware that the deals aren't usually as sweet as they sound.

Ostadar, C. Fermín Calbetón, 13 (☎943 42 62 78). This little bar is the best place to dance with locals and tourists alike to the best dance mix in *parte vieja*. Beer €1.80; mixed drinks €4.50. Open daily 5pm-4am.

Zibbibo, Pl. de Sarriegi, 8 (☎943 42 53 34). One of the best bars in the *parte vieja* that caters almost solely to young tourists. Nice blend of top 40 and techno. *"Grande"* sangría €4.50. Happy Hour Su-Th 10:30-11:30pm. Open daily 2pm-4am. MC/V.

Akerbeltz, C. Koruko Andra Mari, 9. Face Iglesia de Santa María on C. 31 de Agosto, take a left and go up the stairs; it's in the corner at the road's end, just before the port. A tiny, sleek, local bar. Open M-Th 3pm-2:30am, F-Sa 3pm-3:30am.

Molly Malone, C. San Martín, 55 (☎943 46 98 22). An Irish pub with impressive brew selections and a mellow upstairs loft. Beer €3. Open M-F 11am-4am, Sa-Su 3pm-4am.

Bideluze, Pl. de Guipúzcoa, 14 (☎943 42 28 80). Take C. Legazpi 2 blocks. For a relaxed evening out, this cafe has chilled-out music, good coffee (€1.50), and plush red chairs. *Bocadillos* €3-6. Open M-Th 8am-1am, F 8am-2am, Sa-Su 11am-1am.

NEAR SAN SEBASTIÁN

HONDARRIBIA ☎943

Less than 1hr. east of San Sebastián by bus, Hondarribia (pop. 15,000) is a charming miniature of its popular neighbor. Its quiet streets, lined with cafes and art galleries and dotted with parks and modern sculpture, are the perfect place to spend a day away from the elative hustle and bustle of San Sebastián. The suburbanized beach town stretching along Txingudi Bay boasts old wharfs and new shops along a golden sand beach. Compared to chic San Sebastián, Hondarribia is refreshingly small and simple, but not old-fashioned. In the peak days of summer, the beach can become ridiculously crowded with vacationers from Madrid and Barcelona, but it's usually pleasantly calm through June.

📍 PRACTICAL INFORMATION. Green and white **Interurbanos buses** (☎943 64 13 02) to **San Sebastián's** Pl. Guipuzkoa stop in front of the post office at Pl. San Cristóbal; pay onboard (45min.; every 20min. M-Sa 7:30am-10:35pm, Su 7:45am-9:45pm; €2). **AUIF buses** (☎943 63 31 45) go to **Irún** (10min., 10am-8pm, €0.85). The **airport,** Gabarrari Kalea (☎902 40 05 00), is within walking distance of the town center. The **tourist office, Bidasoa Turismo,** Jabier Ugarte Kalea, 6, is right off Pl. San Cristóbal; from the bus stop walk across the plaza. (☎943 64 54 58. Open July-Sept. M-Sa 10am-2pm and 3-8pm. Oct.-June M-F 9am-1:30pm and 4-6:30pm, Sa 10am-2pm. English spoken.) Local services include: **bank,** Kutxa, San Pedro Kalea, 9, across from the post office (open M-Th 8:15am-2:15pm and 4:15-7:30pm; F 8:15am-2:15pm); **emergency** ☎112; **police,** Mayor Kalea, 10 (☎943 64 43 00). The **English Corner,** Itsasargi Kalea, 2, which also runs small-scale, English-language tours of the area, offers **Internet** access. From the bus station, walk back up Bernat Etxepare Kalea with the bay on your right onto Zuloaga Kalea, which becomes Itsasargi Kalea. (☎943 64 54 35. €1 per 15min. Open M-F 11am-2pm and 5-7pm.) The **post office** is at Pl. San Cristóbal, 1. (☎943 64 12 04. Open M-F 8:30am-2:30pm and Sa 9:30am-1pm.) **Postal Code:** 20280.

📬 **ACCOMMODATIONS. Hostal Txoko Goxoa ❷,** Etxenagusia Kalea, s/n, lies in the other direction from Pl. San Cristóbal. From the tourist office, head up Jabier Ugarte Kalea, take the second right onto Juan Laborda Kalea. Follow it uphill until it ends at the city's old walls and take a right. The friendly English-speaking owner will greet you. (☎/fax 943 64 46 58. Private baths. Breakfast €4. July-Sept. singles €34.50; doubles €47.50. Oct.-June €26.20/€41.20. MC/V.) A brand new hotel in a very old building, **Hotel Palacete ❺,** Pl. Gipuzkoa, 5, combines the best of both worlds: simple, elegant interiors with thatched chairs, whitewashed walls, and subtle modern paintings. From the tourist office, walk up Jabier Ugarte Kalea and take the first left onto S. Kompostela Kalea, which runs into Pl. Gipuzkoa. (☎943 64 08 13; fax 64 62 69; www.hotelpalacete.net. Breakfast €6. July-Sept. 15 singles €68; doubles €75. Sept. 16-June €53/€60.) **Hostal Álvarez Quintero ❸,** Bernat Etxepare Kalea, 2, offers conveniently located rooms with large private baths. Other amenities include a comfortable downstairs common room, tennis courts, and a swimming pool. (☎943 64 22 99. Pets allowed. Breakfast €4.30. July-Sept. 15 and *Semana Santa* singles €33; doubles €42; triples €49-58. Sept. 16-Nov. and Mar.-June €27/€35/€42-49. Reception 8am-midnight. MC/V.) **Albergue Juan Sebastián Elcano (HI) ❶,** Ctra. Faro, sits on a hillside overlooking the beach and mountains. From the last bus stop, head to the beach on Itsasargi Kalea, bear left at the coast, and continue straight for several long blocks. At the traffic circle, turn left and follow signs uphill. The hostel has a TV room and tennis and basketball courts. (☎943 64 15 50; fax 64 00 28. Breakfast included. 3-night max. stay when full. Reception daily 9am-noon and 4-8pm. Call ahead in Dec. and Jan. Curfew midnight, but doors open at 1 and 2am. Members only; HI cards €6-10. Sheets €2. Dorms €9, over 30 €13.50. MC/V.) **Camping Jaizkibel ❶** is 1km from town on Ctra. Guadelupe toward Monte Jaizkibel and can be reached only by car or foot. Campground has hot water showers, cafeteria, restaurant, and self-service laundry. Bungalows come with full bath and kitchenette. (☎943 64 16 79. Reception 9am-10pm. €3.70 per person, per tent, and per car. Bungalows for 1-2 people €45-60, for 3-4 €60-78.)

🍴 **FOOD.** Eat like rural royalty at 🔲**Antontxo ❷,** Santiago Kalea, 47, where you'll find unbelievably generous portions served up under the rafters of an old farmhouse. Bright yellow-and-blue wall decorations and reliefs celebrating traditional Basque life complete the experience. The *rabo de buey* (oxtail; €9) is amazing. From Pl. San Cristóbal with your back to the bay, head up Jaizkibel Etorbidea and turn right on Santiago Kalea. (☎943 64 00 59. Entrees €9-16; *menú* €21. Open daily 1-4pm and 8pm-2am.) For a more affordable meal, head to **Maitane ❷,** Jabier Ugarte Kalea, 6, where fish-lovers are pampered but all will be satisfied. (☎943 64 57 11. *Menú* €10. Entrees €6-13. Open daily 9am-11pm.) Several **markets** spill onto San Pedro Kalea, 3 blocks inland from the port. Stock up at **Charter,** Santiago Kalea 19. (☎943 64 15 40. Open M-F 8:30am-1:30pm and 5-7:30pm, Sa 8:30am-1:30pm. Sept. 16-June M-F open until 7:30pm. MC/V.)

🏛️ 🏞️ **SIGHTS & OUTDOOR ACTIVITIES.** The gorgeous stone-and-timber **casco antiguo,** centered around Carlos V's imposing palace in Pl. de Armas (now a *parador nacional*—peek inside to catch a glimpse of the luxury hotel), provides a welcome relief from Coppertone fumes. The **Parroquia de Nuestra Señora de la Asunción,** also in Pl. de Armas, is a lovely 15th-century church where Louis XIV of

France married, by proxy, Habsburg María Teresa of Spain. (Open only for Mass daily at 7pm and tours; check at the tourist office. €3.) There are several possible excursions from Hondarribia. **Monte Jaizkibel,** 6km up Monte Jaizkibel Etorbidea, guards the **Santuario de Guadalupe.** Hiking the mountain—the highest on the Costa Cantábrica—affords incredible views of the coast; on a clear day you can see as far as Bayonne, France. **Jolaski Boats** (☎943 61 64 47) shuttle travelers 5km to **Hendaye,** a French town with a bigger beach. The boats leave from the pier at the end of Domingo Egia Kalea, off La Marina (every 15min.; €2.50). Or, if you're just sick and tired of being able to breathe without special equipment, head to **Scuba Du,** Itsasargi Kalea, 18, where the knowledgeable staff offers English-language scuba lessons and rents equipment. Diving excursions cost €18-24 per person. (☎943 64 23 53 or 608 77 36 95. Open Tu-Sa 10am-1pm and 4:30-8pm, Su 10am-1pm.)

BILBAO (BILBO) ☎944

Bilbao (pop. 370,000) is a city transformed. Over the last decade, it has made a technological, cultural, and aesthetic turnaround. The economic engine of the Basque country and a major shipbuilding center since the 1700s, Bilbao, known affectionately as "Botxo" to Basques, was an important trade link between Castile and Flanders. But what was once all industry—bourgeois, business-minded, and ugly—is now new, avant-garde, and futuristic. Careful investment and 20th-century success showered the city with wide boulevards lined by grandiose buildings, a gleaming new subway system, an overhauled international airport, a stunning new bridge, and a stylish riverwalk, all designed by renowned international architects. Frank Gehry's Guggenheim Museum, its graceful gleaming curves perfectly embodying the spirit of the new Bilbao, has powerfully fueled the city's rise to international prominence. Incredibly, Bibao has managed all these changes without seeming at all self-conscious. Visitors are welcomed to this friendly city with open arms, certainly, but leave feeling that *bilbainos* have worked so hard making Bilbao the beauty it is today for themselves, not the tourists.

▐ TRANSPORTATION

Flights: Airport (☎944 86 93 00), 8km from Bilbao. To reach the airport take the **Bizkai Bus** (☎944 48 40 80) marked **Aeropuerto** from Pl. Moyúa, in front of the Hacienda building (20min.; M-F every 30min. 6:30am-9pm, Sa-Su every hr. 7am-9pm; €1). Buses return from the airport to Pl. Moyúa (M-F every 30min. 6:45am-10:45pm, Sa-Su every hr. 6:30am-10:30pm). **Taxi** approx. €17. **Iberia,** C. Ercilla, 20 (☎902 40 05 00). Open daily M-F 9:15am-1:30pm and 3-6pm, Sa 9:15am-1:30pm.

Trains: Bilbao has three train stations.

RENFE: Estación de Abando, Pl. Circular, 2 (☎902 24 02 02). Info open 7am-11pm. To: **Barcelona** (8¾-10½hr., 1 per day 10:45pm, €43); **Madrid** (5½-8½hr.; M-F and Su 2 per day 4:30, 8:45pm; €37.50); **Salamanca** (5½hr., 1 per day 2:05pm, €24).

FEVE: Estación de Santander, C. Bailén, 2 (☎944 25 06 33). Info open M-F June-Sept. 15 9am-2pm and 4-7pm; Sept. 16-May 7am-10pm. To **Santander** (2½hr.; 3 per day 9:35am, 1:35, 6:35pm; €6). Also has an extensive local route.

Ferrocarriles Vascongados/Eusko Trenbideak (FV/ET): Estación de Atxuri, Cl. Atxuri, 8 (☎902 54 32 10). Trains to **San Sebastián** via **Guernica.** Closed for renovation at press time.

Buses: The following companies are based at the **Termibús terminal,** C. Gurtubay, 1 (☎944 39 50 77; M: San Mamés). **Information booth** open M-F 7am-10pm, Sa-Su 8am-9pm. A bus to **Guernica** leaves daily from **Estación de Abando** (45min.; every 30min. M-F 6:15am-9:45pm, Sa 6:30am-10:30pm, Su 7:30am-10:30pm; €2.05).

ALSA: (☎902 42 22 42). To: **Barcelona** (7¼hr., 4 per day 6:30am-11pm, €34.79); **La Coruña** (5½hr.; 2 per day 10am, 1:45am; €42); **Santander** (1¼hr., 13 per day 6:30am-11pm, €5.43); **Zaragoza** (4hr.; M-F 4-10 per day 6:30am-8:15pm, Su 6:30am-9pm; €16.24).

Continental Auto: (☎944 27 42 00). To **Burgos** (2hr.; M-Sa 7-10 per day 6:30am-10:30pm, Su 8:30am-10:30pm; €10) and **Madrid** (4-5hr.; M-F 10-18 per day 7am-1:30am, Su 8am-1:30am; €22.52).

PESA: (☎902 10 12 10). To **San Sebastián** (1¼hr.; M-F every hr. 6:30am-10:30pm, Sa-Su every 30-60min. 7:30am-10:30pm; €7.75).

La Unión: (☎944 27 11 11). To: **Haro** (1hr., 3-5 per day 8:30am-7:30pm, €7.30); **Logroño** (1¾hr., 3-5 per day 8:30am-7:30pm, €10); **Pamplona** (2hr.; July-Aug. M-Sa 4-6 per day 7:30am-8:30pm, Su 11am-8pm; Sept.-June M-Th and Sa 7:30am-7pm, F 7:30am-8pm, Su 11am-8pm; €10.90); **Vitoria-Gasteiz** (1hr.; 11-22 per day M-F 6:35-10pm, Sa 7:30am-10pm, Su 8:30am-9:30pm; €4.65).

Public Transportation: You can buy a pre-paid Creditrans pass for any amount to spend on transportation via Bilbobús, Bizkaibus, EuskoTran, the Metro, and the funicular. 20% off rides that are less than an hour (except Bilbobús) with the card. Available at Metro ticket machines, ONCE booths, and most kiosks.

Metro (☎944 25 40 25; www.metrobilbao.net). Ultra modern, though it only has two lines. Look for three interlocking red circles to find entrances, and **hang onto your ticket after entering**—you'll need it again to exit. Travel within 1 zone €1, 2 zones €1.10, 3 zones €1.20. 10-trip ticket €5.50/€6.50/€7.50. Trains run July-Aug. M-Th and Su 6am-11pm, F-Sa 6am-11pm and every 20min. 11pm-6am; Sept.-June M-Th and Su 6am-11pm.

Bilbobús (☎944 48 40 80) runs 23 lines across the city (6am-11:30pm; M-F €0.81, Sa-Su €1).

Bizkai Bus (☎902 22 22 65) connects Bilbao to suburbs and the airport.

EuskoTran, Buenos Aires, 9 (☎900 15 12 06), runs brand-new fast, comfortable trains around Bilbao. Service now reaches from Atxuri to the Guggenheim (€1.80, €0.40 with Creditrans).

Taxis: Teletaxi (☎944 10 21 21). **Radio Taxi Bilbao** (☎944 44 88 88).

Car Rental: Europcar, C. Licenciado Poza, 56 (☎944 42 22 26). 21+ with passport and valid driver's license. Open M-F 8am-1pm and 4-7:30pm, Sa 9am-1pm. Airport **branch** (☎944 71 01 33). Open daily 7am-11:30pm.

■*■ ORIENTATION & PRACTICAL INFORMATION

Gran Vía de Don Diego López de Haro connects three of Bilbao's main plazas, heading east from Pl. del Sagrado Corazón, through central Pl. Federico Moyúa, and ending at **Plaza Circular.** Past Pl. Circular, cross the Ría de Bilbao on **Puente del Arenal** and arrive in **Plaza de Arriaga,** the entrance to the **casco viejo** and **Plaza Nueva.**

Tourist Office: Oficina de Turismo de Bilbao, C. Rodríguez Arias, 3 (☎944 79 57 60; www.bilbao.net). English spoken. Open M-F 9am-2pm and 4-7:30pm, Sa 9am-2pm, Su 10am-2pm. Call ahead, as the office may move in 2004. **Branch** near the Guggenheim. Open Tu-F 11am-2:30am, Sa 11am-3pm and 4-7pm, Su 11am-2pm.

Currency Exchange: Banco Santander Central Hispano, Pl. Circular (☎944 25 48 00). **ATM.** Open May-Sept. M-F 8:30am-2pm; Oct.-Apr. M-F 8:30am-2pm, Sa 8:30am-1pm.

Luggage Storage: At **Estación de Abando,** lockers €3. Open 7:30am-11pm. In **Termibús,** lockers €1. Inside storage €1 per bag. Open M-F 7am-10pm, Sa-Su 8am-9pm.

El Corte Inglés: Gran Vía, 7-9 (☎944 25 35 00), in Pl. Circular. Department store, supermarket, salon, bookstore, and **currency exchange.** Open M-Sa 10am-9pm.

English-Language Bookstore: Casa del Libro, Alameda de Urquijo, 9 (☎944 15 32 00). Terrific selection. Open M-Sa 9:30am-9pm. AmEx/MC/V.

Emergency: ☎112. **Police:** C. Luis Briñas, 14 (☎092).

Medical Services: Hospital Civil de Basurto, Av. Montevideo, 18 (☎944 20 50 00).

Internet Access:

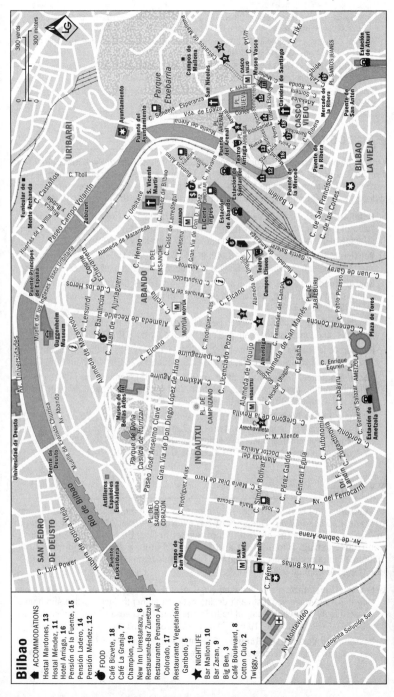

Bilbao

ACCOMMODATIONS
Hostal Mardones, **13**
Hostal Méndez, **11**
Hotel Arriaga, **16**
Pensión de la Fuente, **15**
Pensión Ladero, **14**
Pensión Méndez, **12**

FOOD
Café Bizvete, **18**
Café La Granja, **7**
Champion, **19**
New Inn Urrestarazu, **6**
Restaurante-Bar Zuretzat, **1**
Restaurante Peruano Aji
Colorado, **17**
Restaurante Vegetariano
Garibolo, **5**

NIGHTLIFE
Bar Mallona, **10**
Bar Zaran, **9**
Big Ben, **3**
Café Boulevard, **8**
Cotton Club, **2**
Twiggy, **4**

Ciberteca, C. José María Escuza, 23 (☎944 27 82 26). €0.60 per 10min., €1.20 per 30min., €2.10 per hr. Open M-Th 8am-10pm, F-Sa 8am-midnight, Su 10am-10pm.

L@ser, C. Sendaja, 5 (☎944 45 35 09). English-speaking owner. €0.05 per min. Also sells €5 and €10 phone cards. Open M-F 10:30am-3:30am, Sa-Su 11:30am-3:30am.

Net House, C. Ripa (☎944 23 71 53). €1.50 for first 30min., then €0.05 per min. Open M-F 10:30am-10:30pm, Sa 10:30am-11:30pm, Su 11:30am-11:30pm.

Post Office: Alameda de Urquijo, 19 (☎944 70 93 38; fax 43 00 24). Open M-F 8:30am-8:30pm, Sa 8:30am-2pm. **Postal Code:** 48008.

ACCOMMODATIONS

During **Semana Grande** (August 17-25) rates are higher than those listed below. As for the rest of the year, it shouldn't be hard to find a reasonably priced room if you arrive before noon. **Plaza de Arriaga** and **Calle Arenal** have budget accommodations galore, while other nice options line the river and pepper the new city off **Gran Vía.**

Hotel Arriaga, C. Ribera, 3 (☎944 79 00 01; fax 79 05 16). Large rooms, many with a view of the river. All with private bath, TV, A/C, and phone. English and German spoken. Garage and elevator. Singles €39; doubles €60; triples €72. AmEx/V. ❹

Pensión Méndez, C. Sta. María, 13, 4th fl. (☎944 16 03 64). Many rooms have sinks and balconies. Common baths. Singles €25; doubles €33; triples €45. ❷

Hostal Méndez, C. Sta. María, 13, 1st. fl. (☎944 16 03 64). Affiliated with, though more comfortable than, its *pensión* neighbor. Rooms have full bath and TV. Singles €36-39; doubles €48-50. ❹

Pensión Ladero, C. Lotería, 1, 4th fl. (☎944 15 09 32). Modern common baths, rooms with TVs, and toasty winter heating. Singles €18; doubles €30. ❷

Pensión de la Fuente, C. Sombrerería, 2 (☎944 16 99 89). Has all the basics, but heating and TV will cost you €3 extra. Singles €18; doubles €26-28, with bath €36. ❷

Hostal Mardones, C. Jardines, 4, 3rd fl. (☎944 15 31 05). Some rooms with balconies, all with marble sinks. Singles €32, with bath €38; double with 1 bed €34, with 2 beds €42, with bath €38-45; triples with bath €45-50. ❸

Albergue Bilbao Aterpetxez (HI), Ctra. Basurto-Kastrexana Errep., 70 (☎944 27 00 54). Take bus #58 from Pl. Circular or Pl. Zabálburu. 142 beds. Internet, currency exchange, bike rental, and laundry service. July-Sept. singles €16, over 25 €18; bed in a double or triple €14, over 25 €16. Oct.-June €1 cheaper. MC/V. ❷

FOOD

Restaurants and bars in the *casco viejo* offer a wide selection of local dishes, *pintxos,* and *bocadillos.* The new city has even more variety. **Mercado de la Ribera,** on the riverbank, is the biggest indoor **market** in Spain; it's worth a trip even if you're not eating. (Open M-Th and Sa 8am-2:30pm, F 8am-2:30pm and 4:30-7:30pm.) Pick up **groceries** at **Champion,** Pl. Santos Juanes, past Mercado de la Ribera. (Open M-Sa 9am-9:30pm. MC/V.)

▨ **New Inn Urrestarazu,** Alameda de Urquijo, 9. As its English-Basque name suggests, New Inn is perfect when you just can't decide between authentic local cuisine and home-cooked food: it features plenty of both. Try the Idiazábal cheese (€2.60) or onion rings (€4.75). Open M-Th 7am-11pm, F 7am-midnight, Sa 8am-1am, Su 10am-10pm. ❶

Restaurante Vegetariano Garibolo, C. Fernández del Campo, 7 (☎944 22 32 55). Serves up delicious, creative veggie fare. *Menú* €9.75. Open M-Sa 1-4pm. MC/V. ❷

Restaurante Peruano Ají Colorado, Barrenkale, 5 (☎944 15 22 09). Specializes in *ceviche*, a Basque marinated raw fish salad (€9.65-11.40). M-F luncheon *menú* €12. Open Tu-Sa 1:30-3:30pm and 9-11:30pm, Su 1:30-3:30pm. MC/V. ❸

Restaurante-Bar Zuretzat, C. Iparraguirre, 7 (☎944 24 85 05), near the Guggenheim. High-quality seafood. Don't miss the incredibly sweet cinnamon rice pudding (€3.20). Open M-Sa 7am-11pm, Su 8am-11pm. MC/V. ❷

Café La Granja, Pl. Circular, 3 (☎944 23 08 13). Founded in 1926, this bustling cafe has long served as a crowded local favorite (good thing it's so big). Grab a coffee (€1-3) and a window booth and indulge in some afternoon people-watching. Open M-Th 7am-11pm, F 7am-3am, Sa 10am-3am. ❶

Café Bizvete, Pl. de Santiago, 6 (☎944 16 29 45), in the peaceful courtyard of the Catedral de Santiago. Sandwiches €1.90-3.80, entrees €4-6. 10% surcharge for outside dining, but well worth it. Open M-Sa 8am-9pm. ❶

🏛 🔆 MUSEUMS & SIGHTS

▧**MUSEO GUGGENHEIM BILBAO.** Frank Gehry's Guggenheim can only be described as breathtaking. Lauded in the international press with every superlative imaginable, it has catapulted Bilbao straight into cultural stardom. Visitors are greeted by Jeff Koons's "Puppy," a dog composed of 60,000 flowers standing almost as tall as the museum. The undulating shapes and flowing forms of the building itself are undoubtedly the main attractions. Sheathed in titanium, limestone, and glass, the US$100 million building is said to resemble an iridescent fish or a blossoming flower. The amazingly light, dramatically spacious interior features a towering atrium and a series of non-traditional exhibition spaces, including a colossal 130m by 30m hall. Don't be surprised if you are asked to take your shoes off, lie on the floor, walk through mazes, or even sing throughout your visit to the various eccentric exhibits. The museum hosts rotating exhibits drawn from the Guggenheim Foundation's collection. A cafe on the ground floor serves snacks and drinks; the restaurant on the second floor provides a more decadent dining experience and is a work of modern art in itself. (*Av. Abandoibarra, 2. ☎944 35 90 00; www.guggenheim-bilbao.es. Handicap accessible. Guided tours in English Tu-Su 11am, 12:30, 4:30, and 6:30pm. Sign up 30min. before tour at the info desk. Open July-Aug. daily 9am-8pm; Sept.-June Tu-Su 10am-8pm. Audio tour €3.61. €10, students and seniors €5, under 12 free.*)

MUSEO DE BELLAS ARTES. Although it can't boast the name recognition of the Guggenheim, the Museo de Bellas Artes wins the favor of locals, who claim it to be the superior attraction. Hoarding aesthetic riches behind an unassuming facade, the museum boasts an impressive collection of 12th- to 20th-century art, featuring excellent 15th- to 17th-century Flemish paintings, works by El Greco, Zurbarán, Goya, Gauguin, Francis Bacon, Velázquez, Picasso, and Mary Cassatt, as well as canvases by Basque artists. The sculpture garden in back is perfect for a relaxing stroll. (*Pl. del Museo, 2. Take C. Elcano to Pl. del Museo or bus #10 from Pte. del Arenal. ☎944 39 60 60, guided visits 39 61 37. Open Tu-Sa 10am-8pm, Su 10am-2pm. €4.50, seniors and students €3, under 12 free. W free.*)

MUSEO VASCO. Located appropriately enough in the *casco viejo*, this museum celebrates the region's oldest inhabitants, from prehistoric times to the present, with special attention to Basque craftsmanship. (*Pl. Miguel de Unamuno, 4. ☎944 15 54 23. Open Tu-Sa 11am-5pm, Su 11am-2pm. Temporary exhibition open Tu-Sa 11am-8pm, Su 11am-2pm. €3; students €1.50, seniors and under 12 free. Th free.*)

PAÍS VASCO

OTHER SIGHTS. The best view of Bilbao's surrounding landscape and the perfect place for a picnic is atop **Monte Archanda,** north of the old town and equidistant from both the *casco viejo* and the Guggenheim. *(Funicular to the top every 15min. M-F 7:15am-10pm, June-Sept. also Sa 7:15am-11pm and holidays 8:15am-11pm. €0.69. Handicap accessible lift €0.25.)* A 5-20min. Metro ride to the north leads to various **beaches,** including **Getxo, Sopelana,** and **Plencia (Plentzia).** For Getxo, get off at any stop near Neguri or Algorta, then walk ½km to the beach. Along with Sopelana, Getxo attracts a surfer crowd and lies just a little nearer to the Bay of Biscay; its illuminated **Puente Colgante** (a suspension bridge constructed over 100 years ago) spans the river, leading to a plethora of all-night bars.

♫ NIGHTLIFE & ENTERTAINMENT

Bilbao has a thriving bar scene. In the *casco viejo,* revelers spill out into the streets to sip their *txikitos* (chee-KEE-tos; small glasses of wine), especially on Barrenkale, one of the seven original streets from which the city of Bilbao has grown. Teenagers and twenty-somethings fill C. Licenciado Poza on the west side of town, especially between C. General Concha and Alameda de Recalde, where a covered alleyway connecting C. Licenciado Poza and Alameda de Urquijo teems with bars. Try flower-themed **Twiggy,** across the street from the alley on Alameda de Urquijo, or **Big Ben,** where the dancing is as crazy as the cow on their logo. **The Cotton Club,** C. Gregorio de la Revilla, 25 (entrance on C. Simón Bolívar), decorated with over 30,000 beer caps, draws a huge crowd on Friday and Saturday nights while the rest of the week is a little more low-key. DJ spins W-Th at 11pm and F-Sa at 1pm. Over 100 choices of whiskey for €4.50 per *copa.* (☎944 10 49 51. Beer €2-3.50. Cash only. Open M-Th 4:30pm-3am, F-Sa 6:30pm-6am, Su 6:30pm-3am.) For a mellower scene, munch on *pintxos* (€0.90-1.20) and people-watch at Bilbao's oldest coffee shop (est. 1871), **Café Boulevard,** C. Arenal, 3. This Art Deco cafe was once an important site for literary meetings and one of Miguel de Unamuno's favorite haunts. Put on your dancing shoes and get ready to tango on Fridays at 11pm. (☎944 15 31 28. Open M-Th 7:30am-11pm, F-Sa 8am-2am, Su 11am-11pm. MC/V.) Climb your way to a peaceful drink at **Bar Zaran,** C. Calzados de Mallona, 18, towards Campos de Mallona. Ascend the long stone stairway next to the *casco viejo* Metro entrance. Take your drink outside for great views of Bilbao. (Beer €1.35, red wine €0.35, cigars €0.40-1. Open daily 8am-12:30am.) A bigger scene can be found three doors uphill at **Bar Mallona.**

The massive fiesta in honor of *Nuestra Señora de Begoña* takes place during **Semana Grande,** a nine-day party beginning the Saturday after August 15 with fireworks, concerts, theater—you name it. Pick up a *Bilbao Guide* from the tourist office for event listings. Documentary filmmakers from all over the world gather for a week in October or November for the **Festival Internacional de Cine Documental de Bilbao.** During the summer, the municipal band offers free **concerts** every Sunday morning at the bandstand in Parque del Arenal. *Fútbol* is another outdoor activity; catch an Athletic de Bilbao match at Campo de San Mamés.

GUERNICA (GERNIKA)

Founded in 1366, Guernica (pop. 15,600) long served as the ceremonial seat of the Basque country. Representatives from all seven Basque provinces met in Guernica's *Casa de Juntos,* and under a nearby oak tree Castilian monarchs ritually swear to uphold the *fueros,* ancient laws which guaranteed Basque autonomy.

Like Bilbao, this town has undergone massive reconstruction. Unlike Bilbao, however, Guernica had no choice. On April 26, 1937, at the behest of General Francisco Franco, the Nazi Condor Legion released an estimated 29,000kg of explosives on Guernica, obliterating 70% of the city in three hours. The tragedy marked the first mass civilian aerial bombing, what Winston Churchill dubbed "the first experimental horror of the 20th century." The nearly 2000 people who were killed have been immortalized in Pablo Picasso's masterpiece *Guernica*, which now hangs in Madrid's Museo Nacional Centro de Arte Reina Sofía. Today, Guernica serves not only as a brutal reminder of the atrocities of the past, but also as a hopeful beacon for a more peaceful future and an international site of contemplation and reflection where visitors are challenged with the ideas of peace.

◪ PRACTICAL INFORMATION. Trains (☎902 54 32 10; www.euskotren.es) connect Guernica to **Bilbao** (45min.; every 45min. M-F 5:50am-10:15pm, except 9:45pm; Sa-Su every 30 min. 8:15am-10:15pm, except 8:45am; €2). **Bizkai Bus** (☎902 22 22 65) sends more convenient and more frequent **buses** between Guernica and **Bilbao's Estación Abando** (45min.; M-F every 30min. 6:15am-9:45pm, Sa every hr. 7am-10pm, Su every hr. 9am-10pm; €2.05, with Creditrans card €1.50). To reach Guernica's multilingual **tourist office,** Artekalea, 8, from the train station, walk 3 blocks up C. Adolfo Urioste (past C. Ocho de Enero) and turn right on Barrenkalea. Turn left at the alleyway. (☎946 25 58 92; fax 25 32 12; www.gernika-lumo.net. Open July-Sept. M-Sa 10am-7pm, Su 10am-2pm; Oct.-June M-Sa 10am-2pm and 4-7pm, Su 10am-2pm.) The **post office,** C. Iparragirre, 26, is 2 blocks to the left down C. Iparragirre, one block from the bus station. Turn right at C. Alhóndiga. (☎946 25 03 87. Open M-F 8:30am-2:30pm, Sa 9:30am-1pm.) **Postal Code:** 48300.

◪◪ ACCOMMODATIONS & FOOD. Although Guernica's main attractions can be seen in a daytrip from Bilbao, **Akelarre Ostatua Pensión ❸,** Barrenkalea, 5, offers a delightful place to stay. From the train station, walk 2 blocks up C. Adolfo Urioste and take a right onto Barrenkalea. (☎946 27 01 79. *Semana Santa* and July-Aug. 20 singles €38.50; doubles €50. After *Semana Santa*-June singles €30; doubles €40. Aug. 21-*Semana Santa* singles €28; doubles €36. Slight discount with a stay of 2 nights or more. MC/V.) **Restaurante Boliña ❷,** conveniently located at Barrenkalea, 3, always draws a large local crowd with its classy low-key vibe, friendly waitstaff, and huge portions of delicious food. Gorge yourself in this classy bar/restaurant with dark woods and mellow yellow walls. (☎946 25 03 00. *Menú* M-F 1-3:30pm €8. *Pintxos* €1-1.20. Open daily 8am-1:30am. MC/V.) At **Pedro Bilbao,** C. Ocho de Enero, 3 (☎946 25 09 84), you'll find a variety of delicious pastries and good coffee all for less than €2. Enter on either C. Ocho de Enero or Barrenkalea.

◪ SIGHTS. In January 2003, after a complete overhaul, the modest Gernika Museoa reopened its doors as the **◪Gernika Peace Museum.** Utilizing a variety of multimedia exhibits, this stunning museum asks visitors to examine their own preconceptions of peace in both an historical and a contemporary context. *(Foru Plaza, 1, across from the town hall. From the train station, walk 2 blocks up C. Adolfo Urioste and turn right on Artekalea. ☎946 27 02 13. Guided tours in Basque, Spanish, English, and French at 12 and 5pm, or call for an appointment. Open July-Aug. Tu-Sa 10am-7pm, Su 10am-2pm; Sept.-June Tu-Sa 10am-2pm and 4-7pm, Su 10am-2pm. €4, students and seniors €2.)* The historical focus of Guernica is **El Árbol,** inside the gates of the **◪Casa de Juntos.** Encased in stone columns, the 300 year-old oak marks the former political center of the País Vasco, where medieval Basques gathered to debate community issues and Castilian monarchs ritually swore their respect for the autonomy of the local government. Today, the Vizkaya General Assembly meets here. Next to the oldest tree grows an oak planted in 1860 and, behind it, a "sapling" only 31 years old. (☎946 25 11 38. Open daily June-Sept. 10am-2pm and 4-7pm; Oct.-May 10am-2pm and 4-6pm. Free.) There are two sights worth seeing in Guernica's **Parque de los Pueblos de Europa.** Eduardo Chillida's dramatic sculpture

THE TRAGEDY OF GUERNICA Founded on April 28, 1366, Guernica was virtually erased from the map on April 26, 1937. It was a Monday market day when the church bell rang three times to warn the small town of an aerial attack. The German Condor Legion began to bomb at 4:30pm and didn't stop until 7:45pm. Heavy bombs and hand grenades were dropped first in order to create panic and a stampede. Next, low-flying planes machine-gunned those fleeing and hiding in the fields. These planes forced the townspeople into buildings, which were then wrecked and burned by 12 bombers. The entire center city was effectively destroyed. Strangely, the Casa de Juntos and the oak tree were untouched, as was Franco's war-material factory a few kilometers down the road. Guernica was far behind the lines; the destruction was fueled by a desire to rob the anti-Fascist Basque people of their desire to fight and to test German aviation ability in preparation for World War II.

Many pictures, sketches, and paintings have attempted to capture this day. In a painting now at the Gernika Peace Museum, Sofía Gandarias depicted clocks stopped at 4:30, women holding dead children, and the words "*y del cielo llovía sangre*" (and the sky rained blood). But it was Pablo Picasso who brought the town's tragedy to international fame. The Spanish Republican government had commissioned the artist to paint a mural for the Universal Exhibition in Paris in 1937, and he used the bombing for inspiration. In 10 days he had 25 sketches; he finished the painting—his largest work—in only one month. After much controversy, *Guernica*, Picasso's masterpiece, now resides in Madrid's Reina Sofía (see p. 127). When asked about the meaning of the painting as a whole, he replied, "Let them interpret as they wish." Picasso was even approached by a German ambassador who asked of the painting, "Did you do this?" Picasso answered simply, "No, you did."

Gure aitaren etxea (Our Father's House), a peace monument, was commissioned for the 50th anniversary of the city's bombing; it stands alongside Henry Moore's voluptuous 1986 **Large Figure in a Shelter,** which suggests a female form and symbolizes rebirth. To get to the park from the bus station, follow C. Adolfo Urioste; at the top, follow the arrow to the right and enter the park on the corner. (Open daily June-Aug. 10am-9pm; Sept.-May 10am-7pm. Free.) Paintings and artifacts on display inside the **Museo de Euskal Herria,** C. Allende Salazar, 5, document Basque history. (☎946 25 54 51. Guided tours in English. Open Tu-Sa 10am-2pm and 4-7pm, Su 11am-3pm. Free.) The tourist office offers a **historic tour** of the city's principal attractions July-Sept. M-Sa at 11am (€4); during the rest of the year, call ahead and the office will gladly arrange one (minimum of 2 people). The city holds a **fiesta** the first Saturday of every month June to October.

VITORIA-GASTEIZ ☎945

Vitoria-Gasteiz (pop. 220,000) boasts greenery galore and an impressive newly-opened contemporary art museum. Packed with avenues and parks, Vitoria-Gasteiz possesses a charm that belies its status as a sleek cosmopolitan center. The city's hyphenated name testifies to its regional loyalty; renamed Villa de Nueva Vitoria by the King of Navarra in 1181, the city regained its original name when the Basques recovered their regional autonomy in 1979. Spray-painted road signs with "Vitoria" crossed out are evidence of its continuing Basque pride. An independent spirit is not the only thing to be proud of; plenty of hiking and biking opportunities await visitors, and for those spending some time in the País Vasco, Vitoria-Gasteiz offers many outdoor adventures.

Vitoria-Gasteiz

🏠 ACCOMMODATIONS

Hostal-Residencia Nuvilla, **9**
Hotel Iradier, **10**
Pensión Araba, **8**

🍴 FOOD

Bocatería Boca a Boca, **5**
Museo del Órgano, **11**
Restaurante Argentino La
    Yerra, **1**
El Siete, **4**
La Taberna de los
    Mundos, **6**

⭐ NIGHTLIFE

Cervecería Txistu, **3**
The Man in the Moon, **7**
Scheherazade, **2**

🖥 TRANSPORTATION

Flights: Aeropuerto Vitoria-Foronda (☎945 16 35 00), 9km outside town. Accessible only by car or taxi (approx. €15). Info open M-F 8am-2:15pm. **Iberia** (☎945 16 37 38). Info open 6am-midnight.

Trains: RENFE, Pl. de la Estación (☎902 24 02 02). Info open 7:30am-10:30pm. To: **Barcelona** (8-14½hr.; 2 per day 4:15, 10:55pm; €31.50); **Burgos** (1½hr.; 10 per day 12:15am-6:05pm; €6.95-16); **Logroño** (1½hr., 1 per day 8:10am, €6.35); **Madrid** (4½-7hr., M-F 4-6 per day 7:25am-12:33am, €25.70-35); **San Sebastián** (2hr., 9 per day 4:56am-7:57pm, €7.55-16.50); **Zaragoza** (3hr.; M-Sa 3 per day 7:40am-7:05pm, Su 3:25-7pm; €13.35) via **Pamplona** (1hr., €3.35).

Buses: C. los Herrán, 50 (info ☎945 25 84 00). Open M-F 8am-8pm, Sa-Su 9am-7pm. **ALSA** (☎945 25 55 09; www.alsa.es) to: **Barcelona** (6½-7hr., 2-3 per day 7:30am-11:15pm, €30.19); **Pamplona** (1½hr., M-F 12 per day 6:30am-8:30pm, Sa 8 per day 7am-8:30pm, Su 6 per day 9am-9pm; €5.98); **Zaragoza** (3hr.; 5-7 per day M-Th and Sa 7:30am-9:15pm, F and Su 7:30am-10pm; €27.45). **Continental Auto** (☎945 28 64 66) to: **Burgos** (1½hr., 7-9 per day 7:15am-12:30am, €6.03); **Madrid** (4½-5hr.; M-

PAÍS VASCO

Sa 9-10 per day 6:45am-2:05am, Su 8:45am-2:05am; €18.83-27); **San Sebastián** (1½hr.; M-Th and Sa 8-10 per day 5am-11:30pm, F and Su 5am-1:30am; €6.13). **La Unión** (☎945 26 46 26) goes to **Bilbao** (1hr.; 20 per day 6:30am-10pm; €4.50).

Public Transportation: Tuvisa Buses (☎945 16 10 54) cover the metropolitan area and suburbs (7am-10pm, €0.60). Bus #2 goes from the bus station to C. Florida, but it is probably easier to walk. A **tourist train** makes a 45min. loop of all major landmarks, departing from Pl. de la Virgen Blanca. €3, children €2.50.

Taxis: Radio Taxi (☎945 27 35 00). 24hr. service to Vitoria and surrounding areas.

Car Rental: Europcar, C. Adriano VI, 29 (☎945 20 04 33). 21+. Open 9am-1pm and 4-7:30pm, Sa 9am-1pm. Also an airport **branch** open M-F 1:30-2:45pm.

■▮ ORIENTATION & PRACTICAL INFORMATION

The medieval **casco viejo** is the almond-shaped core of Vitoria-Gasteiz. **Plaza de la Virgen Blanca** marks the center of town.

Tourist Office: Pl. del General Loma, 1 (☎945 16 15 98; www.vitoria-gasteiz.org/turismo). Open M-F 10am-7pm, Su 11am-2pm.

Currency Exchange: Banco Santander Central Hispano, Pl. del Arca, 13. Open May-Sept. M-F 8:30am-2pm, Oct.-Apr. M-F 8:30am-2pm and Sa 8:30am-1pm. 24hr. **ATM.**

Luggage storage: Lockers at the **train station** (€3; buy tokens at the ticket counter 6am-1am) and the **bus station** (€0.63 per piece the 1st day, €0.52 each additional day). Open M-Sa 8am-8pm, Su 9am-7pm.

El Corte Inglés: (☎945 26 63 33), on C. de la Paz. Supermarket downstairs. Open M-Sa 10am-10pm.

Emergency: ☎112. **Police:** C. Aguirrelande, 8 (☎091 or 092).

Medical Services: Hospital General de Santiago, C. de Olaguíbel, 29. (☎945 00 76 00). **Osakidetza Servicio Vasco de Salud,** Av. de Santiago, 7 (☎945 24 44 44), off C. de la Paz. Open M-F 5pm-midnight, Sa 2pm-midnight, Su 9am-midnight. Free medical attention; passport required.

Internet Access: Nirv@na, C. Manuel Iradier, 11 (☎945 14 06 60). €0.60 per 15min. Open M-Sa 11am-2:30pm and 5-10pm, Su 5-10pm. **Ponte Cómodo.com,** C. los Herrán, 37. €2.40 per hr. Copies €0.10. Open M-F 10am-8pm, Sa 11am-8pm, Su 4-8pm. **Cuatro Azules,** C. Postas, 28 (☎945 13 45 13), across from the post office. €0.50 per 7min., €1 per 30min. Open Su-Th 12:30pm-2:30am, F-Sa 12:30pm-4am.

Post Office: C. Postas, 9 (☎945 15 46 92). Open M-F 8:30am-8:30pm, Sa 9:30am-2pm. **Lista de Correos** on C. Nuestra Señora del Cabello. **Postal Code:** 01008.

▮ ACCOMMODATIONS

Vitoria-Gasteiz has only a handful of cheap *pensiones*, although more deluxe hostels abound. If you plan to come during the jazz festival (first two weeks of July) or the *Fiestas de la Virgen Blanca* (Aug. 4-9), make reservations in advance.

Hotel Iradier, C. Florida, 49 (☎945 27 90 66; fax 27 97 11). Ring buzzer to enter. Cozy blue and yellow rooms, some with balconies, have bathroom, TV, and phone. Singles €30; doubles €48; triples €66. IVA included. MC/V. ❸

Hostal-Residencia Nuvilla, C. de los Fueros, 29, 3rd fl. (☎945 25 91 51). Common baths. All have balconies and marble sinks. Singles €21-23; doubles €33; triples €45. Discount after first night. ❷

Pensión Araba, C. Florida, 25 (☎945 23 25 88). Attractive rooms have sinks and TV (some with VCR). Singles €24, with bath €28; doubles €30/€36; triples €40/€48. ❷

Camping: Camping Ibaya (☎945 14 76 20), 3km from town toward Madrid. Follow Portal de Castilla west from the new cathedral. Supermarket, restaurant, hot showers, and laundry. Open year-round. €3.50 per person, per tent, and per car. MC/V. ❶

▊ FOOD

You can't go wrong in the *casco viejo*. The streets around Pl. de España have *pintxos* galore. Buy groceries at **Champion,** C. General Álava, 10 (open M-Sa 9am-9:30pm) or at the huge **Consum,** C. Pío XII, 11 (open M-Sa 9am-9pm).

Bocatería Boca a Boca, C. Nueva Fuera, 13 (☎945 27 84 18). Right across from the Metropolis Sex Shop. The swinging tiki lounge interior is the perfect place to enjoy a Döner Kebab (€3.80) or one of the many *bocadillos* (€2-4). Open M-Th 11am-4pm and 8pm-midnight, F-Sa 11am-4pm and 8pm-4am, Su 8pm-midnight. ❶

Museo del Órgano, C. Manuel Iradier, 80 (☎945 26 40 48), on the corner just before the Pl. de Toros. A favorite among locals, with fresh, filling vegetarian cuisine. M-F 4-course *menú* €8.50, Sa €11.50. Open M-F 1-4pm, Sa 1:30-3:30pm. MC/V. ❷

Restaurante Argentino La Yerra, C. de la Correría, 46 (☎945 26 57 59), in the *casco viejo*. Good beef entrees (€11-18, unless you're brave enough to take on all 800g of the monster €30 steak) and enticing pasta dishes (€7.25). M-F luncheon *menú* (€8). Open Su and Tu-W 1:30-4pm, Th-Sa 1:30-4pm and 9:30pm-midnight. MC/V. ❸

La Taberna de Los Mundos, C. la Independencia, 14 (☎945 13 93 42). Serves excellent, affordable sandwiches with international names (€3-4). Fish and pork entrees €8-11. Open M-W 9am-midnight, Th 9am-1am, F-Sa 10:30am-2am, Su noon-midnight. ❷

El Siete, C. Cuchillería, 3 (☎945 27 22 98). Popular with locals in search of traditional food—and a lots of it. Thirty-eight varieties of sandwiches (€2.50-3.60). *Menú* served M-F 1-4pm (€8.20). Open Su-Th 9am-12:30am, F-Sa 10am-3am. ❶

◉ SIGHTS

The tree-lined pedestrian walkways of the new city and steep narrow streets of the *casco viejo* make for pleasant wanderings. **Plaza de la Virgen Blanca** is the focal point of the *casco viejo* and site of Vitoria-Gasteiz's *fiestas*. Beside Pl. de la Virgen Blanca is the broad, arcaded **Plaza de España,** marking the division of the old town from the new. **Los Arquillos,** a series of arches that rise above Pl. de España, were designed by architect Justo Antonio de Olaguíbel from 1787 to 1802 to connect the *casco viejo* with the rapidly growing new town below.

MUSEUMS & PALACES. The permanent collection at ▊**Artium,** the two year-old contemporary art museum, boasts multimedia works and paintings by 20th-century greats such as Dalí, Picasso, Miró, and Arroyo. Equally as worthwhile, two galleries feature a regular rotation of macabre and unconventional works by such local favorites as surrealists Vicente Ameztoy and Javier Pérez. *(C. de Francia, 24. ☎945 20 90 20. Open Tu-F 11am-8pm, Sa-Su 10:30am-8pm. Adults €3; students, seniors, and under 18 €1.50; under 14 free; W by donation.)* Many of the *casco viejo*'s Renaissance palacios are open to the public as museums. The gorgeous **Palacio de Agusti** houses the **Museo de Bellas Artes,** with works by regional artists. *(Po. Fray Francisco de Vitoria. Open Tu-F 10am-2pm and 4-6:30pm, Sa 10am-2pm, Su 11am-2pm. Free.)* The world's largest deck of playing cards weighs 10kg and measures 94x61.5cm, and you'll find it (along with 20,000 others) at the **Fournier Playing Card Musem.** *(C. de la Cuchillería,*

PAÍS VASCO

FROM THE ROAD

UN FELÍZ MENÚ

When I passed my first McDonald's in Madrid, I pooh-poohed the hordes of American tourists inside, all waiting eagerly for a taste of the deep-fried familiar. Obviously, these people had different ideas about foreign travel. Whereas mine had to do with visiting far-off places and immersing myself in local culture, theirs probably consisted of driving their BMW SUVs through Chinatown listening to Ricky Martin. I shook my head, utterly disappointed in my fellow Americans.

Two days later, I found myself in Vitoria-Gasteiz, confused, tired, alone, and doing my best to order 9-piece Chicken McNuggets and a large Coke. With my shaky Spanish, I managed to get everything ordered and paid for without a hitch. Then I got cocky and inquired about free refills. This was the stupidest question ever: in Spain, Coca-Cola is like pure liquid gold, only more expensive and not as good for you. I didn't know this at the time however, and was attempting to communicate my desire when I heard a voice behind me say "eres tonto" (you're stupid). I turned around and found myself looking down at two little boys, one about 8 years of age and the other about 10. It was the approximate 10 year-old who had spoken. He stood about waist-high, his big brown eyes staring at me accusatorily, as if my very existence personally insulted him. "No," I responded

54. ☎945 18 19 18. Open Tu-F 10am-2pm and 4-6:30pm, Sa 10am-2pm, Su 11am-2pm. Tours can be booked for W and F mornings.) The 15th-century **Casa del Cordón** hosts changing exhibits, many featuring student art. (C. de la Cuchillería, 24. ☎945 25 96 73. Open Tu-F 10am-2pm and 4-6:30pm, Sa 10am-2pm, Su 11am-2pm. Free.)

CATHEDRALS. The apse of the 20th-century neo-Gothic **Catedral Nueva,** in the new town, hosts the ▨**Museo Diocesano de Arte Sagrado,** a collection from Basque churches including a canvas by El Greco. (C. Monseñor Cadena y Eleta. ☎945 18 19 18. Cathedral open M-Sa 11am-2pm. Free. Open Tu-F 10am-2pm and 4-6:30pm, Sa 10am-2pm, Su 11am-2pm.) Construction of the Gothic **Catedral de Santa María** in the casco viejo began in the 12th century; today it flaunts two especially expressive doors. Though the cathedral is closed for a €24 million restoration until 2010, it still offers English tours of the restoration process and archaeological studies. (☎945 25 51 35. Tours Mar.-Sept. €2 , under 12 free.)

🎭🎵 NIGHTLIFE & FESTIVALS

After nightfall, the casco viejo lights up. Bars line C. Cuchillería ("La Cuchi"), C. Herrería ("La Herre"), C. Zapatería ("La Zapa"), and C. de San Francisco. For intimate socializing, crash ▨**Scheherazade,** C. de la Correría, 42, a sumptuous Moroccan tea room with small tables, embroidered cushions, and an intoxicating ambience. Sip a kiwi shake (€1.80) or hot tea with fresh herbs blended to order (€1.50) and let your creative juices flow—crayons and paper are provided. (☎945 25 58 68. Open Su-Th 4:30-11pm, F 4:30pm-midnight, Sa 4:30pm-1am. July-Sept. opens daily 6pm-last customer.) For a pint of English Real Ale brewed on-site (€3), try **The Man in the Moon,** C. Manuel Iradier, 7. Locals come here to practice their English with foreign travelers. Catch the Thursday night jam session (starting around 10pm), or test your knowledge on Wednesdays at the weekly trivia quiz (in English). (☎945 13 43 27. Open daily 8am-3am.) Finally, head over to **Cervecería Txistu,** C. de San Vicente, 1, for a great selection of international beers in a relaxed environment. (Beer €0.60-1.30. Open M-Th 8:30am-1am, F-Sa 8:30am-3am.)

For info on **theater** and special events, pick up the weekly Kalea (€1.40) from tobacco stands or newsstands. During the first 2 weeks of July, world-class jazz grooves into the city for the **Festival de Jazz de Vitoria-Gasteiz.** Tickets for big-name performers cost €10-35, but there are plenty of free performances on the street. Call or visit the **Asociación Festival de Jazz de Vitoria,** C. Florida, 3, for specific info (☎945 14 19 19; www.jazzvitoria.com). On July 24-25, *Las Blusas* or "The Blouses" hold their own festival with wine, music, and games. The blue shirts represent the old shepherds that used to live in Vitoria. Rockets mark the start of the **Fiesta de la Virgen Blanca** (Aug. 4-9) at 6pm on the 4th in Pl. de la Virgen Blanca.

cleverly. He nodded slowly, "Sí." When I again tried to protest, he launched into a flurry of incomprehensible syllables that melted into one another like the ice cubes in my Coke, which sat warming on the counter. I looked questioningly at the 8 year-old, who I took to be the little brother. "He say..." the little brother began, his fresh-scrubbed face heavy with the obvious weight of reluctant translation, "...something bad."

"Oh," I said. I looked back at the 10 year-old. Clearly, he had won our little battle of wits. And he knew it too: a smile tugged at the corner of his precocious little lips. He looked up at me and nodded again, slowly, acknowledging my defeat.

I grabbed my tray and headed to a table as far away as possible from him, his little brother, and their mom.

Only 3 weeks later, I found myself on an hour-long stopover in Vitoria-Gasteiz. In that short time, I had made great inroads towards understanding Spain: its words, ways, and wines, if not its women. In those 3 weeks, I had run the streets of Pamplona, hiked the Pyrenees, and swam in the Cantabrian Sea. I was still no Spaniard, certainly, but nor was I any longer purely an American. No, the boy who had struggled so lamely to order his Chicken McNuggets no longer existed; he had been replaced by a man of the world, an urbane, cosmopolitan sophisticate, capable of adapting to any environment.

When I got to McDonald's I ordered the 9-piece Chicken McNuggets and a McCerveza. Extra grande, *por favor.*

—Chris Starr, 2004

History as Identity

Centuries-old whitewashed farmsteads with red tiled roofs stand strong and sometimes defiant on the deep green hills and Pyrenees mountains. They represent the past, present, and future of Basque culture. Key to understanding Basque society is an appreciation of the shared history, culture, traditions and language of the seven provinces which make up Euskal Herria, the Basque Country. It is also important to remember that there are many versions of history, and that the Basque perceptions of history are plural and contested by various intellectuals and segments of society. To understand the Basque collective past—real and imagined—I will summarize Basque history and identity as written by Basques and non-Basques and highlight the influence of the old foral laws and collective nobility, political factors, and constant emigration, which are significant elements of Basque homeland and diaspora identity. Basque society is heterogeneous and, of course, there are many exceptions to the following generalizations.

Throughout its history, the Basque region of Spain and France—referred to as Vasconia by the Romans—has been a nation and a kingdom, though not a state, thus the confusion for some visitors when determining their travel plans to the Basque Country. The area is not a "country" or "state"" as people tend to think of Canada, Japan, or Argentina. It is a geographical region with a shared ethnicity, which, since the 1512 border divide, includes three provinces under the political domain of France and four under Spain. Euskal Herria (literally, land of the Basques) is currently politically divided, with the provinces of Lapurdi, Behe Nafarroa, and Zuberoa under French administration, and Nafarroa (Navarre), Bizkaia, Araba, and Gipuzkoa as historic territories in Spain.

The Basque Country is small in both territory and population. The total population (which has the lowest per capita birth rate in the European Union) is nearly three million. In today's political terminology, when Basques refer to "the north", *Iparralde*, they are referring to the three French provinces "to the north" of what many see as an artificial political border. "In the south," *Hegoalde*, denotes the four Spanish provinces. Because these are also administratively differentiated in the current Spanish state created under the Constitution of 1978, the Gernika Statutes of Autonomy—passed in a 1979 referendum—established that together Bizkaia, Gipuzkoa, and Araba make up the Basque Autonomous Community of Euskadi. Nafarroa, or Navarre, has its own separate autonomous statutes negotiated between the *Diputación of Navarre* (executive branch) and the central government in Madrid. Nafarroa maintains a permanent right to join politically and administratively with the Basque Autonomous Community. Political realities have affected culture, language development, and Basque identity in each of the seven provinces, and many Basques in Nafarroa identify themselves as specifically Nafarroan.

Ethnic claims to physiognomic distinctiveness are not specific to Basques, and Basque nationalist rhetoric utilizes certain features in physiological makeup that point to uniqueness. Basques differ from their surrounding populations in their blood types, for example; they manifest the highest rate in any European population of the blood type O and the lowest occurrence of blood type B. They also have the highest occurrence of any population in the world of the Rh-negative factor (Cavalli-Sforza and Cavalli-Sforza 1995; Collins 1986: 4-8). Basques use these elements to argue that they are biologically distinct from any other population, and therefore deserve political recognition.

Basque collective myth includes the possibility of a history that stretches to cave populations and human occupation since the Stone Age (Caro Baroja 1971). What is certain is that there are no recorded histories or information describing the Basques specifically until the Romans invaded the Iberian peninsula and documented that the Basque population was organized into small tribal units inhabiting the valleys of the western Pyrenees—and beyond, according to later linguistic studies. They originally did not form a single civic unit and spoke a variety of tribal dialects of Euskera whose diversity persists to the present day. Although until recently Basques have believed otherwise, the latest scientific research demonstrates that the Basque territory was indeed subject to Roman administrative, political, and military domain until approximately the 4th-century AD. Other questions arise regarding the linguistic and cultural Romanization of the existing populations. It seems the agricultural mentality of the colonizers led to the agriculturally richer lower lands in Nafarroa and Araba nearer the rivers experiencing a more intense cultural impact than did the more mountainous and forested areas in Bizkaia and Gipuzkoa (Sayas Abengoechea 1999). Christianity was introduced into the Basque region during Roman

...mes, but it scarcely spread beyond the southern fringes of lower Araba and Nafarroa.

The debut of the Basques as a separate entity in the history of western Europe follows the fall of the Roman Empire and the establishment of the Germanic kingdoms in western Europe. The ra's chronicles describe the staunch resistance by Basques to the Visigothic powers in Toledo and the attempts at assimilation by the Franks from the north (Sayas Abengoechea 1999). The perseverance of the early Basque resistance through the seventh and eighth centuries indiates some kind of civic cooperation may have been established among these tribes. The reality of the resistance and lack of assimilation had a salient effect on the political philosophy of the Basques at the end of the Middle Ages and the following centuries.

Contemporary Spain arose from an unstable alliance of independent Christian kingdoms defending against Islamic invaders. The initial unifying idea behind Spain was that of Christian opposition to the Muslim threat. Unlike León, Aragón, and Catalunya, Castile had no previous political existence and was basically a product of the long *Reconquista* (718-1492). The historic Spanish kingdoms did not have their roots in Roman or Visigothic origins, but in the defensive reaction against Muslims in the early Middle Ages that led to the process of regaining land. During the eighth century, the independent and Christian populations in the northern sections of the peninsula, such as the Basques, began to coalesce around regional nuclei determined by three main factors: geography, ethnic identity, and prevailing politico-military pressures.

Historians write that Basques in Pamplona constituted their own kingdom by the 8th century. By the 12th-century, and as a result of gradually joining with other lands free of Muslim occupations (as were Bizkaia, Gipuzkoa, and Araba), this region came to be known as the Kingdom of Navarre. For the next years all of the Basque-inhabited territory south of the Pyrenees recognized a single Basque political sovereignty for the first and last time in its history thus far. Though remote in time, this period of political unification has had a significant impact on the development of Basque nationalism both in the homeland and in the diaspora. These centuries of political unification were ended in 1200 when the three western Basque territories were militarily occupied by Alfonso VIII of Castile. From this point their development was tied to the powerful kingdom of Castile and their incorporation interpreted as a bilateral pact, with Basque liberties respected as the status quo.

Gradually, the self-government of Basque communities grew as recorded in the Basque fueros, or local laws. For centuries, the Basque provinces maintained exclusively separate legal codes and created their own autonomous political institutions. Under the *fueros*, the popular assemblies, or *biltzarrak*, were granted legislative authority and the Castilian kings and lords were subject to their laws. Although Church leaders and lords both were excluded from the legislative deliberations, upon accession to the throne the king was required to appear before the Basque assemblies and swear to respect their authority. Some examples of the citizens' rights enjoyed from the 1452 *Fuero Viejo de Vizcaya* (Bizkaia) included:

—the freedom of every Bizkaian to engage in commerce;

—rights of due process in all legal proceedings;

—privileged rights to land ownership in Bizkaia;

—exemption from taxes on any maritime activity; and

—exemption from obligatory military service outside the Basque territory.

Another important aspect of distinction between regions in Spain was the concept of universal nobility, which can be traced back to 1053 and the Basque valley of Roncal in Nafarroa. In the Basque provinces, there was a legislated collective nobility and all Basques were considered "noble." Thus, all citizens of the Basque region, regardless of one's origin, enjoyed political and economic rights and could aspire to noble privileges and offices. The Basque fueros and the practice of collective nobility played influential roles in establishing further reaching regional identities beyond that of connection with village or town. The Basques set themselves apart from the Castilian population and control because of this separate political structure, reinforced by their linguistic and ethno-cultural uniqueness.

The importance and influence of the concept of the collective in Basque culture and society is extremely significant to understanding Basque people, politics, and community structure. From the reality of extended collective nobility to all Basques born in the Basque provinces and to those born to Basques abroad, to the traditional foral laws of rights and privileges, economic and political self-rule, and codes of behavior and customs, Basque society exemplifies a reverence for democratic values.

The Basque region entered advanced development during the 11th and 12th-centuries with the growth of maritime and commercial activities. The 15th-century proved to be another time of notable economic development, especially for Bizkaia and Gipuzkoa. The Bay of Biscay, and particularly Bizkaian shipping, dominated the peninsula's trade with northern European ports. The 16th-century was a period of continually expanding economy and social change in the Basque provinces. Bizkaia and Gipuzkoa were the two juridically freest and most egalitarian areas in all of Spain. Throughout most of Castile the peasantry was being crushed by taxes and the social and economic predominance of the aristocracy, while, conversely, in Bizkaia (1526) and Gipuzkoa (1610) the struggle had been won for royal recognition of the "noble" status of all their native inhabitants. Every person enjoyed equality before the law and freedom from most common taxes. In Araba and Nafarroa, different communities were protected by their different *fueros* and some had already established this collective nobility for their residents. Other towns and villages continued this process of emancipation and social mobility through the 17th-century.

During and after the French Revolution, the northern Basque provinces were subjected to military occupation and their ancient foral laws were abolished. Basques were deprived of their lands and livestock, and while some Basques were interned in camps by revolutionary officials, there was also a forced deportation of more than three thousand Basques who were accused of treason with Spain (Jacob 1994:33-35). In 1793 in Baiona (Bayonne) alone, more than sixty death penalties were pronounced for "complicity in illegal immigration or correspondence with priests in exile" (Jacob 1985:83). Emigration was obviously as risky as staying put. Napoleon's rise to power and push to conquer the Iberian Peninsula resulted in several wars being fought in the Basque Country, with Basques themselves recruited and conscripted by both sides.

The integration of the Basques into the Spanish monarchy entered a crisis at the beginning of the 18th-century with a change of dynasty. The Bourbons consolidated the Spanish crown, and, following the French tradition, unified it by dismantling the confederate structure. They implanted a centralized state system with a single parliament, or *Cortes*, and with ministers whose powers extended over all territories. Nevertheless, there remained an exception to the unification: the four Basque territories. The *fueros* of the four territories remained valid and were enforced. This maintained the political differentiation of Vasconia, but simultaneously ushered in a period of tension between the administrations in Araba, Bizkaia, Gipuzkoa, and Nafarroa with that in Madrid that for many Basques remains to this day.

Since the 1200s, Basque emigrants have spread throughout the Iberian Peninsula, and then later to Europe, the Americas, the Philippines, and Australia. It would not be an exaggeration to state that no major Spanish expeditionary force and no ecclesiastical or secular administration in the New World did not have Basques among its members. Basque, and especially Bizkaian, interests controlled more than shipping; they "supplied capital, equipment and goods for trade as well as many of its personnel" (Lynch 1964:35) and several of the previously established Basque commercial interests in Spain opened branch operations with kinsmen in the Indies, especially in Santo Domingo (Bilbao 1958:192-209). *Iparralde* Basques also participated in the American ventures, and vessels from Donibane Lohitzun (St-Jean-de-Luz) were registered with authorities as Bizkaian. Lynch estimates that almost 80% of the New World traffic between 1520 and 1580 was Basque controlled, and between 1580 and 1610 Basques' interests represented at least 50% of the total. This accounts for nearly 100 years of Basque domination in Spanish colonial efforts, pushing Basque maritime specialists toward the New World where they established trade links back to their homeland.

The Basque presence in Madrid and in the American colonies continued to be significant in the 18th-century. The creation of the Gipuzkoan Company of Caracas demonstrated the great Basque mercantile society involvement in the colonization of Venezuela, and the Consulate of Bilbao produced the Ordinances that served as the model for all commercial trade in Spain and the Americas. Basques have often acted as a self-aware ethnic group, maintaining ties to each other and to their homeland. This has resulted in trade networks, collective action, mutual assistance programs, schools for Basque children, and ethnic associations and societies for the maintenance of Basque language, culture, and traditions. In 2003, there are nearly 170 Basque social, cultural, political, and economic organizations in over 20 countries. Several of these have over four hundred years of history, while others were established only in 2003. Despite great distances and differences in times of immigration, transnational ties and maintenance of ethnic identity in these Basque communities have intensified with the globalization of communications. Technology is aiding the strengthening of inter-relationships among Basques living around the world.

Basque Identity as Simultaneously Traditional & Post-Modern

What exactly is meant by "Basque ethnic identity," and what is "Basque ethnicity"? The phenomenon of ethnic identity emerges where the subjects of anthropology, sociology, political science, and psychology converge. It includes the language one speaks and the civic territory in which one lives, and in the case of the Basques, shared ancestry and culture play crucial roles in his determination. Homeland definitions of Basqueness" and "Basque culture" have progressed to more civic and inclusive categories and are no longer linked only to the traditional conservativism of the 1900's father of Basque nationalism Sabino Arana y Goiri. Arana's definitions of who counted as a Basque highlighted shared ancestry, language, and religion. Today, the majority of people living in the Basque Country would define "being Basque" as those people who are born in, or permanently live in the Basque Country; those who speak Basque; those who have Basque ancestry; as well as those around the world who love the Basque culture and work for its protection and promotion.

Despite five centuries of speculation by linguists and philologists concerning the possible relationships between Basque and other languages, no studies have indicated a conclusive relationship between Basque and any other language (Michelena 1985; Tovar 1957; Collins 1986:8-12). This makes Euskera, the Basque language, unique among Western and Central European languages. Euskera is the only surviving pre-Indo-European language of the continent. Visitors will see that most signs in Araba, Bizkaia, and Gipuzkoa are posted in both Basque and Spanish. In the other provinces, Euskera is not heard as often, nor is it as visible. Although the Basque term for "Basque people" is *Euskaldunak*, (those who have the Basque language) defining Basque people as those who speak Basque becomes problematic in that so many of those who live in Euskal Herria no longer utilize Euskera regularly. The Basque language was prohibited as a means of communication in Spain during the Franco dictatorship (1939-1975) and it had been lost in many areas of the hispanicized urban centers in the 1800s. The current system of *ikastola*, or schools where the language of instruction is Euskera, and especially the education system of Araba, Bizkaia, and Gipuzkoa, has significantly reversed the decline in Basque knowledge and usage. Today, the majority of youth in those provinces understand or have studied Euskera, though they do not necessarily use it. The

political parties in power in Navarre have not prioritized the maintainance of Euskera in their territory, and the historic language has suffered immeasurable decline.

According to anthropologist Julio Caro Baroja, the single most important element in stimulating emigration out of Euskal Herria was the rules of inheritance followed in rural Basque society (Caro Baroja 1971; Bilbao 1992). Population density, high fertility, and live birth rates, coupled with the scarcity of available agricultural lands and low agricultural output resulted in limited expansion potential. The lack of industrial and urban growth until the late 1800s also limited possible options for employment and migration within Euskal Herria. Each farmstead could support a single family in agriculture. Those who had rental arrangements were less committed to the land and were more likely to emigrate because of their current instability. Those who owned their property and animals kept their holdings in the same family and Basque common law discouraged fragmentation or division through sales or inheritance. Consequently, most Basque farmsteads remained unchanged for many centuries, with each generation having a single heir.

The *fueros* guaranteed the practice of selecting one of the former owner's offspring to be the new owner, and other siblings could be disinherited, although in practice they were usually provided with dowries. This meant that in every family there were most likely three or four siblings that were candidates for emigration. Even today in certain villages the traditional rules of male primogeniture are followed, in other areas a female is selected, while in parts of Nafarroa the heir or heiress is chosen according to individual merit without reference to gender or birth order (Lafourcade 1999:167-174). Until recently, the remaining siblings would have to depend upon the new owner for employment, accommodation, and care. and although family members, there usually was not enough work to finance the entire extended family. Unmarried siblings had the right to stay with the family farmstead as long as they stayed single, some married other heads of households, others turned to religious professions or the military. For thousands, a more viable alternative to alleviate hardship was emigration.

The Industrial Revolution of the 19th-century disrupted traditional agricultural economic activities and displaced workers from both rural and urban areas. The cheaper manufacture of products left artisans searching for markets, which waited open armed in the Americas. Displacement from rural society, changing urban society, unemployment, unrest, labor strikes, arrests and imprisonments related to a lack of civil rights, all preceded the cataclysm of the Spanish Civil War (1936-1939). After the Republican and Basque nationalist forces were defeated, Franco's victory guaranteed a central policy of Spanish identity-building and Basque nation-destroying. The horrendous indignities suffered, the dismantling of Basque institutions, the outlawing of manifestations of Basque culture, the dictatorial repression and lack of human and civil rights, and multitudes of death warrants, shoved Basques out of their homeland in pursuit of safe havens. Urban and rural dwellers, widowed mothers and children, orphaned teenagers, and republican soldiers—thousands who had the connections and the means to escape the political and military crush—did so. Most evacuated to Iparralde initially, and from there decided their final destinations usually based upon family ties to regions in the New World or information they had obtained from family and village networks. Hundreds of thousands of Basques were exiled from political and economic repression and the majority were never able to return to their homeland. The political factors of Basque identity remain critical and are a part of daily life from choosing which bar or restaurant to frequent, to the purchase of daily newspapers with a certain political bias.

Today's Basques are affected by these historical factors, but also add another layer of identity with a futuristic post-modern 'Basqueness' that includes trilingualism (Basque, Spanish, and English, or Basque, Spanish and French), and the ability to live in the present and not the past. Travelers will notice extraordinary service, business efficiency, high standards in education, and tremendous cultural literacy. Despite political wrangling with Madrid, the Basque provinces consistently rank among the highest in economic output and quality of life indicators.

Rituals & Customs

Basques are fond of entertainment, and visitors have numerous opportunities to witness the many folk festivals laden with ethnic music, dance, and cuisine celebrated throughout the year. Basque folk dances include those of religious processions and festivals, social celebrations, and rival combats. Costumes are extremely colorful, and performances include flowered hoops, sticks and swords, flags and scarves, baskets of fish, wooden chests, and animal skins. Agricultural fairs gather the best produce and livestock for exhibition, as well as cooking competitions. Cuisine is a very important factor of Basque culture, and fresh quality ingredients are essential to any Basque dish at home or in any bar or restaurant. Daily morning shopping for fresh bread, fish, meats, vegetables and fruits is common in almost every household.

Community fiestas honor their local patron saints, and one of the most popular is that of Saint John, on the night of the summer solstice. Thousands of bonfires are lit to celebrate the tradition of purification, summer, and light. Many coastal villages celebrate their festivals with activities on the seacoast. Accordion music is common and a part of every town's festival. Musical instruments particular to the Basque culture include a three-holed flute, a *txistu*, and an *alboka*, made of an animal horn, wood and a pipe of straw. Singing is also another popular aspect to any town festival, and Basque oral poetry competitions are particularly entertaining. Because Basques did not utilize written words to record their history until approximately the 1500s, hundreds of years of Basque history were handed down through song and verse by *bertsolaris*, singers who perform memorized, or in most cases, spontaneous singing in poetic phrase. Festivals also include various sports competitions such as pelota, or handball games, regata rowing races, weight-lifting stones of different shapes and different sizes, and weight-carrying, tug-of-war, wood-chopping, grass-scything, and sheepdog skills competitions.

Tradition is a part of daily life, and not only celebrated once a year for special feast days. In the Basque Country, one can drive to neighboring provinces and experience completely different landscapes, architecture, histories, festivals, economies, and rituals. However, they share a respect for the land, history, art and ancestors.

Dr. Gloria Totoricagüena Egurrola received her Ph.D. from the London School of Economics and Political Science and is currently an Assistant Professor at the University of Nevada, Reno Center for Basque Studies in Reno, Nevada.

ASTURIAS & CANTABRIA

Jagged cliffs and precipitous ravines lend an epic scope to the tiny lands of Asturias and Cantabria, tucked between the País Vasco and Galicia. Though connected by location and landscape, Asturias and Cantabria have distinct provincial personalities. With the world-class resort towns of Santander and Comillas, Cantabria appeals to Spain's vacationing elite. Asturias instead draws hearty mountaineers looking to conquer the peaks of its national parks, including the Parque Nacional Picos de Europa and the Parque Natural de Oyambre.

   The impassable peaks of the Cordillera Cantábrica halted the Moorish advance, enabling Visigoth Christians to make the land their northern stronghold. Asturian hero Don Pelayo officially began *la Reconquista* in 722 AD in the Picos hamlet of Covadonga; the campaign would last until the fall of Granada in 1492. Today, Spain's heir to the throne is titled the Príncipe de Asturias, in honor of the region's preservation of true "Spain" during the Moorish invasions. This legendary spirit of defiance found outlet during and before the Spanish Civil War in blue-collar resistance to the Fascists, most prominently during a bloody miners' revolt. Mountainous terrain has still limited the number of rail lines through the region, leaving lone roads to wind along its steep mountainsides and scalloped shores.

   Asturias is famous for its apples, cheeses, wholesome fresh milk, and *arroz con leche* (rice pudding). *Sidra* (cider) and *fabada asturiana* (a hearty bean-and-sausage stew) grace menus everywhere. True Asturians can be recognized by the way they take their cider, poured from several feet above the glass and downed immediately. Cantabrian cuisine draws from the mountains and the sea, adding anchovies, tuna, and sardines to the mix. Local favorites include *cocido montanés* (bean stew) and *marmita* (tuna, potato, and green pepper stew).

HIGHLIGHTS OF ASTURIAS & CANTABRIA

MARVEL at the breathtaking natural beauty of the **Parque Nacional Picos de Europa** while staying in a remote *refugio* high in the mountains (see p. 548).

PLAY amid the train, rides, mini-zoo, and beautiful palms, pines, and beaches of the renowned Península de la Magdalena in **Santander** (see p. 561).

THANK your lucky stars (or God) that you aren't living during the Inquisition while taking in the gruesome sights at the Museo de la Tortura y de la Inquisición in **Santillana del Mar** (see p. 563).

FROLIC in **Comillas** along the smooth sands of the beach, one of Spain's best. Be sure to check out the one-of-a-kind El Capricho, Gaudí's summer palace (see p. 564).

ASTURIAS

Impenetrable peaks and dense alpine forests define the Asturian landscape, as well as its history. Thanks to the foreboding Picos de Europa, Asturias never fell to bands of marauding Moors in the 8th century, leaving its residents free to dot the countryside with timeless Asturian Pre-Romanesque churches, the cure for the common cathedral. A different sort of invasion is at work today: tourists reveling in the endless outdoor activities in the Parque Nacional Picos de Europa. Although better known for its peaks, Asturias also has a popular coast. Not the swaths of sand and raging waves of Cantabria, Asturian beaches are more often quiet, rocky coves where tropical and alpine vegetation commingle with mountaineers.

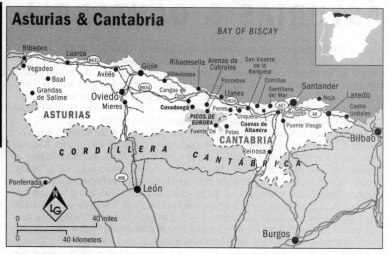

Asturias & Cantabria

BAY OF BISCAY

OVIEDO ☎958

Oviedo's name comes from the Latin *urbis* (city), and for a few centuries, it really was *the* city in Spain. As one of the few places from which to ward off Moorish attacks, it became the epicenter of *la Reconquista*. Oviedo (pop. 200,000) was made the capital of the Kingdom of Asturias as early as 810, but the city has since faded into the background of Spanish political geography. The city center is pleasant enough, with an immense park, lively street musicians, beloved *churrerías*, and the promise of mountains on the horizon. Yet beyond its provincial art museum and miles of pedestrian shopping streets, there's not much to see or do in Oviedo proper. Head up to Monte Naranco instead, or take a bus to one of the smaller nearby gateways to the Picos de Europa.

▐ TRANSPORTATION

Flights: Aeropuerto de Ranón/Aeropuerto Nacional de Asturias (☎985 12 75 00), in Avilés, 28km from Oviedo. **Prabus,** C. Marqués de Pidal, 20 (☎985 25 47 51), runs frequent buses from the ALSA station to the airport. **Aviaco** (☎985 12 76 03) and **Iberia** (☎985 12 76 07) fly to **Barcelona, London,** and **Madrid.**

Trains: Both RENFE and FEVE serve Oviedo from **Estación del Norte,** Av. de Santander.

> **FEVE** (☎985 29 76 56), 3rd fl. Info open daily 9am-10pm or until last train. To: **Bilbao** (7hr., 1 per day 9:08am, €16.70); **El Ferrol** (6½hr.; 2 per day 7:47am, 2:47pm; €15.70); **Llanes** (2hr., 4 per day 9:08am-6:33pm, €5.65); **Ribadeo** (4hr.; 2 per day 7:47am, 2:47pm; €8.15); **Santander** (4½hr.; 2 per day 9:08am, 3:48pm; €10.65).

> **RENFE** (☎985 24 33 64 or 25 24 02), 1st fl. Pay attention to the type of train; a slow local train through the mountains can double your travel time. Info open daily 7:45am-11:15pm. To: **Barcelona** (12-13½hr.; 2 per day 10:57am, 7:48pm; €38.50-51) via **Burgos** (5-6hr., €20.50-27); **Gijón** (30min., every 30min. 5:18am-11:28pm, €1.90); **León** (2-2½hr.; M-F 7 per day 7:30am-11pm, Sa-Su 6 per day 1-11pm; €12-16); **Madrid** (6-9hr.; 3 per day 9:15am, 4:25, 11pm; €32-36) via **Valladolid** (4hr., €22-25).

ASTURIAS & CANTABRIA

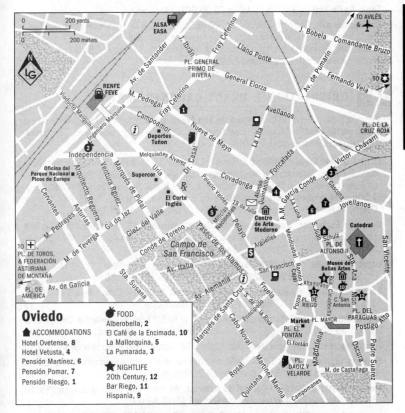

Oviedo

🏠 ACCOMMODATIONS
Hotel Ovetense, **8**
Hotel Vetusta, **4**
Pensión Martínez, **6**
Pensión Pomar, **7**
Pensión Riesgo, **1**

🍴 FOOD
Alberobella, **2**
El Café de la Encimada, **10**
La Mallorquina, **5**
La Pumarada, **3**

⭐ NIGHTLIFE
20th Century, **12**
Bar Riego, **11**
Hispania, **9**

Buses: ALSA (national) and **Económicos/EASA** (regional) buses operate out of the new bus station on C. Pepe Cosmen, s/n (☎902 49 99 49). Open daily 6:30am-12:30am.

ALSA (☎985 96 96 96 or 902 42 22 42). To: **Barcelona** (12hr.; 2 per day 8am, 8pm, Su also 7:30pm; €42.38); **Burgos** (4¼hr.; 2 per day 8am, 8pm; €13.84); **La Coruña** (4½-6¾hr.; M-Sa 4 per day 6:30am-4pm, Su 4 per day 6:30am-7pm; €21.21-28); **León** (1½hr., 7-9 per day 7:30am-10:30pm, €6.88); **Madrid** (5hr.; M-F 12 per day, Sa 10 per day, Su 14 per day 6:30am-12:30am; €47.75); **Santander** (3-4hr., 8-10 per day 12:45am-11:20pm, €10.71-18.25); **Santiago de Compostela** (5½-7hr.; M-Sa 4 per day 6:30, 9:30am, 3, 4pm; Su 4 per day 6:30am, 3, 4, 7pm; €25-32; **Vigo** (7-9hr.; 2 per day 6:30am, 3pm; €29.94); **Valladolid** (4hr., 5 per day 7:30am-12:30am, €14.60).

Económicos/EASA (☎985 29 00 39). To: **Arenas de Cabrales** (2hr.; M-F 5 per day 7:45am-6pm, Sa-Su 2 per day 9:30am, 6pm; €6.90); **Cangas de Onís** (1-1½hr.; M-F 13 per day 6:45am-9:30pm, Sa-Su 7 per day 8:30am-9:30pm; €4.90); **Covadonga** (1¾hr.; M-F 5 per day 6:45am-6:30pm, Sa-Su 5 per day 8:30am-6:30pm; €5.60); **Llanes** (1½-2hr.; M-F 15 per day 6:45am-8:45pm, Sa-Su 13 per day 7am-8:45pm; €7).

Public Transportation: TUA (☎985 22 24 22) runs **buses** 8am-10pm (€0.80). All stops have bus maps. #4 runs from the bus and train stations up C. Uría, turning off just before Campo de San Francisco. #2 runs from all of the stations to the hospital. #2, 3, 5, and 7 run from the RENFE station along C. Uría to the old city.

Taxis: Radio Taxi (☎985 25 00 00 or 25 25 00). 24hr. service.

Car Rental: Avis, C. Ventura Rodríguez, 12 (☎985 24 13 83). From €58 per day. Weekend specials. 25+ with credit card in driver's name. Open M-F 9am-1pm and 4-8pm, Sa 9am-1pm. **Branch** in the train station, Av. de Santander. Open M-F 8am-2pm and 4-8pm, Sa 9am-1pm, Su 9:30am-12:30pm.

■ ▪ ORIENTATION & PRACTICAL INFORMATION

At Oviedo's city center is the **Campo de San Francisco,** a massive park on the slope of a hill. At its downhill base is **Calle Uría,** the city's main thoroughfare. The **cathedral** lies down C. San Francisco from C. Uría.

Tourist Office: Regional Office, C. Uría, 64 (☎985 21 33 85). Offers many brochures on Oviedo and Asturias, including hiking trails in the Parque Nacional Picos de Europa. English spoken. Open M-F 9am-2pm and 4:30-6:30pm, Sa-Su 10am-2pm and 4:30-7:30pm. **Municipal Office,** C. Marqués de Santa Cruz, 1 (☎985 22 75 86). Info on Oviedo. Open M-F 10:30am-2pm and 4:30-7:30pm, Sa-Su 11am-2pm.

Currency Exchange: Banco Santander Central Hispano, Pl. de la Escandalera, s/n (☎902 24 24 24), across from Campo de San Francisco. Open Apr.-Sept. M-F 8:30am-2pm; Oct.-Mar. M-F 8:30am-2pm, Sa 8:30am-1pm.

Luggage Storage: At the **RENFE station** (€1.80 per day). Open daily 7am-11pm. Lockers also at the bus station (€2 per day). Open daily 6:30am-12:30am.

English-Language Bookstore: Librería Cervantes, C. Doctor Casal, 9 (☎985 20 77 61). Open M-F 10am-1:30pm and 4-8pm, Sa 10am-2pm.

Emergency: ☎1006. **Police: Municipal** (☎092 or 985 11 56 57), **Guardia Civil** (☎062 or 985 28 02 04). Both are in the municipal building on C. Quintana, s/n.

24hr. Pharmacy: Farmacia Nestares, C. Uría, 36. Across from El Corte Inglés.

El Corte Inglés: C. Uría, 33. Gigantic department store with supermarket downstairs. Open M-Sa and the 1st Su of every month 9:30am-9:30pm.

Medical Services: Hospital Central de Asturias, Av. de Julián Clavería, s/n (☎985 10 61 00), near the Pl. de Toros. **Ambulance:** ☎985 10 89 00.

Internet Access: CiberCentro La Lila, C. la Lila, 17 (☎984 083 400). 24 very fast computers. 1hr. limit if people are waiting. Free. Open M-F 9am-9pm, Sa 10am-9pm. **Laser Internet Center,** C. San Francisco, 9 (☎985 20 00 66). €3 per hr. Open 24hr.

Post Office: C. Alonso Quintanilla, 1 (☎985 21 41 86 or 902 19 71 97). Open M-F 8:30am-8:30pm, Sa 9:30am-2pm. **Postal Code:** 33060.

▮ ACCOMMODATIONS

Pensiones, hostales, and *hoteles* pack the new city on C. Uría, C. Campoamor, C. Nueve de Mayo (2 blocks to the left of the station), and C. Jovellanos.

Pensión Martínez, C. Jovellanos, 5 (☎985 21 53 44). This modern apartment building offers clean rooms with sinks. Pristine common baths. Singles €18; doubles €21. ❷

Pensión Riesgo, C. Nueve de Mayo, 16, 1st fl. (☎985 21 89 45). A pleasant *pensión* on a pedestrian street in the city center has great prices. Singles €15-18; doubles €26-28, with shower €28-33. ❷

Hotel Vetusta, C. Covadonga, 2 (☎985 22 22 29; fax 22 22 09). A modern 3-star hotel, Vetusta offers jacuzzis and saunas in half of its rooms. Enjoy the dark red walls. Singles €50.50-70; doubles €73-96. AmEx/MC/V. ❺

Hotel Ovetense, C. San Juan, 6 (☎985 22 08 40; fax 21 62 34). Comfortable rooms in a noisy neighborhood only a few steps away from the cathedral. Singles €25-31; doubles €37-43; triples €46-57; quads €61-73. AmEx/MC/V. ❸

Pensión Pomar, C. Jovellanos, 7 (☎985 22 27 91). Spacious, old building has 20 rooms with large windows for your voyeuristic pleasure. Common baths are somewhat dirty. Singles €12; doubles €18-24; triples €27. ❶

🍽 FOOD

If you only have enough euros for one drink in Oviedo, be sure to try *sidra* (cider) by the bottle (€1.50-3.60). It goes fast, and much of it ends up on the floor due to the unconventional pouring method. For the best *sidra* experience, head to the wooden-beamed, ham-hung **sidrerías**, where waiters pour from above their heads and expect you to swallow in one huge gulp. Cheap restaurants line C. Fray Ceferino between the bus and train stations. The indoor **market** at Pl. El Fontán (open M-Sa 8am-3pm) and **Supercor**, C. Uría, 15 (open M-Sa 9:30am-9:30pm), sell fresh produce and groceries.

La Pumarada, C. La Gascona, 8 (☎985 20 02 79). Located on *La Calle de la Sidra,* a lively and festive street on weekend evenings, La Pumarada is both a popular restaurant offering delicious meat and fish entrees (€13-17) and a starting point for Oviedo's nightlife, with friendly waiters serving glasses of traditional *sidra* (€1.95 per bottle). Open Tu-Su 9am-2am. ❸

Alberobella Pasta Fresca, C. Independencia, 22 (☎985 27 57 15). Despite the fast-food appearance, Alberobella concocts delicious and authentic Italian fare, perfect for the *tapas*-weary traveler. Huge pasta dishes €5.20-7.60. Pizza €4.90-8.80. Open M-F 11am-4pm and 6:30-11:30pm, Sa-Su 11am-11:30pm. MC/V. ❷

La Mallorquina, C. Milicias Nacionales, s/n. Sunny pastry cafe also offers light, vegetarian-friendly fare. Salads €7-12. *Menú* €7.50. Open daily 10am-midnight. ❷

El Café de la Encimada, C. San Antonio, 3 (☎985 20 33 17). A beautiful restaurant with brick walls and wooden floors in the midst of the *casco antiguo.* Offers a varied selection of entrees (€10-40). Open daily from 10am-2am. ❺

TOWER OF BABLE Galicians have *gallego*, Catalans have *català*, and Asturians have...*bable*. It's not an official language, but the dialect has returned full force with the sweeping post-Franco reassertion of regional traditions, and it's now taught to school children. The codification of a hodgepodge of more than 10 distinct traditional dialects originating in different corners of Asturias, *bable's* grammar borrows from many but belongs to none. As a result, almost no one is fluent in the tongue (you probably won't hear it on the street), and grandparents tend to express bewilderment at their grandchildren's *bable*-ing.

🔆 SIGHTS

CATEDRAL DE SAN SALVADOR. A recent renovation restored Oviedo's cathedral to its original beauty. Two chapels are roofed with a brilliant blue ceiling above the altar. The **Capilla de Santa María del Rey Casto,** which houses the royal pantheon, was chosen by Alfonso II el Casto in 802 to house the remains of Asturian monarchs and Christian relics rescued from the Moors. An intense metal relief sculpture in the unusual **Capilla de San Pedro** depicts Simon Magus being dropped from the sky by hideous demons. The cathedral complex also includes an 80m **tower**

with great views of the city's rooftops, a *cámara santa* (holy chamber), a **cloister,** and a church **museum.** *(Pl. de Alfonso II. ☎985 22 10 33. Cathedral open daily 10am-8pm. Free. Cámara santa €1.25. Museum ☎985 20 31 17. Museum, cámara, and cloister open M-Sa 10am-2pm and 4-8pm. €2.50, seniors €1.80, children €0.90; Th free.)*

MUSEO DE BELLAS ARTES. The two buildings of the Museo de Bellas Artes in the **Palacio de Velarde** display a wide range of Asturian art and a small collection of 16th- to 20th-century Spanish works. While the upper floors display devotional art on loan from Madrid's Prado, the ground floor has a permanent collection of astonishing modern works by local artists. In addition to the Klimt-esque work of Herme Anglada Camaresa, the highlight is undoubtedly José Ramón Zaragoza's triptych of the myth of Prometheus. *(C. Santa Ana, 1, and C. Rúa, 8, just up C. Santa Ana from Pl. de Alfonso II. ☎985 21 30 61. Open Tu-Sa 11am-2pm and 4:30-8:30pm, Sa 11:30am-2pm and 5-8pm, Su 11:30am-2:30pm. Free.)*

MONTE NARANCO. Asturian Pre-Romanesque style was the first European attempt to blend architecture, sculpture (including human representations), and murals since the fall of the Roman Empire. The style was developed under Alfonso II (789-842) and refined under his son Ramiro I, for whom the *Ramirense* style is named. Two simple yet beautiful examples, **Santa María del Naranco** and **San Miguel de Lillo,** lie 4km outside Oviedo on Monte Naranco. *(☎985 25 72 08. Both open May-Sept. M-Sa 9:30am-1pm and 3-7pm, Su 9:30am-1pm; Oct.-Apr. Su-M 9:30am-1pm, Tu-Sa 9:30am-1pm and 3-7pm. €1.50, children €0.75; M free.)*

OTHER SIGHTS. The tourist offices can provide you with a list of **churches** whose Gothic architecture is the only of its kind. The **Centro de Arte Moderno** hosts temporary exhibits of regional and national cutting-edge artists. *(C. Alonso Quintanilla, 2. Open M-F 5-9pm, Sa 11:30am-2:30pm and 5-9pm, Su 11:30am-2:30pm. Free.)*

🖿 HIKING

Though not the best base for hiking in the Parque Nacional Picos de Europa (see p. 548), Oviedo is definitely the place to stock up on gear and supplies, as shops within the park and in gateway towns can be prohibitively expensive.

■ **Federación Asturiana de Montaña,** Av. de Julián Clavería (☎985 25 23 62), near the bull ring, a 30min. walk from the city center (get a full-sized map of the city from the tourist office). Or, take bus #2 (dir.: Hospital) from C. Uría. Organizes excursions and provides guides, weather conditions, and advice on the best hiking routes. Instructors for everything from paragliding to kayaking. Open M-F 8am-8pm.

Deportes Tuñón, C. Campoamor, 7. Extensive selection of camping and rock-climbing gear, long underwear, and a few maps. Open M-F 10am-1:30pm and 4:30-8:30pm, Sa 11am-2pm. AmEx/MC/V.

🎵 ENTERTAINMENT

The streets south of the cathedral, especially C. Mon and the areas around Pl. Riego, Pl. El Fontán, and Pl. El Paraguas, teem with noisy *sidrerías* and clubs. Stylish **Bar Riego,** on Pl. Riego, serves tasty *batidos* (milkshakes; €2-3.60) on a breezy *terraza.* (Open M-Sa noon-4pm and 8pm-2am.) After a few *chupitos* and *copas,* most students head to one of the several clubs in the area. **20th Century,** C. Mon, 12, and **Hispania,** C. Altamirano, 1, are both very popular among locals and tourists and play mostly pop music. (Mixed drinks €2-3. Open midnight-8am.) Wine connoisseurs follow **la ruta de los vinos** (the wine route) from *bodega* to *bodega* along C. El Rosal. (*Copas* €1.80-3.60.) Between C. Alcalde M. García

Conde and C. Jovellanos, **Danny's Jazz Café**, C. La Luna, 11, hosts a variety of acts. (☎985 21 14 83. Beers €1.80. Mixed drinks €3.60. Open daily 8pm-4am.) On Sept. 19-21, Oviedo throws a **fiesta** in honor of its patron saint, San Mateo.

LLANES ☎985

Perched on a narrow ledge between the heights of the Picos de Europa and the cliffs over the Bay of Biscay, Llanes seems like an apparition. While the small, rocky beaches here are crowded, this is no resort town; rather, it's a small Asturian village rising above the frothing teal sea, only lightly touched by modernity—complete with cows, ruins, and winding streets.

▐ TRANSPORTATION. Trains leave from the FEVE station, C. Alonso Vega, s/n (☎985 40 01 24) to **Oviedo** (2½hr., 6 per day 8:05am-8pm, €5.80) and **Santander** (2hr., daily 6 per day 11:27am-9:10pm, €5.15). To get to the tourist office from the train station, walk down C. Alonso Vega, take a right at its end onto C. Egidio Gavito, walk for two blocks, and turn left onto C. Alfonso IX.

ALSA-Turytrans runs **buses** from the bus station on C. la Bolera, s/n. (☎985 40 24 85. Ticket office open M-F 8am-7:30pm, Sa-Su 8am-1:45pm and 3:15-8pm.) A new station is being built on the same street. To: **Bilbao** (3-4hr., daily 7 per day 2am-6:45pm, €10.41); **La Coruña/Pontevedra/Santiago de Compostela/Vigo** (6-11hr., daily 1 per day 4:55am, €26-35); **Gijón** (2hr., daily 6 per day 8am-9:15pm, €7.19); **Oviedo** (2-3hr.; M-F 15 per day 6:30am-9:15pm, Sa-Su 13 per day 8am-9:15pm; €7); **San Sebastián** (4-5hr., daily 5 per day 2am-4:45pm, €16.34); **Santander** (2hr., daily 8 per day 2am-10:10pm, €5). To reach the town center from the station, take a left onto C. la Bolera, and veer right as it becomes C. Cueto Bajo; at the post office, turn left onto C. las Barqueras, which leads to the Ayuntamiento and tourist office. For a **taxi**, call 24hr. ☎985 40 11 77. For **car rental**, head to **EuropCar**, on Av. de la Paz just before CyberSpacio. (☎985 40 10 07. €53 per day for 350km. 21+ and have had license for 1yr. Open M-F 9am-1:30pm and 4-8pm, Sa 9am-1:30pm.)

▐ PRACTICAL INFORMATION. The **tourist office** is in a 13th-century tower on C. Alfonso IX, directly behind the yellow Casa de Cultura/Ayuntamiento on C. Castillo Mercaderes. Ask here for information on adventure tourism. (☎985 40 01 64. Open July-Sept. M-Sa 10am-2pm and 5-9pm, Su 10am-2pm; Sept.-June M-Sa 10am-2pm and 4-6:30pm.) Services include: **emergency** ☎006; **municipal police**, C. Nemesio Sobrino, s/n (☎985 40 18 87); **Farmacia Mariano Ruiz**, Pl. Parres Sobrino, 1 (open M-F 9:30am-1:30pm and 4:30-8pm, Sa 10:30am-1pm; late-night pharmacy location is posted in the window, though it may be a few towns over); **health center**, Av. de San Pedro, s/n (☎985 40 20 00); **Internet access** at **Cyber Spacio**, Av. de la Paz, 6 (☎985 40 03 44; €3 per hr.; open M-F 9am-midnight); **post office**, C. Pidal, s/n (☎985 40 11 14; open M-F 8:30am-2:30pm, Sa 9:30am-1pm). **Postal Code:** 33500.

▐▐ ACCOMMODATIONS & FOOD. Rooms fill early in July and August, making one-month advance reservations a necessity. **Casa del Río ❷**, Av. de San Pedro, 3, is a restored mansion near the beach with wonderful rooms, some with balconies. Doubles have large windows. (☎985 40 11 91. Reception 24hr. Singles €15; doubles €30-36, with bath and TV €38-50.) The spacious and bright rooms of the well-adorned **Pensión La Guía ❷**, Pl. Parres Sobrino, 1, are right in the center of town. (☎985 40 25 77. Check-out 2pm. Reservations accepted. Doubles with bath €38-50. MC/V.) **Albergue de la Estación ❶**, C. Alonso Vega, s/n, at the FEVE station, is Llanes's only hostel, frequented by Spanish teens enjoying a beach weekend. The owners arrange outdoor excursions in the Picos. (☎985 40 14 58 or 610 52 81 11. Lockout 1:30-5pm. 4- to 8-bed dorms €14 per person. MC/V.) For those looking to splurge on something unique, next door to Casa del Río is **Hotel Don Paco** ❺, Av. de San Pedro, 1, a three-star hotel in a 17th-century manor, complete with welcoming soft beds and antique chandeliers. Its **restaurant** ❹ has a *menú* (€19) updated daily that features local game and dishes with an extra creative kick. (☎985 40 01 50; www.llaneshoteldonpaco.com. Doubles €60-76. IVA not included.) On a small bluff, **Camping Entreplayas** ❶, off Av. de Toró between Playas de Puerto Chico and Toró, is wildly popular, if not for its scenic views, then for the neighboring bar, where campers laze away their days with bikinis and beer. (☎985 40 08 88. €3 per person, per tent, and per car; electricity €2. IVA not included.)

Cafes and *sidrerías* line C. las Barqueras, C. Castillo Mercaderes, and C. Nemesio Sobrino; near the beaches, Av. de Toró and C. Marqués de Argüelles have many local eateries. **Café Bitácora** ❶, C. las Barqueras, 1 (☎985 40 03 88) serves salads (€2-5), entrees, and *platos combinados* (€5-6) in a lively, social setting close to the river. However, the most interesting fare in town is undoubtedly served at **El Latino** ❷, C. Venezuela, 1. From the Ayuntamiento, walk up C. Nemesio Sobrino, turn right on Av. de San Pedro, and then left onto C. Genaro, which becomes Av. de Méjico and brings you to C. Venezuela. This tropical cantina serves all the Mexican favorites, including guacamole, enchiladas, and fajitas. (☎985 40 32 40. Entrees €3-10.82. Restaurant open daily 8pm-2am, bar 10am-2am.) **El Pescador** ❷, C. Manuel Cué, s/n, in the center of the old city, serves delicious Asturian entrees (€6-10) to loyal patrons who fill the restaurant's large outdoor seating sections. (☎985 40 32 93. Open daily 11am-5pm and 7pm-1am.) For groceries, go to **El Árbol,** Av. de Méjico s/n, across from El Latino. (☎985 40 10 50. Open M-Sa 9am-9pm.)

🔲 **BEACHES.** Though some of the most popular beaches in Asturias, these are not the wide swaths of sand that probably come to one's mind. Rather, Llanes's beaches are tucked into coves and inlets along the coast, made all the more idyllic by the occasional rocky outcropping. As these are protected waters, the sea is calm (and rather seaweedy). Compact **Playa de Sablón**, in the center of town, is the most popular—and the most crowded. From the Ayuntamiento, turn right onto C. Alfonso IX, which runs straight to the beach. **Playa de Toró** is by far Llanes's prettiest and most swimmer-friendly beach, though it's still fairly crowded. It's also the only beach with any semblance of waves. From the Ayuntamiento, walk up C. Castillo Mercaderes across the river and at the post office, turn left onto Av. de la Guía, which turns into Av. de Toró. **Playa de Puerto Chico** will please those looking for total seclusion, but only if they can stand the mountains of seaweed and their accompanying stink. Follow the directions to Playa del Sablón, above, and take the steps up the hill to the 🏴**Paseo de San Pedro,** a grassy strip running along the edge of the cliffs above the sea. Plenty of benches, shade trees, and lizards share the wide open and breezy sea views.

CANGAS DE ONÍS ☎985

During the summer months, when the streets are packed with mountaineers and vacationing families, it can seem like the sole purpose of Cangas (pop. 6285) is to help travelers spelunk and hang glide. While it's true that most visitors come to Cangas to get closer to the Parque Nacional Picos de Europa (see p. 548), Cangas is, if not thrilling, a relaxing, history-rich town. In between arranging adventures, visit the town's sights, testaments to its former Paleolithic, Celtic, and Roman residents. The town's accessibility by bus makes it a useful and ideal base for those interested in just a taste of the Picos. Those seeking a central base for extensive exploring should look into *refugios* and *albergues* inside the park.

☞ TRANSPORTATION. ALSA, Av. de Covadonga, 18 (☎985 84 81 33), in the Pícaro Inmobiliario building across from the tourist office, runs **buses** to: **Arenas de Cabrales** (30min.; M-F 5 per day 9am-7:25pm, Sa-Su 2 per day 10:55am, 7:25pm; €2.05); **Covadonga** (30min.; M-F 11 per day 8:30am-7:35pm, Sa-Su 7 per day 9:10am-7:35pm; €0.90); **Madrid** (7hr., 1 per day 2:35pm, €25.49); **Oviedo** (1½-2hr.; M-F 12 per day 6:15am-8:30pm, Sa-Su 6 per day 9:15am-8:30pm; €4.90); **Valladolid** (5hr.; 2 per day 2:35pm, 7:30pm; €14.51). For a taxi, call **Radio Taxi** (24hr. ☎985 84 87 97 or 84 83 73) or wait in front of the Ayuntamiento.

🛈 PRACTICAL INFORMATION. The main street in Cangas de Onís is **Avenida de Covadonga.** The **tourist office,** Jardines del Ayuntamiento, 2, is just off Av. de Covadonga across from the bus stop and has information about the town, accommodations, and adventure tourism offices located in other park border towns. (☎/fax 985 84 80 05. Open daily May-Sept. 10am-10pm; Oct.-Apr. 10am-2pm and 4-7pm. English spoken.) Park information is available at the **Picos de Europa National Park Visitors' Center,** Av. de Covadonga, 43, in the **Casa Dago.** The office has a list of mountain *refugios,* maps, hike suggestions, and a fantastic, three-dimensional model of the park. From the bus stop, walk up Av. de Covadonga toward the large church. (☎/fax 985 84 86 14. Open May-Sept. M-F 9am-2pm and 5-6:30pm, Sa 9am-2pm and 4-6:30pm, Su 9am-2:30pm; Oct.-Apr. M-Sa 9am-2pm and 4-6:30pm, Su 9am-2:30pm.) Services include: **Banco Santander Central Hispano,** Av. de Covadonga, 6 (☎985 84 87 84; open Apr.-Sept. M-F 8:30am-2:30pm, Oct.-Mar. also Sa 8:30am-1pm); **emergency** ☎112; **municipal police** in the Ayuntamiento, Av. de Covadonga, 21 (☎985 84 85 58); **pharmacy,** Av. de Castilla, 24, just off Av. de Covadonga near the *puente romano* (☎985 84 80 38; open M-Sa 9am-2pm and 4:30-7:30pm); **health center,** C. de la Cárcel, s/n (☎985 84 85 71), down C. Emilio Laria from Av. de Covadonga; **Internet access** next to the tourist office (open M-F 4-9pm, €2 per hr); **car rental** at **EuropCar,** C. San Pelayo, 17 (☎985 94 75 02; open daily 9:30am-1:30pm and 6-9:30pm; €66 per day for 350km; V); **post office,** Av. Constantino González, s/n, a right off Av. de Covadonga when heading toward the *puente* (☎985 84 81 86; open M-F 8:30am-2:30pm, Sa 9:30am-1pm). **Postal Code:** 33550.

☞☏ ACCOMMODATIONS & FOOD. A few clean *pensiones* along Av. de Covadonga will gladly accept your euros. **Hospedaje Principado ❷,** Av. de Covadonga, 16, 3rd fl., is a tiny, immaculate *pensión* with a TV in every room. (☎985 84 83 50 or 667 98 31 88; fax 985 84 83 15. Singles €15-19; doubles €20-30, with bath €33-39.) **El Chofer ❷,** C. Emilio Laria, 10, has clean rooms with firm beds and nice sheets that sore bodies will welcome. Oriental rugs, TVs, sinks, and hall baths complete the experience. (☎985 84 83 05. Winter heat. Singles €20-25; doubles €25-35.) **Hotel Puente Romano ❺,** Puente Romano, s/n, overlooking the enchanting bridge at the end of Av. de Covadonga, boasts very comfortable, warm rooms in a serenely set 19th-century manor. Rooms include TV, heat, phone, and private bath. (☎985 84 93 39. Doubles €45-70. IVA not included. MC/V.) **Camping Covadonga ❶,** in Soto de Cangas, 4km up the road toward Arenas de Cabrales, has a cafeteria, bar, supermarket, and showers with hot water. (☎985 94 00 97. €4 per adult, €3.25 per child; €3.74 per tent; €3.50 per car. Open *Semana Santa* and June-Sept. 20.)

Restaurant **Pizzería Eladia ❷,** Av. de Covadonga, 14 (☎985 84 80 00), next to the bus stop, serves pizzas (€6-7), entrees (€7-9), and three course *menús* (€9) on a social terrace where the town action passes. (Open daily 9am-midnight.) Choose from sandwiches, *pinchos, tapas,* and even hamburgers (€2-5) at **Cafetería Reconquista ❶,** Av. de Covadonga, 6. (☎985 84 82 75. Open daily 8am-11pm.) For a do-it-yourself-meal, try **Alimerka Supermercado,** Av. de Covadonga, 15. (☎985 84 94 13. Open Su-M 9am-2pm, Tu-Sa 9am-9:30pm.)

◎ ⚑ SIGHTS & EXCURSIONS. At the far end of Av. de Covadonga is the **Puente Romano,** a medieval bridge with an ornate golden cross hanging from the middle. The bridge is particularly beautiful when viewed at night. From the bridge, following Av. de Covadonga into town, turning left onto C. Constantino González, and crossing the river brings you to the **Capilla de Santa Cruz.** This Romanesque chapel, built in AD 737, sits atop the town's oldest monument, a Celtic *dolmen* (monolith) dating from 3000 BC, which can be seen from the chapel's cave. (Open daily 10am-1pm and 3-6:30pm.) Also of interest is **Cueva de "El Buxu"** (BOO-shoo), whose walls are adorned with 15,000-year-old paintings by Cangas's paleolithic residents. To reach the cave, follow the main road to Covadonga for 3km until the signs for the *cueva* and Cardes, the closest town, direct you left. From here, it's a gradual 1km climb past pastures to the easily missed sign to the caves, by Bar Cueva El Buxu. Buses to Arenas de Cabrales, Covadonga, and Llanes (see **Transportation,** p. 545) run near the cave; ask to be dropped off at the **Cruce de Susierra.** Come by 10am, as only 25 people are allowed in each day. (☎985 94 00 54. Open W-Su Apr.-Sept. 10am-3pm; Oct.-Mar. 9:30am-1pm and 3-5pm. €1.40; W free.) Those with wheels will want to head south from Cangas de Onís along the Río Sella. This route winds through Santillan, Sames, and finally to the **Desfiladero de los Beyos,** an 11km gorge filled with wet rocks and blossoming beech trees.

⛰ ADVENTURE TOURISM. Cangas de Onís is the perfect place to arrange outdoor activities, but it is imperative to reserve at least 2 days ahead of time, 3-5 days in June-August. There are several tourist agencies in town, but all are closed from December to February. **Cangas Aventura,** Av. de Covadonga, 23, sets up various expeditions, including hiking (only in the low season), white-water rafting, *espeleología* (spelunking), ▨ *barranquismo* (canyoning, swimming, and spelunking), canoeing, horseback riding, paintballing, and bungee jumping. (☎985 84 92 61; fax 84 85 61. Open daily 9:30am-10pm. €19-42 per person depending on the activity, time of day, and size of the group. Prices include equipment, a guide, transportation to and from Cangas, and sometimes a bag lunch. Discounts for large groups and multiple activities. Call for departure times and destinations.) **Monteverde,** C. Alférez Provisional, 5, offers the same activities led by very friendly instructors. (☎985 84 80 79; www.hotel-monteverde.com. €22-36 per person.) **Los Cauces,** Av. de Covadonga, 23, offers most of the same activities for similar prices. (☎985 94 73 18 or 84 01 38. €18-33 per person. Open daily 9:30am-10pm.) The tourist office lists other adventure agencies. **Deportes Tuñon,** C. San Pelayo, 31, sells hiking shoes (€40-129), backpacks (€20-180), and other gear. (☎985 94 70 61. Open Tu-Sa 10am-1:30pm and 4-8pm, Su 10am-2pm. MC/V.)

ARENAS DE CABRALES ☎985

Some say the small town of Arenas de Cabrales (pop. 800) sits "as close to the sky as to the ground," and that's not so far from the truth. The town rests on several craggy peaks, and the fog, wandering mountain goats, and breathtaking vistas make Arenas seem almost like a mountain mirage. Outdoor enthusiasts flock to Arenas, eager to take advantage of the excellent hiking and climbing just 6km away in the Parque Nacional Picos de Europa (see p. 548).

▐ TRANSPORTATION. ALSA buses (☎902 42 22 42) head to **Oviedo** (2½hr.; M-F 5 per day 7:25am-7:45pm, Sa-Su 3 per day 8:35am, 5:50, 7:45pm; €6.90), via **Cangas de Onís** (50min., €2), and **Poncebos** (20min.; M-F 4 per day 10:15am, 5:15, 6:15, and 7:15pm, Sa-Su 1 per day 7:15pm; €0.90). Get to **Potes** via **Panes** (30min; M-F 4 per day 11:35am, 3:05, 6:05, and 8:05pm, Sa-Su 1 per day 11:35pm; €1.55). From June to September, buses run to **Llanes** (1-2hr.; 3 per day 10, 11:15am, 7:45pm). Buses to

Poncebos depart from the tourist hut; the others leave from across the street in front of the small park (look for the ALSA sign). Buses always show up, but sometimes are 10-15min. behind schedule. In Panes, buses tend to arrive 10-15min. early and do not wait. For a **taxi**, call Joaquín (☎985 84 64 87 or 689 38 06 03), who claims "un cliente, un amigo" and will go just about anywhere in the Asturian Picos.

🛈 **PRACTICAL INFORMATION.** The **tourist office** is in a hut on the main road just before the bridge. (☎985 84 64 84; http://turismo.cabrales.org. Open July-Sept. 20 Tu-Su 10am-2pm and 4-8pm.) Services include: **emergency** ☎112; **Guardia Civil,** on the main road toward Cangas near the post office (☎985 84 50 04); **Consultorio Médico** (☎985 84 55 04), uphill on the main road across the street from the **ATM** and the pharmacy; **pharmacy** (☎985 84 50 16), next to Cajastur; **Internet access** at **El Mirador Cibercafe** in Poo de Cabrales, 15min. down the road to Cangas de Onís (☎985 84 54 30; open daily 7am-midnight, Su noon-midnight; €3 per hr.); **post office,** near the bus stop towards Cangas de Onís (open M-Sa 9-11am). **Postal Code:** 33554.

THE CHEESE STANDS ALONE

It's an odd selling point, but somehow Arenas de Cabrales has become famous for the unbridled moldy funkiness of its blue cheese. To produce the cheese, locals arduously empty cow, goat, and ewe udders into large tin bins. After allowing the mix to "mature," cheese-makers drain the extra liquid, add a pinch of cow afterbirth and a twist of lamb fetus, store the mush inside cabbage leaves and let them stew in mountain caves in humid darkness. Half a year later the speckled brown wheels rolls out onto the sidestreets of every tourist destination in Asturias. Brave tasters rave about the pungent flavor, the creamy texture, and the "knock you to the floor and have you begging for yo' *madre*" kick.

🖪🖫 **ACCOMMODATIONS & FOOD.** Since many of Arenas's visitors opt for camping, the town has few low-priced lodgings. Family-style ▨**Pensión Covadonga ❷**, down C. Pedro Niembro near the tourist office, offers spotless rooms with incredible mountain views. (☎985 84 68 10. Reserve 2 months ahead. Doubles €24-27.) **El Castañeu ❶**, right next to Pensión Covadonga, offers nice doubles, some with breathtaking views of the Picos. (☎985 84 65 73. Reserve 1 month ahead for Aug. Winter heating. Single next to the common room €10-12, doubles with bath €24-30.) **Hotel Picos de Europa ❸**, Ctra. General, s/n, is located in an orange building visible from the bus stop. It offers spacious, fully equipped rooms along with an outdoor pool. (☎985 84 64 91. One-month advance reservations for Aug.; also recommended for July. Singles €41-65, doubles €53-80, depending on the time of the year.) **Naranjo de Bulnes Camping ❶**, 1km east on AS-114, has campsites and cabins, as well as a cozy TV room, a cafeteria, a bar, and shower facilities. (☎/fax 985 84 65 78. Camping €4.25 per person, €4 per tent, €3.80 per car. Cabins for 1-2 people €29-34; each additional person €6.)

Of the few eateries in Arenas, ▨ **La Panera ❸**, is by far the best. Atop a small hill to the left of Banco Bilbao Vizcaya (BBVA) on the main road, this restaurant has the look and feel of an intimate alpine lodge, complete with a romantic balcony and outdoor terrace with astounding views of the surrounding peaks. The delicious food (*menú* €11, entrees €11-20) is prepared with care and features homemade specialties. (☎985 84 68 10. Open daily noon-4pm and 7:30-11:30pm. MC/V.) For a traditional Spanish *cafetería*, head down the main road to **Cafetería Santelmo ❷**, beside Hotel Picos de Europa. The restaurant offers a wide variety of meats, salads for €7-9, and *tapas* for €3-8. (Open daily noon-4pm and 8pm-midnight. AmEx/MC/V.) The **Casa Tres Palacios** market is opposite the tourist office. (☎985 84 65 05. Open M-F 6:30am-9:30pm, Sa-Su 7:30am-9pm.)

ASTURIAS & CANTABRIA

◪ **ADVENTURE TOURISM. Novedades Cendón,** across the street from the tourist office, sells basic gear and maps. (☎985 84 64 74. Open daily June-Aug. 9am-10:30pm, Sept.-May 10am-8pm. MC/V.) **Pico Urrielly** (☎985 85 67 70), outside of town toward Panes on AS-114, arranges hiking expeditions, spelunking, canoeing, and horseback riding. Prices range from €12-48, depending on the activity, the length of the trip, size of the group, and day of the week. For bike rentals, head to **Viesca Aventura,** on the main road towards Cangas de Onís. (☎605 50 30 00. Open daily 10am-8pm. €15 per day.)

PARQUE NACIONAL PICOS DE EUROPA

Three hundred million years ago, Mother Nature flapped her limestone bedsheet and erected the Picos de Europa, a mountain range of curious variation and chaotic beauty. This accident of nature created a formidable border between the Asturias and Cantabria regions and the rest of Spain. In fact, this jagged barrier is one of the main reasons Asturias never fell to the Moors—residents found protection and divine inspiration in their impenetrable range. Although the mountains and towns here often feel as isolated as they were centuries ago, they are now part of the very civilized Parque Nacional Picos de Europa. Founded in 1918 as the Parque Nacional de Covadonga, Spain's first national park, Covadonga grew into the largest national park in Europe, spanning three massifs and three provinces (Asturias, Cantabria, and Castilla y León).

The ancient crags and summits of the Picos de Europa shelter some of Europe's most elusive and endangered species, including wild horses, boars, bears, and *chamois* (a goat-type animal), as well as long-eared owls, Egyptian vultures, songbirds, and eagles. According to local lore, the mountains are also home to the half-man, half-beast *busgosos;* the bearded and highly unattractive *nuberos* who are responsible for clouds, rain, and snow; and the tiny *trasgus,* who will either tidy up or trash your room at night depending on their mood. The scrub-spotted peaks lure thousands of outdoor enthusiasts who come to explore the myriad caves and caverns carved out by centuries of glacial activity. Gorges and rivers criss-cross the floor of the park, and silent alpine meadows sway in the breeze high above. Highlights include the peaceful Santa Cueva in Covadonga (see p. 551), the sparkling Lagos de Enol y Ercina (see p. 552), and the monumental, vertigo-inducing Teleférico de Fuente Dé (see p. 556).

✜ ORIENTATION

Part of the larger Cordillera Cantábrica, the Picos de Europa consist of three mountainous massifs: the **Occidental** (Cornión), the **Central** (Urrieles), and the **Oriental** (Ándara), with the highest peak, **Torrecerredo** (2646m), rising out of the Central massif. Several rivers wind through the floor of the park; the three largest are the Sella, Dobra, and Cares. The **Garganta del Cares** (Cares Gorge), which cuts a dramatic border between the Macizo Oriental and Macizo Central, the latter of which holds the park's most popular trails and famous peaks: the life-claiming Peña Vieja (2613m) and Pico Tesorero (2570m), the stark Llambrión (2642m), and the mythic **Naranjo de Bulnes** (Picu Urriellu; 2519m).

Those interested in day hikes and guided adventure tourism start in **Cangas de Onís** (see p. 544) and **Potes** (see p. 554); experienced and well-equipped hikers head to **Arenas de Cabrales** (see p. 546), which serves as a good base. Although independent adventures are definitely possible, most visitors opt for guided hikes and expeditions instead of setting out on their own.

⊡ TRANSPORTATION

Getting to the Picos is relatively easy—it's the getting around once there that's difficult. **ALSA buses** link **Cangas de Onís** (see p. 544) and **Arenas de Cabrales** (see p. 546), the gateways in the west and the north, with towns lying just inside the park's borders. The most important are **Covadonga** and **Poncebos; La Palomera buses** link **Potes,** the gateway in the east, with **Fuente Dé** and, with carefully planned connections, Arenas de Cabrales as well. With a bit of creativity and the help of knowledgeable locals, it is possible to reach more towns than bus schedules suggest. It is, however, much more efficient to travel by car as buses run infrequently and make many stops, lengthening journeys. Route **AS-114** runs along the northern edge of the Picos from Cangas de Onís (10km north of Covadonga) through Arenas de Cabrales and on to **Panes,** where it intersects Route N-621. N-621 runs 50km south and west to Potes, where a branch leads to Fuente Dé.

⊠ PRACTICAL INFORMATION

The key to hiking in the Picos is planning ahead. Water sources and campsites are hard to come by, and few of the towns in the park have supermarkets or ATMs.

Although hiking is possible from May to September, the best times to visit are July and August, despite the crowds. In early summer, it is cold and stormy, with snow still a real possibility; September weather can be equally unpredictable. If visiting during July and August, you must make reservations in the gateway cities to the park (Cangas de Onís, Arenas de Cabrales, and Potes) a month in advance, possibly even earlier in August.

Emergency: ☎ 112, but the only phones are in town and at *refugios.*

Park Information: In **Asturias:** Cangas de Onís, Av. de Covadonga, 43 (see p. 544); in **Cantabria:** Fuente Dé, in the Ctra. Potes (☎ 942 73 32 01); and in **Castilla y León:** Posada de Valdeón at Ctra. Cordinanes, s/n (☎ 987 74 05 49; fax 74 05 79). The **Administrative Office** (www.mma.es) is in Oviedo (see p. 538).

Guidebooks: In English, Robin Walker's *Picos de Europa* is the best. In Spanish, the many guides of Miguel Ángel Andrados do fine. The park office in Cangas sells a guide book (in Spanish) listing several hiking trails (€9.02, with maps and photos).

Gear: Basic amenities and hiking gear are available in all of the gateway towns, but **gear** is cheapest in Oviedo (see p. 538). Inside the park, **food and water** are scarce, even in the towns of Poncebos, Covadonga, and Fuente Dé, none of which have supermarkets. Only in Oviedo are **water purification** packets available. The free **maps** of the park provided by tourist offices are insufficient for hiking if you plan on following any trails other than the most touristed. Extensive trail maps can be purchased in just about every store in Cangas de Onís, Arenas de Cabrales, and Potes for €3-4.

REFUGIOS & RANGERS

Before embarking on any hikes in the park, consult the below list of *refugios,* which, in addition to providing shelter in the mountains, also double as ranger stations. The stations are typically open from 8 or 9am to 5 or 6pm. Some *refugios* are known by several names. You can also pick up the most complete and current list at any park office. Most *refugios* cost €3-6 per night.

Macizo Occidental

Casa Municipal de Pastores/Vega de Enol (☎ 985 84 92 61), next to Lake Enol. 26 spots.

Vegarredonda (☎ 985 92 29 52), south of Lago Enol. 68 spots.

Marqués de Villiviciosa/Vega de Ario (☎639 81 20 69 or 650 90 07 60), by Vega de Ario southeast of Lago Enol. 45 spots.

Vegabaño (☎987 29 21 47 or 74 03 26), in the southwest corner of the park. 25 spots.

Macizo Central

Delgado Úbeda/Vega de Urriellu. (☎985 92 52 00 or 94 50 24), by Vega de Urriellu. 100 spots.

Cabaña Verónica, near Pico Tesorero. 2-3 spots, call the Guardia Civíl to reserve (☎942 73 00 07).

El Redondo/Fuente Dé (☎942 73 66 99), by Fuente Dé in the park's southeast corner. 68 spots.

Diego Mella/Collado Jermoso. (☎616 90 43 53), next to Collado Jermoso. 29 spots.

Toño Odriozola/Hotel de Áliva (☎942 73 09 99), in the Ptos. de Áliva. Several hotel-style doubles. The most expensive *refugio* in the park. Doubles €45.

José Ramón Lueja/Jou de Los Cabrones (☎985 84 59 43 or 608 18 15 81), by Jou de los Cabrones. 24 spots.

La Terenosa, by Montaña Terenosa. 30 spots. No reservations; keys in neighboring *cabaña*.

Macizo Oriental

Casetón de Andara (☎942 55 81 57), by Vegas de Andara and Pica del Mancondiú. 18 spots.

TOURS & GUIDED HIKES

For information on adventure tourism outings, see **Cangas de Onís** (p. 544) and **Potes** (p. 554). There are no outfitters in Arenas de Cabrales. The park service offers free guided hikes daily from towns throughout the park. Below is a list of guided hikes, listed with difficulty (L=Low, M=Medium, H=High), map route number, location, schedule, and departure point. Shortly before your hike begins, call the region park office to confirm the information. You can also pick up schedules at any office. Most hikes are day hikes; many others can be done in 2-3 days.

Northwest Sector (by Cangas de Onís)

L: A-1 **Lagos de Covadonga.** (3hr.; Tu, W, F 10:30am; Buferrera parking lot at Los Lagos.)

M: A-3 **Majada del Tolleyu.** (4hr., W 9:30am, Buferrera parking lot.)

M: A-4 **Majada de Belbín.** (4hr., Th. 9:30am, Buferrera parking lot.)

M/H: A-2 **Vega de Comeya.** (5hr., M 9:30am, Buferrera parking lot.)

M/H: A-5 **Vega de Orandi.** (5hr., F 9:30am, Covadonga (Escolanía).)

Northeast Sector (by Arenas de Cabrales):

M: B-2 **Bulnes.** (4hr.; Tu, Sa 10am; info booth at Poncebos.)

M: B-3 **Minas de Ándara.** (4½hr.; W, Su 10am; Hoyo del Tejo, between Sotres and Tresviso.)

M/H: B-1 **Monte Camba.** (4hr.; M, F 10am; Plaza de Tielve.)

H: B-4 **Peña Maín.** (6hr., Th 9:15am, Plaza de Sotres.)

Southeast Sector (Liébana—by Potes and Fuente Dé)

L: C-2 **Hayedo de las Íces.** (4½hr., Tu 10am, Plaza at Espinama.)

L: C-3 **Vega Linares.** (4hr., W 10am, Cosgaya town border.)

L: C-4 **Canal Arredondas.** (4hr., Th 10am, Brez town border.)

L: C-6 **Sierra de Bejes.** (4hr., Sa 10am, Plaza at Bejes.)

L: C-7 **Puertos de Áliva.** (4hr., Su 10am, Fuente Dé at the top of the *teleférico* station.)

M: C-1 **Horcados Rojos.** (4hr., M 10am, Fuente Dé at the top of the *teleférico* station.)

M: C-5 **Espinama-Áliva.** (5½hr., F 10am, Plaza at Espinama.)

Southwest Sector (by Sajambre and Valdeón)

L: D-6 **El Cuebre.** (4hr., Sa 10am, Posada de Valdeón park info booth.)

L: D-7 **El Odrón.** (4hr., Su 10am, Posada de Valdeón park info booth.)

M: D-1 **Majada de Vegabaño.** (4½hr., M 9:30am, Soto de Sajambre at Escuelas.)

M: D-2 **Vega de Llos.** (6hr., Tu 9:30am, Posada de Valdeón park info booth.)

M: D-3 **Monte Piergua.** (4½hr., W 9:30am, Posada de Valdeón park info booth.)

M: D-4 **Valle de Sajambre.** (4½hr., Th 9:30am, Oseja de Sajambre Ayuntamiento.)

M: D-5 **Barbujó.** (6hr., F 9:30am, Plaza at Santa Marina)

⚐ ACCOMMODATIONS

The easiest accommodations are in Cangas de Onís, Arenas de Cabrales, and Potes; however, these limit one to day hiking. For multi-day hikes, the **refugios ❶** (usually cabins with bunks but not blankets; see **Refugios & Rangers**, p. 549) scattered throughout the park are the best option. All of the park offices have a complete list of the Picos's *refugios*. There are only four **campgrounds ❶** in the park (at Caín, Santa Marina, Caldevilla, and Fuente Dé), and they are all in its southern half. However, many towns close to the park borders have campsites, including Cangas de Onís and Arenas de Cabrales. Other lodging options include **albergues ❶** (hostels, usually in ancient, unheated buildings with bunks and cold water) and **casas ❶** (buildings with bunks, hot water, and wood stoves); these, however, are also only in or near towns. In all cases you should bring a sleeping bag. Both *refugios* and camping prices range from €3 to 6 per person and/or tent, and reservations are usually not accepted. It's wise to call ahead to see if space is available. Towns within the park also have **pensiones ❷** and **rooms ❷** in private residences; look for *camas* and *habitaciones* signs (typically €20-30 per double).

⚐ ⚐ HIKING & EXCURSIONS

For multi-day routes, consult one of the Picos de Europa park offices. In addition to the following suggested day hikes, there are numerous free guided hikes arranged through the park offices (see **Tours & Guided Hikes**, p. 550). The following hikes are listed according to the nearest trailhead or town. Before embarking on any hike, secure a good map that has all trails clearly marked. The following are merely suggestions; be sure to gather more information before departing.

COVADONGA

Covadonga is accessible only from Cangas de Onís and Oviedo. ALSA buses (☎ 902 42 22 42) run from Cangas (30min.; M-F 11 per day 8:30am-7:35pm, Sa-Su 7 per day 10am-7:35pm; €0.90) and back (30min.; M-F 10 per day 8:50am-7:15pm, Sa-Su 6 per day 10:30am-8pm; €0.90) and from Oviedo (1¾hr., 1 per day 9:30am, €5). Buses stop in two places: at the Hospedería and uphill at the basilica.

"This little mountain you see will be the salvation of Spain," prophesied Don Pelayo, the first king of Asturias, to his Christian army in 718, gesturing to the rocky promontory above what is now Covadonga. The mountain soon became the site of the first successful battle in the fight against the Moors, although legend claims that it was not geography but the intervention of the Virgin Mary that made victory possible. Don Pelayo became the first king of Asturias, and out of this battle grew *la Reconquista.* Covadonga was also the first national park in Spain, the precursor to the Parque Nacional Picos de Europa established in 1918. Visitors come to Covadonga to see the cliffside basilica and the cave where the Virgin is said to have appeared to Don Pelayo. Nearly 1300 years ago he prayed to the Virgin for help in defeating the Moors from atop a waterfall in the ▓**Santa Cueva.** Today, pilgrims and tourists crowd the quiet, candlelit sanctuary where the Virgin appeared to him. (Open daily in summer 9am-9pm; in winter 9am-7pm. Free.) The **Santuario de Covadonga,** a neo-Gothic basilica built in 1901, towers above the town. (Open daily in summer 9am-9pm; in winter 9am-7pm. Free.) The **Museo del Tesoro,** next to the bus stop, displays the *Corona de la Virgen*, a gold-and-silver crown studded with 1109 diamonds and 2000 sapphires; below it lies a sparkling crown crafted to honor Jesus. (Open M and W-Su 10:30am-2pm and 4-7:30pm. €2, children €1.)

Covadonga's **info office**, at the top of the hill by the Cueva, has details on local accommodations and sights. (☎985 84 60 35. Open daily May-Oct. 10am-2pm and 3-7pm; Nov.-Apr. 11am-2pm and 3-5pm.) Cangas offers cheaper accommodations, but it's hard to resist the friendly atmosphere and stunning views of the mountains at the **Hospedería del Peregrino ❷**, on the main road next to the bus stop. (☎985 84 60 47; fax 84 60 51. Singles €18-29, doubles with hall bath €22-36. AmEx/MC/V.) At **El Huerto del Ermitaño ❷**, savor a carefully prepared meal to the tune of the Cueva's waterfall just across the road. The *menú* (€8.50) features typical Asturian platters with a creative touch. (In a tan building halfway up the hill to the basilica. ☎985 84 60 97. Open daily noon-11:30pm.) For a quick meal, visit **Merendero Covadonga ❶**, right where the main highway meets the road to the Lagos. Enjoy a wide variety of sandwiches (€2), *raciones* (€4), *platos combinados* (€6), and *paellas* (€8) on the outdoor terrace. (☎985 84 60 67. Open daily 9am-9pm, or later if there are enough customers.) The only **groceries** in town arrive for Hospedería guests twice a week (W and Sa) by truck—buy them from the driver at the hostel.

> **⚠ SUGGESTIONS FOR HIKERS.** Always consider the difficulty level and length of route when planning your hike. If you don't get a guide or hike with someone that knows the area, stay on marked trails. Never start a hike without a compass and a map of the area (min. scale 1/25000). Before you start hiking, tell someone where you are heading and when you expect to be back. The best guides are the people you will find during your hikes; don't hesitate to ask them for any information you might need. If you want to spend the night in the *refugios* scattered throughout the park, call ahead and make sure they're open (see p. 549). In case of fog, it is better to sit down and wait rather than walk around without knowing where you are.

▨ LOS LAGOS DE ENOL Y ERCINA

These tarns, or mountain lakes, are accessible from Cangas de Onís and Covadonga (see above). ALSA buses (☎902 42 22 42) run from Cangas past Covadonga, continuing to the lakes (45min.; July-Aug. M-F 6 per day 8:30am-6:45pm, Sa-Su 4 per day 10am-4:40pm; Sept.-June 2 per day; €1.62). In Covadonga, buses leave from the basilica to follow a frightening but spectacular road lined with cliffs and precipitous pastures; the right side of the bus has the best views en route.

Perhaps the most impressive site in the park, the **Lagos de Enol y Ercina** sparkle silently among limestone slopes and open valleys. Free **guided hikes** around the lakes depart from the Buferrera parking lot (3hr., M-F 10:30am). Slightly more difficult hikes are offered W at 9:30am (5hr.) and F at 10am (4hr.).

The first recommended hike goes from the Buferrera parking lot around Lago Enol, on to the **Mirador del Príncipe** and the **Mina de Buferrera**, an old abandoned mine. After the *mina*, the trail leads to the Lago Ercina, the **Monte Palomberu,** and ends up in the parking lot. This is an easy hike that takes 1-2hr. to complete.

Two especially good hikes from the lakes take travelers east to the **Vega de Ario,** which offers a panoramic view of the Urrieles mountains (8-9hr. round trip, medium to high level of difficulty), or south to the **Mirador de Ordiales**, a vantage point overlooking the Pico de las Vidriosas, Río Pomperi, and a frightening gorge (7-8hr. round-trip, rated as a difficult hike). Alternatively, head west 2km to the **Mirador de Rey** lookout point, then wander among the beeches of the **Bosque de Pome** (4-5hr. round-trip). Both lookouts are also accessible by car driving from

Covadonga to Los Lagos. (For more hikes, see **Tours & Guided Hikes,** p. 550.) The **Refugio de Vega de Ario ❶** (1630m) sits just off the trails leading from the lakes, 300m past the intersection. The refuge has 45 spots year-round and provides meals and guides. To get there by car, follow highway AS-114 (the Cangas de Onís-Panes highway), take the *desvío* (exit) for Covadongas y Lagos, go right at Lago Enol, and continue straight to the *refugio*, which finished a year-long renovation in July 2003. (☎639 81 20 69. No reservations accepted.)

PONCEBOS

Poncebos is accessible only from Arenas de Cabrales. ALSA buses run from Arenas de Cabrales (20min.; July-Sept. M-F 6 per day 10:15am-7:15pm, Sa-Su 7:15am; €0.75). By car, take AS-114 to Las Arenas, then turn across the river onto AS-264 to town.

Poncebos is actually the starting point for Arenas's hiking trails 6km away. The walk to the trailhead threads through the feet of surrounding mountains; tight, winding roads make some corners dangerous. To stay overnight in Poncebos, try either **Hostal Poncebos ❷** (☎985 84 64 47; singles €24-36; doubles €39-60; triples €51-72; MC/V) or the comfortable beds in **Hostal-Restaurante-Bar Garganta del Cares ❸** (☎985 84 64 63; dorm-style rooms for 2 with TV €24-30, for 3 €34-42, for 4 €44-54; doubles with bath and TV €45-75; MC/V). All rooms in both hostels have winter heating and windows either facing the mountains or overlooking the river.

Poncebos marks the start of one of the Picos's most famous trails, the 12km **Ruta del Cares.** The Cares gorge's vertical walls drop 200m down to the Río Cares below. The Ruta del Cares is an easy hike (6hr.) that starts in Poncebos and ends in **La Posada del Valdeón.** A shorter alternative is to walk from Poncebos to **Caín** (3hr.) and take a taxi or bus from there to the Posada del Valdeón (Taxi Pidal ☎985 84 51 77 or 616 96 12 01). In **Caín's portion of the trail,** choose from many secluded spots along the river to eat lunch and savor the refreshing breeze and mountain greenery. Stay overnight in Caín at either **La Ruta ❷** (☎987 74 27 02; singles €21; doubles €40; closed Oct. 1 to *Semana Santa*) or **La Posada del Montaña ❹** (☎942 31 86 50; doubles €36, triples €50; reserve a month in advance for Aug.).

The **Poncebos-Bulnes** route follows the Río Tejo to Bulnes, a small village that is seemingly frozen in time. This is also an easy hike and takes approximately 3hr. Consider tucking in at the **Albergue de Bulnes ❶,** which has 20 beds in three rooms, a bar, library, showers, guides, and meals. (☎985 84 59 43.

NO WORK, ALL PLAY

SKY HIGH

While the mountaineers in the Picos tend to shy away from Spain's usual party life, they do indulge every once in a while.

The biggest Picos party is the *Fiesta del Pastor* (July 25) in Vega del Enol, near the glacial lakes of Ercina and Enol. Called the *Romería cerca del cielo* (feast near the sky) for its mountainous location, the crafts, dancing, and games are held to honor the memory of pastoral traditions. As such, it is an event that has broken the barriers of time and outlasted generations. Youth begin the party the night before, spending the night in tents by the Lago de Enol until the games start early on the morning of the 25th.

Around 8am, the rest of the town starts the trek up to the lakes where competitions like *the Escalada a la Porre de Enol* (a type of local alpinism race), the bareback horse race, and the town tug-of-war pit lifelong friends against each other. The winners of the last 12 years are listed in local papers.

As an important town gathering, the *Fiesta del Pastor* is often associated with the social activism of various interest groups in the area, and it is not uncommon to see the winning tug-of-war team's anchor later espousing the importance of curbing wolf litters in order to protct the town's flock of sheep. The gathering is not only a clebration of tradition, but also an airing of citizen grievances aimed at improving life in the

One to three-week advance reservations suggested. Breakfast €3.60. Doubles €38; triples €45; quads €51.) The park service offers free **guided hikes** to Bulnes on Tuesday and Saturday (4hr.; departs at 10am from the small information hut on Poncebos's main highway). The ▓**Poncebos-Invernales de Cabao-Naranjo de Bulnes** route, a killer 17km hike (10-12hr. round-trip), crawls first to Invernales de Cabao and then inches 9km farther to the Picos's most famous mountain, **Naranjo de Bulnes,** named for its unmistakable sunburnt orange face. From here you can see the major *picos* in the area and the dancing blue waves of the Bay of Biscay in the distance. Most climbers start the hike in **Sotres** and continue from there (9-10hr. round-trip). There are two *refugios* in the Naranjo de Bulnes area: **Refugio Vega de Urriellu ❶** and **Refugio Jou de Los Cabrones ❶** (see **Refugios & Rangers,** p. 549). If the trail is open, it's worth going beyond the **Poncebos-Camareña** path, up a rocky slope, to **Puertos de Ondón,** where the view is incomparable.

POTES

Palomera buses (☎942 88 06 11 or 50 30 80) travel to Fuente Dé (45min.; M-F 3 per day 8am, 1, 8pm, Sa-Su 1 per day 1pm; €1.60) and back (M-F 3 per day 8:45am, 5, 8:45pm, Sa-Su 1 per day 1pm). Buses also go to Santander (2½hr.; M-F 3 per day 7, 9:30am, 5:45pm, Sa 2 per day 9:30am, 5:45pm, Su 2 per day 10:30am, 5:45pm; €5.80) via Panes (40min.) and Unquera (1hr.). There are two bus stops coming from Santander. The first is at the town border in front of Hotel Rubio, and the second is at the bus station on the other edge of town. The station shares a building with the tourist office.

The Potes (pop. 2000) tourist brochure prophesies *"…Y Volverás"* (You'll return) and you probably will—this down-to-earth town in the shadow of the mountains makes a great base for outdoor activities in the Picos de Europa. Moreover, its sidewalks brimming with action, cheese, and cafe tables, and its accessibility to worthwhile hikes make saying goodbye that much harder.

Urdón, 15km north of Potes on the road to Panes, is the start of a challenging 6km (4hr.) hike to **Treviso,** a tiny town where chickens outnumber humans. Trail details are on posters all over Potes. Another option for outings from Potes is **Peña Sagra,** about 13km east (2hr.) of the towns of **Luriezo** and **Aniezo.** From the summit, you can survey the Picos and the sea, 51km away. On your way down, visit **Iglesia de Nuestra Señora de la Luz,** where the beautifully carved patron saint of the Picos lives 364 days a year. The Virgin, known affectionately as *Santuca* (tiny saint), is removed from the church and honored on May 2. A 3km uphill hike from the tourist office towards Fuente Dé is the **Monasterio de Santo Toribio de Liébana,** which protects the largest surviving piece of the cross of Christ in the world. The building itself is enchantingly illuminated. (Open daily 9am-1pm and 3:30-8pm. Free.)

The streets of Potes are lined with outfitters specializing in the latest outdoor fads. The tourist office has a list of all the outfitters in town. In summer, book several days in advance for expeditions. **Picos Aventura,** C. Cervantes, 3, organizes horseback riding, mountain biking, paragliding, and canyoning. The office is at the base of the bridge on C. Dr. Encinas. (☎942 73 21 61. €21-61. Open daily 11am-8pm, sometimes later. MC/V.) **La Liébana,** between Potes and Fuente Dé, organizes similar outings. The office is behind the gazebo on the river on C. Dr. Encinas. (☎942 73 10 00; fax 73 10 21. €18-48.) The best horseback riding and paragliding trips are organized through **La Cabaña,** C. La Molina, s/n. (☎942 73 00 50. Tandem paragliding €51 per flight. Horseback riding €18.03-28.24 per person.)

The **tourist office** has information on adventure tourism, *refugios*, and accommodations in town and on free **guided hikes** outside of the park (☎/fax 942 73 07 87. Open daily 10am-2pm and 4-8pm.) Services include: **Banco Santander Central Hispano,** C. Dr. Encinas, 11, at the corner of C. San Marcial with a **24hr. ATM** (☎902 24 24 24; open M-F 8:30am-2pm, Sa 8:30am-1pm); **Guardia Civil** (☎942 73 00 07), on C.

Picos de Europa

Parque Nacional
Picos de Europa

Obispo off C. Dr. Encinas; **Farmacia F. Soberón,** C. Cántabra, s/n (☎942 73 00 08; open daily 9:30am-9:30pm); **health center** (☎942 73 03 60) on C. Eduardo García de Enterría, inside the **Cruz Roja** (Red Cross) building (☎942 73 01 02); **post office,** Pl. de la Serna, s/n (open M-F 8:30am-2:30pm, Sa 9:30am-1pm). **Postal Code:** 39570.

Several hostels are scattered on C. Dr. Encinas and on C. Cántabra, a side street. The cheapest rooms fill early in the day, so make reservations a day or two in advance for June and July and a couple weeks in advance for August. The palatial rooms at ▨**Casa Cayo ❸,** C. Cántabra, 6, a right off C. Dr. Encinas when walking into town from the bus stop, have TVs, phones, bathrooms, and a cozy lounge with an even bigger TV. (☎942 73 01 50. Singles €30; doubles €45. MC/V.) **Hostal Lombraña ❷,** C. el Sol, 2, has small but bright doubles with beautiful views of the mountains. Walking into town from the bus stop, it's on the right just before the bridge and under a medieval tunnel. (☎942 73 05 19. Doubles €25-28. IVA not included.) Closer to Panes off C. Dr. Encinas, **El Fogón de Cus ❷,** C. Capital Palacios, 2, has sunny, spacious rooms and friendly owners. From the bus stop along C. Dr. Encinas into town, the hotel is up a stairway on the right. The adjoining **restaurant ❷** serves hearty mountain fare (*menú* €8.50) on white tablecloths; for a livelier atmosphere, ask for a table in the back room with the TV. (☎942 73 00 60. Singles €15; doubles €24, with bath €25. All rooms have sinks and winter heating. Restaurant open daily 1:30-4pm and 8:30-11pm. AmEx/MC/V.) There are also several *casas de labranza* (farm houses for rent) in the area; ask at the tourist office for details. The closest camping site is the first-class **Camping La Viorna ❶,** about 1km up the road to Monasterio Santo Toribio, which helps organize excursions and has a restaurant, supermarket, and pool. (☎942 73 20 21 or 73 21 01. €3.80 per person, car, and tent. Open *Semana Santa*-Oct. 30.)

Potes can feed plenty of hungry hikers; C. Dr. Encinas, C. Cántabra, and C. San Cayetano are packed with restaurants, *tapas* bars, and cafeterias. A delicious dining option in a dim but joyful atmosphere is riverside **Restaurante La Caseta II ❷,** C. Cántabra, 8, next door to Casa Cayo, where veal, lamb, and game are the specialties. (☎/fax 942 73 07 13. *Menú* €11, entrees €7-10. Open daily 1-4pm and 8pm-midnight.) Supermarket **El Árbol** is across from the bus station. (☎942 73 05 26. Open M 9:30am-8:30pm, Tu-Sa 9:30am-2pm and 5-8:30pm, Su 10am-2pm.)

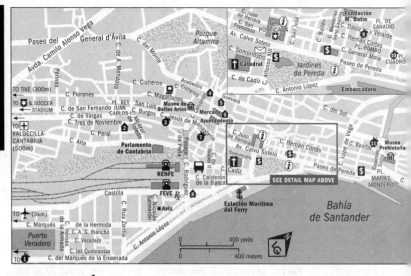

FUENTE DÉ

Fuente Dé is accessible only from Potes on ALSA buses (☎ 902 42 22 42; 45min.; M-F 3 per day 8am, 1, 8pm, Sa-Su 1 per day 1pm; return M-F 3 per day 8:45am, 5, 8:45pm, Sa-Su 1 per day 5pm). The bus stops in front of the Parador de Fuente Dé, just below the teleférico (cable car) base.

Only 23km from Potes, the ⬛**Teleférico de Fuente Dé** is well worth an excursion. The mind-blowing, goosebump-inducing *teleférico*, the third largest cable car system in the world, jets 750m to the mountain top (1834m) in less than 4min. (☎ 942 31 89 50. Open July-Aug. daily 9am-8pm; Sept.-June 10am-6pm. €6, round-trip €9; under 10 round-trip €4.50.) A zig-zagging trail ascends just left of the cable (3hr.). At the top, there are many safe routes along four-wheel-drive tracks. If you're feeling ambitious, take the northern trail to **Sortes**. Another good, less demanding Fuente Dé trek starts and ends at the cable car's lower station (11½km, 4½hr.). The **Somo Waterfall Route** swings through the Berrugas cattle sheds, the soft Bustantivo meadows, and on to the Somo waterfall. From the top of the *teleférico*, it's a 4km walk to **Refugio de Áliva ❹** (1666m), the most expensive and luxurious "refuge" in the park. All rooms come with full baths and heat in winter; there is also a cafe on site. (☎/fax 942 73 09 99. Doubles €45. MC/V.) To return to road-level, retrace your steps to the *teleférico* or walk (3hr.) to **Espinama**, where **Habitaciones Sebrango ❷**, offers respite from the Picos. (☎ 942 73 66 15. Singles €24; doubles €30.) Alternatively, camp at **El Redondo Camping ❶**, just above the base of the *teleférico*. (☎ 942 73 66 99. Bar, market, and hot water showers. Reception open daily 9am-9pm. Spaces €5, adults €5, children €3.)

CANTABRIA

From the spectacle of Santander's *El Sardinero* beaches to the pristine provincial park of Oyambre, it's the shore that makes Cantabria famous. Though they have yet to see the resort build-up of Spain's more famous southern coasts, the region's beach towns are by no means untouched or secluded. The beach scene, particu-

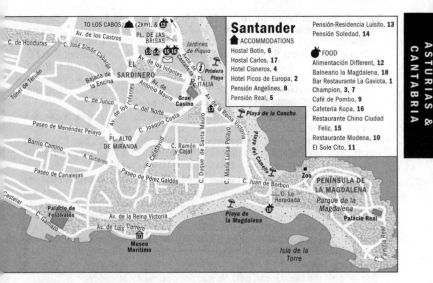

Santander

▲ ACCOMMODATIONS

Hostal Botín, 6
Hostal Carlos, 17
Hotel Cisneros, 4
Hotel Picos de Europa, 2
Pensión Angelines, 8
Pensión Real, 5
Pensión-Residencia Luisito, 13
Pensión Soledad, 14

🍴 FOOD

Alimentación Different, 12
Balneario la Magdalena, 18
Bar Restaurante La Gaviota, 1
Champion, 3, 7
Café de Pombo, 9
Cafetería Kopa, 16
Restaurante Chino Ciudad Feliz, 15
Restaurante Modena, 10
El Sole Cito, 11

larly in Santander, is what lures visitors, but Cantabria also has hiking in the Picos de Europa, Paleolithic cave drawings, some of the world's cleanest surfing waters, and renowned architecture like Gaudí's *El Capricho*.

SANTANDER ☎942

Welcome to Vacationland, Spanish-style. Here in Santander (pop. 185,000), palm trees rub shoulders with pines, pasty Brits bake on the beach next to well-bronzed Spaniards, and the grime of the city center is easily forgotten on the walk down *El Sardinero*'s bougainvillea-filled boardwalks. Santander has been destroyed three times by natural and not-so-natural disasters—a fire at the beginning of the 15th century incinerated everything in sight, an explosion on a dynamite ship in 1893 leveled the city, and in 1941 another fire gutted the peninsular town. The most recent incarnation of Santander has resulted in the ideal city, complete with surf, sand, and sometimes sun. Those looking to get away from it all should avoid Santander, as it is "all" and then some. Those willing to share their beach space with a thousand other sun-starved bodies, however, will reap great rewards. The mountainous horizon with cliff-top lighthouses is the Bay of Biscay at its best.

▐ TRANSPORTATION

Flights: Aeropuerto de Santander, Av. de Parayas (☎942 20 21 00), in nearby Camargo 4km away. Serviced exclusively by Iberia. Accessible only by taxi (€12). **Iberia,** Po. de Pereda, 18 (☎942 22 97 00). Open M-F 9am-1:30pm and 4-7pm.

Trains: FEVE (☎942 20 95 22) and **RENFE** (☎902 24 02 02), Pl. de las Estaciones, s/n. RENFE serves only a few destinations, as Santander is the terminus of a rail line; take a slower FEVE train to larger cities east or west of Santander. Info open daily 7:30am-11pm. To: **Madrid** (6hr.; M-F 5 per day 8:10am-11pm, Sa 6 per day 8:10am-8:05pm, Su 7 per day 8:10am-11pm; €23.30-32.50); **Palencia** (2¼hr.; M-F 5 per day 8:10am-11pm, Sa 6 per day 8:10am-8:05pm, Su 7 per day 8:10am-11pm; €9.85-19.50); **Valladolid** (5hr., M-F 5 per day 8:10am-11pm, Sa 6 per day 8:10am-8:05pm, Su 7 per day 8:10am-11pm; €12.55-22).

Buses: C. Navas de Tolosa, s/n (☎942 21 19 95). Info open M-F 8am-10pm, Sa 8am-1pm. To: **Barcelona** (10hr.; daily 9am, 1:45, 9:30pm; €40); **Bilbao** (1½hr., 15 per day 6am-4pm, €5.43-9.70); **Burgos** (4hr.; daily 12:30am-10:30am; €18); **León** (3½hr.; M-Th and Sa 1 per day 9am; F 2 per day 9am, 4pm; Su 1 per day 7:30pm; €10.37); **Madrid** (6hr.; M 7 per day 12am-7pm, Tu-Su 6 per day 12:30am-7pm; €29.78); **Oviedo** (3½hr.; M-F and Su 9 per day 6:30am-8pm, Sa 6 per day 6:30am-8pm; €10.71-18.25); **Palencia** (M-Th and Sa 2 per day 9am, 5pm; F and Su 3 per day 9am, 4, 5pm; €7.61); **Salamanca** (6hr.; 2 per day 9am, 5pm; €13.74).

Ferries: Brittany Ferries, Estación Marítima, s/n (☎942 36 06 11; www.brittany-ferries.es), near the Jardines de Pereda. Info M-F 9am-3:30pm and 4:30-7:30pm. In summer reserve 2 weeks ahead. To **Plymouth, UK** (2 per week; €85-132, plus €6 for seat reservation). **Los Reginas,** C. Embarcadero, s/n (☎942 21 66 19), by the Jardines de Pereda. **Tours of the bay** (45min., June 6-Sept. 1 3-6 per day, €3).

Public Transportation: Municipal buses (☎942 20 07 71) run throughout the city (every 15min.; July-Aug. 6am-midnight, Sept.-June 6am-10:30pm; night buses run every hr. midnight-6am; €1). Buses #1, 3, 4, 5, 7, and 9 run from the Ayuntamiento stop (buses coming from El Sardinero stop in front of the plaza; buses going to El Sardinero stop in front of Foot Locker) to El Sardinero along Po. de Pereda and Av. de la Reina Victoria, stopping at Pl. de Italia and Jardines de Piquío. Stops are usually not marked with route numbers, but the tourist office offers bus route maps.

Taxis: Radio Taxi (☎942 33 33 33). 24hr. service to greater Santander. Taxis wait outside the train and bus stations, on C. Vargas, and near the Ayuntamiento.

Car Rental: Avis, C. Nicolás Salmerón, 3 (☎942 22 70 25). 25+; must have had driver's license for at least 1yr. and a credit card in the renter's name. From €54 per day. Open M-F 8am-1pm and 4-7:30pm, Sa 9am-1pm.

◆ 🛈 ORIENTATION & PRACTICAL INFORMATION

Santander sits on a peninsula in the Bay of Biscay; its southern shores form the Bay of Santander. There are two main sections to the city: **the center,** around the train and bus stations and the Jardines de Pereda in the east, and **El Sardinero** in the west. The main thoroughfare starts at the Ayuntamiento in the center as **Avenida Calvo Sotelo** and runs along the shore to the Jardines de Piquío in El Sardinero, changing its name to **Paseo de Pereda** and **Avenida de la Reina Victoria** along the way. At the western tip of Santander is **La Península de la Magdalena,** the city's famed park. Santander is surprisingly large; the best way to get around is by city bus.

Tourist Office: Jardines de Pereda (☎942 81 88 12). Bus and city maps. Open July-Sept. daily 9am-9pm; Oct.-June M-F 9am-1:30pm and 4:30-7:30pm, Sa 9am-1:30pm. **Branches** at the port, Pl. Porticada, and El Sardinero; all open July-Sept. 10am-9pm.

Budget Travel: TIVE, C. Canarias, 2 (☎942 33 22 15). Take bus #5 from the Ayuntamiento 6 stops to C. Camilo Alonso Vega. ISIC €5. HI card €10. Open M-F 9am-2pm.

Currency Exchange: Banco Santander Central Hispano, on Av. Calvo Sotelo. **Branch** in El Sardinero at Pl. de Italia. Open May-Sept. M-F 8:30am-2:30pm; Oct.-Apr. M-F 8:30am-2pm, Sa 8:30am-1pm.

Luggage Storage: Lockers at the **RENFE train station,** by the ticket window (€3 per day). Open daily 7am-11pm. Lockers at the **bus station** on the bottom level near *pasaje* 16 (€2.40 per day). Open daily 6am-12am.

Laundromat: Lavatu, Av. de los Castros, 29 (☎942 27 70 00).

Emergency: ☎112. **Police:** Pl. Porticada, s/n, and Av. del Deporte (☎942 20 07 44).

Hospital: Hospital Universitario Marqués de Valdecilla, Av. de Valdecilla, s/n (☎942 20 25 20). **Ambulances:** (☎942 31 30 00, 27 30 58, or 32 06 05).

Pharmacy: Lda. Isabel Ochoa, C. Castilla, 15. Open M-F 10am-2pm and 4-9pm, Sa 10am-3pm. In El Sardinero, **Somacarrera,** Pl. de Italia, 1 (☎942 27 05 96), underneath the Gran Casino. For late-night pharmacies, call ☎942 22 02 60 to find the pharmacist on call. Every pharmacy also posts the weekly schedule of on-call pharmacies.

Internet Access: Divernet Informática, C. Cisneros, 25 (☎942 24 14 25). English spoken. €1.80 per hr. Open M-Sa 9am-10pm, Su 4-9pm. **La Copi,** C. de la Lealtad, 13. Next to the cathedral. Open 9am-1:30pm and 5-8:30pm.

Post Office: Av. Alfonso XIII, s/n (☎942 21 26 73). Open M-F 8:30am-8:30pm, Sa 9:30am-2pm. **Branch** in El Sardinero on Av. Las Cruces, s/n. Open M-F 8:30am-2pm. **Lista de Correos** and fax only at Av. Alfonso XIII branch. **Postal Code:** 39080.

ACCOMMODATIONS

In summer and on weekends, all rooms must be booked over a week in advance; showing up in town without a reservation will most definitely leave you out in the cold. The train and bus stations are loaded with *pensión* hawkers, but beware: this is illegal, and the rooms are often far from the beaches. The highest hotel densities are near the market on Pl. de la Esperanza, across from the train station on C. Rodríguez, and along elegant Av. de los Castros in El Sardinero.

EL SARDINERO

Everyone wants to stay in El Sardinero because of its beaches and promenades. Unfortunately, such popularity means rooms are expensive and hard to come by. From the Ayuntamiento stop in the city center, take bus #1, 3, 4, 5, 7, or 9 to El Piquío (Hotel Colón); Av. de los Castros is directly opposite the beach.

Pensión Soledad, Av. de los Castros, 17 (☎942 27 09 36). Sixteen large rooms with sinks and good views. Breakfast €1.35. Open July-Sept. Singles €19; doubles €31. ❷

Pensión-Residencia Luisito, Av. de los Castros, 11 (☎942 27 19 71). The garrulous owner will tend to your every need. Twelve airy rooms sport flowered sheets, terraces, sinks, and sloping ceilings. Be sure to get a room with a *mirador* (view). TV room on 1st fl. Breakfast €1.50. Open July-Sept. Singles €19; doubles €30. ❷

Hostal Carlos, Av. de la Reina Victoria, 135 (☎942 27 16 16). Big, sunny rooms across in El Sardinero. English and German spoken. June 16-30 singles €37; doubles €51. July 1-Sept. 15 €48/€63. Mar. 16-June 15 and Sept. 16-Nov. 4 €31/€44. MC/V. ❹

■ **Camping: Cabo Mayor,** Av. del Faro, s/n (☎ 942 39 15 42). On the scenic bluff of Cabo Mayor, 2km from Playas Primera and Segunda. From the Ayuntamiento, take bus #8 or 9 to Av. del Faro, 7 stops after El Piquío. From the bus stop, turn left onto Av. del Faro and follow it into the Cabos; the campgrounds are a 10min. walk. Alternatively, head north along coastal Av. de Castañeda, bear right at the rotary, and then turn left onto C. Gregorio Marañón; Av. del Faro is on the right. Pool and tennis courts. Reception 8am-11pm. Open July 15-Sept. 30. €10 per person, €10 per car, €6 per tent. ❶

CITY CENTER

Although the area is loaded with cheap accommodations, only out of desperation should one stay near the stations. By day, the area is grimy, noisy, and far from the beach; by night, it's unsettling. The area north of the Ayuntamiento and Av. de Calvo Sotelo is a far more pleasant area, filled with restaurants, shops, and bars crowded with locals trying to escape the reflective glare of vacationers. At night, catch a cab to El Sardinero (€4), or take a pleasant, if lengthy, stroll.

Hostal Cisneros, C. Cisneros, 8, 1st fl. (☎942 21 16 13). A clean, comfortable option. All rooms have TVs, beautiful wooden headboards, sunny terraces, and bathrooms. Reservations with first night's payment required. July-Sept. doubles €42; Semana Santa-June €38; Oct.-Semana Santa €30. Cash or traveler's checks only. ❹

Pensión Real, Pl. de la Esperanza, 1, 3rd fl. (☎942 22 57 87), in the peach building at the end of C. Isabel II. Communal baths, but all rooms have sinks. English and French spoken. No reservations. June-Sept. doubles €30-36; Oct.-May €24. ❷

Hotel Picos de Europa, C. Arco Iris, 3 (☎942 37 10 15; fax 37 10 35). Fully equipped rooms with TV, bathroom, and telephones in Santander's commercial district. Singles €25; doubles €40. MC/V. ❸

Hostal Botín, C. Isabel II, 1, 1st fl. (☎942 21 00 94 or 630 49 26 06). Crazy 80s comforters keep guests warm and balconies overlook the bustling market. All rooms have TV and sink. Reservations accepted with advance payment. Singles €16-27; doubles €24-45; triples €39-75; quads €48-80. ❷

Pensión Angelines, C. Rodríguez, 9, 2nd fl. (☎942 31 25 84). Immaculate rooms with huge windows and winter heating. Strong shower. TV lounge. July-Aug. singles €18; doubles €27. Sept.-June €12/€21. ❷

☐ FOOD

EL SARDINERO
The best grocery option is **Alimentación Different,** C. Joaquín de la Costa, 18, in the Hotel Sartena shopping complex. (Open M-Sa 9:30am-2:45pm and 5:45-9:30pm, Su 10am-3pm. AmEx/MC/V.) Restaurants in El Sardinero are either expensive or ice cream stands. For more value for your dining euro, head to the city center, where good, cheap food is plentiful.

▩ Restaurante Chino Ciudad Feliz, C. Las Brisas, s/n (☎942 27 32 30). Serves all the westernized Chinese staples while you dine with a view of the sea. Alas, no fortune cookies, but plenty of other post-meal gifts to make your family a happy one. Lunch menú €7.50. Entrees €5.75-9. Open daily 1-4pm and 7pm-midnight. MC/V. ❷

Cafetería Kopa, C. Las Brisas, s/n, in the same building as Ciudad Feliz. Though not the most exciting fare, Kopa has what most restaurants in El Sardinero lack: good Spanish/British food at reasonable prices. Menú €3-10. Open daily 9am-midnight. ❷

Balneario La Magdalena, C. La Horadada, s/n (☎942 03 21 07), on Playa de la Magdalena. A quiet restaurant on the beach with a decent selection of entrees (€7-12). The best place for a late afternoon beer. Open daily 10am-midnight. ❷

CITY CENTER
Seafood restaurants crowd the **Puerto Pesquero** (fishing port), grilling up the day's catch at the end of C. Marqués de la Ensenada. From the main entrance of the train station, turn right onto C. Rodríguez and right again onto C. Castilla; walk eight blocks down and turn left on C. Héroes de la Armada; cross the tracks and turn right after about 100m (20min.). Across the street from the Ayuntamiento, **Champion,** C. Jesús de Monasterio, s/n, has groceries. (Open M-Sa 9:15am-9pm.)

▩ El Sole Cito, C. Bonifaz, 19 (☎ 942 36 06 33, order take-out at 32 51 18). The plates are the only square things in this undeniably hip bistro. Autumn leaves, African masks, flamed tables, and superb food. Try the unthinkably tender croquetas de solomillo (sirloin croquettes, €5). Entrees €5-9. ❶

Café de Pombo, C. Hernán Cortés, 21 (☎ 942 22 32 24). On Pl. de Pombo, just behind Banco de Santander. Coffees. Pastries. Ice creams. Crêpes. Sandwiches. All delicious, all huge, all €1-3, served up in an elegant, comfortable setting. What more could you want? Go-go dancers? This place has zero go-go dancers. ❶

Restaurante Modena, C. Eduardo Benot, 6 (☎942 31 33 71). Delectable Italian standards, from lasagna to *tortellini al quattro formaggio*, served in a sleek dining room. Not particularly budget (pasta €6-10), but the filling, vegetarian-friendly fare and *tiramisú* are worth the extra euros. Open daily 1-4pm and 8pm-midnight. MC/V. ❷

Bar Restaurante La Gaviota, C. Marqués de la Ensenada, s/n (☎942 22 11 32 or 22 10 06), at the corner of C. Mocejón in the *barrio pesquero* (fishermen's neighborhood). An elegant dining room hidden behind a rough exterior. Try the fresh grilled sardines (12 for €3.60) or the *paella mixta* (*ración* €3.60). *Menú* €7.50. Open daily 11:30am-4:15pm and 7:30pm-midnight. MC/V. ❷

🅢 SIGHTS

While Santander is proud of its few official architectural sights and museums, skip them in favor of its beaches and parks unless it rains (which is very likely), in which case Santander's amusing—and free—museums are worth perusing. The tourist office has a list of one- to two-hour walking tours, the best way to get to know the city and feel like you actually did something during the day.

█ PENÍNSULA DE LA MAGDALENA. Although it can feel a bit like an amusement park at times, La Magdalena is Santander's prime attraction and one of the most beautiful parts of the city. The entire peninsula is filled with palms and pines and ringed by bluffs plunging into the sea along slender, calm beaches. The park's centerpiece is the **palacio,** a 20th-century, neo-Gothic mansion Alfonso XIII used as a summer home. Today, the palace houses the elite Universidad Internacional Menéndez Pelayo's summer sessions on oceanography. The peninsula also boasts a mini-zoo (polar bears, penguins, and sea lions, oh my!), sports several models of mermaids and ships, and offers train rides around the park. (☎639 51 36 72. €1.80) Walking, however, is the best way to explore, and the 2km path ends with nourishment: *churrerías* flank the park's entrance. (☎942 27 25 04. Park open daily June-Sept. 8am-10pm; Oct.-May 8am-8:30pm. The palace has no scheduled visiting hours.)

█ LOS CABOS. More peninsular parks lie just north of the El Sardinero beaches. While Cabos Menor and Mayor lack the attractions and action of La Magdalena, their bluffs and vistas are more scenic. Cabo Menor, the more southern of the two, houses Santander's golf course and another mini-zoo; it also has postcard-worthy views of Cabo Mayor's 19th-century lighthouse. (From Pl. de Italia, walk up Av. de Castañeda past Glorieta del Doctor Fleming, and turn right onto Av. de Pontejos, which turns into Av. del Faro and takes you out onto the capes.)

MUSEO DE BELLAS ARTES. Devoted to the works of local artists, Santander's Museo de Bellas Artes is surprisingly impressive. Art history buffs will enjoy the collection of 20th-century pieces; much of the sculpture could easily be mistaken for Giacometti. An entire room is devoted to forays into Cubism (and apparently Juan Gris imitation). The lower two floors feature special exhibitions of more well-known Spanish artists like Picasso and Miró. (C. Rubio, 6. ☎942 23 94 85. From the Ayuntamiento, walk up C. Jesús de Monasterio and turn right onto C. Florida. Open June 16-Sept. 14 M-F 10:30am-1pm and 5:30-8pm, Sa 10:30am-1pm; Sept.15-June15 M-F 10am-1pm and 5-8pm, Sa 10am-1pm. Special exhibitions open until 9pm. Free.)

CATEDRAL DE SANTANDER. Built in the Middle Ages, Santander's Gothic cathedral is often called the city's first monument. The heads of martyred Roman soldiers Emeterio and Celedonio are kept inside the ruins of an oven once used to heat Roman baths; after dropping into the guillotine basket in AD 300 in La Rioja, they were brought to Santander in the 8th century for safekeeping during the Moorish invasion. Occasionally they are taken out for religious processions. (Pl.

Somorrostro, just behind the post office and Banco España. ☎942 22 60 24. Open M-F 10am-1pm and 4-7:30pm, Sa 10am-1pm and 4:30-8pm, Su 8am-2pm and 4:30-8pm. Free tours in Spanish daily at 10:30, 11:30am, 12:45, 4:30, 5:45, 6:30, and 7:30pm.)

MUSEO MARÍTIMO DEL CANTÁBRICO. The top floors of the Museo Marítimo chart the evolution of regional fishing-boats, while the bottom floor highlights the sea's living creatures. *(C. San Martín de Bajamar, beyond the Puerto Chico. ☎942 27 49 62. Open May 2-Sept. 15 Tu–Su 9am-9pm; Sept. 16-May 1 10am-7pm. €6.)*

◢ BEACHES

In Santander, every day is a beach day: rain or shine (but most often rain), locals flock to the beach as soon as work gets out and spend the late afternoon and evening soaking up the last rays of sun. It's easy to understand why, as Santander's beaches, particularly those in El Sardinero, are wide swaths of powdery sand. The water, however, can get very rough; it's not uncommon for five-foot breakers to crash onto the beach. The water is calmer and the beaches rockier on the bay side. The best and most popular beaches are undoubtedly ◪**Playas Primera y Segunda** in El Sardinero. Not only does the soft sand go on forever, but the EU has declared these waters one of the eight cleanest beaches in the world. Primera and Segunda are also the hangout of Santander's surfing crowd, which emerges during and after rain. Calmer waters but no fewer bodies line the southern shore of La Magdalena. Rock-framed **Playa de Bikinis,** on the peninsula itself, is the most secluded and the haunt of Santander's guitar-strumming teens; **Playa de la Magdalena** and **Playa de los Peligros,** stretching from the peninsula to below Av. de la Reina Victoria, are virtually waveless and therefore very popular with families. To escape the beach-going hordes, either head across the bay to **Playas Puntal, Somo,** and **Loredo** lining a narrow peninsula of dunes, or hoof it up to the remote beaches of Los Cabos where ◪**Playa de Matalenas** and **Playa de los Molinucos** await you sans the throngs.

◪ ◪ NIGHTLIFE & FESTIVALS

Exhausted from sunbathing, everyone in Santander seems to hit the sack early. In **El Sardinero,** cafes and bars line the promenade along Playas Primera and Segunda, with street performers offering live entertainment to families and teenagers. Others spend their evenings blowing euros at the **Gran Casino,** Pl. de Italia, s/n. Passport, proper dress (pants and shoes), and a minimum age (18 to gamble) are required. (Open daily 8pm-4am. €3 to enter main casino, games in lobby free.) In the city center, university students and older couples *tapas*-hop around Pl. Cañadío, C. Daoíz y Velarde, and C. Pedrueca; facing Banco de Santander from the tourist office, walk up C. Las Infantes, which runs into C. Pedrueca. Around 2 or 3am, crowds flood **Calle Río de la Pila** and **Calle Casimiro Sainz.**

The July **Concurso Internacional de Piano de Santander** and August **Festival Internacional de Santander** bring crowds of people and myriad music and dance recitals to town. For more info, contact the **Oficina del Festival,** Palacio de Festivales de Cantabria (☎942 21 05 08), on C. Gamazo. The **Baños de Ola** is a turn-of-the-century style celebration of Alfonso XIII's discovery that, lo and behold, playing in the waves is fun. The festival takes place the third week of July on the El Sardinero promenades, with bathers clad in antique swimsuits. That same week, the *barrio pesquero* celebrates the patron saint of fishermen, **Santiago.**

⚡ DAYTRIPS FROM SANTANDER

CUEVAS DE ALTAMIRA

The Altamira caves are on the way to Santillana del Mar on the San Vicente de la Barquera line. La Cantábrica (☎942 72 08 22) sends buses from Pl. de las Estaciones, s/n, in Santander to Altamira (45min., 1 per day 10:30am, €2.) There will be a car from the caves waiting at the bus stop. Or, get some exercise and follow the signs on a beautiful 1km walk from Santillana del Mar up to the caves.

Bison roam, horses graze, and goats butt heads on the ceilings of the limestone ▓Cuevas de Altamira, dubbed the "Sistine Chapel of Paleolithic Art." The large-scale polychromatic paintings are renowned for their scrupulous attention to naturalistic detail and resourceful use of the caves' natural texture. Unfortunately, tourism has caused substantial damage, and the caves are now closed for the forseeable future while scientists try to stop the decay. The **Museo de Altamira** offers a replica of the original cave, complete with handrails and a holographic cave family, as well as a well-done exhibit on human evolution. (☎942 81 80 05. Open June-Sept. Tu-Sa 9:30am-7:30pm, Su 9:30am-5pm. €2.40, Sa afternoon and all day Su free.) If you happen to be spending a day in Madrid at some point during your journey, you can also see replicas of the cave at the Museo Arqueológico Nacional.

SANTILLANA DEL MAR

Santillana del Mar and Comillas are on the Santander-San Vicente de la Barquera line. La Cantábrica (☎942 72 08 22) sends buses from Navas de Tolosa, s/n, in Santander (45min.; M-F 4 per day 10:30am-7:15pm, Sa 3 per day 10:30am-9:30pm, Su 5 per day 10:30am-9:30pm; €1.70). In Santillana del Mar, buses stop on C. Santo Domingo in front of the Museo Diocesano; the return bus stops in front of the stairway across the street.

French philosopher Jean-Paul Sartre proclaimed Santillana del Mar (pop. 4000) the most beautiful town in Spain. He also said that hell is other people, so his enthusiasm for Santillana might well be tempered by the hordes of tourists that flock here daily. Santillana is a tourist town and knows it: the tangled stone streets are crowded with ice cream stands and tourist shops. The crowds are here for a reason, though: Santillana *is* beautiful, and it's worth suffering a few other tourists to see it. If you dislike crowds and commercialism, avoid Santillana altogether.

The town is named for Santa Juliana Cino del Mar, a martyr who refused to renounce her virginity and her faith in God. The **Colegiata de Santa Juliana**, a 12th-century Romanesque church founded by Turkish monks, houses her remains. The sepulchre guards her relics, and the gorgeous high altarpiece is a 15th-century Spanish-Flemish painting depicting the saint's martyrdom. From the bus stop in front of the steps on C. Santo Domingo, walk uphill into town, and veer to the right at the first fork onto C. Cantón, which turns into C. del Río and leads directly to the church. (Open daily 10am-1:30pm and 4-6pm. €2.50, which also gets you into the Museo Diocesano.) From the front of the Colegiata, a trek back up C. del Río leads to the ▓ **Museo de la Tortura y de la Inquisición,** Av. de Jesús Otero, 1. Four words: abdominal-gouging vaginal pear. If this freaks you out, skip this small museum, whose exhibits of terrifying torture methods used during the Spanish Inquisition reveal the darker side of Christianity. (☎942 84 02 73. Open daily 10am-10pm. €3.60.) The **Museo Diocesano,** across the street from the stop on C. Santo Domingo in the Monasterio Regina Coeli, has a mediocre collection of religious relics and artwork. Most interesting is the collection of over 300 miniature crucifixes. (Open daily 10am-1:30pm and 4-6pm. €2.40, includes the Colegiata.)

The **tourist office** is at Av. de Jesús Otero, 22. From the bus stop, walk up C. Santo Domingo and bear right onto C. de la Carrera. Then take the first right onto C. Gándara and right again onto Av. de Jesús Otero. (☎942 81 88 12. Open daily 9:30am-1:30pm and 4-7pm.) From the bus stop, the **post office** is up C. Santo Domingo (keep left at the fork) in Pl. Mayor. (☎942 81 80 40. Open M-F 8:30am-2:30pm, Sa 9:30am-1pm.) **Postal Code:** 39330.

▨ COMILLAS

Buses follow the exact same route as those to Santillana del Mar and depart from Navas de Tolosa in Santander; the trip to Comillas takes 1½ hr. €3.

The beaches of Comillas (pop. 2800) are intoxicating, and most of their visitors intoxicated. From desolate and calm inlets to the wind-swept swaths of sand directly on the Bay of Biscay, Comillas's beaches are its main attraction, drawing everyone from Spanish nobles to foreign visitors. Everyone shuttles serenely to the beaches, amazed simply to have access to the splendor of Comillas. This small resort town's central beach, **Playa Comillas,** is a vast expanse of silky sand and raging waves; on windy days, ten-foot breakers pound the shores.

From the main bus stop, follow C. Marqués de Comillas uphill into town. Pass through Pl. del Generalísimo and veer left onto Cuesta General Mola; after another small square, Corro San Pedro will be on the right. From there, turn left onto C. La Moria, and then follow the footpath downhill to the beach (10min.). Heading in the opposite direction on C. Marqués de Comillas from the bus stop will bring you, 4km later, to **Playa Oyambre,** another expansive beach. It's easier to take the La Cantábrica bus toward San Vicente and ask the driver to let you off at Oyambre.

Comillas is equally proud of its architectural attractions. Most notable—and amusing—is ▨ **El Capricho,** Gaudí's summer palace. While it's not possible to tour the building, most visitors are content to see the bright swirling turrets and gingerbread-esque windows outside. Standing at the bus stop, you can see the colorful palace on the hill; follow the footpath across the street for a closer view. One way to get a peek inside El Capricho is to eat a meal in its **dining hall ❸**. (Reservations ☎924 72 03 65. Entrees €12-13. Open daily 1-3:30pm and 9-11pm.) Next to El Capricho on the same hill are the neo-Gothic **Palacio de Sobrellano,** designed by Catalan architect Doménech i Muntaner, and the **Capilla-Pantheon,** containing furniture designed by Gaudí. (Hours vary; check with the tourist office before venturing over. €3) From the tourist office, turn uphill and sneak a peek at the impressive facade of the **Universidad Pontificia** (closed to the public). On July 15-18, Comillas's **fiestas** go up in a blaze of fireworks, pole-walking, goose-chasing, and dancing.

The **tourist office** is at C. María del Piélago, 2. From the main bus stop, follow C. Marqués de Comillas past the turn-off for the beach, through the plaza, and uphill one block, then follow the signs to the office. (☎942 72 07 68. Open May-Sept. M-Sa 10am-1pm and 5-9pm, Su 11am-1pm and 4:30-7pm.) The **post office** is at C. Antonio López, 6, on the main road uphill from the tourist office turn-off. (☎942 72 00 95. Open M-F 8:30am-2:30pm, Sa 9:30am-1pm.) **Postal Code:** 39520.

GALICIA (GALIZA)

If, as the old Galician saying goes, "rain is art," then there is no gallery more beautiful than the misty skies of northwestern Spain. Galicia looks and feels like no other region of the country. Often veiled in a silvery drizzle, it is a province of fern-laden eucalyptus woods, slate-roofed fishing villages, and seemingly endless white beaches. Rivers wind through hills and gradually widen into estuaries that empty into the Bay of Biscay and the Atlantic Ocean.

A rest stop on the Celts' journey to Ireland around 900 BC, Galicia harbors enduring Celtic influences. Ancient *castros* (fortress-villages), inscriptions, and *gaitas* (bagpipes) testify to this Celtiberian past, and lingering lore of witches, fairies, and buried treasures has earned Galicia a reputation as a land of magic. The rough terrain has historically hampered trade, but ship building, auto manufacturing, and even renowned fashion labels are contributing to the region's gradual modernization and development. Tourists have begun to visit even the smallest of towns, and Santiago de Compostela, the terminus of the Camino de Santiago, continues to be one of the world's most popular backpacking destinations.

Galicians speak *gallego*, a linguistic missing link of sorts between Castilian and Portuguese. While newspapers and street signs alternate between languages, most conversations are conducted in Spanish. Regional cuisine features *caldo gallego* (a vegetable broth), *vieiras* (scallops, the pilgrim's trophy), *empanadas* (turnovers stuffed with assorted fillings), and *pulpo a gallego* (boiled octopus). Regionalism in Galicia doesn't cause quite the stir it does in the País Vasco or Catalunya, but you still may see graffiti calling for *"liberdade."*

HIGHLIGHTS OF GALICIA

TRACE the footsteps of pilgrims following the thousand-year-old Camino de Santiago at the cathedral in **Santiago de Compostela** (see below). Or, if you're adventurous, trek the month-long French route yourself, starting in Roncesvalles (see p. 505).

REVEL on the beach while gulping down the fiery local concoction *la queimada* during the June 23 Fiesta de San Juan in **Vigo** (see p. 577).

EXPLORE the untouched coves and beaches of the **Islas Cíes** (see p. 578), where only 2200 visitors are allowed each day.

SAVOR the region's renowned seafood while sipping a glass of world-famous white wine in **Cambados** (see p. 583), the heart of *albariño* country.

SANTIAGO DE COMPOSTELA   ☎981

Santiago (pop. 94,000) is a city of song. From the impromptu orchestra concerts on Rúa do Vilar to the thumping of all-night discos, from the roving bands of *gaita* players to the cathedral's morning chimes, every street and plaza is filled with musical celebration. Perhaps these are the chords of weary pilgrims, elated to have, at long last, reached the apostle's tomb. Or perhaps these are the tunes of the *Apóstolo*, the city's extravagant two-week *fiesta* in honor of its namesake. But more likely, these are just the sounds of joy at waking up to another day in Santiago, where narrow, Baroque streets empty into vast plazas, where relaxers and revelers spill out of the myriad cafes and bars, and where every day in this sun-blessed (and perhaps Apostle-blessed) city is worthy of celebration.

Galicia

TRANSPORTATION

Flights: Aeropuerto Lavacolla (☎ 981 54 75 00 or 54 75 01), 10km toward Lugo. A bus goes to Santiago, stopping at the bus and train stations and C. General Pardiñas, 26 (8 per day 6:40am-10:30pm, €1.55). Schedule in the daily *El Correo Gallego* (€0.75). **Iberia**, C. General Pardiñas, 36 (☎ 981 57 20 28). Open M-F 9:30am-2pm and 4-7pm.

Trains: R. do Hórreo, s/n (☎ 981 52 02 02 or 24 02 02). To: **Bilbao** (10¾hr., 1 per day 9:04am, €32.50) via **León** (6½hr., €23) and **Burgos** (8hr., €28.50); **La Coruña** (1hr.; M-F 20 per day 6:30am-10:26pm, Sa-Su 14 per day 7:12am-10:26pm; €3.20-11); **Madrid** (8hr.; M-F 2 per day 1:47, 10:25pm, Sa 1 per day 10:30pm, Su 3 per day 1:47, 9:52am, 10:30pm; €36); **Vigo** (2hr.; M-F 20 per day 6:30am-10:05pm, Sa-Su 14 per day 7:33am-10:05pm; €4.90-6.25) via **Pontevedra** (1½hr., €3.20-4.05).

Buses: Estación Central de Autobuses, R. de Rodríguez, s/n (☎ 981 58 77 00), a 20min. walk to downtown. Bus #10 and bus "C Circular" go from the station to the R. de Montero Ríos side of Pr. de Galicia (10min., every 15-20min. 6:30am-10pm, €0.66). Info open daily 6am-10pm.

ALSA (☎ 981 58 61 33, reservations 902 42 22 42). Open daily 7:30am-9:30pm. To: **Bilbao** (11¼hr.; 2 per day 9am, 9:30pm; €39); **Madrid** (8-9hr., 4 per day 8am-9:30pm, €31); **San Sebastián** (13½hr.; 2 per day 8am, 5:30pm; €44).

GALICIA

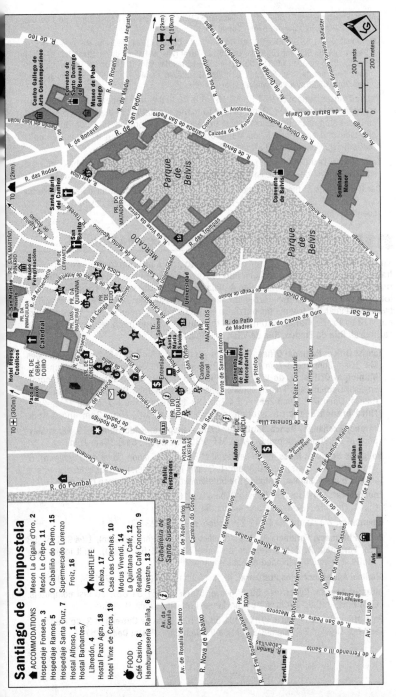

Santiago de Compostela

▲ ACCOMMODATIONS
Hospedaje Fonseca, **3**
Hospedaje Ramos, **5**
Hospedaje Santa Cruz, **7**
Hostal Alfonso, **1**
Hostal Barbantes/
Libredón, **4**
Hostal Pazo Agra, **18**
Hotel Virxe de Cerca, **19**

◆ FOOD
Café Casino, **8**
Hamburguesería Raíña, **6**

Meson La Cigala d'Oro, **2**
Mesón Le Crêpe, **11**
O Cabaliño do Demo, **15**
Supermercado Lorenzo
    Froiz, **16**

★ NIGHTLIFE
A Reixa, **17**
Casa oas Crechas, **10**
Modus Vivendi, **14**
La Quintana Café, **12**
Retablo Café Concerto, **9**
Xaveste, **13**

GALICIA

Arriva/Finisterre (☎981 58 85 11) to **Finisterre** (2½hr.; M-F 7 per day 8am-7:30pm, Sa 4 per day 8am-7:30pm, Su 3 per day 8am-6:15pm; €9.30).

Castromil (☎981 58 90 90 or 902 10 44 44). To: **La Coruña** (1½hr.; every hr. M-F 7am-10pm, Sa 9am-10pm, Su 9:15am-10:30pm; €5.25); **El Ferrol** (2hr.; M-F 6 per day 9:15am-9pm, Sa-Su 4 per day 9:15am-9pm; €6.31); **Noia** (1hr.; M-F 15 per day 8am-10:15pm, Sa 10 per day 8am-8pm, Su 8 per day 8am-8:30pm; €3); **Vigo** (2hr.; every hr. M-F 6am-10pm, Sa 8am-9pm, Su 9am-9pm; €5.85) via **Pontevedra** (1½hr., €4.05).

Public Transportation: (☎981 58 18 15). Bus #6 to the train station (10am-10:30pm), #9 to the campgrounds (10am-8pm), #10 to the bus station. In the city center, almost all buses stop at Pr. de Galicia, where there are 2 stops, one on the R. do Doutor Teixeiro side and one along R. de Montero Ríos. Except for #6 and 9, buses run daily 6:30am-10:30pm every 20-30min. €0.70.

Taxis: Radio Taxi (24hr. ☎981 58 24 90 or 59 84 88). Taxis wait at the bus and train stations and Pr. de Galicia. For late-night service, try near the clubs in Pl. Roxa.

Car Rental: Avis at the train station (☎981 59 61 01). 25+, must have had license for 1yr. Open M-F 7am-1:15pm and 4-7pm, Sa-Su 7am-noon. €85 per day for 350km. Discounts for longer rentals.

ORIENTATION & PRACTICAL INFORMATION

The **cathedral** marks the center of the old city, on a hill above the new city. The **train station** is at the far southern end of town. To reach the old city from the station, either take bus #6 to **Praza de Galicia** or walk up the stairs across the parking lot from the main entrance, cross the street, and bear right onto R. do Hórreo. The **bus station** is at the town's far northern end. The walk is over 20min.; instead, take bus #10 to Pr. de Galicia (10min.). In the old city, three main streets lead to the cathedral: **Rúa do Franco, Rúa do Vilar,** and **Rúa Nova.**

Tourist Office: Regional Office, R. do Vilar, 43 (☎981 58 40 81). English spoken. Open M-F 10am-2pm and 4-7pm, Sa 11am-2pm and 5-7pm, Su and holidays 11am-2pm. **Municipal Office,** R. do Vilar, 63 (☎981 55 51 29; www.santiagoturismo.com). English, German, and French spoken. Open daily 9am-9pm. **Second branch** in Pr. de Galicia. Open M-F 10am-2pm and 4-7pm, Sa 11am-2pm and 5-7pm, Su 11am-2pm. **Third branch** at the bus station in summer. Open M-F 10am-2pm and 5-8pm.

Currency Exchange: Banco Santander Central Hispano, R. do Hórreo, 20. Open May-Sept. M-F 8:30am-2:30pm; Oct.-Apr. M-F 8:30am-2:30pm, Sa 8:30am-1pm.

Religious Services: Mass in the cathedral M-Sa 9:30am, noon (*Misa del Peregrino*), 6, and 7:30pm (vespers); Su 10:30am, 1, 5, and 7pm (vespers). Most nights also offer a special **pilgrim's mass,** featuring the *botafumeiro* (a gigantic incense burner).

Laundromat: ServiLimp, R. Ramón Cabanillas, 16 (☎981 59 29 52). 4.5kg of laundry €5.11. Open M-F 9am-noon and 4-8pm, Sa 10am-2pm.

Emergency: ☎112 or 900 44 42 22. **Police:** ☎981 54 23 23.

24hr. Pharmacy: Farmacia M. Jesús Valdés Cabo, Cantón do Toural, 1 (☎981 58 58 95). **Farmacia R. Bescanses,** Pr. do Toural, 1 (☎981 58 59 90). Built in the mid-1800s, it is an old-fashioned establishment worth seeing.

Medical Assistance: Hospital Xeral, R. das Galeras, s/n (☎061 or 981 54 00 00).

Internet Access: CyberNova 50, R. Nova, 50 (☎981 57 51 88). 26 fast computers. €1.20 per hr. 9am-10pm, €1 per hr. 10pm-1am. Open daily 9am-1am.

Post Office: Tv. de Fonseca, s/n (☎981 58 12 52). **Lista de Correos** at R. do Franco, 6, and **fax.** Open M-F 8:30am-8:30pm, Sa 9:30am-2pm. **Postal Code:** 15701.

ACCOMMODATIONS

Nearly every street in the old city houses at least one or two *pensiones*. The liveliest and most popular streets, however, are R. do Vilar and R. da Raíña. Call ahead in winter when university students occupy most rooms.

Hospedaje Ramos, R. da Raíña, 18, 2nd fl. (☎981 58 18 59), above O Papa Una restaurant. In the center of the *ciudad vieja*, these well-lit rooms are newly renovated with shining floors, tight windows that keep out the noise and weather, and private baths. Reserve 2 weeks in advance during summer. Singles €13.50; doubles €24.50. ❶

Hostal Barbantes/Hostal Libredón, Pr. de Fonseca, 5 (☎981 57 65 20; fax 58 41 33). Two hostels under the same owner share a reception area. Both have spacious, sparkling clean rooms with sunlight and private bath. Barbantes's rooms are newly renovated. The attic room has fantastic views of the city, while others have views of peaceful Pr. de Fonseca. Winter heating and TV. Singles €40; doubles overlooking R. do Franco €45, overlooking Pr. de Fonseca €60. MC/V and AmEx Traveler's Checks. ❹

Hostal Pazo Agra, R. da Calderería, 37 (☎981 58 35 17). Clean rooms with tall ceilings have floor-to-ceiling glass doors opening to balconies. Some have TV. July-Sept. singles €23; doubles €32. Oct.-June €17/€26 and approx. €240 per month. ❷

Hostal Alfonso, R. do Pombal, 40 (☎981 58 56 85). Rooms in this affectionately decorated hostel each have a view of either the park or the cathedral (the quieter side). TV, private bath, winter heat, and fruit. Breakfast included. Reserve a month ahead in Aug. June-Sept. singles €42; doubles €54. Oct.-May €30/€42. AmEx/MC/V. ❹

Hotel Virxe da Cerca, R. da Virxe da Cerca, 27 (☎981 56 93 50). This hotel, situated in a former 18th-century Jesuit house, is peaceful and relaxing. Across the street from the daily market and old city walls, with a garden and a view of the nearby hills and the convent that crowns them. Standard rooms in the new building are less expensive than the *especial* rooms in the old building. Rooms have all the amenities and more. Apr.-Oct. standard singles €72; *especial* €84; doubles €85/€95. Nov.-Mar. singles €60/€72; doubles €72/€84. IVA not included. V. ❺

Hospedaje Santa Cruz, R. do Vilar, 42, 2nd fl. (☎981 58 28 15). Clean rooms in the old city's center near bars and restaurants. Some doubles have private bath. Winter heat. Singles €15; doubles €25, with bath €40. Oct.-May €150 per person per month. ❷

Hospedaje Fonseca, R. de Fonseca, 1, 2nd fl. (☎981 57 24 79). Colorful, sunny rooms. Common kitchen with TV. Winter heating. Shared baths. Singles, doubles, triples, and quads all €12-15 per person. Oct.-May. approx. €150 per person per month. ❶

Camping: As Cancelas, R. 25 de Xullo, 35 (☎981 58 02 66). 2km north of the cathedral. Take bus #6 or #9 from the train station or Pr. de Galicia. Laundry, supermarket, and pool. €4.40 per person, €4.70 per car and per tent, electricity €2.90. ❶

FOOD

Tapas-weary budget travelers appreciate Santiago's selection of restaurants. Bars and cafeterias line the streets with remarkably inexpensive *menús*. Most restaurants are on **Rúa do Vilar, Rúa do Franco, Rúa Nova,** and **Rúa da Raíña**; in the new city, look near Pr. Roxa. End your meal with a *tarta de Santiago*, a rich almond cake emblazoned with a sugary St. James cross. Santiago's **mercado,** near the Convento de San Agostiño, is a sight in its own right. (Open M-Sa 7:30am-2pm.) **Supermercado Lorenzo Froiz,** Pr. do Toural, is one block from Pr. de Galicia. (Open M-Sa 9am-3pm and 4:30-9pm, Sa 9am-3pm and 5-9pm. MC/V.)

THE LOCAL LEGEND

WALK LIKE A HERMIT

One night in 813, a hermit trudged through the hills on the way to his hermitage. Suddenly, miraculously bright visions flooded his senses, revealing the long-forgotten tomb of the Apostle James. Around this *campus stellae* (field of stars) the cathedral of Santiago de Compostela was built, and around this cathedral a world-famous pilgrimage was born.

Since the 9th-century, thousands of pilgrims have traveled the Camino de Santiago. Many have made the pilgrimage in search of spiritual fulfillment: most as true believers, some to adhere to a stipulation of inheritance, a few to absolve themselves of sin, and at least one to find romance (the wife of Bath in Chaucer's *Canterbury Tales* sauntered to Santiago in bright red stockings to find herself a husband).

Clever Benedictine monks built monasteries to host pilgrims along the *camino*, giving rise to the world's first large-scale International tourist route and helping make Santiago's cathedral the world's most frequented Christian shrine. In the 12th-century, an enterprising French monk added a book to the *Codex Calixtinus*, a collection of stories about the apostles, that was filled with information on the quality of water at various rest stops and descriptions of villages and monuments along *La Ruta Francesa* (begining

O Cabaliño do Demo, R. Ayer Ulloa, 7 (☎981 58 81 46). Enjoy a variety of global vegetarian entrees from Middle Eastern to Ethiopian in this creative and resourcefully-decorated restaurant. *Menú* €7.25. Open M-W 2-4pm and 9-11:30pm, Th-Sa 2-4pm and 9pm-midnight. Cafe downstairs open 8am-midnight. ❷

Hamburguesería Raíña, R. da Raíña, 18. An oasis for the starving, broke traveler. Huge hamburgers €1-2.15, entrees €3.80-€4.25, *menú* €4.30. Open daily lunch 1-4pm; dinner M-W 8pm-midnight, Th-Sa 8pm-1am. ❶

Mesón Le Crêpe, Pr. de Quintana, 1 (☎981 57 76 43). Savor crêpes (€4.50-7) at this popular meal spot either on the beautiful terrace or in the softly-lit dining room upstairs. Open daily 1-4pm and 8pm-midnight. MC/V. ❷

Café Casino, R. do Vilar, 35 (☎981 57 75 03). Enjoy a light meal in this time-warp of a vast dining hall (est. 1873) with tall, wood-paneled walls, stained glass windows, and big, comfortable armchairs. A good selection of salads (€4), sandwiches (€2-3), and beer (€2-4). Open Su-Th 9am-2am, F-Sa 9am-4am. MC/V. ❷

Mesón La Cigala d'Oro, R. do Franco, 10 (☎981 58 29 52). Specializes in seafood. The *mariscada* (€55) serves 2 and contains every kind of seafood imaginable. Three-course *menú* €18.75. Open daily 1-3:30pm and 8-11:30pm. AmEx/MC/V. ❹

👁 SIGHTS

🏛 CATEDRAL DE SANTIAGO DE COMPOSTELA
☎981 58 35 48. Open daily 7am-7pm. Free.

Santiago's cathedral has four facades, each a masterpiece from a different era, with entrances opening to four different plazas: Praterías, Quintana, Inmaculada, and Obradoiro. From the southern **Praza das Praterías** (with the spitting sea horse), enter the cathedral through the Romanesque arched double doors. The **Torro de Reloxio** (clock tower), Pórtico Real, and Porta Santa face **Praza da Quintana,** to the west of the cathedral. To the north, a blend of Doric and Ionic columns grace **Praza da Inmaculada,** combining Romanesque and Neoclassical styles. Consecrated in 1211, the cathedral later acquired Gothic chapels (in the apse and transept), a 15th-century dome, a 16th-century cloister, and the 18th-century Baroque **Obradoiro facade** with two towers that soar above the city. This facade faces west toward **Praza do Obradoiro,** an immense plaza scattered with souvenir hawkers and *tunas* (young lute-strumming male students in medieval garb).

Many consider Maestro Mateo's **Pórtico de la Gloria,** encased in the Obradoiro facade, the crowning achievement of Spanish Romanesque sculpture. This unusual 12th-century amalgam of angels, prophets, saints, sinners, demons, and monsters forms a compendium of Christian theology. Unlike most rigid Romanesque statues, those in the Pórtico seem to smile, whisper, lean, and gab. Galician author Rosalía del Castro once remarked, "It looks as if their lips are moving . . . might they be alive?" The revered **remains of St. James** (Santiago) lie beneath the high altar in a silver coffer, while his bejeweled bust, polished by the embraces of thousands of pilgrims, rests above the altar. The **botafumeiro,** an enormous silver censer used in religious rituals and intended to overpower the stench of dirty pilgrims, swings from the transept during high Mass and liturgical ceremonies. Much older than the towers that house them, the **bells** of Santiago were stolen in 997 by Moorish invaders and transported to Córdoba on the backs of Christian slaves. Centuries later, when Spaniards conquered Córdoba, they had their revenge by forcing Moors to carry the bells back.

MUSEUM & CLOISTERS. Inside the museum are several gorgeous, intricate 16th-century tapestries and two unusual statues of the pregnant Virgin Mary. The museum also houses manuscripts from the *Codex Calixtinus* and Romanesque remains from one of many archaeological excavations conducted in the cathedral. The 12th-century *Codex,* five volumes of manuscripts of the stories of the Apostle James, includes travel information for early pilgrims. There is also a room dedicated to the stone choir that once stood inside the cathedral. Maestro Mateo built this impressive structure to represent the "New Jerusalem that descends from heaven" as written in the Apocalypse. (☎981 58 11 55. Museum open June-Sept. M-Sa 10am-1:30pm and 4-7:30pm, Su and holidays 10am-1:30pm; Oct.-Feb. M-Sa 11am-1pm and 4-6pm, Su and holidays 11am-1pm; Mar.-May M-Sa 10:30am-1:30pm and 4-6:30pm, Su and holidays 10:30am-1:30pm. €5, with student ID €3. Ticket includes entrance to crypt.)

OTHER SIGHTS

▧ **PAZO DE RAXOI.** The majestic facade of the Pazo de Raxoi shines with gold-accented balconies and monumental Neoclassical columns. Once a royal palace, it now houses the Ayuntamiento and the office of the president of the Xunta de Galicia (Galician government). At night, floodlights illuminate the remarkable bas-relief of the 844 Battle of Clavijo, when, according to legend, St. James helped the Spanish fight off the Moors. (Across Pr. do Obradoiro, facing the cathedral.)

near the French border in Roncesvalles, Navarra)—in essence, the world's first travel guide.

Nowadays, pilgrims are easily spotted by their crook-necked walking sticks, sunburnt faces, and scallop shells tied onto weathered backpacks. The shells, the emblem of fisherman St. James, were first acquired by pilgrims after visiting the cathedral. Although only pilgrims on their way home used to carry the shell, it has now become a symbol of voyage to Santiago as well.

True *peregrinos* (pilgrims) must cover 100km on foot or horse or 200km on bike to receive La Compostela, an official certificate of the pilgrimage issued by the cathedral. A network of *refugios* and *albergues* offers free lodging to pilgrims on the move and stamps the "pilgrims' passports" to provide evidence of completion of the full distance. At a rate of 30km per day, walking the entire French route (from Roncesvalles in the Pyrenees to Santiago de Compostela, 750-870km), takes about a month and places you in the ranks of such illustrious pilgrims as royal couple Fernando and Isabel, St. Francis de Assisi, Pope John Paul II, and Shirley MacLaine.

For more information and free guides to the Camino de Santiago, contact the Oficina Xacobeo, Av. da Coruña, 6, in Santiago. ☎981 57 20 04. Open M-F 8:30am-2:30pm and 4:30-6:30pm.

MUSEO DAS PEREGRINACIÓNS. This three-story Gothic building is full of creatively displayed historical info about the *Camino* and pilgrimages in general, including statues of the Virgin as a baby-Jesus-toting pilgrim and exhibits on the rituals of pilgrimage and the iconography of St. James. *(Pr. de San Miguel. ☎981 58 15 58. Open Tu-F 10am-8pm, Sa 10:30am-1:30pm and 5-8pm, Su 10:30am-1:30pm. €2.40, children and seniors €1.20, free during special expositions and most of the summer.)*

CENTRO GALLEGO DE ARTE CONTEMPORÁNEO. The expansive galleries and rooftop *terraza* of the sparkling Centro Gallego de Arte Contemporáneo (CGAC) house cutting-edge exhibitions of boundary-bending artists from around the world. *(R. de Ramón del Valle Inclán, s/n. Near the Museo de Pobo Gallego. ☎981 54 66 19; www.cgac.org. Open Tu-Su 11am-8pm. Free.)*

MUSEO DE POBO GALLEGO. Find out everything you have ever wanted to know about traditional Galician living. Exhibits on ship building, pottery, house construction, and *gaitas* (the Galician bagpipe) are highlights, but the museum also includes exhibits dedicated to Galician painting. *(Inside the Convento de Santo Domingo de Boneval. ☎981 58 36 20. Open June 7-Mar. 2 Tu-Sa 10am-2pm and 4-8pm, Su 11am-2pm; Mar. 3-June 6 Tu-Sa 10am-2pm and 4-7pm. Free.)*

MONASTERIO DE SAN MARTIÑO PINARIO. Once a religious center almost as prestigious as the cathedral, the monastery is a mixture of Romanesque cloisters, Plateresque facades, and Baroque sculpture. Its composite style makes it an outstanding architectural example. *(In Pr. de San Martiño Pinario.)*

◑ ▤ FESTIVALS & NIGHTLIFE

The local newspaper *El Correo Gallego* (€0.75) and the free monthly *Compostela Capital* list art exhibits and concert information. Consult any of three local monthlies, *Santiago Días Guía Imprescindible, Compostelán,* or *Modus Vivendi,* for updates on the live music scene. At night, crowds flood cellars throughout the city. To boogie with local students, hit the bars and dance joints off Pr. Roxa. Clubs are open from roughly midnight to 6am. The city celebrates the **Día de Santiago** (July 25) for a full two weeks, from July 15 to 31, in a celebration called *Apóstolo;* on the night of the 24th, a Pontifical Mass is held in the cathedral during **Las Vísperas de Santiago.** The Día de Santiago falls on a Sunday in 2004, making 2004 a Jubilee year; thus, the celebration will likely be especially grand. By tradition, the church grants special graces in these years.

▨ **Casa oas Crechas,** Vía Sacra, 3 (☎981 56 07 51). A smoky stone-and-wood pub with a witchcraft theme. Renowned for its Galician folk concerts. Beer €1.50-1.95. Open daily 4pm-2am and later.

Xavestre, R. de San Paolo de Antaltares, 31. Get to know some *santiaguinos* up close and personally in this crowded bar. Packed with 20-somethings, Xavestre plays the latest hits in Spanish pop music. Mixed drinks €5. Serves hot chocolate on its terrace during the day. Open daily 11am-late.

La Quintana Café, Pr. da Quintana, 1. In a dark stone basement, Quintana fills on weekends with students dancing to popular Spanish and English songs. Beer €3-5, mixed drinks €4. Upstairs and terrace open daily from 10am-late, downstairs 11pm-late.

Retablo Café Concerto, R. Nova, 13 (☎981 56 48 51). Heavenly decor in rich reds, purples, and golds and low prices keep tourists and students coming back to Retablo. Eclectic music selections include techno, pop, and house. Drinks start at €2. Open daily from noon until the last *santiaguino* leaves.

A Reixa, C. Salomé, 3. A low-ceilinged pub dedicated to 60s rock. Homemade drinks and concerts W nights (look for posters throughout the city). Open daily 4:30pm-late.

Modus Vivendi, Pr. de Feijo, 1. Galicia's oldest pub and a clubhouse for revolutionary Galician youth in the 1970s. Today, it entertains Santiago's youth into the wee hours of the night with live music. Beer €2, drinks €4. Open daily 7pm-late.

▶ DAYTRIPS FROM SANTIAGO DE COMPOSTELA

The northern part of the Rías Baixas hide undiscovered hamlets frequented only by pilgrims. These small towns make good daytrips from Santiago, but buses in this area tend to stop frequently, making travel times quite lengthy. Go anyway; otherwise, you'll regret missing the views of the turbulent coastline and the peace of small Spanish fishing towns.

▨ CABO FINISTERRE (CABO FISTERRE)

Arriva/Finisterre buses make daily trips from Santiago to Finisterre (2½hr.; M-F 7 per day 8:15am-7:30pm, Sa 4 per day 8am-7:30pm, Su 3 per day 8am, 12:15, 6:15pm; €9.65) and back (M-F 5 per day 7:50am-4:45pm, Sa 3 per day 7am-4pm, Su 2 per day 1:45, 6:45pm). The bus stop is in front of the harbor's fishing center.

Jutting out precariously from the infamously rocky Costa de la Muerte ("Coast of Death"; Costa da Morte in *gallego*), Cabo Finisterre was once considered Europe's westernmost point, and for centuries it was a crucial port for all naval trade along the Atlantic. Finisterre was also famous due to the ancient belief that it was off these shores that the world ended—hence its name: *finis* (end), *terre* (earth). Even today, it feels like the end of the earth, with the seemingly endless bus ride out to a desolate town on a lonely, wind-swept peninsula. On July 1, 2003, Cabo Finisterre became the first port on the Costa de la Muerte to send out fishermen since the sinking of the oil tanker *Prestige* in November 2002.

The 1½hr. hike from the port to **Monte San Guillermo** is long, but those who complete it are rewarded with incredible views of the tumultuous sea and Finisterre's famous bed-shaped **fertility rocks.** Couples having problems conceiving are advised to make a go of it on the rocks under a full moon (harvest moons are even better). On another hill on San Guillermo are **As Pedras Santas,** two fairly large rocks which cannot be lifted by themselves, but which slide effortlessly side-to-side if you press the right spot. Try it yourself—the contact point is well marked. The **lighthouse** that has beckoned ships for years stands 45min. from the center of town. To reach the **beach,** walk right. The best beach in Finisterre, however, is on the flat isthmus that connects the peninsula with the mainland. The sands are powdery and wide; the waters calm, but frigid. Either walk 4km along the road to Santiago, or take the bus and ask the driver to stop.

The **Albergue de Peregrinos,** C. Real, 2, has maps, brochures, and tourist info. From the bus stop, facing the water, turn left. At the pink statue, turn left again. (☎981 74 07 81. Open M-F 9:30am-1pm and 7-11pm, Sa-Su noon-2pm and 7-11pm.) Nearby, **Tenda Peregrina** also has maps and info on bike rentals and boat trips.

▨ O CASTRO DE BAROÑA

To reach O Castro de Baroña, you'll need to make a connection in Noia. Castromil (☎981 58 90 90) runs buses from Santiago to Noia (1hr.; M-F every hr. 8am-10pm, Sa 12 per day 8am-10pm, Su every 2hr. 10am-10pm; €2.75). From Noia, Hefsel buses stop at O Castro de Baroña (in front of Café-Bar O Castro) en route to Riveira (30min.; M-F 14 per day 6:50am-9:30pm, Sa 7 per day 8am-9pm, Su 11 per day 8am-10pm; €1.30). Be sure to tell the bus driver where you're going, as the stop is easy to miss. From the bus stop, follow signs to the fortress. Catch the bus home across the road from Café-Bar O Castro.

One of Galicia's best-preserved coastal Celtic villages, **O Castro de Baroña,** lies 19km south of Noia. The seaside remains of a 5th-century Celtic **fortress** cover the neck of the isthmus, ascending to a rocky promontory above the sea and then descending to the soft sands of an excellent crescent **beach** where clothing is optional. For those who need a shower, **Café-Bar O Castro ❸**, Lugar Castro de Baroña, 18, in **Porto do Son** (the O Castro bus stop), offers spotless rooms under the care of a very nice owner. (☎981 76 74 30. Doubles €25-30. Open June-Aug.) The nearest town, **Baroña**, 1km north, has a supermarket, restaurant, and bus stop. Should you get stuck in **Noia** on the way back to Santiago, several hotels are a short walk from the bus station on R. da Galicia. From the bus station, walk uphill on R. Pedra Sartaña, turn right onto Rosalía de Castro and then left onto R. da Galicia. The bus station offers **luggage storage**. (€0.75 per bag per day. Open 6:30am-11pm.) The closest hostel to the station, **Hostal Valadares ❷**, C. Alameda, s/n, offers spotless, comfortable rooms with firm mattresses, most with views of the surrounding mountains. TV, winter heat, bath, and breakfast are included. From the bus station, walk uphill on R. Pedra Sartaña and turn left at the street's end. (☎981 82 04 36. Singles €20-25; doubles €30-40.)

MUROS & LOURO

Castromil runs buses between Santiago and Muros (2hr.; M-F every hr. 8am-9pm, Sa 11 per day 8am-9pm, Su every 2hr. 10am-10pm) via Noia.

Muros is a small but lively fishing village recognized in 1970 as a historical site for its unique examples of traditional Gothic urban design, including narrow one-person lanes, arcades, sailor houses, and bite-size plazas. Its neighbor Louro, 4km away, is home to some of the most untouched, soft-sanded beaches in all of Galicia. The combination of the two makes an ideal daytrip—Muros, with its transportation facilities, accommodations, and restaurants, provides the amenities necessary for a day in the surf at Louro. From Muros, after walking around the old city's steep and stringy streets, visitors can walk along the **Paseo Marítimo** (to the right, facing the water) to Louro, encountering wonderful views of sparkling cobalt waters on the way. The first beach in Louro, **Playa San Francisco**, is less than 3km from Muros. Stay overnight right on the beach at **A Vouga Camping ❶**, which has a restaurant, bar, hot showers, and a small market. (☎981 82 76 07. Sites €11, €17, or €20 depending on size. Small tent rental €2.75, large tent €3.40. Electricity €2.40. Call a couple days ahead to reserve a space.)

The Ayuntamiento in Muros houses a small **tourist office** open June-September. (☎981 82 60 50. Open daily 8am-2pm and 5:30-8:30pm.) From the bus stop, facing the water, walk right. The Ayuntamiento is in the plaza where the street bends. For **bike rentals**, try **TriKi** (☎981 76 20 02) farther along the same street. If you'd like to stay in Muros, closer to the restaurants (all with boat-themed furniture), try the American-run **Hospedaje A Vianda ❸**. Some rooms have a view, and all are very clean with winter heat and shared baths. (☎981 82 63 22. Reserve a month ahead for Aug. stays. Doubles €30, with view €37; triples with view €43.)

RÍAS BAJAS (RÍAS BAIXAS)

According to Galician lore, the Rías Baixas (Low Estuaries) were formed by God's tremendous handprint, with each *ría* stretching like a finger through the land. These deep, navy blue bays, countless sandy coves, and calm, cool waters have lured vacationing Spaniards for decades. Only recently have foreign tourists discovered the area's charm. While not nearly as cool or rainy as their Galician neighbors—the Baixas are, after all, the sunniest part of the northern Spanish coast—the Baixas are blessed with an ocean wind that makes for a refreshing break from the scorching heat (and hordes of tourists) of central and southern Spain.

VIGO ☎986

Spanish poet José María Álvarez once wrote that "Vigo does not end, it goes on into the sea." Often called Spain's door to the Atlantic, Vigo (pop. 300,000) began as a small, unobtrusive fishing port; with the arrival of the Citröen manufacturing plant, it exploded into the biggest city in Galicia. While Vigo isn't the place to go to escape city life, the nightlife and shopping are among the best in the region. The city is also a good base for daytrips to nearby villages and beaches.

TRANSPORTATION

Flights: Aeropuerto de Vigo (☎986 26 82 00), on Av. del Aeropuerto, 15km from the city center. The local R9 bus runs regularly from R. Urzáiz near R. Colón to the airport (€0.85). **Iberia** (☎986 26 82 28) and **Air Europa** (☎986 26 83 10) have offices at the airport. Daily flights to **Barcelona, Bilbao, Madrid,** and **Valencia.**

Trains: RENFE, Pr. de la Estación, s/n (☎986 43 11 14), downstairs from R. Urzáiz. Open daily 7am-11pm. To: **La Coruña** (2½hr.; M-F 14 per day 5:45am-8:55pm, Sa-Su 10 per day 5:45am-8:55pm; €10.20); **Madrid** (8-9hr.; M-F and Su 2 per day 1:25, 10:30pm; €38); **Pontevedra** (30min.; M-F 17 per day 5:45am-9:35pm, Sa 11 per day 5:45am-8:55pm, Su 13 per day 5:45am-9:35pm; €2.10); **Santiago de Compostela** (2hr.; M-F 17 per day 5:45am-9:35pm, Sa 11 per day 5:45am-8:55pm, Su 13 per day 5:45am-9:35pm; €6.35).

Buses: Estación de Autobuses, Av. de Madrid, s/n (☎986 37 34 11), on the corner of R. Alcalde Gregorio Espino.

ATSA (☎986 61 02 55) to: **Bayona** (50min.; every 30min. M-Sa 7am-10pm, Su 8am-11pm; €1.85); **La Guardia** (1½hr.; M-F every 30min. 7:30am-9pm, Sa every hr. 8:30am-8:30pm, Su 6 per day 10am-9pm; €4.20); **Túy** (45min.; M-F every 30min. 7:30am-9pm, Sa every hr. 8:30am-8:30pm, Su 4 per day 10am, noon, 6, 9pm; €2.15). Buy tickets onboard.

Auto Res (☎986 27 19 61) to **Madrid** (9hr., 6-8 per day 8:30am-11pm, €28.64-33.10).

Castromil (☎986 27 81 12) to: **La Coruña** (2½hr.; M-F 9 per day 6:30am-8:30pm, Sa 8 per day 7:30am-8:30pm, Su 7 per day 8:30am-8:30pm; €12); **Pontevedra** (45min.; M-F every 30min. 6:30am-9pm and 10:30pm, Sa every 30min. 7:30am-9pm and 10:30pm, Su every 45min. 7:30am-8:30pm; €2.10); **Santiago de Compostela** (1¼hr., every 30min. 6:30am-8:30pm; €6.40).

Ferries: Estación Ría, R. As Avenidas, s/n (☎986 22 52 72), past the nautical club on the harborside walkway. To: **Cangas** (20min.; M-F every 30min. 6:30am-10:30pm, Sa-Su every hr. 6:30am-10:30pm; round-trip €3.20); **Islas Cíes** (50min.; June-Sept. 4 per day 11am-7pm, Oct.-May 3 per day 11am-4pm; round-trip €14.50); and **Moaña** (30min.; every hr. M-Sa 6:30am-10:30pm, Su 8:30am-10:30pm; €1.35).

Car Rental: National, R. Urzáiz, 84 (☎986 41 80 76). 21+, must have had license at least 1yr. Open M-F 8:30am-1:30pm and 4:30-7:30pm, Sa 9am-1pm.

ORIENTATION & PRACTICAL INFORMATION

Gran Vía is Vigo's main thoroughfare, stretching south to north from Pr. de América through Pr. de España and ending at the perpendicular **Rúa Urzáiz.** A left turn onto R. Urzáiz leads to Pta. do Sol and into the **casco antiguo;** most of the city's action is here in the old city and along the waterfront. As you exit the **train station** onto R. Urzáiz (upstairs from the main entrance), go right two blocks to reach Gran Vía. Keep walking on R. Urzáiz for 10min. to reach the waterfront. The city center is a 25min. trek from the **bus station.** Exit right uphill along busy

THE LOCAL STORY

NEVER AGAIN

On November 19, 2002, the oil tanker Prestige *sunk off Spain's northwest coast, spilling millions of gallons of fuel. María Luisa García Fernández, a 15-year Vigo resident, reflects on the spill.*

LG: Did the spill, which you call *"el chapapote"* [crackers], spread to Vigo and the Islas Cíes?

A: Yes, it did. It was a lot of work. Now everything is just about clean, although every once in a while you find *"galletas de chapapote"* [oil crackers]. *"Galletas de chapapote,"* not for eating.

LG: What are *"galletas,"* if not for eating?

A: *"Galletas"* are small stains of fuel that leaked from the *Prestige*. The big ones are removed by machine, but the little ones, which are the *"galletas,"* stay hidden.

LG: There are t-shirts all over Vigo that say *"nunca máis."* Why?

A: "*'Nunca máis'* means that this will not happen again and that we want this neither in Vigo, nor in Galicia, nor in any of Spain, because it is very bad for all of us who live here, particularly those who make a living by fishing. This has affected them significantly. Even though they've received tons of help, they've lost a great deal. They can't go fishing anymore; they can't work. Nunca Máis is an association that was founded after the spill to help those who were affected and to take political action to ensure that a spill like this never happens again."

Av. de Madrid. Eventually, a right on Gran Vía at Pr. de España leads to the intersection with R. Urzáiz. It's easier to take the R4, 7, 12a, or 12b bus from Av. de Madrid in front of the bus station to Gran Vía, R. Urzáiz, or R. Colón (€0.80).

Tourist Office: R. Cánovas de Castillo, s/n (☎986 43 05 77). From the train station, turn right on R. Urzáiz and follow it to R. Colón; veer right. When R. Colón reaches the water, turn left onto R. de Montero Ríos. The office is on the left as the street changes to R. Cánovas de Castillo and curves left. English spoken. Open June-Sept. M-F 9:30am-2pm and 4:30-6:30pm, Sa-Su 9:30am-2pm; Oct.-May M-F 9:30am-2pm and 4:30-6:30pm, Sa 10am-noon.

Currency Exchange: Banco Santander Central Hispano, R. Urzáiz, 20 (☎902 24 24 24). Open Apr.-Sept. M-F 8:30am-2:30pm; Oct.-Mar. M-F 8:30am-2:30pm, Sa 8:30am-1pm.

Luggage Storage: At the **train station** (€3). Open daily 7am-9:45pm. Luggage check-in at the **bus station** (€2.40). Open M-F 9:30am-1:30pm and 3-7pm, Sa 9am-2pm.

Emergency: ☎112. **Police:** Pr. do Rei, s/n (☎986 43 22 11).

Late-Night Pharmacy: C. del Príncipe, 27, left off R. Urzáiz just before it turns into R. Colón. Open daily 9am-1pm and 4-7pm.

Medical Assistance: Hospital Xeral, R. Pizarro, 22 (☎986 81 60 00). **Ambulances:** ☎061, 986 41 62 26, 34 42 29, or 81 60 62.

Internet Access: CiberStation (☎986 22 36 35), Pta. do Sol, across the street from the end of C. del Príncipe. €1.80 per hr. Open daily 10am-1am.

Post Office: Pr. de Compostela, 3 (☎986 43 81 44), a left off R. Colón. **Lista de Correos** and **fax.** Open M-F 8:30am-8:30pm, Sa 9:30am-2pm. Also a **branch** in the basement of El Corte Inglés on Gran Vía.

Postal Code: 36201.

♖ ACCOMMODATIONS

Vigo's inexpensive rooms make the city a logical base for exploring surrounding areas. Most accommodations are clustered in the area around the train station on R. Alfonso XIII (to the right upon exiting the train station) and its side streets.

Hostal Ría de Vigo, R. Cervantes, 14 (☎986 43 72 40), a left off R. Alfonso XIII 4 blocks from the station. Cheerful rooms with private bathrooms, TVs, and balconies overlooking busy R. Cervantes. Check-out 11am. Singles €15; doubles €18.20. Cash only. ❷

Hostal Atlántico, Av. García Barbón, 35 (☎986 22 05 30). From the train station follow R. Alfonso XIII to Av. García Barbón. In a central location near the *casco antiguo,* Hostal Atlántico offers spacious rooms, with comfortable beds, TV, bath, A/C, and phone. Singles €38; doubles €48; triples €60. ❹

Hospedaje La Estrella, C. Martín Codax, 5 (☎986 22 50 35), a left off R. Alfonso XIII, 3 blocks down from the station. Unadorned but large rooms complete with TVs and clean, large bathrooms. Singles €18, with bath €25; doubles €30. ❷

Hotel Celta, C. México, 22 (☎986 41 46 99; fax 48 06 56). From the train station, walk up the stairs to R. Urzáiz and make a right; the first street on your left is C. México. In the center of a restaurant area. Private baths, phone, TVs, and friendly service. July-Sept. singles €38; doubles €48. Oct.-June €32/€45. ❹

GALICIA

🄵 FOOD

Gran Vía and C. Venezuela, four streets uphill from R. Urzáiz off Gran Vía, are brimming with bright *cafeterías* and *terrazas.* Many restaurants lie around the As Avenidas boardwalk by the water, near the more touristy area of the *casco viejo.* For 24hr. cheap hot food or dessert visit **Ecos Cafetería ❶,** R.Urzáiz, 35. For groceries, hit **Supermercado Froiz,** R. do Uruguai, 14. (Open M-Sa 9am-2pm and 5-9pm.)

Cafetería El Coral, on the corner of C. Ecuador and C. Cuba (☎986 41 07 19). From R. Urzáiz, take a left onto Gran Vía and a left again on C. Ecuador. Whether you want an early breakfast or a cheap dinner, El Coral is the place for *cocina gallega.* Entrees €4.50-6; 3-course *menú* €6. Open daily 6:30am-midnight. ❶

Restaurante Curcuma Vegetariano, C. Brasil, 4 (☎986 41 11 27). Serves immense portions of Mediterranean vegetarian dishes like *mousakka* and couscous. Entrees €5-6. Open M-Sa 1-4pm and 8pm-midnight. MC/V. ❶

Tapas Areal, C. México, 36 (☎986 41 86 43). A typical Spanish *tapería* specializing in fish and seafood. Delicious food and a broad selection of wines in a very traditional, dark-paneled setting. Entrees €3-10; *tapas* from €2.50. Open daily 1pm-12:30am. ❷

El Capitán, C. Triunfo, 5 (☎986 22 09 40), off Pr. de la Princesa. In a simple, straightforward dining area, choose from several popular fish specialties (€9-30), including *lubina a la sal* (sea bass in salt) and *besugo* (sea bream). Also has many *tapas* and beef dishes (€8-11) and a fine selection of wine. Open daily 1pm-late. MC/V. ❸

🄹 ENTERTAINMENT

Watch for the magical **Fiesta de San Juan (Xuan)** on June 23, when neighborhoods light huge cauldrons of *aguardiente* (firewater) to make an infusion called *la queimada.* The potent potable consists of *aguardiente,* coffee, lemon, and sugar; the sweet mixture is passed around for all to drink and revel in traditional song while dancing among bonfires on the beach. In honor of its past as a haven for witches, Vigo also hosts **Expomagia,** a celebration of the occult. The festival, which occurs somewhat irregularly, generally happens sometime from May to June.

🄼 NIGHTLIFE

There isn't much to see or do in Vigo besides party. Starting in the late afternoon, students pack the *casco antiguo,* where cafes, bars, and discos abound. The area around **Rúa Areal** and **Rúa Concepción Arenal** is jam-packed with discos, nightclubs, and bars playing the latest Spanish hits for trendy 20-somethings. The area around the train station—R. Cervantes, R. Lepanto, and R. Churruca, in particular—is filled with trendsetting bars and clubs. For the latest hotspots, check the posters hanging around town advertising discos and techno music.

Black Ball, R. Churruca, 8. The perfect bar for anyone who longs for the feathered hair and leisure suits of the 70s. With an incredible collection of vintage kitsch and groovin' music from the likes of James, Jimi, and Janis, Black Ball offers a great atmosphere and cheap mixed drinks (€2.50) to start the night. Open daily 11pm-4am.

Posada de las Almas, Pr. de Compostela, 19. A luscious mix of medieval castle and theater, this club with red silk and velvet curtains and crystal chandeliers attracts a chic crowd in its 30s. Mostly pop. Drinks €6. Open Su-W 6pm-3am, Th-Sa 6pm-4:30am.

La Bola de Cristal, R. Churruca, 12. Like its neighbor Black Ball, La Bola de Cristal specializes in the 1970s. Come for the retro decor; stay for the funk and disco. A mixed-age crowd dances to the beat of The Jackson 5 and Gloria Gaynor. Open daily 11pm-4am.

20th Century Rock American Classic Bar, R. Areal, 18. A bar and Americana museum. With a full-size Cadillac, Harley Davidson motorcycle, and the Statue of Liberty adorning its halls, your beer (€3) or mixed drink (€5) is only an excuse to gaze at the collection. Open Su-Th 7pm-2am, F-Sa 7pm-3:30am.

Versus, R. Areal, 22. Break out your most stylish ensemble for this upscale club. The numerous video screens and dim lighting create a decadent techno-minimalist ambience. The latest pop songs get well-dressed crowds moving as they sip their €6 drinks.

VIP, R. Areal, 20. Frequented by scooter-riding teens sporting tight tops and dark sunglasses, VIP is a mecca of techno music. Different DJs perform nightly in this 2-story club. Open Th-Sa midnight-10am, although doors close at 5:30am.

El 7-4, R. Areal, 74. An energetic place where hetero- and homosexuals alike dance to funk and groove. Open M-Sa midnight-3am.

⚡ DAYTRIPS FROM VIGO

■ ISLAS CÍES (ILLAS CÍES)

Four ferries per day (sometimes more in nice weather) make the 14km trip to and from the islands. Though fairly expensive, the trip is worth it. 40min.; daily June-Sept., Sa-Su only the rest of the year; departs 11am, 1, 5, and 7pm; returns noon, 2, 6, and 8pm; round-trip €14.50, children under 12 free. Ferries usually fill quickly, so buy tickets in advance.

The Romans called them the "Islands of the Gods," and one can hardly doubt that Jupiter had at least a villa in the Islas Cíes. Guarding the mouth of the Ría de Vigo, the three islands—**Illa de Monte Agudo** or del Norte, **Illa do Medio** or del Faro, and **Illa do Sur** or de San Martiño—offer irresistible beaches and cliffside hiking trails for travelers. The islands (pop. 8) were declared a natural park in 1980; only 2200 people are allowed in per day, ensuring wide stretches of uncrowded beach. **Playa de Figueiras** and **Playa de Rodas** gleam with fine sand and sheltered waters. For smaller, wavier, and more secluded spots, walk along the trail beyond Playa de Figueiras, which leads to a plethora of coves and rocky lookouts. A 4km hike to the left of the dock on the main "road" leads to a bird conservatory, two lighthouses, and breathtaking views. On the same trail is a campsite, a restaurant, and a supermarket that sells bottles of water, which will come in handy once you get to *o faro grande* (the big lighthouse). Watch out for territorial seagulls that dive-bomb hikers walking too close to the birds' spotted chicks.

After the last ferry leaves for Vigo, **camp ❶** overnight on the island. Facilities include a small market, bar, bathrooms, and hot water showers. (Reservations ☎986 43 83 58, reception 68 76 30, fax 44 72 04. Open daily *Semana Santa* and June-Sept. 8:30am-1pm and 2:30-7pm. Camping €5.70 per person, ages 3-12 €4.20; individual tent €5.70, family tent €7. IVA not included). Before leaving Vigo, get a "Tarjeta de Acampado" in the **Camping Office** at the Estación Marítima.

CANGAS

Ferries run from Estación Ría (☎986 22 52 72) in Vigo to Cangas (20min.; M-F every 30min. 6:30am-10:30pm, Sa-Su every hr. 6:30am-10:30pm; round-trip €3.20). From Cangas, an equal number return (M-F every 30min. 6am-10pm, Sa-Su every hr. 6am-10pm).

Just across the bay from Vigo, tiny Cangas's main draw is its placid, nearly deserted beach, **Praia de Rodeira.** With your back to the ferry terminal, turn right onto Po. Marítimo, the pedestrian waterside walkway, which brings you to the beach (10min.). The cobalt waters here are virtually waveless, perfect for actual swimming. While there are no snack bars near the beach, restaurants lurk near the ferry station. The most popular is undoubtedly **Restaurante-Bar Celta ❷,** R. Alfredo Saralegui, 28, which serves endless seafood *tapas* to the hungry hordes gathered at long tables along the street. With your back to the ferry terminal, cross the street and head up the stairs to your left; the restaurant is at the top. (*Tapas* €0.75-9.50. Fish entrees €5-10. Open daily 10am-midnight.) On Fridays, Cangas attracts crowds from surrounding towns for its extravagant **market** in the harborside gardens immediately to the left of the ferry terminal.

LA GUARDIA (A GUARDA)

Buses from Vigo (1½hr., every 30min. 7:30am-9pm, €4.20) stop in La Guardia at the corner of C. Domínguez Fontela and C. Concepción Arenal. Bus office open daily 9am-9pm.

Between the mouth of the Río Miño and the Atlantic Ocean, La Guardia (pop. 10,000) thrives on an active fishing industry and the 500,000 tourists who descend annually on its little beach and large mountain. The town itself is a sleepy, pastel-colored maze overlooking a bay; most visitors skip the town and head instead to its majestic **Monte Santa Tecla.** From the bus stop, turn right onto C. Domínguez Fontela and then right onto C. José Antonio. From C. José Antonio, bear right uphill onto C. Rosalía de Castro, which continues to the top (6km). Alternatively, 5min. up the road, take the steps off to the left that mark the start of a shorter, steeper pedestrian pathway through the woods (3km). Three-quarters of the way up the mountain lies the highlight of the climb: the ruins of a **Celtic castle.** The interlocking circles of the foundations of this ancient fortress village overlook frothy seas, moss-laden mountains, and the glimmer of La Guardia below. Near the peak is a **chapel** dedicated to Santa Tecla, the patron saint of headaches and heart disease. Cured worshippers gave the wax body parts inside (hearts, heads, and feet) as gifts to Santa Tecla. To reach the beach from the bus station, turn right onto C. Domínguez Fontela, right onto C. José Antonio, and follow the signs.

TÚY (TUI)

An ATSA bus (☎986 61 02 55) from Vigo stops on C. Calvo Sotelo at Hostal Generosa and returns from the other side of the street (45min., every 30min. 7:30am-9pm, €2.90).

While the medieval border town of Túy (pop. 16,000) offers the novel opportunity to walk into Portugal, it's more notable for its beautiful *casco antiguo* and its views of the Río Miño valley and Portugal. The centerpiece of the old city is the **cathedral;** constructed in 1120, it was the first Gothic structure in Iberia. It now houses the relics of San Telmo, patron saint of sailors, and boasts an impressive organ. One ticket gets you into both the cathedral and the **Museo Diocesano.** (Museo Diocesano ☎986 60 36 00. Cathedral and museum open daily July-Aug. 9am-9pm; Sept.-Dec. 9:30am-1:30pm and 4-8pm; Dec.-May 9:30am-1:30pm and 4-7pm. €2.40.) A 1km metal walkway over the Río Miño extends to Portugal's Valença do Minho (see p. 747). To get to the **tourist office** on Puente

Tripe, s/n, follow Av. de Portugal from **El Puente Internacional** until you approach the little wooden cottage on your left. (☎986 60 17 89. Open July-Sept. daily 9:30am-2pm and 4:30-8pm; Oct.-June M-F 9:30am-1:30pm and 4-6pm.)

BAYONA (BAIONA)

ATSA buses run to Vigo (50min.; every 30min. M-Sa 7am-10pm, Su 8am-11pm; €1.85).

Bayona (pop. 10,000) was the first Iberian town to receive word of the New World when Columbus returned to port in March 1493. The town even boasts a reconstructed version of the famous globe-trotting ship **La Caravela Pinta** in the harbor and reenacts the landing every March. (Open M-Tu and Th-Su 10am-8:30pm. €0.75.) While the ship is Bayona's main historic attraction, most visitors sail straight to its blustery Atlantic beaches, where brightly colored fishing boats bob offshore and only the bravest dare to swim in the icy blue waves. The golden sand, however, is perfect for lounging among myriad other sun worshipers. The 2km pedestrian Po. Alfonso IX loops around the grounds along the shore. As you get off the bus, walk along Po. Alfonso IX to your right to get to sandy and boat-free **Praia Santa Marta** and **Praia Ladeira**. To your left, the path will take you to the rocky and shell-filled **Praia de los Frailes** and **Praia Cruncheira**. The path also leads to the grounds of the 16th-century **Fortress of Monte Real**, now a *parador nacional*, which stands just above the beaches. The fortress is a perfect place to explore if you get bored of the beach.

PONTEVEDRA ☎986

According to legend, Pontevedra (pop. 80,000) was founded by the Greek archer Teucro as a place to convalesce after his Trojan War exploits. Today, it continues the tradition of providing a place to crash by offering reasonably priced beds for visitors flitting about the various high-priced coastal towns. Although it makes a good base, Pontevedra on the whole is not the most interesting town, and the new city is a bit of an eyesore. The old city, however—filled with palm trees, flowering balconies, stately cathedrals, and squares lined with traditional arcaded *gallego* buildings—is pleasant and inviting, making for a surprisingly enjoyable stay.

■ TRANSPORTATION

Trains: Av. Alféreces Provisionales, s/n (☎902 24 02 02), a 20min. walk southeast of the old city. Info open daily 6am-11pm. To: **La Coruña** (3hr.; M-F 11 per day 6:16am-7:12pm, Sa-Su 9 per day 6:16am-9:21pm; €7.20, express €9.10); **Madrid** (11hr.; 2 per day Su-F 12:35 and 9:30pm, Sa 8:45am and 9:30pm; €38.50); **Santiago** (1½hr.; M-F 14 per day 6:16am-10:14pm, Sa 7 per day 6:16am-7:12pm, Su 11 per day 6:16am-10:14pm; €3.25-4.15); **Vigo** (20min.; M-F 14 per day 7:40am-10:56pm, Sa 12 per day 7:40am-10:56pm, Su 11 per day 8:55am-10:56pm; €1:45-2.10).

Buses: Av. Alféreces Provisionales, s/n (☎986 85 24 08). Info open daily 9am-9:30pm. To: **Cambados** (1hr.; M-F 11 per day 8:30am-8:30pm, Sa 9 per day 11:15am-8:30pm, Su 3 per day 12:30, 5:30, 8:30pm; €1.90); **La Coruña** (2½hr.; daily 9 per day 7am-9pm; €9.15); **El Grove/La Toja** (1hr., every 30min. 7:45am-10pm, €3.15); **Madrid** (8hr., 6 per day 9am-11pm, €27.87); **Santiago** (1hr.; daily every hr. 7am-9pm; €5); **Vigo** (1hr.; M-F every 30min. 8am-9:30pm, Sa-Su every hr. 8am-8pm; €4.95).

Taxis: Radio Taxi (24hr. ☎986 85 12 85). €2.40 from the stations to town.

Car Rental: Avis, R. da Peregrina, 49 (☎986 85 20 25). €80 per day for 350km. Ages 23-25 add €10 per day for insurance. Discounts for longer rentals. 23+, must have had license for at least 1yr. Open M-F 9am-1:15pm and 4-7pm, Sa 9am-12:45pm.

☒ ⓘ ORIENTATION & PRACTICAL INFORMATION

Six streets radiate out from **Praza da Peregrina,** the main plaza connecting the new and old cities. The main streets are R. Oliva, R. Michelena, R. Benito Corbal, and R. da Peregrina. **Praza de Galicia** is a 5min. walk from Pr. de la Peregrina; from Pr. da Peregrina, head down R. da Peregrina and veer right at the first fork onto R. Andrés Muruais. The **train** and **bus stations,** located across from each other, are about 1km from the old city. To get to the city center, turn left onto Av. Calvo Sotelo from the bus station entrance; from the train station, walk straight out onto Av. Calvo Sotelo after crossing the highway. Continue on Av. Calvo Sotelo for 10-15min. as it changes to the one-way Av. de Vigo and then R. da Peregrina before depositing you in Pr. da Peregrina.

Tourist Office: R. General Mola, 3 (☎986 85 08 14). From Pr. da Peregrina, get on R. Michelena and take the 1st left onto R. General Mola. English spoken. **Branch** in a hut on Pr. de España. Both open June-Aug. M-F 10am-2pm and 5-7:30pm, Sa 10am-2pm and 4-6pm, Su 10am-2pm and 5-6:30pm; main office also open Sept.-May M-F 10am-2pm and 4-6pm, Sa 10am-12:30pm.

Currency Exchange: Banco Santander Central Hispano, Pr. da Peregrina, 5 (☎986 85 42 16). Open M-F 8:30am-2pm, Sa 8:30am-1pm. 24hr. ATM outside.

Bookstore: Librería Michelena, R. Michelena, 22 (☎986 85 87 46). Selection of books in English in back. Open M-F 9am-1pm and 4:30-8:30pm, Sa 9am-1pm. MC/V.

Emergency: ☎112. **Police:** C. Joaquín Costa, 19 (☎091 or 986 85 38 00).

Pharmacy: R. da Peregrina, 3. Open daily 9am-1pm and 4-8pm.

Hospital: Hospital Provincial, R. del Doutor Loureiro Crespo, 2 (☎061 or 986 85 21 15).

Internet Access: Ciber Las Ruinas, R. del Marqués de Riestra, 21, 2nd fl. (☎986 86 63 25), just off Pr. de España. €1.50 per hr. Open M-F 10am-2:30pm and 5pm-1:30am, Sa 11am-2:30pm and 4pm-1:30am, Su 5pm-1:30am; open until 2am if crowded.

Post Office: R. Oliva, 21 (☎986 84 48 64). **Lista de Correos** and **fax service** available. Open M-F 8:30am-8:30pm, Sa 9:30am-2pm. **Postal Code:** 36001.

⌂ ACCOMMODATIONS

Hotels and hostels are not particularly abundant in Pontevedra, and hostels with private baths are especially hard to come by. Reservations are necessary in August, when Spaniards head to coastal towns and cities.

Casa Maruja, Av. de Santa María, 12 (☎986 85 49 01). From Pr. da Peregrina, walk up R. Michelena through Pr. de España, and turn right onto R. Mestre Mateo. Av. de Santa María will be on the right. Most of the small, homey rooms in this family-run *pensión* have pleasant views with big windows. All have private bath, TV, and winter heat. July-Aug. singles €18; doubles €37; triples €40. Sept.-June €12-16/€25/€30. ❷

Hotel México, R. de Andrés Muruais, 10 (☎986 85 90 06; fax 84 59 39). Follow the directions from the stations (see above), but turn left onto R. de Andrés Muruais before you reach Pr. da Peregrina. Carpeted rooms, laundry service, TV, winter heat, elevator, and a cafeteria. Singles €25-32; doubles €33-49. MC/V. ❸

GALICIA

Casa del Barón-Parador, C. Barón, 19 (☎986 85 58 00; fax 85 21 95), in the *casco antiguo*. The hotel has a beautiful terrace, reading room, bar, and restaurant. Soothingly huge rooms have cable TV, winter heat, A/C, minibar, safe, and phone. Access to windsurfing, horseback riding, and rafting. Rooms €94.24-€109.96. Oct.-June, ages 20-30 €37.70 per person per night in a standard double, breakfast buffet included. Must reserve in advance. AmEx/MC/V. ❹

Hospedaje Penelas, R. Alta, 17 (☎986 85 57 05). Wonderful location close to bars and clubs. One double has a great view of the old city and part of the countryside. Spacious though unadorned rooms with common baths. Singles €13-18; doubles €20-30. ❶

Casa Alicia, Av. de Santa María, 5, 1st fl. (☎986 85 70 79). From Pr. da Peregrina, walk up R. Michelena through Pr. de España, and turn right onto R. Mestre Mateo. Av. de Santa María will be on the right. Small rooms amidst a collection of family photos. Winter heating, hall bathrooms. Doubles €18-21; quads €27. ❷

FOOD

Pontevedra prides itself on seafood. In the evenings, locals crowd tiny bars in the streets around Pr. da Peregrina. C. Figueroa, Pr. da Leña, and C. San Sebastián harbor some of the most popular *marisquerías* and *tapas* bars. For groceries, try **Supermercado Gadis**, C. Benito Corbal, 34. (Open M-Sa 9am-2pm and 5-9pm.)

Bodegón Micota, R. da Peregrina, 4 (☎986 85 59 17). This basement *bodega* serves Spanish takes on global classics like *fajitas* (€7.70), shishkabobs (€9-14), and fondue (€11-14). Also has a good selection of salads (€4-7). *Menú del día* €6.70. Open daily noon-4:30pm and 8pm-1am. ❷

La Algueria Mudejar, C. Churruchaos, 2 (☎986 851 258). On the other side of the Ayuntamiento from Pr. de España. Enjoy fresh food that is a fusion of Spanish elements and Arab art in a warm, welcoming atmosphere. If not the *menú del día* (€7.15), then try one of the special house dishes (€7-21). Open daily noon-4pm and 7:30pm-late; Su open evenings only. MC/V. ❸

Mesón La Peregrina, R. da Peregrina, 16 (☎986 86 27 50). This *restaurante típico* specializes in seafood. Try the 3-course *menú* (€9) or any of the delicious seafood entrees (€4-13). Opens daily 1-4pm and 8pm-midnight. MC/V. ❷

SIGHTS

Pontevedra's primary sight is the extensive **Museo Provincial**, with exhibits covering everything from traditional Galician cooking to contemporary art. (R. Pasantería, 10. From Pr. da Peregrina, walk up Po. de Antonio Odriozola, which runs between the gardens and Pr. da Ferrería; this eventually curves into R. Pasantería and leads to the museum off Pr. da Leña. ☎986 85 14 55. Open June-Sept. Tu-Sa 10am-2:15pm and 5-8:45pm, Su 11am-2pm; Oct.-May daily 10am-1:30pm and 4:30-8pm. €3, EU members free.) In Pr. de España sit the 13th-century Gothic **ruinas de Santo Domingo**. With moss-encrusted sepulchres and the sun filtering through cracks in what remains of the structure, the ruins are an eerie glimpse into the past in the midst of the new city. (Open June 1-Sept. 30 Tu-F 10am-2pm. Free.) The **Basílica de Santa María a Maior** features a golden Plateresque door constructed in the 16th century depicting several sculptures of Mary; at night, it's illuminated by flood-lights. (From Pr. de España take Av. de Santa María, to the left of the Ayuntamiento. ☎986 86 61 85. Open daily 10am-1pm and 5-9pm.) Don't miss the facade of the **Santuario de la Virgen Peregrina** in Pr. da Peregrina. This uniquely shaped Baroque church looks incredibly light.

🎵 🔍 ENTERTAINMENT & FESTIVALS

Sunny days bring a crowd to the white-sand **beaches** of nearby Marín. Monbus buses make the journey from the outer corner of Pr. de Galicia on Av. Augusto García Sánchez (30min., every 15min., €0.90). From the bus stop in Marín, facing the water, head left on C. Angusto Miranda around the track and up the hill. To reach **Playa Porticelo,** turn right on C. Tiro Naval Janer, continue for 15min., and bear right when the road splits. Another 10min. brings you to the larger **Playa Mogor.** The festivals of **Santiaguiño del Burgo** (July 25) and **La Peregrina** (the 2nd week of August, peaking on Sunday) bring city-wide celebration and bullfights.

At night, find bar after pub after *tapería* on the triangle of streets made by R. Princesa, R. Paio Gómez Charino, and R. Tetuán. A popular place among residents of all ages is **Café Teatro,** R. Michelena, 11, a karaoke bar complete with stage and comfy-couch audience seating. (Open daily 10pm-6am.)

🔁 DAYTRIPS FROM PONTEVEDRA

The following towns are perfect daytrips from Pontevedra, as the Monbus lines run often. The towns can also be reached easily from Santiago de Compostela.

🏛 CAMBADOS

26km from Pontevedra. Plus Ultra buses run from Pontevedra to the bus station in Cambados near Pr. Concello (1hr.; M-F 11 per day 8:30am-8:30pm, Sa 6 per day 11:15am-8:30pm, Su 3 per day 12:30, 5:30, 8:30pm; €2.40). Check return schedule at the bus station bar.

Offering a precious glimpse of small-town life and a glass of renowned *albariño* wine, harborside Cambados (pop. 14,000) makes for a quiet daytrip from Pontevedra. The lack of a beach has left Cambados out of the tourist loop; however, the resulting isolation adds to the town's charm, as do its enchanting sights.

Conveniently, all of the sights can be visited in a simple loop-route. Follow your nose to the **Palacio de Fefiñanes,** an attractive 16th-century palace-turned-*bodega* that brims with giant, sweet-smelling barrels of *albariño*. From the tourist office, walk away from the bus station along the tree-covered Po. da Calzada. At the walkway's end, walk up the street on the right, R. Príncipe, lined with stores selling *albariño* at bargain prices. At the street end, turn left onto R. Real, which leads into Pr. de Fefiñanes,

ON THE MENU

KING OF THE WHITES

Like many kings, it is short-lived, inbred, and gets drunk young. It has thousands of devotees who espouse its charm, grace, and taste. Indeed, since its ascension in the 1980s, after wine producers in Galicia shifted their attention to this difficult-to-grow grape, *El Albariño* has become king of Spanish white wines, transforming Galicia's hillsides forever.

The mild temperatures and high rainfall in Galicia have always hampered attempts at growing red wine grapes. However, the sturdy, rot-resistant *albariño* grape thrives in Galicia. Not only is it well-suited to the climate, but its wine, light, with a distinctive perfume and crisp taste, perfectly compliments the region's celebrated seafood. Thanks to the popularity of *albariño*, which is considered the best white wine in Spain and one of the best in the world, wine production is now Galicia's fastest growing industry.

The controversy over *albariño's* bloodlines only adds to its royal mystique. Some claim French monks brought it to Santiago during the 12th- and 13th-century crusades, further asserting that *albariño* is genetically linked to Germany's Riesling grape. However, locals hold steadfastly to the explanation that *albariño* is indigenous to Galicia. No matter what region gave birth to the grape, the Rías Baixas are now the uncontested parents of the regal wine.

crowned by the palace. The mouth-watering 15th-century *bodega* and hotel **Pazo A Capitana** is a short walk from the palace. Its hanging vines, patio fountains, and wine cellars merit, if not a couple of nights, at least a couple of minutes. From Pr. de Fefiñanes, return down R. Real and continue until its end. Turn left up Av. de Vilariño, right on R. Barcelona, and left onto R. Sabugueiro at the street end. (☎986 54 32 10. Open for visits daily 11am-1pm and 4-8pm.) On a quiet hill 10min. away, watching over the town cemetery, lie the beautiful ruins of the **Iglesia Santa Mariña.** From Pazo A Capitana, return down R. Sabugueiro. At the four-way intersection turn left and continue until the street end. The church is up on the left. Walk up the wide, flat stairs just behind it to a *mirador* with a view of the *ría*, including El Grove and La Toja. Just below the church is the new **Museo Etnográfico a do Viño,** Galicia's first wine museum. (☎986 52 61 19. Open Tu-Su 10am-2pm and 4:30-7:30pm). For a second privileged view of the *ría*, walk straight down Po. os Olmos (on the right facing the museum gate), cross the main street, and continue walking through the oldest, most tangled and worn-in section of town until you hit the water and see the **Torre de San Sadorniño.** The remains of this 12th-century fortification stand on a seemingly dissolving island connected to mainland by a tiny bridge. The first Sunday in August brings in famous poets and politicians for the town's well-known **wine festival.** Its shining star, of course, is the *albariño*, whose vines peek out from backyard fences and porch rooftops throughout Cambados.

Visitors may find it helpful to start at the **tourist office** to get a map. With your back to the bus station and the water, walk left. The office, a small cabin-like building, will be on your left. Inquire here about *La Ruta del Vino* (Wine Route) if you have a car. (☎986 52 07 86. Open M-Sa 10am-1:30pm and 4:30-7:30pm.)

EL GROVE (O GROVE) & LA TOJA (A TOXA)

Monbus (☎902 15 87 78) runs buses from Pontevedra to El Grove (1hr.; June-Sept. every hr. 7:45am-10pm, fewer in winter; €3.15); an equal number return (every hr. 6:30am-9pm). Buses also run from Santiago. Buses run from El Grove to Cambados (30min.; daily 7 per day 6:50am-6:15pm, €0.80). Schedules are posted in the El Grove bus station.

Every July and August, affluent Europeans come in Land Rovers and BMWs to the fishing town of El Grove (pop.14,000) and its swanky island partner, La Toja. Sea-saturated El Grove, on a tranquil strait west of Pontevedra, is lined with mussel farms, colorful boats, and clam-diggers. Even though there's no beach in town and few on-the-water activities, the waterfront is the main attraction; from here, tourists gawk at fishermen bringing their catches to the local restaurants and peruse the wares at the Friday morning market. The **tourist office** has plenty of information on boat rides, free bike rentals, sea museums, beaches, La Toja, and the town's popular October seafood festival; the office also offers free posters. With your back to the main entrance of the bus station, walk right, following the water. The tourist office is in a small log-cabin-like building among ice cream and snack stands. (☎986 73 14 15. Open June-Aug. M-Sa 10am-2pm and 4-9pm and Su 11am-2pm; Sept-May same hours but closed Su.)

LA LANZADA

Monbuses (☎902 15 87 78) en route to El Grove stop at La Lanzada (50min; June-Aug. every hr. 7:45am-10pm, €3).

Ten kilometers toward Pontevedra from El Grove, La Lanzada—arguably the best beach in Galicia—seduces bathers with its fine white sands and irresistible waves. This mile-long beach is protected by a dunes and rocky promontories jutting into sea. While most bathers come to relax and lounge beside the Atlantic, quite a few come seeking the elusive "Ninth Wave"; according to pagan legend, women who swim in exactly nine waves at moonlight will forever be cured of infertility.

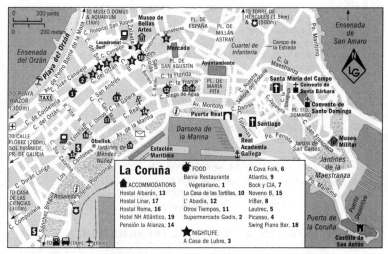

La Coruña

ACCOMMODATIONS
Hostal Albarán, 13
Hostal Linar, 17
Hostal Roma, 16
Hotel NH Atlántico, 19
Pensión la Alianza, 14

★ **FOOD**
Bania Restaurante
Vegetariano, 1
La Casa de las Tortillas, 10
L' Abadía, 12
Otros Tiempos, 11
Supermercado Gadis, 2

A Cova Folk, 6
Atlantis, 9
Bock y CIA, 7
Noveno B, 15
IriBar, 8
Lautrec, 5
Picasso, 4
Swing Piano Bar, 18

★ **NIGHTLIFE**
A Casa de Lubre, 3

RÍAS ALTAS

Thick fogs and misty mornings have kept the Rías Altas secret from most visitors. With the exception of La Coruña, the area's busy capital, the Rías Altas seem to have been nearly forgotten, and that's the very reason to visit: isolated highways and the tiniest of coastal towns mean that the visitors who actually make it here have miles of green estuaries and secluded beaches all to themselves.

LA CORUÑA (A CORUÑA)   ☎981

Unlike most of its Galician neighbors, La Coruña (pop. 255,000) is a big city, complete with highrises, expressways, and urban sprawl. Somehow, though, La Coruña manages to preserve the feel of an old-time fishing port. The center is a maze of tangled, narrow alleys, teeming with raucous bars and popular *marisquerías* (seafood restaurants). The harborside walks echo with Galician legend and lore: Greek hero Hercules supposedly built the lighthouse, and the city's nickname, the Crystal City, was earned for the blinding effect of sunset on its rows of tightly-packed windows. As any proud *coruñese* will tell you, Santiago might be the northwest's most popular city, but La Coruña is the *real* Galicia.

▐ TRANSPORTATION

Flights: Aeropuerto de Alvedro (☎981 18 72 00), 9km south. Served by **Air Europa** (☎981 18 73 08), **ERA** (☎981 18 72 86), and **Iberia** (☎981 18 72 59). Daily charters to **Paris** via **Barcelona** and **London.**

Trains: Estación San Cristóbal, Pr. San Cristóbal, s/n (☎902 24 02 02). Info open daily 7am-11pm. To: **Barcelona** (15-16hr.; 2 per day 7:10am, 6:05pm; €39.50-50); **Madrid** (8½-11hr.; Su-F 2 per day 12:55, 10:22pm; Sa 1 per day 12:55pm; €38); **Santiago** (1hr.; M-F 20 per day 5:55am-10:01pm, Sa 13 per day 5:55am-9:20pm, Su 16 per day 5:55am-10:01pm; €3.88-18); **Vigo** via **Pontevedra** (2-3hr.; M-F 13 per day 6:15am-8:40pm, Sa 8 per day 8:25am-8:40pm, Su 10 per day 8:25am-8:40pm; €2.60-10).

Buses: C. de Caballeros, s/n (☎981 23 96 44 or 23 90 99).

ALSA/Enatcar (☎981 15 11 00 or 902 42 22 42) runs to: **Madrid** (8½hr.; 4-7 per day 5am-10:30pm; €33.20-47); **Oviedo** (4½-6¾hr.; 3 per day 9:30am, 5, 7pm; €21.21); **San Sebastián** (14hr.; 2 per day 9:30am, 6pm; €44.05) via **Santander** (10hr., €30.05).

Castromil (☎981 24 91 92 or 23 92 41) runs to: **Santiago** (50min.-1½hr.; M-F every hr. 7am-10pm, Sa-Su every hr. 8am-10pm; €5.85) and **Vigo** (2-2½hr.; M-F 9 per day 8am-8pm, Sa-Su 8 per day 8am-8pm; €12) via **Pontevedra** (1½-2hr., €10).

IASA-Arriva (☎981 23 90 01) runs to: **Betanzos** (40min.; M-F every 30min. 6:30am-10:30pm, Sa-Su 24 per day 6:30am-10:30pm; €1.80); **Ribadeo** (4hr.; M-F 5 per day, 8am-4pm, Sa 6 per day 8am-4pm, Su 2:15pm; €30.70); **Viveiro** via **Betanzos** and **El Ferrol** (3½hr.; M-Sa 6 per day 6:30am-7:30pm, Su 4 per day 6:30am-7:30pm; €11.30).

Public Transportation: Red **Compañía de Tranvías de la Coruña** buses (☎981 25 01 00) run frequently (7am-11:30pm; €0.80). Buy tickets onboard.

Taxis: Radio Taxi (☎981 24 33 33). **TeleTaxi** (☎981 28 77 77). Both 24hr. With the tourist office and ocean to the right, walk along the sidewalk to the taxi stand.

Car Rental: Autos Brea, Av. Fernández Latorre, 110 (☎981 23 86 45 or 689 53 94 86). 21+, must have had license for 1 year. From €30 per day with unlimited mileage. 3 day min. rental. Open M-F 9am-1pm and 4-7pm, Sa 9am-2pm.

✳🛈 ORIENTATION & PRACTICAL INFORMATION

La Coruña sits on a narrow peninsula between the Atlantic Ocean and the Ría de A Coruña. The new city stretches across the mainland; the peninsula contains the *ciudad vieja* (old city). Beaches are on the Atlantic side and the harbor is on the river. **Avenida de la Marina** runs along the harbor and leads past the tourist office and the obelisk to **Puerta Real,** the entry into **Plaza de María Pita** and the *ciudad vieja.* From the bus station, take bus #1 or 1a straight to the **tourist office** at the Puerta Real stop. To get from the train station to the *ciudad vieja,* take the city bus from the bus station. From the main entrance of the train station on Pr. San Cristóbal, cross the plaza and walk right on R. de Outeiro. Turn left onto R. Estaciones and follow the pedestrian paths over the highway. The bus station and stop for buses #1 and 1a are across the street from the base of the pedestrian stairs. Bus #14 connects the center with the museums and monuments along Po. Marítimo.

Tourist Office: Regional Office, Dársena de la Marina, s/n (☎/fax 981 22 18 22). English spoken. Ask about bike rentals and surfing lessons. Open M-F 10am-2pm and 4-7pm, Sa 11am-2pm and 5-7pm, Su 11am-2pm. **Turismo A Coruña,** Av. Alférez Provisional, s/n, Edificio Atalaya, 1st fl. (☎981 21 61 61). Open M-F 9am-2pm and 4-8pm.

Laundromat: Surf, C. Hospital, 35 (☎987 20 44 20) Wash and dry up to 6kg for €10. Open M-F 9:30am-1:30pm and 4:30-8pm.

Emergency: ☎061. **Police: Municipal,** C. Miguel Servet, s/n (☎981 18 42 25).

24hr. Pharmacy: Telefarmacia (☎981 56 09 92 or 902 13 41 34).

Medical Services: Ambulatorio San José, C. Comandante Fontanes, 8 (☎981 22 63 35). **Ambulance** ☎061.

Internet Access: Cyber, C. Zalaeta, 13 (☎981 20 38 41). Speedy connections €0.75 per 30min., €1.20 per hr. Open daily 10am-2am. **Estrella Park,** C. Estrella, 12. €0.50 per 20min. Open daily 11am-midnight.

Post Office: C. Alcalde Manuel Casas, s/n (☎902 19 71 97). **Lista de Correos** and **fax** service. Open M-F 8:30am-8:30pm, Sa 9:30am-2pm. **Postal Code:** 15001.

🛏 ACCOMMODATIONS

Most accommodations are located near the old city. Bed-hunters should head to C. Riego de Agua and R. Nueva. Reservations are necessary only in August during the city's month-long festival.

Hostal Roma, R. Nueva, 3 (☎981 22 80 75). Mingle with other guests in the common room, complete with TV and tables. Internet on 5 computers (€1 per hr.). Breakfast available. Reception 24hr. Singles €24-30; doubles €36-45. MC/V. ❸

Pensión la Alianza, C. Riego de Agua, 8, 1st fl. (☎981 22 81 14). Small but comfortable rooms in the *ciudad vieja*, with character and an owner to match. Be sure to request a room with a window. Spotless bathroom. Singles €15; doubles €27. ❷

Hostal Albarán, C. Riego de Agua, 14 (☎981 22 65 79). Small rooms with bath, TV, and winter heating. First-floor common room with sofas and a big screen TV. Singles €23-24; doubles €33-37. ❷

Hostal Linar, C. General Mola, 7 (☎981 22 78 37; fax 22 49 11). Sleep in comfort above Linar's Brazilian restaurant in rooms with bath, radio, phone, TV, and heating. July-Aug. singles €25; doubles €43. Sept.-June €21/€30. MC/V. ❷

Hotel NH Atlántico, Jardines de Méndez Núñez, s/n (☎981 22 65 00; fax 20 10 71). Atlántico has everything you need and more. Your stay will be a memorable experience, for both you and your checking account. Rooms €104 plus tax. AmEx/MC/V. ❺

G A L I C I A

⬛ FOOD

The streets around C. Estrella, C. de la Franja, and C. La Galera teem with cheap *marisquerías* and other restaurants. The area around Av. Rubine off Playa de Riazor is fancier. The **market** is in the oval building on Pr. San Agustín, near the old town. (Open M-Sa 8am-3pm.) For groceries, stop by **Supermercado Gadis,** C. del Orzán, 86. (☎981 21 62 63. Open daily 9am-9pm.)

La Casa de las Tortillas, C. del Orzán, 5 (☎981 22 67 18). In a warm, homey setting, La Casa offers dozens of creative varieties of *tortilla española* (€5-7) and salads (€2.50-6). Open Su-Th 8pm-12:30am, F-Sa 8pm-2am. ❶

Otros Tiempos—Cervecería-Jamonería, C. la Galera, 54 (☎981 22 93 98). Founded in 1914. The restaurant's vintage furniture is complemented by black-and-white movie stills, a mounted bull's head, and a lively clientele. Entrees €8-10. *Menú* €8.15. Wide selection of beer (€2-4). Open daily 11am-4pm and 7pm-12:30am. ❷

L'Abadía, C. Riego de Agua, 44 (☎981 22 97 02). A typical *taberna* with a wide variety of beers, *tapas*, sandwiches, and entrees. Huge dishes of meat and eggs accompany exotic salads including pineapple and bananas. Delicious food and reasonable prices. Entrees €4.65-6. Salads €5. Open daily 11am-1am, Th-Sa 11am-2am. ❶

Bania Restaurante Vegetariano, C. de Cordelería, 7 (☎981 22 13 01). Fresh, creative vegetarian cuisine served in a sunny environment. Immense salads €4.90-6.85. Entrees €4.85-7.80. Open M-Sa 1:30-4pm and 9-11:30pm. ❶

👁 SIGHTS

While La Coruña lacks many of the historic monuments of other towns, it has several phenomenal attractions along Po. Marítimo. To visit them all in one afternoon, start from Playa del Orzán and follow waterside Po. Marítimo to the major museums and Torre de Hércules. Trolleys also follow Po. Marítimo with stops at all the museums and the Torre. The route begins at the start of Po. Marítimo, near Puerta Real, and ends at Playa del Orzán. (Trolleys daily every 30 min. noon-9pm, €1.)

LAS TRES CASAS CORUÑESAS

A €7 bono ticket allows same-day admission to all three museums.

🐟**AQUARIUM FINISTERRAE.** Also known as the **Casa de los Peces,** this aquarium is La Coruña's magnificent homage to the sea. Over 200 species of local marine life are displayed in vast aquariums while the downstairs room features exhibitions on marine ecosystems the world over. Don't miss *Nautilus* in the basement. *(On Po.*

Marítimo at the bottom of the hill from the Torre de Hércules. Also reached by bus #14 from the Puerta Real. ☎981 22 72 72. Open July-Aug. daily 10am-9pm; Sept.-June M-Sa 10am-7pm, Su 10am-8pm. €6, children and seniors or with Carnet Joven €3.)

MUSEO DOMUS. The Domus, also called the **Casa del Hombre** (House of Man), is an anthropology, natural history, and science museum rolled into one, featuring interactive, high-tech exhibits on the human body and cultures. Watch "blood" spurt at 50km/h from a model heart; hear "Hello, I love you" in over 30 languages; and spend hours playing with microscopes, computers, and other gizmos. *(Santa Teresa, 1, on Po. Marítimo, between the Aquarium and Playa Orzán. ☎981 21 70 00. Open daily July-Aug. 11am-9pm; Sept.-June 10am-7pm. €2, children and seniors or with Carnet Jovem €1. IMAX supplement €1.20; check at ticket booth for schedule.)*

CASA DE LAS CIENCIAS. Casa de las Ciencias is an interactive science museum designed for kids to learn by doing rather than reading. This four-story building features a giant Foucault pendulum and a planetarium. *(Parque Sta. Margarita. ☎981 18 98 46; www.casaciencias.org. Open daily July-Aug. 10am-7pm; Sept.-June 11am-9pm. Casa €2, children and seniors €1. Planetarium €1; check show schedules.)*

OTHER SIGHTS

TORRE DE HÉRCULES. La Coruña's tourist magnet, the Torre de Hércules looms over rusted ships at the peninsula's end. The tower originally dates from the 2nd century, but was recently renovated. Legend has it that Hercules erected the tower, the world's oldest working lighthouse, upon the remains of his defeated enemy Geryon. The long climb to the top is rewarded with stunning views of the city and bay. *(On Po. Marítimo, a 20min. walk from Puerta Real. From C. Millán Astray, turn left onto C. de Orillamar, which turns into Av. de Navarra and brings you to the tower. Open July-Aug. Su-Th 10am-8:45pm, F-Sa 9am-11:45pm; Apr.-June and Sept. daily 10am-6:45pm; Oct.-Mar. daily 10am-5:45pm. €2, children and seniors €1.)*

MUSEO DE BELLAS ARTES. This museum displays classic Spanish, French, Italian, and Flemish art in a renovated convent; don't miss the Goya display. It also showcases the work of *gallego* artists. *(☎981 22 37 23. Open Tu-F 10am-8pm, Sa 10am-2pm and 4:30-8pm, Su 10am-2pm. €2.40.)*

MUSEO HISTORICO ARQUEOLÓGICO CASTILLO DE SAN ANTÓN. La Coruña flaunts its archaeological treasures here, with displays of Galician fortresses and artifacts from the Megalithic, Bronze, and Roman Ages. *(☎981 20 59 94. Open July-Aug. Tu-Sa 10am-7:30pm, Su 10am-2:30pm; Sept.-June Tu-Sa 10am-7pm, Su 10am-3pm. €2, children and seniors or with Carnet Joven €1.)*

BEACHES

La Coruña's best beaches are long, narrow **Playa de Riazor** and **Playa del Orzán**, which flank Po. Marítimo on the Atlantic side of the peninsula and are separated from one another only by a small walkway. On weekends, the sand along these calm waters is packed with bodies, but crowds thin out on weekdays. Small, secluded beaches, including **Playas del Matadero, de Las Amorosas,** and **das Lapas,** hide farther down Po. Marítimo, although these tend to be rockier and seaweedier.

FESTIVALS

The city's main festival is **Las Fiestas de María Pita,** which lasts the entire month of August. Party-hardy *coruñeses* spend the month celebrating with various concerts, parades, and a mock naval battle to honor María Pita, the woman who single-handedly rallied a defense against the invading army of Sir Francis Drake in 1589 after the town's men had fled the port in fear. Although it is celebrated in many parts of Europe, La Coruña greets **La Noche de San Juan** (June 23) with particular fervor since it coincides with the opening of sardine season. Locals light the traditional *aguardiente* bonfires before spending the night leaping over the flames and gorging on sardine flesh. Contrary to what you might assume, the rite is supposed to ensure fertility. If you drop an egg white in a glass of water on this night, it will supposedly assume the form of your future spouse's occupation.

NIGHTLIFE

In the early evening, *coruñeses* linger in Celtic pubs throughout the old city, barhopping around C. del Orzán, C. del Sol, and the mess of streets near C. de la Franja and C. de la Florida. **IriBar**, C. Panaderas, 34, is La Coruña's sleekest and most cosmopolitan lounge. (Open daily 9pm-4am.) Popular Celtic pubs, playing folk and rock along C. del Orzán, are **Bock y CIA**, C. del Orzán, 2, **A Cova Folk**, C. del Orzán, 38, and **A Casa de Lubre**, C. del Orzán, 68. (All open approx. 11pm-3am.)

When bars die down around 2am, **discos** pick up along the two beaches and on C. Juan Florez. **Sol Pirámide**, C. Juan Florez, 50 (☎981 27 61 57), plays dance music loud enough to rouse the dead, while **Picasso**, C. del Sol, 21, and **Lautrec**, C. del Sol, 12, across the street, attract house-music lovers. (All open daily midnight-5am.) Nearby, fancifully decorated **Atlantis**, C. Fita, 6, off C. del Orzán, hosts concerts and DJs spinning house. (Open Th-Sa midnight-4am.) Popular among university students is the club **Noveno B**, Canton Grande, 6, playing mostly mainstream dance music. (Open daily midnight-5am.) For a more sophisticated (and pricier) scene, *coruñeses* head to the **Swing Piano Bar**, Av. de la Marina, 32, where smoky singers and Benny Goodman tunes entertain martini drinkers. (Open daily 10pm-3am.)

THE NORTHERN COAST

The northern estuaries of Galicia are among the cleanest, loveliest, and emptiest in all of Spain. To explore the Rías Altas often means spending hours on quiet coastal roads in the misty rain; if you want to leave the beaten path, this is where to do it. Though public transportation is reliable, renting a car is more convenient.

Cedeira (pop. 8000), 84km northeast of La Coruña, has Spain's highest coastline and is home to thriving pagan cults with rituals involving worship of the *hierba de amor* (love herb). Hide it among the belongings of the person you desire, and he or she will soon be at your mercy. Every first Sunday of July, the town goes crazy for its annual horse-shearing festival (see **The Beauty of the Beasts**, p. ??). To reach the Cedeira **tourist office**, C. Ezequiel López, 22, walk to the main street outside the bus station and take a right. Follow the street to the small river, cross the bridge, and turn left onto C. Ezequiel López. (☎981 48 21 87. Open Apr.-Sept. M-F 10:30am-1:30pm and 5-8pm, Sa 10:30am-2pm, Su noon-2pm.) **Rialsa buses** (☎981 31 59 55) run from **El Ferrol** via **Valdoviño** (1hr.; M-F 7-9 per day 7:30am-10pm, Sa 6 per day 8:30am-10:30pm, Su 5 per day 11am-10:30pm; €2.60), where connections can be made to and from **La Coruña** (1hr., 6 per day 8:30am-7:30pm, €5.40). **Valdoviño**, Cedeira's neighbor, is home to many gorgeous, isolated beaches and hosts the Pantín Classic **surfing competition** at its famous **Playa de Pantín** every September.

A beautiful old city poised between forest and sea, **Viveiro** (pop. 15,276) is known throughout Spain for its beaches, peaceful atmosphere, and July *fiestas*, especially **Las Rapas das Bestas**. Viveiro's **tourist office**, C. Benito Galcerán, s/n, posts info on accommodations. (☎982 56 08 79. Open daily June 15-Sept. 15 10:30am-1:30pm and 5-8pm; *Semana Santa* 11am-2pm and 4:30-8:30pm.) Ask about adventure tourism and bike rentals here. Exit through the bus station's front entrance and you will see the tourist office, a small wooden cabin, on the left. **IASA buses** connect to: **La Coruña** (4hr., 5 per day 6:30am-7:30pm, €10.75); **El Ferrol** (2¼hr., 4-6 per day 6:30am-7:30pm, €6.85); **Ribadeo** (1½hr.; 2 per day 6:50am, 6:15pm; €4.20). Nearby, Galicia's free-spirited youth camp out on Ortiguera's beaches every second weekend of July for the town's **Celtic Music Festival.** For 25 years, folk bands from every region of Spain and from Ireland, Scotland, and even Sweden have played free concerts. During the festival, a special bus runs from La Coruña to Ortiguera Wednesday through Sunday.

The official boundary between Galicia and Asturias, **Ribadeo** lays claim to one of the most beautiful beaches in Spain, ▩**Praia As Catedrais.** Natural rock archways droop into the sea, and low tide reveals caverns, coves, and warm lagoons perfect for exploring and swimming. The town itself has a quiet, almost ghostly air. The **tourist office,** Pl. de España, s/n, is in Parque de San Francisco. (☎982 12 86 89. Open M-F 10am-2:30pm and 4:30-8:30pm, Sa-Su 10am-8pm.) **IASA buses** run to: **La Coruña** (2½-3½hr.; M-Sa 4 per day 7:15, 8:45am, 1:30, 6:15pm; €10.90); **Santiago de Compostela** (3¼hr., 1 per day 6pm, €12.50); **Viveiro** (1½hr.; M-Sa 3 per day 9, 11:30am, 6pm; Su 2 per day 2:45, 6pm; €4.20).

ISLAS CANARIAS

From the snowy peak of Mount Teide to the fiery volcanos of Timanfaya, the Canary Islands have enchanted humanity since the beginning of time. Homer and Herodotus often referred to them as gardens of astounding beauty, and the lost civilization of Atlantis was said to have left behind these seven islands when it sank into the ocean. The Spanish in the Canaries bears stronger resemblance to the Spanish of Cuba or Puerto Rico than that of mainland Spain, while Canarian fare is marked by a heavy Mediterraneran influence. Remnants of pre-Spanish Guanche culture— names such as Tenerife, for example—stand as reminders of the island before the 1496 Spanish conquest and the subsequent development of plantation economies. Since then, the Canaries have been known as the "Fortunate Isles" for the incomparable and diverse natural beauty among the islands and within each individual island, from volcanic deserts in the east to wind-swept dunes in the south to misty forests in the north. While many beautiful coastlines are now marred by ugly tourist developments, the Canaries reward anyone who steps off the beaten path. Isolated beaches still exist, and the breathtaking rugged landscapes offer an incredible variety of flora and fauna. Set your eyes on these, and on the people who inhabit these strange, seemingly inhospitable islands, and your trip will be unforgettable.

HIGHLIGHTS OF LAS ISLAS CANARIAS

SAMPLE the volcanic beauty of **El Teide National Park** (see p. 606).

LIVE OUT your Martian fantasies amid the barren bliss of the **Parque Nacional de Timanfaya** (see p. 613).

ESCAPE from the hoards of other travelers on distant **La Gomera** (see p. 614).

INDULGE in the **beach paradise** of Morro Jable (see p. 610).

APPRECIATE Canarian culture with the art of **César Manrique** (see p. 611).

✈ GETTING THERE

When properly informed and guided, a trip to the Canaries can be amazing. For island adventure, purchase your tickets to and from the mainland to opposite sides of the Canaries, hop from island to island by boat, make your way through island interiors with cheap rental cars, and stay in rural houses, beach-side apartments, or *hostales*. Otherwise, browse travel agencies in Spain, England, and Germany for advertisements for 8 day/7 night packages to the Canaries, including hotel and airfare, for €300-400. You won't be staying at the Ritz, but expect much more than your average budget hostel. These packages usually restrict you to a specific part of an island and are not the best option for wanderers or backpackers looking to explore.

Located off the western coast of Morocco, the Canaries make for a long haul by boat (15hr. from Cádiz, ES), but a relatively quick flight (2½-3½hr.) from mainland Spain. Competitive fares and quick flights make flying the best option. Many airlines fly direct from Spain, Portugal, Morocco, and northern Europe. Flights from Madrid are the cheapest and most frequent. European tourists, primarily Germans and British, flock to the islands in January and February; airfares during this time are the most expensive. Still, if you plan ahead, getting to the Canary Islands will not break the bank. Prices are the same whether you purchase your tickets in

Spain or abroad. However, buying your tickets from consolidators can cut your costs in half (www.travelocity.com provides good deals). A one-way ticket in the summer should cost no more than €115.

Air Europa (24hr. ☎902 24 00 42; www.aireuropa.com) and **Spanair** (☎902 13 14 15; www.spanair.com) fly to the islands cheaply (round-trip €150-360).

Iberia (24hr. ☎902 40 05 00; www.iberia.com) flies from Madrid and Barcelona to Gran Canaria, Fuerteventura, Tenerife, and Lanzarote (round-trip €170-350).

GETTING AROUND

INTER-ISLAND TRANSPORT

If time is not an issue, traveling between the islands by ferry is the cheapest choice (see the **chart** on p. 594). However, jetfoils and inter-island flights are competitively priced to facilitate transit among the Canaries, and both carry cars. Jetfoils, faster and more comfortable, cost almost twice as much—consider taking them on longer voyages. Prices for ferries and jetfoils vary with accommodation; travelers can choose between a *butaca* (a seat like those on buses) and a *camarote a compartir* (a dorm bed). Tickets can be purchased one-way (*ida*) or round-trip (*ida y vuelta*). All Canary Islands transport companies listed provide substantial student discounts. Three major lines serve the islands. The offices at each city's ports offer timetables and fares, although it is much easier to check times and fares on-line. You can make reservations and check schedules by phone, but be prepared to wait on hold for roughly 30min. Arrive at least 1hr. before departure to buy your ticket.

BY PLANE

Binter Canarias (www.bintercanarias.com or www.bintercanarias.es; verify flight information with parent company **Iberia** ☎902 40 05 00). Almost all islands are connected by daily flights. All prices listed are 1-way, normal fare first, followed by student rate; round-trip is always cheaper. The number of flights per day varies by season; check website for more info. **Gran Canaria** to: **Fuerteventura** (40min., €53/€46); **La Gomera** (40min., €73/€63); **El Hierro** (45min., €79/€68); **Lanzarote** (45min., €60/€51); **La Palma** (50min., €73/€63); **Tenerife Norte** (40min., €45/€39); **Tenerife Sur** (35min., €45/€39).

BY BOAT

Fred Olsen (☎922 62 82 00 or 902 10 01 07; www.fredolsen.es) runs both jetfoils and ferries throughout the Canaries. MC/V.

Naviera Armas (☎902 45 65 00; www.naviera-armas.com). Ferry routes between most islands. MC/V.

Trasmediterránea (24hr. ☎902 45 46 45; www.trasmediterranea.com). Runs ferries from Cádiz, Spain and jetfoils and ferries between islands. 15hr.-2 days; departs from Cádiz Tu, returns W and Sa; round-trip with dorm bed €270. Ticket windows open 1hr. prior to departure. MC/V.

INTRA-ISLAND TRANSPORT

Outside of Gran Canaria and Tenerife, the limits of **public transportation** prevent budget travelers from accessing the natural and cultural treasures of the Canary Islands. On islands such as Lanzarote, Fuerteventura, El Hierro, and La Gomera, buses to national parks and secluded beaches are either limited or nonexistent. Dependency on public transportation will leave you in one of the abysmal capital cities of the smaller islands, where buses run only to and from the main bus sta-

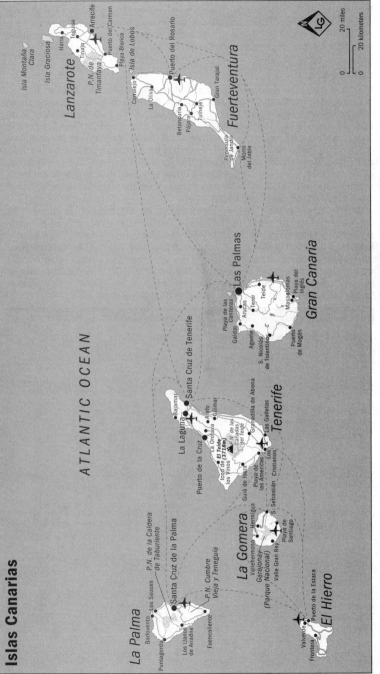

Islas Canarias

ATLANTIC OCEAN

Lanzarote

Isla Montaña
Clara
Isla Graciosa
Haria
Teguise
Tinajo
Arrecife
P.N. de
Timanfaya
Puerto del Carmen
Playa-Blanca
Isla de Lobos

Fuerteventura
Corralejo
La Oliva
Puerto del Rosario
Gran Tarajal
Betancuria
Pájara
Tuineje
Península
de Jandía
Morro
del Jable

Gran Canaria
Las Palmas
Playa de las
Galdar Canteras
Arucas
Teror
Teide
Agaete
Maspalomas
Playa del
Inglés
S. Nicolás
S. de Tolentino
Puerto
de Mogán

Tenerife
La Laguna
Bajamar
Santa Cruz de Tenerife
Tacoronte
Orotava
Tejina
Güímar
La Orotava
Granadilla de Abona
P.N. de las
Cañadas
del Teide
Las Galletas
El Teide
(3718m)
Icod de
los Vinos
Puerto de la Cruz
Playa de
las Américas
Los
Cristianos
Guía de Isora

La Gomera
Vallehermoso
Hermigua
Garajonay
(Parque Nacional)
Valle Gran Rey
S. Sebastián
Playa de
Santiago

La Palma
Barlovento
Los Sauces
Santa Cruz de la Palma
P.N. de la Caldera
de Taburiente
P.N. Cumbre
Vieja y Teneguía
Puntagorda
Los Llanos
de Ariadne
Fuencaliente

El Hierro
Valverde
Frontera
Puerto de la Estaca

20 miles
20 kilometers

tion. Rent a **car** to avoid wasting time in such areas; at €30 per day, a rental car is an invaluable, cost-effective investment, especially for groups of two or more. A car in the Canaries opens up a new world of pristine landscapes, secluded beaches, mountain-top vistas, and remote villages.

CAR RENTAL

Choose a rental car agency with several offices throughout an island so you can pick up and drop off a car in different locations for no extra charge. Reserve ahead of time to ensure good prices, as renting the day of can cost double. Almost all cars are manual. Most agencies follow the same time schedule (9am-1pm and 5-8pm); cars must be picked up and dropped off during these times. Prices quoted are per day (based on 1-2 day rental), including tax, insurance, and unlimited mileage. Prices drop significantly when renting for longer periods of time. Minimum age for rental is 21, and you must have a driver's license, though it need not be an international one. Some agencies allow you to take the car from island to island (via ferry), but this comes with a hefty fee.

CiCAR (Canary Islands Car) is the best option for car rental on all islands. The company has 27 offices throughout the Canaries. Reservations can be made through the main office (☎928 82 29 00; www.cicar.com). Certain offices arrange for a representative to pick you up upon arrival and take you to the car rental office, free of charge. Economy cars are available for €29 per day. Other reliable companies include: **Auto-Reisen** (☎922 63 59 78 or 39 22 16; €26 per day); **Avis** (☎902 13 55 31; €35 per day); **Betacar/Europcar** (☎922 37 28 82; €35 per day); **Felycar** (☎900 21 10 40; €28 per day); **Hertz** (☎902 14 37 89).

ORIGIN	DESTINATION	LENGTH	FREQUENCY	TIME	PRICE
Arrecife	Las Palmas	8hr.	W, F	noon	€28.12
Arrecife+	Las Palmas	8hr.	Tu, Th, Sa	1pm	€29
Arrecife+	Puerto del Rosario	45min.	Th	10:15am	€14
Arrecife+	Santa Cruz, Tenerife	10hr.	Th	10:15am	€34
Corralejo+	Playa Blanca	45min.	5-6 per day	8am-8pm	€11.40
Corralejo*	Playa Blanca	45min.	5 per day	9am-7pm	€12.50
Las Palmas	Arrecife	8hr.	Tu, Th, Sa	Tu-Th midnight; Sa 2:30pm	€28.12
Las Palmas+	Arrecife	10hr.	M, W, F	11:50pm	€29
Las Palmas	Morro Jable	1½hr.	1 per day	M-Sa 10 or 11am; Su 2 or 3pm	€49.33
Las Palmas+	Morro Jable	4hr.	1 per day	M-Sa 7:10am; Su 1:30pm	€26.80
Las Palmas	Puerto Rosario	8hr.	M, W, F	midnight	€28.12
Las Palmas+	Puerto Rosario	8hr.	Tu, Th	11:50pm	€29
Las Palmas	Santa Cruz, LP	8½hr.	Th	11:30pm	€37.06
Las Palmas	Santa Cruz, Tenerife	2hr.	2-3 per day	varies 7:30am-7pm	
Las Palmas+	Santa Cruz, Tenerife	3½hr.	M-F 2 per day; Sa-Su 1 per day	M-F 6:45am, 3:30pm; Sa-Su 7am	€49.33 €14
Las Palmas* (bus to Agate)	Santa Cruz, Tenerife	1½hr.	M-F 6 per day; Sa-Su 6 per day	M-F 7am-8:30pm; Sa-Su 8am-8:30pm	€29.70
Los Cristianos	San Sebastián	1½hr.	1-3 per day	daily 8:30am; M-F 2pm; W, F, Su 7pm	€16.93
Los Cristianos*	San Sebastián	40min.	4 per day	8am-8:30pm	€20.30
Los Cristianos*	Santa Cruz, LP	5hr.	1 per day	Su-F 7am; Sa 8am	€34
Los Cristianos	Valverde, El Hierro	5hr.	Su-F	7pm	€21.73
Los Cristianos*	Valverde, El Hierro	5hr.	Su-F 1 per day	8am	€28.70
Morro Jable	Las Palmas	1½hr.	1 per day	5pm	€49.33
Morro Jable+	Las Palmas	4hr.	1 per day	7pm	€26.80
Playa Blanca+	Corralejo	45min.	5-6 per day	7am-7pm	€11.40
Playa Blanca*	Corralejo	45min.	4-5 per day	8am-6pm	€12.30

ORIGIN	DESTINATION	LENGTH	FREQUENCY	TIME	PRICE
Puerto del Rosario	Las Palmas	8hr.	Tu, Th, Sa	1pm	€28.12
Puerto del Rosario+	Las Palmas	8hr.	W, F	noon	€29
Puerto del Rosario+	Santa Cruz, Tenerife	12hr.	F	2:30pm	€34
San Sebastián	Los Cristianos	1½hr.	1-2 per day	daily 5:15pm; M-F 11:45am	€16.93
San Sebastián*	Los Cristianos	40min.	4 per day	7:15am-6:30pm	€20.30
San Sebastián	Valverde, El Hierro	3hr.	1 per day	M, Tu, Th 5:10pm; W, F, Su 8:45pm; Sa 10:30am	€20.52
Santa Cruz, LP+	Arrecife	19hr.	Th	noon	€37.50
Santa Cruz, LP*	Los Cristianos	5hr.	1 per day	6:30pm; call ahead	€34
Santa Cruz, LP+	Puerto del Rosario	19hr.	Th	noon	€37.50
Santa Cruz, LP+	Santa Cruz, Tenerife	8hr.	Tu, Th-F and Su	Tu and Th 1pm; F noon; Su 5pm	€16
Santa Cruz, Ten.+	Arrecife	10hr.	Th	10pm	€34
Santa Cruz, Ten.+	Las Palmas	3½hr.	1-2 per day	M-F 11:10am, 8:10pm; Sa-Su 7:30pm	€14
Santa Cruz, Ten.+	Puerto del Rosario	10hr.	Th	10pm	€34
Santa Cruz, Ten.+	Santa Cruz, La Palma	8hr.	M-W, Sa	M-W 11:50pm, Sa 1am	€16
Valverde	Los Cristianos	8hr.	Su-F	midnight	€21.73
Valverde*	Los Cristianos	8hr.	1 per day	3:30pm	€28.70
Valverde	San Sebastián	3hr.	Su-F	midnight	€21.73

Unless otherwise noted, ferries are run by Trasmediterránea. * denotes Fred Olsen. + denotes Naviera Armas.

GRAN CANARIA

Often called the "miniature continent," Gran Canaria sports a wide range of land-scapes, from green, tropical vegetation in the north to the rolling dunes of Maspal-omas in the south. Las Palmas is a vibrant and eclectic city with attractive museums and the famous Playa de las Canteras, but European tourists flock primarily to the south, reveling in Gran Canaria's perpetual sunshine and beautiful beaches. Mountain towns in the interior, where daily life does not revolve around tourists, provide visitors with a rare glimpse into the vibrance of local culture. An ideal visit to Gran Canaria is a well-rounded one. Be sure to take it all in; the beach will still be there when you're ready for it.

LAS PALMAS

The urban mecca of the Canaries, Las Palmas (pop. 365,000) features all the quali-ties of any normal big city—shopping, decent eating, theater, cafes, and bars. The city boasts a quaint historic district in the south, equipped with some of the Canar-ies' best museums. Playa de las Canteras, one of Europe's most famous beaches, is packed with locals—tourists prefer the pristine beaches and guaranteed sun on the southern coast.

▐ TRANSPORTATION

Flights: (24hr. ☎928 57 90 00). **Buses** *(guaguas)* run from Parque de San Telmo's Est-ación de Guaguas to the airport (#60; 45min., every hr. 6:30am-1:30am, €1.70).

Buses: Estación de Guaguas (☎928 36 83 35), on the sea side of Parque de San Telmo. Office open M-F 7am-7pm, Sa-Su 8am-1pm. **Líneas Global** (☎902 38 11 10; www.globalsu.net) connects Las Palmas to the rest of the island. For those exploring extensively by bus, the blue **tarjeta insular** pass (€12.20) gives a 20% discount on municipal and island-wide buses. Bus schedules change on weekends, especially on Su; pick up a timetable in the ticket office. To: **Arucas** (#205, 209, 210, 234; every 30min.-1hr. 6am-2am, €1.35-1.70); **Maspalomas-Playa del Inglés** (#5 and 30; 30min.; every 20min. 5:20am-3am; Playa Inglés €4.05, Maspalomas €4.45); **Puerto de Mogán** (#1; 20min., every 20min. 5:40am-7pm, €6.35); **Puerto Rico** (#91; every hr. 6am-8:15pm, €5.45); **Teror** (#216; every 30min. 6am-11pm, €1.70).

Inter-City Buses: Guaguas Municipales, C. León y Castillo, 330 (☎928 44 65 00), are yellow buses (€0.85) that travel within the city. Stops are frequent. Bus #1 runs north to south, 24hr. a day, from Muelle de la Luz to Teatro Pérez Galdós, passing Parque de Santa Catalina and Parque de San Telmo. When in doubt, hop on bus #1. 10-ride *"bono"* available at tobacco shops or at the main bus station (€5.10).

Ferries: Trasmediterránea (☎928 26 56 50) runs jetfoils from Muelle de Santa Catalina. **Naviera Armas** (☎928 26 77 00 or 902 45 65 00) ferries depart from Muelle León y Castillo. Ferry tickets can be purchased at the docks 1hr. before departure. **Fred Olsen** (☎922 62 82 00) ferries to **Tenerife** depart from **Agaete**. A free bus leaves Parque de Santa Catalina 1hr. before the ferry leaves. Buy your ferry tickets and board the bus at the Fred Olsen office in the northwest corner of the park. Tickets also sold at travel agencies for a small fee. For more info, see **Inter-Island Transport,** p. 592.

Car Rental: CiCAR Gran Canary airport office (☎928 57 93 78). Muelle de Santa Catalina office (☎928 26 40 89). **Hertz** (☎928 57 95 77) has offices scattered around the island, including at the airport and in the Jetfoil office at Muelle de Sta. Catalina.

Taxi: Radio Taxi (☎928 46 22 12, 46 18 18, or 42 43 00).

ORIENTATION & PRACTICAL INFORMATION

The bus system is the easiest way to get around Las Palmas. The city is loosely divided into a series of districts, connected by a major highway and avenues running north to south along the east coast. **Avenida León y Castillo** runs parallel through the city center. Bus #1 passes through this thoroughfare. **Playa de Las Canteras** and **Muelle de la Luz** frame the north of the city, packed with accommodations, bars, discos, and sex shops. Farther south through a series of residential neighborhoods lies **Triana,** a shopping district close to the city's main bus station. **Vegueta,** home to the city's historical district, branches south from Triana. Buses #1, 12, 13, 15, and 41 run between **Parque de Santa Catalina** and the quaint, beautiful Vegueta. Pick up the mini-magazine *Info Ocio* at any tourist kiosk for complete listings of cultural activities, restaurants, nightlife, and cybercafes. When in doubt, throughout the Canaries and all of Spain, dial information at ☎1003 from a pay phone to get phone numbers and addresses (free of charge).

Tourist Offices: English spoken. Open M-F 10am-7:30pm, Sa 10am-3pm. **Centro de Iniciaturas y Turismo** (☎928 24 35 93), in Pueblo Canario. Open M-F 10am-1pm and 5-8pm. The **Patronato de Turismo,** C. León y Castillo, 17 (☎928 21 96 00; www.turismograncanaria.com), is also a good resource.

Currency Exchange: Banco Santander Central Hispano, C. Nicolás Estévanez, 5 (☎902 24 24 24). No commission. Open 8:30am-2pm.

Laundromat: Lavasec, C. Joaquín Costa, 46 (☎928 27 46 17). Wash, dry, and iron (up to 7kg) €6. Open M-F 9am-1pm and 4-8pm, Sa 9am-3pm.

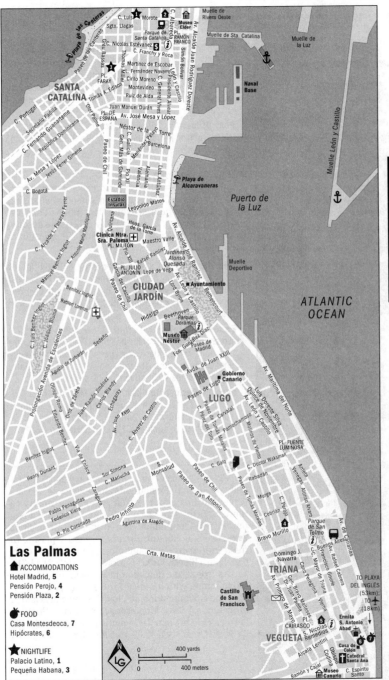

Las Palmas

ACCOMMODATIONS
Hotel Madrid, **5**
Pensión Perojo, **4**
Pensión Plaza, **2**

FOOD
Casa Montesdeoca, **7**
Hipócrates, **6**

NIGHTLIFE
Palacio Latino, **1**
Pequeña Habana, **3**

ON THE MENU

EATING LIKE A BIRD

Canarian cuisine is delightful, though sometimes hard to find in more touristed areas, where food caters to European tourists. Main dishes include a variety of fresh fish (*vieja* is very popular) served *a la plancha* (grilled). *Potaje*, a stew made from pork, corn on the cob, potatoes, beans, and whatever else is in the kitchen, is a heavier dish served more often in colder climes. Most meals are accompanied by delicious *papas arrugadas* (small "wrinkly" potatoes cooked in sea water) and served with a variety of *mojos* (sauces). The most popular of these sauces are *mojo picón* (a spicy red sauce) and *mojo verde* (a green sauce made with parsley). *Gofio*, a remnant of the Guanche culture consisting of ground toasted cereals, is often put in soups or eaten for breakfast with warm milk.

Accompany your meal with a Canarian wine (Lanzarote's *malvasía* wine was lauded by the likes of Shakespeare and Sir Walter Scott), delicious *Arehucas* rum (produced in Arucas, Gran Canaria), or a local beer (*Tropical* is produced in Gran Canaria, while *Dorada* hails from Tenerife).

The islands grow a v ariety of tropical produce such as bananas, avacados, mangos, and cactus fruits—and fruit is often the dessert of choice. Also popular is creamy *bienmesabe*, a dessert usually made from honey, almonds, eggs, and rum.

Emergency: ☎112. **Police:** Parque de Sta. Catalina (☎092 or 928 26 05 51).

Hospital: Hospital Insular (☎928 44 40 00), Pl. Dr. Pasteur. A 24hr. emergency clinic. English spoken.

Internet: Cyber's@Zero, in Parque de Santa Catalina (☎928 27 47 75), offers cheap access and speedy computers. €0.50 per 30min. Open daily 9am-midnight.

Post Office: Av. Primero de Mayo, 62 (☎928 36 13 20). Open M-F 8:30am-8:30pm, Sa 9:30am-2:30pm. **Postal Code:** 35007.

⚐ ACCOMMODATIONS

Without advance notice, it's nearly impossible to find lodging during high season (December-February, especially during *Carnaval*). Try calling the **Reservations Center** (☎928 38 46 46 or 38 47 47; after hours fax 38 48 48).

Hotel Madrid, Pl. Cairasco, 4 (☎928 36 06 64; fax 38 21 76). Elegantly-furnished rooms retain their historical feel. Franco stayed in #3 the night before the Civil War began. Singles €24, with bath €30; doubles €30, with bath €36. ❷

Pensión Perojo, C. Perojo, 1 (☎928 37 13 87). Located in an airy older building, Perojo's rooms are spacious and spotless. The short walk from the old city makes up for lots of street noise. Communal bathrooms. Singles €15; doubles €24; triples €30. ❶

Pensión/Residencia Plaza, C. Luis Morote, 16 (☎928 26 52 12). Location is great, but water pressure is lacking. Laundry €7. 24hr. reception. Singles €17, with bath €20; doubles €23/€26. Extra bed €6. ❷

⚐ FOOD

Las Palmas's cuisine is as international as its fluctuating population. Restaurants along Playa de las Canteras and in Vegueta often cater specifically to tourists. *Info Ocio* has a complete listing of all restaurants in Las Palmas. For groceries, **Mercado de Vegueta,** on C. Mendizábal, is a sensory parade of fresh fruit, dairy, fish, and olive stands. (Open daily 6am-2pm.) **Hipócrates ❷,** C. Colón, 4 (☎928 31 11 71), across from Casa de Colón in Vegueta, offers vegetarian dining with a *menú* for €9.20. (Open daily 1-4pm and 8:30pm-midnight, closed Su evenings and M afternoons.) **Casa Montesdeoca ❸** serves Spanish entrees (€7-14) in a 16th-century courtyard. (☎928 33 34 66. Open M-Sa 12:30-4pm and 8pm-midnight.)

👁 SIGHTS

Las Palmas's sights can be toured in a single day. Begin in the south in Vegueta, Las Palmas's **historic neighborhood;** its colonial and Neoclassical architecture and open markets make for a sweet respite from the new city's commercial buildings. A plethora of small side streets renders maps difficult to follow; from the bus station, head down C. Triana and cross C. Lentini to enter the historic neighborhood.

CASA DE COLÓN. Visit as a last stop before landing in the New World. The museum contains various artifacts of early transatlantic voyages and investigations of pre-Colombian cultures. Multilingual descriptions of exhibits can be found in each room. *(C. Colón, 1. ☎928 31 23 86 or 31 23 84; www.grancanariacultura.com. Open M-F 9am-7pm, Sa-Su 9am-3pm. Free.)*

MUSEO CANARIO. The collection provides a comprehensive background on the Canaries' pre-conquest history. Peruse the extensive collection of Cro-Magnon skulls and mummies, documenting the evolution of man and Guanche society. *(C. Verneau, 2. ☎928 33 68 00. Open M-F 10am-8pm, Sa-Su 10am-2pm. Guided tours run every 45min. 10am-2pm, 6, and 7pm. €3, students €1.20.)*

CATEDRAL DE SANTA ANA. This 16th-century gothic cathedral houses the **Diocesan Museum of Religious Art.** José Luján Pérez, the Canaries' favorite sculptor, designed the Neoclassical facade. *(C. Espíritu Santo, 20. ☎928 31 49 89. Open M-F 10am-4:30pm, Sa 10am-1:30pm. €3.)*

PUEBLO CANARIO. In the white-washed **Pueblo Canario** (Canarian Village), dedicated to the dissemination of Canarian culture, resides the ▨**Museo Néstor,** a collection of painter Néstor Martín-Fernández de la Torre's celebration of body and spirit. As per Néstor's request, on Sunday mornings, Pueblo Canario is filled with traditional Canarian folk dance and music from 11:30am-1pm. *(Take bus #1, 15, or 41. ☎928 24 51 35. Open Tu-F 10am-8pm, Su 10:30am-2:30pm. €2, students free. Call ahead for free guided tours.)*

MUSEO ELDER DE LA CIENCIA Y LA TECNOLOGÍA. The city's new pride and joy, the museum, on the port side of Parque de Santa Catalina, is a state-of-the-art exploration of topics from energy to transport. It also houses a space station, science workshop, and IMAX theater. *(☎928 01 18 28; www.museoelder.org. Open Tu-Su 10am-8pm. €3.)*

📷 🎭 BEACHES & ENTERTAINMENT

The waters along **Playa de Las Canteras** are protected during low tide by a natural reef, turning the sea into a tranquil swimming pool. Locals flock to the far left, where the waves are great for bodyboarding. Surfers and windsurfers head to the far extremes where waves and wind are plentiful. **Medusa Sub,** C. Bernardo de La Torre, 33, specializes in diving, instructional courses, and equipment rental and sales. *(☎928 26 27 86. Open M-F 11am-2pm and 5-9pm, Sa 11am-1pm and 6-8pm.)*

   Nightlife in Las Palmas is unremarkable. Most popular spots (including karaoke bars) are located near Parque de Santa Catalina—be careful at night. Take advantage of year-round outdoor terraces on Pl. de España and along Po. de las Canteras. **Palacio Latino,** C. Luis Morote, 51, is a standard *discoteca*, while **Pequeña Habana,** C. Fernando Guanarteme, 45, sizzles with salsa until 4am on weekends.

▶ DAYTRIPS FROM LAS PALMAS

MASPALOMAS

Buses run to and from the airport (#66; 40min., every hr. 6:15am-9:15pm, €2.95); Las Palmas (#5 and 30; 1hr., every 15min. 5am-2:30am, €4.05-4.45); Puerto de Mogán (#32 and 61; 30min., schedule varies 8:30am-8:30pm, €2.90); Puerto Rico (#32, 39, 61; 30min., schedule varies 7am-8:30pm, €1.45).

Located on the southern tip of Gran Canaria, the 17km of Maspalomas's shoreline offer the best beaches in the Canary Islands. The famed **Playa del Inglés** allows parasailing, surfing, jet-skiing, scuba diving, and deep-sea fishing. The secret has long been out, and planeloads of European tourists swarm the coast every year. The crowds are worth putting up with, though, to see the awesome, wind-swept ▧**Dunas de Maspalomas** beyond the beach, a subtle reminder that the Canaries share their latitude with the Sahara. From Playa del Inglés, head left on the beach and walk approx. 20min.—you can't miss them.

Other good beaches include the flawless, quieter **Playa de Maspalomas** and the rocky **Playa de la Mujer** and **Playa las Meloneras. Water Sports Center,** in the Kabash shopping center, rents jetskis (☎928 76 66 83; €30-36 for 20min.); **Diving Center "Sun-Sub"** (☎928 77 81 65; www.sunsub.com) offers daily diving trips with optional equipment (€28 without equipment). **Happy Biking,** in Yumbo Centrum, rents bikes, equipment, guides, and picnic supplies. (☎928 76 68 32. Open M-Sa 9am-2pm and 6-8pm. €9-24 per day.) Beyond the fantastic beaches, most people come to Playa del Inglés and Maspalomas to eat, drink, and party. Cement buildings and market bazaars house the town's **nightlife.** Once you get over the ostentatious party atmosphere, marvel at the sparkler in your drink, accompanied by a plastic frog and token orange slice. The frequent nightbus between Las Palmas and Maspalomas makes nighttime entertainment that much easier. **Yumbo Centrum,** located between Av. Tirajana and Av. de España and facing Av. de EEUU, houses an entire block of restaurants, gay and straight bars, clubs, Internet cafes, laundromats, and grocery stores. Also near Yumbo Centrum is the **tourist office** is on the corner of Av. de España and Av. EEUU. (☎928 77 15 50. Open in summer M-F 9am-2pm and 3-8pm, Sa 9am-1pm; in winter M-F 9am-9pm, Sa 9am-1pm.)

Residencia San Fernando ❶, C. La Palma, 16, is the only budget accommodation in town, though nicer hotels are affordable through tour packages. Follow Av. Tirajana uphill away from the beach; La Palma is the second right after the highway. The *residencia* is across from Centro San Fernando. The dunes and beach are easily accessible, but rooms are bare. (☎928 76 39 06. Singles €12.50; doubles €18.50.) Dining in Maspalomas is quite awful. Hustlers lure you to tourist-themed restaurants serving over 120 generic entrees. The town's culinary savior is the dirt-cheap **Pepe Chiringo ❶,** at Av. Tirajana and Av. Francia, with heaping portions of chicken breast covered in homemade *alioli* (€3).

ARUCAS

Buses #205, 209, 210, and 234 travel from the Las Palmas station to Arucas (every 30min.-1hr. 6am-2am, €1.35-1.70).

Arucas, a delightful mountain town set on a dormant volcano, has a stunning neo-Gothic church and a genuine, relaxed atmosphere. An enjoyable daytrip from Las Palmas or any point on the island, it is worth tearing yourself away from the beach to take in the town's splendor. While tourist kiosks in Las Palmas and tourist offices in Maspalomas can provide maps and guides for the city, a local **tourist office** is near the church at C. León y Castillo, 22. (☎928 63 35 47; www.arucasturismo.com. Open M-F 10am-5pm.) Overlooking a set of gardens, the **Iglesia de San**

Juan Bautista is a magnificent structure constructed mostly by local stonemasons and artisans between 1909 and 1977. (Open daily 9am-12:30pm and 4-7pm. Free.) A short walk out of town leads to **Montaña de Arucas**, which features breathtaking panoramic views of the island. Since 1884, Arucas has been home to the **Arehucas factory**, which produces the island's delicious rum; see the tourist office for tour information. There is one (and only one) place to stay in Arucas: a little *albergue* called **La Granja Escuela Anatol ❷**, C. Ruz de Pineda, 5, which provides a home for scholars—and for you, too, if you reserve in advance. (☎/fax 928 60 55 44. €20 per person, includes breakfast.)

TENERIFE

The volcanic peak of El Teide (3718m) jets into the blinding blue sky, peering down on Tenerife's diverse landscapes and tranquility. Though Tenerife is the Canaries' second most inhabited island, the land is dotted with countless solitary walking trails less than 10min. outside the capital. The microclimates of the island have generated a land of ever-changing flora and terrain, best characterized by the verdant gardens of the north, the rocky beaches of the south, and the mesmerizing mountainous and volcanic spectacles of the interior. Though the beauty of the island lies more in its people and spectacular vistas than its beaches, sun-worshippers can still get their fix down south. Naturelovers, adventurous backpackers, and families will find Tenerife a rewarding travel destination, a peaceful outlet from the urban sprawl of mainland Europe. For those in search of even greater seclusion, the island provides transportation to the more untouched westernmost islands of La Gomera, La Palma, and El Hierro. Cheap flights from Madrid and Barcelona make Tenerife easily accesible from Iberia.

SANTA CRUZ DE TENERIFE ☎922

The first shots of the Spanish Civil War rang out in this capital of Tenerife in 1936. The Canaries' General-in-Chief, Francisco Franco, would go on to orchestrate the war for the next three years. Today, with more than 250,000 residents, the small port city is a pedestrian utopia, with endless *ramblas*, quaint historical houses, *zumerías*, and lush parks. Santa Cruz de Tenerife has a strong sense of Spanish and Canarian culture that is somehow lost in the capitals of the eastern islands.

▣ TRANSPORTATION

Flights: National flights land at the northern airport, **Los Rodeos** (☎922 63 56 35; www.aena.es/ae.tfn), 6km west of Santa Cruz. From Los Rodeos, buses #102, 107, 108, and 109 run to town (20min., every 20min. 6am-midnight, €1.05). International flights dominate the south's larger **Reina Sofía** airport (☎922 75 92 00 or 75 90 00; www.aena.es/ae.tfs). From Reina Sofía, buses #111 and 341 head to town (every hr. 5am-1:30am, €4.67). **Iberia** (☎922 33 58 79), **Spanair** (☎922 63 58 13), **Air Europa** (☎922 63 59 55), and **Binter Canarias** (☎922 63 56 44) all fly to the island.

Buses: TITSA (24hr. ☎922 53 13 00 or 21 56 99; www.titsa.com) serves all towns from **Estación de Guaguas,** Av. Tres de Mayo, 57, down Av. José Antonio Primo de Rivera from Pl. de España. Some lines do not run during the summer; call ahead or check online for information. To **Los Cristianos/Playa de las Américas** (#110 and 111; 1hr., every 30min.-1hr. 6:15am-8:15pm, €5.71-6.50) and **Puerto de la Cruz** (#102 has stops, #103 runs direct; 1hr.; every 30min.-1hr. 6:50am-9:50pm, then 11pm, 12:45, 3:15, 4:45am; €3.30). A **bonobus ticket** (Card Titsa; €12) deducts 31% of the cost of individual tickets on short rides and 50% for distances greater than 20km.

Ferries: Trasmediterránea (☎922 24 30 11). **Fred Olsen** (☎922 62 82 00) runs a **free bus** from the main station to Los Cristianos for departures to La Gomera and El Hierro 90min. prior to departure. See **Inter-Island Transport**, p. 592.

Car Rental: Local offices include **Auto-Reisen** (☎922 26 22 02), **Avis** (☎922 25 87 13), and **CiCar** (☎922 63 59 25). See **Intra-Island Transport**, p. 592.

Taxis: ☎922 25 88 06.

■▪ 🛈 ORIENTATION & PRACTICAL INFORMATION

Despite its extensive bus system, Santa Cruz is easily navigable on foot. The port city branches out from **Plaza de España**. Directly across from Pl. de España is **Plaza de la Candelaria**; C. del Castillo runs perpendicular to the water into the commercial district. Av. José Antonio Primo de Rivera and Av. Francisco La Rocheoriginate in Pl. de España and run along the waterfront, separating the port and the city. To get to Pl. de España from the **ferry terminals,** turn left onto Av. Francisco la Roche/Av. Anaga, and follow it to the plaza (10min.). From the **bus station,** head right down Av. Tres de Mayo towards the water, then take a left on Av. José Antonio Primo de Rivera, continuing on to the plaza (15min.).

Tourist Office: Pl. de España, s/n (☎922 23 95 92 or 23 98 11), on the corner of Av. José Antonio Primo de Rivera. Facing the monument, it's in the far right corner. Open July-Sept. M-F 8am-5pm, Sa 9am-noon; Oct.-June M-F 8am-6pm, Sa 9am-1pm.

Police: Av. Tres de Mayo, 72 (☎922 60 60 92). Follow Av. Tres de Mayo past the intersection with Av. La Salle; the station is on the right.

Pharmacy: Farmacia La Marina, C. de la Marina, 7 (☎922 24 24 93), one block from Pl. de España. Open M-F 8am-8pm, Sa 9am-1:30pm. Many are also located along C. del Castillo and its extensions.

Hospital: In an **emergency** dial ☎112. In La Laguna, north of Santa Cruz, **Hospital Universitario de Canarias,** Urb. Ofra s/n (☎922 67 80 00 or 67 82 83). Take bus #014 or 015. **Red Cross,** C. San Lucas, 60 (☎922 28 29 24). From C. del Castillo, turn right onto C. San Lucas; it's across from the church.

Internet Access: Tóp Anaga, Av. Francisco La Roche/Av. Anaga, 11 (☎922 28 24 96), next to the 24hr. convenience store. Internet €1 per 30min. Open daily 9am-midnight.

Post Office: Pl. de España, s/n (☎922 53 36 29). Open M-F 8:30am-8:30pm, Sa 9:30am-2pm. **Postal Code:** 38007.

🏠 ACCOMMODATIONS

Budget accommodations in Santa Cruz tend to be overshadowed by one- and two-star hotels. Several affordable places to spend the night are scattered along C. del Castillo and C. Bethencourt Alfonso. The tourist office has lists of accommodations, and their map marks the hotels; make use of their free 2min. phone calls to reserve a room.

▨ **Hotel Horizonte,** C. Sta. Rosa de Lima, 11 (☎/fax 922 27 19 36). From Pl. de España, take C. de la Marina, turn left onto C. Emilio Calzadilla, then right onto C. Sta. Rosa de Lima. The spacious rooms are spotless and all have private baths. Superb service. Singles €18-24; doubles €36-42; triples €48. ❷

Pensión Casablanca, C. Viera y Clavijo, 15 (☎922 27 85 99). C. Bethencourt Alfonso becomes C. Pérez Galdós and then C. de Viera y Clavijo. Funky rooms are cramped but alive with pink, blue, or green color schemes. Common baths. Reservations highly recommended, as the rooms are few. Singles €15; doubles €21. ❶

Hotel Anago, C. Imeldo Seris, 19 (☎922 24 50 90; fax 24 56 44). Take C. General Gutiérrez and turn right on C. Imeldo Seris. Basic rooms, many with balconies. Singles with shower €25.50, with bath €32; doubles €42/ €53. AmEx/MC/V. ❸

❒ FOOD

Eating is a cheap and delicious activity in Santa Cruz. The numerous *zumerías* and sandwich shops lining the city streets serve over 50 combinations of fresh fruit juices and shakes for around €1.60. ◙ **La Hierbita,** C. del Clavel, 19, offers delicious Canarian specialties (entrees €2.75-9), local wines, and homemade desserts. The owners, from La Palma and La Gomera, restored and converted this former *pensión* into a cozy local favorite with multiple dining rooms. From Pl. de España, take C. General Gutiérrez, a right onto C. Imeldo Seris, and another right onto C. Cruz Verde; Clavel is your first left. (☎922 24 46 17. Open M-Sa 11am-4pm and 7-11pm.) Among the best in town, ◙**Zumería Tropicana ❶,** C. Portlier, 71, specializes in vegetarian food (like pumpkin burgers) and drinks made from fruits and vegetables. (☎929 84 44 90. Open 5pm-midnight.) Cafes, restaurants, and bars crowd Pl. de España, but **Avenida Francisco La Roche/Avenida Anaga** has better deals (*menús* from €6) and chic *terrazas*. **Mercado de Nuestra Señora de Africa,** across the river and one block inland from the Museo de la Naturaleza, sells meat and produce.

◉ ♫ SIGHTS & ENTERTAINMENT

The greatest sights of Santa Cruz lie outside the city limits along lookout points off the main highway and smaller side roads. Renting a car allows you to explore the hidden treasures that encircle the city. Within the city itself, the social plazas and beautiful parks are perfect for coffee sipping, people-watching, and deep thinking. Besides **Plaza de España,** the **Plaza de Weyler** is the most popular plaza in the city and a gateway to the great **shopping** that lies southward. **Parque Municipal García Sanabria** doubles as an impressive garden and an open-air sculpture museum with avant-garde works by Pablo Serrano, Rafael Soto, and Gustavo Torner. The **Museo de la Naturaleza y el Hombre,** C. Fuente de Morales, 1, off C. San Sebastián, transports you to the Canaries' archaeological past, detailing everything from prehistoric marine biology to Guanche burial practices. On the lighter side, have a go at sculpting your own ceramic pots in the museum's classroom. (☎922 53 58 16; fax 29 43 45. Open Tu-Su 9am-7pm. €3, students €1.50. 50% discount with *bonobus* pass. Su free.) The intricate woodwork of the 16th-century

THE LOCAL LEGEND

FROM WHENCE THEY CAME

The word *Guanche,* derived from the term for Tenerife's pre-Spanish inhabitants (*Guan Chenech* in the local language meant "man from Tenerife"), today refers to the mysterious peoples that inhabited the Canaries before the 15th-century Spanish invasion. Very little is known of their culture or language even today; the Guanches were either killed, enslaved, or quickly assimilated into Spanish culture and religion. Anthropologists speculate that these light-skinned, often blond peoples were related to the Berbers of northern Africa. When the Spanish arrived in the 1400s, they found a Stone Age civilization of hunter-gatherers. Most interestingly, the Guanches didn't know how to sail, leading scientists to speculate that they either "forgot" how to sail after arriving to the islands or were taken to the islands as passengers on the boats of seafaring peoples.

Today, remnants of Guanche culture can be found in pasttimes such as *lucha canaria,* Canarian wrestling. Guanche artifacts and mummies are studied with great interest, and new discoveries bring scientists closer to an understanding of a people whose culture and language have all but disappeared. For more information, visit the **Museo Canario** in Las Palmas de Gran Canaria.

Iglesia de la Concepción is worth the architectural pilgrimage. To reach Pl. de la Iglesia, turn left onto C. Bravo Murillo from the tourist office. (☎ 922 24 23 84. Mass M-F 9am, 7:30pm; Sa 6, 7:30pm; Su 9, 11am, noon, 1, 6, 8pm. Open M-F 8am-7:30pm.)

🏖️ 🎵 BEACHES & NIGHTLIFE

Many flock to Tenerife for a beach holiday. Though the beaches around Santa Cruz are not spectacular, the black sands of **Almáciga** (bus #246), **Benijo** (bus #246), and **Las Gaviotas** (bus #245), and the artificial golden sand of **Las Teresitas** (bus #910), are all accessible by frequent buses departing from the central bus station.

In Santa Cruz, warm summer **nights** beckon Latin lovers of both sexes. The young'uns of Santa Cruz take a pause to down cheap vodka-colas in the plaza since drinks in the clubs run €4.80. Exploding from Av. Francisco La Roche/Av. Anaga's bar-discos at 4am, the drunken parade of stilettos marches to the sizzling **terrazas del verano** running down Av. José Antonio Primo de Rivera's waterfront. A night at **El Primero,** one of three adjoining outdoor clubs, goes by in a blur of booze promotions, seductive platform dancers, and bursting sequined halters. (Open 11pm until dawn.) **Camel Bar,** Av. Francisco La Roche/Av. Anaga, 41, is a virtual shrine to the phallic-nosed mascot of the tobacco giant, sporting old posters and advertisements urging readers to smoke. Trendy music and a long bar keep the local crowd dancing (open daily 9pm-3:30am). The party at disco-bar **Noctua Anaga,** Av. Francisco La Roche/Av. Anaga, 35, spills out to its streetside tables until dawn. (☎ 922 29 04 61. Open 10am-5am.)

LOS CRISTIANOS & PLAYA DE LAS AMÉRICAS

The white prenumbral sand of Playa de las Américas is the first hint of what awaits visitors to Tenerife's main southern attractions: from the frat-boy nightlife to the fast food chains, just about everything here quivers with a flavor of modern kitsch. Brought in from the Sahara desert, the sand is a tasteful contrast to the nearby gray-sanded Los Cristianos beach. Exploding into full-fledged resorts in the 1960s and 70s, these two popular island towns probably have more sub-par five-star hotels than natives. Paling in comparison with the beaches of Fuerteventura, Playa de las Américas and Los Cristianos still serve as useful bases for exploring other shores in the south, including **Playa del Médano,** one of Tenerife's best and a windsurfing mecca. Most importantly, ferries to La Gomera depart from Los Cristianos.

📧 **TRANSPORTATION.** Although Los Cristianos and Playa de las Américas are actually two separate towns and municipalities (accounting for the high taxi fare between the two, about €3.60), they are considered one by tourists and tourist offices alike. The pedestrian **Paseo Marítima** connects Los Cristianos to its northern neighbor, Playa de las Américas. **Ferries** leave from Los Cristianos, connecting Tenerife to the western islands. **Fred Olsen** (☎ 922 79 05 56) and **Trasmediterránea** (☎ 902 45 46 45) run ferries to **Santa Cruz, San Sebastián,** and **Valverde** (see **Inter-Island Transport,** p. 592). **Buses** run from stops on Av. Juan Carlos in Los Cristianos to **Puerto de la Cruz** (#343; 4 per day 9am-5:45pm, €9.32), the **Reina Sofía airport** (#487; every hr. 7:20am-9:20pm, €1.80), **El Teide** (#342; 1 per day 9:15am, €3.90), and **Santa Cruz** (#110, 111; every 30min. 6am-10pm, then 11:15pm, 12:30, 4:30am; €6.01). In Playa de las Américas, buses stop along Av. Rafael Puig Lluvina. Buses #342, 441, 442, 467, 470, and 487 link Playa de las Américas and Los Cristianos, stopping frequently along the shore. Buses from Santa Cruz run directly from Los Cristianos along the outer highway to Costa

Adeje's bus station. To get to Playa de las Américas, get off at Los Cristianos and take one of the above buses.

⊠ PRACTICAL INFORMATION. To reach the **tourist office** from Los Cristianos bus stop, walk downhill on Av. Juan Carlos and take a right onto Av. de Amsterdam; it's on your left in the Centro Cultural. (☎922 75 71 37. Open M-F 9am-3pm, Sa 9am-1pm.) Services include: **banks,** near Pl. Carmen and Av. General Franco in Los Cristianos (most open M-F 9am-1pm and 4-7pm); **police,** on Av. Valle Menéndez in Los Cristianos (☎922 79 78 50); **Internet access** at **Salon Oper Teide,** C. General Franco (€1 per 30min.; open daily 10am-midnight), a block downhill from the plaza; **post office,** on C. Sabandenos, (follow yellow *correos* signs from Pl. Carmen. (☎922 79 10 56. Open M-F 8:30am-2:30pm, Sa 9:30am-1pm.) **Postal Code:** 38650.

⊠⊠ ACCOMMODATIONS & FOOD. Pl. de las Américas is full of resorts, but unless you want to splurge, stick to Av. General Franco or C. Paloma in Los Cristianos. The many *pensiones* are almost always full; be sure to call ahead. One option is ⊠**Pensión La Playa ❷,** C. Paloma, 9. From Av. General Franco, turn uphill onto C. Estocolmo; C. Paloma is the first left. The basic rooms boast aqua decor and lush plant life. (☎922 79 22 64. Communal bathrooms. Singles €15.03-20; doubles €24.04; triples €30.05.) **Pensión Corisa ❷,** C. Amalia Alayón, 18. From Pl. Carmen, bear right onto C. Amalia Alayón, parallel to Av. General Franco; across from the gas station. The neat furniture forges comfort out of small rooms, and common baths are spotless. (☎922 79 07 92. Singles €18-20; doubles €20-25.) **Food** in both towns caters to international tastes and big budgets but is marginally better in Los Cristianos, away from the beachfront. For groceries, go to **Supermercado Carolina,** Av. General Franco, 8. (☎922 79 30 69. Open M-Sa 8am-8:30pm. V.)

⊠⊠ BEACHES & NIGHTLIFE. Playa de las Américas makes a picture-perfect postcard, but **Playa Vistas** in Los Cristianos is more appealing if heavy crowds aren't your style. Either way, break out the bronzer. Kiosks and parked info-vans fortify the beaches, full of fliers for **water sports** and **scuba diving.** Booths on the far end of Los Cristianos beach offer daily **fishing** excursions for €12. **Water Sports & Charters** (☎922 71 40 34; booking office open daily 9am-7pm) monopolizes the water sports centers on several beaches around Playa de las Américas (parasailing €25-30 for 10min.). Nightlife centers on Playa de las Américas, where a pastiche of vibrant lights, bikini contests, and beer (€2.40) awaits. A battery of two-story discos hawking 2-for-1 drink promotions to thirsty foreigners ensure that the city's nightlife stays charged and energetic. The **Verónicas** complex offers an imitation Ministry of Sound and your standard Shamrock Pub.

PUERTO DE LA CRUZ

Filled with a wholesome energy in its colorful streets, this port town (pop. 25,000) is one of the most enjoyable urban spots in the islands. Once a capital of the wine trade and an important 17th-century connection to the New World, Puerto de la Cruz draws an assorted mix of sailors and visitors; the steep streets are filled with African vendors, Spanish fishermen, tanned Europeans, and some unusually large lizards. Puerto de la Cruz serves as a base for exploring the Orotava region and Teide National Park, as frequent buses depart from this western destination.

⊠⊠ ORIENTATION & PRACTICAL INFORMATION. From the main bus station on C. del Pozo, 1 (☎922 38 18 07), buses leave for: **El Teide** (#348; 1½hr., 1 per day 9:15am, €3.91); **La Orotava** (#101, 345, 350, 352, 353; 25min., every 30min.-1hr. 6:30am-1:10pm, €0.90); **Playa de las Américas** (#343 and #340; 1hr., 4 per day 9am-5:45pm, €9.30); **Santa Cruz** (#101 and 103; 1-2hr.; every 30min. 6:15am-9:40pm, then

11pm, 12:45, 3:15, and 4:45am; €3.30). Puerto de la Cruz expands from Playa San Telmo past **Plaza del Charco,** ultimately reaching the sands of Playa Jardín. To get to Pl. del Charco from the bus station, turn right on C. del Pozo as you exit, continue onto C. Dr. Ingram, and turn left on C. Blanco (10min.). The **tourist office** sits on Pl. Europa. From Pl. del Charco, head toward the port on C. Blanco, and turn right on C. Santo Domingo; the office is on the left at the far end of the plaza. (☎922 38 60 00. Open July-Sept. M-F 9am-7pm, Sa 9am-noon; Oct.-June M-F 9am-8pm, Sa 9am-1pm.) Services include: **emergency** ☎112; **police,** on Pl. Europa (☎922 37 84 48); the **post office,** C. del Pozo, 14, across from the bus station. (☎922 38 58 02. Open M-F 8:30am-2:30pm, Sa 9:30am-1pm.) **Postal Code:** 38400.

ACCOMMODATIONS & FOOD. *Pensiones* are comfortable and plush in Puerto de la Cruz—reserve in advance. The tourist office has a list of accommodations. An excellent option is **Pensión los Geranios ❷,** C. del Lomo, 14. From Pl. del Charco, turn left on C. San Felipe, right on C. Pérez Zamora, and left on C. del Lomo. Marble floors, great location, comfortable rooms, and a friendly owner all add to the charm of this *hostal.* (☎922 38 28 10. Doubles €22-24.) **Cafes** line Pl. del Charco. For something a little more refined, try **La Rosa de Bari ❷,** C. del Lomo, 23, featuring fresh pastas and other Italian fare. (☎922 36 85 23. Entrees €4-9. Open Tu-Su 12:30-2:45pm and 6:30-10:45pm. AmEx/MC/V.)

SIGHTS & ENTERTAINMENT. The parade of flowers, tourists, bathing suits, and palm trees makes Puerto de la Cruz a sight in itself. **Loro Parque** houses the world's largest penguinarium, marine mammal shows, and great ape exhibits. (☎922 37 38 41; www.loroparque.com. Free shuttle from Playa Martiánez. Open daily.) The small **Museo Arqueológico,** C. del Lomo, 9, features exhibits on the processes and ceremonies used by the prehistoric natives to produce pots, urns, jewelry, and decorations. (☎922 37 14 65. Open Tu-Sa 10am-1pm and 5-9pm, Su 10am-1pm. €1, students €0.50.) Far more interesting are the city's **botanical gardens,** C. Retama, 2. To reach them, climb from Playa de San Telmo on C. la Hoya and continue onto C. Calzada de Martiánez until you reach Av. Marqués Villanueva del Prado. Follow the road past the Canary Centre; the gardens are on your left. Buses to La Orotava and Santa Cruz pass by as well. (☎/fax 922 38 35 72. Open daily Apr.-Sept. 9am-7pm, Oct.-Mar. 9am-6pm. Free.) For beaches, **Playa Jardín** is preferable to the smaller **Playa Martiánez.** The amusing **Lago Martiánez** is a nature-based water park designed by César Manrique. (Open daily 10am-7pm. €3.30.)

Party-primed locals and tourists mix in Puerto's nightlife. **Azúcar,** at the intersection of C. Dr. Ingram and C. Blanco, is a Cuban-themed bar and a local favorite. (Drinks €2.40-3.60. Open daily 7:30pm until late.) Tourists are also drawn to the **Fiestas de Julio,** two weeks of live performances and festive meals centered around July 16th's **Fiesta de la Virgen del Carmen,** in which an image of the fisherman's saint is paraded through town and out into the ocean.

DAYTRIPS FROM PUERTO DE LA CRUZ

PARQUE NACIONAL EL TEIDE

Bus #348 departs from the main station in Puerto de la Cruz at 9:15am and returns from the Parador de Turismo of El Teide at 4pm. From Playa de las Americas, bus #342 departs from Torviscas at 9:15am, passing by Los Cristianos at 9:30am, on its way to the park (1½hr., €3.90). The bus returns to Playa de las Americas and Los Cristianos at 3:15pm from El Portillo Visitors Center, 3:40pm from the teleférico, and 4pm from the Parador de Turismo. Renting a car provides flexibility and allows exploration of the wildly different but equally beautiful views of the eastern (from the Puerto de la Cruz) and western (from Los Cristianos) access roads.

Towering 3718m over Tenerife, Spain's highest peak presides over a vast, unspoiled wilderness. El Teide itself forms the northern ridge of a much larger volcano that erupted millions of years ago; the remaining 17km-wide crater, the **Caldera,** only hints at the size of the explosion. El Teide shadows peaceful fields of the most vibrant wildflower fields on earth. In 1798, during the last major eruption, lava seeped down the slopes of **Pico Viejo** (3102m), creating a stunning, 800m crater. **Las Cañadas,** comprised of collapsed craters, is another product of the sinking process. Though dormant, the area's volcanic activity has not yet ceased. Among the 400 species that inhabit the diverse terrain, watch out for the large **Lagarto Tizón,** a stone-camouflaged lizard, lurking in the park.

The park is accessible by **bus** from Puerto de La Cruz or Playa de las Américas. The buses stop first at **El Portillo Visitors Center,** which offers comprehensive park maps and a brief, but excellent, video on the history and geology of El Teide. (☎922 35 60 16. Open daily 9am-4:30pm.) The bus then continues to the **teleférico** (cable car), which climbs the final 1000m to El Teide's peak. (Open daily 9am-5pm; €20.) The bus stops last at the **Parador de Turismo/Cañada Blanca,** which has free brochures, maps, and a restaurant, but is less helpful than the visitors center at El Portillo. (☎922 35 60 16. Open 9am-4pm.)

Call the national park information service in Santa Cruz (☎922 29 01 29 or 29 01 83; open M-F 9am-2pm) to reserve a spot on one of the **free guided hikes** that depart daily or inquire about the most scenic routes for the day. Nine **unguided hiking trails** allow for independent pacing and meandering. The Parador occupies an idyllic setting next to the emblematic **Roques de García** (2140m), rock chimneys and remnants of volcanic eruptions that face their creators, Mt. Teide and Pico Viejo. An enjoyable 3hr. hike circles the huge formations of **Guajara's** peak and leaves plenty of time to spare for bus-riders. Hikes to El Teide's peak require strong legs and an early start to complete in a day, though it is possible. Alternatively, walkers spend the night at **Refugio Altavista ❶,** past Montaña Blanca, and hike the last hour up the mountain to catch the early-morning sunrise. To reserve a spot, contact the office in Santa Cruz. (☎922 23 98 11. Open Mar.-Oct. M-F 9am-2pm. €12, students €3.)

LA OROTAVA

Buses #101, 350, and 353 run from Puerto de la Cruz's main bus station (30min., at least every 30min.-1hr. 6:30am-1:25am, €0.90).

Named after the lush valley that spreads out below its balconies, the small town of La Orotava warrants a daytrip from Puerto de la Cruz. Nobility resided here in the 17th and 18th centuries, leaving a number of elegant squares, streets, and churches renowned for their facades. If you intend to visit the sights, plan a weekday for the jaunt—most establishments here are closed on weekends.

The tourist office map lists over 15 sights; though it would take forever to see them all, the following walking tour should take two hours. From the tourist office, turn left down C. Tomás Zerolo to find **Iglesia de Santo Domingo,** whose chapel houses several notable paintings and the **Museo Iberoamericano de Artesanía** examining handicrafts of Spain and Latin America. (C. Tomás Zerolo, 34 ☎922 32 33 76. Open M-F 9am-6pm, Sa 9am-2pm. €2.10; during Mass free.) Next, **Iglesia de la Concepción,** off C. Cologan, is a National Artistic Monument and perhaps the Canaries' most graceful Baroque building. Rebuilt in the late 18th century after earthquakes ravaged it, the church has a marble dome over the altar and its myriad works. Especially delicate is Angelo Olivari's rendition of the Immaculate Conception. Check out the church's collection of jewels from the Americas. (Open M-Sa 9am-1pm and 4-8pm. Free.) From the church, go uphill on C. Tomás Pérez and right on C. Carrera del Escultor Estévez to the neo-classical **Palacio Municipal** and the **Plaza del Ayuntamiento.** The cobblestones in the plaza are the result of regal egotism—Alfonso XIII ordered the streets paved before he visited. (Open 9am-2pm. Free.) Just up C. Tomás Pérez, the sensory explosion of **Hijuela del Botánico,** behind iron gates, offers celestial walkways through displays of tropical flora.

ISLAS CANARIAS

(Open M-F 8am-2pm. Free.) From the bus station, head downhill on C. Tejar and take a left onto C. Calvario to the **tourist office,** C. Carrera del Escultor Estévez, 2. (☎922 32 30 41. Open M-F 8:30am-6pm.)

FUERTEVENTURA

Named Fuerteventura after the strong winds that whip along the western coast, the second largest island in the archipelago is a varied physical and cultural landscape. The island is home to the Canaries' best stretch of beach in the south, the Canaries' most abysmal city in the east, and some decent beaches in the north. Beyond coastal towns, Fuerteventura is quite undeveloped, providing mountainous serenity. Like Lanzarote, car rental is a must for those venturing to Fuerteventura on their own. For more information, see **Intra-Island Transport,** p. 592.

PUERTO DEL ROSARIO

Until 1957, Fuerteventura's whitewashed capital was known as Puerto de Cabras (Goats' Harbor). The goats knew what was good for them when they migrated out of the city, which has since become the armpit of the Canaries. Unless you long for a depressing vista of dilapidated, crumbling cement buildings, use Puerto del Rosario (pop. 21,000) only as a transportation hub and skip town for the south.

■ TRANSPORTATION. Trasmediterránea (☎928 85 00 95) and **Naviera Armas** (☎928 85 15 42) run ferries to and from Las Palmas; see **Inter-Island Transport,** p. 592. **Tiadhe buses** (☎928 85 21 66) run to: the **airport** (#3 Caleta de Fuste bus; 20min., 13 per day 7am-9:30pm, €0.90); **Corralejo** (#6; 45min., every 30min. 7am-10pm, €2.40); **Morro Jable** (#1; 2hr., every 1½hr. M-Sa 11 per day 6am-7pm, Su 4 per day 6:30am-6pm; €7). For a **taxi,** dial ☎928 85 00 59.

■■ ORIENTATION & PRACTICAL INFORMATION. Calle León y Castillo is the main thoroughfare of Puerto del Rosario, running downhill to the port and ferry station. **Avenida Primero de Mayo,** perpendicular to C. León y Castillo and parallel to the water, is the town's commercial drag. The **tourist office,** Av. de la Constitución, 5, down the street from the bus station and two blocks from Av. Primero de Mayo, has a handy map of Fuerteventura's major towns. (☎928 53 08 44. Open July-Sept. M-F 8am-6:30pm, Sa 9am-1pm; Oct.-June M-F 8am-7pm, Sa 9am-2pm.) In an **emergency,** call ☎112 or the **police,** C. 23 de Mayo, 16 (☎928 85 51 00). A **hospital** (☎928 86 20 00) is on Ctra. Aeropuerto, and a **pharmacy** on Av. Primero de Mayo, 43. (☎928 53 17 21. Open M-F 9am 1pm and 5-7pm.) A back room of the **S.O.S. market,** off Av. Primero de Mayo on C. del Rosario, has two computers offering **Internet access** (€1.20 per 30min.). The **post office** can be found at Av. Primero de Mayo, 58. (☎928 85 04 12. Open M-F 8:30am-8:30pm, Sa 9:30am-1pm.) **Postal Code:** 35600.

■■ ACCOMMODATIONS & FOOD. Unprepared budget travelers may find themselves stuck in Puerto del Rosario for a night until accommodations in more scenic towns open up. Pray that this doesn't happen, or better yet, plan ahead. Most budget accommodations are at the end of C. León y Castillo and its continuation past the port, C. Almirante Lallermand. **Hostal Tamasite** ❷, C. León y Castillo, 9, has clean rooms on the waterfront. Though few have a view, all have TV and phones. (☎928 85 02 80. Singles €27; doubles €36.) Food in Puerto del Rosario is equally basic; *cafeterías* are scattered along Av. Primero de Mayo and C. León y Castillo. *Tapas* suggestions from the friendly owners at **Getaría Taberna** ❷, C. Guise, 3, are a standout in the generic cafeteria scene. It's located in a small alley next to Hostal Tamasite. (Open M-Sa 10am-4pm and 7pm-1am.)

CORRALEJO

Corralejo's center is a zoo of northern European families, car rental shops, and restaurants. To the south, however, sunbathers and those in search of water sports will appreciate the protected sand dunes, which unfold into a silent, crystal ocean. Daily ferries to Playa Blanca in Lanzarote make Corralejo a necessary stop for island hoppers.

◾ TRANSPORTATION. **Fred Olsen** and **Naviera Armas** run daily **ferries** to **Playa Blanca, Lanzarote** (see **Inter-Island Transport,** p. 592). To reach the center from the **port,** take C. General García Escámez and turn left onto C. la Milagrosa, then turn left to reach the end of **Avenida General Franco** (20min.). **Tiadhe** runs **buses** from the **station** on Av. Juan Carlos I (☎928 85 21 66), off C. Lepanto, to **Puerto del Rosario** (#6; 45min., every 30min. 7am-10pm, €2.40). For a **taxi,** call ☎928 86 61 08 or hail one next to Supermercado Los Corales.

◪ ORIENTATION & PRACTICAL INFORMATION. All activity extends from **Avenida General Franco,** where tourists walk from the southern sand dunes to their hotels in the north, by the port. The **tourist office** is in Pl. Pública, off the end of Av. General Franco nearest the port. (☎928 86 62 35. Open in summer M-F 8am-2:30pm, Sa 9am-noon.) Services include: **emergency,** ☎112; **police,** Po. Atlántico (☎928 86 61 07), near the intersection with Av. General Franco; **pharmacy,** at Av. General Franco, 46 (☎928 86 60 20; open M-F 9am-1:30pm, 5-9pm); **Internet access** at **Coolers Internet and Wine Bar,** C. la Milagrosa, 31, behind the tourist office (☎928 86 63 35; €2 per hr.; open Sa-F 9:30am-2:30pm and 7:30pm-2am, Su 9:30am-2am, W closed); and the **post office,** C. Isaac Peral (☎928 53 50 55; open M-F 8:30am-2:30pm, Sa 9:30am-1pm). **Postal Code:** 35660.

◾◪ ACCOMMODATIONS & FOOD. Apartments and hotels line the beach, but budget accommodations are rare. With a convenient and quiet beachfront location, **Hotel Corralejo ❷,** C. la Marina, 1, is the choice for very simple rooms with ocean views. (☎/fax 928 53 52 46. Singles €20; doubles €25; triples €30.) The English-speaking crew at **Hostal Manhattan ❷,** C. Gravina, 24, a left off Av. General Franco when heading toward the port, offers plain, cool rooms, all with bath. (☎928 86 66 43. Singles €22; doubles €30; triples €42; quads €50. MC/V.) **Food** is nothing special, catering almost entirely to tourists. Restaurants line Av. General Franco; breakfast deals abound. For standard supplies, try **Supermercado Los Corales,** Av. General Franco, 40. (☎928 86 70 43. Open M-Sa 9am-9:30pm, Su 2-9pm.)

◪◪ ENTERTAINMENT & BEACHES. The *Fiestas del Carmen,* beginning July 16 and lasting for two weeks, make for a lively visit. During the festival, such decidedly unholy events as volleyball competitions and outdoor dances help celebrate the town's patron saint before she is led on a watery parade through the port. Nightlife in Corralejo is a parade of tipsy tourists and leering locals. Bars tend toward the cliché, with surf or pub themes; most of them are found along Av. General Franco and in the connecting shopping centers. The **Caleta Dorada Complex** and **Centro Commercial Atlántico** are filled with various second-rate bars and pubs.

The main attraction in Corralejo is the **Parque Natural de Corralejo y Lobos,** which contains protected and rugged sand dunes. Adventure companies compete for business along Av. General Franco, catering to all athletic tastes and abilities. **Dive Centro Corralejo,** C. Nuestra Señora del Pino, 36 (☎928 53 59 06), offers dive trips, lessons, and equipment rental. **Catamaran Celia Cruz** rigs daily trips on glass-bottomed catamarans. (☎639 14 00 14; €8-10 per person.) **Ventura Surf,** in the Apartamentos Hoplaco complex on Av. General Franco, rents windsurfing equipment (€37 per day) and offers a 3hr. (€72) beginner's course and an 8hr. course (€126) for those wanting extra assistance. (☎928 86 62 95. Open daily 10am-6pm.)

MORRO JABLE/PENÍNSULA DE JANDÍA

Expanding 30km across the south of Fuerteventura, the Península de Jandía and its crystal blue beaches along Playa de Sotavento and Playa de Barlovento are the top reasons for visiting the island. The heavenly white sands and turquoise waters that frame the southern coast have transformed the former fishing village of Morro Jable into a mecca for accommodations, food, and transport.

☐ TRANSPORTATION. Though there is no designated bus station in town, **Tiadhe** buses (☎928 85 21 66) stop at the Centro Comercial de Jandía before terminating on C. Gambuesas (across from the post office) in Morro Jable. **Buses** run to **Costa Calma** (#5; 1hr., 11 per day 8:30am-9pm, €1.90) and **Puerto del Rosario** (#1; 2hr., 8 per day 6am-7pm, €7). **Taxis** (☎928 54 12 57) stand at the port in Morro Jable. A ride to one of the two main *playas* of Jandía costs €2.50. In addition to rental cars, **Orlando**, in Apartamentos El Matorral, rents four-wheel-drive vehicles for navigating the peninsula's rough dunes. (☎928 54 04 09. 21+. From €33 per day. AmEx/V.)

☑ ORIENTATION & PRACTICAL INFORMATION. Morro Jable hugs the beach across vast expanses of sun and sky, most notably the **Playa de la Cebada** and the **Playa del Matorral. Avenida Jandía,** which becomes **Avenida del Saladar,** connects the east and west sides of the city center. Most hotels and restaurants line these two streets; the town's roads inevitably lead to the beach. The **tourist office**, Av. del Saladar, is in the Centro de Comercial de Jandía, local 88. (☎928 54 07 76; www.rcanaria.es/pajara. Open M-F 9am-3:30pm.) Services include: **emergency,** ☎112; the **police,** C. Hibisco, 1 (☎928 54 10 22); **pharmacy,** C. Senador Cabrera, 23 (☎928 54 10 12; open M-F 9am-1pm and 5-7pm, Sa 9am-1pm); the **Centro Médico Jandía,** at the Jandía Beach Center, Urb. Solana. (☎928 54 04 20 or 928 54 15 43; open 24hr.); Internet access at **Videoclub Canal 15,** C. del Carmen, 41, one street away from C. Maxorata. (☎928 16 60 30. Open M-Sa 11am-1:30pm and 6-10pm. €1 per 30min.) The **post office** on the corner of C. Buenavista and C. Gambuesas. (☎928 54 03 73. Open M-F 8:30am-2:30pm, Sa 9:30am-1pm.) **Postal Code:** 35625.

☐☐ ACCOMMODATIONS & FOOD. Budget accommodations cluster around the city center, most notably along C. Maxorata and C. Senador Velázquez Cabrera. Visitors should not be alarmed by the occasional bugs that also take up residence; they are no indication of cleanliness, or lack thereof. **Hostal Maxorata ❷,** C. Maxorata, 31, has spacious and airy double rooms, some with views of the beach. (☎928 54 04 74 or 686 98 60 51. Doubles with bath €25.) Have an experience down the street at **Hostal Omahy ❷,** C. Maxorata, 47. (☎928 54 12 54. Call ahead for reservations. Doubles with bath €25.) **Restaurants** in the area are tailored to the tourist crowds; Italian bistros, dime-a-dozen seafood joints, and German *konfiterias* line the beach. **Piccola Italia ❶,** toward the beach from Videoclub Canal 15 on C. del Carmen, serves scrumptious and authentic pizzas to a mostly local crowd. (Pizza €6-7. Open M-W and F-Su 1-4pm and 7pm-midnight. MC/V.) For a calm seaside escape, try Morro Jable's best, near the port. **Avenida del Mar ❷,** Av. del Mar, 1, at the end of the string of restaurants, offers fresh fish (€9) served on a fabulous patio. (☎928 84 43 35. Open daily 10:30am-11pm.)

☐☐ BEACHES & ENTERTAINMENT. The main attractions on the peninsula and in Morro Jable are fierce tanning and water sports in the welcoming turquoise waters. Morro Jable's ■**beaches** are lined with bodies in various states of undress from early morning to late night. The most pristine beaches of the peninsula are those in the south along Playa de Sotavento, followed by those in Playa de Barlovento and Playa del Matorral (close to the city center). The beaches are ideal for reflective walks and adventurous drives (where cars are allowed to enter the beach). Blessed with the islands' calmest waters and lushest sea life, Morro Jable offers excellent opportunities to practice **water sports.** Stiff breezes off the peninsula's southern tip justify the innumerable **windsurfing** schools who set up camp on the beach (the coast hosted last year's world freestyle competition in July). **Barakuda Club,** Av. del Saladar, offers **scuba diving** and equipment rental. (☎928 54 14 18. Dives Su-F 9am and 2pm. €32 per dive; €26 with your own equipment. Good package deals available. Open Su-F 8:30am-6pm.) Sparse **nightlife** revolves around the resorts along Av. del Saladar. Start the night with drinks in one of the many bars of the **Centro Comercial de Jandía** and continue in the city's two *discotecas,* **La Cara Disco** and **Stella Discoteque,** two blocks away.

LANZAROTE

Declared a World Biosphere Reserve by UNESCO in 1993, Lanzarote is both a natural and cultural treasure. Volcanic activity from nearly 300 years ago has left the land barren and dry, with an unusual landscape resembling the surface of the moon. Driving through the island can best be described as inspirational, most notably en route to the unique Parque National Timanfaya. Lanzarotan artist César Manrique and the local government made remarkable efforts to develop a tourism industry that compliments, rather than detracts from, the island's natural beauty. When visiting, do not rely on public transportation—the vast majority of the islands' sights can be accessed only by car. Rent a car, pick up an island map at any tourist office, and start exploring.

THE VISION OF CÉSAR MANRIQUE

Born in Arrecife, César Manrique (1919-1992) is a legendary figure throughout the Canaries. In his native Lanzarote, however, his influence is particularly striking. Manrique took part in the new-wave abstract art movement in Spain, living for periods of time in Madrid and New York City. Dreaming of a sustainable tourism for his native island, however, Manrique spent much of his energy during the 1950s and the rest of his life working with the local government to preserve Lanzarote's natural culture, architecture, and landscape while developing a tourism industry to aid the local economy. Today, visitors can see and experience the fruits of Manrique's labor. The **Centros de Arte, Cultura, y Turismo** are all influenced by Manrique, most created by the artist himself. Within the Parque Nacional de Timanfaya, take note of Manrique's uniquely-designed **El Diablo** restaurant (see p. 566).

■ **FUNDACION CÉSAR MANRIQUE.** The fabulous two-story house, once home to the famous artist, was constructed over five large volcanic bubbles and lava caves in the late 1960s, resulting in a series of unprecedented subterranean chambers and rooms connected by volcanic passageways. *(6km north of Arrecife. ☎ 928 84 31 38. Take the highway to Tahiche and turn on Taro de Tahiche, off San Bartolome Rd. Alternatively, from Arrecife take bus #7 to Teguise and ask to be let off at the Fundación. Open July-Oct. M-Sa 10am-7pm; Nov.-June M-Sa 9am-6pm and Su 10am-3pm. €6.50.)*

■ **MUSEO INTERNACIONAL DE ARTE CONTEMPORÁNEO.** The original building, an 18th-century fortress built by Carlos III, was intended to defend the island from pirate attacks. Its simple stonework epitomizes César Manrique's revitalization of the island's history and architecture. Exhibits rotate frequently, but geometric and abstract works (including those by Manrique himself) form part of the permanent collection, affixed to the fort and hanging into the restaurant below. *(Located to the west of Arrecife, off Av. Naos. ☎ 928 81 23 21. A 40min. walk; taxis from Arrecife cost €2.60 and are safer than walking after dark. Open daily 11am-9pm. Free.)*

MONUMENTO AL CAMPESINO. Manrique's monument to the Lanzarotan peasant is a large abstract sculpture of a farmer and camel. The adjacent museum is worth a look. *(Located just off the highway heading north from San Bartolomé, before Mozaga.* ☎928 52 01 36. *Open daily 10am-6pm, restaurant open daily noon-4:30pm, bar open daily 10am-5:45pm. Free.)*

JARDÍN DE CACTUS. Constructed in the style of a Roman amphitheater, Manrique's prickly paradise boasts 1420 species of cactus from around the world as well as a 24ft. cactus sculpture. *(Off the highway in Guatiza. ☎928 52 93 97. Open daily 10am-6pm, bar open 10am-5:45pm. €3.)*

NATURAL WONDERS

JAMEOS DEL AGUA. Built into the natural subterranean tubes formed by volcanic activity 3000-4500 years ago, the Jameos del Agua constitute a natural and architectural marvel. In the luminous underground lake, keep an eye out for tiny endemic blind crabs. You'll see them before they see you. Jameos del Agua is home to the internationally-renowned **Casa de los Volcanes**, dedicated to the study of vulcanology. An auditorium built into the grotto is home to the **Festival de Música Visual de Lanzarote** every October. At night, Jameos del Agua's restaurant fills with well-dressed patrons. (On the northeastern coast 4km north of Arrieta. ☎928 84 80 20. Open M and W-Th 10am-6:30pm; Tu and F-Sa 6:30pm-2am. €6.60 during the day, €7.20 at night.)

LA CUEVA DE LOS VERDES. Part of the same volcanic system as Jameos del Agua, La Cueva was designed in 1964 by Jesús Soto, though the subterranean chambers were used much earlier by Canarians as refuge from pirate attacks in the 17th century. The caves' colorings and textures are stunning. A natural auditorium similar to that of Jameos del Agua is another site of the October music festival. (3km inland from Jameos del Agua in the northeast. ☎928 84 84 84. Open daily 10am-6pm, last entrance 5pm. €6.60.)

MIRADOR DEL RÍO. Manrique successfully designed the Mirador del Río to blend right into its surroundings; the building remains hidden from view almost until you've reached it. The site provides a breathtaking view of La Graciosa island and the rest of the Chinijo archipelago from over 1400ft. above the sea. Take note of Manrique's hanging metal sculptures, designed to absorb sound within the *mirador*. (At the northern tip of the island, 7km north of Máguez. ☎928 52 65 51. Open daily 10am-6pm, bar/cafe open daily 10am-5:45pm. €2.70.)

PUERTO DEL CARMEN

Primarily British tourists flock to Puerto del Carmen, packaged and lobster-tied by one of many tour companies. As Lanzarote's largest tourist destination, the area provides typical beach fare and decent sun-bathing spots. **Avenida de las Playas** squeezes in endless restaurants, bars, and bazaars. Offshore reefs offer some of the islands' best **scuba diving.** For more information try **Lanzarote Dive Service,** Av. de las Playas, 35 (☎928 51 08 02; www.lanzarotedive.com.).

Bus #2 runs between Arrecife and Puerto del Carmen and stops along Av. de las Playas (40min., every 20min. 6:20am-11:20pm, €1.30). **Fred Olsen** (☎902 10 01 07) and **Naviera Armas** (☎902 45 65 00) also run buses to Playa Blanca to meet their ferry departures. The **tourist office** is at Av. de las Playas near the beach. (☎928 51 33 51; fax 51 56 15. Open M-F July-Aug. 10am-4pm; Sept.-June 10am-5pm.) To explore the island to its fullest, rent a car—there are good deals along Av. de las Playas. **Lanzauto,** Av. de las Playas, 19, rents from €20 per day, insurance and unlimited mileage included. (☎928 51 06 18. 21+. Open M-F 8:30am-1pm and 4-8pm, Sa-Su 8:30am-1pm and 6-8pm.)

■ PARQUE NACIONAL DE TIMANFAYA

Known as **Montañas de Fuegos** (Fire Mountains), the barren landscape of Lanzarote's national park erupts with evidence of the six-year explosion that began in 1730. Resembling the surface of the moon, copper *hornitos* (mud-volcanos) and blackened folds of solidified lava carve their way into the loose soil; only lichen seem to survive in the scorching ground. The winding roads leading to the national park entrance provide countless photographic opportunities. Note that no public transportation runs to the park; you need your own car. Exploration of the park itself is achieved through a tri-lingual 30min. **bus tour** (sit on the right for better views). The roller coaster bus tour is made even more entertaining by a melodramatic soundtrack culminating in the theme from *2001: A Space Odyssey*. Buses leave from the main parking lot in front of El Diablo Restaurant. (☎928 84 00 57. Park open daily 9am-5:45pm. €6.60.) The magic tricks of **Islote de Hilario's** geothermal heat are the tour's highlight. Legend has it that the hermit Hilario, who lived here with his lone camel, planted a fig tree whose fruit was consumed by the underground fires; today, park employees demonstrate the effects of the 300°C temperatures below the earth, provoking jets of steam from the ground. The **El Diablo ❹** restaurant that now occupies the *islote* was designed by César Manrique and constructed using only stone, metal, and glass (due to the high tempera-tures). Volcanic heat seeping from the earth powers the kitchen's grill. The panoramic view from the dining room is the best on the island, extending from the arid mountains to the azure sea. (☎928 17 31 05. Open daily noon-3:30pm, bar 9am-4:45pm.)

Self-exploration of the national park is prohibited, but free **walking tours** can be arranged through the Spanish National Park State Network. The 3.5km Termesana trail in English or Spanish gives tourists a rare opportunity to explore the natural vol-canic beauty by foot (M, W, F 10am from Visitor's Center in Mancha Blanca). Walking tours must be arranged ahead of time by phone or in person at the **Visitor's Center in Mancha Blancha**. (5min. from park main entrance. Take the road from Yaiza to Tinajo, km11.5. ☎/fax 928 84 08 39; www.mma.es. Open daily 9am-5pm.) Tours by **camel** are run separately but do nothing more than go up a hill near the park entrance. The visi-tor's center provides detailed directions for exploring two spectacular and accessible craters outside the national park. They also host a challenging guided walk, the *Ruta del Litoral*, along Lanzarote's northern coast, which lasts roughly 6hr. About 7km away, in the town of Tiagua, lies Lanzarote's quaintest accommodations, **■La Casa Rural Molina ❷**. Turn into the driveway directly next to the km13 sign off the highway in Tiagua. Lounge around the country house, sip fresh juice, and peruse the *casa's* library of guidebooks and novels in a quiet and secluded setting. The gay-friendly Molina is an ideal base for exploring the entire island. Have a cool drink and conversa-tion at the bar. The delicious buffet-style breakfast is free. (☎928 52 92 66; www.casalamolina.com. Reservations recommended. Singles €38; doubles €48, with bath €63.) Head even further south towards Mozaga to dine at Lanzarote's most deli-cious restaurant, **■Monumento al Campesino Restaurante ❸**, adjacent to the monument itself. Feast on *papas arrugadas* drowned in homemade Canarian sauces. (☎928 52 01 36. *Tapas* and entrees €4-15. Open daily 10am-6pm.)

TEGUISE

Brushing the side of Mt. Guanapay (452m), Teguise is Lanzarote's prettiest village, per-fect for wandering walks. A 5min. drive or 30min. walk from Pl. de la Constitución, the 16th-century **Castillo Santa Bárbara** offers one of the island's best views. The castle houses the **Museo Etnográfico del Emigrante Canario**, whose centerpiece is a provoking ethnographic chronicle of the island's first 12 emigrant families. The collection, how-ever, barely rivals the castle itself, with its views of the town and the lava landscape. (Exit Pl. de la Constitución on C. Herrera y Rojos; following the main highway, enter at the Castillo Santa Bárbara sign, up the mountain to the castle. ☎619 84 50 76. Open in summer Tu-F 10am-3pm, Sa-Su 10am-2pm; rest of the year Tu-F 10am-4pm, Sa-Su 10am-3pm. €3.)

Back in Teguise itself, across from the church's entrance lies the 18th-century **Casa Museo Palacio Spinola**, named after a wealthy local merchant. César Manrique oversaw renovations to restore the island's official museum. Old photos of festivals and Canarian customs fill the simple rooms. (☎928 84 51 81. Open M-F 9am-4pm, 3pm in summer; Su 10am-3pm, 2pm in summer. €3.) **Iglesia de la Virgen de Guadalupe** resides in the corner of Pl. de la Constitución.

Buses run daily from Arrecife to Teguise (#7, 9, 10; 6 per day 7:40am-8pm, €0.95), stopping in front of the Ayuntamiento. To get to **Plaza de la Constitución,** the center of town, face the Ayuntamiento, turn right on C. Santo Domingo, right again on C. Morales Lemes, then right into the plaza, the site of the Sunday **market.** Teguise is famous for its authentic Canary Islands cuisine, and food stands flood the town on market day.

LA ISLA GRACIOSA

La Graciosa Island makes Lanzarote look like a bustling metropolis. Located off the northeastern coast of Lanzarote, diminutive La Graciosa is inhabited only by a fishing village (pop. 500) and the few visitors that revel in its isolation. **Camping** is allowed on Playa Francesa. The most adventurous can **rent bikes** from La Graciosa Bike (☎928 84 21 38) or Natural Bike (☎928 84 21 42) within the town itself and head for Playa de las Conchas, a rocky and solitary beach 45min. across the island. Double-check ferry schedules or plan to camp; there are no accommodations on the island. (Líneas Romero runs 3-4 daily ferries between Orzola and La Graciosa. ☎928 84 20 70. From Orzola: July-Sept. 4 per day 10am, noon, 5, 6:30pm; Oct.-June 3 per day 10am, noon, 5pm. From La Graciosa: July-Sept. 4 per day 8, 11am, 4, 6pm; Oct.-June 3 per day 8, 11am, and 4pm. Round-trip €13.)

PLAYA BLANCA

Island-hoppers will invariably end up at Playa Blanca, a beach town and transportation hub at the southern tip of Lanzarote, in the transit to Fuerteventura. Budget accommodations are limited in the area. If you need a place to stay, try **Apartamentos Gutierrez ❹**, Pl. Nuestra Señora del Carmen, 8. (☎928 51 70 89. Doubles €36, extra person €40; quads €50.) A **tourist office** is located in the port (☎928 51 90 18; open July-Sept. 9am-1:30pm; Oct.-May 9am-2pm). Playa Blanca is a great spot for **scuba diving;** contact Centro de Buceo "Toninas" for classes and activities. (☎928 51 73 00; www.arrakis.es/~divingtoninas. Open daily 10am-6pm.)

LA GOMERA

Many believe the verdant island of La Gomera, with its terraced gorges and steep mountain passes, to be the most blessed of all the Canaries. La Gomera's relative isolation and small, stony beaches keep the droves of tourists at bay. Surrounded by banana and avocado plantations and freshened by a constant breeze, the island's main town, San Sebastián, is refreshingly provincial, unscarred by daytrippers from Tenerife. La Gomera's crown jewel, however, is the spectacular Parque Nacional de Garajonay and its refuge of laurisilva forests, which died out elsewhere millions of years ago and remain only in the western Canary Islands.

SAN SEBASTIÁN DE LA GOMERA

Heading off to find the mythical Middle Passage to India, Christopher Columbus dropped anchor here for a few days. He gathered water from the well, prayed at the church, and fell in love with a girl before "discovering" the Americas. May your stay be as storied. These days most explorers breeze through this charming town on their way to the beaches in the south. Still, as a transportation hub filled with affordable accommodations, good restaurants, and a welcoming feel, San Sebastián makes an excellent base for discovering the rest of La Gomera.

█ TRANSPORTATION

Flights: Though most people arrive in La Gomera via ferry from Tenerife, the island's new **airport** (☎922 87 30 00) has a few daily flights from Tenerife and Gran Canaria.

Buses: The main bus stop is by the ferry station on the port. 3 lines start in the port and branch out across the island (€5). Not all buses actually stop at the **bus station**, Vía de Ronda, on the corner of Av. de Colón (☎922 14 11 01), so the port is your best bet. Line 1 to **Valle Gran Rey** with stops in **Parque Nacional de Garajonay** (M-Sa 10:10am, 2:30, 6:30, and 9:30pm; Su 10:10am, 6:30pm). Line 2 to **Playa Santiago** and **Alajeró** (M-Sa 10:10am, 2:30, 6:30, 9:30pm; Su 10:10am, 6:30pm). Line 3 to **Vallehermoso**, stops in **Aguio** and **Hermigua** (M-Sa 10:10am, 2:30, 6:30, 9:30pm; Su 10:10am, 6:30pm). Line 5 to the island's new **airport** (M-Sa 6:30am, 1pm).

Ferries: Trasmediterránea (☎922 87 13 24) and **Fred Olsen** (☎922 87 10 07) run daily ferries to **Los Cristianos** and **El Hierro**. See **Inter-Island Transport**, p. 592.

Car Rental: CiCar (☎922 14 11 46; open M-F 9am-10pm, Sa-Su 9am-noon and 2-7pm) and **Hertz** (☎922 87 15 44; open daily 8am-1pm and 3-7pm), both in the port terminal. 21+. AmEx/MC/V.

Taxis: ☎922 87 05 24.

██ █ ORIENTATION & PRACTICAL INFORMATION

Navigating San Sebastián is a breeze. From the port, **Paseo de Fred Olsen** becomes **Avenida de los Descubridores** and runs along the entire coast, intersected midway by **Calle Real,** the town's main drag, at **Plaza de las Américas.** To get to the plaza from the **port,** turn left on Po. de Fred Olsen; the plaza is on the right (5min.). If you arrive after sunset, consider taking a quick taxi into town (€2), as the streets aren't clearly named and are difficult to maneuver in the dark. **Buses** stop at the port, meeting most ferries (though they're quick to leave once the ferry has arrived). If you've rented a **car,** turn right on Vía de Ronda and left on Ctra. General de Sur (TF-713) to head out of town toward Valle de Gran Rey. Use extreme caution driving the island; blind corners on narrow mountain passes and wide-turning buses can be treacherous—honk that horn.

Tourist Office: C. Real, 4 (☎922 14 15 12 or 87 02 81; www.gomera-island.com), behind Pl. de las Américas. Open M-Sa 9am-1pm and 4-6pm, Su 10am-1pm. **Park Service,** Ctra. General de Sur (TF-713), 20 (☎922 80 09 93). Go left on Av. de Colón from C. Real, and continue across the bridge following signs to Valle Gran Rey; the office is on the right at the 2nd bend. Open daily 9:30am-4:30pm.

Currency Exchange: Banco Santander Central Hispano, C. Real, 7. Open M-F 8:30am-2pm, Sa 8:30am-1pm. **Banks** line Pl. de las Américas.

Laundromat: Lavandería HECU, C. Real, 76 (☎922 14 11 80). Open M-F 8:30am-1:30pm and 5-8pm, Sa 8:30am-1:30pm. €4.20 wash, €4.20 dry.

Emergency: ☎112.

Pharmacy: Pl. de la Constitución, 14 (☎922 14 16 05), next to the tourist office in Pl. de las Américas. Open M-F 9am-1:30pm and 5-8pm, Sa 9-1:30pm.

Hospital: Nuestra Sra. de Guadalupe (☎920 14 02 02). From Pl. de las Américas, walk away from the port, turn right on Av. del Quinto Centenario, left across the bridge, and take the 1st right.

Internet Access: CiberGomera, C. República de Panamá (☎922 87 17 51), on the corner with C. Real. €1 per 30min. Open M-Sa 11am-1pm and 4:30-9:15pm.

Post Office: C. Real, 60 (☎922 87 10 81). Open M-F 8:30am-2:30pm, Sa 9:30am-1pm. **Postal Code:** 38800.

ACCOMMODATIONS

San Sebastián's budget accommodations are more affordable than anywhere in the Canaries. *Pensiones* offer double rooms in old Canary-style homes; most have communal baths. For longer stays, *apartamentos* are a better option. *Pensión* signs hang out of windows on C. Real. Pricier hotels reside on C. Ruiz de Padrón.

Pensión Victor, C. del Medio, 23 (☎607 51 75 65 or 81 32 01; fax 922 87 13 35). A renovated 250-year-old house with flower beds and vines along the outdoor patio. High wood-beamed ceilings and common baths. Ask for the room with the terrace. Noisy restaurant downstairs has tasty sandwiches (€1.20). Singles €16-18; doubles €20-24. ❷

Apartamentos San Sebastián, C. del Medio, 20 (☎922 14 14 75 or 653 96 21 66; fax 87 13 54). Breezy, newly furnished apartments with 2 twin beds, kitchen, TV, and living room. Reception (open 8:30am-1pm and 4-8pm) is in the currency exchange office to the right when facing the entrance. Apartment €35; economical for pairs. ❸

Pensión Colón, C. Medio, 59 (☎922 87 02 35). Tiled floors and austere rooms surround a quiet courtyard; avoid stuffy rooms without windows. Singles €20; doubles €25. ❶

FOOD

San Sebastián is filled with authentic Canarian restaurants and cheap *tapas* bars. Nicer options surround Pl. de la Constitución, and typical bars and *mesones* line C. Ruiz de Padrón and C. del Medio. **Bar-Restaurante Casa del Mar ❶,** Po. de Fred Olsen, 1, serves excellent local fare; try the *bacalao a la vizcaína*—delicious cod in tomato and zucchini sauce with local potatoes. (☎922 87 03 20. Entrees €4.80-8. Open W-M noon-4pm and 7-11pm. **Bar-Restaurant Cubino ❷,** C. Virgen de Guadalupe, 2, off Pl. de la Constitución, serves delicious seafood and meat dishes in healthy portions to a local crowd. (☎922 86 03 83. Entrees €4-9. Open W-M 9am-4pm and 7pm-midnight.) Buy groceries at **Hiper Trebol,** in the market complex at the intersection of C. Colón and Av. del Quinto Centenario. (Open M-F 9am-9pm, Sa-Su 9am-3pm.) A **produce market** fills the plaza on Wednesdays and Saturdays.

SIGHTS

The few sights in San Sebastián are centered on a foreigner: Christopher Columbus. **Iglesia de la Asunción,** where Columbus prayed before he left, is the only church on C. Real . The carved woodwork adorning the simple church is typical of Canarian architecture. Nearby, the **Casa de Colón,** C. Real, 56, hosts a permanent collection of ceramics from the Andean Chimú civilization of the 11th-15th centuries, as well as rotating exhibits. (Open M-F 10am-1pm. Free.) The **Torre del Conde,** a small 15th-century fort, looms over the beach. In 1488, the wife of the murdered governor Hernán Peraza bolted herself inside as she watched the citizens take control of the port. Now it displays Gomeran cartography. (Open Tu-F 10am-1pm.) The tourist office is inside **La Casa de la Aguada,** which features the well from which Columbus drew water to "baptize the Americas."

No Canarian city would be complete without a **beach.** Although there is a small patch of black sand in front of Pl. de las Américas, **Playa de la Cueva** is better: more sand, calmer waters, caved cliffs, and a view of Tenerife. From Pl. de las Américas, follow Po. de Fred Olsen toward the port and curve left away from the wharf.

NEAR SAN SEBASTIÁN

■ PARQUE NACIONAL DE GARAJONAY

Take the bus (line #1) to Valle Gran Rey and get off at Pajarito; if you bear right, the trailhead is 1km up the road. A car greatly facilitates exploration of the park, but several of the best trails are reachable by bus.

Blanketed in thick mist and fog that produces a "horizontal rain" year-round, Gara-jonay National Park sustains some of the last **laurisilva forest** on earth. Once ubiquitous in the Mediterranean basin, these moss-filled forests fell victim to the Ice Age millions of years ago. Hikers in Garajonay wade through lush ferns, myriad streams, and drip-ping plants to reach a stunning mountaintop view of the other islands. The park main-tains numerous trails and **three self-guided paths,** most originating from **Contadero.** Remnants of volcanic activity, **Los Roques,** line the roadside. The **visitors center** (☎922 80 09 93) is in **Agulo,** 9km outside the park (open daily 9:30am-4:30pm). It provides info on the park's three self-guided hikes. To get to the visitors center, take bus #3 from San Sebastián (45min., 4 per day 10:30am-9:30pm) and get off at the Las Rosas stop. The **Park Service,** Ctra. General de Sur (TF-713), 20, in San Sebastián, has the same info. (☎922 80 09 93. Open daily 9:30am-4:30pm.) Both offices make the reservations required for the **free guided tours** (Sa 10am, meet in La Laguna Grande; tour in Spanish only) and carry the booklet whose descriptions corresponds to the numbered wooden signs on the park trails.

VALLE GRAN REY

Green terrace farms step back from sandy beaches into the deep gorge of the "Valley of the Great King." The mellow shores keep the tourist population con-tent with sunbathing, cliff-exploring, and water sports, while farmers work the peaceful valley. Because of its beaches, Valle Gran Rey is probably the nicest place to base a stay in La Gomera, but it can be slightly expensive.

Bus #1 runs from San Sebastián to Valle Gran Rey's three small villages: **La Calera, La Playa,** and **Vueltas,** in that order. (2hr.; M-F 4 per day 10:10am-9:30pm, Su 10:10am and 6:30pm; €5.) La Calera sits up higher in the valley, while La Playa and Vueltas cover the shores below. The three are geographically aligned in a triangular form less than a kilometer long. Street signs are nonexistent, but the area is easy to navi-gate—for help, stop at the **tourist office** in La Playa. From the La Playa bus stop, face the beach, head right on the main road, and turn left on C. Noria. (☎/fax 922 80 54 58. Open in winter M-Sa 9am-1:30pm and 4-6:30pm, Su 10am-1pm; in summer M-Sa 9am-1pm and 4-6pm, Su 10am-1pm.)

The most popular beaches are **Playa de Argaga** and **Playa las Arenas,** a short walk left of Vueltas when facing the beach. The sandy **Playa de Calera** and **Playa de Puntilla,** which stretch left from La Playa, have calm waters. **Playa del Inglés** features more waves, nearby cliffs, and naked bodies, a 10min. walk from La Playa. With your back to the tourist office turn right, take your first right, and follow the road, as it becomes dirt, to the beach.

Valle Gran Rey's charm and scenery are best experienced with an overnight stay, though call ahead as the area is no secret to tourists. The few *pensiones* in the area offer only doubles. *Apartamentos* provide more creature comforts; one place to inquire is the **San José ❷** restaurant, just to the right of the tourist office in La Playa. (☎922 80 53 31. Single apartment €20; double apartment €24.) **Casa Bella Cabellos ❶** on C. la Alameda in La Calera offers great views from modern, balconied apartments, and simple wooden doubles in an antique home. From the bus stop, head back up the valley and take the first left (almost an uphill U turn), follow the road past the San Sebastián bar, then bear right at the "do not enter sign," and follow the road up the hill until it flattens out. It's on the left. (☎922 80 51 82. 3 night min. House rooms €20. Double with fridge €25; quad with kitchen €35.) Also in La Calera, **Pensión Parada ❶** offers simple doubles (a bath for every 2 rooms) right next to the bus stop and a 10min. walk from the beach. (☎922 80 50 52; fax 28 13 10. Doubles €24.)

PORTUGAL

A place where rows of olive trees give way to ancient castles and working docks are flanked by trendy nightclubs, Portugal is a destination overflowing with diversity and contradictions that will delight any traveler. Today's Portugal is a product of its varied history that ranged from rule over one of the most glorious trading empires in the world to vassal status under the Moors, Spanish, and French. The relics of that history are a major reason to come to Portugal, but modern Portugal hosts comparable attractions of its own, from Lisboa's nightlife to the hiking trails in the pristine mountains of Trás-Os-Montes. Sheltered from many of the modernizing forces of the 20th century by an oppressive fascist dictatorship, Portugal is emerging from the shadows with a unique mix of the cosmopolitan and the traditional. That mixture makes Portugal a colorful and worthwhile choice for those tired of the more conventional travel spots in Europe.

HISTORY

In the 14th and 15th centuries, Portugal was one of the most powerful nations in the world, ruling a wealthy empire that stretched from America to Asia. Although the country's international prestige declined by 1580, Portuguese pride did not. Over the following centuries, Portugal struggled to assert its national identity and its uniqueness from Spain. Modern Portugal, with its stable democracy and fast-growing economy, has proven the strength of its national character.

EARLY HISTORY. Settlement of Portugal began around 5500 BC when neolithic cultures arrived from Andalucía. Other than some banging of stones, their impact was negligible, leaving the real work of settling Portugal to be done hundreds of years later. Several tribes inhabited the Iberian Peninsula during the first millennium BC, including the **Celts,** who began to settle in northern Portugal and Spanish Galicia in the 9th and 8th centuries BC, and the **Phoenicians,** who founded several fishing villages along the Algarve and ventured as far north as modern-day Lisboa. The **Greeks** and **Carthaginians** soon followed, settling the southern and western coasts. After their victory over Carthage in the Second Punic War (218-201 BC) and their defeat of the Celts in 140 BC, the **Romans** gained control of Portugal, integrating the region into the Iberian province of Lusitania. Six centuries of Roman rule, which introduced the *Pax Romana* and "Latinized" Portugal's language and customs, also paved the way for Christianity.

VISIGOTHS & MOORS (469-1139). Rome's decline in the 3rd and 4th centuries AD heavily impacted the Iberian Peninsula. By 469, the **Visigoths,** a tribe of migrating Germanic people, had crossed the Pyrenees, and for the next two centuries they dominated the peninsula. In 711, however, the Muslims (also known as the **Moors**) invaded Iberia, toppling the Visigoth monarchy. Muslim communities settled along Portugal's southern coast, an area they called the *al-Gharb* (Algarve), and after nearly four centuries of rule, the Muslims left a significant legacy of agricultural advances, architectural landmarks, and linguistic and cultural customs.

THE CHRISTIAN RECONQUISTA & THE BIRTH OF PORTUGAL (1139-1415). Though *la Reconquista* officially began in 718, it didn't pick up steam until the 11th-century, when Fernando I united Castilla and León, providing a strong base from which to reclaim territory. In 1139, **Dom Afonso Henriques** (Afonso I), a noble from the frontier territory of Portucale (a region centered around Porto), declared

Portugal

ATLANTIC OCEAN

0 — 50 miles
0 — 50 kilometers

Valença do Minho
Vila Nova de Cerveira
Parque Nacional da Peneda-Gerês
Caminha
Rio Minho
Viana do Castelo
Rio Lima
MINHO
Serra do Gerês
Caldas de Gerês
Parque Natural de Montesinho
Bragança
Rio Cávado
Barcelos
Braga
TRÁS-OS-MONTES
Guimarães
Rio Tâmega
Amarante
Serra do Marão
Vila Real
Oporto
DOURO LITORAL
DOURO ALTO
Espinho
Rio Douro
COSTA VERDE
BEIRA ALTA
Ovar
Aveiro
Viseu
BEIRA LITORAL
Luso
Rio Mondego
Buçaco
Guarda
Coimbra
Serra da Estrêla
Parque Nacional da Serra da Estrêla
COSTA DA PRATA
Figueira da Foz
Conimbriga
Rio Zêzere
Serra da Gardunha
BEIRA BAIXA
Leiria
Castelo Branco
Nazaré
Batalha
Fátima
Serra de Aire
São Martinho do Porto
Alcobaça
Tomar
Castelo de Vide
Ilhas Berlengas
Caldas da Rainha
Rio Tejo
Serra de São Mamede
Marvão
Cabo Carvoeiro
Óbidos
Crato
Portalegre
Peniche
Santarém
ESTREMADURA
RIBATEJO
Ericeira
Vila Franca de Xira
Estremoz
Elvas
Mafra
SPAIN
Sintra
Queluz
Lisboa
Cascais
ALTO ALENTEJO
Estoril
Évora Monte
Parque Nacional de Arrábida
Setúbal
Évora
Cabo Espichel
Tróia Peninsula
Rio Sado
Serra de Ossa
Sesimbra
Alcácer do Sal
COSTA AZUL
Santiago do Cacém
Sines
Beja
BAIXO ALENTEJO
Rio Guadiana
COSTA DOURADA
Rio Mira
Mértola
Serra de Monchique
Lagos
Silves
ALGARVE
Portimão
Albufeira
Tavira
Cabo de São Vicente
Sagres
Faro
Vila Real de Santo António
Olhão
Golfo de Cádiz

PORTUGAL

independence from Castilla and León. Soon thereafter, he declared himself the first king of Portugal, and although the kingdom of Portugal was recognized by Spain in 1143, the papacy did not officially recognize the kingly title until 1179.

With the help of Christian military groups like the Knights Templar, the new monarchy battled Muslim forces, capturing Lisboa in 1147. By 1249, *la Reconquista* under **Afonso III** defeated the last remnants of Muslim power with successful campaigns in the Alentejo and Algarve. The Christian kings, led by **Dinis I** (1279-1325), promoted use of the Portuguese language (instead of Spanish) and with the **Treaty of Alcañices** (1297) settled border disputes with neighboring Castilla, asserting Portugal's identity as the first unified, independent nation in Europe.

PORTUGAL SAILS THE OCEAN BLUE (1415-1580). João I (1385-1433), the first king of the House of Aviz, ushered in unity and prosperity never before seen in Portugal. DOm João increased the power of the crown, thereby establishing a strong base for future Portuguese expansion and economic success. The Anglo-Portuguese alliance, which he secured with the **Treaty of Windsor** (1386), would come to influence Portugal's foreign policy well into the 19th century.

The 15th century was one of the greatest periods in the history of maritime travel and naval advances. Under the leadership of João's son, **Prince Henry the Navigator,** Portugal established itself as a world leader in maritime science and exploration. Portuguese adventurers captured the Moroccan city of Ceuta in 1415, discovered the Ilhas Madeiras in 1419, happened upon the uninhabited Azores in 1427, and began to exploit the African coast for slaves and riches a few years later.

Bartolomeu Dias changed the world forever when he rounded Africa's Cape of Storms, later renamed the Cape of Good Hope, in 1488. Dias opened the route to the East and paved the way for Portuguese entrance into the spice trade. The Por-

---

ISLANDS IN THE BIG STREAM Paradise on earth? Start with water, water, everywhere. Add some volcanic eruptions, plus hearty, friendly, and pleasingly relaxed inhabitants. Pepper it with astounding beauty, alluring beaches, and filter out pollution, persecution, and stress. Voilà!—you have Portugal's Atlantic islands, the **Azores** and **Madeiras,** considered by many to be the world's most beautiful and most serene. The **Madeiras**—Madeira, Porto Santo, and Desertas—rise abruptly from the ocean off Africa's northwestern coast. Once an important stop-over for explorers, today their climate, colorful fauna, tropical fruits, and luxurious hotels make them a strong contender for the ideal resort spot. Immortalized in *Moby Dick,* the nine islands of the **Azores** boast rolling hills, lush fauna, cavernous lakes, glimmering seas, and friendly inhabitants. Tranquil and tempting, the Azores will leave the particularly melodramatic to muse (as does one brochure), "Is this the home of God?"

---

tuguese monarchs may have rejected **Christopher Columbus,** but they funded a number of other momentous voyages. In 1497, they supported **Vasco da Gama,** who led the first European naval expedition to India; successive expeditions added numerous East African and Indian colonies to Portugal's collection. Three years after da Gama's voyage, **Pedro Álvares Cabral** claimed Brazil for Portugal, establishing a far-flung empire. Portugal's monarchy peaked with **Dom Manuel I the Fortunate** (1495-1521). Known as "the King of Gold," Manuel controlled a spectacular empire. Competition from other commercial powers took its toll, however, and the House of Aviz lost its predominance in 1580.

THE HOUSES OF HABSBURG & BRAGANÇA (1580-1807). In 1580, Habsburg King of Spain **Felipe II** claimed the Portuguese throne, and the Iberian Peninsula was briefly ruled by one monarch. For 60 years, the Habsburgs dragged Portugal into several ill-fated wars, including the Spanish-Portuguese Armada's crushing loss to England in 1588. Inattentive King Felipe didn't even visit Portugal until 1619, and by the end of Habsburg rule, Portugal had lost its once vast empire. In 1640, the **House of Bragança** engineered a nationalist rebellion against King Felipe IV. After a brief struggle they assumed control, asserting Portuguese independence from Spain. To secure sovereignty, the Bragança dynasty went to great lengths to reestablish ties with England. In 1661, Portugal ceded Bombay to England, and the marriage of Catherine of Bragança to England's Charles II cemented the Portuguese-British alliance. Nearly half a century later, **João V** (1706-1750) restored a measure of prosperity, using newly mined Brazilian gold and diamonds to finance massive building projects, including construction of extravagant palaces. The momentous **Earthquake of 1755** devastated Lisboa and southern Portugal, killing over 50,000 people. Despite the damage, dictatorial minister **Marquês de Pombal** was able to rebuild Lisboa while instituting national economic reforms.

NAPOLEON'S CONQUEST & FAMILY MATTERS (1807-1910). Napoleon took control of France in 1801 and set his sights on the rest of Europe. When he reached Portugal, his army encountered little resistance. The Portuguese royal family fled to Brazil. **Dom João VI** returned to Lisboa in 1821, only to face an extremely unstable political climate. Amidst turmoil within the royal family, João's son **Pedro** declared independence for Brazil the following year, becoming the country's first ruler. The **Constitution of 1822,** drawn up during the royal family's absence, severely limited the power of the monarchy, and after 1826, the **War of the Two Brothers** (1826-1834) between constitutionalists (supporting Pedro, the new king of Brazil) and monarchists (supporting Miguel, Pedro's brother) reverberated through Portugal. Eight gory years later, with Miguel in exile, Pedro's daughter **Maria II** (1834-1854) ascended the throne at a mere 15 years old. Conflict continued during the **Portuguese Civil War** in 1868. The next 75 years brought continued tensions between liberals and monarchists.

FROM THE FIRST REPUBLIC TO SALAZAR (1910-1974). Portugal spent the first few years of the 20th century trying to recover from the political discord of the 19th. On October 5, 1910, 20 year-old **Dom Manuel II** fled to England. The new government, known as the **First Republic,** earned worldwide disapproval for its expulsion of the Jesuits and other religious orders, and the conflict between the government and labor movements heightened domestic tensions. Portugal's decision to enter **World War I** (even though on the side of the victorious Allies) proved economically fatal and internally divisive. The weak republic wobbled and eventually fell in a 1926 military coup. General **António Carmona** took over as leader of the provisional military government, and in the face of financial crisis, he appointed **António de Oliveira Salazar,** a prominent economics professor, minister of finance. In 1932, Salazar became prime minister, but soon devolved into a dictator. His *Estado Novo* (New State) granted suffrage to women, but did little else to end the country's authoritarian traditions. While Portugal's international economic standing improved, the regime laid the cost of progress squarely on the shoulders of the working class, the peasantry, and colonial subjects in Africa. A terrifying secret police (PIDE) crushed all opposition to Salazar's rule, and African rebellions were quelled in bloody battles that drained the nation's economy.

REVOLUTION & REFORM (1974-2000). The slightly more liberal **Marcelo Caetano** dragged on the unpopular African wars after Salazar's death in 1970. By the early '70s, international disapproval of Portuguese imperialism and the army's dissatisfaction with colonial entanglements had led General António de Spinola to call for decolonization. On April 25, 1974, a left-wing military coalition calling itself the Armed Forces Movement overthrew Caetano in a quick coup. This **Revolution of**

PORTUGAL

the Carnations sent Portuguese dancing into the streets; today every town in Portugal has its own Rua 25 de Abril. The Marxist-dominated armed forces established a variety of civil and political liberties and withdrew Portuguese claims on African colonies by 1975, resulting in a flood of over 500,000 refugees into the country.

The socialist government nationalized several industries and appropriated large estates in the face of substantial opposition. The country's first elections in 1976 put the charismatic socialist prime minister **Mario Soares** into power. When a severe economic crisis exploded, Soares instituted "100 measures in 100 days" to shock Portugal into economic shape. Through austere reforms, he helped stimulate industrial growth. The landmark year 1986 brought Portugal into the European Community (now the European Union), ending its age-old isolation from more affluent northern Europe. Despite challenges by the newly formed Social Democratic Party (PSD), Soares won the elections in 1986, becoming the nation's first civilian president in 60 years. Soares was eventually replaced by the Socialist former mayor of Lisboa, **Jorge Sampaio,** in 1995.

CURRENT EVENTS

The European Union declared Portugal a full member of the EU Economic and Monetary Union (EMU) in 1999, and the nation continues in its quest to catch up economically with the rest of Western Europe. In 1999, Macau, Portugal's last overseas territory, was ceded to the Chinese. Portugal and Indonesia have agreed to cooperate over the reconstruction of East Timor, an ex-Portuguese colony that Indonesia invaded in 1975, with Portugal as an intermediary between the EU and Indonesia in their mutual efforts to promote stability and democracy in the former colony. In 1997, Portugal celebrated the dark 500th anniversary of the explusion of the Jews. **Jorge Sampaio** returned to the presidency after the January 2001 parliamentary elections, but Socialist prime minister **Antonio Guterres** resigned in December of 2001 after his party suffered heavy losses in Parliamentary elections. President Sampaio then appointed **Jose Manuel Durao Barroso** as prime minister to represent the newly merged parties.

PEOPLE & CULTURE

LANGUAGE

Thanks to the Romans, who colonized Iberia late in the third century BC, practiced Romance speakers will find Portuguese an easy conquest (though pronunciation may be difficult). Although this softer sister of Spanish is closely related to the other Romance languages, modern Portuguese is an amalgam of diverse influences. A close listener will catch echoes of Italian, French, Spanish, Arabic, and even English and Slavic. Portugal's global escapades spurred the spread of its language. Today, Portuguese (the world's 6th most-spoken language) binds over 200 million people worldwide, most of them in Portugal, Brazil, Mozambique, and Angola. Prospective students of the language should note the differences between Brazilian and continental Portuguese, mainly in pronunciation and usage.

Some may be heartened to know that English, Spanish, and French are widely spoken throughout Portugal, especially in tourist-oriented locales. Look to the *Let's Go* glossary for terms used in this guide (see **Glossary,** p. 814).

RELIGION

Though constitutional freedom of religion mandates no state religion in Portugal, it might as well; roughly 97% of the Portuguese population practices Roman Catholicism. Composing the remaining 3% are Protestants, Jehovah's Witnesses, and Mormons, along with 35,000 Muslims and a mere 700 Jews. A major force in the shaping of Portugal's history, the Catholic Church is a respected and powerful influence in modern-day Portugal as well; attendance is high at Sunday masses, and festivals honoring patron saints (*romarias*) are celebrated everywhere.

FLORA & FAUNA

The push to conserve nature, landscape, and heritage in harmony with the growing needs of a burgeoning population has recently been responsible for the establishment of protected areas. The Costa Azul boasts a natural park and two reserves among other protected areas. The chalky hills of the **Serra da Arrabida** date back 180 million years, while the Natural Reserve of the **Sado Estuary** protects river birds, the European otter, and bucks, amidst the diverse species of the estuary. Bird-watching is especially rewarding in the **Tejo Estuary,** where the bird population in winter months reaches 80,000,largely due to the gathering of half the **avocets** in Europe. The protected **Arriba Fossil Area** of the Costa da Caparica showcases sedimentary rock as river bank, dating back 15 million years, where one can see fossilized fauna from the Miocene epoch.

FOOD & DRINK

LOCAL FARE

The Portuguese season their dishes with the basics: olive oil, garlic, herbs, and sea salt. Despite their historic role in bringing Eastern flavorings to Europe, they use relatively few spices. Portugal's miles of coastline ensure that **seafood** forms the core of Portuguese cuisine; it is usually prepared as simply as possible to emphasize freshness. Seafood lovers will enjoy *choco grelhado* (grilled cuttlefish), *linguado grelhado* (grilled sole), and *peixe espada* (swordfish), to name a few. The more adventurous should try the *polvo* (boiled or grilled octopus), *mexilhões* (mussels), and *lulas grelhadas* (grilled squid). **Meat** is treated in the opposite manner from seafood; the taste is extensively embellished and even masked by heavy sauces. Pork, chicken, and beef appear on most menus and are often combined in *cozida à portuguesa* (boiled beef, pork, sausage, and vegetables). True connoisseurs add a drop of *piri-piri* (mega hot) sauce on the side. An expensive delicacy is freshly roasted *cabrito* (kid). No matter what you order, leave room for *batatas* (potatoes), prepared countless ways—including *batatas fritas* (fried potatoes)—which accompany each meal.

The availability of excellent produce means that **sopas** (soups) are usually made from local vegetables. Savory and substantial, soups can serve as a cheap alternative to a full meal. Common varieties include *caldo de ovos* (bean soup with hard-boiled eggs), *caldo de verdura* (vegetable soup), and the tasty *caldo verde* (a potato and kale mixture with a slice of sausage and olive oil). **Sandes** (sandwiches) such as the *bifana* or *prego no pão* (meat sandwich) may be no more than a hunk of meat on a roll. Cows, goats, and ewes please the palate by providing raw material for Portugal's renowned **queijos** (cheeses). Vegetarians should accustom themselves to cheese sandwichs and Portugal's delectable *broa* bread.

Portugal's favorite dessert is **pudim**, or *flan*, a rich, caramel custard similar to *crême bruleé*. Satisfy your sweet tooth with **marzipan** made with almonds from the groves of the Algarve. For something different, try *pêras* (pears) drenched in sweet port wine and served with raisins and hazelnuts on top. Most common are countless varieties of inexpensive, high-quality **sorvete** (ice cream)—look for vendors posting the colorful, ubiquitous "Olá" sign. *Pastelarías* (bakeries) are in most towns, and tasty **pastries** make for a cheap breakfast.

MEALS & DINING HOURS

Portuguese eat their hearty midday meal—*almoço* (lunch)—between noon and 2pm and *jantar* (dinner) between 9pm and midnight. Both meals entail at least three courses. There are no greasy lumberjack breakfasts to be found in Portugal—a pastry from a *pastelaría* (bakery) and coffee from a café suffices for *pequeno almoço* (breakfast). If you get the munchies between 4 and 7pm, snack bars sell **sandes** (sandwiches) and sweet cakes. It is advisable to make reservations when dining in some of the more upscale city restaurants.

EATING OUT

A full meal costs €6-15, depending on the restaurant's location and quality. **Meia dose** (half portions) cost more than half-price but are often more than adequate—a full portion may satisfy two. The ubiquitous **prato do dia** (special of the day) and **ementa** *(menú)* of appetizer, bread, entree, dessert, and beverage will stifle the loudest stomach growls. The **ementa turística** (tourist *menú*) is usually not a good deal—restaurants with menus translated into multiple languages are more likely to charge exorbitant prices. Standard pre-meal bread, butter, cheese, and pâté may be dished without your asking, but these pre-meal munchies are not free (€1-3 per person). You may appreciate them, however, since chefs start cooking only after you order; be prepared to wait. In restaurants (but not cafes), a service charge of 10% is usually included in the bill. When service is not included, it is customary to leave 5-10% as a tip. Vegetarians may find themselves somewhat left out in the cold in Portugal, but given the availability and high quality of fresh produce, making special requests to chefs may prove fruitful. Smoking is still generally accepted in most establishments, although there has been a recent move in parliament to institute no smoking zones in some areas.

DRINK

The exact date marking the birth of Portuguese wine is unknown, though 5000 BC is often used as an estimate. Though it does not quite rival the internationally-renowned French and German wines, the quality and low cost of Portuguese *vinho* (wine) is truly astounding; the reds are perhaps the most recognized. The pinnacle, **vinho do porto** (port), pressed (by feet) from the red grapes of the Douro Valley and fermented with a touch of brandy, is a dessert in itself. Chilled, white port can be a snappy aperitif, while ruby or tawny port makes a classic after-dinner drink. A six-month-long heating process gives **Madeira** wines their unique "cooked" flavor. Try the dry Sercial and Verdelho before the main course, and the sweeter Bual and Malmsey after. Sparkling *vinho verde* is picked and drunk young and comes in either red or white. The red may be a bit strong, but the white is deliciously brash by any standard. The latter is exported rather than consumed and is classified as a semi-sparkling wine. The Adega Cooperatives of Ponte de Lima, Monção, and Amarante produce the best of this type. Excellent local table wines include Colares, Dão, Borba, Bairrada, Bucelas, and Periquita. If you can't decide, experiment with the **vinho de casa** (house wine); either the *tinto* (red) or the *branco* (white) is a reliable standby. Tangy **sangría** comes filled with fresh orange slices and makes even a budget meal festive at a minimal expense (usually around €2.50 for a half-pitcher). Your Portuguese drinking vocabulary should contain the following terms: *claro:* new wine, *espumante:* sparkling wine, *rosado:* a rosé wine, *vinho de mesa:* table wine, and *vinho verde:* a young wine. Bottled Sagres and Super Bock are excellent beers. If you don't ask for it *fresco* (cool), it may come *natural* (room temperature). A tall, slim glass of draft beer is a **fino** or an **imperial,** while a larger stein is a **caneca.** To sober up and wake up, order a **bica** (cup of black espresso), a **galão** (coffee with milk, served in a glass), or a **café com leite** (coffee with milk, served in a cup). See the Glossary for more wine terms.

CUSTOMS & ETIQUETTE

Portuguese are generally friendly, easygoing, and receptive to foreign travelers. Even if your Portuguese is a little rusty, a wholehearted attempt at speaking the native tongue will be appreciated.

TABOOS. Be cautious of shorts and flip-flops; they may be seen as disrespectful in some public establishments or in more rural areas, even during a heat wave. Though dress in Portugal is obviously more casual in the hot summer months than in the cold of winter, strapless tops on women and collarless t-shirts on men are generally unacceptable. Skimpy clothes are always a taboo in churches, as are tourist visits during masses or services.

PUBLIC BEHAVIOR. On any list of Portuguese values, politeness would be at the top. Be sure to address Portuguese as *senhor* (Mr.), *senhora* (Mrs.), or *senhora dona* followed by the first name (for older and respected women). To blend in, it is a good idea to be as formal as possible upon a first meeting. Introduce yourself in detail, giving more than just your name. You'll be welcomed openly and made to feel at home if you mention who you are, where you're from, and what you are doing in Portugal. Don't be surprised if you get pecked on both cheeks by younger Portuguese, but handshakes are generally the standard introductory gesture.

THE ARTS

ARCHITECTURE

Portugal's signature **Manuelino** style celebrates the prosperity and imperial expansion of Dom Manuel I's reign (see **Portugal Sails the Ocean Blue,** p. 620). Manueline works routinely merge Christian images and maritime motifs. Their rich and lavish ornaments reflect a hybrid of Northern Gothic, Spanish Plateresque, and Moorish influences. The Manueline style found its most elaborate expression in the church and **Torre de Belém,** built to honor Vasco da Gama. Close seconds are the **Mosteiro dos Jerónimos** in Belém and the **Abadia de Santa Maria de Vitória** in Batalha.

Though few Moorish structures survived the Christian *Reconquista,* their style influenced later Portuguese architecture. One of Portugal's most beautiful traditions is the colorfully painted ceramic tiles which grace many walls and ceilings. Carved in relief by the Moors, these ornate tiles later took on Italian and northern European designs. Though many of the tiles are blue, their name doesn't come from *azul* (Portuguese for blue), but rather from the Arabic word *azulayj,* meaning "little stone." Numerous museums showcase collections of **azulejos,** including Lisboa's Museu do Azulejo and Coimbra's Museu Machada do Castro.

PAINTING & SCULPTURE

The Age of Discovery (1415-1580) was an era of vast cultural exchange with Renaissance Europe and beyond. Flemish masters such as **Jan van Eyck** brought their talent to Portugal, and many Portuguese artists polished their skills in Antwerp, Belgium. Dom Manuel's favorite, High Renaissance artist **Jorge Afonso,** created realistic portrayals of human anatomy. Afonso's best works hang at the Convento de Cristo in Tomar and Convento da Madre de Deus in Lisboa. In the late 15th century, the talented **Nuno Gonçalves** led a revival of the primitivist school.

Portuguese Baroque art featured even more diverse styles and themes. Woodcarving became extremely popular in Portugal during the Baroque period. **Joachim Machado** carved elaborate crèches in the early 1700s. On canvas, portraiture was head and shoulders above other genres. The prolific 19th-century artist **Domingos António de Sequeira** depicted historical, religious, and allegorical subjects using a technique that would later inspire French Impressionists. Porto's **António Soares dos Reis** brought his Romantic sensibility to 19th-century Portuguese sculpture.

In the 20th century, Cubism, Expressionism, and Futurism trickled into Portugal despite Salazar-instituted censorship. More recently, **Maria Helena Vieira da Silva** has won international recognition for her abstract works, and the master **Carlos Botelho** has become world-renowned for his wonderful vignettes of Lisboa life.

LITERATURE

Portugal's literary achievements—mostly lyric poetry and realist fiction—can be traced back to the 12th century, when the lyrical aspects of Portuguese were standardized by poet-king **Dinis I.** Dom Dinis made Portuguese the region's official language, one of the first "official" non-Latin Romance vernaculars. **Gil Vicente** (1465-1537), court poet to Manuel I, is considered the Portuguese Shakespeare with his dramas about peasants, nature, and religion. The witty realism of his *Barcas* trilogy (1517-1519) influenced contemporaries the real Shakespeare and Cervantes.

Portuguese literature blossomed during the Renaissance, most notably in the letters of **Francisco de Sá de Miranda** (1481-1558) and the lyrics of **António Ferreira** (1528-1569). An explorer during the Age of Discovery, the humanist **João de Barros** (1496-1570) penned *Décadas da Ásia*, a history of Portuguese conquest in Goa. Influenced by the *Décadas*, **Luís de Camões** (1524-1580) celebrated Vasco da Gama's sea voyages to India in Portugal's greatest epic, *Os Lusíadas* (*The Lusiads*, 1572), modeled on the *Aeneid* (see **Ladies' Man**, p. 652).

Spanish hegemony, intermittent warfare, and imperial decline conspired to make the literature of the 17th and 18th centuries somewhat less triumphant than that of past eras. The 19th century, however, saw a dramatic rebirth with poet **João Baptista de Almeida Garrett** (1799-1854) and historian **Alexandre Herculano** (1810-1877), who were both exiled because of their liberal political views. Garrett, whose famous play *Frei Luís de Sousa* (1843) marks him as a reviver of drama, and Herculano integrated Portuguese literature with the Romantic school of fiction they encountered while in exile.

When political thinkers dominated the rise of the literary intelligentsia in the **Generation of 1870,** literature shifted from romantic to realist. The most visible figure to influence this shift was novelist and life-long diplomat (residing almost always outside Iberia) **José Maria Eça de Queiroz.** He conceived a distinctly Portuguese social realism and documented 19th-century Portuguese society, sometimes critical of its bourgeois elements. His best works were *O Crime do Padre Amaro* (*The Sin of Father Amaro*) and *Os Maias* (*The Mayas*).

Fernando Pessoa (1888-1935), Portugal's most famed writer of the late 19th and early 20th centuries, wrote in English and Portuguese under four different names: Pessoa, Alberto Caeiro, Ricardo Reis, and Alvaro de Campos. His semi-autobiography, *Livro do Desassossego (The Book of Disgust)* is his only prose work, posthumously compiled and viewed as a modernist classic. Other influential writers of the 20th century include **Aquilino Ribeiro,** author of *O Homem que Matou o Diabo* (*The Man Who Killed the Devil*), and **José Maria Ferreira de Castro,** widely known for his realist fiction, especially his novel *A Selva (The Jungle)*.

Contemporary writers like **Miguel Torga** have gained international fame for their wonderfully satirical novels. **José Saramago,** winner of the 1998 Nobel Prize for literature, is perhaps Portugal's most important living writer. His work, written in the realist style and laced with irony, has achieved new acclaim in the post-Salazar era. After Salazar's reign, female writers have emerged with a vengeance. In **Novas Cartas Portuguesas** *(New Portuguese Letters),* the "Three Marias" expose the mistreatment of women in a male-dominated society. Other acclaimed post-Salazar authors include **António Lobo Antunes** and **José Cardoso Pires.** Antunes has achieved the status of Saramago but with a different style, one known for its scattered form and psychoanalytic themes. Pires's works often comment on the repression of the Salazar regime, and his novel *Balada da Praia dos Cães (Ballad of Dogs' Beach)* exposes the terror of Salazar's secret police.

MUSIC

Named after fate, **fado** (FA-doo) is a musical tradition unique to Portugal, identified with a sense of *saudade* (yearning or longing) and characterized by tragic, romantic lyrics and mournful melodies. Solo ballads, accompanied by the acoustic *guitarra* (a flat-backed guitar like a mandolin), appeal to the romantic side of Portuguese culture. **Amalia Rodrigues** (1920-1999) gained international renown as a singer of *fado* and Portuguese folk music.

Apart from its folk tradition, the music of Portugal has yet to achieve international fame. Portuguese opera peaked with **António José da Silva** (1705-1739), a victim of the 1739 Inquisition. The Renaissance in Portugal led to the development of pieces geared for solo instrumentalists and vocals. Coimbra's **Carlos Seixas** thrilled 18th-century Lisboa with his genius and contributed to the development of the sonata form. **Domingos Bomtempo** (1775-1842) introduced symphonic innovations from abroad and helped establish the first Portuguese Sociedade Filarmónica, modeled after the London Philharmonic, in Lisboa in 1822.

Although the Portuguese Civil War decreased patronage and stifled experimentation, folk music and dancing are still popular in rural areas. In the late 19th century, Joly Braga Santo led a modern revival of Portuguese classical music. The Calouste Gulbenkian Foundation in Lisboa has also kept Portuguese music alive, sponsoring a symphony orchestra since 1962, and hosting local folk singers (including Fausto and Sérgio Godinho), ballets, operas, and jazz festivals. The Teatro Nacional de São Carlos, with its own orchestra and ballet company, has further bolstered Portuguese music. The Teatro has spawned a group of talented young composers, including Filipe Pires, A. Vitorino de Almeida, and Jorge Peixinho, all of whom have begun to make their mark in international competitions.

THE MEDIA

Portugal's most widely read daily newspapers are *Público* (www.publico.pt), *Diário de Notícas* (www.dn.sapo.pt), and *Jornal de Notícas* (www.jn.sapo.pt). If you haven't mastered Portuguese, check out *The News*, Portugal's only online English language newspaper, at www.the-news.net. Those interested in international news stories can also pick up day-old foreign papers at larger newsstands.

Portuguese TV offers four main channels: the state-run Canal 1 and TV2, and the private SIC (Sociedade Independente de Communicação) and TVI (TV Independente). Couch potatoes can also enjoy numerous cable channels, most of which air Brazilian and Portuguese soap operas and subtitled foreign sitcoms.

PORTUGAL

SPORTS

Futebol (soccer to Americans) is the game of choice for just about all Portuguese sports fans. Team Portugal has had its moments in the sun—the national team ousted Denmark en route to the semifinals at the 1996 European Championships and garnered a third-place finish in 2000 at the UEFA European Championship in Belgium with the help of 2001 FIFA World Player of the Year, Luis Figo—but has also fallen short at crucial moments, such as the World Cup '98 qualification matches. Games create a crazed fervor throughout Portugal, and fans will be rewarded as Portugal hosts the European Championships in 2004. Lisboa's **Benfica** fields some of the best players in the world, now under the watchful eye of former Spanish national team coach, José Antonio Camacho.

Native Portuguese have also made names for themselves in long-distance running, where marathon-queen **Rosa Mota** dominated her event for years. For recreation other than jogging and pick-up soccer, native Portuguese often turn to the sea. Wind, body, and conventional **surfers** make waves along the northern coast; **snorklers** and **scuba divers** set out on mini-explorations to the south and west.

NATIONAL HOLIDAYS

The following table lists the national holidays for 2004.

DATE	FESTIVAL
January 1	New Year's Day
January 6	Epiphany
March 4	Carnival
April 13-20	Holy Week
April 17	Senhor Ecce Homo (Monday Thursday)
April 18	Good Friday
April 20	Easter
April 25	Liberation Day
May 1	Labor Day
June 22	Corpus Christi
June 10	Portugal Day
August 15	Feast of the Assumption
October 5	Republic Day
November 1	All Saints' Day
December 8	Feast of the Immaculate Conception
December 25	Christmas
December 31	New Year's Eve

RECOMMENDED READING

FICTION: PORTUGUESE & FOREIGN. For Portuguese classics in most every genre, check out **Literature** (p.626). The more famous works have been translated into English. *Selected Letters and Journals*, by Lord Byron, narrates the days Byron spent in Portugal. The classic *The Lusiads*, by Luís de Camões, chronicles Portuguese exploration during the Age of Discovery. *The Last Kabbalist of Lisboa*, by Richard Zimler, is a fantastic murder mystery exploring the world of Portugal's 16th-century Jewish mystics. *The Gospel According to Jesus Christ* and *Blindness* are some of the finest works by Noble Prize-winning José Saramago.

HISTORY & CULTURE. David Birmingham's *A Concise History of Portugal* (1991) packs an amazing quantity of historical and cultural information in one handy volume. Elanea Brown's *Roads to Today's Portugal: Essays on Contemporary Portuguese Literature, Art, and Culture* (1983) provides a good introduction to 20th-century Portuguese culture. Though somewhat outdated, A.H. de Oliveira Marquês's *History of Portugal* is among the most comprehensive Portuguese history texts available. *Modern Portugal* (1998), edited by António Costa Pinto, covers 20th-century Portuguese history from the rise of Salazar to the evolution of the nation's resilient democracy. *Europe's Best-Kept Secret: An Insider's View of Portugal* (1997), by Costa Matos, is a witty account of Portuguese culture and history, including amusing anecdotes about peculiar Portuguese personalities. Finally, for a more literary rather than historical examination of Portuguese life and customs, read José Saramago's *Journey Through Portugal.*

PORTUGAL ESSENTIALS

The information in this section is designed to help travelers get their bearings once in Portugal. For information about general **travel preparations** (including passports, money, health, packing, and more), consult the **Essentials** chapter (p. 9), which also has important info for those with **Specific Concerns** (p. 51). See **Alternatives to Tourism** for opportunities to work and study in Portugal (p. 57).

ENTRANCE REQUIREMENTS

Passport (p. 11). Required for all citizens of Australia, Canada, Ireland, New Zealand, South Africa, the UK, and US.

Visa (p. 13). Required only for citizens of South Africa.

Work Permit (p. 13) Required for all foreigners planning to work in Portugal.

Driving Permit (p. 49). Recommended for those planning to drive.

EMBASSIES & CONSULATES

Embassies and consulates are usually open Monday through Friday, mornings and late afternoons, with *siestas* in between—call for specific hours.

Australia: Embassy: Av. da Liberdade, 200, 2nd fl., 1250-147 **Lisboa** (☎213 10 15 00, fax 10 15 55; www.portugal.embassy.gov.au).

Canada: Embassy: Av. da Liberdade, 196-200, 3rd fl., 1269-121 **Lisboa** (☎213 16 46 00; fax 16 46 92). **Consulate:** R. Frei Lourenço do Santa Maria, 1, 1st fl. Partado 79, 8001 **Faro** (☎289 80 37 57; fax 88 08 88).

Ireland: Embassy: R. da Imprensa à Estrela, 4th fl., Ste. 1, 1200 **Lisboa** (☎213 92 94 40; fax 97 73 63).

New Zealand: Embassy: Refer to New Zealand Embassy in Spain: Pl. de la Lealtad 2-3rd fl., 28014 **Madrid** (☎915 23 02 26; fax 23 01 71). **Consulate:** Av. Antonio Augusta de Aguiar, 9th fl., 1097 **Lisboa** (☎213 50 96 90; fax 57 20 04).

South Africa: Embassy: Av. Luis Bivar, 10A, 1069-024 **Lisboa** (☎213 19 22 00; fax 53 57 13). **Consulate:** R. Antonio José Da Costa, 78-1st fl., 4150-090 **Porto** (☎226 07 60 10; fax 09 98 20).

United Kingdom: Embassy: R. São Bernardo, 33, 1249-082 **Lisboa** (☎213 92 40 00; fax 92 41 83). **Consulate:** Av. da Boavista, 3072, 4100-120 **Porto** (☎226 18 47 89; fax 10 04 38).

United States: Embassy: Av. das Forças Armadas, 1600-081 **Lisboa** (☎217 27 33 00; fax 27 91 09). **Consulate:** same address (☎/fax 217 27 23 54).

TRANSPORTATION

Portugal is easily accessible by plane. Long-distance trains run from **Madrid** (p. 97) to Lisboa, and buses run from **Sevilla** (p. 232) to Lagos. Closer to the border, trains run from **Huelva** (easily accessible from Sevilla, p. 253) and **Cáceres** (p. 212) to Portugal. Trains and buses run from **Badajoz** (p. 223), only 6km from the border, to Elvas and elsewhere. **Ciudad Rodrigo** (p. 188) lies only 21km from the border. In the north, trains run from **Vigo** (p. 575) to Porto; from **Túy** (p. 579), you can walk across the Portuguese border to Valença do Minho.

BY PLANE

Most major international airlines serve Lisboa; some serve Porto, Faro, and the Madeiras. **TAP Air Portugal** (in US and Canada ☎800-221-7370, in UK 845 601 09 32, in Lisboa 218 43 11 00; www.tap.pt) is Portugal's national airline, serving all domestic locations and many major international cities. **Portugália** (www.pga.pt) is a smaller Portuguese airline that flies between Porto, Faro, Lisboa, all major Spanish cities, and other Western European destinations. Offices are located in Portugal (☎218 42 55 59), Spain (☎913 93 64 39), and the UK (☎087 0755 0025), with other locations in Belgium, France, Germany, and Italy.

BY TRAIN

Caminhos de Ferro Portugueses (☎808 20 82 08; www.cp.pt) is Portugal's national railway, but for long-distance travel outside of the Braga-Porto-Coimbra-Lisboa line, the bus is better. The exception is around Lisboa, where local trains are fast and efficient. Most trains have first- and second-class cabins, except for local and suburban routes. When you arrive in town, go to the station ticket booth to check the departure schedule; trains often run at irregular hours, and posted schedules *(horarios)* aren't always accurate. Unless you own a Eurailpass, the return on **round-trip tickets** must be used before 3am the following day. Don't ride without a ticket; if you're caught *sem bilhete*, you'll be fined exorbitantly. Children under 12 and adults over 65 receive a 50% discount. **Youth discounts** are only available to Portuguese citizens. Though there is a Portugal Flexipass, it is not worth buying.

BY BUS

Buses are cheap, frequent, and connect just about every town in Portugal. **Rodoviária** (national info ☎213 54 57 75), the national bus company, has recently been privatized. Each company name corresponds to a particular region of the country, such as Rodoviária Alentejo or Minho e Douro, with notable exceptions such as EVA in the Algarve. Private regional companies also operate, among them **AVIC, Cabanelas,** and **Mafrense.** Be wary of non-express buses in small regions like Estremadura and Alentejo, which stop every few minutes. Express coach service *(expressos)* between major cities is especially good; inexpensive city buses often run to nearby villages. Schedules *(horarios)* are usually printed and posted, but double-check with the ticket vendor to make sure they are accurate.

Portugal's main **Euroline** affiliates are Internorte, Intercentro, and Intersul. **Busabout** coach stops in Portugal are at Porto, Lisboa, and Lagos. Every coach has a guide to answer questions and make travel and hostel arrangements en route.

BY CAR

Portugal has the highest rate of automobile accidents per capita in Western Europe. The new highway system (IP) is quite good, but off the main arteries, the narrow, twisting roads are difficult to negotiate. Speed limits are ignored, recklessness is common, and lighting and road surfaces are often inadequate. Buses and trucks are safer options. Moreover, parking space in cities borders on nonexistent. **Gas** comes in super (97 octane), normal (92 octane), and unleaded. Gas prices may be high by North American standards—US$0.60-0.90 per liter. Portugal's national automobile association, the **Automóvel Clube de Portugal (ACP),** Shopping Center Amoreiras, Lojas 1122 **Lisboa** (☎213 71 20), provides **breakdown** and **towing service** and **first aid**.

BY THUMB

In Portugal, **hitchhikers** are rare. Beach-bound locals occasionally hitch in summer, but otherwise stick to the inexpensive bus system. Rides are easiest to come by between smaller towns. Best results are reputedly at gas stations near highways and rest stops. *Let's Go* does not recommend hitchhiking (see p. 51).

MONEY

THE EURO (€)		
US $1 = €0.91		€1 = US $1.10
AUS $1 = €0.59		€1 = AUS $1.69
CDN $1 = €0.66		€1 = CDN $1.52
DH 1 = €0.09		€1 = DH 10.74
NZ $1 = €0.53		€1 = NZ $1.90
UK £1 = €1.44		€1 = UK £0.70
ZAR 1 = €0.12		€1 = ZAR 8.06

Official **banking hours** are Monday through Friday 8:30am to 3pm, but play it safe by giving yourself extra time. For more information on money, see p. 15. **Taxes** are included in all prices in Portugal and are not redeemable like those in Spain and Morocco, even for EU citizens. **Tips** are customary only in fancy restaurants or hotels. Some cheaper restaurants include a 10% service charge; if they don't and you'd like to leave a tip, round up and leave the change. Taxi drivers do not expect a tip unless the trip was especially long. **Bargaining** is not customary in shops, but you can give it a shot at the local *mercado* (market) or when looking for a *quarto*.

SAFETY & HEALTH

EMERGENCY Dial ☎112 for **POLICE, MEDICAL,** or **FIRE.**

In Portugal, the highest rates of crime have been in the Lisboa area, especially on buses, in train stations, and in airports. Exercise the most caution in the Alfama district, the Santa Apolonia and Rossio train stations, Castelo de São Jorge, and in Belém. The towns around Lisboa with the most reported crimes in recent years are Cascais, Sintra, and Fátima. Thieves try to distract people by staging loud arguments, passing a soccer ball back and forth on a crowded street, asking for direc-

PORTUGAL

tions, pretending to dance with their victim, or spilling something on their victim's clothing. Motorists should be wary of Good Samaritans who have been known to help ailing motorists by the side of the road and then steal their cars.

Portugal poses no particular health risks to travelers. The public health system in Portugal is quite good, and many doctors speak English. A private clinic might be worth the money for convenience and quick service; most travel insurance providers will pick up the tab. For small medical concerns, Portuguese *farmacías* offer basic drugs and medical advice and are easy to find in most towns. For general **health** information, see p. 22.

ACCOMMODATIONS

PENSÕES & HOTELS

Pensões, also called **residencias,** are a budget traveler's mainstay. They're far cheaper than hotels and only slightly more expensive (and much more common) than crowded youth hostels. Like hostels, *pensões* generally provide sheets and towels and have common rooms. All are rated on a five-star scale and are required to visibly post their category and legal price limits. (If you don't see this information, ask for it.) During high season, many *pensões* do not take reservations, but for those that do, booking a week ahead is advisable.

Hotels in Portugal tend to be pricey. Room prices typically include showers and breakfast, and most rooms without bath or shower have a sink. When business is weak, try bargaining in advance—the "official price" is just the maximum allowed. **Pousadas,** like Spanish *paradores*, outperform standard hotel expectations (and, unfortunately, rates). They are castles, palaces, or monasteries converted into luxurious, government-run hotels. "Historical" *pousadas* play up local crafts, customs, and cuisine and may cost as much as expensive hotels. Most require reservations. Priced less extravagantly are *regional pousadas*, situated in national parks and reserves. For info, contact **ENATUR**, Av. Santa Joana Princesa, 10, 1749-090 Lisboa (☎ 218 44 20 01; fax 44 20 85; www.pousadas.com).

YOUTH HOSTELS

Movijovem, Av. Duque de Ávila, 137, 1069 Lisboa (☎707 20 30 30, fax 217 23 21 02; www.pousadasjuventude.pt), the Portuguese Hostelling International affiliate, oversees the country's HI hostels. All bookings can be made through them. A bed in a *pousada da juventude* (not to be confused with plush *pousadas*) costs €10-15 per night and slightly less in the off-season (breakfast and sheets included). Lunch or dinner usually costs €4.50, snacks around €1. Rates may be higher for guests 26 and older. Though often the cheapest option, hostels may lie far from the town center. Check-in hours are 9am to noon and 6pm to midnight. Some have lockouts 10:30am to 6pm, and curfews might cramp club-hoppers' style. The maximum stay is eight nights unless you get special permission. An **HI card** is usually mandatory to stay in an affiliated hostel. Although they are sold at Movijovem's Lisboa office, it is more convenient to get an HI membership before leaving home. To reserve a bed in the high season, obtain an **International Booking Voucher** from Movijovem (or your country's HI affiliate) and send it from home to the desired hostel four to eight weeks in advance. In the off-season (Oct.-Apr.), double-check to see if the hostel is open. Large groups should reserve through Movijovem 30 days in advance. For more info, see **Youth Hostels,** p. 30.

ALTERNATIVE ACCOMMODATIONS

Quartos are rooms in private residences, similar to *casas particulares* in Spain. These rooms may be your only option in smaller, less touristed towns, or the cheapest one in bigger cities. The tourist office can usually help you find a *quarto*. When all else fails, ask at bars and restaurants for names and addresses, but try to verify the quality of the rooms. Prices are flexible and can drop with bargaining.

CAMPING

In Portugal, over 150 **official campgrounds** *(parques de campismo)* feature amenities and comforts. Most have a supermarket and cafes, and many are beach-accessible. Given the facilities' quality and popularity, happy campers are those who arrive early; urban and coastal parks may require reservations. Police are cracking down on illegal camping, so don't try it. Tourist offices stock *Portugal: Camping and Caravan Sites*, a free guide to official campgrounds. Otherwise, write the **Federação Portuguesa de Campismo e Caravanismo,** Av. Coronel Eduardo Galhardo, 24D, 1199-007 Lisboa (☎218 12 68 90; fax 218 12 69 18; www.fpcampismo.pt).

KEEPING IN TOUCH

Most useful communication information (including **international access codes, calling card numbers, country codes, operator** and **directory assistance,** and **emergency numbers**) is listed on the **inside back cover.**

TELEPHONES. Portugal's national telephone company is **Portugal Telecom.** Though phone offices exist in most cities, all services are available in phone booths on the street and in post offices. Pay phones are either coin-operated or require a phone card. The country uses the **Credifone** and **Portugal Telecom** systems. For both systems, the basic unit for all calls (and the price for local ones) is €0.10. Telecom phone cards, using "patch" chips, are most common in Lisboa and Porto and increasingly elsewhere. Credifone cards, with magnetic strips, are sold at drugstores, post offices, and locations posted on phone booths, and are most useful outside these two big cities. Private calls from bars and cafes cost whatever the proprietor decides; a posted sign usually indicates the rates. City codes all have a two before them, and local calls do not require dialing the city code.

Calling cards probably remain the best method of making international calls (see p. 37 for more details). The numbers to access major calling card services (including AT&T, MCI, Canada Direct, BT Direct, Ireland Direct, Telstra Australia, Optus Australia, Telekom New Zealand, and Telkom South Africa) are listed on the **inside back cover.** To **call home with a calling card,** contact the operator for your service provider in Portugal by dialing the appropriate toll-free access number (see p. 37).

MAIL. Mail in Portugal is somewhat inefficient—**Air mail** *(via aerea)* can take from one to two weeks (or longer) to reach the US or Canada. It is slightly quicker for Europe and longer for Australia, New Zealand, and South Africa. **Surface mail** *(superficie),* for packages only, takes up to two months. **Registered** or **blue mail** takes five to eight business days (for roughly 3 times the price of air mail). **EMS** or **Express Mail** will probably get there in three to four days for more than double the blue mail price. **Stamps** are available at post offices *(correios)* and at automatic stamp machines outside post offices and in central locations around cities. Also at post offices, **fax** machines are available for public use.

EMAIL. Cybercafes are common in cities and most smaller towns, and are listed in the **Practical Information** section. When in doubt, try the library, where there is often at least one computer equipped for Internet access.

LISBOA

It's sunset, and the glow cast over the Rio Tejo is matched only by that of the *vinho do Porto*. Welcome to Lisboa, where locals and visitors translate a history of eminence and glory into a passion for the best in food, wine, and music. The city's compactness and simple themes allow even the most inexperienced visitor to explore the city in the better part of a week. But don't be deceived; many have tried and failed to define Lisboa according to such categories.

Part of the difficulty in describing Lisboa has to do with its multi-layered history. Half a dozen civilizations claim parenthood of the city, starting with the Phoenicians, Greeks, and Carthaginians. The Romans arrived in 205 BC. Under Julius Caesar's reign, Lisboa became the most important city in Lusitania; in 1255, it was made the capital of the kingdom of Portugal. The city and the Portuguese empire reached their apex at the end of the 15th-century when Portuguese navigators pioneered explorations of Asia, Africa, and South America. A huge earthquake on November 1, 1755, touched off the nation's fall from glory—close to one-fifth of the population died in the catastrophe and two-thirds of Lisboa crumbled. Under the authoritarian leadership of Prime Minister Marquês do Pombal, the city recovered with a massive reconstruction effort. In the 20th-century, Lisboa saw more than its share of changes. During WWII, Portugal's neutrality and Atlantic connections made the city a frequent meeting spot for spies on both sides. In 1974, when Mozambique and Angola won independence, hundreds of thousands of refugees converged on the city. Today, Portuguese of African, Asian, and European origin peacefully coexist. The wells, temples, castles, and cathedrals contributed by each of Lisboa's past civilizations constitute a consequential part of its personality; nevertheless, Lisboa's diverse history still doesn't quite capture the city's uniqueness.

Above all, travelers feel the difference in Lisboa because of the rare combination of glorious history and bittersweet memory. The Portuguese have an infamous word for it: *saudade*. Anyone interested in patriotic discourse is invited to ask locals for their perception of the term. Unique to the Portuguese, *saudade* involves an almost aching, wistful longing; as a noun it is a possession of the people of Lisboa and Portugal. Travelers hear it in the traditional *fado* music, drink it in the celebrated wines, and above all, see it in the Portuguese faces. That is the glory of Lisboa—it can fill you with wonder and break your heart all at once. So while the ornate cathedrals, hip clubs, and captivating history might initially bring travelers to Lisboa, *saudade* keeps them there—and brings them back.

The neighborhoods of Alfama, Bairro Alto, and Baixa are not to be missed. They are home to Lisboa's most definitive sights and are representative of the history that continues to flavor the city today. Whether you seek the open spaces of lush parks or the intensity of labyrinthine streets, Lisboa's neighborhoods await.

HIGHLIGHTS OF LISBOA

SEE grown men cry over traditional **fado** (see p. 644).

VISIT the city within the city at the **Parque das Nações** (see p. 659).

EXPERIENCE a different breed of **bullfighting** (see p. 645).

GET LOST in labyrinthine **Alfama**, the former Arabic quarter (see p. 656).

ESCAPE into Portugal's sweet, pastry-filled past in **Belém** (see p. 660).

DEFY gravity walking atop the walls of an 8th-century castle in **Sintra** (see p. 668).

Lisboa & Vicinity

Santarém
Lourinhã
Campelos
Torres Vedras
Sobral de Monte Agraço
ATLANTIC OCEAN
Ericeira
Vila França de Xira
Mafra
Alverca
Infantado
Odivelas
Loures
Sintra
Amadora
Rio Tejo
Cabo da Roca
LISBOA
Paisagem Protegida da Sintra e Cascais
Queluz
Montijo
Cascais
Estoril
Almada
Barreiro
Costa da Caparica
Seixal
Maräteca
Setúbal
Paisagem Protegida da Serra da Arrábida
Tróia
Sesimbra
Cabo Espichel
Baía de Setúbal

0   20 miles
0   20 kilometers

LISBOA

✳ HOW TO USE THIS CHAPTER. Lisboa is divided into several neighborhoods. We have grouped together all of each area's accommodations, food, sights, museums, and nightlife listings. General information on these aspects of Lisboa, as well as shopping and specific listings for camping and entertainment (including sports, theater, concerts, and film) appears after the practical information.

✴ INTERCITY TRANSPORTATION

BY PLANE

All flights land at **Aeroporto de Lisboa** (☎218 41 35 00), on the city's northern edge. Walk out of the terminal, turn right, and follow the path around the curve to the bus stop. Take **bus** #44 or 45 (15-20min., every 12-15min. 7am-9pm, €1) to Pr. dos Restauradores and Rossio; the bus stops in front of the tourist office at Pr. dos Restauradores, located inside the Palácio da Foz. Or take the express **AeroBus** #91 to the same locations (15min., every 20min. 7am-9pm, €1); it's a better option during rush hour. A **taxi** from downtown costs about €6 (plus a €1.50 baggage fee) at

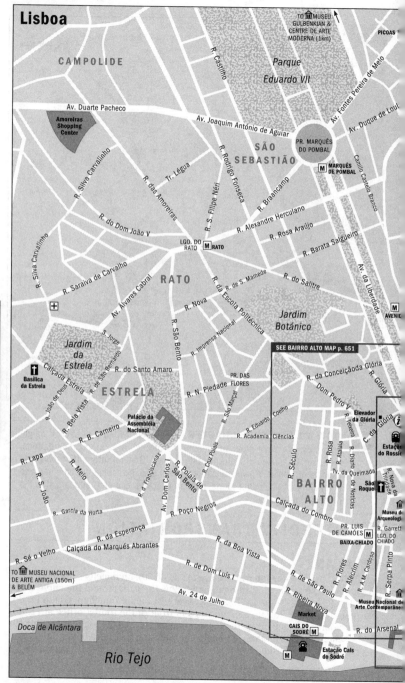

Lisboa

LISBOA

CAMPOLIDE

TO 🏛 MUSEU
GULBENKIAN &
CENTRE DE ARTE
MODERNA (1km)

PICOAS

*Parque
Eduardo VII*

Av. Duarte Pacheco

Amoreiras
Shopping
Center

Av. Joaquim António de Aguiar

Av. Fontes Pereira de Melo

Av. Duque de Loul

SÃO
SEBASTIÃO

R. Castilho

R. Silva Carvalinho

R. das Amoreiras

Tr. Légua

R. Rodrigo Fonseca

R. Braancamp

PR. MARQUÊS
DO POMBAL

M MARQUÊS
DE POMBAL

Camilo Castelo Branco

R. do Dom João V

R. S. Filipe Néri

R. Alexandre Herculano

R. Rosa Araújo

R. Barata Salgueiro

R. Silva Carvalinho

R. Saraiva de Carvalho

LGO. DO
RATO M RATO

RATO

R. de S. Mamede

R. do Salitre

Av. da Liberdade

M
AVENIE

Av. Álvares Cabral

R. Nova

R. da Escola Politécnica

*Jardim
Botánico*

✚

R. Saraiva de Carvalho

S. Jorge

R. São Bento

R. Imprensa Nacional

SEE BAIRRO ALTO MAP p. 651

*Jardim
da
Estrela*

Calçada Estrela

R. de São Bernardo

R. do Santo Amaro

ESTRELA

PR. DAS
FLORES

R. N. Piedade

R. da Conceiçãoda Glória

R. Glória

Dom Pedro V

✝
Basílica
da Estrela

R. João de deus Estrela

R. Bela Vista

R. São Marçal

R. Eduardo
Coelho

Elevador
da Glória

C. da Glória

ⓘ

R. B. Carneiro

Palácio da
Assembléia
Nacional

R. Academia Ciências

R. Século

R. Rosa

R. Teixeira

R. Diario

R. Atalaia

Estação
do Rossi

R. Lapa

R. Melo

R. d Franciscanas

Av. Dom Carlos I

R. Polais de
São Bento

Tv. da Queimada

São
Roque

R. Nova da
Trindade

✝

R. S. João

R. Garcia da Horta

R. Poço Negros

BAIRRO
ALTO

C. de Noticias

Museu de
Arqueologi
🏛

R. da Esperança

Calçada do Marqués Abrantes

R. da Boa Vista

Calçada do Combro

PR. LUIS
DE CAMÓES M

BAIXA-CHIADO

R. Garrett
LGO. DO
CHIADO

R. Serpa Pinto

R. Sé o Velho

TO 🏛 MUSEU NACIONAL
DE ARTE ANTIGA (150m)
& BELÉM

R. de Dom Luís I

R. de São Paulo

R. Flores

R. Alecrim

R.A.M. Cardoso

🏛

Av. 24 de Julho

R. Ribeira Nova

Museu Nacional de
Arte Contemporâne

Market

Doca de Alcântara

CAIS DO
SODRÉ M

M

🚇
Estação Cais
do Sodré

R. do Arsenal

Rio Tejo

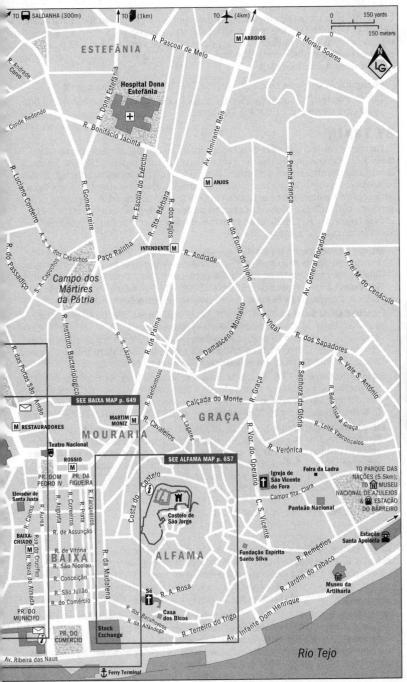

TO 🚇 SALDANHA (300m) TO 🚌 (1km) TO ✈ (4km)

0 ___ 150 yards
0 ___ 150 meters

ESTEFÂNIA

R. Pascoal de Melo

Ⓜ ARROIOS

R. Morais Soares

R. Andrade Corvo

. Conde Redondo

Hospital Dona Estefânia ✚

R. Dona Estefânia

R. Bonifácio Jácinta

R. Almirante Reis

R. Penha França

Ⓜ ANJOS

R. Luciano Cordeiro

R. A. S. A. dos Capuchos

R. do passadiço

R. Gomes Freire

R. Escola do Exército

R. Sta. Bárbara

R. dos Anjos

R. do Forno do Tijolo

Av. General Ropadas

R. Frei M. do Cenáculo

Paço Rainha

S. A. Capuchos

INTENDENTE Ⓜ

R. Andrade

Campo dos Mártires da Pátria

R. Instituto Bacteriológico

R. S. Lázaro

R. da Palma

R. Damasceno Monteiro

R. A. Vidal

R. dos Sapadores

R. Vale S. António

R. Bela Vista à Graça

R. das Portas São

Antão

R. Bentormoso

Calçada do Monte

GRAÇA

R. Lágres

Graça

R. Senhora da Glória

R. Leite Vasconcelos

SEE BAIXA MAP p. 649

✉

Ⓜ RESTAURADORES

MARTIM MONIZ Ⓜ

R. Cavaleiros

R. Voz do Operario

R. Verónica

MOURARIA

SEE ALFAMA MAP p. 657

Teatro Nacional 🎭

ROSSIO Ⓜ

PR. DA FIGUEIRA

Costa do Castelo

ⓘ

Igreja de São Vicente de Fora ✝

Feira da Ladra ■

TO PARQUE DAS NAÇÕES (5.5km); TO 🏛 MUSEU NACIONAL DE AZULEJOS & 🚉 ESTAÇÃO DO BÁRREIRO

PR. DOM PEDRO IV

R. Faqueiros

Campo Sta. Clara

Elevador de Santa Justa

R. Correeiros

R. Prata

R. Aurea

C. S. Vicente

Panteão Nacional

Castelo de São Jorge 🏰

BAIXA-CHIADO Ⓜ

R. de Assunção

R. da Madalena

Estação Santa Apolónia 🚉

Rua do Crucifixo

R. Nova do Almada

R. de Vitória

ALFAMA

BAIXA

R. São Nicolau

R. Conceição

Fundação Espírito Santo Silva

R. Remédios

R. São Julião

R. A. Rosa

Sé ✝

Museu da Artilharia

R. do Comércio

R. Jardim do Tabaco

PR. DO MUNICÍPIO

ⓘ

R. dos Bacalhoeiros

Casa dos Bicos

R. da Alfândega

R. Terreiro do Trigo

PR. DO COMÉRCIO

Stock Exchange

Av. Infante Dom Henrique

Av. Ribeira das Naus

Rio Tejo

⚓ **Ferry Terminal**

LISBOA

low traffic hours, but trips are billed by time, not distance. Ask at the **tourist office** (☎218 45 06 60) inside the airport about the **voucher** program, which allows visitors to buy pre-paid vouchers for taxi rides from the airport, avoiding potential problems with fare dishonesty. Major airlines have offices at Pr. Marquês do Pombal and along Av. da Liberdade.

Portugália, Aeroporto de Lisboa, Ed. 70, Rua C (☎218 42 55 00; www.pga.pt).

TAP Air Portugal, Aeroporto de Lisboa, Ed. 19, Rua C, ground level (☎218 41 50 00; www.tap-airportugal.pt). Open M-F 9am-6pm.

BY TRAIN

Train service in and out of Lisboa is potentially confusing, as there are three stations in Lisboa and one across the river in Barreiro, each serving different destinations. Long distance trains in Portugal tend to be quite slow; buses, although more expensive, are both faster and more comfortable. However, the two train lines with service to locations near Lisboa (to Cascais and Sintra, with stops along the way) are both reliable. Contact **Caminhos de Ferro Portuguêses** (☎800 20 09 04 for Lisboa connections, 808 20 82 08 elsewhere; www.cp.pt) for further information about Portugal's rail system.

Estação do Barreiro, across the Rio Tejo, serves points south. Station accessible by ferry from the Terreiro do Paço dock off Pr. do Comércio. Ferries leave every 30min. and take 30min.; ferry ticket included in the price of connecting train ticket (otherwise €0.50). To: **Évora** (2½hr., 7 per day 6:50am-11:50pm, €7.50); **Lagos** (5½hr., 5 per day 7:35am-7:45pm, €14); **Setúbal** (1½hr., every hr. 7:55am-6:50pm, €4.50).

Estação Cais do Sodré (☎213 47 01 81), just beyond the end of R. do Alecrim, a 5min. walk from Baixa. M: Cais do Sodré. Take the Metro or bus #1, 44, or 45 from Pr. dos Restauradores or bus #28 from Estação Santa Apolónia. To: the monastery in **Belém** (10min., every 15min. 5:30am-2:50am, €1); **Cascais** and **Estoril** (30min., every 20min., €0.90); the youth hostel in **Oeiras** (20min., every 15min., €1.05).

Estação Rossio (☎213 46 50 22). M: Rossio or Restauradores. Services points west. **Information** on ground level open daily 10am-1pm and 2-7pm; domestic window open 7am-3:30pm; international window open 9:15am-noon and 1-5:30pm. English spoken. To **Sintra** (45min., every 15-30min. 6am-2am, €1.25.) via **Queluz** (€0.80).

Estação Santa Apolónia (☎218 88 40 25), Av. Infante Dom Henrique, runs the international, northern, and eastern lines. All trains to Santa Apolónia also stop at **Estação Oriente** (M: Oriente) by the **Parque das Nações.** The international terminal has **currency exchange** and an **info desk** (English spoken). To reach downtown, take bus #9, 39, 46, or 90 to Pr. dos Restauradores and Estação Rossio. To: **Aveiro** (3-3½hr., 4 per day 9:05am-8:05pm, €19); **Braga** (5hr.; 2 per day 7:55am, 5:55pm; €15.50); **Coimbra** (2½hr., 8 per day 8:05am-8:05pm, €16); **Madrid** (10hr., 1 per day 10:05pm, €51.50); **Porto** (4½hr., 8 per day 7:55am-8:05pm, €21).

BY BUS

The bus station is the **Arco do Cego,** Av. João Crisóstomo, around the block from M: Saldanha. Exit the Metro onto Av. da República, walk one block up from Pr. Duque de Saldanha, and take a right onto Av. João Crisóstomo. The bus station is a beige building on the corner of Av. João Crisóstomo and Av. Defensores de Chaves. All Saldanha buses (#36, 44, 45) stop in Pr. Duque de Saldanha (€0.60).

Rede Expressos (☎213 10 31 11; www.rede-expressos.pt). To: **Braga** (5hr., 6 per day 7am-12:15am, €14.50); **Caldas da Rainha** (1¼hr., 10 per day 7am-11pm, €5.90); **Coimbra** (2½hr., 16 per day 7am-12:15am, €9.40); **Évora** (2hr., 13 per day 7am-9:30pm, €9.80); **Faro** (5hr., 9 per day 5am-1am, €14.50); **Pen-**

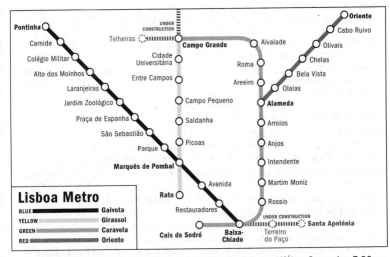

Lisboa Metro

BLUE	■■■■■■■	Gaivota
YELLOW		Girassol
GREEN		Caravela
RED	■■■■■■■	Oriente

iche (2hr., 11 per day 7am-7:30pm, €6.20); **Portalegre** (4½hr., 8 per day 7:30am-9:55pm, €10.80); **Porto** (4hr., 7 per day 7am-12:15am, €13.50) via **Leiria; Tavira** (5hr., 5 per day 5am-1am, €14.50).

ORIENTATION

The city center is made up of three neighborhoods: **Baixa** (low district, resting in a valley), **Bairro Alto** (high district), and hilly **Alfama**. The suburbs extending in both directions along the river represent some of the fastest-growing sections of the city and are interesting for their contrast with the historic districts. Other areas of urban interest several kilometers from downtown include **Belém** (see p. 659), **Alcântara**, home to much of Lisboa's party scene, and the **Parque das Nações**, the site of the 1998 World Exposition and host of a number of attractions.

On the other side of Baixa (to the right with your back to the river) is **Alfama**, Lisboa's famous medieval Moorish neighborhood and the lone survivor of the 1755 earthquake. The city's oldest district, Alfama is comprised of a labyrinth of narrow alleys and stairways beneath the Castelo de São Jorge. Expect to get lost. Without a detailed map, expect to get doubly lost. The twisting streets either change names every three steps or don't have street signs at all. A street-indexed **GeoBloco Planta Turística de Lisboa** and the **Poseidon Planta de Lisboa** (including Sintra, Cascais, and Estoril) are good maps and well worth the money (both sold in Estação Rossio and at newsstands, €10).

LOCAL TRANSPORTATION

Lisboa and its surrounding areas have an efficient public transportation system with subways, buses, trams, and funiculars run by **CARRIS** (☎213 61 30 00; www.carris.pt). Use it to full advantage—no suburb takes longer than 90min. to reach. If you don't speak Portuguese, taxi drivers try to charge an exorbitant fare or keep your change. If you opt for a taxi anyway, make sure you know the approximate fare in advance.

Buses: €1 within the city; pay on the bus. If you plan to stay in Lisboa for any length of time, consider a *passe turístico*, good for unlimited travel on all CARRIS transports. 1-, 3-, 4-, and 7-day passes available (€2.35/€5.65/€9.95/€14.10). Passes sold in CARRIS booths located in most network train stations and the busier Metro stations (e.g., M: Restauradores). Open daily 7am-8pm.

Subway: The Metro (☎213 55 84 57; www.metrolisboa.pt) covers downtown and the modern business district with 4 lines. A red "M" marks Metro stops. €0.65, unlimited daily use ticket €1.40. Book of 10 tickets €5.10, one week pass €4.80. Trains run daily 6:30am-1am, though some stations close earlier. As you pass through various stations, enjoy the murals, poetry, and sculptures that celebrate talent in Portugal.

Trams: €1. Many date from before WWI. Line #28 is great for sightseeing in Alfama and Mouraria (stop in Pr. do Comércio). Line #15 heads from Pr. do Comércio and Pr. da Figueira to Belém and the nightlife districts Av. 24 de Julho and Docas de Santo Amaro.

Funiculars: €1. Funiculars are elevators that link the lower city with the residential areas in the hills. One goes up Elevador da Glória from Pr. dos Restauradores to Bairro Alto.

Taxis: Rádio Táxis de Lisboa (☎218 11 90 00), **Autocoope** (☎217 93 27 56), and **Teletáxis** (☎218 11 11 00). Along Av. da Liberdade and Rossio. Luggage €1.50.

Car Rental: A car is an unnecessary burden if your travels take you only to Lisboa, though one can be useful for daytrips. Agencies have offices at the airport, train stations, and downtown; contact them for specific locations. **Avis,** R. Castilho, 149 (☎800 201 002, fax 217 54 78 52); **Budget,** R. Castilho, 167B (☎213 19 55 55; fax 55 69 20); **Hertz,** R. Castilho, 72A (☎800 238 238 or 218 43 86 60; fax 87 41 64).

⑦ PRACTICAL INFORMATION

TOURIST & FINANCIAL SERVICES

Tourist Office: Palácio da Foz, Pr. dos Restauradores (☎213 46 33 14). M: Restauradores. The largest tourist office has information about the entire country. Open daily 9am-8pm. The **Welcome Center,** Pr. do Comércio (☎210 31 28 10) is the main office for the city. Sells tickets for sightseeing buses and the "Lisboa Card," which includes transportation and entrance to most sights for a flat fee (€12.75 for 24hr., €21.50 for 48hr., €26.55 for 72hr.; children €5.70/€8.55/€11.40). English spoken. Open daily 9am-8pm. **Branch** at the airport (☎218 45 06 60), just outside the baggage claim area. English spoken. Open daily 8am-midnight. Look for kiosks that read "Ask me about Lisboa" at Santa Apolónia, Belém, and other locations for more info.

Budget Travel: Movijovem, Av. Duque d'Ávila, 137 (☎217 23 21 00; www.pousadasjuventude.pt). M: São Sebastião. Open daily 9am-7pm. V.

Embassies: See **Embassies & Consulates,** p. 629.

Currency Exchange: Banks are open M-F 8:30am-3pm. **Cota Câmbio,** Pr. Dom Pedro IV, 41 (☎213 22 04 80). Open M-Sa 9am-8pm. The main post office, most banks, and travel agencies also change money. Exchanges line the streets of Baixa. Ask about fees first—they can be exorbitant.

American Express: Top Tours, Av. Duque de Loulé, 108 (☎213 19 42 90). M: Marquês do Pombal. Exit the Metro and walk up Av. da Liberdade toward the Marquês do Pombal statue, then turn right. English spoken. Open M-F 9:30am-1pm and 2:30-6:30pm.

LOCAL SERVICES

Luggage Storage: At **Estação Rossio** and **Estação Santa Apolónia.** Lockers €4.50 for 24hr. Open daily depending on the schedule of the station (usually 6:30am-1am). The lockers at Estação Cais do Sodré are confusing and not the most secure.

English-Language Bookstore: Livraria Británica, R. Luís Fernandes, 14-16 (☎213 42 84 72), in Rato (see **Lisboa Overview**, p. 580). Walk up R. São Pedro de Alcântara from Bairro Alto; keep straight as it becomes R. Dom Pedro V and then R. Escola Politécnica. Turn left on R. São Marcal, then right after 2 blocks onto R. Luís Fernandes (20min.). Open M-F 9:30am-7pm. AmEx/MC/V.

Library: Biblioteca Municipal Central, Palácio Galveias (☎217 97 38 62). M: Campo Pequeño. Open M-F 10am-7pm, Sa 11am-6pm.

Shopping Centers: Colombo, Av. Lusíada (☎217 11 36 36), in front of Benfica stadium. M: Colégio Militar-Luz. The largest shopping mall in Portugal, with over 400 shops, a 10-screen cinema, and a small amusement park. Open daily 10am-midnight. **Centro Comercial Amoreiras de Lisboa**, Av. Eng. Duarte Pacheco (☎213 81 02 00 or 81 02 40), near R. Carlos Alberto da Mota Pinto. M: Marquês do Pombal. Take bus #11 from Pr. dos Restauradores. 383 shops including a huge **Pão de Açúcar** supermarket, English bookstores, and cinema. Open daily 10am-11pm. **Centro Comercial Vasco da Gama**, Av. Dom João II (☎218 93 06 01). M: Oriente. Open daily 10am-midnight.

El Corte Inglés, Av. António Augusto de Aguiar at Av. Duque d'Ávila (☎213 71 17 00). Portugal's first branch of the Spanish department store giant has everything, including electronics, designer clothes, groceries, and the largest movie theater in Lisboa (14 screens). M: São Sebastião. Open M-Th 10am-10pm, F-Su 10am-11:30pm.

Laundromat: Lavatax, R. Francisco Sanches, 65A (☎218 12 33 92). Wash, dry, and fold €2 per kg. Open M-F 8:30am-1pm and 3-7pm, Sa 8:30am-1pm.

EMERGENCY & COMMUNICATIONS

Emergency: ☎112. **Police:** R. Capelo, 13 (☎346 61 41, ext. 279). English spoken.

Late-Night Pharmacy: ☎118 (directory assistance). Look for the green cross at every intersection, or specifically at **Farmácia Azevedos**, Pr. Dom Pedro IV, 31 (☎213 43 04 02), at the base of Rossio in front of the Metro.

Medical Services: Hospital Inglês, R. Saraiva de Carvalho, 49 (☎213 95 50 67). **Cruz Vermelha Portuguesa** (Red Cross), R. Duarte Galvão, 54 (ambulance ☎219 42 11 11 or 217 71 40 00).

Telephones: Portugal Telecom, Pr. Dom Pedro IV, 68 (☎808 21 11 56). M: Rossio. Has pay phones and booths for international calls. Pay the cashier after your call or use a phone card. **Phone cards** come in 50 units (€3), 100 units (€6), or 150 units (€9). Buy them here or at neighborhood bookstores and stationers. Local calls cost at least 2 units. Minutes per unit vary with type of call and type of phone. PT cards should only be purchased for local use, as better deals for non-local calls can be found elsewhere. Office open daily 8am-11pm. V.

Internet Access: Web C@fé, R. Diário de Notícias, 126 (☎213 42 11 81). €2 per 15min., €2.50 per 30min., €3.50 per 45min., €4 per hr. Open daily 4pm-2am. **Abracadabra**, Pr. Dom Pedro IV, 66 (☎213 42 62 88). €1 per 15min., €3 per hr. Open daily 8am-9:30pm. **Cyber.bica**, R. Duques de Bragança, 7 (☎213 22 50 04), in Bairro Alto. €0.75 per 15min., €3 per hr. Open M-Th 11am-midnight, F 11am-2am.

Post Office: Main office, Pr. dos Restauradores (☎213 23 89 71; fax 23 89 76). Open daily 8am-7pm. **Branch**, Pr. do Comércio (☎213 22 09 21; fax 22 09 27). Open M-F 8:30am-6:30pm. Cash only. **Postal Code:** Central Lisboa 1100.

ACCOMMODATIONS

The local government enforces a price ceiling on *pensões* and hostels, but some try to ignore it. If prices seem inflated, ask for the printed price list (it should be openly displayed, but some define "open" differently than others). During low sea-

LISBOA

son, prices generally drop €5 or more, so try bargaining. Many establishments have rooms with only double beds and charge per person. Expect to pay €15-25 for a single and €25-45 for a double, depending on amenities.

Several hotels are in the center of town on Av. da Liberdade, while many more convenient budget hostels are in Baixa along the Rossio and on R. da Prata, R. dos Correeiros, and R. do Ouro (R. de Aurea). Lodgings near Castelo de São Jorge are quieter and closer to the sights. If central accommodations are full, head east to the hostels along Av. Almirante dos Reis. Be careful at night, especially in Alfama; many streets are isolated and poorly lit. While these areas are certainly not lairs of crime and debauchery, it pays to exercise caution.

YOUTH HOSTELS

Pousada da Juventude de Lisboa (HI), R. Andrade Corvo, 46 (☎213 53 26 96). M: Picoas. Exit the Metro station, turn right, and walk 1 block. Spacious rooms with fantastic meal options (enormous breakfast included, lunch, and dinner available; €5). HI card required. Due to finish renovations March 2004. June-Sept. dorms €15; doubles with bath €35. Oct.-May €12.50/€25. Reserve ahead all year long. MC/V. ❷

Pousada da Juventude de Parque das Nações (HI), R. de Moscavide, 47-101 (☎218 92 08 90; fax 92 08 91). M: Oriente. Exit the station and go left on Av. Dom João II for about 20-30min., walking past the Parque das Nações until the street intersects with R. de Moscavide. The hostel is the striped building on the corner, inside the Instituto Português da Juventude. Internet €0.50 for 15min. HI card required. June-Sept. dorms €12.50; doubles €35. Oct.-May €10/€28. ❶

CAMPING

Camping is popular in Portugal, but campers can be prime targets for thieves; common sense in preparing for security should be followed. Info on campgrounds is available from the tourist office in the free booklet *Portugal: Camping and Caravan Sites*. There are 30 campgrounds within a 45min. radius of the capital; listed below is the only one in Lisboa proper.

Parque de Campismo Municipal de Lisboa (☎217 62 31 00), on the road to Benfica. Take bus #14 to Parque Florestal Monsanto; the campsite is at the entrance of the park. Pool and supermarket. Reception daily 9am-9pm. July-Aug. €4.80 per person, €5 per tent, €3.20 per car. Sept.-June prices vary, but generally run €3.20-3.70. ❶

ACCOMMODATIONS BY PRICE

UNDER €15 (❶)			
Pensão Beira Mar	A	Pensão Estrela	A
Pousada da Juventude Parque Naçoes	PN	Pensão Estação Central	B
Campismo Municipal de Lisboa	E	Residencial Florescente	B
		Pensão Ninho das Águias	A
€15-25 (❷)		Pousada da Juventude de Lisboa	E
⌨ Casa de Hóspedes Globo	BA	Pensão Royal	B
Residencial Duas Nações	B	**€26-35 (❸)**	
		Pensão Londres	BA

A Alfama **B** Baixa **BA** Bairro Alto **E** Elsewhere **PN** Parque das Nações

🗎 FOOD

Lisboa has some of the least expensive restaurants and best wine of any western European capital. A full dinner costs about €9-11 per person and the *prato do dia* is often only €4-6. One meal will probably be enough to keep you full all day. Until then, just snack on surprisingly filling, incredibly cheap, and addictively delicious Portuguese pastries; *pastelarias* are everywhere. Incidentally, calorie-counters should proceed with caution in any Portuguese eatery besides supermarkets. In Lisboa, the closer to the industrial waterfront, the cheaper the restaurant. The south end of Baixa, near the port, and the area bordering Alfama are particularly inexpensive. In Baixa, moving just a block off R. de Augusta, the main pedestrian street, can save you a few euros. Lisboa abounds with seafood specialties such as *amêjoas à bulhão pato* (steamed clams), *creme de mariscos* (seafood chowder with tomatoes), and a local classic, *bacalhau cozido com grão e batatas* (cod with chick peas and boiled potatoes, doused in olive oil). For a more diverse food selection, head up to the winding streets of Bairro Alto, where restaurants specialize in everything from shark to traditional food from Góia, a former Portuguese colony on the coast of India.

SUPERMARKETS

Pingo Doce (☎213 42 74 95). A small branch of Portugal's major supermarket chain and the only one in central Lisboa. Open M-Sa 8:30am-9pm.

Mercado Ribeira (☎213 46 29 66), on Av. 24 de Julho. A vast market complex inside a warehouse, just outside Estação Cais do Sodré. Accessible by bus #40 or tram #15. M: Cais do Sodré. Go early for the freshest selection. Open M-Sa 6am-2pm for produce, 3-7pm for flowers.

Supermercado Pão de Açúcar, Amoreiras Shopping Center de Lisboa, Av. Duarte Pacheco (☎213 82 66 80). Take bus #11 from Pr. dos Restauradores or Pr. da Figueira. Open daily 9am-11pm.

FOOD BY TYPE

PORTUGUESE		INTERNATIONAL	
🏨 Martinho da Arcada ❸/❶	B	Chimarrão ❷	PN
Casa das Sandes ❶	B	Sul ❸	BA
Churrasqueira O Cofre ❷	A	Restaurante Ali-a-Papa ❸	BA
Churrasqueira Gaúcha ❷	B	Restaurante Calcuta ❸	BA
O Eurico ❷	A	Restô ❷	A
A Lanterna ❶	B		
Lua da Mel ❷	B	**VEGETARIAN**	
Pastelaria Anunciada ❷	B	Restaurante Ali-a-Papa ❸	BA
Restaurante Bomjardim ❷	B	Restaurante Calcuta ❸	BA
Restaurante Tripeiro ❷	B		

🍎 **A** Alfama **B** Baixa **BA** Bairro Alto **E** Elsewhere **PN** Parque das Nações

🔆 SIGHTS

To refer to the wonders that attract visitors to Lisboa as "sights" is a bit misleading. From the most modern of art to the most natural of beauty, Lisboa is a city to be experienced—taken in with all the senses. While it's wildest side may be more nightlife than wildlife, *parques* sprinkled throughout the city neutralize the energy of electrified crowds and crawling commercial districts. Each intricate neighborhood unravels at the feet of the curious to reveal its history and a spirit very much of the moment.

THE LOCAL STORY

SINGING YOUR SORROWS

If your heart is broken, *fado* will not only captivate it but nurse it back to health. The melodies and lyrics of *fado* drip with the wrenching pain of unrequited passion. *Let's Go* Portugal researcher Peter Brown had an opportunity to interview one of Lisbon's famed *fado* singers, Sara Reis.

LG: So, what makes *fado* different from other traditional songs about heartbreak?

SR: *Fado* comes from the Latin, *fatum,* which means destiny. it's a feeling that is born with us. Either you understand it or you don't. I do because I was born in the middle of *fadistas.* At home I never heard Rock 'n' Roll, and by the time I reached age 7, I was already singing *fado.* To feel *fado* in its totality is to understand life—it's love, death, birth, passion, hatred. It's very complex. In order to really feel *fado,* you have to have reached a certain level of maturity and suffering. There you have it. *Fado* is nostalgia. In my opinion, it is one of the most revolutionary kinds of music. It was created by and for the people. In private rooms, the original *fadistas* would sing about murder and prostitution.

LG: That makes sense. Now, with so much suffering in the world, so much pain, why did *fado* come about in Portugal? What makes it specifically Portuguese?

SR: I've heard a lot of different answers to that question during

✆ NIGHTLIFE

Bairro Alto is the first place to go for nightlife, especially before 2am. In particular, **Rua do Norte, Rua do Diário de Notícias,** and **Rua Atalaia** have many small bars and clubs packed into three short blocks, making club-hopping as easy as crossing the street. Several gay and lesbian establishments are between Pr. Luis de Camões and Tv. da Queimada, as well as in the **Rato** area near the edge of Bairro Alto past Pr. Príncipe Real. For later hours, the options outside Bairro Alto are flashier and more diverse; **Docas de Santo Amaro** hosts a strip of waterfront bars, clubs, and restaurants while the **Avenida 24 de Julho** and the **Rua das Janelas Verdes** in the **Santos** area above have some of the most popular clubs and discos. Newer expansions include the area along the river across from the **Santa Apolónia** train station, where the glitzy club Lux is located. At clubs, jeans and sneakers are generally not allowed—some places have uptight fashion police at the door. Inside, beer runs €3-5. Some clubs also charge a cover (generally €10). There's no reason to show up before midnight; crowds flow in around 2am and stay past dawn.

♫ ENTERTAINMENT

Agenda Cultural and *Follow Me Lisboa,* free at the tourist office and at kiosks in the Rossio, on R. Portas de Santo Antão, have information on concerts, movies, plays, and bullfights. They also have lists of museums, gardens, and libraries.

FADO

Lisboa's trademark entertainment is the heart-wringing *fado,* an expressive art combining elements of singing and narrative poetry (see **Music,** p. 627). *Cantadeiras de fado,* cloaked in black dresses and shawls, perform emotional tales of lost loves and faded glory. Their melancholy wailing is expressive of *saudade,* an emotion of nostalgia and yearning; listeners are supposed to feel the "knife turning in their hearts." On weekends, book in advance. Bairro Alto has many *fado* joints off R. da Misericórdia and on side streets radiating from Igreja de São Roque; it's the best place in the city for top-quality *fado.* All of the popular houses have high "minimum consumption" requirements. To avoid these, explore nearby streets; various bars and small venues often offer free shows with less notable performers. Otherwise, treat yourself to a fancy serenaded dinner; the *casas de fado* offer some of the most elegant dining in town. These places are touristy, but do feature Portugal's top names in *fado*. All have acts every 20 minutes.

Machado, R. Norte, 91 (☎213 22 46 40). Founded in 1937, Machado is one of the larger *fado* restaurants and features some of the best known *cantadeiras* and guitarists. Dinner is not cheap, in either sense of the word. Entrees €19-30. Minimum consumption €15. Open Su and T-Sa 8pm-3am; *fado* starts at 9:15pm. AmEx/MC/V. ❹

O Faia, R. Barroca, 56 (☎213 42 67 42), between R. Atalaia and R. Diário de Notícias. Elegant and expensive. Some of Portugal's better known *fadistas* perform nightly. Minimum consumption €18, includes 2 drinks. Entrees €18 and up; *menú* €35. Open M-Sa 8pm-2am; *fado* starts at 9:30pm. AmEx/MC/V. ❹

O Forcado, R. da Rosa, 221 (☎213 46 85 79). A traditional restaurant that features *fado* from Coimbra and Lisboa, as well as folk music and dance. Decorated with bullfighting pictures and *azulejos*. Prides itself on its menu as well, with part of the restaurant removed from the performance area. Minimum consumption €15. Entrees €18-20. Open Su-Tu and Th-Sa 8pm-1:30am; *fado* starts at 9:15pm. AmEx/MC/V. ❹

Cristal Fados, Tv. da Queimada, 9 (☎213 42 67 87). Less famous singers and less luxurious meals; have dinner without blowing your budget. Minimum consumption €7. Entrees €8-11. Open 8:30pm-1am; *fado* Th-Su. AmEx/MC/V. ❸

BULLFIGHTING

The drama that is Portuguese bullfighting differs from the Spanish variety in that the bull is not killed. These spectacles take place most Thursdays from late June to late September at **Praça de Touros de Lisboa,** Campo Pequeno. (☎217 93 21 43. Open daily 10pm-2am.) The Praça de Touros is due to re-open in May after a series of renovations; call ahead or check at the tourist office (☎213 46 33 14) to confirm it's open. Take the Metro to Campo Pequeno or bus #1, 44, 45, or 83. True aficionados should include Setúbal (see p. 669) in their travels plan, as it is the capital of Portuguese bullfighting and hosts some of the most celebrated *matadores*.

FUTEBOL

Lisboa has two professional teams featuring some of the world's finest players: **Benfica** at Estadio da Luz (☎217 26 61 29; M: Colégio Militar Luz) and **Sporting** at Alvalade Stadium (☎217 56 79 14; M: Campo Grande). Check the ABEP kiosk in Pr. dos Restaura-

these 42 years. I read a lot, and nobody has ever come to a conclusion. But my own opinion is simple.

Just by virtue of the fact that in 1500 we were already exploring the world, and shipwrecks, and forced labor by prisoners. These people were far from home and family. They were treated so badly, whether by nature or their captains.

LG: Do you think *fado* has anything to do with Portugal's influence on the African continent?

SR: I think that obviously there was a lot of mixing going on. We've got some Arab blood in us, some Spanish blood. So I wouldn't be surprised. There's always a mix.

LG: Can somebody who has never had a broken heart sing *fado*?

SR: Sweetheart, I have already heard young girls no older than 16 sing about life in a way that would move you with emotion. And, on the other hand, I've heard old *fado* singers 50 years old sing from here (points to her head). It all depends on the sensibility and ability of the person.

Modern fadistas, *including* **Amália Rodrigues** *and* **Argentina Santos,** *have been securing* fado *as a cultural fixture since legendary* fadista **Maria Severa** *made* fado *quintessentially Portuguese in the early 19th century.*

NO WORK, ALL PLAY

SAINTLY INTERVENTION

The *Festa de Santo António*, the largest of Portugal's many saints' days, transforms the entire coutnry on the 13th of June. Smaller towns throughout the country decorate with multi-colored banners and ribbons hung between the narrow streets, so characteristic of the country. Lisbon itself is transformed by decorations, concerts, and events. So why all the commotion? It's difficult to say, but locals claim to honor Santo António's kind dedication to the poor during his life, and his eager support of losers of all kinds (that is, he's the saint who blesses those who misplace their belongings). But who really needs an excuse to throw a party anyhow? Even the government participates in the fun and games, paying for and televising the weddings of 20 or so lucky winners who agree to wed on the saint's feast day. But whether flinging ribbons on your home, marrying off a family member, or simply attending a concert, the 13th of June is, for many, easily the greatest and most anticipated holiday in Portugal, especially if you are the father of the bride, and desire a little divine guidance as you lose your daughter and your money in planning the wedding.

dores or the sports newspaper *A Bola* for games. The EuroCup championship is scheduled to be played throughout Portugal in 2004 (see p. 628).

THEATER, MUSIC & FILM

Teatro Nacional de Dona Maria II, Pr. Dom Pedro IV, stages performances of classical Portuguese and foreign plays and houses the **Orquesta Nacional** (☎213 47 22 26; €3.50-10, 50% student discount). At Lisboa's largest theater, **Teatro Nacional de São Carlos**, R. Serpa Pinto, 9, near the Museu do Chiado in Bairro Alto, **opera** reigns from late September through mid-June. (☎ 213 46 59 14. Open daily 1-7pm.)

São Jorge movie theater (☎212 42 25 23) is at the corner of Av. da Liberdade and Av. dos Condes, across from the Pr. dos Restauradores tourist office. Ten-screen cinemas are also located in the **Amoreiras** (☎217 81 02 00; M: Marquês Pombal) and **Colombo** (☎217 11 36 36; M: Colegio Militar Luz) shopping centers and on the top floor of the **Centro Vasco da Gama** (☎218 93 06 01; M: Oriente). The largest theater, with 14 screens, is part of the new **El Corte Inglés** shopping complex (☎213 71 17 00; M: São Sebastião). American films are shown with Portuguese subtitles.

◘ FESTIVALS

Those who love to mingle with the public will want to visit Lisboa in June. Open-air *feiras*—smorgasbords of eating, drinking, live music, and dancing—fill the streets. After savoring *farturas* (huge Portuguese pastries) and Sagres beer, join in traditional Portuguese dancing. On the night of June 12, the streets explode into song and dance in honor of St. Anthony during the **Festa de Santo António.** Banners are strung between streetlights, and confetti falls in buckets during a parade along Av. da Liberdade; young crowds absolutely pack the streets of Alfama, and grilled *sardinhas* (sardines) and *ginginha* (wild cherry liqueur) are sold everywhere. Lisboa also has a number of commercial *feiras*. Bookworms burrow for three weeks in the **Feira do Livro** (in Parque Eduardo VII behind Pr. Marquês do Pombal from late May to early June). The **Feira Internacional de Lisboa** occurs every few months in the Parque das Nações, while in July and August the **Feira de Mar de Cascais** and **Feira de Artesania de Estoril** (celebrating famous Portuguese pottery) take place near the casino. Year-round *feiras* include the **Feira de Oeiras** (Antiques) on the fourth Sunday of every month and the **Feira de Carcanelos** for clothes (Th 8am-2pm). Packrats should catch the **Feira da Ladra** (flea market), held behind Igreja de São Vicente de Fora in the Graça neighborhood (Tu and Sa 7am-3pm). Take bus #104 or #105 or tram #28.

BAIXA

Baixa, Lisboa's old business hub, is the center of town, with neatly layed streets, cafes, and shoe stores. Its grid begins at **Praça Dom Pedro IV** (better known as **Rossio**) and ends at **Praça do Comércio** on the **Rio Tejo.** The *praças* work well as decorative bookends to new Lisboa, completely rebuilt after the earthquake of 1755 decimated it (if Mr. Richter had had a scale back then, records show that this quake would have tipped 8.9). Praça do Comércio was actually built on the site of the former Royal Palace, and hence bears the nickname *Terreiro do Paço* (the Palace Lot). For tourists, a central train station and the main Portuguese tourist office make Rossio the city's focal point. Linked to Rossio is **Praça dos Restauradores,** where buses from the airport stop, and those to other destinations start. Pr. dos Restauradores lies just above Baixa, and from it, sprawling **Avenida da Liberdade** runs uphill to the new business district around **Praça do Marquês do Pombal.**

▟ ACCOMMODATIONS

Dozens of *pensões* surround the three connected *praças* that form the heart of downtown Lisboa. Staying in this area is quite convenient, as it serves as a good base for visiting sights in and around the city. Most *pensões* are on the top floors of buildings (a bane to luggage-laden travelers), often overlooking noisy streets. Few if any are especially memorable, though they do differ slightly in amenities. If you didn't reserve at least a week ahead in summer, don't despair; it's usually possible to track something down without too much effort.

Pensão Royal, R. do Crucifixo, 50, 3rd fl. (☎213 47 90 06). M: Baixa-Chiado. This new *pensão* has airy rooms with TVs and baths for among the most reasonable prices in Baixa, not to mention bright pink and electric blue bedspreads and curtains. Convenient access to Baixa's historic districts and Bairro Alto's nightlife. May-Oct. dorms €15; singles €20; doubles €30. Nov.-Apr. €10/€15/€25. ❷

Residencial Duas Nações, R. da Vitória, 41 (☎213 46 07 10), on the corner of R. Augusta, 3 blocks from M: Baixa-Chiado. Hotel-style lodging equipped with elevator has large rooms that look out onto the main pedestrian street of Baixa. Breakfast included. May-Sept. singles €20, with bath €35; doubles €25, with bath €45; triples with bath €55. Oct.-Apr. €15/€30/€20/€40/€45. AmEx/MC/V. ❷

Pensão Estação Central, Calçada da Carmo, 17, 2nd-3rd fl. (☎213 42 33 08). M: Rossio. Small, plain rooms, but inexpensive and centrally located. TV lounge with a rug depicting the Last Supper draped on the wall. Rooms without bath have shower. June-Sept. singles €15, with bath €20; doubles €30/€35. Oct.-May €10/€15/€25-30. ❷

Residencial Florescente, R. das Portas de Santo Antão, 99 (☎213 42 66 09). M: Restauradores. Rooms with marble baths, French doors, small terraces, phone, and TV. June-Sept. singles €25, with bath €40; doubles €30/€45-60; triples €45/€60. Oct.-May €20/€35/€25/€40-55/€40/€55. AmEx/MC/V. ❷

Pensão Prata, R. da Prata, 71, 3rd fl. (☎213 46 89 08). M: Baixa-Chiado. Basic, simple rooms, some with small bath. July-Sept. singles €25, with bath €30; doubles €30/€35; triples €35. Oct.-June €18-20/€20-25/€20/€25/€30. Must pay ahead. ❷

Hospedagem Estrela da Serra, R. dos Fanqueiros, 122, 4th fl. (☎218 87 42 51). The 5-floor hike doesn't pass by unnoticed, but neither does the resulting view; half the rooms have terraces with a view of all of Baixa. June-Aug. singles €15; doubles €20. Sept.-May €10/€15. ❷

■ FOOD

Despite the fact that Baixa is home to Lisboa's most tourist-oriented restaurants, a little hunting and insider tips uncover prices that compete with anything in Portugal. Look for *pastelarias*—more than pastry shops, they are less touristy and have good deals for lunch. R. das Portas de Santo Antão has a great seafood selection, but be warned; they love tourists and have the colorful signs and steep prices to match. To flee the tourist scene, Calçada de Santa Ana, above Pr. da Figueira, offers amazing selection and prices (everything locals love for under €6).

Martinho da Arcada, Pr. do Comércio, 3 (☎218 87 92 59). Founded in 1782, this is the oldest restaurant in Lisboa. The restaurant side offers mildly expensive entrees (€11-15) in an elegant dining room; but the price also allows guests to see photos and read poems of the restaurant's most celebrated regular: renowned Portuguese poet Fernando Pessoa. A less expensive option (and one of the best in town) is found in the cafe side of the establishment, with *pratos do dia* (€4) from noon-3pm. Open M-Sa 7am-10pm. Serves meals noon-4pm, 7-11pm. AmEx/MC/V. ❸/cafe ❶

Casa das Sandes, R. da Vitória, 54. Offers sandwiches locals know and love (such as salmon, lemon, and cream cheese) and others that travelers will immediately recognize (club, tuna, and turkey). Serving baguettes taken to the terrace outside, the franchise offers great seating and the lowest prices in town (a large sandwich runs €3-5). Open daily 10am-10pm. ❶

Lua da Mel, R. da Prata, 242 (☎218 87 91 51). Caramelized everything draws crowds to this diner-style pastry shop. Pastries €0.60-1. Try the house specialty, also its namesake. Serves fairly affordable meals (€7-9) on the terrace and inside and daily specials (€5-6), inside only. Open M-Sa 7am-midnight. ❷

Pastelaria Anunciada, Lgo. da Anunciada, 1-2 (☎213 42 44 17). Specialties include *bacalhau à minhota* (codfish; €7) and *cozida à portuguesa* (boiled carrots, meats, potatoes, and more; €4.90). Open daily 6:30am-10pm, serves meals noon-10pm. ❷

Restaurante Tripeiro, R. dos Correeiros, 70A (☎213 25 71 03). Specializes in fish, but offers plenty of other options with large portions and piles of vegetables on the side. Entrees €6-9. Open M-Sa noon-3pm, 7-10pm. ❷

A Lanterna, Calçada de Santa Ana, 99 (☎218 86 42 04), up the hill from R. Portas de Santo Antão, toward Alfama. A pleasant escape from the tourist traps and inflated prices on the streets below. Entrees €3.50-4.50. Open M-Sa 9am-9:30pm, meals served noon-3pm and 7-9:30pm. ❶

Restaurante Bomjardim, Tv. Santo Antão, 10-11 (☎213 42 43 89 or 42 74 24). Two restaurants with the same name and same management (facing each other on the *travessa*) boast the titles of *Rei dos Frangos* (king of chicken) and *Rei da Brasa* (king of the grill). Their Highnesses deliver with style and distinctive flavor. *Frango assado* €8.42. Other grilled meats €7-9. Open daily noon-11:30pm. AmEx/MC/V. ❷

Churrasqueira Gaúcha, R. Bacalhoeiros, 26C-D (☎218 87 06 09). South American-style grilled meat dishes. Entrees €7-10. Open M-Sa 9am-12am. AmEx/MC/V. ❷

◎ SIGHTS

Although Baixa claims few historic sights per se, the lively pedestrian traffic and dramatic history surrounding the neighborhood's three main *praças* make it a monument in its own right. Beware the thousands of cooing pigeons, spoiled by the statues of so many distinguished leaders on which to make their mark.

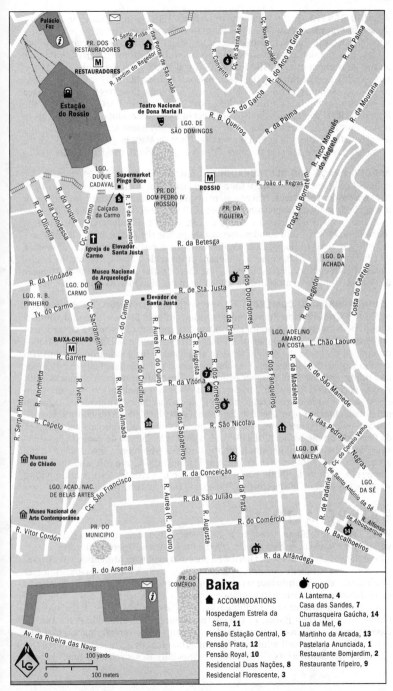

LISBOA

Baixa

♠ ACCOMMODATIONS

Hospedagem Estrela da
  Serra, **11**
Pensão Estação Central, **5**
Pensão Prata, **12**
Pensão Royal, **10**
Residencial Duas Nações, **8**
Residencial Florescente, **3**

🍎 FOOD

A Lanterna, **4**
Casa das Sandes, **7**
Churrasqueira Gaúcha, **14**
Lua da Mel, **6**
Martinho da Arcada, **13**
Pastelaria Anunciada, **1**
Restaurante Bomjardim, **2**
Restaurante Tripeiro, **9**

AROUND ROSSIO. Begin your tour of Lisboa's 18th-century history in its heart: **Rossio,** or **Praça Dom Pedro IV** as it is more formally known. The city's main square was once a cattle market, public execution stage, bullring, and carnival ground. Today, it is the domain of tourists and ruthless local motorists circling Pedro's statue. Another statue, of Gil Vicente, Portugal's first great dramatist (see **Literature, p.** 626), peers from atop the **Teatro Nacional de Dona Maria II** (easily recognized by its large columns) at one end of the *praça.* Adjoining Rossio is the elegant **Praça da Figueira,** which lies on the border of the hilly streets of Alfama. Nearby, the **Museu Nacional de Arqueologia** uses artifacts of iron, stone, and precious metals to depict Portugal's ancient history. Aficionados of early European history will come away satisfied; others may find it a bit dry. *(From the Mosteiro, go right; once inside the complex, the entrance is around the corner. Open Tu 2-6pm, W-Su 10am-6pm. €2, students €1.)*

AROUND PRAÇA DOS RESTAURADORES. Anyone who mistakes Portuguese for a dialect of Spanish or Portugal for a province of Spain has obviously never been to **Praça dos Restauradores,** where a giant obelisk celebrates the hard-earned (read: a king died) independence from Spain in 1640 after its 60-year captivity. The obelisk is accompanied by a bronze sculpture of the "Spirit of Independence." The less monumental tourist office and numerous shops line the *praça* and C. da Glória— the hill that leads to Bairro Alto. Pr. dos Restauradores is also the start of **Avenida da Liberdade,** one of Lisboa's most elegant promenades. Modeled after the boulevards of 19th-century Paris, this mile-long thoroughfare ends at **Praça do Marquês do Pombal;** from there an 18th-century statue of the Marquês overlooks the city.

AROUND PRAÇA DO COMÉRCIO. The grid of pedestrian streets on the other side of Rossio from Pr. dos Restauradores caters to people-watchers and window shoppers, as well as the politicians flitting in and out of its many government buildings. After the earthquake of 1755 leveled this section of Lisboa, the Marquês do Pombal designed the streets to serve as a conduit for goods from the ports on the Rio Tejo to the city center. Pombal envisioned an enlightened city of efficiency and utility, and the final product is just that. The grid forms perfect blocks, with streets designated for specific trades: *sapateiros* (shoemakers), *correeiros* (couriers), and *bacalhoeiros* (cod merchants) each had their own avenue. Although much has changed over the last 250 years (good luck finding a cod merchant), Baixa remains first and foremost a commercial center. Baixa's roads lead to **Praça do Comércio** on the banks of the Tejo, also known as **Terreiro do Paço** (Palace Lot) ever since the earthquake shook the royal palace which once stood there to the ground in 1755. Mother Nature and the Marquês did a fine job, and the Pr. do Comércio, with its 9,400 lb. statue of **Dom João I,** serves as a wide and inviting space between the Tejo's crowds of boats and the city's crowds of people.

BAIRRO ALTO

When people talk about "going to Lisboa," they often mean going to Bairro Alto, and they often mean going at night. It's the only place in Lisboa that never sleeps, where the streets are crowded until well past midnight with pretentious intellectuals, teens, and idealistic university students. Even though the area is known for its celebrated *casas de fado* and scores of hip bars and clubs, there is still enough to behold during the daytime to warrant a visit.

A mix of narrow streets, idyllic parks, and Baroque churches, Bairro Alto is harder to reach than Baixa. At the center of the neighborhood is **Praça Luis de Camões,** which adjoins **Largo do Chiado** at the top of R. Garrett, a good place to rest and orient yourself while sightseeing. Travelers quickly learn to curse the expanses of *escadinhas* (little stairs), especially in search of a hotel before

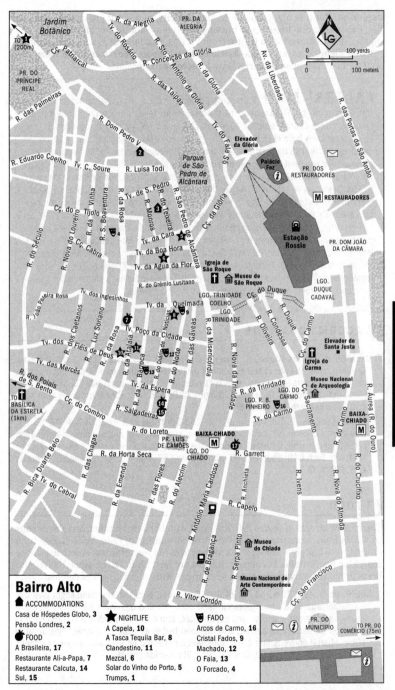

LISBOA

Bairro Alto

⌂ ACCOMMODATIONS
Casa de Hóspedes Globo, **3**
Pensão Londres, **2**

🍖 FOOD
A Brasileira, **17**
Restaurante Ali-a-Papa, **7**
Restaurante Calcuta, **14**
Sul, **15**

★ NIGHTLIFE
A Capela, **10**
A Tasca Tequila Bar, **8**
Clandestino, **11**
Mezcal, **6**
Solar do Vinho do Porto, **5**
Trumps, **1**

🍷 FADO
Arcos de Carmo, **16**
Cristal Fados, **9**
Machado, **12**
O Faia, **13**
O Forcado, **4**

exploring. But it is a good place to stay for city views and proximity to night-life; those who don't feel up to braving steep hills and the accompanying steps might find the Elevador da Glória from Pr. dos Restauradores a helpful respite.

Other nightlife areas include **Avenida 24 de Julho** and **Docas de Santo Amaro**, as well as the developments across from **Estação Santa Apolónia**.

LADIES' MAN
Pr. Luis de Camões, in the heart of Bairro Alto off R. Garrett, is marked by a monument to the man considered Portugal's greatest poet. Camões's 16th-century epic *Os Lusíadas* chronicled his nation's discoveries in lyric verse. Most likely born in Lisboa in 1524 (accounts of his life vary slightly), this swashbuckling stud had so many affairs with ladies of the court that he fled to North Africa to escape their vengeful husbands (official sources say his politics got him banished). Camões led an adventurous life for a poet, enlisting as a common soldier in the army in 1547. His service took him all over the globe, including the Arab and Indian coasts and numerous stops in Portugal's expanding empire; all the while he was working on his verses. By the time he made his way back to Lisboa in 1570, Camões had lost an eye in battle, been jailed and injured in a sword duel, and survived a shipwreck off the coast of Cambodia (clutching his precious poetry the whole time, of course). Two years later (1572) he published *Os Lusíadas;* despite its success he died in poverty somewhere in Asia in 1580. Portugal was never able to recover his body, but Camões is remembered with an honorary tomb just outside Lisboa in Belém's Mosteiro dos Jerónimos and on streets across the country which bear his name.

⌂ ACCOMMODATIONS

⌘ **Casa de Hóspedes Globo,** R. Teixeira, 37 (☎/fax 213 46 22 79). From the park entrance, cross the street and go 1 block on Tv. da Cara, then turn right. A popular spot for young travelers. All rooms newly renovated with phones, most with TV, and all but 2 with bath. Laundry €10 per load. Singles €20, with bath €22.50; double with bath €30-35; triple with bath €40. ❷

Pensão Londres, R. Dom Pedro V, 53, 2nd-5th fl. (☎213 46 22 03 or 46 55 23; www.pensaolondres.pt). Rooms with phones, some with TVs and panoramic views. High ceilings and marble bathrooms add to the classy charm. Breakfast included. Singles €29, with bath €48; doubles €40, with shower €52, with bath €67; triples €76; quads €86. MC/V. ❸

⌂ FOOD

The narrow streets of Bairro Alto are lined with bars, restaurants, and the famous *casas de fado*, restaurants that also house the singers of *fado*. Prices range from modest to definitely *im*modest, as in the *casas de fado*. Budget eaters and those searching for veritable Portuguese locales are best off in Baixa, since Bairro Alto hosts predominantly international restaurants with international clienteles.

Sul, R. do Norte, 13 (☎213 46 24 49). Dark wood paneling and candlelight give this restaurant and wine bar a romantic feel; cool jazz and tree-trunk bar stools give it a swank one. The mix is unique and comfortable, and definitely worth a visit. Creative presentation on each plate served, and the food tastes as good as it looks. Fills up after 10pm when it converts into a bar. International-themed entrees with a slew of famous house sauces €7.50-13.50. Open Tu-Su 7:30pm-midnight. ❸

Restaurante Calcuta, R. do Norte, 17 (☎213 42 82 95), near Lgo. Camões. Indian restaurant with wide selection of vegetarian options (€4.50-5). Meat entrees €6.50-9. Tourist menu (full meal of nan, chicken curry, dessert, etc.) €12.50. Open M-F noon-3pm and 7-11pm, Sa-Su 7-11pm. MC/V/AmEx. ❸

Restaurante Ali-a-Papa, R. da Atalaia, 95 (☎213 47 41 43). Serves generous helpings of traditional Moroccan food in a quiet atmosphere. Vegetarian options available. Entrees €7.50-12. Open M-Sa 7-11pm. MC/V/AmEx. ❸

A Brasileira, R. Garrett, 120-122 (☎213 46 95 41). Another former romping ground of early 20th-century poets and intellectuals (their successors continue to gather today), the cafe almost doubles as a tourist site. The *esplanade* out front is a hotspot throughout the day and night, and the restaurant below serves a famous *bife à brasileira*, steak and eggs served in cream sauce (€11). Mixed drinks €5. Open daily 8am-2am. ❸

⊙ SIGHTS

■ **BASÍLICA DA ESTRELA.** Directly across from the Jardim da Estrela, the Basílica da Estrela dates from 1796. Its dome, poised behind a pair of tall belfries, peaks out from surrounding buildings and trees to take its place in the Lisboa skyline. Half-mad Dona Maria I, desiring a male heir, promised God anything and everything if she were granted a son. When a baby boy was finally born, she built this church, and admirers of beautiful architecture and ornate wall paintings have been grateful ever since. Ask the sacristan to show you the 10th-century nativity. *(Pr. da Estrela. Accessible by Metro, or tram #28 from Pr. do Comércio. ☎213 96 09 15. Open daily 8am-12:30pm and 3-7:30pm. Free.)*

PARKS. For a perfect picnic, head to the **Parque de São Pedro de Alcântara.** The Castelo de São Jorge in Alfama stares back from the cliff opposite the park, and Bairro Alto twinkles below. *(A 5min. walk from Pr. Luis de Camões.)* More greenery awaits uphill along R. Dom Pedro V at the **Parque Príncipe Real,** which connects to the extensive Jardim Botánico. Across from the basílica on Lgo. da Estrela, the wide paths of the ■**Jardim da Estrela** wind through flocks of pigeons and lush flora. A perfect spot for lovers, photographers, and children, the park leaves ample room to do as you please amid the plentiful park benches, shady cypress trees, and intoxicating aroma of tropical flowers. *(M: Rato. With your back to the Metro stop, take R. Pedro Álvares Cabral, the 2nd road from the left in the traffic circle, for 10min. Open 8am-9pm.)*

ELEVADOR DE SANTA JUSTA. The Elevador de Santa Justa, a historic elevator built in 1902 inside a Gothic wrought-iron tower, once served as transportation up to Bairro Alto, but now just takes tourists up to see the fantastic view and back down again. *(Elevator runs M-F 7am-11pm, Sa-Su 9am-11pm. €1.)*

MUSEU NACIONAL DE ARTE ANTIGA. This museum hosts a large collection of Portuguese art as well as a survey of European painting, ranging from Gothic primitives to 18th-century French masterpieces. *(R. das Janelas Verdes, Jardim 9 Abril. Buses #40 and 60 stop to the right of the museum exit. Tram #15, from Pr. da Figueira or Pr. do Comércio, also stops nearby. ☎213 91 28 00. Open Tu 2-6pm, W-Su 10am-6pm. €3, students €1.50. Free Su before 2pm.)*

MUSEU DO CHIADO. The Museu do Chiado's collection features works from Portugal's most famous post-1850 artists. However, its own interesting twist is to juxtapose works from the Fascist era with pre- and post-Salazar works. The museum also hosts important exhibits. *(R. Serpa Pinto, 4. ☎213 43 21 48. Open Tu 2-6pm, W-Su 10am-6pm. €3; students, seniors, and teachers €1.50. Free Su before 2pm.)*

IGREJA DE SÃO ROQUE. When the Church decided to bring Sr. Roque's bones and other relics to Lisboa from Spain in the 1500s, they had not intended to build a church in his name. But when the pesky rodents and their epidemic-inducing germs miraculously dissipated upon his arrival, Mr. Roque became São Roque, and a church with all the bells and whistles of the era was quickly built. Inside, the **Capela de São João Baptista** (fourth from the left) blazes with agate, lapis lazuli, and precious metals. The chapel caused a stir upon its installation in 1747 because it took three ships to transport it from Rome, where it was built. *(Lgo. Trinidade Coelho. ☎213 23 53 83.)* Next door, **Museu de São Roque**, with its own share of gold and silver, features European religious art from the 16th to 18th centuries. *(☎213 23 53 82. Open Su and T-Sa 10am-5pm. €1, students and seniors free. Su free.)*

 NIGHTLIFE NEAR BAIRRO ALTO

SOUTH OF BAIRRO ALTO: AVENIDA 24 DE JULHO & SANTOS

Kapital, Av. 24 de Julho, 68 (☎213 24 25 90). The classiest club in Lisboa has a ruthless door policy that makes admission a competitive sport. Don't expect to get in, especially if you're an unaccompanied male. For the best chance, go with Portuguese regulars, smile politely, and keep your mouth shut. Three floors, with a nice terrace on top and a dance floor on the bottom. At closing time, take the back tunnel directly into neighboring Kremlin to continue partying. Cover usually €15. Open M-Sa 11pm-6am.

Kremlin, Escandinhas da Praia, 5 (☎213 95 71 01), off Av. 24 de Julho. Run by the same management, but a more mixed crowd including Kapital rejects and post-Kapital migrants. Door policy is harsh but not impossible. Set in a former bishop's residence, Kremlin has giant plastic statues and 3 rooms throbbing with house and dance music. Cover usually €5 for women and €10 for men, includes 1 drink. Open Tu-W midnight-6am, Th midnight-8am, F-Sa midnight-9:30am.

WEST OF BAIRRO ALTO: DOCAS DE SANTO AMARO

Speakeasy, Docas de Santo Amaro (☎213 95 77 308; www.speakeasy-bar.com), between the Santos and Alcântara stops near the river. More of a concert with waiters and beer than a bar, Speakeasy is Lisboa's premiere jazz and blues center. Live shows nightly, with famous national and international performers once a month. Beer €3. Open M-Sa 8pm-4am.

Salsa Latina, Gare Marítima de Alcântara (☎213 95 05 55), across the parking lot from the cluster at Doca de Santo Amaro. Sophisticated crowds come for the live salsa dancing on weekends (lessons available by appointment). Terrace with a view of the river. Minimum consumption €10. Open M-Th 8-11pm, F-Sa 8pm-4am.

Indochina, R. Cintura do Porto de Lisboa, Armazém H (☎213 95 58 75), 10min. walk from the Santos station. Part of a three-club strip (along with **Blues** and **Dock's**). The Far East decorations give this club, otherwise patronized by older teens and early twenty-somethings, a classy feel. Cover €10 for men, €5 for women. Open Th-Sa 11:30pm-6am.

OP Art, R. da Cozinha Economia, 11 (☎213 95 67 87), almost directly under the 25 de Abril bridge on the Lisboa side. By day it's a cafe, by night it's a bar, and by early morning, it slaps on a strobe light and starts blasting electronica. Also the only cafe/bar/disco right on the river. Beer €3. Open Su and Tu-Sa noon-4am.

SÃO SEBASTIÃO

Besides being home to Lisboa's first El Corte Inglés, a true cultural mecca, this section of town boasts two excellent art museums, both subsidiaries of the largest foundation for the arts in Portugal, **A Fundação Calouste Gulbenkian.**

🌀 SIGHTS

■ **MUSEU CALOUSTE GULBENKIAN.** When oil tycoon Calouste Gubenkian died in 1955, he left his extensive art collection (some of it purchased from the Hermitage in St. Petersburg, Russia) to his beloved Portugal. Though the philanthropist was of Armenian descent and a British citizen, it was Portugal's neutrality in World War II that appealed to him. He came in 1942, booked a room at the local luxury hotel, and stayed there for the next thirteen years. The collection is divided into sections of ancient art—Egyptian, Greek, Roman, Islamic, and Oriental—and European pieces from the 15th to 20th centuries. Highlights include the Egyptian room, Rembrandts, Monets, Renoirs, and a Rodin. *(Av. Berna, 45. M: São Sebastião. Bus #18, 46, 56.* ☎ *217 82 30 00; www.museum.gulbenkian.pt. Open Su and Tu-Sa 10am-6pm. €3, seniors, students, and teachers free.)*

CENTRO DE ARTE MODERNA. Though not as famous as its neighbor, this museum houses an extensive modern collection dedicated to promoting Portuguese talent. Other notable 20th-century artists are also represented. Don't miss the sculpture gardens that separate the two museums. *(R. Dr. Nicolau Bettencourt. M: São Sebastião. From the station, head downhill past a palace, or take bus #16, 31, or 46.* ☎ *217 95 02 41. Open Su and Tu-Sa 10am-5pm. €3, free for seniors, students, and teachers.)*

🌀 NIGHTLIFE

Trumps, R. Imprensa Nacional, 104B (☎ 213 97 10 59), down R. Dom Pedro V from Bairro Alto, on the 5th street to the left after Pr. Príncipe Real. Lisboa's biggest gay club, Trumps doesn't get going until after 1:30am. Enormous dance floor, lounge areas, pool tables, and live shows. Come Sunday for the weekly foam party. Minimum consumption €10. Shots €6. Beer €4. Open Su and Tu-Th 11:30pm-4:30am, F-Sa midnight-6:30am.

Clandestino, R. da Barroca, 99. Cavernous bar with messages from former patrons sprawled all over the rock walls. Groups of young people chat at low tables while rock plays in the background. Listen for at least one song from Pearl Jam; it's Clandestino's trademark. Beer €1.50. Small mixed drinks €3. Open Su and Tu-Sa 10pm-2am.

Portas Largas, R. da Atalaia, 105 (☎ 213 46 63 79), at the end of Tv. da Queimada. The original rendezvous point for Bairro's gay community, but also a popular bar for others (almost completely gay in summer, very mixed in winter). Portuguese music before midnight and techno afterwards. Open July-Sept. 7pm-3:30am, Oct.-June 8pm-3:30am.

Mahjong, R. da Atalaia, 3 (☎ 213 42 10 39). The suffering artist/poet/musician hangout *par excellence*, complete with foosball table. The intellectually inclined come for the cheap shots (€2) and simple, almost austere, interior. Open daily 9:30pm-4am.

A Tasca Tequila Bar, Tv. da Queimada, 13-15 (☎ 213 43 34 31). This classy Mexican bar is an ideal place for some after-dinner cocktails and schmoozing before heading off to the louder bars and discos. Cocktails €5. "Quickies" (specialized shots including Blow Job, Orgasmo, and Multi-Orgasmo) €2.50. Open daily 6pm-2am.

A Capela, R. da Atalaia, 45. A popular bar in the later hours. With gold walls and red velvet cushions, it offers more room and seats than many other bars in the district. Large beer €3. Mixed drinks €5. Open daily 9pm-2am.

Mezcal, on the corner of Tv. Agua da Flor and R. Diário de Notícias. This tiny Mexican bar with the cheapest drinks in Bairro Alto is the perfect stop before hitting more upscale establishments. Find the answer to late-night munchies here with tacos, burritos, and nachos (€2-4). Sangria €1.75. *Caipirinhas* €2.75. Shots €2. Their specialty: €2 margaritas. Open daily 7pm-2am.

Solar do Vinho do Porto, R. São Pedro de Alcántara, 45 (☎213 47 57 07), at the top of the steps through the large doorway. Product of a government institute created in 1933 to certify and promote port wine, Solar is a mature setting ideal for sipping and playing grown-up. Complete with fancy cheeses, plush red chairs, and tuxedoed waitstaff. Port runs from €1-20 per glass, depending on age and quality. Open M-Sa 2pm-midnight.

ALFAMA

Alfama, Lisboa's medieval quarter, was the lone neighborhood to survive the infamous 1755 earthquake. The area descends in tiers from the dominating **Castelo de São Jorge** facing the Rio Tejo. Between Alfama and Baixa is the **Mouraria** (Moorish quarter), ironically established after Dom Afonso Henriques and the Crusaders expelled the Moors in 1147. In Alfama, Portuguese grandmothers gossip and schoolboys play soccer amid the few camera-toting tourists who survive the maze of Alfama's enchanting streets without ending up in one of its not-so-enchanting dark alleys. Muggers make nighttime visits imprudent; even during the day, handbags should be left securely in hotels or lockers. Though the constant hike that is sightseeing in Alfama is half the fun, visitors can also hop on tram #28 from Pr. do Comércio (€1), which winds past most of the neighborhood's sights.

♦ ACCOMMODATIONS

Alfama has fewer accommodations options and less competition for prices, but staying here can be a nice change of pace (especially after the Baixa grid).

Pensão Ninho das Águias, Costa do Castelo, 74 (☎218 85 40 70). Climb the spiral staircase, greet the funny squawking bird at the entrance, and ring the bell to get into the garden. Among the very best views Lisboa has to offer, especially from rooms #5, 6, 12, 13, and 14. All rooms have phones. English spoken. May-Aug. singles €25; doubles €38, with bath €40; triple €50. Sept.-Apr. €25/€30/€33/€38. ❷

Pensão Estrela, R. dos Bacalhoeiros, 8 (☎218 86 95 06). An under-utilized option in the lower part of Alfama. Breezy rooms with the basic amenities, including TV, look out on the busy square below. Bargain in low season. Check-out 11am. June-Sept. singles €20; doubles €30; one triple €45. Oct.-May €13-15/€20-25/€38. One floor up, the similar **Pensão Verandas** (☎218 87 05 19) has comparable rooms and prices. ❷

Pensão Beira Mar, R. Terreiro do Trigo, 16 (☎218 87 15 28). Probably the cheapest option in Alfama for solo travelers. Some rooms with a view of the river cost a bit more. June-Aug. singles €15; doubles €30-40; quads €60. Oct.-May €10/€15-20/€40. Be tough and bargain for lower prices in low season. ❶

♦ FOOD

The winding streets of Alfama conceal a number of tiny, unpretentious restaurants, often packed with the neighbors and friends of the owners. Lively chatter bounces between buildings through the damp, narrow alleys. Whatever you do, watch the clock—labyrinthine Alfama grows dangerously dark after nightfall.

O Eurico, Lgo. de S. Cristóvão, 3-4 (☎218 86 18 15), at C. do Marques de Tancos. Run by owner Eurico Ferreira since 1969, this simple restaurant serves generous portions of grilled meats and is packed with workers at lunchtime. Entrees €5-7. Open M-F 9am-10pm, meals served noon-4pm and 7-10pm; Sa noon-4pm. ❷

Churrasqueira O Cofre, R. dos Bacalhoeiros, 2C-D (☎218 86 89 35). A display case shows what's available for grilling. Outside seating in summer. Entrees €6.50-11. Open daily 9am-midnight, meals served noon-4pm and 7-11:30pm. AmEx/MC/V. ❷

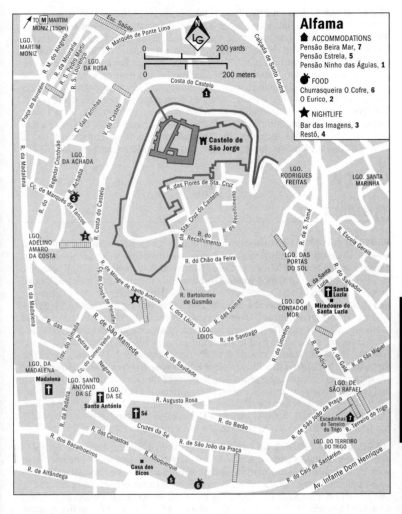

Alfama

🏠 ACCOMMODATIONS
Pensão Beira Mar, 7
Pensão Estrela, 5
Pensão Ninho das Águias, 1

🍴 FOOD
Churrasqueira O Cofre, 6
O Eurico, 2

⭐ NIGHTLIFE
Bar das Imagens, 3
Restô, 4

LISBOA

👁 SIGHTS

CASTELO DE SÃO JORGE. At the end of a winding uphill walk lies the Castelo de São Jorge, which offers spectacular views of Lisboa and the ocean. Built in the 5th-century by the Visigoths and enlarged in the 9th-century by the Moors, this castle was again improved and converted into a playground for the royal family between the 14th and 16th centuries. Wander around the ruins, soak in the views, explore the ponds, or gawk at the exotic birds in the gardens. For shoppers, the castle also includes a string of souvenir shops and restaurants. (☎ 218 82 36 70. Castle open daily Apr.-Sept. 9am-9pm; Oct.-Mar. 9am-6pm. Free.)

LOWER ALFAMA. Rua da Alfândeo, which begins two blocks away from Pr. do Comércio, connects Baixa and lower Alfama. Veer right when you see **Igreja da Madalena** in Lgo. da Madalena on the right. Take R. de Santo António da Sé and follow the tram tracks to the small **Igreja de Santo António,** built in 1812 over the beloved saint's alleged birthplace. The construction was funded with money collected by city children, who fashioned miniature altars bearing saintly images to place on doorsteps—a custom reenacted annually on June 13, the saint's feast day and Lisboa's largest holiday. *(☎218 86 91 45. Open daily 8am-7pm. Mass daily 11am, 5, and 7pm.)* In the square beyond the church is the solid 12th-century **Sé de Lisboa.** Although the cathedral interior lacks the excessive ornateness of the city's other churches, its sheer age and relic-filled treasury make it an intriguing visit. *(☎218 86 67 52. Open M 10am-5pm, Tu-Su 10am-6pm. Treasury open 10am-1pm and 2-5pm. €2.50.)*

GRAÇA

👁 SIGHTS

PANTEÃO NACIONAL. Formerly the Igreja da Santa Engrácia, the pantheon houses a tale of irony, abandon, and (somewhat less dramatic) architecture, in addition to the remains of such national figures as *fado* queen Amália Rodrigues. In 1680, the people of Graça wanted to reward their namesake with the largest domed church in Lisboa; unfortunately, faith outstripped funds, and the project had to be abandoned before the dome's completion, leaving an enormous building with an equally large sunroof. Over the next 280 years, the church changed hands between Catholic monks and enterprising factory owners, and, eventually, the dictatorial regime of Salazar, who finished the dome in 1966 and dedicated it as the National Pantheon (burial ground for illustrious statesmen). The collapse of the dictatorship in 1975 led to a final twist of irony, when the new liberal government relocated the remains of the prominent martyrs of the fascist era to the Pantheon and barred entrance of any statesmen who participated in the dictatorship. Today the building's architecture is one of the most interesting and inspiring in all Lisboa. *(To reach Graça and the Panteão, take the #12 bus or the #28 tram from the bottom of R. dos Correeiros. ☎218 85 48 20. Open Su and Tu-Sa 10am-5pm. €2.)*

IGREJA DE SÃO VICENTE DE FORA. Built between 1582 and 1629, the *Igreja* is dedicated to Lisboa's patron saint. Ask the church attendant to see the *sacristia* with inlaid walls of Sintra marble, and be sure to admire the geometrically confused walls at the base of the center dome. *(From the bottom of R. dos Correeiros in Baixa, take bus #12 or tram #28; €1. Open Tu-Sa 9am-6pm, Su 9am-12:30pm and 3-5pm. Free. Chapel next door with scenic view €3.)* At the **Feira da Ladra** (flea market), in the expanse between the Panteão and Igreja de São Vicente, the din of curious and talkative passersby drowns out the cries of merchants hawking new and used goods, from Beatles paraphernalia to African sculpture. *(Open Tu and Sa 7am-3pm.)*

MUSEO NACIONAL DO AZULEJO. Housed within the 16th-century Convento da Madre Deus, the museum is devoted to the art of the *azulejo* (tile), which was first introduced by the Moors (see **Architecture,** p. 625). Through a Manueline doorway, the Baroque interior of the former convent is an explosion of oil paintings, and *azulejos* of greater variety than can be found anywhere else in Portugal. The opulent excess continues in the choir and **Capela de Santo António.** *(East of Alfama in Xabregas. R. Madre de Deus, 4. From Pr. do Comércio, take bus #104 or #105; €1. ☎218 10 03 40. Open Tu 2-6pm, W-Su 10am-6pm. €3, students €1.50.)*

NIGHTLIFE

Restô, R. Costa do Castelo, 7 (☎218 867 334). In early evening, the moderately priced restaurant ❷ serves Argentine steaks (€12), New Zealand lamb chops (€15), and Spanish *tapas* (€4). Between 10pm-midnight, Restô fills with a young crowd come to drink and soak in the twilight view of the city from the huge outdoor patio. Live Portuguese guitar Su and F-Sa. *Caipirinhas* €4. Beer €1.25. Open daily 7:30pm-2am.

Bar das Imagens, Calçada de Marquês de Tancos, 11-13 (☎218 88 46 36). An outdoor patio between the castle wall and the final descent to Baixa. The DJ brings hip-hop to a whole new level, while tasty finger foods and "Mocktails" (non-alcoholic fruit cocktails; €3.50) get people pumped for the more popular *caipirinhas* (€4.50). Live Portuguese folk music Sundays. Open Su 3-9pm, W-Sa 4pm-2am.

Lux/Frágil, Av. Infante D. Henrique, A (☎218 82 08 90). Take a taxi to the area across from the Sta. Apolónia train station to get to this enormous 3 fl. plus terrace complex. In a class and location all its own, Lux continues to be the hottest spot in Lisboa since opening in 1998. Top two levels are dominated by large bars and seating, while the subterranean level is dedicated to the mass of dancers. Minimum consumption €10. Open Tu-Sa 6pm-6am; arrive after 2am if you want company.

LISBOA OUTER DISTRICTS

PARQUE DAS NAÇÕES

*From Lisboa, ride to the end of the red Metro line (Oriente, €0.65). The Oriente stop has escalators to the park's main entrance at the **Centro Vasco da Gama** (☎218 93 06 01; open daily 10am-midnight; free luggage storage (open daily 9:30am-8pm). Alternatively, city buses #5, 10, 19, 21, 25, 28, 44, 50, 68, and 114 all stop at the Oriente station (€1). ☎218 91 93 33; www.parquedasnacoes.pt. **Cable cars** connect one end of the park to the other. (8min.; M-F 11am-7pm, Sa-Su 10am-8pm; €3, under 18 and over 65 €1.50). **Oceanário** open daily Apr.-Sept. 10am-7pm; Oct.-Mar. 10am-6pm. €9, under 13 and over 65 €5. **Pavilhão do Conhecimento** ☎218 91 71 12. Open Tu-F 10am-6pm, Sa-Su 11am-7pm. €5, under 18 and over 65 €2.50. **Torre Vasco da Gama** open daily 10am-8pm. €2.50, under 18 and over 65 €1.25.*

Until the mid-1990s, this area was a muddy wasteland with a few run-down factories and warehouses along the banks of the Tejo. However, the city rapidly transformed the land to prepare for the 1998 World Exposition. Afterward, the government took a risk and pumped millions of euros into the land to convert it into the Parque das Nações (Park of Nations). Fortunately, the gamble paid off. Today, the park is packed day and night with people enjoying its futuristic yet graceful setting and, above all, its bewildering diversity. The park has everything from an enormous movie theater to an indoor neighborhood of restaurants, a shopping mall, and a science museum. If the proposed construction goes according to plan, the park will soon become a small city. The park entrance leads through the Centro Vasco da Gama shopping mall to the center of the grounds, where several information kiosks provide maps.

The biggest attraction is the ■Oceanário, the largest oceanarium in Europe. The new aquarium has interactive sections showcasing the four major oceans (down to the sounds, smells, and climates). All of these connect to the main tank, which houses fish, sharks, and other creatures. Visitors get within an arm's length of playful sea otters and penguins. The multilevel design allows for unique views of sea life from underneath the tank. Kids will enjoy the **Pavilhão do Conhecimento** (Pavilion of Knowledge), an interactive science museum. Other pavilions scattered throughout the park, including the **International Fairgrounds,** have rotating exhibits during the year. The **Atlantic Pavilion** (site of many big concerts), the **Virtual Reality Pavilion,** with a ride that challenges the senses, and the 145m **Torre Vasco da Gama** (the city's tallest building) grab visitors' attention with striking 21st-century architecture. The entire city can be seen from the observation tower.

■ **Chimarrão,** Edifício Lisboa, Fracção A (☎218 95 22 22). Look for the giant sign along the river near the Parque das Nações. Not for vegetarians, or even those who eat meat sparingly. After being seated, diners are introduced to two odd but committed friends: a card with a picture of a cow divided into 28 parts and a wooden tube painted on one side and green on the other. Green means go, and tuxedoed waiters will bring as many of the 28 parts as you can handle. Particular favorites include filet mignon and Brazilian *picanha*, a spicy and tender steak. Also includes salad bar, beans, rice, and juicy grilled pineapple. €24 per person. Open daily 11am-11pm. ❶

BELÉM

To get to Belém, take tram #15 from Pr. do Comércio (15min.), bus #28 or 43 from Pr. da Figueira (15min.), or the train from Estação Cais do Sodré (10min., every 15min., €0.90). If taking the tram or the bus, get off at the "Mosteiro dos Jeronimos" stop, one stop beyond the regular Belém stop. From the train station, cross the tracks, then cross the street and go left. The Padrão dos Descobrimentos is by the water, across the highway on your left (use the underpass), while the Mosteiro dos Jerónimos is to the right, through the public gardens.

Belém is more an outlying suburb farther west than a neighborhood of Lisboa, but its concentration of monuments and museums makes it a crucial stop on any tour of the capital. The town epitomizes Portuguese tradition in all its glory: a religious structure that redefines ornamentation, loads of monuments and museums that showcase the seafaring discoverers of centuries past, and unbelievable pastries.

■**MOSTEIRO DOS JERÓNIMOS.** Established in 1502 to give thanks for the success of Vasco da Gama's expedition to India, the Mosteiro dos Jerónimos was granted UN World Heritage status in the 1980s. The combination of excruciatingly minute Renaissance detail amidst Gothic arches and architecture is a sight to behold. The main door of the church, to the right of the monastery entrance, is a sculpted anachronism: Prince Henry the Navigator mingles with the Twelve Apostles on both sides of the central column. The symbolic tombs of Luís de Camões (see **Ladies' Man,** p. 652) and navigator Vasco da Gama lie in opposing transepts. Inside the monastery, the octagonal cloisters of the courtyard continue with the almost haunting attention to detail that flows in pleasant contrast with the simple rose gardens in the center. (*☎213 62 00 34. Open Su and Tu-Sa 10am-5pm. €3, students €1.50. Free Su 10am-2pm. Cloisters open Su and Tu-Sa 10am-5pm. Free.*)

■**TORRE DE BELÉM.** The best-known tower in all of Portugal, the Torre de Belém rises from the north bank of the Tejo and is surrounded by the ocean on three sides. Built under Manuel I from 1515-1520 as a harbor fortress, it originally sat directly on the shoreline; today, due to the receding beach, it is accessible only by a small bridge. Nevertheless, this symbol of Portuguese grandeur has a cameo in dozens of paintings, postcards, and photographs calling people to Lisboa from abroad. This member of the UN's World Heritage list offers panoramic views of Belém, the Tejo, and the Atlantic beyond. (*A 10min. walk along the water from the monastery away from Lisboa. Take the underpass by the gardens to cross the highway. ☎213 62 00 34. Open Su and Tu-Sa 10am-6pm. €3, students and seniors €1.50.*)

MUSEU DA MARINHA. The Museu da Marinha displays Portuguese shipping prowess. Model ships and naval tools track the development of Portugal's constant nautical fascination. (*At the far end of the Mosteiro complex. ☎213 62 00 19. Open Su and Tu-Sa Apr.-Sept. 10am-6pm; Oct.-May 10am-5pm. €3, students and seniors €1.50.*)

CENTRO CULTURAL DE BELÉM. Contemporary art buffs will bask in the glow of this luminous complex. With three pavilions holding rotating world-class exhibitions, posh meetings, and a huge auditorium for concerts and performances, the center provides the only modern entertainment in a sea of imperial landmarks. *(Across the street from the monastery museums. ☎ 213 61 24 00; www.ccb.pt. Open daily 9am-10pm. Exhibitions 11am-7:15pm; prices vary.)*

PADRÃO DOS DESCOBRIMENTOS. Along the river is the Padrão dos Descobrimentos, built in 1960 to celebrate the 500th anniversary of Prince Henry the Navigator's death. The great, white monument features Henry leading celebrated compatriots (among them Vasco da Gama and Diogo Cão) as they wistfully ponder their famous journeys. The view here is better than that from the *Torre*, with the added bonus of an elevator (rather than stairs) that transports visitors 50m up to a small terrace. The Padrão also hosts temporary exhibits. *(Across the highway from the Mosteiro. ☎ 213 03 19 50. Open Tu-Su 9am-5pm. €2, students €1.)*

PALÁCIO NACIONAL DA AJUDA. A short bus ride up the emerald hills above the town brings you to this palace, home of the Portuguese royal family for 110 years. Constructed in 1802, the 54 chambers are a telling display of opulence and decadence as befits the current resident: the Portuguese Ministry of Culture. *(Lgo. da Ajuda. Take tram #18 (Ajuda) to the palace's back door, or walk up Calçada de Ajuda (20min.). ☎ 213 63 70 95. Open Su-Tu and Th-Sa 10am-4:30pm. Guided tours €3, students €1.50.)*

⚡ DAYTRIPS FROM LISBOA

Lisboa, with all its history and passion, can be daunting after several days. If Nature calls, respond with daytrips to some of the following coastal towns. The beaches and related outdoor activities are a great escape from the city's museum/cathedral/bar crawl. Pay close attention to transportation links as you plan; many of these places lie en route to other, larger destinations such as Sintra and Setúbal. (See **Near Lisboa,** p. 665.)

ESTORIL

Trains from Lisboa's Estação Cais do Sodré (☎ 213 42 48 93; M: Cais do Sodré) run to Estoril (30min., approximately every 20min. 5:30am-2:30am, €1.20) continuing to Cascais (also a pleasant 20min. walk along the beach from Estoril). Stagecoach bus #418 to Sintra departs from Av. Marginal, in front of the train station (35min., every hr. 6:10am-11:40pm, €2.50).

Even though Estoril is home to one of Europe's largest casinos, the beaches, lined with bars and restaurants, are its best asset. One of the city's five beaches, **Praia Estoril Tamariz,** greets visitors upon arrival. When exiting the train station, use the underpass; take a left to get to the beach or a right to go to the casino and the rest of town. **Casino Estoril** in Pr. José Teodoro dos Santos is well worth a visit even for non-gamblers, offering free shows and concerts as well as a fashionable game room and over 1200 slot machines. A nightly show, *O Egoísta* (The Selfish Guy), includes comedy, dance, and music starting at 10pm. Every Wednesday at 11:30pm in the Wonder-Bar, the *fado* concert features some of Portugal's most acclaimed singers. Be sure to reserve at least a day in advance. (☎ 214 66 77 00; www.casino-estoril.pt. Dress code: no sneakers, jeans, shorts, swimwear, or hats allowed anywhere in the casino; jackets required for the game room (with tie during the winter), and can be borrowed at the entrance if you leave an ID. Slots and game room 18+. Passport required. Open daily 3pm-3am.)

The **tourist office,** on Arcadas do Parque, is across the street from the train station and to the left of the park. (☎ 214 66 38 13; www.estorilcoast.com. Wheelchair accessible. Open M-Sa 9am-7pm, Su 10am-6pm.) If you need a place to stay after the casino closes, the cheapest alternative in town is easily **Pensão Mariluz ❷,** R.

Maestro Lacerda, 13. From the train station, turn right and follow Av. Marginal three blocks until it intersects Av. dos Bombeiros Voluntários. Turn left and walk 5min. In an old house, the spacious rooms offer an inexpensive respite from gambling losses and overpriced seafood. (☎214 68 27 40. June-Aug. singles €20, with bath €25; doubles €40/€45. Sept.-May €5-10 less. Prices negotiable year-round.) For those coming off a high-euro winning streak, the lovely **Pensão Pica Pau ❹**, R. Dom Afonso Henriques, 48, is the best place to crash. From the train station, take a left and walk past the tourist office, take the next right after the church onto R. Fausto Figueiredo. Walk to the junction and take a right. *Azulejos* line each hallway, and the private bar, posh swimming pool, and personal safes in each room give the *pensão* a beach resort feel. (☎214 66 71 40; fax 67 06 64. July-Sept. singles €50; doubles €75. May, June, and Oct. €40/€60. Nov.-Mar. €35/€50.)

CASCAIS

To get to Cascais from neighboring Estoril, take a right onto the walkway at Praia Estoril Tamariz and walk along the coast about 20min. Trains from Lisboa's Estação Cais do Sodré (☎213 42 48 93; M: Cais do Sodré) head to Cascais via Estoril (30min., approximately every 20min. 5:30am-2:30am, €1.30). Stagecoach bus #417 leaves from outside the train station for Sintra (40min., every hr. 6:35am-7:08pm, €2.80). To visit Praia de Guincho, a popular windsurfing beach considered by many to be best on the coast, take the circular route bus #405/415 to the Guincho stop (22min., every 1-2hr. 7:39am-5:34pm, €1.80). The last bus to Cascais is at 8:01pm.

Although the town is pleasantly serene during the off-season, the summer crowds seem to define the flavor of Cascais rather than spoil it. In balmy weather, the beaches, especially **Praia da Ribeira, Praia da Rainha,** and **Praia da Duquesa,** are filled with tanners. To reach Praia da Ribeira, simply take a right upon leaving the tourist office and walk down Av. dos Combatantes de Grande Guerra until you see the water. As is often the case, the better beaches require a little more effort; Praia da Rainha and large Praia da Duquesa are a short walk out of town towards Estoril. Those in search of shade should head to the expansive **Parque Municipal da Gandarinha** (open daily 10am-6pm). About 1km outside Cascais, another 20min. walk up Av. Rei Humberto de Itália, lies the natural wonder **Boca de Inferno** (Mouth of Hell), so named because of the cleft carved in the rock by the Atlantic surf and the haunting sound of the waves pummeling the cliffs. As the sun sets, the nightlife picks up on **Largo Luís de Camões,** the main pedestrian square.

To get to the **tourist office,** Av. dos Combatantes de Grande Guerra, 25, from the train station, cross Largo da Estaçaõ and take a right at McDonald's onto Av. Valbom; the office is at the end of this shop-lined street. (☎214 86 82 04. Open M-Sa 9am-7pm, Su 10am-6pm.) Sleeping in Cascais isn't the cheapest thing in the world; try staying at a base in Lisboa or at the youth hostel outside nearby Oeiras. But if the town's late-night scene convinces you of more central accommodations, consider **Residencial Valborn ❹**, Av. Valborn, 14. Enormous rooms with aquamarine bathtubs and breakfast included. (☎214 86 58 01. July-Sept. singles €48; doubles €63. Apr.-June and Oct. €43/€58. Nov.-Mar. €30/€35.)

QUELUZ

The best way to get to Queluz is by train. Take the Sintra line from Lisboa's Estação Rossio (M: Rossio) or Estação Sete Rios (M: Jardim Zoológico) and hop off at the Queluz-Belas (not Queluz-Massomá) stop (25min., every 15min., €0.80). To get to the palace, exit the train station through the ticket office and head left on Av. António Ennes, continuing straight as the street becomes Av. da República. Follow the signs until you see the expansive pink palace; the entrance is to the left of the statue of Dona Maria I.

Queluz itself is unexceptional, but the **Palácio Nacional de Queluz** makes it a worthy stop en route to Sintra. In the mid-18th-century, Dom Pedro III turned an old hunting lodge into a summer residence with the help of Portuguese architect Mateus

Vicente de Oliveira and French sculptor Jean-Baptiste Robillon. While the well-ordered garden makes the palace feel like a miniature Versailles, the *azulejo*-lined canal is purely Portuguese. Highlights include the **Sala dos Embaixadores,** with its gilded thrones, marble floors, and Chinese vases, and the **Quarto Piquenique,** with gilded honeycombed ceiling. Of historical interest is the **Quarto Don Quijote** where Dom Pedro I, the first and last emperor of Brazil, drew his final breath. (Open M and W-Su 10am-5pm. Palace €3, garden €0.50; seniors and students €1.50.)

MAFRA

Mafrense buses, labeled with a green and white "M," run from Lisboa's Campo Grande and stop in the square across from the palace; Mafrense buses serve Lisboa (1-1½hr., every hr. 5:30am-9:30pm, €2.75) and Ericeira (20min., every hr. 7:30am-midnight, €1.25). Don't take the train from Lisboa's Estação Santa Apolónia unless you're up for the 7km walk to Mafra; the station is out where cabs are rare.

An attractive stop on the way to Ericeira from Lisboa, Mafra is home to one of Portugal's most impressive sights and one of Europe's largest historical buildings, the ▨**Palácio Nacional de Mafra.** Built by Dom João V as a "hunting palace," the building took 50,000 workers and 30 years to build. The massive structure includes a monastery, palace, library, and a cathedral patterned after the famous basilica in Rome. The monastery has its own hospital and infirmary, as well as a **Sala de Penitencia,** where the Franciscan monks punished themselves—note the whip on the wall and the skull above the bed. The palace on the third floor features two towers, one for the queen and one for the king. The **Sala do Trono** (Throne Room), where the king gave his speeches, is covered with murals representing his eight ideal virtues. Look for the **Sala da Caça** (Hunting Room), decorated garishly in antlers and heads of all kinds; even the chairs and tables are made of elk antlers. The **Sala dos Jogos** (Game Room), which contains billiard and lion-pocketed snooker tables, also boasts one of the original precursors of foosball. The most impressive space in the palace is the **biblioteca** (library) containing 40,000 volumes from the 16th- to 18th-centuries, many of which were bound by the monks. Note the drawer-steps at the bottom of each Brazilian bookcase that allowed the monks to reach the top shelf. From the balcony of the **Sala de Bênção** (Blessing Room), which overlooks the cathedral, Dom João V blessed the people of Mafra; the windows on the opposite wall look down into the church, allowing the royal family to view Mass from their quarters. The **Basílica do Palácio do Convento** below is renowned for its bell towers and its unique collection of six organs. For the tour of the palace and the monastery, enter through the door to left of the main steps of the palace. (☎261 81 75 50. Open M and W-Su 10am-5pm, last entrance at 4pm. Daily 1hr. tours in English 11am and 2:30pm. €3, students and seniors €1.50, under 14 free. Free Su before 1:30pm.)

To reach the **tourist office,** simply walk to the entrance on the other side of the palace; the recently-renovated office is now inside the palace compound. Besides maps and brochures, the office has free **Internet access.** (☎261 81 71 70. Open M-F 9am-7pm, Sa-Su 9:30am-1pm and 2:30-6pm.) If you get hungry, try **Restaurante O Brasão ❷,** Tr. Manuel Esteves, 7, across the street from the Palácio Nacional. Try their *picanha brasileira,* €11. (☎261 81 56 87. Open daily 11am-midnight.)

ERICEIRA

Mafrense buses run from Lisboa's Campo Grande (1¼-1½hr., every hr. 6:30am-11:20pm, €4). Ask the driver to drop you at the stop nearest the center, or just get off at the bus station. Buses run to: Lisboa (1½hr., every hr. 5:15am-9:05pm, €4); Mafra (25min., every hr. 5:15am-9:05pm, €1.45); Sintra (50min., every hr. 6:30am-8:30pm, €2.80).

Ericeira is a pleasant fishing village whose beaches have been discovered by surfers. Despite its rising popularity, the town seems to handle the attention responsibly, more or less maintaining its traditional way of life while visitors frolic in the waves of the internationally-renowned beaches. Beachgoers find their way quickly to nearby **Praia do Norte**, a long beach to the right of the port, and **Praia do Sul** on the left. Although the waves close to town are great for novices, experienced surfers head beyond Praia do Norte to the more pristine **Praia de São Sebastião, Praia da Ribeira d'Ilhas** 3km away (site of a former World Surfing Championship), or the motherlode: **Praia dos Coxos** (Crippled Beach) just beyond Praia da Ribeira d'Ilhas. **Utilmar,** near the town center at R. 5 de Outubro, 25A, rents surfboards and bodyboards. (☎261 86 23 71. €15 per day, €25 with wet-suit. AmEx/MC/V.)

To get to the **tourist office,** R. Dr. Eduardo Burnay, 46, from the bus station, cross the road (EN 247-2), turn left, and walk uphill. Take the second right onto Calçada do Rego and take a right at the fork onto R. Paróquia. After three short blocks take a left onto R. 5 de Outubro, which runs to Pr. da República. The tourist office is the white building with blue trim on the opposite end of the square. The dedicated staff hosts nightly parties with live music in the plaza until midnight; note the constant change in schedule. The office also rents out bikes during the summer. (☎261 86 31 22. Open July-Sept. daily 9:30am-midnight; Oct.-June Su-M 9:30am-7pm, Sa 9:30am-10pm. Bike rental Apr.-Sept. half-day 9:30am-2:30pm or 2:30-8pm, €4; full day 9:30am-8pm, €7.)

If you choose to stay or if you miss the last bus back to Lisboa (9:05pm), you might have some trouble finding a cheap room in summer. Check with the tourist office for a list of rooms in private homes. The cheapest option, and a favorite of those staying to hit the waves for more than a day, is **Hospederia Bernardo ❷**, R. Prudêncio Franco da Trinidade, 11. This place is a combination apartment (€400-500 a week for 3 people), hotel-style *residencial* with all the amenities (singles €25; doubles €40), and hostel with a common kitchen (€15 per person). Prices drop €5-10 Sept.-May and are negotiable. (☎261 86 23 78.) One of the most suitable places to stay is **Residencial Fortunato ❹**, R. Dr. Eduardo Burnay, 7, a few blocks past the tourist office. All rooms have bath, TV, gleaming tile, and shiny wood. (☎261 86 28 29. July-Sept. 15 singles €40-48; doubles €45-55. May-June €36/€40. Sept. 16-Oct. €35/€40. Nov.-Apr. €30/€35.) **Restaurante O Jogo da Bola ❷**, Tr. do Jogo da Bola, 3, just behind the tourist office, is a popular stop for cheap beer and seafood, among other local dishes. (☎261 88 46 46. Entrees €4.50-11; seafood €11-20; beer €0.60-0.85. Open Su-Tu and Th-Sa noon-2am.) More seafood restaurants and several bars can be found along **Rua Dr. Eduardo Burnay,** which runs from Pr. da República. In the evening, head over to **Neptuno Pub,** R. Mendes Leal, 12. Face Pr. da República from the tourist office and take a left onto Tr. do Jogo da Bola, and take the first left. This friendly Irish pub offers live, traditional *fado* music every Friday night starting at 11pm. They pull off the weird combination of pub/fado well, keeping tourists and locals entertained (in that order). Beer €2 and up. (☎261 86 20 17. Open daily 7pm-2am. Sometimes opens at noon during summer.)

SESIMBRA

To get to Sesimbra, take a Transtejo ferry from Lisboa to Cacilhas (10min., every 15min. 5:50am-9:30pm, €0.60) from the dock at Pr. do Comércio and then catch a TST bus to Sesimbra (45min.-1hr., 15 per day 6:40am-12:40am, €2.60). Alternatively, TST buses go directly to Sesimbra (1hr., 7 per day 8am-7:30pm, €2.90) from Lisboa's Pr. de Espanha (M: Pr. de Espanha), but heavy traffic can delay them. TST buses leave from Sesimbra's main bus station on Av. da Liberdade (☎212 23 31 03) to: Cacilhas (45min.-1hr., every 30min. 5:40am-12:30am, €2.60); Lisboa (1hr., 7 per day 6:30am-6:10pm, €3.10); Setúbal (45min., 9 per day 6:20am-6:50pm, €2.50).

The agenda in Sesimbra is refreshingly simple: go to the beach, gape at the Moorish castle, eat seafood, and relax. Although the welcoming atmosphere invites guests to stay at their leisure, it certainly doesn't lay out the red carpet for travelers from abroad. And that is Sesimbra's charm—it has beaches and sights and food that draw tourists, but hasn't been changed by the attention (yet). For those who pride themselves on being outdoorsy, a steep hour-long hike to the **Moorish castle** rewards one with a luminous view of the ocean and surrounding mountains. To reach the castle from the beach, follow the yellow and green signs and take R. Gen. Humberto Delgado to the marked path. (☎212 268 07 46. Castle open June-Sept. 7am-8pm; Oct.-May 7am-7pm. Free.)

To get to the **tourist office,** Lgo. da Marinha, 26-27, from the bus station take a left onto Av. da Liberdade and walk downhill to the end, then take a right. (☎212 28 85 40. Open daily June-Sept. 9am-8pm; Oct.-May 9am-12:30pm and 2-5:30pm.) Inexpensive rooms are difficult to find, especially in summer, but **Residencial Mateus ❷,** Av. da Liberdade, across the street from Mini-Preço, is the exception. The place has rooms that absolutely complement the Sesimbra feel, with old wooden furniture, long bathrooms, and live-in owners. (☎212 23 30 39. June-Aug. €20 per person, Sept.-May €15 per person.) Restaurants cluster in the plaza above the tourist office along Lgo. da Marinha. Don't miss **Casa Isaías ❷,** R. Coronel Barreto, 2, up the street from Lgo. do Município, at the end of the block on the right. Isaías grills fish (€5-8) in an outdoor brick oven. (☎914 57 43 73. Open M-F noon-10pm; serves food noon-3pm and 7-10pm.)

NEAR LISBOA

SINTRA   ☎219

No visit to Portugal is complete without at least a day among the palaces and sheer bucolic beauty of Sintra. The town is adept at welcoming those exasperated with Lisboa's crazy city life; sultans, kings, and wealthy citizens have found the same pleasures that backpackers and travelers find today. Of course, the former left behind castles, palaces, and mansions that attract the latter even more than Sintra's natural endowments. Many daytrippers from Lisboa find comfort among the town's geranium- and bougainvillea-lined streets and surrounding hills.

▊ TRANSPORTATION

Trains: Estação de Caminhos de Ferro, Av. Dr. Miguel Bombarda (☎219 23 26 05). To Estação Rossio and Estação Sete Rios in **Lisboa** (45min., every 15min. 6:07am-2:07am, €1.20).

Buses: Stagecoach buses (☎214 83 20 55; fax 86 81 68) on Av. Dr. Miguel Bombarda run to **Cascais** (#417; 40min., every hr. 7:20am-8:30pm, €2.80) and **Estoril** (#418; 40min., every hr. 6:50am-midnight, €2.50). **Mafrense** buses, just down the street, go to **Ericeira** (50min., every hr. 7:25am-8:25pm, €2.30).

▊▊ ORIENTATION & PRACTICAL INFORMATION

Situated 25km northwest of Lisboa and 10km north of Estoril, Sintra is split into three parts: the modern **Estefânia** around the train station, where most budget accommodations and banks are located; **Sintra-Vila,** where the historic sights settle on the mountainside; and **Portela de Sintra,** where shops and municipal offices cluster. To get to the old town from the train station (a 15min. walk), take a left out of the train station's ticket office, and turn right down the small hill at the next intersection. One block down the hill, turn left again at the fountain in front of the castle-like **Câmara Municipal,** following the road as it curves past the **Parque da Liberdade.** From there, head up the hill to **Praça da República;** the Palácio Nacional de Sintra is the large white building on the right.

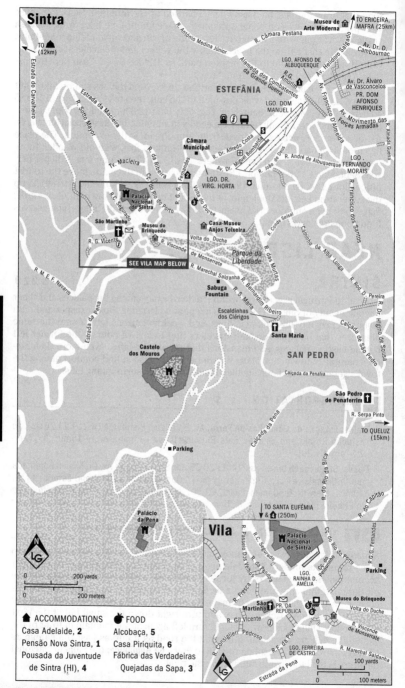

Sintra

TO ▲
(12km)

Museu de Arte Moderna

TO ERICEIRA, MAFRA (25km)

R. António Medina Júnior

R. Câmara Pestana

Estrada do Carvalheiro

Av. Dr. D. Cambournac

LGO. AFONSO DE ALBUQUERQUE

Alameda dos Combatentes da Grande Guerra

R.G. Amorim

Av. Dr. Álvaro de Vasconcelos

ESTEFÂNIA

PR. DOM AFONSO HENRIQUES

Estrada da Macieira

LGO. DOM MANUEL I

Av. Movimento das Forças Armadas

Tv. Macieira

Câmara Municipal

R. Dr. Alfredo Costa

LGO. FERNANDO MORAIS

R. da Ribeira

Cç. do Rio do Porto

Av. Dr. Miguel Bonhardt

R. André de Albuquerque

R. Francisco dos Santos

Palacio Nacional de Sintra

LGO. DR. VIRG. HORTA

R. João de Deus

São Martinho

Volta do Duche

Museu do Brinquedo

Casa-Museu Anjos Teixeira

Caminho da Alda Longa

R. G. Vicente

R. Visconde de Monserrate

Volta do Duche

R. das Murtas

Parque da Liberdade

SEE VILA MAP BELOW

R. M.E.F. Navarro

R. Marechal Saldanha

R. Bernardim Ribeiro

R. das Murtas

Calçada de São Pedro

Estrada da Pena

Sabuga Fountain

R. S. Maria

R. Dr. Higino de Sousa

Escaldinhas dos Clérigos

Santa Maria

SAN PEDRO

Castelo dos Mouros

Calçada da Penalva

Calçada da Pena

São Pedro de Penaferrim

R. Serpa Pinto

TO QUELUZ (15km)

Parking

R. do Rio da Bica

R. do Capitão

Palácio da Pena

TO SANTA EUFÉMIA & ▲ (250m)

Vila

N
LG

0   200 yards
0   200 meters

Palacio Nacional de Sintra

R. Passeio D'S Velhos

R.C. Segurado

R. da Ribeira

Cç. do Rio do Porto

R.G.G. Fernandes

Parking

R. Fresca

LGO. RAINHA D. AMÉLIA

Cç. do Pelourinho

São Martinho

Museu do Brinquedo

R. Gil Vicente

PR. DA REPÚBLICA

Volta do Duche

R. Consiglieri Pedroso

R.F. da Pipa

LGO. FERREIRA DE CASTRO

R. Visconde de Monserrate

R. Marechal Saldanha

N
LG

Estrada da Pena

0   100 yards
0   100 meters

L I S B O A

🏠 ACCOMMODATIONS
Casa Adelaide, **2**
Pensão Nova Sintra, **1**
Pousada da Juventude
de Sintra (HI) **4**

🍎 FOOD
Alcobaça, **5**
Casa Piriquita, **6**
Fábrica das Verdadeiras
Quejadas da Sapa, **3**

Tourist Office: Pr. da República, 23 (☎219 23 11 57), in Sintra-Vila. ATM inside. Open daily June-Sept. 9am-8pm; Oct.-May 9am-7pm.

Currency Exchange: Banco Totta e Açores, R. Padarias, 4 (☎219 10 68 70; fax 10 68 71). On the popular uphill side street off the main *praça* in Sintra-Vila. Open M-F 8:30am-noon and 1-3pm. **ATMs** also line Av. Heliodoro Salgado in modern Sintra.

Emergency: ☎112. **Police:** R. João de Deus, 6 (☎219 23 09 35).

Medical Services: Centro de Saúde, R. Dr. Alfredo Costa, 34, 1st fl. (☎219 10 69 00); **Hospital Fernando Fonseca (Amadora-Sintra)** in nearby Amadora (☎214 34 82 00), 20min. by train (€1.10).

Internet Access: Loja do Arco, R. Arco do Teixeira, 2 (☎219 10 61 51; fax 10 61 49; www.rigra.pt). €2.50 for first 30min., €1.25 each additional 15min.

Post Office: Av. Movimento das Forças Armadas, 1 (☎219 23 91 51; fax 23 91 56). Internet access. Open M-F 8:30am-6pm. **Postal Code:** 2710.

ACCOMMODATIONS

Sintra makes a good base for daytrips to surrounding historical sights and coastal towns, as accommodations are quite affordable. Reserve months ahead if possible.

Pousada da Juventude de Sintra (HI), Santa Eufémia at S. Pedro de Sintra (☎219 24 12 10; fax 23 31 76). Take bus #435 from the train station to São Pedro (15min., €1.20) and then hike 2km, or hail a taxi in front of the train station (€9-€10). Dining room, sitting room, TV with VCR, stereo, and winter heating. The rooms are on the high end of the youth hostel price range—cleaner than most, yet plain. Breakfast included. HI membership required. June 16-Sept. 15 dorms €10.50 per person; doubles €24, with bath €25. Sept. 16-June 15 €8.50/€20/€24. MC/V. ❶

Casa Adelaide, R. Guilherme G. Fernandes, 11 (☎219 23 08 73). Enter through the back. Well-kept, rustic rooms in an older home. Ask for private bath; the price is the same either way. Singles €25; doubles €25; triples €30. €5-10 less in winter. ❷

Pensão Nova Sintra, Lgo. Afonso de Albuquerque, 25 (☎219 23 02 20; fax 10 70 33). The *pensão* is the yellow building above a row of shops. Offering space and luxury, all nine rooms include TV, bath, and phone. The open patio at the restaurant and bar is a good place to relax. Singles €45; doubles €60. ❹

Camping: Parque de Campismo da Praia Grande, Av. Maestro Frederico de Freitas, 28 (☎219 29 05 81), on the coast 12km from Sintra. Take bus #441 from Portela de Sintra to Praia Grande. Reception daily until 7pm. Campsite is 200m from the beach, surrounded by the forest, and near the Serra de Sintra. €3 per person. ❶

ON THE MENU

PASTRIES WITH A PAST

There's a lot of history packed into those little cheese pastries proudly sold in the *pastelarias* of Sintra. *Queijadas* date back to the 13th century and were once used as a form of currency to pay landlords. The *queijada's* ascent to fame began in 1756, when a woman named Maria made the pastries to sell at the entrance of town. After the railroad tracks linking Sintra to Lisbon were completed in 1887, famous writers began to pass through. Some were so impressed by the little sweet that it soon made its way into many classic works of Portuguese literature. Maria's descendants still run the oldest pastry shop in Sintra, and they have joined with the three prestigious names of the *queijada* tradition—Preto, Gregorio, and Piriquita—to form an association for the protection of the authenticity and integrity of *queijadas de Sintra*. All shops use the same ingredients to prepare the pastries: cheese, wheat flour, sugar, egg yolk, and cinnamon, in a shell made of flour and water. However, according to Francisco Barreto das Neves, the current grandfather of the *Sapa* tradition and self-proclaimed head of quality control, there are countless variables in the production process that make the *queijadas* different in every shop.

◻ FOOD

Pastelarias (pastry shops) and restaurants crowd **Rua João de Deus** and **Avenida Heliodoro Salgado.** In the old town, **Rua das Padarias** (near the Palácio Nacional) is lined with great lunch spots. On the 2nd and 4th Sundays of every month, take bus #435 from the train station to nearby São Pedro (15min., €1.10) for the spectacular **Feira de São Pedro,** featuring every kind of local food you can imagine without the unfortunate price embellishments seen in town.

▨ **Fábrica das Verdadeiras Queijadas da Sapa,** Volta do Duche, 12 (☎219 23 04 93). Founded in 1756 and at its current location since 1890, Sapa is still run by the same family. Owners proudly display media references to their legendary *queijada* recipe on the front wall. Try a pastry (€0.60) or buy a *pacote* (package) for the road (€3.25). Open Tu-F 9am-6pm, Sa-Su 9am-7pm. ❶

Casa Piriquita, R. Padarias, 1 (☎219 23 06 26), up a small side street off Pr. da República. One of the four classic pastry shops of Sintra, Piriquita has the advantage of being right in the central tourist area. Bright yellow tiles cover the facade, and *fado* music floats into the narrow street. The counter is flanked by a marble-floored coffee and tea room. Try one of their *queijadas* (€0.60) or their premium *travasseiros* (almond cream-filled pastry; €90). Open Su-M and W-Sa 9am-10pm. ❶

Alcobaça, R. Padarias, 9 (☎219 23 16 51). Stacks of fresh seafood in the window. Shellfish lovers will enjoy the *arroz de marisco* (seafood and rice; €8). Other entrees, including grilled meats, €5-10. Open daily noon-11pm. Closed Dec. 12-26. MC/V. ❷

◉ SIGHTS

▨ **CASTELO DOS MOUROS.** You're not likely to forget a walk along the walls of this 8th-century Moorish castle—in any case, bring your camera because the views are more photogenic than almost anything in Portugal. On a clear day, the view extends to Lisboa and the Atlantic. The view-struck are usually also sun-struck; a bottle of water is recommended. *(Bus #434 runs to the top from outside the tourist office. €3.90 for an all-day bus pass. If you want to walk (1-1½hr.), start at the Museu do Brinquedo off Pr. da República and follow R. Visconde de Monserrate up the hill; continue straight as it becomes R. Bernardim Ribeiro, then take a right up the Escadinhas dos Clerigos and walk to the fork at the end. Turn left onto the Calçada da Santa Maria (toward the church), then right when you see a sign for Casa do Adro. Take another right at the first side street and follow it up the mountain to the castle. Open June-Sept. 9am-8pm, Oct.-May 9am-7pm. €3, seniors €1.)*

PALÁCIO NACIONAL DE SINTRA. Also known as the Paço Real or Palácio da Vila, the palace presides over Pr. da República. Once the site of a summer residence for Moorish sultans and their harems, the Paço Real and its gardens were built in two stages. Dom João I built the main structure in the 15th-century; a century later, Dom Manuel I created the best collection of *azulejos* in the world. He added various wings to create a mix of Moorish, Gothic, and Manueline styles. The palace has more than 20 rooms, including the *azulejo*-covered **Sala dos Árabes** and the majestic gilded **Sala dos Brasões.** You may notice a bird theme: doves symbolizing the Holy Spirit line the walls of the **Capela,** magpies cover the ceiling of the **Sala das Pegas,** and swans grace the ceiling of the **Sala dos Cisnes.** *(Lgo. da Rainha Dona Amélia. ☎219 10 68 40. Open Th-Tu 10am-5:30pm. Closed holidays. Buy tickets by 5pm. €3; seniors, students €1.50. Free Su before 2pm.)*

PALÁCIO DA PENA. Built in the 1840s by Prince Ferdinand of Bavaria, husband of Portugal's Dona Maria II, this royal retreat embraces romantic and fantastic style with its excessive detail. The prince, nostalgic for his country, rebuilt and embellished the ruined monastery with the assistance of a Prussian engineer, combining the artistic heritages of both Germany and Portugal. The result is a Bavarian castle decorated with Arabic minarets, Gothic turrets, Manueline windows, and a Renaissance dome. Interior highlights include the chapel, a fully furnished kitchen, incredible views from the Queen's terrace, and her majesty's toilet—crafted entirely in *azulejos*. *(About 1km uphill from the Castelo dos Mouros. ☎219 10 53 40. Open Su and Tu-Sa July-Sept. 10am-6:30pm; Oct.-June 10am-5pm. €5, seniors and students €3.)*

MUSEU DE ARTE MODERNA. Works by Andy Warhol and Gerhard Richter, dominate the collection, housed in a 19th-century building. *(Av. Heliodoro Salgado. ☎219 24 81 70. Open Su and T-Sa 10am-6pm. €3, students €1.50, under 10 free. Free Th.)*

MUSEU DO BRINQUEDO. The toy museum, which grew out of the private collection of João Arbue's Moreira (a local engineer and toy enthusiast), displays a fascinating three-floor assortment of over 20,000 toys in Sintra's old fire station. According to Moreira, the unifying idea of his museum is to show the history of humanity by way of toys; this philosophy unifies his eclectic collection of cars, trains, Legos, dolls, lead soldiers, and many other items. The collection includes trinkets from all over the world as well as traditional Portuguese playthings. Especially intriguing is the second floor, which presents the entire history of war from the dawn of man to WWII. *(R. Visconde de Monserrate, 28. ☎219 24 21 71. Open Su and Tu-Sa 10am-6pm. €3, under 3 and seniors €1.50.)*

SETÚBAL
☎265

No question about it, Setúbal is a port city. You can smell it in the air and see it on the menus. But unlike the port cities in the Algarve, Setúbal leaves travelers with more options that just beaches and *bacalhau* (codfish). Here to commune with Mother Nature? The wild dolphin population in the Reserva Natural do Estuário do Sado can take care of that. Fleeing from campy tourist traps in a quest to discover "Portugal?" Setúbal gets your back there, too, with central city squares full of traditional *lojas* (individual stores), cobblestones, and, of course, statues of obscure Portuguese statesmen. Whatever your fancy, Setúbal is well-equipped to tickle it and should take no more than a day to do so.

▮ TRANSPORTATION

Trains: leave from either **Estação Praça de Quebedo,** which is the most convenient to the city center, or **Estação de Setúbal** (☎265 23 88 02), in Pr. do Brasil (a 10min. walk down the same street) for **Faro** (4hr.; 3 per day 9:20am, 6:55, 8:25pm; €11) and **Estação do Barreiro** (50 min., every hr. 5am-1am, €1.50), where you transfer to a boat to get to **Lisboa.**

Buses: Setubalense, Av. 5 de Outubro, 44 (☎265 52 50 51). From the local tourist office, walk up R. Santa Maria to Av. 5 de Outubro and turn left; the station is about 2 blocks down on the right, in the building with "Rodoviária" written vertically down the front. To: **Évora** (express bus 1½hr., 1 per day 10:20am, €8.20; other buses 2-2½hr., 6 per day 6:30am-7pm, €5); **Lisboa's** Praça de Espanha (1hr., 26 per day 7am-10:30pm, €3.10); **Faro** (4hr., 5 per day 5:50am-1:50am, €12.80); **Sesimbra** (45min., 9 per day 7:20am-8:00pm, €2.40).

Ferries: Transado, Doca do Comércio (☎265 23 51 01), off Av. Luísa Todi at the eastern end of the waterfront. To **Tróia** (15min.; every 20 min. around the clock; €1, children 5-10 €0.50, under 5 free).

Taxis: Rádio Táxi (☎265 23 33 34), Av. Luísa Todi and by the bus and train stations.

▮▮ ▮ ORIENTATION & PRACTICAL INFORMATION

Setúbal's spine is **Avenida Luísa Todi,** a long boulevard parallel to the Rio Sado. Inland from the river and the *avenida* lies a dense district of shops and restaurants centered around **Praça de Bocage.** Another major thoroughfare, **Avenida 5 de**

Outubro, runs along the opposite side of the main district from Av. Luísa Todi to Pr. de Bocage. Perpendicular to Av. 5 de Outubro, **Avenida da Portela** runs past the train and bus stations.

Regional Tourist Office: Posto de Turismo da Costa Azul (☎265 53 91 20), on Tv. Frei Gaspar, just off Av. Luísa Todi near Lgo. da Misericórdia. Wheelchair accessible. Open May-Sept. Su 9:30am-12:30pm, M-Sa 9:30am-7pm; Oct.-Apr. M-Sa 9:30am-6pm. **Municipal branch,** R. Santa Maria, 2-4 (☎265 53 44 02). From the bus station, turn left (with your back to the big Rodoviária sign) and walk down Av. 5 de Outubro for 2 blocks; then take a right on R. Santa Maria and it's on your right. More convenient location to train and bus stations than the regional office and offers the same information. Open June-Sept. daily 9am-7pm, Oct.-May M-F 9am-7pm.

Currency exchange: Banks line Av. Luísa Todi. All open M-F 8:30am-3pm. **Caixa Geral de Depositos** (☎265 53 05 00), on Av. Luísa Todi.

Bike Rentals: Planeta Terra (☎919 47 18 71). Rents street, hybrid, and mountain bikes starting at €7.50 per day. Service includes delivery; even so, reserve ahead.

Emergency: ☎112. **Police:** Av. Luísa Todi (☎265 52 20 22), at Av. 22 de Dezembro.

Medical Services: Hospital São Bernardo (☎265 52 21 33), R. Camilo Castelo Branco.

Internet Access: Instituto Português da Juventude (☎265 52 12 00), Lgo. José Afonso. 30 min. free. Open daily 9:30am-5:30pm. **Ciber Centro,** Av. Bento Gonçalves, 21A (☎265 23 48 00). €2.50 per 30min., students €2.25. Open M-F 9am-11pm.

Post Office: (☎265 52 86 20), on Av. Mariano de Carvalho at Av. 22 de Dezembro. **Posta Restante.** Open M-F 8:30am-12:30pm and 2:30-6:30pm. **Postal Code:** 2900.

ACCOMMODATIONS

There are a few good *pensões* along **Avenida Luísa Todi** and near **Praça de Bocage.** Alternatively, ask at either tourist office for a list of *quartos* in private houses.

Residencial Bocage, R. São Cristóvão, 14 (☎265 54 30 80), off Pr. de Bocage. Fully loaded suites without fully loaded prices. Rooms include phone, TV, A/C, and breakfast. Singles Jan.-July and Sept.-Dec. €27.50, Aug.€37.50; doubles Nov.-Mar. €32.50, Apr.-July and Sept.-Oct. €37.50, Aug. €45. ❸

Pensão O Cantinho, Beco do Carmo, 1-9 (☎265 52 38 99), in an alley off Av. Luísa Todi behind Lgo. do Carmo. The rooms above the restaurant are startlingly cheap, and for no good reason; they're simple, clean, and spacious. Reserve a month ahead in summer. Singles €5-10, with bath €15; double with bath €23. ❶

FOOD

Setúbal is full of restaurants offering town specialties (including grilled fish and fried calamari) at very affordable prices; there's no reason to pay more than €8 for a memorable meal. A row of seafood places lines **Avenida Luísa Todi** just up the street from Doca do Comércio; you can watch as they cut and fry your fish on grills set up along the sidewalk. Pick up **groceries** and fresh baked goods at **Pingo Doce,** Av. Luísa Todi, 249. (☎265 52 61 05. Open daily 8am-10pm.)

Snack-Bar Dona Pança, R. José António Januário Silva, 32 (☎265 52 54 98), a block off Av. Luísa Todi, through the big arch. The Portuguese answer to eat-and-go cafeterias, with five main dishes and about every kind of salad you can imagine. Eat for €5-6 in the well-lit dining area with the crowd of locals on their lunch break, or come later in the day for a quieter dinner. Open M-Sa 8am-8pm. ❶

Novo 10, Av. Luísa Todi, 422-426 (☎265 52 54 98). A place of professional action. Hang out with people in suits during their lunch break and enjoy fantastic service and huge selection from a traditional menu. Meat lovers won't leave disappointed; the variety of pork and beef is among the best in town. (€9-15). Open daily noon-2am. ❸

O Cantinho, Beco do Carmo, 1-9 (☎265 52 38 99), off Av. Luísa Todi in an alley behind Lgo. do Carmo. Quality grilled seafood and other traditional dishes. Fish meals run €5-7.50. Be sure to try the *baba do camelo* ("camel's drool," a dessert made of condensed milk and eggs)—it's MUCH better than the name suggests (small bowl €0.60). Open M-W and F-Su 9am-11pm; meals served noon-3pm and 7-10pm. ❷

📷 🎭 SIGHTS & FESTIVALS

The most impressive sight in town is not really *in* town. The 16th-century **Forte de São Filipe** sits just outside the city. Designed by Italian engineer Filipe Terzi, the fortress was built during the Spanish occupation of Portugal in 1582 and took almost 20 years to finish. A phenomenal view of the Rio Sado rewards visitors, but not before making them earn it; the walk is 20min. uphill from the base of the mountain, not to mention the additional 30min. from the town center. To get there, follow Av. Luísa Todi to its end (toward the beaches), turn right onto Escadinhas do Castelo, then ascend R. Estrada do Castelo.

During the last week of July and first week of August, the **Feira de Santiago** in Lgo. José Afonso brings a carnival, folk music, and an enormous outdoor market with local snacks and souvenirs. Coinciding with the fair, Portuguese bullfighting (in which they don't kill the bull at the end of the fight) in the Pr. dos Touros sees its heyday. (Pr. dos Touros is on the opposite side of town, by the train station).

🏔 OUTDOORS

BEACHES. Outside of town are the beaches along the peninsula of **Tróia.** The beaches may be the entire reason to come to Setúbal at all, since Tróia is the first in a 70km stretch of beach territory. *(A brief ferry ride (15min., every 15-45min; €1, children 5-10 €0.50, under 5 free) away from Doca do Comércio.)*

PARKS. To the west of Setúbal is the well-known and well-loved **Parque Natural da Arrábida,** a large nature preserve that includes rolling hills and rocky beaches. The state unfortunately does not allow individual exploration beyond the well-groomed roads built to zig-zag through the park. Guides, however, are available in great quantity and variety; pick your favorite mode of transportation, and they likely will have it. For walking tours, **SAL** is your best bet. With various hikes ranging from 10 to 18km, the guides are prepared to entertain with legends, historical secrets to the convents and castles in the area, and descriptions of flora and fauna. The Portuguese guides are versatile and can adapt to language needs as requested. *(SAL ☎265 22 76 85; www.sal.jgc.pt. Tours Sa and Su throughout the year, excluding July and Aug. when they take place on select nights.)*

Other areas just outside Parque da Arrábida are also of interest. The nearby **Reservado Natural do Estuário do Sado** has a wild dolphin population, and **Vertigem Azul** offers a choice of either a sight-seeing cruise (€30), canoeing (€30), or a jeep excursion for €64. *(☎265 238 000; www.vertigemazul.com.)* Outdoor adventurers can also contact **Mil Andanças,** Av. Luísa Todi, 121, for somewhat pricy mountain biking, hiking, canoeing, and other nature trips. *(☎265 53 29 96.)*

ALGARVE

Behold the Algarve: a vacationland where happy campers from the world over bask in the sun. Nearly 3000 hours of annual sunshine have transformed this former fishermen's backwater into one of Europe's favorite vacation spots. In July and August, tourists mob the Algarve's resorts, packing bars and discos from sunset at 10pm until long after sunrise. Still, not all is excess in the Algarve. The region between Faro and the Spanish border remains relatively untouched, and to the west of Lagos towering cliffs shelter immaculate beaches. During low season, the resorts empty and wildlife of a different sort arrives, as roughly one-third of Europe's flamingos migrate to the wetlands surrounding Olhão.

With nearly a hundred miles of coastline, the Algarve has perfected the art of delicious seafood; local favorites include *sardinhas assadas* (grilled sardines) and *caldeirada* (seafood chowder). Almonds and figs also make their way into most regional cooking, especially in divine desserts like *figos cheios* (figs filled with a thick paste made of ground almonds, cacao, cinnamon, and lemon peel).

LAGOS   ☎282

In the 17th century, travelers ventured here for the indigo and sugar markets; today they come for the meat market that Lagos becomes after the sun goes down. Come for two days and you'll be tempted to stay a month or even longer. Just ask any one of the innumerable expatriate bartenders, surf guides, or restaurant owners. They came, they saw, and they decided to stay to contribute to the tourist culture that dominates every aspect of a commercial life that goes back centuries; the Algarve's capital for almost 200 years, Lagos launched many of the caravels that brought Portugal power and fortune in the 15th and 16th centuries. And then came the late 20th century and the golden age of tourism. Today no one cares much for its history, but the legendary beaches and swinging northern European bars keep people coming back year after year.

▐ TRANSPORTATION

To reach Lagos from northern Portugal, you must go through Lisboa; origins in the east transfer in Faro.

Trains: (☎282 79 23 61), across the river (over the pedestrian suspension bridge) from the main part of town. To: **Beja** (4hr.; 2 per day 8:20am, 5:15pm; €8) via Faro; **Évora** (6hr.; 2 per day 8:20am, 5:15pm; €12.50) via Faro; **Faro** (1¾hr., 9 per day 6:06am-10:30pm, €4.10); **Lisboa** (4-4½hr., 5-6 per day 6:55am-11:45pm, €13.55); **Silves** (40min., 9-12 per day 6:06am-11:45pm, €1.60); **Vila Real de Santo António** (4hr., 8-9 per day 6:55am-11:45pm, €5.60).

Buses: The **EVA** bus station (☎282 76 29 44), off Av. dos Descobrimentos, is just before R. Porta de Portugal (when walking into town) and across the channel from the train station and marina. To: **Albufeira** (1¼hr., 7 per day 7am-6pm, €3.40); **Faro** (2½hr., 6 per day 7am-5:15pm, €3.80); **Huelva, ES** (4¾hr.; 2 per day 7:30am, 2pm; €9.98); **Lisboa** (5hr., 12 per day 7:40am-11:30am, €14.50); **Portimão** (40min., 14 per day 7:15am-7:15pm, €1.90-2.50); **Sagres** (1hr., 17 per day 7:15am-8:30pm, €2.80).

Taxis: Lagos Central Taxi (☎282 76 24 69) 24hr. service to Lagos and environs.

Car Rental: 21+ for vehicles, 16+ for motorbikes.

Marina Rent A Car, Av. dos Descobrimentos, 43 (☎282 76 47 89). July-Aug. cars start at €45 per day; May-June and Sept. €35; Oct.-Apr. €30. Tax and insurance included. Rent for two days and get a third free. AmEx/MC/V.

Motoride, R. José Afonso lote 23-C (☎282 76 17 20), rents bikes (€10 per day) and scooters (€28 per day). 16+; license required. Open daily 9:30am-7pm.

Hertz-Portuguesa, Rossio de S. João Ed. Panorama, 3 (☎282 76 98 09), behind the bus station off Av. dos Descobrimentos. Cars start at €45 per day, tax and insurance included. MC/V.

ORIENTATION & PRACTICAL INFORMATION

Running the length of the channel, **Avenida dos Descobrimentos** carries traffic to and from Lagos. From the **train station,** walk through the pink marina and cross the pedestrian suspension bridge; turn left onto Av. dos Descobrimentos. Exiting the **bus station,** walk straight until you hit Av. dos Descobrimentos and turn right. **Praça Gil Eanes** is the center of the old town. The **tourist office** is on the corner of R. Lima Leitão, which extends from Pr. Gil Eanes. Follow R. Silva Lopes to R. General Alberto da Silveira to reach the grotto-lined beach of **Praia Dona Ana.**

Tourist Office: Municipal office (☎282 76 41 11), on R. Lima Leitão. Open July-Aug. M-Sa 10am-8pm; June and Sept. M-Sa 10am-8pm; Oct.-May M-F 10am-6pm.

Luggage Storage: Futebol Mania, R. Professor Luís de Azevedo, 4, off R. Cândido dos Reis. (☎962 74 63 42). €5 per day.

Currency Exchange: Cota Cambios, Pr. Gil Eanes, 11 (☎282 76 44 52). Open June-Sept. daily 8:30am-10pm; Oct.-May M-F 9:30am-7:30pm, Sa-Su 10am-7:30pm.

English-Language Bookstore: Loja do Livro, R. Dr. Joaquim Telo, 3 (☎282 76 73 47). Small selection of English and other foreign language books including best-sellers and travel guides. Open June-Aug. M-F 10am-1pm and 3-11pm, Sa 10am-1pm; Sept.-May M-F 10am-1pm and 3-7pm.

Laundromat: Lavandaria Miele, Av. dos Descobrimentos, 27 (☎282 76 39 69). Wash and dry €6.50 per 5kg. Open M-F 9am-1pm and 3-7pm, Sa 9am-1pm.

Emergency: ☎112. **Police:** R. General Alberto da Silveira (☎282 76 29 30).

Pharmacy: Farmácia Silva, R. 25 de Abril, 9 (☎282 76 28 59).

Medical Services: Hospital, R. Castelo dos Governadores (☎282 77 01 00).

Internet Access: The Em@il Box (Caixa de Correio), R. Cândido dos Reis, 112 (☎282 76 89 50). €1.25 per 15min., €3.50 per hr. Open M-F 9:30am-8pm, Sa-Su 10am-3pm. Several bars in Lagos have a computer or two; check along R. Lançarote de Freitas as well as at the youth hostel.

Post Office: R. das Portas de Portugal (☎282 77 02 50), between Pr. Gil Eanes and the river. Fax €4.10 for two pages. Open M-F 9am-1pm and 3-6pm. **Postal Code:** 8600.

ACCOMMODATIONS

In the summertime, *pensões* (and the youth hostel) fill up quickly; reserve more than a week in advance. If full, the youth hostel will happily refer you to a *quarto* near the hostel (close to the nightlife) for about the same price. Locals trying to rent rooms in their homes will probably greet you at the station. Though these rooms are often inconveniently located, they can be the best deals in town, at €10-15 per person in summer. Haggle with owners; room quality varies greatly.

Pousada da Juventude de Lagos (HI), R. Lançarote de Freitas, 50 (☎282 76 19 70; fax 76 96 84). Friendly staff and lodgers congregate in the courtyard and form the core of bar-hoppers later in the evenings. In July-Aug., book through the central **Movijovem** office (☎213 59 60 00) as early as you can. June 16-Sept. 15 dorms €15; doubles with bath €42. Sept. 16-June 15 €10/€28. MC/V. ❷

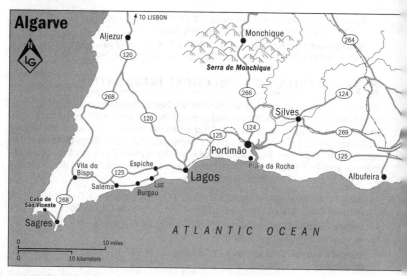

Algarve

TO LISBON

Aljezur

Monchique

264

120

Serra de Monchique

268

266

124

120

Silves

125

124

269

Portimão

125

Vila do Bispo

Espiche

125

Praia da Rocha

Albufeira

Salema

Luz

Lagos

Burgau

Cabo de São Vicente

268

Sagres

ATLANTIC OCEAN

0   10 miles

0   10 kilometers

Olinda Teresa Maria Quartos, R. Lançarote de Freitas, 37, 1st and 2nd fl. (☎282 08 23 29). Clever Sra. Olinda converted her large home into the answer to the crowded hostel, mirroring the prices and dorm-style atmosphere. Doubles or dorm rooms with shared kitchen, terrace, and bath. If the owner is not in, check at the youth hostel. June 16-Sept. 15 dorms €15; doubles €24. Sept. 16-June 15 €10/€30. ❷

Residencial Rubi Mar, R. da Barroca, 70 (☎282 76 31 65; fax 76 77 49). Eight centrally located, make-yourself-at-home rooms. Breakfast included. July-Oct. doubles €40, with bath €45; quads €75. Nov.-June €28/€33/€50. Prices fluctuate; call ahead. ❹

Residencial Lagosmar, R. Dr. Faria da Silva, 13 (☎282 76 37 22). Friendly 24hr. reception and comfortable rooms all with bath, TV, and phone. July-Aug. singles €60; doubles €70; extra bed €22. June and Sept. €35/€40/€13. Nov.-Feb. €22/€25/€9. Mar.-May and Oct. €30/€35/€11. MC/V. ❺

Residencial Caravela, R. 25 de Abril, 8 (☎282 76 33 61), just up the street from Pr. Gil Eanes. Sixteen small and basic but well-located rooms off a courtyard, some with balconies. Singles €24; doubles €32.50, with bath €36; triples €50. ❷

Camping: Camping Trindade (☎282 76 38 93), just outside town. Follow Av. dos Descobrimentos toward Sagres. €3 per person, €3.50 per tent, €4 per car. ❶

Camping: Camping Valverde (☎282 78 92 11), 6km outside Lagos and 1.5km west of Praia da Luz. Grocery store, restaurant, and pool. Free showers. €4.70 per person, €3.95 per tent, €6 per car. ❶

⬛ FOOD

Tourists can peruse multilingual menus around Pr. Gil Eanes and R. 25 de Abril, but the cheapest dining options in Lagos are the local produce **market** (Sa only) on Av. dos Descobrimentos and **Supermercado São Toque,** R. das Portas de Portugal, 61. (☎282 76 28 55. Open July-Sept. M-F 9am-8pm, Sa 9am-7pm; Oct.-June M-F 9am-7:30pm, Sa 9am-7pm.) You'll pay more on R. de Silva Lopes and R. 25 de Abril.

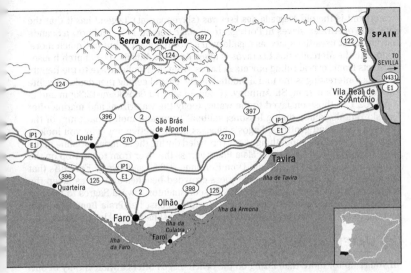

■ **Casa Rosa,** R. do Ferrador, 22 (☎968 37 71 15). A backpacker's culinary mecca, this Lagos mainstay serves whopping portions for next to nothing. Gorge on a wide range of entrees with many vegetarian options (€3.50-7). Monday all-you-can-eat spaghetti (€5). Free Internet for diners. Happy Hour 10-11pm. Open daily 6pm-midnight. ❶

Mediterraneo, Tr. Senhora da Graça, 2 (☎282 76 84 76). Mediterranean and Thai cuisine, including great seafood and meat dishes, salads, and desserts. The town's best vegetarian option. Eat indoors or outside. Entrees €7.50-9. Open Tu-Sa 7-10pm. ❷

Mullen's, R. Cândido dos Reis, 86 (☎282 76 12 81). A funny combination of great Portuguese and international cuisine, stereotypical Irish pub (complete with stacked barrels of beer), and jazz. People come from afar to try the legendary duck in orange sauce, as well as the spicy *frango grelhado.* Entrees €7-9.50. Open noon-2am. ❷

Snack-Bar Caravela, R. 25 de Abril, 14 (☎282 76 26 83), just off Pr. Gil Eanes. Well-touristed, but for good reason—it's a great place to people-watch, and their pizza is the best in town. Outdoor seating. Seafood and meat dishes €6-10, pizzas and pasta €4.50-7.10. Caravela is famous for its supreme strawberry ice cream. Open daily June-Sept. 9am-midnight; Oct.-Mar. 9am-11pm. AmEx/MC/V. ❷

A Forja, R. dos Ferreiros, 17 (☎282 76 85 88). Few traditional Portuguese restaurants exist in Lagos, but locals swear by A Forja, affectionately known as "Blue Door." Serves Algarvian seafood with all its tricks but sans the steep prices. Entrees €5.49-12.47. Open daily noon-3pm and 6:30-10pm. ❷

🔵🔵 SIGHTS & BEACHES

Although sunbathing and non-stop debauchery have long erased memories of Lagos's rugged, sea-faring past, most of the city is still surrounded by a nearly intact 16th-century wall enclosing interesting sights worth the sacrifice of a little time at the beach or bar. The **Forte da Ponta da Bandeira,** a 17th-century fortress holding maritime exhibitions, overlooks the marina. (☎282 76 14 10. Open Tu-Sa 10am-1pm and 2-6pm, Su 10am-1pm. €1.85, students €1, under 13 free.) Also on the

ALGARVE

waterfront is the old **Mercado dos Escravos** (slave market). Legend has it that the first sale of African slaves in Portugal took place here in 1441, and now a Scandinavian artist uses the space as a gallery. It's worth a glance, but not much more. Opposite the Mercado dos Escravos is **Igreja de Santo António**. The church houses artifacts from several ruling powers in Lagos, from the Neolithic age to the Republic. Most interesting is the mural painted on the chapel ceiling that depicts the life of the church's patron, St. Anthony. (Open Su and Tu-Sa 9:30am-12:30pm and 2-5pm. €2.) To those enslaved to the water, today the waterfront and marina offer jet-ski rentals, scuba diving lessons, sailboat trips, and motorboat tours of the coastal rocks and grottoes. Lagos's **beaches** are seductive any way you look at them. Flat, smooth, sunbathing sands (crowded during the summer, pristine in the low season) line the 4km-long **Meia Praia**, across the river from town. Hop on the 30-second ferry near Pr. Infante Dom Henrique (€0.50 each way). For cliffs that plunge into the sea hiding smaller, less-crowded beaches and caves, keep the ocean on your left and follow Av. dos Descobrimentos toward Sagres to **Praia de Pinhão** (20min.). Five minutes farther down the coast lies **Praia Dona Ana**, with sculpted cliffs and the grottoes that appear on at least half of all Algarve postcards.

■ WATER ACTIVITIES

If you're up for more than lazing on the beach, Lagos offers a wide variety of outdoor sports—from scuba diving, to surfing, to (booze) cruising.

Grotto Boat Tours: Companies offering tours of the coastal cliffs and grottoes (caves) set up shop on Av. dos Descobrimentos. Most tours 45min.; €25 and up for 2 people. Smaller boats are preferable, as they can maneuver into rock caves and formations.

Surf Experience: R. dos Ferreiros, 21 (☎282 76 19 43; www.surf-experience.com). One or 2-week surfing trips including lesson, transportation, and accommodations in Lagos. All levels welcome. Daytrips when space available. Apr.-Nov. 1 week €435; 2 weeks €747. Dec.-Mar. €388/€700. Board and wet suit rental 1 week €78; 2 weeks €117.

Booze Cruise: (☎963 01 26 92) This extremely popular cruise offers swimming, snorkeling, tours of the nearby grottoes, a live DJ, and, of course, cheap drinks. Cruises on M, W, and Sa. €15. For tickets, call or purchase at the youth hostel.

■ NIGHTLIFE

You're tan, you're glam, now go find yourself a (wo)man. The streets of Lagos pick up as soon as the sun dips down. On alternate Sundays 4-10pm, **Bahia Beach Bar** on Meia Praia hosts live music, volleyball, and a crowd packed with workers from Lagos's bars and restaurants. In town, the area between **Praça Gil Eanes** and **Praça Luis de Camões** is filled with cafes. **Rua Cândido dos Reis, Rua do Ferrador,** and the intersection of **Rua 25 de Abril, Rua de Silva Lopes,** and **Rua Soeiro da Costa** are packed with bars and clubs that rarely close until well past 5am.

Eddie's, R. 25 de Abril, 99 (☎282 76 83 29). Hospitable, easy-going bar popular with backpackers. Busy at night, but still comfortable. Beer €2. Happy hour 4-9pm. Open M-Sa 4pm-2am, Su 8pm-2am.

Taverna Velha (The Old Tavern), R. Lançarote de Freitas, 34 (☎282 76 92 31). Backpackers, expats, and rugby enthusiasts mingle with the amicable staff. The only air-conditioned bar in Lagos, with free nightly showings of American movies at 5:30pm, a Simpsons double-header immediately following, and regular rugby parties. Happy Hour with 2-for-1 drinks 9pm-midnight. Beer €1.25-2.50. Excellent strawberry-banana daiquiris (€7.50 per pitcher). Subs €3.50. Open Apr.-Jan. 14 M-Sa 4pm-2am, Su 8pm-2am.

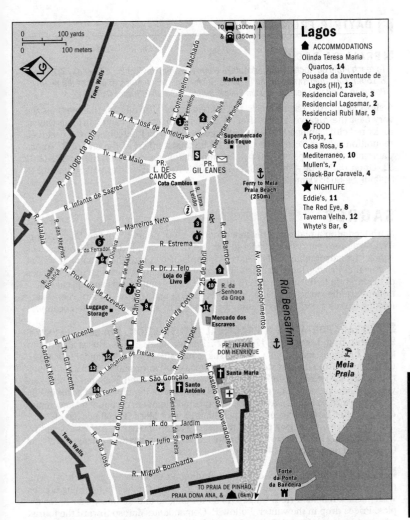

ALGARVE

Metro Bar, R. Lançarote de Freitas, the newest club in town, boasts a cosmopolitan atmosphere with acid jazz, customer cards for discounts and priority seating, and the only bar in town tailored to gay audiences (although not exclusively). Scheduled to open July 2003. Prices and schedule pending.

The Red Eye, R. Cândido dos Reis, 63. 20-something Brits and Aussies flood in around midnight for classic rock and cheap liquor. Some dancing, but mostly a pick-up scene. Mixed drinks €2.50-3.50; 1½ pint coladas €4.50. Open daily 8pm-2am.

Whyte's Bar, R. do Ferrador, 7. A Lagos institution. Live DJ keeps this small bar packed all night long. Dancing on basement level during the summer. If you're brave enough, try the 9 Deadly Sins shot drinking contest. Beer €3. Huge variety of mixed drinks €2.50-3.50. Happy hour nightly. Open daily July-Sept. 7pm-2am; Oct.-June <8pm-2am.

⚡ DAYTRIP FROM LAGOS

▨ PRAIA DA ROCHA

To reach Praia da Rocha from Lagos, take a bus to Portimão (40min., 14 per day 7:15am-8:15pm, €2), then switch to the Praia da Rocha bus, which stops in front of the nearby Portimão Honda dealership (10min., every 30min. 7:30am-8:30pm, €1.30).

A short jaunt from Lagos, locals and tourists agree that this beach is perhaps the very best the Algarve has to offer. With vast expanses of sand, surfable waves, rocky red cliffs, and plenty of secluded coves, Praia da Rocha has a well-deserved reputation (and the crowds to match). The **tourist office,** at the end of R. Tomás Cabreina, offers maps and lists of accommodations and restaurants. (☎282 41 91 32. Open daily May-Sept. 9:30am-7pm; Oct.-Apr. M-F 9:30am-12:30pm and 2-5:30pm, Sa-Su 9:30am-12:30pm.)

SAGRES   ☎282

Marooned atop a plateau at the most southwestern point in Europe, Sagres (pop. 2500) was for centuries considered the end of the world. Battered by ceaseless winds, the surrounding cliffs plunge hundreds of feet into the Atlantic. It was at Sagres that Prince Henry founded his school of navigation and organized voyages of exploration to the far reaches of the globe. Large tour groups and upscale vacationers are discouraged by the desolate location and relative lack of recreation, making Sagres a perfect destination for travelers in search of uncharted beauty.

▣⚡ TRANSPORTATION & PRACTICAL INFORMATION. **EVA buses** (☎282 76 29 44) run from **Lagos** (1hr., 17 per day 7:15am-8:30pm, €2.60). Buses also run to **Lisboa** (July-Sept. daily 4pm, €14.50). The **tourist office** on R. Comandante Matoso, up the street from the bus stop, dispenses maps and information on Sagres's illustrious history. (☎282 62 48 73. Open Tu-Sa 9:30am-1pm and 2-5:30pm.) Local services include: privately-run **emergency** (☎112) in Pr. da República and **police** in Vila do Bispo (☎282 63 91 12). At **Turinfo,** helpful staff members recommend accommodations, offer Internet access (€3 per 30min.), rent **bikes** (€9.50 per day, €6 per half-day), give info on **jeep tours** of the nearby nature preserve, A Costa Vicentina (€38, including lunch), provide **scuba** advice, and offer **currency exchange.** (☎282 62 00 03; Open daily 10am-12:30pm and 1:30-6:30pm.)

▨▣ ACCOMMODATIONS & FOOD. Finding a bed in Sagres is not hard; windows everywhere display multilingual signs for rooms, many in boarding houses with guest kitchens. Prices range €15-30 for singles and doubles; €25-40 for triples. Prices drop in the winter. Follow R. Comandante Matoso toward the tourist office and take a left on R. Patrão António Faustino to reach ▨**Atalaia Apartamentos ❷.** The beautiful, fully-furnished rooms with bath, TV, and refrigerator, and apartments with kitchen, bath, living room, and terrace, are great deals. (☎282 62 42 28. Apartments: July-Sept. up to 3 people €50, 4-6 people €80; Apr.-June €30/€60; Oct.-May €25/€50. Rooms: doubles July-Sept. €40; Apr.-June €25; Oct.-May €20.) Open-air **camping** is strictly forbidden, so head to the **Orbitur Campground ❶,** 2.5km on the way to Cabo de São Vicente, just off EN 268. (☎282 62 43 71; fax 62 44 45. June-Sept. €4 per person, €3.20 per tent, €1.75-2.24 per car. Oct.-May €2.50/€2-3/€2-2.25. Reception open daily 9am-7pm.) For groceries, try the **market** on R. Mercado, which intersects R. Comandante Matoso (open M-Sa 7am-1pm), or **Alisuper,** a larger supermarket on R. Comandante Matoso (☎282 62 44 87; open daily 9am-8pm). **O Dromedário Bistro ❷,** on R. Comandante Matoso, whips up innovative crepes (€4.10-6.50) and vegetarian dishes (€4.80-7). The bar is a night hotspot (☎282 62 42 19; open 10am-midnight; bar open until 2am. Closed Tu and Jan.-Feb.)

🎵 🎷 **SIGHTS & ENTERTAINMENT.** Near town stands the 🏛 **Fortaleza de Sagres,** the outpost where Prince Henry received the big shots of Portuguese navigation and talked about his fancy instrumentation, including the **Rosa dos Ventos,** a large circle used to measure air pressure and wind speed. The pentagonal 15th-century fortress and surrounding paths yield vertigo-inducing views of the cliffs and sea. (Open May-Sept. 10am-8:30pm; Oct.-Apr. 10am-6:30pm. Closed May 1 and Dec. 25. €3, under 25 €1.50.) Six kilometers farther west lies desolate **Cabo de São Vicente,** which features the second most powerful lighthouse in Europe, a towering structure that overlooks the southwestern tip of the continent and shines over 100km out to sea; tours are not available, though occasionally a caretaker can be persuaded to give one. On weekdays, take the bus from the bus station on R. Comandante Matoso near the tourist office (10min.; 11:15am, 12:30, 4:15pm; €1). On weekends, you're on your own—it's an hour on foot, less by bike (see **Turinfo**).

Several **beaches** fringe the peninsula, most notably **Mareta,** at the bottom of the road from the town center. Rock formations jut into the ocean on both sides of this sandy crescent. Though not as picturesque as the coves of Salema and Luz, Mareta is popular for its length and isolation; just remember, Sagres is known for its wind, and the beach is no exception. Just west of town lies one of the best beaches for windsurfing, **Praia de Martinhal.** Less windy **Praia da Beliche** is located 3km outside of town on the way to Cabo de São Vicente.

Although Sagres may seem dead on arrival, its pulse picks up around 10pm in the summer. At night, the young crowd fills the lively +**Rosa dos Ventos** in Pr. da República. (☎282 62 44 80. Beer €1. Mixed drinks €3. Famous sangría €5.50. Open 10am-2am. Closed W.) Another hotspot is **Água Salgada,** on R. Comandante Matoso, 75m beyond the tourist office, going away from the fortress, which has an extensive drink menu. (☎282 62 42 97. Beer €1. Mixed drinks €4.50. Open 10am-2am. Closed Tu from Sept.-May.) Next door is **O Dromedário** (see **Accommodations & Food,** above), where trendy young locals let loose and a request-taking DJ keeps the party raving. (☎282 62 42 97. Beer €1. Mixed drinks, including daiquiris and coladas, €3.50-5. Open daily 10am-2am.)

SILVES ☎282

Rustic Silves, once the Moorish capital of the Algarve, has bragging rights for a couple of very different reasons. Here the Moors built a beautiful sandstone castle, perfectly preserved today, that overlooks the Algarvian countryside. But Silves is not content simply to remember its history; with its annual Beer Festival, attended by scores of vendors and thousands of drinkers, the town continues to make its mark in a very current way. Above all, visitors come to Silves to flee the over-touristed areas of the Algarve and to experience the quintessential Portuguese environment that prevails.

🚆 **TRANSPORTATION.** The train station, **Estação Cams Ferro** (☎282 44 23 10), is 1km out of town; arrive in Silves by **bus.** If you do take a train, catch the "Estação" bus from the train station to town (10min., 6 per day 7:15am-7:40pm, €0.42). **Trains** run to: **Faro** (1hr., 6-11 per day 6:30am-11:16pm, €2.70); **Lagos** (40min., 10-13 per day 6:05am-12:15am, €1.40); **Lisboa** (4-5hr.; 2 per day 9:25am, 11:03pm; €10-12.50) usually via **Funcheira; Portimão** (20min., 10-13 per day 6:05am-12:15am, €0.90). **Buses** depart from the bus stop next to the municipal market on route EN 124 for **Portimão** (30min., 11 per day 7:15am-6:10pm, €1.95) and from the bus stop on the other side of the road, farther away from the castle, for **Albufeira** (40min., 8 per day 6:40am-6:25pm, €2.70) and **Lisboa** (4hr., 4 per day 8:20am-6:20pm, €14).

🗺 ⓘ **ORIENTATION & PRACTICAL INFORMATION.** The **EVA bus office,** on R. Francisco Pablos, is just next to the municipal food market. (☎282 44 23 38. Open M-F 8am-noon and 2-6pm.) To get to the **tourist office,** R. 25 de Abril, 26-28, from

ALGARVE

Lgo. António Enes, follow R. Francisco Pablos to its intersection with R. 25 de Abril and continue up the steps. (☎282 44 22 55. Open May-Sept. daily 9:30am-1pm and 2-5:30pm; Oct.-Apr. M-F 9:30am-1pm and 2-5:30pm.) The **Centro de Saúde** is located just outside of town on R. Cruz de Portugal (☎282 44 00 20).

⌐◖ ACCOMMODATIONS & FOOD. Inexpensive lodging is hard to come by in Silves. Ask at the tourist office or in any restaurant or bar for help in finding a private *quarto* (about €35-40 for a double). **Residencial Sousa ❶**, R. Samora Barros, 17, just down the steps from the tourist office, offers small, simple, and altogether genuine rooms. There is no reception desk; ask one of the cafe workers next door for assistance if the owner isn't around. (☎282 44 25 02. July-Aug. singles €15; doubles €30; triples €45. Sept.-June €12.50/€25/€36. Discounts for longer stays.) Camping is available in the neighboring town of Armação de Pera, accessible by bus (20-30min., 6 per day 7:50am-7:15pm, €1.80). For fresh fruits, vegetables, and fish, try the **mercado municipal** on Lgo. António Enes (open M-Sa 7am-1pm). For spectacular views of the town and tasty brick oven pizza, try ◪**Café Inglês ❷**, R. do Castelo, 11, between the cathedral and the castle walls. During summer months, check out the roof-top bar. (☎282 44 25 85. Pizza and entrees, with many vegetarian options €5.75-10, salads €2.50-8, desserts €1.75-3.25. Open daily 9:30am-midnight, rooftop bar open June-Sept. 7pm-2am. AmEx/MC/V.) Other restaurants and cafes can be found along the river near the bus stop and the bridge.

◪ ◪ SIGHTS & ENTERTAINMENT. Start at the **Museu Municipal de Arqueologia,** R. das Portas de Loulé, 10, built around a 12th-century Moorish well. The museum chronicles the past occupations of Portuguese residents through the artifacts they left behind. (Open M-Sa 9am-6pm, €1.50.) From there, head up R. da Sé to the **Sé Antiga** (old cathedral). Thought to have been built in the 13th century on the site of a mosque, this small cathedral has undergone a series of renovations, most of them after the 1755 earthquake, but still has an impressive Gothic ceiling. (Open daily 8:30am-8:30pm. Mass M-F 9am, Su 8:30am, 10:15am, and noon. Free.) Just up the hill from the cathedral lies the **castelo.** The structure dates from the 12th century; archaelogical digs within the castle's walls continue to turn up artifacts. It offers great views and occasional art shows in a downstairs room. (☎282 44 56 24. Open daily 9am-8pm. €1.50 for castle walls and garden. Art exhibits extra.) From the castle, turn left onto R. do Castelo and then right down R. Gregório Mascarenhas to get to the Fábrica do Inglês, which hosts the **Museu da Cortiça** (Cork Museum). Silves once served as the center of Portugal's cork industry, and this museum provides a look at both tradition and industrialization in Portugal, with photographs, machines, and plenty of cork in various processing stages. (☎282 44 04 80. Open daily June-Aug. 9:30am-12:45pm and 2-9:45pm; Sept.-May 9:30am-12:45pm and 2-6:15pm. €1.50, children 6-12 €1, under 6 free.) In the same complex as the cork museum, subdued Silves comes to life for 10 days in the end of June with the **Festival da Cerveja** (Beer Festival), when locals and travelers crowd the old mill to swig beers of every kind and color. (☎282 44 04 40. Held at the end of June into early July, usually open 6pm-1am. Tickets €5, includes 2 beers.)

ALBUFEIRA ☎289

Welcome to a land where summer populations more than double and locals dedicate themselves to one single enterprise: hosting the tourists. Sandwiched between two hills, sprawling hotel and condominium development decorate the town, and the international night scene brings such stellar (impersonation) performances as the Rolling Stones and Neil Diamond. But don't let the hype and glamour of Swedish hotels and English pubs scare you off; you are in the Algarve, and that means fabulous beach space. Soak it up, especially since your hotel is most likely only a 5min. walk from the shore.

TRANSPORTATION. EVA buses connect the **train station** (☎289 57 26 91) to the town center 6km away (10min., every hr. 7:05am-8:20pm, €1.30). To: **Faro** (45min., 9-14 per day 5:15am-11:52pm, €1.80); **Lagos** (1hr., 10 per day 7:45am-11:45pm, €3.30); **Lisboa** (4-5½hr., 5 per day 7:45am-7:10pm, €12.05); **Olhão** (1½hr., 6 per day 5:15am-11:55pm, €2.10); **Tavira** (2hr., 13 per day 5:15am-11:52pm, €3.30); **Vila Real de Santo António** (2¼hr., 6 per day 5:15am-11:55pm, €4.60). The EVA **bus station** (☎289 58 97 55) is in nearby Caliços. Buses head to: **Faro** (1hr., 9-15 per day 6:20am-7:45pm, €3.30); **Lagos** (1½hr., 7 per day 9:15am-6pm, €4.25); **Lisboa** (3½-4hr., 6 per day 6:45am-7:30pm, €14.50); **Tavira**, via Faro (1½hr.; 2 per day 7:20am, 2:40pm; €2.40). Or grab a ride from **Táxi Rádio** (☎298 58 32 30).

ORIENTATION & PRACTICAL INFORMATION. Albufeira spreads along the Atlantic with R. Latino Coelho, R. Bernardino Sousa, and R. da Bateria bordering the coast. **Rua 5 de Outubro** and **Avenida da Liberdade** run perpendicular to the ocean and separate the town's busy cafe- and bar-filled section to the east from the slightly more sedate area to the west. From the new "bus station," a parking lot in a field outside of the city, it is at least a 30min. trek to the town center. Take the city bus marked "local" from the bus station to Av. da Liberdade (every 20min., 9am-8pm, €1.30). To reach the **tourist office**, R. 5 de Outubro, 8, follow Av. da Liberdade downhill to Tr. 5 de Outubro and take a right. Turn left when this small street intersects R. 5 de Outubro. The English-speaking staff at the tourist office offers maps, a list of rooms, and brochures on water sports, including fishing and scuba diving. (☎289 58 52 79. Open daily June-Sept. 9:30am-7pm; Oct.-May 9:30am-5:30pm.) Local services include: **banks,** surrounding the touristy Lgo. Eng. Duarte Pacheco; **laundromat,** (☎289 58 89 56) at the Bellavista Comercial building on Av. dos Descobrimentos, a short drive from town or 20min. walk; **emergency** ☎112; **police,** (☎289 51 22 05) on Av. 25 de Abril; **pharmacy,** Farmácia Piedade (☎289 51 22 54) on R. João de Deus, also posts listings of on-call pharmacies; **Centro de Saúde,** (☎289 58 75 50) in nearby Caliços. **Internet access** and **used books** can be found at **Windcafe.com** in the Shopping Center California, R. Cândido dos Reis, 1. (☎289 58 64 51. Open June-Sept. M-F 10am-10pm, Sa-Su noon-10pm; Oct.-May closes at 8pm.) The **post office** is next to the tourist office on R. 5 de Outubro. (☎289 58 08 70; fax 58 32 30. Open M-F 9am-12:30pm and 2:30-6pm.) **Postal Code:** 8200.

ACCOMMODATIONS & FOOD. Most lodgings in Albufeira are booked solid by package tours from late June through mid-September. But cheer up! The trick to Albufeira is learning to find and **haggle** with the old women who live above the sqaure. Find the streets R. Cemitério Velho, R. do Saco, R. Igreja Nova, and R. Igreja Velha. Simply looking expectantly at anyone around and saying "Rooms?" will automatically start the process. Don't pay more than €15-20 for a single in the summer and €25-30 for a double, and be sure to see the room before you agree. There are a few pensions closer to the center of town. ■**Pensão Dianamar ❸**, R. Latino Coelho, 36, is close to the beach, but removed from the commotion. It features a charming courtyard, guest kitchen, TV lounge, roof terrace with a gorgeous view of the sea (for a few extra euros), and clean and comfortable rooms with bath and balconies. (☎289 58 78 01; www.dianamar.com. July singles €28-35; doubles €38-45; Aug. €30-40/€50-65; June and Sept. €25-30/€35-43; Mar.-May and Oct. €20-25/€30-33. Closed Nov.-Feb.) **Residencial Capri ❸**, Av. da Liberdade, 83, offers basic white-walled rooms, many with verandas and all with TVs and bathrooms. Ask

Mark, the young owner, for info on the hottest local clubs. (☎289 51 26 91. June-July singles €35; doubles €40; triples €45. Aug.-Sept. and Mar.-May €30/€35/€40. Oct.-Apr. €25/€30/€35. Prices are not fixed, so call ahead to be sure.) Open-air camping is illegal, but weary travelers can pay for the ritz and glitz of **Parque de Campismo de Albufeira ❶,** 2km outside town on the road to nearby Ferreiras, home of the train station. It's more like a shopping mall or a commune than a campground, with three swimming pools, a restaurant, tennis courts, a supermarket, and a disco. (☎289 58 76 29; fax 58 76 33. June-Sept. €4.85 per person, €4.35 per car, €4.65 per tent. Oct.-May 15-50% discount. AmEx/MC/V.)

For fresh produce and seafood, check out the **mercado municipal.** Follow R. da Figueira from the main bus station and take a right on Es. Vale Pedras. (Open Tu-Su 8am-1pm; Th offers the most variety.) Restaurants and cafes abound in Albufeira, mostly congregating around, and often in, the local bars on R. Cândido dos Reis. Light meals run €5-6, and more interesting local dishes creep up to €9-10. If you're in the mood for a quick fix to interrupt your busy day at the beach, then the local pick **Snack Bar Amorim ❶,** R. 5 de Outubro, opposite the tourist office, is the answer. This quintessential Portuguese cafe/diner offers sandwiches, *biftoques* (steak), and about every kind of omelet/egg combination imaginable. And the price is right: €3.50-5 per meal. (☎289 51 26 69. Open M-Sa 8:30-2am.)

🏖 **BEACHES.** Albufeira's spectacular slate of **beaches** ranges from the popular **Galé** and **São Rafael** (4-8km toward Lagos) to the chic local favorite **Falésia** (10km toward Faro), both accessible by car, taxi, or bus. Check the tourist office for seasonal schedules. To get to the centrally-located **Inatel beach** from the main square, Lgo. Eng. Duarte Pacheco, follow Av. 25 de Abril to its end and continue down R. Gago Coutinho until you hit sand. Beautiful but packed **Praia de Albufeira** awaits through the gate to the tourist office. Explore beyond these popular options, as the farther you venture, the greater the reward in lack of crowds and quantity of sand.

🎭 **ENTERTAINMENT.** Bars and restaurants line all the streets of Albufeira, but especially R. Cândido dos Reis. Clubs blast everything from salsa to techno as soon as the sun sets—and continue until it rises. The locals recommend **Atrium Bar** (R. Cândido dos Reis, at the entrance), the place to be for karaoke. The interesting contrast between the professional musicians outside the bar and the amateurs blasting away inside (karaoke nightly 9pm-4am) remind guests that you don't necessarily need talent to hit a groove. (Beer €3, mixed drinks €6. Light food served until 11pm.) **Classic Bar,** R. Cândido dos Reis, 10 (www.ruadosbares.com), is a popular spot with elaborately decorated drinks and a gaggle of tourists grooving to everything the nightly DJ gives them, but mostly Latin and English pop. (☎289 51 20 75. Beer €2-3. Mixed drinks €5-6. Open daily June-Sept. noon-4am; Oct.-May noon-midnight. **Café Latino,** R. Latino Coelho, 61, in the old town, is popular with Portuguese youth and has a pool table, a terrace with a seaside view, and a grungy feel. Recently added "culture nights" expose guests to music and dance of the region. (☎289 58 51 32. Beer €1.25. Coffee €0.75. Open Tu-Su 9am-midnight.) Many of the hottest clubs are just outside of Albufeira (€3-6 by taxi), including **Locomia, IRS Disco,** and **Kiss Disco** (all open daily 2am-6am).

FARO ☎289

Many northern Europeans begin their holidays in Faro (pop. 55,000), the Algarve's capital and largest city, though few stay long enough to absorb its charm and local color. While here, visitors often take advantage of the town's unusual diversity, such as a modern shopping district, museums of all sorts, a quiet historical neighborhood within the walls of the perfectly preserved *cidade velha,* and calm beaches on the estuary's islands.

▐ TRANSPORTATION

Flights: Aeroporto de Faro (☎ 289 80 08 00; flight info 80 08 01), 5km west of the city, has a **police station, bank, post office, car rental companies,** and **tourist info booth.** Open daily 10am-midnight. Buses #14 and 16 run from the street opposite the bus station to the airport (20min.; M-F 24 per day 7:10am-9:40pm, Sa-Su and holidays 20 per day 8am-9:40pm; €0.90).

Trains: Lgo. da Estação (☎ 289 82 64 72), near the center of town next to the bus station, not to be confused with a secondary station 2km away but still in Faro. To: **Albufeira** (45min., 6 per day 7:20am-11:15pm, €1.80); **Beja** (3hr.; 2 per day 9:05am, 5:30pm; €8); **Évora** (5hr.; 2 per day 9:05am, 5:30pm; €10.50); **Lagos** (2hr., 6 per day 8:05am-9:05pm, €4.10); **Lisboa** (5-6hr., 6 per day 7:20am-11:15pm, €13.55); **Vila Real de Santo António** (1½hr., 13 per day 6:15am-12:36am, €3.30).

Buses: EVA, Av. da República (☎ 289 89 97 00). To: **Albufeira** (1hr., 8-17 per day 6:30am-6:45pm, €3.30); **Beja** (3-3½hr., 7 per day 7:45am-4pm, €10); **Lagos** (2hr., 8 per day 7:30am-5:30pm, €4); **Olhão** (20min., every 20-40min. 7:15am-7:30pm, €1.20); **Tavira** (1hr., 11 per day 7:15am-7:30pm, €2.40); **Vila Real de Santo António** (1½hr., 9 per day 7:15am-6:20pm, €3.50). **Renex,** Av. da República (☎ 289 81 29 80), provides long-distance service to: **Braga** via Lisboa (8½hr., 9 per day 5:30am-1:30am, €21); **Lisboa** (4hr., 11-15 per day 5:30am-1:30am, €15); **Porto** via Lisboa (7½hr., 6-13 per day 5:30am-1:30am, €20). €2-2.50 discount for ISIC holders.

Taxis: Táxis Rotáxi (☎ 289 89 57 95). Beige, poorly-marked taxis gather near Jardim Manuel Bívar (by the tourist office) and at the bus and train stations.

▐▌ ORIENTATION & PRACTICAL INFORMATION

Faro's center hugs the **Doca de Recreio,** a marina lined with luxuriously apportioned ships and bordered by the Jardim Manuel Bívar and **Praça Dr. Francisco Gomes.** From the train or bus stations, follow Av. da República around the harbor. Enter the **cidade velha,** or old city, through the **Arco da Vila,** a stone arch next to the tourist office, on the far side of the garden bordering Pr. Dr. Francisco Gomes.

Tourist Office: R. da Misericórdia, 8 (☎ 289 80 36 04). From the bus or train station, turn right down Av. da República along the harbor, then left past the garden. English and French spoken. Open daily May-Sept. 9:30am-7pm; Oct.-Apr. 9:30am-5:30pm. **Regional office,** Av. 5 de Outubro, 18-20 (☎ 289 80 04 00). Open M-F 9am-7pm.

Currency Exchange: Cota Cambios, R. Dr. Francisco Gomes, 26 (☎ 289 82 57 35). Open June M-F 8:30am-8pm, Sa-Su 10am-6pm; July-Sept. M-F 8:30am-9pm, Sa 10am-8pm, Su 10am-7pm; Oct.-May M-F 8:30am-6:30pm, Sa 10am-2:30pm.

Laundromat: Sólimpa, R. Batista Lopes, 30 (☎ 289 82 29 81). Wash and dry €7 for 4kg, €2 per additional kg. Open M-F 9am-1pm and 3-7pm, Sa 9am-1pm.

Emergency: ☎ 112. **Police:** R. Polícia da Segurança Pública (☎ 289 82 20 22).

Hospital: R. Leão Penedo (☎ 289 89 11 00), just north of town.

Internet Access: Free at the **Instituto Português de Juventude,** next to the youth hostel. 30min. limit. Open M-F 9am-7pm. Also at the **Ciência Viva** museum, R. Comandante Francisco Manuel (☎ 289 89 09 20; www.ualg.pt/ccviva), near the old city. From Pr. Dr. Francisco Gomes, walk through the gardens and turn right, heading toward the docks. €2, students €1. W 50% off. Open July-Sept. 15 Tu-Su 4-11pm; Sept. 16-June Tu-F 10am-5pm, Sa-Su 3-7pm.

Post Office: Lgo. do Carmo (☎ 289 89 25 90), across from Igreja de Carmo. Open M-F 8:30am-6:30pm, Sa 9am-12:30pm. **Postal Code:** 8000.

ALGARVE

⌐ ACCOMMODATIONS

Lodgings surround the bus and train stations. Most of the low-end budget *pensões* are plain but adequate.

Pousada da Juventude (HI), R. Polícia de Segurança Pública (☎289 82 65 21), near the police station. Sleep easy at the cheapest place here. Bunk beds, sunny TV atrium, and kitchen. Lockers provided. Breakfast included. June 16-Sept. 15 dorms €9.50; doubles €23, with bath €26.50. Sept. 16-June 15 €7.50/€18/€21. AmEx/MC/V. ❶

Pensão-Residencial Central, Lgo. Terreiro do Bispo, 12 (☎289 80 72 91), near the pedestrian area up R. 1 de Maio. Clean, bright rooms, all with bath and TV, some with terraces. Doubles €30-50, depending on size and whether it has a terrace. ❸

Pensão-Residencial Oceano, R. Ivens, 21, 2nd fl. (☎289 82 33 49). From Pr. Dr. Francisco Gomes, head up R. 1 de Maio; it's 1 block up on the right. Rooms with bath, phone, and TV. July-Sept. singles €35; doubles €45; triples €60. Oct.-June €25/€35/€45. AmEx/MC/V. ❸

Residencial Madalena, R. Conselheiro Bívar, 109 (☎289 80 58 06; fax 80 58 07), close to the train and bus stations. Follow R. Gil Eanes to R. Infante Dom Henrique and take a right. Twenty-one warmly-decorated rooms with dark wooden moldings and big windows. All have TV and large, free-standing closets. Breakfast included. July-Sept. 15 singles €30, with bath €40; doubles €50. Sept. 16-June €15/€25/€35. ❸

Pensão São Filipe, R. Infante Dom Henrique, 55, 2nd fl. (☎/fax 289 82 41 82). From the train station, go up R. Ventura Coelho 3 blocks and turn right onto R. Infante Dom Henrique. Close to the center of town, this place offers 10 charming rooms, all with TV and fans, some with bath. July-Sept. singles €40, with bath €45; doubles €40/€50. Apr.-June €25/€30/€25/€35. Jan.-Mar. and Nov.-Dec. €20/€25/€20/€30. ❹

⌐ FOOD

Almonds and figs are native to the Algarve; local bakeries take good advantage of this and transform them into delicious marzipan and fig desserts. Faro has many cafes along **Rua Conselheiro Bívar** and **Praça Dr. Francisco Gomes.** At the **mercado** in Lgo. Dr. Francisco Sá Carneiro, locals barter fresh seafood. (Open daily 8am-1:30pm.) Stroll to R. Santo António, a pedestrian district with more (expensive) fresh seafood than you can shake a credit card at. Budget travelers might also opt for the supreme of local favorites: the **Minipreço** grocery store, Lgo. Terreiro do Bispo, 8-10. (☎289 80 77 34. Open M-Sa 9am-8pm.)

Mister Frango, R. Cruz das Mestras, 51 (☎289 82 84 44). From R. de Santo António, turn left on R. de Portugal and follow it for 2 blocks. The name says it all. *Frango assado* (roasted chicken) as only the Portuguese can make it, and at the best price around. €5 buys you a half chicken, rice, and fries. Ask for the not-so-hot hot sauce, *piri piri*, for a nice kick. Open noon-2:30pm and 7-10:30pm. ❶

Sol e Jardim, Pr. Ferreira de Almeida, 22-23 (☎289 82 00 30). Great restaurant featuring salads and soups (€1-7.40) and—what else?—fresh seafood (€5.50-10). Casual atmosphere seeks to please an international crowd with draping flags and diverse music. Traditional Portuguese music performed every F night (approx. 8:30pm) in July and Aug. Open daily 10:30am-3:30pm and 6:30-10:30pm. AmEx/MC/V. ❷

Creperia, Pr. Ferreira d'Almeida, 27 (☎914 63 93 55), at the end of R. 1 de Maio. Delight in a variety of gourmet crepe options, from asparagus and cream to hot chocolate, kiwi, banana, and apple (€2-5). Open July-Sept. M-Sa 8:30am-midnight, Su 6pm-midnight; Oct.-June M-Sa 8:30am-8pm, Su 4-8pm. ❶

Cervejaria A Baía, Lgo. Dr. Silva Nobre, 7 (☎289 822 845), off R. de Santo António and R. Vasco da Gama. Not just another in a string of seafood restaurants, A Baía offers specials *à Algarvia* at low prices (€6-10). Take advantage of the two-sided terrace and the diverse selection of fresh fruit. Open daily 11am-3:00pm and 7-10:30pm. ❷

🔾 SIGHTS

Faro's *cidade velha* is an uncorrupted haven for those looking for the Old World. It is a medley of ornate churches and museums punctuated by shops selling local handicrafts in addition to housing multi-generational families.

█ CAPELA DOS OSSOS. Step into **Igreja de Nossa Senhora do Carmo** to inspect the small Capela dos Ossos (Chapel of Bones), built from the remains of monks originally buried in the church's former cemetery. More than 1245 skulls and multitudes of bones are arrayed in geometric designs on the walls and ceiling. A sign above the door reads "Stop here and think if this fate will befall you." *(Lgo. do Carmo. ☎289 82 44 90. Open May-Sept. daily 10am-1pm and 3-6pm; Oct.-Apr. M-F 10am-1pm and 3-5pm, Sa 10am-1pm. Church free, chapel €0.75.)*

MUSEU REGIONAL DE FARO. Showcasing the history of the Algarve from various perspectives and time periods, the museum includes a Roman mosaic of Neptune, Moorish candles, Christian art, and a trip through the 20th century. This former convent has beautiful architecture and a comfortable, cool cloister. *(Pr. Afonso III, behind the cathedral in cidade velha. Open June-Sept. M and Sa 2-6pm; Tu-F 10am-6:30pm; Oct.-May M and Sa 2-5:30pm, Tu-F 9:30-5:30pm. €2, families €5.)*

CEMITÉRIO DOS JUDEUS. So you've seen a million cathedrals and churches (however beautiful) since coming to Portugal. Now is your chance to add some diversity to your repetoire in this, the only cemetery of its kind in all of Europe. The cemetery includes the graves of "Little Jerusalem," a community of the descendants of Jewish exiles fleeing the Spanish Inquisition. After returning from North Africa, they settled in Faro and established, among other things, this obscure but interesting cemetery. *(Rua Leão Penedo, between the hospital and the soccer stadium. A 20min. walk from the tourist office. Open M-F 9:30am-12:30pm. Free.)*

CATEDRAL (SÉ). A narrow road leads through an Arab *portico* to the Renaissance Sé, in a square lined with orange trees and blindingly white buildings. The Capela do Rosário is decorated with 17th-century *azulejos*, while the choir stands in front of an altar of striking ornamentation. The cloister is an ideal spot to relax with a book. *(☎289 806 632. Open M-F 10am-6pm, Sa 10am-1pm. €1.50.)*

🔾🔾 BEACHES & NIGHTLIFE

Faro's sandy beach, **Praia de Faro,** hides on an islet off the coast with the **Parque Natural da Ria Formosa** on one side. Take bus #16 from the bus station or the stop in front of the tourist office, just across the garden from Pr. Dr. Francisco Gomes. (5-10min., every hr. 8am-8:40pm, €1.) Ferries go to nearby **Ilha do Farol,** a less crowded beach. (45min., June-Sept. every 2hrs. 7am-7:30pm, €1.30.)

Sidewalk **cafes** crowd the pedestrian walkways off the garden in the center of town, and several **bars** with young crowds liven R. Conselheiro Bívar and its side streets. **O Conselheiro,** in the middle of R. Conselheiro Bívar with the well-lit sign, is the place for fun and (drinking) games. The bar also has themed parties on weekend evenings, a nightly DJ, and professional dancers to boot. (Beer €1.50, mixed drinks €4. Open July-Sept. daily 10pm-2am; Oct.-June Th-Sa 10pm-2am.)

OLHÃO
☎ 289

Olhão (ol-yow-n), 8km east of Faro, is the largest fishing port in the Algarve. For hundreds of years, the few inhabitants of the area have been fishermen, and modern locals continue the tradition, helping to create one of Portugal's most productive fishing industries. Locals pride themselves on their "genuineness;" don't be surprised if restaurants and other places aren't in the hurry you might see elsewhere. Still, there is more to Olhão than tuna and cuttlefish. Beyond this no-frills town lie gorgeous beaches and the Parque Natural da Ria Formosa (see **Daytrips from Olhão**), with its numerous species of exotic birds.

⊑ TRANSPORTATION. The **train station** is on Av. dos Combatentes da Grande Guerra, one block from Av. da República. (☎289 72 17 00. Open daily 6am-9:30pm.) **Trains** run to: **Faro** (10min., 17 per day 6:54am-10:39pm, €0.80); **Tavira** (30min., 6 per day 6:27am-12:45am, €1.20); **Vila Real de Santo António** (1¼hr., 6 per day 6:27am-12:45am, €2.10). The **bus station** is on R. General Humberto Delgado, one block from Av. da República. (☎289 70 21 57. Open daily 7am-8pm.) **EVA buses** run to: **Faro** (20min., 11 per day 7:35am-7:50pm, €0.85); **Tavira** (40min., 11 per day 7:35am-7:50pm, €1.75); **Vila Real de Santo António** (1½hr., 9 per day 7:35am-6:40pm, €3.10).

◪ ⁊ ORIENTATION & PRACTICAL INFORMATION. To reach the **port** from the train station, turn left on Av. dos Combatentes da Grande Guerra and take a right on **Avenida da República** past the Palácio da Justiça (10-15min.). From the bus station, turn right on R. General Humberto Delgado and then take another right onto Av. da República (5-10min.). Once on Av. da República, go straight until reaching Olhão's main church. Veer left on R. do Comércio and continue as far as possible. From the end of R. do Comércio, turn left on R. Olhanense and follow the street until it reaches Av. 5 de Outubro and the sea. The **tourist office** is on Lgo. Sebastião Martins Mestre, a small road that intersects the end of Av. da República, opposite the Câmara Municipal. Its English-speaking staff has maps, ferry schedules, and sometimes free **luggage storage** during the day—ask nicely. (☎289 71 39 36. Open M-Sa 9:30am-noon and 1-5:30pm.) In an **emergency,** call ☎112. The **post office** is at Av. da República, 17. (☎289 70 06 03. Open M-F 8:30am-6pm.) **Postal Code:** 8700.

⁊⁊ ACCOMMODATIONS & FOOD. Pensão Bela Vista ❷, R. Teófilo Braga, 65-67. Exit the tourist office and follow Tr. da Lagoa to R. Teófilo Braga. Nine comfortable, modern rooms have TVs, and some come with baths. (☎289 70 25 38. June-Sept. singles €20, with bath €25; doubles €35/€40-45. Oct.-May €5 less.) From the train or bus station, take Av. da República and turn right on R. 18 de Junho. After four blocks, turn left again. Here you'll find **Pensão Boémia ❸,** R. da Cerca, 20. Boémia is away from the shore at the center of town, but has all the modern amenities. Its cheerful, sunny, and immaculate rooms all have bath, TV, and A/C, and some have large terraces and refrigerators. The friendly owner will give you all the info you need in English, French, German, or Portuguese to explore the town and beaches. (☎/fax 289 71 45 13. July-Aug. singles €40; doubles €50. June and Sept. €30/40. Oct.-May €20/30. AmEx/MC/V.) Olhão's year-round campground is the **Parque de Campismo dos Bancários do Sul e Ilhas ❶,** off the highway outside of town and accessible by "Câmara Municipal de Olhão" buses (9 per day 7:45am-7:15pm) which leave from in front of the gardens on Av. 5 de Outubro. Amenities include a swimming pool, tennis court, market, bar, and restaurant. (☎289 70 03 00; fax 70 03 90. Showers included. July-Aug. €3.45 per person, €2.35-5.50 per tent, €2.85 per car. Sept.-June €2.95/€2.15-4.65/€2.40.)

Supermercado São Nicolau, R. General Humberto Delgado, 62, lies up the block from the bus station. (Open M-Sa 8am-8pm.) The **market** is housed in two red brick buildings adjacent to the city gardens along the river, near Pr. Patrão J. Lopes. (Open daily 7am-1:30pm.) Many eateries on Av. 5 de Outubro grill the day's catch. At busy **Casa de Pasto O Bote ❷**, Av. 5 de Outubro, 122, pick your slippery, silvery meal, caught only hours before, from the trays of fresh fish and watch it char-grilled right before your eyes. Meats are also offered, but the seafood draws the crowds. (☎289 72 11 83. Entrees €8. Open M-Sa 11am-4pm and 7pm-midnight.)

🏃 DAYTRIPS FROM OLHÃO

ILHAS ARMONA, CULATRA & FAROL

Ferries go to Armona from Olhão's dock (15min.; July-Aug. 13 per day 7:30am-8pm; June and Sept. M-F 9 per day 7:40am-7:30pm, Sa-Su 11 per day 8am-7:30pm; Oct.-May 3 per day 8:30am, noon, 5pm; last return in July-Aug. 8:30pm; June 8pm; €1). Another fleet serves Culatra (30min.; June-Aug. every 2hr. 7am-7:30pm, Sept.-May 4 per day 7am-6:30pm, last return June-Aug. 8pm; €1) and Farol (45min.; June-Aug. every 2hr. 7am-7:30pm, Sept.-May 4 per day 7am-6:30pm, last return in June-Aug. 8:20pm; €1.30).

Long expanses of uncrowded, sandy beach and sparkling sapphire sea surround **Ilhas Armona** and **Culatra,** the two major islands off the coast of Olhão. Armona is the closest, followed by Culatra and then **Farol,** off the far end of Culatra; all three are easy daytrips from Olhão. The farther away you go, the quieter the beaches become, and, of course, the better they are. Farol is easily your most handsome bet. Even so, none of the three has the volume of tourists seen in other sections of the Algarve, and the inconvenience of getting there will soon be forgotten when you pass the clearing. The islands and sandbars just offshore fence off the Atlantic, creating the **Parque Natural da Ria Formosa,** an important wetland habitat for an amazing variety of sea creatures. During the winter, roughly one-third of Europe's flamingo population can be found here. If you miss the last ride back from Armona, bungalows are available at **Camping Orbitur ❺** on the central path 5min. from the dock, but at these prices, it's probably better not to get stranded. (☎289 71 41 73. July-Aug. 4-night minimum stay €324; 2-day minimum the rest of the year. June and Sept. €39 per day, Oct.-May €33 per day.) While in Armona, check out the international **Restaurante Santo António ❷** (☎289 70 65 49), at the entrance to the beach 15min. from the dock. Be greeted in half a dozen languages, and then try their specialty: swordfish. (Meals €6-9. Open Apr. 15-Sept. 15 9am-11pm.)

TAVIRA ☎281

Tiny Tavira (pop. 11,000) was once the most populous city in the Algarve. Now, residents are outnumbered by tourists, drawn by the winding streets along the Rio Gilão and desperate for the stunning nearby beaches. Look for two main vestiges of the town's more important past, the pointed rooftops known as "treasure" roofs and the beautiful latticed doorways, remnants of the Moorish influence once felt in the Algarve. Much more than a beach town, Tavira is a gentle place to spend time relaxing among the local fisherman, good restaurants, and a history that extends back to the first inhabitants of the peninsula.

🚆 TRANSPORTATION

Trains (☎281 32 23 54; info ☎808 20 82 08) go to: **Faro** (40min., 15-20 per day 6:26am-10:12pm, €1.80); **Olhão** (30min., 12-17 per day 6:26am-10:12pm, €1.20); **Vila Real de Santo António** (30min., 12 per day 6:55am-1:10am, €1.20). For **Albufeira,** transfer in

ALGARVE

Faro; for **Lagos,** transfer in Faro or Tunes. **EVA buses** (☎281 32 25 46) leave from upriver from Pr. da República for: **Faro** (1hr., 12-13 per day 6:50am-7:10pm, €2.40); **Lisboa** (4-5hr., 5 per day, €15); **Olhão** (45min., 12-13 per day 6:50am-7:10pm, €1.80); **Vila Real de Santo António** (40min., 6-10 per day 6:55am-7:20pm, €2.30).

🛈 PRACTICAL INFORMATION

From the **train station,** it's a short 5-10min. walk down Av. Dr. Teixeira de Aze-vedo to the town center. Alternatively, catch the local **TUT bus** (10min., every 30min. 7:25am-7:15pm, €0.50) or call a taxi (☎281 32 15 44; approx. €3.50). The **tourist office** on R. Galeria, 9, is staffed by English-, French-, and Spanish-speaking experts. (☎281 32 25 11. Open July-Aug. M-F 9:30am-1pm and 2-5:30pm, Sa-Su 9:30am-1pm and 2-7pm; Sept.-June M-F 9:30am-1pm and 2-5:30pm.) Rent **bikes** and **scooters** from **Loris Rent** on R. Galeria next to the tour-ist office. (☎281 32 52 03 or 964 07 92 33. Hybrid bikes €4-5 per day. Scooters €20-24 per day. Open M-Sa 9am-1pm and 3-6pm.) The tourist office provides free **luggage storage** during the day, while Residencial Bela Fria, across from the bus station, charges €0.75 per day for non-guests. Wash up at **Lavanderia Lavitt** laundromat, R. das Salinas, 6, on the far side of town behind the Repsol gas station. (wash €3.20 for 6kg, €4.25 for 8kg, and €5.35 for 10kg; same to dry. Detergent €0.35; service €1.10-1.65.) Local services include: **emergency** (☎112); **police** (☎281 32 20 22); **Centro de Saúde** (health center; ☎281 32 90 00). Free **Internet access** is available at **Sala Internet Câmara Municipal de Tavira,** on the corner of R. da Liberdade and Pr. da República. (Open M-F 10am-10pm, Sa 10am-8pm.) A faster connection is available across from the bus station at **Ciber Café Bela Fria,** R. dos Pelames, 1. (€1 per 15min. Open daily 9am-2am. Closed for lunch 12-1pm Oct.-May.) The **post office,** R. da Liberdade, 64, is one block uphill from Pr. da República. (Open M-F 9am-6pm.) **Postal Code:** 8800.

🛏 ACCOMMODATIONS

Like elsewhere in the Algarve, accommodations fill quickly in the summer. It's wise to reserve a week or two in advance or try to stay in Faro or elsewhere and make a daytrip. ◪**Pensão Residencial Lagôas Bica ❷,** R. Almirante Cândido dos Reis, 24, is an excellent choice. Cross the pedestrian bridge from the side of town with the bus station and continue straight down R. A. Cabreira; turn right and go down one block. This *pensão,* run by a warm and hospitable woman, has well-furnished rooms, an outdoor patio, a lounge, and a fridge for guest use. Don't let the lack of TV and A/C deter you; you won't find anything else this good and this cheap in town. (☎281 32 22 52. July-Sept. singles €18; doubles €28, with bath €38. Oct.-May €3 less.) Each bright, spacious room at **Pensão Residencial Imperial ❹,** Lgo. Dr. José Pires Padinha, 24, has a marble bathroom and TV; 5 rooms have A/C. Breakfast included during the summer. (☎281 32 23 34. July- Aug. singles €40; doubles €50; June and Sept. €30/€40; Oct.-May €20/€30.) At **Residencial Bela Fria ❺,** located across from the bus stop at R. dos Pelames, 1, breakfast is included with your pleasant, air condi-tioned room containing bath, phone, and TV. All rooms have either a view of the river or of the churches and castle; the pretty roof terrace also affords river views. Each guest receives 15min. free Internet access in the adjoining café. Breakfast included. (☎/fax 281 32 53 75. Transportation to Faro airport €25, minimum 4 people. July singles €50; doubles €70; extra bed €18. Aug. €60/€90/€18. June and Sept. €35/€50/€15. Oct.-May €25/€35/€12.50. MC/V.)

◖ FOOD

Food does not come quite as cheaply in Tavira as it does in other parts of the country, but the traditional flavor of grilled seafood and fish is worth the price. For grilled fish and other sea specialties, head to ☒**Vela II ❷**, Campo dos Mártires da República, 1. It's a little tricky getting there: from Pr. da República, walk until you pass through Lgo. Dr. José Pires Padinha and keep going until you see Tr. das Unhas on your right. Follow it until R. Poço do Bispo; the restaurant is on the right. This local hot spot combines *Algarvio* cuisine with quantities that travelers with large appetites can appreciate; it's all-you-can eat, and the only restaurant like it in town. Each order (€6.50) includes potatoes, olives, and bread. Locals love it, so expect competition for seating during lunchtime. (☎281 32 36 61. Open M-Sa noon-3pm and 7-10pm.) **Restaurante Bica ❷**, R. Almirante Cândido dos Reis, 22, is the best option for dishes that didn't start their life swimming. Cross the river at the footbridge, turn right, then take the second left. Bica has been part of the Tavira restaurant scene for 50 years, and their experience with lamb, chicken, pork, and seafood shows. (☎281 32 38 43. €6-8 per plate. Open Su-F noon-3pm and 7-10pm.) The **mercado municipal** has a slew of fresh fruit and fish at wholesale prices. (15min. along the river from the tourist office. Open daily 7am-2pm.)

◉ SIGHTS

The sights in Tavira offer a three-way mix of sun-burnt beaches, millenia of history, and, a little outside of town, Mother Nature hanging out and relaxing. But let's be serious. You're here for the beach, and with good reason.

■**MOINHO DA ROCHA.** The natural waterfall hidden between a vineyard and orange, almond, fig, and olive orchards is not normally considered one of Tavira's "attractions." However, the waterfall has been a favorite spot for diving, swimming, and picnicking for decades. *(5km outside the city at the source of the Rio Gilão. A bike, scooter, or 30-45min. hike will take you there.)*

ILHA DE TAVIRA. The water is warm, the sand is dazzling, and the wind is the best in the Algarve. **Vasco's** at the beach entrance offers **wind-surfing** gear and lessons during July and August. *(July-Aug., take the TUT from the bus station (8am-8pm; €1) to the dock, and then the boat (10 min., every 10min. 8am-11pm, €1 round trip). Sept.-June, make the 2km trek to the dock, following the river all the way to the end.)*

CASTELO DE TAVIRA. The castle is one of the oldest in all of Portugal, and almost every civilization that passed through contributed to it. Begun in the Neolithic age as a wall and improved subsequently by Phoenicians, Moors, and Christians, the castle now hosts a beautifully manicured garden of trees, shrubs, and flowers. Also offers the best (and only) view of the city and surrounding area. *(From R. da Liberdade, turn right at the post office. Open M-F 8am-5pm, Sa-Su 10am-7pm. Free.)*

IGREJA DE SANTA MARIA DO CASTELO. Santa Maria is most striking for its architecture and various dazzling altars lined with *azulejos* and decorated with gold trimming. The **Museu de Arte Sacra** inside houses sculptures of Christ dating from the 17th century. *(Directly behind the castle. Open M-F 9am-1pm and 2:30-5:30pm. Museum €1 for two students, seniors, or children; otherwise €1 per person.)*

IGREJA DE SANTIAGO. Igreja de Santa Maria do Castelo's little brother was once a mosque. Its impressive preservation distinguish it from other churches in the area. Multi-colored marble altars and golden ornamentation are also worth your time. *(Mass Su 7pm. Open M-F 9am-6pm. €1.)*

ALGARVE

ALENTEJO

The vast Alentejo region dominates the lower central section of Portugal and appeals to travelers desiring to escape the commotion of Lisboa or the wilds of the Algarve for a more historic Portuguese setting. Its arid plains stretch to the horizon, punctuated only by olive trees. The region is known for its wine and its cork—more than two-thirds of the world's cork comes from here. Évora, Elvas, and other medieval towns preserve their pristine state in the Alto Alentejo, while Beja remains the only major town on the seemingly endless Baixo Alentejo plain. The Alentejo is best in the spring; be prepared for fiery temperatures in summer.

HIGHLIGHTS OF ALENTEJO

FLOAT Upon the island in the sky that is the walled city of **Marvão** (see p. 697).

GET BONED at Evora's **Capella dos Ossos** (see p. 694).

CHECK OUT Europe's oldest aqueduct in **Elvas** (see p. 696).

ÉVORA   ☎266

Évora (pop. 35,000) is the capital and largest city of the Alentejo region. The historic center is home to palaces, churches, and Roman ruins as well as a medieval and innovative approach to recycling (see the *Capela dos Ossos*, below). University of Évora (UÉ) students liven up the town, especially during the *Queima das Fitas*, a week-long graduation celebration with live music, dancing, and drunkenness. The festivities during the last week of May culminate with the burning of little ribbons with messages from friends and family.

▐ TRANSPORTATION

Trains: Lgo. da Estação de CP, next to Av. dos Combatentes de Grande Guerra (☎/fax 266 70 21 25). To: **Beja** (1½hr., 4 per day 7:45am-7:15pm, €5.80); **Faro** (5hr.; 2 per day 7:35am, 7:15pm; €10.50); **Lisboa** (2½hr., 5 per day 5:30am-7.15pm, €8.05).

Buses: Av. São Sebastião (☎266 76 94 10), 300m outside the town wall. More convenient than trains. Normal buses often stop in several smaller towns and serve as local transportation while in bigger ones. Express buses stop only in major cities, can be faster, and cost twice as much. To: **Beja** (1½hr., 6-8 per day 8:45am-12:45am, €4.35, €7.35); **Elvas** (1½-2hr., 5 per day 8am-9:05pm, €4.80-€8.50); **Faro** (5hr., 4 per day 8:45am-6pm, €11.80); **Lisboa** (3hr., every 1-1½hr. 6:30am-8pm, €5.05- €8.80); **Portalegre** (1¾-3hr., 3-5 per day 10:25am-5:40pm, €5.55-9.80); **Braga** (7¾-9¾hr., 4-6 per day 6am-8pm, €17) via **Porto** (6-8½hr., 5 per day, €15.50-€16); **Setúbal** (1¾hr., 8 per day 6:30am-6pm, €5.05-€8.50).

Taxis: ☎266 73 47 34 or 73 47 35. Taxis hang out 24hr. in Pr. do Giraldo.

▌▐ ORIENTATION & PRACTICAL INFORMATION

To reach Pr. do Giraldo from the **bus station** (15min. walk), turn right up Av. São Sebastião, and continue straight when it turns into R. Serpa Pinto at the city wall. No direct bus connects the **train station** to the center of town. To walk, go up Av. Dr. Baronha and continue straight as it turns into R. da República at the city wall, until you reach **Praça do Giraldo**. To avoid the hike, hail a taxi (€3).

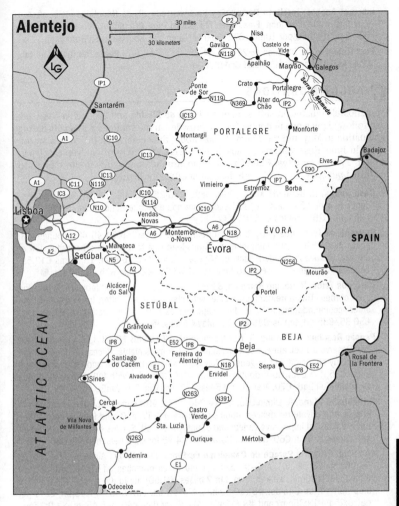

Tourist Office: Pr. do Giraldo, 73 (☎266 70 26 71). Wheelchair accessible. Tours conducted in various European languages. Consult desk for a list of guides. Open Apr.-Sept. M-F 9am-7pm, Sa-Su 9am-5:30pm; Oct.-Mar. 9am-6pm.

Currency Exchange: 24hr. **ATM** outside the tourist office. Several banks line **Praça do Giraldo,** all open M-F 8:30am-3pm. **Crédito Predial Português,** Pr. do Giraldo, 67 (☎266 74 50 40).

Emergency: ☎112. **Police:** R. Francisco Soares Lusitano (☎266 74 69 77).

Hospital: Hospital do Espírito Santo (☎266 74 01 00), Lgo. Senhor Jesus da Pobreza, near the city wall and the intersection with R. Dr. Augusto Eduardo Nunes.

Internet Access: Instituto Portuguêse da Juventude, R. da República, 105; often a long line in the afternoon. Free. Open M-F 9am-11pm. **Oficin@,** R. Moeda, 27 (☎266 70 73 12). €0.50 per 10min. €2.50 per hr. Open Tu-F 8pm-3am, Sa 9pm-2am.

Post Office: R. de Olivença (☎266 74 54 80; fax 74 54 86). **Posta Restante** and **fax.** Open M-F 8:30am-6pm. **Postal Code:** 7000.

ACCOMMODATIONS

Most hostels cluster on side streets off **Praça do Giraldo** and are well-advertised; just follow signs when in doubt. They're crowded in the summer, especially during graduation in May and the *Feira de São João*, the celebration of Evora's patron saint, in June. Reservations are absolutely necessary. Prices often drop €2.50-5 in winter. Private *quartos*, €20-25 per double, are pleasant summer alternatives to crowded *pensões*, so check with the tourist office for listings.

Casa Palma, R. Bernardo Matos, 29A (☎266 70 35 60). This homey, well-kept residence is over 100 years old, and each room has a unique atmosphere. Singles €15, with bath €25; doubles €25/€30. ❶

Pousada da Juventude (HI), R. Miguel Bombarda, 40 (☎266 74 48 48). Lounge with pool table, kitchen, and laundry room. Stairs lead to a terrace with a beautiful view of the city. Breakfast included. Lockout 10:30am-4pm. June 16-Sept. 15 dorms €12.50; doubles with bath €35. Sept. 16-June 15 €10/€28. €2 more without HI card. ❶

Casa dos Teles, R. Romão Ramalho, 31 (☎266 70 24 53). It's not labeled, so just ring the doorbell. This unremarkable hostel with clean rooms is often less crowded than other accommodations in Évora. June-Sept. singles €20-25, with bath €25-30; doubles €30-35/€35-40; triples €35-40. Oct.-May €5 less. ❷

Pensão Residencial Giraldo, R. dos Mercadores, 27 (☎266 70 58 33). All rooms have TVs. Reserve a week ahead. 10% discount for 2 or more nights. Prices are complex and constantly changing, but in general: July-Sept. singles €25, with shower and external toilet €35, full bath €50; doubles €35/€40/€60; triples with full bath €70; quads €65, with full bath €70. Mar.-June €5 less, €7 less Oct.-Feb. AmEx/MC/V. ❸

Residencial Diana, R. Diogo Cão, 2-3 (☎266 70 51 90). A more upscale alternative to hostels and private residences. Rooms complete with TV, A/C, and Renaissance-esque art. Breakfast of impressive variety and quantity included. Singles €45, with fridge, bar, and complete bath €60; doubles €50/€70. €4.95 for extra person. AmEx/MC/V. ❹

Camping: Orbitur's Parque de Campismo de Évora, Estrada das Alcáçovas (☎266 70 51 90; fax 70 98 30). A 3-star campground which branches off at the bottom of R. Raimundo. A 30min. walk to town, but 2 buses (€1.50) run to the nearby Vila Lusitano stop from Pr. do Giraldo: #5 (10-20min.; M-F 10 per day 7:45am-7:15pm, Sa 3 per day 8:25am-12:35pm) and #8 (15min.; M-F 6 per day 9:40am-5:45pm, Sa 9:25am, Su 2:50, 7:05pm). Taxi €3.50. Has a washing machine, market, tennis court, and bank. Reception 8am-10pm. Prices vary with season. €2.50-3.80 per person, €1-1.70 per child; €2-5 per tent; €3.50 per car. AmEx/MC/V. ❶

FOOD

Restaurants are scattered near **Praça do Giraldo,** especially along **Rua dos Mercadores,** but many are tourist-oriented; to find local favorites, wander a bit away from the center. The **market,** near Pr. da República, sells crafts and other regional goods as well as cheese and produce (open Tu-Su 6am-1pm).

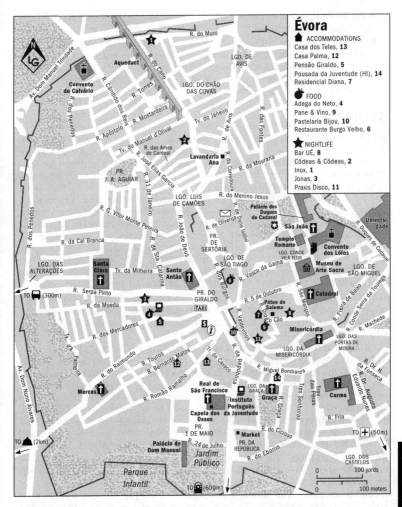

Évora

🏠 ACCOMMODATIONS
Casa dos Teles, **13**
Casa Palma, **12**
Pensão Giraldo, **5**
Pousada da Juventude (HI), **14**
Residencial Diana, **7**

🍎 FOOD
Adega do Neto, **4**
Pane & Vino, **9**
Pastelaria Bijou, **10**
Restaurante Burgo Velho, **6**

⭐ NIGHTLIFE
Bar UÉ, **8**
Côdeas & Côdeas, **2**
Inox, **1**
Jonas, **3**
Praxis Disco, **11**

Restaurante Burgo Velho, R. de Burgos, 10 (☎266 22 58 58), prides itself on large portions of Alentejo dishes and excellent service. In this small restaurant, higher prices buy the attentive service, attractive decor, and cool, quiet surroundings. Entrees €5-8.50. Open M-Sa noon-3pm, 7-10pm. ❷

Pane & Vino, Páteo do Salema (☎266 74 69 60). It may seem strange eating Italian food in the middle of the Alentejo, but this popular restaurant more than fills you with the best (and only) authentic pastas and pizzas around. Students, families, and travelers rendezvous in the spacious dining room and bar. Pizzas and pasta (€5-8) are accompanied by pricier meat entrees. Open Tu-Su noon-3pm, 6:30-11pm. ❷

ALENTEJO

Adega do Neto, R. dos Mercadores, 46. Locals flock here for mercurial service and typical *alentejano* dishes under €6. Entrees €5. Open M-Sa noon-3:30pm and 7-10pm. ❶

Pastelaria Bijou, R. da República, 15. A variety of excellent pastries displayed beneath the long, marble countertop can be enjoyed in air-conditioned comfort. Ask for a *bolo de berlim* (sugar-coated cake with delicious cream) or a *romana* (flaky pastry with sweet potato and almond spread) for a taste of their baking expertise. Pastries €0.65-1.40. Coffee €0.40-0.60. Open daily 7am-7pm. ❶

👁 SIGHTS

◾**CAPELA DOS OSSOS.** The Capela dos Ossos (Chapel of Bones) warmly welcomes visitors: *"Nós ossos que aqui estamos, pelos vossos esperamos"* (We bones that are here are waiting for yours). In order to provide a hallowed space to reflect on the profundity of life and death, three Franciscan monks built this chapel of remains of over 5000 people. The hip bone's connected to the thigh bone all over the walls and ceiling, while the three founders lie unexposed in stone sarcophagi right of the altar. For thrills and chills, read the sign below the one undecomposed corpse in the chapel: legend has it that it is a son cursed by his mother for disobedience and cruelty—then call your mother and tell her you love her. *(Pr. 1 de Mayo. Follow R. da República from Pr. do Giraldo, then take a right into Pr. 1 de Mayo; enter the chapel through the door of the Convento de São Francisco to the right of the church steps. ☎266 70 46 21. Open Apr. and June-Sept. M-Sa 9am-1pm and 2:30-6pm, Su 10am-1pm; May and Oct-Mar. M-Sa 9am-1pm and 2:30-5:30pm, Su 10am-1pm. €1, photos €0.50.)*

TEMPLO ROMANO. Columns still stand in Lgo. Conde do Vila Flor as a reminder of Évora's long history as a central city in several empires. The small temple dates back to the time of Roman occupation in the 2nd and 3rd centuries and was allegedly built in honor of the goddess Diana. *Open 24hrs.*

IGREJA DE SÃO JOÃO DE EVANGELISTA & PALÁCIO DE DUQUES DE CADAVAL. Also known as the Igreja de Loíos, immediately facing the Templo Romano is the Igreja de São João de Evangelista (1485). The church and ducal palace are owned by the Cadaval family, descendants of the original dukes, who restored the buildings with their personal fortunes in 1957-8. The interior of the church is covered with dazzling *azulejos*, and a beautiful cloister equipped with an outdoor cafe open to tourists. The restoration offers a glimpse of the magnificent sheen of the original gold and *azulejos*. *(Lgo. Conde do Vila Flor. Open Tu-Su 10am-12:30pm and 2-6pm. €2.50 for church, €4.20 for church and next door exhibition hall.)*

BASÍLICA CATEDRAL. The 12th-century cathedral also known as the Sé towers castle-like above Évora. It's darker than other churches in the city, but no less ornate or impressive. The 12 Apostles adorning the doorway are masterpieces of medieval sculpture. The **cloister** was designed in the 14th-century Romanesque style, with stairs spiraling to the terrace with a marvelous view of the city. The **Museu de Arte Sacra,** in a gallery above the nave, houses the cathedral's treasury and a 13th-century ivory *Virgem do paraíso*, and displays the original holy garb worn by bishops of the Sé in centuries past. *(From the center of Pr. do Giraldo, head to the end of R. 5 de Outubro. Cathedral open daily 9am-12:30pm and 2-5pm. Free. Cloisters open daily 9am-noon and 2-4:30pm. Museum open Tu-Su 9am-noon and 2-4:30pm. Cloisters and museum €2.50. July-Sept. 15 ticket includes visit to the tower. For just the cloister on M €1.50.)*

🎙 NIGHTLIFE

Évora's nightlife is fueled largely by the students from the university who fill the bars after midnight and then move on to the clubs. Even so, families and non-students also find plenty of evening space in and around Pr. do Giraldo, where people stay and socialize until well past midnight. Wednesday nights are student nights at most establishments, so expect considerably larger crowds then.

Jonas, R. Serpa Pinto, 115 (☎964 82 16 47). Wooden walls and dim lighting give this bar a cavernous feel, while the blue-lit room upstairs is made for chilling. Down-to-earth staff and different nightly drink specials keep the 20- and 30-somethings coming. Crowd starts filtering in around 1am to dance to everything from Smashing Pumpkins to techno. Popular Brazilian *caipirinhas* €2.50. Open M-Sa 11pm-3am.

Praxis, R. Valdevinos. This warehouse-turned-disco is the only disco in town, but it doesn't let it go to its head. With four different bars for hard dancing, quiet socializing, weekly live music, and even strippers twice a month, Praxis knows how to deliver a party in style. Beer €1.50. Mixed drinks €4. Minimum consumption €5 for men, €3 for women. Open daily 10pm-4am.

Côdeas & Côdeas, on the corner of R. do Cano and R. das Amas do Cardeal. From Pr. do Giraldo, follow R. João de Deus until it hits Lgo. Luis de Camões; turn right and take your second left, following it one block until it turns into R. do Cano. The only place in town for live jazz, this cozy bar sets the scene for the artistically inclined. Has a limited bar, but patrons come mainly for the live music 5 nights a week and the friendly, inter-active environment. Open Tu-Su 6pm-3am.

Bar UÉ, R. Diogo Cão, 19 (☎266 74 39 24). It's a university bar, although non-students are welcomed as occasional guests. Has a homey terrace for conversation and strate-gizing the rest of the night's gameplan; Bar UÉ is definitely not the last stop, but the place to meet people before heading elsewhere. Open Tu-Su noon-2am; serves food 1-3pm and 7:30-9:30pm.

ELVAS ☎268

Even if you're just stopping over in Elvas on your way elsewhere, a day here is not a wasted one. The quiet, hilly town 13km from the Spanish border has an inviting main square and steep streets that lead to the fortified city walls. But before you write it off as yet another cathedral-intensive suburb to a 500-year-old castle, give Elvas (and yourself) a chance to see a rare combination of beautiful architecture and a vibrant local personality.

▆ TRANSPORTATION. The nearest **train station** (☎268 62 28 16) is 3km away in Fontainhas and services **Badajoz, ES** (17min., 1 per day 12:08pm, €1.10). A **taxi** (☎268 62 22 87) is the only transport from the train station to town (€5). **Buses** are the best transportation option (☎268 62 28 75) and go to: **Albufeira** (6hrs., 1 per day 6:40am, €13); **Beja** (3½hr., 1 per day 6:40am, €9.90); **Caia,** on the border (30min.; 2 per day 6:40am, 2pm; €1.35); **Évora** (1½hr., 4 per day 6:40am-4:25pm; at 6:40am and 8:05am, €8.50; 1 and 4:25pm, €4.80.); **Faro** (6½hr., 6:40am, €13); **Lisboa** (3hr., 5-7 per day 5am-6:30pm, €10.80); **Portalegre** (1½hr., M-F 7am, €4).

▆ ▐ ORIENTATION & PRACTICAL INFORMATION. Buses stop at the entrance to the city walls. The **tourist office** (*posto de tourismo*) is in Pr. da República. (☎268 62 22 36. Open Apr.-Oct. M-F 9am-6pm, Sa-Su 10am-12:30pm and 2-5:30pm; Nov.-Mar. daily 9am-5:30pm.) To get to the tourist office from the bus station (5min. walk), take a right and go through Lgo. da Misericórdia; continue up to R. da Cadeia, and after a series of fountains take a left into Pr. da República— the *posto de turismo* will be on the right. If the 3km trek doesn't scare you away, take a right onto Estrada das Fontainhas and then take a left onto Estrada de Campo Maior at the traffic circle; continue straight and then take a right, passing under the giant Portas de Olivença, and go up R. de Olivença until it reaches Pr. da República. Services include: **emergency** ☎112; **police,** R. André Gonçalves (☎268 62 26 13); **Hospital de Santa Luzia,** Estrada Nacional, 4. (☎268 62 22 25). For **Internet access,** the tourist office has free access for those in a hurry: one computer avail-able with a 5-minute limit. Otherwise, check out **O Livreiro de Elvas,** R de Olivença,

ALENTEJO

4-A, a little bookstore with 2 computers in the back room; just watch your head as you enter the back. (☎268 62 08 82. €0.80 for 15min., €1.40 for 30min. Open M-F 9:30am-1pm and 3:15-7:15pm, Sa 9:30am-1pm.) The **post office** is one block behind the tourist office. (☎268 62 26 96. Open M-F 9am-6pm.) **Postal Code:** 7350.

☎☐ ACCOMMODATIONS & FOOD. António Mocisso e Garcia Coelho ❷, R. Aires Varela, 15. From the tourist office, take a right out of the *praça* (to the right of Banco Espírito Santo) and then your first left; go left at the end of the street and the reception will be on the right. Large rooms with TVs (however small), and private baths. If you're taller than five feet, beware the entrance to the bathroom. Reservations recommended throughout the year, but especially June-September. A breakfast of bread and jam, coffee, and juice is served from 8-10am; new arrivals should not come before noon. (☎268 62 21 26. Singles €20; doubles €30; triples €40; quads €50.) A more excluded, resort-style experience can be had at **Quinta de Torre das Arcas, ❶,** in an orange, olive, and fig orchard 5km from Elvas accessible via the bus to Varche and a 10min. walk. During the orange season (Dec.-May), guests are encouraged to help themselves to as many sacks of oranges as they'd like. Includes swimming pool. (☎268 62 60 30. €3 per person, €1.50 per child under 12, €4-5.50 per car and tent. Owner also rents apartment-style rooms. Minimum rental €30 for one, €50 for 2, €70 for 3.) **Parque de Campismo ❶** is ideal for a small group willing to rough it for a night. Take the first right from the bus station; follow the road until the sign. (☎268 62 89 97. €2.50 per car or tent).

For fresh fish, fruits, and vegetables, try the **mercado municipal** on Av. de São Domingos (open M-Sa 6am-1pm). The traveler with a penchant for Portuguese cuisine and the spending money to back it up will appreciate **O Lagar ❷,** R. Nova da Vedoria, 7. Leaving Pr. da República on the opposite side of the castle, turn right on R. da Cadeia, take the second left on R. do Tabolado next to the fountain, and finally right onto R. Nova da Vedoria. Considered by some locals the best restaurant in Elvas (with a bar to match), the menu preserves the reputation with variety and excellence from tiger shrimp to grilled veal, *gaspacho* to the celebrated *bacalhau à bras.* (☎268 62 47 93. Entrees €7.50-15. Open 12-4pm and 7pm-midnight; closed Th.) *Frango assado* is Portugal's other white meat, and Elvas does it up right. Converted fans will be filled at **Canal 7 ❶,** R. dos Sapateiros, 16. Exit Pr. da República on R. dos Sapateiros to the left of Banco Espírito Santo and follow the curving road to the left toward the oven. Take your *frango assado* outside; €2 gets you a half chicken to go (dine-in €3.95). Other entrees include their specialty *leitão* (grilled suckling pork; €6.50). (☎268 62 35 93. Entrees €3.50-7. Open 11am-3pm, 6-10pm; Su take-out only. Closed Tu.)

◎ SIGHTS. Elvas's main sight, the **Aqueduto da Amoreira,** emerges from a hill at the entrance to the city. Begun in 1529 and finished in 1622, the colossal structure is Europe's largest aqueduct—its 843 arches extend almost 8000m. The **castelo,** above Pr. da República, has a breathtaking view of the aqueduct and the infinite rows of olive trees on the horizon; a stairwell to the right of the entrance leads up to the castle walls. (Castle open 9:30am-5:30pm. €1.30; seniors and 14-25 €0.70, under 14 free.) The **Igreja de Nossa Senhora da Assunção,** better known as the **antiga Sé,** in Pr. da República has *azulejos* and a beautiful ribbed ceiling. (☎268 62 59 97. The hours are tricky and change regularly; call ahead. Mass Su 6pm.) Behind the cathedral and uphill to the right is the **Igreja de Nossa Senhora da Consolação dos Aflitos.** Its octagonal interior has beautiful geometric tiles, and the view even bests that of the castelo. Informal tours given in Portuguese and Portaño upon request. (Open Tu-Su 9:30am-noon and 2:30-5pm.)

NEAR ELVAS

CASTELO DE VIDE

Situated 600m above sea level on the edge of the Serra de São Mamede, Castelo de Vide (pop. 4500) is a quaint town of whitewashed houses and cobblestone streets. The **castelo,** completed in 1280, overlooks the historic center and offers impressive views. (Open daily July-Sept. 9am-6pm; Oct.-June 9am-5pm. Free.) The **burgo medieval** (medieval quarter) is Castelo de Vide's best attraction. Located just below the castle, the old town consists of steep and narrow alleys overflowing with potted plants, roses, and sunflowers. The quarter shows the serenity of unpolluted Alentejo, which is hard to come by in Èvora or Beja. The town center surrounds two 19th-century plazas, evidence of Castelo's former popularity as a spa resort.

Since Castelo de Vide and neighboring Marvão can be done in half a day, staying in the pricy *residenciais* is not recommended. Stranded travelers may find the **Albegueria El Rei Dom Miguel ❷,** R. Bartolomeu Álvares de Santa, 45, a satisfying option. Huge rooms stick to the historic themes of the town and include continental breakfast, TV, radio, A/C, and telephone. The hall decorations are also impressive. (☎245 91 91 90. Singles €25; doubles €50.) For food, the very local and very tasty **O Miguel ❶,** R. Almeida Sarzedas, 32-34, is the best bet. The plentiful trays of local cuisine are a great complement to the already provincial feel. The *javeli de cachatrito* (shredded pork) is the chef's specialty. (☎245 90 18 82. Entrees €4-7. Open M-Sa noon-2:30pm and 7:30-10pm.)

The **tourist office,** R. Bartolomeu Álvares de Santa, 81, offers maps, helps find accommodations, and provides short-term **luggage storage.** (245 90 13 61. Open daily July-Sept. 9am-5:30pm.) Services include: **emergency** ☎122; **police** on Av. Anamenha (☎245 90 13 14); the **health center** (☎245 90 11 05), behind the tourist office.

MARVÃO

If Castelo de Vide lacks bone-rattling attraction, then Marvão more than makes up for it. The ancient walled town (pop. 190) sits almost as if on an island overlooking the ocean of the Alentejo plains. The hills and meadows of the **Parque Natural de São Mamede** make the view even more worthwhile. Almost all of the town's whitewashed houses lie within the 17th-century walls. Marvão's 13th-century **castelo,** atop the ridge at the west end of town, hasn't been seized in 700 years. Prior to the castle's construction, however, Marvão passed through several different owners, among them the Romans, the Visigoths, and the Moors. Remnants of these early days are on display at the **Museu Municipal,** near the castle in the **Igreja de Santa Maria.** (☎245 99 32 72. Open daily 9am-12:30pm and 2-5:30pm. €1, students €0.75.)

Buses run to **Castelo de Vide** (25min., M-F 2 per day 7:15am, 1:05pm, €0.80) and **Portalegre** (50min.; M-F 2 per day 7:05am and 1:10pm; €1.60-5). Ask at the tourist office about express buses to **Lisboa** (5½hr., 1 per day 7:30am, €12); buy tickets one day ahead. To get to the **train station** (☎245 99 22 88), 9km north of town in Beirã, with service to Lisboa and Madrid, take a taxi (☎245 99 32 72). Taxis are also the most convenient way to **Castelo de Vide** (€10). Arriving by bus, you'll be dropped just outside the town wall. Enter through a gate and proceed up R. Cima until you see the stone whipping post in Pr. Pelourinho. From here, R. Espírito Santo leads toward the *castelo* and the **tourist office.** (☎245 99 38 86. Open Aug.-Sept. M-F 9am-6:30pm, Sa-Su 10am-12:30pm and 2-6:30pm; Oct.-July daily 9am-12:30pm and 2-5:30pm.) Services include **emergency** ☎112 and **police** ☎245 99 36 17.

ALENTEJO

BEJA
☎**284**

An oasis amid the vast and monotonous wheat fields of the southern Alentejo, Beja is a relaxed, friendly town proud of its varied history and architecture. Originally called Pax Juliato to commemorate Julius Caesar's peace with the Lusitanian tribes, it changed hands more than a dozen times between Romans, Moors, and Christians. Although full of history and interesting sights and scenery, the city is not considered a tourist "hot spot" and therefore maintains a tranquility that travelers will come to appreciate.

🖪 TRANSPORTATION. Trains run from the station (☎284 32 50 56) 1km outside of town to: **Évora** (1½hr., 5 per day 5:22am-8:40pm, €6.50); **Faro** (3½hr.; 2 per day 9:30am, 9:13pm; €8) via **Funcheira; Lisboa** (2½-3hr., 4 per day 5:30am-7:20pm, €8.50). The **bus station** (☎284 31 36 20) is on R. Cidade de São Paulo, near the corner of Av. do Brasil. Buses to: **Évora** (1½hr., 8 per day 7:10am-7:15pm, €7.50); **Faro** (3½hr., 4 per day 10:10am-7:20pm, €10); **Lisboa** (3¼hr., 6 per day 7:10am-7:30pm, €9.80); **Picalho**, a border town with connections to most major destinations in Spain (1½hr., 5 per day 10:50am-9:15pm, €6.70); **Portalegre** (3-4hr., 2 per day, €10).

🖪 PRACTICAL INFORMATION. The **tourist office**, R. Capitão J. F. de Sousa, 25, provides luggage storage and walking tour maps. To get to the tourist office from the bus station, take a left onto Av. do Brasil. Make the third right onto Av. Vasco da Gama and follow it to the center of town, bending left, until you hit R. Capitão J. F. de Sousa, a pedestrian avenue. (☎/fax 284 31 19 13. Open M-F 9am-8pm, Sa 10am-1pm and 2-6pm.) **Banks** are open M-F 8am-3pm. **ATMs** abound near the station and on R. de Sousa around the tourist office, but one can exchange traveler's checks only in expensive hotels, banks, and travel offices of which you are a client; bring an alternate source of cash. The bus station provides **luggage storage** on weekdays (€1.75 per day). Services include: **emergency** ☎112; **police** on R. D. Nuno Álvares Pereira (☎284 32 20 22), one block downhill from the tourist office. To get to the **post office**, Lgo. dos Correios, take a left out of the tourist office, then a right on R. Infantaria 17. **Poste Restante** and **fax service** (€2.20 per page) are available. (☎284 31 12 70. Open M-F 9am-6pm.) **Postal Code:** 7800.

🖪 ACCOMMODATIONS. Beja is a perfectly pleasant place to stay for the night, and there are several satisfying options for accommodations. Most are located within a few blocks of the tourist office. **🖪Pousada de Juventude de Beja (HI) ❶**, R. Professor Janeiro Acabado, is one such option. From the front of the bus station, turn left, and then left again on R. Cidade de São Paulo, then right on R. Professor Janeiro Acabado; the hostel is on the left. The squeaky clean Pousada has everything you need: a living room with TV and foosball, laundry room, and a kitchen. Each guest receives a personal cabinet with lock, so your stuff is safe while you eat the hearty included breakfast. (☎284 32 54 58; fax 32 54 68. Open 8am-noon and 6pm-midnight. Check out at 10:30am. June 16-Sept. 15 dorms €9.50; doubles €21, with bath €23; Sept. 16-June 15 €7.50/€18/€19. €2 more without HI card.) The recently renovated three-star **Residencial Bejense ❸**, R. Capitão J. F. de Sousa, 57, boasts *azulejo*-lined hallways, marble bathrooms, TVs, phones, and A/C. Escape your room for the lounge, replete with big screen TV and bar. Take a left out of the tourist office and walk just a little bit down the street. (☎284 31 15 70; fax 284 31 15 79. Guests can check in as early as noon with check-out the same hour next day. Singles €28; doubles €40, with 3rd bed €50. AmEx/MC/V.)

🖪🖪 FOOD & NIGHTLIFE. Beja is one of the best places to taste authentic (and affordable) cuisine *à Alentejana*, such as *biftoques* (pork steaks with special spices) and *bacalhau à bras* (grilled codfish with egg and caramelized onions).

Restaurants are everywhere, and most have similar menus within the range of €5-6. A **market** next to the *castelo* at the end of town has fresh produce and fish at great prices (open M-Sa 6am-1:30pm). Diners consider **Casa de Pasto Imperial ❶**, R. Tomás Vieira, 14, the paragon of unaltered Alentejo cooking. Leaving the tourist office, turn right and walk the rest of the block, turning right again on R. Dr. Brito Camacho. Walk up the hill 2 blocks until Lgo. de S. João, and then bear right on R. Tomás Vieira. Try the *bolo de bolacha* (cookie cake) for dessert and you'll agree. (Open M-Sa 11am-3pm and 6-10pm. Entrees €4.40-6.) At night, locals head to **Kara's**, at the end of R. Dr. Brito Camacho. A live DJ spins nightly in the well-decorated interior of Kara's industrialesque building. (Beer €1.50.18+. Open Tu-Sa 11:30pm-4am.) Looking for even cheaper beer? Head for the mother ship at **UFO's**, in the Centro Comercial do Carmo. Follow R. de Sousa from the tourist office, taking your first left onto R. dos Reis. Turn left after 2 blocks. Bigger and popular earlier in the evening, UFO's features karaoke Tuesdays and live music twice a week. (Beer €1.25. Welcomes age 16 and up.)

◪ SIGHTS. Beja's sites are scattered, but follow a pretty basic trail. Walking tour maps from the tourist office lead you at a leisurely pace to every beautiful historic sight. The **Convento de Nossa Senhora da Conceição** makes an excellent starting point. Take a right from the tourist office and walk into Pr. Diogo Fernandes de Beja. Go right on R. Dr. Brito Camacho, through Lgo. de São João to Lgo. da Conceição; the museum is on the right. Inside, the church's 18th-century *azulejo* panels depict the lives of Mary and St. John the Baptist. The nearby panels of *talha dourada* (golden carvings) are remarkably ornate and worth a careful examination. (Lgo. de Conceição. ☎284 32 33 51. Open Tu-Su 9:30am-12:30pm and 2-5:15pm. €0.50, Su free. Ticket includes the **Museu Regional de Beja** on the second floor of the convent, which displays intriguing artifacts from ancient times.)

One block downhill from the Convento-Museu is the 13th-century **Igreja de Santa Maria da Feira,** transformed into a mosque during the Moorish invasion and back into a church when the city reverted to Portuguese control; the result is a notable mix of architectural styles. (Lgo. de Santa Maria. Open daily for mass 6-6:30pm and Su noon. Free.) From here, take your second left to R. Cadeia Velha and then right at Pr. da República; follow it until you reach the **Hospital da Misericórdia,** one of the first hospitals of its kind in Portugal. Patients enjoyed a beautiful cloister and chapel. (Open M-F 9:30am-12:30pm and 2-5pm. Once inside the building, go to the right, as the left side of the building houses a modern health clinic and pharmacy.) After leaving the hospital, turn left and check out the looming **Castelo de Beja,** built by the Moors in the 12th century on the remains of a Roman fortress. The castle still has an enormous marble keep, vaulted chambers, stones covered with cryptic symbols, and ivy-covered walls. Two hundred years later, Dom Dines improved the castle by adding the **Torre de Menagem,** which provides an impressive view of the vast *Alentejano* plains (Castel open May-Sept. Tu-Su 10am-1pm and 2-6pm; Oct.-Apr. 9-11:30am and 1-3:30pm. Free; €1.25 to climb the tower, €0.65 students and seniors). On the other side of town lies a beautiful garden, the Jardim Gago Coutinho e Sacadura Cabral. Named for Portuguese aviators, the garden is lined with orange trees and benches—a shady end for your trek through Beja. (Open daily sunrise-sunset.)

ALENTEJO

RIBATEJO & ESTREMADURA

The fertile region of the Ribatejo ("Above the Tejo") is perhaps the gentlest and greenest in the entire country. Known as the "Heart of Portugal," the Ribatejo is famous for lush wetlands and pastures that sharply contrast with the arid plains of the Alentejo to the west. The beauty is not only of the natural variety, however. With ornate monasteries in Alcobaça and Batalha, the spooky medieval town of Óbidos, and the hallowed sanctuary at Fátima, the Ribatejo boasts some of the country's finest sights. Nearby, serrated cliffs and whitewashed fishing villages line Estremadura's Costa de Prata (Silver Coast), whose beaches rival even those of the Algarve. Throngs of tourists and summer residents storm seafront Nazaré and Peniche. Smaller, less touristed towns with sparkling beaches line the coast, and the ruggedly beautiful Ilhas Berlengas lie just offshore.

SANTARÉM ☎243

Perhaps the most versatile of Ribatejo's cities, Santarém (pop. 30,000) invites guests to an internationally renowned summer festival as well as a slew of attractions ranging from bullfighting to the best view of the Tejo in all of Portugal. Once a ruling city in the ancient Roman province of Lusitania and later a flourishing medieval center, Santarém has a long history of prosperity. While here, visitors enjoy not only the fruits of that prosperity in the form of large churches and museums, but also the impressive range of architectural trends that it produced.

▣ TRANSPORTATION

Trains: Station, Estrada da Estação (☎243 32 11 99), 2km outside town. **Bus** service to and from the station (10min., every 30min.-1hr. 7:30am-7pm, €1.30). To: **Coimbra** (2hr., 11 per day 6:25am-1:10am, €10); **Faro** via Lisboa's Estação do Barreiro (4hr., 6 per day, €16.10); **Lisboa** (1hr., 37 per day 4:40am-3:55am, €4.10); **Portalegre** (3hr., 4 per day 8:50am-9pm, €11.60); **Porto** (4hr., 4 per day 9:55am-8:55pm, €12); **Tomar** (1hr., every hr. 6:20am-1:25am, €3.30).

Buses: Rodoviária do Tejo, Av. do Brasil (☎243 33 32 00). To: **Braga** (5hr.; 2 per day 10:45am, 6:45pm; €13.80); **Caldas da Rainha** (1½hr., 5 per day 7:20am-6:20pm, €4.10); **Coimbra** (2hr.; 2 per day 10:45am, 6:45pm; €9.90); **Faro** (7hr., 4 per day 10:30am-4:30pm, €15.50); **Leiria** (1½hr., 3 per day 10:45am-6:45pm, €8.80); **Lisboa** (1¼hr., 9 per day 7am-6:45pm, €5.70); **Óbidos** (1½hr., 4 per day 7:20am-10:45pm, €4.30); **Porto** (4hr.; 3 per day 10:45am, 1:50, 6:45pm; €12.70).

Taxis: Scaltaxis (☎243 33 29 19) has a stand across the park from the bus station.

▣▣ ORIENTATION & PRACTICAL INFORMATION

The densely packed streets between **Praça Sá da Bandeira** (the main square) and **Portas do Sol** park (above the Tejo) form the core of Santarém. **Rua Capelo e Ivens,** which begins at the *praça*, is home to the tourist office and many *residencials*.

Tourist Office: R. Capelo e Ivens, 63 (☎243 30 44 37). Maps and info on festivals, accommodations, and transportation. Informative brochure on festivals, sites, and history. Friendly English-speaking staff. Open daily 9am-12:30pm and 2-5:30pm.

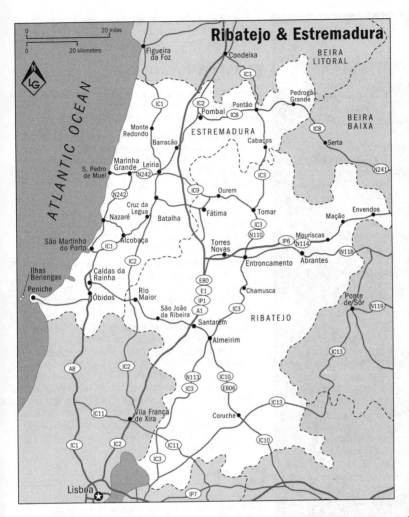

Ribatejo & Estremadura

Currency Exchange: Caixa Geral de Depósitos (☎243 33 30 07), at R. Dr. Texeira Guedes and R. Capelo e Ivens. €7.50 commission. Open M-F 8:30am-3pm.

Luggage Storage: At the bus station. €2 per bag. Open M-F 9am-1pm and 3-7pm.

Emergency: ☎112. **Police:** Av. do Brasil (☎243 32 20 22), near the bus station.

Hospital: Av. Bernardo Santareno (☎243 30 02 00). Take R. Alexandre Herculano until it becomes Av. Bernardo Santareno. English spoken.

Internet Access: Instituto Português da Juventude, downstairs from the youth hostel, M-F 9am-8pm (30min. limit; free). **E-planet,** Av. Madre Andaluz, 16B (☎914 95 47 80). From the youth hostel, turn left and walk 5min. down the road. €1.50 per 30min. Open daily 2pm-2am.

THE LOCAL LEGEND

G-RATED

The story of Santarém's founding could have been a Disney movie. All the elements are there: beautiful girl, frustrated love, bitter jealousy, a little bit of magic, and no sex whatsoever. The daughter of two 7th-century nobles, Iria was sent to a convent at an early age to live a life of purity and devotion. Soon Iria fell in love with a noble named Britaldo. The two contented themselves with innocent hand-holding and tried to live happily ever after. Enter Remígio, a former teacher of Iria's, now madly in love with her as well. Cue the jealous rage. Remígio decided, if he can't have Iria, no one can, and slips a potion into her soup that makes her look pregnant. Needless to say, sex is a convent no-no, so the townspeople cast Iria into the river. Her nun friends form a search party and eventually find her body washed up on the shore. Before anyone can give her a proper burial, the river rises, giving the girl a watery grave. Santarém was founded on this tragic site, "Santarém" being derived from "Santa Iria." A statue of her by the river marks the spot where Iria is said to lie still.

Post Office (☎243 30 97 00), on the corner of Lgo. Cândido dos Reis and R. Dr. Texeira Guedes. Open M-F 8:30am-6:30pm, Sa 9am-12:30pm. **Postal Code: 2000.**

ACCOMMODATIONS

Prices are fairly high year-round, increasing during the Ribatejo Fair (10 days starting in early June). The tourist office can help find a room in a private house.

Residencial Beirante, R. Alexandre Herculano, 5 (☎243 32 25 47). Hotel-style rooms with all the perks, including phone, A/C, TV, buffet breakfast, and even a blow dryer in the tiled bathrooms. Call ahead in summer. Singles €25; doubles €40. ❸

Residencial Muralha, R. Pedro Canavarro, 12 (☎243 32 23 99; fax 32 94 77). Comfortable rooms, all with TV, most with large private bath. Reserve a week ahead in summer. Singles €15, with bath €25-33; doubles €35. Be insistent about the €15 singles. ❷

Pensão José Rodrigues, Tr. do Froes, 14 (☎243 32 30 88). An elderly lady and her more elderly mother rent cheap, clean rooms in a central location. Popular during the summer, so call ahead. Singles €15; doubles €25. Prices drop in winter. ❶

Pousada da Juventude de Santarém (HI), Av. Grp. Forcados Amadores de Santarém, 1 (☎/fax 243 39 19 14), near the bullring. Follow Av. Dom Afonso Henriques as it curves past the stadium-style bullring; the hostel is upstairs from the Instituto Português da Juventude. Rooms are clean and comfortable. Breakfast included (8:30-10am). Reception 8am-noon and 6pm-midnight. Check-in after 6pm and check-out before 11am. Lockout 11am-6pm. HI card required, available at front desk (€2). June 16-Sept. 15 dorms €9.50; doubles with bath €23. Sept. 16-June 15 €7.50/€19. ❶

FOOD

Eateries cluster around the parallel R. Capelo e Ivens and R. Serpa Pinto. The **municipal market** in the pagoda on Lgo. Infante Santo near Jardim da República, sells fresh produce. (Open M-Sa 8am-2pm.) **Supermercado Minipreço,** R. Pedro Canavarro, 31, is on the street leading from the bus station to R. Capelo e Ivens. (Open M-Sa 9am-8pm.) The local favorite for meals is **O Saloio ❶,** Tr. do Montalvo, 11, off R. Capelo e Ivens, where they grill an assortment of meats (duck, salmon, lamb, beef) and serve up a mean *caldeirada*. (☎243 32 76 56. Entrees €5-8. Open M-Sa 10am-9pm.) **Pastelería Eureka ❶,** R. Capelo e Ivens, 12, makes a wide variety of pastries (€0.60), not to mention some of the best bread in town. (☎243 32 23 16. Open M-F 8am-7pm, Sa 8am-1:30pm.)

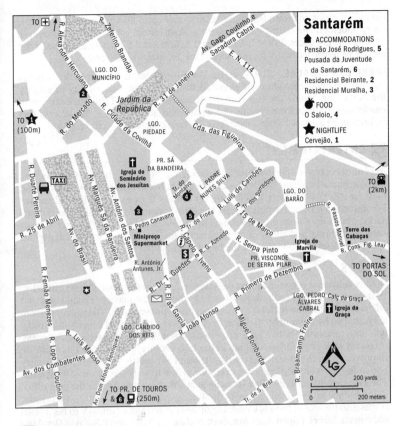

Santarém

🏠 ACCOMMODATIONS
Pensão José Rodrigues, **5**
Pousada da Juventude
  da Santarém, **6**
Residencial Beirante, **2**
Residencial Muralha, **3**

🍎 FOOD
O Saloio, **4**

⭐ NIGHTLIFE
Cervejão, **1**

👁 SIGHTS

🏛 PORTAS DO SOL. This paradise of flowers and fountains surrounded by Moorish walls is best visited on a clear day, when the walls offer a striking view of the Alentejo plains and the river below. *(Take R. Cons. Figueiredo Leal and bear left on Av. 5 de Outubro after the abandoned art deco theater. Open daily 8am-11pm. Free.)*

PRAÇA VISCONDE DE SERRA PILAR. Centuries ago, Christians, Moors, and Jews gathered for social and business affairs in this *praça*. *(Take R. Serpa Pinto from Pr. Sá da Bandeira.)* The 12th-century **Igreja de Marvila**, off the *praça*, was revamped in the late 17th century with traditional ornamentation of the era. Don't be fooled, then, by the white-washed simplicity outside; the *azulejo*-covered interior is dazzling, as is the Manueline entrance. *(Open Su and Tu-Sa 9:30am-12:30pm and 2-5:30pm. Free.)* The early Gothic purity of nearby **Igreja da Graça** contrasts sharply with Marvila's overflowing exuberance. Within Graça's chapel lies Pedro Álvares Cabral, the explorer who "discovered" Brazil and one of the few to live long enough to return to his homeland. *(Open Su and Tu-Sa 9:30am-12:30pm and 2-5:30pm. Free.)*

IGREJA DA NOSSA SENHORA DA CONCEIÇÃO. Better known as the **Igreja do Seminário,** this church hosted a school for Jesuit priests for centuries. The austere facade dominates Pr. Sá da Bandeira, Santarém's main square. Stone friezes

RIBATEJO & ESTREMADURA

carved as ropes separate the three stories, and Latin biblical mottos embellish every doorway. The ceiling mural inside the main chapel is an interesting example of religious art. *(Open Su and Tu-Sa 9:30am-12:30pm and 2-5:30pm. Free. If closed, enter through the door to the right of the entrance and ask the sacristan to unlock it.)*

TORRE DAS CABAÇAS. The medieval Torre das Cabaças (Tower of the Gourds) was named after the eight earthen bowls installed in the 16th century to amplify the bell's ring. Inside the tower is the Museu de Tempo (Time Museum), with clocks and sundials from various times and civilizations. *(Take R. São Martinho from Pr. Visconde de Serra Pilar. Open Su and Tu-Sa 9:30am-12:30pm and 2-5:30pm. €1.)*

🎭 ENTERTAINMENT

Around the corner and two blocks down from the bus station is **Cervejão,** Av. António Maria Baptista, 10. The name means "big beer," and lots of it can be found here. (☎243 26 43 33. Beer €0.65. Whiskey shots €2. Open M-Sa 11am-midnight.) For unrestrained daytime partying, try the **Feira Nacional de Agricultura** (also known as the *Feira do Ribatejo*). Thousands of people come for a 10-day orgy of markets, bullfighting, and hilarious farmers racing their tiny horses for personal glory. This party goes for 10-14 days at the beginning of June.

ÓBIDOS

Óbidos delivers a versatile tourist package; in fact, her 200 residents do little else. Visitors come first to see exactly what hides behind the massive castle walls that enclose the entire town. But it's more than just another castle. The town's personality, shaped by the tourist attention over the years, has turned a medieval stronghold into an alluring native enterprise not to be missed. The **castelo** on the coast, originally a Moorish fortress rebuilt in the 12th century, gradually lost its strategic importance as the ocean receded. Although the castle itself—now a luxury *pousada*—is open only to guests, everyone is free to walk the 1.5km of its ■ **walls.** The 17th-century *azulejo*-filled **Igreja de Santa Maria,** to the right of the post office in the central *praça*, displays Josefa de Óbidos's vivid canvases off the main altar. It was also the site of the 1441 wedding of 10-year-old Dom Afonso V to his 8-year-old cousin, Isabel. (Open daily Apr.-Sept. 9:30am-12:30pm and 2:30-7pm; Oct.-Mar. 9:30am-12:30pm and 2:30-5pm. Mass Su at noon. Free.)

The **tourist office** is a small, green cottage just up the steps from the bus stop, across from Porta da Vila. (☎262 95 92 31; fax 95 50 01. Open May-Sept. M-F 9:30am-7pm, Sa-Su 10am-7pm; Oct.-Apr. M-F 9:30am-6pm, Sa-Su 10am-6pm.) There are several private rooms for rent in Óbidos, as advertised by the signs on and around R. Direita, but it may be difficult to find a good price. **ÓbidoSol ❷,** R. Direita, 40, is a charming 17th-century home that has three rooms with window seats, an *azulejo*-covered common bath, and a large living room. Reservations recommended, especially during the summer. (☎262 95 91 88. June-Sept. singles €25; doubles €30. Oct.-May €20/€25. Request a €5 discount if you are traveling alone.) "Typical" **restaurants** (most with typical tourist prices) and several **markets** cluster on and around R. Direita. Eat light and save your euros for Óbidos's signature *ginja*; stores on R. Direita sell bottles for €7.

Buses stop outside the town gate and are more convenient than trains. Connections to: **Caldas da Rainha** (20min., 24 per day 7:35am-8:35pm, €1.30); **Lisboa** (1¼hr., M-F 4 per day 7:05am-4:10pm, €6.20); **Peniche** (40min.; M-F 10 per day 8:10am-7:40pm, Sa 7 per day 8:10am-7:40pm, Su 5 per day 9:40am-7:40pm; €2.50). On weekends you must stop in Caldas da Rainha to go to Lisboa (1½hr., 5-7 per day 7am-9pm, €5.50). No bus schedules are posted here, so ask at the tourist office.

PENICHE ☎262

Many travelers en route to the Ilhas Berlengas overlook Peniche, a seaport town 22km west of Óbidos, and miss this lively city close to popular beaches. Home to Portugal's second largest fishing fleet, Peniche used to dedicate an entire festival just to the sardine; it has since broadened its horizons and now celebrates fishing and seafood in general.

▐ TRANSPORTATION

Buses: Peniche is accessible only by bus. The station is on R. Dr. Ernesto Moureira (☎262 78 21 33), on an isthmus outside the town walls. To: **Alcobaça,** via Caldas da Rainha (1¾hr., 3 per day 10:45am-5:10pm, €4.65); **Caldas da Rainha** (1hr., 8 per day 8am-7:30pm, €5.20); **Leiria,** via Caldas da Rainha (2hr., 3 per day 10:45am-5:10pm, €8.90); **Lisboa** (2hr., 12 per day 6am-8:45pm, €5.50); **Nazaré** (1½hr., 4 per day 10:45am-5:10pm, €4.30); **Porto** (6½hr., 3 per day 7am-6pm, €12.70); **Santarém,** via Caldas da Rainha (1½hr., 3 per day 7am-5:10pm, €9.90).

Taxis: (☎262 78 44 24 or 78 29 10) in Pr. J. Rodrigues Pereira and Lgo. Bispo Mariana.

■ ▐ ORIENTATION & PRACTICAL INFORMATION

Most of Peniche's services are situated in or around the grid of streets between **Largo Bispo Mariana** and the **fortaleza** on the coast. **Praça Jacob Rodrigues Pereira** marks the center of town, near the tourist office and the start of **Avenida do Mar,** which runs along the river to the docks and fishing port.

Tourist Office: R. Alexandre Herculano (☎/fax 262 78 95 71). From the bus station, take a left and cross the river over Ponte Velha to the right. Turning left on R. Alexandre Herculano, walk alongside the public garden, and follow signs to the office. English spoken. Open daily July-Sept. 9am-8pm; Oct.-May 10am-1pm and 2-5pm; June 9am-7pm.

Bank: Caixa Geral de Depósitos, on R. Alexandre Herculano, down the street from the tourist office. Open M-F 8:30am-3pm.

Emergency: ☎112. **Police:** R. Heróis Ultramar (☎262 78 95 55).

Hospital: R. Gen. Humberto Delgado (☎262 78 09 00). From the tourist office, turn right onto R. Alexandre Herculano and take the 1st left onto R. Arquitecto Paulino Montez; walk past the post office, then take a right on R. Gen. Humberto Delgado.

Internet Access: Espaço Internet, R. Heróis Ultramar, is the city-run, slow option for Internet access. Turn right from the tourist office onto R. Alexandre Herculano, then take your first left onto R. Arquitecto Paulino Montez. Walk 5min.; R. Heróis Ultramar is the 4th left. Open M-Sa 10am-1pm and 3:30-8pm.

Post Office: R. Arquitecto Paulino Montez (☎262 78 00 60). From the tourist office, turn right on R. Alexandre Herculano, left on R. Arquitecto Paulino Montez, and walk 3 blocks. **Posta Restante** and **fax.** Open M-F 9am-6pm. **Postal Code:** 2520.

▐ ACCOMMODATIONS

Peniche's budget accommodations are located above restaurants of the same name; look for signs to find a *residencial* on or behind Av. do Mar. They fill quickly, though, especially from June to August; try to arrive early in the day. Persistent elderly matrons renting rooms in their private houses gather in Pr. Jacob Rodrigues Pereira and meet the buses as they arrive. Rooms in private houses may be the best budget options, but insist on seeing them first and inquire about hot water and amenities. Learn the sport of bargaining: rarely accept their first offer.

Residencial Marítimo, R. António Cervantes, 14 (☎262 08 34 07 or 78 28 50), off the *praça* in front of the fortress. Newly renovated rooms, all with 42-channel TVs and private, beautifully tiled bathrooms. Buffet breakfast included. Reserve ahead. Aug. singles €25; doubles €45; July €20/€35; Sept.-June €15/€25. ❷

Residencial Maciel, R. José Estévão, 38 (☎262 78 46 85), just off the *praça*, behind the church. Eleven elegant, spacious rooms with complimentary bottled water and cable, sports-laden TV. Quite chic for Peniche. Buffet breakfast included. June-Sept. singles €40; doubles €50. Oct.-May €20/€30. ❹

Peniche Praia, Municipal Campground (☎262 78 34 60), 2km outside town, at least a 30min. walk from the center. From the bus station, turn left onto Av. Porto de Pesca to reach EN 114, following it through the traffic circle and past the waterpark; the campsite is on the left. Or take a taxi (approx. €3 from downtown). About a 15min. walk from the beautiful rock formations of Peniche and decorated with old fishing boats. Free hot showers and swimming pool. Open year-round. €3 per person, €1.50 per child age 6-12, under 6 free. €3-3.80 per tent. €2.70 per car. ❶

🍴 FOOD

Restaurants lining **Avenida do Mar** serve excellent fresh grilled seafood. Despite the multilingual menus, the prices are reasonable and there are plenty of locals mixed in among tourists. Peniche's *sardinhas* (sardines) are exceptional, as are the seafood *espetadas* (skewers). The outdoor cafes on **Praça Jacob Rodrigues Pereira** are lively, particularly on Sundays, when the rest of town is quiet. The **market,** on R. António da Conceição Bento, stocks fresh produce (open Tu-Su 7am-1pm).

Restaurante Mira Mar, Av. do Mar, 42 (☎262 78 16 66). One of the best of the string of nearby restaurants. The place gets loud and busy at dinner time, especially 9-10pm. Entrees €4.50-8. Excellent *crème de marisco* (shellfish chowder; €2). Open 10am-11:30pm; meals served noon-4pm and 7-11pm. AmEx/MC/V. ❷

Ristorante Il Boccone, Av. do Mar, 4 (☎262 78 24 12). Fantastic pizza (€5-8) and enormous pasta dishes (€4.50-10) provide a welcome reprieve from seafood. Open Tu-Su noon-4pm and 6:30pm-midnight. ❷

Café Oceano, Pr. Jacob Rodrigues Pereira, 12-13 (☎262 78 23 15). Popular cafe with outdoor seating. Polish off a sandwich (€2-4.50) followed by coffee (€0.40-0.85) or a scoop of gourmet ice cream (€1) inside the cafe or out on the terrace. Specialty *pasteis de Peniche* (almond pastries; €0.70). Open daily 8am-midnight. ❶

📷 SIGHTS

FORTALEZA. António Salazar, Portugal's longtime dictator, chose Peniche's formidable 16th-century fortress for one of his four high-security political prisons. Today it houses the **Museu de Peniche,** highlighted by a chilling walk through the cells of Salazar's prison, including replicas of the torture room, interrogation chamber, and descriptions of the horrors inmates faced. In an annex outside the museum, a small anti-Fascist exhibition traces the dictatorship and underground resistance from the seizure of power in 1926 to the coup that toppled the regime on April 25, 1974. (*Campo da República, near the dock where boats leave for the Ilhas Berlengas. Fortaleza open Tu-Su 10:30am-noon and 2-6pm. Free. Museum ☎262 78 01 16. Open Tu-Su 10:30am-noon and 2-6pm. €1.50, under 16 free.*)

BEACHES. For sun and surf, head to any of the town's three beaches. The beautiful but windy **Praia de Peniche de Cima,** along the north crescent, has the warmest water. It merges with another beach at **Baleal,** a small fishing village popular with tourists. The southern **Praia do Molho Leste,** besides being worthy on its own, marks the entrance to **Super-tubos,** the beach so nicknamed because of its huge waves. Beyond it is crowded **Praia da Consolação.** The strange humidity at this beach and its hot rocks supposedly cure bone diseases. Watch out for elderly visitors seeking relief from their afflictions, often wearing nothing but expectation on their faces. *(Buses 7am-7pm, €1.10. Check with the tourist office for changes.)*

◗ ◖ FESTIVALS & NIGHTLIFE

Peniche may seem sleepy during the day, but the town's nightlife heats up from the after-dinner hours until late, especially during the summer. For daytime party-seekers, Peniche's biggest festival takes place on the Saturday before the first Sunday of August, when boats bedecked in wreaths of flags and flowers process into the harbor to launch the two-day **Festa de Nossa Senhora da Boa Viagem,** celebrating the protector of sailors and fishermen. The town lets loose with carnival rides, live entertainment, wine, and seafood, continuing the festivities that begin two weeks before the launch. Mid-September brings the **Sabores do Mar** festival, and with it a huge celebration of everything seaworthy, including *fado*, pottery displays, and special discounts on restaurant fare.

◙ **Adego do Becas,** R. Lgo. da Ribeira, 24 (☎262 18 91 14), at the end of Av. do Mar, behind the last restaurant on the right. Hugely popular with locals, it combines two favorites famously: beer and steak. €1 beers and €6 steaks, prepared in a variety of ways, keep people coming in droves. The basement dance floor and the rooftop terrace also attract those looking for versatile party space. The barbecue pit, however, is the main draw. Open daily 1pm-4am.

Bar No. 1, R. Afonso Albuquerque, 14 (☎262 78 45 41), close to the intersection with R. José Estévão. Popular with both tourists and locals, the owner mans the DJ booth midnight-2am, and people respond, turning the tiny space into a miniature dance floor. The bar hosts 10 small exhibits of local art annually. Beer and shots €1-1.50. Mixed drinks €3. Open daily noon-2am.

◗ HIKING

To truly enjoy the ocean air, hike around the peninsula (8km, 2hr.). Start at Papôa, just north of Peniche. From Pr. Jacob Rodrigues Pereira, take R. Alexandre Herculano and then Av. 25 de Abril and follow the signs along the coast. Stopping occasionally at the wall at the edge of the road, you can observe the hundreds of playful fish. At Papôa, stroll out to the tip, where majestic orange cliffs rise from a swirling blue sea. Nearby lie the sparse ruins of an old fortress, Forte da Luz. As you pass the campsite (20-30min. later), the pancake-shaped rocks piled atop one another inspire interesting stories of origin. The endpoint of the peninsula, Cabo Carvoeiro, is the most popular of Peniche's natural sights, as the view of the Ilhas Berlengas below is unparalleled. On your way, you'll pass the Cruz dos Remédios, a stone cross of unknown origin.

◗ DAYTRIP FROM PENICHE

ILHAS BERLENGAS (1HR.)
Several companies operate boats from Peniche's public dock. Largest is Viamar ferry (☎262 78 56 46; fax 262 78 38 47. Ticket booth open 8:30am-5:30pm), which offers 3 crossings per day. (40min.; July-Aug. 3 per day 9:30, 11:30am, 5:30pm; return trips at 10:30am, 4:30, 6:30pm; to stay overnight, buy a €12 1-way ticket each way. May 15-June and Sept. 1-15

RIBATEJO & ESTREMADURA

10am, returns 4:30pm; same-day round-trip ticket €17, children 5-12 €12, under 5 free.) Reserve 3-4 days in advance. Arrive 1hr. in advance, 2½hr. in Aug. The crossing from Peniche to the island is notoriously rough; expect to witness or experience sea sickness. (Inhale as the boat goes up and exhale as it goes down.) Trips by Berlenga Turpesca (☎262 78 99 60) include visits to the Berlenga caves, although scheduling can be difficult. €17.

The rugged Ilhas Berlengas rise out of the Atlantic Ocean 12km northwest of Peniche. The main island of Berlenga and archipelago of several smaller islands (the Farilhões, Estelas, and Forcados), are inhabited by thousands of screeching seagulls. The **Reserva Natural da Berlenga** is home to wild black rabbits, lizards, and a very small fishing community. Unfortunately for visitors, the *reserva* is off-limits to non-researchers. Nevertheless, the islands' real prize is the rock formations that compose them. Deep gorges, natural tunnels, and rocky caves carve through the main island, and the main path (2km) allows for some scrambling and exploration. The only beach accessible by foot lies in a small cove by the landing dock. For beach-goers willing to brave the cold, dips in the calm water bring abrupt respite from the heat. Hikers can trek to the island's highest point for a gorgeous view of the 17th-century **Forte de São João Batista**, now a luxury hostel run by the Associação Amigos da Berlenga (AAB). The entire hike lasts no more than 1hr.

NAZARÉ   ☎262

Had someone set out with the intention of planning the perfect Portuguese tourist town, they could not have done better than Nazaré. The town capitalizes on its historic relationship with the sea, dazzling the crowds with embellished menus, clothing, crafts, and more. But with all the effort given to emphasizing this history, the beach is the major draw for visitors. The town rests directly on a 3km expanse of perfect sand and waves. Many visitors come from the urban regions of Portugal itself, making annual trips over the course of a lifetime. Whatever the case, the attention of everyone in town focuses for 3 months a year on the guest of honor: the tourist, who will enjoy feasting on seafood chowder and dried fruits.

▐ TRANSPORTATION

Buses: Av. Vieira Guimarães (☎808 20 03 70), perpendicular to Av. da República. More convenient than trains (6km away). To: **Alcobaça** (20min., 6 per day 7:10am-6:45pm, €1.30); **Batalha** (50min., 6 per day 7:10am-6:45pm, €2.80); **Caldas da Rainha** (1¼hr., 10 per day 6:30am-7:15pm, €2.80); **Coimbra** (2hr., 5 per day 6:25am-7:25pm, €8.80); **Fátima** (1½hr., 3 per day 7:10am-5:10pm, €3.50); **Leiria** (1¼hr., 6 per day 7:10am-6:45pm, €3.10); **Lisboa** (2hr., 8 per day 6:50am-8pm, €7.30); **Peniche** (1½hr., 6 per day 8:35am-6pm, €4.10); **Porto** (3½hr., 7 per day 6:25am-7:25pm, €8.90); **São Martinho do Porto** (20min., 10 per day 6:50am-8pm, €1.40); **Tomar** (1½hr., 3 per day 7:10am-5:10pm, €4.90).

Taxis: Praça de Taxi, ☎262 55 13 63 (main line).

▟ ▞ ORIENTATION & PRACTICAL INFORMATION

All of the action in Nazaré takes place along the beach. Its two main squares, **Praça Sousa Oliveira** and **Praça Dr. Manuel de Arriaga**, are near the cliffside away from the fishing port. The cliffside funicular and a winding road leads up to the **Sítio**, the old town, which preserves a sense of calm and tradition less prevalent in the crowded resort below. To get to the tourist office from the bus station, take a right toward the beach and then a right onto Av. da República; the office is a 5min. walk along the shore between the two *praças*.

Tourist Office: (☎262 56 11 94), beachside on Av. da República. Provides maps as well as information on entertainment and transportation. Open daily July-Aug. 10am-10pm; June 15-30 10am-1pm and 3-8pm; Apr.-June 15 10am-1pm and 3-7pm; Sept. 10am-8pm; Oct.-March 9:30am-1pm and 2:30-6pm.

Bank: Major banks lie on and around Av. da República. Open M-F 8:30am-3pm.

Emergency: ☎112. **Police** (☎262 55 12 68), 1 block from the bus station at Av. Vieira Guimarães and R. Sub-Vila.

Hospital: Hospital da Confraria da Nossa Senhora de Nazaré (☎262 56 11 16), in the Sítio district on the cliffs above the town center. **Centro de Saúde** (☎262 55 27 43), Urbanizacão Caixins in the new part of town.

Internet Access: Centro Cultural, Av. Manuel Remigio (☎262 56 19 44), the continuation of Av. da República in the direction of the fishing port. Free Internet access. Open M-Sa 9:30am-1pm and 2-7pm, Su 4-7pm.

Post Office: Av. da Independência Nacional, 2 (☎262 56 91 06). From Pr. Sousa Oliveira, walk up R. Mouzinho de Albuquerque. 1 block past Pensão Central. **Fax** and **Posta Restante.** Open M-F 9:30am-12:30pm and 2:30-6pm. **Postal Code:** 2450.

ACCOMMODATIONS

In Nazaré reside the most aggressive room-renters in Portugal; insistent old ladies swarm arriving buses at the station and line Av. da República, waving colored signs and relentlessly proffering their homes to sleepy tourists. Use the buyer's market to your advantage, and bargain with the same aggressive attention with which they court you. Agree on a price before seeing the room, but don't settle the deal until afterward. In summer, take nothing over €25. For less stressful lodging, look above the restaurants in Pr. Dr. Manuel de Arriaga and Pr. Sousa Oliveira.

Vila Turística Conde Fidalgo, Av. da Independência Nacional, 21-A (☎262 55 23 61), 3 blocks uphill from Pr. Sousa Oliveira. The best option for families and groups. Private apartments come with kitchen, refrigerator, microwave, and more. Large, comfortable rooms have flowered curtains and white metal beds. Reception 9am-1am. Reserve ahead in summer; 50% pre-payment required if far in advance. Aug. singles €40; doubles €45, with kitchen €70; July €30/€35/€60; Sept.-June €15-20/€25-30/€25. ❷

Pensão Ideal, R. Adrião Batalha, 98 (☎262 55 13 79), between the 2 main *praças*. Five rooms with high ceilings and comfortable beds share a clean bath with picturesque 1970s linoleum. See if they are offering *pensão completa:* a double room and 3 meals in the restaurant for 2 people (€70). Reception 10am-10pm in the restaurant downstairs. July-Sept. 15 singles €30; doubles €40-45; Sept. 16-June €15-20/€25-30. ❸

Camping: Vale Paraíso, Estrada Nacional 242 (☎262 56 18 00), 2½km out of town in a wooded area. Take the bus to Alcobaça or Leiria (10min., 12 per day 7am-7pm). Also rents bungalows and apartments. Swimming pools, restaurant-bar, supermarket, occasional Internet access (€2 per 30min., €3 per hr.), and laundry (€7 per load). Pool open June-Sept. day pass €2; Apr.-May and Oct. free; Nov.-Mar. closed. June-Sept. €3.80 per person, €3-4.70 per tent, €3 per car; Oct.-May €2.90/€2.50-3.70/€2.50. Free showers. AmEx/MC/V. ❶

FOOD

For groceries, check out the **market** across from the bus station. (Open daily July-Sept. 8am-1pm; Oct.-June Tu-Su 8am-1pm.) **Supermarkets,** such as **Supermercado Ecoloja,** line R. Sub-Vila, parallel to Av. da República. (☎262 56 18 87. Open daily June-Aug. 9am-10pm; Sept.-May 9am-8pm.)

■ **Casa Marquês,** R. Gil Vicente (☎262 55 16 80), directly behind Pr. Dr. Manuel Arriaga. Slightly hidden yet overwhelmingly popular, Marquês is packed with locals and tourists. The adroit cook has prepared their special *caldeirada* (€7) for over 25 years, making it one of the best recipes in a town known for the best *caldeirada* in Portugal. Chipper waiters serve other traditional dishes for €5-8. Open daily 11am-midnight. Closes sometimes between 5-7pm for cleaning. ❷

O Borgas, R. Mouzinho de Albuquerque, 4 (☎262 57 91 03), near Pr. Sousa Oliveira. Bright and roomy, this upscale restaurant serves fish, but specializes in steak. *Bife na lage,* seasoned steak grilled on a heated rock at the diner's table, is their specialty (€10). Other entrees €8-12. Open daily 1pm-midnight. MC/V. ❸

Pastelaria Batel, R. Mouzinho de Albuquerque, 2 (☎262 55 11 47). The best-known pastry shop in Nazaré, with a 34-year history. The place to try sweet local specialties. All pastries €0.70. Try the *tamares* (little boats with creamed egg filling capped with chocolate), *sardinhas* (flaky pastry, not fish), and *Nazarenos* (almond pastry). Open June-Aug. daily 8am-2am; Sept.-May M-Tu, Th-Su 8am-2am. ❶

🏖 🎭 BEACHES & ENTERTAINMENT

Nazaré's main attraction is the expansive **beach**. After catching some rays, take the **funicular** (3min.; every 15min. 7:15am-9:30pm, every 30min. 9:30pm-midnight; €0.70 1-way, €1.60 for 6 trips) which runs from R. Elevador off Av. da República to the **Sítio,** a clifftop area of Nazaré. For centuries, the Sítio constituted the whole of Nazaré; the tide below could not be trusted. Now, uneven cobbled streets, weathered buildings, and staggering views provide the perfect ambience for an afternoon picnic. Around 6pm, fishing boats return to the **port** beyond the far left end of the beach; eavesdrop as local restaurateurs spiritedly bid in an incomprehensible code for the most promising catches at the **fish auction** (M-F 6-9:30pm).

Cafes in Pr. Sousa Oliveira teem with people past midnight. The intimate bar **Ta Bar Es,** R. de Rio Maior, 20-22, off R. Mouzinho de Albuquerque near Pr. Dr. Manuel de Arriaga, is a mellow haven from the sun by day, but livens up with live *bossa nova* and traditional Portuguese music most summer evenings after 11pm. Ta Bar Es also serves a variety of pizzas for €5-7. (☎262 56 23 19. Coffee €0.50. Before 7pm beer €1; mixed drinks €3. After 7pm beer €1-2.50; mixed drinks €3.50. Open daily 2pm-4am. Closed Nov. 1-15.)

On Saturday afternoons in May and June, locals dress in traditional outfits and haul the fishing nets out of the water, enacting the old-fashioned technique in an event known as **Arte Xávega,** followed by an exciting fish auction open to the public. During the summer, look out for late-night **folk music** gatherings on the beach. **Bullfights** are also popular; Nazaré is on the schedule that brings *corridas* to a different city in the province each summer weekend (usually Sa 10pm; tickets start at €27). Bullfights occur the first 3 Saturdays in June, July, and August.

▶ DAYTRIPS FROM NAZARÉ

ALCOBAÇA

Buses are the best way to reach Alcobaça. The bus station on Av. Manuel da Silva Carolino (☎262 58 22 21) offers service to: Batalha (30min., 8 per day 7:30am-7:10pm, €2.15); Coimbra (2hr., 1 per day 4:25pm, €8.80); Leiria (1hr., 8 per day 7:30am-7:10pm, €2.60); Lisboa (2hr.; M-F 5 per day, Sa-Su 3 per day 6:30am-6pm; €7.70); Nazaré (25min., 12-15 per day 7:30am-8:20pm, €1.35); Porto (3½hr., 1 per day 4:25pm, €9.80).

A sleepy town in the hills not too far from the coast, Alcobaça welcomes thousands of visitors each year for one reason: its dominatint ■**Mosteiro de Santa Maria de Alcobaça,** the oldest church in Portugal. The town was founded in 1153, follow-

EAT YOUR HEART OUT, DON JUAN

There's love, and then there's *love*. Dom Pedro I was in the latter. While a prince, he fell head-over-heels for Inês de Castro, the daughter of a Spanish nobleman and lady-in-waiting to his first wife. Pedro's father, Afonso IV, objected to the romance, fearing that such an alliance would open the Portuguese throne to Spanish domination. Despite his father's opposition to the marriage, Pedro fled with Inês to Bragança, where the couple secretly wed. Soon thereafter, the disgruntled Afonso had Inês killed. Upon rising to the throne two years later, Pedro personally ripped out the hearts of the men who had slit his young wife's throat and proceeded to eat them. Henceforth, the hardy king became known as Pedro the Cruel. In a macabre ceremony, he had Inês's body exhumed, dressed her meticulously in royal robes, set her on the throne, and officially deemed her his queen; according to legend, he even made his court kiss her rotting hand. She was eventually reinterred in an exquisitely carved tomb in the king's favorite monastery, the Mosteiro de Santa Maria de Alcobaça. The king later joined her. The inscription on their tombs reads, *"Até ao fim do mundo"* (until the end of the world).

ing Dom Afonso Henriques's expulsion of the Moors, as a grant from the king to Cistercian monks. Afonso was attempting to secure Christianity in the region and expected the monastery to do just that. Slaves and monks began construction in 1178, with additions continuing over the course of several centuries. Today it is the largest building of the Cistercian order in Europe. In the smaller naves adjacent to the towering central one, the **tombs** of Dom Pedro I and his wife Inês de Castro display sophisticated carvings, immortalizing one of Portugal's great, twisted royal love stories (see **Eat your heart out, Don Juan,** p. 711). Surrounding the monastery's cloisters are numerous Gothic rooms, most notably the **Sala dos Monges** (Monk's Hall), and the immense **kitchen** and **refectory,** where the monks could roast more than 6 oxen at a time. (☎262 50 51 20. Monastery open daily Apr.-Sept. 9am-7pm; Oct.-Mar. 9am-5pm. Cloisters open daily Apr.-Sept. 9am-6:30pm; Oct.-Mar. 9am-4:30pm. €3, students 14-25 €1.50, under 14 free. Su before 2pm free.)

The **Museu da Vinha e do Vinho,** 5min. from the bus station on Estrada de Leiria (which branches off Av. dos Combatentes de Grande Guerra on the way out of town), houses a comprehensive exhibit about the history and methods of Portugal's wine industry, and modern innovations. The best exhibit, however, is participatory and involves free samples. (☎262 58 22 22. Open year-round M-F 9am-12:30pm and 2-5:30pm. €1.50, students €0.75. Weekend visits for large groups available with reservation.)

The **tourist office** sits on the corner of Pr. 25 de Abril. Turn right out of the bus station and right onto Av. dos Combatentes de Grande Guerra, following the road towards the monastery. Keeping the main garden to your left; the office is one block up and on the right. The staff hands out accommodation lists, maps, and guides to Alcobaça and surrounding areas. (☎262 58 23 77. Open daily Aug. 10am-7pm; May-July and Sept. 10am-1pm and 3-7pm; Oct.-Apr. 10am-1pm and 2-6pm.) Alcobaça can easily be appreciated as a daytrip, but should you have to spend the night, **Pensão Corações Unidos ❶,** R. Frei António Brandão, 39, off Pr. 25 de Abril, has 20 rooms with flower bedspreads and newly renovated bathrooms. (☎/fax 262 58 21 42. Reception 8am-midnight. Breakfast included. July-Sept. singles €12.50, with bath €17.50; doubles €30/€35. Oct.-June €10/€15/€25/€30.) Their **restaurant ❶** serves *frango na púcara* (chicken in thick sauce with vegetables; €6)

SÃO MARTINHO DO PORTO

Buses run to Nazaré (20min., 7 per day 9:30am-7:30pm, €1.35) and other towns. Schedules are posted in the tourist office. The bus stops on the main road leading into town.

Countless ages of crashing surf hollowed out surrounding coastal cliffs to create the bay of São Martinho do Porto. Nearly enclosed on all sides by rolling hills and steep cliffs, the town lies at the base of the inlet, while its windless, swimmer-friendly **beach** sweeps 3km along and around the bay, forming an almost perfect semi-circle. Its red-roofed houses and palm-studded hillside give São Martinho do Porto an almost Mediterranean charm; it's an ideal escape from crowded Nazaré and Peniche. Vacationers disturb the peace somewhat in July and August.

The **tourist office**, on Lgo. Frederico Ulrich at the end of Av. 25 de Abril, provides a list of private rooms, which are generally the cheapest accommodation option. (☎262 98 91 10. Open June-Sept. Tu-Su 10am-1pm and 3-7pm; Oct.-May Tu-Su 10am-1pm and 2-6pm.) If a day at the beach calls for a night of quality relaxation, then **Pensão Atlântica ❹**, R. Miguel Bombarda, 6, just behind the tourist office, is the town's best bet. Newly decorated rooms come complete with cable TV, throw rugs, enormous bathrooms, and a varying buffet breakfast. Avoid staying here in August, and you'll get a steal. (☎262 98 01 51. Reserve ahead for July and Aug. July 15-Aug. 31 singles €50; doubles €75. May-June €30/€50; Sept.-Apr. €20/€30.)

LEIRIA   ☎244

Welcome to the transport hub of the Ribatejo. Although the bus station alone is one of the largest spaces in town, there's more lurking in Leiria than first meets the eye. Its accommodations, from hostels to hotels, are among the very best in quality and price that Portgual has to offer. The impressive ancient castle that peers over the city also catches visitors' attention. This year, however, Leiria gains another monument of national importance. In preparation for the Euro Cup 2004 soccer championship, the government has built a new stadium for the two games that the city will host on June 7 and June 16. Even if *futebol*'s not your game, Leiria makes a practical base for exploring the nearby region, with frequent buses to Alcobaça, Batalha, Fátima, and the beaches of the Costa da Prata.

▐ TRANSPORTATION

Trains: Leiria's train station is 3km outside town (☎244 88 20 27, national scheduling 808 20 82 08). Buses run between the station and the tourist office (15min., every hr. 7:05am-7:20pm, €0.80). To: **Coimbra** (2hr., 6 per day 7:15am-10:15pm, €3.60); **Figueira da Foz** (1hr., 3 per day 10:30am-5:45pm, €3.70); **Lisboa** (1¾hr., 9 per day 3am-11pm, €7.55-8.45).

Buses (☎244 81 15 07), off Pr. Paulo VI, next to the main park and near the tourist office, in an exhaust-filled warehouse-esque building; the ticket office is down the steps in back. Buses are the most convenient transport out of Leiria. Express buses are twice the price of regional buses. To: **Alcobaça** (50min., 6 per day 7:10am-6:30pm, €2.60); **Batalha** (20min., 9 per day 7:10am-7:10pm, €1.20-1.95); **Coimbra** (1hr., 11 per day 7:15am-2am, €6.50); **Fátima** (1hr., 20 per day 6:40am-7:05pm, €2-4.80); **Figueira da Foz** (1½hr., M-F 8 per day 7:55am-8:30pm, €3.85-6.50); **Lisboa** (2hr., 11 per day 6am-11pm, €7.80); **Nazaré** (1hr., 6-9 per day 7:20am-7:20pm, €2.60-6); **Porto** (3½hr., 10 per day 7:15am-2am, €10.20); **Santarém** (2hr., 5 per day 7:10am-7:15pm, €4.45-8.80); **Tomar** (1½hr., 6 per day 6:45am-6pm, €3.10-6.70).

Taxis: ☎244 81 59 00 or 88 15 50. Taxis gather at the Jardim Luís de Camões.

◀▌ ▐ ORIENTATION & PRACTICAL INFORMATION

The **Jardim Luís de Camões** lies at the center of Leiria. The castle is a 20min. climb from town.

Tourist Office: (☎244 84 87 70; fax 83 35 33), in the Jardim Luís de Camões, across the park from the bus station. Maps, accommodations lists, and a precise model of Batalha's monastery, made entirely of sugar. Free short-term **luggage storage.** Open daily May-Sept. 10am-1pm and 3-7pm; Oct.-Apr. 10am-1pm and 2-6pm.

Laundromat: Ecosec Lavanderia (☎244 83 36 38), R. Capitão Mouzinho Albuquerque, 7, in the alley behind the Centro Comercial Maringá, on the opposite side of the garden. €2.50 per kg, €2.80 for shirts and pants.

Emergencies: ☎ 112. **Police:** Lgo. São Pedro, next to the castle (☎244 85 98 30).

Hospital: Hospital de Santo André (☎244 81 70 00), on R. Olhalvas, along the road to Fátima. For non-emergency illness, go to the closer **Serviço Atendimento Permanente** (☎244 81 13 90), Av. General Norton de Maxos. 30min. walk from the tourist office.

Internet Access: The city offers a convenient (and free) service within the pedestrian mall, known as Leiria Digital (☎244 81 50 91), Lgo. de Santana. Twelve computers with Windows XP and fast connections. 1hr. time limit enforced only when people are waiting. Open M-F 10:30am-9:30pm, Sa 3-8pm.

Post Office: Downtown office (☎244 82 04 60), in Lgo. Santana on Av. dos Combatentes da Grande Guerra, between the tourist office and the youth hostel. Label **Posta Restante** mail "Estação Santana." Open M-F 8:30am-6pm. **Main office,** Av. Heróis de Angola, 99 (☎244 84 94 10), a bit farther away, past the bus station toward the mall. Open M-F 8:30am-6:30pm, Sa 9am-12:30pm. **Postal Code:** 2400.

▐ ACCOMMODATIONS

Staying in Leiria, even during high season, is a chance to score big with amenities without spending your week's lunch money. The list below includes the best options, although the laws of the market have kept services and prices fairly consistent throughout the town.

▨ **Pousada da Juventude de Leiria (HI),** Lgo. Cândido dos Reis, 9 (☎/fax 244 83 18 68). From the bus station, walk to the cathedral and exit Lgo. da Sé (next to Lgo. Cónego Maia) onto R. Barão de Viamonte. Lgo. Cândido dos Reis is 6 blocks ahead. Large guest kitchen, TV room, and game room with pool table (€2 per hr.). Also includes an elegant garden courtyard. Breakfast included 8:30-10am. Reception daily June 16-Sept. 15 8am-midnight; Sept. 16-June 15 8am-noon and 6pm-midnight. Lockout noon-6pm (bag drop-off still available). June 16-Sept. 15 dorms €10.50; doubles €27. Sept. 16-June 15 €8.50/€21. AmEx/MC/V. ❶

Residencial Dom Dinis, Tr. Tomar, 2 (☎244 81 53 42; fax 82 35 52). Turn left after exiting the tourist office, cross the bridge over the Rio Lis, walk 2 blocks, and turn left again. Twenty-four comfortable rooms with huge bathtubs, telephone, and cable TV. Buffet breakfast 8-10:30am. Singles €21; doubles €33; triples €42. AmEx/MC/V. ❷

Pensão Alcôa, R. Rodrigues Cordeiro, 24 (☎244 83 26 90), off Pr. Rodrigues Lobo, and next to the restaurant of the same name. All 16 rooms come with small bath and cable TV. Breakfast included 8:30-10:30am. June 16-Sept. singles €22; doubles €32; triples €38. Oct.-June 15 €20/€30/€35. ❷

▐ FOOD

The **mercado,** on Av. Cidade de Maringá, sells fresh produce (open M-F 8am-4pm, Sa 8am-1pm). Groceries and fresh baked bread are at **Supermercado Ulmar,** Av. Heróis de Angola, 56, just past the bus station. (☎244 83 30 42. Open M-Sa 8am-9pm, Su 10am-1pm and 3-8pm.) Budget restaurants line side streets between the park and the castle; other quality finds are near Pr. Lobo and the youth hostel.

Restaurante Alcôa, R. Rodrigues Cordeiro, 24 (☎244 83 26 90), off Pr. Rodrigues Lobo and below the pensão of the same name. Besides a host of traditional Portuguese options, Alcôa offers one of the best deals in town, with a full meal (appetizer, salad, potatoes, main dish, and dessert) all for €4.95. Other entrees €5-8. Open June-Sept. daily noon-3pm and 7-10pm. Oct.-May M-Sa noon-3pm and 7-10pm. ❶

Restaurante O Rocha, R. Dr. Correria Mateus, 54-58 (☎244 83 31 03). One in a series of popular, moderately priced restaurants in a corner of the pedestrian mall. Entrees €5-8. Large half portions €4-5. Open M-Sa noon-3pm and 7:30-10:30pm. ❷

👁 🏖 SIGHTS & BEACHES

From the main square, follow the signs past the austere **Sé** (cathedral) to the city's most significant monument, the **Castelo de Leiria.** Built by Dom Afonso Henriques after he snatched the town from the Moors, this granite fort presides atop the crest of a volcanic hill on the north edge of town. The passing centuries have been good to it, leaving what is left in an adventurous state of depair. The preserved **Torre de Menagem** (homage tower) houses rusty swords, old armor, and artifacts found on-site. Before discos and clubs took over the nightlife, the **Sala dos Namorados** (Lovers' Hall) set the stage for medieval courting. Old habits die hard for some, and local couples still come to the garden for cuddling and smooching. From the Sala dos Namorados, the terrace opens onto a panoramic view of the town and river. *(☎244 81 39 82. Castle open Apr.-Sept. M-F 9am-6:30pm, Sa-Su and holidays 10am-6:30pm; Oct.-Mar. M-F 9am-5:30pm, Sa-Su 10am-5:30pm. €1; students €0.50.)*

Nearby beaches are accessible via buses running from the station July-Sept. 14 to **Praia de Viera** (45min., 9 per day 7am-6:35pm, €2.30; last return 7:25pm); **Praia Pedrógão,** popular with locals and populated by stately residences (1hr., 6 per day 8:25am-6:35pm, €2.40; last return 6:15pm); and more secluded **São Pedro de Muel** (45min.; M-F 8 per day 7:55am-6:30pm, Sa 7 per day 6:55am-5:30pm, Su 7 per day 7:55am-5:30pm; €2; last return 7:15pm).

BATALHA   ☎244

The only reason to visit Batalha (pop. 7500) is the gigantic **Mosteiro de Santa Maria da Vitória,** rivaling Belém's Mosteiro dos Jerónimos in its monastic splendor.

🚍 TRANSPORTATION. Buses stop in Lgo. 14 de Agosto de 1385 across the street from the monastery. Inquire at the tourist office for info or call the bus station in Leiria (☎244 81 15 07). Buses from Batalha to: **Leiria** (20min., 10 per day 7:50am-8:25pm, €1.20-1.45); **Lisboa** (2hr., 6 per day 7:25am-6:55pm, €6.60); **Nazaré** (1hr., 13 per day 7:35am-6:50pm, €2.85) via **Alcobaça** (45min., €2.25); **Tomar** (1½hr.; 3 per day 8:05am, noon, 6pm; €2.85) via **Fátima** (40min., €1.55).

🔲 🅿 ORIENTATION & PRACTICAL INFORMATION. The **tourist office** is on Pr. Mouzinho de Albuquerque along R. Nossa Senhora do Caminho, just across from the monastery. Its friendly staff offers maps and bus information, as well as accommodation lists and free short-term **luggage storage.** (☎244 76 51 80. Open daily May-Sept. 10am-1pm and 3-7pm; Oct.-Apr. 10am-1pm and 2-6pm.) In case of **emergency** call ☎112 or the **police** at ☎244 76 51 34, on R. Mouzinho de Albuquerque, across the street from the bus stop. The **Centro de Saúde** (health center) is on Estrada da Freiria (☎244 76 52 46). **Internet** access is available at **Cafeteria Online,** R. Nossa Senhora do Caminho, down the pedestrian path from the tourist office, in the opposite direction from the rotary. (1 computer; €2 per 30min., €2.50 per hr.)

The **post office,** in Lgo. Papa Paulo VI near the freeway entrance, has **fax** (€2.20 per page) and **Posta Restante.** (☎244 76 91 00; fax 76 91 06. Open M-F 9:30am-1pm and 2:30-6:30pm.) **Postal Code:** 2440.

⌂⌂ ACCOMMODATIONS & FOOD. Pensão Residencial Gládius ❷, Pr. Mouzinho de Albuquerque, 7, has seven comfortable rooms, all with TV and bath. Two rooms have a view of the plaza. (☎244 76 57 60. Reception 9am-11:30pm. June-Sept. singles €20; doubles €30; triples €40. Oct.-May €15/€25/€35.) **Pensão Vitória ❷,** on Lgo. da Misericórdia next to the bus stop, has three rooms, each with one double bed; solo travelers can ask for a discount. (☎244 76 56 78. Reception 9am-11:30pm. Rooms €20.) The **restaurant** below offers daily specials for €5-8 and *frango assado na brasa* (roasted half-chicken with rice, potatoes, and salad; €4.50). Meals are served daily noon-3pm and 7-11pm. Several inexpensive *churrasqueiras* (barbecue houses) line the squares flanking the monastery.

◎ SIGHTS. Batalha's **▓Mosteiro Santa Maria da Vitória** puts it on the map, and for good reason. Its flamboyant facade soars upward in Gothic and Manueline style, opulently decorated and topped by dozens of spires. The **Capela do Fundador,** immediately to the right of the church, shelters the elaborate sarcophagi of Dom João I, his English-born queen Philippa of Lancaster, and their more famous son Prince Henry the Navigator. The rest of the complex is accessible via a door in the nave of the church; enter through the broad Gothic arches of the **Claustro de Dom João I,** the delicate columns of which initiated the Manueline style. Adjacent to the cloister lies the **Tomb of the Unknown Soldier,** always guarded by two silent and oppressed-looking men in uniform. Through the **Claustro de Dom Afonso V** are the **Capelas Imperfeitas** (Unfinished Chapels), the best part of the monastery. The ornate buttresses were designed to support a massive dome, but construction of the Mosteiro dos Jerónimos in Belém diverted attention, manpower, and funds from Batalha; the result is a circular hall with a sunroof. (Open daily Apr.-Sept. 9am-6pm; Oct.-Mar. 9am-5pm. €3, under 25 and seniors €1.50, under 14 and Su before 2pm free. Church free.)

⚠ CAVES. A 20min. drive outside town brings you to a series of spectacular underground *grutas* (caves) in Estremadura's natural park. The **Grutas de Mira de Aire** are the deepest, though **Grutas de Santo António** and **Alvados** are equally impressive. Although exploration of the caves takes only an hour or two, the bus schedules from Batalha can be tricky and require careful planning. From Batalha, take a bus to **Porto do Mós** (20min.; 3 per day 8:35am, 12:35, 6:40pm; €2.65; last bus back to Batalha 6:30pm). If a 16km hike from Porto do Mós doesn't sound like a good time, then wait a couple hours for the bus to **Alvados** (10min., 6 per day 7:35am-6:40pm), which is still 5km from the caves. Before planning anything, check with the tourist office to confirm schedules, as more buses may be allocated. (Caves open daily July-Aug. 9:30am-8:30pm; June and Sept. 9:30am-7pm; Oct.-Mar. 9:30am-5:30pm; Apr.-May 9:30am-6pm. €3.50, students and seniors €2.50.)

FÁTIMA   ☎249

Until May 13, 1917, when the Virgin Mary appeared to three peasant children, Fátima was a quiet sheep pasture. Now the once-obscure village has become a religious center, defined by its total immersion in holy fervor. A sign at the entrance of the town's holy Santuário complex states, "Fátima is a place for adoration; enter as a pilgrim." Only Lourdes rivals this site in popularity with Catholic pilgrims, as the miracles believed to have occurred here attract an endless international procession of religious groups. The plaza in front of the church, larger than St. Peter's Square in the Vatican, floods with pilgrims on the 12th and 13th of each month and stays busier than any other Portuguese monument throughout the year.

▐ TRANSPORTATION

Trains: The **Caxarias** station (☎249 72 07 01), 10km out of town, is closer than the Fátima station (☎249 56 61 22), 22km away. From Caxarias to: **Coimbra** (1hr., 14 per day 5:25am-1:55am, €4.10); **Lisboa** (2½hr., 9 per day 6:50am-11:30pm, €5.70); **Porto** (4hr., 12 per day 5:25am-1:55am, €9.50); **Santarém** (1½hr., 10 per day 6:50am-9:35pm, €3.30). **Buses** run between Caxarias and Fátima (30min., 7 per day 7:50am-7:50pm, €2) as well as between the Fátima train and bus stations (45min., 5 per day 6:10am-6:35pm, €2.40).

Buses: Av. D. José Alves Correia da Silva (☎249 53 16 11). To: **Batalha** (30min.; 3 per day 9am, 12:35, 6:35pm; €1.55); **Coimbra** (1½hr., 9-13 per day 7:45am-7:40pm, €8.30); **Leiria** (1hr., 13 per day 7:45am-8pm, €2.30-4.80); **Lisboa** (1½-2½hr., 11-17 per day 7am-5pm, €7.80); **Nazaré** (1½hr.; 3 per day 9am, 1:55, 6:25pm; €3.50); **Porto** (3-3½hr.; 11 per day 7:45am-9:30pm, Sa last bus 5:30pm; €10.80); **Santarém** (1hr., 7 per day 7:30am-5:45pm, €6.50); **Tomar** (1¼hr.; 3 per day 8:30am, 12:30, 6:35pm; €2.70).

Taxis: ☎249 53 21 92, or catch one next to the bus station.

✦ ▐ ORIENTATION & PRACTICAL INFORMATION

Activity in Fátima centers around the basilica complex. The **Santuário de Fátima** is the huge, open *praça* that fills with visitors on special occasions and the 12th and 13th of each month. The bus station and tourist office are on **Avenida D. José Alves Correia da Silva**, below the Santuário. The **tourist office** is in a lovely stone building with a wooden roof on Av. D. José Alves Correia da Silva. From the bus station, take a right and walk approximately 10min. (☎249 53 11 39. Open daily June-July, and Sept. 10am-1pm and 3-7pm; Aug. 10am-7pm; Oct.-May 10am-1pm and 2-6pm.) The Santuário has its own information office, on the left side when facing the basilica. (☎249 53 96 00. Open M-Sa 9am-6pm, Su 9am-5pm.) Several major **banks** have branches along the commercial center of R. Jacinta Marto (open 8:30am-3pm). Services include: **emergency** ☎112; **police,** Av. D. José Alves Correia da Silva (☎249 53 97 30); **Centro de Saúde,** on R. Jacinta Marto (☎249 53 18 36); **Internet access** at **X-Medi@,** R. S. João de Deus, 13 (☎249 53 22 60), in the Edificio Varandas de Fátima, a few blocks behind and to the right of the basilica. The **post office** is on R. Cónego Formigão. (☎249 53 18 10. Open M-F 8:30am-6pm.) **Postal Code:** 2495.

▐ ▐ ACCOMMODATIONS & FOOD

Scores of *residencials* surround the basilica complex; prices vary little. During the grand pilgrimages of the 12th and 13th of every month, population and prices rise. It's always best to reserve one week ahead, and a month ahead on summer weekends and holidays. The plain but comfortable rooms of **Residencial São Francisco ❶**, R. Francisco Marto, 100, near the Santuário, all come with TV, phone, and private bath, and half have private balconies. (☎249 53 30 17; fax 53 20 28. Reception 7:30am-midnight. Light breakfast included 8-9:30am. Singles €20; doubles €30; triples €40.) **Residência São Jorge ❷**, R. Santa Cruz, 4, off R. Jacinta Marto near the wax museum, has hotel-like rooms with TV, private bath, and flower-lined balconies. During the day, enter through the religious souvenir shop next door on the left. (☎/fax 249 53 14 64. Reception 7:30am-12:30am. Lockout 12:30am. Singles €20; doubles €30; triples €45. AmEx/MC/V.)

Restaurants and snack bars cluster in commercial centers along R. Francisco Marto, R. Santa Isabela, and R. Jacinta Marto. Close to the wax museum, **O Terminal ❷**, R. Jacinta Marto, 24, offers among the biggest portions for the best price in town. Local favorites, such as grilled lamb, run €7-9, while the *pratos do dia* are €5-6. (☎ 249 53 19 77. Open daily 9am-midnight; meals served 11:30am-3:30pm and 7-10pm.) On the other side of the Santuário, well-established **Restaurant Alfredo ❷**, R. Francisco Marto, 159 CV, serves huge plates with more elegance. Entrees €6-9. Don't miss their *bacalhau no forno*, a specialty. (☎ 249 53 12 49. Open daily noon-3pm and 7-10pm.)

🔘 SIGHTS

▧ SANTUÁRIO DE FATIMA. The modern holy sanctuary is a visually overwhelming site. Many of the devout travel the length of the plaza on their knees, all the way from the cross to the *capelinha*, praying for divine assistance or giving thanks to the Virgin Mary. After decades of fervent speculation, the Vatican disclosed the closely guarded "third secret" of Fàtima in 2000, ending fears that it revealed the apocalypse. The Virgin is also said to have prophesied the 1981 assassination attempt on Pope John Paul II in St. Peter's Square. The Pope now credits the Virgin with saving his life and had the bullet placed in her crown here.

At the end of the plaza rises the **Basílica do Rosário** (erected in 1928), featuring a crystal cruciform beacon atop the tower's seven-ton bronze crown. Inside are the tombs of two of the children who witnessed the apparitions; Francisco lies in the right nave, while Jacinta is in the left. Lúcia, the third and oldest child, still lives in Coimbra, a devout nun. *(Open daily 7:30am-10:30pm. Mass daily at 7:30, 9, 11am, 3, 4:30, and 6:30pm. Free.)* To the left is the **Capelinha das Aparições,** where the miracles allegedly took place. Sheltered beneath a metal and glass canopy, the *capelinha* was built in 1919 and continues to house "Perpetual Adoration," which consists of Mass during the day and a fire that never dies. The faithful from all over the world make pilgrimages to the site and perform Mass at the chapel; an international Mass is held there every Thursday at 9am, and a candlelight procession occurs every evening at 9:30pm from April to October.

MUSEUMS. The **Museu de Arte Sacra e Etnologia** exhibits Catholic icons from various centuries. *(R. Francisco Marto, 5. ☎ 249 53 94 70. Open Apr.-Oct. Tu-Su 10am-7pm; Nov.-Mar. noon-5pm. €2, seniors and students €1.)* The **Museu Fátima 1917 Aparições** uses light, sound, and special effects to re-create the apparition and is one of the only places in town where the message of the Virgin is readily accessible to the public. *(R. Jacinta Marto. To the left of the basilica, through the park, in the complex beneath Hotel Fátima. ☎ 249 53 28 58. Open daily Apr.-Oct. 9am-7pm; Nov.-Mar. 9am-6pm. €2.50, under 12 €1.50.)*

TOMAR ☎ 249

Visitors come to Tomar mainly to walk quietly and wide-eyed through the versatile Convento de Cristo, which includes a castle, a fortress, a convent, and several beautiful gardens. Around the year 1160 D. Afonso Henriques enlisted the Knights Templar (a kind of sanctified swat team) to build a fortified castle at Tomar, then the weak spot between Lisboa and Coimbra. When the Knights fell out of favor with the Pope two hundred years later, sheepish Portuguese royalty quickly founded a new religous order and gave them the Templar's property, thus today's unique collage of menacing medieval walls and piously ornate architecture. The rest of the town lazes beside the Rio Nabão, stirring only for the legendary **Festival dos Tabuleiros** every four years (due again in 2007).

⌐ TRANSPORTATION

Trains: Av. dos Combatentes da Grande Guerra (☎249 72 07 55). Tomar is the northern end of a minor line, so most destinations require a transfer at Entroncamento or Lamarosa; check your ticket twice and pay attention to the stops. Ticket office open Su-F 5:30am-8:30pm and 9:30-10:30pm, Sa 5:30-8:30pm. To: **Coimbra** (2½hr., 8 per day 6:05am-6:05pm, €5.60-6.40); **Lisboa** (2hr., 18 per day 5:05am-10:05pm, €5.60-6.40); **Porto** (4½hr., 7 per day 8:05am-8:05pm, €8.50-9.50); **Santarém** (1hr., 12 per day 5:05am-10:05pm, €3.30-3.70).

Buses: Rodoviária Tejo, Av. dos Combatentes da Grande Guerra (☎968 94 35 50). Express buses are twice the price of regular buses. To: **Coimbra** (2½hr., 1 per day 7am, €9.20); **Fátima** (30min., 3 per day 7:50am-5:20pm, €2.60-5.20); **Figueira da Foz** (4½hr., 1 per day 7am, €9.40); **Lagos** (9hr.; 1 per day M-Sa 9:15am via Santarém and Évora, 10:15am via Lisboa, Su 10:15am via Lisboa; €17.50); **Leiria** (1hr.; M-F 2 per day 7:15am, 5:45pm; Sa 1 per day 7am; €3.10); **Lisboa** (2hr., 4 per day 9:15am-6pm, €6.50); **Nazaré** (1½hr., 3 per day 7:50am-5:20pm, €5); **Porto** (4hr., 1 per day 7am, €11.60); **Santarém** (1hr., 1 per day 12:30pm, €4.65).

Taxis: Vitorino e Marguerita, Ltd. ☎963 04 23 06. **Autotáxi Capítulo** ☎917 20 14 35. Taxis cluster near the bus and train stations, as well as across the river on R. Santa Iria.

❖❷ ORIENTATION & PRACTICAL INFORMATION

The **Rio Nabão** divides Tomar, leaving almost everything travelers need—the train and bus stations, accommodations, and sights—on the western bank. The lush **Parque Mouchão** straddles the two banks, while the ancient **Ponte Velha** (Old Bridge) connects them. From the **Ponte Nova** (New Bridge), **Avenida Dr. Cândido Madureira** leads to **Praça Infante Dom Henrique,** behind which lie the trails of the **Parque da Mata Nacional dos Sete Montes.** (Park open daily 10am-6pm. Free.) The **bus and train stations** sit side by side on **Avenida dos Combatentes da Grande Guerra** at the edge of town. The pedestrian-only **Rua Serpa Pinto** cuts across town from the river to the castle and connects Ponte Velha to **Praça da República,** the main square.

Tourist Office: Av. Dr. Cândido Madureira (☎249 32 24 27). From the bus/train station, head down Av. General Bernardo Faria toward the city past several municipal buildings. Turn left 3 blocks later onto Av. Cândido Madureira. Short-term **luggage storage** available. Open daily July-Sept. 10am-8pm, Oct.-June 10am-6pm.

Emergency: ☎112. **Police:** R. Dr. Sousa (☎249 31 34 44).

Hospital: Hospital Nossa Senhora da Graça, Av. Dona Maria de Lourdes Melo e Castelo, (☎249 32 01 00), on the other side of the river (25min. walk.)

Internet Access: Espaço Internet, R. Antorim Rosa, between R. Marquês de Pombal and Av. Norton de Matos, on the other side of the river. 30min. limit.

Post Office: Av. Marquês de Tomar (☎249 31 04 00; fax 31 04 06), across from Parque Mouchão. **Posta Restante** and **fax** available. Open M-F 8:30am-6pm, Sa 9am-12:30pm. **Postal Code:** 2300.

⌐ ACCOMMODATIONS

Finding accommodations is a problem only during the **Festival dos Tabuleiros. Rua Serpa Pinto** is lined with quality lodging, while cheaper options lie closer to the bus and train stations.

▨ **Residencial União,** R. Serpa Pinto, 94 (☎249 32 31 61; fax 32 12 99), halfway between Pr. da República and the bridge. The nicest budget accommodation in Tomar, in a central location. 28 rooms all have TV, phone, regal red carpet, and private bath. Anyone with the urge is welcome to take advantage of the piano to the right of reception. Well-stocked bar. Buffet breakfast included. Reception 8am-midnight. Reservations recommended for July and Aug. Apr.-Sept. singles €25; doubles €37.50; 3rd person in a double €5 more. Oct.-Mar. €20/€30/€2.50. ❷

Residencial Luz, R. Serpa Pinto, 144 (☎249 31 23 17; www.residencialluz.com). 14 clean, comfy rooms, most with private bath, TV, and phone. Antique *aficionados* can request the room with the 1973 big screen TV. May 16-Sept. singles €20, with bath €22; doubles €30/€32.50; quad with bath €45-60. Oct.-May 15 €15-18/€18-20/€23-25/€25-30/€35-45. ❷

Casa de Dormidas, R. de D. Aurora de Macedo, 46 (☎249 31 19 03 or 32 28 78). Go to the Casa Costa shop on Av. Dr. Cândido Madureira, 18, near the traffic circle, and speak with owner José Costa. The older rooms are ideal for those who like big spaces and aren't particular about how they look. Singles €15; doubles €20. For the absolute rock bottom deal in town, ask about his rooms without bath at **Casa de Dormidas Convento,** Av. dos Combatentes da Grande Guerra, 7. Singles €10; doubles €15. ❶

◨ FOOD

Parque Mouchão, across from Av. Marquês de Tomar, is the perfect spot for a picnic. The **market,** across the river on the corner of Av. Norton de Matos and R. Santa Iria, provides all but the red-checkered blanket. (Open Tu and Th-F 8am-2pm. The larger market on Friday has a flea market as well.) Several inexpensive **mini-markets** line the side streets between the tourist office and Pr. da República.

Salsinha Verde, Pr. da República, 19 (☎249 32 32 29), in the corner, to the left when facing the town hall. Students pop *petingas* (small fish; €0.15) at the bar. Local cuisine served in the dining room €3.50-7. Cheaper *pratos do dia* (€3). Pray that your trip lands you here on a Tuesday, when the cook makes his legendary *bacalhau com natas* (creamy codfish). It tastes much better than it sounds. Open daily 8am-midnight. ❶

Ristorante/Pizzeria Bella Italia, R. Everard, 91 (☎249 32 29 96), near the river, between the bridges. The family owners serve delicious pastas (€4-7) and pizzas (€4-9) in stuff-yourself portions. Specialties include *pasta mista* (€12; serves 2). The tiramisú (€2.50) is quite popular. Open W-M noon-3pm and 7-11pm. ❶

◉▢ SIGHTS & FESTIVALS

From the tourist office, take a right and bear left on the dirt path. The 10min. leisurely ascent leads to the reason you should come to Tomar, ▨**Convento de Cristo,** which displays an intriguing range of architecture and landscaping. The first structure was built by the Moors to defend themselves from pesky invaders; that clearly failed, and the Knights Templar fortified it in 1160 after the Moorish defeat. Successive architectural enterprises really deserve the credit for its beauty, since the centuries added an eclectic collection of cloisters, convents, and buildings. The most impressive aspect of the convent is the grounds that surround its entrance; *azulejo*-covered benches beckon visitors to sit and gaze at the orange trees and the views of the nearby national forest. Upon entering, an ornate octagonal canopy protects the high altar of the **Templo dos Templares,** modeled after the Holy Sepulchre in Jerusalem. Below stands the **Janela do Capítulo** (chapter window), an exuberant tribute to the Age of Discovery. One of Europe's masterpieces of Renaissance architecture, the **Claustro dos Felipes** honors Felipe II of Castile, who was crowned here as Felipe I of Portugal during Iberia's unification (1580-1640). Stairs spiral upward to sweeping views of the **Terraço da Cera.** Tucked behind the

Palladian main cloister and the nave is the **Claustro da Santa Bárbara,** where grotesque gargoyle rain spouts writhe in pain as they cough up a fountain. On the northeast side of the church is the Gothic **Claustro do Cemitério.** (☎249 31 34 81. Open daily June-Sept. 9am-6pm, Oct.-May 9am-5pm. €3, under 14 free.)

The **Museu Luso-Hebraico Abraáo Zacuto** is Portugal's most significant reminder of its historic presence in the European Jewish community. This synagogue, built between 1430 and 1460 and given up in 1496 when the Jews faced exile or conversion to Christianity, now houses a small museum of international Jewish history, with a collection of tombstones, inscriptions, and pieces from around the world. (R. Dr. Joaquim Jaquinto, 73. Open daily 10am-1pm and 2-6pm. Free.) During October 19-23, handicrafts, folklore, *fado,* and raisins storm the city during the **Feira de Santa Iria,** which includes the **Feria das Passas** (Raisin Fair). The **Feria de Artesanato** has taken place during the first half of July ever year since 1984. The biggest party in Tomar, however, is the **Festival dos Tabuleiros,** which takes place once every four years as an act of thanks for good harvests. Six thousand people swarm the town for a week to watch young girls walk in a 4km procession bearing the traditional *tabuleiro* (tray) stacked on their heads. The *tabuleiro* itself must be as tall as its bearer and is composed of bread, paper flowers, ribbons, and shafts of wheat. Tomar also hosts four summer **bullfights;** look for large, brightly colored posters advertising the *corridas.*

THE THREE BEIRAS

The Three Beiras region offers a versatile sampling of the best of Portugal: the pristine beaches of the coast, the rich greenery of the interior, and the ragged peaks of the Serra da Estrela. The Beira Litoral (Coastal Region) encompasses the Costa da Prata (Silver Coast) beginning at the party town of Figueira da Foz and passing through up-and-coming Aveiro on the way to Porto. The soil in this region yields some of Portugal's best farmland, and the countryside is dotted with red-roofed farmhouses surrounded by expanses of corn, sunflowers, and wheat. Coimbra, Portugal's major university town, contributes an opinionated and vibrant population, making it a popular center for discussion and rendezvous among travelers. And fortunately for those seeking unsullied Portugal, Beira Alta offers the mountainous extremes of the region, while lowland Beira Baixa is "just right," although Goldilocks is not included. Both regions have retained their wealth in tradition if for no other reason than that many wimp out before getting there.

HIGHLIGHTS OF THE THREE BEIRAS

LIVE your favorite childhood fairy tale in the enchanting **Buçaco Forest** (see p. 728).

SEE the sinking Convento de Santa Clara-a-Velha in **Coimbra** (see p. 726).

RISK IT ALL at **Figueira da Foz's** famed casino (see p. 728).

COIMBRA   ☎239

Going off to the university in Portugal before the 20th century meant coming to Coimbra, the original Portuguese college town. But even though scores of universities have cropped up throughout the country, Coimbra presides over them, drawing backpackers and youth from across the globe. Just don't feel the draw in August; when the students leave, the town slows down to a crawl.

⌨ TRANSPORTATION

Trains: Info ☎808 208 208. **Estação Coimbra-A (Nova)** is 2 blocks from the lower town center. **Estação Coimbra-B (Velha)** is 3km northwest of town. Regional trains stop first in Coimbra-B, then continue to Coimbra-A, departing in reverse order. Long-distance trains arriving from/departing for cities outside the region stop in Coimbra-B only. If your train stops only at Coimbra-B, it is easiest to take a connecting train to Coimbra-A (4min., immediately after trains arrive, €0.70 or free if transfer). Trains to: **Braga** (3hr.; 2 per day 9:55am, 9:20pm; €7-8); **Figueira da Foz** (1¼hr., 24 per day 5:20am-12:20am, €1.55); **Lisboa** (3hr., 23 per day 5:35am-2:20am, €8.50-9.50); **Porto** (2hr., 21 per day 5:10am-3:10am, €5.60-6.40).

Buses: AVIC, R. João de Ruão, 18 (☎239 82 01 41). To **Condeixa** (25min., 14 per day 7:35am-7:35pm, €1.45) and **Conímbriga** (30min.; 1 per day 9:35am, returns 6pm; €1.55). RBL (☎239 82 70 81), near the end of Av. Fernão de Magalhães 15min. past Coimbra-A. Buses to: **Évora** (4hr.; 2 per day 9:30am, 4:15pm; €12.40); **Faro** (8hr., 3 per day 9:25am-2:10am, €17); **Lisboa** (2½hr., 17 per day 7:30am-2:15am, €9.40); **Luso** and **Buçaco** (45min.; M-F 7 per day 7:35am-7:20pm; Sa 2 per day 9am, 12:45pm; Su 2 per day 10:15am, 5:30pm; €2.50-2.70); **Porto** (1½hr., 10 per day 8:30am-9:30pm, €8.10).

The Three Beiras

Peso da Regua
Lamego
BEIRA ALTA
Oporto
A4
IP3
N102
Furadouro
São João de Madeira
Castro Daire
Vila Nova de Paiva
Pinhel
Ovar
IC2
Tamanhos
E80 IP5
Viseu
E80 IP5
E80 IP5
Aveiro
IP1
Águeda
IC12
Guarda
A1
IP3
IC7
IP2
Luso
Santa Comba Dão
Oliveira do Hospital
Seia
Buçaco Forest
IC12
Raiva IC6
Coimbra
IC6
Covilha
IC6
IC1
IC2
BEIRA LITORAL
Fundão
Figueira da Foz
Conímbriga
BEIRA BAIXA
IC1
Pombal
IP2
IC8
Pontão
IC8
IC8
Leiria
Proença-a-Nova
Castelo Branco
IP2
IP1
A1

ATLANTIC OCEAN
COSTA DA PRATA
SPAIN
35 miles
35 kilometers

Public Transportation: SMTUC buses and street cars. Three-trip ticket €1.40 at kiosks and vending machines; one-way €1.20 on the bus. Book of 11 €4.80; 3-day pass €6.20 sold at vending machines at Lgo. da Portagem, Pr. da República, and elsewhere.

Taxis: Politaxis (☎239 49 090). Outside Coimbra-A and the bus station.

Car Rental: Avis (☎/fax 239 83 47 86, reservations toll-free 800 20 10 02), in Coimbra-A. 21+. Open M-F 8:30am-12:30pm and 3-7pm. From €75 per day.

◪ ◪ ORIENTATION & PRACTICAL INFORMATION

Coimbra's steep cobbled streets rise in tiers above the **Rio Mondego**. Of the three major parts of town, the most central is **Baixa**, site of the **tourist office** and the Coimbra-A **train station**, and set within the triangle formed by the river, **Largo da Portagem**, and **Praça 8 de Maio**. The historic **university district** looms atop the steep hill overlooking Baixa. On the other side of the university, the area around **Praça da República** is home to cafes, a shopping district, and the youth hostel.

Tourist Office: Regional office, Lgo. da Portagem (☎239 85 59 30). Open June-Sept. M-F 9am-7pm, Sa-Su 10am-1pm and 2:30-5:30pm; Oct.-May M-F 9am-6pm, Sa-Su 10am-1pm and 2:30-5:30pm. English-speaking staff distributes maps. **Municipal offices,** Lgo. Dom Dinis (☎239 83 25 91). Open M-F 9am-6pm, Sa-Su 9am-12:30pm and 2-5:30pm; and Pr. da República (☎239 83 32 02). Open M-F 10am-6:30pm.

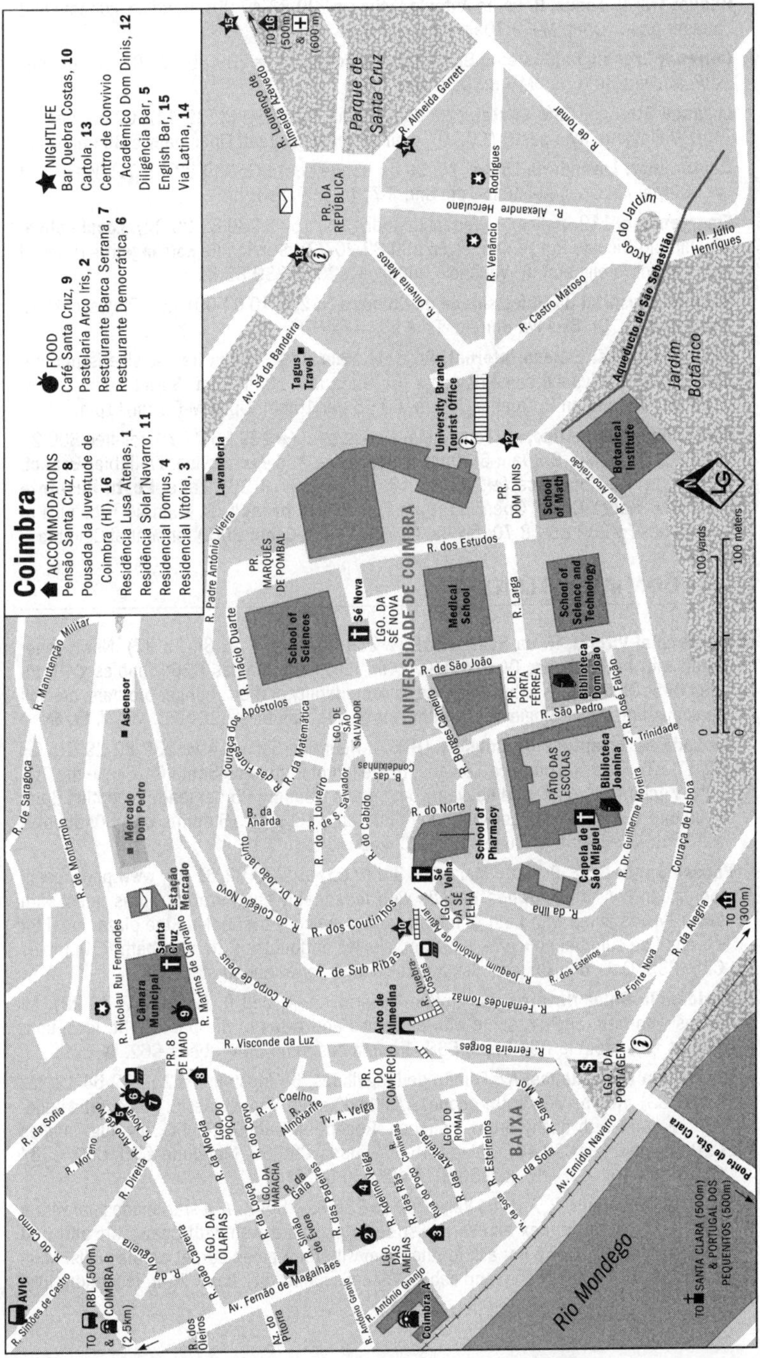

Coimbra

▲ ACCOMMODATIONS
Pensão Santa Cruz, **8**
Pousada da Juventude de
  Coimbra (HI), **16**
Residência Lusa Atenas, **1**
Residência Solar Navarro, **11**
Residencial Domus, **4**
Residencial Vitória, **3**

● FOOD
Café Santa Cruz, **9**
Pastelaria Arco Iris, **2**
Restaurante Barca Serrana, **7**
Restaurante Democrática, **6**

★ NIGHTLIFE
Bar Quebra Costas, **10**
Cartola, **13**
Centro de Convívio
  Académico Dom Dinis, **12**
Diligência Bar, **5**
English Bar, **15**
Via Latina, **14**

Budget Travel: Tagus, R. Padre António Vieira (☎239 83 49 99). Handles students and budget travel. Open M-F 9:30am-6pm.

Currency Exchange: Montepio Geral, Lgo. da Portagem (☎239 85 17 00). €5 commission above €50. Open M-F 8:30am-3pm.

Luggage Storage: Café Cristal, Lgo. das Ameias, 5 (☎239 82 39 44). €2 per bag for 4hr. While here, try a pastry (€0.70); their selection is great. Open daily 5:30am-10pm.

Laundromat: Lavandaría Lucira, Av. Sá da Bandeira, 86 (☎239 82 57 01). Wash and dry €2 per kg. Open M-F 9am-1pm and 3-7pm, Sa 9am-1pm.

Emergency: ☎112. **Police:** R. Venâncio Rodrigues, 15 (☎239 82 20 22). **Local police,** R. Olímpio Nicolau Rui Fernandes (☎239 82 20 22). **Serviço de Estrangeiros** (Special division for foreigners), R. Venâncio Rodrigues, 25 (☎239 82 81 34).

Hospital: Hospital da Universidade de Coimbra (☎239 40 04 00), Lgo. Professor Mota Pinto and Av. Dr. Bissaya Barreto. Take bus #7 or 29.

Internet Access: Espaço Internet, Pr. 8 de Maio. This city-run free service is popular and requires advance same-day sign up. Open M-F 10am-8pm, Sa-Su 10am-10pm. **Central Modem,** on R. Quebra-Costas. €0.55 per 15min. Open M-F 1am-11pm.

Post Office: Main office, Av. Fernão Magalhães, 223 (☎239 85 07 70; toll-free 800 20 68 68). Open M-F 8:30am-6:30pm. **Telephones** and **fax** service available. **Branch office,** Pr. da República (☎239 85 18 20; fax 85 18 26). Label **Posta Restante** "Estação Santa Cruz." Open M-F 9am-6pm. **Third branch,** R. Olímpio Nicolau Rui Fernandes (☎239 85 18 70; fax 85 18 76). **Postal Code:** 3000 for central Coimbra.

ACCOMMODATIONS

Residencial Vitória, R. da Sota, 11-19 (☎239 82 40 49; fax 84 28 97). Newly renovated with bath, phone, TV, and A/C. 24hr. reception. Singles €25; doubles €40; triples €45. Older rooms, which lack the slick modernity of their younger brothers, are still spacious and calm. Singles €10, with shower €15; doubles €20-€25. MC/V. ❷/❶

Pousada da Juventude de Coimbra (HI), R. Henrique Seco, 14 (☎239 82 29 55; fax 82 17 30). From R. Lourenço Azevedo, to the left of Parque de Santa Cruz, take the 2nd right. Kitchen, TV room, and heavenly bathrooms. Laundry €5 per load. Reception 8am-noon and 6pm-midnight. Lockout noon-6pm. June 16-Sept. 15 dorms €10.50; doubles with bath €29. Sept. 16-June €8.50/€24. ❶

Pensão Santa Cruz, Pr. 8 de Maio, 21, 3rd fl. (☎/fax 239 82 61 97; www.pensaosantacruz.com). A family-owned *pensão* with reasonably comfortable rooms, most with cable TV and some with bath. 2 rooms share a balcony overlooking the plaza, ideal for viewing free summer concerts. July-Sept. singles or doubles €20, with bath €30; triples €25/€35. Oct.-June €5 less. Ask about iscounts for extended stays. ❷

Residência Solar Navarro, Av. Emídio Navarro, 60-A, 2nd fl. (☎239 82 79 99). All rooms with bath and TV, some with balconies and views of the park. 24hr. reception. Singles €15; double €30; triple €38; 1 enormous room with 5 beds €62. ❶

Residência Lusa Atenas, Av. Fernão de Magalhães, 68, upstairs (☎239 82 64 12; fax 82 01 33). Rooms with bath, phone, A/C, and cable TV in a classic, aristocratic building. TV room with cushy brown couches. Reception 8am-midnight. July-Aug. singles €20-25; doubles €30-40; triples €45-50; quads €55-60. May-June €20/€30/€38/€50. Sept.-Apr. €18-20/€25-30/€38-40/€40-50. ❸

Residencial Domus, R. Adelino Veiga, 62 (☎239 82 85 84). A 3-star *residencial* with a more economical annex across the street. Decorated well with cheap art and bed frames unique to the room; ask for the room with retro green carpet on the walls. Main rooms all have bath, phone, and cable TV; annex rooms lack bath. 24hr. reception. July-

Sept. main rooms: singles €30; doubles €40; triple €50. Annex: singles €23; doubles €30. Oct.-June main rooms €23/€35/€38; annex €20/€23. The annex also serves as an apartment for €50-60 per night. Discounts for extended stays beyond 3 nights. ❸

Hotel Bragança, Lgo. das Ameias, 10 (☎239 822 17). The hotel is luxurious, complete with room service and complimentary mints. A great deal during the low season. May-Sept. singles €33-50, double €65. Oct.-Apr. singles €25-40; double €50 ❹.

🍴 FOOD

Check out the areas around R. Direita off Pr. 8 de Maio, the side streets between the river and Lgo. da Portagem, and the university side of Pr. da República. Restaurants offer steamy portions of *arroz de lampreia*. The cheapest meals around are at **UC Cantina** (under €3), the university student cafeteria, on the right side of R. Oliveiro Matos. An international student ID is mandatory. Get fruits and veggies at the enormous **Mercado Dom Pedro V** on R. Olímpio Nicolau Rui Fernandes (open M-Sa 8am-1pm). Discount fiends will appreciate **Supermercado Minipreço,** R. António Granjo 6C, in the lower town center. (☎239 82 77 57. Open M-Sa 8:30am-8pm, Su 9am-1pm and 3-7pm.)

▨ **Restaurante Barca Serrana,** R. Direita, 46 (☎239 82 06 16). A popular and inexpensive lunch spot. Enjoy local entrees such as *leitão* for €3-7 in the dining room in back or at the wide counter. The two daily specials are the steal of the town (€3.50). Open M-F 9am-11pm, Sa 9am-4pm. ❷

▨ **Pastelaria Arco Iris,** Av. Fernão de Magalhães, 22 (☎239 83 33 04). A colorful and almost unending variety of pastries (€0.55-0.85) are displayed in glass cases. Coffee €0.50-0.90. A large selection of sandwiches is also available (€1-2.50). Travelers can live off the *bolos de passa* (raisin buns, €0.70), which are as big as your forearm. Open M-Sa 7:15am-8:30pm, Su 8am-8:30pm. ❶

Café Santa Cruz, Pr. 8 de Maio, 5 (☎239 83 36 17). Formerly part of the cathedral, this is the city's most famous cafe—a popular place for coffee (€0.50-1) and people-watching. Features a vaulted ceiling and gargoyle birds holding lamps in their beaks. Best on summer nights, when the weather is cool and the people are gathering. Sandwiches €1.25-2.50. Open May-Sept. M-Sa 7am-2am, Oct.-Apr. M-Sa 7am-midnight. ❶

Restaurante Democrática, Trav. de R. Nova, 15 (☎239 82 37 84). A popular spot for traditional fare in a large, laid-back setting. Entrees €6-12. Try their exotic *arroz de polvo* (€8) for a sampling of local tradition. Open M-Sa noon-3:30pm and 7-10pm. ❷

🔆 SIGHTS

OLD TOWN. Take in Coimbra's old town sights by making the steep 15min. climb from the river up to the university. Begin at Pr. 8 de Maio and the **Igreja de Santa Cruz,** the centerpiece. The 16th-century church boasts an enormous and ornate center dome and *azulejo*-lined walls. *(Open M-Sa 9am-12:30pm and 2-6pm, Su 4-6pm. Check the schedule at the main door for Mass times.)* The ascent continues at the ancient **Arco de Almedina,** a remnant of the Moorish town wall, one block uphill from Lgo. da Portagem. The gate leads past several university bookstores to a street aptly named R. Quebra-Costas (Back-Breaker Street). Up a narrow stone stairway looms the 12th-century Romanesque **Sé Velha** (Old Cathedral). Although the gilded altar is certainly impressive, the real winner is the sheer enormity of the interior. Don't miss the peaceful cloister upstairs from the main nave. *(Open M-Th 10am-1pm and 2-6pm, F-Su 10am-1pm. Cathedral free. Cloisters €1, students €0.75.)* Follow the signs to the nearby 16th-century **Sé Nova** (New Cathedral), whose exterior was completed by architects for the resident Jesuit community. Bring sunglasses; the opulently gilded main alter can be blinding. *(Open Tu-Sa 9am-noon and 2-6:30pm. Free.)*

UNIVERSIDADE DE COIMBRA. Though many buildings have since been built from 1950s reinforced concrete, the original law school still retains its spot on the architectural Dean's List. Enter the center of the old university through the **Porta Férrea** (Iron Gate), off R. São Pedro, to the **Pátio das Escolas**, which sports an excellent view of the rural outskirts of Coimbra. *(Uphill from the new cathedral. Open daily May-Sept. 9am-7:30pm; Oct.-Apr. 9:30am-12:30pm and 2-5:30pm.)* The staircase at right leads up to the **Sala dos Capelos** (Graduates' Hall), where portraits of Portugal's kings (6 of whom were born in Coimbra) hang below a 17th-century ceiling. *(Open daily 9:30am-12:30pm and 2-5pm. €2.50.)* The **university chapel** smells funny, but gives an idea of the religious life of the students. At the end of the row of buildings, the mind-boggling, gilded 18th-century **Biblioteca Joanina** surprises visitors with its ostentation. *(☎239 85 98 00. Open daily May-Sept. 9am-7:30pm; Oct.-Apr. 9:30am-noon and 2-5:30pm. A limited number of people allowed at a time, so there is generally up to 1hr. wait. €2.50, teachers and students free. A ticket for all university sights can be purchased for €4 from the office in the main quad.)*

ACROSS THE RIVER. Cross Ponte de Santa Clara to discover the 14th-century **Convento de Santa Clara-a-Velha.** Don't be surprised to see huge cranes trying to lift it by inches; more than half of its structure is submerged in the morass, which annoys the Câmara Municipal. The multi-million dollar attempt to rescue it will continue indefinitely. Before this round of repairs, another renovation revealed an ancient church founded in 1330 by Dona Isabel, wife of Dom Dinis. Isabel's Gothic tomb was relocated uphill to the ornate **Convento de Santa Clara-a-Nova.** *(☎239 44 16 74. Interior closed through summer 2003 for massive renovation. Call ahead to see if it has reopened. Church open M-Sa 9am-noon and 2-6pm. Cloisters and sacristy €1.)*

NIGHTLIFE

After dinner, outdoor cafes surrounding Pr. da República buzz with animated conversation from midnight to 2am, after which crowds move on to the bars and clubs farther afield. The scene is best October through July, when the students are in town. Bars and clubs are listed in chronological order by peak hour. Figueira da Foz (see p. 728) offers more nightlife options and makes a popular "night trip."

Quebra Costas, R. Quebra-Costas, 45 (☎239 821 661). Specializing in 12 different salads during the day, this artistic joint blasts jazz and funk to an eager and enthusiastic crowd in their 20s and 30s at night. Admire the modern art on the wall, or wonder about the half-car in the main room. Beer €1-3; mixed drinks €4-5. Open daily midnight-4am.

Centro de Convívio Acadêmico Dom Dinis, Lgo. Dom Dinis (☎239 83 85 38). A conference center by day, the university-owned *Centro* wakes with a DJ M-Th and live music F-Sa 1-3am. ISIC or college ID required. Beer €1. Best Oct.-July after midnight, especially Th. Open Sept.-July M-Sa 10:30pm-3am.

Via Latina, R. Almeida Garrett, 1 (☎239 82 02 93). Large dance club popular with students on weekends and older residents M-Th. Latin music Sa-Th, house F. Two 1100L tanks of Super Bock fuel the whole operation. Best place for dancing. Tu is ladies' night (3 drinks with entrance). Beer €1.50. Mixed drinks €3.50-4. Min. consumption M-Th €2.50 for men, €1.50 for women; F-Sa €5/€3.50. Open M-Sa 11pm-7am.

Cartola, Pr. da República (☎239 836 236). Good luck finding a seat; this place brims with young folk after 9pm. Coffee €0.50. Beer €1. Open M-Sa 7am-2am, Su 8am-1am.

English Bar, R. Lourenço de Almeida Azevedo, 24 (☎919 50 94 39). The bottom floor restaurant serves traditional English pub grub and plays Latin music, while a top floor DJ spins classic rock to an age 20-40 bar-side crowd. Huge backyard patio. Beer €1.50-2; mixed drinks €3-4. Best F-Sa at midnight. Bar-restaurant open daily 2:30pm-4am; dance floor upstairs open 10pm-4am.

Pitchclub, Lgo. da Sé Velha, 4-8 (☎239 83 81 64). This recently renovated club is one of Coimbra's newest dance spots. Stone, wood, and metal walls reverberate with house, Brazilian, African, and pop. Serves vegetarian options during the day. Salads €2-5. Beer €1. Mixed drinks €2.50. One-drink minimum after 11pm. Open June-Sept. 15 M-Sa 11am-4am; Sept. 16-May M-Sa 9pm-4am.

Diligência Bar, R. Nova, 30 (☎239 82 76 67). Shamelessly touristy during the summer, yet still intimate and pleasant. Local *fado* performed nightly after 10pm. Although not as professional as its Lisboa counterparts, it gives an idea of the traditional music. Dinner is expensive, but people come for more than food. Entrees €8-15. Sangría €9.50 per jug. Open daily 6pm-2am.

◘ FESTIVALS

Students run wild during the **Queima das Fitas** (Burning of the Ribbons), Coimbra's infamous week-long festival in the first or second week of May. The festivities begin when graduating seniors set fire to narrow ribbons received from friends and family to commemorate their graduation and receive wide, ornamental replacements. Live choral music echoes in the streets during the **Festas da Rainha Santa,** held the first week of July, and the city's largest fireworks display lights up the sky. During even-numbered years, two processions of the statue of Rainha Santa (one at the beginning, one at the end) more visibly reflect the festival's religious roots. The firework-punctuated **Feira Popular** in the second week of July offers carnival rides and games across the river.

◙ DAYTRIPS FROM COIMBRA

CONÍMBRIGA

AVIC buses (☎239 82 37 69) run each morning from Coimbra (30min.; M-F 2 per day 9:05, 9:35am; Sa-Su 1 per day 9:35am; €1.65) and return in the afternoon (M-Sa 2 per day 1, 6pm; Su 1 per day 6pm). Buses run more frequently to Condeixa, 2km away from Conímbriga (25min.; 6-30 per day M-F 6:35am-10pm, Sa-Su 7:05am-6:05pm; €1.40). Come in the morning and leave at 1pm; if that doesn't work, heading to Condeixa is mildly complicated but still doable. Follow the signs and walk along the highway for approx. 10min., then turn left on the street heading to Condeixa. Follow it for another 25min. until the bus stop. Taxis are a more expensive but secure bet (☎239 94 12 43).

The **Ruínas de Conímbriga** is Portugal's largest preserved Roman site. Highlights include a 3rd-century town wall, an ancient, luxurious villa, and baths complete with sauna and furnace room. Stunningly well-preserved mosaics are visible under the shelter of a glass canopy. (Open daily Mar. 16-Sept. 15 9am-8pm; Sept. 16-Mar. 15 9am-6pm. Ticket office closes 30min. before the ruins. €3, under 25 and seniors €1.50, under 14 free.) The ticket for the ruins includes the nearby **Museu Monográfico de Conímbriga** and its displays of regional artifacts. (☎239 94 11 77. Open Su and Tu-Sa same hours as the ruins.) The **tourist office** is inside the museum. (☎239 94 47 64; fax 94 14 74. Open daily 9am-12:30pm and 2-5:30pm.)

BUÇACO FOREST & LUSO

Buses run from Coimbra to Buçaco (45min.; M-F 7 per day 7:35am-7:20pm; Sa 2 per day 9am, 12:45pm; Su 2 per day 10:15am, 7:20pm; €2.70) before continuing on to Viseu. Buses back to Coimbra depart a few blocks from the Luso tourist office, across from the natural springs (35min.; M-F 5 per day 7:35am-6:35pm; Sa 2 per day 10:35am, 6:35pm; Su 1 per day 4:35pm; €2.50).

Home to Portugal's most revered forest, Buçaco (Bussaco) is a favorite weekend retreat for many residents of Coimbra. The forest has drawn wanderers in their escape from the city for centuries. Benedictine monks settled the Buçaco area in the 6th century, established a monastery, and remained in control until the 1834 disestablishment of all religious orders. The forest owes its fame, however, to the Carmelites, who arrived here barefoot and dead set on a life of seclusion, nearly 400 years ago. Selecting the forest for their *desertos* (isolated dwellings for penitence), the Carmelites planted over 700 types of trees and plants brought from around the world by missionaries. In the center of the forest, adjoining the old Carmelite convent, is Dom Carlos's exuberant **Palácio de Buçaco**. Now a luxury hotel, the building is a flamboyant display of neo-Manueline architecture. The *azulejos* on the outer walls depict scenes from Camões' *Os Lusíadas*, the great Portuguese epic about the Age of Discovery (see **Literature**, p. 626). In the forest itself, landmarks include the lovely **Fonte Fria** (Cold Fountain), the **Vale dos Fetos** (Fern Valley), and the **Porta de Rainha** (Queen's Gate). A 1hr. hike along the Via Sacra leads past 17th-century chapels to a sweeping panorama of the countryside from the **Cruz Alta** viewpoint. The tourist office in Luso has detailed maps describing the other 5 hikes, ranging from a 3hr. historic hike to 1hr. nature walks.

FIGUEIRA DA FOZ

Two words: bars and beaches. Figueira da Foz appeals to young pilgrims in search of the vacation Holy Land. The 3km beach, covered with recreational distractions from a bike track to beach soccer, is within spitting distance of a stretch of bars that keep crowds rocking until those with day jobs start waking up. As if that weren't enough, Figueira's infamous casino makes losing money an art.

F TRANSPORTATION. Trains run from **Coimbra** (1½hr.; M-Sa 20-24 per day 5:20am-12:20am, Su 17 per day 6:19am-12:20am; €1.55). From Figueira station, it's an easy 25min. to the tourist office and beach. With the river on your left, follow Av. de Saraiva de Carvalho as it becomes R. 5 de Outubro at the fountain and then curves into Av. 25 de Abril. For those wanting to save energy for the waves, the local **AVIC bus** goes to the center (7min., every 30min. until midnight, €0.80).

ORIENTATION & PRACTICAL INFORMATION. Packed with hotels, beachfront **Avenida 25 de Abril** runs the length of Figueira, turning into **Avenida Foz do Mondego** after the fortress before becoming **Avenida de Saraiva de Carvalho** as it nears the train station. Four blocks inland and parallel to Av. 25 de Abril, **Rua Bernardo Lopes** is lined with semi-affordable hostels and restaurants, as well as the heart of the city's nightlife. The **tourist office**, Av. 25 de Abril, 24, is next to Hotel Mecure, facing the beach. (☎233 40 28 27; fax 40 28 28. Open June-Aug. daily 9am-midnight; Sept. daily 9am-11pm; Oct.-May M-F 9am-5:30pm, Sa-Su 10am-12:30pm and 2:30-6:30pm.) The **police** are on R. Joaquim Carvalho (☎233 42 88 81), by the bus station. Take the "Gala" or "Hospital" bus (from in front of the market on R. 5 de Outubro; €0.80) or catch a cab (approx. €5) to the **Hospital Distrital de Figueira da Foz** (☎233 40 20 00), across the river in the Gala district. Two blocks behind the tourist office is the Internet cafe **Net Center**, R. da Liberdade, 25. (☎233 41 83 35. €1 per half hour. Open M-Sa 10am-11pm, Su 3-11pm.)

ACCOMMODATIONS & FOOD. Several *pensões* line R. Bernardo Lopes and R. Miguel Bombarda; prices are steep, and if you don't win at the casino, Coimbra is a much better bet. Partying all night and taking the morning train is not unusual. Comfortable **Pensão Residencial Bela Figueira ❸**, R. Miguel Bombarda, 13, is two blocks from the tourist office. The modern rooms are clean and close to the beach. (☎233 42 27 28. Doubles €30-60. AmEx/MC/V.) To reach the **Parque Municipal de Campismo da Figueira da Foz Municipal ❶** on Estrada Buarcos, walk up Av. 25 de Abril with the beach on your left, turn right at the rotary on R. Alexandre Herculano, then left at Parque Santa Caterina. A taxi from the bus or train station runs €3. The well-kept grounds have an Olympic-size pool (€1.75 per day), tennis courts (€2 per hr.), market, and currency exchange. (☎233 40 28 10. 2-person min. Reception June-Sept. 8am-8pm; Oct.-May 8am-7pm. Quiet hours midnight-7am. Showers €0.55 for 7min. Sites €1 per person, €2-2.50 per tent, €1.50 per car.)

Eating in Figueira da Foz is not cheap; bring a picnic basket and save your dough for the nightlife. Several restaurants and snack bars are scattered along **Rua Bernardo Lopes** and the beach. A local **market** offering fruit, bread, and beach gear sets up beside the public garden between Av. Foz do Mondego and R. Dr. Francisco A. Dinis. (open daily June-Sept. 15 7am-7pm; Sept. 16-May M-Sa 7am-4pm.) Fill your picnic basket at **Supermercado Ovo**, on the corner of R. Francisco António Dinis and R. Bernardo Lopes. (☎233 42 00 52. Open M-Sa 8:30am-8pm, Su 9am-2pm.) At **Restaurante Andaluz ❷**, R. Maestro David de Sousa, 91, the dark wood interior creates a striking contrast to the sunny beach outside. Excellent generous meals are served at some of the most reasonable prices in this resort town. *Pratos de dia* €6-10. (☎233 42 04 54. Open for meals daily noon-3pm and 7-10pm. Bar open until midnight. Beer €0.70. AmEx/MC/V.)

SIGHTS & ENTERTAINMENT. Just up from the public gardens on R. 5 de Outubro, the **Museu Municipal Dr. Santos Rocha,** in Parque Abadias, displays ancient coins and the fashions of Portuguese nobility along with a large collection of Portuguese sculpture. (R. Calouste Gulbenkian. ☎233 40 28 40. Open Tu-Su 9:30am-5:15pm. Free.) On R. Joaquim Sotto Mayor, the continuation of R. da Liberdade running parallel to the beach, the modest exterior of **Palácio Sotto Mayor** conceals the shameless extravagance within; lavish green marble columns line the main hallway, and gold leafing covers the ceiling. Sotto Mayor made his fortune as a Portuguese banker in the volatile Brazilian markets in the 19th century. (☎233 42 20 41. Open June-Aug. Tu-Su 2-6pm; Sept.-May Sa-Su 2-6pm. €1.) The drinking shenanigans that normally characterize Figueira's party life switch to a more religious tone with the **Festa de São João,** usually starting in mid-June and continuing through the first week of July. The party includes the biggest display of fireworks in the area, as well as a somber procession where the sea receives the official blessing of the Catholic Church for the good of the community. On the night of June 23, the eve of the **Dia de São João,** crowds of locals dance in the streets and on the beach, gleefully bonking each other on the head with plastic noisemakers. After a spectacular fireworks display at 1am, crowds congregate around bonfires along the beach until the 5am *banho santo* (holy bath), when the brave take a dip in the ocean, and the not-so-brave take pictures and applaud. The popular **casino complex,** on R. Dr. Calado, at the corner of R. Bernardo Lopes, houses a nightclub, huge showroom, and arcade. (☎233 40 84 00. Entrance 18+ with ID. Casino open daily 3pm-3am. Entrance to slot machines and bingo free. Game room open daily July-Aug. 4pm-3am; Sept.-June M-F 5pm-3am, Sa-Su 4pm-3am. Day pass €5.50, €11 on Saturdays. No shorts or sneakers.)

◪ NIGHTLIFE. The quality of bars and clubs is not on par with Lisboa, but for the hordes of beach-goers, that matters little. Easy socializing makes Figueira da Foz a night-time hot spot. The summer crowds get thick between 10pm and 2am and linger until dawn. Many bars and clubs with nightly summer hours are open only Friday and Saturday during the rest of the year. On winter weekdays, nightlife remains back in Coimbra. Crowds fill several nearby bars before hitting the small but up-and-coming club scene. **Rolls Bar** is an Irish pub at R. Poeta Acácio Antunes, 1E. The clever owners include guests in the price-making process, Wall Street style. A screen shows the price of drinks, like the price of stocks, and popularity makes them rise or fall. (Beer €1.50-2.50; mixed drinks €3-4. 1 drink min. Open July-Aug. daily 5pm-6am; Sept.-June M-Sa 5pm-6am.) Grab a Bacardi (€4) at Cuban bar **Havana**, R. Cândido dos Reis, 86. It's best around 11pm, although crowds filter in from 8pm on. Come on a Saturday and be surprised at the huge discounted drink parties, during which a specific drink is honored and consumed by liters. (☎233 43 48 99. Beer €1. Open Tu-Su 8pm-4am.) The new **Beach Club**, Esplanada Silva Guimarães, 3, on the terrace above the tourist office, features a downstairs dance floor and a chill bar and sandwich menu upstairs. Enter through the door to the left of the downstairs bar. (☎233 42 08 82. Beer €1. Popular martinis €2. Open daily 11am-4am.) End the night and bring on the morning at **Discoteca Bergantim**, R. Dr. Lopes Guimarães, a block from the beach. Crowds groove to pop and rock 5-7am; don't bother coming before 4am. (☎233 42 71 29. Beer €1.50; mixed drinks €4. Minimum €4 for women, €5 for men. Open July-Aug. daily 2-8am, Sept.-June F-Sa 2-8am.)

DOURO & MINHO

Plenty of Europeans lament the loss of the "old country," as if the big cities and big governments of the last century squashed the soul of the continent. Be that as it may, the march of progress must have lost its beat when it neared the regions of Minho and Douro. The sweeping vineyards that surround little villages make the traveler forget the teeming beaches and bustling cities of the south. Just like the rest of the country, the history of the area goes back to the Neolithic period— but only the very eccentric come to Douro and Minho to poke around old museums. Instead, the regions bring salvation to nature lovers. The purples, blues, and greens of the fruit orchards, vineyards, and olive trees are worthy of the most melodramatic romantic poetry. The mountain ranges that enclose the country are tough enough for hiking, camping, or just strolling. So although many come to get goofy with the *vinho do porto* and other local wines, the natural environment is not to be missed. Wine can be shipped; the Minho and Douro cannot.

HIGHLIGHTS OF DOURO & MINHO

TASTE famed wine of **Porto** for free by visiting its numerous port lodges (see p. 737).

MEDITATE in the spectacular Igreja do Bom Jesus, which was built to provide residents of **Braga** a pilgrimage site closer than Jerusalem(see p. 741).

IMAGINE yourself living the life of a medieval duke at the exquisite Paço dos Duques de Bragança in **Guimarães** (see **p. 742**).

CRAWL through ancient Celtic ruins on Monte de Santa Luzia while contemplating the picturesque surroundings of **Viana do Costelo** (see p. 747).

PORTO
☎ 22

Magnificently situated on a gorge cut by the Douro River just 6km from the sea, Portugal's second-largest city is characterized by an elegance reminiscent of Paris or Prague and feels more vibrant than Lisboa. The wine cellars that dot the banks of the Rio Douro are easily the most sought after attractions of the city, with free tours and samples. But Porto has more to offer than fine wine. It's a city with personality, totally distinct from heart-wrenching, *fado*-wailing Lisboa. A visit to Porto is not a nostalgic glance at the past, but a very comfortable stroll through the present; clever museums, a bustling stock exchange, and the wide variety of olives added to the sugary port wine form a package that locals prize and tourists relish.

▚ TRANSPORTATION

Flights: Aeroporto Francisco de Sá Carneiro (☎229 41 25 34), 13km from downtown. City bus #56 goes to the airport from R. do Carmo, but makes multiple stops. The **aerobus** from Av. dos Aliados near Pr. da Liberdade is more efficient. (40min., every 30min. 7am-6:30pm, €2.60.) Buy tickets on board. **Taxis** are even quicker (15-20min., €18-20). **TAP Air Portugal,** Pr. Mouzinho de Albuquerque, 105 (☎226 08 02 31), flies to most major European cities, with six daily shuttles to Lisboa (35min., €100-150).

Trains: Estação de Campanhã (☎225 36 41 41), on R. da Estação 2km east. To: **Aveiro** (1¼hr., 30 per day 5:05am-11:15pm, €1.70); **Braga** (1½-1¾hr., 21 per day 5:20am-11:20pm, €2.50); **Coimbra** (2hr., 17 per day 5:05am-12:05am, €5.60); **Faro** (9hr.; Tu, Th, and Su 1 per day 10:10pm; €19); **Lisboa** (3½-4½hr., 14 per day 6am-8:05pm, €15-21); **Madrid, ES** (13-14hr., 1 per day 6:10pm, €60), transfer at Entroncamento;

DOURO & MINHO

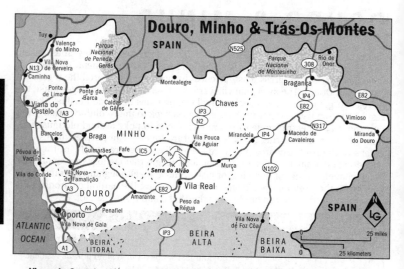

Viana do Castelo (1½-2hr., 12 per day 5:35am-12:35am, €2.30); **Vigo, ES** (2½hr.; 2 per day 7:40am, 6:55pm; €12.75). Buses #34 and 35 connect Campanhã to downtown (every 30min., €0.90). **Estação de São Bento** (☎222 00 27 22), Pr. Almeida Garrett, serves trains with mostly local and regional routes. Frequent connections to **Estação São Campanhã** (5-10min., every 20-30min. 5:55am-11:10pm, €0.75).

Buses: Several companies operate out of garages through the downtown area.

Internorte, Pr. Galiza, 96 (☎226 05 24 20) has service to **Madrid, ES** (10½hr.; Tu, Th, and Sa-Su 1 per day 9am; €34), as well as other international cities. Book 3 days ahead. Open M-F 9am-12:30pm and 2-6:30pm, Sa 9am-12:30pm and 2-4pm, Su 9am-12:30pm and 2-5:30pm.

Rede Expressos, R. Alexandre Herculano, 366 (☎222 05 24 59), sends buses to: **Braga** (1¼hr., 8 per day 9:25am-12:15am, €4.70); **Bragança** (5hr., 7 per day 7:15am-8:15pm, €8.20); **Coimbra** (1½hr., 11 per day 7:15am-12:45am, €7.50); **Lisboa** (4hr., 12 per day 7:15am-12:45am, €14); **Viana do Castelo** (1¾hr.; 2 per day 10:55am, 6:40pm; €8.20).

REDM, R. Dr. Alfredo Magalhães, 94 (☎222 00 31 52), 2 blocks from Pr. da República, has buses to **Braga** (1hr.; M-F 26 per day 6:45am-8pm, Sa-Su 9-12 per day 7:15am-8pm; €3.30).

Renex, Campo Mártires da Pátria (☎222 00 33 95), has express service via Lisboa to **Lagos** (8½hr., 6 per day 9am-1:15am, €18) and **Vila Real de Santo António** (9½hr., 5 per day 9am-1:15am, €20).

Rodonorte, R. Ateneu Comercial do Porto (☎222 00 43 98), goes to **Vila Real** (1¾hr.; M-F 16 per day 6:50am-10:30pm, Sa 7 per day 6:50am-9:20pm, Su 7 per day 6:50am-10:30pm; €5.50) via **Amarante** (1hr., €4.25).

Public Transportation: STCP (☎808 20 01 66) operates **tram** and **bus** lines throughout the city (both €0.55). Tickets purchased on the bus cost twice as much. Buy bus tickets beforehand at small kiosks around the city or at the **STCP** office, Pr. Almeida Garrett, 27 (open M-F 8am-7:30pm, Sa 8am-1pm). Buy 1-day unlimited tickets (€2.10) onboard.

Taxis: Taxis assemble on Av. dos Aliados and along the river in Ribeira. As in other larger cities, ask for a quote before getting in, and make sure the taxi has an electronic meter. **Radiotáxis,** R. de Alegria, 1802 (☎225 07 39 00).

ORIENTATION & PRACTICAL INFORMATION

Porto's heavy traffic and chaotic maze of one-way streets fluster travelers who come by car; if that's you, ditch the car in a safe parking lot and make the trek by foot. The city center is easy to navigate: hillside **Praça da Liberdade** is joined to

DOURO & MINHO

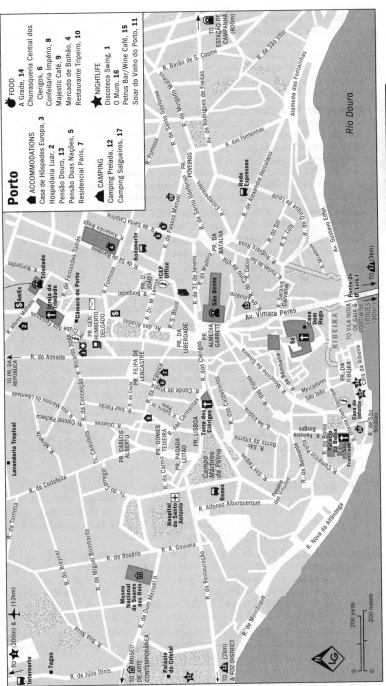

Porto

▲ ACCOMMODATIONS
Casa de Hóspedes Europa, 3
Hospedaria Luar, 2
Pensão Douro, 13
Pensão Duas Nações, 5
Residencial Paris, 7

♣ FOOD
A Grade, 14
Churrasqueria Central dos Clérigos, 6
Confeitaria Império, 8
Majestic Café, 9
Mercado de Bolhão, 4
Restaurante Tripeiro, 10

NIGHTLIFE
Discoteca Swing, 1
O Muro, 16
Petrus Bar/Wine Café, 15
Solar do Vinho do Porto, 11

▲ CAMPING
Camping Prelada, 12
Camping Salgueiros, 17

Praça General Humberto Delgado by **Avenida dos Aliados,** and the rest of the city radiates from these two squares. Between the Rio Douro and the city center lies the **Ribeira** district, where much of Porto's sights and nightlife are located on steep, narrow sidestreets. Directly across from Ribeira, the two-level **Ponte de Dom Luís I** spans the river to **Vila Nova de Gaia,** where the port wine cellars are located. Back on the other side of the river, 5km west of the center, is the **Foz** district, where beaches and nightclubs are the main attraction.

Tourist Office: Main office, R. Clube dos Fenianos, 25 (☎223 39 34 72). Open Aug.-Sept. daily 9am-7pm; Oct.-July M-F 9am-5:30pm, Sa-Su 9:30am-4:30pm. **Ribeira branch,** R. Infante Dom Henrique, 63 (☎222 00 97 70); same hours, same services. **ICEP (National Tourism) office,** Pr. Dom João I, 43 (☎222 05 75 14). Open July-Aug. daily 9am-7:30pm; Apr.-June and Sept.-Oct. M-F 9am-7:30pm, Sa-Su 9:30am-3:30pm; Nov.-Mar. M-F 9am-7pm, Sa-Su 9:30am-3:30pm. **Airport branch** (☎229 41 25 34). Open daily 8am-11:30pm. 24hr. multilingual **computer info stands** in the main shopping centers and the larger squares; one sits in front of McDonald's in Pr. da Liberdade.

Budget Travel: Tagus, R. Campo Alegre, 261 (☎226 09 41 46). English-speaking staff offers advice and student rates. Open M-F 9am-6pm, Sa 10am-1pm.

Currency Exchange: Portocâmbios, R. Rodrigues Sampaio, 193 (☎222 00 02 38). Open M-F 9am-6pm, Sa 9am-noon. **Automatic exchange machine** up Av. dos Aliados.

American Express: Top Tours, R. Alferes Malheiro, 96 (☎222 07 40 20). Handles all AmEx functions. Open M-F 9:30am-1:30pm and 2:30-6:30pm.

Luggage Storage: Free in the **tourist office** during the day. At **Estação de São Bento** (€12 per 48hr.). The lockers are a bit fussy at times. Open daily 5:15am-midnight.

Laundromat: Lavanderia Tropical, R. Bragas, 329 (☎222 05 13 97). Wash and dry €3 per kg. Open M-F 8:30am-6:30pm, Sa 9:30am-1pm. Closed the first 2 weeks in Aug.

Emergency: ☎112. **Police:** R. Clube dos Fenianos, 11 (☎222 08 18 33).

Late-Night Pharmacy: Rotation list posted on the door of every pharmacy (and printed in many newspapers) gives the address and phone number of pharmacy on 24hr. duty.

Hospital: Hospital de Santo António (☎222 07 75 00), on R. Alberto Aires Gouveia.

Internet Access: Portweb, Pr. Gen. Humberto Delgado, 291 (☎222 00 59 22). €1.20 per hr. Coffee €0.50. Open M-Sa 10am-2am, Su 3pm-2am. Plays classic MTV.

Post Office: Pr. Gen. Humberto Delgado (☎223 40 02 00). **Fax,** phone, and **Posta Restante.** Most services closed after 6pm. Open M-F 8:30am-9pm, Sa-Su 9am-6pm. **Postal Code:** 4000 for central Porto.

▐▛ ACCOMMODATIONS & CAMPING

Hostels in Porto are rarely charming and often overpriced. For the best deals, look west of Av. dos Aliados, or on R. de Fernandes Tomás and R. Formosa, perpendicular to Av. dos Aliados. Prices usually dip in the low season.

■ **Pensão Duas Nações,** Pr. Guilherme Gomes Fernandes, 59 (☎222 08 96 21; fax 08 16 16). The best combination of low price and comfortable rooms in town. To "keep the youngsters upbeat," the owner repaints the walls twice a year in bright colors. Rooms have large windows with small terraces and TV. Laundry €7 per load. Internet €0.50 per 15min. Reserve ahead. Singles €12.50-€15, with bath €20; doubles €22/€25-30; triples €30/€35; quads €40/€45; 1 room with 6 beds and bath €11 per person. ❶

Hospedaria Luar, R. Alferes Malheiro, 133 (☎222 087 845). Recently constructed rooms offer huge spaces, cable TV, and private bath. Ask the owner about doing a load of laundry for €5. Singles €20-25; doubles €25-30. ❷

Residencial Paris, R. da Fábrica, 27-29 (☎222 07 31 40). To sleep among Porto's history, this is the place, in business since 1888. The charming old building with marble staircases also houses a classic upright piano and a luxury breakfast room with a buffet. All rooms come with private bath, TV, and phone; half with full balconies. Apr.-Oct. singles €35; doubles €45. Nov.-Mar. €30/€40. ❹

Casa de Hôspedes Europa, R. do Almada, 398 (☎222 00 69 71). Above a restaurant of the same name. Nothing extravagant, but convenient and clean. Singles €15, with bath €25; doubles €20/€30. AmEx/MC/V. ❶

Pensão Douro, R. do Loureiro, 54 (☎222 05 32 14), closer to the river than many of the other *pensões*. The old-fashioned rooms come with couches and lots of space; for those interested in spending little, staying close to the action, and bypassing the amenities. Singles €12.50, with bath €15-20; doubles €17.50/€20-30. ❶

Camping: Camping Prelada (☎228 31 26 16), on R. Monte dos Burgos, in Quinta da Prelada, 4km from the town center and 5km from the beach. Take bus #6, 50, 54, or 87 from Pr. da Liberdade (only #50 and 54 run at night). Reception 8am-1am. €3 per person, €3-3.50 per tent, €2.60 per car. ❶

Camping: Camping Salgueiros, R. do Campismo (☎227 81 05 00; fax 81 01 36), near Praia Salgueiros in Vila Nova de Gaia. A less accessible and less equipped campsite, but also less expensive and closer to the beach. To get there, catch the green Espírito Santo bus from Pr. da Batalha in front of the Teatro Nacional de São João (€1.10). €1.50 per person, €1.50-2 per tent, €0.75 per car. ❶

DOURO & MINHO

🗒 FOOD

Quality budget meals can be found near Pr. da Batalha on **Rua Cimo de Vila** and **Rua Cativo**. Places selling *bifanas* (small pork sandwiches) line R. Bomjardim. Ribeira is the place to go for a high-quality, affordable dinner, particularly on **Cais da Ribeira, Rua Reboleira,** and **Rua Cima do Muro.** Local *azeitarias* (olive houses) offer a fantastic selection of olives tucked between the tourist traps. Adventurous eaters can try the city's specialty, *tripas à moda do Porto* (tripe and beans), if chewy and greasy cow innards sound appealing. The 🖾**Mercado de Bolhão** has an enormous selection, including fresh bread, cheese, meat, and olives. The upper level has fresh produce. (Open M-F 8:30am-5pm, Sa 8:30am-1pm.)

🖾 **Confeitaria Império,** R. de Santa Catarina, 149-151 (☎222 00 55 95). Founded in 1941, this *pastelaría* has a huge selection of excellent pastries and inexpensive lunch specials (€3) served in the back dining room. Try the *especialidade Império* pastry (€0.60). Open M-Sa 7:30am-8:30pm. A new **branch** at R. de Fernandes Tomás, 755, is the largest self-service cafe in the city, selling a variety of meals and snacks. ❶

Majestic Café, R. de Santa Catarina, 112 (☎222 00 38 87). One of the best snapshots of 19th-century bourgeois opulence, the cafe is the oldest and best-known in the city. The management knows it, so be careful with the overpriced sandwiches, cigars, and pastries. Best for a coffee and a look around at the chandeliers and sculptures of cherubim grinning like they know something you don't. Sandwiches €4-10. Elaborate pastries €4-6. Fine cigars €6-23. Open M-Sa 9:30am-midnight. AmEx/MC/V. ❷

Churrasqueria Central dos Clerigos, R. da Fábrica, 69 (☎222 57 49 21). A lively and cheerful restaurant lined with *azulejos*, this *churrasquería* offers assorted grilled fish and meat dishes accompanied by generous portions of salad and other extras. *Pratos do dia* are perfect for experimenting cheaply with local cuisine. Entrees €2.50-7. Open M-Sa noon-3:30pm and 7:30-10:30pm. ❶

A Grade, R. de São Nicolau, 9 (☎223 32 11 30), in Ribeira. A welcoming restaurant furnished with old-fashioned wooden tables, benches, and wine bottles. Tasty lunch *menú* (€6-7). Entrees are €5-10, while specialties like *polvo assado no forno* (octopus) and *cabrito assado no forno* (goat) run €10-11. Open daily M-Sa 9am-midnight. ❷

Restaurante Tripeiro, R. de Passos Manuel, 195 (☎222 00 58 86). Well-prepared dishes, including regional specialties. Perfect for a night of classy dining without the touristy atmosphere. Entrees €8-15. Open M-Sa noon-3pm and 7-10pm. ❸

🅞 SIGHTS

Your first brush with Porto's rich stock of fine artwork may be, of all places, at Estação de São Bento, home to a celebrated collection of *azulejos*. Up Av. dos Aliados in Pr. General Humberto Delgado, the formidable **Câmara do Porto** (City Hall) is a monument to Porto's late 19th-century greatness.

🅿 PALÁCIO DA BOLSA. The elegant *Palácio da Bolsa* (Stock Exchange) was built from 1842 to 1910 over the ruins of the Convento de São Francisco after it was destroyed by fire in 1832. At the entrance is the **Pátio das Nações** (Hall of Nations), which served as the trading floor of the stock exchange until 1991 when the building was given to the Commerce Society of Oporto. The domed ceiling is decorated with the coats of arms of 20 countries friendly with Portugal. Leading up to the top floor is the **Escadaria Nobre** (Noble Staircase), decorated with carved granite and topped with two giant bronze chandeliers each weighing over one metric ton. Among the exquisitely decorated rooms is the **Sala dos Retratos** (Portrait Room), which features a wooden table that took a man and his pocket knife three painstaking years to carve. The most striking room of the *Palácio* is the opulent **Sala Árabe** (Arabian Hall). The green crests on the ceiling proclaim "Allah above all," and its gold and silver walls are covered with the oddly juxtaposed inscriptions "Glory to Allah" and "Glory to Dona Maria II." Note that the door to the hall is set slightly off-center—an intentional alteration to symbolize that only Allah is perfect. The various rooms of the *Palácio* are now used for occasional ceremonies and official receptions. (*R. Ferreira Borges.* ☎223 39 90 00. *Open daily Apr.-Oct. 9am-7pm, Nov.-Mar. 9am-1pm and 2-6pm. Multilingual tours every 30min. €5, students €3.*)

SÉ. Fortified on the hilltop slightly south of the train station is Porto's imposing Romanesque *Sé* (cathedral). Built in the 12th and 13th centuries, the Gothic, *azulejo*-covered cloister was added later in the 14th century. The **Capela do Santíssimo Sacramento,** to the left of the high altar, shines with solid silver and plated gold and is used as the bishop's study. During the Napoleonic invasion, crafty townspeople whitewashed the altar to avoid vandalism. Climb the staircase to the Renaissance chapter house for a splendid view of the old quarter. (*Terreiro da Sé.* ☎222 05 90 28. *Open M-Sa 9am-12:30pm and 2:30-6pm, Su 2:30-6pm. Cloister €1.25.*)

IGREJA DE SÃO FRANCISCO. The Gothic and Baroque eras of ecclesiastical architecture favored gilded wood, no question. But they outdid themselves with this church. In all of Portugal, few if any chapels approach its detail and sheer quantity of glittering handiwork. Under the floor, thousands of human bones are stored in preparation for Judgment Day. (*R. Infante Dom Henrique.* ☎222 06 21 00. *Open daily 9am-6pm. €3, students €1.50.*)

MUSEU DE ARTE CONTEMPORÂNEA. This museum rotates exhibits of contemporary Portuguese art and architecture, as well as international photography and sculpture. Its 44 colossal acres of manicured gardens, fountains, and old farmland tumbling down toward the Douro River are also easy on the eyes. (*R. D. João de Castro, 210.* ☎226 15 65 00. *Several km out of town, on the way to the beach. Bus #78 leaves from*

Av. dos Aliados; ask the driver to stop at the museum (30min., return buses run until midnight). Museum open Tu-W, F, Sa 10am-7pm, Th 10am-10pm. Park closes at 7pm daily. Museum and park €5, park only €2.50. Free Su before 2pm.)

IGREJA E TORRE DOS CLÉRIGOS. The 18th-century **Igreja dos Clérigos** is decorated with Baroque and Rococo carvings. Its **Torre dos Clérigos** is the city's tallest landmark, reaching a height of 75.6m. Atop the 200 steps await spectacular views of Porto and the Rio Douro valley. *(R. dos Clérigos. ☎222 00 17 29. Church open M-Th 10am-noon and 2-5pm, Sa 10am-noon and 2-8pm, Su 10am-1pm. Tower open daily Sept.-July 9:30am-1pm and 2:30-7pm, Aug. 9:30am-7pm. Church free, tower €1.)*

MUSEU NACIONAL DE SOARES DOS REIS. A former royal residence, this 18th-century museum houses an exhaustive collection of 19th-century Portuguese painting and sculpture, much of it by Soares dos Reis, often called Portugal's Michelangelo. *(R. Dom Manuel II, 44. ☎223 39 37 70. Open Tu 2-6pm, W-Su 10am-6pm. €3, seniors and students €1.50. Free Su until 2pm.)*

JARDINS DO PALÁCIO DE CRISTAL. Beautiful gardens lie outside the *Palácio do Cristal* (Glass Palace). Take a gander at the geese, swans, ducks, peacocks, and fountains. *(R. Dom Manuel II. ☎226 05 70 80. Open daily until dark.)*

DOURO & MINHO

🎇 PORT LODGES

Everyone knows why you're here. All of the port lodges are located across the river in the nearby suburb, **Vila Nova da Gaia.** Cross the lower level of **Ponte de Dom Luís I.** Many lodges offer free tasting tours on which you can note the differences between British and Portuguese lodges. Remember: you still need to cross the bridge to get back to the city.

🍷 **Taylor's,** R. do Choupelo, 250 (☎223 74 28 00). Easily the most inviting of the lodges, Taylor's plays up its 300-year history. The wonderful staff will wow you with service and knowledge of port, and free sampling induces inebriation. A warning to those who don't respect the sanctity of the port: Taylor's doesn't look kindly upon those looking for a free ride, and burgeoning connoisseurs are encouraged. The outdoor garden, complete with squawking peacocks, adds to the relaxed ambience. Free tours (every 20-30min.) and tasting. Open Aug. M-Sa 10am-6pm, Sept.-July M-F 10am-6pm; last visit starts 5pm.

Sandeman, Lgo. Miguel Bombarda, 3 (☎223 74 05 33), just off Av. Diogo Leite. The bigshot of Vila Nova da Gaia, with costumed guides, a souvenir shop, and a museum. Tours (every 15min.) last about 30min. €2.50, under 16 free. Tickets are good for a €3 discount at the gift shop. Open Apr.-Oct. daily 10am-12:30pm and 2-6pm; Nov.-Mar. M-F 9:30am-12:30pm and 2-5pm. AmEx/MC/V.

Calém, Av. Diogo Leite, 26 (☎23 74 66 60), right along the river with the enormous sign. Those with a heavy thirst can expand the two-wine sample to a five-wine selection. Tours every 15-20min. Open daily 10am-6pm. AmEx/MC/V.

🎇 NIGHTLIFE

For whatever reason, Porto is not a party house after hours. Most people congregate around the bar-restaurants of **Ribeira,** where spicy Brazilian music plays until 2am. The narrow streets and poor lighting, however, can be spooky; don't go alone. Pr. da Ribeira, Muro dos Bacalhoeiros, and R. Nova da Alfândega harbor most of the bars and pubs. Be cautious, as Pr. da Ribeira and Cais da Ribeira can be unsafe at night. Most clubs are located along the river in **Foz** and in the new industrial zones; nightlife in Porto is hard to follow without a car. Bus #1 runs all night from Pr. da Liberdade to the beach at Matosinhos, passing Foz along the way. A taxi to Foz from downtown costs about €4.

Solar do Vinho do Porto, R. Entre Quintas, 220 (☎226 09 47 49). Twin sister of the *Solar* in Lisboa, this is a good choice if you're still not tired of port. Nicer than the lodges, since it's exclusively for tasting and sipping. Once a manor house, the upscale lounge has a terrace with river view. Port €1.50-€15. Open M-Sa 2pm-midnight. MC/V.

O Muro, Muro dos Bacalhoeiros, 87-88 (☎222 08 34 26), a pedestrian street in Ribeira. A remarkable restaurant during the day, O Muro later attracts night owls with a great view of the river and the complimentary olives and *tremoço*, a local edible seed, that come with each beer. Beer €1. Open Tu-Su noon-2am.

Petrus Bar/Wine Café, R. Fonte Taurina, 97 (☎919 86 77 80). During the day, Petrus is a cool escape from the sun. At night, cool jazz, soul, and blues stream from the lounge. The patio is a perfect spot to enjoy the view of the port lodges across the river. Live music on the patio Sa 3-7pm, inside W 10am-2pm. Beer €1.50-2.50. Mixed drinks €3.50. Open daily 10:30am-5am.

Discoteca Swing, Pr. Engenheiro Amaro Costa, 766 (☎226 09 00 19). Guest DJs rock the weekends, while regular house, new wave, and Latin go strong during the week. Th is ladies' night with 3 free drinks. No cover M-W, €7.50-€12.50 Th-Su. Beer €3. Mixed drinks €7.50. Open daily midnight-7am, but the fun starts around 1am.

◗ FESTIVALS

Porto hosts the **Fantasporto Film Festival** (2 weeks during February), screening international fantasy, sci-fi, and horror flicks for crowds of film enthusiasts. Early June brings the **Festival Internacional de Teatro de Expressão Ibérica,** which stages free performances of Portuguese and Spanish drama. Porto's biggest party, however, is the **Festa de São João** (June 23-24), when locals storm the streets for free concerts, folklore, *fado*, and (of course) wine. Although not as big a production as in Lisboa, the northern version is still a guaranteed entertainer.

BRAGA
☎253

In Braga (pop. 160,000), a fountain graces every plaza, loudspeakers channel music to the streets, and gardens breathe freshness into urban air. A city impressive enough on its own, it is a shame that Braga goes by a nickname—"Portuguese Rome"—that identifies it through another country's city. The AD 1926 coup that paved Salazar's path to power was launched from here, and the city retains conservative tendencies to this day. During Holy Week, religious processions cross flower-carpeted streets and somber devotion explodes into fireworks and dancing. Those who come to Braga expecting just to pass through often end up staying for several days, as the city makes a convenient base for worthwhile daytrips.

▤ TRANSPORTATION

Trains: The train station is closed for construction into 2005.

Buses: The bus station is the **Central de Camionagem** (☎253 61 60 80 or 68 31 33), a few blocks north of the city center. **Rodoviária** runs to: **Coimbra** (3hr., 6-9 per day 6am-11:30pm, €8); **Faro** (12-15hr., 9 per day 6am-11:30pm, €17); **Guimarães** (1hr., every 30min. 7am-8pm, €1.90); **Lisboa** (5¼hr., 8-9 per day 9:30am-11:30pm, €12). **Rede Expressos** runs to **Porto** (1¾hr., every 45min. 6:45am-8pm, €3.80). **Hoteleira do Gerês** runs to **Caldas de Gerês** (1½hr., 17-18 per day 6am-11:30pm, €7.50).

Taxis: ☎253 61 40 19.

DOURO & MINHO

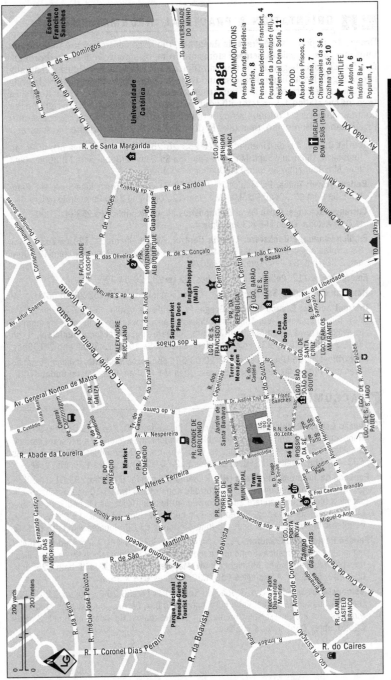

Braga

ACCOMMODATIONS
Pensão Grande Residência Avenida, **8**
Pensão Residencial Francfort, **4**
Pousada da Juventude (HI), **3**
Residencial Dona Sofia, **11**

FOOD
Abade dos Priscos, **2**
Café Vianna, **7**
Churrasqueira da Sé, **9**
Cozinha da Sé, **10**

★ **NIGHTLIFE**
Café Astoria, **6**
Insólito Bar, **5**
Populum, **1**

DOURO & MINHO

✈ ⓘ ORIENTATION & PRACTICAL INFORMATION

Braga's focal point is the **Praça da República**, the large central square full of fountains and cafes. **Avenida Liberdade** stems out from the square. Pedestrian thoroughfare **Rua do Souto** begins at the tourist office corner of Pr. da República, eventually becoming R. Dom Diogo de Sousa and then R. Andrade de Corvo, before leading straight to the currently under-construction **train station.** To get to Pr. da República from the **bus station,** take a left with your back to the entrance, and turn right up the commercial street. Continue straight under the modern building's overpass onto Pr. Alexandre Herculano, then take R. dos Cháos straight ahead into the square.

Tourist Office: Av. da Liberdade, 1 (☎253 26 25 50; www.cm-braga.pt), in Pr. da República. Open July-Sept. M-F 9am-7pm, Sa-Su 9am-12:30pm and 2-5:30pm; Oct.-June M-F 9am-7pm, Sa 9am-12:30pm and 2-5:30pm.

Budget Travel: Tagus, Pr. Município, 7 (☎253 21 51 44). Open June-Sept. M-F 9am-6pm, Sa 9am-12:30pm; Oct.-May M-F 9am-12:30pm and 2:30-6pm. AmEx/MC/V.

Currency Exchange: Caixa Geral de Depósitos, Pr. da República (☎253 60 01 00), next to Café Astória. Open M-F 8:30am-3pm.

English-Language Bookstore: Livraria Central, Av. da Liberdade, 728 (☎253 26 23 83). Small selection of books and travel guides in English. Open M-F 9am-12:30pm and 2:30-7pm, Sa 9am-1pm. AmEx/MC/V.

Emergency: ☎112. **Police:** R. dos Falcões, 12 (☎253 20 04 20).

Hospital: Hospital de São Marcos, Lgo. Carlos Amarante, 6e (☎253 20 90 00).

Internet Access: Espaço Internet Braga, Pr. Conde de Agrolongo, 177 (☎254 26 74 84). Ten computers. Free. 1hr. limit if there are people waiting; go in the early morning to avoid a crowd. Open M-F 9am-7:30pm, Sa 9am-1pm. **Videoteca Municipal,** R. do Raio, 2 (☎253 26 77 93). Free; 1hr. limit. Open M-Sa 10am-12:30pm and 2-6:30pm.

Post Office: Av. da Liberdade (☎253 20 03 64). For **Posta Restante,** indicate "Estação Avenida." Phone, fax, and other services. Open M-F 8:30am-6pm. **Postal Code:** 4700.

🏠 ACCOMMODATIONS

Pensão Grande Residência Avenida, Av. da Liberdade, 738, 2nd fl. (☎253 60 90 20). Handsome rooms with phones and cable TV overlook the avenue or a backyard garden. Breakfast included. June-Sept. singles €20, with bath €25; doubles €27/€37; triples €33. Oct.-May singles €15/€20; doubles €22.50/€27.50; triples €30. MC/V. ❷

Pousada da Juventude de Braga (HI), R. Santa Margarida, 6 (☎/fax 253 61 61 63). A taxi from the train station costs €4. Crowded dorm rooms, with 8-10 beds each, are offset by a friendly atmosphere and a convenient location. Fills with school groups Apr.-May and tourists June-Aug. Reception 8am-midnight. June 16-Sept. 15 dorms €9.50; doubles with bath €26.50. Sept. 15-June 15 dorms €7.50; doubles with bath €21. ❶

Pensão Residencial Francfort, Av. Central, 7 (☎253 25 25 48). A large red tiled building in a premium location. Some of the rooms overlook the fountain in Pr. da República. Reception 8am-midnight. Midnight curfew. May-Sept. singles €20, with bath €25; doubles €20/€35. Oct.-Apr. singles €13/€20; doubles €18/€25. ❷

Residencial Dona Sofía, Lgo. S. João do Souto, 131 (☎253 26 31 60; fax 61 12 45). The spacious rooms in this 3-star hotel come with bar, TV, A/C, phone, bath, and large windows and are an excellent break from budget rooms. Breakfast included. Singles €45; doubles €55; suites €70. ❹

Camping: **Camping Parque da Ponte** (☎253 27 33 55), 2km down Av. da Liberdade from the center, next to the stadium and the municipal pool. Buses every 20min. 6:30am-11pm. Laundry facilities. €1.80 per person, €1.40 per tent, €1.50 per car. ❶

◨ FOOD

Braga has many cafés and several superb restaurants. A **market** sets up in Pr. do Comércio. (Open M-Sa 7am-3pm.) For fast meals, head to the food court of the **BragaShopping** mall, facing the plaza (☎253 20 80 10). Supermarket **Pingo Doce** is in the basement. (Open daily 10am-11pm.)

Churrasqueira da Sé, R. D. Paio Mendes, 25 (☎253 26 33 87). An efficient and popular restaurant, serving delicious and generous half-portions to lunchtime crowds (€5). *Prato do dia* €3.50-7.50. Open Th-Tu 9:30am-3pm and 6:30-9:30pm. ❶

Abade de Priscos, Pr. Mouzinho de Albuquerque, 7, 2nd fl. (☎253 27 66 50). Named after a priest who died in the 1930s and who is still widely considered to have been Portugal's best chef, this restaurant serves traditional Portuguese cuisine. Small menu of excellent entrees prepared with care (€7-10). Open M 7:30-9:30pm, Tu-Sa noon-2:30pm and 7:30-9:30pm. Closed last 3 weeks of July. ❷

Café Vianna, Pr. da República, 87 (☎253 26 23 36). This marble and velvet-lined cafe is packed at midnight in summer. *Prato do dia* €4.25. Sandwiches €3.50-5. Open May-Sept. daily 8am-2am. Oct.-Apr. closed Su. AmEx/MC/V. ❶

Cozinha da Sé, R. D. Frei Caetano Brandão, 95 (☎253 27 73 43). This spot boasts excellent service and some of the most affordable and well-prepared fish dishes in Braga. Entrees €6-10. Open Tu-Su 12:30-3pm and 7:30-10pm. AmEx/MC/V. ❷

◉ SIGHTS

IGREJA DO BOM JESUS. Braga's most famous landmark crowns a hillside 5km outside of town. This 18th-century church was built in an effort to recreate Jerusalem in Braga, providing Iberian Christians with a pilgrimage site closer to home. To visit, take either the 285m ride on the antique cable car (8am-8pm, €1) or a 25-30min. walk up the granite-paved pathway. On the way up, check out the 365-step zig-zagging **staircase** depicting, among other things, the stations of the cross, fountains representing the five senses ("smell" spouts water through a boy's nose), and stony prophets. The church, a few small cafes, and stunning sunset views await at the top. **Café Esplanada** (open daily 8am-midnight) is a popular place to wait for the sunset with a drink or sandwich. *(Buses labeled "#02 Bom Jesus" depart at 10 and 40min. past the hr. in front of Farmácia Cristal, Av. da Liberdade, 571. Buses stop at the bottom of the stairway; the last bus from Bom Jesus leaves at 9pm. €1.09.)*

CATHEDRAL. Braga's **Sé**, Portugal's oldest cathedral, has undergone a series of renovations since its construction in the 11th and 12th centuries. Guided tours (in Portuguese, French, or English, depending on the guide) of its treasury, choir, and chapels run frequently during visiting hours. The treasury showcases the archdiocese's most precious paintings and relics. On display is the *Cruz do Brasil*, an iron cross from the ship Pedro Álvares Cabral commanded when he discovered Brazil on April 22, 1500. Perhaps most curious is the cathedral's collection of *cofres cranianos* (brain boxes), one of which contains the 6th-century cortex of São Martinho Dume, Braga's first bishop. Near a Renaissance cloister lie the cathedral's two historic chapels. The more notable, **Capela dos Reis,** guards the 12th-century stone sarcophagi of Dom Afonso Henriques's parents and mummified remains of a 14th-century archbishop. Also of interest is the choir—its organ has 2,424 fully functional gold pipes. (☎253 26 33 17. Mass daily 5pm. Open daily June-Aug. 8:30am-6:30pm, Sept.-May 8:30am-5pm. Cathedral free. Treasury and chapels €2.)

🔾 FESTIVALS

Braga's biggest festival of the year is the **Festa de São João**, a week-long celebration peaking the night of June 23. The biggest bash is supposedly in Porto, but the *bracarenses* don't fall too far behind; traditional folk music, good food, colorful lights and decorations, concerts, and general revelry take over Av. da Liberdade and Lgo. São João da Ponte. Don't be surprised to see locals running around beating each other on the head with toy hammers. Few seem to remember the bizarre ritual's origin, but older folks relate that it's a tribute to São João, Protector of the Head.

🔾 NIGHTLIFE

The cafés in **Praça da República** fill with people after midnight. The upstairs bar of **Café Astória**, Pr. da República, 5, next door to Café Vianna, is a popular student hangout after midnight. The bar has red velvet curtains and couches and a large balcony overlooking the plaza. (☎966 08 36 97. Beer €0.75. Open M-Sa 8am-6am, Su 10am-6am.) Nearby is the **Insólito Bar,** Av. Central, 47, between Pr. da República and the youth hostel. Live music in the large yard out back attracts a university crowd of students and professors. (☎968 01 62 40. Beer €1. Mixed drinks €2.50. Minimum consumption M-Th €1, F-Sa €2.50. Open M-Sa 10pm-4am. Closed Aug.) Another nightspot is **Praça Conde de Agrolongo** (a.k.a. Campo da Vinha). Here, **Populum** is popular. (€1.50 minimum consumption. Open Th-Sa 10pm-5am.) Bars on **Rua do Taxa** and around **Universidad do Minho**, 10min. down Av. Central off Pr. da República, begin to fill up around midnight. The area around Pr. do Comércio between Tr. do Carmo and R. Alferes Ferreira is quite dangerous at night; be cautious after dark.

🔾 DAYTRIPS FROM BRAGA

MOSTEIRO DE TIBÃES

A city bus labeled "Sarrido" heads 6km from Braga to the monastery. Buses leave from the bus stop at the corner of Pr. Conde de Agrolongo and Av. Visc. Nespereira (25min.; every hr. at 5min. and 35min. past the hr., 8:05am-7:35pm; €1.10).

Surrounded by unspoiled forest, this peaceful 11th-century Benedictine monastery has suffered from centuries of neglect. Stones rattle underfoot in the weathered cloister. The monastery is undergoing much-needed restoration; check with the tourist office in Braga or the monastery office to find out which areas are open for visits. Adjoining the cloister is an exceptionally well-preserved church. (☎253 62 26 70. Open Tu-Su 10am-noon and 1-6:30pm. €4, age 14-25 €2, under 14 free.)

GUIMARÃES

REDM buses (☎253 51 62 29) run from Braga to Guimarães (40min.; M-F 19 per day 7:15am-8:35pm, Sa-Su 13-15 per day 8am-8:35pm; €2.15), and return (40min.; M-F 19 per day 6:30am-8:30pm, Sa-Su 13-15 per day 6:55am-8:30pm; €2.15).

Ask any native about Guimarães (pop. 60,000), and they will tell you that it was the birthplace of the nation. Guimarães was the hometown of the first king of Portugal, Afonso Henriques, and the site of his initial court in the 12th century. It was also where the Portuguese *Reconquista* began. One of Portugal's most gorgeous palatial estates, the ◨**Paço dos Duques de Bragança** (Ducal Palace), is modeled after the manors of northern Europe. The museum inside includes furniture, silverware, tapestries, and weapons once used at the palace. Don't miss the elaborate Pastrana tapestries in the **Sala dos Pasos Perdidos** (Hall of Lost Footsteps) or the interesting display of archaic weaponry in the **Sala das Armas** (Arms Room). Up a few steep steps from the courtyard is the **capela**. (Palace open daily 9:30am-12:30pm and 2-5:30pm. €3, ages 15-25 and seniors €1.50. Su mornings free.) Overlooking the city is the **Monte da Penha**, home to an excellent campsite as well as picnic areas, mini-golf, and cafes. To get there, take the **teleférico** (skyride) which runs from Lgo. das Hortas to the mountaintop. (☎253 51 50 85. Open Apr.-July and Sept. M-F 11am-7pm, Sa-Su 10am-8pm; Aug. daily 10am-8pm. €1.50, round-trip €2.50.)

The **train station** is a 10min. walk down Av. Afonso Henriques from the tourist office. The **bus station** (☎253 51 62 29) is in the **GuimarãeShopping** complex, on Alameda Mariano Felgueiras. To get there, follow Av. Conde Margaride downhill. The main **tourist office** is on Alameda de São Dâmaso, 83, facing Largo do Toural. From the bus station, take Av. Conde Margaride to the right, walk uphill, and turn right at the fork onto R. Paio Galvão; the tourist office is two streets across from the far corner of Largo do Toural. The English-speaking staff distributes maps and brochures and offers short-term **luggage storage**. (☎253 41 24 50. Open June-Sept. M-Sa 9:30am-7pm; Oct.-May M-Sa 9:30am-6pm.) Other services include: **emergency** ☎112; **police** on Alameda Alfredo Pimenta (☎253 51 33 34); **hospital** on R. dos Cutileiros (☎253 51 26 12). Follow the crowds for lunch at **Restaurante O Pinguim** ❷, Tr. do Picoto, off R. Picoto. From Lgo. Navarros de Andrade, go up Av. Humberto Delgado (across the square from the post office) and take a left onto R. Picoto up the hill, then another left off the street as it curves to the right. Their specialty is *bacalhau à pinguimu*, a salted cod dish (€12.25, serves 2). Other entrees run €4.75-9. (☎253 41 81 82. Open Tu-Su 8am-10:30pm; serves meals 11:30am-3:30pm and 7-10:30pm. AmEx.)

BARCELOS

REDM buses (☎253 80 83 00) leave from Av. Dr. Sidónio Pais, 245, across from Campo da República, and run frequently to Braga (40-50min.; M-Sa 6:30am-7:20pm, Su 6:50am-7:20pm; €1.60).

Though Barcelos is known throughout Portugal for its famous rooster, the town also hosts one of the largest weekly markets in Europe—vendors from the entire region come on Thursdays to sell everything from produce to local ceramics. This market, the **Feira de Barcelos**, was inaugurated in 1412 by Dom João I. Vendors begin arriving at the huge **Campo da República** late Wednesday night to set up, and by 8am on Thursday, the market is going at full force. Old ladies carry live roosters by the feet, artisans display traditional ceramics, and aggressive pastry sellers work from trucks on the square's edge along Av. da Liberdade. Even if you miss market day, it's still worth the trip. The **Templo do Bom Jesus**, in main Lgo. da Porta Nova is an octagonal Baroque church dating from 1704 with a golden altar. In Lgo. do Município is the 17th-century **Igreja Matriz**, a Gothic church. Behind the church is the 14th-century **Paço Condal**, site of the famous monument to the Barcelos cock. The Paço has also hosted the **Museu Arqueológico** since 1920. (All sights open daily 9am-noon and 1-5pm. Free.)

The **tourist office** is in the Torre da Porta Nova, part of the town's original 15th-century wall and the only remaining of three towers that once marked the entrance to the ancient city. The office provides short-term **luggage storage**. (☎/fax 253 81 18 82; www.camaramunicipal.bcl.pt. Open Mar.-Oct. M-F 10am-6pm, Sa 10am-12:30pm and 2:30-5:30pm, Su 2:30-5:30pm; Nov.-Feb. M-F 9:30am-5:30pm, Sa 10am-12:30pm and 2:30-5pm.) Services include: **emergency** (☎112) and the **police** on Av. Dr. Sidónio Pais (☎253 80 25 70).

PARQUE NACIONAL DE PENEDA-GERÊS

A crescent-shaped nature reserve along the Spanish border, the Parque Nacional de Peneda-Gerês became Portugal's first protected area in 1971. This park consists of the northern Serra da Peneda and the southern Serra do Gerês. The main base is Caldas de Gerês, a spa town in the south. The park is one of the most popular destinations for Portuguese vacationers in July and August, but those who venture farther away from Caldas de Gerês can find areas to relax any time of year.

TRANSPORTATION & PRACTICAL INFORMATION. Empresa Hoteleira do Gerês (☎253 61 58 96) runs **buses** between **Gerês** and **Braga** (1½hr.; M-Sa 10-17 per day 6:30am-7:55pm, Su 7 per day 7:15am-8:25pm; €3). To get to the **tourist office** from the bus stop, walk uphill along Av. Manuel Francisco da Costa; the office is surrounded by a semicircle of shops. The English-speaking staff provides info on the national park and **luggage storage.** (☎253 39 11 33. Open M-Sa 9:30am-12:30pm and 2:30-6pm, Su 9:30am-12:30pm.) The **police** (☎253 39 11 37) are off Av. Manuel Francisco da Costa. The **post office** is located off the rotary that leads uphill into the center. (☎253 39 00 10; fax 39 00 16. Open M-F 9am-12:30pm and 2-5:30pm.)

ACCOMMODATIONS & FOOD. There are plenty of *pensões* in Gerês. One option is **Casa de Ponte ❷**, on Av. D. João V. From the bus stop, head downhill until you see the hostel on the left corner where the road splits, next to the Escola Primaria. The English-speaking owner offers rooms with baths and TV. Most also have porches overlooking the garden. (☎253 39 11 25. Midnight curfew. Aug.-Oct. singles €25; doubles €40; triples €45. May-July €20/€30/€35. Nov.-Apr. €15/€20/€35.) For camping, try **Camping Vidoeiro ❶**, 1km out of town by the river. Facing the tourist office, take the uphill road to the left. (☎253 39 12 89. Open May 15-Oct. 15. Reception 8am-7pm. €2 per person, €1.75-2.25 per tent, €2.25 per car.) Meals are available at the *pensões* throughout town. **Restaurants** and **cafes** lie along Av. Manuel Francisco da Costa, around the corner from the bus stop.

HIKING. The main **park information office** is located in **Braga,** on Av. António Macedo. (☎253 20 34 80; fax 61 31 69. Open M-F 9am-12:30pm and 2:30-5:30pm.) The **Gerês branch office** (☎253 39 01 10), on Av. Manuel Francisco da Costa uphill from the municipal tourist office, can assist with hike planning. More casual hikers tend to stay south where the few roads provide scenic and manageable journeys, while more dedicated visitors head to the northern trails. In both areas, numerous hamlets and villages offer accommodations, campsites, and food. The most popular hike, because of its accessibility and its 5km distance, is the **Trilho da Preguiça.** It begins just north of Gerês proper and follows the Río Gerês. Another hike follows the road toward **Portela do Homem,** a small town on the Portuguese-Spanish border with a river pool at the bottom of the **Minas dos Carris** valley.

Southeast of Gerês, the **Miradouro do Gerês** overlooks the **Caniçada** reservoir—beware the en masse migration of weekend picknickers. The village of **Rio Caldo,** at the base of Caniçada reservoir just 8km south of Gerês, offers windsurfing and waterskiing. The main attraction in Gerês proper is **Empresa das Aguas do Gerês,** open May to October. Along with famed waters, the spa complex includes a pool, tennis, horseback riding, hiking, canoeing, and nautical sports. Next door, **Parque das Termas** has flourine mineral waters. (☎253 39 11 13. €0.85, under 12 €0.40. Pool open Apr.-July and Sept. 10am-6pm; Aug. 10am-8pm. €3.50; under 7 €2.)

VIANA DO CASTELO ☎258

Although it is visited mainly as a beach resort, Viana do Castelo (pop. 20,000) also has a lively historic district centered around the Praça da República, excellent and unique culinary specialties, and intriguing architecture including a bridge designed by Gustave Eiffel. The surrounding hilltops and the nearby Monte de Santa Luzia offer excellent views of the fertile landscape and the sea. Those intending to pass through en route to Galicia soon discover the town's charm.

⌐ TRANSPORTATION

Trains: The station (☎258 82 13 15) is at the top of Av. dos Combatentes da Grande Guerra, under the Santa Luzia hill. Trains to: **Porto** (2hr., 13-14 per day 5am-8pm, €4.10); **Valença do Minho** (1hr., 7 per day 7:45am-8:38pm, €2.20); **Vigo, Spain** (2½hr., 7 per day 7:50am-8:38pm, €8.15); **Vila Nova de Cerveira** via **Caminha** (1hr., 7 per day 7:44am-8:30pm, €1.80).

Buses: The station is the **Central de Camionagem** (☎258 82 50 47), on the eastern edge of town and a 20min. walk from the center. **REDM** runs to **Braga** (1½hr.; M-F 9 per day 6:50am-7:05pm, Sa 6 per day 6:50am-6:35pm, Su 4 per day 8:15am-6:35pm; €3.20). **AVIC** (☎258 82 97 05) and **Auto-Viação do Minho** (☎258 80 03 41) go to **Lisboa** (5½hr.; Su-F 3 per day 8am-11:45pm, Sa 7am and 2:30pm; €18) and **Porto** (2hr.; M-F 9 per day 6:45am-6:30pm, Sa-Su 4-6 per day 8:20am-6:30pm; €3.50-5.25). **A.V. Minho** (☎258 80 03 41) runs to **Valença do Minho** (1hr.; M-F 1:30, 5:15, 7:15, and 8:15pm, Sa 5:15pm; €5).

Taxis: Táxis Vianenses (☎258 82 66 41 or 82 20 61).

✳❓ ORIENTATION & PRACTICAL INFORMATION

Wide **Avenida dos Combatentes da Grande Guerra** runs from the **train station** to the port. Most accommodations and restaurants are on or near the Avenida. The **historic center** stretches east of the Avenida around **Praça da República,** while the fortress and sea lie to the west, and **Templo de Santa Luzia** lies to the north. Beaches, sights, and stations are within a 20min. walk from Pr. da República.

Tourist Office: Trav. do Hospital Velho, 8 (☎258 82 26 20), on the corner of Pr. da Erva. From the train station, take the 4th left at the sharp corner onto R. da Picota, then a right onto Pr. da Erva. Open May-July and Sept. M-Sa 9am-12:30pm and 2-5pm, Su 9:30am-1pm; Aug. daily 9am-7pm; Oct.-Apr. M-Sa 9am-12:30pm and 2:30-5:30pm.

Currency Exchange: Montepio Geral, Av. dos Combatentes da Grande Guerra, 332 (☎258 82 88 97), near the train station. Open M-F 8:30am-3pm. On-site 24hr. **ATM.**

Emergency: ☎112. **Police:** R. de Aveiro (☎258 82 20 22).

Hospital: Hospital de Santa Luzia, Estrada Sta. Luzia (☎258 82 90 81).

Internet Access: Free at the **Biblioteca Municipal** (public library) on R. Cândido dos Reis (☎258 80 93 02), up from Pr. da República. Five computers. ID required. Strict 30min. limit. Open M-F 9:30am-12:30pm and 2-7pm, Sa 9:30am-12:30pm. Also available at the **post office.** A €5 card lasts about 3hr.

Post Office: Av. dos Combatentes da Grande Guerra (☎258 80 00 80). **Posta Restante** and **fax.** Open M-F 8:30am-6pm, Sa 9am-12:30pm. **Postal Code:** 4900.

♠♣ ACCOMMODATIONS & CAMPING

Accommodations in Viana do Castelo are easy to find. Check the side streets off Av. dos Combatentes da Grande Guerra if you have trouble finding a place.

▧ **Pousada de Juventude de Viana do Castelo (HI),** R. de Límia (☎258 80 02 60; fax 80 02 61), right on the marina, off R. da Argaçosa and Pr. da Galiza. Rooms with balconies and great views. Lounge with a pool table and ping-pong. Bar, common kitchen, and dining hall. Breakfast (8:30-10am) included. Lunch (1-2pm) and dinner (7:30-8:30pm) €4.75 each. Laundry €5 per load. Internet access €1.50 per 30min., €2.50 per hr. Reception 8am-midnight. Checkout 10:30am. Reservations recommended. June 16-Sept. 15 dorms €12.50; doubles with bath €35. Sept. 16-June 15 €10/€28. ❶

■ **Pensão Dolce Vita,** R. Poço, 44 (☎258 82 48 60), across from the tourist office. In an excellent location. Sleek, newly renovated rooms with two twin beds, TV, bath, A/C, and plenty of light. €40 per room; €30 for one person. MC/V. ❸

Pensão Guerreiro, R. Grande, 14 (☎258 82 20 99; fax 82 04 02), off Av. dos Combatentes da Grande Guerra. June-Sept. 15, Dec. 16-31 and Apr. singles €19; doubles €25; triples €30; quads €37; rest of year €6 less. ❷

Residencial Viana Mar, Av. dos Combatentes da Grande Guerra, 215 (☎/fax 258 82 89 62), 2min. from the train station. Large, hotel-like *residencial* with TV and A/C. Singles €22.50, with shower €25, with bath €30; doubles €32.50/€35/€45. AmEx/MC/V. ❷

Pousada de Viana do Castelo, Monte Santa Luzia (☎258 82 88 89; fax 82 88 92). Built in 1918 atop a mountain, this gorgeous hotel features beautiful views of Monte Santa Luzia and Viana from plush seating in its vast balcony, restaurant, and bar. A 25min. walk or €5 cab ride from the center of town, but there's no hurry to stray too far from the swimming pool, tennis courts, mountain bikes, and snooker anyway. Doubles: Apr.-Oct. Su-Th €139, with view €149, F-Sa €152/€170; Nov.-Mar. Su-Th €94/€104, F-Sa €104/€115. Under age 30 and over age 60 discounts. ❺

Camping: Orbitur (☎258 32 21 67; fax 32 19 46), at Praia do Cabedelo. Catch a TransCunha "Cabedelo" bus (6 per day 7:35am-6:45pm, €0.75) from the bus station or from Lgo. 5 de Outubro. A well-equipped campsite with free showers. Apr.-Sept. €3-3.50 per person, €2.50-5 per tent, €2.50-3 per car. Oct.-Nov. and Jan.-Mar. €2/€1.50-2.75/€1.75. Closed Dec. 1-Jan. 15. ❶

☐ FOOD

People eat well in Viana do Castelo. The local specialties are *arroz de sarabulho* (rice cooked with blood and served alongside sausages and potatoes) and *bacalhau à Gil Eanes* (cod cooked with milk, potato, onion, garlic, and oil). Most budget restaurants lie on the small streets off Av. dos Combatentes da Grande Guerra. The **municipal market** is on Av. Rocha Páris, in front of Pr. Dona Maria II. (☎258 82 26 57. Open M-Sa 8am-3pm.) A **weekly market,** attracting many of the same vendors as the market in Barcelos, is held Friday mornings off Av. Capitão Gaspar de Castro, on the same road as the bus station. For groceries, go to **Pingo Doce** on R. de Aveiro. (Open daily 9am-10pm.)

■ **Restaurante Dolce Vita,** R. Poço, 44 (☎258 82 48 60), at the corner of Pr. da Erva, across the square from the tourist office. Brick-oven pizzas with generous, fresh toppings (€4.50-5.25) are served to a bustling crowd. Portuguese dishes and pastas €4.50-10. Open daily noon-3pm and 7:30-10:30pm. MC/V. ❶

Confeitaria Natário, R. Manuel Espregueira, 37 (☎258 82 23 76), just off Av. dos Combatentes da Grande Guerra. People line up at 10:30am to catch the meat and fish pastries hot out of the oven (€0.60-1). Their delicious specialty is *bolos de berlim* (€0.75), a sweet pastry made with fresh egg cream. Open M and W-Su 9am-10pm. ❶

Ruela Bar, Av. Campo do Castelo, 11 (☎258 81 10 72), on the street below the castle, across from the square. Popular with students for its *prato do dia* (€3.50), as well as its burgers and sandwiches (€1-2.50). Open M-Sa 11:30am-3pm and 6pm-midnight. ❶

A Matriz, R. do Tourinho, 82 (☎258 33 12 16), on the corner with R. Sacadura Cabral. Enjoy the quiet, soothing setting with excellent fish and meat dishes. Entrees €6-12. Open M-Sa noon-3:30pm and 7-10pm. ❷

👁 SIGHTS

Viana do Castelo's **Praça da República** is a stately representative of Portugal's impressive squares. Its centerpiece is a 16th-century fountain encrusted with sculptures and crowned with a sphere bearing a cross of the Order of Christ. The small **Paço do Conselho** (1502), formerly the town hall, seals off the square to the east. Diagonally across the plaza, granite columns support the playful and flowery facade of the **Igreja da Misericórdia** (1598, rebuilt in 1714), which is known for its *azulejo* interior. The ⬛**Monte de Santa Luzia,** overlooking the city, is crowned by magnificent Celtic ruins and the **Templo de Santa Luzia,** an early 20th-century neo-Byzantine church. Though the cable car no longer runs, you can always reach the hilltop by walking up the long stairway beginning behind the train station. (20-30min.) The view of Viana from the hill is fantastic, especially from the top of the church; take the elevator (€0.65) up the tower, or climb the narrow stairway that leads to the **Zimbório** at the very top. (Templo open daily in summer 8am-7pm; in winter 8am-5pm. Mass daily at 4pm. Free.)

🏖 BEACHES

Sunbathers, swimmers, and windsurfers alike fill the beaches of Viana do Castelo and its neighboring towns. **Praia Norte,** at the end of Av. do Atlântico at the west end of town, is easy to reach and has swimming pools. **Praia da Argaçosa,** a small beach on Rio Lima next to the youth hostel and marina, is popular with sunbathers in summer. To get to **Praia do Cabedelo,** a great beach for surfing and windsurfing, take the ferry that leaves from the dock in front of Av. dos Combatantes de Grande Guerra. (10min.; 11 per day 9:15am-7pm to the beach, 9:20am-7:05pm from the beach; €0.80, bike €0.40 extra.) A short train ride north of Viana leads to the **Praia do Bico** in Afife, frequented by surfers (10min.), and the large **Praia de Âncora** (15min.). Farther north are the beaches of **Moledo** and **Caminha.**

🎭 NIGHTLIFE & FESTIVALS

The cafes and bars around Pr. da República fill up in the evening. The most popular place in Viana is **Bar Glamour,** R. da Bandeira, 183, down the street from the plaza and away from the main avenue. The interior dance floor features mainstream dance music, and the garden hosts live music on Thursdays and karaoke on Tuesdays. (☎258 82 29 63. Minimum consumption Su-Th 1 drink. Cover F-Sa €2.50. Open daily 10pm-4am.) Another bar popular with a similar crowd is the nearby **Casting Bar,** R. Nova San Bento, 120-124. (☎258 82 73 96. Open Th-Sa 10pm-4am.) Viana's biggest festival of the year is the **Festa de Nossa Senhora da Agonia,** celebrated with parties and performances in the plaza from August 20 to 24.

🔁 DAYTRIP FROM VIANA DO CASTELO

VALENÇA DO MINHO

*Valença do Minho is a 1hr. **bus** ride from Viana do Castelo. **A.V. Minho** (☎258 80 03 41) runs buses back to Viana do Castelo (1hr.; M-F 6:20, 7:50, 11:50am, Sa 7:50am, Su 7:50pm, Oct.-June also Su 4:40 and 6:50pm; €5). A **train** (☎808 20 82 08) back to town takes around the same time (1hr., 5 per day 5:20am-8:15pm, €2.20). To get to the fortaleza from the **bus station,** take a right onto the road parallel to the station and pass the rotary and modern sculpture. Take the first left uphill until you reach another rotary. Cross this rotary and make your way uphill toward the fortaleza. To get to the fortaleza from the **train station,** walk through the rotary in front of the station and take a* *right at the end of the street. Up this hill is another rotary. Cross the rotary and from here make your way uphill. You should be able to see the fortaleza.*

Valença's sizeable 17th century **fortaleza,** once a barrier to outsiders, is now the main attraction. Wide-eyed tourists, busy locals, vibrant merchandise, and patient cars jumble together in the *fortaleza's* streets, creating a unique atmosphere found only in a walled-in town. Walking through the bustling streets of this town on the border with Spain gives a feel of the crowds of years past. The hill top location also offers panoramic views of the neighboring countryside and Río Miño. Just outside the walls is **El Puente Internacional,** built in 1886. Walk across into Spain's **Túy,** whose *casco viejo* also makes a worthwhile trip (see p. 579).

TRÁS-OS-MONTES

The country's roughest and most isolated region, Trás-Os-Montes ("behind the mountains") is a land of extremes. *Trasmontanos* describe their seasons as "nine months of winter and three months of hell." The region's isolation, beauty, and tranquility are its biggest draws. Rocky hilltops give way to fields of grapes and corn, which in turn are followed by arid stretches, good only for growing olives. *Trasmontanos* themselves are quite possibly the friendliest people in Portugal.

Trás-Os-Montes has long been home to Portugal's political and religious exiles. Dom Sancho I practically had to beg people to settle here after he incorporated it into Portugal in the 12th century, and it was here that the Jews chose to hide during the Inquisition. Today, it is one of the last outposts of traditional Portugal. The gastronomic specialties, served in generous portions, hint at the region's rustic character: *cozido à portuguesa* is made from sausages, pig parts, carrots, and turnips, and it takes some serious hikes to burn off the hearty *feijoada à trasmontana* (bean stew). The most prized dish is probably *posta a mirandesa*, locally bred beef that locals claim is the most tender in the world.

BRAGANÇA ☎273

Wedged in a narrow valley between two steep slopes, Bragança (pop. 40,000) is a steadfast wilderness outpost. While most visitors come for clean air, blue skies, and olive-covered hillsides—or the massive 12th-century castle—the people of Bragança make it unique; its substantial distance from the rest of Portuguese civilization seems to have preserved an almost archaic sense of hospitality and festivity. The town is in the middle of an extensive revitalization project that includes new commercial centers and an updated bus station. Bragança is the perfect base for exploring the Parque Natural de Montesinho, which extends north into Spain.

⌐ TRANSPORTATION

Trains: No train service. Nearest station is **Mirandela**, 1hr. away and accessible by bus.

Buses: The bus station is 2km from the center of town, on Av. Dom Sancho I. (Offices open M-F 5:30am-6pm, Sa 7am-5pm, Su 7am-9pm.) The new station, scheduled to open no sooner than 2005, will be at the top of Av. João da Cruz. **Rodonorte** (☎273 30 01 83) runs to **Braga** via **Mirandela** and **Vila Real** (4-5hr.; M-F 3 per day 6am-11am, Sa 1 per day 7:25am, Su 2 per day 2, 5pm; €10.70). **Rede Expressos** (☎273 33 18 26) runs to: **Coimbra** (6hr.; M-F 6 per day, Sa 5 per day 6am-9:30pm; €10.50); **Lisboa** (8hr.; M-F 8 per day, Sa-Su 6 per day 6am-9:30pm; €14); **Porto** (5hr.; M-F 8 per day, Sa-Su 6 per day 6am-11pm; €8.80); and **Vila Real** (2hr.; M-F 6 per day, Sa-Su 3 per day 2-7pm; €6.75). **Santos** (☎279 65 21 88) goes to **Lisboa** via **Vila Real** and **Porto** (8hr; M-F 4 per day 6, 8am, 2, 5pm; Sa 1 per day 2pm; Su 3 per day 2, 5, 9pm; €14). **Autocares F. Ledesma** (☎980 52 83 71) runs to **Madrid** via **Zamora, ES** (5hr.; Tu and F 2 per day 12:30, 1:30pm; Su 1 per day 5:45pm; €37).

Taxis (☎273 32 21 38). Near the post office and temporary bus station. €3-4 to town.

✦ ☑ ORIENTATION & PRACTICAL INFORMATION

To get to the center of town from the bus station (20min. walk), exit the station by turning right. Take the first left onto Av. 22 de Maio and continue straight. Take a right onto R. Santo António and a quick right onto hostel-lined **Avenida João da Cruz.**

Continue straight, merging onto downward-sloping R. Almirante dos Reis, which leads to more budget *pensaões* and the **Praça da Sé** at the heart of the old town. To reach the **fortress,** situated on a hill west of Pr. da Sé, take R. dos Combatentes da Grande Guerra, walk uphill, and enter through the opening in the stone walls.

Tourist Office: Av. Cidade de Zamora (☎273 38 12 73). From Pr. da Sé, take R. Abilio Beca and take the 2nd left onto R. Marqués. Turn right onto Av. Cidade de Zamora. Short-term **luggage storage.** Open May-Sept. M-F 10am-6pm, Sa 10am-12:30pm and 2-5pm, Su 10am-1pm; Oct.-Apr. M-F 10am-12:30pm and 2-5pm, Sa 10am-12:30pm.

Currency Exchange: BCP Sotto Mayor 24, Av. João da Cruz, 53. Also has Western Union services. Open M-F 10am-5pm. 24hr. **ATM at Crédito Predia Português,** R. Almirante dos Reis, 30.

English-Language Bookstore: Livraría Mário Péricles, R. dos Combatentes da Grande Guerra, 180 (☎273 32 25 49). Open M-F 9:30am-noon and 2-7pm, Sa 9:30am-1pm.

Emergency: ☎112. **Police:** R. Dr. Manuel Bento (☎273 30 34 00).

Hospital: Hospital Distrital de Bragança, Av. Abade de Baçal (☎273 31 08 00), before the stadium on the road to Vinhais.

Internet Access: CyberCentro (☎273 33 12 80), 2nd fl. of the new *mercado municipal* between the bus station and Pr. da Sé. €0.54 per hr. Open M-Sa 11am-11pm.

Post Office: (☎273 31 00 71), on the corner of R. Almirante dos Reis and R. 5 de Outubro. Open M-F 8:30am-5:30pm, Sa 9am-12:30pm. **Postal Code:** 5300.

▌ ACCOMMODATIONS

Plenty of cheap *pensaões* and *residenciales* line Pr. da Sé and R. Almirante dos Reis; the youth hostel is near the bus station.

Pensão Poças, R. Combatentes da Grande Guerra, 200 (☎273 33 14 28 or 33 12 16). From Pr. da Sé, walk toward the castle and bear right. Clean common baths with showers. To avoid street noise, ask for a room that does not overlook R. Combatentes da Grande Guerra. Includes breakfast (8:30-11am). Reception in restaurant. Singles with or without bath €10; doubles €20; triples €30. AmEx/MC/V. ❶

Pousada de Juventude—Bragança (HI), Forte de São João de Deus (☎273 30 46 00; fax 32 61 36), off Av. 22 de Maio. A 20min. walk from Av. João da Cruz, but near the temporary bus station. From the station, turn right and take the first left onto Av. 22 de Maio. The 24 dorms with 4 beds each come accompanied by a kitchen, playroom, sitting room, and terrace seating. Laundry facilities. Check-in 6pm-midnight. June 15-Sept. 14 dorms €12.50; doubles with bath €35. Sept. 15-June 14 €10/€28. MC/V. ❶

Camping: Parque de Campismo Municipal do Sabor (☎273 33 15 35), 6km from town on the edge of the Parque Natural de Montesinho, on the road to Portelo (N103-7). The #7 STUB bus (yellow and blue) toward Meixedo goes by the campground, leaving from the Caixa Geral de Depósitos on Av. João da Cruz (10min.; M-F 12:44 and 6pm, also Sept.-June 2:10pm; Sa 1:35pm; €0.75). If you choose to hike, be careful—roads are narrow and curvy. Reception 8am-midnight. Open May-Oct. €1.50 per person and per car, €1.50-2.25 per tent. Electricity €1. ❶

▐ FOOD

The region is celebrated for its *presunto* (cured ham) and *salsichão* (sausages), as well as the local delicacy, *alheiradas,* sausages made with bread and various meats. You can find these and fresh produce at the stores that surround the *mercado municipal,* two blocks down from Pr. da Sé.

⚅ Restaurante Poças, R. Combatentes da Grande Guerra, 200 (☎273 33 14 28), off Pr. da Sé. Share seating with both locals and fellow travelers. Meals include appetizers of bread, pates, and black olives. Entrees €5-9. Open 8am-midnight; serves full menu noon-3pm and 7-10:30pm. AmEx/MC/V. ❷

Restaurante Dom Fernando, R. Rainha D. Maria II, 197 (☎273 32 62 73), inside the castle walls, upstairs above the bar. Given its location, this restaurant should be more touristy, more expensive, and less good. Fortunately, it's not. Entrees €4.50-8.50. *Menú* €9. Open June-Sept. daily 9am-10pm; Oct.-May M-W and F-Su 9am-10pm. ❷

Solar Bragançano, Pr. da Sé (☎273 32 38 75). A Victorian setting with chandeliers dripping crystal and a beautiful garden on the back patio of a renovated mansion. Entrees (€6.50-15) include wild game. Excellent vegetarian soups (€2) and vegetarian omelettes available. Open daily noon-3:30pm and 7:30-10pm. ❸

⊙ SIGHTS

Uphill from Pr. da Sé is the old town and its 12th-century **castelo.** The castle is encircled by massive restored walls that provide phenomenal views of Bragança and Spain. Inside the walls, the castle's **Museu Militar** has a wide range of military paraphernalia that traces Portugal's war history, from the medieval treaties with Spain to the Portuguese efforts in WWI and the African campaigns. (Open M-W and F-Sa 9-11:45am and 2-4:45pm, Su 9-11:45am. €1.50. Free Su mornings.) The venerable **pelourinho** (pillory) in the square behind the castle bears a coat of arms. At the base of the whipping post is a granite pig, a vestige of pagan ideology and the place where sinners and criminals were bound during the Middle Ages. The **Domus Municipalis,** behind the church across the square from the castle, once served as the city's municipal meeting house. Today, it is the only existing example of Roman civil architecture on the Iberian Peninsula.

⚑⚐ NIGHTLIFE & FESTIVALS

Students from the polytechnic institute ensure good nightlife in the city. At **Central Pub,** R. do Poço, 18, above Pr. da Sé, on a cross street between R. Almirante dos Reis and R. 5 de Outubro, an elegant upstairs pub plays 60s music and rotates art exhibitions every three weeks. Fast-forward a decade at the disco/bar downstairs. (☎273 33 13 09. Open daily

NO WORK, ALL PLAY

ON THE PROWL

The *Festa dos Rapazes*, an ancient ritual enacted in the villages of the Parque Natural de Montesinho, is certainly not lacking for erotic innuendo. The festival, which coincides with the winter solstice, has regional variations but the general idea is the same everywhere. On December 26th or January 6th, the single young men of the villages dress up as *caretos*, wearing shaggy colored suits and diabolic painted masks, and prowl around in groups in search of lone females. Upon finding a *rapariga*, they surround her and one of the *caretos* grabs and shakes her, knocking the bells attached to his belt against her hips (the verb is *chocalhar*). The *festa* continues today, as shy young men use the event to meet and flirt with local girls.

Fortunately for all involved, festivals and ritual gatherings are thought to be times when the natural order of things is suspended. According to anthropologist Ernesto Veiga de Oliveira, the festival "is a time of great licentious freedom where all excesses are authorized." And Caro Baroja asserts that "the inversion of the normal order of things has a predominant role." All scholarly theory aside, this makes for one hell of an excuse to get wild. So loose your inhibitions, defy the norm, and, go ahead, find your inner animal. You know you want to.

1-3pm.) A popular student hangout, especially after 1am on weekends, is **Zona+,** Av. Sá Carneiro, 2A, below Confeitaria Veneza through the door to the right. (☎933 37 63 95. Open M-Sa 10pm-3am.)

The most important festival in Bragança is the **Festa de Nossa Senhora das Graças,** celebrated annually from early August until the climactic day, August 22nd; fireworks mark the night of the 21st. During the **Festa do Estudante,** *tunas* (student music groups) gather to play for the entire town.

▶ DAYTRIP FROM BRAGANÇA

PARQUE NATURAL DE MONTESINHO

Inquire at the information office in Bragança, R. Cónego Albano Falcão, 5 (in Bairro Salvador Nunes Teixeira). Walk downhill from the tourist office on Av. Cidade de Zamora, take the 1st left on a paved street and the 1st left again; it's at the end of the street on the right. Park trails are unmarked, but the office has maps and can help plan hikes. (☎273 38 14 44; fax 38 11 79. Open M-F 9am-12:30pm and 2-5:30pm.) The info office (☎273 38 12 34 or 38 14 44) rents Casas Abrigos (traditional houses, also called Casas de Naturaeza). Doubles €25-38; quads €50. Getting to the park can be complicated. Buses to the border village of Rio de Onor leave from Bragança on Av. João da Cruz, in front of Banco Nacional Ultramarino near Pr. da Sé (Sept.-June M-F, and the 3rd, 12th, and 21st of summer months, 2:09pm; return bus runs year-round Su-F 6:50pm).

One of the largest protected areas in Portugal, the **Parque Natural de Montesinho** covers 290 square miles between Bragança and the Spanish border. The park consists of 88 traditional *aldeias* (villages). Rich with tradition, these villages preserve age-old communal customs and enact ancient rituals, from the carving of pigs to lively festivals such as the **Festa dos Rapazes.** Some of the villages can be reached in a day's hike or bike ride, but visitors with more time often design multi-day hikes between villages.

Old mountain paths lead through rolling woodlands of oak, chestnut, pine, and cherry trees. *Pombais pombales* (pigeon lofts) dot the landscape, and the land is home to many rare and endangered species including the Iberian wolf, royal eagle, and black stork, among others. Trout fishing, hiking, and horseback riding are popular. The riverbanks are ideal for picnics. If you have only one day to visit the park, the most worthwhile trip is to **Rio de Onor,** a village near the northeast corner, on the border with Spain. Here the Portuguese and Spanish have lived together for centuries, intermarrying and even speaking their own hybrid dialect, *rionorés.* A subtle stone post, with a "P" for "Portugal" carved into one side and an "E" for "España" on the other, marks the border. Villagers cross into Spain for groceries and back into Portugal for coffee at **Cervejaria Preto,** a bar that's not hard to find, as it's the only one in town. You can eat on the stone tables overlooking the river.

VILA REAL ☎259

Vila Real (pop. 25,000) presides over the edge of the gorges of the Corgo and Cabril Rivers in the foothills of the Serra do Marão. The small, historic town center is surrounded by new neighborhoods reaching into the hills, a lively main street, and a few cafes. As the principal commercial center for the southern farms and villages of Trás-Os-Montes, Vila Real is a good point of departure for excursions into the fields and slopes of the Serra do Alvão and Serra do Marão.

▐ TRANSPORTATION. Trains run from Av. 5 de Outubro (☎259 32 21 93) to **Porto** (4½hr., 5 per day 7:20am-7:45pm, €7). To get to Vila Real's center, walk up Av. 5 de Outubro, over the iron bridge onto R. Miguel Bombarda, and turn left on R. Roque da Silveira. Continue to bear left until Av. 1 de Maio. Trains take longer than buses and require transfers at Régua. **Rodonorte buses,** R. Dom Pedro de Castro (☎259 34

07 10), are on the square directly uphill from the tourist office. To: **Bragança** (2hr., 5-9 per day 8:45am-11pm, €7.50); **Guimarães** (1½hr.; M-F 4 per day 6:25am-5:20pm, Sa 10am, Su 3 per day 4:30-7pm; €5.80); **Lisboa** (6½hr.; M-F 3 per day 8am, 1:10, 5:20pm; Sa 3 per day 9:30am, 1:10, 5:20pm; Su 5 per day 9:30am-10:40pm; €13.50); **Porto** (1¾hr.; 8-13 per day M-F 6:25am-8:20pm, Sa 8am-7pm, Su 8am-10:30pm; €5.50). Taxis cluster along Av. Carvalho Araújo; try **Rádiotáxi** (☎259 37 31 38).

■✴ ORIENTATION & PRACTICAL INFORMATION. Vila Real's old neighborhood is centered around **Avenida Carvalho Araújo,** a broad tree-lined avenue that runs downhill from the bus station to the Câmara Municipal. Most of the town's cafes, shops, and *residenciais* are here. The bus stops at Rodonorte Station on **Rua Dom Pedro de Castro;** go right upon exiting to get to the main avenue. The **tourist office,** Av. Carvalho Araújo, 94, is to the right and downhill from the bus station, across the street. Its English-speaking staff offers free short-term **luggage storage.** (☎259 32 28 19; fax 32 17 12. Open May-Sept. M-F 9:30am-7pm, Sa-Su 9:30am-12:30pm and 2-6pm; Oct.-Apr. M-F 9:30am-12:30pm and 2-6pm, Sa 10am-12:30pm and 2-4:30pm.) The **Currency exchange** is at **Realvitur,** Lgo. Pioledo, 2 (☎259 34 08 00), 4 blocks uphill from the tourist office and to the right. (Open M-F 9am-7pm, Sa 9am-1pm.) The **post office,** Av. Carvalho Araújo (☎259 33 03 00), is across the street from the tourist office. (Open M-F 8:30am-6pm, Sa 9am-12:30pm.)

◨◪ ACCOMMODATIONS & FOOD. Rooms in Vila Real are cheap and plentiful, making the town a convenient place to stay as either a stopover or as a base for exploring the region. Several cafes along Av. Carvalho Araújo advertise rooms. **Residencial São Domingos ❶,** Tr. de São Domingos, 33 (☎259 32 20 39), is the last of 3 *residenciais* on a side street off Av. Carvalho Araújo, to the right of the cathedral. Its rooms are old, but you can't argue with cable TV and the unbeatable prices. All rooms but 1 have private bath, TV, and phone. (Singles €7.50-13; doubles €23; triples €30.) Hikers come in groups to the **Pousada da Juventude,** R. Dr. Manuel Cardona (☎259 373 193), in the building behind the Instituto Português da Juventude. Besides traditional *hostal* rooms and prices, the *hostal* provides free Internet access at the Instituto next door. Breakfast 8:30-10am. June 16-Sept. 15 singles €9.50; doubles €26.50. Sept. 16-June 15 €7.50/€21. Reception 8am-midnight. Camp at **Parque de Campismo Municipal de Vila Real ❶,** R. Dr. Manuel Cardona (☎259 32 47 24), beside the river and past the youth hostel, at the end of the street on the right. The site offers free showers and space to throw a tent or park a car, and little else. (Reception June-Aug. 8am-10pm; Sept.-May 8:30am-5pm. Open Jan. 16-Dec. 15. €2.75 per person, €1.75 per tent and per car.) Rugged campers will enjoy the wild of the nearby Serra do Alvão.

Eating well in Vila Real is no challenge on a budget. **Avenida Carvalho Araújo** and the parallel **Rua Antonio de Azevedo** are good places to look; restaurants on **Rua Teixeira de Sousa** tend to be more touristy, but there are some cheaper ones there as well. The cafes along Av. Carvalho Araújo and in the square at the bottom of the avenue offer what humble nightlife options the town has to offer. The Mercado da Praça, R. D. Maria das Chaves, 75, hosts a large local market twice a week (Tu and F 8am-noon) and a regular market Monday-Saturday (8am-7pm). Churrasqueira Real ❶, R. Teixeira de Sousa, 14, midway up the street, is very popular, and has a large selection of grilled meats. Ask for your *frango* to be *guarnecido* for €2 more; your chicken will come with a huge serving of traditional salad, rice, and potatoes. (☎259 32 20 78. Entrees €2.50-8.50. Open Tu-Su 9am-11pm; meals noon-2pm and 7-9:30pm. Another **branch** at R. Dom Pedro de Castro, 15.) Restaurante Museu dos Presuntos ❶, Av. Cidade de Orense, 43, at R. D. Afonso III and R. Morgado de Mateus, is a bit of a hike from the town center, but worth it for the *presunto* combinations. *Presunto* is essentially the by-product of a full pig hung from a hook and left to sit in a vat of salt for a month. From the tourist office, cross Av. Carvalho Araújo, take a right, and continue up R. Dom Pedro de Castro. Past the

Rodonorte station, bear right onto R. Dom Pedro de Menezes and take a right onto R. D. Afonso III. The restaurant is at the end of the street across the intersection. (☎259 32 60 17. Open M-Th and Sa-Su 12:30-2:30pm and 7-9:30pm, F 7-9:30pm.)

👁 🗺 SIGHTS & EXCURSIONS

The **Parque Natural do Alvão** is a protected area reaching to the edge of the mountainous Serra country 15km north of Vila Real. The expanse includes a remote community that has maintained its rural appeal, including impressive homes still representative of the design and building materials of several centuries ago. Getting to the park without a car can be problematic, but there are other options. The local bus leaves at 1pm from the Rodonorte bus station (€1.55) and drops people off at Lamas de Ôlo, the beginning of the Serra. Unfortunately, there is no return bus. Travelers can then spend a few hours on the trails (the park information office provides detailed maps with specific hikes ranging from 4-18km), and then hike 15km downhill on the major road. Or, assuming adequate preparation, the mountains offer beautiful and convenient free camping. Among other very unique flora and fauna, the endangered Iberian wolf (usually harmless and fairly rare) lives in the Serra. For maps and more specific hiking info, visit the **park information office,** Lgo. dos Freitas, at the bottom of Av. Carvalho Araújo behind the Câmara Municipal. (☎259 30 28 30; fax 30 28 31. Open M-F 9am-12:30pm and 2-5:30pm.)

MOROCCO المغرب

On a clear day, you can stand on a hill in southernmost Andalucía and gaze across the Strait of Gibraltar, where the faint ridges of the Atlas Mountains—and North Africa—beckon along the horizon. The North African influence permeating Andalucía often piques the curiosity of travelers, who take advantage of the proximity of the two continents to travel to Morocco. This path is well-trodden, serving for centuries as a trade route for language, religion, and culture. Fortunately for the modern traveler, the trek has only become easier.

A host of influences—African, European, and Middle Eastern—carved Morocco's identity. Now, the country teeters between the past and present as both a civilization descended from nomads and a modern nation that has struggled against imperial powers for its sovereignty.

HISTORY

PREHISTORY TO THE ROMAN ERA. Archaeological evidence along Morocco's Atlantic coast suggests that regions of the country have been settled for anywhere from 100,000 to 1,000,000 years. The influences of numerous foreign civilizations pervade Morocco's early history. Each faced a similar problem: it was impossible to exert any control over the land without a reliable overland route. As a result, the majority of the country remained unexplored for centuries. The **Berbers** arrived between 4000 and 2000 BC; evidence of the use of early Berber tools can still be found in rock carvings scattered throughout the High Atlas Mountains. Though the **Phoenicians** began to explore the area in the 12th century BC and developed colonies along the coast, they exerted little control or influence over the area. The **Romans** sacked Carthage, near modern Tunis in Tunisia, then eventually became dependent on North Africa's agricultural supply and created the province of Mauritania Tingitana in what is now Morocco. When the *Pax Romana* deteriorated in the 4th century AD, the Romans abandoned Morocco. By 420 the country was ruled by the Vandals, followed by a brief period of **Byzantine** rule.

THE RISE & FALL OF ISLAM (AD 669-1554). Morocco achieved stability in the late 7th and early 8th centuries when Muslim armies invaded North Africa. In 669, **Uqba bin Nafi al-Fihri** spread the religion of the prophet Mohammed to Morocco. The Berbers could not hold off the Muslim troops, so they made peace with the leader Musa ibn Nusayr, and many converted to Islam. This set the stage for the Arab invasion of Spain less than fifty years later. However, Arab rule was short-lived in Morocco, ending in 740. Although Arabs remained in North Africa, they would not regain power until the 20th century. Instead, a series of local Muslim dynasties rose up to take control of the area, claiming descent from Mohammed to legitimize their rule. **Idris ibn Abdullah,** after fleeing Arabia, founded the first truly Moroccan state in 789. Idris was poisoned in 791, and his kingdom did not last. Over the next few centuries, Morocco was conquered by one minor dynasty after another, the most important of which were the **Almoravid dynasty** that founded Marrakesh in 1062 and the **Almohad Dynasty** that conquered it in 1160.

A golden age during the reign of the Berber **Merinid** (ruled from the 13th to 15th centuries) and then **Wattasid** dynasties (1472-1549) promoted a cultural and intellectual boom and tied Morocco to Spain. As Muslim influence in Christian Iberia waned, however, the Spanish became aggressive. During the Spanish Inquisition in

MOROCCO

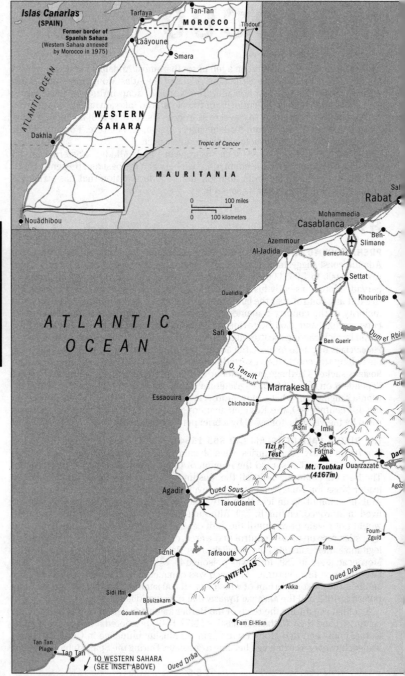

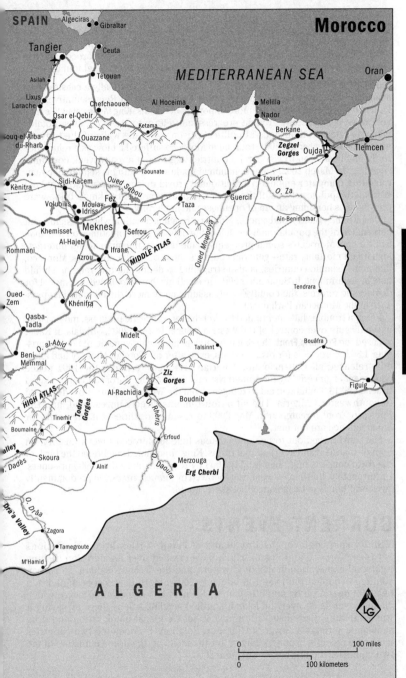

Morocco

in comparison to those in neighboring countries. Morocco's relations with neighbors are strained, particularly with Algeria, where illegal arms shuttling resulted in the closing of the Morocco-Algeria border in 1994. Southern Europe, also aligned against Islamist infiltration, has been taking a greater interest in Morocco and has advocated tighter border controls in light of a steady flow of illegal immigration.

MODERN MOROCCO (1999-2003). Today Morocco is nominally a **constitutional monarchy;** though assisted by a parliament and Chamber of Representatives, the king and his advisers make the more important decisions. **King Mohammed VI's** five-year reign has generally brought progress and reform to Morocco, most notably when he released thousands of political prisoners. In the wake of the terrorist attacks of **September 11,** 2001, tourism in Morocco suffered a blow as a reluctance to fly and hesitation to visit Arab countries aggravated already weak consumer spending. In March 2002, King Mohammed made waves with his semi-public marriage to a computer engineer. Traditionally, royal marriages were strictly kept secrets; the public release of the name and photograph of the king's bride were presented as heralding an era of openness and modernity.

Despite the country's advances, Morocco remains a nation where a significant percentage of the population lives below the poverty line, sometimes on less than US$1 a day. Morocco's social problems—among them unemployment, illiteracy, high infant mortality rate—generally outpace those of similar countries. Morocco, like many Islamic countries, is also struggling to define the role religion should take in government. In September 2002, in elections that were billed as a model for democratic reforms, the country's only Islamic party more than doubled its presence in the Moroccan Parliament.

Foreign troubles have continued to overshadow domestic progress, most visibly in the dispute over control of the **Western Sahara.** In June 2002, officials in Rabat accused the **Polisario Front,** the Saharawi independence movement, of holding prisoner 1,362 Moroccans for over 20 years, even after the Foreign Ministry had allegedly released all Polisario and Algerian prisoners to honor the 1991 peace agreement engineered by the United Nations. In 2002, the European Union moved to send US$13.3 million in aid to refugees from the Western Sahara, now displaced to southwestern Algeria. The situation remains largely unresolved, and the Polisario Front threatened in May 2003 to resume hostilities if its demands for independence are not met.

May 2003 turned out to be a momentous time in Morocco's recent history, on both the national and international fronts. King Mohammed celebrated the birth of the royal couple's first child in May 2003 by releasing more than 9000 prisoners. Unfortunately, this happy event was followed by **terrorist attacks** on predominantly "western" hotels in Casablanca that same month.

CURRENT EVENTS

Military sparring over the tiny island of **Perejil** further strained relations between Morocco and Spain, which have clashed over immigration, fishing rights, oil exploration in disputed waters, and the Western Sahara. Moroccan soldiers occupied the island in late July 2002 before it was reoccupied in a peaceful operation by an elite team of Spanish commandos. Morocco, which claims sovereignty over the island, justified sending troops there by saying it was maintaining an observation post to tackle illegal immigration and drug smuggling across the Strait of Gibraltar. Relations between the two countries have only recently begun to thaw; after the incident, the prime ministers of the two countries did not meet until June 2003.

General instability in the region s was further compounded by the May 2003 terrorist suicide bombings in Casablanca. The attacks, which targeted Jewish and Spanish sites, killed 31 civilians and 12 of the 14 bombers, who were linked to a radical Islamic group. Although the bombings did not target Americans, the US State Department warns that the potential for transnational **terrorism** remains high. Western sources have linked the attacks to **al-Qaeda,** an allegation that Moroccan authorities have yet to confirm. Regardless, the attacks are symptomatic of the growing influence of radical politics in the country.

PEOPLE & CULTURE

LANGUAGE

Morocco is paradise for polyglots. Although Classical Arabic *(al-Fusha)* is the official language of Morocco, it is rarely spoken and has become an almost exclusively written language. Most Moroccans speak the modern dialect called *Darija,* a compacted **Arabic** peppered with **Spanish** and **French,** as well as French proper. Whether Arabic, French, or Spanish, each language absorbed into Morocco has been sprinkled and spiced. In this book, **city names** appear first in English, then in Arabic. (Fez, for example, is written neither as Fès, the French spelling, nor Faas, the Arabic spelling.) A massive naming shift from French to Arabic is underway on **street signs,** so some of the streets mentioned may go by a different title (here they are listed in both French and Arabic when necessary). *Rues* and *avenues* may become *zanqats, derbs,* or *sharias.* For a brief pronunciation guide, consult the **Moroccan Phrasebook,** p. 814.

RELIGION

The Arab prophet Mohammed founded the religion of **Islam** in AD 622. Informed of his prophetic calling by the angel Gabriel, Mohammed is believed by Muslims to be the end of a long chain of visionaries that includes Abraham, Moses, Elijah, and Jesus. Mohammed led his followers until his death in 632, during which time his words and deeds were recorded in *hadith* (sayings) that comprise the *Sunna,* or examples of Mohammed. Following his death, the issue of who would rule divided Muslims into two branches, the Sunni and the Shi'a. The **Sunni** wanted Mohammed's successor chosen from a community of men; they believe strongly in God's will and predestination, while the **Shi'ites** insisted on his successor being a blood relative of their prophet and believe in free will.

At the heart of the Islamic faith is the Arabic word *islam,* which translates literally to either peace or submission, depending on who you ask. The believer, or *Muslim,* accepts complete submission to the will of God *(Allah)* as embodied in the Qur'an (book of recitation). This Arabic text is considered by Muslims to be a miracle—perfect, immutable, and untranslatable; it replaces all earlier revealed books and is the definitive form of God's word. Unlike the Christian conception of Jesus, the Islamic view considers Mohammed a human messenger of God. All practicing Muslims must adhere to the five pillars of Islam: the formal profession of faith, prayer toward Mecca five times daily, alms-giving, fasting during the month of Ramadan, and, if possible, a pilgrimage to Mecca.

Moroccan Islam is somewhat unique. While there is the inevitable difference between popular and orthodox Islam in Morocco, there is less of a gap between the religious intellectuals and the general public than in other Arab countries. **Sufism** is a mystical twist to Islam that is based on the belief that Muslims will find

RAMADAN 101 It is believed that Mohammed received the Qur'an during the month of **Ramadan**. Fasting during this holy month is the fourth pillar of Islam. Between dawn and sunset, Muslims are not permitted to smoke, have sexual intercourse, or let any food or water pass their lips; exceptions are made for pregnant or menstruating women, the sick, and travelers (though all must make up the fast at a later date). Fasting is meant to teach Muslims to resist temptation and thereby control all their unchaste urges. Ideally, Muslims read the Qur'an during the daylight hours. By experiencing hunger they are meant to better understand the plight of the poor and to be more thankful for the food which God has provided them. It is insensitive to eat in public during Ramadan. Ramadan inspires a sense of community. As soon as the sun sets, the fast is broken and a night of feasting and visiting of friends and relatives begins. The revelry lasts until dawn, when the fast begins again.

the truth of God's love and knowledge through a personal experience with God. Sufis were once quite politically powerful; they are still a large presence, but their influence in politics has faded.

Morocco has had its share of Islamic fundamentalist movements, but they have been substantially weaker than those in other North African countries due to the popular belief that the king is a religious as well as political leader. Nevertheless, recent events seem to indicate that fundamentalism is on the rise. More than 99% of Moroccans are Sunni Muslim, though Morocco also has a small **Jewish** minority and an even smaller **Christian** one. Islam is the official state religion.

FOOD & DRINK

Moroccan chefs lavish aromatic and colorful spices on their dishes—pepper, ginger, cumin, saffron, honey, and sugar are culinary staples. The distinctive Moroccan flavor comes from a unique blend of spices, known as *ras al-hanut*. However, no matter how delicious everything may seem, be prepared to get sick at least once, as Morocco is full of things to which tourists are not immune. Taking extra precautions may help. Bottled mineral water is the way to go, as is peeling all fruits and vegetables. The truly cautious may avoid salads as well, or ensure that their vegetables are washed in purified water. Most food sold on the street, especially meat, can be quite risky.

TYPICAL FARE

Moroccan cuisine consists mainly of couscous, *tajine*, and soups. **Tajine** is a stew steamed in a cone-shaped clay dish. It consists of meat (chicken, lamb, or pigeon) along with an assortment of vegetables, olives, and prunes. Vegetarian forms of *tajine* are common as well. **Couscous** is a semolina-grain pasta about the size of sesame seeds served with meat or vegetables. The most popular of the Moroccan soups is **harira,** a salty chickpea soup, sometimes containing meat (it is served every day during Ramadan). **Baguettes** and **honey-soaked pastries** are everywhere, as are delicious Moroccan breads.

Other common dishes include **poulet** (chicken), which can be prepared either *rôti* (roasted on a spit with olives) or *limon* (with lemon). Pricier and harder-to-find specialties include **mechoui**, whole lamb spitted over an open fire, and **pastilla,** a combination of pigeon or chicken, onions, almonds, eggs, butter, cinnamon, and sugar under a pastry shell. For a lighter treat, slurp sweet natural **yogurt** with mounds of peaches, nectarines, or strawberries, or try an oily Moroccan **salad** with finely chopped tomatoes, cucumbers, and onions. Snackers munch briny olives, roasted almonds, dried chickpeas, and cactus buds. Oranges abound as the cheapest, sweetest, safest fruit in the country.

EATING OUT

The restaurant scene in Morocco depends on whether you're in a big city or small town. As eating out isn't common practice for locals, eateries in large, modern cities cater mainly to foreign tourists, featuring comprehensive menus of typical French or Moroccan cuisine. Seeking out **authentic** regional cuisine in larger cities often requires an adventurous expedition into the maze of the medina. Tiny restaurants hide the most tantalizing dishes. A complete meal includes a choice of entree (*tajine*, couscous, or perhaps a third option), salad or *harira*, a side of vegetables, and yogurt or an orange for dessert. Less expensive *tajine* is made with *kefta* (a ground beef cooked in an array of herbs and spices) and often served on a baguette, as is *merguez* (a spicy beef or lamb sausage). Almost every Moroccan main course includes meat; *cous aux légumes* (couscous with vegetables) will usually be the closest **vegetarian** option. The best bet for strict vegetarians is to cook with produce from the market or to request an omelette at restaurants. Lunchtime runs from noon to 2pm, dinner 7 to 9pm. If a service charge isn't automatically included, a 10% **tip** will definitely suffice.

DRINKING

Although tap water is drinkable in most parts of the country, **bottled and purified water** is a safer bet. If you get a bottle that isn't completely sealed, return it—chances are the bottle has been filled with tap water. Orange juice and other fruit drinks are popular, but make sure that they are diluted with purified water.

Despite the Islamic prohibition against **alcohol,** Morocco is a wine-lover's paradise. While the two best wines are the Cabernet Medallion and Beauvillion (about 80dh), the less expensive Vabernet du President, Amazir, and Guerraine Rouge are also quite good (all 35dh). Moroccan, French, and Spanish **wines** are available in supermarkets and restaurants (but not in the medina). Watery local **beer,** usually Stork or Flag Speciale, isn't particularly good. Moroccan **bars** are entirely male and focus on heavy drinking; otherwise, they are pricey, tourist-oriented, and tend to attract less-than-savory types. More pleasant are the many coffee houses where you can get inexpensive Moroccan **coffee** and **tea.** Espresso is widespread, as is regular coffee, usually sweetened with sugar and milk. Green tea, a staple of the Moroccan diet, is sipped with fresh mint leaves and lots of sugar.

CUSTOMS & ETIQUETTE

TABOOS. Avoid clothing that exposes too much flesh: modest clothing (covering legs and shoulders) for both men and women is recommended, particularly in more rural areas. Even properly dressed non-Muslims are barred from entering many of Morocco's active mosques. Topics to avoid in conversation with Moroccans include sex, Israel and Palestine, the Royal Family, and the Western Sahara.

M O R O C C O

PUBLIC BEHAVIOR. Tourists in larger areas are susceptible to the advances of Moroccans offering to guide them. If you refuse, be polite but insistent. Western women will find that their presence attracts attention from Moroccan men. The best way to react is not at all; toning down public visibility is always smart.

 Non-Muslims are prohibited from entering Moroccan mosques (except for the Hassan II mosque in Casablanca), though visitors may glimpse the splendor of interior courtyards from doorways. Out of respect, non-Muslim guests should keep their distance during services (five times daily; Fridays at midday).

TABLE MANNERS. A traditional Moroccan meal begins with hand washing. Dinner may be served from a communal dish at a low, round table. Avoid directly using your left hand when eating, as this hand is considered reserved for personal hygiene. In more personal settings, such as dining in the home of a Moroccan, vocally praising the food is important; belching may also be appropriate.

THE ARTS

In Morocco, art lives daily in the form of architecture and crafts such as carpets, pottery, jewelry, and embroidery. Morocco has entranced Western painters for centuries; Orientalism, in the works of painters like Eugene Delacroix, began here.

ARCHITECTURE

Diverse architectural forms define Moroccan landscapes and cityscapes. An intense climate, combined with Berber austerity and Islamic privacy, give **Berber architecture** an enclosed and stark nature. *Kasbahs*, the monumental houses of the Berbers, feature central courtyards, narrow passageways, animal shelters, simple high towers, thick walls, and plain facades. *Qsour* (plural of *qsar*, or fortified Berber villages) house densely packed "apartments." Built of *pisé* (packed earth), many are gradually turning to ruins, unable to withstand wind and sand storms.

In the 10th century, Fez residents built the first Moroccan **mosques** (sometimes called *djemmas* or *masajid*), al-Andalus and the Qairaouine. The *qibla* (wall) contains the *mihrab* (prayer niche), which faces Mecca. There are two basic designs for mosques: Arab-style, based on Muhammad's house with a pillared cloister around a courtyard, and Persian-style, with a vaulted arch on each side. Attached to most mosques, Qur'anic schools *(madrasas)* have classrooms, libraries, and a prayer hall around a central courtyard and fountain.

In order to avoid idolatry, Muslim artists are forbidden from portraying figures of people, animals, or even plants. The result is a style of incredibly ingenious geometric and calligraphic decorations. Colorful patterns swirl across tiles, woodwork, stone, and ceramic. In less doctrinaire times, Almoravid artists slipped in designs that vaguely resemble leaves and flowers. **Calligraphy,** used in particularly elegant renderings and illuminations of the Qur'an, became another outlet for creativity as well as religious devotion. Sultans reserved their most dazzling designs for **imperial palaces,** with long, symmetrical reception and dwelling rooms studded with decorative gates, hidden gardens, and tiny pools and fountains.

CRAFTS

Carpet connoisseurs differentiate between rugs and *kilims*. While rugs are knotted, *kilims* are woven. The most valuable carpets will be older, with detailed embroidery, and colored with vegetable pigments. A sniff test will differentiate currant crimson from Red #5. Higher-quality rugs will also be woven of wool or linen. Berber patterned carpets from the Rif or Middle and High Atlas mountains are filled with colorful markings. Those from Rabat and other coastal cities are modeled on the famed Turkish carpets.

Fez has been the center of a renowned **leather** industry since the 15th century. High-quality Moroccan leather can be purchased here for a fraction of its international price. Fez is also the center for Moroccan **pottery,** famous for its classic blue-and-white designs. Saharan and Berber **terra cotta** ware are also common, and the south is known for its distinctive **silver jewelry,** often inlaid with colorful stones or glass. Morocco is also known for its intricate woodwork.

All of the above are to be found in Moroccan **souqs** (markets). Those in more touristed areas target foreign travelers for the sale of craftwork; the wise will make for local *souqs* to do their real purchasing. Bargaining in Morocco is serious business, as much a cultural art form as an everyday engagement. Approach with vigor: a reasonable final price should be about 50% of your seller's original quote. To avoid unnecessary hassle, declare that you've finished your shopping already or claim penniless student status. If your heart is set on a certain pair of slippers and their price refuses to drop, try walking out the door and down the block: the owner is quite likely to chase after you with a better offer. Even if he doesn't, you'll find the same item two stores down. (See also **Bargaining for Dummies,** p. 792.)

MUSIC

In the north, a hybrid genre known as **Andaloussi** is played on instruments like the *bendir* (tambourine), *oud* (lute), and *darbuqa* (percussion), putting classical poetry to complex musical structures. Originally developed in Granada in the 9th century, Arab-Andalucian music thrived in Morocco after the Muslim expulsion from Spain in the late 15th century and is still performed today. **Berber** music dates back to before the arrival of the Arabs; often emphasizing a storytelling aspect to music, it may be accompanied by *ahidous*, a ritual group dance. **Gnawa** music, a style of religious music derived from sub-Saharan Africa, is performed in a ceremony to deter evil spirits, characterized by a trance-like rhythm. Moroccan popular music is heavily influenced by **Rai,** a rebellious, polyglot pop born in urban Algeria. Artists such as **Cheb Mimoun** and **Cheb Mara** joined the Maghreb canon that includes such international superstars as **Cheb Mami, Rachid Taha,** and **Cheb Khaled.**

SPORTS

Moroccans are deeply passionate about **soccer,** and there are intense rivalries between competing clubs, including Raja Casablanca, COD Meknes, and MAS Fez. The national team, the Atlas Lions, has secured Morocco first place in the Arab league according to FIFA. **Basketball** runs a distant second but is still popular. Team sports remain limited to men. **Skiing** is common in the High Atlas Mountains (late December to early March) and is possible in the Middle Atlas Mountains as well. **Hiking** is available everywhere, **water sports** are popular on the Atlantic coast, and **biking** takes place nationwide.

Despite the popularity of soccer and basketball, Morocco's greatest athlete may well be distance runner **Hicham el-Guerrouj,** a four-time gold-medalist in the 1500m at the World Championships and the recipient of the IAAF's Athlete of the Year award in 2001 and 2002.

NATIONAL HOLIDAYS

Moroccans celebrate several secular and Islamic holidays. The dates of all Muslim holidays, which begin at sundown before the day listed, are based on the lunar calendar and are valid for 2004 only. The Gregorian year 2004 is the year 1424-1425 on the Islamic calendar, since an Islamic year is 11 days shorter than the Gregorian year. Be aware that many establishments are closed during most holidays, particularly religious ones (if the holidays fall near a weekend, establishments are likely to remain closed for an extended period.)

DATE	FESTIVAL
January 1	New Year's Day
January 11	Independence Manifesto
February 1	'Eid al-Adha (Festival of the Sacrifice)
February 21	Al Hifra (Islamic New Year)
May 1	Labor Day
August 14	Reunification Day
August 20	Anniversary of the King's and People's Revolution
August 21	Young People's Day
November 6	Anniversary of the Green March
November 18	Independence Day
October 16-November 13	Ramadan (month of fasting)
November 14	'Eid al-Fitr

RECOMMENDED READING

LITERATURE ABOUT MOROCCO. Most literature about Morocco focuses on the country's intoxicating culture and landscape. *In Morocco*, by Edith Wharton, gives episodic descriptions of Rabat, Salé, Fez, and Meknes. Walter Harris's *Morocco That Was* is a turn-of-the-century journalist's diary, featuring a wry account of a Brit's kidnapping by the international bandit Raissouli. *The Voices of Marrakesh*, by Bulgarian Nobel Prize recipient Elias Canetti, eloquently records a European Jew's encounter with Moroccan Jews. For insight into the country's social history, pick up *The House of Si Abd Allah*, edited by noted scholar Henry Munson, which recounts an oral history of a Moroccan family. No Moroccan reading list would be complete without *The Sheltering Sky*, *The Spider's House*, and *Days: Tangier Journal*, all by Paul Bowles. These books give a gorgeous introduction to Morocco and to Bowles.

MOROCCAN LITERATURE IN ENGLISH. For a more authentic taste of contemporary Moroccan life, read *Love With a Few Hairs*, *The Lemon*, and *M'hashis*, by Muhammad Mrabet and translated by Paul Bowles. *The Battle of Three Kings*, by Youssef Necrouf, gives an entertaining account of medieval violence and intrigue under the Saadian dynasty. In *Dreams of Trespass (Tales of a Moroccan Girlhood)*, Fatima Mernissa tells her story of growing up in a Fez harem in the 1950s.

MOROCCO ESSENTIALS

The information in this section is designed to help travelers get their bearings once they are in Morocco. For info about general **travel preparations** (including passports and permits, money, health, packing, international transportation, and more), consult the **Essentials** section at the beginning of this guide. Essentials also contains tips for travelers with specific concerns (p. 51).

ENTRANCE REQUIREMENTS
Passport (p. 11). Required of all foreign travelers.
Visa (p. 13). Required in addition to passport for citizens of South Africa.
Driving Permit (p. 767). For all those planning to drive in Morocco.

EMBASSIES & CONSULATES

In Morocco, most embassies and consulates are open Monday through Friday from around 8am to noon; some reopen after lunch until 6pm. For Moroccan embassies abroad, see **Embassies & Consulates,** p. 9

Australia, Ireland, & New Zealand: In an emergency, contact any Commonwealth embassy.

Canada: Embassy: 13 Bis, Jaafar As-Saddik, B.P.709, Agdal, **Rabat** (☎037 68 74 00).

South Africa: Embassy: 34 rue de Saadiens, **Rabat** (☎037 70 67 60; fax 70 67 56), opposite the mausoleum.

United Kingdom: Embassy: 17 bd. de la Tour Hassan, B.P. 45, **Rabat** (☎037 72 96 96; fax 70 45 31; www.britain.org.ma). **Consulates:** 43 bd. d'Anfa, B.P. 13, #762, **Casablanca** (☎022 22 16 53); bd. Mohammed V, B.P. 2122, **Tangier** (☎039 94 15 57; fax 94 22 84).

United States: Embassy: 2 av. de Mohammed El Fassi, **Rabat** (☎037 76 22 65, afterhours 76 96 39; fax 76 56 61). **Consulate:** 8 bd. Moulay Youssef, **Casablanca** (☎022 26 45 50; fax 20 41 27).

TRANSPORTATION

BY PLANE

Royal Air Maroc (RAM; in Casablanca ☎022 31 41 41 or 33 90 00, in the US 800-344-6726, in the UK 7 439 43 61), Morocco's national airline, flies to and from most major cities in Europe, including Madrid and Lisboa. Domestically, a network of flights radiates from the Mohammed V Airport outside Casablanca. Planes fly daily to Agadir, Fez, Marrakesh, Tangier, and occasionally to Ouarzazate.

If you hope to see a lot of Morocco in a short time, flying can be a convenient and affordable option; you don't have to commit to a flight until the day before, and the price of the ticket always remains the same, whenever you buy it. Royal Air Maroc and its competitor, **Regional Airlines,** fly to all major domestic cities. Regional Airlines (in Casablanca ☎022 54 34 17; www.regionalmaroc.com) flies from Barcelona, Las Palmas, Lisboa, Madrid, and Málaga, and offers many domestic routes, including Agadir, Casablanca, Laayoune, Tangier, and Oujda.

BY FERRY & HYDROFOIL

For travel from Spain to Morocco, the most budget-minded mode is by sea. Spanish-based **Trasmediterránea** (in Spain ☎902 45 46 45; www.trasmediterranea.es/homei.htm) runs ferries on a shuttle schedule from **Algeciras** (☎956 65 62 44; Recinto del Puerto, s/n) to **Ceuta,** known within Morocco as Sebta (☎956 50 94 11; Muelle Cañonero Dato, 6), and **Tangier.** Trasmediterránea is represented in Tangier by **Limadet** (☎039 93 50 76; 3 rue Ibn Roched). "Fast" ferries run from Algeciras to Ceuta. **Comarit** (☎956 66 84 62; www.comarit.com; Av. Virgen del Carmen, 3-1°Cial) runs from Algeciras to Tangier and offers **vehicle transport.** Check online for Comarit's unpredictable weekly schedule.

BY TRAIN

Trains in Morocco are faster than buses, more comfortable, fairly reliable, and prompt. Second-class train tickets are slightly more expensive than corresponding CTM bus fares; first-class tickets cost around 20% more than those second-class.

The main line runs from Tangier via Rabat and Casablanca to Marrakesh. A spur connects Fez, Meknes, and points east. There is one *couchette* train between Fez and Marrakesh. Tickets bought on board cost at least 10% more and may cause trouble with the conductor. No student fares are available. Be wary of old schedules that show times for the Atlantic coast, south of Casablanca—this route has been out of service for a few years now. **InterRail** (see p. 45) is valid in Morocco, but Eurail is not. Fares are so low, however, that InterRail is not worth it.

BY BUS

In Morocco, bus travel is less frequent and less reliable than in Spain or Portugal. Plan well ahead if you plan to use buses as your method of transport. They're not all that fast or comfortable, but they are extremely cheap and travel to nearly every corner of the country. **Compagnie de Transports du Maroc (CTM),** the state-owned line, has the fastest, most luxurious, most reliable, and generally most expensive buses (though "expensive" here means just a few more dirham). In many cities, CTM has a station separate from other lines; reservations are usually not necessary. *Let's Go* lists CTM stations in each city. Several dozen private companies operate as well. Though they may offer more frequent departures, the comfort level is so low, you'll probably wish you had waited for the next CTM. Other private companies, called **cars publiques** (a.k.a. *souq* buses), have more departures and are slower, less comfortable, and cheaper. In bus stations, each company has its own info window; window-hop for information on destinations and schedules.

The **baggage check** at CTM bus depots is usually safe. Your bags, however, may not be accepted for storage if you don't have padlocks on the zippers. Private bus companies also have baggage checkrooms; they're generally very trustworthy.

BY TAXI

Two separate packs of taxis prowl Moroccan streets: intra-urban *petit taxis* and inter-urban *grand taxis*, both dirt cheap by European standards. *Petit taxis*, small Renaults or Fiats that can each hold a strict maximum of three passengers, are all painted in one color depending on the municipality (red in Fez, blue in Meknes, etc.) and can't leave the city or take you to the airport. Make sure the driver turns the meter on; they are required to do so by law. If the driver won't turn it on, agree on the price before you go (around 50% of what the driver asks is fair). There is a 50% surcharge after 8pm. Don't be surprised if the driver stops for other passengers or picks you up with other passengers in the car, but if you are picked up after the meter has been started, note the initial price.

Grand taxis, typically beige or dark-blue Mercedes sedans, are the most expensive way to travel, but do go just about everywhere. Unlike their *petit* cousins, they don't usually cruise for passengers, congregating instead at a central area in town. They hold up to six passengers (four in the back, two in the front), but if you plan on taking a long ride, you might buy two spaces to allow for extra room. A taxi won't go until it is filled with passengers going in the same direction. Ask other passengers what they are paying to avoid being ripped off.

BY CAR

There are two reasons to rent a car in Morocco: large group travel and travel to areas not reached by Morocco's public transportation system. Otherwise, rental is unnecessary. Roads can be very dangerous; reckless passing maneuvers, excessive speed, shoddy maintenance, and poorly equipped vehicles are all common.

Hertz, Avis, and **Europcar** all rent cars; expect to pay about 400dh per day for an economy car, including taxes and insurance. Large local firms such as **Afric Car, Moroloc,** and **Locoto** offer cars for considerably less money but are also less reliable. Both international and local firms are easy to find in all major cities. Before you leave the lot, make sure that you have a full spare tire and a complete toolkit.

Once in your car, you face a myriad of complications, the most serious being **security checks.** Virtually any trip you take will bring you to at least one checkpoint. Expect to be pulled over and asked to produce your passport and proof of rental. One tactic if pulled over is to immediately ask for directions, either in French or Arabic. You also may be stopped for **traffic violations,** real or not. The fine is payable on the spot in dirhams and may be negotiable; asking for a receipt could be construed as provocative. Whatever you do, **do not travel with drugs in your car.**

Routes goudronées (principal roads), marked "P," are paved and connect cities. **Pistes** (secondary roads), designated "S," are very rough. If traveling in the **desert,** be sure to bring at least 10L of bottled water for each person and for the radiator. Move rapidly over sand; if you start to bog down, put the car in low gear and step on the gas. If you come to a stop in soft sand, push. **Gas** costs about 10dh per liter.

Driving in Morocco without the **Michelin map** of Morocco all but ensures that you will get lost. Even with the map, you still should inquire about road conditions. One place to make such inquiries is the automobile association, **Touring Club du Maroc,** 3 av. des F.A.R., Casablanca (☎022 20 30 64).

BY THUMB

Almost no one in Morocco **hitches,** although flagging down buses and trains can feel like hitchhiking. Transportation is dirt cheap by European and North American standards. If Moroccans do pick up a foreigner, they will most likely expect payment for the ride. Hitching is more frequent in the south and in the mountains, where transportation is irregular. *Let's Go* does not recommend hitchhiking.

MONEY

DIRHAM (DH)	
US $1 = 9.79DH	1DH = US $0.10
EUR €1 = 10.75DH	1DH = EUR €0.09
AUS $1 = 6.35DH	1DH = AUS $0.16
CDN $1 = 7.07DH	1DH = CDN $0.14
NZ $1 = 5.66DH	1DH = NZ $0.18
UK £1 = 15.44DH	1DH = UK £0.06
ZAR 1 = 1.33DH	1DH = ZAR 0.75

In Morocco, **banking hours** are Monday through Friday 8:30 to 11:30am and 2:30 to 4:30pm, during Ramadan from 9:30am to 2pm. In the summer, certain banks close at 1pm and do not re-open in the afternoon. Do not try the **black market** for currency exchange—you'll be swindled. As in Europe, **ATMs** are the best way to change money. Also know that it is very difficult to change back upon departure.

Taxes are generally included in prices, though in malls and *grandes surfaces* (larger superstores) you will find a 7% **Value-Added Tax (VAT)** on food and a 22% tax on luxury goods. **Tipping** a small amount after restaurant meals is unnecessary, but a nice gesture given the extreme degree of poverty of many Moroccan citizens.

Bargaining is a legitimate part of the Moroccan shopping experience—it is most commonly accepted in outdoor markets. There are guidelines to consider when bargaining. Tailor your bargaining to the situation—offering 40% of the asking price may be too much or too little, depending on where the seller started. Decide what the item is actually worth to you, and use that as a benchmark. Do not appear overly eager, instead point out imperfections in the item, or mention that you saw the item elsewhere at a lower price. Walk away when the seller has quoted a "minimum" price. Do not try to bargain in supermarkets or established stores.

SAFETY & SECURITY

Morocco has received a bad rap among travelers. While the **crime rate** is higher than in Spain or Portugal, there is more to Morocco than just hustlers and drugs. Nevertheless, visitors should be suspicious of offers for free food or drinks, as they have been known to be drugged. Large cities like Tangier and Fez are filled with fake guides offering tours of the city for a small price; they should be avoided.

Debates between the Moroccan government and the Algerian-based Polisario Front over possession of the Western Sahara resulted in a **guerrilla war** until the late 1980s. The UN called a cease-fire in 1991, but there are still unexploded **land mines** in the area. Travel to Western Sahara is difficult and not recommended; those interested must obtain clearance information from the Moroccan embassy.

Women travelers will probably have extra difficulties traveling through Morocco without a male companion. At the very least, they should never travel alone. Visitors will feel safer and more comfortable (and will avoid offending local sensibilities) by not wearing short skirts, sleeveless tops, and shorts; moreover, females should always wear bras. Regardless, non-Moroccan women may be gawked at, commented upon, approached by hustlers, followed in a crowd, or even groped on the street. Moroccan woman may "hiss" at indecently clad female travelers. The best response to male harassers may be silence, but yelling *"shuma"* (meaning shame) may well embarrass them, especially in the presence of onlookers. If an uncomfortable situation persists, look out for a policeman.

HEALTH

All travelers in Morocco face a different set of health issues than in Spain and Portugal; **food and waterborne diseases** in particular are common causes of illness. The CDC recommends that travelers drink only bottled or boiled water, avoiding tap water, fountain drinks, and ice cubes. It is also advisable to eat only fruit and vegetables that are cooked and that you have peeled yourself. Stay away from food sold by street vendors, and check to make sure that dairy products have been pasteurized. There is only a slight **malaria** risk in Morocco, but it would still be wise to take extra precaution against insect bites. Consider getting a vaccine before leaving. For further information, see **Health,** p. 23.

While there is a public health system in Morocco, travelers should seek out private clinics, which offer the most dependable and affordable care. There are few English-speaking doctors, though French is widespread; learn a few basic words of medical vocabulary in French in case of an emergency. Private clinics are found in large cities and university towns with medical schools, such as Casablanca and Rabat. Travelers with significant medical problems that might need sudden and immediate attention are advised to stay in larger cities for accessibility reasons.

ACCOMMODATIONS

HOTELS

Although there is an official star system for rating hotels in Morocco, the number of stars reflects little more than price. Hotels that are not part of the system are not necessarily worse—their standards vary greatly—but are usually cheaper. Rooms can vary widely even within a particular hotel, so ask to see another room if you don't like the first, or find another hotel, often next door. Cheap hotels in Morocco are really cheap—as little as 50dh per night. *Let's Go* listings are generally divided between medina and *ville nouvelle* establishments. Medina hotels are usually cheaper than their *ville nouvelle* counterparts, but less comfortable and with fewer amenities. Hot showers, when available, may cost extra (usually less than 10dh). Cold showers are usually free. Many hotels offer laundry service.

YOUTH HOSTELS

The **Federation Royale des Auberges de Jeunesse (FRMAJ)** is the Moroccan Hosteling International (HI) affiliate. Beds cost 30-40dh per night, and there is a surcharge for non-members everywhere but in Casablanca. Some hostels sell HI memberships on the spot. Call ahead for reservations. To reserve beds in high season, get an International Booking Voucher from FRMAJ (or a nearby HI affiliate) and send it to the hostel four to eight weeks in advance. You'll probably need to bring your own sleepsack and towel, and there are usually curfew and lock-out times. For hostel addresses, write FRMAJ, Parc de la Ligue Arabe, B.P. 15998, Casa Principale, Casablanca 21000 (☎022 47 09 52; fax 22 76 77). For more info on international youth hostel associations, see **Accommodations, p. 30.**

CAMPING

Camping is popular and cheap (about 15dh per person), especially in the desert, mountains, and beaches. Like hotels, conditions vary widely. You can usually expect to find restrooms, but electricity is not as readily available. Use caution if camping unofficially, especially on the beaches, as theft is a problem.

KEEPING IN TOUCH

Most useful communication information (including international access codes, calling card numbers, country codes, operator and directory assistance, and emergency numbers) is listed on the inside back cover of this book.

TELEPHONES. Morocco has recently invested hundreds of millions of dollars into modernizing its telephone system, markedly improving services. Pay phones accept only phone cards. Available at post offices, cards are usually in denominations too large to be practical. Entrepreneurial Moroccans hang around phone banks and let you use their phone cards. You pay for the units used—typically 2dh per unit. To use the card, insert and dial 00. Once the dial tone turns into a tune, dial the number.

 Country Code: 212. International dialing prefix: 00.

Phone offices *(téléboutiques)* are located in most cities. If you can't find one, head to the post office—they always have at least one phone for international calls. To make a collect call, ask the desk attendant at the local telephone office to place a call *en P.C.V.* ("ahn PAY-SAY-VAY"). Write down your name and the country, state, city, and telephone number you want to call. Collect calls can also be made from payphones; simply dial 12 and ask to call *en P.C.V.* Remember that the initial zero (0) in **city codes** is dialed only when calling from another area within Morocco; from outside of Morocco the number is omitted. Local calls do not require dialing any portion of the city code.

The best way to make international calls is with a **calling card** (see **By Telephone,** p. 35). To **call home with a calling card,** contact the operator for your service provider in Morocco by dialing the appropriate toll-free access number (see p. 37).

MAIL. Sending something **air mail** (*par avion*) can take a week to a month to reach the US or Canada (about 10dh for a slim letter, postcards 4-7dh). Less reliable **surface mail** (*par terre*) takes up to two months. **Express mail** (*recommandé* or *exprès postaux*), is faster than regular air mail and more reliable. Post offices and *tabacs* sell **stamps.** For fast service (2 days to the US), your best bet is DHL (www.dhl.com), which has drop-off locations in major cities, or FedEx, (www.fedex.com).

EMAIL. Cybercafes are common in major cities and more touristed towns. *Let's Go* lists Internet access where applicable.

EXPLORING MOROCCO

For many travelers weary of visiting Spanish and Portuguese cathedrals, a short excursion across the Strait of Gibraltar into Morocco becomes an unexpected highlight of their trip. In Morocco, passersby don't pass you by; everyone wants to know your name. Fruits and vegetables are sold right off the street—next to stinking fish. Old men squat on the side of the road, wrapped in hooded garments. Excitement and adventure need not be planned or paid for lavishly; just step outside your hotel door and wander down an ancient medina street. While Morocco offers a manageable, if at times stressful, introduction to both the Islamic and African worlds, it's the proud and hospitable nation's own unique blend of languages, landscapes, and people which defy any preconceptions and exceed all expectations. The country, still largely inhabited by an ancient race of people known as Berbers, has a fascinating history as the crossroads between two rich continents. Physically, the nation contains unparalleled raw beauty in the form of lush valleys, enormous desert dunes, ancient imperial cities, and North Africa's highest mountains. Finally, there is Morocco in its modern mutation, a nation that struggles to balance a youthful and striving face with its traditional ways.

Coverage of Morocco is included here to provide a guide for a brief visit during more extensive travel in Spain and Portugal, featuring the accessible highlights rather than an exhaustive survey. So, as the draw of North Africa pulls you south through Andalucía, skim across the Strait and immerse yourself in Morocco.

HIGHLIGHTS OF MOROCCO

BROWSE with Berbers in the Meknes **medina** (see p. 779).

MARVEL at Casablanca's **Hassan II mosque,** the world's third largest and the only one in Morocco open to Westerners (see p. 798).

SPICE things up in the markets and shops of ancient **Marrakesh** (see p. 804).

! EDITOR'S NOTE. Due to the May 2003 Casablanca bombings, *Let's Go* did not send a researcher for the 2004 edition. The following coverage was last updated in August 2003.

THE MEDITERRANEAN COAST

Northern Morocco is comprised of Mediterranean ports, beaches, and the jagged Rif Mountains. The most accessible region from Spain, the Mediterranean coast is a common point of entry into the country. Precisely because of its proximity to Europe and the prevalence of European influence throughout its history, this area where French, Spanish, and Arabic architecture, lifestyles, and language overlap is rarely considered "real Morocco." The Mediterranean cities provide a taste of the country, but they may not leave visitors with the most favorable impression. Those interested in observing true Moroccan culture should keep pushing south.

TANGIER طنجة ☎039

For travelers venturing out of Europe for the first time, Tangier (pop. 500,000) can be stressful. Many make the city out to be a living nightmare, but despite the very real difficulties, it remains the best way to enter from Spain. While it is not one of Morocco's main tourist attractions, Tangier interests visitors with its complex history and edgy urban pace. For centuries, the region bounced from one imperial power to the next, culminating in 1923 with the declaration of Tangier as an "international zone" loosely governed by the US and eight European powers. Law enforcement dwindled, and the city began to attract rich heiresses, drug users, spies, and Beat Generation poets. When Morocco declared its independence from France in 1956, the new government tried to change Tangier's image, closing down most of the brothels and increasing police presence. Nevertheless, rising tourism (thanks to expanded ferry service) has propelled Tangier forward.

▐ TRANSPORTATION

Flights: Royal Air Maroc, pl. de France (☎039 37 95 08). **Iberia,** 35 bd. Pasteur (☎039 93 61 78), flies daily to **Madrid. British Airways,** 83 rue de la Liberté (☎039 93 52 11) to **London.** A **taxi** to the airport, 16km away, is 80-100dh for up to 6 people.

Trains: Mghagha Station (☎039 95 25 55), 6km from the port. *Petit taxi* to the station 15dh. To: **Casablanca** (6hr., 4 per day 8am-11pm, 117dh); **Fez** (5½hr., 4 per day 8am-11pm, 96dh); **Meknes** (5hr., 4 per day 8am-11pm, 80dh).

Buses: Private buses leave from av. Yacoub al-Mansour at pl. Jamia al-Arabia, 2km from the port. Ask blue-coated personnel or check boards for ticket info. Luggage 5dh. *Petit taxi* from the port to the terminal 8dh. To: **Casablanca** (6hr., every hr. 5am-1am, 69dh); **Chefchaouen** (2 per day 7am, 2:45pm); **Ceuta** (40min., 7 per day 6:15am-5:45pm, 10dh); **Fez** (6hr., 11 per day 11:30am-9:30pm, 63dh); **Marrakesh** (10hr.; 3 per day 6:45am, 4:20, 8:30pm; 115dh); **Meknes** (5hr., 8 per day 6am-5:45pm, 57dh). **CTM buses** (☎039 93 11 72) to: **Agadir** (3 per day 11am, 4:30, 9pm); **Casablanca** (6 per day 11am-midnight); **Chefchaouen** (1 per day 12:30pm); **Fez** (3 per day 3, 7, 9pm); **Marrakesh** (2 per day 11am, 4:30pm); **Meknes** (3 per day 3, 7, 9pm).

Ferries: The cheapest and most convenient option is to buy a ticket at the port agent, 46 ave. d'Espagne (☎039 94 26 12), though ticket agencies are located throughout the city. You'll need a boarding pass (available at any ticket desk) and a customs form (ask uniformed agents). Near the terminal, pushy men with ID cards will try to arrange your ticket and fill out your customs card for 10dh; just do it yourself. To **Algeciras** (2½hr., every hr. 7am-9pm, 210dh) and **Tarifa** (35min., 3-5 per day, 200dh).

Taxis: Prices subject to bargaining; a fair price is 20dh per person for 6 passengers. Found everywhere, especially by the main bus stop, the Grand Socco, and the intersection of bd. Pasteur and bd. Mohammed V.

Car Rental: Avis, 54 bd. Pasteur. Open daily 8am-noon and 2-7pm. **Hertz,** 36 bd. Mohammed V (☎039 93 30 31). Open M-Sa 8:30am-noon and 2-6:30pm, Su 9am-noon. From 250dh per day with a 20% tax for a Fiat Palio or Fiat Uno. 25+. International license not required.

▟ ORIENTATION

Avenue d'Espagne runs from the port along the waterfront to the train station 6km away and makes Tangier easy to navigate. Many of the *ville nouvelle* hotels are located about 1.5km down av. d'Espagne away from the ferry terminal (a *petit taxi* should cost 5dh, but if you don't have a lot of baggage and you have your wits about you, it's better to walk). Hustlers tend to prey on fresh meat here. Adjacent to the ferry terminal area on av. d'Espagne is the **CTM bus station. Rue du Portugal** heads uphill here and divides the *ville nouvelle* from the medina. You can enter the medina and easily find some of its accommodations by turning right above the

Tangier

🛏 ACCOMMODATIONS
Auberge de Jeunesse (HI), 14
Hôtel Continental, 2
Hôtel El Muniria (Tanger Inn), 9
Hôtel and Restaurant L'Marsa, 11
Pension Amal, 5
Pension Miami, 6
Pension Palace, 4

🍴 FOOD
Brahim Abdelmalek, 13
Restaurant Africa, 7
Restaurant Hammodi, 1

☕ CAFÉS
Café Central, 3
Café de Paris, 8
Negresco, 12
Tanger Inn, 10

CTM station, continuing uphill on rue Salah Idine al-Ayoubi. Soon you will reach the large, busy rotary known as the **Grand Socco** (Pl. du 9 Avril 1946), the center of activity directly above the medina. From the Grand Socco, you can head down into the medina via **rue al-Siaghin,** which leads to the **Petit Socco,** or walk down bustling **rue d'Italie,** which skirts the medina's western wall. The *ville nouvelle's* main commercial road is **boulevard Pasteur,** which connects the main square, **place de France,** with **boulevard Mohammed V,** containing many banks, the post office, and cafes.

⁇ PRACTICAL INFORMATION

Tourist Office: 29 bd. Pasteur (☎039 94 80 50). Some English, French, and Spanish spoken. List of accommodations available. Open M-F 8:30am-7:30pm.

Currency Exchange: BMCE, 21 bd. Pasteur (☎039 93 11 25). No commission here, but other Moroccan banks charge fees for exchanging traveler's checks. Open M-F 8:15am-2:15pm. **BMCE branch** on most ferries and one in the port complex, although these only change cash. Major banks line bd. Pasteur and bd. Mohammed V, several of which have **ATMs.** Travel agencies near the port are required to change money at official rates. There are **Western Union** locations at pl. de France and the main post office.

Luggage Storage: At the **train station** (5dh per bag). Open 24hr. Also at the **bus station** (4dh per bag). Open daily 5:30am-12:30am.

English-Language Bookstore: Librairie des Colonnes, 54 bd. Pasteur (☎039 93 69 55). English classics, French and Spanish fiction, and literature on Moroccan culture. Open M-F 9:30am-12:30pm and 4-7pm, Sa 9:30am-1pm.

Police: ☎ 19, at the port and main train station.

Medical Services: Red Cross, 6 rue al-Mansur Dhabi (☎039 94 25 17), runs a 24hr. English-speaking medical service. **Ambulance:** ☎039 31 27 27.

Internet Access: Cyber Café Adam, 2 rue Ibn Roched. 10dh per hr. Open daily 8:30am-2am. **Espace Net** and **Euronet** are on rue du Mexique.

Post Office: 33 bd. Mohammed V (☎039 93 25 18). **Poste Restante.** Open M-Th 8:30am-6:30pm, Sa 8:30am-12:15pm. Parcels are received around the corner from main entrance, on the back side of the building.

⁇ ACCOMMODATIONS

Whether you stay in the *ville nouvelle* or the medina, you are bound to meet hustlers "welcoming" you to Morocco. Accommodations in the *ville nouvelle* are often more comfortable. Reserve ahead, be cautious, and have a sense of where you're going when you hit town. Rates may decrease in winter.

MEDINA

The most convenient hostels are near **rue Mokhtar Ahardan** off the Petit Socco. From the Grand Socco, take the first right down rue al-Siaghin to the Petit Socco, a small intersection. Rue Mokhtar Ahardan begins at the end of the Petit Socco closest to the port. At night, the smaller streets off the medina can be unsafe.

Pension Amal, 5 rue Mokhtar Ahardan (☎039 93 36 00). Rooms are clean and plain, if a bit dingy. Free cold showers. Singles 50dh; doubles 100dh. ❶

Pension Palace, 2 rue Mokhtar Ahardan (☎039 93 61 28). Stark rooms inhabited by students. The courtyard starred in Bertolucci's adaptation of *The Sheltering Sky.* Singles 40dh; doubles 80dh, with bath 120dh; triples 120dh/150dh; quads 120dh/200dh. ❷

Hôtel Continental, 36 Dar Baroud (☎039 93 10 24), overlooking the port. From the ferry terminal, bear right around the CTM station and follow the many signs. A grand hotel furnished with a mix of Moroccan ornament and Art Deco. Home to newbie visitors and aging hippies. Breakfast included. Showers hot only in the mornings. Reservations recommended. Singles 284dh; doubles 365dh; triples 435dh. ❺

VILLE NOUVELLE
Hotels line av. d'Espagne as it heads away from the port. The best values lie a few blocks uphill toward bd. Pasteur and bd. Mohammed V.

Hôtel El Muniria (Tanger Inn), rue Magellan (☎039 93 53 37). William Burroughs wrote *Naked Lunch* in room #9 (now the owner's room). Ask for room #4, where Jack Kerouac and Allen Ginsberg stayed. A great deal for Tangier, with spacious rooms, hot showers, and towels. Singles 100dh; doubles 130dh. ❸

Auberge de Jeunesse (HI), 8 rue El-Antaki (☎039 94 61 27). A backpacker hotspot. New, firm dormitory beds. Common area with TV. Hot showers 5dh. Office open M-Sa 8-10am, noon-3pm, and 6-11pm; Su 8-10am and 6pm-midnight. Closes around 10:30pm in winter. 29.50dh; HI members 27dh. ❶

Pension Miami, 126 rue Salah Idine al-Ayoubi (☎039 93 29 00). 45 rooms, high carved ceilings, and a balcony on each floor. Basic communal bathroom. Hot showers 10dh. Singles 50dh; doubles 80dh; triples 120dh; quads 160dh. ❶

Hôtel L'Marsa, 92 av. d'Espagne (☎039 93 23 39). Clean rooms with closets, some with terrace. Hot showers outside 7dh. Laundry 5dh per piece. Singles 50dh; doubles 100dh; quads 200dh. MC/V. ❶

☐ FOOD

MEDINA
Begin at the **Grand Socco,** where you can stall-hop for delights of all types, and then head toward the Petit Socco for a slew of inexpensive local eateries. On the corner near pl. de France sprawls a huge **market.** The best pastries in town are at **Café Patisserie Charaf,** 28 rue Smarine, just below the Grand Socco in the medina.

Restaurant Hammadi, 2 rue de la Qasbah (☎039 93 45 14). Specialties are *tajine* (40dh) and couscous (45dh). Beer and wine served. Entrees 40-60dh. 10% tax added to each meal. Open daily 11am-3pm and 7pm-midnight. MC/V. ❷

Restaurant Dar Tagine, 29 rue du Commerce, Petit Socco (☎068 425 500). When coming down the hill from the Grand Socco, take the first left; the restaurant is on the left. Some of the best Moroccan cuisine in the city. Elegant and immaculate Moroccan-style decor. Set price for 5-course meal is 110dh. Open daily. MC/V. ❹

VILLE NOUVELLE
The restaurants along av. d'Espagne tout unspectacular and overpriced *menus touristiques* for 50dh and up. Beachfront restaurants run by the high-end hotels are just what you'd expect—expensive and boring. You're better off scouting around **place de France.** Hot sandwiches can be found all along bd. Pasteur.

L'Marsa, 92 av. d'Espagne (☎039 93 19 28). This popular restaurant/cafe has outdoor dining and a mixed Italian and Moroccan menu. Praiseworthy pizzas (23-35dh), pasta, and Italian ice cream (12-25dh). Women traveling alone should avoid the rooftop terrace, a choice pick-up spot for Moroccan men. Entrees 25-70dh. Open daily June-Aug. 5am-3am; Sept.-May 5am-midnight. MC/V. ❷

Restaurant Africa, 83 rue Salah Idine al-Ayoubi (☎039 93 54 36). A quiet, dimly lit place by Moroccan standards. Omelettes (15dh) and *tajine* (30dh). Beer served. Big 4-course *menu du jour* 50dh. Entrees 25-80dh. Open daily 9am-12:30am. ❷

Brahim Abdelmalek, 14 rue du Mexique (☎039 93 17 96). King Hassan II lunched here. You can too, for less than 15dh. Owner claims to have invented Moroccan sandwich craze in 1960. (See **The Local Story.**) Open daily 10:30am-3am. ❶

⊙ SIGHTS

▧ OLD AMERICAN LEGATION. The Old American Legation is an austere and refined escape. In 1821, this became the first foreign property acquired by the United States. The museum contains correspondence between George Washington and his "great and magnanimous friend" Sultan Moulay ben Abdallah, among other exhibits. (Morocco was the first nation to recognize America's independence, thus forever solidifying friendly relations between the countries.) Visit the room dedicated to famous expat writer Paul Bowles, featuring photographs from Tangier's storied "interzone" days. The friendly curators will give excellent tours on request, but calling first is recommended. *(8 rue d'America. Enter the medina via the large white steps on rue du Portugal and look for the yellow archway emblazoned with the US seal. ☎039 93 53 17. Open M-F 10am-1pm and 3-5pm. Donation suggested.)*

DAR AL-MAKHZEN. An opulent palace, currently under renovation, with hand-woven tapestries, inlaid ceilings, and foliated archways, Dar al-Makhzen was once home to the ruling pasha of Tangier and is now the Museum of Moroccan Art. The collection includes intriguing exhibits of ceramics, carpets, silver jewelry, weapons, and musical instruments, with plaques in French and English. *(Currently undergoing renovations; call to see if it has reopened. Enter the medina from the porte de la Qasbah gate and stick to the rampart wall until you reach pl. de la Qasbah. The museum is to the right. ☎039 93 20 97. Open W-M 9am-12:30pm and 3-5:30pm. 10dh.)*

MARKETS. The medina's commercial center is the **Grand Socco.** This busy square and traffic circle are cluttered with fruit vendors, parsley stands, and *kebab* and fish stalls. Off rue de Fès is the small, colorful **Fez Market,** where local merchants cater to Tangier's Europeans. *(2 blocks down rue de Fès on the right.)* Rif Berbers come to the **Dradeb district** every Thursday and Sunday bearing pottery, olives, mint, and fresh fruit, but unless Tangier is your only stop, buy crafts elsewhere. *(West of the Grand Socco along rue Bou Arrakia and rue de la Montagne.)*

OTHER SIGHTS. Rue Riad Sultan runs alongside the **Jardins du Soltane,** where artisans weave carpets, and continues to **place de la Qasbah,** a sunny courtyard with a promontory offering spectacular views of Spain and the Atlantic Ocean. With your back to the water, walk toward the far right corner of the plaza; just around the corner to the right the **Mosque de la Qasbah** rears its octagonal minaret. Outside the medina, 17th- and 18th-century bronze cannons hide in the **Jardins de la Mendoubia,** a welcome escape from the excitement of the Soccos. *(Through white gate #50.)*

◪ CAFES

The most popular evening activity in Tangier is sipping mint tea in front of a cafe on pl. de France or bd. Pasteur. **Café de Paris,** 1 pl. de France, hosted countless meetings between spies during WWII. Coming from the Grand Socco, look to the left. (☎039 93 84 44. Tea and coffee 5-6dh. Open daily 7am-11:30pm.) Inside the medina, **Café Central** was a favorite of William S. Burroughs (off the Petit Socco; same hours and prices). **Café Hafa,** near the *qasbah*, has a great view of Spain on a clear day. Cafes tend to attract a male crowd, but female tourists should not be afraid to grab a table and an orange juice—it's perfectly acceptable. ■**Kandinsky Plaza,** 30 route Malabata, a chic cafe and gourmet ice cream shop, is popular with men and women, foreign and Moroccan. For no-hassle beer, head to the **Tanger Inn,** rue Magellan (open 9pm-late); for a quiet drink, try **Negresco,** 20 rue du Mexique, off pl. de France. The city's longest-running bar is full of expats and backpackers. (☎039 93 80 97. Beer 15-18dh. Mixed drinks 30-35dh. Open daily 10am-midnight.)

CEUTA (SEBTA) سبتمة ☎039

Travelers hoping to avoid Tangier altogether may opt to ferry to the Spanish enclave Ceuta and from there cross the Moroccan border, only 5km away. Most visitors don't stay in Ceuta (pop. 70,000), moving on immediately to Tetouan (35min. away) or Chefchaouen (allow 4hr.). If you're trapped in Ceuta, try the helpful **tourist booth** (☎956 50 62 75) in the ferry terminal, which has a map. If you need to spend the night, accommodation options do exist.

BORDER CROSSING. To reach the Moroccan border from Ceuta, grab a taxi from the town center (€4.80) or take **bus #7** (€0.47); to reach the bus stand from the ferry (5min. away), exit the terminal and take a left onto the main street. At the end of the street, near a roundabout with a fountain in the middle (and near the water), take a right up the hill, and then another right to the stand. Taxis and buses stop short of the border; you must cross on foot and have your passport stamped. Expect to be accosted by guides wanting to escort you to their cousin's rug emporium. Just head straight to the parking lot, where **grand taxis** await (see p. 777). **Cash** exchange is also available at the border; do it here rather than in Ceuta. From the border, full *grand taxis* to Tetouan are 15-20dh per person. From there you can connect to the more mellow Chefchaouen by catching a bus or taxi. If you are heading to **Algeciras** (see p. 280) from Ceuta, there are sixteen **fast-ferry** departures (35min., 7:30am-10:30pm, €21). Don't forget about the 2hr. time difference between Spain and Morocco.

CHEFCHAOUEN (CHAOUEN) شفشوان ☎039

Mellow, whitewashed Chefchaouen (pop. 30,000) lies high in the Rif Mountains. Chefchaouen's relaxed atmosphere and cool mountain air refresh even the weariest of travelers, who are attracted by its manageable, Mediterranean medina and the proximity to *kif* (hashish) farms. There are also some breathtaking natural wonders within hiking distance.

◧ TRANSPORTATION. The **bus station** (☎039 98 95 73) is far downhill from town. **Buses** heading south fill up, so get tickets early. **CTM** and other **buses** go to: **Fez** (5hr.; 2 per day 1:15, 3pm; 45-55dh); **Ouazzene,** the best bet for connections (1hr.; 3 per day 7am, 1:15, 3:30pm; 18dh); **Tangier** (via Tetouan, 28-33dh); and **Tetouan** (1½hr., 7 per day 6:45am-6pm, 16-18dh). To get to **Ceuta,** you must go through Tetouan. Private companies also have daily buses to Fez and Meknes. There is a **second bus station** only four blocks downhill from pl. Mohammed V, on rue Mohammed Abdallah, that has buses to several locations at better prices than CTM. **Grands taxis** are the easiest way to get to **Ceuta** (24dh), although they often take a while to fill. **Taxis** leave a block downhill from pl. Mohammed V.

🔃 PRACTICAL INFORMATION. From both **bus stations,** head up the steep hill and turn right after several blocks onto the large road, which leads to tree-filled, circular pl. Mohammed V; it's about a 20min. walk to the center of town (or a few dirham for a taxi). Cross the plaza and continue east on **avenue Hassan II,** the *ville nouvelle's* main road. Here you'll find currency exchange at **BMCE** (open M-F 8:15am-2:15pm), the **post office** with **telephones** (open M-F 8:30am-12:15pm and 2:30-6:30pm), and **Internet access** at **IRIC,** 10 av. Hassan II. (☎039 98 97 15. 10dh per hr. Open daily 9am-midnight.) Chefchaouen has no tourist office. Av. Hassan II ends at Bab al-Ain, the main gate into the **medina.** From Bab al-Ain, the main street twists uphill to **place Uta al-Hammam,** the plaza at the heart of the medina. **Hospital Mohammed V** is a block west from pl. Mohammed V, and **police** are at ☎19.

🝔🝓 ACCOMMODATIONS & FOOD. Chefchaouen has a slew of colorful budget hotels. Inside the medina, head uphill from Bab al-Ain; hotels are clustered along this street and around pl. Uta al-Hammam. The best of the lot is ▧**Hotel Andalus ❶,** 1 rue Sidi Salem, directly behind Credit Agricola on pl. Uta al-Hammam, in the medina. Friendly owner Ahmed takes great pride in this clean, comfortable, and relaxing pension. With cheap rates, a gorgeous terrace, and a large common room, it's one of Morocco's best deals. (☎039 98 60 34. Singles 30dh; doubles 60dh; triples 90dh; quads 120dh; lovely terrace 20dh. Prices include hot shower.) Tucked in the corner of whitewashed walls and next to a *hammam,* **Pensión la Castellana ❶,** 4 Sidi Ahmad Bouhali, caters almost exclusively to backpackers and encourages long stays. Walk to the end of pl. Uta al-Hammam to get there. (☎039 98 62 95. Communal kitchen and common room with stereo. Free hot showers. Singles 30dh; doubles 60dh; triples 90dh; quads 120dh.) **Pension Znika ❶,** 4 rue Znika, in the medina, has well-kept rooms. (☎039 98 66 24. Singles 30dh, doubles 60dh, triples 90dh.) **Hotel Rif ❶,** rue Hassan II, is just outside the medina walls. Follow rue Hassan II to the right around the medina; it's on the left after a few blocks. Rif has clean rooms, great views, a TV lounge, and terraces decorated in an odd combination 16th-century Moroccan and 1970s Americana motifs; they also can help with **mountain hikes**—just ask for affable owner Younes. (☎/fax 039 98 69 82. Singles 50dh, with shower 90dh; doubles 80dh/120dh; triples 120dh/160dh. MC/V.) For a quick bite, **Chez Aziz ❶,** just outside Bab al-Ain, has cheap, tasty snacks. (Open daily noon-midnight.) Inside the medina, outdoor seating is available in pl. Uta al-Hammam at various restaurants. More upscale choices are along av. Hassan II.

🝓 SIGHTS. Chefchaouen's steep ▧**medina** is one of Morocco's best. It's uncrowded and more relaxed than those of larger cities. Enter through Bab al-Ain and walk uphill toward pl. Uta al-Hammam, the center of the medina. In the *place* are several outdoor cafes, the 16th-century **Grand Mosque** with its red-and-gold minaret, and a 17th-century *qasbah* built by Moulay Ismail, Morocco's famous rogue. Inside the *qasbah* stands the 15th-century **Tower of Homage.** *(Open daily 9am-1pm and 3-6:30pm. 10dh.)* Chefchaouen's **souq** operates Mondays and Thursdays outside the medina and below both av. Hassan II and av. Allal ben Abdalallah.

🝕 HIKING. For trailhead or map info, see Ahmed at Hotel Andalus or Younes at Hotel Rif. To obtain a friendly guide, contact Mouden Abdeslam (mobile ☎062 11 39 17). Follow the **Oued Ras al-Ma** (still known as Hippie River from the days when Chefchaouen attracted many) upstream into the hills for just a few kilometers for spectacular results. For a view of the city, hike to the Hotel Asmaq (follow signs for the *ville nouvelle*). Behind the hotel, there's a path that winds up the peak to the left, and then runs down into the valley. Try reaching the "Spanish mosque" about halfway up the peak to the right of the medina, or the spectacular rocky arch

known as **Pont de Dieu** (God's Bridge). Most of the hikes are 1hr. round-trip, though
it takes a full day to reach Pont de Dieu. Consider taking a taxi to the base of the
bridge. Finally, with much planning or a guide, an **overnight hike** to villages in the
mountains where Berbers will host you can be unforgettable.

THE MIDDLE ATLAS الاطلس المتوسط

The Middle Atlas is Morocco's heartland, where traditional culture and political
dynasties were formed. Home to the Roman ruins of Volubilis and the imperial cities of Meknes and Fez, the region is full of historical points of interest. Modernization creates stunning contrasts; thousands of satellite dishes face skyward from
Fez's medieval medina homes.

MEKNES مكناس ☎ 055

After uniting Morocco under his brutal rule, the rogue Sultan Moulay Ismail
chose Meknes as his seat of power in 1672 and tried to turn this relative backwater into a capital to rival Versailles. Though less arresting than Morocco's
other imperial cities, Meknes remains a pleasant and manageable city where
visitors can take leisurely enjoyment of a few impressive monuments left by
Moulay Ismail as well as the nearby world-renowned ruins of Volubilis. Named
for the Berber tribe Meknassa, this provincial capital has the largest Berber
population in Morocco.

▣ TRANSPORTATION

Trains: The **Main Station** is far from the center of town. Use **al-Amir Abdelhader Station,**
rue d'Alger (☎ 055 51 61 35). To: **Casablanca** (3¾hr., 7 per day 8am-3:30am, 81-
119dh); **Fez** (50min., 9 per day 9:55am-2am, 16.50dh); **Marrakesh** (8hr., 7 per day
8am-3:30am, 153-228dh); **Tangier** (4hr., 4 per day 7:50am-2:15am, 75-117dh).

Buses: CTM, av. des F.A.R. (☎ 055 51 47 59). To: **Casablanca** (4hr., 8 per day 8:30am-
3am, 63dh); **Fez** (1hr., 9 per day 4am-11pm, 18dh); **Marrakesh** (8hr., 1 per day 7pm,
132dh); **al-Rachidia** (6hr., 1 per day 10pm, 80dh) via Fez; **Tangier** (5hr., 3 per day 2-
7pm, 70dh). **Private buses** depart from a station on av. du Mellah just outside Bab al-
Khemis. A *petit taxi* is necessary. To: **Casablanca** (12 per day 5:30am-4pm); **Erfoud** (1
per day 9pm); **Fez** (2 per day 10am, 5:30pm); **Marrakesh** (4 per day 5:30am-
6:30pm); **al-Rachidia** (4 per day 9am-2pm); **Tangier** (6 per day 4:45am-3pm).

Taxis: *Grands taxis* cluster, among other places, on av. des F.A.R., across from Hotel Continental, next to the private bus station, and outside the al-Amir Abdelhader train station. To **Fez** (17dh) and **Moulay Idriss** (8dh).

✳ ⁊ ORIENTATION & PRACTICAL INFORMATION

The **Oued Bou Fekrane** divides Meknes into three "boroughs": the **medina,** the neighboring **Dar El-Kebira** (imperial city), and the modern **ville nouvelle.** Trains and CTM
buses deposit passengers in the *ville nouvelle.* Tree-lined **avenue Mohammed V**
intersects av. Hassan II at a large roundabout surrounded by cafes and shops.
Local buses #5, 7, and 9 (1.50-2.30dh) shuttle between the CTM bus station and
Bab al-Mansur (20min. walk); a *petit taxi* costs 8dh. The private bus station
deposits passengers at Bab al-Khemis.

Tourist Office: 27 pl. Administrative (☎055 52 44 26). Some English spoken. Brochure with basic map of city. Guides are necessary only if you want more historical information about the sites. Tours half day 120dh, full day 150dh. Open July-Sept. M-F 8am-6:30pm; Oct.-June M-F 8:30am-noon and 2:30-6:30pm. **Syndicat d'Initiative** (☎055 52 01 91), on Esplanade de la Foire. Open M-F 8:30am-noon and 3-6pm.

Currency Exchange: BMCE, 98 av. des F.A.R. (☎055 52 03 52), has **ATMs.** Exchange window open daily 10am-2pm and 4-8pm. **Hôtel Rif,** on Zenkat Accra, cashes traveler's checks for a fee. **Banks** line both av. Mohammed V and av. Hassan II.

Late-Night Pharmacy: Red Crescent Emergency Pharmacy (☎055 52 33 75), in pl. Administrative, across from the Petrol station. Open daily 8:30am-8:30pm.

Hospitals: Hôpital Moulay Ismail (☎055 52 28 05 or 52 28 06), on av. des F.A.R.

Internet Access: Cyber Paris, on Zankat Accra. 6dh per hr. Open daily 9am-late. In the medina, try **Meetnet,** 38 rue Roumazine. 6dh per hr. Open Sa-Th 10:30am-11:45pm, F 10:30am-12:20pm and 3-11:45pm.

Post Office: pl. Administrative. **Poste Restante** at the side entrance. Open M-Sa 8am-3:30pm. **Branch** on rue Dar Smen, near the medina.

ACCOMMODATIONS

MEDINA

Rue Roumazine and rue Dar Smen house most of the medina's budget hotels, although even backpackers opt for plusher accommodations in the *ville nouvelle.*

Maroc Hôtel, 7 rue Roumazine (☎055 53 00 75). Clean, small rooms. Cold showers and squat toilets. Breakfast 20dh. Hot showers 10dh. 60dh per person. ❷

Hôtel de Paris, 58 rue Roumazine. Basic and clean. Shower and *hammam* next door, both 6dh. Singles 35-40dh; doubles 70dh; triples 90dh; nice terrace for 20dh, but beds are rough. ❶

Camping: Municipal Camping Agdal (☎055 55 53 96), on the ramparts of the medina behind Agdal Basin. Follow signs from Bab Mansour (15min. walk) or Bab Bou Amir. Cheap rates and proximity to Meknes's tourist sights outdo many hotel options. Set in a beautiful, wooded park. Hot showers (7dh), kitchen and restaurant. Reception daily 8am-1pm and 4-8pm. 17dh per adult, 12dh per child, 10dh per tent, 17dh per car. ❶

VILLE NOUVELLE

The *ville nouvelle* offers greater comfort and easier access to banks, CTM buses, and trains. Most cheap hotels lie near av. Mohammed V and bd. Allal ben Abdallah.

■ **Majestic Hôtel,** 19 av. Mohammed V (☎055 52 20 35). Comfortable rooms, cozy lounge, modern bathrooms, and free hot showers. The friendly and helpful owner takes pride in the Majestic's constant upkeep. Breakfast 24dh. Backpacker dorm on terrace 60dh, includes breakfast. Singles 112-189dh; doubles 150-225dh; triples 217-292dh. Prices depend on bathroom options. Low season 10% discount. ❸

Hôtel Continental, 92 av. des F.A.R. (☎055 52 54 71). Offers spacious rooms with red drapes, lounge and cafe area on 2nd floor, and friendly reception. Singles with shower 109dh, with shower and toilet 137dh; doubles 141dh/162dh. ❸

Hôtel Touring, 34 rue Allal ben Abdallah (☎055 52 23 51). This hotel is dark but clean and spacious. Singles 65dh, with shower 85dh; doubles 90dh/110dh. ❷

Hôtel de Nice, 10 Zankat Accra (☎055 52 03 18). Clean and bright rooms with bath. Singles 185dh; doubles 217dh. ❹

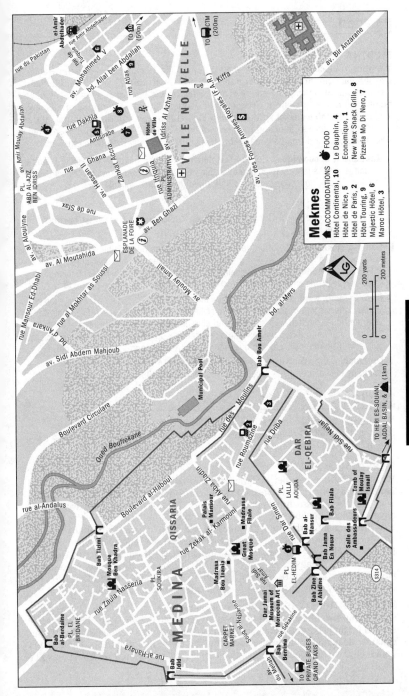

EXPLORING
MOROCCO

Meknes

■ ACCOMMODATIONS
Hôtel Continental, 10
Hôtel de Nice, 5
Hôtel de Paris, 2
Hôtel Touring, 9
Majestic Hôtel, 6
Maroc Hôtel, 3

● FOOD
Le Dauphin, 4
Economique, 1
New Mex Snack Grille, 8
Pizzeria Mo Di Nero, 7

▶ FOOD

MEDINA

Vendors in **place El-Hedim** sell *merguez* (spicy Moroccan sausage) sandwiches, freshly-made potato chips, corn on the cob, and fresh orange juice. Other inexpensive fare sizzles in the one-man *brochetteries* on **rue Dar Smen.** Few places have menus, let alone English or French copies—most have their options on display. The daily **vegetable market** sprouts beside Bab al-Mansur. As a rule of thumb, if the establishment looks clean and food is cooked in front of you, it's a pretty safe bet. Avoid cooked food that has been left sitting out, especially rotisserie chicken.

> **Restaurant Economique,** 123 rue Dar Smen, under the hand-painted sign. Friendly manager serves tasty staples at reasonable prices. Try the excellent chicken with vegetables (25dh). *Couscous* or *tajine* 25dh. Open daily 7am-10pm. ❶

VILLE NOUVELLE

Like the very concept of the *ville nouvelle* itself, most of the best options are imported from abroad.

> ▨ **New Mex Snack Grille,** 20 rue de Paris, tucked away in an alley between Festival des Glaces and Lahlon Optique. For a break from Moroccan cuisine, shockingly good Tex-Mex fare (34-45dh) in a very refreshing, air-conditioned atmosphere. Friendly manager also serves pizzas and sandwiches (30-45dh). Open daily 11:30am-11pm. ❷

> **Pizzeria Mo Di Nero,** 14 rue Antisirabe (☎055 51 76 76). This gourmet pizza shop and eatery offers some of the best Western-style food in Morocco (27-70dh). Brick walls, marble tables, stuffed wild animals, and chic black-and-white photos somehow mix to make a romantic date spot. Non-smoking section upstairs. Try the house specialty, pizza with shrimp, chicken, and mushrooms. Open daily noon-3pm and 7-11pm. ❷

> **Le Dauphin,** 5 av. Mohammed V (☎055 52 34 23). A glitzy Moroccan restaurant specializing in seafood. Highly recommended. Set *menù* 130dh. Open daily. ❺

◉ SIGHTS

Meknes's best sights cluster around magnificent **Bab al-Mansur,** which has become a national symbol. Through the gate lie the remainders of Meknes's imperial past, and in front of it thrives the medina and the lively place El-Hedim.

IMPERIAL MEKNES

Weakened by war, weather, and the Great Earthquake of 1755, the ramparts of the **Dar El-Kebira** (Imperial City) testify to Meknes's former glory. Sultan Moulay Ismail, who, along with Hassan II, is perhaps Morocco's most revered visionary, personally supervised the building of over 25km of protective **walls** for his city within a city. Strolling about the site with a pick-ax and whip in hand, the sultan criticized and occasionally decapitated workers who displeased him. Gathering materials from sights all over Morocco, including Roman marble from the ruins at Volubilis, Moulay Ismail created a radiant city. Ismail razed part of the medina to create **place El-Hedim** (Plaza of Destruction), an approach to **Bab al-Mansur,** Morocco's finest gate. Today, only the walls and several large monuments remain.

▧ **TOMB OF MOULAY ISMAIL.** The tomb, along with its accompanying **mosque,** is one of only two Muslim buildings in all of Morocco open to non-Muslims. After several bright yellow antechambers lies a larger courtyard. At the far left end is an ornately designed room from which you can view the tomb itself. The tomb is flanked by two functioning grandfather clocks, a consolation prize from Louis XIV after he refused Moulay Ismail's proposal to his daughter. Don't feel sad for ol' Moulay—he already had over 300 lovers. Photographs are allowed. *(Through the two blue arches, and then immediately to the left. Open Sa-Th 9am-noon and 3-6pm, F 3-6pm. Free, but donations requested in the crypt.)*

SALLE DES AMBASSADEURS. Standing by itself in an open court is the green-tiled roof of the recently restored Salle des Ambassadeurs, where Ismail conducted affairs of state. Ask the guard to unlock the doors to the so-called **Christian Dungeon**, a 6 square kilometer underground storehouse and granary for the sultan, his entourage, and their horses. This storehouse is said once to have housed 50,000-100,000 Christian prisoners. Since the "dungeon" remains a cool 15°C even in summer, it is the perfect place to avoid the midday sun. *(From pl. El-Hedim, go through Bab al-Mansur or one of the nearby smaller gates, walk straight, and follow the wall on the right around the bend. Open daily 9am-noon and 3-6pm. 10dh.)*

OTHER IMPERIAL CITY SIGHTS. A short trek from Moulay Ismail's tomb is the **Heri Es-Souani** (storehouse), a cool granary with immense cisterns designed to withstand prolonged sieges. Trees and birds have invaded, giving it a jungle-like feel. Do not, under any circumstances, pay for guided tours; they're overpriced and unnecessary. *(Open daily 9am-noon and 3-6pm. 10dh.)*

MEDINA

Meknes's medina is more pleasant, tranquil, and compact than those of the other imperial cities. Facing the Dar Jamaï Museum of Moroccan Art, take the alley to the left of the entrance. Push straight ahead to **Souq al-Nejjarine**, a major street. Heading left here brings you first to the **textile souq**, the **carpenters' souq**, and the **carpet market**. The rest of the medina is best explored like any other: wander until you get lost, then try to find your way out.

GREAT MOSQUE & MADRASA BOU INANIA. While everything except the view of the green-glazed minaret of the Great Mosque is off-limits to non-Muslims, the breathtaking 14th-century Madrasa Bou Inania, across from it, is not. A college of theology and Muslim law, this *madrasa* typifies traditional Merenid architecture—the courtyard combines arch, stucco, and mosaics with characteristic flair. Upstairs are a number of cells, each of which snugly hosted at least two students. The roof, which you may have to unlock yourself, offers a splendid view of the minaret of the Great Mosque and the rooftops of Meknes. *(Madrasa open daily 9am-noon and 3-6pm. 10dh.)*

◪ DAYTRIP FROM MEKNES

VOLUBILIS تجولولوبييليس

*There are no direct buses to Volubilis: a **taxi** is the most reliable and convenient method of transport. While you can hire a grand taxi near the private bus station in Meknes, you need a 6-person party to get the cheapest fare, and taxis rarely fill up; alone it will cost 100dh. The surest way is to take a grand taxi to **Moulay Idriss** (45 min., 8dh per place). Even taxis to Moulay Idris can take a long time to fill. From Moulay Idriss, either walk if it's not too hot (4km, 40min., straight from the junction with Moulay Idriss and then left at the sign for Oualili), or save your energy and take another taxi from Moulay Idriss (10dh total). Alternatively, you can also try grabbing a **bus** from Meknes to Ouezzane (every hr. 7am-7pm, 10dh) and asking the driver to drop you off near the ruins. To get back to Meknes, hop on a tour bus or wait by the parking lot for a taxi; they are infrequent but not rare. Don't try to return too late; rides become scarcer the later it gets. Leave yourself at least 1.5hr. to enjoy the ruins. Open daily sunrise-sunset (20dh; bring exact change).*

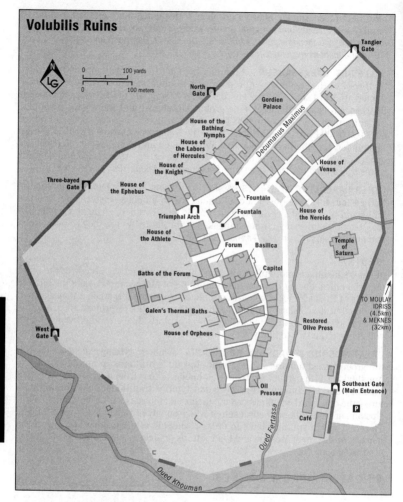

Volubilis Ruins

0   100 yards

0   100 meters

Tangier Gate

North Gate

Gordien Palace

Decumanus Maximus

House of the Bathing Nymphs

House of the Labors of Hercules

House of Venus

House of the Knight

Three-bayed Gate

House of the Ephebus

Fountain

Triumphal Arch

Fountain

House of the Nereids

House of the Athlete

Forum   Basilica

Temple of Saturn

Capitol

Baths of the Forum

TO MOULAY IDRISS (4.5km) & MEKNES (32km)

Galen's Thermal Baths

House of Orpheus

Restored Olive Press

West Gate

Southeast Gate (Main Entrance)

Oil Presses

P

Café

Oued Fertassa

Oued Khouman

The dramatic ruins of Volubilis, the best-preserved Roman site in Morocco and perhaps all of North Africa, lie 33km from Meknes. Surrounded by beautiful countryside and containing an extensive collection of **Roman mosaics,** Volubilis has deservedly earned must-see status. Once a major center for the olive oil trade, the city flourished under Roman rule, reaching its zenith in the 2nd and 3rd centuries AD when it became capital of the kingdom of Mauritania. The Romans, who viewed their North African possessions as a bread basket for their European citizens, ordered the deforestation of the area to make room for grain crops; from that point on, local resources dwindled and the city began to decline. When Moulay Idriss took control of the city in the 18th century, he siphoned off much of the residential population to Fez and Meknes and claimed many of the city's pillars and stones for his own palace. The Lisboa Earthquake of 1755, which wreaked devastation all along the Atlantic seaboard, finally sealed the city's fate.

When US General George C. Patton visited the ruins, he declined an offer of a guided tour—he believed he had been stationed here as a Roman centurion in his previous life and thus knew his way around. If you've been equally lucky, stop reading here. Otherwise, head past the ticket office and over a bridge, take a left, and climb the steps to the top, where among the ruins of a housing and industrial area are several **olive presses.** In this area you'll also find the **House of Orpheus,** which includes a few well-preserved mosaics, one of which depicts the Orpheus myth. Nearby is a small building containing a restored olive press and then further on are the towering columns of the **capitol** (dating from 218 AD) and arches of the **basilica.** The basilica, despite its name, served as the courthouse during Roman times. Follow the path to the **House of the Athlete** on the left, named for its mosaic depicting the victor of a *desultor* race (which involved mounting a moving horse). In the middle of town looms the **Triumphal Arch,** built in AD 217 to celebrate Emperor Caracalla and his scheming mother Julia Domna. Julia assured her son's power by helping him murder his rival Gota in AD 212. The gate marks the beginning of the town's main street, **Decumanus Maximus.** The houses along the street, including the **House of the Ephebus** and the **House of the Knight,** have impressive mosaics of Dionysus, Hercules, Orpheus, and other mythical figures. From the top of the hill is an amazing panoramic view of Volubilis. The **Tangier Gate,** with the **Gordien Palace** just before it, is atop the hill. Walk down the hill and head toward the only tree in front. Under it is the **Cortege of Venus,** which holds several mosaics including *Chariot Race, Bacchus Surrounded by the Four Seasons, Diana Bathing,* and the *Abduction of Hylas by Nymphs,* all dating as far back as the late 2nd or early 3rd century AD. Cross the stream back to the ticket gate to see the ruins of a **temple** dedicated to Jupiter, Juno, and Minerva.

The ruins are more peaceful and scenic in the early morning or late afternoon. Be sure to bring a hat, sunscreen, water, and sunglasses (if possible) if you are visiting in the afternoon, as the sun can be ferocious. You may be nearly alone at the ruins; the isolation makes you feel like you've stumbled onto the ruins yourself. Bring a picnic; there is only one small, overpriced cafe. Volubilis is one place where you might seriously consider hiring a guide (through the ticket office for roughly 20-30dh per person)—placards labeling sights are very brief.

FEZ فاس ☎ 055

Fez's bustling, colorful medina epitomizes Morocco—no visit to the country is complete without seeing it. Artisans bang out sheets of brass, donkeys strain under crates of Coca-Cola, children balance trays of dough on their heads, and tourist groups struggle to stay together. The scent of *brochettes* on open grills combine with whiffs of hash, the sweet aroma of cedar shavings, and the stench of fresh fish brought in at daybreak from the coast. Since UNESCO designated Fez a World Heritage Site in 1981, the city's walls have been largely restored. Founded in the 8th century by Moulay Idriss I, Fez rose to prominence with the construction in the 9th century of the Qairaouine, one of the world's first universities. Fez emerged as the most prominent city in the Maghreb, nurturing (or destroying) political dynasties and handing down legal rulings to the rest of the region. Modern Fez is an expansive city containing a conspicuously middle-class *ville nouvelle,* but remains at the artistic, intellectual, and spiritual helm of the nation.

EXPLORING MOROCCO

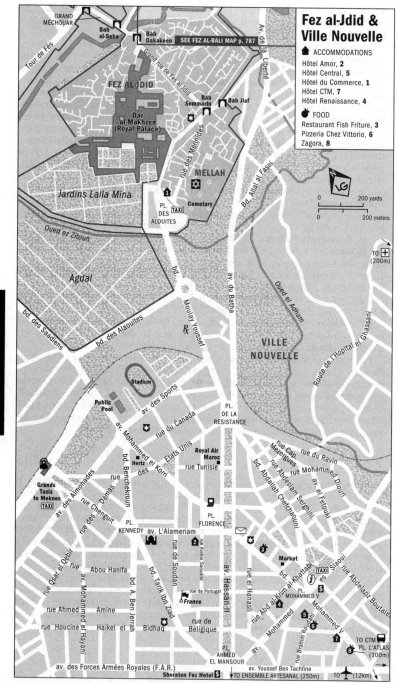

Fez al-Jdid & Ville Nouvelle

🏠 ACCOMMODATIONS
Hôtel Amor, **2**
Hôtel Central, **5**
Hôtel du Commerce, **1**
Hôtel CTM, **7**
Hôtel Renaissance, **4**

🍴 FOOD
Restaurant Fish Friture, **3**
Pizzeria Chez Vittorio, **6**
Zagora, **8**

SEE FEZ AL-BALI MAP p. 787

EXPLORING
MOROCCO

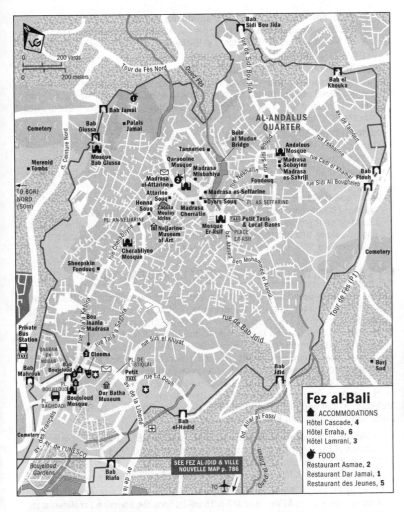

Fez al-Bali

⛺ ACCOMMODATIONS
Hôtel Cascade, **4**
Hôtel Erraha, **6**
Hôtel Lamrani, **3**

🍴 FOOD
Restaurant Asmae, **2**
Restaurant Dar Jamai, **1**
Restaurant des Jeunes, **5**

SEE FEZ AL-JDID & VILLE NOUVELLE MAP p. 786

▐ TRANSPORTATION

Flights: Aérodrome de Fès-Saïs (☎055 62 47 12), 12km out of town on the road to Immouzzèr. Take bus #16 from pl. Mohammed V (3dh) or a *grand taxi* (120dh). **Royal Air Maroc,** 54 av. Hassan II (☎055 62 55 16), flies daily to **Casablanca.**

Trains: av. des Almohades (☎055 93 03 33), a 5min. taxi ride to the *ville nouvelle* (5dh) or a 10min. ride to the medina's Bab Boujeloud (10dh). 2nd-class trains are comfier than buses. To: **Casablanca** (4½hr., 8 per day 7am-2:45am, 97-144dh); **Marrakesh** (9hr., 7per day 7:15am-2:40am, 171-255dh); **Meknes** (1hr., 8 per day 7am-2:45am, 17-24dh); **Tangier** (5hr., 4 per day 7am-1:35am, 96-141dh).

Buses: CTM (☎055 73 29 92) stops near pl. l'Atlas. To: **Casablanca** (5hr., 9 per day 6am-2:30am, 85dh); **Chefchaouen** (4hr.; 2 per day 11am, 11:45pm; 50dh); **Marrakesh** (8hr., 2 per day, 130dh); **Meknes** (1hr., 7 per day 6am-9pm, 18dh); **Tangier**

(6hr., 3 per day 11am-1am, 85dh). The **private bus station** is just outside the medina near Bab Boujeloud. To: **Casablanca** (25 per day 4:30am-1pm); **Marrakesh** (4 per day 3-9pm); **Meknes** (6 per day 6am-8pm); **al-Rachidia** (5 per day 7:30am-9pm); **Tangier** (8 per day 6:30am-10pm).

Public Transportation: Pl. Mohammed V and pl. de la Résistance are the major hubs for city buses. Important routes include: bus #9 and 11 from the Syndicat d'Initiative to **Bab Boujeloud** and **Dar Batha**; #3 from the train station and pl. Mohammed V to **Bab Ftouh**; #4 from pl. de la Résistance to **Bab Smarine** in Fez al-Jdid. 2.20dh; fares increase 20% July-Sept. 15 after 8:30pm, Sept. 16-June after 8pm.

Car Rental: Avis, 50 bd. Abdallah Chefchaouni (☎055 62 67 46). **Hertz** (☎055 62 28 12), bd. Lalla Meryem. Open M-Sa 8:30am-noon and 2-6:30pm, Su 9am-noon. Both agencies charge 250-500dh per day with a 20% tax, not including mileage. 23+ for the smallest cars (Fiat Palio or Uno), otherwise 25+, though many offices don't ask for proof of age. International license not required.

Taxis: Some prices are fixed, such as *grands taxis* to Meknes (400dh) and Volubilis/Moulay Idriss (800dh round-trip). A loop of Fez and around the medina costs 200dh. See the tourist office if you have questions. Stands at the post office, Syndicat d'Initiative, Bab Boujeloud, and Bab Giussa (Fez al-Bali). *Petits taxis* should always use a meter. Fares increase 50% July-Sept. 15 after 8:30pm, Sept. 16-June after 8pm.

■★ 🛈 ORIENTATION & PRACTICAL INFORMATION

Fez is large and spread out, but manageable. It is essentially three cities in one: the fashionable, French-built **ville nouvelle**, 1.5km from the medina; the Arab **Fez al-Jdid** (New Fez), containing the Jewish cemetery and the palace of Hassan II, next to the medina; and the enormous medina of **Fez al-Bali** (Old Fez) housing nearly 500,000 residents. The *ville nouvelle* is most convenient for services and quiet accommodations; its two central streets are **avenue Hassan II** and **boulevard Mohammed V,** which intersect at **place Florence**, the center of activity. Walking down bd. Moulay Youssef from the *ville nouvelle* brings you to pl. des Alaouites in Fez al-Jdid, directly in front of the king's palace, **Dar al-Makhzen.** At the end of Grand rue de Fès al-Jdid, a right through Bab Dakakeen leads to Fez al-Bali and **Bab Boujeloud.**

Tourist Office: Syndicat d'Initiative, pl. Mohammed V (☎055 62 34 60). Helpful *Fassi* (citizens of Fez) answer almost any question. Limited English. Hire official local guides here for 120dh half-day or 150dh full-day; national guides for 150dh half-day, 250dh full day. Open M-F 8:30am-noon and 2:30-6:30pm, Sa 8:30am-noon.

Currency Exchange: BMCE, pl. Mohammed V. Handles MC/V and traveler's checks transactions and has **ATMs**. Open M-F 8:15am-2:15pm. The **Sheraton Fez Hôtel,** at the end of av. Hassan II, 4 blocks from the post office, has after-hours exchange.

Luggage Storage: 24hr. storage at the **train station** (2.50dh per bag per day) and **CTM station** (5dh per bag per day).

Police: ☎19.

Late-Night Pharmacy: Municipalité de Fès, av. Moulay Youssef (☎055 62 33 80), 5min. uphill from the royal palace. Open daily 8pm-8am.

Hospital: Ghastani (☎055 62 27 76), at the end of av. Hassan II.

Internet Access: Soprocon, off pl. Florence. 10dh per hr. Open daily 9am-11pm.

Post Office: At the corner of av. Hassan II and bd. Mohammed V in the *ville nouvelle.* **Branches** at pl. l'Atlas and in the medina at pl. Batha. All open July-Sept. 15 M-F 8:30am-2:30pm; Sept. 16-June M-F 8:30am-12:15pm and 2:30-6:30pm.

ACCOMMODATIONS

VILLE NOUVELLE

Rooms here are convenient to local services and more comfortable than those in the medina. The cheapest lodgings are just off bd. Mohammed V, between av. Mohammed es-Slaoui near the bus station and av. Hassan II near the post office.

Hôtel Central, 50 rue Brahim Roudani (☎055 62 23 33). Clean rooms with better-than-average furnishings. Singles 59dh, with shower 89dh; doubles 89dh/119dh; triples 150dh/180dh. ❷

Hôtel Amor, 31 rue Arabie Saoudite (☎055 62 27 24). A good choice for those with a little more to spend. All rooms are clean, nicely furnished, and have private bath. Singles 164dh; doubles 198dh. ❹

Hotel CTM (☎055 62 28 11), between pl. Mohammed V and the CTM bus station. Look for the huge sign on the pinkish wall. Clean and cheap rooms with rock-hard beds. Singles 60dh, with shower 80dh; doubles 80dh/100dh. ❷

Hôtel Renaissance, 29 rue Abd al-Krim al-Khattabi (☎055 62 21 93). All rooms have a window or a view of the terrace. Squat toilets. Hot showers 6dh. Singles 50dh; doubles 90dh; triples 120dh; quads 140dh. ❶

FEZ AL-JDID

Fez al-Jdid has only one hotel of note, but the location is perfect—close to the medina without the annoyance of hustlers.

Hôtel du Commerce, pl. des Alaouites (☎055 62 22 31), by the Royal Palace. Friendly owners, comfortable rooms, and affordable prices. Offers views of palace grounds. Cold showers. Singles 50dh; doubles 90dh. ❶

FEZ AL-BALI

Head to the area around Bab Boujeloud for budget rooms. Although accommodations are less pleasant than those in the *ville nouvelle* and hustlers may seem to have tourist radar, they're still perfect for that 24hr. medina experience.

▨ **Hôtel Cascade,** 26 Serrajine Boujeloud (☎055 63 84 42), just inside Bab Boujeloud and to the right. Friendly staff, free hot showers, free luggage storage, a modern toilet, a tap for hand-washing clothes, and a laundry service (30dh for 15-20 pieces). Popular with backpackers and families. Rooms are clean and basic. The terrace provides a bird's-eye view of Bab Boujeloud and the medina. 50dh per person; terrace 20dh. ❶

Hôtel Lamrani, Tala'a Seghira (☎055 63 44 11). Enter Bab Boujeloud; take the 1st right, then left and through the arch. Unusually clean, with in-room sinks. Head here when the Cascade is full. Nearby *hammam* 6dh. Singles 40-60dh; doubles 80-120dh; triples 150-180dh. ❶

Hôtel Erraha (☎055 63 32 26). Follow the alley on the right of the cafe just before Bab Boujeloud. Basic rooms. Singles 50dh; doubles 80dh; triples 120dh. ❶

FOOD

VILLE NOUVELLE

Cheap sandwich dives, cafes, and juice shops line both sides of bd. Mohammed V. The *ville nouvelle* is stricken with more than its fair share of western-style fast food joints that offer a time-out for those overwhelmed by real Moroccan fare. For those in search of local eats, poke through stalls of fresh food at the **central market** on bd. Mohammed V. (Open daily 7am-1pm.)

Restaurant Fish Friture, 138 bd. Mohammed V (☎055 94 06 99). A small and relaxing maritime-themed restaurant with friendly service. Good for lunch or dinner with excellent fish brochettes (60dh) and other Moroccan standards (entrees 35-50dh; set *menús* up to 130dh). Open daily 10am-3pm and 6pm-midnight. MC/V. ❷

Zagora, 5 bd. Mohammed V (☎055 94 06 86). Look for the red neon sign. Elegant, air-conditioned restaurant with Moroccan fare. Set *menú* includes soup or puff pastry, couscous, brochettes or chicken pastilla, and dessert (140dh). Open 9:30am-11:30pm. MC/V. ❺

Pizzeria Chez Vittorio, 21 rue Brahim Roudani (☎055 62 47 30). This dark, cool restaurant with charming Italian countryside decor serves beer, wine, and spirits. Pizzas, ravioli, and spaghetti 45-50dh. Meat entrees 90-100dh. ❸

FEZ AL-BALI

Food stalls line Tala'a Kebira and Tala'a Seghira, near the Bab Boujeloud entrance to Fez al-Bali and a couple minutes further down. A feast of *harira* (spicy lentil soup), roasted peppers and eggplant, potato fritters, and bread will set you back only 10dh at the stalls inside, while a good *kefta* (ground meat) sandwich goes for 15dh. Directly across from Hôtel Cascade and Restaurant des Jeunes by Bab Boujeloud, **La Qasbah** ❷ has a pleasant rooftop terrace perfect for a quiet meal (*tajine* and couscous 40dh; 60dh for the house specialty *pastilla*). For some of the cheapest eateries in Morocco, go left from Tala'a Kebira at Madrasa el-Attarine and head into the medina toward pl. Achabine. Also, consider splurging on one of the Moroccan specialty restaurants listed below.

Restaurant des Jeunes, 16 rue Serrajine (☎055 63 49 75). A tourist favorite. Regional favorites. Set *menú* 35dh. Open daily 6am-midnight. ❶

Restaurant Asmae, 4 Derb Jeniara (☎055 741 210), located near the Qaraouine Mosque. Choose from 4-course meals (120-250dh). Open daily noon-midnight. ❺

Restaurant Dar Jamai, 14 Funduq Lihoudi (☎055 63 56 85), 100m from the Palais Jamai. Traditional feasting and royal treatment at affordable prices in this pillow-filled hideaway. 4-course *menú* 100dh. Open daily noon-11pm. ❹

🄶 SIGHTS

FEZ AL-BALI

Fez's medina is the handicraft capital of the country. With over 9000 streets and nearly 500,000 residents, the crowded medina is possibly the most difficult to navigate in all Morocco. But it is also the most rewarding, containing fabulous mosques, *madrasas*, and *souqs* and unparalleled frenzy. Craftsmen work at trades completely untouched by modern industry and machinery. The medina is quieter and less crowded between noon and 3pm. If you definitely want to make a purchase at the medina, it's best to wait until after 5pm, when shop owners will be more flexible with prices for some quick money before closing.

WITH A GUIDE. This approach is simple and recommended in spite of the cost: hire an official guide. **Official guides** are available at the Syndicat d'Initiative. They'll save you time, discourage hustlers, and provide detailed explanations. (Don't assume that they'll help you bargain for goods, though.) You can choose between a local or national guide for either a half-day (3hr.) or full-day (5+hr.) tour. Both types are adequate, though national guides have earned a higher qualification and therefore can provide tours of the whole country. Local guides cost 120-150dh and national guides 150-200dh. Based in Fez, national guide Hassan El-khader is highly recommended (☎ 067 33 44 11). He offers friendly and informative tours of Fez in English or French. Though much cheaper, **unofficial guides** are illegal, often lack historical knowledge, and usually take travelers only to shops from which they will get a 25% commission. Whichever type of guide you hire, nail down an itinerary and price beforehand and establish your aversion to shopping.

WITHOUT A GUIDE. To keep hustlers and merchants at bay, ignore calls or hisses and simply say "non, merci" or "la shukran" to those who approach you directly. Remember: walking downhill will take you farther into the medina, while trekking uphill will lead you out to Bab Boujeloud. Without a guide, there are two classic approaches to exploring the medina. The first is to head to the main gateway Bab Boujeloud and wander down **Tala'a Kebira** from there. Virtually all of the sights in Fez's medina lie along Tala'a Kebira (Grand Tala'a), old Fez's main street and an essential reference point for anyone attempting to navigate the medina. Tala'a Kebira heads downhill from Bab Boujeloud to the Qaraouine Mosque area. **Bab Boujeloud** is the main entrance to the medina; faux guides tend to gather here. Once you pass the gate, however, they will tend to leave you alone. Built in 1912 by the Frenchman Maréchal Lauyote to gain the confidence of the locals, the *bab* is tiled in blue on one side (the color of Fez) and green on the other (the favorite color of Mohammed and consequently the color most identified with Islam). The square just inside the *bab* is where the Moroccan revolution against the French occupation began. Down to the right is **Tala'a Seghira,** Fez's other main street, lined mostly by shops catering to locals (i.e., the famed underwear *souq*). The second classic approach is to taxi inside the medina to the more centrally located **place er-Rsif** nearby the Qaraouine Mosque. This choice puts you right near the center of the sights described below. The final option, though you'll be vulnerable to hustlers, is simply to get lost in the magnificent atmosphere that is Fez's medina. When you're done, ask merchants or women how to get to Tala'a Kebira and follow it back uphill to Bab Boujeloud.

■ **BOU INANIA MADRASA.** At the head of the main thoroughfare Tala'a Kebira is the spectacular Bou Inania Madrasa and mosque, a school built in 1326 for teaching the Qur'an and Islamic sciences. The intricacy of the cedar and stucco work make this arguably the best *madrasa* in Morocco and perhaps even the world. Classes were held in the courtyard and the adjacent salons, and students lived three or four to a 2x2m cell on the upper floor. When the Merenid Sultan Abou Inan was presented with the totals for the construction, he threw them into the canal, claiming that no price tag could be placed on beauty. *(Closed for renovations in 2002; reopening date uncertain. Open daily 9am-5:30pm. 10dh.)*

■ **MADRASA EL-ATTARINE.** Tala'a Kebira ends at Madrasa el-Attarine, which dates from 1324. Though often overlooked by visitors, this could be the most peaceful place in the old city. Built by Abou Siad, a Merenid, it is one of the smallest *madrasas* in Morocco, but is notable for its details and mosaics. The intricacies of the carvings are spectacular—they rival the Bou Inania's both in beauty and in style. *(Open daily June-Aug. 9am-6pm; Sept.-May 9am-5pm. 10dh.)*

FUNDUQS. Plunging ahead down Tala'a Kebira, you'll notice a series of *funduqs* (old inns now used as factories) on the left side. First is the drum *funduq*, where skins are stretched over hoops to produce the right tone. Next is the *funduq* for honey, olive oil, and butter, which was formerly a mental hospital. Last, you'll sniff the products of the **sheepskin funduq,** just after the parking lot on the left.

EXPLORING MOROCCO

BARGAINING FOR DUMMIES You'll have to do it for everything from carpets to camel treks, so you might as well do it right. Know that you never have to buy anything just because you look in the shop; feel free to say nothing interests you, and move on. Once you've found something you want, let the shopkeeper be the first to offer a price. You'll be expected to make a counter-offer; don't be intimidated by the shopkeeper's enthusiasm or claim that he's "making you a good price." Decide what you want to ultimately pay (anywhere from one-tenth to half of the initial price) then offer one-third to half of *that*. The shopkeeper may respond by laughing or calling you a Berber (the true skinflints), at which point you may choose to politely but firmly walk out. (Generally, you should leave at least once when haggling over a big purchase.) Invariably, you will be dragged back in. You can gauge the seller's willingness to negotiate by how quickly (and by how much) he drops his price. If you're with a friend, it can be useful to play good-cop/bad-cop with the storekeeper, one of you always saying the item is too expensive or that you need to move on. If you're at an impasse, you can try any of the following: 1) You've seen the same thing elsewhere for X (lower) price. 2) You like it but it's flawed; point out blemishes. 3) You're a student/budget traveler (sellers scale their prices to what you look like you can pay). 4) Tell them you've made your final offer.

In larger *souqs*, the same goods are often available at several stores, so don't be afraid to try a couple of negotiations until you find a price you like. By the fourth haggle of your day, you will be much more comfortable. Be wary of shopkeepers trying to sell you something that is somehow "unique"—there are no special years, months, or weeks on the calendar of Berber carpet makers, so don't pay as if there were.

NEJJARINE MUSEUM OF ART. The easiest way to get to the **place an-Nejjarine**, with its tiled fountain, is to go all the way down Tala'a Seghira until it turns into Tala'a Kebira. Turn around, facing the direction you just came from, and go down the steps that are about 10m in front of you. At the bottom of the steps, follow the path to the small square; the museum is just off this small courtyard. The displays are of tools, instruments, decorated doors, etc. Today, its rooftop **salon de thé** (tea room) offers a tranquil escape from the rushing traffic of peddlers and tourists, as do its ◼bathrooms, Morocco's finest. *(Open daily 10am-5pm. 10dh.)*

SPICE SOUQ & OTHER MARKETS. Back on Tala'a Kebira, the **attarine (spice) souq**, perhaps the most exotic market, awaits. Off to the right at the beginning of the spice *souq* is the **henna souq**, which sells the plant used to temporarily tattoo women at weddings. At the far end is the **Maristan Sidi Frej**, built in 1286, where the depressed were treated with music, sexual stimulation, and herbs and spices. It was the model for the first Western psychiatric hospitals in southern Spain. Toward the end of the *attarine souq* are passageways leading into a **cloth market**, selling slippers and *djellabas* (robes), and a **dried fruit market.**

QARAOUINE MOSQUE. Exit the *madrasa*, turn left, and then left again; a few meters down is a little opening into the Qaraouine Mosque. It contains 14 gates and six fountains (3 for men and 3 for women) and can hold up to 20,000 worshippers (second only to the Hassan II mosque in Casablanca). Founded in 857 by Fatima al-Fihri, a woman, the mosque is also one of the oldest universities in the world. It trained students in logic, math, rhetoric, and the Qur'an while Europe stumbled through the Dark Ages. You can thank (or curse) the mosque for educating Pope Sylvester II, who introduced algebra and the modern number system. Non-Muslims can take pictures through the portals but may not enter. Its library holds what some think is the oldest manuscript of the Qur'an in North Africa.

⬛ METAL SOUQ & TANNERIES. Keeping the mosque on the right, you'll eventually come to pl. Seffarine, known for its fascinating **metal souq,** which deafens travelers with incessant cauldron-pounding. There are several potential routes from here. To reach the **tanneries,** turn sharply left and continue to bear left (follow the worn, hexagonal cobblestones). Once the smell becomes intense, head right down a microscopic alley (a tannery *"guardien"* has probably grabbed you by now; 10dh is the basic fee). From a balcony above, you may view skins being soaked in green liquid, rinsed in a washing machine/cement-mixer hybrid, dunked in diluted pigeon excrement or waterlogged wheat husks (for suppleness), and saturated in dye. The dyeing process takes one week (except for the expensive yellow color of saffron, which is dyed by hand and takes 2 days). The entire tanning process takes up to two weeks for one piece. Beware—the pervasive odor of the tanneries is not for the faint of stomach and can be overpowering on the hottest days. To exit the medina or reach **place al-Rcif,** a major bus and taxi hub, follow the street heading away from the mosque to its end, turn left, and then right.

DAR BATHA MUSEUM. The beautiful Dar Batha Museum, located by Hotel Batha, with its well-kept garden, makes an excellent diversion for those tired of the endless, winding medina streets. The building itself, a 19th-century palace, may be the highlight of the museum. The spacious Andalusian mansion headquartered Sultan Hassan I and his playboy son, Moulay Abd al-Aziz, during the last years of decadence before the French occupation. The museum, which hosts Moroccan music concerts in September, chronicles Fez's artistic history. The keynote is the display of ceramics with the signature "Fez blue" (derived from cobalt) on a white enamel background. *(Start at Bab Boujeloud, head straight down Tala'a Seghira, take the first right past the movie theater, then turn right again at pl. I'lstiqlal, home to the museum. Open W-Th and Sa-M 8:30am-noon and 2:30-6pm, F 8:30-11:30am and 3-6pm. 10dh.)*

FEZ AL-JDID

Fez al-Jdid, built by the Merenids in the 13th century, was once known as a place for the peaceful coexistence of Christians, Muslims, and Jews. Today, its principle attraction is the gaudy **Dar al-Makhzen,** the former palace of Hassan II, shunned by King Mohammed VI for its excess. Tourists may enter the grounds but not the guarded palace. Near the palace is the *mellah,* or Jewish quarter. Today, there are few Jews left in Fez, as the majority left for Israel in 1948. The placement of the ghetto near the palace is not arbitrary, as here the Jews could be easily protected and—more importantly—easily taxed. Diagonally off the plaza, **grande rue des Merinides** runs up to Bab Smarine and its seven bronze gates installed by King Hassan II in 1968. Just before the beginning of the main street is a peaceful, 17th-century **Jewish cemetery,** the resting place for over 12,000 people. *(Cemetery open daily dawn-dusk; free, though a donation may be requested.)* Off this boulevard, the meter-wide streets open into miniature underground tailors' shops and half-timbered houses. The **jewelers' souq** glitters at the top of grande rue des Merinides. Cackling chickens, salty fish, and dried okra abound in the **covered market,** inside Bab Smarine at the entrance to Fez al-Jdid proper.

Bear left at the end of rue des Fez al-Jdid into the **Petit Méchouar;** on the left is **Bab Dakakeen,** the back entrance to the Dar al-Makhzen. **Bab al-Seba,** an imperial gate, opens onto the **Grand Méchouar,** a roomy plaza lined with street lamps. From here it's an easy walk to Bab Boujeloud—turn through the opening to the right of Bab al-Seba, continue straight for 250m, veer to the right, and pass through a large arch at the end of the road. The entrance to the refreshing **Boujeloud Gardens,** a refuge from the midday sun, is on the right. *(Open Tu-Su. Free.)* The gardens were a gift from Hassan I to the people of the medina. Inside is the delightful **Café Restaurant**

Noria, known as Lovers' Café, a pleasant place for female travelers (as well as male) to relax under the grape-leaf arbor. Coffee 5dh. Couscous 35dh. **Bab Boujeloud** lies another 300m down the street.

OUTSIDE THE MEDINA

For fantastic views of Fez, head to the hills on either side of the city. The ramparts of the Borj Nord (Arms Museum), Merenid Tombs, and Palais des Merenides provide good vantage points. All three are located on the same hill overlooking Fez. Be careful after dark, as aggressive hustlers are known to frequent the area.

BORJ NORD & THE MERENID TOMBS. To reach Borj Nord and the nearby tombs (they can be spotted from the ground), grab a *petit taxi* from the medina (5dh) or exit the medina through a small gate to the right on pl. Baghdadi when walking from Bab Boujeloud toward Fez al-Jdid. Turn right on the main road, walk past the bus station 200m, then take a small path that winds its way up the hillside; the tombs are to the right and Borj Nord is to the left. The **Palais des Merenides,** a five-star hotel, overlooks the tombs from one of the most picturesque hillsides in the Maghreb. From here, the medina reveals itself with the delicate beauty that inspired Paul Bowles and countless other Orientalist writers. The panorama is particularly impressive in the half-light of dawn or dusk; during calls to prayer, when over a hundred *muezzin* summon the faithful, the experience is almost mystical.

■ ⌂ SHOPPING & CRAFTS

The medina of Fez is world-famous, particularly for its twice-baked blue pottery and its tannery. In general, try to get an idea of prices before heading into a shop, and don't be afraid to walk away once inside. The quality of products—from *djellabas* to rugs—can vary widely. Don't pay top dollar for something that's a dirham a dozen (for more bargaining strategy, see **Bargaining 101,** p. 792). The following quality shops are located in the medina, with the exception of the pottery shop. They are as interesting for their managers and buildings as they are for their products. If you're looking to buy, discreetly return without your guide to avoid commission charges.

▨ **Société Fakhkhari,** 16 Quartier des Potiers, Route Sidi Harazem (☎055 64 93 22), outside the medina in the hills by Borj Sud. Take a tour (ask for Ahmed) of fascinating work areas and buy a fresh piece of pottery from the 450° oven. A *petit taxi* here 7-10dh.

▨ **Berber House,** 51 Derb Sidi Moussa (☎055 74 12 68). From Zaouia Moulay Idriss II, turn left after the wooden bar and go straight for 50m. Specializes in Berber tribe blankets and *kilims* and sells cheaper blankets made on location. Open daily 9am-9pm.

El Haj Ali Baba, 10 Hay Lablida (☎055 63 66 25). This shop offers wonderful views of the enormous tannery and dye wells below and sells a vast array of goods.

Dar Zaouia, 4 Derb Jeniara Blida (☎055 63 55 12). A 15th-century house now filled with modern rugs and Berber *kilims* instead of harems. Open daily 8:30am-7:30pm.

Herboriste Ibn Sina, 6 Zaouia Fondouk Lihoudi (☎055 63 74 17). Herbal medicine recipes kept in the family and dispensed in little bottles. Open daily 8am-9pm.

THE ATLANTIC COAST

The towns along Morocco's Atlantic coast are undoubtedly more laid-back than their conservative cousins in the interior. Men and women alike sunbathe, swim, surf, and windsurf. The west coast contains Morocco's industrial boom towns, including Casablanca, the country's commercial center bearing little resemblance to the romanticized film version. If you're headed to the coast, your best bets are peaceful and tranquil smaller cities like Essaouira.

CASABLANCA الدار البيضاء ☎ 022

Though sprawling Casablanca (known as "Casa") is famous in the West, there is little to see here other than the grandiose Hassan II Mosque. Unfortunately, there is no Rick's Café Américain in the *qasbah*, and no one looking at you, kid, except the hustlers who prowl the port and medina. Casa is little more than a transportation hub. In the country's economic capital and Africa's largest port, Western dress predominates, and women participate actively in city life. With its early 19th-century French boulevards, parks, and decaying Art Deco buildings, Casablanca can feel more like a European city whose sun has set until one visits the spectacular modern wonder that is the Hassan II Mosque, the world's third largest mosque.

▐ TRANSPORTATION

The **Casa Port train station** is near the youth hostel and the city center; the **Casa Voyageurs train station** is a 50min. walk from Casa Port or a 30dh *petit taxi* ride. The **private bus station** is even farther away. To get from Casa Port to the convenient downtown **CTM bus station,** cross the street and follow bd. Mohammed el Hansali to the head of pl. des Nations Unies. At the rotary, take a sharp left onto the wide av. de l'Armée Royale and watch for Hôtel Safir on the right; the station is behind and to the right of the hotel. Expect to be offered "help" when disembarking in Casablanca, and be wary of *petit taxi* drivers with inflated rates; demand drivers turn on the meter. Alternatively, walk a few blocks from the station for a taxi. Accommodations are almost all within walking distance, but be careful at night.

> **Flights: Aéroport Mohammed V** (☎ 022 53 90 40) handles all flights. Trains run between the airport terminal and the Casa Port train station (45min., 9 per day 5:15am-8:45pm, 30dh), stopping at Casa Voyageurs en route. Make sure to get on a train that runs to Casa Port. **Royal Air Maroc** (☎ 022 31 41 41), at the airport and 44 av. des F.A.R. Open M-F 8:30am-12:15pm and 2:30-7pm, Sa 8:30am-noon and 3-5pm.

> **Trains: Casa Voyageurs** (☎ 022 24 38 18), 4km outside the city center on bd. Ba-Hmad. Southbound service to: **Fez** (5¼hr., 8 per day 7:15am-11:15pm, 97dh) via **Meknes** (4½hr., 81dh); **Marrakesh** (3½hr., 8 per day 4:55am-1:30am, 75dh); **Tangier** (6hr., 4 per day 6:15am-12:15am, 116dh; possible transfer at Sidi Kacem).

> **Buses: CTM** is worth the extra money and effort in Casablanca; the private bus station is a long taxi ride away from the city center. **CTM,** 23 rue Léon l'Africain (☎ 022 45 80 00), off rue Chaouia. To: **al-Jadida** (1½hr., 5 per day 6:30am-3pm, 25dh); **Essaouira** (5½hr., 2 per day 5:30am and 7pm, 110dh); **Fez** (6hr., 11 per day 7am-10pm, 80dh); **Marrakesh** (4hr., 10 per day 7:30am-11pm, 70dh); **Meknes** (5hr., 10 per day 7am-2am, 68dh); **Tangier** (6½hr., 4 per day 6am-11:30pm, 120dh).

> **Car Rental: Avis,** 19 av. des F.A.R. (☎ 022 31 24 24). Open M-F 8am-7pm, Sa 8am-noon and 2-5pm, Su 8am-noon. **Hertz,** 25 rue Arabi Jilali (☎ 022 84 09 39), same hours. 25+, 23+ for small cars. **Budget,** 15 av. des F.A.R. (☎ 022 31 31 24). Min. age 21. Open M-F 8:30am-noon and 2:30-7pm, Sa 9am-noon and 3-6pm, Su 9am-noon.

> ▐❗ In Casablanca, **petit taxi** drivers are particularly flagrant in failing to turn on the meter and taking scenic routes. Be sure to double-check the meter and have a sense of the route. The daytime meter should start at 1.40dh, the nighttime meter at 2.10dh. Taxi drivers are required by Moroccan law to use their meter.

✦ 🔢 ORIENTATION & PRACTICAL INFORMATION

The city has two main squares, **place des Nations Unies,** below the landmark clock tower and a 5min. walk from Casa Port, and **place Mohammed V.** Pl. des Nations Unies spreads out in front of the Hyatt Regency at the intersection of bd. Mohammed V, av. Hassan II, and av. des Forces Armées Royales (F.A.R.). Pl. Mohammed V lies six blocks away from the port along av. Hassan II.

Tourist Office: Syndicat d'Initiative et de Tourisme, 98 bd. Mohammed V (☎022 22 15 24), at rue Chaouia. English spoken. Offers an overpriced guided tour of Casablanca for 450dh, including taxi. Open M-F 8:30am-noon and 2:30-6:30pm, Sa 9am-1pm, Su 8:30am-noon and 3-5:30pm. **Office de Tourisme,** 55 rue Omar Slaoui (☎022 27 95 33 or 27 11 77), has similar services. Open M-F 8:30am-noon and 2:30-6:30pm.

Currency Exchange: When the many **banks** in the city are closed, try the airport and larger hotels, which change money at Morocco's official rates. The **Hyatt Regency, Hôtel Suisse,** and **Hôtel Safir,** near the bus station and the other big hotels near pl. des Nations Unies are all safe bets. 24hr. **ATMs** are everywhere.

American Express: Voyages Schwartz, 112 rue du Prince Moulay Abdallah (☎022 22 29 47). Offer standard services, but won't receive wired money. Open M-F 8:30am-noon and 2:30-6:30pm, Sa 8:30am-noon.

English-Language Bookstore: American Language Center Bookstore, bd. Moulay Youssef (☎022 27 95 59), at pl. de l'Unité Africaine. Vast array of novels and reference books. Open M-F 9:30am-12:30pm and 3:30-6:30pm, Sa 9:30am-noon.

Emergency: ☎19. **Police** on bd. Brahim Roudani.

Late-Night Pharmacy: Pharmacie de Nuit, pl. des Nations Unies (☎022 26 94 91). Open nightly 8pm-8am. Other pharmacies with normal day-time hours (8am-12:30pm and 2:30-8pm) are on almost any city block.

Medical Assistance: Croix-Rouge Marocaine, 19 bd. al-Massira al-Khadra (☎022 25 25 21). **S.O.S. Medicins,** 81 av. des F.A.R. (☎022 44 44 44).

Internet Access: EuroNet, 51 rue Tata. 10dh per hr. Open daily 8am-11pm.

Post Office: bd. de Paris. **Poste Restante** and telephones. M-Th 8:30am-noon and 2:30-6:30pm, F 8:30-11:30am and 3-6:30pm.

🏠 ACCOMMODATIONS

Most travelers don't stay in Casablanca for more than one night. For budget deals, look along **rue Chaouia** and **rue Allah Ben Abdallah;** avoid the overpriced medina. It's worth the effort to scout out the room first or visit a couple hotels before choosing, as quality of rooms and beds can vary significantly even within hotels. Casa is very noisy, so try to get a room away from the street.

Auberge de Jeunesse (HI), 6 pl. Ahmed Bidaoui (☎022 22 05 51), 10min. from Casa Port. Head right along bd. des Almohades, which runs outside the medina wall, and go left up a small ramp-like street; blue signs point the way. If you don't mind the lack of privacy, this is the best budget option. Pleasant lounge, clean dorms, and modern bathrooms. Hot showers in winter. Breakfast included (8-10am). Reception open daily 8-10am and noon-11pm. Lock-out 10am-noon; be sure to check out by 10am. Dorms 45dh; doubles 120dh; triples 180dh. ❶

Hôtel Colbert, 38 rue Chaouia (☎022 31 42 41). Friendly staff maintains spotless rooms. Usually booked, so arrive early. Singles 90dh, with shower 125dh; doubles 130dh, with shower 165dh; each additional person 36dh. ❷

Hôtel des Negociants, 116 rue Allah Ben Abdallah (☎022 31 40 23). A relatively new addition to the block, and it shows—rooms and bathrooms sparkle. Singles 105dh, with shower 168dh; doubles 165dh, with shower 207dh. ❸

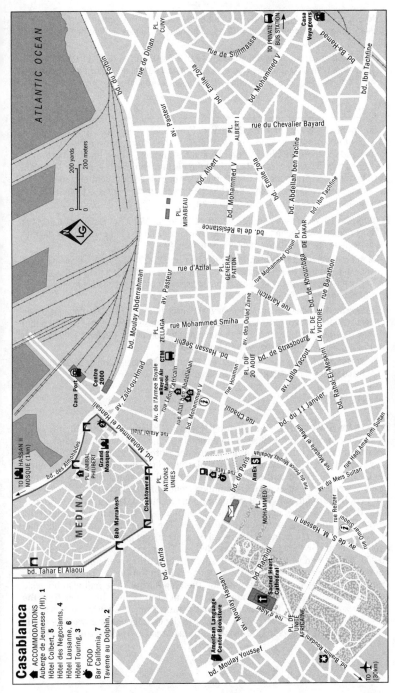

Casablanca

ATLANTIC OCEAN

MEDINA

ACCOMMODATIONS
Auberge de Jeunesse (HI), **1**
Hôtel Colbert, **5**
Hôtel des Negociants, **4**
Hôtel Lausanne, **6**
Hôtel Touring, **3**

FOOD
Bar California, **7**
Taverne au Dolphin, **2**

TO HASSAN II
MOSQUE (1km)

bd. Tahar El Alaoui

bd. des Almohades
PL. AMIRAL PHILIBERT
Grand Mosque
Clocktower
Bab Marrakesh
PL. NATIONS UNIES

bd. Mohammed el Hansali
rue Arabi Jilali
av. Zaid-ou-Hmad
bd. Moulay Abderrahman

Casa Port
Centre 2000

bd. du Gordon
rue de Dinan
PL. CUNY
rue de Sijilmassa
TO PRIVATE BUS STATION
Casa Voyageurs
bd. Ba-Hamad

bd. Emile Zola
bd. Mohammed V
av. Pasteur
PL. ALBERT I
rue du Chevalier Bayard
bd. Ibn Tachfine

bd. Albert I
bd. Mohammed V
PL. MIRABEAU
bd. de la Résistance
bd. Abdellah ben Yacine
bd. Ibn Tachfine

rue d'Azilal
av. Pasteur
PL. GENERAL PATTON
rue Mohammed Diouri
PL. DE DAKAR
bd. de Khouribga
rue Barathon

rue Mohammed Smiha
PL. ZELLAGA
bd. Hassan Seghir
av. des Oulad Ziane
rue Karatchi
rue Houman
av. Lalla Yacout
bd. de Strasbourg
PL. DE LA VICTOIRE

CTM
Royal Air Maroc
rue Léon l'Africain
rue Allal ben Abdallah
bd. Mohammed V
rue Chaoui
bd. du 20 AOUT
bd. Rahal-El-Meskini

bd. de Paris
AmEx
PL. MOHAMMED V
rue du prince Moulay Abdallah
av. du Mers Sultan
rue Hadj Amar Riffi Sultan

bd. d'Anfa
av. d. S. M. Hassan II
rue Omar Slaoui
rue Retzer

American Language Center Bookstore
av. Moulay Hassan
bd. Rachidi
Sacred Heart Cathedral
rue d'Alger
PL. DE UNITE AFRICAINE
bd. Brahim Roudani

bd. Moulay Youssef
bd. Moulay Hassan

TO (30km)

200 yards
200 meters

EXPLORING MOROCCO

Hôtel Lausanne, 24 rue Tata (☎022 26 86 90). Catch up on Egyptian soap operas and Arab news in modern rooms with TV and hot showers. Singles 229dh; doubles 273dh; triples 350dh; quads 427dh. ❺

Hôtel Touring, 87 rue Allah Ben Abdallah (☎022 31 02 16). A budget hotel that offers little more than the necessities; tables and electrical outlets are welcome bonuses. Hot showers 2dh. Singles 62dh; doubles 78dh; triples 114dh. ❷

☐ FOOD

Cosmopolitan Casa offers everything from French *haute cuisine* to fast food, but most restaurants are geared toward the city's wealthy business clientele. The casual and inexpensive ▨rotisserie chicken restaurants, which line the bottom of **rue Chaouia** in the *ville nouvelle* around the corner from rue Allah Ben Abdallah, are safe bets. For fresh meats and produce, try haggling at the **central market,** 7 rue Chaouia (open daily 8am-1pm). Two blocks away from the center is **L'Oliveri,** at 132 av. Hassan II, the best ice cream shop around.

▨ **O'Dissea,** 19 av. Hassan II (☎022 22 49 21). A trendy Moroccan restaurant painted in bright colors with mahogany highlights. Delicious *menú* (try the catch of the day) for 48dh. Also has a *patisserie* and ice cream shop. ❷

Restaurant Snack Bar California, 19 rue Tata (☎022 29 49 44). A welcoming atmosphere for women. Its spectacular vegetarian couscous (40dh) is a rarity in Casa. A darling of the travel guidebooks; locals probably wouldn't be caught dead here. Entrees 20-50dh. Open daily 10am-1am. ❷

Taverne au Dauphin, 115 bd. Mohammed el Hansali (☎022 22 12 00). Entrance on the right side of building. House specialties include *crevettes grillées* (grilled shrimp; 55dh) and *filet de lotte* (fish filet; 70dh). Limited selection of non-seafood options. Beer 15dh. Open M-Sa noon-3pm and 7-11pm. V. ❸

Point Central, 89 rue Allah ben Abdallah. Tajine and couscous dishes 18-28dh. Open M-F noon-2pm and 8-9:30pm, Sa 8-9:30pm. ❶

☉ SIGHTS

▨ **HASSAN II MOSQUE.** The glorious Hassan II Mosque is the third largest mosque in the world. If you're within striking distance of Casa, it warrants a special trip or detour. Built on the orders of former Moroccan king Hassan II, it's very easy to find; from anywhere in Casa, look toward the sea and spot the minaret (200m high, the tallest in the world). Begun in 1980 and inaugurated in 1994, this massive structure cost over US$800 million (much of it collected from the Moroccan people through "universal voluntary conscription"). Designed by a Frenchman, the mosque was constructed by 3300 master Moroccan craftsmen who worked day and night to complete the project. The prayer hall, much larger than St. Peter's Basilica in Rome, combines glass, marble, and precious wood and holds over 25,000 under the glow of 56 chandeliers. The plaza accommodates another 80,000. At one end of the prayer hall, silver electric gates weighing over 34 tons open only once a year—during the birthday celebration for the prophets—for a grand entrance by his living descendant, the king himself. The hall also boasts a retractable roof, a heated floor, and a 20 mi. long laser beam that shoots from the minaret toward Mecca. Hassan II graciously wanted his mosque to be accessible to non-Muslims (unlike every other mosque in the country); take advantage of the tour which offers access to otherwise restricted areas in order to truly appreciate the Moroccan craftsmanship and awe-inspiring beauty of this national and religious monument. *(Walk past the medina along the coastal road for about 15min., or take a petit taxi (no more than 10-15dh though drivers will often ask for an unmetered 20dh). Tours take 1hr. and are given M-Th and Sa-Su 9, 10, 11am, and 2pm. Tours in English, French, and Arabic. 100dh, students 50dh. Elevator up the side of the minaret 10dh.)*

AL-JADIDA الجديدة ☎ 023

Al-Jadida (pop. 150,000) is one of Morocco's largest Atlantic beach towns. With its quiet Cité Portugaise, palmy boulevards, and some of the country's most pleasant beaches, al-Jadida serves as a prime destination for foreign and domestic tourists.

⌐ TRANSPORTATION

Trains: The train station is 5km outside the city center, in a remote area. When arriving in al-Jadida, move as quickly as possible to the taxi stand outside, as taxis seldom come unless there's a train arriving. *Petit taxi* 12dh. There are 2 outgoing trains to **Casablanca** (5:30am, 3:40pm; 25dh), with connecting service to **Fez, Marrakesh, Meknes,** and **Tangier.**

Buses: CTM, on bd. Mohammed V, sends **buses** to **Casablanca** (2hr., 4 per day 8:30am-4:30pm, 24dh) and **Essaouira** (3hr., 8:15am, 54dh). The CTM bus to Essaouira begins in Casablanca and often has few seats left by the time it arrives in al-Jadida; buy a ticket in advance. Slightly cheaper and less reliable **non-CTM buses** run from the same station to: **Casablanca** (almost every hr. 4:15am-7:30pm, 21dh); **Essaouira** (5 per day 7:30am-5pm); **Marrakesh** (every hr. 4am-4pm, 35dh).

Taxis: Many **petit taxis** in al-Jadida don't have meters, so agree on a price beforehand.

✈ 🛈 ORIENTATION & PRACTICAL INFORMATION

From the **bus station,** exit left on bd. Mohammed V and continue up to the city center (10min.). First you'll reach **place Mohammed V,** the center of town, which joins bd. Mohammed V at the post office. Most services, including the tourist office and post office, are nearby. Straight ahead from pl. Mohammed V is **place al-Hansali** (a pedestrian square), which is packed at night, and finally **place Mohammed ben Abdallah,** which connects bd. Suez to the conspicuous, walled **Portuguese city.**

Tourist Office: Syndicat d'Initiative, in pl. Mohammed V next to Bata Shoes. Extremely friendly service. Some English spoken. Open Th-Tu 9am-12:30pm and 3-7pm.

Currency Exchange: There are many banks in and around pl. Mohammed V. **Wafabank,** on pl. Mohammed V, has a 24hr. **ATM.** Bank open M-F 8:15am-2:15pm.

Police: ☎ 19. Stations at the bus station, by the city beach, and on av. al-Jamia al-Arabi.

Late-Night Pharmacy: Pharmacie de Nuit (☎ 023 35 52 52). From pl. Mohammed V, face the post office; take av. Jamai al-Arabia to the left of the post office; walk about 100m and take the 2nd left into the small arcade area. Open nightly 9pm-8am.

Medical Assistance: Hospital, rue Roux (☎ 023 34 20 04 or 023 34 20 05), near rue Boucharette in the south of town. **Ambulance:** ☎ 023 34 37 30. **Clinique Ennakil,** on av. Jamai Ababia, is preferable to the hospital.

Internet Access: Cyber Abir, off rue Zerktouni, past Hotel el-Jadida. 8dh per hr.

Post Office: Pl. Mohammed V. **Poste Restante** at the 1st window to the right. Open M-F 8:30am-noon and 2:30-6:30pm.

ACCOMMODATIONS

Al-Jadida has a decent number of budget hotels. As usual, ask to see a room before you commit; rooms vary in quality even within a hotel. Reserve in July and August.

Hôtel Bourdeaux, 47 rue Moulay Ahmed Tahiri (☎023 37 39 21). A few narrow streets away from pl. al-Hansali; follow signs at the end of the pl. al-Hansali toward the medina (about 100m). Don't be fooled by the less-than-clean streets; step inside to find the best of the budget hotels, with bright, clean, and modern rooms. Rooftop lounge. Hot shower 5dh. Singles 41dh; doubles 57dh; triples 78dh. ❶

Hôtel de Provence, 42 rue Fquih Mohammed Errafil (☎023 34 23 47; fax 35 21 15). From the bus station, turn left off av. Mohammed V (away from the beach) at the post office. Just outside the busiest part of the medina, this quiet, upmarket hotel is popular with older travelers. Spotless rooms include shower, toilet, towels, and nice sheets. Hotel has restaurant, bar, currency exchange, and parking. Continental breakfast (33dh). Singles 186dh; doubles 229dh; triples 384dh. MC/V. ❹

Camping: Caravaning International, 1 av. des Nations Unies (☎023 34 27 55). From pl. Mohammed V, take av. Jamia al-Arabi to left of post office; take the 6th right. Clean and well-kept campground with electricity, showers, and bungalows (231dh for 2). 14dh per adult, 20dh per tent, 8.5dh per car plus 6dh *emplacement* and 10% tax. ❶

FOOD

Cheap eateries serve *brochettes* on **place Mohammed V.** Restaurants cluster in and around **place al-Hansali,** and many cafes dot the waterfront. On Sundays, a **souq** selling everything from fruit to cow lungs is by the lighthouse near rue Zerktouni.

Snack Ramses, around the corner from Hotel Magreb and Hotel France, toward the waterfront. A heaping plate of fresh fried fish, calamari, and shrimp will fill you up for 24dh. Open daily noon-4am. ❶

La Broche, 8 pl. al-Hansali (☎023 37 26 49), next to Paris Cinema. Moroccan standards, veggie options, and *paella* (20-60dh). Open M-Sa noon-3pm and 7-11pm. ❶

Snack Le Dauphin, 18 av. Fquih Mohammed Errafil, by pl. Mohammed V. A cheery spot with tasty Lebanese-style schwarma (23dh). Open daily 11am-2:30am. ❶

SIGHTS & BEACHES

CITÉ PORTUGAISE. In 1502, Portuguese traders completed the lovely ramparted Cité Portugaise at the heart of al-Jadida. In 1769, Moroccan forces, in a siege led by Sultan Sidi Mohammed ben Abdallah finally sent them packing, but not before the retreating Portuguese blasted the old town walls to bits. After Sultan Moulay Abd al-Rahman renovated the ramparts in the 19th century, the city was rebuilt as a Jewish settlement (*mellah*) mostly populated by merchants. The city is much smaller and quieter than Morocco's other ancient cities, with only a few shops on the main thoroughfare. Don't be afraid to venture into the quaint neighborhoods. Enter through the first fortified gate off pl. Mohammed ben Abdallah at the top of bd. Suez. Up rue Mohammed Hachemi Bahbai on the left, a yellow plaque marks the entrance to the famed **Portuguese cistern,** a Gothic structure lucky enough to have survived the Portuguese bombardment. It was designed in 1514 as an arsenal and later converted into a cistern. The water, illuminated by a shaft of light from the roof, reflects the cistern's columns and arches. The riot scene in Orson Welles's *Othello* was filmed here. *(Open Oct.-Apr. 9am-1pm and 3-6pm; May-Sept. 9am-1pm and 3-7:30pm. Guided tour available but unnecessary.)*

BEACHES. The favorite **Sidi Bouzid**, 5km to the south, is sprawling and chic with wide beaches and good swimming. Take a *grand taxi* (5dh per person) or the #2 bus (2.50dh) from near the Cité Portugaise. The bus stops 10min. short of the beach just outside the walls of the Cité Portugaise and makes frequent return trips. A taxi may be preferable, as the bus makes many stops and can be crowded. The splendid **Oualidia**, about 78km south of al-Jadida (20dh per person in a *grand taxi*, or get one of the buses headed to Safi or Essaouira to drop you off), may be Morocco's best beach.

ESSAOUIRA الصويرة   ☎ 044

Essaouira is one of Morocco's most enchanting communities. Piracy boosted this port in the 18th century, when Sultan Muhammad ben Abdallah leveled the Portuguese city of Mogador. In the late 1960s, Jimi Hendrix and Cat Stevens triggered a mass hippie migration. Essaouira achieved international fame as an expat enclave and music center. Though most of the hash smoke has cleared, Essaouira remains one of Morocco's most laid-back cities. The miles of beautiful beaches are often too windy for sunbathing (the wind is calmest in the early morning), but the fortified medina and splendid scenery provide ample diversion. In mid-June, acclaimed musicians descend on the town for the annual Festival of Essaouira, a celebration of the local, African influenced *Gnaoua* music and international jazz.

⊏ TRANSPORTATION

Buses: CTM runs from the station outside the medina, a 15min. walk from pl. Moulay Hassan. To **Casablanca** (6½hr.; 2 per day 11:15am, midnight; 88dh/105dh) and **al-Jadida** (3½hr., 1 per day 11:15am, 76dh). **Supratours** buses leave from Bab Marrakesh, across the square from Agence Supratours (☎044 47 53 17), to **Marrakesh** (2½hr.; 2 per day 6:10am, 4pm; 55dh). Buy tickets at the office. Private companies make daily runs to the **Casablanca** and **Meknes** in addition to the cities listed above.

■ ⚡ ORIENTATION & PRACTICAL INFORMATION

Buses arrive at the **bus station,** about 1km from the medina along bd. Industrie. Exit the rear of the station (where the buses park) and walk to the right, passing two *souqs* (or deserted wastelands, depending on the hour), to reach the medina gate, **Bab Doukkala** (10min.). The gate opens onto **avenue Mohammed Zerktouni,** one of two main arteries; the other is the parallel **rue Sidi Mohammed ben Abdallah.** To reach the city center from Bab Doukkala, continue on av. Mohammed Zerktouni as it becomes av. l'Istiqlal (at an intersection surrounded by *souqs*). Walk until you see a clock tower and gate on the right. Go through the gate, pass through the square, and follow the road as it winds to **place Moulay Hassan.**

Tourist Office: Syndicat d'Initiative du Tourism, rue de Caire (☎044 47 50 80). From the top of pl. Hassan (away from the port), take a right and follow the road as it zig-zags 1 block beyond a gate. Some English spoken. Open M-F 9am-noon and 2:30-6:30pm.

Currency Exchange: Banks cluster around pl. Moulay Hassan. **Crédit du Maroc,** pl. Moulay Hassan (☎044 47 58 19), cashes traveler's checks and has an **ATM.** Open M-F 8:30am-2:15pm. **BMCE** (same hours as above) with ATM is at the end of pl. Moulay Hassan, near rue Mohammed Ben Abdallah.

Luggage Storage: Available 24hr. at the bus station (5dh per bag).

Police: ☎ 19, in the *ville nouvelle* near the tourist office.

Hospital: av. al-Moquamah (☎044 47 27 16), next to the post office.

Bookstore: Galerie Aida, 2 rue de la Skala (☎044 47 62 90), off pl. Moulay Hassan. An interesting collection of crafts, used books, and art. Open daily 10am-8pm.

Internet Access: Several teleboutiques offer Internet access. **Mogador Informatique,** av. Oqba ben Nafil, 3rd fl. (☎044 47 50 65), 2 blocks away from the post on the left. Wait for Computer #4; the others are painfully slow. 10dh per hr. Vague hours, usually daily 9am-midnight. **Cyber Espace** is at the top of pl. Moulay Hassan (15dh per hr.).

Post Office: av. al-Moqamah at Lalla Aicha, the first left after Hôtel les Isles walking away from the medina by the shore. **Poste Restante.** Open 8:30am-noon and 2:30-6:30pm.

🏠 ACCOMMODATIONS

Once Morocco's best kept secrets, Essaouira has lost its anonymity. There are a number of nice, cheap hotels, but reservations may be necessary in summer.

Hotel Cap Sim, 11 Ibn Roched (☎044 78 58 34). Standing in pl. Moulay Hassan facing Crédit du Maroc, make a left on rue de la Skala, the street along the ramparts right next to Banque Populaire. Make a right just before the archway and follow the street around to the hotel. A beautiful new hotel decorated with local art. Rooms are bright and clean with huge modern baths. Singles or doubles 158dh, with shower 258dh. MC/V. ❸

Hôtel Smara, 26 rue de la Skala (☎044 47 56 55). Standing in pl. Moulay Hassan, facing Credit du Maroc, make a left on rue de la Skala, next to Banque Populaire (3min.). Rooms are a little damp, what with ocean waves crashing only 100m away. Arrive early—this is the most popular hotel among backpackers. Breakfast 10dh. Laundry 2dh per piece. Some English spoken. Breakfast served on terrace with a view of the sea. Singles 62dh; doubles 94dh, with ocean view 124dh; triples 156dh; quads 196dh. ❷

Hôtel Souiri, 37 rue Attarine (☎044 47 53 39), off rue Sidi Mohammed ben Abdallah. The comfort is worth the extra dirham. Modern and well-decorated. Singles 95dh, with shower 220dh; doubles 150dh/310dh; triples 225dh/375dh. MC/V. ❸

Hôtel Tafraout, 7 rue Marrakesh (☎044 47 62 76). In pl. Moulay Hassan, walk past the restaurants and cafes and take a left onto the busy rue Sidi Mohammed ben Abdallah. Look for the sign a few blocks up. Newly renovated rooms. Hot showers 7dh. Singles 100dh, with shower 150dh; doubles 150dh/250dh. Extra bed 50dh. ❸

🍴 FOOD

Informal dining is near the port and **place Moulay Hassan.** ▓**Fish grilles,** fried sardines (with fish, bread, and tomatoes; 20dh), and grilled shrimp (25dh) are sure bets. **Berber cafes** near Porte Portugaise and av. l'Istiqlal have low tables, straw mats, and fresh fish *tajine* (20dh). Establish prices before eating.

Restaurant Laayoune (☎044 47 46 43). From the top of pl. Moulay Hassan (away from the port), take a right and continue past rue Sidi ben Mohammed Abdallah. Follow the road as it turns right; the restaurant is ahead on the left. Outstanding Moroccan food at reasonable prices, served in a beautiful, well-decorated setting. Fills up at night; be prepared to wait. 4 set *menús* 45-72dh. Open daily noon-4pm and 7-11pm. ❷

Chez Sam (☎044 47 65 13), past the food stalls, at the very end of the port. Pricy and touristy. Ocean view and one of the town's few liquor licenses. Almost identical **La Coquillage** is next door. Steaming heap of mussels 50dh. Fish dishes 80-100dh. *Menús* 85-200dh. Open daily noon-3pm and 7:30-10:30pm. AmEx/MC/V. ❹

🄶 SIGHTS

While many flock to Essaouira to simply sit back, relax, and do nothing at all, the ramparts, shops, museums, and the beaches can distract one for hours on end.

RAMPARTS & PORT. Essaouira has two *skalas* (forts) that sit high atop fortifications. Buttressed by formidable ramparts, dramatic, sea-sprayed **Skala de la Qasbah,** up the street from Hôtel Smara away from the main square, is the nicer of the two (it's also free). Visitors can go up the large turret and artillery-lined wall to where the cannons, gifts to the sultan from European merchants, face the sea and the medina. The other fort, **Skala de Port,** has a view of the port and medina. *(10dh.)*

MEDINA SHOPS & MUSEUMS. Follow the sound of pounding hammers and the scent of *thuya* wood to the **carpenters' district,** comprised of cell-like niches set in the **Skala Stata de la Ville.** The craftsmen here inlay cedar and *thuya* with lemonwood and ebony to create some of the best woodwork in Morocco. On sale are unique masks and statues, as well as the more typical boxes, drums, chess sets, dice, and desk tools. For a quality overview of Essaouira's goods and prices, go to the cooperative **Afalkai Art,** 9 pl. Moulay Hassan (open daily 9am-8pm) and browse the many shops lining **rue Abd al-Aziz al-Fechtaly** (off rue Sidi Mohammed ben Abdallah). For silver jewelry, head to the *souq,* located just outside the medina walls on Av. Oqba ben Nafil. Look for the sign that says "*bijoux*" above the entrance on the right, about a block from rue de Caire on the right. **Museum Mohammed ben Abdallah,** on rue Derb Laalouj, is in the former residence of a *pasha.* It features antique woodwork and important manuscripts, including a 13th-century Qur'an. (☎044 47 53 00. *Open M and W-Su 9am-noon and 3-6:30pm. 10dh.*) Galleries dot the medina—the best one, **Galerie du Frederic Damgaard,** near the clock tower, displays modern art crafted by local artists. *(Open daily 9am-1pm and 3-7pm. Free.)*

BEACHES. Though infamous for its winds, the wide beach of Essaouira is still one of Morocco's finest. Join locals at the free courts for basketball and volleyball along its pedestrian walkway. To get to the sand, head to the port and veer left; you can't miss it. Windsurfing clubs cluster on the beach and rent boards. Try **Fanatic Fun Center** for good rental deals. (☎044 34 70 13. *Windsurfing boards with harness and wet-suit 100dh per hr., 300dh for a half day; bodyboards 20dh per hr., 150dh per day; jet-skis 60dh per 15min; windsurfing lessons 180-230dh per hr. depending on skill level.)*

PURPLE ISLES HAZE While certain stimulants are still available (especially for foreigners), Essaouira's heyday of "good times" was in the early 1970s when Jimi Hendrix and fellow hippies took over the isles. The fort on the beach, **Borj al-Berad,** and the inland ruins supposedly inspired Hendrix's song *Castles Made of Sand.* When he tried to buy the Berber village-turned-hippie-colony of **Diabat,** the Moroccan government decided that it had had enough of Hendrix and his long-haired expat friends and expelled most non-Moroccans. Today, the village residents have almost forgotten their raucous past; the Purple (Isles) Haze has burned away.

PURPLE ISLES. Just off-shore from Essaouira are the famed Purple Isles, where rare birds still hang out and get high. Dominated by the **Isle of Mogador**, the Isles are now a nature reserve for the rare Eleanora's falcons. A Berber king from Mauritania, Juba II, set up dye factories here around 100 BC, producing the purple dye used to color Julius Caesar's cape, among other things, and giving the Isles their name. In 1506, the Portuguese, under Dom Manuel, built a fortress, and Moulay Hassan added a prison. Visiting the Isles is possible, but requires permission from the municipal office, which can take a few days. A tip may expedite the process.

THE HIGH ATLAS الاطلس الاعلى

Hollywood has deemed southern Morocco one of the most beautiful regions in the world, as evidenced by the numerous movies filmed here over the last fifty years—*Lawrence of Arabia, Kundun, The Mummy, Spy Game,* and *Black Hawk Down,* to name a few. The terrain in the mountains and their foothills is the most varied in the country. At the feet of the High Atlas lies Marrakesh, a city overflowing with unique architecture, exotic bazaars, and magical energy. Falling southeast from the Atlas ranges and stretching through Ouarzazate to the sand-dune seas of the Sahara is Morocco's desert. Mountainous and desolate, its deep reds and oranges are softened only by the rare, green veins of oases that creep through the valley floors. Set into this landscape are fantastic Berber towns and *qasbahs,* where *pizid* (mud and straw) castles tower over the road. Excursions are possible by local transportation, but a rental car is best for exploring this region.

MARRAKESH مراكش ☎ 044

The imperial city of Marrakesh has always exerted an unshakable grip on the traveler. Djema'a al-Fna, the medina's main square, is home to lively crowds of snake charmers, musicians, boxers, acrobats, mystics, dentists, scribes, and storytellers practicing their crafts. Marrakesh's *souqs* and craftwork are some of Morocco's best and, in general, the bustling city is more tourist-friendly (and tourist-ridden) than the rest of Morocco. The Almoravid dynasty founded the city in 1062, elevating an infamous highwayman's outpost to the status of cultural capital and infusing it with Andalusian influences from their Spanish empire.

❗ In Marrakesh, **petit taxi** drivers are particularly notorious about taking scenic routes or failing to turn on the meter. Be sure to double check the meter to make sure it's on—don't be afraid to insist—and have a clear sense of the route. If the driver doesn't oblige, get out and find another who will.

▐ TRANSPORTATION

Flights: Aéroport de Marrakesh Menara (☎ 044 44 79 10 or 44 78 65), 5km south of town. Taxi from town 10dh per person. Bus #11 from the Koutoubia Mosque to the airport (about 7am-10pm, 3dh). Domestic and international flights on **Royal Air Maroc,** 197 av. Mohammed V (☎ 044 42 55 00). Open M-F 8:30am-12:15pm and 2:30-7pm.

Trains: Av. Hassan II (☎ 044 44 65 69). Going away from the medina on av. Mohammed V, turn left on av. Hassan II (40min.). A taxi to or from pl. Djema'a al-Fna costs 10dh. To: **Casablanca** (4hr., 8 per day 5:15am-9pm, 111dh); **Fez** (8hr., 6 per day 5:15am-5pm, 225dh); **Meknes** (7hr., 6 per day 5:15am-5pm, 228dh); **Tangier** (8hr., 3 per day

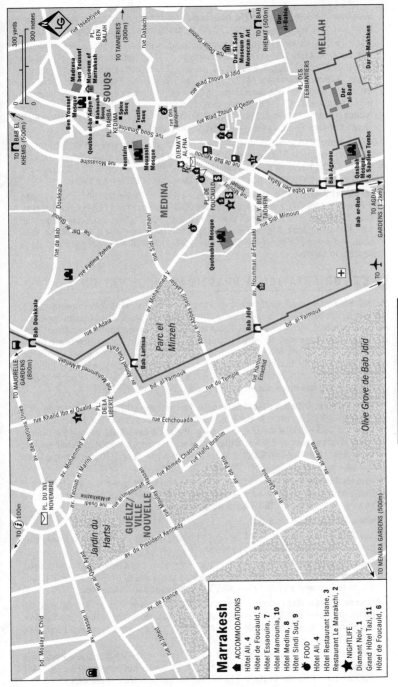

Marrakesh

ACCOMMODATIONS
Hôtel Ali, **4**
Hôtel de Foucauld, **5**
Hôtel Essaouira, **7**
Hôtel Mamounia, **10**
Hôtel Medina, **8**
Hôtel Sindi Sud, **9**

FOOD
Hôtel Ali, **4**
Hôtel Restaurant Islane, **3**
Restaurant Le Marrakchi, **2**

NIGHTLIFE
Diamant Noir, **1**
Grand Hôtel Tazi, **11**
Hôtel de Foucauld, **6**

9am-9pm, 188dh). An **overnight train** leaves for Tangier at 9pm with stops in Casablanca and Rabat. For a *couchette* (200dh including train fare) book 1 day in advance.

Buses: (☎044 43 39 33), outside the medina walls by Bab Doukkala. Arrive 30min.-1hr. early, as seats fill quickly. **CTM** is window #10. To: **Casablanca** (4hr.; 2 per day 12:30, 3:30pm; 70dh); **Fez** (10hr., 1 per day, 135dh); **Meknes** (8-9hr., 1 per day 11pm, 145dh); **Ouarzazate** (4½hr., 1 per day 5pm, 70dh); **Zagora** (4-5hr., 1 per day 10:30pm, 79dh). **Private companies** run frequently to destinations throughout Morocco, including **al-Jadida** (9 per day 6am-4pm); **Asni** (every 30min. 8am-5pm, 10dh); **Casablanca** (every hr. 4am-8pm); **Essaouira** (8 per day 4am-5pm); **M'hamid** and **al-Rachidia** (2 per day 4am, 5pm); **Zagora** (4 per day 10am-10pm).

Grands Taxis: Start from Bab er-Rob, where you can share a taxi to Asni or Setti Fatma. 15dh per person for 6 passengers; slightly more for smaller groups. As always, you have to wait for the taxi to fill up. If you already have a group assembled, there's no need to head to Bab er-Rob; take one of the *grands taxis* waiting at Djema'a al-Fna.

Car Rental: Avis, 137 bd. Mohammed V (☎044 43 37 27). **Hertz,** 154 bd. Mohammed V (☎044 43 99 84). Both agencies charge 250dh per day for a Fiat Palio or Fiat Uno, plus 2.50dh per km. 25+, small cars 23+, though many offices don't require proof of age. No international license required. Open M-F 8am-noon and 3-6:30pm, Sa 9am-noon and 3-6pm, Su 9am-noon. Many hotels (like Hôtel Ali) also arrange rentals. Don't hesitate to bargain.

■ ? ORIENTATION & PRACTICAL INFORMATION

EXPLORING MOROCCO

Marrakesh and its medina are more spacious than Morocco's other imperial cities, but just as crowded and noisy. Most of the excitement, as well as budget food and accommodations, centers around **Djema'a al-Fna** and the **medina** streets directly off it. The **bus** and **train stations,** administrative buildings, and luxury hotels are in the **ville nouvelle** down av. Mohammed V. Also in *ville nouvelle* are most of the car rentals, newsstands, banks, and travel agencies. Bus #1 runs between the minaret and the heart of *ville nouvelle* (1.50dh). Or take one of the many *petits taxis* (10dh) or horse-drawn carriages (15dh, sometimes more at night).

Tourist Office: Office National Marocain du Tourisme (ONMT), av. Mohammed V (☎044 43 61 79), at pl. Abdel Moumen ben Ali; 35min. walk from Djema'a al-Fna. *Petit taxi* 15dh. Helpful if you speak French. There is a better map on sale for 15dh at many tobacco shops and hotels. **Official guides,** a worthwhile option in Marrakesh, can be booked here (half-day 120dh, full day 150dh). Open daily 8:30am-noon and 2:30-6:30pm; summer 7:30am-3pm; Ramadan 9am-3pm.

Currency Exchange: Banks with 24hr. **ATMs** line av. Mohammed V and av. Hassan II in Guéliz and cluster in the medina around the post office. Many of the busier hotels will change money 24hr. Try **Hôtel Ali** or **Hôtel Essaouira.**

Police: (☎19), off Djema'a al-Fna.

Late-Night Pharmacy: (☎044 44 54 26), off Djema'a al-Fna, on the way to av. Mohammed V, on the right. Open Tu-Su 9pm-6am.

Medical Emergency: Doctor on call until 10pm at the late-night pharmacy. Avoid the government-run *polyclinique,* as you will be pushed to the end of the line; ask your consulate to recommend a private physician. See **Embassies and Consulates,** p. 765.

Internet Access: Many good Internet cafes with A/C are on rue de Bab Agnaou, the pedestrian street off Djema'a al-Fna. **Cyber Bab Agnaou, Cyber Mohammed Yassine,** and **Hanan Internet Cyber Café** each charge 10dh per hr. Open daily 8am-11pm. Also **Hôtel Ali** (10dh per hr.). Open daily 8am-11pm.

Post Office: pl. du 16 Novembre (☎044 43 09 77). A madhouse. Unreliable **Poste Restante.** Open M-F 7:30am-3pm. **Branch** (☎044 44 09 77) in Djema'a al-Fna. Open M-F 7:30am-3pm. **DHL** and **FedEx** at 113 av. Mohammed Abdelkrim el Khattabi.

ACCOMMODATIONS

Marrakesh's inexpensive accommodations are in abundant supply near Djema'a al-Fna. It's always worthwhile to see your room before taking it. Many places allow you to sleep on the rooftop terrace for about 20dh, a good option in the summer when rooms get hot, and a nice way to meet other travelers.

■ **Hôtel Ali,** rue Moulay Ismail (☎044 44 49 79; fax 44 05 22). A self-contained tourist compound. Suites with soap, towels, usually A/C, and toilet paper. English spoken. Also has a restaurant, Internet cafe, and currency exchange, and arranges expeditions in the High Atlas (350dh per day). If it's full, don't agree to go to far away Hôtel Farouk. Ali gets quite hectic in summer; head to Essaouira or Sindi Sud (see below) for a more laid-back atmosphere. Breakfast included. Dorms or terrace 40dh. Singles with fan and shower 100dh; doubles with A/C and shower 150dh; triples with A/C 200dh. ❸

■ **Hôtel Essaouira,** 3 Derb Sidi Bouloukat (☎044 44 38 05). From Djema'a al-Fna, facing the post office, head down the road in the left corner, just beyond Café de France, through an archway. Take the first right after the Hôtel de France and look for the signs. A colorful and stylish hotel with a cafe and laundry basins. One of the best sleeping terraces in town. Hot showers 5dh. Luggage storage 5dh per day. 40dh per person, but there are few singles; doubles 80dh; terrace 25dh. ❶

Hôtel Sindi Sud, 109 Riad Zitoun al-Qedim (☎044 44 33 37), just off the intersection with Derb Sidi Bouloukat, across from Hôtel Essaouira. This 2-year-old hotel is a great value for your money. Popular with American Peace Corps workers, it has clean, well-furnished rooms, a nice indoor courtyard, laundry basins, and friendly staff. Hot shower and breakfast included. 40dh per person; terrace 25dh. ❶

Hôtel Medina, 1 Derb Sidi Bouloukat (☎044 44 29 97). Laid-back atmosphere, spotless beds, and a colorful courtyard adorned with traditional mosaic patterns. Laundry basins, drying lines, and a terrace cafe. Breakfast 14dh. Hot showers 5dh. 40dh per person, students 35dh; terrace 20dh. ❶

FOOD

For delicious dinner bargains, take a chance and head for the **food stalls** in Djema'a al-Fna. Dozens of stalls deal from early evening until after midnight. Follow the crowds to the best *harira* (2dh), *kebabs* (2dh each), and fresh-squeezed orange juice (2.50dh). On the other end of the price spectrum, Marrakesh also boasts many **"palace restaurants"** where music, outrageous portions, and liquor combine for a memorable, if expensive, evening (usually 300-600dh per person). **Restaurant Yacout** ❺ is pricy (500-600dh per person) but superb. (☎044 38 29 00. Reservations required.) For lunch, the restaurants off rue de Bab Agnaou are popular with tourists. For pastries, try **Patisserie des Princes** on rue de Bab Agnaou or the understated **Mik Mak** next to Hôtel Ali. Two **markets** peddle fresh produce along the walls surrounding the city, far from Djema'a al-Fna.

■ **Hôtel Ali,** rue Moulay Ismail (see **Accommodations,** above). A tasty all-you-can-eat Moroccan buffet dinner situated 4 floors above the bustle of Djema'a al-Fna on the rooftop of Hôtel Ali. Try to arrive early before the food gets too cold, though lines may be long. A hearty breakfast is served on the 1st fl. as well. A good place for women traveling alone. 60dh, 50dh for Ali guests. Served daily 6:30-10pm. ❷

Restaurant Le Marrakchi, 52 rue des Banques (☎044 44 33 77). If you have a few extra dirham to spend, this excellent restaurant has authentic Moroccan decor and great views of Djema'a al-Fna and the Koutoubia Mosque. Ask to sit near the front windows. Live music and belly dancing. Moroccan menus from 250-450dh. ❺

Hôtel Restaurant Islane, av. Mohammed V (☎044 44 00 81). Brick-oven pizza and pasta (60-80dh) served on the rooftop with a nice view of the mosque. Slightly overpriced, but a refreshing break from typical Moroccan fare. Good for women traveling alone. Open daily noon-3pm and 7-11pm. MC/V. ❸

🔎 SIGHTS

DJEMA'A AL-FNA. Welcome to Djema'a al-Fna (Assembly of the Dead), one of the world's most frantically exotic squares, where sultans once beheaded criminals and displayed the remains. Crowds of thousands participate in the bizarre bazaar that picks up in the late afternoon and peters out after midnight. Individuals consult with potion dealers and fortune tellers; crowds encircle preachers, storytellers, and musicians; women have their children blessed by mystics; and promoters encourage bets on boxing matches between young boys (and girls).

SEEING RED One may see the hands, feet, and hair of Moroccan women decorated with the original temporary tattoo, *henna*. Stemming from the Arabic words meaning "tenderness" and "good luck," henna is made from the leaf of the *tafilat* plant, ground into a powder and mixed with warm water or tea to make a paste. The dye comes in different colors, including red, black, and green, and it has three main uses: as a medicine; for pregnant women in their seventh month; and for marriage ceremonies and the **Festival of the Girls** on the 27th day of Ramadan. The application of the design to the skin, which can take hours, is both an art and a ceremony unto itself. The intricate motifs are painted freehand or with a pattern and are left to sit anywhere from a couple of hours to an entire day before being rubbed off. The resulting decorations may last on the skin for weeks. Tourists can get a henna hand tattoo in Marrakesh for 10-15dh. beware: a synthetic dye (PPD) found in some forms of henna tattooing can cause **severe blisters** and **permanent scarring.** If you have sensitive skin, patch test the henna first, or ask the artist for a simple mix of henna powder and lemon juice.

MEDINA & SOUQS. Second only to Fez in size, Marrakesh's medina contains a fantastic array of crafts and artisans. The best place in Morocco to buy spices, the medina is also where you'll find the most colorful iron and sheepskin lampshades. A worthwhile survey of the medina (primetime, which you'll want to avoid if you don't like packed crowds, is 5-8pm) begins at the *souqs*. If you get lost, ask a merchant for directions, or a child will lead you out for a few dirham. From Djema'a al-Fna, enter the medina directly across from the Café-Restaurant-Hôtel de France. This path runs to the medina's main thoroughfare; turn toward the enormous **souq smarine** (textiles) by taking a quick left after the **pottery souq;** look for the sign on the arched gate. Berber blankets and yarn pile up in the alleyways of the **fabric souq.** Head through the first major orange gateway and make a quick right to the Rahba Kedina, a small plaza containing the **spice souq,** complete with massive sacks of saffron, cumin, ginger, and orange flower, as well as the apothecaries' more unusual wares—goat hoof for hair treatment, ground-up ferrets for depression, and live chameleons for sexual frustration. Nearby is **La Criée Berbère** (the Berber Auction), once a slave-trading center. Nowadays it hosts aggressive carpet merchants. Farther on are the bubbling vats of the **dye souq.** Fragrant whiffs of cedar signal the nearby **carpentry souq,** where workers carve chess pieces with astounding speed. Go left through these stalls to see the 16th-century **Mouassin Fountain** bathe its colorful, but grime-covered, carvings. On the road going right where the **souq attarine** (perfume) forks, an endless selection of colorful leather footwear glows at the **babouche souq** (untinted yellow is traditional for men; women wear the fancier models). The right fork at the end of the street leads to the **cherratine souq,** which connects the *babouche souq* to the **souq al-kebir,** the leather *souq*. Those with strong stomachs can visit the **tanneries;** continue through the *souqs* and take a right after the Madrasa ben Youssef; head straight for 10min. through a run-down stretch of the medina; the tanneries are on your right.

Among the shops that stand out from the rest in terms of quality of products and information is **Chateau des Souks,** which sells Berber rugs and carpets. *(44 rue Souq Smarine. ☎044 42 64 10.)* At **Herboristerie Avenzoar** you can hear fascinating explications of the healing qualities of herbs and spices in fluent English. *(78 Derb N'Khel, off the Rahba Kedima. ☎044 042 69 10.)* **Caverne de Tissage** sells traditional Moroccan pieces in untraditional fabrics like silk, cashmere, and velvet. *(rue Rahba al-Qedim, off the Rahba Kedima. ☎044 42 67 90.)*

⬛AL-BAHIA PALACE. The ruthless late-19th-century grand vizier Si Ahmad Ibn Musa, also known as Ba Ahmed, constructed this palace, naming it al-Bahia (The Brilliance). Serving as the de facto seat of government for the man who ruled in the sultan's stead, al-Bahia was built in an effort to assert Morocco's historical and cultural significance and thus stave off European domination. Today, its impressive ceilings are beautifully preserved, although little artwork or furniture adorn its halls. Occasionally it serves as a gallery for modern art. *(From pl. des Ferbiantiers, then turn left and follow the road as it curves to a red archway, which opens onto a long, tree-lined avenue leading to the palace door. Open Sa-Th 8:30-11:45am and 2:30-5:45pm, F 8:30-11:30am and 3-5:45pm. 10dh. Sometimes closed for restoration.)*

MADRASA BEN YOUSSEF. In 1565, Sultan Moulay Abdallah al-Ghalib raised the Madrasa ben Youssef in the medina center, the largest Qur'anic school in the Maghreb until its closing in 1960. One of the most beautiful buildings open to non-Muslims, the Madrasa was designed in the Andalusian architectural style, including the calligraphy, courtyard, and intricate floral designs. Visitors can roam the students' cells and appreciate the size of their hostel rooms. *(From rue Souq Smarine, bear right onto rue Souq al-Kebir and follow it to its end. Open June-Aug. Tu-Su 9am-1pm and 2:30-6pm; Sept.-May Tu-Su 9am-6:30pm. 20dh, children 10dh.)*

DAR SI SAID. This 19th-century palace was built by Si Said, brother of grand vizier Ba Ahmed and chamberlain of Sultan Moulay al-Hassan. It houses the **Museum of Moroccan Art,** with Berber carpets, pottery, jewelry, Essaouiran ebony, and Saadian woodcarving. One of the best classical Moroccan art museums in the country, it's well worth a visit. *(From rue Riad Zitoun al-Jdid, take the second right heading toward Djema'a al-Fna and the first left onto the alley where the museum resides. Open W-Th and Sa-M 9-11:45am and 2:30-5:45pm, F 9-11:30am and 3-5:45pm. 10dh. Summer travelers may find the museum closed for renovations in late June.)*

MUSEUM OF MARRAKESH. Featuring both thematic exhibits on Moroccan culture and private collections, this is one of Morocco's best museums. The building itself, a 19th-century palace, is lavishly decorated and contains a traditional *hammam* for visitors to explore. There is also a pleasant cafe and shop on site. *(Off the open plaza at the end of rue Souq Smarine in the back of the medina, around the corner from the Madrasa and Qoubba al-ba'Adiyn. ☎044 39 09 11. Open daily 9am-6pm. 30dh, students 10dh.)*

KOUTOUBIA MOSQUE. Almost every tour of Marrakesh begins at the 12th-century Koutoubia Mosque, whose magnificent ⬛**minaret** stands 70m over the Djema'a al-Fna. Crowned by a lantern of three golden spheres, the minaret is the oldest (and best) surviving example of the art of the Almohads who made Marrakesh their capital from 1130 to 1213. At their peak, their rule stretched from Spain to Tunisia, and one of the minaret's two siblings is *La Giralda* in Sevilla (see p. 241). The name Koutoubia comes from the Arabic *koutoubiyyin* (of the books), because the design of the minaret was inspired by one of the first four authorized editions of the Qur'an. After 5pm, visit the beautiful Koutoubia rose garden; when in full bloom, it's perfect for an evening stroll. *(Entrance forbidden to non-Muslims.)*

QOUBBA AL-BA'ADIYN MONUMENT. Beside Madrasa ben Youssef protrudes the unpainted cupola of 12th-century Qoubba al-ba'Adiyn, the oldest monument in town, the only relic of the Almoravid dynasty and the original from which all other Moroccan buildings have borrowed their unique style. Though excavated in the mid-20th century, much remains hidden either underground or by other structures. Ask the guard to open an ancient wooden door to the subterranean cisterns. *(From rue Souq Smarine, bear right onto rue Souq al-Kebir and turn left at the madrasa. Open daily 9am-5:30pm. Bang on the door if it's closed. 10dh, plus 5-10dh tip for the custodian-guide.)*

SAADIAN TOMBS. Modeled after the interior of the Alhambra in Granada, the Saadian Tombs served as the royal Saadian necropolis during the 16th and 17th centuries, until Moulay Ismail walled them off to efface the memory of his predecessors. In 1912, the burial complex was rediscovered during a French aerial survey. The first room after the entrance is home to the mother of Sultan Ahmed al-Mansur (the Victorious). Next door is his own tomb, the most impressive **Hall of the Twelve Columns** where the trapezoidal tombs of the Sultan and his sons rise from a pool of polished marble. The walls of the **mausoleum,** dating from the late 16th century, brim with illuminated mosaic tilework. The sultan's four wives, 23 concubines, and the most favored of his hundreds of children are buried in the third room; the unmarked tombs belong to the women. The minaret of the Mosque of the Qasbah, al-Mansur's personal mosque, towers above the complex. *(English tours. Open daily 8:30-11:30am and 2:30-5:45pm. 10dh.)*

GARDENS. Since the 12th century, rulers have dealt with the sun by constructing massive irrigated gardens. Only the most extravagant and least Moroccan of these gardens, the ◙**Majorelle Gardens,** allows a true escape from the heat. Designed by French painter Jacques Majorelle in the 1920s, the gardens are owned and maintained today by fashion designer Yves Saint-Laurent. On the same site is the small **Museum of Islamic Art.** *(Bear left onto bd. de Safi and turn right onto av. Yacoub al-Mansur; the gardens are on the left. Better yet, take a petit taxi for 10dh. Open daily June-Aug. 8am-noon and 3-7pm, Sept.-May 8am-noon and 2-5pm. Gardens 20dh; museum 10dh.)* The luxurious **gardens at Hotel La Mamounia,** Marrakesh's most extravagant hotel (once frequented by Sir Winston Churchill), can be visited in the morning, though you must act and dress smartly. *(av. Houmman el Fetouaki, just before exiting through Bab Jdid. Open to the public until 2pm, although the doormen will often turn you away even earlier.)*

◨ NIGHTLIFE

Most travelers hang around Djema'a al-Fna or one of the terrace cafes that overlooks it for most of the night. Alternatively, try the **bars** at the **Grand Hôtel Tazi** (☎044 44 27 87) on rue de Bab Agnaou, and **Hôtel de Foucauld** (☎044 44 54 99) on av. Mohammed V, where locals and tourists mix with the help of 15dh *Spéciale Flag.* (Both bars open at 9pm. Cover 50dh.) International karaoke bar **Safran et Cannelle** is at av. Hassan II (☎044 43 59 69). Marrakesh has the closest thing in Morocco to a club scene. Try **Diamant Noir,** in Hôtel Marrakesh on av. Mohammed V in the *ville nouvelle,* or the city's best and largest club, **Paradise,** at the far end of the *ville nouvelle.* Both are a taxi ride away from Djema'a al-Fna.

◨ DAYTRIP FROM MARRAKESH

Travelers should make every effort to push farther south for excursions into the High Atlas Mountains or east toward the Cascades d'Ouzoud. Morocco's most dramatic landscape lies beyond the High Atlas in the *qasbah*-filled oases of the southern deserts. **Hôtel Ali** (see **Accommodations,** p. 807) organizes trips (1-4 days) to the

Cascades, into the mountains, and through the gorges and deserts of the south. Prices depend on group size, averaging around 300-400dh per person per day (usually includes transport, room, and meals).

CASCADES D'OUZOUD

Travel options to the Cascades are rental car, grand taxi, or bus. A car is the easiest, fastest way (3hr., 167km northeast on S508). Buses for Azilal (window #18) run from the main station in Marrakesh (3½hr., 2 per day 8:30am-2pm, 40dh). Ask to be dropped off at the turn-off for the Cascades and then join a grand taxi (10dh) for the rest of the way or, to be safe (as you could wait quite a while for a taxi to fill up), continue to Azilal and grab a place in one of the taxis headed to the falls (40min., 15dh). The return trip may be difficult. If you miss one of the two evening buses running from Azilal to Marrakesh (2:30 and 7:30pm), organize a group to share a grand taxi back to Marrakesh from either Azilal or, if you're lucky, the falls themselves (400dh). Alternatively, arrange a round-trip grand taxi from Djema'a al-Fna for about 550dh, or try round-trip transportation from Hôtel Ali.

The Cascades d'Ouzoud (Ouzoud Falls) adorn posters in hotel rooms across Morocco for good reason: they are the stuff lazy vacations are made of. At the Cascades, you can swim in refreshing pools, search for Barbary apes in the surrounding valley trees, or kiss behind a waterfall. Once you get beyond the unnecessary guides at the top of the waterfall, you can find relative tranquility by the river below where the falls crash into a large pool. You can also jump from the rock precipices high above the pools, or swim directly underneath the falls, but don't try anything too risky. From the top of the falls, take the path to the left and descend the stairs. You are better off crossing the river (water taxi is 2dh) and hiking down to the many more secluded pools below. Spending the night at the Cascades can be highly enjoyable, as there are plenty of excellent campgrounds (10-20dh per person, 5dh per tent) where you can fall asleep to the sound of rushing water and be completely free to explore the surrounding valley (no tent is necessary as thin mattresses and blankets are provided). If you must have a roof above your head, **Hôtel Challal d'Ouzoud ❷** is the best option with clean, well-furnished rooms. (☎ 023 45 96 60. Singles 65dh; doubles 120dh; triples 180dh; terrace 25dh.)

EXPLORING MOROCCO

APPENDIX

CLIMATE

In the following charts, the first two columns for each month list the average daily minimum and maximum temperatures in degrees Celsius and Fahreinheit. The rain column lists the average number of days of rain that month.

SPAIN	JANUARY			APRIL			JULY			OCTOBER		
	°C	°F	Rain	°C	°F	Rain	°C	°F	Rain	°C	°F	Rain
Barcelona	4-13	40-55	5	8-17	47-62	9	19-27	66-81	4	12-21	54-70	9
Bilbao	6-13	42-55	8	8-17	46-62	8	16-25	60-77	5	12-21	53-69	8
Madrid	0-11	32-51	8	6-17	42-63	9	16-32	61-90	2	8-20	47-68	8
Santiago de Compostela	5-10	41-50	21	8-18	46-64	7	13-24	55-75	1	11-21	52-70	10
Sevilla	6-16	42-61	8	10-22	50-71	7	19-35	66-95	0	13-26	56-78	6

PORTUGAL	JANUARY			APRIL			JULY			OCTOBER		
	°C	°F	Rain	°C	°F	Rain	°C	°F	Rain	°C	°F	Rain
Faro	7-16	45-61	9	10-19	50-67	9	18-28	64-83	0	14-23	61-72	6
Lisbon	8-14	46-58	15	8-17	46-63	15	15-24	63-81	2	14-22	58-72	9
Porto	5-13	41-56	18	9-18	48-64	18	15-25	59-76	5	11-21	52-69	15

MOROCCO	JANUARY			APRIL			JULY			OCTOBER		
	°C	°F	Rain	°C	°F	Rain	°C	°F	Rain	°C	°F	Rain
Fez	4-16	39-61	8	9-23	49-73	9	18-36	64-97	1	13-26	55-79	7
Marrakesh	4-18	39-64	7	11-26	52-79	6	19-38	66-100	1	14-28	57-82	4
Tangier	8-16	46-61	10	11-18	52-64	8	18-27	64-81	0	15-22	59-72	8

TIME DIFFERENCES

Spain is 1 hour ahead of Greenwhich Mean Time (GMT) and 6 hours ahead of US EST. **Portugal** and **Morocco** are on GMT and 5 hours ahead of EST. Thus, when it is noon in New York, it is 5pm in Portugal and Morocco and 6pm in Spain. Spain and Portugal, together with the rest of Europe, switch to Daylight Savings Time about one week before the US does; they switch back at the same time. Morocco does not switch, and thus is 4 hours ahead of US EST and 2 hours behind Spain in the summer.

ADDRESSES

SPAIN & PORTUGAL: "Av.," "C.," "R.," and "Tr." are abbreviations for street, "Po." and "Pg." for promenade, "Pl." and "Pr." for plaza, and "Ctra." for highway. A building's number follows the street name; "s/n" stands for *sin numero* (without number).

MOROCCO: "av.," "bd.," "rue," and "calle" mean street; "pl." is a plaza. The building number comes before the street name, when there is one. When hunting for an address, note that many streets are being renamed in Arabic; *rue* and *avenue* may be replaced by *zankat*, *derb*, or *sharia*.

SPANISH PHRASEBOOK

Spanish pronunciation is fairly intuitive. Most consonants are the same as English. Important exceptions are: *j* ("h" in *hello*), *ll* ("y" in *yes*), *ñ* ("ny" in *canyon*), and *rr* (trilled "r"). The consonant *h* is always silent; *x* retains its English sound.

ENGLISH	SPANISH	ENGLISH	SPANISH
	The Bare Minimum		
Yes/No	Sí/No	**Do you speak English?**	¿Habla (usted) inglés?
Hello	Hola (Sí on the phone)	**I don't understand**	No entiendo
Good morning	Buenos días	**I don't speak Spanish**	No hablo español
Good afternoon	Buenas tardes	**What/When**	¿Qué?/¿Cuándo?
Good evening/night	Buenas noches	**Where/How**	¿Dónde?/¿Cómo?
Goodbye	Adiós/Hasta luego	**Who/Why**	¿Quién?/¿Por qué?
Please/Thank you	Por favor/Gracias	**How are you?**	¿Cómo está (usted)?
Excuse me	Perdón/Perdóname	**good/bad/so-so**	bien/mal/así así
Help	Socorro/Ayuda	**What time is it?**	¿Qué hora es?
No smoking/Got a lighter (cigarette)?	No fumar/¿Tiene fuego (un cigarillo)?	**How much does it cost?**	¿Cuánto cuesta?
here/there/left/right/straight	aquí/allí/izquierda/derecha/recto	**Can you drop me off here?**	¿Usted me puede dejar aqui?
open/closed	abierto/cerrado	**My name is...**	Me llamo...
hot/cold	caliente/frío	**What is your name?**	¿Cómo se llama?
Where is a late-night pharmacy?	¿Dónde está una farmacia de guardia?	**Is there a telephone that I could use?**	¿Hay un teléfono que podría usar?
Where is the toilet?	¿Dónde está el lavabo?	**I'm sick.**	Estoy enfermo/a.
	Accommodation & Transportation		
I want/I would like	Quiero/Quisiera	**How do I reach...?**	¿Cómo llego a...?
I would like a room.	Quisiera un cuarto.	**One ticket to...**	Un billete para...
Do you have any rooms?	¿Tiene cuartos libres?	**bus (train) station/airport**	estación de autobús (tren)/aeropuerto
I would like to reserve a room, please.	Quisiera reservar una habitación, por favor.	**How much is the fare to...?**	¿Cuánto vale el billete a...?
bath/shower/water	baño/ducha/agua	**train/plane/bus**	tren/avión/autobús
key/sheets	llave/sábanas	**round-trip**	ida y vuelta
air conditioning	aire acondicionado	**How long is the trip?**	¿Cuánto dura el viaje?
hotel/hostel/camp-grounds/inn	hotel/hostal or albergue/camping/posada	**At what time does it leave/arrive?**	¿A qué hora sale/llega?
	Food & Dining (also see Glossary, p. 813)		
breakfast	desayuno	**the check, please**	la cuenta, por favor
lunch	almuerzo	**drink**	bebida
dinner	cena	**dessert**	postre
Can I get this without the meat?	¿Me puede preparar este plato sin carne?	**Can you please bring me...?**	¿Me puede traer...por favor?
	Days		
Sunday	domingo	**today**	hoy
Monday	lunes	**tomorrow**	mañana
Tuesday	martes	**day after tomorrow**	pasado mañana
Wednesday	miércoles	**yesterday**	ayer
Thursday	jueves	**day before yesterday**	antes de ayer/anteayer
Friday	viernes	**week**	semana
Saturday	sábado	**weekend**	fin de semana

APPENDIX

PORTUGUESE PHRASEBOOK

Portuguese words are often spelled like their Spanish equivalents, although the pronunciation is quite different. In additional to regular vowels, Portuguese has nasal vowels as in French; vowels with a *til* (*ã*, *õ*, etc.) or before an *m* or *n* are pronounced with a nasal twang. At the end of a word, *o* is pronounced *oo* as in *room*, and *e* is sometimes silent (usually after a *t* or *d*). The consonant *s* is pronounced *sh* or *zh* when it occurs before another consonant. The consonants *ch* and *x* are pronounced *sh*, although the latter is sometimes pronounced as in English; *j* and *g* (before an *e* or *i*) are pronounced *zh*. The combinations *nh* and *lh* are pronounced "ny" as in *canyon* and "ly" as in *billion*.

ENGLISH	PORTUGUESE	PRONOUNCIATION
Yes/No	Sim/Não	seeng/now
Hello	Olá	oh-LAH
Good day, afternoon/night	Bom dia, Boa tarde/noite	bom DEE-ah, BO-ah tard/noyt
Goodbye	Adeus	ah-DAY-oosh
Please	Por favor	pur fah-VOR
Thank you	Obrigado (male)/Obrigada (female)	oh-bree-GAH-doo/dah
Sorry/Excuse me, please	Desculpe	dish-KOOLP
Do you speak English?	Fala inglês?	FAH-lah een-GLAYSH?
I don't understand.	Não entendo.	now ayn-TAYN-doo
Where is...?	Onde é que é ...?	OHN-deh eh keh eh...?
How much does this cost?	Quanto custa?	KWAHN-too KOOSH-tah?
Do you have a single/double room?	Tem um quarto individual/duple?	tem om KWAR-toe een-dee-vee-du-AHL/DOO-play?
Help!	Socorro!	so-KO-ro!

MOROCCAN PHRASEBOOK

Moroccan Arabic, though it is historically related to Classical Arabic, is difficult to understand even for those who have studied the Classical language. Particularly daunting is the language's seeming lack of vowels. The consonants *'ayin* (written ') and *hha'* (written *hh*) are pronounced deep in the throat; *'alif* (written ') is a glottal stop. Some consonants, the so-called "emphatics," are pronounced with the throat constricted and the tongue tensed; often this constriction spreads over entire syllables or words. *Let's Go* recommends that you stick with French.

ENGLISH	MOROCCAN ARABIC PRONUNCIATION	FRENCH
Hello (polite)	assa-LAA-mu-'a-LEY-kum / 'a-LEY-kum as-sa-LAAM (response)	Bonjour (day) / Bonsoir (night)
Hello/How are you?	la-BAS?	Ça va?
Fine, thanks	la-BAS, al-HAM-du-lil-lah	Tres bien, merci
Yes/No	EE-yeh/LA	Oui/Non
Please	min FAD-lak (m), min FAD-lik (f)/'AF-fak (m), 'AF-fik (f)/al-LAH-yikhaleek	S'il vous plaît
Thank you	shukran/mercee	Merci
I want (I would like)...	bgheet...	Je voudrais...
I need/I don't need	khuss-NEE/ma-khuss-NEESH	J'ai besoin de/Je n'ai pas besoin de
Where is...?	feen...?	Où est...? / Où se trouve...?
When is...?	fo-QASH...?	A quelle heure est...?
bus/taxi/train	u-tu-BEES/TAK-see/MA-shina	bus/taxi/train

ENGLISH	MOROCCAN ARABIC PRONUNCIATION	FRENCH
hotel/bathroom	u-TEEL/twa-LET or ham-MAM	hôtel/toilette
Is there a room?	wesh kayn beet?	Est-ce qu'il y a une chambre libre?
I don't speak Arabic (French)	ma-kan-tkal-LAMSH al-'arabi (al-fransawee)	Je ne parle pas arabe (français)
Do you speak English?	wesh-kat-TKAL-lim in-GLEE-zee?	Parlez-vous anglais?
How much does it cost?	sh-HAL ta-MAN?	Combien ça coute?
Let's work on a better price.	DIR-I-na shee taman mezyan / wa-TSOW-wab m'ana (very colloquial)	Faites-moi un bon prix.
A lot/A little bit	bez-ZAF/sh-WEEY-ya	Beaucoup/Un peu
Cheap/Expensive	ri-KHEES/GHEH-lee	Pas cher/cher
I'm not interested	ma bagh-EESH	Je ne suis pas interessé
Excuse me	SMEH-li	Pardon
Help!	an-NAJ-da! an-qee-DOO-nee!	Au secours!

ARABIC NUMERALS

0	1	2	3	4	5	6	7	8	9	10
٠	١	٢	٣	٤	٥	٦	٧	٨	٩	١٠
sifir	waahid	itnayn	talaata	arba'a	khamsa	sitta	sab'a	tamaniya	tis'a	'ashara

GLOSSARY

In the following glossary we have tried to include the most useful shortlist of common terms possible, particularly words we use in the text and those that you will encounter frequently in food menus. Non-Castilian words are specified as **C** (Catalan), **B** (Basque), or **G** (Galician), respectively. In the Morocco glossary section, **A** stands for Moroccan Arabic and **F** refers to French.

SPAIN: TRAVELING

abadía: abbey
abierto: open
ajuntament (C): city hall
albergue: youth hostel
alcazaba: Muslim citadel
alcázar: Muslim palace
arena: sand
autobús/autocar: bus
avenida: avenue
avinguda (C): avenue
ayuntamiento: city hall
bahía: bay
bakalao: Spanish techno
bandera azul: blue flag, EU award for clean beaches
baños: baths
barcelonés: of Barcelona
barrio viejo: old quarter
biblioteca: library
buceo: scuba diving
cabo: cape
cajero automático: ATM
calle: street
cambio: currency exchange
capilla: chapel
carrer (C): street
casa particular: lodging in a private home
caseta: party tent for Sevilla's *Feria de Abril*

castell (C): castle
castillo: castle
catedral: cathedral
cerrado: closed
calabacín: zucchini
caldo gallego: white bean and potato soup
carretera: highway
casco antiguo/viejo: old city, old district
churrigueresco: ornate Baroque architecture style
ciudad vieja: old city
ciutat vella (C): old city
colegio: school
consigna: luggage storage
Correos: post office
corrida: bullfight
cripta: crypt
cuarto: room
encierro: running of the bulls
entrada: entrance
ermida (C): hermitage
ermita: hermitage
església (C): church
estación: station
estanco: tobacco shop
estanque: pond
estany (C): lake
extremeño: of Extremadura
fachada: facade
feria: outdoor market or fair

ferrocarriles: trains
fuente/font (C): fountain
gallego: of Galicia
gitano: gypsy
glorieta: rotary
iglesia: church
igrexa (G): church
IVA: value-added tax
jardín público: public garden
judería: Jewish quarter
kiosco: newsstand
librería: bookstore
lista de correos: poste restante
litera: sleeping car (in trains)
llegada: arrival
madrileño: Madrid resident
madrugada: early morning
manchego: from La Mancha
menú: full meal with bread, drink, and side dish
mercado/mercat (C): market
mezquita: mosque
mirador: lookout point
moll (C): wharf, pier
monestir (C): monastery
monte: mountain
mosteiro (G): monastery
Mozárabe: Christian art style
Mudéjar: Muslim architectural style
muelle: wharf, pier

APPENDIX

murallas: walls
museo/museu (C): museum
palau (C): palace
parador nacional: state-owned luxury hotel
parte viejo: old town
paseo, Po.: promenade, stroll
passeig, Pg. (C): promenade
plaça, Pl. (C): square, plaza
plateresque: architectural style noted for its facades
platja (C): beach
plaza, Pl.: square
praza, Pr. (G): square
puente: bridge
rastro: flea market
real: royal
REAJ: the Spanish HI youth hostel network
Reconquista: the Christian reconquest of the Iberian peninsula from the Muslims
refugio: shelter, refuge
reina/rey: queen/king
retablo: altarpiece
ría (G): estuary
río: river
riu (C): river
rua (G): street
sacristía: part of the church where sacred objects are kept
sala: room or hall
salida: exit, departure
selva: forest
Semana Santa: Holy Week, leading up to Easter Sunday; **Setmana Santa** in Catalan
sepulchro: tomb
serra (C): mountain range
seu (C): cathedral
sevillanas: type of flamenco
SIDA: AIDS
sierra: mountain range
Siglo de Oro: Golden Age
sillería: choir stalls
tienda: shop or tent
tesoro: treasury
torre: tower
universidad: university
v.o.: *versión original*, a foreign-language film subtitled in Spanish
valle: valley
zarzuela: Spanish light opera

SPAIN: FOOD & DRINK

a la plancha/a brasa: grilled
aceite: oil
aceituna: olive
adabo: battered
aguacate: avocado
ahumado/a: smoked
ajo: garlic
al horno: baked
albóndigas: meatballs
alioli: Catalan garlic sauce
almejas: clams
almuerzo: midday meal
alubias: kidney beans
anchoas: anchovies
anguila: eel
arroz: rice

arroz con leche: rice pudding
asado: roasted
atún: tuna
bacalao: salted cod
bistec: steak
bocadillo: sandwich
bodega: wine cellar
bollo: bread roll
boquerones: anchovies
brasa: chargrilled
cacahuete: peanut
café con leche: coffee w/milk
café solo: black coffee
calamares: calamari, squid
caldereta: stew
calimocho: red wine and coke
callos: tripe
camarones: shrimp
caña: small beer in a glass
canelones: cannelloni
cangrejo: crab
caracoles: snails
carne: meat
cava (C): champagne
cebolla: onion
cena: dinner
cerdo: pig, pork
cereza: cherry
cervecería: beer bar
cerveza: beer
champiñones: mushrooms
choco: cuttlefish
chorizo: spicy red sausage
chuleta: chop, cutlet
chupito: shot
churros: fried dough sticks
cocido: cooked; stew
conejo: rabbit
coñac: brandy
copas: drinks
cordero: lamb
cortado: coffee with little milk
croquetas: fried croquettes
crudo: raw
cuba libre: rum in Coca-Cola
cuchara: spoon
cuchillo: knife
cuenta: the bill
desayuno: breakfast
dorada: sea bass
empanada: meat/pastry pie
ensaladilla rusa: vegetable salad with mayonnaise
entremeses: hors d'oeuvres
escabeche: pickled fish
espagueti: spaghetti
espárragos: asparagus
espinacas: spinach
fabada asturiana: bean soup with sausage and ham
flan: crème caramel
frambuesa: raspberry
fresa: strawberry
frito/a: fried
galleta: cookie
gambas: prawns
garbanzos: chickpeas
gazpacho: cold tomato soup with garlic and cucumber
guindilla: hot chili pepper
guisantes: peas
helado: ice cream

horchata: sweet almond drink
horneado: baked
huevo: egg
jamón dulce: cooked ham
jamón ibérico: Iberia ham
jamón serrano: cured ham
jatetxea (B): restaurant
jerez: sherry
langosta: lobster
langostino: large prawn
lechuga: lettuce
lomo: pork loin
manzana: apple
manzanilla: dry, light sherry
mejillones: mussels
melocotón: peach
menestra de verduras: vegetable mix/pottage
merienda: tea/snack
merluze: hake
migas: fried breadcrumb dish
mojito: white rum and club soda with mint
morcilla: blood sausage (black pudding)
muy hecho: well-done (steak)
natillas: creamy milk dessert
olivas: olives
paella: rice and seafood dish
pastas: small sweet cakes
patatas bravas: potatos in spicy tomato sauce
patatas fritas: French fries
pavo: turkey
pechuga: chicken breast
pepino: cucumber
pescaíto frito: tiny fried fish
picante: spicy
pimienta: pepper
piña: pineapple
pintxo (B): Basque for tapa
plancha: grilled
plátano: banana
plato del día: daily special
plato combinado: entree and side order
poco hecho: rare (steak)
pollo: chicken
pulpo: octopus
queso: cheese
rabo de toro: bull's tail
ración: small dish
rebozado: battered and fried
refrescos: soft drinks
relleno/a: stuffed
salchicha: pork sausage
sangría: red wine punch
seco: dried
sesos: brains
setas: wild mushrooms
sidra: cider
solomillo: sirloin
sopa: soup
taberna: tapas bar
tapa: bite-sized snack
tenedor: fork
ternera: beef, veal
terraza: patio seating
tinto: red (wine)
tortilla española: potato omelette
tostada: toast

trucha: trout
trufas: truffles
tubo: tall glass of beer
txakoli (B): fizzy white wine
uva: grape
vaca, carne de: beef
verduras: green vegetables
vino: wine
vino blanco: white wine
vino tinto: red wine
xampanyería (C): champagne bar
yema: candied egg yolk
zanahoria: carrot
zarzuela de marisco: shellfish stew
zumo: fruit juice

PORTUGAL: TRAVELING

alto/a: upper
autocarro: bus
bairro: neighborhood, district
baixo/a: lower
berrões: stone pigs found in Trás-Os-Montes
biciclete tudo terrano: mountain bike
bilhete: ticket
bilheteria: ticket office
câmara municipal: town hall
camioneta: coach
capela: chapel
casa de abrigo: shelterhouse, usually in parks
castelo: castle
centro de saúde: state-run medical center
chegadas: arrivals
cidade: city
claustro: cloister
conta: bill
coro alto: choir stalls
Correios: post office
cruzeiro: cross
Dom, Dona: courtesy titles, usually for kings and queens
domingo: Sunday
entrada: entrance
esquerda: left (abbr. E, Esqa)
estação rodoviária: bus station
estrada: road
feriada: holiday
floresta: forest
fortaleza: fort
grutas: caves
horario: timetable
igreja: church
ilha: island
intercidade: inter-city train
lago: lake
largo: small square
ligação: connecting bus/train
livraria: bookstore
miradouro: lookout
mosteiro: monastery
mouraria: Moorish quarter
mudança: switch/change
obras: construction
paco: palace
paragem: stop

partidas: departures
pelourinho: stone pillory
pensão (s.), pensões (pl.): pension(s)/guesthouse(s)
ponta: bridge
porta: gate
pousada da juventude: youth hostel
pousada: state-run hotel
praça: square
praça de touros: bullring
praia: beach
PSP: Polícia de Seguranca Pública, the local police force
quarta-feira: Wednesday
quarto de casal: room with double bed
quinta-feira: Thursday
quiosque: kiosk; newsstand
res do chão: ground floor, abbr. R/C
residencial: guesthouse, more expensive than *pensões*
retablo: altarpiece
ribeiro: stream
ria: estuary
rio: river
romaria: pilgrimage-festival
rossio: rotary
rua: street
sábado: Saturday
saída: exit
sé: cathedral
segunda-fiera: Monday
selos: stamps
sexta-feira: Friday
terça-feira: Tuesday
termas: spa
tesouro: treasury
tourada: bullfight
turismo: tourist office
velha: old
vila: town

PORTUGAL: FOOD & DRINK

açorda: thick soup with bread
adega: wine cellar, bar
aguardente: firewater
alface: lettuce
alho: garlic
almoço: lunch
ameijoas: clams
Antigua: aged grape brandy
arroz: rice
arrufada de Coimbra: raised dough cake with cinnamon
assado: baked
azeitonas: olives
bacalhau: cod
bacalhau à Gomes de Sá: cod with olives and eggs
bacalhau à transmontana: cod braised with cured pork
balcão: counter in bar or café
batata: potato
batido: milkshake
bem passado: well done
bica: espresso
bifinhos de vitela: veal filet with wine sauce

bitoque de porco: pork chops
bitoque de vaca: steak
bolachas: cookies
branco: white (wine)
cabrito: kid
café com leite: coffee with milk, in a mug
café da manhã: breakfast
caldeirada: shellfish stew
caldo: broth/soup
caldo verde: cabbage soup
camarões: shrimp
caneca: pint-size beer mug
caracóis: snails
carioca: cafe mixed with hot water; like American coffee
carne: meat
carne de vaca: beef
cebola: onion
cerveja: beer
chocos: cuttlefish
chouriço: sausage
churrasqueira: BBQ house
cogumelos: mushrooms
conta: bill
couvert: cover charge added to bill for bread
cozido: boiled
doce: sweet
ementa: menu
ervilhas: green peas
esacalfado: poached
espadarte: swordfish
espetadas: skewered meat served with melted butter
esturjão: sturgeon
fatia: slice
feijao: bean
frango: chicken
frito: fried
galão: coffee with hot milk
garrafa: bottle
gasosa: lemonade
gelado: ice cream
ginja: wild cherry liqueur
grao: chick peas
grelhado: grilled
guisado: stewed
hamburger no prato: hamburger patty with fried egg
imperial: tall thin beer glass
jantar: dinner
lagosta: lobster
lampreia: lamprey
laranja: orange
leitão: roasted pork
linguado: sole
linguiça: very thin sausage
lula: squid
maca: apple
manteiga: butter
mariscos: shellfish
massapão: marzipan
mexilhões: mussels
no churrasco: barbequed
no forno: baked
ovos: eggs
padaria: bakery
panado: breaded
pao: bread
passa: raisin
pastelaria: pastry shop

peru: turkey
pimentos: peppers
polvo: octupus
porço: pork
posta: slice of fish or meat
prato do dia: dish of the day
presunto: ham
quiejo: cheese
recheado: stuffed
salmão: salmon
sande: sandwich
seco: dry
sobremesa: dessert
sopa juliana: soup with shredded vegetables
sumo: juice
tasca: bistro/cafe
tigelada: sweet egg dessert
tinto: red (wine)
tomatada: rich tomato sauce
tosta: grilled cheese
tosta mista: grilled ham and cheese sandwich
toucinho do ceu: "Bacon of Heaven," an egg dessert
verdures: vegetables
vinho branco: white wine
vinho de casa: house wine
vinho verde: young wine
vitela: veal

MOROCCO: TRAVELING

adhan (A): call to prayer
aguelmane (A): lake
alcazaba (A): citadel
alcázar (A): palace
al-kebir (A): leather
aourir (A): small mountain
attarine (A): perfume
aujourd'hui (F): today
azrour (A): rock
auberge de jeunesse (F): youth hostel
azib (A): shepherd's hut
bab (A): gate
billet (F): ticket
borj (A): tower
bus (F): bus
chambre (F): room
chameau (F): camel
chaud (F): hot
compris (F): included
consigne (F): left luggage
coûter (F): to cost
dar: palace
demain (F): tomorrow
djebel (A): mountain peak
djellaba (A): traditional Moroccan garment
djoutia (A): flea market
douche (F): shower
droite (F): right
erg (A): sand dune
fassi (A): resident of Fes
fermé (F): closed
froid (F): cold
gare (F): train station
gare routière (F): bus station
gauche (F): left

gîte (F): gov't approved Berber houses used as shelters
hadj (A): Mecca pilgrimage
hammam (A): public bath
hier (F): yesterday
litham (A): veil
louer (F): to rent
madrasa (A): school
makhzen (A): government
medina (A): old Arabic city
mellah (A): Jewish quarter
mihrab (A): prayer niche
msalla (A): prayer area
mosquée (F): mosque
moussem (A): festival
muezzin (A): responsible for calling Muslims to prayer
musée (F): museum
nouveau/nouvelle (F): new
oued (A): river
ouvert (F): open
palais (F): palace
piscine (F): pool
poste (F): post office
qasbah (A): family fortress
qsar, qsour (pl.) (A): fortified village with curved, white-washed houses
rue (F): street
salle de bain (F): bathroom
smarine (A): textiles
souq (A): market
timbre (F): stamp
tmer (A): dates
toilette (F): toilet
train (F): train
vieux/vielle (F): old
ville (F): city
voiture (F): car
zelidj (A): decorative tiles

MOROCCO: FOOD & DRINK

agneau (F): lamb
bastilla (A): pigeon pie
beurre (F): butter
bière (F), birra (A): beer
blanc (F): white
boeuf (F): beef
boulettes de viande (F): meatballs
brochettes (F): shish-kebab, usually lamb
couscous (F): semolina grain
couscous bidaoui (A): couscous with 7 vegetables
cornes de gazelles (F): pastry horns with marzipan
crevettes (F): shrimp
ejben (A): cheese
forsheta (A): fork
frites (F): French fries
fromage (F): cheese
glace (F): ice cream
harira (F): spicy lamb-based bean soup
huile (F): oil
kebab (A): skewered meat
kefta (F): Moroccan burger
l-habra (A): steak

l'houli (A): mutton
légume (F): vegetable
lehmama (A): pigeon
louz (A): almonds
malka (A): spoon
mechoui (A): roast lamb
merguez (A): spicy sausage
moos (A): knife
oignons (F): onions
pain (F): bread
pastilla (A): chicken, almond paste, and spices in a pastry
poisson (F): fish
poulet (F): chicken
qahwa: coffee
qniya (A): rabbit
rouge (F): red
salon de thé (F): tea room
shrab (A): wine
tajine (F): Moroccan stew
viande (F): meat
vin (F): wine

AVERAGE TRAVEL TIMES IN SPAIN & PORTUGAL

	Algeciras	Badajoz	Barcelona	Bilbao	Córdoba	Granada	León	Málaga	Madrid	Pamplona	Sala-manca	San Sebastián	Santiago	Sevilla	Toledo	Valencia	Zaragoza
Algeciras																	
Badajoz	10hr.																
Barcelona	19½hr.	13½hr.															
Bilbao	11-13hr.	10-11½hr.	8-11hr.														
Córdoba	5-6hr.	6hr.	11hr.	9-11hr.													
Granada	5-7hr.	7½-9½hr.	12-13hr.	10-12hr.	3hr.												
León	11hr.	8½hr.	11½hr.	7hr.	7-9hr.	10hr.											
Málaga	5½hr.	7-8hr.	13hr.	11-13hr.	2½-3hr.	2hr.	9-11½hr.										
Madrid	6hr.	4½hr.	7hr.	5-7hr.	2-6hr.	5hr.	4½-5½hr.	4-6hr.									
Pamplona	11hr.	9½hr.	6-8hr.	2hr.	9hr.	10hr.	4hr.	9-11hr.	5hr.								
Salamanca	9hr.	5½hr	11½hr.	5½-6½hr.	6-8hr.	8hr.	3hr.	7-9hr.	3hr.	6-7hr.							
San Sebastián	12-14hr.	10-12hr.	7-10hr.	11hr.	10-12hr.	11-13hr.	5¼hr.	12-14hr.	6-8hr.	1-2hr.	5½-6½hr.						
Santiago de Campostela	14hr.	12-13hr.	15hr.	11hr.	11-13hr.	13hr.	5½hr.	12-14hr.	7½-8hr.	12hr.	7-8hr.	12hr.					
Sevilla	4-5hr.	4½hr.	13-16hr.	8-11hr.	1½hr.	3-5hr.	7-9hr.	2½-3hr.	2½-3½hr.	8hr.	8hr.	9-11hr.	11hr.				
Toledo	6hr.	5hr.	7hr.	6-8hr.	3-5hr.	14hr.	6hr.	5-6hr.	1½hr.	9hr.	4hr.	7-9hr.	12hr.	3hr.			
Valencia	13-15hr.	10hr.	4-6hr.	12hr.	7hr.	8hr.	10-13hr.	11hr.	5-7½hr.	10hr.	8-10½hr.	10hr.	11hr.	9hr.	5-7½hr.		
Zaragoza	9hr.	8hr.	4hr.	4hr.	6-8hr.	8hr.	5½-6hr.	7-9hr.	3hr.	2hr.	7hr.	4hr.	11-12hr.	8½hr.	4hr.	6hr.	

	Braga	Coimbra	Évora	Faro	Fátima	Lisbon	Porto
Braga		4hr.	9-10hr.	12-15hr.	5½hr.	8½hr.	2hr.
Coimbra			6hr.	12hr.	1½hr.	3hr.	3hr.
Évora				6hr.	5½hr.	3hr.	7hr.
Faro					7½hr.	5hr.	8½hr.
Fátima						2½hr.	3½hr.
Lisbon							6hr.
Porto							

INDEX

MAP INDEX

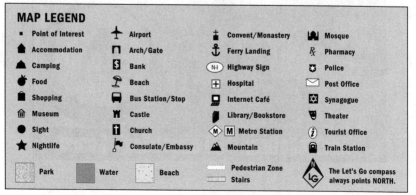

MAP LEGEND

▪ Point of Interest	✈ Airport	⚏ Convent/Monastery	☾ Mosque
▲ Accommodation	⊓ Arch/Gate	⚓ Ferry Landing	℞ Pharmacy
▲ Camping	$ Bank	(N-I) Highway Sign	✚ Police
🍎 Food	🏖 Beach	✚ Hospital	✉ Post Office
🛍 Shopping	🚌 Bus Station/Stop	💻 Internet Café	✡ Synagogue
🏛 Museum	♜ Castle	📖 Library/Bookstore	♥ Theater
● Sight	🏢 Church	⟨M⟩ M Metro Station	(i) Tourist Office
★ Nightlife	🚩 Consulate/Embassy	⛰ Mountain	🚉 Train Station

Park	Water	Beach	▬▬▬ Pedestrian Zone
			▦▦▦ Stairs

The Let's Go compass always points NORTH.